The RUSSELL-COOKE VOLUNTARY SECTOR LEGAL HANDBOOK

3rd edition

18·6·2014

DIRECTORY OF SOCIAL CHANGE

The vision of the Directory of Social Change is of an independent voluntary sector at the heart of social change. We work towards this by providing practical, challenging and affordable information and training to meet the current, emerging and future needs of the sector. We also promote independence for the sector by campaigning for an independent voluntary sector and championing the needs of small- to medium-sized voluntary and community organisations.

Further copies of this book and a copy of the current booklist may be obtained by contacting:

Directory of Social Change
Publications Department
24 Stephenson Way, London NW1 2DP
08450 77 77 07; fax 020 7391 4808
publications@dsc.org.uk
www.dsc.org.uk

Directory of Social Change Northern Office

Federation House, Hope Street, Liverpool L1 9BW
0151 708 0136

The RUSSELL-COOKE VOLUNTARY SECTOR LEGAL HANDBOOK

3rd edition

James Sinclair Taylor
Mary Cheves, Jane Klauber, James McCallum,
David Mears & Andrew Studd
of the Charity Team
Russell-Cooke Solicitors

Edited by Sandy Adirondack

DIRECTORY OF SOCIAL CHANGE

Published by the Directory of Social Change
24 Stephenson Way, London NW1 2DP
tel 08450 77 77 07, fax 020 7391 4808
publications@dsc.org.uk
www.dsc.org.uk

Registered charity no. 800517

First published 1996 as *The Voluntary Sector Legal Handbook*

Second edition 2001

Third edition 2009 as *The Russell-Cooke Voluntary Sector Legal Handbook*

ISBN 978 1 903991 87 9

British Library Cataloguing in Publication Data

A catalogue record for this book is available from the British Library

Designed by Sandy Adirondack
Cover design by Ian Findlay
Printed by Page Bros, Norwich

This book does not give a full statement of the law, nor does it fully reflect changes after 30 June 2009. It is intended for guidance only, and is not a substitute for professional advice. No responsibility for loss occasioned as a result of any person acting or refraining from acting can be accepted by the publisher, authors or editor.

Legal updates cross-referenced to *The Russell-Cooke Voluntary Sector Legal Handbook* can be accessed via www.rclh.co.uk.

CONTENTS

ACKNOWLEDGEMENTS

It would not be possible to produce a book of this size and complexity without the assistance of very many people.

As well as the authors, other solicitors at Russell-Cooke Solicitors who contributed include Thomas Cadman, Deborah Nathan, Tamsin Priddle and Sukanya Ransford in the Charity Team, and Jessica Asher, Richard Frimston, John Gould, Paul Greatholder, Scott Leonard, Rachel Morris, Lee Ranford and Guy Wilmot in other teams.

We are very grateful to all those who contributed or checked our text and provided helpful advice:
Simon Bass, Churches Child Protection Advisory Service;
Shirley Briggs, PEACe (Personnel Employment Advice and Conciliation Service) at London Voluntary Service Council;
Charlie Cattell, independent consultant;
Andy Cawdell, Dovetail Management Consultancy;
Deborah Clarke, ACRE;
Euan Drysdale, Keegan and Pennykid Insurance Brokers Ltd;
Rahel Geffen, London Voluntary Service Council;
Peter Gotham, Gotham Erskine LLP;
Bill Hyde, Community Transport Association;
Sabha MacManus, barrister;
Gareth Morgan, Kubernesis Partnership;
Mark Restall, independent trainer;
Shivaji Shiva, formerly of the Charity Team at Russell-Cooke Solicitors;
Ian Oakley Smith, PricewaterhouseCoopers;
Kate Sayer, Sayer Vincent;
Ian Snaith, Leicester University and Cobbetts LLP;
Gill Taylor, independent consultant;
Paul Ticher, independent consultant;
Kevin Yip, Health@Work.

We remain grateful to those who provided advice and assistance on the first and second editions, or helped in the initial stages of this third edition: Phil Allen, Paul Bater, Simon Chrystal, John Claricoat, Karen Cobham, Sally Collett, Jonathan Dawson, Lindsey Driscoll, James Dutton, Martyn Fisher, Graham Goodchild, Mark Harvey, Roger Jenkinson, Kate Kirkland, Mark Lattimer, Stephen Lee, John Littman, Stephen Lloyd, Christina Morton, Helen Mountfield, Hilary Phillips, Jonathan Pinkney-Baird, Richard Poynter, Christine Rigby, Sue Smith, Dr Michael Stuart, Jo Szwarc, Robert Venables, Lauren Vodopia and Andrew Watt.

Special thanks are due to the partners of Russell-Cooke Solicitors for supporting the effort needed to produce this edition.

Sandy would like to thank Jane Young for her outstanding editorial, indexing, proofreading and technical input and unfailing good humour, and Peter Firkin and Aidan Merritt for ongoing support.

John Martin and the publications team at the Directory of Social Change have been patiently supportive.

Many other friends and colleagues provided support in all sorts of ways: providing information, listening to us, and telling us repeatedly that the first and second editions were so useful that we really did need to do a third one.

James Sinclair Taylor
Sandy Adirondack
Mary Cheves, Jane Klauber, James McCallum
David Mears, Andrew Studd

London, August 2009

The Charity Team is a specialist unit within **Russell-Cooke Solicitors**. Acting for over 600 voluntary sector organisations across the UK, the team advises over the whole field of charity law. Its work touches on most aspects of life in the voluntary sector, from day to day problems to strategic and constitutional issues, including registration, constitutions and governance; property acquisition, sale and management; employment; fundraising and trading; contract negotiation; litigation; copyright, trade mark registration and use of the internet; and tax including VAT.

Russell-Cooke Solicitors is a broad-based Top 100 London legal firm with 150 partners and solicitors. The firm's highly regarded specialist lawyers' breadth of experience and mix of charitable, private and public sector clients reflect the complex legal needs of contemporary clients. Many of the firm's teams are leaders in their fields, with peer group accolades in diverse areas. The firm is highly regarded by the leading legal directories.

James Sinclair Taylor leads the Charity Team, advising on regulatory, structural, governance, employment and commercial issues. He is also involved in training senior staff and trustees, and lectures widely. Much of his work is involved with development and growth, particularly contractual and funding issues, restructuring, and mergers. He has been a trustee of a wide range of charities, and has contributed to a variety of publications.

Jane Klauber heads the team's employment work, dealing with contract and policy reviews and with disciplinary issues, redundancy and dismissals. She has many years of experience defending employment tribunal claims. She is a trustee of two children's and parenting charities.

James McCallum and **Mary Cheves** advise organisations on all aspects of property acquisition, development, disposal, charges, planning and lettings. Their work also involves the variation of trusts and schemes, and release of permanent endowment. Mary is a trustee of the Shaftsbury Young People charity.

David Mears supports organisations on fundraising, tax, contractual, constitutional, and trademark and other and intellectual property issues. He is a trustee of a council for voluntary service.

Andrew Studd advises charities and social enterprises on corporate and charity law issues, governance, service delivery and other commercial contracts. He has particular expertise in mergers and collaborative working arrangements. He sits on the finance and audit committee of an international development charity and lectures on legal matters affecting the wider third sector.

They can be contacted at:
  The Charity Team at Russell-Cooke LLP
  2 Putney Hill, London SW15 6AB
  tel 020 8394 6480; fax 020 8780 1194
  james.taylor@russell-cooke.co.uk
  www.russell-cooke.co.uk

Sandy Adirondack has been a freelance trainer and consultant in the voluntary sector since 1980, working primarily with community-based and user-based organisations and now specialising in governance and legal aspects of voluntary sector management. She is author of *Just About Managing? Effective management for voluntary organisations and community groups* (London Voluntary Service Council 1989, 4th edition 2005), often called 'the voluntary sector's management bible', and the *Good Governance Action Plan for Voluntary Organisations* (National Council for Voluntary Organisations, 2002). She has written, edited or contributed to many other publications on campaigning and voluntary sector management, governance and law, and provides a legal update for voluntary organisations on her website. She can be contacted at:

  39 Gabriel House, 10 Odessa Street, London SE16 7HQ
  tel 020 7232 0726; fax 020 7237 8117
  sandy@sandy-a.co.uk
  www.sandy-a.co.uk

INTRODUCTION AND GLOSSARY

Since the second edition of *The Voluntary Sector Legal Handbook* was published in 2001, a vast number of legal changes have affected charities and voluntary organisations. But just as significant is the increased accessibility of legal information on the internet. The progress of draft legislation can be tracked, new legislation is online within a day or two of parliamentary approval, government departments and other bodies provide guidance, and case law decisions are available to anyone. The lay person now has unprecedented access to information about legal rights and obligations and how they are interpreted by the courts.

Equally important is the changing language of the law. While many statutes and much guidance are still incomprehensible, there is a noticeable trend towards plain English. So not only is information available, but people can understand it. Some of the time, at least.

But organisations still need a starting point, something to guide them to what they should know, and that's where this book comes in. We hope it will continue to be an essential source of basic information for staff and governing bodies, and a guide to when they really should find out more or seek professional legal or financial advice. When professional advice is necessary, we hope the book will provide an understanding of the legal context in which the advice is given.

This book covers the law as it applies to England, and to Wales where that area of law has not been devolved to the Welsh Assembly. For devolved law, organisations should contact Wales Council for Voluntary Action (www.wcva.org.uk). Much law is the same or very similar in Scotland and Northern Ireland, but there are significant differences. Organisations based or operating in these nations should contact the Scottish Council for Voluntary Organisations or the Northern Ireland Council for Voluntary Action (www.scvo.org.uk and www.nicva.org).

Readers must, of course, be aware that large areas of law are summarised and some are not covered at all, and the law will continue to change. No book can replace good legal advice from suitably experienced legal advisors.

We are aware that with heavy usage, the spine of a book this size may break. To avoid this, organisations may want to remove the cover, punch holes in the pages, and put the pages into ring binders or a lever arch file.

BASIC TERMINOLOGY

To minimise confusion, we use the following terminology throughout the book.

- **Charity** and **charitable**: to refer only to charities, regardless of whether they are registered with the Charity Commission or other charity regulator, and never to refer to an organisation which is not legally charitable.

- **Incorporated organisation**: an organisation registered as a company limited by shares or guarantee, community interest company, charitable incorporated organisation (CIO) or industrial and provident society, or incorporated by charter or statute.

- **Unincorporated organisation**: an organisation, typically an association or trust, which is not incorporated.

- **Legal structure** or **legal form**: the form of the organisation, which determines whether it is incorporated or unincorporated and also determines the nature of its governing document.

- **Governing document:** the document(s) setting out the organisation's objects and basic rules – regardless of whether this is the articles (and in many cases also the memorandum) of association of a company, the rules of an industrial and provident society, the trust deed of a trust, the constitution of an association or a charitable incorporated organisation (CIO), a Charity Commission scheme, or any other format.

3

- **Governing body**: the body legally responsible for the management of the organisation – regardless of whether it is made up of directors (in a company), trustees (in a charity) or people who fulfil neither of those roles, and regardless of whether it is called a board, management committee, executive committee, council of management, or anything else.
- **Governing body members**: members of the governing body who under the governing document have the right to vote on decisions. This excludes anyone defined by the governing document as a non-voting member of the governing body, an observer, or someone otherwise defined as not having the right to take part in decisions.
- **Charity trustees**: Governing body members of a charity, regardless of whether the charity is incorporated or unincorporated.
- **Company directors**: Governing body members of a company, regardless of whether it is a company limited by guarantee or by shares or a community interest company.
- **Members of the organisation**: the individuals or in some cases organisations defined as members by the organisation's governing document, and entitled to attend and vote at the AGM and other general meetings and to exercise other rights of members granted under the governing document.
- **Beneficiaries**: the people the organisation is set up to work with or for.

LEGISLATION IN PROGRESS

As we go to press (August 2009) neither the Charities Act 2006 nor the Companies Act 2006 has been fully implemented. We have therefore had to include, in many cases, both the old legislation and the new. We have indicated, as best we can, when the new legislation is likely to come into effect but these dates should not be treated as definitive. Where we do not give a definite or expected implementation date, it means the legislation is already in effect.

FINDING OUT MORE AND KEEPING UP TO DATE

Legislation. To understand what the law really says, there is no substitute for reading the statutes and statutory instruments (SIs). Draft legislation can be tracked at www.parliament.uk for bills and the Office of Public Sector Information website at www.opsi.gov.uk for draft SIs. All new Acts and SIs are online at www.opsi.gov.uk within a few days of parliamentary approval.

The statute law database at www.statutelaw.gov.uk will, when complete, include all legislation still in force (going back to 1267!), as amended – unlike the OPSI website which contains legislation only since 1988.

Statutes and SIs can be purchased from The Stationery Office (TSO). *Halsbury's Statutes*, a multi-volume series, contains all statute law and is available in many public reference libraries.

Case law. Similarly, to understand how the law is interpreted there is no substitute for looking at relevant cases. The British and Irish Legal Information Institute has at www.bailii.org many decisions from UK courts and tribunals, as well as the European court of justice and the European court of human rights.

Important decisions are reported in a variety of law journals but these can be difficult for lay people to access. Anyone involved in an important or contested legal issue may find it worthwhile to ask their solicitor to obtain copies of key cases for them, or to recommend cases that can be looked up on the internet. These can provide an understanding of the relevant legal issues.

Website updates for this book. At **www.rclh.co.uk** readers can access legal updates from the Charity Team at Russell-Cooke Solicitors, cross-referenced to the relevant sections in this book. Sandy Adirondack also provides cross-referenced updates at **www.sandy-a.co.uk/legal.htm**. The websites cannot update the entire book, but should cover the main changes.

PART I
THE ORGANISATION
Chapters 1-11

Part I explains how to set up a voluntary organisation, and issues in deciding whether to become incorporated or remain unincorporated and whether to be charitable or non-charitable. These decisions determine the organisation's legal form or legal structure, and its charitable status or lack of it.

This part also explains how to change to another legal form if this becomes desirable, and looks at issues around setting up branches and other complex structures or undertaking mergers.

Chapter 1
SETTING UP AN ORGANISATION

For sources of further information see end of chapter.

1.1 STARTING UP

1.1.1 The voluntary and community sector

There is no statutory definition of **voluntary organisation** or **community group**, nor is there even any agreed definition in common use. But these terms generally mean a group or organisation which:

- is **voluntary** in the sense of being set up and continuing to operate because the people involved want to, rather than being set up by statute;

- has a governing body (committee or board) whose members are likely to be **volunteers**, receiving no payment other than reimbursement of expenses;

- is set up for the **benefit of the public or a community**, which may be local, national or international, or a community of interest such as people with a particular illness, political or social concern or hobby;

- is set up on a **not for profit** basis, which means it is not set up primarily for financial gain, and has rules saying that if it does make a profit or surplus, this has to be used for the organisation's purposes rather than being shared among the members. Not for profit organisations are sometimes but not always **charitable**.

This chapter explains the decisions about **legal form** (**legal structure**) and **charitable status** that need to be made to set up such an organisation.

Voluntary organisations, especially those working internationally, are sometimes referred to as **non-governmental organisations** (NGOs). **Community groups** (sometimes defined as purely voluntary, without staff) may be differentiated from voluntary organisations (defined as having paid staff). They may be collectively referred to as **voluntary and community organisations** (VCO) or the **voluntary and community sector** (VCS). Voluntary organisations and social enterprises [below] are sometimes collectively referred to as the **third sector**.

1.1.2 Social enterprises

At the time of writing (mid 2009) there is no statutory definition of what constitutes a **social enterprise**, **community business** or **community enterprise** – but all these terms are descriptions of how an organisation operates or wishes to be viewed. They have nothing to do with an organisation's legal form.

All three terms are generally used to refer to businesses with a social purpose, which are run in a commercial way but with a constitutional requirement that all or most profit must be reinvested in the business or be used for charitable purposes or for the benefit of the community or environment.

The term **social enterprise**, in particular, also encompasses charities or other voluntary organisations which earn much or most of their income through charging for their goods or services. An example is a community nursery that earns most of its income through the fees charged to parents, employers or the local authority, rather than being funded primarily through grants or donations.

For more about social and community enterprise, see **51.1**.

1.1.3 Deciding whether to be charitable

At an early stage the people involved in setting up an organisation will need to decide whether to be charitable. **Charitable status** does not come from registering with the Charity Commission; it comes from the organisation's purposes [**chapter 5**]. If the organisation is set up for purposes which are wholly and exclusively charitable and it operates for the benefit of the public, it is in virtually all cases legally a charity. It is subject to charity law, entitled to the privileges of charitable status, and subject to the restrictions on charities. This is explained in **chapter 4**, and in the charity registration materials available from the Charity Commission [see end of chapter].

The people involved in setting up the organisation should consider the advantages and disadvantages of charitable status [**4.2, 4.3**]. If the organisation wants the advantages of charitable status and is willing to operate within the restrictions on charities, it needs to be careful to define its purposes in ways which are wholly and exclusively charitable [**5.2**] and for the benefit of the public [**5.3**]. Otherwise, it will find that it is not entitled to the benefits of charitable status.

Conversely, if the organisation does not want to be subject to the restrictions of charity law, it needs to define its purposes in ways which are not legally charitable. Otherwise, it could find itself subject to charity law without intending this.

If the organisation is legally charitable and is based in England or Wales, it must register with the Charity Commission if it meets all the requirements for registration [**8.1.1**]; it does not have a choice. If it meets all the requirements but its annual income from all sources is below the registration threshold (£5,000 as at 1/8/09) it can choose whether to register.

1.1.3.1 Operating as a charity in Scotland or Northern Ireland

If the organisation is charitable and intends to operate in Scotland or Northern Ireland it may have to register with the **Office of the Scottish Charity Regulator** and/or **Charity Commission for Northern Ireland** [see end of chapter and **8.4**].

The definitions of what is charitable are slightly different in Scotland and Northern Ireland than in England and Wales. The purposes as set out in the governing document will need to comply with charity law in Scotland and/or Northern Ireland if applicable, and certain other clauses also need to be worded appropriately.

1.1.4 Decisions about legal form

1.1.4.1 Legal forms for voluntary organisations

As well as the decision about charitable status, the people involved in setting up the organisation will need to decide whether to **incorporate** (to register as a company limited by guarantee, community interest company, industrial and provident society or, when the structure becomes available, charitable incorporated organisation) or whether to remain **unincorporated** (not registered in one of these legal forms).

If the organisation is being set up for charitable purposes and will be unincorporated, a decision will need to be made about whether to become a **charitable trust**. If it is decided not to become a trust – or if no decision is made one way or the other – the default position is that the organisation is a **charitable unincorporated association**.

A non-charitable organisation usually cannot become a trust, so if it does not incorporate it is by default a non-charitable **unincorporated association**.

The advantages and limitations of incorporating or remaining unincorporated and the differences between the various legal forms are explained in **chapters 2** and **3**, and the process of setting up in the agreed form is described below.

1.1.4.2 Legal forms for social enterprises

The term **social enterprise** might be used for a charitable or other voluntary organisation which raises some or all of its income by charging for goods or services [**1.1.2**]. The people involved in setting it up will need to make the same decisions as for any voluntary organisation [above].

But some social enterprises are set up to run like a commercial business, but with the proviso that all or most of the profits must be used for social or community purposes. The people involved will need to decide whether to remain unincorporated as an unincorporated association, incorporate as a company limited by shares or company limited by guarantee, accept some limitation on profit distribution and set up a company limited by shares or guarantee as a community interest company, or set up an industrial and provident society. These options are explained in **chapter 3**.

Sometimes individuals set up a business primarily to make a profit for themselves and/or their shareholders or investors, but with the intention of using some of the profits for 'good causes'. If the people involved want the business to be incorporated, it will be a company limited by shares, cooperative industrial and provident society, or **limited liability partnership** [**3.6**]. If they do not want to incorporate, they will be an unincorporated **partnership** [**11.3**]. A single person operating in this way and not incorporating as a company is a **sole trader**.

This book does not cover the choices available to social enterprises which are set up as to run as businesses, although some of the issues are covered in **chapter 3** on incorporated structures and **chapter 51** on trading companies.

1.2 SETTING UP AN UNINCORPORATED ASSOCIATION

1.2.1 Coming into existence

Unincorporated associations and their advantages and disadvantages are explained in **2.2**.

Unlike other legal forms which generally require legal recognition before they come into being, an unincorporated association is usually assumed to exist as soon as two or more people start doing something together for a common purpose which is not primarily for business, with the intention (even if it is not explicit) of creating a legal relationship between them. A relationship which is purely family or friendship will not create an unincorporated association.

Unincorporated associations may be made up of individuals, organisations, or both individuals and organisations.

Intention to create a legal relationship will generally be implied (assumed) if the people involved call themselves a 'group' or anything else which signifies that they intend to be bound in some sort of membership, and/or if they develop rules, even informal and non-written ones, for matters such as who can be a member, what the group is doing and how they are doing it. It is not necessary to have a name, a constitution, a bank account, or even any money, so there is a risk of creating an association inadvertently and then suffering the legal consequences of having done so [**2.2.4**].

In a case in 1996, the court of appeal ruled that an unincorporated association did not formally come into existence until its first annual general meeting – even though the organisation had already been operating and had a bank account and a constitution. This was a surprising decision, and legal advice may be necessary in situations where the legal existence (or not) of an unincorporated association is significant.   *Hanuman v The Guyanese Association for Racial Unity & Democracy (1996)*
Court of Appeal LTA 96/5434/G, 13 June 1996 (unreported)

1.2.2 Drawing up a draft constitution

At some point, either early on or after a group has been in existence for a while, there may be pressure to adopt a **governing document** – a **constitution** or a less formal written set of rules. This often arises when the group needs to open a bank account, seek funding, or clarify who is eligible for membership.

The governing document is a legally enforceable agreement between the association's members. Even if nothing is written, the orally agreed rules by which the association operates form the agreement. And even if nothing has been agreed orally, any rules which have been consistently used over a long period form the agreement.   *Re Buckinghamshire Constabulary Widows & Orphans' Fund Friendly Society No.2 [1979]*
1 WLR 936,952; John v Rees [1970] Ch 345,388

Before drawing up even a draft constitution the people involved in the association should consider whether they want to be charitable [**1.1.3**], because this will affect what should or should not be in the governing document. They should also decide whether they want to incorporate [**3.1.3**], become a trust [**2.3.10**], or remain an association [**2.2.5**], as this will affect the governing document's form.

The Charity Commission provides a list of approved constitutions for charitable associations of specific types. If none of the approved ones is appropriate, the Charity Commission and Charity Law Association [see end of chapter] have model constitutions for charitable associations, or a solicitor with voluntary sector experience can create a tailor-made constitution.

If it is not going to be charitable, an unincorporated association does not need to comply with any requirements in drawing up its governing document. However, it is sensible to ensure the governing document includes all the provisions the association is likely to need. **Chapter 7** explains what should be in an unincorporated association's governing document – whether it is charitable or not – and additional clauses which might be included.

Model governing documents for non-charitable associations are harder to find, and advice may be necessary to ensure it includes everything it needs to, and does not include anything which could inadvertently make the association charitable.

The constitution of an unincorporated association can be in any language. If it is registering as a charity, it will have to supply a certified English translation to the Charity Commission. Even if it is not registering as a charity it may want to have a certified translation available for funders, bank managers and others outside the organisation.

1.2.3 Adopting the constitution

The **draft constitution** should be formally adopted by the members of the association at a general meeting called in accordance with the rules in the constitution. When the constitution is adopted it should be signed and dated. This is generally done generally by the chairperson and secretary, unless the constitution indicates otherwise. For example, if it says that the first members of the association are the signatories to the constitution, all the people who are intended to be the first members should sign it. This signed copy should be kept in a safe place.

1.2.4   Charity registration

If the association is charitable and is required to register with the Charity Commission, the constitution and supporting documents must be submitted [**8.2.4**]. Charities not registered with the Commission may need to apply to HM Revenue and Customs for recognition of their charitable status [**8.1.2**, **8.1.3**]. If a charity is to operate in Scotland or Northern Ireland, it may need to register there [**8.4**].

1.2.5   Circulating the constitution

A copy of the agreed constitution should be given to all members of the governing body (committee) and senior staff. A copy or summary should be given to all members of the organisation or be easily available to them.

Procedures should be put in place to ensure all new members of the association get a full or summarised copy of the constitution or know where they can see it, and all new members of the governing body get a copy of the full constitution as soon as they are elected or appointed.

1.2.6   Other registrations

When setting up, consideration should be given as to whether it is necessary to register with other bodies [**1.9**].

1.2.7   First meeting of the committee

At its first meeting after adoption of the constitution the governing body (or the members of the organisation) should:

- arrange for minutes to be taken;
- consider any further appointment of governing body members, if the constitution allows;
- elect or appoint a chairperson, treasurer and possibly other officers [**14.2**], unless the constitution names the first officers or says their appointment must be done at a general meeting or through another process;
- decide on frequency and procedure for calling meetings of the governing body, unless this is set out in the constitution [**19.12**];
- declare and record any conflicts of interest of governing body members – this is obligatory for charitable associations [**15.2**], and good practice for non-charitable associations;
- if the organisation is taking over from a previous body, ensure legal advice has been or will be taken and proper steps are being taken to transfer any assets, liabilities, contracts of employment, leases or agreements [**10.1.2**];
- appoint an independent examiner or auditor, if required [**55.1**];
- decide on the organisation's financial year [**54.2.1**];
- select bankers and account signatories, pass a resolution in the bank's required wording, and complete the mandate forms to open bank accounts;
- agree any contracts the organisation will enter into, for example with landlord or employees, and for telephone, gas, electricity, photocopier etc;
- agree insurances [**chapter 23**];
- appoint solicitors, if necessary [see **64.8.4** for how to find a suitably experienced solicitor];
- admit any members who have applied for membership of the organisation (if the constitution requires this);
- consider and if appropriate agree dates for the annual general meeting and other general meetings (meetings of all the members);
- arrange for registers (lists) of members of the organisation and members of the governing body to be created and maintained;

- ensure that stationery, financial and fundraising documents, emails and websites carry correct details [**18.1**];
- carry out any other business required by the constitution for the first meeting;
- consider arrangements for correspondence and other communications;
- and last but not least, consider what the organisation is actually going to do.

Proper minutes must be kept and should be signed at the next meeting as an accurate record [**19.12.7**].

1.3 SETTING UP A TRUST

1.3.1 The trust deed

The types of trust and their advantages and disadvantages are covered in **2.3**.

The Charity Commission provides a list of sources of approved **trust deeds** (also called **declarations of trust**), and the Charity Commission and Charity Law Association [see end of chapter] have models. **Chapter 7** explains what must be in a trust deed for a charitable trust, and optional clauses.

A trust should not be set up without legal advice, because the trust may fail (be declared **void** or invalid) if there is any uncertainty about the intentions of the people who set up the trust, or about whether they intended the money or property to be used solely for charitable purposes [**2.3.5**].

Individuals often set up personal or family charitable trusts as a tax-effective way of donating to charities [**50.7**]. A charitable trust can also be set up under the terms of a will. A solicitor can advise on setting up these types of trust.

1.3.2 Execution and stamping

The persons setting up the trust and those who will be the trustees **execute** the trust deed by signing and dating it in the presence of a witness. The signatures can be separately witnessed, so everyone does not have to sign at the same time.

If the deed covers assets which include stocks and shares, it must be sent to HM Revenue and Customs' Edinburgh stamp office [see end of chapter]. If it covers land, whether leasehold or freehold, it will be subject to the stamp duty land tax procedure [**61.10.1**]. Deeds which cover only cash do not have to be stamped unless they were executed before 1 December 2003.

1.3.3 Charity registration

After the deed is executed the charity registration process must be carried out if the trust is charitable and is required to register with the Charity Commission [**8.1.1**]. If it is based in England or Wales and is excepted or exempt from registration with the Commission, it may need to register with HM Revenue and Customs charities unit [**8.1.2**, **8.1.3**]. If it is to operate in Scotland or Northern Ireland, it may also need to register there [**8.4**].

1.3.4 Circulating the trust deed

A copy of the trust deed should be given to every trustee (member of the governing body). A procedure should be put in place to ensure a copy is given to all new trustees as soon as they are appointed.

1.3.5 Other registrations

The people involved in setting up the trust must consider whether they must register with other bodies [**1.9**].

1.3.6 First meeting of the trustees

At their first meeting the trustees should consider the same matters as at the first meeting of an association's committee [**1.2.7**].

1.4 SETTING UP A CHARITABLE INCORPORATED ORGANISATION

At the time of writing (mid 2009) the **charitable incorporated organisation** form [**3.2**] was expected to become available in April 2010. The CIO combines the advantages of charitable status and incorporation, but without the dual registration and dual accountability of charitable companies [**3.3.4**]. However, it may also have disadvantages compared with the charitable company structure [**3.2.3**].

Charities Act 1993 ss.69E-69M, to be inserted by Charities Act 2006 sch.7 (expected April 2010)

Full details will be available from the Charity Commission [see end of chapter], with model constitutions for a **foundation model** (where the CIO's only members are its current trustees) and a **non-foundation** or **association model** (where there is a wider membership). There will be different procedures for:

- a new organisation;
- an existing unincorporated association or trust, which will need to go through a process similar to changing from unincorporated status to a charitable company [**10.1**] to set up and transfer its assets to the CIO;
- conversion of a charitable company or charitable industrial and provident society (IPS), which will be relatively straightforward because it involves changing from one incorporated structure to another [**10.3.1**, **10.5.3**];
- conversion of a community interest company [**10.4.2**];
- two or more CIOs amalgamating to create a new CIO [**11.5.4**].

An exempt charity [**8.1.2**] cannot become a CIO. A charitable IPS with a share capital cannot become a CIO unless all shares have been paid up in full.

Charities Act 1993 s.69G(2), to be inserted by Charities Act 2006 sch.7 [expected April 2010]

1.5 SETTING UP A LIMITED COMPANY

Companies limited by guarantee and the advantages and disadvantages of this structure are explained in **3.3**. From 1 October 2009, the **Companies Act 2006** ss.7-38 significantly changed the documentation for registering a company and the form of the governing document. Basic details are in GP1 *Incorporation and names*, available from Companies House [see end of chapter] along with further information about registration and the necessary forms.

Before setting up a charitable company information should also be obtained from the Charity Commission [see end of chapter]. Before setting up any type of company, it may be sensible to consult an experienced solicitor or advisor.

1.5.1 Buying an off the shelf company

A ready-formed **off the shelf company** can be bought from a company formation agent (listed under 'company registration agents' in the Yellow Pages or on the internet) or through an accountant or solicitor. Off the shelf companies are nearly always limited by shares rather than by guarantee, so great care must be taken to get the right structure if this method of setting up is used.

Registration agents keep their fees low by providing a very basic service. The purchaser of the company is expected to specify exactly what they want and to understand the duties and responsibilities of companies and company directors.

An off the shelf company can be useful if a company is needed in a very great hurry, for example to sign a lease. The company name can later be changed [**6.7.1**] and the governing document can be amended [**7.5.3**]. But in the meantime the organisation is likely to be operating an inappropriate company, so this step should be taken only in exceptional circumstances.

1.5.2 The promoters

The persons involved in setting up the company are called the **promoters**. The promoters might or might not be involved in the company when it is finally set up. A solicitor or other person who assists the formation by acting in a professional capacity is not a promoter.

1.5.3   Company constitution

Under the **Companies Act 1985** and earlier Companies Acts, a company's governing document was in two parts: the **memorandum of association**, which set out the company's objects and powers and the limit on members' liability, and the **articles of association**, which set out its internal rules and procedures.

From 1 October 2009 the **memorandum of association** is a simple formation document, signed or authenticated by the **subscribers** [1.5.4] to say they wish to form a company. All of the provisions formerly in the memorandum, such as the objects clause and the limitation of members' liability, are now in the **articles of association**. For companies formed before 1 October 2009, anything in the memorandum is treated under company law as if it is in the articles.

Companies Act 2006 ss.18-20,28; Companies (Registration) Regulations 2008 [SI 2008/3014]

Statutory model articles are available for most types of company, including companies limited by guarantee. These may be adapted and submitted as part of the company registration process, but if not submitted the statutory articles apply by default. *Companies Act 2006 ss.19,20; Companies (Model Articles) Regulations 2008 [SI 2008/3229]*

Voluntary organisations should take advice before using the Companies Act articles, as they may not contain appropriate provisions. Organisations which wish to be charitable should instead consider using model articles from the Charity Commission or Charity Law Association [see end of chapter], or other articles which they know will meet the requirements of both company and charity law. Memoranda and articles from before 1 October 2009 must not be used.

Regardless of whether Companies Act, Charity Commission, CLA, other approved articles or tailor-made articles are used, it is essential to ensure that key provisions are suitable for the new company. These include the objects and powers, membership structure and criteria [12.2], members' meetings and decision making, proxies, election or appointment of the governing body, and governing body meetings and decision making. Particular issues apply to the choice of company name [6.4], and to companies which are being set up as a community interest company [3.4] or trading company [51.5.1].

A company whose registered office must be in Wales [17.1.1] may, if it wishes, submit its articles in Welsh, and from 1 October 2009 a certified translation into English is no longer required. Articles in any other language must be accompanied by a certified translation into English. *Registrar of Companies & Applications for Striking Off Regulations 2009 [SI 2009/1803] regs.6,7*

Chapter 7 explains some of the obligatory and optional clauses for the articles for all companies limited by guarantee, whether charitable or non-charitable.

1.5.4   The subscribers

The **subscribers** are at least one person, but generally more, who state in the memorandum of association that they want to form the company. They are the company's founder members, but have no special rights unless these are stated in the articles. The subscribers' details must be entered in the register of members [18.5.2] as the first company members.

The memorandum of association for a company limited by guarantee is:

Company not having a share capital

Memorandum of association of *[name of company]*

Each subscriber to this memorandum of association wishes to form a company under the Companies Act 2006 and agrees to become a member of the company.

Name of each subscriber   *Authentication by each subscriber*

Dated _____

Companies (Registration) Regulations 2008 [SI 2008/3014] sch.2

Authentication consists of a signature if the memorandum is submitted on paper, or personal details provided to Companies House for authentication if incorporation is done electronically [1.5.7].

The subscribers' addresses are given in part 4 of form **IN01**, the application for registration [1.5.5].

Typically the subscribers are the people who want to start the company, but in the case of an off the shelf company [**1.5.1**] an employee of the agent who forms the company may be the sole subscriber. Any subscriber who is not intended to carry on as a company member should resign their membership as soon as the company is sold to the organisation which purchases it, but there must always be at least one member.

The subscribers may be the first directors, but do not have to be.

1.5.5 Applying for registration

The memorandum [**1.5.4**], the articles (unless Companies Act articles are to be used in their entirety), form **IN01** and any necessary continuation sheets for IN01 are sent to Companies House with the registration fee (£20 as at 1/8/09 for a paper registration and £15 if the incorporation is done electronically) [**1.5.7**]. The organisation should keep copies of all documents and forms posted to Companies House, and print-outs of documents submitted electronically.

1.5.5.1 Registration details

IN01 is the application to register the company. Part 1 includes details of the company's name [**6.4**]; evidence of consent, where required, to use certain words in the name [**6.4.4**]; an indication of whether the company is exempt from having to use the word 'limited' in its name [**6.4.5**], as most voluntary organisations are, and does not want to use the word as part of its name; details of the registered office [**17.1.2**]; and an indication of whether the articles include any **entrenched provisions** requiring a majority of more than 75% to amend [**7.5.3**].

1.5.5.2 First directors and secretary

Part 2 of form **IN01** includes details of the first directors [**13.1.3**] and the first company secretary if there is to be one [**14.3**]. If there is not enough space for all the directors, continuation sheets should be used. The information submitted must also be entered in the company's register of directors and secretaries [**18.5.4**, **18.5.6**]. If the secretary or any director is a corporate body rather than an individual, the relevant sections of the form should be used.

The directors must provide a service address at which company documents can be served, and their usual residential address. Service addresses are available to the public via Companies House and the company's register of directors. Residential addresses, where these are different from service addresses, must be kept in the company's register of residential addresses [**18.5.5**], but this must never be made available to the public, nor are residential addresses which are different from service addresses made public by Companies House. *Companies Act 2006 ss.12,165,240-246*

The directors (and secretary, if there is one) must each sign to show they consent to serve.

Unless the articles specify otherwise, the first directors constitute the governing body only until new directors are elected (usually at the first annual general meeting, or at a general meeting held before this) or until new directors are appointed under the procedures set out in the articles.

1.5.5.3 Statement of capital or guarantee

Part 3 of **IN01** applies only to companies limited by shares, and contains a **statement of capital and initial shareholdings**. Part 4 applies to companies limited by guarantee, and contains the **statement of guarantee**, signed by each subscriber to the memorandum [**1.5.4**], stating the amount each agrees to contribute to the company's winding up costs if required [**3.3.1**]. This amount will be specified in the articles of association. *Companies Act 2006 ss.10,11*

1.5.5.4 Statement of compliance

Form **IN01** ends with part 5, in which all the subscribers or the person setting up the company on behalf of the subscribers confirms that all the legal requirements for setting up the company have been met. Those who sign are certifying that the memorandum of association is in the proper form, the articles have been properly drawn up (if Companies Act model articles are not being used), the objects as set out in the articles accurately reflect what the company is being set up to do, the directors and secretary named in **IN01** can legally hold these posts [**13.3.3**, **14.3.1**], and all other company registration requirements have been complied with.

Companies Act 2006 s.13

1.5.6 Same day registration

For those who need a company in a hurry, immediate registration is possible by attending at or delivering documents to Companies House in London, Birmingham, Cardiff, Leeds, Manchester, Edinburgh or Belfast, and paying an increased fee (£50 as at 1/8/09, £30 if done electronically).

1.5.7 Electronic incorporation

Electronic incorporation may be cheaper and faster than paper incorporation. The memorandum, articles (unless Companies Act articles are being used), form **IN01** and any other documents are sent by secure email. There is no need for any forms to be signed, but the directors, secretary and subscribers have to provide details for personal authentication purposes.

At the time of writing (mid 2009), approved software is required in order to submit these documents directly to Companies House. An online electronic incorporation service is provided by many formation agents [**1.5.1**] who charge their own fees in addition to the standard registration fee.

1.5.8 Certificate of incorporation

When Companies House is satisfied that the company's name is acceptable [**6.4**] and that all the paperwork is in order, a registration number is allocated and a **certificate of incorporation** is issued. Except for same day registration [**1.5.6**], this generally takes about two weeks from the time the forms are sent in. The most common cause of delay is a small error in the paperwork.

The company comes into existence as a body corporate, under the name specified in the memorandum, from the date on the certificate. A private company can start operating as soon it is incorporated. A public company (plc) also needs a **trading certificate** before it can start operating, but voluntary organisations are not plc's so this does not apply to them.

1.5.9 Charity registration

If the company is charitable it must submit its articles and the other required documents to the Charity Commission for registration as a charity [**8.1.1**], or if it is excepted or exempt from registration may have to apply to HM Revenue and Customs for recognition as a charity [**8.1.2**, **8.1.3**]. If it intends to operate in Scotland or Northern Ireland it may need to register there [**8.4**]. It may start its activities immediately, without waiting for charity registration.

1.5.10 Circulating the constitution

At least one copy of the signed articles should be kept in a safe place. A copy, perhaps with a summary of the main points, should be given to all company directors (voting members of the governing body), and procedures should be put in place to ensure it is given to all new directors in future.

It is good practice to give the articles, or a summary of the main points, to all company members and to have procedures in place to ensure it is given to all new members when they join. Any company member who requests it must be sent the full **company constitution**, which includes the (memorandum and) articles, the statement of guarantee or statement of capital and initial shareholdings [**1.5.5.3**], certain resolutions and agreements, certain court orders, and either the statement of guarantee or a current statement of capital.

Companies Act 2006 s.32

It is also good practice to give all directors Companies House leaflet GBA1 *Directors and secretaries guide* which summarises their responsibilities under company law. It is available free from Companies House [see end of chapter].

1.5.11   Other registrations

The company is likely to have to register with HM Revenue and Customs and other bodies [**1.9**].

1.5.12   First meeting of the directors

At their first meeting after incorporation the directors should deal with the matters set out at **1.2.7**, and also:

- receive the certificate of incorporation, articles, statement of proposed directors and secretary and statement of guarantee;
- consider any further appointment of directors, if the articles allow, and ensure they complete the statutory notification [**18.5.4**] and it is submitted to Companies House within 14 days;
- if the company was off the shelf [**1.5.1**] or for any other reason the directors named in the statement of proposed directors are not to remain directors, ensure the statutory notification of ceasing to be a director [**18.5.4**] is completed and submitted for them;
- appoint an independent examiner or auditor if required under the articles or charity or company law [**54.2.7, 54.3.7**];
- ensure steps are taken to notify any party with whom contracts may be made that the organisation is incorporated;
- confirm the location of the registered office and ensure the company's registered name is visible to visitors at the registered office and other places where the company operates [**17.1.3**];
- approve the location for the statutory registers if they are not to be kept at the registered office [**18.5**], and instruct the company secretary or a director to file the relevant forms;
- decide when the company's financial year will end (accounting reference date) and instruct the company secretary or a director to file the notice of accounting reference date [**54.3.1**], unless the ARD is to be the last day of the month in which the anniversary of incorporation falls;
- ensure that these decisions are minuted, and the company's statutory registers are updated to reflect the decisions [**18.5**].

1.6   SETTING UP A COMMUNITY INTEREST COMPANY

A **community interest company** (CIC) is a company limited by guarantee or by shares which complies with additional community interest requirements [**3.4**]. The registration process is the same as for an ordinary company limited by shares or guarantee [**1.5.5**] except that:

- the articles of association must comply with the requirements for CICs;
- as well as the documents required for ordinary company registration [**1.5.5**], form **CIC36**, setting out the company's **community interest statement** and certain other information, must be submitted;
- an additional fee (£15 as at 1/8/09) must be paid;
- before the registrar of companies considers the application for company registration, the CIC regulator examines the documents, in particular CIC36, and confirms that the company meets the requirement for registration as a CIC;
- same day and electronic incorporation are not possible.

Details are available from the CIC regulator [see end of chapter].

1.7   SETTING UP AN INDUSTRIAL AND PROVIDENT SOCIETY

Industrial and provident societies (likely to be renamed cooperatives and community benefit societies) and the advantages and disadvantages of this structure are explained in **3.5**.

The **rules** of an IPS must follow a prescribed format (**form A**), available from Mutual Societies Registration in the Financial Services Authority [see end of chapter]. Unlike company legislation, IPS legislation does not provide detailed models. It simply provides a list of what must be included in the rules.

Industrial & Provident Societies Act 1965 sch.1

The rules may also include other matters, and may specify the documentation to be used for any procedure set out in the rules, for example a membership application form or committee nomination form.

IPSA 1965 s.13(1),(4)

1.7.1   Model rules

Registration as an industrial and provident society is quicker and less expensive if **model rules** from a **promoting body** are used. Model rules are available for a range of voluntary organisations, including transport schemes, housing associations, credit unions, and licensed bars in village halls or community centres. Mutual Societies Registration [see end of chapter] has a list of promoting bodies.

If the rules are exactly as in the model, the registration fee is £40 (as at 1/8/09). If the rules are amended in any way the fee is £120, £350 or £950, depending on the number of amendments. In addition, a promoting body will add its own fee.

1.7.2   Applying without model rules

If there is no relevant promoting body or if the organisation does not want to register through a promoting body, it is sensible to contact an experienced solicitor or other advisor or Mutual Societies Registration (MSR) to obtain confirmation that the organisation is appropriate for registration as a society, and to get confirmation from MSR that the proposed rules are acceptable. The fee for registration without model rules is £950 (as at 1/8/09). Unlike Companies House, MSR scrutinises rules in detail and the registration process can take several weeks.

1.7.3   Consulting HM Revenue and Customs

Industrial and provident societies whose objects are wholly charitable [**5.2**] have been **exempt charities** which do not register with the Charity Commission [**8.1.2**]. From late 2009 some charitable IPSs will remain exempt, those which are no longer exempt will have to register if their annual income is over £100,000, and those with income not over £100,000 will become **excepted** [**8.1.3**]. Excepted IPSs will not have to register with the Commission but from late 2010 will be able to do so if they wish. The £100,000 registration threshold will be reviewed in 2011 and may be reduced.

Charities Act 1993 s.86A, sch.2, to be inserted/amended by Charities Act 2006 ss.11-14, sch.5 [expected Nov/Dec 2009]

IPSs which are exempt charities get recognition of their charitable status through HM Revenue and Customs charities unit [see end of chapter]. Unless they are using model rules which have been accepted as charitable, they should send their rules to HMRC at the same time as they are submitted to Mutual Societies Registration, to ensure the proposed purposes will be considered charitable.

1.7.4   Adopting the rules

When the rules have, if necessary, been agreed in principle by Mutual Societies Registration and for a charitable IPS are acceptable to HM Revenue and Customs, or if model rules are being used, the members must formally adopt the rules at a general meeting.

1.7.5   Applying for registration

An application (**form A**) is submitted to Mutual Societies Registration along with two bound printed copies of the rules and the registration fee. Form A lists all the clauses which must be included in the rules.

For **cooperatives** and **community benefit societies** [**3.5.1**, **3.5.2**], form A and both copies of the rules must be signed by at least three members of the society, the secretary (who can be one of the members) and, if model rules are being used, the promoting body.

A **secondary IPS** is made up of other IPSs. It only needs two member societies and a secretary. Form A and both copies of the rules must be signed by the secretary of the secondary society, the secretary of at least two member societies and, if model rules are being used, the promoting body.

For a **credit union**, form A must be signed by 21 members, the secretary (who may be one of the members), and the promoting body.

1.7.6 Certificate of registration

Mutual Societies Registration sends a certificate of registration (**form B**) to the society, with its registration number and date of registration. Form B is conclusive evidence that the organisation is registered as an industrial and provident society. *Industrial & Provident Societies Act 1965 s.2(3)*

Form B is also conclusive evidence that the society's rules are registered, except for companies which have converted to the IPS structure [**10.3.4**]. These need a separate certificate to show that their rules are registered.

If Mutual Societies Registration does not register the society on the basis that it is not a genuine cooperative or business operating for the benefit of the community, the decision cannot be appealed. But if a refusal to register is based on any other grounds, the members of the organisation may appeal against the decision. *IPSA 1965 s.18(1)(a),(2)*

1.7.7 Circulating the rules

All directors should have a copy of the rules, and members should have either a full copy or summary. Procedures should be in place to ensure new members get a copy of the rules as soon as they join.

A copy of the rules must be given to any person who requests it, at a charge not exceeding 10p. At the time of writing (mid 2009) the government intended to raise the maximum to £1. *Industrial & Provident Societies Act 1965 s.15(1)*

1.7.8 Other registrations

The society will have to register with HM Revenue and Customs and possibly other bodies [**1.9**].

1.7.9 First meeting of the directors

The first meeting of the society's directors should consider the same business as the first meeting of company directors [**1.5.12**].

1.8 SETTING UP A COMMUNITY AMATEUR SPORTS CLUB

In the past, sports clubs set up to promote participation in a single sport could not be registered as charities. As a way of promoting sport, since 2002 many such clubs been allowed to register with HM Revenue and Customs as **community amateur sports clubs** (CASCs) and get many, but not all, of the tax advantages enjoyed by charities. These include tax relief on gift aid donations [**50.2**], mandatory 80% rate relief [**63.2.3**], and in some cases relief from corporation tax on profits [**56.5**]. *Finance Act 2002 sch.18*

Clubs promoting a single sport may now be eligible for charity registration [**5.2.10**], so the people involved in setting one up need to decide whether to opt for charitable status, with all of the advantages but also with the limitations of being charitable [**4.2**, **4.3**], or register as a CASC and get fewer advantages but without the restrictions on charities.

To be eligible for registration as a CASC, the club must be formally constituted. This is generally as an association [**2.2**] but could be as a company limited by guarantee [**3.3**] or industrial and provident society [**3.4**]. Details of CASC registration are available from the HMRC charities unit [see end of chapter]. Once registered as a CASC there is, at the time of writing, no way of deregistering.

1.9 OTHER REGISTRATION REQUIREMENTS

In addition to obligatory registration with the Charity Commission for most organisations with wholly charitable objects [**8.1.1**], most organisations must be registered with other bodies as well.

Business Link [see end of chapter] produces *The no-nonsense guide to government rules and regulations for setting up your business* and a range of other start-up information which is also relevant for voluntary organisations. Some of these registrations are listed below and at the relevant points in this book. But not all potential registrations are covered in this book. New organisations, or organisations undertaking a new type of work, should take advice from an experienced solicitor and/or the relevant professional body.

1.9.1 HM Revenue and Customs registrations

An organisation may need to register with several different parts of **HM Revenue and Customs**:

- for PAYE, if it employs anyone for whom it must operate PAYE [**30.4**];
- for corporation tax if it carries out trading [**56.2.1**];
- if it is a charity and will want to recover tax on gift aid donations [**50.2**];
- if it is required to register for VAT or chooses to register voluntarily [**57.2**].

1.9.2 General registrations

Most organisations will need to register with the **information commissioner**, for data protection [**43.3.7**].

1.9.3 Registration for specific activities

Depending on the services and activities provided by the organisation, the organisation may need to register with bodies which regulate those activities. Some of the main examples are given here, but this list is not exhaustive.

1.9.3.1 Registered social landlords

Housing associations and other registered social landlords (RSLs) based in England which receive funding from the **Homes and Communities Agency** or other public sources must be registered with the HCA. A separate register is maintained in Wales.

Housing & Regeneration Act 2008 s.111

RSLs are subject to particularly complex regulatory requirements, which are beyond the scope of this book. Information is available from the **National Housing Federation**.

1.9.3.2 Provision of care and accommodation

From April 2009 adult care services in England, and some care services serving both adults and children, are registered and inspected by the **Care Quality Commission** [see end of chapter]. Services in Wales are regulated by the **Care and Social Services Inspectorate Wales**. The rules cover care homes that provide personal and/or nursing care, adult placement schemes, domiciliary care (home care) agencies, and nurses' agencies [**41.3.3**].

1.9.3.3 Work with children and young people, and adult learning

Ofsted (the Office for Standards in Education, Children's Services and Skills) [see end of chapter] is responsible for regulating and inspecting services for children, young people and learners of all ages.

Children's services regulated by Ofsted [**41.3.1**] include day care services for children under eight (including playgroups, nurseries, clubs, and organisations providing out of school activities); playschemes operating for more than 14 days in any year; any person paid or rewarded for looking after children under eight for more than two hours a day; social care services for children, children's homes, residential family centres, and adoption and fostering services and agencies.

Regulated services for learners include independent schools, further education colleges and 14-19 provision, work-based learning and funded training, education and training in prisons and other secure establishments, and adult and community learning.

1.9.3.4   Immigration advice

Organisations which provide any immigration advice to members of the public must register with the **Office of the Immigration Services Commissioner** [see end of chapter]. Not for profit organisations do not register as such, but must apply for a certificate of exemption. All immigration advisors, even if they are not registered with OISC, must comply with its code of standards.

Registration is not necessary for employers or their staff who provide immigration advice or services only to their own employees or prospective employees, if the advice relates only to that employee or their immediate family.

1.9.3.5   Other registrations

Other possible registration requirements include:

- the **Community Legal Service** [see end of chapter] if the organisation provides legal information, advice or specialist legal services to the public, even if this is only part of its work;
- the **Office of Fair Trading** if the organisation gives advice about debts, sells goods or services on credit or makes loans to consumers;
- the **Financial Services Authority** if the organisation arranges or provides advice on insurance, mortgages or other financial products, sells those products, helps people fill in application forms, checks application forms, or acts as an intermediary making introductions to providers of such products;
- the **Adventure Activities Licensing Service** [see end of chapter], if the organisation offers adventure activities such as caving, climbing and water sports to under-18s;
- the local authority's **environmental health department**, for premises where food will be prepared, sold or provided [**40.10.1**];
- the local authority's **licensing department**, for the sale of alcoholic beverages or provision of public entertainment [**47.2**];
- the **Performing Right Society**, **Phonographic Performance Limited**, **Video Performance Limited** and/or the **Mechanical Copyright Protection Society**, for the performance of live or recorded music [**47.6**];
- the **local authority**, for premises where there are amusement machines or where other forms of gaming take place [**49.8**].

Even where the organisation does not have to register when it is set up, it may need to register or get a licence or permission later if it undertakes a new activity or service, or for a one-off activity such as a public event [**chapter 47**], a public collection [**49.2**] or a lottery [**49.6**].

Resources: LEGAL STRUCTURES AND CHARITABLE STATUS

See next page.

Resources: LEGAL STRUCTURES AND CHARITABLE STATUS

Charities. Charity Commission: www.charitycommission.gov.uk, 0845 300 0218, email via website.

Charity Law Association: www.charitylawassociation.org.uk, admin@charitylawassociation.org.uk.

HM Revenue & Customs charities unit: www.hmrc.gov.uk/charities, 0845 302 0203, email via website.

Office of the Scottish Charity Regulator: www.oscr.org.uk, 01382 220446, info@oscr.org.uk.

Charity Commission for Northern Ireland (temporary details): www.dsdni.gov.uk/ccni.htm, vcu@dsdni.gov.uk.

Community amateur sports clubs. HM Revenue & Customs charities unit, as above.

Community interest companies. CIC regulator: www.cicregulator.gov.uk, 029 2034 6228, cicregulator@companieshouse.gov.uk.

Companies. Companies House: www.companieshouse.gov.uk, 0303 1234 500, enquiries@companieshouse.gov.uk.

Department for Business, Innovation & Skills: www.bis.gov.uk.

Cooperatives. Co-operatives UK: www.co-operatives-uk.coop, 0161 246 2900, info@cooperatives-uk.coop.

Industrial and provident societies. Financial Services Authority Mutual Societies Registration: www.fsa.gov.uk (at the time of writing, access is via Doing business with the FSA / Small firms / Mutual societies), 020 7066 8002, mutual.societies@fsa.gov.uk.

General information about setting up a voluntary organisation. National Council for Voluntary Organisations: www.ncvo-vol.org.uk, 0800 2 798 798, helpdesk@askncvo.org.uk.

Wales Council for Voluntary Action: www.wcva.org.uk, 0800 2888 329, help@wcva.org.uk.

This book does not cover Scotland and Northern Ireland. Information and advice are available from:

Scottish Council for Voluntary Organisations: www.scvo.org.uk, 0800 169 0022, enquiries@scvo.org.uk.

Northern Ireland Council for Voluntary Action: www.nicva.org, 028 9087 7777, nicva@nicva.org.

Setting up a social enterprise. Office of the Third Sector: www.cabinetoffice.gov.uk/third_sector/social_enterprise, email via website.

Social Enterprise Coalition: www.socialenterprise.org.uk, 020 7793 2324, membership@socialenterprise.org.uk.

Setting up in general. Business Link: www.businesslink.gov.uk, 0845 600 9 006.

Specific registrations. Adventure Activities Licensing Service: www.aals.org.uk, 029 2075 5715, email via website.

Care and Social Services Inspectorate Wales: www.cssiw.org.uk, 01443 848450, cssiw@wales.gsi.gov.uk.

Care Quality Commission: www.cqc.org.uk, 03000 616161,

Community Legal Service: www.legalservices.gov.uk, 020 7759 0000.

Financial Services Authority (for insurances): www.fsa.gov.uk.

HM Revenue & Customs stamp office (for some trusts), Grayfield House, Spur X, 4 Bankhead Avenue, Edinburgh EH11 4BF.

National Housing Federation: www.housing.org.uk, 020 7067 1010, info@housing.org.uk.

Office for Standards in Education, Children's Services & Skills (Ofsted): www.ofsted.gov.uk, 08456 404040, enquiries@ofsted.gov.uk.

Office of Fair Trading: www.oft.gov.uk, 08457 22 44 99, enquiries@oft.gsi.gov.uk.

Office of the Immigration Services Commissioner: www.oisc.gov.uk, 020 7211 1500, info@oisc.gov.uk.

Statute law. www.opsi.gov.uk and www.statutelaw.gov.uk.

Much but not all case law. www.bailii.org.

Updates cross-referenced to this book. www.rclh.co.uk.

Chapter 2
UNINCORPORATED ORGANISATIONS

2.1 UNINCORPORATED ORGANISATIONS

An **unincorporated organisation** is a group of persons bound by a common purpose and a set of rules or procedures, and not incorporated as a company, industrial and provident society or charitable incorporated organisation, or by statute or royal charter.

For voluntary organisations, the main forms of unincorporated organisation are the **unincorporated association** (typically a membership organisation) and the **trust** (typically used when a small number of people will manage money or property for a specific purpose or purposes, without a need for a wider membership).

If the purposes of an unincorporated organisation are wholly and exclusively charitable and it operates for the benefit of the public, it is then a **charitable association** or **charitable trust**.

Unlike **incorporated organisations** [**chapter 3**], unincorporated organisations are not recognised for legal purposes as being legal entities. The law recognises only the persons who make up the organisation. So Anyville Community Association or Anyville Community Trust are not legal entities; rather, the law sees them as 'the members of Anyville Community Association acting together', or 'the members of the governing body of Anyville Community Association acting together on behalf of the members of the association', or 'the trustees of Anyville Community Trust acting together'.

For how to set up an unincorporated association or trust see **1.2** and **1.3**.

2.2 UNINCORPORATED ASSOCIATIONS

2.2.1 What unincorporated associations are

An **association** has been defined in law as 'two or more persons bound together for one or more common purposes, not being business purposes, by mutual undertakings each having mutual duties and obligations, in an organisation which has rules which identify in whom control of it and its funds rests and on what terms, and which can be joined or left at will'. These rules, often embodied in a

23

constitution, create a contract between the members which can be enforced in the courts. *Conservative & Unionist Central Office v Burrell [1981] EWCA Civ 2*

How an association is formed is explained in **1.2.1**.

An association is **unincorporated** if it is not **incorporated** by registration as a company or in some other manner [**chapter 3**]. An association might be called a club, society, trust, organisation, campaign, project, federation, forum or anything similar. It might even be called a company (as in the case of an unincorporated theatre company). What an organisation is called has no significance in terms of its **legal form** (also referred to as **legal structure**). If it is not part of another organisation [**9.2**], is not formally set up as a trust, company, industrial and provident society or charitable incorporated organisation, and is not incorporated under statute or royal charter, it is generally an unincorporated association.

2.2.2 Regulation of unincorporated associations

There is no statute law relating to unincorporated associations as a whole, although there is some case law and there are some statutes regulating specific types of unincorporated association, most notably trade unions. If an association is charitable [**4.1**], it must comply with charity law.

Associations established to promote science, literature or fine arts or to provide adult education are in some very limited situations regulated by the Department for Business, Innovation and Skills under the **Literary and Scientific Institutions Act 1854**.

2.2.3 Advantages of unincorporated associations

2.2.3.1 Flexibility

The main advantage of the unincorporated association structure is that it is **uncomplicated** and **flexible**. Associations can be set up or wound up quickly, easily and cheaply.

An association can have a **simple governing document** (constitution) which the members can, if they wish, draw up themselves without involving lawyers or other advisors. They can create their own constitutional rules and procedures, and if the association's purposes are not charitable these rules and procedures will not have to comply with external requirements. If the people setting up the association want the benefits of charitable status it is advisable to obtain advice, to ensure the governing document meets the requirements of charity law [**7.1.3**].

If the governing document includes procedures for **amendment**, an association's rules can usually be changed quickly and easily. If the association is charitable, prior Charity Commission approval is needed for some changes [**7.5.1**] and all changes, even those for which prior approval is not required, must be notified to the Commission if the charity is registered.

An association can usually be **wound up** simply by complying with the procedures in its governing document [**24.8, 24.9**], and notifying the Charity Commission if it is a registered charity. Incorporated bodies are more difficult to dissolve.

2.2.3.2 Privacy

An association may have the advantages of **privacy** and **absence of external accountability**. No one outside the association needs to know who its members are, what they do, how they operate or how much money they have – unless it has to register with a registration or regulatory body [**1.9**], is charitable and has to register with the Charity Commission [**8.1.1**], or has to meet the requirements of funders or the expectations of donors and supporters.

2.2.4 Disadvantages of associations

2.2.4.1 Personal liability

The overwhelming disadvantage of unincorporated associations is that the members of the governing body, and in some cases all the members of the association, can be held **personally liable** for the organisation's debts [**22.2.2**].

If **creditors** – the people to whom the association owes money – take legal action, the claim will be against the individuals who authorised or incurred the debt, rather than against the organisation. Similarly if a person suffers loss or damage and wants to bring legal action against the organisation, the lawsuit will be brought against some or all of the members of the governing body or other individuals who authorised or carried out the activities which caused the loss.

There are ways to reduce the risk to individuals [**22.7**], but it cannot be removed.

2.2.4.2 Entering into contracts and taking legal action

An unincorporated association is not a legal entity, so it **cannot enter into legal agreements** or take legal action in its own right. If it rents a telephone line, hires staff, opens a bank account or orders goods or services, those contracts are entered into by individuals – the signatories and/or the members of the governing body who authorised the transaction – and they could be held personally liable if there is **breach of contract**. If the individuals cease to be members of the governing body or the association, this does not end their legal liability, unless the legal agreement is transferred to a new signatory [**21.5.1**].

If an unincorporated association wants to take **legal action** [**65.4**], the action must be brought in the name of an individual or individuals.

If the association is charitable and does not want to become incorporated as an organisation, the governing body can be incorporated [**2.4**]. This makes the governing body a legal entity but does not confer limited liability.

2.2.4.3 Holding property and investments

Because land, buildings, other property and investments must be held by individuals or by a body which is recognised as a legal entity, they cannot be directly held by an unincorporated association. Unless it is a charitable association which has incorporated its governing body [**2.4**], the association should appoint individuals or a corporate body to hold the assets on its behalf. These are called **nominees** (**holding trustees** or **custodian trustees**) or a **nominee company** [**20.4**]. A nominee agreement or trust deed should be prepared to record the terms on which the property is held.

Holding trustees may be the same people as the governing body members, but the roles are different. Where the governing document of a charitable unincorporated association refers to 'trustees', legal advice may be needed to clarify whether it means holding trustees or the members of the governing body as charity trustees.

2.2.4.4 Gifts to non-charitable associations

A gift or grant given to an unincorporated association in effect creates a **trust** [**2.3.1**], with the association's members entrusted to use the money or property for the purposes of the association. Except in very exceptional circumstances, a trust can be created only for identifiable individuals or for charitable purposes [**2.3.5**]. If property or any other significant gift is being given to a non-charitable association, legal advice may be needed to ensure that the terms are worded in a way that makes clear that the purposes for which the gift is given are charitable in law, or that if the purposes are non-charitable, the gift is given 'for the benefit of the members of the association for the time being' or for other identifiable beneficiaries. If the wording is not correct, the donation could be declared invalid.

Re Astor's Settlement Trust [1952] Ch 534

2.2.5 Choosing to be an unincorporated association

An unincorporated association may be an appropriate legal form if:

- the organisation does not expect to own significant property or to employ staff, will have a secure income, and will not undertake risky or financially burdensome activities; and
- it wants to be a membership organisation; and/or
- it wants more privacy than it could get as a company or industrial and provident society (but some of this privacy will not be available if it is charitable).

If it is financially secure and does not intend to have a membership, a trust may be more appropriate [**2.3.10**].

If the organisation will have long-term financial commitments such as hiring staff, or if it owns land or buildings, or if it is in situations of financial risk such as dependence on grant funding, it should consider incorporation [**chapter 3**].

2.3   TRUSTS

2.3.1   What trusts are

Early in the development of English law the courts, particularly the church courts, felt that moral obligations should be recognised even where they were not enshrined in statute law, a contract [**21.1.1**] or a deed [**20.3**]. These courts began to enforce promises under a type of law known as **equity** [**64.2.3**].

Within equity, promises are enforced as a **trust** where money or property of any sort is given by a **settlor** or **donor** to a **trustee**, with the intention that the trustee holds it not as their personal property, but on behalf of a **beneficiary**.

For a trust to be enforced there must be a benefit for a third party. A trust is not created when the intention is merely to benefit the settlor and/or trustee. Nor is a trust generally created if either of them has the right to revoke the intention to benefit the third party, for example if the settlor is entitled to cancel the benefit by diverting it to him or herself. However this rule is subject to many exceptions.

As soon as the property has been given to the trustees it belongs to them, not to the settlor, even if the settlor is a trustee. The trustees own the property (the **legal interest**), but they are required to use it only for the defined beneficiaries or purposes. The beneficiaries have the **beneficial interest** in the property.

2.3.2   Types of trustee

Trustees may be individuals or incorporated bodies, and may have a variety of roles and titles.

Administrative trustees use the trust's assets to carry out the trust's purpose. For example in a private (not charitable) trust set up to pay a child's school fees, the administrative trustees invest the money and use the proceeds to pay the fees.

Charity trustees [**2.3.6.1**] are the administrative trustees for a charitable trust, charitable association or charity established by charter. But under charity law, the term **charity trustee** also refers to the members of the governing body of *any* charity, even if it is set up as a company, industrial and provident society or charitable incorporated organisation.

Holding trustees [**2.2.4.3**, **20.4.4**], often called nominees, simply hold an asset or assets for the administrative trustees, unless they are given specific powers under the document that appoints them. There must always be at least two holding trustees.

A **custodian trustee** [**20.4.2**] is an incorporated body specially authorised to hold assets.

Managing trustee is sometimes used to distinguish administrative or charity trustees, who are responsible for managing the trust, from holding or custodian trustees who simply hold property on behalf of the trust but do not manage it.

A **constructive trustee** is a trustee not through the deliberate creation of a trust, but rather where he or she acquires property and because of the circumstances, is not entitled to retain it. A person who fundraises for any purpose becomes a constructive trustee in respect of the donations received [**48.2.1**].

2.3.3   Trusts established by trust deed or will

A trust comes into being, without any formalities, as soon as money or property is given to a person to be used for an identifiable beneficiary or for a charitable purpose. The term **trust** defines the **relationship between parties**, rather than an organisational form.

However most trusts are formally created under the terms of a will, or through a **trust deed** or **declaration of trust** [**1.3.1**]. Organisations which are formally set up as trusts are sometimes called **strict trusts** or **simple trusts**. The trust deed or declaration needs to be executed, and may need to be stamped by the HM Revenue and Customs stamping office [**1.3.2**].

Where trusts are set up for charitable purposes they are referred to in this book as organisations with the legal form of a trust.

2.3.4 Private and public trusts

A **private trust** is intended to benefit one person or a specific group of private individuals (for example, a trust set up under a will for the benefit of the deceased person's children). A trust intended to benefit the public or a section of the public, rather than identifiable beneficiaries, is a **public trust**. A public trust must in virtually all cases be **charitable** [**4.1**].

2.3.5 Valid trusts

For a public or private trust to be valid, it must be clear that the donor(s) intended to set up a trust (**certainty of intention**), and it must be clear what the trust's property is. A trust cannot be required to accumulate its income, without spending it, for more than the common law **perpetuity period**, which is 21 years after the death of the donor (**rule against excessive accumulations**). A trust which does not meet these requirements is void (invalid).

Perpetuities & Accumulations Act 1964 s.13

Other rules apply in different ways to private and public trusts. For a *private* trust where the gift, the selection of beneficiaries, or the use of the trust funds is conditional on something happening, the event must happen within the **perpetuity period** of 80 years or a lifetime plus 21 years. This **rule against perpetuities** (also known as the rule of inalienability or **rule against perpetual trusts**) does not apply if the gift is given for charitable purposes or is given to one charity on condition that it be given to another charity if a specific event occurs (a **gift over**).

Perpetuities & Accumulations Act 1964 ss.1,3

A *private* trust must have identifiable beneficiaries (referred to as **certainty of objects**). These might be defined by name, by reference to an individual or employer or in any other way, but they must be capable of being identified. A *public* or *charitable* trust cannot be for named individuals.

A *private* trust may have one or any number of beneficiaries. A *public* or *charitable* trust must benefit the public or a section of the public, rather than only a small group [**5.3.2**].

A *public* or *charitable* trust must have stated purposes or objects. These do not have to be precisely defined, so long as it is clear that they are completely charitable as defined by law [**5.2**] or fall into the very small number of objects which are allowed for non-charitable public trusts. A *private* trust needs to have defined beneficiaries, but does not need stated objects.

A trust which does not define identifiable beneficiaries and is set up for a purpose which is not charitable is called a **trust of imperfect obligation** and is nearly always void (invalid). There are a few exceptions, such as trusts to maintain individual tombs or monuments, or to support one or more specific animals ('my beloved dog Fifi'), but these are anomalous. Apart from these, it is not possible to set up a trust without identifiable beneficiaries for non-charitable purposes.

2.3.6 Common confusions about trusts and trustees

The terms **trust** and **trustee** are used in many different ways and can cause great confusion within voluntary organisations. All charities hold their assets **on trust**, in the sense that they have a special duty to apply those assets only for their charitable purposes, but only some charities are set up with the **legal form** of a trust. However, even those which are not set up as trusts may have 'trust' in their name. The fact that something is called 'trust' does not mean it has the legal form of a trust.

2.3.6.1 Trustees under charity law and trust law

For the purposes of **charity law**, members of the governing body of *all* charitable bodies are **charity trustees** and are subject to charity law even if they are actually called committee members, directors, governors or something else.

Charities Act 1993 s.97

Trustees of charitable unincorporated associations, trusts, and bodies established by charter are all subject to relevant aspects of **trust law**, and in particular have statutory duties and powers under the **Trustee Act 2000 [15.6, 58.1.2]**. Governing body members in companies and other incorporated bodies, even if charitable, do not have these powers except in situations where property is held on trust.

2.3.7 Regulation of trusts

A *private* trust does not need to be registered with any regulatory or supervisory body, and so long as the trustees fulfil the terms of their trust, they are not externally accountable to anyone. If they do not fulfil the terms of their trust, the beneficiaries can take legal action against them.

A *charitable* trust must comply with the requirements for charity registration and accountability [**8.1, 8.3**]. The terms of the trust are enforceable not by the beneficiaries but by the Charity Commission, or by the high court in proceedings involving the attorney general or in some cases brought by persons with an interest in the charity [**65.8**].

Rules providing for the appointment of new trustees and some matters relating to the powers of trustees are contained in the **Trustee Acts 1925** and **2000**, the **Trusts of Land and Appointment of Trustees Act 1996** and the **Trustee Delegation Act 1999** [**15.6**]. Investments by trustees are controlled by the governing document and legislation [**58.1.2**].

2.3.8 Advantages of the trust form

Organisations set up as trusts share with unincorporated associations the advantages of simplicity, flexibility and ease of creation and winding up [**2.2.3**].

The **number of trustees** can be small. For private trusts it is possible to have only one trustee, although it is usual to have at least two if the trust property includes land. The Charity Commission usually presses for a minimum of three trustees for charitable trusts.

Trustees are generally appointed by the existing trustees or sometimes by an outside body, rather than being elected. This creates a **self perpetuating governing body**, which may (or may not) be perceived as an advantage.

2.3.9 Disadvantages of the trust form

As in an unincorporated association [**2.2.4.1**], the trustees of a trust are **personally liable** for the trust's debts if it cannot meet them.

Because trustees are usually appointed rather than elected, the trust form is typically **undemocratic**. It is not well suited for a membership organisation, although it can be adapted to have members and give them the right to elect the governing body.

Trust governing documents can include a power of amendment [**7.5.1**]. But if the power is limited or is not included, they cannot not be altered except by an order of the court or, in the case of a charitable trust, an order or scheme of the Charity Commission. Inflexibility can be avoided by including a power of amendment and a wide objects clause [**5.7.1**].

Unlike unincorporated associations, the trustees **can hold land or investments** without having to appoint separate holding trustees, a custodian trustee or a nominee company [**20.4**]. But it is the trustees, rather than the trust itself, who hold the trust's property. If a trustee changes, a new trustee must be appointed to hold the property. To overcome this, property can be held by a corporate body (a custodian trustee or nominee company) or the trustee body can be incorporated and can then hold property as a corporate body [**2.4**].

2.3.10   Choosing the trust form

A trust may be a suitable legal form if:

- the organisation will have very substantial assets or very secure funding and/or will not have long-term financial commitments, so it can with some certainty ensure it will be able to meet all its financial obligations;
- it will not employ staff; and
- it will not have a large membership.

2.4   INCORPORATING THE GOVERNING BODY

Trustee incorporation is a process by which the governing body (the charity trustees) of a charitable unincorporated association or charitable trust can incorporate, without incorporating the organisation as a whole as a company limited by guarantee, industrial and provident society or charitable incorporated organisation. The process of applying to the Charity Commission is explained in CC43 *Incorporation of charity trustees*.   *Charities Act 1993 ss.50-62*

This gives them **legal personality** and **permanent succession** [**3.1.1**], with the right to own property, enter into legal agreements and take legal action in the name of the trustee body as a whole rather than in the name of individuals.

It does not, however, limit the liability of members of the governing body or the organisation. They still have the same responsibilities and individual liabilities as in an unincorporated organisation [**2.2.4**].

Trustee incorporation might be appropriate if the organisation:

- is a registered, exempt or excepted charity [**8.1**];
- owns or expects to own property or investments and/or is involved or expects to be involved in leases or long-term contracts; and
- does not consider that it needs the additional protection it would get by incorporating the charity as a company, industrial and provident society or charitable incorporated organisation.

2.5   CHARITY SCHEMES

Many older charities are now regulated by a **scheme**, made by the court or more commonly by the Charity Commission [**7.5.2**]. Under this procedure the charity is given a new governing document or the old one is varied (changed). The governing body under a scheme has the powers and duties of the type of body it was before the scheme – generally an association or trust.

2.6   FRIENDLY SOCIETIES

Friendly societies developed in the 18th century as mutual aid or self help associations. Under the **Friendly Societies Act 1974**, registration was available to some self help and benevolent organisations. The **Friendly Societies Act 1992** ended registration under the 1974 Act. Since 1 February 1993 only mutual assurance societies have been able to register as friendly societies, and the structure has been changed from unincorporated to incorporated. The structure is no longer available for voluntary organisations, and is not included in this book.

Resources: UNINCORPORATED ORGANISATIONS

See end of **chapter 1**.

Statute law. www.opsi.gov.uk and www.statutelaw.gov.uk.

Much but not all case law. www.bailii.org.

Updates cross-referenced to this book. www.rclh.co.uk.

Chapter 3
INCORPORATED ORGANISATIONS

For sources of further information see end of chapter 1.

3.1   INCORPORATION

Before deciding whether to incorporate, the main points to be aware of are:

- an **incorporated organisation** exists as a legal entity separate from its members, and can own property, enter into contracts and take other legal action in its own right, rather than having to do it in the name of individuals or an incorporated body as an unincorporated organisation must do;

- there are a number of forms of incorporation, but some are not appropriate for voluntary organisations;

- previously most voluntary organisations which chose to incorporate became a **private company limited by guarantee**, with smaller numbers becoming a **community benefit society** (a form of **industrial and provident society**); now an organisation which is going to charge for its goods or services also has the option of becoming a **community interest company** (CIC), and from 2010 a charitable organisation will be able to choose to become a **charitable incorporated organisation** (CIO);

- some bodies become incorporated by **statute** or by **royal charter**;

- in most incorporated organisations the members have **limited liability**, so they are protected from unlimited personal liability if the organisation cannot meet its financial obligations;

- members of the governing body (company or IPS directors or CIO trustees) are generally protected by limited liability if the organisation cannot meet its financial obligations, but may in some situations be made personally liable;

- incorporation requires a certain amount of paperwork, and the people responsible for managing may be fined if the organisation does not comply with the requirements;

- a form of incorporation for trustees of charitable associations and trusts allows them to act as a legal entity, but without giving limited liability [**2.4**].

For how to set up an incorporated organisation see **1.4-1.7**.

3.1.1 Advantages of incorporation

For most organisations, the overriding advantage of incorporation is the limited liability it provides to the members of the organisation and its governing body. But there are other advantages as well.

3.1.1.1 Legal personality

When an organisation incorporates, it takes on **legal personality** (legal personhood) as a **corporate body** or **body corporate**. Unlike an unincorporated organisation it can, in its own right, enter into contracts, rent or own property, take legal action and be sued. It is considered to be a **legal person**, and within the bounds of common sense can do anything a human person can do. So when documents refer to **people** or **individuals** they always mean only human persons, whereas **persons** generally means corporate bodies as well as individuals.

Because an incorporated organisation can enter into legal agreements in its own right, there is no need to appoint holding trustees, custodian trustees or a nominee company [**20.4**] to hold its land, buildings or investments.

3.1.1.2 Limited liability

Incorporation nearly always gives **limited liability** to members of the organisation and its governing body. Because an incorporated organisation enters into contracts in its own right, it is liable for its own debts. If it does not or cannot pay its bills, the people to whom it owes money (its creditors) take legal action against the organisation. Very occasionally they may be able to take action against the members of its governing body, but not against the members of the organisation.

If an incorporated organisation cannot meet its financial obligations, it goes into insolvent liquidation [**24.5**], and its assets are sold and distributed among its creditors. The organisation is insolvent, but the members of the organisation and in almost all cases the members of its governing body are protected from any personal liability for its debts.

3.1.1.3 Permanent succession

An incorporated organisation has **permanent succession**, so there is no need to transfer contracts, leases or other legal agreements to new signatories whenever the persons who signed them cease to hold their position in the organisation.

3.1.1.4 Permanence

An incorporated organisation is **permanent**. Unlike an unincorporated association which may simply fade away if its members cease to meet, it continues to exist until it is formally dissolved [**24.1.4**] or struck off [**24.4**]. This is generally an advantage, but can be a disadvantage if the final governing body members forget it still exists and fail to comply with their ongoing duties under company, IPS or CIO law.

3.1.2 Disadvantages of incorporation

3.1.2.1 Cost

Incorporation is likely to involve **legal costs**, unless the people involved in setting up the organisation can do it themselves, get help from a council for voluntary service or similar organisation, or get *pro bono* help [**64.8.4**]. As well as setting-up costs, **ongoing costs** such as audits, if required, may be more expensive than for an unincorporated organisation.

For companies there is a registration fee (£20 as at 1/8/09) and an annual filing fee (£30 as at 1/8/09), with lower fees for filing electronically. If the company is a community interest company, there is an additional £15 registration fee and an additional £15 annual filing fee (both as at 1/8/09).

For industrial and provident societies the registration fee is higher (£40 as at 1/8/09 if approved model rules are used; £120 to £950 if model rules are used with amendments or model rules are not used). The annual fee (as at 1/8/09) ranges from £55 to £425, depending on the IPS's total assets.

At the time of writing (mid 2009) it was intended that there would be no fee to register a charitable incorporated organisation (CIO).

3.1.2.2   External accountability

Incorporation also means **accountability**: for companies to the registrar of companies and for community interest companies to the CIC regulator as well, and for industrial and provident societies to the Financial Services Authority.

These regulatory bodies must make specified information available to the public. Non-charities, in particular, may consider it a disadvantage to have to make public details of their financial position and names of their governing body members. Charities have to do this anyway, regardless of whether they are incorporated.

3.1.2.3   Paperwork

Primarily because of limited liability and public accountability, incorporation involves **detailed paperwork** [**chapter 18**] and compliance with the relevant legislation. An organisation needs to have the capacity to keep various **registers** (lists) up to date, notify the registration body every time certain changes are made, and send in annual accounts and returns. Failure could lead to the members of the governing body, and in some cases the company secretary and senior managers, being fined.

3.1.2.4   Public access to records

Information about a company's directors and (if it has one) secretary, including for a community interest company, is publicly available at Companies House and via its website [**18.5.4**, **18.5.6**]. In addition a company's registers of directors and secretaries must be open to members of the public [**18.5.4**], and its register of company members must be open to any member of the public who explains why they want it [**18.5.2**]. The company can apply to the court not to provide access to the register of members if they do not believe the reason is valid.

Until 30 September 2009, directors' residential addresses had to be available at Companies House and the company's registered office, unless the director had been given consent to use a **service address** (an address at which legal documents may be served). From 1 October 2009 any company director may use a service address [**18.5.5**] as the address that will be made public.

Access rules for industrial and provident societies are less intrusive [**18.6.1**, **18.6.2**] than for companies.

For charitable incorporated organisations, trustees' names will generally be available via the Charity Commission. At the time of writing (mid 2009) it had not been decided whether other information about them or about the CIO's members would have to be made public [**18.7**].

3.1.2.5   Limitations on limited liability

The ordinary members of an incorporated body are protected from personal liability for its debts. But incorporation does not protect governing body members from all liability. They may be held **personally liable** if, for example:

- they fail to comply with certain **statutory duties** [**15.3**];
- they allow the organisation to continue operating when it is, or is going to become, **insolvent** [**24.2.4**];
- they act **outside their powers**;
- they **fall below the required standard** in respect of their duties;
- if the organisation is charitable, they are **in breach of their duties as charity trustees** [**15.6**].

The protection of limited liability is extensive, but it is not absolute. For more about the duties and potential liabilities of governing body members, see **chapters 15** and **22.**

3.1.2.6 Permanent endowment

Permanent endowment [58.8.1] is money given to a charitable organisation on condition that it not be spent, or property given on condition that it not be disposed of (or if it is disposed of, the proceeds cannot be spent).

Trust law generally prevents permanent endowment held by a charitable unincorporated association or trust from being disposed of. But assets subject to these conditions and held by a charitable company or industrial and provident society or by a charitable incorporated organisation are not protected in the same way. In the case of a company, IPS or CIO liquidation, the assets would be available for sale to meet the organisation's liabilities [24.5-24.7].

For this reason a charitable trust or unincorporated association which holds permanent endowment and becomes incorporated, or an incorporated body which receives permanent endowment, will generally be required to agree with the Charity Commission **special trust** arrangements for holding it. In relation to such arrangements the governing body of the incorporated organisation will be trustees for the purposes of the **Trustee Act 2000 [58.1]**.

3.1.2.7 Winding up

Because an incorporated organisation is permanent, it must go through a formal process to bring it to an end [24.4-24.7]. It cannot simply fade away or pass a resolution to dissolve itself, as unincorporated associations often do. Failure to wind up an incorporated body can lead to it being struck off the register of companies [24.4.2] and/or unexpected liabilities for governing body members well into the future.

3.1.3 Choosing to incorporate

It is sensible to consider incorporation if an organisation:

- employs or expects to employ staff;
- owns or expects to own land, buildings, investments or other substantial assets;
- is or expects to be involved in activities, leases or contracts where there is financial risk; and/or
- is finding it difficult to recruit governing body members because they want the protection from personal liability that comes with incorporation.

Incorporation may not be suitable if an organisation:

- does not employ staff, own property or investments, or have long-term leases or contracts;
- does not expect to last a long time;
- does not have the administrative capacity (or desire) to comply with paperwork requirements and external rules about how it operates (although if it is charitable, it will have many of these even if it is unincorporated);
- does not want its details of members and governing body to be public;
- is not a charity, and does not want to make its accounts publicly available; or
- does not want to put onto the members of its governing body the extra responsibilities and liabilities involved with incorporation. But without incorporation, they will have all the responsibilities and risks which arise from *not* being incorporated.

3.1.4 Profit, not for profit and incorporation

The phrases **not for profit, non-profit** or **non-profit-making** may be used to describe charities, some cooperatives and community interest companies, social or community enterprises and sometimes even some organisations that are normal businesses. But these phrases have no legal meaning.

Not for profit, **non-profit**, or **non-profit-making** generally imply that the governing document prevents or restricts distribution of profit or surplus to members of the organisation, and prevents or restricts payments or benefits to members of the governing body – although in some cases payments may be allowed. In addition, the governing document is likely to include restrictions on the use of assets on dissolution.

For profit generally means operating with the explicit purpose of making money for the organisation's owners (including shareholders, in a company limited by shares), members and/or directors.

For profit, not for profit and similar terms do not define legal structures, but may affect the structure chosen by an organisation. A for profit body is likely to have the structure of **partnership** [**11.3**], **limited liability partnership** [**3.6**], company limited by shares [**3.3.1.3**] or cooperative industrial and provident society [**3.5.1**]. A not for profit organisation will generally be an unincorporated association or trust [**2.2**, **2.3**], charitable incorporated organisation [**3.2**], company limited by guarantee [**3.3.1.4**] or community benefit IPS [**3.5.2**].

A community interest company [**3.4**] or prescribed community benefit society [**3.5.2.1**] operates in the for profit world, but with not for profit restrictions on the use of its profits and assets.

3.1.4.1 Distribution of profit and assets

For charities and community interest companies, constitutional restrictions on the distribution of profits and assets are externally enforced by the Charity Commission, CIC regulator, regulators for specific types of charities such as the Homes and Communities Agency for registered social landlords, and ultimately by the courts. Such enforceable **non-distribution provisions** are sometimes called an **asset lock**, because profits and other assets are 'locked into' being used for the organisation's purposes.

Non-charitable community benefit IPSs can amend their rules to put in an asset lock, called a **restriction on use**, that cannot be altered or removed. A society which does this becomes a **prescribed community benefit society** [**3.5.2.1**]. Compliance is enforced by the Financial Services Authority.

Co-operatives & Community Benefit Societies Act 2003 s.1

For other non-charitable organisations, there is no external regulator to prevent distribution of profit or assets. The courts can enforce constitutional restrictions if a claim is brought, but may not be able to stop the organisation's members from amending the governing document to remove or change the non-distribution provisions.

3.1.5 Social enterprise and incorporation

A social or community enterprise [**1.1.2**] may use almost any type of structure, either unincorporated or incorporated. Most are likely to register as a community interest company (CIC) [**3.4**], ordinary (non-CIC) company limited by guarantee or company limited by shares [**3.3**], community benefit industrial and provident society [**3.5.2**] or prescribed community benefit society [**3.5.2.1**].

3.1.6 Incorporation without limited liability

Trustee incorporation [**2.4**] enables the governing body of a charitable trust or charitable association to incorporate itself. This gives the trustee body legal personality and enables it to enter legal agreements, own property or take legal action as a corporate body, but does not give the trustees limited liability.

3.2 CHARITABLE INCORPORATED ORGANISATIONS

The Charities Act 2006 created a new form of incorporated organisation, the **charitable incorporated organisation** (CIO). At the time of writing (mid 2009), the CIO form was expected to become available in April 2010.

Charities Act 1993 ss.69A-69Q, sch.5B, to be inserted by Charities Act 2006 sch.7 [expected April 2010]

Many of a CIO's key aspects are like those of a company limited by guarantee [**3.3.1.4**]: it is incorporated, it must have a principal office, it must have at least one member, and members may be liable to contribute up to a maximum amount on winding up.

But unlike a company limited by guarantee the CIO structure can be used only by an organisation which is legally charitable, a CIO is registered only with the Charity Commission rather than with Companies House as well, and there is provision for the members not to be liable to contribute anything on winding up.

3.2.1 Regulation of CIOs

CIOs are regulated by the Charity Commission, which has considerable powers to control their activities. These include, for example, that an amendment to a CIO's constitution does not take effect until the change has been registered with the Commission [**7.5.4**], and that the Commission may refuse an application for two CIOs to amalgamate if their purposes, rules governing application of property on dissolution, and member or trustee benefits are not substantially the same [**11.5.4**].

3.2.2 Advantages of the CIO structure

CIOs have all the advantages of incorporation [**3.1.1**], but without the burdens of dual registration with both the Commission and Companies House and having to comply with two sets of law. Conversion from a charitable company to a CIO is relatively straightforward [**10.3.1**].

At the time of writing (mid 2009), CIO trustees' duties set out in legislation were less comprehensive than those set out in company legislation [**15.3, 15.5**]. However, taken together with other statutory and non-statutory charity trustee duties, the overall package of duties of CIO trustees will not be substantially different from those of directors of a charitable company limited by guarantee.

Governing body members of companies and industrial and provident societies must exercise their powers in good faith in a manner most likely to further the purposes of the organisation [**15.3.2, 15.4**], but there is no statutory obligation on the ordinary members of a company or IPS to do so. In a CIO, this requirement applies not only to governing body members, but also to ordinary members. This may be seen as an advantage, if members can actually be made to observe the duty.   *Charities Act 1993 sch.5B para.9, to be inserted by Charities Act 2006 sch.7 [expected April 2010]*

CIO registration requirements will ensure that it is set up with an effective and detailed **constitution** which will generally be based on a model constitution.

Annual returns, accounts and reports will only have to be submitted to **one regulator** rather than two, and will only have to comply with one set of requirements. But for most CIOs the administrative burden will only be slightly lower than for a charitable company.

CIO legislation allows a **simple method of merger** similar to that for industrial and provident societies [**11.5.6**], but not available to companies. But this procedure only allows for mergers of CIOs. At the time of writing it was unclear how an unincorporated association, company limited by guarantee or IPS that wants to merge with a CIO would do so.

3.2.3 Disadvantages of the CIO structure

The idea of a CIO has been discussed and carefully considered for a long period, but any legislation creating an entirely new legal form may produce unexpected results. For an established charity of a reasonable size already incorporated as a company or industrial and provident society, it is not at all clear whether the process of internal discussion, decision making, adoption of a new governing document and the process of applying for conversion will be worth the modest potential advantages. However an unincorporated organisation considering incorporation, or a new organisation setting up from scratch and wanting to incorporate, may find the CIO's advantages over a charitable company more attractive.

Company registration takes only a few days and can be done in one day [**1.5.6**]; the company can then start operating even if charity registration takes several weeks or months. If a CIO is setting up from scratch (rather than converting from an existing unincorporated organisation) it will not be able to operate until it is registered by the Charity Commission. If registration is delayed this could leave the organisation unable to operate.

At the time of writing (mid 2009) the simplified administrative procedures brought in by the **Companies Act 2006** had not been fully implemented, and the detailed procedures for the CIO had not been confirmed. So it remained unclear whether a CIO will be administratively more straightforward than a charitable company, or *vice versa*, or whether there will not be much difference.

For example, written resolutions [**7.5.4**] to amend a CIO's constitution require agreement by 100% of the CIO's members, while written resolutions to amend a company's articles require only 75% of the vote (not even 75% of all the members). This is an example of a requirement that could make the CIO unattractive when compared with a charitable company. On the other hand companies must allow proxy voting [**19.8.3**], but at the time of writing it was not expected that CIOs would have to – so this could make the CIO more attractive.

3.2.4 Choosing the CIO structure

When the CIO structure becomes available, it may be suitable if:

- the organisation has decided to incorporate [**3.1.3**];
- the organisation is legally charitable [**4.1**];
- it does not want to deal with two regulators (the Charity Commission and Companies House) and two sets of administrative requirements;
- it does not mind the Commission having greater control of constitutional changes than it would for a charitable company;
- it has weighed up the relative advantages and disadvantages of the charitable company and CIO structures;
- the people involved in setting up or converting the organisation do not mind using a structure with no previous track record.

3.3 COMPANIES

A company is a membership organisation in which the **company members** generally elect **directors** as the governing body. Although the term is usually associated with businesses, the company structure also has a long history of being used effectively by charities and other not for profit organisations.

3.3.1 Types of company

The members of a company may have limited or in some cases unlimited liability. A voluntary organisation which incorporates as a company will become a **limited liability company**. A limited liability company can be **public** or **private**.

3.3.1.1 Public limited companies

A **public limited company** must have share capital of at least £50,000 or the prescribed euro equivalent, and states as part of its company registration process that it is a public limited company. It is identified by the words 'public limited company', the initials 'plc', or the Welsh equivalent in its name. A plc can raise money by selling shares publicly on a stock exchange, and the shareholders become company members. Plc's operating in two or more EU member states can form a **European company**, also known as a *societas europeas* or **SE**.

Members (shareholders) may be individuals or corporate bodies. They provide the company's working capital (**share capital**), and generally hope to make money for themselves through **dividends** (a proportion of profits paid to shareholders).

Shares may generally be sold or transferred. Normally each share carries one vote in the company, so members with multiple shares are entitled to multiple votes.

If the company becomes insolvent, members' personal liability is limited to the amount, if any, they still owe on their shares.

3.3.1.2 Private limited companies

If a company is not public, it is a **private limited company** (usually identified by 'limited', 'ltd' or the Welsh equivalent). A private limited company may be **limited by shares** or **limited by guarantee**.

3.3.1.3 Private companies limited by shares

Like a public limited company [**3.3.1.1**] a **private company limited by shares** (sometimes abbreviated as CLS) has members (**shareholders**) who each purchase at least one share in the company. Private companies limited by shares can invite people to invest in them through buying shares, subject to rules set out in the **Financial Services and Markets Act 2000**. But unlike plc's they cannot raise money by selling their shares on a stock exchange.

3.3.1.4 Company limited by guarantee

A **company limited by guarantee** (sometimes abbreviated as CLG) does not issue shares. Instead the members promise (guarantee) to contribute a sum, usually between £1 and £10, if the company becomes insolvent and is wound up. Their personal liability to the company is limited to this amount [**12.4.1**].

The vast majority of voluntary organisations which incorporate become private companies limited by guarantee and not having a share capital. A few companies limited by guarantee registered before 1980 have a share capital.

A voluntary organisation which incorporates as a private limited company can choose not to use 'limited' or 'ltd' as part of its name [**6.4.5**].

3.3.1.5 Community interest company

A **community interest company** (CIC) is a company limited by guarantee or company limited by shares whose governing document requires it to comply with a **community interest test** and certain other requirements [**3.4**]. CICs must comply with all relevant company law, plus additional rules relating to CICs.

3.3.2 Regulation of companies

Companies are regulated by a variety of Acts, of which the most important are the **Companies Acts 1985, 1989** and **2006, Company Directors Disqualification Act 1986, Insolvency Act 1986, Enterprise Act 2002** and **Companies (Audit, Investigations and Community Enterprise) Act 2004**. Most (but not all) of the Companies Acts 1985 and 1989 and some of the other legislation was replaced by the **Companies Act 2006**.

As well as statutes there are many statutory instruments (regulations containing the detailed rules for implementing the statutes) and a substantial body of case law. Members of the governing body, as directors of the company, are responsible for ensuring the requirements of company law are met.

Information about CICs is provided by the CIC regulator [see end of **chapter 1**]. Questions about general company law can sometimes be answered by Companies House [see end of **chapter 1**] or the Insolvency Service [see end of **chapter 24**] but they will often advise the enquirer to consult a legal advisor. Many solicitors are reasonably well versed in company law, but may not be aware of differences in the treatment of companies limited by guarantee or community interest companies. It is generally sensible to consult a legal advisor who is a voluntary sector or CIC specialist [see **64.8.4** for how to find a specialist advisor].

If asked to do so by the company itself or by at least 20% of the company's members, the secretary of state for business, innovation and skills can appoint inspectors to investigate a company's affairs. The secretary of state can also require anyone involved in a company to provide and explain any documents.

Companies Act 1985 ss.431-437

3.3.3   Advantages of the company structure

For the main advantages and disadvantages of incorporation, see **3.1.1** and **3.1.2**. Specific advantages of the company structure are that it is flexible and can be adapted for any size and type of voluntary organisation, and that it is widely understood by solicitors and funders.

A company can be formed very rapidly, often within a few hours [**1.5.6**].

The company structure is **intrinsically democratic**, giving company members the right to elect and remove directors. But there is nothing to stop an organisation from adapting it in an undemocratic way, for example having only three company members who keep electing themselves as directors, or having directors who under the articles of association serve for life or until they resign.

The company structure is **suitable for any size** of organisation. A private company only needs to have one member and one director, who can be the same person. For a charitable company, however, the Charity Commission generally presses for a minimum of three directors.

A company normally has a detailed governing document (the memorandum and articles of association, or for companies formed after 1 October 2009 the articles of association), which can be an advantage in dealing with the problematic situations which organisations get themselves into. Even where there is nothing in the governing document, company law sets out many key procedures and requirements or a model set of articles is deemed to apply. *Companies Act 2006 s.20; Companies (Model Articles) Regulations 2008 [SI 2008/3229]*

There is a **statutory right to amend** the articles and the objects clause by special resolution, although some amendments of a charitable company's governing document require prior consent from the Charity Commission [**7.5.3**].

3.3.4   Disadvantages of the company structure

As indicated above [**3.1.2**], the main disadvantages of becoming a company are the cost, the paperwork, and the risk of fines for the company or potential personal liability for directors if the paperwork is not dealt with on time or for not complying with other aspects of company legislation.

The company's officers (its directors, the company secretary if there is one and in some cases senior management) could, for example, each be fined for failure to circulate a resolution properly submitted by members, failure to submit the annual accounts to Companies House within the required period, or any other of the dozens of criminal offences within company law. But companies and their officers are generally prosecuted for breach of company law only if a default has been deliberate and persistent, so the risk of legal action and the resultant fines or imprisonment is very low.

Perhaps more significantly, failure to comply with company law can result in the company being removed from (struck off) the register of companies, thus ending the limited liability of the members and directors. A company which has been struck off can be reinstated, but this requires application to the court and is an expensive procedure.

For some organisations, public access to the registers of members and directors [**18.5.2**, **18.5.4**] may be a disadvantage.

Companies need to comply with detailed company regulations concerning their annual accounts. All charities with annual income over £25,000 need to comply with similar requirements, so incorporation does not make a significant difference for them. But for non-charitable unincorporated associations, incorporation brings the obligation to prepare accounts according to company law. [For more about accounting see **chapter 54**.]

Other disadvantages may arise from misunderstandings about what it means to be a company. Members or supporters may not understand that 'company' is simply a legal structure and can be used for not for profit as well as well as profit-making bodies. Or people who would happily 'just be a committee member' might not like the idea of being a company director, even though they are almost certainly more at risk on the governing body of an unincorporated organisation.

3.3.5 Choosing the company limited by guarantee structure

The company limited by guarantee structure is suitable if:

- the organisation has decided to incorporate [**3.1.3**];
- it wants a flexible structure suitable for any size of organisation;
- the people involved are prepared to ensure that the administrative responsibilities are dealt with;
- the people involved do not mind the public generally having access to the registers of members and directors; and
- the CIO and industrial and provident society structures are not suitable, or are suitable but have been rejected [**3.2.4**, **3.5.6**].

3.3.6 Choosing the company limited by shares structure

The vast majority of businesses which incorporate becomes companies limited by shares. A community interest company (CIC) should register as a company limited by shares if it intends to raise capital by issuing shares.

The company limited by shares structure is unlikely to be suitable for charities or other voluntary organisations, but **trading companies** or **trading subsidiaries** set up by charities and other organisations [**51.3.2**] are usually incorporated as private companies limited by shares. The parent organisation or, in the case of an unincorporated organisation, a person or persons appointed by the parent organisation, generally own all the shares.

A charity or other voluntary organisation which wants to set up a company limited by shares must get specialist legal advice. In particular, the relationship between a charity and a company limited by shares must be very carefully worked out to ensure the affairs and accounts of the two bodies are kept completely separate, the charity's assets are not used for non-charitable purposes, and the tax and VAT arrangements are appropriate [**chapter 51**].

Most company law which applies to companies limited by guarantee also applies to private companies limited by shares. But there are some significant differences, and share companies must comply with many additional requirements which are not covered in this book.

3.4 COMMUNITY INTEREST COMPANIES

The company limited by guarantee structure was perceived as having a number of problems when used for non-charitable organisations, particularly the risk that the company members would amend the governing document to allow profits or assets to be used for private gain, rather than for social or community purposes. To overcome these problems, the **community interest company** structure became available in 2005 as a non-charitable structure for social enterprises and not for profit organisations.

As companies, CICs have limited liability and are subject to company law, but with a **community interest test** [**3.4.1**], **asset lock** [**3.1.4.1**] and caps on dividends and interest they can pay [**3.4.3**], to ensure the capital and income are used in the interests of the community. CICs cannot be charitable – even if their objects are wholly charitable – so they lack many of the advantages of charitable status, but are subject to lighter touch regulation than charities.

Companies (Audit, Investigations & Community Enterprise) Act 2004 ss.26,30,31

A CIC must be in the form of a company limited by shares or company limited by guarantee [**3.3.1**]. As at 31 March 2009 74% of CICs were registered as companies limited by guarantee and 26% were limited by shares.

New companies that wish to become CICs apply to the registrar of companies in the normal way [**1.5.5**] but must submit additional information [**1.6**] and be approved by the CIC regulator before the company is incorporated. Existing non-charitable companies can convert into CICs by applying to the CIC regulator [**10.3.2**]. It is also possible to convert an industrial and provident society or a charitable company into a CIC [**10.5.2**, **10.3.3**].

If the CIC structure proves to be unsuitable any CIC can convert to an industrial and provident society, and a CIC with charitable objects can convert to a charitable company or charitable incorporated organisation [**10.4**]. It is not possible to convert from a CIC to an unregulated company free of restrictions such as the asset lock, dividend cap and interest cap [**3.4.3**].

3.4.1 Community interest test

To be approved for registration, a CIC must be able to show that its objects are for a community interest purpose, and all of its activities are going to be carried out for the benefit of the community or a section of it.

This **community interest test** is satisfied if a reasonable person might consider that such activities are being carried on for the benefit of the community.

Companies (Audit, Investigations & Community Enterprise) Act 2004 s.35

Political activities, defined as seeking to change the law or policies of government or public bodies or support for political parties, are not treated as being carried on for the benefit of the community unless these activities can reasonably be regarded as incidental to other activities which are for the benefit of the community.

Community Interest Company Regulations 2005 [SI 2005/1788] reg.3

'Section of the community' is defined as any group of individuals who share a common characteristic which distinguishes them from other members of the community, and where a reasonable person would consider that they constitute a section of the community. Activities which benefit *only* the members of a particular body, rather than the wider community, or which benefit only employees of a particular employer will not pass the community interest test.

CIC Regs 2005 regs.4,5, amended by Community Interest Company (Amendment) Regulations 2009 [SI 2009/1942] reg.4

3.4.2 Regulation of CICs

CICs have to comply with all the requirements of company law. In addition they are regulated by the CIC regulator, whose powers include approving any change to the objects other than to convert to a charity; intervening where the remuneration paid to directors amounts to a breach of the directors' duties or where there is misconduct, mismanagement or misuse of the company's property; removing or appointing a director; and investigating the CIC's affairs, requiring an audit, or ordering the transfer of property or shares. There is a right of appeal.

Community Interest Company Regulations 2005 [SI 2005/1788] regs.13,16; Companies (Audit, Investigations & Community Enterprise) Act 2004 ss.42-49

3.4.3 Advantages of the CIC structure

CICs have all the advantages of incorporation [**3.1.1**].

Model governing documents are available from the CIC regulator. Provided the community interest test is satisfied registration is straightforward, as is conversion from an existing non-charitable company. Conversion from a charitable company may be less straightforward [**10.3.3**].

If the CIC is a company limited by shares, it can issue shares to raise capital to support its activities. Strict rules govern share issues by all companies [**59.6**], and the dividends that can be paid by a CIC are subject to a **dividend cap** limiting how much can be distributed.

Community Interest Company Regulations 2005 [SI 2005/1788] regs.17-20,22

CICs can raise loans and debentures (a form of loan secured on the CIC's assets), but the level of interest on loans and debentures, where it is related to the performance of the company, is subject to an **interest cap**.

CIC Regs 2005 regs.21,22

Members of a CIC's governing body may be paid, but such payments must be reasonable and must not violate the community interest test or the asset lock principles [**16.3**]. There is no statutory definition of what is reasonable, and any CIC which wants to pay its directors should seek advice from the CIC regulator.

CICs are subject to lighter touch regulation than a charitable company. But because CICs, like charities, are regulated and are subject to an asset lock, they have reputational and public trust advantages over unregulated organisations which claim to be acting for the public benefit.

3.4.4   Disadvantages of the CIC structure

CIC registration is slower than for a non-CIC company, as the CIC regulator has to be satisfied before Companies House will register the CIC.

CICs have none of the tax advantages of being a charity, so CICs are subject to corporation tax on their profits and capital gains [**56.2**], are not eligible for reliefs from stamp duty on the transfer of investments [**58.7.2**] or stamp duty land tax on the transfer of land [**61.10.1**], cannot benefit from gift aid and other forms of tax-effective giving [**chapter 50**], and bequests to CICs are not exempt from inheritance tax [**50.6**].

Some rating authorities may be willing to grant discretionary relief from non-domestic rates to some CICs, but CICs are not eligible for mandatory 80% rate relief as charities are [**63.2.3**].

Some funders, in particular charitable funders, may not be able to fund CICs.

The dividend cap and interest cap raise complex issues.

CICs are more lightly regulated than charities, but they do have to file accounts complying with company law as well as a CIC report demonstrating the CIC's community benefit, and have to comply with other company and CIC regulations and the requirements of the regulator.

There may be reputational advantages to CICs, but it is likely to be some time before the structure and the protections inherent in it are widely understood.

3.4.5   Choosing the CIC structure

A CIC may be suitable if:

- the people involved want to make it clear to all that the organisation will be working for the benefit of the community rather than for private gain;
- they want to be sure that if the organisation winds up, the remaining assets will be preserved for community benefit rather than be at risk of being distributed to members or used for other purposes outside the original intention;
- the organisation is not eligible for charitable status, or is eligible but the advantages such as tax relief do not outweigh the advantages of being a CIC;
- the people involved want, or may in future want, to pay governing body members and are willing for the amount to be limited to what is 'reasonable'; and/or
- the organisation wants, or may in future want, to raise money by issuing shares, and will not be disadvantaged by the dividend cap.

3.5   INDUSTRIAL AND PROVIDENT SOCIETIES

At the time of writing (mid 2009), the government had proposed renaming industrial and provident societies as **cooperatives** and **community benefit societies** [**3.5**]. In this book we still refer to IPSs. IPS members agree to purchase one or more shares, and their liability is limited to the amount unpaid on the purchase of the shares.

IPSs are much less common than companies. Unlike the company structure, which is available to virtually any sort of organisation, the IPS structure is available only to *bona fide* cooperative societies, and to voluntary organisations carrying on an industry, trade or business for the benefit of the community.

Industrial & Provident Societies Act 1965 s.1(1),(2)

3.5.1   Cooperatives

A *bona fide* (genuine) **cooperative**:

- carries on a business or trade for the mutual benefit of its members;
- is democratically run by its members, with each member having one vote at general meetings; and
- has **rules** which reflect the principles agreed in 1966 by the International Co-operative Alliance Commission on Cooperative Principles.

Workers' co-ops and consumer co-ops allow for the profits of the business to be distributed to the members. Other co-ops are set up on a not for profit basis, which means that profits cannot be distributed, but must be used solely for the objects of the co-op. An example is a housing co-op where any profit or surplus from the rents must be used to improve or increase the housing. This type of co-op may be, on paper, virtually indistinguishable from a charitable housing association. But it does not have charitable status, because it provides housing only to its members rather than 'for the benefit of the public' [**5.3.2**].

A co-op is not obliged to register as an IPS. Depending on the sort of co-op it is, it may be unincorporated as a partnership or association, or may incorporate as a company limited by shares or by guarantee, community interest company or limited liability partnership [**3.6**].

Since August 2006, cooperatives operating in two or more EU member states can register as a **European cooperative society** (**SCE**).

European Cooperative Society Regulations 2006 [SI 2006/2078]

This book does not cover cooperatives. For more information contact the Financial Services Authority or Co-operatives UK [see end of **chapter 1**].

3.5.2 Community benefit societies

If an organisation is not a genuine cooperative, it can register as an industrial and provident society only if:

- it is carrying on some sort of industry, trade or business which is in the interests of the community at large;
- it will benefit people other than, or in addition to, its own members;
- all profits made from the business will be applied solely for the benefit of the community, with none distributed as profits or dividends to members or anyone else; and
- there are convincing special reasons why it should be registered as an IPS rather than a company limited by guarantee.

There is no statutory definition of 'special reasons' but such reasons could include that the organisation wants to operate on the basis of one member one vote; or that it is part of a group structure of IPSs.

These organisations are called **community benefit societies**, sometimes shortened to **bencoms**. If the organisation is being paid for its services or activities, it is likely to be considered to be carrying on a trade or business and will be eligible for registration as a community benefit society if it meets the other criteria. Payments might come, for example, as rents, fees or admission charges, or as payments by customers or under a contract or service agreement, or as membership subscriptions and other charges paid by members of a social or recreational club.

The meaning of 'business' is not interpreted strictly when community benefit societies are registered, and it may be possible to register community organisations which are not trading in a conventional sense. The Financial Services Authority or Co-operatives UK [see end of **chapter 1**] or a specialist solicitor can advise.

3.5.2.1 Prescribed community benefit societies

Non-charitable community benefit societies can pass a special resolution to amend their rules, creating an **asset lock** [**3.1.4.1**] so assets cannot be distributed to members but must be used in perpetuity for the benefit of the community. This creates within IPS law a **prescribed community benefit society**, a structure equivalent to a community interest company [**3.4**].

Co-operatives & Community Benefit Societies Act 2003 s.1; Community Benefit Societies (Restriction on Use of Assets) Regulations 2006 [SI 2006/264]

These provisions do not apply to charitable community benefit societies and registered social landlords, because they are already subject to such restrictions.

3.5.2.2 Charitable community benefit societies

Under the **Charities Act 1993**, industrial and provident societies set up for charitable purposes were exempt charities [**8.1.2**], unable to register with the

Charity Commission and outside the Commission's jurisdiction. But under provisions of the **Charities Act 2006**, expected at the time of writing (mid 2009) to come into effect in 2010, most IPSs set up exclusively for charitable purposes [**5.2**] and operating for the benefit of the public will come within the Charity Commission's jurisdiction, and those with annual income over £100,000 in their last financial year will have to register with the Commission. The threshold will be reviewed in 2011 and may be reduced.

Most charitable IPSs which are not required under the **Charities Act 2006** to register with the Commission will become excepted charities, under the jurisdiction of the Commission but not required to register. Others, in particular registered social landlords, will remain exempt. They are eligible for the tax benefits available to charities [**4.2.1**] by applying to HM Revenue and Customs for recognition as a charity. Most of the provisions of the Charities Acts do not apply to exempt charities but some do.

It is unlawful for an exempt IPS, even if it is recognised as charitable by HMRC, to say it is a registered charity. It can, however, say 'a charity exempt from registration' or similar wording and/or use its HMRC charity reference number.

3.5.3 Regulation of IPSs

IPSs register with Mutual Societies Registration in the Financial Services Authority, under the **Industrial and Provident Societies Act 1965**. For the registration process, see **1.7**. The FSA has a supervisory responsibility for IPSs, and can appoint an inspector to investigate a society's affairs.

3.5.4 Advantages of the IPS structure

IPSs have all the advantages of incorporation [**3.1.1**].

The legislative requirements are less detailed, intrusive and cumbersome than for companies, and the risk of prosecution for non-compliance is low.

Members of the society and persons with an interest in its funds have a right to see its register of members, but the register is not open to the public in general as it is for a company.

For a larger membership organisation costs can be lower than for companies, as full accounts do not have to be sent to every member but can instead be advertised or displayed at the society's premises. But company law allows the accounts to displayed on the company's website rather than being posted to all members [**18.3.6**], so this may balance the IPS advantage.

IPSs can use a straightforward merger process called transfer of engagements [**11.5.6**] which is not available to companies.

The use of model rules produced by promoting bodies [**1.7.1**] could eliminate the need to write a governing document, and reduces the registration fee.

3.5.5 Disadvantages of the IPS structure

3.5.5.1 Unfamiliarity

The industrial and provident society structure remains unfamiliar and not well understood, and it is surprisingly difficult to get detailed information about the requirements even from the registration body, the Financial Services Authority. Non-specialist legal advisors are unlikely to know anything about IPSs.

It can be difficult to explain to funders that an exempt IPS has charitable status even though it is not registered with the Charity Commission, and this may become more difficult as many but not all formerly exempt charities are required to register with the Commission.

3.5.5.2 Governance structure

IPSs must generally be democratic, and any constitutional provision which is not democratic – such as places on the governing body which are filled by outside bodies rather than being elected by the IPS's members – may be challenged during the registration process.

3.5.5.3 Slower registration

The registration process for IPSs is slower and more expensive than for companies, and the governing document will be scrutinised before registration. After registration, however, the requirements are generally less strict.

If model rules are used the process is quicker and cheaper (though still slower and more expensive than registration as a company) if the model rules are used *exactly* as they are. Any deviation increases the registration fee and delay.

It can be difficult to convince HM Revenue and Customs that a charitable IPS is indeed charitable, and there can be problems in getting the tax benefits to which the society should be entitled.

3.5.5.4 Cost

The cost of registration and the annual fee are substantially higher than for a company [**1.7.5**].

3.5.6 Choosing the IPS structure

An industrial and provident society may be a suitable structure if:

- the organisation is charging for all or some of the services it provides;
- suitable model rules already exist through a promoting body;
- it wants to avoid the detailed requirements of company law;
- it is charitable and if not required to register with the Charity Commission, it will not be affected by not having a Commission registration number; *and*
- it can make a convincing case as to why it should be registered as an IPS rather than a company.

3.6 OTHER INCORPORATED BODIES

Some organisations are incorporated under **royal charter** or by **statute**. These bodies must comply with much company legislation but there are some differences. This book does not deal with them, and organisations with these structures should contact a specialist advisor.

A **limited liability partnership** (LLP) has the internal form of a partnership [**11.3**] but is incorporated under the **Limited Liability Partnerships Act 2000**. It is used primarily by professional firms which want the protection of limited liability, and is unlikely to be appropriate for voluntary organisations.

European Commission proposals for a **European association**, an incorporated structure for associations (membership bodies) operating in two or more EU member states, were dropped in 2005 but may be revived. In 2009 the Commission consulted on proposals for a **European foundation**, for non-membership charities operating in two or more member states.

At the time of writing (mid 2009) the European Commission had proposed a **European private company** structure, to make it easier to operate in more than one EU state. It is unclear whether this would be available for companies limited by guarantee, but it could be appropriate for trading companies.

Resources: INCORPORATED ORGANISATIONS

See end of **chapter 1**.

Statute law. www.opsi.gov.uk and www.statutelaw.gov.uk.

Much but not all case law. www.bailii.org.

Updates cross-referenced to this book. www.rclh.co.uk.

Chapter 4

CHARITABLE STATUS, CHARITY LAW AND REGULATION

For sources of further information see end of chapter 1.

4.1 DEFINING CHARITABLE STATUS

In England and Wales an organisation, regardless of its legal structure, is a charity if it is established for charitable purposes only [**5.2**], operates for the benefit of the public [**5.3**], and is subject to the high court in the exercise of its jurisdiction in respect of charities [**4.4.5**].   *Charities Act 2006 s.1*

An organisation in England or Wales does not become a charity by registering with the Charity Commission or anyone else; by definition it *is* a charity, has charitable status and must comply with charity law if it meets the above criteria.

An organisation which does not want to be subject to charity law must word its purposes so they are not wholly and exclusively charitable. Alternatively, it can set itself up as a type of organisation that can have charitable purposes but is defined by statute as not being charitable: a **community interest company** (CIC) [**3.4**], or a **community amateur sports club** (CASC) registered with HM Revenue and Customs [**1.8**]. Even if they have charitable purposes, CICs and CASCs are not subject to charity law. CICs are not entitled to the tax reliefs and other benefits available to charities [**4.2**], but CASCs are entitled to some of these.

4.1.1 Charitable status and registration

Most charities in England and Wales are required to register with the Charity Commission [**chapter 8**]. Those which are not registered with the Commission can get recognition of their charitable status through HM Revenue and Customs.

4.1.2 Charitable status and legal structure

In general, charitable status is completely separate from an organisation's legal structure. Regardless of whether an organisation is an **unincorporated association** [**2.2**], **trust** [**2.3**], **company limited by guarantee** [**3.3**] or **industrial**

45

and provident society [**3.5**], it is also a charity if its purposes are charitable and it operates for the benefit of the public (unless it is a CIC or CASC). For these organisations it is not possible to be 'a charity' on its own, without also having another legal status.

Charitable incorporated organisations (CIOs) are different, with a single structure that combines both incorporated and charitable status [**3.2**].

4.1.2.1 Charities as trusts

Under charity law, the members of the governing body of all charities, regardless of their legal structure, are **charity trustees**, and have duties under charity law [**15.6**]. *Charities Act 1993 s.97*

The governing body members of a trust, charitable association or body established by charter hold money, property and other assets **in trust** [**2.3.1**] for the charity's beneficiaries, and have a range of duties and powers as **trustees** under the **Trustee Act 2000** [**15.6, 58.1.2**]. In some situations governing body members of charitable companies, industrial and provident societies or charitable incorporated organisations may also have these duties and powers.

4.2 ADVANTAGES OF CHARITABLE STATUS

4.2.1 Tax benefits

The tax advantages of charitable status include:

- for associations and incorporated organisations, exemption from **corporation tax** on profits or surplus and capital gains (gains from the sale of assets), and for trusts, exemption from income tax and capital gains tax [**56.4**], provided the profits or capital gains are used wholly for the charity's purposes;
- exemption from having to pay **stamp duty land tax** on land transactions [**61.10.1**] and **stamp duty** on most other transactions [**58.7.2**];
- mandatory 80% relief on **non-domestic rates** for property used wholly or mainly for charitable purposes, and the possibility of up to 20% further discretionary relief [**63.2.3**];
- the right to reclaim tax on donations made under **gift aid** [**50.2**];
- the right to receive donations through **self assessment tax returns** [**50.3**];
- donors able to make donations free of tax through a **payroll deduction** scheme [**50.4**];
- donors do not generally pay **inheritance tax** on legacies to a charity or capital gains tax on assets donated to a charity [**50.6.2, 50.5.1**];
- eligibility for **zero rate VAT** instead of standard rate on some goods and services purchased by the charity [**57.5**];
- for a charity which is registered for VAT, **the right to charge zero rate VAT** instead of standard rate for some goods and services [**57.10**].

To qualify for these fiscal benefits, the organisation and its activities must fall within the definition of charity for tax purposes [**56.4.1**].

4.2.2 Other advantages

Further advantages of charitable status are:

- many funders are allowed (or choose) to fund only charities;
- charities have, for the most part, a good public image, and most people think of charity as 'a good thing', so it may be easier to raise money or obtain co-operation and help as a charity;
- the Charity Commission provides help and guidance to charities on some matters;
- charities are subject to scrutiny by the Charity Commission or other bodies, which can help prevent abuse.

4.3   RESTRICTIONS ON CHARITIES

All charities must comply with certain restrictions:

- the charity's resources can be used only for its **purposes** and within its powers as set out in the governing document, and any use of the charity's resources outside its purposes or powers may be a **breach of trust** for which the members of the governing body can be held personally liable [**22.4**];

- in general, **members of the governing body cannot be paid** for serving on the governing body or for any other goods or services they provide to the charity, unless this is authorised by the governing document, statute, the Charity Commission or the court [**16.3**];

- members of the governing body cannot profit in any other way or benefit from the charity unless this is similarly authorised [**chapter 16**];

- charities can charge for charitable activities or services which they provide for their beneficiaries, and for goods produced or services provided by their beneficiaries, but there are limits on other **trading** they can undertake [**51.1.3**];

- although charities can undertake non-party **campaigning** and **political activities** which are directly related to their purposes, there are limits on other campaigning and political activities they can undertake [**46.4**];

- there may be restrictions on how a charity's funds can be **invested** [**58.4**];

- a charity must comply with statutory requirements in dealing with its **property** [**61.11.1, 61.12**].

Other aspects of charitable status possibly perceived as disadvantageous are:

- charities are public bodies, open to **public scrutiny**;

- all charities must prepare **annual accounts**, and most must prepare annual reports [**54.2**];

- charities may have to have their **accounts examined or audited** and may have to submit the accounts to the Commission [**54.2.7**] (but many non-charities have to have their accounts audited anyway, to comply with funders' or constitutional requirements or company law);

- charity trustees are required to act 'with **prudence**' which may inhibit some activities, such as investing in some ethical investments [**58.6.2**];

- the Charity Commission has considerable powers to investigate complaints, and if there is serious mismanagement to step in and even take legal action against the charity, the charity trustees and employees [**4.5.9**].

4.4   REGULATION OF CHARITIES

4.4.1   Charity legislation

4.4.1.1   Early legislation

Charity regulation is not new. The preamble to the **Charitable Uses Act 1601** gave examples of the purposes for which charitable property could be used [**5.2.1**]. The purpose of this Act was 'to redress the misemployment of lands, goods and stocks of money', making it very clear that misuse of charity assets is not a new phenomenon. It was repealed in stages over the next three centuries.

The **Charitable Trusts Act 1853** set up a permanent Charity Commission, and a series of other Charitable Trusts Acts sought to ensure charities were properly managed. Most of these were replaced by the **Charities Act 1960**, which consolidated and extended charity law but did not define charitable purposes.

After the repeal of the 1601 Act, the legal definition of charitable status was based on case law [**4.4.3**]. Until the **Charities Act 2006** [**4.4.1.4**], the **Recreational Charities Act 1958** was the only statute defining charitable purposes.

4.4.1.2   Charities Act 1992

The **Charities Act 1992** increased the powers of the Charity Commission, clarified requirements for charity registration, accounting and reporting, introduced new administrative requirements and made it an offence for trustees not to comply with some of them, and regulated professional and commercial involvement in fundraising. It also included, in part 3, rules for public collections. but these were never implemented and will be replaced by the **Charities Act 2006 [49.2.3]**.

4.4.1.3 Charities Act 1993

The **Charities Act 1993** consolidated existing statute law relating to charity management and administration, including most of the Charities Act 1992, and did not include anything new. Parts 2 and 3 of the Charities Act 1992, on professional fundraisers and public collections, were not included in the 1993 Act.

4.4.1.4 Charities Act 2006

The **Charities Act 2006** updated charity law and regulation by amending and supplementing the 1992 and the 1993 Acts. Key provisions include a statutory definition of **charitable purposes [5.2.3]**, an obligation to show that a charity is operating for the **public benefit [5.3.1]**, extension and redefinition of the role of the **Charity Commission [4.5]**, a **charity tribunal** to hear appeals against the Commission's decisions **[4.5.11]**, the **charitable incorporated organisation [3.2]** as a new form of incorporation,, new regulation of **public collections** and other forms of fundraising **[49.2.3]**, and a reserve power for the government to control fundraising by charities **[48.1]**.

Implementation of the **Charities Act 2006** is in stages between 2007 and 2010, with a review in 2011.

4.4.1.5 A consolidated Charities Act?

At the time of writing (mid 2009) the Office of the Third Sector was working on a bill to consolidate the **Charities Acts 1992, 1993** and **2006**, and perhaps the **Recreational Charities Act 1958** and other legislation into a single Charities Act. The government hoped this would become law in 2010.

4.4.2 Other legislation

Governing body members of charitable trusts **[2.3]**, schemes **[4.5.5]**, and charitable unincorporated associations **[2.2]** have duties and powers under trust law, including the **Trustee Act 2000**. In some situations governing body members of incorporated charities may also have these duties. The duty of care under the **Trustee Act 2000 [58.1.2]** has been extended to the exercise of many of the new powers given to trustees by the **Charities Act 2006 [15.6]**.

All charities are also subject to all relevant aspects of UK and European law. These statutory obligations are outlined throughout this book.

4.4.3 Case law

Governments have for hundreds of years recognised the need to ensure that charity management and administration are effective. But between 1601 and 2006 they resisted the temptation to define too closely what is and is not charitable, preferring to rely on case law decisions about whether a new purpose was **within the spirit and intention** of the **Charitable Uses Act 1601 [5.2.1]**.

Even with the statutory definition of charitable purpose in the **Charities Act 2006**, this principle is preserved. Many charitable purposes are defined, but other purposes will be charitable if they are **analogous** to or **within the spirit** of the statutorily defined purposes.   *Charities Act 2006 ss.2(2)(m),2(4)*

The Charity Commission refers to case law not only when deciding whether a new purpose is or is not charitable, but also in determining whether it meets the **public benefit test [5.3.1]**.

4.4.4 Charity Commission and government

The **Charity Commission [4.5]** is a non-ministerial government department, acting on behalf of Parliament and the courts. Cabinet Office ministers appoint Charity Commission board members (charity commissioners) and report annually to Parliament on the general work of the Commission.

The Commission is responsible for the regulation of charities, but the **Office of the Third Sector** in the Cabinet Office is responsible for charity legislation.

The **Charity and Third Sector Finance Unit**, part of HM Treasury, is responsible for strategic policy development on third sector issues within the Treasury, including taxation and public sector spending. It works closely with the Cabinet Office and HM Revenue and Customs.

4.4.5 Charitable status and the high court

To be a charity in England or Wales, the organisation has to be 'subject to the control of the high court in the exercise of the court's jurisdiction with respect to charities'. The court's jurisdiction is England and Wales.   *Charities Act 2006 s.1(1)(b)*

Factors taken into account in determining whether an organisation is regulated by the laws of England and Wales include the residence of the original trustees and whether the organisation's property is based in England or Wales, but these factors are not conclusive. For charitable companies, the determining factor is where the company is registered.   *Gaudiya Mission v Brahmachary [1997] EWCA Civ 2239*

The high court retains final jurisdiction in charity matters, and if individuals or an organisation do not accept the Commission's or charity tribunal's view or ruling, they can apply to the court. Applications are expensive and therefore rare.

4.4.6 Charitable status in Scotland and Northern Ireland

The Charities Acts cover charities based or operating in England and Wales. They do not cover charities in Scotland or Northern Ireland, although some aspects of charity law, such as the statement of recommended practice for charity accounts, [**54.2.3**] cover all of the UK.

Charities based in Scotland, or based elsewhere but with significant operations in Scotland, must register with the **Office of the Scottish Charity Regulator** (OSCR) [**8.4**]. A **Charity Commission for Northern Ireland** (CCNI) began operating in 2009, with the first charity registrations expected in April 2010.

A **regulatory forum**, with representatives from the Charity Commission, OSCR and CCNI, as well as the Department of Community, Rural and Gaeltacht Affairs in the Republic of Ireland, seeks to ensure consistent regulatory approaches.

Guidance is available from the Charity Commission and OSCR for charities operating in England and Wales as well as Scotland, and from the Commission and CCNI for charities in England and Wales which operate in Northern Ireland.

4.4.7 The charity's governing document

A governing document has the force of law, so every charity must carefully comply with the requirements in its constitution, trust deed, memorandum and articles of association or other governing document. In particular, if a charity acts outside its defined purposes or powers [**5.8**], the trustees can be personally liable for **breach of the charity's trust**. The administrative procedures are also important, because the improper appointment of a trustee, for example, or a meeting called with inadequate notice could be held to be invalid.

This is why it is essential to get good advice when drawing up the governing document, and to ensure the document is regularly updated. **Chapter 7** looks at the process of drawing up and reviewing a governing document.

4.5 THE CHARITY COMMISSION

The Charity Commission covers only England and Wales, with staff divided between offices in London, Liverpool, Taunton and Newport, south Wales.

The statutory objectives of the Charity Commission are to promote increased public trust and confidence in charities, awareness of the public benefit requirement [**5.3.1**], compliance by trustees with their legal duties in running charities, the effective use of charitable resources, and accountability of charities to donors, beneficiaries and the public.   *Charities Act 1993 s.1B, inserted by Charities Act 2006 s.7*

To achieve these objectives, the Commission's functions are to determine whether organisations are or are not charities, encourage their better administration, identify and investigate misconduct and misadministration and take protective action, issue public collections certificates [**49.2.3**], provide information and advice to the government, and evaluate its own performance.

Charities Act 1993 s.1C, inserted by Charities Act 2006 s.7

The Commission produces free material on many charity matters, available from the Commission or its website [see end of **chapter 1**]. Its detailed internal operational guidance and research papers are also on its website.

4.5.1 Registers of charities and mergers

The Charity Commission maintains a **register** of all charities in England and Wales except those which are exempted or excepted from having to register [**8.1.2**, **8.1.3**]. Inclusion in the register is conclusive proof for all purposes that an organisation is charitable.

Charities Act 1993 ss.3,4(1)

The Commission must keep the register up to date and remove any organisation which is no longer charitable, was registered in error, ceases to operate or no longer exists. Updating is done via an **annual update form** [**54.2.10**] which all registered charities are required to submit, or changes can be submitted online during the year. Trustees of registered charities are required to notify the Commission of changes in the charity's name, purposes or address, or the name or address of the contact person.

Charities Act 1993 s.3(4),(7)(b)

Information about the register is available from the Commission. Details about every charity on the register are on the Commission's website [see end of **chapter 1**], or requests for information can be made in person at Commission offices, or by phone or letter. The online register usually contains the names of trustees and the charity's annual accounts and reports.

The Charity Commission removes charities which have not been in contact for an extended period, but includes them as removed charities on its website.

A separate register of charity mergers is also maintained [**11.5.4**].

4.5.2 Information and advice

The Charity Commission provides considerable information on its website, and provides informal information and advice, either about charity law in general or about a specific situation, through its helpline or in writing. It can also provide formal advice on any matter relating to the 'proper administration' of a charity.

A charity which feels it is getting inconsistent or even incorrect advice from Commission staff should consult the Commission's operational guidance (available on its website) and discuss the issues with relevant staff. If it is still dissatisfied it should seek legal advice, use the Commission's review procedure, or in the case of a decision appeal to the charity tribunal [**4.5.11**].

4.5.2.1 Section 29 advice and guidance

The charity trustees and other people connected with a charity will not be held liable for a breach of trust [**22.4**] arising from any situation related to their duties as trustees if they ask the Commission for an opinion under the **Charities Act 1993** s.29; provide, to the best of their knowledge, the full facts; and act on the Commission's formal advice. It is important to realise that most advice given by the Commission is informal guidance and is not given under section 29.

Charities Act 1993 s.29, amended by Charities Act 2006 s.24

4.5.3 Official custodian for charities

The **official custodian for charities** is a person appointed by the Commission to serve as a **custodian trustee** [**20.4.2**], holding charity land on behalf of unincorporated charities.

If the Commission believes that any of a charity's assets are at risk of being misused, it can make a direction [**4.5.4**] vesting the assets (not only land) in the official custodian.

4.5.4 Orders and directions

The Charity Commission has power to authorise some actions which are outside the trustees' powers but are considered to be in the best interests of the charity. It does this by making an **order** or a **scheme** [**4.5.5**] at the request of the charity's trustees. Orders can be obtained reasonably quickly, but schemes can be very slow.

Charities Act 1993 s.26

An order might be made, for example:

- to allow appointment of a trustee, former trustee or connected person [**16.3.2- 16.3.4**] to a paid position;
- to prevent payment to, or require reimbursement of money or benefits paid to, a trustee or connected person [**16.3, 16.6.1**];
- to allow, on a one-off basis, a benefit to someone who is not within the charity's defined beneficiary group;
- to appoint trustees, if the governing document does not specify how this is to be done or if the trustees are unable to appoint;
- to discharge trustees, if they have ceased to be active but have not resigned;
- to relieve a trustee or auditor from personal liability for breach of trust [**22.7.7, 55.7**].

It is a breach of trust, for which the members of the governing body and others involved with the management of the charity may be held personally liable, to take action outside the charity's purposes and powers unless this is authorised by statutory provisions or the Charity Commission.

As well as orders the Commission also has power under the Charities Acts to make **directions**, for example to bring two or more charities together for registration purposes (a **uniting direction** – see **9.4.2**) or to require any action to protect a charity or direct how its property is used.

Charities Act 1993 ss.19A,19B, inserted by Charities Act 2006 ss.20,21

4.5.5 Schemes

A **scheme** is the procedure by which the Commission or a court alters or extends the purposes of a charity, or authorises acts which are expressly prohibited under the charity's governing document or under other conditions. The procedure may also be used for other amendments to the governing document. A scheme is not always necessary for amendment [**7.5**].

Charities Act 1993 ss.13-18, amended by Charities Act 2006 ss.15-18

4.5.6 Consents and other powers

The Commission has many other powers in relation to individual charities (but not exempt charities, **8.1.2**). These include power to require a charity to change its name [**6.8.2**], determine who is or is not a member of a charity [**12.1.2**], authorise *ex gratia* payments [**53.3.1**], authorise charity proceedings [**65.8**], authorise mortgages or the disposal of property [**61.11.1, 61.12**], require information or documents, or obtain a search warrant.

Charities Act 1993 s.9(1); s.31A, inserted by Charities Act 2006 s.26

4.5.7 Monitoring

The Commission's computerised monitoring system for annual returns, supported by examination of annual accounts and reports, is designed to identify charities at risk or in need of assistance and to enable the Commission to help charities avoid serious problems. If the monitoring shows cause for concern, an approach is made to the trustees. The intention is to clarify the issues involved, provide advice and assistance, and take action as appropriate to resolve any difficulties and ensure that the charity functions effectively.

Circumstances which might lead to Commission enquiries include lack of trustee meetings or other signs of poor governance, lack of expenditure, exceptional expenditure in certain areas, excessively high payments to staff, unauthorised payments or other benefits to trustees, high fundraising expenses compared to funds raised, activities outside the purposes as set out in the governing document, loans to or from associated bodies, high reserves without an appropriate reason for holding them, or potential insolvency.

4.5.8 Serious incidents, complaints and disputes

The Charity Commission requires trustees of charities with annual income over £25,000 to confirm in their annual report that no serious incidents have occurred during the year which have not been reported to the Commission. Incidents that should be reported by the trustees when they occur – not at the end of the year – include fraud, theft or significant loss of funds or other property; significant donations from an unknown or unverified source; any known or alleged links to a banned organisation [**46.6.1**] or to terrorist or other unlawful activity; someone who is disqualified from acting as a trustee serving in that role [**13.3.2**]; charities not having adequate policies and procedures in place to comply with the law on safeguarding [**chapter 41**] and to protect vulnerable beneficiaries; and suspicions, allegations and incidents of abuse or mistreatment of beneficiaries.

The Charity Commission intervenes in disputes or takes action on complaints affecting charities only when it believes that there is a serious risk of harm to or abuse of a charity. This could include significant financial loss to a charity, serious harm to beneficiaries, sham charities, terrorism or other threats to national security, or deliberate use of a charity for private gain.

It cannot intervene in contractual disputes with third parties, or in internal disagreements or disputes about how the charity should be run (provided it is operating within its governing document and charity law). The Commission can, however, be asked for advice in these situations [**4.5.2**]. Where there are internal disputes within a charity, the Commission recommends mediation [**65.2.2**].

Any person connected with the charity or any member of the public may contact the Commission if they believe there is cause for concern. The procedure is set out in CC47 *Complaints about charities*, available from the Commission. The Commission does not normally respond to anonymous complaints, but will try to respect a complainant's wishes for confidentiality as much as possible.

4.5.9 Section 8 inquiries

Only if a situation cannot be informally resolved, or if there are indications of serious problems, will a **section 8 inquiry** be initiated. The procedure is explained in CC47 *Complaints about charities*. Such an inquiry might concern one charity or several. An inquiry cannot be undertaken in relation to an exempt charity [**8.1.2**] unless requested by its principal regulator.
*Charities Act 1993 s.8,
to be amended by Charities Act 2006 sch.5 [expected Nov/Dec 2009]*

Trustees and others connected with the charity can be required to attend an inquiry or to provide accounts and any other relevant information, and the Commission can obtain warrants to allow it to enter premises and remove documents. It is a criminal offence knowingly to conceal, destroy or falsify relevant documents or other information or to give false evidence to the Commission.
Charities Act 1993 s.11; s.31A, inserted by Charities Act 2006 s.26

The purpose of an inquiry into an individual charity is not to punish the charity or its trustees, but to identify current or potential problems and to help the charity strengthen its management and administration. But if the inquiry shows that mismanagement or maladministration has already occurred, or that charity property is at risk of not being used properly, the Commission has power to suspend any trustees, officers or employees for up to 12 months ('officers' include members of the governing body, the company secretary, and senior executives or managers), suspend from charity membership a trustee, officer or employee who is a member of the charity [**12.8.5**], and/or appoint additional trustees.

The Commission can direct any action in the interests of the charity or on how its assets are to be used [**4.5.4**], freeze the charity's bank accounts and other assets held by third parties, transfer any of the charity's assets (not only land) to the official custodian for charities [**4.5.3**] for safekeeping, and appoint an **interim manager** (formerly called a receiver and manager) to run the charity's affairs temporarily, with powers and duties specified by the Commission. The interim manager cannot be a Commission employee.
Charities Act 1993 s.18(1)

If the investigation shows that serious mismanagement or maladministration has already occurred, the Commission may also remove the responsible trustees, officers, agents (persons authorised to act on behalf of the charity) or employees permanently; make a scheme [**4.5.5**] to reorganise the charity, even if the trustees do not cooperate; and bring the results of its investigations to the attention of the police or other bodies. *Charities Act 1993 s.18(2)*

The Commission maintains a list, available for public inspection, of everyone removed in this way or by the court. It is an offence for anyone on the list to serve as trustee of any charity. *Charities Act 1993 s.72*

The Commission publishes the findings of inquiries on its website, and some in its annual report. These make instructive reading on how things can go wrong.

4.5.10 Legal proceedings and enforcement

Some orders and directions of the Charity Commission, for example those requiring documents or other information to be provided, property transferred or payments made, are enforceable as if they were high court orders. Non-compliance is treated as contempt of court and is punishable by a fine or imprisonment.

Non-compliance with some Charities Act requirements is an offence punishable by a fine. In other cases the Commission can make an order requiring a default (for example a failure to apply for registration) to be made good. Such orders are also enforceable as if they were high court orders.

Although the Commission has extensive powers and there are penalties for some non-compliance, it reserves these for wilful breaches of the rules. An innocent mistake, even where it has serious consequences, rarely causes the Commission to take penal action.

4.5.11 Complaints and appeals

An informal complaint about any aspect of the Charity Commission's service, including a complaint about the way a decision has been made, can be made initially to the Commission's **case review panel**.

If this is not considered appropriate or the outcome of the case review is unsatisfactory, a formal complaint may be made initially to the customer service manager in the relevant Commission office. This must be made within six months of the action or decision complained about. If the customer service manager's response is unsatisfactory, an appeal can be made to the head of customer service within one month. A further appeal can be made to the **independent complaints reviewer**, who does not have power to require the Commission to change its decision or action, but can look at how the decision was made. At the time of writing (mid 2009) the role of the independent complaints reviewer was being reviewed.

At the time of writing (mid 2009) the possibility of a **charities ombudsman** was being discussed.

Most key orders or decisions by the Commission, as listed in schedule 1C to the **Charities Act 1993**, can be appealed to the **charity tribunal**, part of the general regulatory chamber in the first-tier tribunal [**64.7**]. Appeals from the tribunal are to the high court. *Charities Act 1993 sch.1C, inserted by Charities Act 2006 sch.4; Charity Tribunal Rules 2008 [SI 2008/221]*

Resources: CHARITABLE STATUS, CHARITY LAW AND REGULATION

See end of **chapter 1**.

Statute law. www.opsi.gov.uk and www.statutelaw.gov.uk.

Much but not all case law. www.bailii.org.

Updates cross-referenced to this book. www.rclh.co.uk.

Chapter 5
THE ORGANISATION'S OBJECTS

5.1   OBJECTS AND POWERS

Objects are the **purposes** for which an organisation is established, as set out in its governing document (constitution, trust deed, memorandum or articles of association etc). The objects clause generally defines who the organisation is intended to benefit (**beneficiaries** in a charitable organisation), and may also include the geographical area covered (**area of benefit** or **beneficial area**).

Powers define what the organisation can do in order to achieve the objects. For example, the payment of rent or salaries does not *directly* achieve the object of relieving poverty, advancing the education of the public, or whatever else the organisation seeks to achieve. Acquiring premises and hiring staff are *means to an end*, rather than the end. For more on powers, see **7.4.3**.

Action outside the objects or powers is *ultra vires* ('beyond the powers'). The person(s) who authorise or undertake an *ultra vires* action could be required to make good any losses to the organisation and in some cases, to third parties [**5.8**].

If the objects or powers as set out in the governing document are very narrow, there is a risk that the governing body or the organisation's members could unintentionally find themselves acting *ultra vires*. This is why many organisations have relatively wide objects [**5.7.1**] and why the powers clause in many governing documents gives power to do anything which is lawful and achieves, or helps to achieve, the objects [**7.4.3**]. But even a catch-all powers clause such as this does not entitle the organisation to do anything it wishes. Everything the organisation does must be in furtherance of the objects.

Objects are described in detail in this chapter. Powers are covered throughout the book, and especially in **7.4.3-7.4.8** and **chapter 15**.

5.2   CHARITABLE PURPOSES

To be charitable, an organisation's purposes as set out in its objects must be wholly and exclusively charitable – although occasionally charities might in the past have been registered with ancillary objects which are not charitable [**5.2.20**]. The purposes must fall within one or more of the charitable purposes defined in the **Charities Act 2006** [**5.2.3**], and the organisation must satisfy a **public benefit test** [**5.3.1**]. *Charities Act 2006 ss.1-3*

Two types of organisation are defined by statute as being not charitable even if their objects are wholly charitable and they operate for the benefit of the public. **Community interest companies** (CICs) by definition are not charitable [**3.4**], nor are **community amateur sports clubs** (CASCs) which are registered as such with HM Revenue and Customs [**1.8**]. However, amateur sports clubs are charitable if they are registered with the Charity Commission [**5.2.10**].

To help new charities write their objects in a way which is legally charitable, example objects for a range of charitable purposes are available from the Charity Commission [see end of **chapter 1**]. Using an example object will speed the charity registration process [**8.2**], but most organisations should nonetheless take advice to ensure the object accurately reflects their purposes and will cover their proposed and potential activities. Even a small variation in the wording can make a difference as to whether an organisation is accepted as a charity, so advice should also be sought before making any change to an example object.

If an organisation's proposed activities do not clearly fit within one of the charitable purposes set out in the **Charities Act 2006**, or are at the boundaries of what is regarded as legally charitable, the people involved should seek advice from a solicitor with charity law experience.

5.2.1   The Statute of Elizabeth I

The preamble to the **Charitable Uses Act 1601** (often referred to as the Statute of Elizabeth I) contained a long list of activities then seen as charitable. This list came to be used as the starting point for making decisions on what is and is not charitable. An **analogy** or **stepping stones** approach was taken, to show that a proposed purpose was sufficiently close to one of the 1601 purposes, either directly or by analogy. For example provision of a crematorium was held to be charitable because it is analogous to provision of burial grounds, which is analogous to the upkeep of churchyards, which is analogous to 'the repair of churches' in the 1601 Act. By this rather tortuous route, activities which could never have been foreseen in 1601 could be defined as charitable. *Scottish Burial Reform Cremation Society v Glasgow City Corporation [1968] UKHL 3*

5.2.2   The Pemsel case: the four heads of charity

In the centuries following 1601, the Charitable Uses Act was gradually repealed. But in a landmark case in 1891, known as the **Pemsel case**, Lord Macnaghten drew on the 1601 Act and an 1804 definition of charitable objects to divide charitable purposes into four **heads** or categories: the **relief of poverty**, the **advancement of education**, the **advancement of religion**, and **other purposes beneficial to the community**. These four heads remained the basis for decisions about charitable status until implementation of the charitable status provisions in the **Charities Act 2006**. *Income Tax Special Purpose Commissioners v Pemsel [1891] UKHL 1*

5.2.3 Charities Act 2006: the statutory purposes

As a result of pressure to clarify and modernise the four heads of charity, the **Charities Act 2006** introduced statutory charitable purposes from April 2008:

- prevention or relief of poverty [**5.2.4**];
- advancement of education [**5.2.5**];
- advancement of religion [**5.2.6**];
- advancement of health or the saving of lives [**5.2.7**];
- advancement of citizenship or community development [**5.2.8**];
- advancement of the arts, culture, heritage or science [**5.2.9**];
- advancement of amateur sport [**5.2.10**];
- advancement of human rights, conflict resolution or reconciliation or the promotion of religious or racial harmony or equality and diversity [**5.2.11**];
- advancement of environmental protection or improvement [**5.2.12**];
- relief of those in need by reason of youth, age, ill health, disability, financial hardship or other disadvantage [**5.2.13**];
- advancement of animal welfare [**5.2.14**];
- promotion of the efficiency of the armed forces of the Crown, or the efficiency of the police, fire and rescue services or ambulance services [**5.2.15**];
- other purposes currently recognised as charitable under charity law or under the **Recreational Charities Act 1958** s.1 [**5.2.17**] and any purposes that can reasonably be regarded as analogous (similar) to, or within the spirit of, another charitable purpose [**5.2.16**]. *Charities Act 2006 s.2*

An overview of these purposes is set out below. Further information about all of them is available from the Charity Commission [see end of **chapter 1**].

5.2.4 Prevention or relief of poverty

The first purpose, **prevention or relief of poverty**, includes relief, support, help or services for people who are poor, either to help them directly or to help them to become self supporting. 'Poor' applies not only to people who are destitute or are receiving means tested welfare benefits, but also to those who are suffering financial hardship compared to their normal standard of living.

Examples include making grants or loans or providing services to individuals, or to organisations that assist people in financial need, relieving poverty in deprived areas, and providing legal, debt management or financial advice.

5.2.5 Advancement of education

Charities for the **advancement of education** include places of education, such as schools, colleges and universities and charities supporting their work such as parent teacher associations, scholarship and educational prize funds, and student unions; charities that educate the public about a particular subject; pre-school education; training organisations, including training for unemployed people; museums, which must meet a criterion of merit [**5.2.9**]; professional bodies; physical education and out of school education for children and young people; and research projects.

Scholarship funds and research grants, to be charitable, must not only benefit the individuals who receive them, but must have a clear public benefit. Scholarships must be shown to encourage high standards of learning, thus promoting the advancement of education in general. Charities which promote research may be required to publish their findings, so the public gets the benefit of the research.

5.2.6 Advancement of religion

Religion, in relation to charitable purpose, includes religions which involve a belief in more than one god or do not involve belief in a god. *Charities Act 2006 s.2(3)(a)*

Advancement of religion as a charitable purpose includes, for example, advancing a particular religion; promoting general religious purposes and supporting religious bodies; maintaining and promoting public worship; providing and maintaining places of worship and items within them; maintaining churchyards and other religious burial places; and supporting clergy, former clergy, their families, lay workers, and people such as caretakers employed at a place of worship.

Because there must be some element of public benefit, prayer and contemplation on their own have been held not to be charitable.

Many faith groups carry out a wide range of activities for other charitable purposes, such as the relief of poverty, the advancement of education or the promotion of conflict resolution. These activities fall within the 'advancement of religion' purpose if they are an 'outworking' of religion. If the activities cannot be shown to be an expression of the religion they may need to be carried out through a separate charity registered under the relevant other purpose, or it may be possible to amend the religious charity's objects to cover the other purposes. Charity Commission consent is likely to be needed for this amendment [**7.5**].

5.2.7 Health or the saving of lives

The **advancement of health** encompasses conventional as well as complementary, alternative and holistic approaches to the prevention or relief of sickness, disease or human suffering. It also includes the promotion of health. Activities within this charitable purpose include providing medical treatment, care and healing; supporting the work of medical treatment centres, such as a hospital league of friends; providing items, services, facilities and comforts to ease the suffering or assist the recovery of people who are ill, convalescing, disabled or infirm; medical research; providing services and facilities for medical practitioners; and promoting activities that have a proven beneficial effect on health.

The **advancement of the saving of lives** includes activities to save people whose lives are in danger and to protect life and property. This overlaps with promoting the efficiency of police and rescue services [**5.2.15**], and includes providing rescue services, or assisting the police and public sector services; assisting victims of war or natural disasters; providing life saving or self defence classes; providing street lighting or security cameras in public places; and repairing sea and flood defences.

5.2.8 Citizenship or community development

The **advancement of citizenship or community development** relates to social and community infrastructure. This includes the promotion of volunteering, the voluntary sector, and/or the efficiency and effectiveness of charities and the effective use of charitable resources. Other examples under this heading include the promotion of civic responsibility and good citizenship; urban or rural regeneration; community capacity building; and social investment.

5.2.9 The arts, culture, heritage or science

This is a broad heading, encompassing **advancement of the arts, culture, heritage or science**. Charitable **arts** activities include events such as concerts and arts festivals; facilities such as theatres, cinemas and concert halls; activities such as drama societies and art or craft classes; and the promotion of various forms of the arts.

Museums and art galleries need to satisfy a **criterion of merit**, with 'sufficient evidence that the collections and exhibits and the use made of them either will educate the minds of the public whom the museum or art gallery intends to serve, or at least will be capable of doing so ... an idea, emotion or experience which is enlightening and which is, or is capable of being, of value to them.' More information is in Charity Commission publication RR10 *Museums and art galleries*.

Heritage covers local or national history and traditions, and includes the preservation of historic land, buildings and archaeology, as well as activities to preserve or maintain a tradition where there is a demonstrable public benefit in doing so.

The advancement of **science** includes scientific research, learned societies and institutions.

5.2.10 Amateur sport

The **advancement of amateur sport** covers sports or games which promote health by involving physical or mental skill or exertion, and which are undertaken on an amateur basis. It also includes the promotion of community participation in healthy recreation.

Amateur sports clubs, such as tennis or football clubs, are charitable if they are registered with the Charity Commission, as are other bodies which promote a particular amateur sport, and multi-sports centres. But **community amateur sports clubs** which are registered as CASCs with HM Revenue and Customs are, by statutory definition, not charitable. CASCs registered with HMRC enjoy some, but not all, of the tax advantages of charities [**1.8**]. *Finance Act 2002 sch.18; Charities Act 2006 s.5(4),(5)*

5.2.11 Human rights, conflict resolution, harmony or diversity

This very broad category, the **advancement of human rights, conflict resolution or reconciliation, or the promotion of religious or racial harmony or equality and diversity**, covers many purposes previously regarded as too 'political' to be charitable. For more about charities dealing with issues such as these, see **5.3.6**.

The advancement of human rights in the UK and abroad includes raising awareness of human rights issues, securing the enforcement of human rights law, and providing relief for victims of human rights abuse. Charity Commission publication RR12 *The promotion of human rights* clarifies the boundaries on promoting human rights in countries whose domestic law provides little or no protection for such rights.

Identifying the causes of conflict, seeking to resolve such conflict, and relieving the suffering, poverty and distress caused by conflict are charitable. Restorative justice at a local, national or international level, bringing together the parties to a particular conflict or offence, is charitable. So is mediation, conciliation or reconciliation between individuals, organisations, authorities or groups involved or likely to become involved in a dispute or interpersonal conflict.

The promotion of religious or racial harmony or equality and diversity includes promoting the elimination of discrimination, promoting good relations between persons of different racial or religious groups, and helping people understand the religious beliefs of others.

5.2.12 Environmental protection or improvement

The **advancement of environmental protection or improvement** includes preservation and conservation of the natural environment and the promotion of sustainable development. Before registering such a charity the Charity Commission may require independent expert evidence to show that the particular species, land or habitat to be conserved is worthy of conservation. Charity Commission publication RR9 *Preservation and conservation* provides more information.

5.2.13 Relief of disadvantage

This category covers a wide range of provision for the **relief of those in need, by reason of youth, age, ill health, disability, financial hardship or other disadvantage**. It covers specialist advice, care, support, equipment, accommodation, or other services, as well as services or support for carers. Many of these activities would also fall within other charitable purposes, such as the prevention or relief of poverty or the advancement of health. But many activities, such as those intended for persons in need solely because they are young or elderly, may fall only within this charitable purpose.

There is no statutory definition of 'youth' or 'age'. Before registering a charity intended for a specific age group, the Charity Commission will need to accept that there is a clear reason, based on need, for the charity's services to be limited to the intended age group. Any such restrictions must also fall within exemptions allowed under legislation prohibiting discrimination in the provision of goods or services on the basis of age [**5.6.6**].

5.2.14 Animal welfare

The **advancement of animal welfare** includes the prevention or suppression of cruelty to animals, and the prevention or relief of suffering by animals. This includes animal sanctuaries, veterinary care and treatment, and the care and re-homing of animals that are abandoned, mistreated or lost.

5.2.15 Armed forces or emergency services

People are often surprised to learn that the **promotion of the efficiency of the armed forces of the Crown**, as a means of defending the country, is charitable. This includes ensuring the forces are properly trained and equipped, and providing facilities and benefits for the armed forces. Examples of activities within this charitable purpose include providing training or training facilities, educational resources, sports facilities, or band instruments and equipment; providing or maintaining military memorials, churches, chapels or museums; encouraging contact between military units or between serving and former personnel; and encouraging recruitment to the armed forces.

Promotion of the efficiency of the police, fire and rescue services or ambulance services was added to the **Charities Act 2006** in the final stages of its passage through Parliament. This overlaps with the advancement of the saving of lives [**5.2.7**], and includes charities that provide rescue services, such as lifeboats, mountain rescue, fire, ambulance, air ambulance and first aid services, or which assist the work of the police and emergency services.

5.2.16 Other charitable purposes

Any purpose not explicitly included under one of the categories in the **Charities Act 2006**, but recognised as charitable at the time of its implementation in April 2008, is charitable. New purposes can be recognised as charitable if they are analogous (similar) to, or within the spirit of, another charitable purpose.

The Charity Commission gives the following examples of purposes recognised as charitable under this heading:

- providing or maintaining public works or facilities such as bridges, highways, libraries, cemeteries, crematoria or public conveniences, or providing public services such as water and lighting;
- the relief of unemployment;
- promoting industry and commerce, or agriculture and horticulture;
- gifts for the benefit of a particular locality or its inhabitants, the beautification of a town, or civic societies;
- the promotion of the moral or spiritual welfare or improvement of the community;
- the preservation of public order;
- the rehabilitation of ex-offenders and the prevention of crime;
- the promotion of ethical standards of conduct and compliance with the law in the public and private sectors.

Some of these may also come, in part, under other headings.

5.2.17 Recreational charities

Charities registered under the **Recreational Charities Act 1958** are brought within the 2006 Act by being included in the 'other charitable purposes' category. The Recreational Charities Act covers village halls, community centres, women's institutes, and other facilities for recreation and leisure activities.

Such provision is charitable only if it is 'in the interests of social welfare'. This means the facilities must be intended to improve the conditions of life of the people for whom they are primarily intended, and must be intended for people who need them because of their youth, age, infirmity, disability, poverty or social and economic circumstances; or available to the public at large, or only to women or men. Until 27 February 2008, such facilities could be available only to women, but not only to men. *Recreational Charities Act 1958 s.1, amended by Charities Act 2006 s.5(2)*

The criteria for recreational charities are explained in the Charity Commission's RR4 *The Recreational Charities Act 1958*.

Miners' welfare organisations, which were defined as charitable under the Recreational Charities Act, retain their charitable status after 1 April 2010 only if they meet the Charities Act 2006 statutory definition of charity [**5.2**].

Charities Act 2006 s.5(3) [expected 1/4/10]

5.2.18 Charitable purposes in Scotland

Until the **Charities and Trustee Investment (Scotland) Act 2005** came into effect in April 2006, organisations based in Scotland were recognised as charitable by HM Revenue and Customs, using criteria based on English charity law. Scotland now has its own definition of charitable purposes, and its own definition of public benefit [**5.3.8**].

Charitable purposes as defined in Scottish law are broadly similar to those in the Charities Act, with the following differences:

- 'advancement of health' and 'the saving of lives' are separate purposes, rather than combined;
- 'advancement of public participation in sport', rather than advancement of amateur sport;
- 'the provision of recreational facilities or the organisation of recreational activities, with the object of improving the conditions of life for the persons for whom the facilities are primarily intended' is a purpose in its own right, rather than being included in the catch-all at the end;
- 'advancement of human rights, conflict resolution or reconciliation', 'the promotion of religious or racial harmony' and 'the promotion of equality and diversity' are separate purposes, rather than combined;
- 'youth' is not included in the 'relief of those in need' purpose (but it is presumably included within 'age' anyway);
- 'promotion of the efficiency of the armed forces of the Crown, or the efficiency of the police, fire and rescue services or ambulance services' is not included, although some aspects would be included under 'the saving of lives';
- 'any other purpose that may reasonably be regarded as analogous to any of the preceding purposes' is used, rather than the wider catch-all in the Charities Act.

Charities & Trustee Investment (Scotland) Act 2005 s.7

The **Office of the Scottish Charity Regulator** (OSCR) registers Scottish charities, and charities based elsewhere which operate in Scotland [**8.4**].

5.2.19 Charitable purposes in Northern Ireland

As in Scotland, charities based in Northern Ireland have been recognised as charitable by HM Revenue and Customs. But in 2008 Northern Ireland got its own Charities Act, with its own charity law and a **Charity Commission for Northern Ireland** (CCNI) that is expected to start registering charities in April 2010.

Charitable purposes in NI are the same as under the **Charities Act 2006**, with the following differences:

- 'promotion of the efficiency of the armed forces of the Crown, or the efficiency of the police, fire and rescue services or ambulance services' is not included;
- 'the advancement of peace and good community relations' is explicitly included along with the advancement of human rights, conflict resolution or reconciliation or the promotion of religious or racial harmony or equality and diversity.

Charities Act (Northern Ireland) 2008 s.2

5.2.20 Ancillary objects

Despite the requirement that a charity's objects must be wholly and exclusively charitable, it used to be possible to be accepted as a charity even if some ancillary objects were not in themselves charitable. **Ancillary** means related to the main object, but incidental or secondary to it.

If such purposes are to be included now, they must be written into the governing document as powers [**7.4.3**]. This enables the organisation to carry out that type of activity, but only in furtherance of its charitable objects.

5.3   CHARITIES: THE PUBLIC BENEFIT REQUIREMENT

Charities must be for the benefit of the public or a section [**5.3.2**] of the public. Under the **Charities Act 2006**, the longstanding presumption that organisations established for the relief of poverty, the advancement of education or the advancement of religion operate for the benefit of the public unless proved otherwise has been abolished. Such organisations now have to show – as do organisations established for all other charitable purposes – that they benefit the public.

Charities Act 2006 s.3

The approach to public benefit is different under the **Charities Act 2006** than under comparable legislation for Scotland and Northern Ireland [**5.3.8**], which could have implications for English and Welsh charities operating there.

5.3.1   The public benefit test

Public benefit is not defined in the **Charities Act 2006**, but is based on case law with the Charity Commission determining how it is interpreted. The Commission's approach is based on two broad principles:

- There must be an identifiable benefit or benefits. It must be clear what the benefits are, the benefits must be related to the aims, and benefits must be balanced against any detriment or harm.
- Benefit must be to the public, or a section of the public. The beneficiaries must be appropriate to the aims, and where benefit is to a section of the public, the opportunity to benefit must not be unreasonably restricted by geographical or other restrictions, or by ability to pay any fees charged. People in poverty must not be excluded from the opportunity to benefit. Any private benefits must be incidental.

Guidance on public benefit is available from the Charity Commission, along with guidance for specific sectors such as fee-charging charities and charities for the relief of poverty or the advancement of education, religion, or moral or ethical belief systems. The guidance will be developed over time through Charity Commission decisions and, almost certainly, challenges through the charity tribunal.

As part of the charity application process [**8.2.4**], information must be provided about how the **public benefit test** is satisfied. If public benefit cannot be demonstrated, the application for registration must be rejected.

In addition, charity trustees must have regard to the guidance when exercising any powers or duties to which the guidance is relevant, so a copy of the Commission's summary guidance should be provided to all governing body members and senior staff, should be available at all governing body meetings, and should be referred to as appropriate.

The trustees' annual report must set out how the charity provides benefit for the public [**54.2.8**]. The Charity Commission has examples of what might be included in the annual report.

5.3.1.1   Assessing public benefit

A charity's assessment of its public benefit should be based on questions such as:
- What benefit(s) does the organisation provide? How do those benefits help fulfil the organisation's purpose(s)?
- Who is the organisation primarily set up to benefit? Does the organisation provide wider benefits to the community or society generally? If so, how?
- What criteria does the organisation use to select beneficiaries? Is anyone excluded from being a beneficiary? If so, who is excluded and why?
- Does the organisation have a membership where someone must be a member to benefit? If so, is it open to anyone to join? If not, who can join and why?

- Does the organisation provide facilities for, or services to, the public? If so what, if any, restrictions are there on who can have access or what can be accessed?

- Does the organisation charge for its services? If so, how are charges set? Is everyone charged the full rate? How are people on low incomes able to benefit from the organisation?

- Does anyone receive private benefits from the organisation? If so, what benefits do they receive? How do those benefits contribute towards achieving the organisation's purposes, and/or to what are they incidental?

5.3.1.2   Review of charities

Following the removal of the presumption of public benefit for charities for the relief of poverty, the advancement of education or the advancement of religion, the Charity Commission was at the time of writing (mid 2009) reviewing existing charities where concerns had been raised, or where there was potential for concerns to be raised, about whether they meet the public benefit test.

Where the Commission identifies grounds for concern, it works with the charity to find ways it can benefit a sufficient section of the public. If necessary the Commission can take regulatory action to ensure compliance with the public benefit rules and, in extreme cases, can require the charity's assets to be redirected to other charitable purposes.

5.3.2   Section of the public

The definition of **section of the public** varies depending on the purpose for which the charity is established. So long as the beneficiaries are defined in a broad way or covering a wide geographic area, it may not matter that only a few people qualify. For example an organisation set up to help people with a rare illness is almost certainly charitable, even if only a few people have the illness.

A specialist legal advisor or the Charity Commission should be consulted before attempting to set up any charity which will be restricted to a relatively small group or to a group defined by reference to an individual or an employer.

5.3.2.1   Clubs and self help groups

An organisation set up solely as a members' club or for the self improvement of narrowly defined members is not charitable. Even if its objects are charitable, a club or self help group will be considered charitable only if can show that it also provides some benefit to others who are not members, and/or that it is open to all members of the public who meet the criteria for membership and that these constitute a sufficient section of the public.

5.3.3   Private benefit

Individual or private benefit obviously occurs in charities. But it must arise directly from the achievement of the charity's objects, for example education provided to a child or services provided to a person with a disability, or it must be legitimately incidental to the achievement of charitable objects, for example a local business gaining new customers as a result of urban regeneration.

5.3.4   Disaster appeals and appeals for individuals

A legally enforceable trust will always be implied (assumed to be created) when funds are sought for a particular purpose [**48.2.1**]. If there is no formal declaration of trust, the terms of the appeal form the basis for the trust.

The attorney general has drawn up special guidelines (reprinted in Charity Commission booklet CC40) for **disaster appeals** and appeals for individuals or groups of individuals. The guidelines clarify the distinction between:

- the establishment of a **charitable trust**, which is eligible for all the tax benefits of charitable status [**4.2.1**] but under which individuals cannot be named and can only receive funds or benefits appropriate to their needs, with any surplus being used for other appropriate charitable purposes;

- a **non-charitable (private) trust**, which is not entitled to tax reliefs but which can distribute funds or benefits in any way defined by the appeal or other document setting out the terms of the trust.

An inappropriately worded appeal could result in the loss of tax benefits, and an appeal which does not indicate what will happen to surplus funds could result in any surplus having to be returned to donors. The Charity Commission [see end of **chapter 1**] will give advice as a matter of urgency on disaster appeals.

5.3.5   Provision of public services

In the **Wigan and Trafford decisions** in 2004, the Charity Commission said that charities can fundraise for and deliver services that the public sector has a statutory duty to provide. Previously the Commission had said that charitable funds could be used only to supplement statutory services. The decision involved Trafford Community Leisure Trust and the Wigan Leisure and Culture Trust, which operate sports facilities, leisure facilities, and other public services, such as cemeteries and libraries, that were previously provided by the local authorities.

The Commission's view is that charity law does not prevent charities providing services on behalf of a public sector body, provided the charity is operating within its objects and powers and is independent of the government or other funder, and the trustees are acting in the interest of the charity and its beneficiaries. Further information is in CC37 *Charities and public service delivery*, from the Commission [see end of **chapter 1**].

5.3.6   'Political' charities

A number of rulings by the courts have made it clear that seeking to achieve a political purpose cannot in itself be charitable. This is because charities must exist for the public benefit, and the courts will not decide whether a particular political purpose is or is not for the public benefit.   *Bowman v Secular Society Limited [1917] AC 406; National Anti-Vivisection Society v Inland Revenue Commissioners [1947] UKHL 4*

However, once a 'political' purpose has become enshrined in law, its promotion or education in its principles is likely to be accepted as charitable. Promotion of racial harmony, for example, was accepted as charitable after the **Race Relations Act 1976** was passed, as was the promotion of human rights in the wake of the **Human Rights Act 1998**. These and similar 'political' purposes have been defined as charitable under the **Charities Act 2006 [5.2.11]**.

Political purposes that cannot be charitable include promoting the interests of a political party whether local, national or international, or seeking to change or oppose changes to the law or government policy at home or abroad. But it is crucial to differentiate between **political objects** or purposes, which are not acceptable for a charity, and **campaigning** or **political activities,** which may be acceptable if they are directly related to achieving the charity's objects [**46.4**].

Education and research on political matters generally and on forms of government can be charitable, if the education or research are made available to the public. In these cases it will be necessary to show that educational programmes are objective and balanced, and do not constitute propaganda.
Re The Trustees of the Arthur McDougall Fund [1956] 3 All ER 867

5.3.7   Charities working internationally

When an organisation with international activities seeks to register as a charity, the Commission considers whether it would be charitable if its activities were carried out in England and Wales. If so, it is presumed to be for the public benefit in the country where it will operate and will be registered, unless it would be 'contrary to public policy' to do so. A charity cannot be set up for objects which are unlawful in the country where it is working.

The Commission will need to be satisfied that the organisation will be able to monitor the work carried out abroad and the use of funds sent or raised abroad. Its legal and good practice guidance is set out in *Charities working internationally*, free from the Commission [see end of **chapter 1**].

Activities undertaken abroad by a UK charity are generally eligible for UK tax relief [**4.2.1**].

A UK charity operating internationally may be required to register in the country or countries where it operates. Even where it is not obliged to register, there may be tax or other advantages in doing so.

5.3.8 Public benefit in Scotland and Northern Ireland

Unlike charity legislation in England and Wales [**5.3.1**], the legislation for charities in Scotland includes a **statutory definition** of public benefit. In assessing whether the public benefit test is met, two criteria must be considered:

- the extent of any benefit gained by members of the organisation or other people, or the disbenefit incurred by the public as a result of the organisation's activities compared to the benefit to the public; and
- whether any conditions, such as charges or fees, restrict people from obtaining the organisation's benefits, and if so whether these are unduly restrictive.

Charities & Trustee Investment (Scotland) Act 2005 s.8

Northern Ireland follows the Scottish statutory approach rather than English case law approach to public benefit.   *Charities Act (Northern Ireland) 2008 s.3*

English or Welsh charities registered in Scotland need to ensure that all of their activities – not just those in Scotland – meet the public benefit test for Scotland. At the time of writing (mid 2009) it was not expected that the same rule would apply to English or Welsh charities registered in Northern Ireland.

At the time of writing the case law approach to public benefit in England and Wales and the statutory approach in Scotland had already led to situations where an organisation could be recognised as charitable in one jurisdiction but not another. The long-term implications of this situation were unclear.

5.4 CHARITIES: THE REQUIREMENT TO BE NOT FOR PROFIT

Charities must be set up on a **not for profit** or **non-profit basis**. This does not mean that charities cannot charge for their goods or services, or cannot make a profit. It does mean that charities cannot be set up specifically for commercial or profit-making purposes, and that under the terms of their governing document they must be **non-profit-distributing**. Any profits or surplus made by the organisation must be used solely for the purposes of the organisation, and must not be distributed as profits, dividends, bonuses etc to members of the organisation or members of the governing body, as they can be in a business.

In addition, all other assets or resources must be used for the purposes of the organisation, and if the organisation is wound up, any remaining assets must be used for its purposes or similar purposes.

'Charitable' does not intrinsically mean providing services free or below cost. So long as it is set up for charitable purposes, can show it is operating for the benefit of the public and that any private gain is necessarily incidental, an organisation is charitable (unless it is a community interest company, or a community amateur sports club registered with HM Revenue and Customs) even if it charges a commercial rate for its charitable activities or services. However, where charges are so high that the charity cannot demonstrate that it is operating for the benefit of the public, it will not be registered as a charity and if already registered, could be required to change how it operates [**5.3.1**].

If a charity charges for its charitable activities and services and makes a profit, it will not be charged income or corporation tax on the profits so long as they are used solely for the charity's purposes [**56.4.1**]. But there can be VAT implications if a charity charges anything at all for its activities or services, even if it does not charge a commercial rate or does not make a profit [**57.1**].

5.5 NON-CHARITABLE OBJECTS

Non-charitable associations may be set up for any lawful purposes, without having to meet the specific requirements for charities.

From 1 October 2009, the objects of a newly registered **non-charitable company** are **unrestricted** unless they are specifically restricted in the articles of association. The objects of a non-charitable voluntary sector company are always **restricted** in the articles.

Companies Act 2006 s.31(1)

Community interest companies [**3.4**] are by definition not charities. Provided they meet the community interest test they can be set up for any purposes, even charitable purposes, but cannot legally be charitable. A CIC's objects are likely to be restricted.

Non-charitable industrial and provident societies may be set up for any purposes which meet the requirements for IPS registration [**3.5**].

5.6 EQUAL OPPORTUNITIES AND THE OBJECTS

In general it is unlawful for organisations to discriminate on the basis of race, sex, disability, religion or belief or sexual orientation in providing access to services, facilities, goods or premises [**chapter 42**]. At the time of writing (mid 2009) there was no legislation on age discrimination in the provision of goods and services, but this was expected to be included in the **Equality Act** [**28.1.12**].

Exceptions in the legislation allow charities and some other organisations to have constitutional objects which limit their membership or their beneficiary group. Before drawing up an objects clause which seeks to limit membership or the beneficiary group in a potentially discriminatory way, it is sensible to take legal advice to ensure the proposed objects do not contravene the relevant legislation.

In some situations, even organisations which do not have a membership or beneficiary group defined in this way can provide activities for a specified racial group or groups, for one sex or people of a particular sexual orientation, people with a specific disability or disabilities, or people of a particular religion or belief. Again, advice should be taken before limiting activities of services to a specific group, to ensure it is lawful to do so.

5.6.1 Racial groups

Charities are allowed to limit their beneficiary group on racial grounds (race, ethnic origin, national origin, nationality) [**12.3**, **42.3**], provided the beneficiary group is not defined by reference to colour. This is why the Charity Commission cannot register groups which define their beneficiary group simply as 'black'.

Race Relations Act 1976 s.34

Non-charitable clubs and associations are allowed to define their main object as enabling the benefits of membership to be enjoyed by people of a particular racial group, not defined by reference to colour. An example is a cultural association open only to members of a particular ethnic group and providing its services only to its members.

Race Relations Act 1976 s.26

Even where an organisation's governing document limits its membership or beneficiaries to a particular racial group, it can provide ancillary (related) services to people of other racial groups.

5.6.2 Sex

Charities are allowed to limit their beneficiary group to members of one sex [**12.3**, **42.4**]. Non-charitable membership organisations set up on a not for profit basis may restrict their membership, and the services they provide to members, to one sex.

Sex Discrimination Act 1975 ss.34,43

Single-sex organisations can provide ancillary services to people of the other sex.

5.6.3   Religion or other belief

A charity may limit its beneficiaries to people of a particular religion or belief [**12.3**, **42.5**]. Other non-commercial organisations may under some circumstances be able to restrict membership or the provision of goods, facilities or services.

Equality Act 2006 s.57

5.6.4   Sexual orientation

A charity can be set up for beneficiaries of a specific sexual orientation (heterosexual, gay, lesbian, bisexual) and can provide services only to that group [**12.3**, **42.6**]. Any organisation can offer persons of a particular sexual orientation access to services to meet their specific educational or welfare needs.

Equality Act (Sexual Orientation) Regulations 2007 [SI 2007/1263]

5.6.5   Disability

There is no explicit provision in the **Disability Discrimination Act 1995** to allow a charity to be set up specifically for people with a particular disability or disabilities, but the Act makes clear that charities whose beneficiaries are defined by reference to any physical or mental capacity are not unlawful [**42.7**].

Disability Discrimination Act 1995 s.18C (formerly Disability Discrimination Act 1995 s.10)

5.6.6   Age

At the time of writing (mid 2009) it was not unlawful to discriminate on the basis of age in the provision of goods and services (except vocational training), but it was expected to become unlawful [**42.8**]. Organisations seeking to restrict membership or services to people in particular age groups should take advice to ensure it is lawful to do so.

5.7   THE OBJECTS CLAUSE

When setting up any organisation it is important to ensure the objects as set out in the governing document are clear, and are suitable for the organisation's planned activities and for its development well into the future. This is especially important for charities and community interest companies, because if their objects are not properly worded, considerable time is likely be added to the charity or CIC registration process. In addition, they may need consent from the Charity Commission or CIC regulator to change their objects in future, and the consent may not be forthcoming [**7.5**].

For an organisation which is not a charity or CIC it is somewhat less critical if the objects clause is not quite right. Provided the governing document contains an amendment clause which allows for the objects to be amended [**7.4.26**], there is generally no need for external consent, although under some funding agreements the funder may have to agree to the change.

5.7.1   Breadth of the objects

If a charity's purposes, beneficiaries or area of benefit are narrowly defined, the founders can ensure the charity will not get sidetracked into other activities or into working with other beneficiaries. But it is also very limiting. Unless the governing document contains power to change the objects and the Charity Commission allows a change – which it will do only if there is good reason within what is allowed under charity law – the charity will not be able to broaden its activities or beneficiary group.

Widely defined objects allow the charity flexibility. Despite the wide objects, the charity does not have to be all things to all people; it is completely free to make its own policy decisions limiting its activities to specific types of work, beneficiary groups or geographic areas. But it can at any time alter its policies if it wants to take on new activities or start working with a new client group.

With widely defined objects, however, the charity may end up doing something completely different from what the founders intended, or it may be difficult to set priorities. One solution may be to define the objects relatively broadly but with a statement that it will 'particularly' pursue a more limited objective. This makes clear the intentions and priorities of the founders, without unduly limiting the charity's future development.

There is no right level of specificity. The people involved in each potential charity must define the limits themselves, in consultation with their advisor or solicitor.

During the process of applying for registration as a charity [**8.2**], the Charity Commission may suggest narrowing wide objects to reflect more closely the founders' plans, or widening narrow objects to allow for future development. It is not always necessary to make these changes. Provided all the objects are clear, are charitable in law and will benefit the public, the Charity Commission cannot insist that they be changed.

5.7.2 Altering the objects clause

If the objects clause is too narrow or is inappropriate for other reasons, it may be possible to amend it [**7.5**]. Such alteration must not be made unless the governing document allows it. Even where the governing document allows such change, it may say that the change requires the prior consent of the Charity Commission, or there may be a statutory requirement to obtain consent from the Charity Commission or another regulator [**7.5**].

The Charity Commission allows charitable objects to be altered only if there is good reason to do so. Any change must be *cy près* (as near as possible to the original objects), but can take into account the social and economic conditions at the time of the amendment [**7.5**].

5.8 ACTING OUTSIDE THE OBJECTS OR POWERS

The possible adverse consequences of acting *ultra vires* – outside the organisation's objects or powers as set out in the governing document, or outside other constitutional requirements or limitations – mean that it is essential for those running an organisation to be aware of *and understand* the organisation's governing document, and in particular the objects and powers. This includes the members of the governing body, members of sub-committees and senior staff.

An *ultra vires* act is a **breach of trust** or **breach of fiduciary duty** [**22.4**], and may also be a breach of a statutory duty [**22.3**]. The members of the governing body, and anyone else who authorised the act or allowed it to take place, could be held personally liable for any costs or losses arising from the act.

The *ultra vires* rules could mean that a third party entering into a contract with an organisation could find that the contract is invalid because the governing body did not have the power to enter into it. If the organisation is unincorporated the contract will actually be with the members of the governing body, rather than with the organisation itself, so they would be responsible for fulfilling the contract. For incorporated bodies, the statutory rules described below protect the interests of the person who entered into the contract with the organisation.

5.8.1 Companies

Under the **Companies Act 1985** *ultra vires* acts by a company or its directors were void (invalid), but in a company that was neither a charitable company nor a community interest company some *ultra vires* acts could be authorised or ratified by a special resolution by the company members. There is no comparable provision in the **Companies Act 2006**, because companies are assumed to have unrestricted objects unless they are explicitly restricted [**5.5**]. Where the objects are restricted, any action outside the objects is void.

From 1 October 2009 any transaction with a third party which the directors, or anyone authorised by them, enter into on behalf of a non-charitable company is generally valid, even if it is *ultra vires* and even if the person who is dealing with the company knew it was *ultra vires*. The exceptions to this are transactions with directors or their associates, where special rules apply [**5.8.1.3**].

Companies Act 2006 ss.40,41

5.8.1.1 Charitable companies

An action which is outside the objects or powers of a charitable company is valid only if the third party enters into an *ultra vires* transaction without knowing that the company is a charity, or the third party does not know that the transaction is *ultra vires* but pays the charitable company full money or money's worth in relation to the transaction, or the transaction involves the transfer of property to someone who has paid a full price for it and was not informed that the transaction might be invalid. *Companies Act 2006 s.42*

The Charity Commission may make an order or scheme [**4.5.4**, **4.5.5**] to authorise an *ultra vires* act by a charitable company.

5.8.1.2 Community interest companies

In the absence of specific *ultra vires* rules for community interest companies, they are subject to the same company law rules as any other non-charitable company [**5.8.1**]. All actions are, however, subject to the community interest test [**3.4.1**].

5.8.1.3 Transactions involving directors or connected persons

An *ultra vires* transaction by the directors of any company, whether charitable or non-charitable, is voidable (can be invalidated) by the company members if it is with a person who is a director of the company, a director of the company's holding (parent) company, connected with such a director as a family member or business associate [see **15.2.5** for definition of connected person], or connected with certain other companies or firms with which the director is associated.

The company may require the director, connected person, and/or the directors who authorised the transaction, to repay any gain they have made from the transaction, or repay to the company any losses it has suffered as a result of the transaction. However a person connected with a director does not have to repay any losses if he or she did not know, when entering into the transaction, that the directors were exceeding their powers. *Companies Act 2006 s.41*

5.8.2 Charitable incorporated organisations

The trustees of a charitable incorporated organisation [**3.2**] will have a statutory duty to operate within its constitution and in accordance with any constitutional limitations on their powers, including limitations arising from a resolution by the CIO's members.

Any transaction or arrangement with a third party which the CIO's trustees, or anyone authorised by them, enter into on behalf of the CIO is generally valid, even if it is *ultra vires*, provided that a third party pays the CIO full money or money's worth in relation to the transaction and does not know that the transaction is outside the CIO's or trustees' constitutional powers, or the transaction involves the transfer of property to someone who has paid a full price and who was not informed that the transaction might be invalid. *Charities Act 1993 sch.5B paras.5-8, to be inserted by Charities Act 2006 sch.7 [expected April 2010]*

An act outside a CIO's objects or powers can be authorised by a Charity Commission order or scheme [**4.5.4**, **4.5.5**].

5.8.3 Industrial and provident societies

At the time of writing (mid 2009), the government had proposed renaming industrial and provident societies as **cooperatives** and **community benefit societies** [**3.5**]. In this book we still refer to IPSs.

An *ultra vires* act by the governing body of an IPS can be ratified by a special resolution [**19.7.5**] of the society's members. For a charitable IPS, any such ratification must have the prior written consent of the Charity Commission, even if the society is not registered with the Commission. In a non-charitable IPS, the members can also pass a further special resolution granting relief from personal liability arising from the *ultra vires* act. *Industrial & Provident Societies Act 1965 ss.7A,7D, inserted by Co-operatives & Community Benefit Societies Act 2003 s.3*

Rules on transactions with third parties and governing body members or connected persons are similar to the rules for companies [**5.8.1.3**]. *IPSA 1965 ss.7B,7E*

5.8.4 Trusts

In a charitable trust, action outside the objects or powers must be authorised by an order or scheme of the Charity Commission [**4.5.4**, **4.5.5**]. If this is not done, trustees could be held personally liable for any *ultra vires* act. This liability would be enforced by the courts or through the Charity Commission. In a private (as opposed to charitable) trust the liability may be enforced by the beneficiaries.

5.8.5 Unincorporated associations

A charitable association must act within its objects or powers unless it obtains a Charity Commission order or scheme [**4.5.4**, **4.5.5**] authorising an *ultra vires* act or authorising amendment of its objects or powers.

For non-charitable associations, there is no statute law governing their objects or powers. If all the members agree and there is no breach of grant conditions, leases etc, a non-charitable unincorporated association can do anything it wants, even if it is *ultra vires*. But if any member disagrees with the action:

- the member can insist that the governing document or other rules are followed, and could get an injunction to stop the others from taking the action;
- members who approved or undertook the action could be held liable to repay to the organisation any money which had been used for that purpose; and/or
- members who enter into a contract outside the organisation's objects or powers could be held personally liable for the contract, without being able to claim the funds from the organisation.

In a non-charitable association it may be possible to amend the governing document to make further acts lawful [**7.5.1**].

Resources: THE ORGANISATION'S OBJECTS

See end of **chapter 1**.

Statute law. www.opsi.gov.uk and www.statutelaw.gov.uk.

Much but not all case law. www.bailii.org.

Updates cross-referenced to this book. www.rclh.co.uk.

Chapter 6

THE ORGANISATION'S NAME

For sources of further information see end of chapter 1.

6.1 CHOOSING A NAME

When choosing a name for an organisation:

- **non-charitable associations** must not use any name whose use is prohibited [**6.3**];

- **charitable associations**, **trusts**, **companies** and **charitable incorporated organisations** (CIOs) must comply with the rules on charity names [**6.2**];

- **companies** and **industrial and provident societies** (IPS), whether charitable or non-charitable, must follow the rules on company names [**6.4**].

A charity, company or IPS which does not comply with the relevant rules could be required to change its name.

Even where there is no statutory restriction on using a name, any organisation which uses a name which is the same as, or very similar to, another organisation's name could have a claim brought against it for **passing off** [**44.5**] or infringement of **trade mark rights** [**44.4**]. Before choosing any name it is sensible – even if it is not legally required – to consult the registers of charities [**6.2**], companies [**6.3**], trade marks [**44.4.5**] and domain names [**44.4.6**] to avoid the risk of trade mark infringement or a passing off claim. Websites such as www.start.biz provide free checks of registered companies, registered business names [**6.5.2**], trade marks and domain names, but do not check the register of charities.

It is important to choose a name which reflects not only what the organisation is now, but what it might become. There is no point calling it 'Anyville Dance Centre' if in a few years it will be serving a wider geographic area, and will have drama and music activities as well as dance. However the mere fact that the name is Anyville Dance Centre does not stop it from operating outside Anyville or carrying on activities other than dance. It is limited to Anyville and dance only if its objects and area of benefit, as defined in its governing document, are limited in this way [**5.1**].

6.2   CHARITY NAMES

A registered charity's name must not be the same as, or in the Charity Commission's opinion too like, the name of any other registered or unregistered charity. Names can be checked on the register of charities on the Charity Commission website or at its offices [see end of **chapter 1**].   *Charities Act 1993 s.6(2),(7)*

Entering a charity's abbreviated name, informal name or any other **operating name** [**6.5.4**] on the register of charities helps prevent other charities from using those names as well as the registered name.

A charity's name must not be offensive, give a misleading impression of the charity's purposes or activities, or give a misleading impression that the charity is connected with the government, a local authority, an individual or a group. The name needs explicit Charity Commission approval if it includes certain words or expressions; a list of these is available from the Commission.

Charities (Misleading Names) Regulations 1992 [SI 1992/1901]

A charity must also comply with the requirements for its legal structure [**6.3**, **6.4**]. Companies House will not incorporate a charitable company until its promoters have received any necessary approval from the Commission for the use of words in the charity's name.

6.2.1   Charitable incorporated organisations

The same charity rules will apply to the names of charitable incorporated organisations when the structure becomes available (expected April 2010).

6.3   TRUSTS AND UNINCORPORATED ASSOCIATIONS

Apart from a few words which are protected by specific legislation [**6.4.4.3**], a *non-charitable* unincorporated association or trust which is not carrying on a business can use virtually any name it chooses. If it is carrying on a business, it is an offence to use a name with *limited*, *ltd* or the Welsh equivalent as the last word, or to use words that indicate a specific legal structure, such as *community interest company*, *CIC* or *limited partnership* anywhere in the name. Even if an unincorporated organisation is not carrying on a business, it should avoid breaching these rules.   *Company & Business Names (Miscellaneous Provisions) Regulations 2009 [SI 2009/1085] regs.13,14*

A *charitable* association or trust must comply with charity law rules [**6.2**].

Organisations should be very careful about using a name already used by another organisation if there is any risk of an action for **passing off** [**44.5**] being brought.

6.4   COMPANY AND IPS NAMES

Strict rules apply to company and industrial and provident society names. Details are in GP1 *Information and names* from Companies House.

6.4.1   The registered name

Companies and industrial and provident societies are legal entities which must be identified for all legal purposes by their full name (called **registered name** or **corporate name**). This name must be used *exactly* as it is on the certificate of registration. Words which are written out in the registered name cannot be abbreviated, and words which are abbreviated cannot be used in full. Nor is it allowed to put in or take out commas or full stops, or to use & instead of *and* (or *vice versa*). An exception is that all names are shown on a company certificate of registration in uppercase (capital) letters, and the capitalisation can be ignored.

The registered name must be on certain paper and electronic documents [**18.1.1**, **18.1.2**] and publicly displayed at the organisation's registered office and any premises where it carries on its work [**17.1.3**, **17.2.2**].

6.4.2 Using symbols in names

Symbols that can be used in company and industrial and provident society names are &, @, £, $, €, ¥, numerals and a range of punctuation marks, including brackets, exclamation marks, question marks, / and \. The following symbols can also be used, but not as one of the first three permitted characters in a name: *, =, #, % and +.

Company & Business Names (Miscellaneous Provisions) Regulations 2009 [SI 2009/1085] reg.2, sch.1

6.4.3 Similarity to other names

6.4.3.1 'The same' names

The registered (corporate) name of a company or industrial and provident society cannot be **the same as** any other name on the register of company and IPS names kept by Companies House.

Companies Act 2006 ss.66,1099

Some words and symbols are not taken into account when deciding whether a name is the same. For example, the following are ignored: punctuation and spaces; *the* as the first word of a name; *company, and company, co, limited, ltd, unlimited, public limited company* etc and their Welsh equivalents as the last word of a name; and *and* and &. Under regulations in effect from 1 October 2009, symbols and their written equivalent are treated as the same, for example £ and *pound*, $ and *dollar*, € and *euro*, ¥ and *yen*, % and *per cent*, and numerals and the written equivalent (such as *1* and *one*). *At* and @ are treated as the same unless @ is part of an email address.

Company & Business Names (Miscellaneous Provisions) Regulations 2009 [SI 2009/1085] reg.7, sch.3

As part of the company or IPS registration process, Companies House or Mutual Societies Registration consults the register and advises if the proposed name is 'the same as' another. However it is sensible to check the register before this, on the Companies House website, in person at Companies House or main reference libraries, or by ringing Companies House.

If a company or IPS is a registered charity, its name must not be the same as or too similar to that of any other charity [**6.2**].

6.4.3.2 'Too like' names

A company or industrial and provident society name is rejected only if it is 'the same as' one on the register. Sometimes, therefore, a name is registered which is very similar to another. If an existing company or IPS thinks a new organisation's name is 'too like' its own and could cause confusion, it can object to the registration within 12 months. The new company or IPS could then be required to change its name [**6.8.1**]. It is therefore sensible to check beforehand for similar names as well as names which are 'the same'.

Companies Act 2006 ss.67,68

6.4.3.3 Names where a person has goodwill

Any organisation – even if it is not a registered company or industrial and provident society – can object to a company's or IPS's name, if it can show that it has **goodwill** in the name. Application is made to a **company names adjudicator** in the UK Intellectual Property Office [see end of **chapter 44**]. The applicant has to show that it has been operating under that name, or that it has been operating under a name similar enough that the public could be misled into thinking it has a connection with the company or IPS. It may also have to be able to show that the company's or IPS's main intention in choosing the name was to obtain payment from the applicant or prevent the applicant from registering the name.

Companies Act 2006 ss.69-74; Company Names Adjudicator Rules 2008 [SI 2008/1738]

6.4.4 Misleading and sensitive names

A company or industrial and provident society cannot use a name which is offensive or constitutes a criminal offence; includes **sensitive words and expressions** as specified in regulations, without authorisation from the secretary of state for business, innovation and skills or other authorities; or contains words or expressions whose use is governed by other legislation.

Companies Act 2006 ss.53-56

6.4.4.1 Sensitive words

The complete list of 'sensitive' words and expressions which need approval from the secretary of state (for companies) or the Financial Services Authority (for industrial and provident societies), or from other bodies is in GP1 *Incorporation and names,* from Companies House [see end of **chapter 1**].

An organisation intending to use a word requiring authorisation may need supporting evidence, for example an organisation wishing to use *national* in its name may need a letter from a government department or large organisation confirming that the new organisation is genuinely national or pre-eminent, or documentation showing that it has already used the word in its name for a long time and should therefore be allowed to continue using it.

6.4.4.2 Misleading names

A company or industrial and provident society needs to be careful not to use a name which is seriously misleading or gives a misleading impression of its activities. If it does, it could be required to change the name [**6.8.1**].

6.4.4.3 Protected names

The names of a few associations (British Legion, Girl Guides Association, National Society for the Prevention of Cruelty to Children, Royal Life Saving Society, Scout Association, and Venerable Order of St John of Jerusalem) are protected and cannot be used by any other organisation.   *Chartered Associations (Protection of Names & Uniforms) Act 1926*

6.4.5 Indication of company type or legal form

6.4.5.1 Community interest companies

The name of a private **community interest company** [**3.4**] must end with *community interest company* or *CIC*, or the Welsh equivalent. The name of a public limited company registered as a CIC must end with *community interest public limited company*, the initials CIPLC or the Welsh equivalent.
Companies (Audit, Investigations & Community Enterprise) Act 2004 s.33

6.4.5.2 Other companies

A **public limited company** [**3.3.1**] which is not a CIC must end its name with *public limited company* or *plc*. Most **private limited companies** [**3.3.1**] which are not CICs must end their name with *limited, ltd* (with no full stop) or *ltd.* (with a full stop), or with *cyfyngedig* or *cyf* if its name is in Welsh.
Companies Act 2006 ss.58,59

The name of a company or industrial and provident society cannot include the word *limited, unlimited* or *public limited company*, or their abbreviation or Welsh equivalent, anywhere except at the end of the name.   *Companies Act 2006 s.65*

6.4.5.3 Companies exempt from having to use 'limited'

A private company limited by guarantee which is not a community interest company does not have to use *limited, ltd* or the Welsh equivalent at the end of its name if its objects are the promotion or regulation of commerce, art, science, education, religion, charity or any profession; its memorandum or articles require the company's profits or other income to be used to promote its objects [**7.4.9**]; its articles prohibit payments of dividends or any return of capital to its members [**7.4.9**]; and its articles require all the company's assets to be transferred, if the company is wound up, to another body with similar or charitable objects.
Companies Act 2006 ss.60-64; Company & Business Names (Miscellaneous Provisions) Regulations 2009 [SI 2009/1085] reg.3

A company exempt from using *limited, ltd* or the Welsh equivalent under the **Companies Act 1985** or earlier Acts remains exempt under the 2006 Act, provided it does not change its name, or amend its articles in a way which would make the exemption no longer apply.

A company which does not want to use *limited* etc in its name on registration must indicate this on form **IN01** when applying for registration [**1.5.5**].

A qualifying company which is registered with *limited*, *ltd* or the Welsh equivalent and subsequently decides it does not want to use it may do so by notifying Companies House on form **NE01** .   *Companies Act 2006 s.60*

A company which does not use one of these words at the end of its name must disclose that it is a limited liability company on its stationery and many other paper and electronic documents [**18.1.1**].

6.4.5.4 Industrial and provident societies

An industrial and provident society must generally end its name with *limited,* or *cyfyngedig* if its rules are in Welsh. Societies established for charitable or benevolent purposes may apply to Mutual Societies Registration, part of the Financial Services Authority [see end of **chapter 1**], for exemption from having to use *limited* as part of their name.   *Industrial & Provident Societies Act 1965 s.5*

6.5 USING OTHER NAMES

6.5.1 Company and IPS business names

Many companies and industrial and provident societies (IPS) operate under abbreviations or names other than their registered name, or allow projects or parts of the organisation to operate under other names. Any name other than the full registered name – even if the difference is only very slight – is a **business name** (often called **trading name** or **operating name**). It is called a business or trading name even if the organisation is not actually carrying on a business or trade.

For example if the registered name is 'The West Anyville Neighbourhood Team Limited', then any other name used for all or some of its work instead of, or in addition to, its registered name – such as The West Anyville Neighbourhood Team (without 'Limited'), WANT, Anyville Under Fives, WANT Enterprises – would all be business names.

Anyone who enters into agreements on behalf of the organisation must be aware of the difference between registered and business names. The consequences of getting this wrong can be serious, because a contract signed under a business name is not legally a contract with the company or IPS, but is a contract with the signatories for which they are personally liable, and a cheque which does not have the registered name on it is personally guaranteed by the person who signs it.

6.5.1.1 Permitted business names

A business name cannot end in *limited* or *ltd*, so 'WANT Limited' cannot be used.

A word needing approval from the secretary of state or other body for use in a registered name [**6.4.4**] also needs approval for use in a business name.
Companies Act 2006 ss.1192-1196

A word cannot be used in a business name if it gives a inappropriate indication of type of company, or a misleading impression of the company's or IPS's activities [**6.4.4.2**, **6.4.5**].

The rules about 'same as' and 'too like' names do not apply [**6.4.3**, **6.4.3.2**], so the legislation does not prevent a company or IPS from using a business name which is the same as, or very similar to, someone else's registered name or trading name. But this opens the organisation to the risk of legal action for passing off [**44.5**]. When choosing a business name, it is sensible to check the register of company names to be sure the name is not too similar to a registered name.

The registered name must be on certain documents [**18.1.1**, **18.1.2**] and at the organisation's premises [**17.1.3**, **17.2.2**]. If a business name is also included on these documents or premises, it must be clear which is the registered name.

6.5.2 Voluntary registration of business names

A business name does not have to be registered in any way. It is, however, possible to register it with a commercial **business names registration agency**. The agency will generally check that the business name is not the same as any other registered company name and is not registered as a business name or domain name; and may check that the business name does not infringe any UK trade mark rights [**44.4**].

Such registration is optional and is not linked in any way with any official registration. Even without such registration, free checks on company, business and domain names and trade marks can be carried out on some business name registration websites [**6.1**].

6.5.3 Unincorporated organisations

The names of non-charitable unincorporated associations do not have to be registered with any registration body. It is however possible to register the name voluntarily with a commercial business names registration agency [above].

6.5.4 Charity operating names

A charity which uses any names other than its full registered name should (but does not have to) register these **operating names** or **working names** with the Charity Commission. This includes acronyms and names used for fundraising purposes, and could include project names.

6.6 NAMES AS INTELLECTUAL PROPERTY

Logos, names, designs etc are part of the organisation's **intellectual property** and its **goodwill**, and as such are valuable assets which should be protected against exploitation and unauthorised use [**44.9**].

Organisations' names, logos, designs, brand names, symbols, slogans, abbreviations etc can generally be registered as **trade marks** (for goods) or **service marks** (for services) [**44.4**]. This provides very effective protection.

A logo, design, symbol or other visual representation of the organisation's name is automatically **copyright** if it has any artistic merit, however small [**44.2.1**]. But a name cannot, in itself, be copyright.

Even if a name is not copyright or registered as a trade mark, a case for **passing off** can be brought if it is used for a similar purpose [**44.5**].

6.7 CHANGING A NAME

Changing an organisation's name does not change its legal status, so it is not necessary to undertake any formal procedures to transfer the assets, liabilities and contracts to the renamed organisation. Nor does a name change alter any legal proceedings the organisation is involved in.

It is, however, important to notify everyone with whom the organisation has any dealings, in particular banks, HM Revenue and Customs and other registration bodies, and the Land Registry if the organisation owns any registered land [**60.6.3**]. Registered charities, companies and industrial and provident societies must ensure that the new name is on all required documents and premises [**18.1**, **17.1.3**]. Cheques and financial documents must be used only with the new name.

6.7.1 Companies

So long as the name meets all the usual requirements for a company name [**6.4**], any company, including a community interest company, may change its registered name by a special or written resolution [**19.7.4**, **19.10.2**], or if the articles allow, by a simpler procedure such as a resolution by the directors or ordinary resolution by the company members.   *Companies Act 2006 ss.77-81*

A charitable company should check with the Charity Commission to ensure the proposed new name meets charity requirements, and for all companies it is sensible to search trade marks and domain names [**6.1**]. A company which is a registered social landlord requires consent from the Homes and Communities Agency.

The change of name must be submitted to Companies House within 15 days after being passed, on form **NM01** (change of name by resolution), **NM04** (change by means provided for in the articles), or **NM05** (change by resolution of the directors). Where it has been changed by special or written resolution, form **Res CA2006** or **Written Res CA2006** must be submitted. A fee (£10 as at 1/8/09) must be sent in with the notice.

The name change takes effect from the date Companies House issues a revised certificate of incorporation, usually within five working days of receiving the documents. For a higher fee (£50 as at 1/8/09) the certificate can be issued on the same day the documents are received at any Companies House office.

The old name can be used as a business name [**6.5.1**] but must not have *limited* or *ltd* at the end. All new documents, including cheques, which are required to include the registered name must be changed immediately to the new name.

6.7.1.1 Conditional change of name

A change of name can be conditional on an event taking place, for example a merger. Any such name change must be made by special resolution [**19.7.4**], and the notification to Companies House must be on **NM02** within 15 days of the resolution being passed. If the condition has been satisfied at the time NM02 is submitted, the fee (£10 as at 1/8/09) must be sent in with the form. If the event does not occur until later, **NM03** and the fee must be submitted when it happens. A revised certificate of incorporation will not be provided until Companies House is told on NM02 or NM03 that the event has occurred. *Companies Act 2006 s.78*

6.7.2 Industrial and provident societies

An IPS must provide, in its application to change its name (**form C**), its reasons for the change. The Financial Services Authority [see end of **chapter 1**] must be satisfied that the change is necessary and will not lead to confusion for people dealing with the organisation. Approval is usually granted only if there is a good reason for the name change. *Industrial & Provident Societies Act 1965 s.5(3)(b)*

If there is a procedure in the IPS's rules for passing a resolution to change its name, this procedure must be followed. If there is no such provision in the rules, the usual procedures for amending the rules must be followed. *IPSA 1965 s.5(3)(a)*

6.7.3 Charitable incorporated organisations

A charitable incorporated organisation changes its name by amending its constitution with a 75% majority of votes cast at a general meeting, or with 100% agreement of all the CIO's members if the resolution is passed otherwise than at a general meeting. The change of name does not take effect until it has been registered with the Charity Commission [**6.7.6**]. *Charities Act 1993 sch.5B para.14, to be inserted by Charities Act 2006 sch.7 [expected April 2010]*

6.7.4 Trusts

If a trust deed includes a procedure for alteration, the name can be changed using that procedure. This will involve passing a resolution of the trustees and preparing a **supplemental deed** [**20.3**]. If there is no procedure for amending the trust deed, a charitable trust can ask the Charity Commission for a scheme [**7.5.2**].

6.7.5 Unincorporated associations

If the constitution of an unincorporated association includes a procedure for amendment, the name can be changed in this way. If there is no such procedure, the name of an association can be changed by agreement of all the members [**7.5.1**], or a charitable association may change it by a Charity Commission scheme [**7.5.2**].

6.7.6 Charities

Change of a charity's name does not require the Charity Commission's prior consent unless its governing document requires this. But it is sensible to check with the Commission beforehand, since a registered charity must notify the Commission anyway, and can be required to change its new name. *Charities Act 1993 s.3(7)(b)*

The notification is made by sending the Commission:

- for a charitable association, a copy of the resolution and the minutes of the meeting at which it was passed, signed by the chairperson or secretary to certify that it is an accurate copy;
- for a charitable trust, a certified copy of the supplemental deed;
- for a charitable incorporated organisation, a copy of the resolution within 15 days of its being passed, with an amended copy of the CIO's constitution;
- for a charitable company, a copy of the new certificate issued by Companies House.

If a charitable trust or association does not have the power to amend its governing document, the Commission has to make a scheme [**7.5.2**].

So long as its objects are not changed, a charity which changes its name can still retain all property given to it under its previous name. However there could be problems with legacies left to the charity under its former name, and advice should be sought about how to reduce the risk of such problems.

6.8   COMPULSORY CHANGE OF NAME

Any organisation can be required by the court to change its registered name or any other name it uses if it is found guilty of passing off or infringement of trade mark rights [**44.4**, **44.5**]. In addition, companies, industrial and provident societies and charities can be required to change their name if it is the same as or too similar to another company/IPS or charity name.

6.8.1   Companies and IPSs

The secretary of state for business, innovation and skills can require a company or industrial and provident society to change its registered name within 12 months of registration, if the name is the same as or too like the name of another registered company or IPS; within five years of registration, if the company or IPS gave misleading information at the time of registration; or at any time, if the name is so misleading that it could cause harm to the public, or it does not use limited in its name and ceases to be eligible for this exemption.

Companies Act 2006 ss.64,67,68,75,76

A **company names adjudicator** can require any company or IPS to change its name if someone successfully claims they have goodwill in the name [**6.4.3.3**].

6.8.2   Charities

The Charity Commission can require a registered charity to change its name within 12 months of registration, if its name is the same as or too like the name of another charity, whether registered or not. *Charities Act 1993 s.6*

It can require any charity other than an exempt charity [**8.1.2**] to change its name at any time if the name gives a misleading impression or includes a word that is not allowed [**6.2**] or is offensive. In this situation the trustees can choose the new name and change it by a resolution of the directors, but the new name must be approved by the Commission. The name change must be notified to Companies House in the usual way [**6.7.1**].

Resources: THE ORGANISATION'S NAME

See end of **chapter 1**.

Statute law. www.opsi.gov.uk and www.statutelaw.gov.uk.

Much but not all case law. www.bailii.org.

Updates cross-referenced to this book. www.rclh.co.uk.

Chapter 7
THE GOVERNING DOCUMENT

For sources of further information see end of chapter 1.

7.1   THE IMPORTANCE OF THE GOVERNING DOCUMENT

If a group is set up informally, rules may be made up as they are needed, and perhaps changed whenever anyone feels like it. But as the group gets larger or seeks public recognition and funding, there will be pressure to put in writing what the organisation is and the rules by which it operates. This is the organisation's central document, its **governing document** or **governing instrument**, usually referred to as its **constitution**.

Because it is so important, all members of a governing body should receive a copy as soon as they are elected or appointed, and should understand that they have a legal duty to ensure the organisation complies with it. If the governing document is very long or complex, they should also receive a summary of the main points.

In a membership organisation it is good practice to give the members a copy of the full version or a summary. If this is not practical, a copy should be posted in a visible place or copies should be easily available on request.

Companies and industrial and provident societies have a statutory obligation to provide a copy of their governing document to anyone who requests it [**1.5.10, 1.7.7**], and this is also likely to apply to charitable incorporated organisations.

It is good practice to include with the governing document standing orders [**7.4.25**] and other rules and policies that relate to provisions in the governing document.

7.1.1 Form of the governing document

The form of the governing document depends on the legal structure of the organisation [**chapters 2** and **3**]:

- for an **unincorporated association**, the governing document is generally called the **constitution** or **rules**;
- for a **trust**, it is generally a **trust deed** or **declaration of trust**, but could be a will or similar document;
- for an **industrial and provident society**, it is the **rules**;
- for a **charitable incorporated organisation**, it is a **constitution**;
- for a **company**, including a community interest company, formed before 1 October 2009 the governing document is in two parts: the **memorandum of association**, setting out the company's objects, powers and the liability of its members; and the **articles of association**, setting out its administrative procedures, but from 1 October 2009 the provisions in the memorandum are treated as if they are in the articles;
- for a company formed on or after 1 October 2009, the governing document is a single document, the **articles of association**, and the memorandum is simply a registration document [**1.5.4**].   *Companies Act 2006 ss.8,18,28*

The term **constitution** is often used to refer to all governing documents, of whatever form.

The fact that an organisation is charitable affects the content of the governing document, in particular the objects clause [**5.1**], but does not affect the form.

7.1.1.1 Company constitution

The **Companies Act 2006** introduces the concept of a **company constitution**. A company constitution includes not only the articles of association (including, for companies formed before 1 October 2009, the memorandum of association), but also all special resolutions passed by the company [**19.7.4**], and all written resolutions agreed by the company members which, had they not been passed in writing, would have had to be passed as a special resolution [**19.10.2**]. Certain other resolutions or agreements may also need to be notified to Companies House and be provided to anyone who asks for the company's governing document.

Companies Act 2006 ss.17,.29

Companies formed before 1 October 2009 do not have to revise their memorandum and articles until they make any amendment [**7.5.3**]. At that point they have to submit the resolution to Companies House, with new articles which include the amendment(s) plus all the provisions in the memorandum that have now become part of the articles (everything except the list of subscribers), Alternatively the new articles can just include the amendment(s), and the memorandum provisions can be attached as an annex. If the only amendment is a change of name [**6.7.1**] this does not trigger an obligation to produce or submit revised articles.

7.1.2 Legal nature of the governing document

7.1.2.1 Under statute

For incorporated organisations, legislation defines the nature of the governing document, what it must include, who it must be provided to, and other rules:

- for companies set up from 1 October 2009, the **Companies Act 2006**, and for companies set up before that the **Companies Act 1985** or **1948**;
- for community interest companies, the **Companies Acts** and the **Companies (Audit, Investigations and Community Enterprise) Act 2004**;
- for charitable incorporated organisations, the **Charities Act 2006** and the CIO regulations;
- for industrial and provident societies, the **Industrial and Provident Societies Act 1965**.

7.1.2.2   As a contract

In unincorporated associations, companies (including community interest companies), charitable incorporated organisations and industrial and provident societies the governing document is a type of contract, setting out the mutual rights and obligations of members and the organisation, the rights and obligations of the members in relation to each other, and the powers and obligations of the governing body in relation to the members and the organisation. As contracts, the terms of these governing documents are enforceable in the courts.

7.1.2.3   As a trust

In an organisation set up as a trust [**2.3**], the governing document is generally a trust deed or declaration of trust, or in some cases a will, conveyance or similar arrangement. This sets out the terms of the **trust** between the trust's donors or funders, the governing body (the trustees), and the beneficiaries. Any action outside these terms may be a **breach of trust** for which the trustees could be held personally liable.

In all charitable organisations, even if they are not set up as trusts, the governing document embodies the trust between donors or funders, the charity trustees, and the charity's beneficiaries, and the trustees can be liable for breach of trust.

7.1.3   Getting it right

A governing document:

- must comply with the statutory requirements [**1.4**, **1.5.3**, **1.7.1**] or, if applicable, trust law [**1.3.1**];
- should reflect not only what the organisation is going to do now but what it might become [**5.7.1**];
- should embody the desired governance style, which might be democratic (sometimes called the **association** model) or controlled by the people who set up the organisation and their successors (the **foundation** model);
- should not be unduly restrictive, and should allow for amendment unless there are acceptable default statutory procedures for this [**7.4.26**];
- should include provision for dissolving the organisation, unless there are acceptable default statutory procedures for this [**7.4.27**], and should indicate what happens to any remaining assets;
- after it is agreed, should be reviewed every three to five years to be sure it is still appropriate and the organisation is complying with it;
- should and in some cases must include all amendments with every copy, either attached to the end or retyped with the amendments included.

7.2   GETTING ADVICE

7.2.1   Using a legal advisor

There is no obligation to consult a legal advisor to set up any kind of voluntary organisation, but doing so may speed up the process, and can ensure the governing document is appropriate and meets any legal requirements [see **64.8.4** for how to find a legal advisor].

It is sensible to consult an advisor if charitable status is desired or a decision needs to be made about whether the organisation should be charitable, or the governing document is not based on a well proven model. Legal advice should also be sought if it is important that the process not be delayed, or if the organisation is likely to need advice on other legal matters such as contracts of employment, property, or setting up a separate trading arm.

Most solicitors can help set up a trust or company, but one who specialises in the voluntary sector is far more likely to be able to advise on how to phrase the objects and powers so they are acceptable to the Charity Commission, what forms of membership and governing body are most appropriate, and similar issues.

Specialist advice is also important when setting up a **community interest company**. **Industrial and provident societies** are generally set up through a promoting body, using model rules [**1.7.1**]. Advice from an advisor with expertise in IPSs is essential if setting up an IPS without going through a promoting body.

Even if legal advice is not necessary when the organisation is first set up, it may be needed later if the organisation wants to change its legal structure or develop a more detailed governing document.

7.2.1.1 The cost

Solicitors and other advisors with voluntary sector experience should be able to give a good estimate of the likely cost of drawing up the governing document and, if necessary, registering the organisation. If they quote an hourly rate, they should be able to indicate how long the process is likely to take. If they quote a flat fee, it is important to clarify what is included and whether there are likely to be any extras, such as disbursements (expenses).

It may be tempting to use a solicitor who will deal with the governing document free or at reduced cost, but this could be a false economy if he or she does not have a clear understanding of relevant areas of the law and experience of issues affecting voluntary organisations.

7.2.1.2 The process

Unless only two or three people are involved in setting up the organisation, development of the governing document should be delegated to a small group. They should have a clear indication of what sorts of issues they can agree on their own and what needs to go back to the larger group for discussion and decision.

Before meeting a solicitor or other legal advisor, the people involved should:
- be familiar with the process of setting up a voluntary organisation, and the decisions that need to be made as part of the process [**chapter 1**];
- be familiar with the choice of legal forms [**chapters 2 and 3**] and the pros and cons of charitable status [**chapter 4**];
- send the advisor background material, especially on the proposed objects [**chapter 5**], and any model or draft governing document they have;
- prepare for the meeting by writing a list of questions and issues and if possible, send this to the advisor beforehand.

At the meeting it is important to ensure the advisor is made aware of any values or issues which are particularly important for the group, and to ask for clarification of anything which is not clear. Both parties should make full notes and should agree a timetable for progress, with critical dates highlighted.

If notes are written up or a report to a meeting of the group is minuted, a copy should be sent to the advisor.

7.2.2 Guidance

Virtually all councils for voluntary service and other voluntary sector support bodies can offer general information and support about setting up an organisation and drawing up a governing document. This may be very helpful in the early stages, but for a trust, company, charitable incorporated organisation or industrial and provident society it may be necessary to consult a legal advisor at a later stage, unless the support body can provide detailed technical advice.

7.2.3 Do it yourself

It may be tempting simply to adopt another organisation's governing document, but this may lead to the organisation ending up with something inappropriate to its needs or that does not meet current regulatory requirements. Another temptation is to cobble together sections from a number of governing documents. This can create a document which is internally inconsistent and therefore unworkable.

Even organisations which for cost or ideological reasons want to draw up their own governing document, may decide to have the final version checked by a legal advisor. If the motive for doing it themselves was cost, they may find that this approach saves very little. Even at final draft stage a good advisor will need to become thoroughly familiar with the organisation. Because the governing document will be unfamiliar, it may take the advisor as much time to consider it as to create one from precedents (previously used models) with which he or she is familiar. In addition the advisor may raise fundamental questions, such as whether to incorporate, which put the process back to square one, or may have to break the bad news that the draft does not comply with statutory requirements.

7.3 THE LANGUAGE OF CONSTITUTIONS

Many governing documents, especially older ones, use unfamiliar terminology. Most of the terms used in governing documents are explained in this chapter or in the relevant section of this book, so they should become comprehensible, but if in doubt ask for an explanation from a solicitor or voluntary sector advisor. Sometimes the same term may have a different meaning in different governing documents, or different terms may be used to describe the same thing.

Governing documents, even for companies and trusts, do not need to be written in legal jargon. Models which are reasonably clear and straightforward are now available from the Charity Law Association, Charity Commission, umbrella bodies for some types of organisations, and other sources [**8.2.2**].

7.3.1 Should and shall, may and must

For all governing documents, clarity is essential. For example, a common confusion arises from the use of the word 'should'. Anything which *shall* be done *must* be done. Anything which *may* be done is optional. Beware of anything which says it *should* be done. It is often unclear whether this is intended to mean 'must' or 'it is good practice'. If something must be done, use *must* or *shall*.

7.3.2 Terms relating to people

7.3.2.1 Governing body

The **governing body** is the body which, under the governing document, is responsible in law for managing the organisation [**15.1**]. It is unlikely to be called this in the governing document; instead, it will be called the **board of directors**, **board of trustees**, **board of governors**, **management committee**, **executive committee**, **council of management** or a similar name.

Regardless of what they may be called in the governing document or in practice, all the voting members of the governing body of a charitable organisation are **charity trustees**, and all the voting members of the governing body of a company are **company directors**. If the organisation is a charitable company, governing body members are charity trustees as well as company directors.

7.3.2.2 Officers

The term **officers** is used in a number of ways. In company law it includes the company directors and possibly shadow directors [**13.1.3**], as well as **honorary officers** (chairperson, vice chair, secretary, treasurer etc), the company secretary, and senior management.
Companies Act 2006 ss.1121(2),1173(1)

The term is used in a similar way for industrial and provident societies.

In unincorporated associations and trusts 'officers' typically refers only to honorary officers, and in many company and IPS governing documents the term is used in this way as well.

7.3.2.3 Secretary

Similarly the term **secretary** has a specific meaning as the person responsible for various administrative matters under company or industrial and provident society law. A **company** or **IPS secretary** may be a member of the governing body, but could be an employee or someone such as a solicitor or accountant who is not directly connected with the organisation or its governing body.

Private companies, whether limited by shares or guarantee, are no longer required to have a company secretary unless this is required by the articles. If a company does not have a secretary, the duties normally done by the secretary must be carried out by a director or directors, or someone appointed by them.

Companies Act 2006 s.270

In trusts, **trust secretary** often refers to a person who is not a member of the governing body but attends meetings to take minutes. It may also refer to the chief executive.

In associations – and sometimes in trusts or companies as well – **secretary** refers to a member of the governing body who is elected by the governing body or at a general meeting to carry out certain administrative duties. This is often called an **honorary secretary**, to distinguish it from company secretary or a person employed as a secretary.

7.3.2.4 Agents

As well as being 'officers', members of the governing body of an incorporated organisation are **agents** of the organisation, acting on behalf of the incorporated organisation. An agent is anyone who has authority, in general or for specific purposes, to act on behalf of the organisation (or anyone else). The person or organisation on whose behalf an agent acts is the **principal** [see **20.5** for more about agents and principals].

Governing body members of an unincorporated association may be agents acting on behalf of the organisation's members, or principals acting in their own right.

7.3.2.5 Servants

The term **servants** as used in governing documents refers to employees who carry out the work of the organisation as directed by an officer (as defined above). This is an outmoded term and does not need to be used.

7.3.3 Terms relating to property

The governing document might refer to:

- **demise**: to lease property, or the lease itself;
- **bequest**: personal property (money or goods) left to the organisation under a will;
- **devise**: real property (land or buildings) left to the organisation under a will;
- **endowment**: money or property which produces an income for the organisation, through interest, dividends or rent;
- **permanent endowment**: money or property given on condition that the capital or principal sum of money is not spent or that the investments or property are not sold or disposed of, or that if they are sold the proceeds from the sale are not spent.

7.3.4 Latin and French terms

Some governing documents contain Latin or other phrases which have a specific meaning in law. Some of the more common ones are:

- *ad hoc* (Latin, literally 'for this'): for a specific purpose, usually short term e.g. 'The management committee may set up standing [permanent] or *ad hoc* [temporary] sub-committees';
- *cy près* (Norman French, 'so near'): as near as possible, applied to changes in a charity's objects or purposes when the original objects can no longer be met [**7.5.2.1**];
- *ex gratia* (Latin, 'out of gratitude' or 'as a favour'): a payment made where there is no legal obligation to do so but the organisation feels a moral obligation [**53.3**];
- *ex officio* (Latin, 'by virtue of office'): holding a position by virtue of holding another position, e.g. 'The chair is a member *ex officio* of all sub-committees';
- *inter alia* (Latin, 'among others'): among other things, e.g. 'a governing document may contain, *inter alia*, rules for general meetings';

- *inter se* (Latin, 'among themselves'): between or among themselves, e.g. 'The members of the committee shall decide *inter se* or by drawing lots which one-third of their number shall retire';
- *intra vires* (Latin, 'within powers'): actions authorised by the organisation's governing document or in any other way;
- *mutatis mutandis* (Latin, 'changing the things that need to be changed'): the rules relating to one situation are adapted for another, e.g. 'The rules relating to meetings of the governing body shall be applied *mutatis mutandis* to meetings of its committees';
- *sine die* (Latin, 'without a date'): with no date set, e.g. 'If a date within seven days is set for an adjourned meeting no notice of the adjourned meeting need be given, but at least seven days' notice must be given for a meeting adjourned *sine die* or to be held more than seven days after the original meeting';
- *status quo* (Latin, 'the situation which is'): the current situation;
- *ultra vires* (Latin, 'beyond powers'): with no legal authority; actions which are not authorised by the organisation's governing document or in any other proper way [**5.8**].

7.3.5 General terms

It is not only Latin or ancient French terms which cause difficulty; even English words can be unfamiliar.

These presents means this document; **heretofore** means before this; **hereinafter** means after this; **whereas** means 'here's why we are doing this'. **From time to time** means 'when they choose to do it' (as in 'Members must pay the subscription as determined from time to time by the executive committee'), rather than once only or at a set time. **For the time being** means 'at the time the action takes place', as in 'Notice must be sent to all members for the time being'. **Save that** or **saving that** means except.

Determine and **determination** can mean the same as **terminate** and **termination** – or the same as **decide** and **decision**. In something like 'The board has power to determine membership' it is necessary to look at the context to determine whether determine means 'decide' or 'terminate'.

7.3.6 Interpretation

Within the governing document there may be an **interpretation** section which defines what is meant by some of the terms used in the governing document. Use of capital letters within the governing document usually signals that the word has been defined in the interpretation section.

There may be a section stating 'the masculine imports [or includes] the feminine', meaning that wherever the governing document says 'he', it means 'he or she'. 'He or she', 's/he' or other non-sexist language, can be used throughout the governing document. 'They' can also be used to avoid the cumbersome 'he or she', but can be confusing because it is a plural implying more than one person. 'She' can be used throughout, either by women's organisations or where 'the feminine includes the masculine'.

There may be a section which says that if words or expressions are not specifically defined in the interpretation section (if there is one), and if they do not obviously have a different meaning, they should be interpreted as they would be within the **Interpretation Act 1978** as it applies to an Act of Parliament. This Act sets out what words mean when they are used in statutes. The section does not have to be included, and certainly should not be included unless the people who draw up the governing document are clear that they are using words exactly as they would be used within the Interpretation Act.

The articles of association of a company usually say that words or expressions in the articles have the same meaning as in the Companies Acts. Again, it is important to ensure that if this clause is included, words are used in this way.

7.4 WHAT A GOVERNING DOCUMENT INCLUDES

Although there are significant differences in governing documents for organisations with different legal structures, most cover the following matters.

7.4.1 Name and location

The governing document generally starts with the name of the organisation [**6.1-6.4**]. This clause is followed, for a company or industrial and provident society, by the country where the **registered office** will be located, or for a charitable incorporated organisation the country where the **principal office** will be [**17.1.1**, **17.2.1**, **17.4.1**]. For companies, the country where the registered office must be located is called **domicile**.

7.4.2 Objects or purposes

The **objects** clause [**chapter 5**] is the most important clause in the governing document, covering the objects or **purposes** for which the organisation is established; if appropriate, the **beneficiaries** (clients, users) the organisation is set up to serve or work with; and if appropriate, the **area of benefit** (geographic area).

7.4.3 Powers

Strictly speaking, a voluntary organisation has the right to carry out only activities *directly* related to its objects as set out in its governing document. Its right to undertake secondary activities, such as fundraising necessary to achieve its objects, is set out in its **powers**. A power may be given by **statute**, **implied** (implicit) in case law or common law, **express** (explicit) within an organisation's governing document, or included in a **general** catch-all power.

If a power to do something does not exist, *the organisation may not be able to do it*. If it does it anyway, the action could be *ultra vires* (outside its powers) and the individuals who authorised or undertook the action could be personally liable to repay to the organisation all funds used for it or losses caused by it [**5.8**].

In a company, charitable incorporated organisation or industrial and provident society the powers unless indicated otherwise are those of the incorporated body. In an unincorporated association the powers rest with the members of the organisation or, if specified in the governing document, with the governing body. In a trust the powers rest with the trustees.

7.4.3.1 Statutory powers

Powers given under **statute** automatically apply to organisations of that type or their governing body. Members of a company, for example, always have power to remove a company director, even if there is no such clause in the articles [**13.5.6**]. Similarly, trustees of trusts and charitable unincorporated associations have certain investment powers [**58.1.2**] under the **Trustee Act 2000**.

Some statutory powers can be varied or excluded by the governing document. Trustees, for example, may have under the governing document investment powers narrower than those allowed by legislation [**58.1.2**]. Other statutory powers, such as company members' right to appoint a proxy [**19.8.3**], always exist and anything in the governing document that alters or excludes them is void (invalid).

7.4.3.2 Implied powers

Some powers may exist because a court would find that they were so directly and necessarily linked to the achievement of the organisation's objects or to other activities imposed on the organisation that they must be assumed – for example the power to open a bank account. Such powers can be exercised even if they are not explicit in statute or in the governing document. But **implied powers** are likely to be narrow, and should only be relied upon after taking legal advice.

7.4.3.3 General power

A well drafted governing document should contain a **general power**, such as 'power to do any other acts the committee thinks fit' or 'power to do any lawful act necessary for the achievement of the objects'. This gives the organisation the right to undertake acts which are not specifically mentioned, so long as the action is lawful, is for the purpose of achieving the objects, is not one for which explicit power has to be given in the governing document, is not explicitly prohibited by the governing document, and falls within the wording of the general power.

Without a general power in its governing document, the organisation may not in future be able to do what it wants to do without amending its governing document or going to the Charity Commission for a scheme [**7.5.2**].

A charitable incorporated organisation has statutory power, subject to anything in its constitution, to do anything which is calculated to further its purposes or is conducive or incidental to doing so.   *Charities Act 1993 sch.5B para.1(1), to be inserted by Charities Act 2006 sch.7 [expected April 2010]*

If in doubt about whether an action falls within implied or general powers, advice should be sought from the Charity Commission or an experienced solicitor.

7.4.3.4   Express powers

If a power does not exist under statute and cannot properly be implied in case law or common law, and there is no general power in the governing document, the organisation is able to do something only if there is an **express** (expressed, explicit) power to do so within its governing document. This is the reason for the long lists of powers in many voluntary organisations' governing documents.

If, for example, the governing document does not include an express power to set up committees and delegate decision making powers to them, and if there is no statutory or general power to do so, the governing body will not be able to delegate any of its decision making powers to committees [**15.8.1**].

Even with a general power, it is good practice to list powers in detail, in order to avoid future doubt about whether an action is allowed.

Some powers, such as the power to pay a charity trustee for serving as a trustee, must be explicit [**16.3.3**]. These powers cannot be implied within a general power.

7.4.3.5   Powers requiring consent

Even with a statutory or express power, some powers require the **consent** of a third party. A charitable company, for example, has a statutory right, subject to certain limitations, to amend its governing document, but must get prior consent from the Charity Commission before making some amendments [**7.5.3.2**]. A charity may have a constitutional power to sell or mortgage property, may require Charity Commission consent before doing so [**61.11.1**, **61.12**]. Consent from a funder may be required before amending the governing document, or organisations affiliated to an umbrella or parent body and using its name and logo may need the consent of that body before making any amendments [**11.2**].

7.4.3.6   Powers subject to special duties

The exercise of some powers, most notably in relation to investment and property, may be subject to specific statutory requirements or to requirements arising from **fiduciary duty**, **duty of care** and **duty of prudence** [**15.1.1**, **58.1**].

7.4.4   Powers relating to money
7.4.4.1   Raising funds

Unless there is an explicit and broad power to raise funds, advice should be sought from the Charity Commission or a specialist solicitor before relying on a general or implied power.

7.4.4.2   Trading

Many charity governing documents explicitly prohibit **trading** or do not explicitly give any power to trade. In these cases the charity is allowed to charge for goods or services provided directly in furtherance of the charity's objects [**56.4.5**]. But a charity can charge for other goods, services or activities only if it has power to do so, even if the trading is allowed under tax law [**56.4**].

A charity's governing document may say that the charity must not engage in **substantial** or **permanent trading**. This prohibits only continuous or large-scale trading for fundraising purposes. It does not refer to charges made for goods or services provided directly in furtherance of the charity's objects [**56.4.5**], and would not prevent fundraising events and activities which are not 'permanent' and which fall within the tax exemptions for charities [**56.4.6, 56.4.7**].

Or a charity's governing document may say that the charity must not engage in **taxable trading**. This allows it to undertake any trading – even for fundraising purposes, and even if permanent and relatively substantial – provided the trading falls within the tax exemptions [**56.4**].

7.4.4.3 Borrowing

Raising money through loans or other forms of borrowing may be *ultra vires* unless there is an explicit power, or such power can be clearly implied. The power to borrow money or to charge the organisation's property (use it as security for a loan or mortgage) should be explicit if the organisation is ever likely to need to borrow [see **chapter 59** for more about borrowing].

7.4.4.4 Financial transactions

A governing document generally includes the power to operate bank accounts and undertake financial transactions to carry out the organisation's business, although if this power is not explicit it would be likely to be implied.

7.4.4.5 Investment

Statutory investment powers were widened by the **Trustee Act 2000** for the governing body of trusts, charitable unincorporated associations and bodies established by charter [**58.1**], and where a charitable company or other incorporated body holds assets in trust. The statutory powers may be restricted by an organisation's governing document.

The governing documents of companies and industrial and provident societies normally include wide investment powers.

The wording of the investment clause is very important for any organisation which might want to invest in or make loans to a trading subsidiary [**51.4.4, 51.4.5**].

It may also be important to include power to appoint investment managers with powers to make investment decisions and hold assets [**58.3.2**]. This would normally require such decisions to be made within a policy set by the governing body [**58.6**], and provide for regular reporting and review.

7.4.4.6 Insurance

There is no need for a specific power in the governing document where there is a **statutory obligation** or **statutory power** to insure [**23.2.1**]. Taking out other insurances requires either an express power to do so or a general power. Insurances are covered in more detail in **chapter 23**.

7.4.4.7 Set-up costs

For new organisations the governing document often includes the power to pay the costs of setting up and, if required, registering the organisation.

7.4.5 Powers relating to property

If the organisation is likely ever to own or use land, buildings or other property, such as vehicles or major equipment, the governing document should include a full range of powers to buy, let, take in exchange, mortgage, build, sell, etc [**60.2**]. Where there are no explicit powers, the governing body of a trust or charitable unincorporated association has statutory powers to acquire and manage land [**60.2.3**], and there are powers to manage land under the **Trusts of Land and Appointment of Trustees Act 1996**.

For an unincorporated association, the governing document may usefully make provision as to whether the title to any property is to be held by **holding trustees**, the **official custodian for charities**, another **custodian trustee** or in some other way [**20.4**].

Industrial and provident societies have a statutory power to acquire, maintain and alter land and buildings. This statutory power may be excluded in the governing document.

Industrial & Provident Societies Act 1965 s.30(1)

7.4.6   Power to employ staff and agents

Even if it is not explicit in their governing document, companies and industrial and provident societies have an implied power to employ staff. Charitable incorporated organisations will have power to employ staff under their statutory general power [**7.4.3.3**].

Ferguson v Wilson [1866] 2 Ch App 77;
Burnley Equitable & Co-operative Society v Casson [1891] 1 QB 75

The governing bodies of trusts and charitable unincorporated associations have statutory power to employ and pay agents, including staff [**20.5**], nominees and custodians [**20.4**] to transact any business or carry out any other act necessary for the organisation's work. This might be a solicitor, banker, stockbroker, or other person, including staff. The trustees must properly supervise the appointed person.

Trustee Act 2000 ss.11-23,32

For non-charitable associations, if the power to employ staff is not explicit in the governing document, it may be covered by a general power.

For charities and many non-charitable organisations, there is generally a proviso that members of the governing body cannot be employed or remunerated by the organisation. For charities this is likely to apply even if it is not explicit [**7.4.6**].

7.4.7   Ancillary powers

Many governing documents include a range of powers enabling the organisation to undertake activities which do not directly further its objects, but are related or **ancillary**. These might include, for example, the power to undertake research, produce publications, hold conferences, and set up branches or advisory committees. If they are not explicit, these powers may be covered under a general power.

7.4.8   Power to undertake joint activities

The governing document is likely to include powers to support, cooperate with, join or amalgamate with other charities, voluntary organisations and statutory or public authorities which carry out work related to the organisation's own objects.

Charities have a statutory right to undertake joint activities with other charities, local authorities and joint boards carrying out the functions of local authorities, provided the activities promote the charity's work or make it more effective.

Charities Act 1993 s.78(2)

7.4.9   Restrictions

The governing document may set out restrictions on activities or on how the organisation's property and income can be used.

7.4.9.1   Restrictions on payments by charities

The governing document of a charitable organisation usually contains some or all of the following restrictions [see **chapter 16** for more information]. The following restrictions apply even if they are not express:

- The charity's income and property must be used only to promote its objects or for activities allowed in its objects. Any other use is a **breach of trust**.
- None of the charity's money or property can be paid or given as a dividend, bonus or other form of profit to any member of the charity.
- If the charity is wound up, any assets remaining after all its debts have been paid must be given to another charitable organisation with the same or similar purposes, unless the governing document allows disposition for different charitable purposes or the Charity Commission authorises this.

Charities have a statutory power to pay a trustee or person connected with a trustee [**15.2.5**] for services provided to the charity, but not for services as a trustee or as an employee. This power applies only if nothing in the governing document explicitly prohibits a payment of that type to that person, and only if certain rules are complied with [**16.3.2**].*Charities Act 1993 ss.73A-73C, inserted by Charities Act 2006 ss.36,37*

Apart from this power under the Charities Act, the members of a charity's governing body and persons connected with them cannot receive any direct or indirect 'benefit in money or money's worth' from their charity, unless it is reimbursement of genuine out of pocket expenditure incurred in carrying out their duties for the charity [**16.3.1**], or the governing document authorises it or the Charity Commission gives consent [**16.3**].

This means that unless it is covered under the statutory power above, is explicitly allowed under the governing document or is authorised by the Commission:

- a member of the governing body cannot be paid a salary or fee by the charity;
- spouses and civil partners of governing body members, other close relatives, business partners, and companies in which any of these people or the governing body member has an interest cannot be paid for work done for the charity;
- members of the governing body or persons connected with them cannot receive any benefit from the charity, unless it is a benefit generally available to the community such as using a village hall.

If the intention is to provide charitable services or other benefits to governing body members or persons connected with them, or to pay them beyond what is allowed under the statutory power above, this must be explicitly included in the governing document. Similarly if the intention is for the governing body to include beneficiaries or users of the charity, it is advisable to make clear in the governing document that this is allowed [**16.5**].

Provisions that may be allowed in charity governing documents, or if not in the governing document may be permitted by the Charity Commission on a one-off basis, include:

- power to pay members of the governing body for serving as a trustee [**16.3.3**];
- consent for an employee or employees to be governing body members [**16.4.1**];
- consent for members of the governing body to be beneficiaries (clients, users etc) of the charity, or charitable benefits to be given to governing body members [**16.5**];
- power to pay interest on money lent to the charity by a member of the charity or its governing body, although there is likely to be a limitation on the rate of interest which can be paid [**16.2.3**, **16.3.8**];
- power to pay reasonable rent to a member of the charity or its governing body [**16.2.3**, **16.3.7**];
- consent to purchase goods or services from a company in which a governing body member owns shares, although this generally applies only if the member's holding is less than 1% of the company's issued share capital [**16.3.5**].

A charity's governing document cannot be amended to include any of the above powers unless the Charity Commission gives prior consent.

Re French Protestant Hospital [1951] 1 All ER 938; Charities Act 1993 s.64

7.4.9.2 Restrictions on charitable companies

The memorandum or articles of association of a charitable company may say that the company must not become involved in the regulation of relationships between employers and employees, which means it cannot become a trade union. This type of restriction is now redundant and can be deleted after obtaining consent from the Charity Commission.

The memorandum or articles may also say that in relation to charity law, the members of the governing body are personally accountable in the same way as if the charity were not incorporated. This means that despite having limited liability in general, they may still be held personally liable for misuse of the charity's funds or property, breach of charity law, or other breaches of trust. This applies even if it not explicit in the company's governing document.

7.4.9.3 Restrictions on community interest companies

Community interest companies can pay governing body members, provided the payment is reasonable [**16.3**]. Authorisation for such payment should be included in the governing document if the CIC is ever likely to want to use it.

The governing document of a community interest company limited by shares will include provision for paying dividends to shareholders which are other bodies with an **asset lock** [**3.1.4**]. It may also allow payment of dividends to other shareholders including individual investors, but these will be subject to a **dividend cap**, set by the CIC regulator, on the level of dividends and on how much of the CIC's assets can be paid as dividends.

7.4.9.4 Restrictions on prescribed community benefit societies

Restrictions similar to those for community interest companies may be included in the rules for non-charitable community benefit societies, in particular if they are prescribed societies [**3.5.2**].

7.4.9.5 Other non-charities

A non-charitable voluntary organisation's governing document might have restrictions (and exceptions) virtually the same as a charity's, and might include a prohibition on amending certain clauses.

Non-charitable **trading subsidiaries** or **trading companies** set up by charities may have particular restrictions in their governing document [**51.5.1**]. For example, a charity's trading company might have a restriction requiring it to pay all profits to the parent charity. Such restrictions should not be necessary if the trading company is wholly owned by the charity, and should in general be avoided.

7.4.10 Conflict of interest

A member of a governing body must be careful to avoid conflicts of interest and conflicts of loyalty, and must comply with the statutory rules on such conflicts [**15.2, 15.3.5**].

These general and statutory duties may be buttressed by particular restrictions and procedures set out in the governing document, or the governing document may include a clause authorising conflicts of interest or of loyalty in situations where they would otherwise not be allowed [**15.3.5**].

7.4.11 Membership

If the organisation has a membership [**12.1**] the governing document may set out the requirements for membership, including eligibility, rights and benefits of membership, any right of members to resign, and any right of the organisation to terminate membership. If there are different classes of membership, these may be specified. The governing document might set out a process for applying for membership and for the application to be approved.

Instead of specifying classes of membership, eligibility, rights or benefits and application procedures, the governing document may say that these are to be decided by the members at a general meeting, or by the governing body. These rules may then be set out in **standing orders** [**7.4.25**].

7.4.12 General meetings

If the organisation has a membership, the governing document should set out the requirements for members' meetings [**19.2**]. These are likely to include a requirement to have an **annual general meeting**, including the amount of notice which must be given for the AGM and the business which must be transacted at an AGM.

Under the **Companies Act 2006** companies are not required to hold an AGM unless the articles of association explicitly require one, the members request it, or certain resolutions are being passed [**19.2.1**]. Even where not explicitly required by the articles, it will generally be good practice for a voluntary sector company to hold an AGM unless it has a very small membership. *Companies Act 2006 ss.281-287*

The governing document may also include any requirements relating to other meetings of the members, which might be called **general**, **special**, **ordinary** or **extraordinary** meetings; procedures by which members of the organisation can require (**requisition**) a general meeting to be held; procedures for general meetings, for example chairing, quorum, proxies and voting; and the majority required to approve resolutions at meetings.

The governing document may also specify whether decisions may be made by telephone or electronic means [**19.1.2**] or by the requisite number of members signing a written resolution [**19.10**], so that a meeting does not need to be held. For companies, there is a statutory right to use some of these procedures.

7.4.13 Governing body

The governing document should set out provisions for the **governing body** [**chapter 13**] and is likely to include:

- what the governing body is going to be called (board, board of trustees, board of directors, committee, management committee, executive committee, council, council of management, or whatever);
- who the first members of the governing body are or how they are to be selected;
- who is eligible to serve on the governing body;
- the maximum and minimum number of people on the governing body;
- how the members of the governing body are elected or appointed, how long they serve, whether they can be re-elected or reappointed, and how they can be removed;
- how vacancies are filled;
- whether and how others can be appointed or co-opted as non-voting members of the governing body or observers;
- powers of the governing body.

Governing documents often do not make it clear that the voting members of the governing body are charity trustees if the organisation is a charity, and/or company directors if the organisation is a company. This should be made clear to everyone on a governing body.

7.4.14 Governing body meetings

The governing document may specify how often the governing body must meet [**19.12**] and the quorum and procedures for its meetings, or may specify that the governing body decides how it will operate. It may also specify that decisions may be made by telephone or electronic means, or by a written resolution signed by all or a specified number of the members.

7.4.15 Committees and delegated powers

Members of the governing body have the right to delegate decision making to individuals, committees, employees or others only if this is authorised by statute, by the governing document, or (for charities) by the Charity Commission. Even where they have power of delegation, the members of the governing body remain ultimately responsible for ensuring the organisation is properly managed and decisions are properly made.

The governing document should generally state that the governing body may delegate some or all or its powers to committees [**15.8**]. (If the governing body is called a board these are likely to be called **committees**, but if the governing body is itself called a management committee, executive committee or something similar, the delegated bodies are generally called **sub-committees**.)

The governing document may state that any such committee must include a minimum number of members of the governing body, and should make clear whether people who are not members of the governing body can serve as members of committees and if so whether they have voting rights in making decisions or recommendations, or serve only as advisors or observers.

Sometimes the governing document states that any committee must act only within the authority delegated to it by the governing body, and must keep proper minutes and make them available to the governing body, and/or must report back as soon as reasonably practical. These rules apply even if they are not explicit.

The governing document may also specify that some powers can be delegated to individual officers or members of the governing body.

If the power to delegate decision making does not exist, the governing body may delegate only the right to make proposals or recommendations. It is then up to the governing body to make the decision.

7.4.16 Officers

The governing document may say that certain officers (sometimes called **honorary officers**) must be elected or appointed, and should indicate whether this is to be done by the organisation's members or by the governing body [**chapter 14**]. The officers usually include a chairperson, vice-chair and treasurer, and may also include a secretary. The governing document may set requirements, for example that officers must be members of the organisation or live in the area of benefit.

References to a **secretary** in a company's articles of association mean the company secretary [**14.3**] unless the articles clearly indicate otherwise.

The governing document may list other officers, and may also say how long officers serve, whether they can be re-elected or reappointed, and how they can be removed. Care should be taken not to confuse a maximum term for serving as an officer with a maximum term for serving on the governing body.

7.4.17 Minutes

There is often a clause in the governing document requiring **minutes** to be kept of all general, governing body, and committee meetings. Even if this clause is not there, minutes should, and in most cases must, be kept [**19.11**, **19.12.7**].

7.4.18 The seal

The governing document may include provision for a **seal**, a stamping device used when an incorporated body enters into a legally binding agreement [**20.1.3**]. Companies, charitable incorporated organisations and industrial and provident societies are not required to have a seal, but many do. An IPS can have and use a seal only if its rules include provision for how it is used.

7.4.19 Bank accounts

The governing document may specify how money is to be held, and how cheques and other transactions are to be authorised. If this is not set out in the governing document, charities have a statutory power to delegate authorisation of financial transactions to two or more governing body members.   *Charities Act 1993 s.82*

7.4.20 Accounts and audit

The governing document may specify in detail – especially for unincorporated associations – the types of financial records which must be kept, the type of annual accounts to be prepared and how the accounts are to be checked or audited. Or the governing document may simply say that accounts are to be prepared in accordance with the relevant provisions of the Charities Acts or Companies Acts. Even if this is not included, all charities and companies must do so anyway.

Where legislation that has been repealed or amended (such as the **Charities Act 1992** or the **Companies Act 1985**) is referred to in the governing document, the reference automatically means the new legislation.

Accounting and audit procedures are covered in **chapter 54**. If the Charities Act or Companies Act does not require a full audit, but the governing document does, the organisation must generally comply with the governing document. However, it may be possible to amend it [**7.5**] so the organisation only has to comply with the relevant legislation.

If the governing document does not require an audit but legislation does, the organisation must comply with the legislation. Funders may require a full audit even if this is not required under legislation or the organisation's governing document.

7.4.21 Property and insurance

The governing document may make provision for aspects of property acquisition, management, insurance and disposal, for example that any land not required may be sold or leased. Advice should be taken if the organisation wants to engage in property transactions and does not have explicit power to do so.

7.4.22 Indemnity

The governing document should say that members of the organisation, members of the governing body, officers [**7.4.16**] and staff have a right to be indemnified (repaid) out of the organisation's assets:

- in trusts and unincorporated associations, for any liability incurred in connection with their position, unless they have acted negligently or fraudulently; or
- in companies, for costs incurred in defending legal proceedings brought against them in that capacity – but only if judgment is given in their favour, or if the court grants relief from liability for negligence, default, breach of duty or breach of trust [**22.7.4**].

For more about the right to be indemnified see **22.7.8**.

7.4.23 Notices

The governing document usually sets out how notices (official communications required by statute or the governing document, such as notice of meetings) are given, and who is entitled to receive them [**19.3**, **19.12.2**]. For companies, extensive rules govern electronic communications [**18.2**], and similar rules will apply to charitable incorporated organisations.

7.4.24 Branches

If the organisation is to have branches or affiliates [**9.2**, **11.2**], the governing document might set out how these are to be set up and rules for the relationship between the main organisation and its branches or affiliates.

7.4.25 Standing orders

The governing document may say that the members of the organisation or the governing body may make **standing orders**, **by-laws**, **regulations**, **rules** or **secondary rules** about specified matters, or about any matters relevant to how the organisation operates. These rules might cover matters such as eligibility for membership, membership application procedures, subscriptions, procedures for governing body nomination and election, procedures for general and governing body meetings, or terms of reference for committees. Standing orders, rules etc cannot contradict anything in the governing document, or exempt the organisation from a statutory duty.

Unincorporated associations and trusts generally have no power to make standing orders unless this is explicit in the governing document. An exception is literary or scientific institutions, in which the governing body has a statutory power to make by-laws.   *Literary & Scientific Institutions Act 1854 s.24*

In a company, even if there is no express power to make standing orders, the members may pass an **ordinary resolution** [**19.7.4**] setting out how the provisions of the governing document are to be implemented or covering any other matter, or they may authorise the governing body to make such rules. The members of an industrial and provident society have a statutory right to make such rules.   *Industrial & Provident Societies Act 1965 s.13(4)*

Any rules and procedures relating to company or IPS governing body meetings can either be adopted by ordinary resolution of the organisation's members, or by the governing body.

Unlike amendments [**7.5**], standing orders do not generally need to be sent to registration bodies or circulated with copies of the governing document. However some standing orders may form part of a **company constitution** [**7.1.1.1**] and may need to be sent to Companies House and included with copies of the articles.

Standing orders can be changed in the same way they are made.

7.4.26 Amendment

Companies and charitable incorporated organisations (CIOs) have statutory procedures for amending the governing document [**7.5.3**, **7.5.4**]. It is not necessary to include these in the governing document unless it is desired to require a longer notice period or higher proportion of the vote than the statutory procedure.

For other organisations, the governing document should include an amendment procedure. If it does not, the governing document of a non-charitable association can generally be altered only by unanimous agreement of every member, and the governing document of a charitable association or trust can generally be altered only by a Charity Commission scheme. Amendment is covered in **7.5**.

7.4.27 Dissolution

Company law, industrial and provident society law and the law relating to charitable incorporated organisations provide procedures for dissolution (winding up the organisation). For other organisations the governing document should specify how dissolution is authorised, and what happens if the organisation has assets left after meeting its financial obligations. Dissolution is covered in **chapter 24**.

7.5 ALTERING THE GOVERNING DOCUMENT

Alteration of a governing document is a particularly complex area, and in many cases legal advice may be necessary.

A general rule relating to amendments is that they should be within the spirit of the original objects or intentions. Dissatisfied members who feel that an amendment is contrary to those intentions may be able to ask the courts to decide whether the amendment is lawful. *Hole v Garnsey [1930] AC 472,496,500*

Once an amendment has been properly approved, it should (and for companies must) be attached to or included with all copies of the governing document, or the governing document should be reprinted including the new provisions. It is sensible to put 'as amended [date]' on the front of the amended version.

7.5.1 Trusts and unincorporated associations

Amending the governing document of an association or trust depends on whether it contains a power of amendment, and whether the organisation is charitable or non-charitable. Failure to follow the proper procedure could result in a claim for breach of trust against governing body members, or court action by members of an association.

7.5.1.1 Unincorporated charities: amendment of administrative provisions

Any of the administrative powers and procedures in the governing document of a charitable association or trust can be amended by following the amendment procedure in the governing document if there is one. *Charities Act 1993 s.74D, inserted by Charities Act 2006 s.42*

If there is no amendment procedure, such an amendment can be made by the governing body passing a resolution. If the organisation is an unincorporated association with a body of members separate from the governing body, the resolution of the governing body must then be approved at a general meeting of the association's members. This approval must be with a majority of at least two-thirds of those voting or, if the meeting makes decisions without voting, there must have been no expression of dissent when the question of whether to agree was put to the meeting.

The amendment takes effect from the date specified in the original resolution passed by the governing body, or the date agreed by the association's members if their agreement is required.

Registered charities must send a copy of the resolution(s) and amended governing document to the Charity Commission. *Charities Act 1993 s.3B(3), inserted by Charities Act 2006 s.9*

7.5.1.2 Unincorporated charities: amendment of objects

The governing body of an unincorporated charity with annual income no more than £10,000, which does not hold land designated for specific purposes, may amend any or all of the charity's **purposes** (objects). The new purposes must be charitable and must consist of or include purposes similar to the ones that are being replaced, and the trustees must be satisfied it is in the interests of the charity for the purposes to be changed. The resolution must be passed by at least two-thirds of the governing body members voting on it. In an unincorporated association, a resolution to amend the objects does not require further approval by the members of the organisation. *Charities Act 1993 s.74C, inserted by Charities Act 2006 s.41*

The governing body must send a copy of the resolution and their reasons for passing it to the Charity Commission, which may require the charity to give public notice of the resolution, with a 28-day period for representations to be made to the Commission by any person appearing to be interested in the charity.

Provided the Commission approves the resolution, it takes effect 60 days from when it was received by the Commission. A copy of the amended governing document must be sent to the Commission.

An unincorporated charity which does not have an amendment procedure and is not entitled to use the statutory provisions to amend its objects must apply to the Charity Commission for a *cy près* scheme [**7.5.2.1**].

7.5.1.3 Unincorporated charities: other amendments

Amendments to provisions relating to payments or other benefits to members of the governing body of a charitable association or trust, or to persons connected with them [**15.2.5**], require prior Charity Commission consent even if the governing document includes an amendment procedure. Consent should also be sought before changing the investment provisions, any provisions relating to permanent endowment [**58.8.1**], or provisions on distribution of the charity's assets when the charity is wound up.

7.5.1.4 Unincorporated non-charities

If a non-charitable association has only one object, it may not be possible to change it. In this case the association would have to be wound up if the original object was no longer appropriate. *Thellusson v Viscount Valentia [1907] 2 Ch 7; Doyle v White City Stadium Ltd & British Boxing Board of Control [1935] KB 110, 121*

Apart from this, if the governing document of a non-charitable association allows for amendment, any amendment can be made provided it is not prohibited by the governing document, is not in itself unlawful, and does not have implications for funds received from funders and donors. The constitutional procedures must be strictly followed. In particular, the amendment power may not apply to alteration of the objects clause or certain other clauses; in this case, alteration of those clauses must be treated in the same way as for an organisation without power of amendment.

Where there is no power of amendment, amendment of a non-charitable association's governing document requires 100% agreement of all of the organisation's members (not just 100% of those who vote on the resolution). *Abbatt v Treasury Solicitor [1969] 1 WLR 1575,1583*

If it is impossible to get 100% agreement there may be two options, each of which is potentially risky and requires legal advice. If the amendment is controversial but there is provision to wind up the organisation [**24.8**], it may be possible to set up a new organisation, transfer the assets of the old organisation to the new one, wind up the old one, and start again. Alternatively if the amendment is non-controversial and no one is likely to object to the change, it may be possible for it to be agreed by **acquiescence**. Under this procedure the amendment is agreed by a simple majority [**19.8.5**] at a general meeting, and is then notified to all the members who were not at the meeting, making clear that if none of those members object to the change it will be put into place. It is important to get specialist legal advice before using either of these approaches.

7.5.2   Charity Commission schemes

If a charitable association's or trust's governing document does not contain an amendment procedure and the desired amendment is not covered under the statutory amendment procedures for unincorporated charities [**7.5.1**], or if the governing document of a charitable association, trust or company expressly prohibits amendment of certain parts of the governing document, the Commission must authorise the alteration, and if necessary make a **scheme** [**4.5.5**] for it. A scheme is an agreed and approved way to alter the provisions under which the charity was originally set up.

Schemes are explained in the Charity Commission's CC36 *Changing your charity's governing document*. The Commission has a standard form for a resolution applying for a scheme. Except for very small charities [**7.5.2.3**], the resolution must be passed at a meeting of the charity's members or its trustees. Except in relation to exempt charities, application may also be made by the attorney general.
Charities Act 1993 s.16(4)

Trustees are under an obligation to request a scheme if one is necessary in order to ensure that the charity's assets are effectively used. If the charity has been in existence for at least 40 years and the Commission believes a scheme is necessary but the trustees refuse to apply for one, the Commission has power to make a scheme anyway.
Charities Act 1993 s.13(5),16(6)

7.5.2.1   Cy près schemes

The general presumption is that a charity's objects cannot be changed, because money and other property has been given to the charity in trust [**4.1.2**] to be used only for the purposes for which the charity was established. However, trustees of unincorporated charities with annual income no more than £10,000 may change the objects provided certain criteria are met [**7.5.1.2**]. Other unincorporated charities must apply to the Charity Commission for a *cy près* **scheme**, and charitable companies and charitable incorporated organisations must apply to the Commission for consent to change their objects.

Cy près is a Norman French expression meaning 'as near as possible'. It means that if a charity's objects or purposes have to be changed, the new ones must be in the spirit of the original ones, and as close to it as possible. But under the **Charities Act 2006**, the Commission can also take into account the social and economic conditions at the time of the proposed amendment. *Charities Act 1993 s.14B, inserted by Charities Act 2006 s.18*

A *cy près* amendment is possible if:

- the original purposes of the charity have been fulfilled as much as they can be;
- the original purposes cannot be carried out, or cannot be carried out according to the instructions given, within the spirit of the original objects or effectively in relation to current social and economic circumstances;
- the original objects only cover part of the charity's property (for example, if a charity raises more money than can be used for the specified purposes);
- the charity can operate more effectively if it amalgamates with other charities;
- the area of benefit (geographical area) defined in the objects has changed, for example because of local government reorganisation;
- the area of benefit and/or the definition of the beneficiaries is no longer appropriate;
- all or some of the objects are being adequately provided for by other means;
- all or some of the objects for which the charity was established have ceased to be charitable in law; or
- all or some of the original objects are no longer suitable or effective.
Charities Act 1993 s.13, amended by Charities Act 2006 s.15

96

A *cy près* scheme is frequently slow and expensive to undertake.

If a scheme is very complex or contentious, the Charity Commission may advise trustees to apply to the high court for a scheme.

7.5.2.2 Administrative schemes

An **administrative scheme** is one which is not a *cy près* scheme. If a charitable association's or trust's governing document does not contain amendment procedures and the change it wants to make is not covered under the statutory provisions for unincorporated charities [**7.5.1.1**], it must apply to the Charity Commission. Such a scheme is straightforward and involves convincing the Commission that the change is in the best interests of the charity and its beneficiaries, is in keeping with the spirit of the original trusts, and is workable.

Rather than making schemes to deal with specific alterations, the Commission's emphasis now is on making schemes which give trustees the power to amend the governing document. Such powers of amendment generally exclude the power to amend the charity's objects, to dissolve the charity or to spend its permanent endowment, and will require the charity to get authorisation before making any amendments relating to remuneration of trustees or powers of investment.

7.5.2.3 Very small charities

If a charity's annual income is less than £500 and it is not an exempt charity [**8.1.2**], application for a Charity Commission scheme does not have to be made by a resolution of the charity's members or its governing body. It may be made by one trustee of the charity or by any person 'interested in the charity', or, if it is a local charity, by any two or more inhabitants of the area of benefit.

Charities Act 1993 s.16(5)

7.5.3 Companies

All companies have the right to alter their articles by special resolution or written resolution [**19.7.4**, **19.10.2**]. Some amendments require consent or special procedures. Charitable companies, for example, must obtain Charity Commission consent for some changes [**7.5.3.2**]. The liability of members (for example, the amount of the members' guarantee) cannot be increased without the written consent of all the affected members. Where a company has different classes of membership with different rights [**12.2**], any change to those rights requires not only a special resolution, but also written consent from at least 75% of the members of that class, or a special resolution passed at a separate general meeting of that class.

Companies Act 2006 ss.21,25,28,631

Because of the statutory right of amendment, company governing documents often do not contain an amendment clause. If there is such a clause, it must be carefully followed if its requirements are more strict than the statutory provisions (for example if it requires a longer notice period or a higher percentage of the vote than the statutory provisions). If the statutory provisions are stricter than those in the governing document, the statutory provisions apply.

Within 15 days of passing a special resolution or written resolution relating to amendment, the company must send a copy of the resolution to Companies House, with an amended copy of the articles [**7.1.1.1**], a copy of the Charity Commission's consent if this was required, and form **CC04** if the objects were changed. A change to the objects does not take effect until it is registered by Companies House. If the company is charitable, a copy of the special resolution and the amended articles must also be sent to the Charity Commission.

Companies Act 2006 ss.26,30,31(2); Charities Act 1993 s.64(3), s.38(3), inserted by Charities Act 2006 s.9

7.5.3.1 Entrenched provisions

A company can now state in its articles of association that certain articles or parts of an article can only be amended or repealed if certain conditions are met or a specified procedure is complied with. These conditions must be more restrictive than a special resolution [**19.7.4**], for example that a change requires a higher proportion of the vote than the 75% needed for a special resolution. But a **provision for entrenchment** cannot say that something can never be amended or repealed.

Companies Act 2006 ss.22-24

Provision for entrenchment can only be put into the articles when a company is set up, or by an amendment agreed by 100% of the company's members. When a provision for entrenchment is put into the articles, either on formation or by amendment, Companies House must be notified on form **CC01**, and if the relevant article is ever amended or repealed the special resolution must be accompanied by form **CC03** or **CC02** stating that the entrenchment provision has been complied with.

7.5.3.2   Charitable companies

Charitable companies must obtain prior Charity Commission consent for **regulated alterations**. These are changes to the objects clause, relating to use of property when the company is dissolved, or relating to the provision of benefit to directors or members of the company or persons connected with them.

Charities Act 1993 s.64, amended by Charities Act 2006 s.31; Companies Act 2006 s.21

7.5.3.3   Community interest companies

A community interest company amends its governing document in the same way as a non-charitable company [**7.5.3**]. If the objects have been amended, a completed form **CIC14**, signed by every company director, must be sent to Companies House with the special resolution and amended governing document. CIC14 contains the community interest statement and a statement of the steps that have been taken to bring the proposed alteration to the notice of persons affected by the CIC's activities. Companies House will only register a change of objects when the CIC regulator has approved it, and the change does not take place until it is registered.   *Community Interest Company Regulations 2005 [SI 2005/1788] regs.13-16*

7.5.4   Charitable incorporated organisations

The constitution of a charitable incorporated organisation can be amended at a general meeting of the CIO's members, with at least 75% of the votes cast. If the resolution is passed otherwise than at a general meeting, for example by written resolution, it requires agreement of every member. A copy of the resolution and a revised constitution must be sent to the Commission within 15 days of being passed. The resolution does not take effect until it is registered by the Commission. The Commission can in some circumstances refuse to register the change.

Charities Act 1993 sch.5B para.14,15, to be inserted by Charities Act 2006 sch.7 para.2 [expected April 2010]

The Charity Commission's prior written consent is required for any change to the objects, provisions for use of the charity's property on dissolution, or any provision authorising a benefit to members of the governing body, members of the CIO or persons connected with them [**15.2.5**]. 'Benefit' does not include payments to governing body members and connected persons which are allowed under the Charities Act [**16.3**]. Even where the Commission has given prior consent, the amendment still does not take effect until a copy of the resolution and amended constitution have been sent to the Commission and registered by it.

At the time of writing (mid 2009), the rules for CIO **entrenched provisions** were expected to be similar to those for companies [**7.5.3.1**].

7.5.5   Industrial and provident societies

An industrial and provident society's rules must include provision for amendment. The legislation does not specify what the procedure should be, but typically amendment requires a two-thirds majority of members present and voting at a general meeting.   *Industrial & Provident Societies Act 1965 sch.1 para.5*

Alteration of the objects or powers of an IPS, whether charitable or non-charitable, requires the prior consent of the Financial Services Authority. For charitable IPSs, Charity Commission rather than FSA consent is likely to be required if the IPS is registered with the Commission [**8.1.2**].

Two signed copies of any amendment must be sent to Mutual Societies Registration in the FSA, with the appropriate forms (available from MSR). The amendment does not come into force until MSR has registered it.   *IPSA 1965 s.10*

7.6 ALTERNATIVES TO AMENDMENT

Alteration of the governing document may be slow, expensive or impossible, especially where a change to the objects is desired. In this situation it may be appropriate to set up a new organisation with additional or broader objects and transfer the organisation's activities to the new body, or for a charitable, trading or campaigning organisation to be set up with the new objects.

Before doing this, careful consideration must be given to:

- whether the original organisation has power to create the new organisation;
- whether the new organisation is intended to be short term and therefore perhaps needs only a simple unincorporated structure [**chapter 2**], or whether it is likely to be complex, risky or long term and should therefore be incorporated [**chapter 3**];
- the possible need to obtain Charity Commission consent if the original organisation is charitable;
- possible restrictions on the use of the original organisation's funds for any purposes which are not within its objects, which may mean that funds cannot be transferred to the new organisation if its objects are completely different, or that transferred funds need to be ringfenced within the new organisation;
- the additional administrative burden in running a separate organisation; and
- the relationship between the original and new organisations [**51.5**].

7.7 CHARITIES AND COMPANIES ACTS 2006 AMENDMENTS

Some changes in the **Charities Act 2006** and **Companies Act 2006** apply regardless of what is in the articles of association, but others apply only if the articles do not specify otherwise, or if the articles explicitly say they do apply. To take full advantage of the changes, companies and charities should review their governing documents. Specialist advice is likely to be necessary or advisable.

As well as making amendments to reflect or take advantage of statutory changes, the governing document review provides a good opportunity to consider whether the objects, powers, and provisions relating to membership of the organisation, the governing body, meetings and other matters remain appropriate and workable – and whether the organisation is complying with them.

7.7.1 Possible company amendments

When reviewing its governing document, a company limited by guarantee should consider:

- including provision to change the company's name without requiring a special resolution [**6.7.1**];
- removing any prohibition on company directors being elected as a block or any requirement that they be elected individually, so they can be elected as a block if this is appropriate [**13.4.2**];
- whether it wants to amend, in the articles, the definition of mental incapacity under which a director would have to cease serving as a director [**13.5.2**];
- whether it wants to remove the requirement in the articles, if there is one, to have a company secretary [**14.3**];
- amendments necessary to authorise particular conflicts of interest [**15.3**];
- seeking Charity Commission consent to an amendment to allow the directors, in a charitable company, to authorise transactions where a director has a conflict of interest [**15.3.6**];
- an amendment to allow the directors, in a charitable company, to authorise a person with a conflict of duties or other situational conflict of interest to serve on the governing body [**15.3.8**];
- removing any provisions in the articles about when notices are treated as having been delivered, so the company can use the statutory deemed delivery provisions [**18.3.1**];

- including provision to allow company notices and other information to be provided on the company's website [**18.3.6**];
- if the articles require an annual general meeting or other general meetings, whether this should be removed [**19.2.1**] (if this is removed, everything linked to the AGM or other general meetings, such as governing body elections and laying the accounts before a general meeting, must also be amended or removed);
- amending the notice period for AGMs and general meetings at which special resolutions are being decided to 14 days [**19.3.4**] (it cannot be less than this);
- removing any provision that says proxy voting is not allowed, any restriction on who may be a proxy or any restriction on a proxy's right to attend, speak or vote at a general meeting, as all company members now have a statutory right to appoint a proxy to attend, speak and vote on their behalf regardless of anything in the articles [**19.8.3**];
- explicitly including procedures for proxy voting, even though this is not necessary as it is a statutory right;
- including provision for written resolutions by company members [**19.10.2**], if it is not already there, to make clear that this right applies not only to decisions required under the Companies Act but to all decisions made by company members;
- if the articles say that written resolutions require agreement by 100% of the members, amending this to make clear that for matters that would be passed as special resolutions they require agreement by 75% of members entitled to vote, and for ordinary resolutions they require agreement by a simple majority of members entitled to vote [**19.10.2**];
- including provision for written resolutions by governing body members [**19.12.6**];
- removing any restrictions on the indemnities that can be provided by the company to company directors and other officers [**22.7.8**].
- removing any restrictions which prevent summary financial statements, rather than the full audited annual accounts, being circulated to company members and other entitled to receive the accounts [**54.3.8**].

Further amendments may be appropriate for companies limited by shares.

7.7.2 Possible charity amendments

A charity – whether incorporated or unincorporated – should consider seeking Charity Commission consent:

- to amend the objects, if appropriate, to fit in with the new statutory charitable purposes [**5.2.3**];
- to remove any prohibition on governing body members and persons connected with them being paid for services provided to the charity (other than as an employee or trustee) [**16.3.2**];
- to remove any prohibition on the charity purchasing trustee indemnity insurance or directors' and officers' insurance [**23.10**];
- to remove any requirements to get Charity Commission consent for amendments other than those relating to the objects, provision of benefits to trustees or connected persons, and the dissolution clause.

Resources: THE GOVERNING DOCUMENT

See end of **chapter I**.

Statute law. www.opsi.gov.uk and www.statutelaw.gov.uk.

Much but not all case law. www.bailii.org.

Updates cross-referenced to this book. www.rclh.co.uk.

Chapter 8
REGISTERING AS A CHARITY

For sources of further information see end of chapter 1.

8.1   WHO HAS TO REGISTER

8.1.1   Compulsory registration

Every organisation based in England and Wales which meets the legal definition of a charity [**4.1**] must register with the Charity Commission unless it is **exempt** or **excepted** from registration [**8.1.2**, **8.1.3**].

Charities Act 1993 s.3A, inserted by Charities Act 2006 s.9

An organisation is likely to be charitable and have to register if:

- all of its main purposes are charitable as defined by the **Charities Act 2006**, the Charity Commission or the courts [**5.2.3**];
- it is set up with the intention of benefiting the public or a section of the public, rather than simply benefiting private individuals;
- all money raised by the organisation will be used only for the organisation's purposes; and
- its income is more than £5,000 per year [**8.1.3.1**].

An organisation which is charitable but is not registered, and is not exempt or excepted from registration, may be required to register with the Commission before it can receive the tax benefits to which it is entitled [**4.2.1**], and some funders may also require registration. If the Commission becomes aware of the charity's existence it may direct the members of the governing body to register; failure to do so can lead to contempt of court proceedings.

Being 'a charity' is only one aspect of an organisation. The organisation is also defined by its **legal structure** or **legal form**, such as **unincorporated association** [**2.2**], **trust** [**2.3**], **company limited by guarantee** [**3.3**], **charitable incorporated organisation** [**3.2**] or **industrial and provident society** [**3.5**].

In registering as a charity, there are three separate processes: drawing up the governing document (constitution) [**chapter 7**]; formally establishing the organisation as an association, trust, company, charitable incorporated organisation or industrial and provident society [**chapter 1**]; and registering the organisation as a charity.

8.1.2   Exempt charities

Exempt charities are subject to the jurisdiction of a regulatory body other than the Charity Commission. When the relevant provisions of the **Charities Act 2006** come into effect, exempt charities which have a **principal regulator** who will monitor them for compliance with charity law will remain exempt from registration with the Charity Commission. At the time of writing (mid 2009) principal regulators were expected to be appointed in late 2009 for most universities in England, Kew Gardens, and museums and galleries. Decisions were expected to be made in spring 2010 about principal regulators for further education corporations in England, and industrial and provident societies [**3.5.2**] in England that are registered social landlords.

Rules relating to the regulation of exempt charities are set out in the **Charities Act 1993**, amended by the **Charities Act 2006** sch.5. Some of these are:

- exempt charities must keep accounting records [**53.1.1**], but generally prepare accounts under legislation other than the Charities Act;   *Charities Act 1993 s.46*

- exempt charities do not need to comply with most Charities Act rules on the sale, leasing, mortgage or disposal of land [**61.11.1, 61.12**];   *CharA 1993 ss.36-39*

- exempt charities are not subject to inquiry by the Charity Commission under s.8 of the Act [**4.5.9**] unless the principal regulator requests it;   *CharA 1993 s.8(1), to be amended by ChA 2006 sch.5 para.2 [expected Nov/Dec 2009]*

- the Commission can, if asked to do so by the charity or by order of the court, make orders and schemes [**4.5.4, 4.5.5**] in relation to exempt charities;   *CharA Act 1993 s.16(4), to be amended by CharA 2006 sch.5 para.4 [expected Nov/Dec 2009]*

- before exercising its powers in relation to an exempt charity, the Commission must consult the charity's principal regulator.   *CharA 1993 s.86A, to be inserted by CharA 2006 s.14 [expected Nov/Dec 2009]*

Exempt charities set up under statute may gain formal recognition of their charitable status by statute. Other exempt charities gain recognition by applying to HM Revenue and Customs charities unit [see end of **chapter 1**]. Information about exempt charities is in the Charity Commission's CC23 *Exempt charities*.

8.1.2.1   Charities ceasing to be exempt

Where there is no principal regulator, previously exempt charities will, from late 2009 to mid 2010, come under the jurisdiction of the Charity Commission. If their annual income is over £100,000 they will be required to register with the Commission, or if income is below this they become **excepted** charities [**8.1.3**].
    Charities Act 1993 s.3A, sch.2, to be inserted/amended by Charities Act 2006 s.9 [expected Nov/Dec 2009]

At the time of writing (mid 2009) universities in Wales, students unions in England and Wales, and colleges of the universities of Oxford, Cambridge and Durham were expected to become excepted charities in late 2009. Further education corporations in Wales, charitable industrial and provident societies in Wales, and charitable IPSs in England which are not registered social landlords, were expected to become excepted by June 2009. A decision was expected to be made by June 2010 about whether foundation and voluntary aided schools in England and Wales would be excepted, or would be exempt with a principal regulator.

At the time of writing it was unclear whether charitable industrial and provident societies whose rules allow the payment of dividends to non-charities would have to remove or amend this provision in order to retain their charitable status.

8.1.3   Excepted charities

Some charities are **excepted** from the need to register, either by statute or by Charity Commission orders. These included some small funds of the Scout and Guide Associations, some armed forces charities, and charities which hold only property (no other assets) for foundation schools and voluntary schools which are now in the state sector. But from 1 January 2009 such charities ceased to be excepted if their annual income is over £100,000, and have to register with the Commission.   *Charities Act 1993 s.3A, inserted by Charities Act 2006 s.9; School Standards & Framework Act 1998 s.23; Charities Act 1993 (Exception from Registration) Regulation 2008 [SI 2008/3268]*

Places of worship registered under the **Places of Worship Registration Act 1855** s.9 and denominational groups listed in regulations from 1996 are excepted from registering with the Charity Commission until 1 October 2012 if their income is not more than £100,000. If their income is over £100,000 they must register with the Commission. Worship groups and other places of worship which are not covered by the 1855 Act or excepted by the 1996 regulations must register with the Commission if their income is over £5,000.   *Charities (Exception from Registration) Regulations 1996 [SI 1996/180] & (Amendment) Regulations 2007 [SI 2007/2655]*

An excepted charity:

- does not have to register with the Commission but may, if the Commission agrees, register voluntarily and thereby get a charity number, and if voluntarily registered, may at any time ask to be removed from the register;
  Charities Act 1993 s.3A(6), inserted by Charities Act 2006 s.9

- must keep accounting records and produce annual accounts [**53.1.1**, **54.2**];

- if not registered voluntarily, may not have to comply with the Charities Act requirements on examination and audit of accounts, unless this is required by the governing document or funders [**54.2.7**];

- does not have to submit annual accounts to the Commission, unless specifically required to do so by the Commission or unless voluntarily registered with the Commission and having an annual gross income over £25,000;

- is subject to Charities Act requirements on sale, leasing, mortgage or disposal of land [**61.11.1**, **61.12**]; and

- is subject to the Commission's supervisory powers [**4.5.4-4.5.11**].

The registration threshold is likely to be reduced after review in 2011.

8.1.3.1   Very small charities

A charity is excepted from registration if its income from all sources is £5,000 or less per year. Charities with lower income can register voluntarily but at the time of writing (mid 2009) this provision is not expected to become available until late 2009 or 2010. Charities which have a particular need to register with the Commission before then can ask the Commission to consider registering them.

A charity with annual income of £5,000 or less which does not want to register voluntarily with the Commission should simply follow the steps for setting up an unincorporated association [**1.2**] or trust [**1.3**]. Care should be taken to monitor income and to register when it exceeds £5,000 per year.   *Charities Act 1993 s.3A(2), inserted by Charities Act 2006 s.9*

8.2   THE REGISTRATION PROCESS

Organisations should obtain CC5 *Registration application pack* from the Charity Commission or its website at an early stage in setting up, but cannot apply for registration as a charity until they have adopted their governing document [**chapter 7**] and, if necessary, have had the trust deed executed or have registered as a company [**1.3**, **1.5**].

Assistance from an experienced solicitor or voluntary sector support body can make registration smoother and quicker, especially if the organisation is not using an approved or model governing document [**8.2.2**] or its objects are unusual or on the fringes of what might be considered charitable in law [**5.2.3**]. If they do not get appropriate advice, such organisations may face delays when they apply for registration, and may need to amend their governing document.

8.2.1   Promoters

The person or persons setting up the charity are sometimes called the **promoters**. It is their responsibility to:

- obtain information from the Charity Commission [see end of **chapter 1**], especially CC21 *Registering as a charity*, CC22 *Choosing and preparing a governing document* and CC5 *Registration application pack*;

- choose a legal structure [**chapters 2** and **3**];

- if appropriate, obtain model governing documents [**8.2.2**] from the Charity Commission or the Charity Law Association [see end of **chapter 1**], an approved governing document, or examples of governing documents from other organisations with the same legal structure (association, trust, charitable incorporated organisation, company), similar objects and a similar organisational and membership structure;
- get legal and professional advice, if necessary [see **64.8.4** for how to find an appropriate legal advisor];
- draw up the governing document, or have it drawn up for them.

Anyone may be a promoter. But if they are to be the first trustees (governing body members) they must not be disqualified from acting as a charity trustee [**13.3.2**], and must be meet the minimum age requirement for a governing body member for that type of charity [**13.2**]. This will be either 16 or 18, depending on the charity's legal form.

8.2.2 Model and approved governing documents

The Charity Commission's registration pack includes guidance on the minimum requirements for a governing document and suggests that if an approved (sometimes called standard) or model governing document is adopted the registration process will be easier. Charitable incorporated organisations (CIOs) are required to use a Charity Commission model unless there is good reason not to.

Charities Act 1993 s.69B(5), to be inserted by Charities Act 2006 sch.7 para.1 [expected April 2010]

The Commission has approved governing documents as **precedents** for various types of organisation. These are available from umbrella or parent bodies such as ACRE (for village halls), Age Concern, Community Matters (for community associations), national Mind, Samaritans, YMCA, and a wide range of other organisations. The registration pack contains a list.

If an approved governing document is not available or is not suitable, **model governing documents** for charitable unincorporated associations, trusts and companies are available from the Commission and from the Charity Law Association [see end of **chapter 1**]. Models for CIOs are available from the Commission, and are also likely to be available from the CLA. The Commission's model governing documents are free of charge. The CLA charges for its models, but many practitioners feel they are more comprehensive than the Commission's.

Charitable associations, trusts and companies do not have to use an approved or model governing document. However, those which try to draw up their own without legal advice are likely to find that registration is a lengthy process, and they may have to amend their newly adopted governing document before the Commission will accept it. **Chapter 7** summarises a typical governing document.

8.2.3 Establishing the organisation

To establish the organisation before registering with the Commission:
- an association must formally adopt its governing document at a meeting of the members [**1.2.3**];
- a trust must execute its trust deed [**1.3.2**];
- a charitable incorporated organisation (CIO) must draw up its constitution [**1.4**];
- a company must register with Companies House [**1.5.5**];
- an industrial and provident society must register with the Financial Services Authority [**1.7.5**].

8.2.4 Application form and supporting information

After the organisation has been established, the trustees must fill in the Charity Commission's application (**CC5a**). The form is intended to enable the Commission to decide whether the organisation's purposes and intended activities are wholly and exclusively charitable [**5.2.3**] and to assess whether and how the organisation will operate for the benefit of the public [**5.3.1**]. The form also clarifies whether the organisation needs to register or whether it is exempt or excepted from registration [**8.1**], and provides information to be held on the register of charities [**4.5.1**].

The application form and two copies of the governing document are sent to the Commission, with evidence that the organisation's income is or is expected to be at least £5,000 per year, and a copy of the certificate of incorporation if the organisation is registered as a company limited by guarantee.

Other information which might help the Commission in the registration process, should also be submitted, which could include publicity about the organisation and its activities; a list of planned activities; longer-term plans, if available; accounts of any other organisations which are or will be controlled by the organisation which is registering; or contracts with any fundraisers or others who are not directly employed by the organisation but are paid to raise money for it.

Charities engaging in various specified activities should supply additional information. For example:

- if the charity will work with children or vulnerable adults, the Commission requires confirmation that criminal record checks have, if legally required, been carried out on the proposed trustees, and if checks are available to the organisation but not legally required that they have been carried out or an explicit decision has been made that it is not necessary to do so [**41.6.1**];
- research charities must give full details of how the research is to be conducted, supervised and evaluated;
- charities set up to fundraise for charitable purposes should give details of the fundraising methods to be used;
- charities engaging in counselling must give details of the proposed counsellors' qualifications or training.

The organisation will often be asked to supply a business plan setting out its proposed activities, expenditure budget and anticipated income.

If the trustees do not understand any question or are not certain how to reply or what information to submit, they should seek legal advice or contact the Commission's registration department. It is an offence knowingly or recklessly to supply false information on the questionnaire or in any other way.

The Commission may ask for additional information, and may ask to meet with the trustees. This may be because the Commission does not have enough information to be certain that the organisation is indeed charitable in law, or to explore any other concerns or ambiguities.

8.2.5 Declaration by trustees

All the charity trustees must complete a declaration (**CC5c**) in which they certify that they are willing to act as charity trustees, are not disqualified from doing so [**13.3.2**], and have read specified information supplied with the registration pack.

The Commission checks trustees' names and addresses against an address verification system and the electoral roll, and if the trustee is not listed may ask for proof of address. The Commission will also check the Insolvency Service to see if the trustee is an undischarged bankrupt [**13.3.2**], and Companies House to see whether the trustee is disqualified from serving as a company director [**13.3.3**].

8.2.6 Consultation with HM Revenue and Customs

Because a charity is entitled to tax benefits [**4.2.1**], HM Revenue and Customs has the right to object to its registration. If the Commission thinks this might happen it consults HMRC at this stage, before registration.

8.2.7 Consideration of the application

Some applications can be processed very quickly – within a week, for applications made online and using a model or approved governing document [**8.2.2**]. But in other cases the registration process can be lengthy and difficult. In particularly complex cases, the Commission or the attorney general may take questions of charity law to the charity tribunal, before the Commission makes a decision.

If the Commission is not satisfied that the organisation is being established for exclusively charitable purposes or that it will operate for the benefit of the public, it may propose changes to the objects. These suggestions are open to negotiation, but this is most effectively done by an experienced solicitor. If the organisation agrees to make these changes, either before or after negotiation, it will have to amend its governing document [**7.5**]. Otherwise it will have to resign itself to not being allowed to register as a charity, or seek a review or appeal against the Commission's decision [**8.2.10**].

Changes to internal procedures may also be suggested. These changes reflect the Commission's views on good governance, but may not reflect the charity's values and priorities, and may not be in its best interests in the longer term. Failure to comply with these suggestions should not affect registration, unless the Commission considers that the changes are necessary to ensure the organisation is exclusively charitable and is working for the public benefit.

8.2.8 Decision of the Commission

After its consideration and, if necessary, discussions with the trustees the Charity Commission will inform the trustees either that the organisation has been registered as a charity, the organisation is not set up for exclusively charitable purposes and/or does not meet the public benefit test and therefore cannot be registered, or the application is complex and will require further consideration.

8.2.9 Entry on the register

When the charity is registered it receives its registration number and a certificate setting out the details as entered in the index to the register. This certificate should be kept in a safe place.

Entry on the register is conclusive proof for all purposes that the organisation is legally a charity.   *Charities Act 1993 s.4(1)*

8.2.10 Reviews and appeals against decisions

If registration is refused, there is an internal review procedure [**4.5.11**]. If that fails, the organisation can further appeal to the board of the Charity Commission, or to the **charity tribunal**, part of the first-tier tribunal [**64.7**]. Reviews or appeals on questions of charitable status are complex and legal advice is essential.

To appeal against a refusal to register on the grounds of charitable status, the organisation must have enough assets to make it eligible for compulsory registration, so must have an annual income of at least £5,000. An organisation with income below this level can appeal only against a decision not to consider the organisation for registration.   *Charities Act 1993 s.4(4); ss.2A-2D, sch.1B,1C,*
inserted by Charities Act 2006 s.8

If the organisation remains dissatisfied after appealing, an appeal may be brought in the upper tribunal. However few recent appeals have been successful.

The attorney general or any person affected by the registration of an organisation may appeal *against* a registration. Objections usually come only from HM Revenue and Customs or the rating authority.

8.3 AFTER REGISTRATION

8.3.1 Registered status on documents

As soon as it is registered, a charity whose annual income is over £10,000 must include a statement saying that it is a registered charity on all its cheques, most other financial documents, fundraising materials, and many other documents [**18.1.5, 18.1.3**]. It is an offence to issue cheques and certain documents without the statement, or allow them to be issued. Until new paper and cheques are printed the statement can be handwritten or typed, or put on with a rubber stamp or sticker.

8.3.2   Trustees' duties

All governing body members have a very wide range of common law and statutory duties [**chapter 15**], but charity trustees have special responsibilities [**15.6**]. It is each trustee's responsibility to know, understand and comply with these duties, and to take all reasonable steps to ensure the trustee body as a whole complies with them as well.

8.4   REGISTRATION IN SCOTLAND AND NORTHERN IRELAND

Charities based in England and Wales but operating in Scotland are likely to need to register with the **Office of the Scottish Charity Regulator** if they occupy premises or land in Scotland or carry out regular or significant activities there. Information is available from OSCR [see end of **chapter 1**]. The definition of what is charitable and the public benefit test are slightly different in Scotland than in England and Wales [**5.2.4**, **5.3.8**], and an organisation which plans to operate there should take advice to ensure its governing document complies with Scottish as well as English legislation.

The **Charity Commission for Northern Ireland** [see end of **chapter 1**] is expected to start registering charities there in April 2010. The definition of what is charitable in NI is similar to but not quite the same as in England and Wales; the definition of public benefit is similar to but not quite the same as in Scotland. All charities operating in NI will need to register with the CCNI even if they are registered with the Charity Commission or OSCR, but it will be a 'light touch' rather than full registration. Advice should be sought from the CCNI and, if appropriate, a specialist solicitor.

8.5   LOCAL AUTHORITY REGISTERS, REVIEWS AND REGISTRATION

The Charity Commission is required to provide information about any or all charities in their area to any local borough, district or county council which asks for it. The council may then keep an index of local charities.   *Charities Act 1993 s.76*

Borough, district and county councils have the right to undertake reviews of charities in their area involved in similar types of work, and to make recommendations about the charities to the Commission. This might include, for example, recommendations that small charities be merged. Such reviews cannot be undertaken without the consent of the charities' trustees, and cannot include ecclesiastical charities.   *Charities Act 1993 s.77*

Resources: REGISTERING AS A CHARITY

See end of **chapter 1**.

Statute law. www.opsi.gov.uk and www.statutelaw.gov.uk.

Much but not all case law. www.bailii.org.

Updates cross-referenced to this book. www.rclh.co.uk.

Chapter 9
BRANCHES, SUBSIDIARIES AND GROUP STRUCTURES

9.1 THE RANGE OF RELATIONSHIPS

Faced with the need or desire to grow, to replicate activities in other locations, to develop new activities or to undertake new forms of campaigning or fundraising, organisations can choose from a rich variety of organisational solutions. This may involve complex relationships with external bodies [**chapter 11**], but even within one organisation or group structure there may be equally complex relationships involving projects, branches, subsidiaries and connected bodies.

Unfortunately, in many cases the 'solution' develops piecemeal, and relationships which initially seemed straightforward become legal, financial and managerial nightmares, with potentially dangerous confusion about responsibilities and obligations. This can result in misuse of charitable assets for purposes for which they were not intended; unexpected tax, VAT or business rate liabilities; and one part of the group or organisation becoming liable for other parts' actions or debts.

Another potentially problematic relationship is created when an independent organisation uses another organisation's charity number for its fundraising [**48.5**].

These relationships are considered in the Charity Commission's OG34, *Reporting and linked charities: Registration reporting and accounting*.

9.2 PROJECTS, BRANCHES AND SPECIAL TRUSTS

Projects and branches may be systematically developed, or may emerge spontaneously from the interests of staff members, service users or supporters. Clarity is needed about whether the parent organisation's governing body is responsible for the activities of the branch or project, and those responsible for the branch or project are accountable to the parent; or whether the branch or project is independent and has its own governing body fully responsible for all its operations.

Particular problems can arise if a non-independent project's or branch's objectives or activities do not fall within the objects of the parent organisation and are therefore in breach of trust [**15.6.2**] or *ultra vires* [**5.8**].

9.2.1 Clarifying the situation

The questions below can help clarify whether the branch or project is an integral part of the parent organisation [**9.2.3**], is legally separate from the parent [**9.2.2**], or in the highly undesirable situation of being semi-autonomous [**9.2.4**].

- Does the branch or project use the name of the parent organisation for its activities and fundraising? Or does it use a different name?
- If the parent organisation is a registered charity, does the branch or project use its charity number? Or does the branch or project have its own charity number?
- Does the branch or project have its own committee, and if so, do its members accept that they are accountable to the parent organisation and are, in effect, a sub-committee of the parent? Or do they act as an independent body?
- Does the branch or project need authorisation from the parent organisation before deciding how to spend its money and what activities to run, or can it make its decisions without needing authorisation?
- Does the branch or project account for its income and expenditure to the parent organisation?
- If the branch or project has employees, who is legally the employer [**29.1**]? This is not necessarily the same as who operates PAYE.

To complicate matters, branches or projects may be separate for legal purposes, but for accounting purposes may have to have their accounts consolidated with those of the parent organisation. Or they may be part of the parent, but may be treated as separate for VAT purposes. And to make it even worse, some branches or projects may be separate, and others not. Advice from a solicitor, accountant or the Charity Commission may be necessary to disentangle the relationships.

9.2.2 Separate entities

If a branch or project is **separately registered** with its own company or charity number, it is a separate organisation.

It may choose to **affiliate** to the main organisation, or may agree to comply with conditions set by the main organisation in exchange for being able to use its name and logo and to get support from it [**9.3**]. For accounting, tax or VAT purposes it may form a **group** with the main organisation [**9.4**]. It may be a **subsidiary** of the main organisation, if it is controlled by the it [**9.4**]. But regardless of these relationships, the 'branch' or 'project' is legally separate and is fully responsible for its finance, funding, employees and other legal and financial obligations; can use the main organisation's name only by agreement; and cannot use the main charity or company number of the main organisation.

Even where the 'branches' or 'projects' are separately registered and are therefore legally separate, the main organisation could be held liable for their actions if the separation is not absolutely clear or if, for example, contracts originally held by the main organisation were not transferred to the new one when it became independent.

If there is any possibility of the main organisation being seen as responsible for an independent body, it is sensible for both parties to seek legal advice to ensure the position is clear.

9.2.3 Integrated branches, projects or trusts

A branch, project or special trust [**9.2.3.2**] which is not legally separate is part of the parent organisation, even if it is given considerable freedom of action. The parent organisation will need to recognise that it is fully responsible and potentially liable for the activities of the branch or project or expenditure of the special trust fund, and will have to take appropriate steps to monitor and control it.

9.2.3.1 Branches and projects

It is likely to be helpful to create a **branch** or **project manual** or other written record of what a branch or project can and cannot do, covering issues such as:

- terms of reference for any branch or project committee and its relationship to the main governing body;
- which decisions are delegated to the branch or project;
- how funds and assets of the branch or project are properly safeguarded and accounted for;
- procedures to ensure the parent body's policies, procedures and safeguards are properly implemented and monitored in the branch or project;
- procedures for ensuring the activities and risks of the branch or project are appropriately managed and insured;
- membership arrangements, in particular whether voting members can join the parent organisation through membership of a branch or project or only by direct application to the parent;
- procedures for effective communication between the parent and the branch or project;
- a clear statement that the branch or project accepts that final control of the branch legally rests with the parent organisation, including, where necessary, power to wind up a branch or project and transfer assets.

The obligation to include the branch's or project's finances with the parent's may take the parent to the level where it has to prepare more detailed accounts or have a full audit [**54.2.7**, **54.3.7**], and/or register for VAT [**57.2.1**].

Because the branch or project is legally part of the parent organisation, its assets legally belong to the parent. If the branch or project stops operating, any money or property passes to the parent unless there is a formal agreement specifying otherwise.

9.2.3.2   Special trusts

Many charities hold assets or funds whose use has been limited to some particular purpose. These are **restricted funds** and may be referred to as **special trusts**. Where the restrictions prevent disposal or use of the capital, such trusts are often called **endowments** or **permanent endowment** [**58.8.1**].

Examples are a recreational charity which receives a field on condition it is maintained forever as a football pitch, or a legacy to fund scholarships with the condition that only the interest earned, rather than the bequest itself, can be used.

The gift or grant might impose elaborate controls for the control of the fund or asset, including a requirement for a committee to oversee its use. Funders sometimes use this mechanism when they want to ensure a large grant is used in a particular way. However, no separate charity is created. The committee might exercise day to day control, but as with a branch or project committee [**9.2.3.1**], final responsibility still rests with the governing body of the parent organisation.

Charities Act 1993 s.97

The Charity Commission has power to say that a special trust must be treated and registered as a separate charity [**9.4.2**].

9.2.4   Semi-autonomous branches or projects

Some organisations allow their branches or projects to achieve a **semi-autonomous status**, where the branches or projects use the parent body's name and charity number, particularly for fundraising purposes, but in all other ways act independently with their own committee, bank accounts, premises, employees etc. The branches or projects may be in regular contact with the parent organisation and cooperate with it, but do not see themselves as accountable to it.

Semi-autonomous status is fraught with potential difficulties. For example:

- if the 'branch' gives the impression when raising funds that the money will be used only within the objects of the parent organisation, it is a breach of trust to use the funds for any other purposes;
- the members of the parent organisation's governing body could be found to be negligent in failing to ensure the proper application of funds raised in their name and for which they are legally trustees;

- unless there is a clear agreement about use of the name, it may be difficult to stop that use if the parent organisation is in dispute with a branch or project;
- the members of the parent organisation's governing body could find themselves liable for the debts of the branch or project.

The governing body of the parent organisation must either ensure the branch is clearly within its control (albeit with considerable but explicit delegated powers) or allow the branch to become truly independent [**9.3**], perhaps with an affiliation, franchise or licensing agreement, or other form of link [**11.2**].

9.2.5 Fundraising and supporters' groups

Fundraising or 'friends' groups which raise money solely for a specific named charity generally do not have to register as a separate charity, because they do not have discretion as to how the funds they raise will be used. They are treated in the same way as a branch or project of the charity for which they are raising funds [**9.2.3**].

9.2.5.1 Informal fundraising groups

An informal group which occasionally fundraises for one charity is not treated as part of the charity for which it is fundraising. But even an informal fundraising group may need to register as a charity [**8.1.1**] if it raises funds for a charitable purpose or purposes, rather than for a specific named charity; raises funds for a number of charities, rather than always for one named charity; or has discretion about how it uses the funds it raises.

Where a group raises funds for a named organisation which is not itself registered as a charity, such as a school or hospital, it is not always clear whether registration is necessary. Advice should be sought from the Charity Commission or an experienced solicitor.

9.2.5.2 Responsibilities of the fundraising group

Anyone who raises funds for any organisation(s) or purpose(s) holds the funds as a **constructive trustee** [**48.2.1**], must comply with all relevant legislation on fundraising [**chapters 47** and **48**], and must use the funds only for the purpose(s) for which they were collected. If the funds are collected for charitable, benevolent or philanthropic purposes, those involved in raising the funds are subject to the control of the Charity Commission, even if they have not registered their fundraising group as a charity.

The individuals involved in the fundraising group are responsible for ensuring the group complies with all its legal obligations, and could be held personally liable if the group does not.

9.3 PROJECT OR BRANCH BECOMING INDEPENDENT

Parent organisations may be happy for their offshoots to move to independent status once they are viable, either as a planned move or because of the difficulties in maintaining adequate control. Decisions about independence may be reached through negotiation between the parent and the affected branches or projects, but the final decision must always be made by the parent's governing body.

The process of becoming independent is complex and raises most of the same issues that occur when an unincorporated organisation becomes incorporated [**10.1**]. Issues likely to need particular attention include:

- ensuring the new organisation adopts an appropriate legal form and draws up an appropriate governing document [**chapter 1**];
- ensuring the new organisation is registered with the Charity Commission if necessary [**8.1**], and all other relevant authorities [**1.9**];
- drawing up a formal transfer of funds and other assets [**10.1.2**];
- separating funding and contractual arrangements and liabilities;
- the transfer of staff under TUPE [**29.7**] and resolving pension issues;

- data protection issues around the transfer of information to the new organisation about clients, donors and other individuals [**43.3.4**];

- agreeing any use by the new organisation of the parent body's name, logo, policies, procedures, research and other intellectual property [**chapter 44**];

- agreeing whether the parent body will continue to provide premises, facilities, training or other support, and/or will continue to require key principles or standards to be observed, and if necessary putting these arrangements into a contract, licence or the new organisation's governing document.

Specialist legal advice will ensure the separation, handover and new registration are done properly, and will reduce the risk of later problems.

9.3.1 Ongoing control

Before releasing a branch or project to become independent the parent should carefully consider the safeguards which should be put in place, through requiring adoption of a particular form of governing document and/or embodying the controls in an agreement. Safeguards could include requirements that:

- the objects and other key clauses of the new organisation's governing documents cannot be changed without the consent of the parent organisation;

- the new organisation can operate only in specified geographic areas;

- if the new organisation is wound up, any surplus funds must be transferred to the parent organisation or be used in a specified way;

- the parent organisation must be provided with annual returns or reports and given access on request to other information about the new organisation;

- the parent organisation has the right to be represented on the governing body of the new organisation as either a voting member or an observer;

- the parent organisation has powers of veto to remove officers or members of the governing body if this is considered necessary (for example, if an officer of the new organisation brings the parent organisation into disrepute);

- the new organisation must cease using any name associating it with the parent organisation if it breaches the requirements.

If a branch or project which becomes independent is to continue to use the parent organisation's name or logo in any form, the parent should carefully consider what forms of ongoing monitoring or control are appropriate. This is best done by a legal agreement licensing the branch to use the logo or other copyright or trademarked material [**44.11**].

9.3.2 Ongoing support

If the parent organisation does not want to retain such control over its former branches, it may set up looser ties such as a **franchise** or **federation** [**11.2**].

If this is not appropriate, the parent organisation may maintain a link by providing advice, encouragement, training or consultancy services. Within this model the original organisation has no legal link with its former branches or projects, other than any contractual arrangement to provide services. This is the weakest sort of structure, and may lead to a final break-up of any links.

9.4 GROUP OR PARENT STRUCTURES

In legal terms, a **group** exists when an organisation (which may be referred to as a **holding company**) has one or more **subsidiaries** which it controls, or when one organisation can, by agreement, control another. Group members remain separate legal entities. Each of their governing bodies has legal responsibilities but ultimately they can be directed by the holding company. The control is usually exercised by the main organisation having a right to appoint or remove all or a majority of the members of the governing body of the subsidiary.

A structure with integral branches [**9.2.3.1**] is not a group because the branches are all legally part of one organisation. A federation [**11.2.2**] is not a group because the organisations which make up the federation are independent of each other. An affiliation structure [**11.2.1**] may or may not be a group, depending on the level of control exercised by the main organisation on the governing bodies of the affiliated organisations.

The creation of a group can have important implications for tax, VAT and accounting, as well as employment (especially in relation to rights dependent on the number of employees that 'associated employers' have), and data protection (for the sharing of personal data within the group). It is therefore essential to be clear about what constitutes a group for these purposes and when one exists.

9.4.1 Companies, other incorporated bodies and groups

For company law purposes, a group exists if one corporate body (the **parent undertaking**) is legally able to control one or more undertakings (the **subsidiary undertakings**). Special accounting regulations apply to groups [**54.3.2**].

9.4.1.1 Parent undertakings

The parent undertaking does not necessarily have to be a registered company; it can be any corporate body, including an industrial and provident society or charitable incorporated organisation. If the parent body is a company it may be called a **parent company** or **holding company**. *Companies Act 2006 s.1159(1),(4)*

A **parent undertaking** is a corporate body which:

- holds a majority of the voting rights of another undertaking;
- is a member of another undertaking, and has the right to appoint or remove a majority of its governing body;
- is a member of another undertaking, and has an agreement with the other members of the second undertaking which gives it control of a majority of the voting rights; or
- has a right to exercise dominant control over another undertaking because of provisions contained in the governing document of the second undertaking, or because the two undertakings have a control contract. *Companies Act 2006 s.1162(2)*

A parent/subsidiary situation may also exist if the parent has a **participating interest** in another undertaking, defined as owning 20% or more of the shares or holding 20% or more of the voting rights in an undertaking, and either the parent actually exercises a dominant influence over the other undertaking, or the parent and the other undertaking are managed on a unified basis.

9.4.1.2 Subsidiary undertakings

A **subsidiary undertaking** is a body subject to one of the above types of control. It need not be a company and does not even need to be incorporated. The term includes all corporate bodies, including industrial and provident societies and charitable incorporated organisations, as well as unincorporated associations which carry on a trade or business, whether on a for profit or not for profit basis. *Companies Act 2006 s.1161(1)*

An undertaking is a wholly owned subsidiary if its only members are its parent undertaking, the parent undertaking's other wholly owned subsidiaries, and/or persons who are acting on behalf of the parent undertaking or its wholly owned subsidiaries. *Companies Act 2006 s.1159(2)*

9.4.2 Charity groups

Accounting and reporting by charities: Statement of recommended practice (Charities SORP) requires accounts to contain information about **connected charities**, and requires the accounts of a charity's subsidiaries to be consolidated with those of the primary charity [**54.2.3**].

9.4.2.1 Connected charities

Two charities are **connected** if they have common, parallel or related objects and activities; and they have either **common control** or **unity of administration** (or **shared management**). *Charities SORP 2005 app.1 para.9.1*

Common control exists if the same person or persons, or persons connected with each other through family or business relationships, have the right to appoint a majority of the charity trustees of both or all the charities, or hold a majority of the voting rights in the administration of both or all the charities.

A person may be either an individual person or a corporate body. A charity is not necessarily connected with another simply because a person is a trustee of both. To be connected, one charity subordinates its interests to another charity because of this relationship.   *Charities SORP 2005 app.1 para.50.1(d)*

Unity of administration and **shared management** are not defined in SORP.

Charities may also be connected if they come together under one umbrella organisation, or are part of a federal structure. The Charity Commission may make a **uniting direction** for connected charities [**9.4.2.2**].

9.4.2.2   Subsidiary undertakings and uniting directions

With a subsidiary relationship, the governing bodies of parent and subsidiary remain separately and independently accountable for the discharge of their duties as charity trustees and/or company directors. They therefore need to remain aware of the potential for conflicts of interest [**15.2.3**].

A parent charity's subsidiary undertakings are defined in the same way as in the **Companies Acts** [**9.4.1**]. Charity Commission consent is not needed to set up a subsidiary if the parent charity has the necessary powers, but legal advice should be sought.

Where one charity controls another charity as a subsidiary, the Commission may:

- treat each charity as a **distinct charity**, with each being separately registered with its own number, and each being a **reporting charity** providing separate accounts and reports to the Commission; *or*
- make a **uniting direction**, making the subsidiary a **linked charity**. A linked charity shares the same number with the parent charity, normally with an additional number e.g. 1234567(2).   *Charities Act 1993 s.96(5),(6)*

A linked charity may not be technically a subsidiary. The advantage of the uniting direction is that the reporting (parent) charity accounts for all the charities linked to it. This arrangement may be used where, for example, there are several small charities with similar objects, and one charity is formed as the reporting charity with all the others linked to it – thus removing the need to submit multiple reports and returns.

Subsidiaries, linked charities and uniting directions are explained in the Charity Commission's operational guidance OG34B.

9.4.2.3   Special trusts

A **special trust** is created when money is given to a charity as a restricted fund which can only be used for a specific purpose, or when money or property is given as permanent endowment, with a condition that the money cannot be spent or the property cannot be sold [**58.8.1**]. An incorporated body (charitable company, charitable incorporated organisation or charitable industrial and provident society) cannot hold permanent endowment, so the Charity Commission will require any special trust for its permanent endowment to be treated and registered as a separate charity. Special trusts will normally be linked with the main charity under a uniting direction [above].

9.4.2.4   Affiliates treated as branches

Where one charity is able to exert a substantial degree of influence over another, the influenced charities may have to be treated in the same way as non-independent branches and their accounts may have to be consolidated with those of the main charity [**54.2.2**]. This would apply, for example, in the sort of affiliation arrangement where the main charity prescribes the governing document for the affiliated charities [**9.3.1**] and exercises substantial control over the work of affiliates, even if the affiliated charities are themselves separately registered. Advice should be sought from the organisation's auditor or the Charity Commission.

9.4.3 Unincorporated non-charitable parent bodies

A 'group' exists only if the parent body is incorporated and/or is charitable. If the parent body does not fall into these categories, it may choose to consolidate its accounts with those of its subsidiaries, and should do so if failure to consolidate would give a misleading picture.

9.5 SETTING UP A SUBSIDIARY

A subsidiary may enable an organisation to achieve all of its objectives, or to achieve them in the most efficient way. But the complexity of a group structure increases cost and administration, so subsidiaries should be set up only if necessary and only if the advantages warrant the extra work and cost.

9.5.1 Typical group structures

A huge range of structures is possible, with combinations of charities, non-charities or both. Vital underlying principles are that a charity cannot generally use its funds to create or subsidise a non-charitable body, and a charity's finance and financial records must be separate from those of any non-charity [**51.5.8**].

9.5.1.1 Charity with for profit subsidiary

A common voluntary sector group structure consists of a charitable organisation which sets up a **trading subsidiary** to undertake commercial activities as a way of raising funds for the charity. The trading subsidiary is likely to take the form of a company limited by shares, with the charity holding all the shares [**51.3.2**]. Such a subsidiary may also be set up to obtain VAT benefits in the delivery of charitable services [**57.1.2**].

The subsidiary's profits are subject to tax, but if all or most of the pre-tax profits are passed to the charity through gift aid, the tax is avoided or reduced [**51.7**].

Where a charity's activities border on the non-charitable it may run all or most of its charitable activities through a subsidiary, thus avoiding the need to constantly decide which organisation should run which activity. Or a charity whose activities are exempt from VAT if run by a charity but subject to VAT if run by a non-charity, may run the activities through a non-charity in order to register for VAT and be able to recover VAT on its expenditure for the activity [**57.10**].

9.5.1.2 Charity with non-charitable not for profit subsidiary

If a charity wants to take on activities which are not themselves charitable, for example some types of political activities, it can set up a non-charitable not for profit organisation. This might take the form of an unincorporated association or, if limited liability is important, a company limited by guarantee. In either case the charity generally retains the right to appoint all or most of the members of the subsidiary organisation's governing body, but cannot use its assets or resources to create or subsidise the non-charitable organisation.

9.5.1.3 Non-charity with charitable subsidiary

A business or non-charitable organisation may want to set up a charity in order to take advantage of tax benefits for the charitable aspects of its work [**4.2.1**].

If the charity is likely to be fairly inactive – existing primarily to channel funds to the primary organisation for its charitable activities – and will not be exposed to significant financial risks, the legal form is likely to be a charitable trust. If the charity will itself undertake activities, the structure will probably be a charitable trust, charitable company limited by guarantee or charitable incorporated organisation (CIO). The primary organisation will generally control appointment of all or most of the charity's trustees.

9.5.1.4 Charity with charitable subsidiary

A charity may have a charitable subsidiary as a result of a merger, or may set one up because its own objects are too narrow to allow it to undertake an activity or

115

because it wants to separate activities to manage risk. Where a charity is setting up a charitable subsidiary, a decision will need to be made about whether the new charity is separately registered or linked [**9.4.2.2**].

9.5.1.5 Non-charity with charitable and trading subsidiaries

Various structures may be combined in more complex configurations. An example is a non-charitable voluntary organisation – perhaps an organisation set up primarily for political objects, or a professional association providing services primarily for its members – which sets up a charitable subsidiary to support and raise funds for those of its activities which are properly charitable.

Even though the primary organisation is not charitable, its governing document may prohibit it from undertaking trading activities, or it may feel it is inappropriate to be involved in these. To overcome this, it sets up a trading subsidiary.

The trading subsidiary would then raise funds for the non-charitable organisation, but these would be subject to tax. So any funds which were to be used solely for charitable purposes could be passed to the charity through gift aid, thus taking advantage of tax relief on gift aid donations. The charity could then make a grant to the non-charitable organisation for those parts of its activities which are charitable, or the charity itself could undertake these functions.

9.5.2 Issues in group arrangements

As well as the VAT [**57.2.3, 57.2.4**], accounting [**54.2.2 54.3.2**] and data protection [**43.3.4**] implications of group structures, there are also internal issues.

9.5.2.1 Control

A parent may exercise control of a subsidiary by a variety of means, most commonly through:

- **absolute control** of votes at general meetings of members, where the parent owns 100% of the shares of a company limited by shares or is the only member of a company limited by guarantee;
- **majority control** of votes at general meetings, for example where the parent owns a majority of the shares of a company limited by shares;
- the subsidiary's **governing document** giving the parent the right to nominate all or most of the members of the subsidiary's governing body or the right to remove them; or
- a **contractual agreement** between the parent and subsidiary.

It is not unusual for the parent/subsidiary relationship to break down. One such scenario is when a charity creates an independent members' club to run its bar and social activities, and the club members become a powerful voting bloc controlling the charity.

Another scenario is when a trading subsidiary is highly dependent on key staff in the parent organisation who develop specialist expertise. The staff may come to exercise *de facto* control of the subsidiary because only they have the contacts and expertise to ensure its continued success, and may unduly influence or override the decisions of the subsidiary's governing body.

Or the governing body of a subsidiary may become entrenched, fail to change and develop with the parent organisation, and fail to respond to directions of the parent – but the parent may be powerless to remove them. This can be avoided by including appropriate provisions in the subsidiary's governing document.

9.5.2.2 Conflict of loyalties

Some **conflict of loyalties** (also called **duality of interest**) is inherent in the legal rules governing the separate parts of a group structure. Every member of a governing body must make decisions in the best interests of the organisation they govern [**15.2.3**], and those decisions might conflict with directions given by a parent organisation.

Charity trustees, in particular, must act always in the best interests of the charity and its beneficiaries, even if this involves disregarding the directions of the parent body [**15.6.3**] or the needs of its subsidiary [**51.5.2**]. Similarly, company directors must act in the interests of the company [**15.5.2**], and can be in a position of conflict of loyalties only if this is allowed [**15.3.8**].

There is no easy way around this conflict of loyalties. It can be prevented by not having anyone sitting on the governing bodies of both the parent and a subsidiary or on the governing bodies of two or more subsidiaries, but this may be impractical and undesirable if a truly integrated group is to be maintained. It may be more appropriate to have some overlap to ensure integration, but to have some members of the subsidiary governing body who are not on the governing body of the parent organisation, and *vice versa*.

It is essential to ensure that meetings clearly separate business for one part of the group from business for other parts. Confusion can also be reduced by having separate terms of reference or role descriptions for each governing body, and by ensuring each part of the group has its own clear mission statement and business plan highlighting its objectives.

9.5.2.3 Funding subsidiaries

A trading subsidiary's need for capital raises important issues [**51.4**] which need careful consideration when the subsidiary is established and throughout its life. The Charity Commission's CC35 *Trustees, trading and tax*, available from the Commission [see end of **chapter 1**] explains the issues.

9.5.2.4 Liability for subsidiaries

The isolation of risk within a part of the group is a great advantage, but this advantage can only be retained if care is taken. Even something as minor as using the wrong headed paper or email signature may result in a contractual liability being inadvertently taken on by one member of the group for another member.

Organisations – especially those which are charitable – should take legal advice before guaranteeing loans, overdrafts, leases or other liabilities of subsidiaries. The parent organisation may well not have power to take on such liabilities [**59.5.3**]. Even if it does, it may not want to jeopardise its own future.

9.5.2.5 Closure or liquidation

When setting up any group, thought needs to be given to what will happen if any member of the group ceases to exist or goes into liquidation [**chapter 24**]. This is likely to be particularly important where significant assets are being accumulated within a charity which is a subsidiary of a non-charity. When a charity is wound up, its assets have to be passed to another charity or used for charitable purposes, unless the governing document specifies otherwise, for example that assets given by a non-charitable parent revert to the parent. Failure to include this provision would prevent the assets being passed to a non-charitable parent.

If a subsidiary fails, the governing body of the parent organisation may feel morally bound to meet the subsidiary's debts. Such debts should be paid only after legal advice, because in most cases there will be no legal obligation to pay, and such non-obligatory payments may well be in breach of the governing body's duties.

Resources: BRANCHES, SUBSIDIARIES AND GROUP STRUCTURES

See end of **chapter 1**.

Statute law. www.opsi.gov.uk and www.statutelaw.gov.uk.

Much but not all case law. www.bailii.org.

Updates cross-referenced to this book. www.rclh.co.uk.

Chapter 10

CHANGING LEGAL FORM

For sources of further information see end of chapter 1.

10.1 CHANGING FROM UNINCORPORATED TO INCORPORATED

Many organisations are set up, right from the beginning, as incorporated bodies. But many more start off as unincorporated associations or trusts, and decide to become incorporated when they get larger, take on employees or premises, enter into complex contracts, or want the protection of limited liability. For the pros and cons of incorporation and the available structures, see **chapter 3**.

An unincorporated association or trust cannot simply change into an incorporated body. Instead, it has to set up a completely new company, industrial and provident society (IPS) or, when the form becomes available (expected April 2010), charitable incorporated organisation (CIO). Then all of the assets and legal obligations of the existing organisation have to be transferred to the new body, and usually the existing organisation is dissolved.

If the new organisation is a company or IPS it will have a company or IPS number. If it is a charitable company, an IPS that has to register with the Charity Commission [**8.1**] or a CIO it will have a new charity number, because legally it is a new charity.

Guidance and forms for converting from an unincorporated charity to a charitable company or CIO are available from the Charity Commission [see end of **chapter 1**]. Guidance and forms for becoming an IPS are available from Mutual Societies Registration at the Financial Services Authority [see end of **chapter 1**].

10.1.1 Power to transfer assets

Most recent constitutions for unincorporated associations and trust deeds for charitable trusts include a procedure for dissolving the organisation and transferring its assets to another organisation with the same or similar objects. This procedure must be strictly followed.

If the new organisation's objects are different from the original organisation's, or are similar but wider or narrower (for example, extending the beneficiary group from children 'up to five years of age' to 'up to eight years of age', or *vice versa*) advice should be sought from a specialist solicitor or the Charity Commission.

Advice should also be sought if the organisation holds any money that it is not allowed to spend or property that it is not allowed to sell (**permanent endowment**), or if it holds money or property that has to be used for a specific purpose (**restricted funds** or **special trusts**). Even with a constitutional power to transfer assets, this may not be able to be transferred [**10.1.2.4**].

The governing document of some organisations may require all assets to be transferred, on dissolution, to a named body. This is called a **gift over**. To ensure that assets are not lost when the original organisation is wound up, consent should be sought from the named recipient before any transfer to a new incorporated body.

10.1.1.1   No power to dissolve or transfer assets

If a *charitable* association or trust does not have a transfer or dissolution procedure and its annual income is no more than £10,000, it has a statutory power to transfer all of its assets to another charity or charities. Under these provisions – which do not apply if the charity holds land which must explicitly be used for the purposes, or any particular purpose, of the charity – a decision to transfer the assets can be made by a two-thirds majority of the trustees voting on the resolution. The trustees must be satisfied it is in the interests of the charity to make the transfer, and the assets can be transferred only to a charity with the same or similar purposes. After making any such resolution, the trustees must send a copy to the Charity Commission, with a statement of their reasons for passing it.

Charities Act 1993 s.74, amended by Charities Act 2006 s.40

A charitable association or trust with annual income over the threshold, or holding land or other assets which must be used for a specific purpose, should contact an experienced legal advisor or the Commission for guidance.

Where the unincorporated organisation is going to become a charitable incorporated organisation, virtually all of its property can be transferred to the CIO by resolution of the trustees, even if there is no power to transfer [**10.1.2.1**].

If a *non-charitable* association does not have a transfer or dissolution procedure, any transfer of assets must generally be agreed by *all* of the association's members. This applies even though the assets are going to be used by the same people for the same purposes. Other procedures may be possible [**24.8**], but advice should be sought first from a specialist solicitor.

10.1.2   Transfer of assets, liabilities and responsibilities

Everything must be legally transferred from the old organisation to the new. If this is not done, there could be problems later about the ownership of assets or who is responsible for outstanding liabilities.

In all but the simplest situations, a formal **transfer deed** will need to be drawn up setting out the relationship between the old and new organisations [**20.3**]. The deed generally transfers the original organisation's assets and liabilities to the new one. Legal advice should be sought before drawing this up. The deed may:

- include information and assurances about the extent of assets and liabilities transferred (**warranties**);
- give promises by the new organisation, for example to protect members of the old body against later claims (**indemnities**);
- authorise the new organisation to enforce obligations or collect monies due to the old organisation, generally by **power of attorney**;
- oblige each party to preserve and make available for inspection key records or documents;
- provide for any steps that need to be taken after the transfer date, such as notification to various parties [**10.1.3**].

10.1.2.1   Relevant charity mergers

Where an unincorporated charity transfers its assets to a new incorporated charity and then winds up, the transfer is likely to be a **relevant charity merger**

[**11.5.4**]. In relevant charity mergers it is possible to transfer some, or in some cases most or even all, of the charity's assets through a **vesting declaration**, a form of transfer deed. But liabilities and certain types of asset cannot be transferred in this way, and a separate transfer deed will be needed for these. The Charity Commission must be notified when a vesting declaration is used.

Similarly, most unincorporated charities which want to become a charitable incorporated organisation (CIO) can use a straightforward procedure to transfer their assets, unless they hold **designated land** – land which must be used for a specific purpose or purposes. But a transfer deed is needed to transfer the liabilities, and designated land if there is any. *Charities Act 1993 s.74; s.690, to be inserted by Charities Act 2006 sch.7 para.1 [expected April 2010]*

Before winding up, the original organisation must ensure that all its assets, liabilities and obligations will be transferred or discharged. This may take some time, and the original organisation and the new one may have to run in parallel for a period [**10.1.4.3**].

10.1.2.2 Funding arrangements

To avoid jeopardising grants, any plan to incorporate should be discussed with funders at a very early stage, and written assurances should be obtained that the grant will be seamlessly transferred to the new incorporated body when it starts to operate, and that grant funds already held by the unincorporated organisation can be transferred to the new body.

Contractual arrangements must also be transferred to the new organisation as a **novation** [**10.1.2.8**]. This should also be discussed with purchasers prior to making any final decision to incorporate, because in most cases, consent of the funder or purchaser will be needed.

10.1.2.3 Property and investments

If the original organisation owns or occupies land or buildings, they must be transferred through a vesting declaration (if it is a **relevant charity merger** [**10.1.2.1**] and the property is not prohibited from being transferred in this way) or by an legal agreement. The transfer of a lease or tenancy agreement [**62.2.7**] may require consent of the landlord or superior landlord (one above the landlord with whom the organisation has the lease or licence). These transactions should be done by an experienced solicitor.

Investments must also be formally transferred.

Movable property such as equipment, furniture and vehicles can be transferred through a vesting declaration or by **delivery**, simply by handing it over. Some guarantees on equipment such as computers or photocopiers are invalidated if ownership is transferred, so legal advice should be taken before transferring any item subject to such conditions.

10.1.2.4 Permanent endowment

If a charitable organisation holds money or property which is **permanent endowment** [**58.8.1**], this will normally have to be held by a separate charitable trust, usually with the new incorporated body as trustee.

10.1.2.5 Debts

Any loans, mortgages and other borrowings will have been entered into by the original organisation, and must be transferred to the new one. Failure to do so will leave the original signatories and/or the governing body members of the original organisation personally liable for the debt.

Occasionally an organisation in financial difficulties wishes to transfer its assets and liabilities to a new incorporated body. It cannot do this if the transferred liabilities will exceed the transferred assets and the new organisation does not have adequate assets of its own to cover the difference. In this situation the new organisation would be insolvent, and it is not permissible to set up an insolvent incorporated body.

10.1.2.6 Pension scheme debt

In some situations the original organisation may become liable for a very large **exit debt** if it operates or is a member of an under-funded defined benefit or final salary pension scheme [**30.6.5**]. It is essential for organisations with such pension schemes which are considering changing from unincorporated to incorporated to take advice at a very early stage from their pension provider and legal advisor.

10.1.2.7 Contracts of employment

The transfer of employees is covered by the **Transfer of Undertakings (Protection of Employment) Regulations** (TUPE) [**29.7**], so the original organisation's staff must be consulted before any transfer to the new organisation is agreed [**29.7.3**].

Employees' contracts, statutory rights and virtually all contractual rights are transferred automatically to the new body. New contracts do not need to be issued, but employees must be notified in writing of the identity of the new employer. There is no break in employment, so employment rights related to length of service are not affected [**26.5**].

In relevant charity mergers [**10.1.2.1**], contracts of employment are not transferred under the vesting declaration, so TUPE rules must be followed.

10.1.2.8 Other contracts

Contracts are not covered, in relevant charity mergers, under the vesting declaration [**10.1.2.1**].

To transfer contracts (other than employment contracts) to the new organisation, the original organisation must seek the consent of the other party or parties to the contracts. This is called a **novation agreement**, and ideally contains clauses releasing the original signatories from their obligation for the contract.

However, a supplier or purchaser cannot be forced to agree to such a transfer. If the supplier or purchaser of goods or services will not agree, the new organisation faces difficult decisions, particularly if the contract cannot be terminated or can be terminated only on disadvantageous terms. The organisation should therefore ensure, prior to conversion, that any vital contracts can be transferred.

Many organisations simply ignore the issue, on the assumption that problems will not arise so long as the supplier is paid or the purchaser gets whatever it has paid for. But problems can arise if the new organisation does not meet these obligations. The contract cannot be enforced against the new organisation because it is not legally a party to it and has not taken on any obligation for it, and it cannot be enforced against the original organisation if it no longer exists. So the original signatories, or members of the governing body of the original organisation, could find themselves liable.

One solution is for the transfer deed [**10.1.2.3**] to include promises by the new organisation to indemnify the original signatories against any claim, and appointing the new organisation as an agent with power to enforce the original signatories' rights. Whether this is entirely effective will depend on the wording of the original agreement.

10.1.2.9 Software licences and other IP rights

Software and copyright licences and other intellectual property rights [**chapter 44**] need to be transferred from the individuals who held them on behalf of the old organisation to the new one, in the same way as other contracts [above].

10.1.2.10 Registrations

All bodies with which the original organisation is registered must be notified. In some cases the original organisation's registration will be transferred to the new organisation; for others the new organisation must register and the old organisation's registration must be terminated. Re-registration may trigger fees or greater obligations, which should be understood prior to conversion.

Possible registrations are listed at **1.9**. If the original organisation is registered for VAT, consent must be obtained from HM Revenue and Customs to transfer the activities to the new organisation as a **going concern**.

10.1.2.11   Gift aid and deeds of covenant

Donors with gift aid declarations and deeds of covenant [**50.2**] should be notified of the change and the new charity number.

Provided the new organisation is essentially the same as the old, gift aid declarations can usually simply be transferred if the donors have been notified and do not object. If the organisation has changed its name or objects, donors with gift aid declarations should be asked to make new declarations.

Donors with deeds of covenant should assign (transfer) the deed to the new organisation by deed, or replace it with a gift aid declaration and standing order. HM Revenue and Customs may allow assignment without each donor having to individually agree. Where the organisation's objects have changed, income from assigned covenants should be ringfenced and used only for the original objects.

Advice is available from HM Revenue and Customs [see end of **chapter 50**].

10.1.2.12   Legacies

Where the transfer from unincorporated to incorporated is a **relevant charity merger** [**10.1.2.1**] and the merger is entered in the Charity Commission's **register of mergers** [**11.5.4**], most legacies to the original charity will take effect as a gift to a successor incorporated charity. However, if the successor body has different objects, or if the legacy is worded in a way that precludes it being given to any body other than the original one, the gift may fail. The same may happen with a merger which is not a relevant charity merger or is not entered in the register of mergers.

To avoid these risks, organisations should seek to ensure that known legators make new wills or codicils. The new organisation's governing document should make clear that it is the successor to the original organisation, and the organisation should take legal advice about whether further steps are needed to safeguard legacies from unknown donors or those who do not change their wills.

10.1.2.13   Bank accounts

All bank, building society and other accounts must be in the full registered name of the new organisation, exactly as it is on the certificate of incorporation (if a company) or certificate of registration (if a charitable incorporated organisation or industrial and provident society). Even where the name remains exactly the same, accounts will generally be closed and new ones opened. Cheques and other financial documents must contain the required details of name and status [**18.1**] even if it has to be written on by hand.

10.1.2.14   Insurances

Insurances must be transferred to the new organisation, or the old policies cancelled and new ones taken out. It may be necessary to continue some of the old policies, if there is any risk of potential liability relating to that insurance. It is essential to take advice from the insurers and a legal advisor on these matters.

10.1.2.15   Indemnities

There is always the possibility of liabilities or claims against the old organisation. But with all the assets of the old organisation having been transferred to the new incorporated body, there will be no funds to meet these. To avoid the risk of personal liability, the old organisation should obtain an **indemnity** for current and former members of the old organisation and its governing body.

In drawing up the terms of this indemnity, especially any limitation of liability, there is a conflict of interest between the new and old organisations. Careful drafting will be necessary, and in some situations the members or governing body members of the old organisation may want to take independent legal advice.

10.1.2.16   Membership

There is no way that membership can be automatically transferred, so members of the original organisation must apply for membership of the new body and be entered in a new register of members [**18.5.2**, **18.6.1**, **18.7**]. Members may need to be reassured that the organisation is still essentially the same even though it will have a new legal structure.

10.1.2.17   Policies and procedures

The new organisation must formally adopt (or change) all of the original organisation's policies, procedures, activities etc. This can be done through a minuted decision at the first meeting of the new organisation's governing body [**1.5.12**].

10.1.2.18   Written and electronic documents

Specified information must be included on cheques, stationery, email footers, websites, leaflets, posters and other materials [**18.1**]. Printed stickers with the new details can be used, so long as they completely cover all reference to the old name and/or charity number. It is unlawful to continue to use stationery or to send out emails with the old charity number, or without the new company/CIO/IPS number, charity status (if appropriate) and other required details.

10.1.3   Notification of incorporation

When the transfer takes place, accounts for gas, electricity, telephone, non-domestic rates and credit cards, as well as insurances and accounts with contractors, advisors, suppliers etc have to be transferred to the new organisation. HM Revenue and Customs (for corporation tax registration, PAYE, gift aid and other tax recovery, and VAT if the organisation is registered for VAT) must be notified. All other relevant registration bodies [**1.9**] must also be notified.

Even if the new company, IPS or CIO is going to have exactly the same name as the existing organisation all these notifications must be made, because everyone who does business with the new organisation or who may have any claim against it must know that they are now dealing with an incorporated body rather than the former unincorporated organisation.

A protective measure is to advertise the change in the *London Gazette*, which effectively gives notice of the change to everyone (but does not remove the need to get the specific consents outlined in **10.1.2**). A solicitor can advise on this.

Failure to take the above steps or to provide notification of the change may mean that potential personal liability remains for individuals. A supplier whose bill was not paid, for example, could say they thought they were still supplying the unincorporated organisation, and could claim against the person(s) who authorised an order or contract rather than claiming against the new organisation.

10.1.4   The process

The initial discussions for these steps can be undertaken well in advance and the paperwork can be drawn up, but no date should be set for any transfers until:

- it is clear that there are no adverse consequences;
- if required, the Charity Commission has authorised the transfer of assets to the new body;
- the original organisation has passed at a meeting of its governing body or a general meeting of its members a resolution [**19.7**, **19.12.5**] to proceed with the transfer on the agreed terms;
- the new organisation has been registered as a company, charitable incorporated organisation or industrial and provident society [**1.4-1.7**];
- the new organisation has registered with the Charity Commission, if it is a charitable company or a charitable industrial and provident society required to register [**8.2**];
- the new organisation has passed at a meeting of its governing body or a general meeting of its members a resolution to accept the transfer on the agreed terms.

The first meeting of the new organisation's governing body should deal with all the matters normally considered at an ordinary first meeting [**1.5.12**].

Even where the new organisation seamlessly carries on the previous body's functions, it is legally a completely new and separate body. So not only do the tangible assets and liabilities need to be transferred, but the new body must also re-adopt policies, procedures and delegation of responsibilities.

10.1.4.1 Transferring the assets

The original organisation must pass, in accordance with its governing document, a resolution to transfer its assets to the new company, CIO or IPS, or must carry out such other procedures as are required by its governing document to make this decision. It may be convenient to do this earlier, perhaps when the decision to become incorporated is first taken. That meeting may resolve not only to form the new incorporated body but also to make the transfer of assets and liabilities and to dissolve the existing body [below], at a date or dates to be decided by the governing body. Such a resolution may be conditional, for example on consent being given by funders and/or the Charity Commission.

To save on audit costs, many organisations choose to delay the transfer until the end of the financial year.

10.1.4.2 Dissolving the original organisation

To dissolve the original organisation, the proper procedures must be followed [**24.8, 24.9**]. This is generally a resolution passed in accordance with its governing document [**7.4.27**]. The accounts of the existing association or trust will have to be prepared up to the date of winding up, and if necessary be independently examined or audited [**54.2.7**].

When its final accounts have been prepared and if necessary examined or audited, the old organisation holds a final general meeting or takes the other steps required under its governing document to accept the accounts and to dissolve itself. If the resolution to dissolve was already passed and the governing body authorised to set the date [**10.1.4.1**], it may not be necessary to hold this final meeting.

If the original organisation was a charity the Charity Commission must be notified and final accounts filed, so it can be deregistered.

10.1.4.3 Retaining the original organisation as a shell

If the original body is being retained, for example to hold permanent endowment or to ensure legacies are not lost, its governing document is likely to need amending to enable the organisation to function in its new role. The new incorporated body, for example, may become the sole member or trustee of the original organisation, so procedures for meetings, quorums etc are likely to need to be changed.

10.2 CHANGING FROM ONE INCORPORATED STRUCTURE TO ANOTHER

Changing from one incorporated structure to another does not give any advantage in terms of limited liability and permanent succession [**3.1.1**], since both are incorporated. There may, however, be other reasons to consider such a change.

Most of the procedures required for transferring assets, liabilities and responsibilities [**10.1.2**] are required for a change from one incorporated structure to another, but some will be simpler than when converting from unincorporated to incorporated. The basic procedures for each type of transfer are set out below, but legal advice should be sought.

Where an organisation changes from one incorporated structure to another – even though it is still basically the same organisation – it may become liable for a large **exit debt** if it operates or is a member of an under-funded defined benefit or final salary pension scheme [**10.1.2.6**]. Advice about this should be taken at a very early stage.

10.3   CHANGING FROM COMPANY TO ANOTHER STRUCTURE

10.3.1   Changing from charitable company to CIO

While proposals for the **charitable incorporated organisation** [3.2] were being developed, the assumption was that charitable companies would rush to convert as soon as the CIO structure became available. However the rules for CIOs as set out in the **Charities Act 2006** sch.7, combined with the simplification of company law under the **Companies Act 2006**, mean that at the time of writing (mid 2009) it is unclear whether the CIO will provide enough advantages to justify converting from a charitable company.

When the CIO structure becomes available (expected April 2010), a charitable company wishing to convert must pass a special resolution [19.7.4] or a written resolution signed by every company member who would be entitled to vote on a special resolution [19.10.2]. Even though company law rules allow such written resolutions to be passed by only 75% of the members, a resolution to convert from company to CIO requires 100% of the members. The company must also pass an ordinary resolution agreeing the CIO's proposed constitution. *Charities Act 1993 s.69G(5),(6), to be inserted by Charities Act 2006 sch.7 para.1 [expected April 2010]*

The articles of association of the original company limited by guarantee will specify the amount company members could be required to contribute if the company is wound up [3.3.1]. (For companies registered before 1 October 2009, this will have been in the memorandum of association, but will have become part of the articles from 1 October 2009 [7.1.1].) If the guarantee amount is £10 or less, the guarantee is **extinguished** on conversion to a CIO, and should not be included in the CIO's constitution. If the original guarantee is more than £10, a guarantee must be included in the CIO's constitution, and cannot be less than the original guarantee. *CharA 1993 s.69G(8)-(10), to be inserted by CharA 2006 sch.7 para.1 [expected April 2010]*

The CIO's proposed constitution, the resolutions agreeing to convert to a CIO and accepting the proposed constitution, and other specified documents are sent to the Charity Commission. The Commission consults the registrar of companies, and decides whether to accept the application for conversion. If the application is accepted the Commission notifies the registrar of companies, and the conversion takes effect when the registrar of companies cancels the company's registration.

Slightly different rules apply where the converting company is a company limited by shares, or a company limited by guarantee with a share capital. In this case, the company can convert only if all shares are fully paid up.

Charitable companies which are exempt from registering as a charity [8.1.2] cannot convert to a CIO.

10.3.2   Changing from non-charitable company to CIC

The main reasons for converting from non-charitable company (whether limited by guarantee or by shares) to **community interest company** are:
- the company may want an **asset lock** [3.1.4], to ensure the assets must always be used for the benefit of the community;
- a company limited by shares may find it easier to obtain grants or loans if there is not only an asset lock, but also a cap on dividends;
- it may want to make clear to everyone. or at least everyone who understands what a CIC is, that it is operating for the benefit of the community, rather than purely as a profit-making business.

The company must pass special resolutions [19.7.4] to alter the company's memorandum and/or articles to state it is to be a CIC, to comply with the requirements for CICs [1.6], and to change the name of the company so it ends with CIC or one of the other acceptable forms of wording [6.4.5]. The resolutions, the new memorandum and articles and form **CIC37**, containing the community interest statement and declarations, are sent to the registrar of companies with the registration fee (£25 as at 1/8/09). The registrar consults the CIC regulator, who must confirm the company is eligible for registration as a CIC. The conversion takes effect when the registrar of companies gets this approval and records the changes.

Companies (Audit, Investigations & Community Enterprise) Act 2004 ss.37,38

Special provisions protect the rights of company members, especially when a company limited by shares converts to a CIC. Information about this and all aspects of converting to a CIC is available from the CIC regulator [see end of **chapter 1**].

10.3.3 Changing from charitable company to CIC

The process for changing from charitable company to CIC is the same as for a non-charitable company [**10.3.2**], except that:

- the resolution changing the company's name (to include CIC or equivalent at the end) requires the Charity Commission's prior written consent;
Companies (Audit, Investigations & Community Enterprise) Act 2004 s.39

- the resolution amending other parts of the memorandum and/or articles may require the Commission's prior written consent [**7.5.3**]. *Charities Act 1993 s.64, amended by Charities Act 2006 s.31*

Even if the objects remain charitable, a CIC cannot be a charity [**3.4**], so the charitable company ceases to be a charity when it becomes a CIC, and ceases to be entitled to the tax relief, rate relief and other advantages of charitable status [**4.2.1**]. Giving up charitable status is a serious step, and should be contemplated only after taking specialist legal advice. Failure to take such advice could put the trustees in breach of their duty of trust to the charity [**15.6**].

The Charity Commission will give consent for the necessary resolution(s) to become a CIC only if it is convinced that the company fully understands the implications of losing the advantages of charitable status [**4.2**], conversion will provide the organisation with benefits it cannot obtain as a charity, and the balance of advantage favours conversion. Such advantages might be the ability to raise funds by attracting different types of financing, being able to trade without the restrictions of charity trading, and/or adopting wider objects.

When a charitable company becomes a CIC all the property it holds at that time (other than money) becomes subject to a trust for the charitable purposes of the company immediately before conversion, usually with the CIC as trustee. This trust has to register with the Commission unless it is excepted or exempt from registering [**8.1**], and the property can only be used for the trust's charitable purposes. This could have practical implications if the property is likely to be used for both the original charitable purposes and any new non-charitable purposes of the CIC, and specialist advice should be sought.

10.3.4 Changing from company to IPS

Reasons for changing from a company to an industrial and provident society might include:

- the regulatory requirements are less burdensome [**3.5.4**];
- at the time of writing (mid 2009) charitable IPSs do not register with the Charity Commission, and even when this changes and some have to register, those with annual income not more than £100,000 are unlikely to have to register until 2012 or later [**8.1.2**];
- the statutory status of 'democratic society for the benefit of the community' or community benefit society may sound more ideologically acceptable than 'private company limited by guarantee without a share capital';
- an IPS's register of members does not have to be open to the general public, as a company's does [**18.6.1**];
- an IPS's register of directors does not have to be open to the general public, as a company's does, and is not available the way a company's is at Companies House [**18.6.2**];
- for large membership organisations the costs of circulating company paperwork can be considerable, while an IPS can simply advertise in the press or at its place of business that accounts are available or that a general meeting is to be held, and paperwork only has to be sent to members who ask for it. However, company law provisions allowing accounts and other paperwork to be provided electronically [**18.3**] may mean that this is not a significant factor.

To convert, the procedures set out in the **Industrial and Provident Societies Act 1965** s.53 must be followed. If model rules are not being used, or are being used but with amendment, the rules must be agreed by Mutual Societies Registration, as with a new registration [**1.7.2**]. The company passes a special resolution [**19.7.4**] agreeing to convert into an IPS and appointing three company members to sign the new IPS rules with the secretary. The resolution and rules are sent to Mutual Societies Registration. When the new IPS is registered, a copy of the resolution and the IPS registration are sent to Companies House. As soon as Companies House registers the special resolution, the conversion takes effect.

A company which becomes an IPS cannot use the word 'company' in its new name. *Industrial & Provident Societies Act 1965 s.53(5)*

10.4 CHANGING FROM CIC TO ANOTHER STRUCTURE

10.4.1 Changing from CIC to charitable company

A CIC cannot become an ordinary (non-CIC) non-charitable company, but can become a charitable company. To do this it must:

- pass special resolutions to change its name and make any other necessary changes to the governing document [**19.7.4**];

- obtain a statement from the Charity Commission that in its opinion, the converted company will have charitable status and will not be exempt from registering with the Commission;

- not submit its application for the change until the time allowed for company members to object to the constitutional changes has elapsed, or if any company members have objected, the changes have been confirmed by the court.
Companies (Audit, Investigations & Community Enterprise) Act 2004 ss.54,55

Further information is available from the CIC regulator [see end of **chapter 1**].

10.4.2 Changing from CIC to CIO

Conversion of a community interest company into a charitable incorporated organisation is similar to conversion from charitable company to CIO [**10.3.1**], but the CIC regulator must be notified and must confirm that the company is eligible to cease being a CIC. Where the CIC is limited by shares rather than guarantee, it can convert only if all the shares are fully paid up.
Charities Act 1993 s.69J, to be inserted by Charities Act 2006 sch.7 para.1 [expected April 2010]

10.4.3 Changing from CIC to IPS

CICs were originally prohibited from converting to an industrial and provident society, but from 1 October 2009 can convert to an asset-locked IPS [**3.5.2**].
Companies (Audit, Investigations & Community Enterprise) Act 2004 s.53 &
Community Interest Company Regulations 2005 [SI 2005/1788] reg.6A, amended/inserted by
Community Interest Company (Amendment) Regulations 2009 [SI 2009/1942] reg.5

10.5 CHANGING FROM IPS TO ANOTHER STRUCTURE

10.5.1 Changing from IPS to company

Reasons to change from industrial and provident society to company may include:

- a private company only needs one member, while an IPS needs a minimum of three individual members;

- an IPS which is a cooperative [**3.5.1**] might want to stop being a co-op;

- companies are not required to hold an annual general meeting, and can pass most resolutions in writing;

- a charitable community benefit IPS [**3.5.2**] might want to register with the Charity Commission and get a charity registration number, which at the time of writing (mid 2009) it cannot do [**8.1.2**].

The ways of converting, as set out in the IPS legislation, are by setting up a company and then **amalgamating** the IPS with it, setting up a company and then

transferring engagements (transferring all the IPS's assets and liabilities to it), or **converting** the IPS to a company.   *Industrial & Provident Societies Act 1965 ss.50-52*

In amalgamation and transfer the IPS and new company exist side by side; in conversion the IPS becomes the company.

The IPS must pass a special resolution [**19.7.5**], subject to an additional requirement that at least half of the qualifying members voted on the resolution.

Industrial & Provident Societies Act 2002 s.1

Specialist legal advice should be sought. In particular if the IPS is amalgamating or transferring engagements, all property owned by the IPS must be legally transferred to the company, but if it is converting, this is not necessary. The wording of the resolution is crucial, and should be approved in advance by Mutual Societies Registration in the Financial Services Authority.

10.5.2   Changing from IPS to CIC

An industrial and provident society can convert to a community interest company under the procedure for conversion to a company [**10.5.1**], but with the additional requirements for CICs [**3.4**]. If the IPS is charitable, regardless of whether it is or is not registered with the Charity Commission, it must first contact the Commission to discuss the implications of the proposed conversion, because the CIC will not be charitable.

10.5.3   Changing from charitable IPS to CIO

The procedure for converting from a charitable industrial and provident society to a charitable incorporated organisation is basically the same as for conversion from a charitable company to CIO [**10.3.1**], except with the Financial Services Authority as the current regulator rather than the registrar of companies. However the society cannot convert if any of its shares are not fully paid up, or if it is an exempt charity [**8.1.2**].   *Charities Act 1993 s.69G, to be inserted by Charities Act 2006 sch.7 para.1 [expected April 2010]*

10.6   CHANGING FROM INCORPORATED TO UNINCORPORATED

A decision to deregister as a company, industrial and provident society or charitable incorporated organisation and start (or resume) operating as an unincorporated association is extremely unusual and should never be taken lightly, because the members of the organisation and its governing body will be giving up the protection of limited liability [**3.1.1**].

The organisation will have to wind up as required under company, IPS or CIO law [**24.3-24.7**], and all assets and liabilities will need to be transferred to the members of the new governing body, holding trustees or a custodian trustee [**20.4**]. Particular care may need to be given to the appointment of holding trustees to take on any property or investments.

If the old organisation is charitable, it will have to apply for charitable status as a new unincorporated organisation. If the old organisation is a CIC, it will have to ensure that the new organisation is charitable so it has an asset lock.

Resources: CHANGING LEGAL FORM

See end of **chapter 1**.

Statute law. www.opsi.gov.uk and www.statutelaw.gov.uk.

Much but not all case law. www.bailii.org.

Updates cross-referenced to this book. www.rclh.co.uk.

Chapter 11

COLLABORATIVE WORKING, PARTNERSHIPS AND MERGERS

For sources of further information see end of chapter 1.

11.1 COLLABORATIVE WORKING

Collaboration or **collaborative working** refer to organisations working together while remaining separate. They may do this in a variety of ways including group structures or subsidiaries [**9.4**], affiliated or federal structures, partnerships or contractual arrangements.

Before becoming involved in any form of collaborative working, the organisation needs to ensure that collaboration will bring real benefits, and that:

- it has the powers to work with other organisations [**7.4.3**];
- arrangements for the joint working are clearly documented;
- it is clear where risk and liability fall, and they are appropriately managed and if necessary insured;
- everyone involved is aware of the potential for conflicts of interest, and arrangements are in place for these to be disclosed and managed [**15.2**];
- staff implications including TUPE if applicable [**29.7**] are considered;
- data protection and confidentiality arrangements are in place [**chapter 43**];
- appropriate arrangements are in place for the ownership, control and safeguarding of funds or assets used or created in the process, including intellectual property [**chapter 44**].

For the issues that should be considered see **11.3.2**, the Charity Commission's CC34 *Collaborative working and mergers*, the Office of the Third Sector's *Work-*

ing in a consortium: A guide for third sector organisations involved in public ser-vice delivery, and *Due diligence demystified* from the National Council for Voluntary Organisations [see end of **chapter 1** for contact details].

11.1.1 Partnerships and collaboration with the private sector

Partnerships with commercial bodies can bring substantial benefits, particularly for fundraising. But the risks inherent in the organisations' widely divergent core purposes need careful consideration before entering into such arrangements [**11.3**]. The Charity Commission's RS2 *Charities and commercial partners*, most of which is applicable to non-charities as well as charities, looks at these issues.

11.1.2 Partnerships and collaboration with the public sector

Joint working arrangements with public sector bodies can have many advantages for voluntary organisations and their service users, but can also be fraught with difficulties [**11.4**]. Particular problems arise when the public body seeks to exercise undue influence over the organisation. Organisations entering into collaborative arrangements with public sector bodies should read the Charity Commission's RR7 *The independence of charities from the state*.

11.1.3 Partnerships for service delivery

Increasingly the scale and range of services required by funders or purchasers lead organisations to form alliances to meet the requirements. This can be a fruitful way to obtain grants or contracts that would not be available to the organisation on its own, but can raise significant legal and managerial issues [**11.3**].

11.1.4 Shared services and facilities

Many organisations seek to reduce costs or increase efficiency by sharing services or facilities. This may involve setting up a formal or informal purchasing consortium to drive down costs; sharing buildings, facilities and space; or outsourcing services to one of the collaborators, a commercial partnership or a specially created organisation. This approach is sometimes called a **cluster** or **charity cluster**, and where space is being shared it is sometimes called **co-location**.

The legal risks with each of these arrangements depend on its exact nature. Key issues are likely to include VAT liabilities, lease and licence arrangements, insurance, and enforceable quality standards in service provision.

11.2 NETWORKS OF INDEPENDENT ORGANISATIONS

Independent organisations may become involved in a range of networks and joint activities with other independent organisations, some of which have legal implications. These include affiliated structures, federations, franchises, partnerships and joint local authority committees. A particular issue is that payments between organisations may have VAT implications [**57.2.4, 57.13.1**].

11.2.1 Affiliated structures

The term **affiliated structure** is used here to refer to a structure where a number of independent organisations agree to be bound by rules set by another organisation. The organisations are independent, but choose to accept certain obligations as a condition of affiliation, for example adopting a common governing document or operating within a policy framework set by the main body.

An affiliation agreement should make clear what the affiliate is obliged to do, what the main organisation will provide, and under what circumstances affiliation may be terminated by either party. It is especially important to be clear about situations in which the affiliate could be required to give up use of the main organisation's name and logo.

Depending on the nature of the affiliation relationship, the organisations may constitute a **group** for company and charity accounting purposes [**9.4**].

The term 'affiliation' is often used to refer not to this type of close relationship, but to a looser federal relationship [below].

11.2.2 Federal structures

A **federal structure** is one where independent organisations come together for coordination, joint lobbying and policy work, setting standards, mutual support, information and/or training. The federation is a membership association, with the organisations as its members.

A federation might be set up by one or more organisations, or by a parent body creating a structure within which it can support independent former branches or projects, but without the control needed for an effective affiliated structure.

11.2.3 Licensing

The main body may allow independent bodies to use intellectual property, typically a name, logo or particular technique or practice under licence [**44.11**]. This may not involve the same level of control as in an affiliation [**11.2.1**] or franchise [below]. But as with those approaches, there should be absolute clarity about how the intellectual property can and cannot be used, what happens in case of misuse, and how the arrangement can be terminated.

11.2.4 Franchising

The concept of **franchising** developed in the business world and has been successfully transferred to the voluntary sector. The **franchisor** develops a blueprint which provides the **franchisee** with the information needed to set up a project, contains detailed guidance about the steps involved, and provides complete details about what is required to run the project. The franchisor normally retains the right to terminate the arrangement if the franchisee's behaviour becomes unsatisfactory or the quality of service does not meet the agreed standards.

The blueprint is normally backed by training, information, advice, access to commonly needed supplies or services at preferential rates, opportunities for networking and cooperation with other franchise operators, and an agreement not to compete or cover the same geographic area.

For the franchisee, the main advantages are the franchisor's name and reputation, which may make it easier to build credibility and attract funding; not needing to reinvent the wheel in developing services and management procedures; and access to resources such as tailor-made insurance packages. For the franchisor, the process enables replication of good practice – and can also bring in income.

Franchise arrangements often contain elements found in licences and federal structures. The franchise contract is likely to be detailed and needs very careful development, so it is essential to take legal advice.

11.3 PARTNERSHIPS

The term **partnership** is used in many ways. In the business world, the most common is where two or more individuals carry on a business in common with a view to making a profit, and do not register their enterprise as a company. This type of partnership is the commercial equivalent of an unincorporated association [**2.2.1**], and is governed by the agreement between the parties or, if there is no agreement, by the **Partnership Act 1890**. Business partnerships may also obtain limited liability under the **Limited Liability Partnerships Act 2000**.

In voluntary sector usage the term **partnership** covers a wide range of joint ventures and collaboration between voluntary organisations, or between voluntary organisations and commercial businesses, local authorities, central government or other statutory bodies. Such partnerships take many forms: federal structures [**11.2.2**], contractual relationships, informal associations, the creation of separate bodies or, in some cases, local authority joint committees.

11.3.1 Collaboration or partnerships without creating a new organisation

Most simply, a 'partnership' might operate as an informal group of representatives from various organisations who come together for a common purpose. Such a group might be called an **action group**, **steering committee**, **coordinating group**, **consultative group**, **forum**, **network**, **consortium** or similar name.

There are few legal implications so long as the members of the group merely share information or discuss ideas. But if the group starts to take any action with legal or financial implications, an unincorporated association [**2.2**] or legal partnership may inadvertently be created, with the partners each having unlimited liability for the partnership's or association's liabilities.

11.3.1.1 Lead body arrangement

In some arrangements, policy and direction for the work are set by the partnership, but one organisation – often called the **lead body** or **accountable body** – receives the funding and is accountable for it, and sub-contracts all or part of the work to the members of the partnership.

Problems can arise if, for example, the lead body disapproves of decisions made by the group, or there are differences between the lead body and other members of the group about how the work should develop or be shared, or a member organisation fails to deliver and the lead body finds itself liable to a funder. These arrangements become even more complex if the lead body provides the premises or employs the staff.

To reduce the risk of these problems arising, the relationships between the participating organisations may be set out in either a legally binding contract [**11.3.3**] or a **memorandum of understanding** which explicitly states that it is not intended to be legally binding [**21.1.1**]. Separate sub-contracts or memoranda of understanding may govern the relationship between the lead body and individual organisations to whom work is sub-contracted.

11.3.1.2 Joint responsibility arrangement

If the group undertakes activities jointly without a lead body, they will probably be operating as an **unincorporated association** [**2.2.1**]. The members of the group – incorporated bodies, or individuals representing unincorporated bodies – could be held responsible for the actions of the group. However if both the paperwork and practice make clear that they are acting jointly only on the basis of a non-legally binding cooperation, a court may in some situations say that members of the group are liable only for activities in which they are involved, and not for claims arising from activities undertaken by another member.

11.3.2 Partnership organisations and joint ventures

Partnership arrangements are sometimes implemented by creating a new organisation, in which the 'partners' become members of the new organisation with the right to elect or nominate the governing body. There arrangements are sometimes called **joint ventures**. The new organisation is formally independent of the bodies which set it up, although it generally retains close links with them.

Development trusts, social care consortia and similar bodies which bring together charities, local authorities and businesses are typical examples. So are arrangements where a number of small organisations wish to run a joint trading venture such as a charity shop, or if an organisation wishes to share the risks and capital expenditure of a large commercial venture.

The relationship between the partners is set out in the governing document of the new body, and is elaborated in a more detailed **partnership agreement**, **joint venture agreement** or, for a non-charitable commercial arrangement, a **shareholders' agreement**. Such an agreement typically sets out:

- objects of the venture, and limitations on other activities;
- if applicable, shares of ownership and/or profit or surplus;
- right to positions on the governing body;

- special governance rules, for example that a quorum must include a representative from each partner or a specified proportion of the partners, or that key decisions such as budget setting are subject to special controls;
- provision for resolving deadlocks or disputes;
- provision for withdrawal of a partner;
- valuation provisions for bringing in new partners or, in a commercial venture, buying out partners;
- restrictions on competitive behaviour, but these must not fall foul of anti-competition legislation [**21.2.10**].

The initial glow of goodwill and the pressure of time and work often mean that the parties do not think about such issues until a dispute arises – when it is too late.

If one or more local authorities is involved in the new organisation, it could be a subject to controls on local authority regulated bodies [**11.4.3**]. The implications of this should be considered before drawing up the governing document or appointing members of the governing body.

11.3.3   Contractual arrangements

If two or more organisations choose to work together without setting up a new organisation, they may enter into a contractual relationship with each other. This can be done in a variety of situations:

- **joint service delivery**, for example where one body provides accommodation and contracts with another to provide care for the residents;
- **support services**, where one organisation contracts with another for the provision of human resources, information technology or similar support;
- **lead body arrangements**, where one body receives the funding and sub-contracts parts of the collaborative project to partners.

The formal arrangement between the parties might be called a contract, service agreement, management agreement, memorandum of agreement or any such term. There could also be a supporting tenancy or licence agreement. Depending on the nature of the agreement, it might or might not be legally binding [**21.1.1**].

To reduce the risk of problems it is wise to seek legal advice and draw up a proper agreement between the parties right from the beginning.

11.4   STRUCTURES INVOLVING PUBLIC SECTOR BODIES

Many local authorities, health authorities and other public sector bodies have very close links with voluntary organisations. Where these links simply involve sharing information and consulting, there are no structural implications for the organisations. However, other relationships may have legal implications.

11.4.1   Local authority committees and joint committees

Local authorities have powers to create **committees**, and to create **joint committees** with one or more other local authorities. These committees may in turn appoint **sub-committees**. Such bodies may include persons who are not members of the appointing authority or authorities, including voluntary organisations or individuals associated with voluntary organisations.

Local strategic partnerships are non-statutory bodies that are led by local authorities but involve a range of statutory, private and voluntary sector bodies. With a remit to agree strategies for meeting local needs, they do not usually involve creating a separate organisation.

11.4.2   Organisations created by public sector bodies

Local authorities, health authorities and other public sector bodies have a long history of setting up voluntary organisations and, more recently, social enterprises [**1.1.2**]. An organisation set up in this way might be charitable or non-charitable, depending on its purposes. The parent authority would typically maintain a close working relationship with the independent organisation, perhaps by providing a long-term contract [**chapter 52**] under which the organisation provides services to on behalf of the public sector.

These relationships can cause difficulties. Anyone serving on the governing body of the new organisation is under an obligation to act always in the best interests of that organisation and, if it is charitable, its beneficiaries [**15.3.2, 15.6.3**]. If the person is an employee, officer or member of a local or health authority or other public body this can create a conflict of loyalties [**15.2.3**].

Another potential difficulty is that if the organisation is incorporated as a company or industrial and provident society, it may be a **local authority regulated company** [see below]. Even if it does not fall into this category, any organisation which has close structural links with a public sector body needs to be aware of the potential legal implications.

11.4.3 Local authority interests in companies

At the time of writing (mid 2009) specific restrictions called **propriety controls** apply to companies (including community interest companies) and industrial and provident societies which are **influenced** [**11.4.3.3**] or **controlled** [**11.4.3.2**] by one or more local authorities. Such bodies are called **regulated companies**. The rules are set out in the **Local Government and Housing Act 1989** pt.V, the **Local Authorities (Companies) Order 1995** *[SI 1995/849]* and various Local Authorities (Companies) (Amendment) Orders.

11.4.3.1 Controls under the 2007 Act

Part 12 of the **Local Government and Public Involvement in Health Act 2007** will, when implemented, replace the restrictions under the 1989 Act and will allow propriety controls to apply to any organisation – including trusts as well as incorporated bodies – whose financial information has to be included in the local authority's statement of accounts. At the time of writing (mid 2009), regulations setting out the organisations covered and the nature of the controls had not been drawn up, but the government intended to bring them into force in 2010.   *Local Government & Public Involvement in Health Act 2007 ss.212-218 (pt.12)*

Further information is available from the Department for Communities and Local Government [see end of chapter].

11.4.3.2 Local authority controlled companies

At the time of writing a company or industrial and provident society is a **local authority controlled company** if it is a subsidiary of the local authority as defined by the Companies Act [**9.4.1**], or the local authority has the power to control a majority of the votes at a general meeting of the organisation, or the local authority has the power to appoint or remove a majority of the organisation's board of directors, or the company or IPS is under the control of another local authority controlled company.   *Local Government & Housing Act 1989 s.68*

If two or more local authorities act jointly in relation to an organisation and together are able to control the organisation, the organisation is held to be under the control of each authority.   *Local Government & Housing Act 1989 s.73*

11.4.3.3 Local authority influenced companies

A company or IPS is a **local authority influenced company** if people **associated** with the local authority [below] hold 20% or more of the total membership voting rights, make up 20% or more of the directors or hold 20% or more of the total voting rights at a meeting of the directors; and in addition the company or IPS has a **business relationship** with the local authority.   *Local Government & Housing Act 1989 s.69*

A person is **associated** with a local authority if he or she is a member of the local authority or has been at any time in the previous four years; is an officer of the local authority; or is employed by a local authority controlled company and is also a director, manager, secretary or similar officer of the company.   *LGHA 1989 s.69(5)*

It does not matter whether the person associated with the local authority is a member of the organisation or its governing body in a personal capacity, or as a representative of the local authority.

If the local authority has the right to 20% or more of the places, but does not take up these places, the organisation is not a local authority influenced company.

Business relationship is defined in a variety of ways. Those most likely to apply to voluntary organisations are where:

- in any 12 month period, payments from the local authority or a local authority controlled company account for more than half of the organisation's income;
- local authority capital grants or shares or stock owned by the local authority exceed more than half the net assets of the organisation;
- more than half the organisation's turnover is derived from assets in which the local authority has an interest; or
- the organisation occupies local authority land or buildings at less than market rent, or intends to enter into such an arrangement.   *Local Government & Housing Act 1989 s.69(3)*

Payments from the local authority include grants of all types, fees for services provided under a service agreement or contract, or any other payment made by the local authority to the organisation.

An example of a local authority influenced company is a voluntary sector company or IPS which receives more than half its income from a local authority and/or occupies local authority premises at below market rent, and where 20% or more of its members or the members of its governing body are associated with the local authority.

11.4.3.4   Regulated companies

The restrictions apply only to **regulated companies**. A body is a regulated company if it is:

- a local authority controlled company [**11.4.3.2**];
- a local authority influenced company [**11.4.3.3**], and also registered as an industrial and provident society;
- a local authority influenced company, and the local authority, if it were a company, would have the right to exercise a dominant influence over the company, or has exercised such an influence; or
- a local authority influenced company, and the local authority, if it were a company, would have to prepare group accounts in respect of the influenced company.   *Local Authorities (Companies) (Amendment) Order 1996 [SI 1996/621]*

The effect of these rules is to exclude many influenced companies from the restrictions.

11.4.3.5   Implications of being regulated

The rules on local authority regulated companies deal primarily with how such bodies are financed by local authorities. They:

- require the company to state on business letters, notices and other documents that it is influenced or controlled by a local authority or authorities, and name the authorities;
- limit payments to directors of the company;
- prevent the organisation from publishing material which the local authority would be prevented from publishing [**45.2.6**];
- require certain information to be provided to local authority members, the local authority's auditors and the Audit Commission;
- require controlled companies to obtain Audit Commission consent to the appointment of auditors;
- specify that the local authority's capital spending powers are reduced if a controlled or influenced company borrows money or receives certain grants.
    Local Authorities (Companies) Order 1995 [SI 1995/849]

11.4.3.6   Exemption

It is possible to apply for a **direction** to exempt the company and local authority (or authorities) from the relevant provisions of the Act. Information is available from the Department for Communities and Local Government [see end of chapter].   *Local Government & Housing Act 1989 ss.68(1),69(1)*

Directions made in 1995 exempted area museum councils, regional or area arts boards, Groundwork trusts, building preservation trusts, citizens advice bureaux, registered housing associations, and companies which received less than £2,000 from the local authority in the previous year.

11.4.3.7   Avoiding the restrictions

An organisation which may be caught by these restrictions should take specialist legal advice to clarify its position, the position of the local authority and the possible implications, and if appropriate to decide whether to apply for exemption.

Alternatively it may be able to alter its membership or governing document [**7.5.3**] so the local authority no longer has the right to control or influence it.

If very specific circumstances, a local authority can pass a resolution stating that an organisation is not local authority controlled or influenced during a specified financial year. Among the criteria are that the organisation does not receive any grants at all from the local authority during the financial year, the organisation pays full market rent during the year for any land it occupies in which the local authority has an interest, and the company directors during the year are appointed for fixed terms of at least two years.   *Local Government & Housing Act 1989 s.68(6)*

11.5   MERGERS

11.5.1   Forms of merger

Merger is the process of formally bringing together two or more organisations. Merger includes arrangements where:

- both organisations wind up and transfer their assets and liabilities to a new organisation [**11.5.1.1**];
- an existing organisation (the **transferee**) takes over some or all of the assets and liabilities of the other (the **transferor**), either directly or into a subsidiary [**11.5.1.2**];
- the organisations create a group structure or extend an existing group structure, with the merging organisation becoming a subsidiary [**11.5.1.3**];
- an incorporated organisation becomes the sole corporate trustee of an unincorporated organisation.

Whatever mechanism is adopted, the bodies concerned must ensure that the action is within their powers [**7.4.3**]. Merger or takeover always involves complex financial, tax, VAT, managerial and organisational issues, as well as company and/or charity law issues if applicable. Specialist advice and support are vital for both (or all) bodies.

The charities team at Russell-Cooke Solicitors [**page 2**] maintains a register of voluntary organisations seeking merger partners.

11.5.1.1   Creating a new organisation

For some mergers it may be appropriate to create a new organisation, with the existing organisations transferring their assets and liabilities to it and then winding up. This may reduce the sense that one organisation is being taken over by the other, make it easier to work towards a new organisational culture, and reduce the risk of a transfer of liabilities attached to the old organisations. If both (or all) transferors are charities and are wound up after the merger, this is a **relevant charity merger** under the **Charities Act 2006** [**11.5.4.1**].

11.5.1.2 Merging into an existing organisation

Rather than creating a new organisation, it may be easier to amend the transferee's governing document and perhaps change its name, then transfer the transferor's assets and liabilities and wind it up. This means that only one set of staff transfer under TUPE [**29.7**] and have their terms and conditions protected – unlike creating a new organisation, where all staff have TUPE protection. If both organisations are charities, this is a **relevant charity merger** [**11.5.4.1**].

11.5.1.3 Group structures

In some situations it may be appropriate for both or all organisations to continue, but within a new or existing group structure [**9.4**]. One or more organisations may become subsidiaries of another, or all may become subsidiaries of a parent.

Legal advice will be needed about the company and/or charity law implications of this arrangement, as well as the tax and VAT implications.

11.5.2 Transferring assets and liabilities

Where the merger involves a transfer of assets and liabilities, either to an existing organisation or to a new one, the process is similar to the transfer from an unincorporated organisation to an incorporated body [**10.1**]. But a merger situation is more complex, because:

- the organisations may have different objects, so the assets of each may need to be ringfenced for its own objects within the new body;
- different membership and governance structures will need to be brought together in a way acceptable to both;
- the organisations are likely to have different funding sources, and different financial systems and procedures;
- bringing the organisations together may take them into higher brackets for the purposes of company accounts and audit [**54.3.2**], charity accounts and audit [**54.2.2**], VAT registration [**57.2.1**] and/or employment law requirements dependent on number of employees [**26.6**];
- the organisations are likely to have different contracts of employment, and the fact that each set of employees retains its existing terms and conditions [**29.7**] can lead to problematic differentials;
- transferred staff may bring with them employment claims relating to their previous employer;
- key stakeholders, such as funders, staff, members, service users and any regulators, may oppose the process;
- even where on paper the organisations look quite similar, they may in reality have very different organisational cultures and ways of doing things.

The due diligence process [**11.5.9**] should focus on these organisational and management issues as well as on legal and financial factors.

11.5.3 Pension scheme debt

Where an organisation changes its legal structure or winds up – even if it is doing so only to become part of another organisation – it may become liable for a large **exit debt** if it provides a defined benefit or final salary pension scheme [**30.6.5**]. Organisations considering any form of merger should take advice at a very early stage from their solicitor and pension provider. It may be possible to make arrangements under which the debt will not **crystallise** (become due).

11.5.4 Charity mergers

While there is no need in most cases for charities to seek consent from the Charity Commission before merging, they may need Charity Commission consent to change provisions in their governing document to make the merger possible, particularly the dissolution provisions.

The Commission has powers to assist mergers, in particular to make declarations transferring land and leases.   *Charities Act 1993 s.16(1)*

11.5.4.1 Relevant charity mergers

Relevant charity mergers are mergers of two or more charities where the transferor ceases to exist, or all the transferors cease to exist and a new charity is created. This includes an unincorporated charity winding up after transferring its assets to a newly created incorporated body [**10.1**]. *Charities Act 1993 s.75C(4), inserted by Charities Act 2006 s.44*

The Charity Commission maintains a register of relevant charity mergers [**4.5.1**]. If there is a **vesting declaration** [**11.5.4.2**], the trustees must notify the Commission of the merger. If there is no vesting declaration the trustees of the new merged charity can ask for voluntary registration of the merger. *Charities Act 1993 ss.75C,75D, inserted by Charities Act 2006 s.44*

Where a merger is on the register, any gift made to the transferor which takes effect after the date of registration is treated as a gift to the transferee, unless the donor has explicitly indicated otherwise, or the transferor has permanent endowment [**58.8.1**] and the gift is intended to be part of that endowment. *Charities Act 1993 s.75F, inserted by Charities Act 2006 s.44*

11.5.4.2 Transfer of charity property

In a relevant charity merger [above], the transferor's trustees can transfer some or possibly all of the charity's assets (but not its liabilities) to another charity by making a **vesting declaration**, a form of deed [**20.3**]. Details of what can and cannot be transferred are available from the Charity Commission.

Circumstances in which a vesting declaration cannot be used are where land is held as security, for example under a mortgage; where land is held under a lease or agreement which requires the consent of a third party before the lease or agreement can be assigned (transferred) to someone else; or where there is any form of restriction on the transfer of shares, stock annuities or other property held by the transferor. In these situations legal advice will be required to ensure the transfer is properly done. *Charities Act 1993 s.75E, inserted by Charities Act 2006 s.44*

Unincorporated charities with annual income of not more than £10,000 may be able to transfer all of their property to another charity by a resolution of the trustees, without needing to do it by deed. And where an unincorporated charity holds funds as permanent endowment [**58.8.1**], it may be possible for the trustees to pass a resolution removing the restriction on spending the capital. This could make it easier to transfer the capital as part of the merger. *Charities Act 1993 ss.74-75A, inserted by Charities Act 2006 ss.40,41*

11.5.4.3 Amalgamating to form a new CIO

After provisions for the **charitable incorporated organisation** come into effect (expected April 2010), two or more CIOs can apply to the Charity Commission for **amalgamation** into a new CIO. Each of the transferring CIOs must pass a resolution approving the amalgamation, either with a 75% majority of votes at a general meeting, or by unanimous agreement of every member of the CIO. *Charities Act 1993 ss.69K,69L, to be inserted by Charities Act 2006 sch.7 para.1 [expected April 2010]*

Each transferring CIO must give notice of the proposed amalgamation to people affected by it, inviting them to make representations to the Charity Commission.

When the Commission agrees the amalgamation, all the property, rights and liabilities of the old CIOs are passed to the new CIO, the old CIOs are dissolved, and any gifts intended for the old CIOs will be treated as gifts to the new CIO.

Only CIOs can amalgamate to form a new CIO. At the time of writing (mind 1009) it appeared that a charitable company, industrial and provident society or community interest company would be able to form part of a new CIO only by first converting to CIO status [**10.3.1**, **10.4.2**, **10.5.3**] and then amalgamating.

11.5.4.4 Merging with an existing CIO

Rather than creating a new organisation, a CIO can resolve to transfer all its property, rights and liabilities to another CIO. The rules are similar to those for amalgamation [**11.5.4.3**]. *Charities Act 1993 s.69M, to be inserted by Charities Act 2006 sch.7 para.1 [expected April 2010]*

A charitable company, industrial and provident society or community interest company does not have to convert to a CIO before transferring all its assets and liabilities to a CIO. But doing so may avoid any restrictions on the transfer of charity property [**11.5.4.2**].

An unincorporated charity of any size can, by resolution of the trustees, transfer all of its property to one or more CIOs, provided the charity does not hold any land which must be used for a specified purpose. *Charities Act 1993 s.69O, to be inserted by Charities Act 2006 sch.7 para.1 [expected April 2010]*

11.5.5 Community interest companies

At the time of writing (mid 2009), a community interest company can transfer its assets only to a charity or another CIC. It was expected this would be extended to include prescribed community benefit societies [**3.5.2**]. Any transfer requires consent from the CIC regulator.

11.5.6 Industrial and provident societies

Two or more industrial and provident societies can pass special resolutions **19.7.5**] to become **amalgamated** as one IPS. All assets and liabilities transfer automatically to the new IPS. Alternatively one IPS can by special resolution **transfer its engagements** to another IPS, or can by special resolution agree to convert itself into, amalgamate with or transfer its engagements to a company registered under the Companies Acts [**10.5**]. *Industrial & Provident Societies Act 1965 ss.50-52*

11.5.7 Cross-border company mergers

Limited liability companies in two or more EU member states can merge to create a single company operating under the laws of the country in which it has its registered office. This makes it easier for a company to operate across the EU. *Companies (Cross-Border Mergers) Regulations 2007 [SI 2007/2974]*

11.5.8 Transfer without winding up transferor

Rather than winding up, it may be necessary or advisable to keep the original organisation in existence short term or longer term, for example if a significant guarantee or warranty is invalidated if equipment is transferred during the guarantee period, or if legacies are likely to be received that can be given only to the original organisation. Specialist advice should be sought in these circumstances.

11.5.9 Due diligence

Whatever the form of merger, each organisation must ensure it is not involving itself with a partner with an unacceptable level of actual or potential exposure to financial, legal, employment, property or other risks. This is common sense but is also a duty, arising from each governing body's duty of care [**chapter 15**].

The process of finding out about potential risks is called **due diligence**, and is normally carried out with the assistance of experienced solicitors and accountants. Where the risk of liability or other risks exist it may be sensible to ringfence risk by avoiding full merger, and opting for some form of group structure with the transferor becoming a subsidiary [**9.4**].

An organisation undertaking due diligence focuses primarily on the other organisation, but should also look in depth at its own situation, because it will have to be transparent in disclosing this as part of the other organisation's due diligence.

While due diligence focuses primarily on legal and financial risks, it should also look at other areas of risk such as reputation, or risks arising from different organisational cultures, management structures and ways of operating [**11.5.2**].

The sorts of issues that should be considered as part of due diligence include:

- **history**: the history and activities of both organisations, including any change in legal structure or charitable status, previous mergers or takeovers, and whether work or projects have been taken on from other organisations;

- **consents**: regulatory bodies, funders, purchasers of services, the organisations' members and others who will need to give consent for each organisation's part in the merger, and any likely objections;

- **corporate governance**: a close examination of both organisations' governing documents, in particular their objects, power to merge or transfer assets, and winding up provisions; registers of members and governing body members and their role in the merger; whether regulatory requirements as a charity, company etc have been complied with (for example, submission of annual accounts and returns); whether there are or have been any regulatory investigations; an examination of each organisation's minutes of general and governing body meetings for the past year (or more) and other relevant governance documents to identify recent issues and ensure decisions have been properly made;

- **activities**: whether activities and services are and have been within each organisation's objects and the terms of its contracts or funding agreements; relationships with funders and major donors; current registrations, and whether re-registrations will be necessary as part of the merger; recent, current and potential complaints or litigation about any aspect of the organisation's work;

- **employment**: a close examination of both organisations' contracts of employment, employment policies and procedures, and contracts with self employed people and other contractors; a thorough understanding of the TUPE [**29.7**] and pension implications of the merger [**11.5.3**]; procedures under which both organisations will consult employees about the proposed merger; recent past, current and potential disciplinary issues; past, current and potential claims by employees and other workers;

- **accounts**: a close examination of both organisations' accounts and if necessary financial records for the past three years, financial reports since the annual accounts were prepared, financial projections, and a full understanding of the other organisation's current and future financial situation;

- **assets and property**: land, buildings and other assets owned or rented by each organisation; ownership; current value; mortgages or other claims on the property; any grant or funding conditions attached to the transfer of assets; recent, current or potential disputes relating to any assets;

- **VAT and tax**: whether the other organisation is or should be registered for VAT or tax, and any actual or potential liabilities; VAT and tax implications of the merger;

- **finance and funding**: current and projected sources of income for both organisations; current, future and potential liabilities; liabilities contingent on the merger (such as pension scheme debt [**30.6.5**], or rent due if a lease is surrendered), and legal costs;

- **contracts and funding agreements**: a close examination of both organisations' current agreements, in particular issues which could be affected by the merger; a full understanding of both organisations' future plans for funding;

- **health, safety and environmental issues**;

- **intellectual property**;

- **insurances**;

- **any other issues** that could create liabilities or problems for the merging organisations.

Resources: COLLABORATIVE WORKING, PARTNERSHIPS AND MERGERS

See end of **chapter 1**.

Local authority controlled and influenced companies. Department for Communities and Local Government: www.communities.gov.uk, 020 7944 4400, contactus@communities.gov.uk.

Statute law. www.opsi.gov.uk and www.statutelaw.gov.uk.

Much but not all case law. www.bailii.org.

Updates cross-referenced to this book. www.rclh.co.uk.

Once the organisation is set up, its members (if it is a membership organisation) and its governing body must ensure it operates effectively and legally. The governing body might be called a board of directors, board of trustees, board of governors, management committee, executive committee, council of management or any similar name. Regardless of what it is called, the governing body as a whole and its individual members have a range of legal duties for running the organisation, which are explained in this part.

This part also looks at the types of legal agreement organisations are likely to enter into, liability for those agreements and for other aspects of the organisation's work, insurance, and winding up the organisation.

information and how long records should be kept; records which must be kept by companies, industrial and provident societies, charitable incorporated organisations, trusts, associations and charities

Chapter 12
MEMBERS OF THE ORGANISATION

For sources of further information see end of chapter 1.

12.1   DEFINING MEMBERSHIP

An organisation's **members** are individuals or organisations, who are defined as members by the governing document or under other criteria for membership. Companies, charitable incorporated organisations, industrial and provident societies and unincorporated associations must all have members; trusts hardly ever do [see **chapters 2** and **3** for explanations of these legal forms].

The governing document (constitution, trust deed, articles of association etc) is the legal basis for members' rights and obligations. In incorporated bodies (companies, CIOs and IPSs) the governing document is a contract between the member and the organisation; in unincorporated associations it is a contract between all the members. Membership rights and obligations may also arise from statute law for that type of organisation. The relevant legislation will make clear whether that particular aspect of statute law takes precedence over what is in governing document, or if the governing document takes precedence.

Members have a constitutionally defined role in the organisation, occasionally acting as the governing body itself [**13.1**] or more commonly as the people who elect all or most of the members of the governing body.

12.1.1 Common issues about membership

Members must be distinguished from others, such as **supporters**, **service users** or **participants**, who may be called members but do not have any constitutional role in the organisation. These 'members' are entitled only to such benefits as the governing document indicates or the governing body agrees to give them. These might include, for example, the right to receive a newsletter or use the organisation's facilities, but without any constitutional right to take part in decisions.

Members of the organisation must also be distinguished from the **members of the governing body** [**12.9**]. The organisation's members and the members of the governing body are sometimes one and the same – and in a **foundation model** charitable incorporated organisation (CIO) [**1.4**] they always are. But usually the governing body is smaller than the overall membership, and may include people who are not members of the organisation.

Governing body members may believe they automatically become members of the organisation on election or appointment to the governing body, but this occurs only in a foundation model CIO or if the governing document explicitly says that it does [**13.1, 13.4**].

12.1.2 Membership records

An accurate list or database of members (legally called a **register**) is vital and is often a statutory requirement [**18.5.2, 18.6.1, 18.7**]. Members generally have a key role in governance, so failure to keep accurate membership records can cause serious problems. Where it is not clear who the members are, the governing body may not have been properly elected and decisions at general meetings or, where allowed, by written resolution may not have been properly made.

Where there is doubt or a dispute about who the members of a membership charity are, the Charity Commission has power to determine authoritatively – or appoint a person to determine – who the members are. The Commission can exercise this power only if the charity applies for a decision, or if the Commission has started an inquiry into the charity under s.8 of the **Charities Act 1993**.

Charities Act 1993 s.39A, inserted by Charities Act 2006 s.25

12.1.3 Constitutional provision

Voluntary organisations have hugely varied membership provisions. When drawing up or reviewing the governing document, it is important to think carefully about the role and function members are expected to fulfil, and consider whether the membership arrangements as set out in the governing document [**7.4.11**] help or hinder achievement of the organisation's goals.

12.1.4 Eligibility for membership

Membership eligibility criteria range from the very specific (having a particular illness) to the very broad ('anyone who supports our objects'). The governing document or membership regulations may set any criteria for membership so long as they do not discriminate unlawfully on the basis of racial group, sex, disability, religion or other belief, sexual orientation or age [**12.3**]. **Eligibility** should be distinguished from procedures for **admission** to membership [**12.5**].

The governing body should develop clear policies about the optimum number of members and the extent to which members should be actively recruited.

Some people may be prohibited from being members of the governing body of an organisation [**13.3, 16.3**], but they can be members of the organisation itself unless this is prohibited by the governing document or internal rules.

12.1.5 Rights, benefits and obligations

In considering membership classes a distinction must be made between:

- **membership rights**: rights which exist in law or are granted by the governing document, for example the right to vote at general meetings;
- **membership benefits**: additional benefits conferred on some or all classes of membership, such as the right to use the organisation's facilities;

- **membership obligations**: obligations in law or in the governing document, such as an obligation to pay a subscription or an amount if the organisation is wound up. Members who do not meet their obligations may become ineligible for membership, or could be sued for what they owe the organisation. Members of an organisation may in some cases be held personally liable for the organisation's actions or debts [**22.2.2**].

A charity's governing document often prevents members benefiting financially from the charity. This restriction is not suitable where the members are also the charity's beneficiaries and receive services which have a financial value. The provision may also cause problems when a charity whose members are themselves organisations winds up and must distribute its assets to other similar charities, but is prohibited from distributing them to its own member organisations.

12.1.6 Rights akin to membership

A governing document may provide for some non-members to have rights similar to those of members, for example the right to appoint some officers or members of the governing body, to attend meetings or to approve constitutional changes. Non-members with such rights might include honorary members or patrons [**12.2.7**], a president, funders or other outside bodies.

12.2 CLASSES OF MEMBERS

Where there is more than one class or type of member, the governing document or standing orders [**7.4.25**] should clearly set out the rights and obligations of each class. There is no consistency about what members might be called or their rights and obligations, so the examples here are purely illustrative.

12.2.1 Full membership

Full members (sometimes called **individual** or **ordinary** members, or simply members) have full voting rights and are usually, under the governing document, eligible to become members of the governing body.

12.2.2 'Open' membership

Some organisations have governing documents which state that everyone, or everyone who lives in a certain area or meets some other criterion, is entitled to membership. People who are entitled to membership in this way may have rights, but have no obligations as members unless they have formally joined the organisation or have taken action in a way which implies they have consented to be a member, for example by voting in the organisation's election.

12.2.3 Junior or youth membership

If the governing document does not set an age limit, minors (under 18 years of age) can be full members of a company, association or charitable incorporated organisation. At the time of writing (mid 2009) there was a statutory minimum age limit of 16 for industrial and provident societies, but the government intended to remove this. *Industrial & Provident Societies Act 1965 s.20*

12.2.4 Family membership

Where an organisation offers **family membership**, the governing document or membership regulations should be clear what is meant by 'family' and who it includes. It is essential to be clear whether every member of the family has a vote or whether there is only one vote per family.

12.2.5 Organisational, corporate and group membership

Many organisations make provision for other organisations to be members. The term **corporate member** generally refers to corporate bodies (companies, industrial and provident societies, charitable incorporated organisations, local authorities, other public bodies and most businesses). The term **group member** generally refers to unincorporated organisations, and **organisational member** might refer to either or both. In practice the terms are used interchangeably, but membership affects incorporated and unincorporated bodies differently.

Some organisational members, for example larger ones, may be entitled under the governing document to more than one vote. This is not possible in industrial and provident societies, which must operate on the basis of one member one vote.

12.2.5.1   Corporate bodies as members

An incorporated body can become a member of any other organisation if its objects or powers allow this. The incorporated body then appoints an individual or individuals to be its **representative(s)** at meetings of the organisation of which it is a member. A representative acts on behalf of the corporate member because it is the corporate body, not the individual, which is the member. The governing document might state that corporate members can appoint an **alternate** as well as their representative.

If a company or charitable incorporated organisation is a member of another organisation, any documents which must be signed by 'the member' must be signed by a person authorised by that company or CIO to sign.   *Companies Act 2006 s.43*

If an industrial and provident society is a member of an organisation, any documents must be signed by two members of the IPS's governing body and its secretary.   *Industrial & Provident Societies Act 1965 s.19(2)*

Unless the governing document specifies otherwise, corporate bodies, acting through their representatives, have all the rights of members. Provided the representative acts within his or her powers, the obligations and liabilities of membership rest with the corporate body and not with the representative.

12.2.5.2   Unincorporated organisations as 'members'

Because unincorporated associations and trusts are not legal 'persons' [**2.2.1**], they cannot be members of another organisation. If they want to join an organisation, they must generally appoint a **nominee** to join on their behalf [below].

In practice many organisations ignore this and allow unincorporated organisations to join in the same way as corporate bodies, and to appoint a representative to act on behalf of the organisation. While the organisation might treat these individuals as representatives, in law they would be treated as nominees.

At the time of writing (mid 2009), it appeared likely that there would be statutory provisions for unincorporated organisations as members of a charitable incorporated organisation (CIO).

12.2.6   Nominees

The governing document may contain provisions for unincorporated or other organisations to nominate members who join on their behalf. This nominee, not the appointing organisation, is the member, and has the same rights and liabilities as any other individual member. The nominee and the appointing organisation should have a clear agreement about whether the nominee is expected to act on the basis of the appointing organisation's views, or her or his own.

12.2.7   Other types of membership

Voluntary sector governing documents use a wide variety of labels to describe types of members, and the same labels may be used in quite different ways by different organisations. The key issue is always what rights and obligations, if any, are given to a particular type of membership.

Some typical classes of membership are:

- **branch members**: could refer either to groups set up as branches of the organisation [**9.2**], or members of those branches;
- **affiliates**: may refer to organisational members [**11.2.1**, **11.2.2**, **11.3.2**], or to individuals or organisations who do not meet the criteria for full membership;

- **associate members**: may refer to individuals or organisations who do not meet the criteria for full membership, meet the criteria but choose not to become full members, or are in a trial period prior to full membership;

- **honorary members**: may refer to individuals invited to become members even though they do not meet the criteria for membership, or people whom the organisation wishes to honour or recognise;

- **patrons**: generally refers to well known or illustrious individuals who lend their name and support to the organisation, who may or may not have membership rights;

- **co-opted members**: may refer to individuals invited to become members under provisions in the governing document, with their rights and obligations, if any, as specified in the governing document;

- *ex officio* **members**: people who under the governing document are automatically members – with or without voting rights – by virtue of the position they hold, for example a local headteacher, the local MP or councillors;

- **life members**: typically defined as those who remain members of the organisation until they die or resign, without needing to renew their membership.

12.2.8 Subscribers

The term **subscribers** may refer to individuals or organisations who pay a subscription in order to receive the organisation's publications and/or have access to its activities and services. Under the governing document they may or may not be members with the rights and obligations of membership.

Under company law 'subscribers' has a specific meaning [**1.5.4**], as the persons who sign the memorandum of association and become the first members of the company.

12.2.9 Supporters or 'friends'

Supporters or **friends** are typically individuals or organisations who want to support the organisation. They may pay a subscription and receive mailings or other benefits in return, and depending on the governing document may or may not be members with the rights and obligations of membership.

12.2.10 Observers

In addition to the various classes of members and supporters, some people might be invited to attend the organisation's meetings as **observers**. Observers generally have no right to participate unless invited to do so, and have no right to vote.

12.3 EQUAL OPPORTUNITIES AND MEMBERSHIP

In general, the law prohibits discrimination on the basis of racial group (race, colour, ethnic origin, nationality or national origin), sex, sexual orientation, disability, religion or belief when selecting members of an organisation, providing benefits or services to them, or terminating membership.

There are some exceptions to these non-discrimination provisions. An organisation can use **racial group** or **sexual orientation** as a factor in membership if:

- it has fewer than 25 members, and is not an organisation of workers or employers or a trade or professional organisation; or

- the main object of the organisation is to enable people of a particular racial group, which must not be defined by reference to colour, to enjoy the benefits of membership, or to enable people of a particular sexual orientation to enjoy the benefits of membership. *Race Relations Act 1976 ss.11(2),(3), 25, 26; Equality Act (Sexual Orientation) Regulations 2007 regs.16-18 [SI 2007/1263]*

A not for profit organisation can be set up to provide services to one **sex**, and can limit its membership to people of that sex. *Sex Discrimination Act 1975 s.34*

An organisation whose purpose is to practice, advance, teach or provide activities within the framework of a **religion or philosophical belief** can restrict its

membership on the basis of religion or belief. It can also restrict its membership on the basis of sexual orientation, if this is necessary to comply with the organisation's doctrine or to avoid conflicting with the strongly held religious convictions of a significant number of the religion's followers. *Equality Act 2006 s.57;*
Equality Act (Sexual Orientation) Regulations 2007 reg.14 [SI 2007/1263]

At the time of writing (mid 2009) there was no legislation relevant to membership restrictions on the basis of age, but provisions which could affect membership were expected to be included in the **Equality Act** [**28.1.12**].

For more about limiting membership within the objects clause in the governing document, see **5.6**; for more about equal opportunities in the provision of goods, services and facilities see **chapter 42**.

12.4 RIGHTS AND OBLIGATIONS ARISING FROM LEGAL STRUCTURE

The organisation's legal structure may create membership rights and obligations in addition to those arising from the governing document.

12.4.1 Companies

In all companies, including community interest companies, members agree contractually to join together and to be bound by the articles of association (or, for companies formed before 1 October 2009, the memorandum and articles of association). The company members are the **subscribers** to the memorandum of association [**1.5.4**], and individuals and corporate bodies who agree to become members and whose names are entered in the register of members [**18.5.2**].
Companies Act 2006 s.112

In a company limited by shares, the shareholders are the company members. Typically each share gives a right to vote, so shareholders have as many votes as they have shares.

In a company limited by guarantee, the members guarantee to contribute a specified amount to the company's winding up costs if necessary [**3.3.1**], and each member has only one vote unless the governing document specifies otherwise. Typically the guarantee is for a nominal £1 or £10.

For a private company, whether limited by shares or guarantee, the minimum number of members is one. Voluntary sector companies nearly always have more than one member, but a trading company [**51.3.2**] might have its parent charity as its sole member. *Companies Act 2006 s.7(1)*

The company structure requires two tiers: the **company members**, and the **directors** [**13.1.3**] who are generally but not always elected by the company members. Where there is no intention to have members additional to the directors, the company can be set up with the directors at any given time as the only company members.

12.4.1.1 Rights and obligations of company members

Company members have substantial rights under the Companies Acts, including receiving information about how the directors are running the company on their behalf [**54.1**], deciding key issues including removal of directors [**13.5.6**] and amendment of the governing document [**7.5.3**], requiring a general meeting to be called [**19.2.2**], and approving certain transactions and payments by the company [**15.3**]. *Companies Act 2006 ss.188-239*

But apart from paying for their share in a share company, or paying the amount due under the guarantee if called upon to do so when a company limited by guarantee is wound up, company members have no obligations to the company. They can therefore exercise their powers in any way they like and make decisions in their own interests, even if this is not in the best interests of the company. The courts may however intervene in some circumstances to protect other shareholders or members [**12.10.1**]. *North-west Transportation Co Ltd v Beatty [1887] 12 AC 589*

12.4.2   Charitable incorporated organisations

A charitable incorporated organisation (CIO) must have at least one member. Those who apply to set up the CIO, called **applicants**, are its first members. Where CIOs **amalgamate [11.5.5]**, the members of the amalgamating bodies become the members of the new CIO. CIOs may have more than one class of members, with the voting rights of each class set out in the governing document.

Depending on the wording of the constitution, CIO members may be liable to contribute up to a specified amount if the CIO is wound up, or may have no liability. Where a CIO is formed by conversion from a company limited by guarantee and the company members' guarantee is £10 or less, the guarantee is **extinguished** and does not carry over into the CIO's constitution. For other conversions from company limited by guarantee or industrial and provident society, the CIO's constitution must include an obligation for members to contribute. This cannot be less than the amount for which they were liable under the former status.
Charities Act 1993 s.69G(8-10), to be inserted by Charities Act 2006 sch.7 para.1 [expected April 2010]

At the time of writing (mid 2009), regulations had not been finalised setting out the rights of members in CIOs. These will include at least the right to amend the CIO's constitution [7.5.4] subject to any necessary consent from the Charity Commission, and may include other rights.

One difference between CIOs and charitable companies is that CIO members must exercise their powers as members in a way they decide in good faith would be most likely to further the purposes of the CIO. In a company, only the directors have this duty.   *Charities Act 1993 sch.5B para.9, to be inserted by Charities Act 2006 sch.7 para.2*

12.4.3   Industrial and provident societies

Every industrial and provident society has shareholders who are its members. The rules must state the maximum shareholding. In a community benefit IPS [3.5.2] this can be anything up to a statutory maximum which in most cases is £20,000 per member, but the shares are usually only a token of membership with a nominal value of £1. At the time of writing (mid 2009) the government intended to remove the £20,000 maximum on the total amount of withdrawable shares.
Industrial & Provident Societies Act 1965 s.6(1)

An IPS must have at least three members at all times unless it is a credit union (21 members) or a secondary IPS made up solely of other IPSs, in which case it must have at least two IPSs as members.   *IPSA 1965 s.16(1)(a); Credit Unions Act 1979 s.6*

At the time of writing (mid 2009) IPS members cannot be under 16 years old. Members under 18 years old have the same rights as other members, but cannot be the treasurer or a member of the governing body. The government intended to modify these minimum age provisions.   *IPSA 1965 s.20*

Unless the rules forbid it, corporate bodies can be members of an IPS unless it is a credit union. At the time of writing the government intended to remove the restriction on corporate bodies becoming members of credit unions.   *IPSA 1965 s.19(1)*

Unlike the members of most companies limited by shares, each member of an IPS can have only one vote, regardless of the size of shareholding.

Joint membership is possible unless the rules prohibit this. Joint members have only one vote; clear provision should be made as to who exercises this.

12.4.3.1   IPS members' rights and obligations

Members' obligations in an IPS are limited to the obligation to pay any sum due on shares, and any fine or other penalty imposed by the rules. The rights of members are similar to those of companies [12.4.1.1].

12.4.4   Trusts

Generally trusts do not have members in the conventional sense, and the only 'members' are the trustees. However it is possible to create a trust similar to an unincorporated association where, for example, the power to appoint or replace trustees is vested in individuals who would have some of the rights of members. Other rights or obligations will depend on the governing document.

12.4.5   Unincorporated associations

In an unincorporated association, the obligations of members arise from the fact that the constitution is a contract between all the members. Therefore each member potentially has unlimited liability for the acts of the organisation, and could be required to contribute to paying its debts if the organisation does not have enough funds [**22.2.2**].

There is no statute law governing membership obligations or rights in associations, so the rights of members depend on the governing document and common law [see, for example, **chapter 19** for the common law relating to meetings].

12.5   ADMISSION PROCEDURES

Procedures for agreeing new members vary widely. Membership may be automatic on application for anyone who meets the membership criteria, or may be subject to approval by the members or governing body, a membership committee or an individual such as a membership secretary. The eligibility, application and admission procedures in the governing document or internal regulations must be strictly followed. It is good practice to keep records of the agreement to join – usually an application form – as well as evidence of compliance with any further membership requirements, such as minutes showing approval of the application.

Care must be taken not to discriminate unlawfully in admitting, or not admitting, people to membership [**12.3**]. Some governing documents, for example, require members to be proposed and seconded by an existing member. This may constitute unlawful racial discrimination, if all the existing members are of one racial group.   *Re Handsworth Horticultural Institute (1993) Birmingham County Court, The Guardian 29 Jan 1993*

Where it appears that an applicant's motives may be destructive, a membership charity may consider these motives and the impact on the organisation.
Royal Society for the Prevention of Cruelty to Animals v Attorney General & others [2001] EWHC 474 (Ch)

12.5.1   Companies

The first members of a company are the **subscribers** (signers) of the memorandum of association. Thereafter, admission rules are set out in the articles of association. A person admitted under the rules in the articles becomes a member only when entered in the register of members [**18.5.2**]. A company must always have at least one member.   *Companies Act 2006 s.112*

12.5.1.1   Community interest companies

The first members of a community interest company are the subscribers to the memorandum of association. Thereafter all members must provide application information as specified by the directors, comply with any additional admission procedures in the articles of association, be approved by the directors, and be entered in the register of members.   *Community Interest Company Regulations 2005 sch.1 para.2*

12.5.2   Charitable incorporated organisations

The constitution of a charitable incorporated organisation must include the rules for becoming a member, and indicate who the first members will be.
Charities Act 1993 s.69B(2), to be inserted by Charities Act 2006 sch.7 para.1 [expected April 2010;

12.5.3   Industrial and provident societies

The rules of an industrial and provident society must set out the membership criteria for individual and organisational members and the admission procedure. The rules usually authorise membership decisions to be delegated to the governing body, a committee or officer. The governing document may include the possibility of an appeal to a general meeting.   *Industrial & Provident Societies Act 1965 sch.1 para.4*

To join a community benefit IPS a member purchases at least one share and receives a share certificate, and the member's name and details are added to the register of members [**18.6.1**].

12.5.4 Unincorporated associations

If an association's governing document or membership rules state that membership is open to anyone who agrees with the objects, then anyone who says they agree and who pays any necessary subscription cannot generally be refused admission. Apart from this there is no general right to membership of an association even if a person is eligible, and no reason for refusing membership needs to be given. *Nagle v Feilden [1966] 2 QB 633,644,653; McInnes v Onslow-Fane [1978] 1 WLR 1520,1529,1531; Woodford v Smith [1970] 1 WLR 806*

If an unincorporated association does not have a procedure in its governing document or rules about how members are admitted, any membership decision must be made by all the members. This is because such a decision is, in effect, a variation (change) of the contract between all the members [**2.2.1**].

Unless its governing document requires it, an unincorporated association is not obliged to keep a register of members or keep it up to date. But it is poor practice not to do so, and can lead to serious issues about who the members are.

12.6 SUBSCRIPTIONS AND RAISING MONEY FROM MEMBERS

12.6.1 Membership subscriptions

Many governing documents contain provision for membership to be conditional on payment of a monthly, annual or one-off subscription. If there is to be a subscription, the governing document normally provides for it to be fixed by a general meeting or the governing body. If an amount is specified in the governing document, it can be changed only by amendment [**7.5**].

The governing document may provide that non-payment results in suspension of certain rights or termination of membership. Ultimately, subscriptions can be recovered like any other debt [**21.7**].

Even if the governing document does not require payment of a subscription as a condition of receiving membership *rights* (granted by statute law or the governing document), the organisation may charge a subscription to receive membership *benefits* (additional rights given as a result of a decision by the membership or governing body). If members receive benefits in return for payment of a subscription, the subscription may be subject to VAT [**57.10.1**].

12.6.2 Issuing shares

Some industrial and provident societies and companies (including community interest companies) limited by shares may issue shares to raise funds, with shareholders becoming members. In an IPS, each member can have only one vote regardless of how many shares they hold. But a company can issue differing classes of shares with differing voting or other rights [**59.6**], so the company will need to consider whether it is appropriate for those who contribute more funds to obtain more voting control over the company.

Share issues are subject to detailed regulations, and legal advice should always be sought.

If issuing shares is inappropriate, raising money through other means such as debentures [**59.5.2**] or loans to the organisation [**59.4**] may be possible.

12.7 ASSIGNMENT OR TRANSFER OF MEMBERSHIP

The governing document of most voluntary organisations prohibits the transfer of membership to another person. This is in contrast to companies limited by shares, where the right to transfer shares and therefore membership is normal although it may be subject to restriction.

Examples of where an organisation which does not issue shares might have constitutional provision for membership to be assigned (transferred) are where membership brings valuable rights, as in some sports associations, or where members must invest in or make a loan to the organisation, for example to fund construction of facilities. Difficult issues can arise, such as how much control the organisation has over assignment, and whether membership can be assigned at a premium or profit. Where membership is linked to loans, matters may be simplified by drawing up a loan agreement for any capital input, and separating the loan from membership rights. This should be done only with appropriate legal advice.

12.8 RESIGNATION AND TERMINATION

The membership clause in the governing document should include procedures for resignation or removal of members, or should give the members, governing body or a membership committee power to make such regulations. It may also provide procedures for appeal against removal. All procedures must be strictly followed, and any human rights issues [**64.3**] should be considered.

Companies, charitable incorporated organisations and industrial and provident societies must keep their registers of members [**18.5.2**, **18.6.1**, **18.7**] up to date by entering the date of resignation or termination of membership, as must unincorporated associations whose governing document requires a register. Even where there is no obligation to keep a register, one should be kept.

12.8.1 Minimum number of members

12.8.1.1 Incorporated bodies

Private companies limited by guarantee or shares and charitable incorporated organisations must always have at least one member [**12.4.1**, **12.4.2**], and most industrial and provident societies must have at least three [**12.4.3**]. If the number of members falls below this minimum or any minimum set in the governing document (whichever is higher), the organisation is operating unlawfully and new members must be admitted under the procedure in the governing document [**7.4.11**] – even if they are admitted only to wind up the organisation.

If this is not possible, advice must be sought from the Charity Commission (for charitable companies, CIOs, and IPSs registered with the Commission), the Financial Services Authority (for other IPSs), or a specialist solicitor.

12.8.1.2 Unincorporated associations

Associations must have at least two members [**2.2.1**], but the governing document may set a higher minimum and/or may prohibit a member from resigning if the resignation would bring the number of members below this minimum.

If the number falls below the minimum, new members must be admitted under the procedures in the governing document. If this is not possible and the organisation is charitable, the Charity Commission should be consulted. If the organisation is not charitable and has no money or other assets it may spontaneously dissolve (fizzle out), but if it is has assets and only one member or no members, advice should be sought because these assets will belong to the Crown [**24.8**].

12.8.2 Resignation

Unless the governing document specifies otherwise, a member of an unincorporated association has a right to resign at any time by following the procedure in the governing document or membership rules, or by notifying the secretary. Resignation is then automatic, from the date the letter or other communication is received, and cannot be revoked unless the rules allow this. Action will need to be taken if the resignation brings the numbers below the required minimum [**12.8.1.2**]. *Finch v Oake [1896] 1 Ch 409,415*

A charitable incorporated organisation's constitution must include provision about how a member resigns from membership.

Charitable incorporated organisations and companies must always have at least one member [**12.8.1.1**], so the final member cannot resign and has a duty to take action to admit enough members to form a quorum for a general meeting.

The rules of an industrial and provident society must include procedures for deciding whether and if so how members can withdraw. The 'whether' implies that members do not automatically have a right to withdraw, unless this is explicit in the rules. *Industrial & Provident Societies Act 1965 sch.1 para.9*

12.8.3 Lapsing

The governing document might provide that once a person becomes a member, membership lasts until resignation, automatic termination or expulsion. Or it may say that in order to remain a member, certain criteria must be fulfilled, for example paying a membership subscription within a defined period. If members do not take the action necessary to meet these criteria, their membership **lapses**.

Care is needed that such lapsing arrangements do not risk leaving the organisation without the required minimum number of members [**12.8.1**], or with too few to form a quorum for a general meeting.

12.8.4 Automatic termination

The governing document or membership rules may specify that membership terminates automatically in certain circumstances, for example if the member moves away from the area or ceases to meet other eligibility criteria.

12.8.5 Death

When a member of a share company, including a community interest company, limited by shares, dies, his or her shares and the accompanying membership of the company normally pass to the executor or administrator of the estate.

Shares in an industrial and provident society also pass to the executor or administrator of the estate. The society's rules must include procedures for dealing with this. Members have a right, during their lifetime, to nominate a person to succeed to their interest in the society when they die, and the society must keep a record of this. *Industrial & Provident Societies Act 1965 sch.1 para.11; s.23(1),(5)*

Death terminates membership of a company limited by guarantee, charitable incorporated organisation or unincorporated association unless the governing document allows membership to pass to another person.

12.8.6 Dissolution of a member organisation

Where an organisation, rather than an individual, is a member of an organisation, the winding up of the member organisation is similar to the death of an individual member. In a company limited by shares or an industrial and provident society the shares owned by the member organisation are part of that organisation's assets, and are dealt with as part of its liquidation.

In a company limited by guarantee, charitable incorporated organisation or unincorporated association, a member organisation which is incorporated ceases to be a member if it is wound up, and its representative is no longer able to exercise membership rights on its behalf [**12.2.5.1**]. But if the member organisation is unincorporated and has appointed a nominee to become a member [**12.2.5.2**], the nominee continues to be a member of the other organisation unless its governing document says otherwise.

12.8.7 Suspension and expulsion

12.8.7.1 Suspension by the organisation

A member may be suspended or expelled from an organisation only if there is a power to do so in the governing document or membership rules, the rules are strictly followed, the organisation acts in good faith, the provisions of the **Human Rights Act** are not breached [**64.3**] where they are relevant, and the rules of **natural justice** are followed. Natural justice means that the person to be suspended or expelled has the right to know the reasons for the action, to put his or her case in response to the accusation, and to have any decision made by an unbiased body. *John v Rees [1970] Ch 345,397; Dawkins v Antrobus [1881] ChD 615,620*

If a suspension or expulsion is not carried out properly, the member can bring a claim in court to have it declared invalid, and may be awarded damages. An exception is a short-term suspension needed in order to investigate possible wrongdoing, for example suspending the treasurer while the accounts are checked after an allegation of fraud. In situations such as this the organisation's rules must be followed and those initiating the suspension must act in good faith, but the person being suspended does not have to be given an opportunity to present his or her case before being suspended.

Lewis v Heffer [1978] 1 WLR 1069,1073

12.8.7.2 Suspension by the Charity Commission

When the Charity Commission exercises its power to suspend or remove from office a trustee, officer, agent or employee of a charity [**13.3.2**], it also has power, if that person is a member of the charity, to remove the person from membership.

Charities Act 1993 s.18A, inserted by Charities Act 2006 s.19

12.9 MEMBERS AND THE GOVERNING BODY

Members of the organisation may have substantial statutory and constitutional powers, including rights to direct the organisation, remove members of the governing body [**13.5.6**] and amend the governing document [**7.5**]. The governing document should clearly state which rights and powers are reserved for the members, and which are granted to the governing body.

As well as knowing the constitutional and statutory requirements, the people involved in the organisation should have a clear understanding of the reasons behind the governance arrangements, and the respective roles of members and the governing body should be regularly reviewed to ensure they remain appropriate.

12.10 DISSATISFIED MEMBERS

In most organisations, individuals or minorities of members who do not like the way the majority or the governing body is operating have very little recourse, because the courts or Charity Commission generally will not intervene in an organisation's internal business unless the members or the governing body are acting outside the organisation's objects or powers [**5.8**] or unlawfully. In other cases the only action open to dissatisfied members may be to leave the organisation.

12.10.1 Rights in companies

In companies, individual members have a statutory right to take action in certain situations. A company member can make a **derivative claim** in relation to an actual or proposed act or omission involving negligence, default (failure to do what they were required to do), breach of duty or breach of trust by a director [**15.3**]. But to prevent unmeritorious claims, the member(s) must get the consent of the high court to proceed with their action.

Companies Act 2006 ss.260-264

In addition, individual company members may take legal action if the company's affairs are being or have been conducted in a manner which is unfairly prejudicial to the interests of some or all members, or an actual or proposed act or omission by the company is or would be prejudicial.

Companies Act 2006 ss.994-996

Resources: MEMBERS OF THE ORGANISATION

See end of **chapter 1**.

Statute law. www.opsi.gov.uk and www.statutelaw.gov.uk.

Much but not all case law. www.bailii.org.

Updates cross-referenced to this book. www.rclh.co.uk.

Chapter 13
MEMBERS OF THE GOVERNING BODY

For sources of further information see end of chapter 1.

13.1   MAKE-UP OF THE GOVERNING BODY

The **governing body** are the persons who are responsible in law for managing the organisation. Governing bodies have many names, such as **board of directors**, **board of trustees**, **board of governors**, **management committee**, **council of management**, **executive committee**, **steering committee** or **steering group**. Regardless of what it is called:

- in any company, including a community interest company, the members of the governing body are the **company directors**;

- in a trust or charitable association and in some other charities they are **trustees** for the purposes of the **Trustee Act 2000** and most other trust law;

- in any charity, regardless of its legal form and regardless of whether it is registered with the Charity Commission, the members of the governing body are **charity trustees** for the purposes of charity law.

What matters is not what the governing body is called, but the powers and duties it has under the organisation's governing document (constitution etc) and under charity, company, industrial and provident society, trust and/or general law.

If a group is not formally constituted and does not have a governing document, the governing body are the persons who control the group's activities.

In a company, charitable incorporated organisation (CIO), industrial and provident society or unincorporated association, all or most of the governing body members are typically elected by the members of the organisation. But there is no legal reason why the whole membership should not itself be the governing body. This can be appropriate for very small organisations, or where a high premium is put on members' direct involvement in governing the organisation.

Just as there is no standardisation in what the governing body is called, so there is no standardisation in how large it is, who is on it and how they get onto it. Especially where there is a complex web of decision making groups, it may not be straightforward to work out which is the governing body. But it is important to be clear about this, because it has implications for decision making, legal responsibility and potential liability.

13.1.1   Voting members

To be a full member of the governing body, a person must have a legal right to take part in decisions. Anyone who becomes a member of a governing body under the provisions in the governing document is a full **voting member** of the governing body, unless the governing document explicitly says that he or she is not.

Confusion sometimes arises about the rights of co-opted members [**13.4.1.6**], representatives of other organisations [**13.4.1.3**, **13.4.1.4**], people who serve *ex officio* [**13.4.1.2**], and others who are not appointed or elected in the usual way. There is often an assumption that anyone who is not elected at a general meeting is non-voting and therefore not a full member of the governing body, but this is not the case. Where the governing document allows co-option or any other method of becoming a member of a governing body, those members are full voting members of the governing body unless the governing document says otherwise.

13.1.2   Non-voting members

The governing document sometimes specifies that some 'members' of the governing body do not have voting rights or are observers or advisors on the governing body. This might apply, for example, to funders' representatives or the organisation's employees. 'Members' defined by the governing document as **non-voting** generally have a right to participate in discussions, but are not entitled to vote or participate in decisions in other ways. **Observers** generally have no right to participate in discussions or decisions but they may, with the consent of the person chairing the meeting, participate in discussions. **Advisors** are there to give advice, either generally or on specific matters. They must not take part in decisions.

Anyone who does not have a vote will not count towards the quorum [**19.12.4**] unless the governing document states that they do.

In general, persons who do not have a vote are not legally considered to be members of the governing body and are not liable for the organisation's actions. However, a person who in fact takes part in decisions could be held liable for those decisions in the same way as other governing body members.

13.1.3   Companies and CICs

13.1.3.1   Company directors

Not very helpfully, a **company director** is defined in company law as 'any person occupying the position of director, by whatever name called'. When a company or community interest company (CIC) is set up, the first directors are notified to Companies House as part of registration [**1.5.5**], and their details must be entered in the register of directors [**18.5.4**]. *Companies Act 2006 s.250*

Subsequent directors are elected or appointed under the provisions in the articles for electing or appointing voting members of the governing body. Before, or as soon as being, elected or appointed they must consent to be a director by completing company form **AP01**.

All company directors are **officers** and **agents** of the company [**7.4.16**, **14.1.1**, **20.5**]. In most voluntary sector companies the directors are not paid by the company, but if they are paid solely for their services *as directors* they are not generally classed as **employees** for employment law purposes (although under tax law they will be taxed as employees, and if the company is charitable, the rules on charity trustees serving as employees [**16.4.1**] will apply). Directors who are paid in another capacity, for example as a chief executive, finance officer or care worker, are generally classed as employees in that capacity.

If the company is charitable, its directors are also charity trustees [**13.1.7**].

13.1.3.2 Shadow directors

A **shadow director** is a person who does not have voting rights on the board but 'in accordance with whose directions or instructions the directors of the company are accustomed to act'. If a person gives professional advice, for example as a solicitor or accountant, and it is only on that advice that the directors act, the person is not a shadow director.   *Companies Act 2006 s.251*

Under company law, shadow directors are treated in the same way as ordinary directors. For example they must complete the same forms as company directors [**18.5.4**], must comply with the rules governing conflicts of interest [**15.3.5**], and are liable in the same way as company directors if the organisation becomes insolvent and is involved in fraudulent or wrongful trading [**24.2.4**].

An employee, funding body representative, consultant or other person who dominates or controls the board could be a shadow director. Even a person who gives advice rather than 'directions or instructions', but not as a professional advisor, can be a shadow director. But the tests for shadow directorship require the person virtually to control the directors. This is different from providing information, options and recommendations, and making clear that the decision rests with the directors.   *Secretary of State for Trade & Industry v Deverell [2001] Ch.340*

A chief executive or other employee of a charitable company who is a shadow director would be a charity trustee, and might not be able to be paid by the charity.

13.1.4 Industrial and provident societies

The rules of an industrial and provident society must specify how members of the board or committee, managers and officers are elected. Their names must be entered in the register of officers [**18.6.2**].   *Industrial & Provident Societies Act 1965 sch.1 para.6*

Governing body members of charitable IPSs which are exempt or excepted from registering with the Charity Commission have some duties as charity trustees [**13.1.7**]. In IPSs registered with the Commission, governing body members have the full range of charity trustee duties [**15.6**].

13.1.5 Unincorporated associations

In a small unincorporated association with a single-tier organisational structure, where there is only one identifiable group of people (whether called 'the members', 'the committee' or anything else), those people will be the governing body.

However, the governing document often explicitly states that the members of the association are to elect or appoint a committee. If this committee is empowered to take decisions on behalf of the members or to manage the association, it is clearly the governing body. In situations where it is less clear that management responsibility is being delegated, the committee is usually considered to be the governing body on the assumption that by electing such a committee, the members are authorising them to manage the organisation on their behalf.

But it could perhaps be argued that the full membership is the governing body, and the committee is only a sub-committee. If there is a dispute about the powers held by the committee, it will be necessary to get specialist legal advice.

13.1.6 Trusts

In a trust the original trustees are generally named in the trust deed [**1.3.1**]. The deed may have provision for the appointment of subsequent trustees. If it does not, the remaining trustees may appoint new trustees [**13.4.1.5**].

13.1.7 Charities

The voting members of the governing body of a charity [**4.1**] are **charity trustees**, regardless of the charity's legal form and whether it is registered with the Charity Commission, and regardless of what the governing body members are called in the governing document or in practice. Charity trustees are 'the persons having the general control and management of the administration of a charity'.   *Charities Act 1993 s.97*

Charity trustees are not the same as **holding trustees** [**20.4.4**], who hold property and investments on behalf of unincorporated organisations. But the same people may hold both roles.

Some, but not all, charity trustees are also trustees for the purposes of the **Trustee Act 2000**, and have specific duties and powers under the Act [**58.1**].

13.1.8 Charitable incorporated organisations

The constitution of a charitable incorporated organisation (CIO) must indicate who the first trustees will be, and set out the provisions for eligibility and election or appointment of further trustees. Details of all trustees must be entered in the CIO's register of trustees [**18.7**].

Charities Act 1993 s.69B(2), to be inserted by
Charities Act 2006 sch.7 para.1 [expected April 2010]

13.2 NUMBER ON THE GOVERNING BODY

The **minimum** number of people who must be on the governing body is specified in law and/or in the organisation's governing document. If different numbers are specified, the higher number prevails.

A governing body without the minimum number or without enough members to make a quorum [**19.12.4**] cannot take any action, other than to elect or appoint new governing body members (if it has that power) or to call a general meeting where the members of the organisation can elect new governing body members.

There is no **maximum** number of governing body members set out in law, but the governing document may set a maximum. It is generally advisable not to have too large a governing body, because of the difficulty in making decisions efficiently. On the other hand, it needs to be large enough to have the expertise necessary to understand the organisation and the environment within which it operates, and to make appropriate decisions based on this understanding.

13.2.1 Trust law

A trust may have only one trustee, if that trustee is a corporate body such as a local authority or other trust corporation. Otherwise, in order to sell land, a trust must have at least two trustees. *Trustee Act 1925 s.14(2)*

The Charity Commission is unlikely to register a trust with fewer than three individuals as trustees, but will register one with a single corporate body as trustee.

13.2.2 Company law

A private company – which virtually all voluntary sector and community interest companies are – must have at least one director. A sole director must be a **natural person** (human being), or where there is more than one director at least one must be a natural person. Companies which had on 8 November 2006 a sole director which was a corporate body have a grace period until 1 October 2010 before they need to have at least one human director. *Companies Act 2006 s.155;*
Companies Act 2006 (Commencement No.5) Order 2007 [SI 2007/3495] sch.4 para.46

Where a charitable company has individuals as directors, the Charity Commission generally requires at least three. The Commission has allowed a corporate body to be a sole director, but under the above provisions of the **Companies Act 2006**, there will have to be at least one individual in addition to the corporate body.

13.2.3 Industrial and provident societies

An industrial and provident society must consist of at least three individuals or two societies [**12.4.3**]. The governing body cannot be any smaller than this.

Industrial & Provident Societies Act 1965 s.2

13.2.4 Charitable incorporated organisations

At the time of writing (mid 2009) regulations were not finalised setting out the minimum number of trustees for a charitable incorporated organisation.

13.2.5 Unincorporated associations

An unincorporated association must have at least two members [**1.2.1**] but apart from this the only rules about minimum or maximum numbers on the governing body are those in the governing document.

13.3 ELIGIBILITY AND DISQUALIFICATION

A person may be prohibited from serving on a governing body because he or she does not meet criteria set down in the organisation's governing document or rules and is thus ineligible to serve on its governing body; does not fulfil statutory criteria; has been disqualified by the Charity Commission or court from serving; or does not meet some other external requirement, for example in relation to working with children. It is good practice to alert prospective members of the governing body to factors which would disqualify them [**13.3.2.5, 13.3.3.3**].

13.3.1 The governing document

A governing document may set out eligibility requirements, for example that a member of the governing body must live in a particular area or be a member of the organisation. The governing document may also specify that a governing body member must stand down in certain situations [**13.5**].

13.3.2 Charity law

To serve as a charity trustee or a holding trustee [**20.4.4**] for a charity, a person must meet any requirements set out in the governing document; be capable of understanding the responsibilities involved in trusteeship, including acting prudently and safeguarding the charity [**15.6**]; be properly elected or appointed; and not be disqualified from serving as a charity trustee [**13.3.2.5**].

13.3.2.1 Minors

In charities set up as trusts, trustees must be at least 18 years of age. Although this does not strictly apply to charities set up as unincorporated associations, the Charity Commission generally requires members of a charitable association's governing body to be 18 or over. *Law of Property Act 1925 s.20*

In charitable companies, the minimum age for a director is usually 16 [**13.3.3.1**].

At the time of writing (mid 2009) it was not yet clear whether the minimum age for trustees of a charitable incorporated organisation (CIO) would be 16 or 18.

13.3.2.2 Trustee benefits and conflicts of interest

Charity law generally requires that trustees must not profit or benefit from their trust [**15.6.6**], and that they must not be in a position where they may have a conflict of interest [**15.6.4**]. These principles have important implications, particularly for charities which want to have employees, users/beneficiaries or persons closely connected to them, as trustees, or which want to pay trustees for serving on the governing body or other work done for the charity [**chapter 16**].

13.3.2.3 Capacity

To be a charity trustee, a person must be capable of understanding what trusteeship means and carrying out the duties of trustees [**15.6**]. **Lack of capacity** is defined as not being able to make a decision in relation to a particular matter, even after all practicable steps have been taken to help the person do so, because of an impairment or disturbance in the functioning of the mind or brain. *Mental Capacity Act 2005 ss.1-3*

Unless a court has said that they are incapable of managing their own affairs, persons with mental ill health, a learning disability or a disability which affects memory or communication can be charity trustees. However it is crucial to ensure that they receive appropriate induction and ongoing training and support, that they are able to take part in decisions based on a reasonable understanding of the issues, and that they have enough understanding of financial and legal issues to understand the risks involved. The chair and treasurer, in particular, must ensure issues, options and implications are appropriately explained.

Where capacity varies depending on a person's mental state, the organisation should have guidelines for dealing with situations where a governing body member appears incapable of acting appropriately as a trustee.

The organisation's governing document may include provisions for removing a person from the governing body in case of incapacity [**13.5.2**].

13.3.2.4 Charities working with children and vulnerable adults

It is an offence to serve on the governing body of a children's charity or an educational institution while barred or disqualified from work with children, or to serve on the governing body of a vulnerable adults' charity while barred or disqualified from working with vulnerable adults [**41.6.1**]. It is also an offence for anyone knowingly to offer such a position to a person who is barred or disqualified from work with children or vulnerable adults.

Trustees of charities working with children or vulnerable adults are in some situations required to have criminal record checks before becoming a trustee, and when registration under the vetting and barring scheme is introduced in late 2009 and 2010, most but not all such trustees will have to be registered with the scheme [**41.7**]. Even where it is not a statutory requirement, it is good practice for charities working with children or vulnerable adults to carry out such checks, and the Charity Commission recommends this. Detailed guidance on good practice is available from the Commission [see end of chapter].

The purpose of the checks is for the trustees to satisfy themselves that each potential trustee is suitable to work with a charity of this type. A criminal record does not in itself disqualify a person from being a trustee, unless it is an unspent conviction involving deception or dishonesty [below].

13.3.2.5 Disqualification under charity law

The grounds for disqualification under charity law apply to trustees and holding trustees of all charities, including those which are exempt or excepted from registering with the Charity Commission [**8.1.2**, **8.1.3**]. They are:

- having been convicted for any offence involving dishonesty or deception, unless the conviction is spent under the terms of the **Rehabilitation of Offenders Act 1974** [**41.8**];
- having been declared bankrupt or (in Scotland) having assets sequestered, unless the bankruptcy or sequestration has been discharged or permission has been granted under the **Company Directors Disqualification Act 1986** s.11 for the person to act as director of a charitable company;
- having made a composition or arrangement, including an **individual voluntary arrangement** (IVA), with creditors which has not been discharged;
- having been removed by the Charity Commission or the high court from being a trustee of or for any charity;
- having been removed by the court of session in Scotland from being involved in the management of any charitable body;
- being subject to a disqualification order under the **Company Directors Disqualification Act 1986** [**13.3.3.3**], unless permission has been given to act as a director of a charitable company;
- being subject to an order made under the **Insolvency Act 1986** s.429(2)(b) for failure to make payments under a county court administration order, unless permission to act as a charity trustee has been granted by the court which made the order.

Charities Act 1993 s.72

13.3.2.6 Charity Commission waiver

Any person disqualified on any of these grounds may apply to the Charity Commission for a waiver either in relation to a particular charity or type of charity, or in general. However, a Commission waiver cannot override a disqualification provision in a charity's governing document. Nor is a waiver possible in relation to a charitable company if the person is an undischarged bankrupt or is prohibited from being a charity trustee by a disqualification order under the **Company Directors Disqualification Act 1986**, and permission has not been granted for him or her to act as director of any other company. *Charities Act 1993 s.72(4)*

If a person has been disqualified for more than five years following removal as a charity trustee by the Commission, high court or court of session, the Commission must grant any request for a waiver unless it has a good reason not to.

Charities Act 1993 s.72(4A), inserted by Charities Act 2006 s.35

13.3.2.7 Serving while disqualified

It is an offence, punishable by a fine and up to two years imprisonment, to serve as a trustee of or for a charity while disqualified. For some types of disqualification, trustees of charitable companies are subject to penalties under company law [**13.3.3.3**] rather than charity law. *Charities Act 1993 s.73(1),(2)*

Any person who serves as a trustee while disqualified may be required by the Charity Commission to repay to the charity any payments received as remuneration or for expenses while disqualified, or the monetary value of any benefits received while disqualified. *Charities Act 1993 s.73(4)*

A charity's governing document may specify that the trustee automatically ceases to be a member of the governing body as soon as he or she becomes disqualified. If it does not specify this, the person should resign or, if necessary, be removed from the governing body under the procedure in the governing document or under the provisions of the **Trustee Act 1925** [**13.5.5**] or **Companies Act** [**13.5.6.1**]. While waiting for removal the person remains a trustee but must not attend meetings or take part in any way in managing the charity.

People who are disqualified and are not trustees can be invited to attend trustee meetings in a non-voting capacity, but need to be careful not to act in ways which could be seen as influencing or taking part in decisions.

13.3.2.8 Protecting trustees and the organisation

To ensure an individual does not inadvertently serve while disqualified, the Charity Commission recommends requiring all charity trustees, when elected or appointed, to sign a declaration that they are not disqualified from serving as a charity trustee. A model form is available from the Commission [see end of chapter]. The charity can make clear that the person may be able to apply to the Charity Commission for a waiver if he or she is disqualified [**13.3.2.6**].

The Commission also recommends in CC30 *Finding new trustees* that charities check the register of bankruptcies and individual voluntary arrangements on the Insolvency Service website and the register of disqualified directors on the Companies House website [see end of chapter], and the register of trustees removed by the Charity Commission or courts, which is kept at Commission offices. Charities working with children and vulnerable adults may have a statutory duty to ensure their trustees are not barred from working with those groups [**41.6.1**].

13.3.3 Company law

To serve as a company director an individual must meet any requirements set out in the articles of association, be properly elected or appointed as set out in the articles, not be disqualified from being a company director, and in a charitable company not be disqualified from serving as a charity trustee [**13.3.2.5**].

13.3.3.1 Minors

Company directors must be at least 16 years old, unless the government makes regulations allowing younger directors. *Companies Act 2006 ss.157,158*

13.3.3.2 Capacity

Company law requires all directors to exercise the level of reasonable care, skill and diligence expected of a director [**15.3.4**]. This means that each director must have the capacity to do this. This is potentially a higher test than for charity trustees, who must be capable of managing their own affairs [**13.3.2.3**] but are not required to be capable of serving as a company director. *Companies Act 2006 s.174*

161

13.3.3.3 Disqualification

The **Company Directors Disqualification Act 1986** sets out the reasons for which a court must or may disqualify a person from serving as a company director for a specified period. Disqualification also extends to taking any part in promoting, forming or managing a company.

A person who is an undischarged bankrupt or, in Scotland, has had an estate sequestered, or fails to make payments under a county court administration order cannot be involved in setting up or managing a company or serve as director without permission from the court.   *Company Directors Disqualification Act 1986 ss.11,12(2)*

A person may be disqualified by the court because of **general misconduct** in connection with companies if the person is persistently in default in sending annual returns, accounts or other documents [**54.3.5**] to the registrar of companies; the person is convicted of an indictable offence in relation to the promotion, formation, management or liquidation of a company, or with the receivership or management of a company's property; or it appears, while winding up a company, that the person has been guilty of fraudulent trading [**24.2.4**].   *CDDA 1986 ss.2-5*

A person may also be disqualified if found liable for wrongful trading [**24.2.4**] while a company was being wound up.   *CDDA 1986 s.10*

The court must disqualify for **unfitness** a person who is or has been director or shadow director [**13.1.3.2**] of a company which has become insolvent, either while he or she was a director or afterwards, and the court believes that the person's conduct as a director makes him or her unfit to be involved in managing a company.   *CDDA 1986 ss.6-9*

Companies House maintains a public register of persons disqualified from serving as company directors. Information is provided by telephone, or the register can be searched at Companies House or on its website [see end of chapter]. The Insolvency Service register should also be checked [**13.3.2.5**].

13.3.3.4 Serving while disqualified

It is a an offence, punishable by a fine and up to two years imprisonment, to be involved in promoting, forming or managing a company while disqualified.
Company Directors Disqualification Act 1986 s.13

In addition, a person who acts while disqualified becomes personally liable for all the debts of the company incurred while he or she was involved in managing it. A person who knowingly acts or is willing to act on instructions given by a person who is subject to a disqualification order or is an undischarged bankrupt becomes personally liable for all the debts of the company incurred while he or she acted or was willing to act on such instructions.   *CDDA 1986 s.15*

To protect individuals from these risks, it is good practice to ask all directors to confirm before election or appointment that they are not disqualified from serving as a company director [**13.3.2.8**].

A company's governing document usually specifies that the director ceases to be a member of the governing body as soon as he or she becomes disqualified. If it does not specify this, the person should resign or be removed from the governing body [**13.5.6.1**]. While waiting for removal the person remains a director but must not take part in any way in managing the company.

After resignation or removal there is no prohibition on the disqualified person attending board meetings in a non-voting capacity, but he or she must not take a significant role because of the risk of being seen as managing while disqualified.

13.3.4 Industrial and provident societies

At the time of writing (mid 2009) a person under the age of 18 may not serve on the governing body of an industrial and provident society, or as its manager or treasurer. The government had announced its intention to allow under-18s to serve on IPS governing bodies unless the IPS's rules prohibit it.
Industrial & Provident Societies Act 1965 s.20

At the time of writing, it was expected that the **Company Directors Disqualification Act 1986**, [**13.3.3.3**] would be extended to cover industrial and provident societies. In the meantime, many IPS governing document disqualify anyone subject to company disqualification, or who is an undischarged bankrupt. Charitable IPSs, even if not registered with the Charity Commission, must comply with charity rules on eligibility for and disqualification from trusteeship [**13.3.2**].

13.3.5 Charitable incorporated organisations

Charitable incorporated organisations are subject to charity rules on eligibility and disqualification of trustees [**13.3.2**]. At the time of writing (mid 2009) it was not clear whether the disqualification provisions of the **Company Directors Disqualification Act 1986** [**13.3.3.3**] or similar rules would apply to trustees who have been involved in managing insolvent CIOs.

13.3.6 Trusts and unincorporated associations

Charitable trusts and charitable associations must comply with charity rules on eligibility and disqualification in relation to their trustees and any holding trustees [**13.3.2, 20.4.4**].

Non-charitable associations do not have to comply with any requirements other than those set out in their governing document.

13.4 JOINING THE GOVERNING BODY

The process by which governing body members are appointed or elected, and the length of time they serve, depend on the organisation's governing document and, to a lesser extent, its legal structure.

For **companies**, all changes relating to directors must be entered in the register of directors [**18.5.4**] and must be notified to Companies House within 14 days. **Charitable incorporated organisations** must enter changes relating to trustees in the register of trustees [**18.7**].

When new governing body members are appointed or elected in a **trust**, the trust's assets should be vested in the new trustees [**20.4.5**]. In an **association**, if members of the governing body are holding trustees [**20.4.4**] for property or investments, it may be necessary to vest these in new trustees when the governing body members change. Otherwise the original trustees continue to hold the assets – which can cause problems if the organisation loses touch with them or they die.

13.4.1 Appointment

13.4.1.1 By founders

An organisation's **founders** may name, in the governing document, some or all members of the first governing body.

In a trust the trustees named in the trust deed serve, unless the trust deed indicates otherwise, until they resign, are removed or die.

In a company, the first directors are notified to Companies House when the company is registered [**1.5.5**]. If it is known beforehand who all the directors will be, the form includes all of them. If it is not known, interim directors are listed on the form and serve until new directors are appointed or elected.

In a charitable incorporated organisation, the first trustees are the applicants who apply for registration of the CIO.

Where the governing document refers to the first governing body members as 'directors' or 'trustees' but then refers to 'management committee members' or something similar, it is a common mistake to think that the initial directors or trustees remain there forever, and that the management committee is separate from them. This is not the case. Unless the governing document explicitly names someone as a **permanent director** or says they serve until they resign, are removed or die, the directors or trustees named when setting up serve only as the first governing body, until they are replaced by the election or appointment of new governing body members under the provisions in the governing document – usually at the first annual general meeting.

13.4.1.2 Ex officio

Some people may be entitled to a place on the governing body *ex officio*, by virtue of a position they hold. Unless the governing document specifies otherwise they retain their place on the governing body only for as long as they hold the relevant position, and are then replaced by the new post holder.

13.4.1.3 Nomination

The governing document may give an external body the right to appoint one or more members of the governing body. These appointees may be called **representative**, **nominated** or **nominative members** of the governing body. The individual, not the appointing organisation, is the member of the governing body.

13.4.1.4 Corporate body representatives

A **corporate body** (but not an unincorporated organisation) may under the terms of the governing document be a member of a governing body. Local authorities, for example, are often trustees for charitable trusts.

The corporate body, rather than an individual who acts on its behalf, is the governing body member and has the duties and liabilities of governing body membership. Despite this, the individual could be held liable on the basis that he or she had the powers and duties of a trustee.

13.4.1.5 Appointment by existing members of governing body

The governing document may give the members of the governing body the power to appoint further members. A maximum may be set.

If a charity is set up as a trust [**2.3**] and its governing document gives the trustees or other persons the right to appoint and discharge (remove) trustees, the change may be done by producing a **memorandum** stating that the trustee has been appointed or discharged. *Charities Act 1993 s.83*

The memorandum typically gives the name of the trust and says:

> At a meeting of the trustees held on [date], it was resolved, in exercise of the power in clause ____ of the charity's trust deed/constitution, that the following should be appointed as trustees: [names/addresses] in place of [name/address] who wished to retire [or has died].

The memorandum must be signed and delivered [**20.3.2**] by the person who chaired the meeting at which the appointment or discharge was made, or by another person authorised by the meeting to sign. The memorandum must be witnessed by two people who were at the meeting. Additional procedures are needed to transfer investments and land [**20.4.5**].

If a trust's governing document does not contain rules for appointment of further trustees, the trustees have power to replace trustees when they retire or die, but not to appoint additional trustees or discharge trustees. *Trustee Act 1925 s.36*

13.4.1.6 Co-option

The governing document may give the members of the governing body and/or the members of the organisation power to **co-opt** (appoint) people onto the governing body. If permitted, this process may be used to fill places which were not filled by election, fill vacancies which arise between elections (**casual vacancies**), or bring people with specific skills or experience onto the governing body.

The governing document should set out how long co-opted members of the governing body serve, and whether they can be co-opted again. Unless the governing document says otherwise, co-opted members of the governing body have the same voting rights, other rights and obligations as other governing body members.

If the governing document does not allow co-option it may be amended in the usual way [**7.5**], or people may be invited to attend meetings as observers.

13.4.1.7 By the Charity Commission

The Charity Commission may appoint or discharge charity trustees if requested by trustees to do so, or if it considers it necessary for the proper management of the charity, or if a defunct charity is being revived. *Charities Act 1993 s.16(1)(b)*

13.4.2 Election

In membership organisations, some or all members of the governing body are generally **elected** by those members who have the right to take part in elections [**12.2**]. Procedures set out in the governing document must be carefully followed.

Where an organisation has a small membership, all the members of the organisation may comprise the governing body. If the governing document requires an AGM to be held and/or requires the organisation's members to elect the governing body, these procedures must be followed – even though the members of the organisation simply elect themselves as members of the governing body.

13.4.2.1 Nomination

Some governing documents specify that anyone standing for election to the governing body must be **nominated** by another member or members; others allow individuals to nominate themselves. Some require nominations to be made a specified period before the AGM; others allow nominations from the floor on the day of the election; others require nomination only if the candidate is not a current member of the governing body or approved by the governing body. Standing orders [**7.4.25**] may be put in place to clarify nomination arrangements, provided they do not contradict anything in the governing document.

In designing nomination procedures, a balance often needs to be drawn between ensuring that nominees are well supported and good notice is given of who they are, and the reality of the last-minute struggle to find people willing to stand.

13.4.2.2 Uncontested elections

In many organisations, candidates for an uncontested post are automatically elected. However, some organisations have a procedure for uncontested elections which allows members to vote against the candidate, or requires a minimum number of votes in favour of him or her. This can reduce the risk of a person considered unsuitable being elected simply because no one else was nominated.

13.4.2.3 Voting methods

The governing document may require members to vote in person, or may allow voting by postal ballot or proxy [**19.8.3**, **19.8.4**]. Proxies must always be allowed in companies, even if the articles of association explicitly state that proxy voting is not allowed [**19.3.6**, **19.8.3**].

In a company, if an election is uncontested, one motion may be used to approve two or more directors unless the articles prohibit this.   *Companies Act 2006 s.160*

For contested elections (more candidates than places), members may vote by choosing the candidates they want on a **first past the post** system (the ones with the most votes win), or by voting in order of preference on a **single transferable vote** (STV) system. The Electoral Reform Society [see end of **chapter 19**] can provide advice on STV, and Electoral Reform Services can manage elections for any organisation.

13.4.2.4 Open voting

While many governing documents allow only members formally admitted to the organisation to vote in elections, some allow wider participation. Community associations, for example, may allow voting by 'anyone who lives or works in X parish', or a residents' association may allow any resident of the estate to vote.

13.4.2.5 Electoral colleges

The governing document may specify that groupings within the organisation – for example members who live in the Midlands, a youth section or a service users' group – elect one or more members of the governing body. These groupings are sometimes called **electoral colleges**. Especially in large organisations this procedure can make it easier for people to vote for people they know, and can make it more likely that minority interests will be represented on the governing body. However it may also create a governing body which is too large and cumbersome to make decisions effectively.

13.4.3   Alternates

If the governing document allows, a governing body member may be able to temporarily delegate his or her authority to an **alternate**. This could happen, for example, if a member of the governing body is hospitalised or is going to be away. The alternate is a substitute and serves only until the original member returns.

An alternate should not be confused with a permanent change of representative where a body has the right to appoint a member of the governing body [**13.4.1.3**], or where a corporate body is itself a member of the governing body and changes the person acting on its behalf [**13.4.1.4**].

13.4.3.1   Companies

The articles of association of both charitable and non-charitable companies may allow appointment of **alternate directors**. Virtually all the statutory requirements for company directors apply to alternates. Alternates must not be disqualified from serving as a director [**13.3.3.3**], their name must be entered in the register of directors, and the appointment and revocation must be notified to Companies House in the usual way [**18.5.4**]. Alternate directors are not agents [**20.5**] of the director who appointed them, and are liable for their own acts.

13.4.3.2   Trusts and charitable associations

Trustees are required to act personally [**15.6.8**], so the Charity Commission is generally unwilling to approve a governing document for a charitable trust or association which allows appointment of alternate trustees. However a trustee may delegate any or all powers and duties for a period of up to one year [**15.8.2**]. The original trustee is liable for the acts of the appointed person.

13.4.3.3   Non-charitable associations

A governing document for a non-charitable association which allows alternates should make clear that the alternate is not acting as an agent [**20.5**]. If this is not made clear the original member could be held liable for the acts of the alternate.

13.5   LEAVING THE GOVERNING BODY

A person may leave a governing body by:
- **retiring**, when the term of office comes to an end;
- **resigning**, before the end of the term;
- being **replaced** by the body which appointed him or her;
- becoming **disqualified** from serving as a director and/or trustee [**13.3.3.3**, **13.3.2.5**], and resigning or being removed from the governing body;
- being **removed** for a reason set out in the governing document;
- in a trust, being **replaced** by the other trustee(s);
- being removed by a vote of the members, under provisions in the governing document or statute law;
- being removed by the Charity Commission or the high court;
- dying, or in the case of a corporate body, being dissolved [**24.3-24.7**].

13.5.1   Restrictions on retirement and resignation

Governing documents sometimes contain restrictions relating to retirement or resignation. Examples include a prohibition on a member of the governing body resigning if this would bring the governing body below the quorum for meetings, and provision for retiring members of the governing body to be automatically re-elected or re-appointed at the end of their term if there is no one to replace them.

A trustee of a trust cannot resign if the resignation would leave less than two individual trustees or a trust corporation.   *Trustee Act 1925 s.39(1)*

The Charity Commission is likely to take the view that members of the governing body who resign leaving a charity without an effective governing body remain liable to discharge their duties as charity trustees.

166

13.5.2 Incapacity

The governing document may say that a person automatically ceases to be a member of the governing body if he or she 'suffers from mental disorder', 'becomes incapable by reason of mental disorder, illness or injury of managing and administering his or her own affairs', or similar wording. It is then up to the organisation to determine whether the person is incapable of serving on the governing body, probably based on the **Mental Capacity Act 2005** [**13.3.2.3**].

Unless the governing document specifies otherwise, an incapacitated person remains a member of the governing body until resigning or being removed, or coming to the end of his or her term. In extreme cases it may be possible to obtain a court order excluding the person from attending meetings until they recover.

13.5.2.1 Companies

The articles of association of many companies (and the governing documents of some other organisations) provide for a person to cease being a director if he or she is, or may be, suffering from mental disorder, and is either is admitted to hospital under the **Mental Health Act 1983** or **Mental Health (Scotland) Act 1960**, or is subject to a court order in matters concerning mental disorder.

The model articles under the **Companies Act 2006** do not refer to hospitalisation or legislation, but state that a person ceases to be a director as soon as a registered medical practitioner who is treating the person gives a written opinion to the company stating that the person has become physically or mentally incapable of acting as a director, and may remain so for more than three months; or because of the person's mental health, a court makes an order wholly or partly preventing the person from personally exercising any powers or rights he or she would otherwise have. *Companies (Model Articles) Regulations 2008 [SI 2008/3229] sch.1 para.18, sch.2 para.18*

Companies formed under the **Companies Act 2006** do not have to use the model articles, but may wish to adopt this article. Companies formed under earlier Acts may wish to replace their existing article with this new one [**7.5.3**].

13.5.3 Non-attendance

The governing document may state that a governing body member is automatically removed, or may be removed if the other governing body members agree, if he or she is absent from meetings for a specified time or from a certain number of meetings without consent of the governing body. If the governing document does not contain this provision, it can be amended in the usual way [**7.5**].

Unless the governing document specifies otherwise, membership continues even if the member never attends meetings. However for charity trustees and company directors, persistent non-attendance could constitute a breach of their duties, and could even lead to personal liability for the organisation's debts and disqualification as a company director [**19.12.1**, **13.3.3.3**].

13.5.4 Misconduct

Unless the governing document allows, the members of the governing body generally have no power to remove another governing body member, even one who engages in misconduct. In limited circumstances, the trustees of a trust or charitable association may be able to remove and replace a trustee [below]. If the misconduct threatens a charity's assets, the Charity Commission may be asked to investigate, and has power to remove trustees [**4.5.9**].

13.5.5 Replacement by trustees

Unless the governing document specifies otherwise, trustees of a trust may replace a trustee who is out of the UK for a continuous period of more than 12 months, wishes to be discharged from responsibilities as a trustee, refuses to act as a trustee, is unfit to act as a trustee, is incapable of acting as a trustee, or is under the age of 18. *Trustee Act 1925 s.36*

'Unfit' is not defined but generally applies to matters covered by the charity trustee disqualification rules [**13.3.2.5**]. Incapacity includes dementia etc [**13.5.2**].

This procedure is not available for incorporated bodies whether charitable or non-charitable (companies, industrial and provident societies and charitable incorporated organisations), or for non-charitable unincorporated associations. Even in a charitable association or trust, legal advice should be sought before using it.

13.5.6   Removal by members of the organisation

13.5.6.1   Companies

Members of a company always have a right to remove a director and to appoint a replacement by ordinary resolution with special notice [**19.7.4**]. The right to remove a director cannot be taken away or amended by anything in the articles or by any agreement with directors, and applies even to 'permanent' directors. Any such decision must be made at a general meeting of the members; it cannot be made by written resolution.   *Companies Act 2006 ss.168,288(2)*

Notice of intention to put a resolution to remove a director and/or appoint a replacement must be delivered to the company's office at least 28 days before the meeting. As soon as the company receives this notice of intention, it must send a copy to the director whose removal is proposed.   *Companies Act 2006 s.169*

This director has a right to be heard at the meeting, and to make written representations of a reasonable length to the company and request that these be notified to members. The company must send the representations to every member to whom notice of the meeting is sent. If the representations are received too late to be sent out or the company does not send them, the director can require them to be read out at the meeting.

The company or any aggrieved person may apply to the high court for a ruling that the right to make representations is being abused. If this is granted, the representations do not need to be circulated or read out.

13.5.6.2   Other membership organisations

Provision for removal of governing body members must be included in the rules of an industrial and provident society. IPSs and associations often have provisions similar to those for companies. At the time of writing (mid 2009) it was not clear whether members of a charitable incorporated organisation (CIO) would have a statutory right to remove trustees, or would have this right only if it is included in its constitution.

13.5.7   Vote of no confidence

Members of the organisation or governing body may call for a vote of **no confidence**, in the hope of putting a person or persons in a position where they will resign from the governing body. Unless it meets the requirements of any statutory removal provisions or provisions in the governing document, such a vote has no meaning legally and there is no obligation on the person to resign, even if 100% of those voting say they have no confidence.

Resources: MEMBERS OF THE GOVERNING BODY

See end of **chapter 1**.

Checks on governing body members. Charity Commission register of removed trustees: www.charitycommission.gov.uk, 0845 300 0218, email via website.

Companies House disqualified directors register: www.companieshouse.gov.uk/ddir.

Insolvency Service individual insolvency register: www.insolvency.gov.uk/bankruptcy/bankruptcysearch.htm.

Statute law. www.opsi.gov.uk and www.statutelaw.gov.uk.

Much but not all case law. www.bailii.org.

Updates cross-referenced to this book. www.rclh.co.uk.

Chapter 14
OFFICERS, COMMITTEES AND SUB-COMMITTEES

For sources of further information see end of chapter 1.

14.1   WHO'S WHO

As with so many other aspects of organisational description, the terms used to describe voluntary organisations' officers and committees are inconsistent, overlapping and confusing, and it is important to be clear about how they are used in each individual organisation. For example:

- the governing body might be called a **management committee** or **executive committee**;
- the governing body might be called something else, such as a **board of directors**, **board of trustees**, **board of governors** or **council of management**, and a body called a management committee or executive committee might be a **committee** of that board or council;
- if the governing body is called a board, the sub-groups it sets up are likely to be called **committees** [14.6] – but if the governing body is itself called a committee, the sub-groups it sets up are likely to be called **sub-committees**;
- people called **committee members** might be company directors and/or charity trustees, or might not – depending on whether the committee is or is not the governing body, and on whether the organisation is a company or charity;
- a person called a **director** might be a member of the governing body, or might be the chief executive or the head of a department or team;
- a **president** [14.2.3] might have special responsibilities for example as a chairperson, or might be a figurehead with no responsibilities;
- a **secretary** might be elected at the AGM to deal with the organisation's paperwork [14.2.5], or be a company secretary [14.3] appointed by the board, or be an employee carrying our secretarial and administrative duties.

This chapter looks at these roles and relationships – whatever they are called.

14.1.1 Officers of a company

In most voluntary organisations the term **officers** is used narrowly, to refer only to honorary officers [below]. In company law, however, the term refers to a much wider group, including the **company directors** (the voting members of the governing body), the **honorary officers**, **shadow directors** [**13.1.3**], the **company secretary** if there is one [**14.3**], and the **chief executive** and other senior management.

Companies Act 2006 ss.1121,1173

A company's officers have certain rights and duties under company law, which are referred to throughout this book.

14.1.2 Honorary officers

In general usage, the term **officer** or **honorary officer** refers to the elected or appointed **chairperson**, **vice-chair**, **treasurer**, **honorary secretary** and others who have special responsibilities which distinguish them from the other members of the organisation or its governing body.

When the term 'officers' is used in a governing document, standing orders or other contexts, it is important to be absolutely clear whether it refers only to honorary officers or to a broader group, or even to staff.

There is no statutory obligation to have honorary officers, but governing documents often specify that the organisation must have certain officers. Even if it is not required by the governing document it is generally sensible to have at least a chairperson and treasurer, and possibly a vice-chair. If a company wants to have a secretary to deal with minutes and/or correspondence this post should be called honorary secretary to distinguish it from the company secretary [**14.3**].

Some governing documents provide for other posts such as **president** or **patron**. These might be members of the governing body, or purely honorary posts with very limited or no rights [**14.2.3**, **12.2.7**].

In drawing up or reviewing a governing document, an important decision is whether the chairperson and other officers are to be elected by the members of the organisation or by the governing body. Appointment by the governing body can help ensure that the people chosen for these posts are suitable to oversee the organisation's finances and responsibilities, and are not chosen simply because they are the only people nominated or are the most popular.

14.1.3 Vacancies

A **casual vacancy** occurs if a post is not filled by the usual election or appointment process or if the post falls vacant between elections, usually because the post holder resigns, is removed or dies. If the governing document contains a procedure for filling casual vacancies, this must be followed. If there is no such procedure, the body which would ordinarily have elected or appointed the officer may be able to appoint someone to serve in an **acting** capacity until the next scheduled election. 'Acting' indicates that they were not elected in the usual way.

14.2 DUTIES AND POWERS OF HONORARY OFFICERS

The duties of honorary officers and their powers (if any) are not, in general, set out in statute or case law. They arise primarily from the organisation's governing document, its standing orders [**7.4.25**], and resolutions of the governing body. It is therefore important for anyone elected or appointed as an officer to clarify what is required and expected in that particular organisation, and these expectations should be set out in a role description.

14.2.1 Chairperson

The role of chairperson carries no legal rights or responsibilities except in relation to chairing meetings [**19.5.2**]. Additional responsibilities may be set out in the governing document, standing orders, formal delegation of powers or a role description, or may have developed through custom and practice. In addition to chairing meetings, typical responsibilities of the chairperson include guiding the organisation's strategic development, overseeing the governing body's agenda and the work of the chief executive, and representing the organisation publicly.

14.2.1.1 Chair's action

Chair's action is where a decision must of necessity be made before the next meeting, and the chairperson has the authority to make it. There is no implicit right to take chair's action. A chairperson may do so only if the governing document or standing orders allow such action, or the chairperson has been explicitly authorised to take such action, generally through a delegation of powers [**14.6.2**] recorded in the minutes of the governing body. All decisions taken under chair's action must be reported to the next meeting.

A chair cannot be authorised to take decisions which under the governing document must be made by the governing body or the members of the organisation.

The organisation's custom and practice may be for the chairperson to make decisions between meetings even without explicit authorisation. While common, this leaves legal doubts as to the legitimacy of such action, so explicit authorisation is preferable. A chairperson who makes decisions or authorises actions without proper authority may be acting unlawfully and can be held personally liable unless the decision is subsequently ratified by the governing body.

14.2.2 Convenor

The term **convenor** is used in a variety of ways. Especially in Scotland, it may be synonymous with chairperson. In other organisations it may be a person who arranges meetings but does not chair them, or a person who chairs meetings but does not take on the typical chairperson's role of overseeing the organisation.

14.2.3 President

The term **president** is also used in a variety of ways. Depending on the provisions in the governing document, the president may be the same as a chairperson; may represent the organisation publicly, but not chair meetings; or may have a figurehead role with no responsibilities.

14.2.4 Vice-chair

A **vice-chair** typically stands in when the chairperson is not available to chair meetings. Depending on the organisation, the vice-chair may take on other roles, to ease the burden on the chairperson. It is good practice to keep the vice-chair as fully briefed as the chairperson, so they can chair meetings or represent the organisation at short notice if necessary. Some organisations use the vice-chair position as a way of training people to take on the position of chairperson.

14.2.5 Honorary secretary

The term **honorary secretary** typically refers to the person responsible for dealing with correspondence and/or organising and minuting meetings, but the position may involve other duties. There is no obligation to have an honorary secretary unless this is required by the governing document or standing orders.

14.2.6 Treasurer

Even if the governing document does not require the organisation to have a **treasurer** it is good practice for the governing body to appoint one, so a named person has specific responsibility for monitoring the organisation's finances and keeping the governing body informed. The appointment of a treasurer does not relieve the other members of the governing body of their responsibility for overseeing the finances.

No matter how trustworthy and reliable the treasurer, it is not good practice to allow her or him sole control of the finances, because it does not provide opportunity for mistakes or fraud to be detected [**53.1.4**].

14.3   COMPANY SECRETARY

Private companies – which the vast majority of voluntary sector and community interest companies are – do not need to have a **company secretary** unless the articles of association require one. Where the articles simply refer to the duties of a company secretary ('nominations must be sent to the secretary' 'the secretary must call a meeting'), without an explicit clause saying there must be a secretary, there does not have to be one. Public companies (plc's) must have a secretary.

If a company does not have a company secretary, anything authorised or required to be sent to the secretary may be sent to the company and anything required to be done by the secretary can be done by the directors or someone authorised by them.   *Companies Act 2006 ss.270,271*

Where the articles require a secretary, the company may wish to amend them [**7.5.3**] to remove the requirement. But even if there is no constitutional obligation to have a secretary, it may be sensible for the governing body to appoint one to ensure that the administrative responsibilities set out in company law and the articles of association are properly carried out.

A secretary has no executive or management responsibilities unless these are explicitly delegated by the governing body. So a secretary cannot, for example, authorise expenditure, borrow money, alter the registers or appoint auditors without the authority of the directors or the company members.

A secretary who attends general meetings has no vote unless he or she is a member of the company, and a secretary who attends meetings of the governing body has no vote unless he or she is also a company director.

Although the secretary, if there is one, may have no say in the company's decisions, he or she is an officer for the purposes of company law [**14.1.1**] and can be held liable in the same way as a director for breach of company law duties [**22.3**].

14.3.1   Who can be company secretary

The secretary, if there is one, is normally appointed by the governing body (the company directors), but the articles of association may require the appointment to be made in another way. Unless the articles specify otherwise the secretary may be a member of the governing body, an employee, the company's accountant or solicitor, a company, or anyone else. Two persons can be appointed as joint secretary. The secretary may be paid, but if the company is charitable and the secretary is a member of the governing body, there may be restrictions [**16.3.2**].

In public companies (plc's), the secretary must be properly qualified and/or have relevant knowledge and experience. This does not apply to private companies. But the directors would be failing in their duty of care to the company [**15.3.4**] if they appoint someone – whether called the secretary or anything else – who does not have the ability to carry out the required tasks, or who does not have access to relevant advice to enable her or him to carry out the tasks.

Appointing the organisation's accountant or solicitor as secretary or to carry out the administrative tasks of company and charity law may seem like a good idea, but someone within the organisation must provide all necessary information to them. The forms and paperwork are not difficult, so it may make more sense and be less expensive to appoint a member of the governing body, senior employee or reliable volunteer to carry out the tasks.

Where under company law or the articles of association something must be done or signed by a director and the company secretary, if there is one, it must be done by two persons. A director who is also secretary cannot in this situation act in both roles simultaneously.

14.3.2   Duties

The company directors are ultimately responsible for ensuring the administrative requirements of company law are complied with, regardless of whether there is a company secretary. In the sections below, the term 'secretary' refers to the company secretary, if there is one, or to any other person who in a company without a secretary is responsible for carrying out the duties.

14.3.2.1   When a company is set up

As soon as a company is registered [**1.5.8**] the secretary must:

- open a **register of members** [**18.5.2**], and if it is not to be kept at the company's registered office, notify Companies House on the appropriate form;

- open a **register of directors and secretaries** and a **register of directors' residential addresses**) [**18.5.4-18.5.6**], and file the appropriate forms with Companies House for any directors who were not named when the company was formed and for any initial directors who are resigning immediately;

- open the relevant **register of charges** [**18.5.11**] if there are any mortgages or debentures, and notify the charges to Companies House;

- display the company's full registered name at the company's **registered office** [**17.1.3**];

- arrange for **printed materials** such as stationery and chequebooks to be produced with the necessary details [**18.1.1**];

- add the same details to the organisation's **website** and the footers used on its outgoing **emails**;

- arrange for safekeeping of the **seal** if there is one [**20.1.3**], registers, minute books and the certificate of incorporation.

There are additional responsibilities in companies limited by shares, which are not covered in this book.

14.3.2.2   Taking over as a company secretary

A company secretary appointed for an existing company, or a person appointed to take on these duties, should obtain from the outgoing postholder:

- the original of the certificate of incorporation and any certificate changing the company's name;

- a copy of the memorandum and articles of association and any amendments;

- the company's register of members, registers of directors and directors' residential addresses, minutes books and other statutory records [**18.5.1**];

- copies of forms for the appointment or resignation of company directors or changes in their details which have been submitted to Companies House;

- copies of other forms which have been submitted;

- contact details for company directors and key staff;

- copies of the company notepaper, cheques, and forms used for invoices, receipts, orders and other financial documents;

- printouts from the company's website and outgoing emails, showing company and (if applicable) charity registration details;

- correspondence files of the previous company secretary or person holding the files;

- the previous year's annual accounts, reports and company return [**54.3**] and, for a charitable company, the previous year's charity return [**54.2.10**];

- an up to date company search [**14.3.2.3**], unless it is absolutely certain the company's documentation at Companies House is completely up to date;

- blank copies of company forms to notify Companies House of changes in directors or their details, if this is done on paper rather than electronically;

- the company seal, if there is one [**20.1.3**].

If any of these items is missing the secretary or person taking on the duties of a secretary should alert the governing body and take action to find or replace the missing items.

The secretary or other person should also:

- if they are company secretary, complete and sign form **AP03** and send it to Companies House within 14 days of being appointed;

- find out when the end of the accounting year (accounting reference date) is, and ensure that the appropriate form has been filed if necessary [**54.3.1**];

- check correspondence and email files and if necessary notify key people of the change of name and any change of address for correspondence;

- if one does not already exist, create a diary with all the key dates (end of financial year, deadline for submitting annual accounts, dates for general and governing body meetings, deadlines for giving notice of general and governing body meetings, etc);

- locate the originals of the certificate of incorporation and any certificates recording a change of name, if these are not to hand;

- find out who the company's accountant (if there is one), auditor and solicitor are, and make introductory contact with them;

- if there is no solicitor, ask the governing body how they expect the secretary or person carrying out these duties to obtain advice on company matters.

14.3.2.3   Company search

A company search provides a company record showing what information has been registered at Companies House. Searches can be done on the Companies House website, in person at Companies House offices [see end of **chapter 1**], by post to Companies House, or through a company registration agent (listed in the Yellow Pages). Companies House charges small fees for the information.

The company record should be compared with the company's registers and documents to ensure that Companies House has an accurate record of all the company's directors, including co-optees, representatives and others who have a vote on the governing body [**13.1.3**]; current name and a current address for all company directors, and for the company secretary if there is one; current registered address for the company; up to date version of the articles of association (memorandum and articles, for companies formed before 1 October 2009), with all amending resolutions included; details of all charges or mortgages on the company's property; and up to date accounts and returns.

If there are discrepancies, the appropriate information and forms must be filed to notify the changes.

It is particularly important for a new secretary to check that annual returns and annual accounts have been filed, as there are penalties for late submission [**54.3.8**, **54.3.11**]. If the company is charitable, the secretary should check that the accounts and return have been sent to the Charity Commission [**54.2.9**, **54.2.10**]. This information is easily obtained, free of charge, from the Companies House and, if applicable, Charity Commission websites.

14.3.2.4   Maintaining the registers

The secretary must ensure the **register of directors** [**18.5.4**] is up to date and includes all required details for all voting members of the governing body. These can be obtained from the copies of the companies form they signed when they became directors, and forms which have been submitted to Companies House to update their details. A new secretary's name and details must be entered in the **register of secretaries** [**18.5.6**]. The **register of directors' residential addresses** [**18.5.5**] must be up to date and must be kept in a way that ensures the information is not disclosed.

The **register of members** [**18.5.2**] and index, if there is one, must be kept up to date. This involves ensuring that:

- the proper procedures have been followed to admit members to the company (for example ensuring that applications have been approved as required under the articles, and that membership decisions have been minuted);

- if there are more than 50 company members, the register is alphabetical or there is an alphabetical index [**18.5.3**];

- the register contains up to date addresses for members;

- the register cannot be altered without proper authority.

If any company members have lapsed, for example by failing to pay subscriptions or no longer qualifying for membership, the secretary should inform the governing body and take steps to remove them from membership. But the date they ceased to be a member cannot be entered without the governing body's authority.

Even if members resign, die or move away their names may not be removed from the register until at least 10 years after they cease to be a member [**18.5.2**].

The register of directors' residential addresses must be kept at the company's registered office. If the other registers are kept at an **inspection place** [**17.1.2**] rather than the registered office, Companies House must be notified on form **AD02** and **AD03**, or if they are being moved from an inspection place to the registered office Companies House must be notified on form **AD04**. Arrangements should be made, if not already in place, to ensure availability of the registers that need to be available for inspection by company members and the public [**18.5**].

14.3.2.5 Disclosure of status

The secretary should know the location of the original certificate of incorporation and any certificates altering the company's name. If the original is lost, a duplicate should be obtained from Companies House.

The secretary should ensure the full name of the company, as it appears on the certificate of incorporation or on any subsequent certificate of name change, appears on all relevant paper and electronic documents, along with all other required information [**18.1.1**]. If the company uses a name other than the registered name, this must also appear on some paper and electronic documents. If the company is a registered charity, additional information about its charitable status must appear on some documents [**18.1.5**]. Other information such as VAT registration and registration with regulatory authorities may also need to be shown.

The secretary must ensure that the full name of the company is displayed at the registered office [**17.1.3**]. If the registered office is not the company's usual address or the secretary's address, the secretary must ensure there are clear and workable arrangements for post to be forwarded as soon as it is received at the registered office.

14.3.2.6 Memorandum and articles of association

The secretary should become familiar with the articles of association, and for companies formed before 1 October 2009 the memorandum of association. In particular the secretary should alert the governing body immediately if there is any possibility that the company's activities might be outside its objects or powers.

If the memorandum or articles have been amended, the secretary should ensure that all amendments were properly passed [**19.7.4**], where necessary the Charity Commission's consent was obtained [**7.5.3**], and proper notice of the amendments, with Charity Commission consent if necessary, was sent to Companies House and a copy of the amended version was sent to the Charity Commission.

If amendments have simply been attached to the memorandum and articles, the secretary should consider having the whole thing retyped. If this is done, a copy of the new version must be sent to Companies House and, for charitable companies, the Charity Commission. It is useful to include a summary of amendments made during the history of the company.

14.3.2.7 Meetings and decision making

For meetings of the governing body (board of directors) and general meetings of the company members [**19.2.3**] the secretary must ensure:

- proper notice is given as required under company law or, if longer, the articles of association [**19.3**];
- decisions at meetings are made with the appropriate type of resolution [**19.7.4**] and with proper voting procedures [**19.8**];
- proper minutes are kept and entered in the minutes book [**18.5.9**, **19.11**];
- all necessary changes are made to the registers after the meeting (for example members' names and the date of admission to membership entered in the register of members, and changes of director entered in the register of directors);
- written resolutions are properly passed [**19.10.2**];
- all necessary information and forms are sent to Companies House, the Charity Commission or other bodies within the required period.

14.3.2.8   Legal information

The secretary can perform a valuable role in helping to ensure that directors are aware of their legal obligations. To do this effectively, the secretary should seek to ensure the company has access to legal advisors with experience not only in company law, but also in charity law if the company is charitable, employment law, property law if applicable, and perhaps also with experience in any specialist field within which the company operates, such as housing or the arts.

A secretary might want to suggest to the company directors that the company asks a suitably experienced solicitor to undertake an annual **compliance review** of the company's affairs, to ensure the company is keeping up with the changing requirements of the law and its governing document is still appropriate.

14.3.3   Vacancy

In a company which is required to have a company secretary, any vacancy must be immediately filled. If the company is not required to have a secretary, the directors should decide whether to appoint a replacement and if not, how to ensure the secretary's tasks are carried out. Details of the retirement and replacement (if any) must be entered in the register of secretaries and notified to Companies House on form **TM02** and **AP03**.

A company secretary may be removed at any time by the body which elected or appointed him or her. If the secretary is an employee, the normal procedures for dismissal [**34.5**] or variation of contract [**26.9**] must be followed.

14.3.4   Liability

The company secretary has personal liability if he or she fails to perform duties required under the Companies Acts. Usually such liability arises only if the default was knowing or deliberate. The company can generally insure against such liability, but if the company is charitable and the secretary is also a member of the governing body, the rules on trustee indemnity insurance apply [**23.2.4**].

14.4   IPS SECRETARY

Although industrial and provident society law does not explicitly state that societies must have a secretary, it requires certain acts to be done by the secretary. The duties are less onerous than those of a company secretary, but are similar.

14.5   CHARITABLE INCORPORATED ORGANISATION SECRETARY

At the time of writing (mid 2009) it was not expected that a charitable incorporated organisation (CIO) would be required to have a secretary. However, the trustees must ensure the work that would be carried out by a secretary is done. The duties of a company secretary [**14.3**] can be adapted for CIOs.

14.6   COMMITTEES AND SUB-COMMITTEES

The term **committee** as used here means a group set up by the members (in a membership organisation) or the governing body to undertake specific tasks. If the governing body is itself called a committee, the group is a **sub-committee**. A governing body may delegate to a committee only if this is allowed by law or the governing document [**15.8**]. Committees are accountable to the body which set them up.

A **standing committee** is one which is permanent, usually set up by the governing document or under standing orders [**7.4.25**]. A committee set up for a specific short-term purpose is sometimes called a **working group** or an **ad hoc** ('for this purpose') committee. A group which sets up a committee may disband it at any time, but a committee set up under the provisions of the governing document can be disbanded only if the governing document allows.

14.6.1   Terms of reference

Committees must act only within the **terms of reference** set by the governing document, standing orders or the body which set up the committee. In relation to the committee's work, the **substantive** terms of reference generally cover the purpose(s) of the committee; the topics, issues or areas of work it is authorised to cover; its tasks; whether it can make decisions about those matters, or can only make proposals or recommendations to the body to which it is accountable; and how often it must report to the body to which it is accountable.

Administrative terms of reference generally include how the committee's members are elected or appointed, how long they serve and how they are removed; how often it must meet, its procedures and similar administrative matters; and how its work is funded, whether it controls a budget for its work, and if not, how expenditure is authorised. Committees must always act within agreed policies and budgets and must properly minute their decisions [**19.11**].

14.6.2   Delegated powers

Decision making powers can be delegated to a committee or individuals only if there is statutory power to do so, or an explicit power in the governing document [**15.8**]. Committee meetings are governed by the governing document and common law [**19.13**]. The body which appointed the committee or delegated to an individual remains liable for their acts and must supervise their work [**15.8.3**].

14.6.3   Management or executive committee

The term **management committee** or **executive committee** often refers to the governing body as a whole. But a governing body may be called something else and may, especially if it is very large, appoint a (sub-)committee called a management or executive committee which has delegated powers to act on behalf of the governing body. This sort of committee usually includes the honorary officers [**14.1.2**], chief executive or other senior employee, and perhaps a small number of other key individuals.

A variation is when the governing body is very small – perhaps a trust with only three or four trustees – and they appoint a larger and more representative executive or management committee with some decision making powers.

14.6.4   Advisory committee

A committee which can only make proposals or recommendations to the main body and has no decision making powers may be called an **advisory board** or **advisory committee**.

14.6.5   Steering committee

A **steering committee** is usually a working party or *ad hoc* group set up to start a new project or organisation. If the project is completely within an organisation, the steering committee is simply an internal committee. If it is a group working together to set up a new organisation, it is in effect an unincorporated association [see **11.3.1** for more about this situation, and the implications for liability].

Typically a steering committee hands over to the first governing body when the organisation is set up. If steering committee members have entered into legal agreements in their own names or in the name of their organisations, it may be necessary to transfer these to the new governing body [**20.4.5, 21.5.1**].

Resources: OFFICERS, COMMITTEES AND SUB-COMMITTEES

See end of **chapter 1**.

Statute law. www.opsi.gov.uk and www.statutelaw.gov.uk.

Much but not all case law. www.bailii.org.

Updates cross-referenced to this book. www.rclh.co.uk.

Chapter 15

DUTIES AND POWERS OF THE GOVERNING BODY

15.1   THE RANGE OF DUTIES

Concerns about mismanagement at the highest levels in the corporate, public and voluntary sectors have led to a growing consensus about what constitutes good governance. Some of this consensus has always been enshrined in trust and charity law, some has been codified in legislation, and some is embodied in voluntary governance codes. Breach of legal duties brings the risk of liability [**chapter 22**]. Breach of good governance practice and non-statutory codes, on the other hand, may bring criticism and impede success, but does not lead to liability.

15.1.1   Statutory and other legal duties

Statutory and other legal duties may arise:

- through particular activities carried out by the organisation such as being an employer, occupying premises, providing services, collecting information about individuals, organising public activities or engaging in fundraising;

- by being registered as a company of any type, charitable incorporated organisation or industrial and provident society [**chapter 3**];
- by being registered as a charity, or by meeting the legal definition of being a charity [**5.2.3**] even if not registered as a charity;
- by being a trust [**2.3**], whether charitable or non-charitable.

Duties as trustees arise from **charity law** and **trust law**. Trustee is defined differently for different aspects of law, so a person may be a trustee in some contexts but not others.

Contractual duties can arise:

- from the organisation's governing document, which in a membership organisation forms a contract between the organisation and its members and/or among the members;
- from legally binding agreements [**chapter 21**] such as contracts of employment, leases, and contracts to purchase or provide goods or services.

Legal compliance requires an understanding of the governing body's legal duties, and in particular the difficult areas where there can be an overlap or incongruity between different statutory duties or between statutory and trustee duties.

Moral obligations may arise because of promises made or a belief that the organisation 'should' do something, even when there is no legal obligation to do so. *Ex gratia* payments [**53.3**] are an example of an organisation fulfilling what it sees as a moral duty.

15.1.2   Frameworks for good governance

Legal duties provide the basic framework for good governance, but must be buttressed by good practice. This depends to a large extent on the nature of the organisation and its values, but the Charity Commission's CC10 *Hallmarks of an effective charity* and CC3 *The essential trustee*, and *Good governance: A code for the voluntary sector*, available from the National Council for Voluntary Organisations provide useful starting points [see end of **chapter 1** for contact details].

15.2   CONFLICT OF INTEREST

A **conflict of interest** exists when a member of a governing body has any interest, duty or obligation which may directly or indirectly conflict with the duty they owe the organisation. These can include where a member of the governing body or a **connected person** [**15.2.5**]:

- has a financial interest in, or stands to gain or lose from, a contract, transaction or other arrangement with the organisation;
- uses the organisation's services or facilities, so stands to gain or lose from decisions about them;
- has a personal obligation, for example, to family members who may benefit from the actions or inaction of the organisation;
- obtains information from the organisation which he or she may wish to use in a way which would or could provide a personal benefit;
- has obligations arising from a role – such as employee or trustee – in another organisation, or from holding a position such as local authority councillor.

In *A guide to conflicts of interest for trustees*, available from the Charity Commission [see end of **chapter 1**], the Commission distinguishes between:

- **direct financial gain or benefit** to the governing body member;
- **indirect financial gain or benefit** to a person closely connected with the governing body member, such as a close relative or business partner;
- **non-financial gain** where the governing body member or a connected person uses the organisation's services or takes part in its activities; and
- **conflict of duties or loyalties**, where a governing body member is 'wearing two hats' and has duties in both roles which conflict with each other [**15.2.3**].

Duties in relation to conflict of interest are different under company law [**15.3**], charity and trust law [**15.6**] and industrial and provident society law [**15.4**], and may be different yet again under the organisation's governing document. Given this complexity, it is not always clear what applies in any particular situation.

Breach of conflict of interest rules could invalidate a transaction, or result in the governing body member(s) being required to repay to the organisation the value of anything paid or provided to a governing body member or a connected person. Legal advice from a specialist will often be necessary.

15.2.1   Pecuniary interest

Financial interest, **gain** or **benefit** apply not only to money, but to anything with a monetary value. This is sometimes called a **pecuniary interest**. A potential gain may arise **directly**, for example where the organisation purchases goods or services from the governing body member or from a business owned by the governing body member, or the governing body member receives goods or services from the organisation free of charge or below cost, such as disability aids, hospice care, nursery places, or anything else provided by the organisation.

15.2.2   Indirect financial benefit and situational conflicts

Most conflict of interest duties apply not only directly to governing body members, but also to situations where a governing body member may receive an **indirect benefit**. Examples of indirect financial benefit include:

- goods or services purchased by the organisation from a person connected to a governing body member [**15.2.5**], such as a close family member or business partner, or from a business in which the governing body member or person connected with them has a financial interest;

- a governing body member who owns property adjacent to the organisation's, whose value could be affected by decisions made by the organisation;

- a governing body member who is an employee of a competitor organisation, whose own job could depend on which organisation gets a grant or contract;

- a governing body member who gets paid work, customers or some other advantage through contacts made or information gained at the organisation.

15.2.3   Conflict of duties or loyalties

The terms **conflict of duties**, **conflict of loyalties** or **duality of interest** are often used to describe situations where the governing body member may not have any kind of financial interest, whether direct or indirect, but is 'wearing two hats' and as a result has conflicting obligations or duties.

Examples of situations that may create loyalties or duties include:

- being an employee or governing body member of an organisation, or of its subsidiary or parent body;

- being a governing body member or employee of another organisation;

- professional, advisory, counselling, patient or client relationships;

- family or couple relationships;

- being connected with a body that provides funding to, competes with, or purchases goods or services from the organisation.

15.2.4   Dealing with conflicts of interest

The obligation to declare, avoid or take other action on conflicts of interest may arise from a statutory obligation, for example under the **Companies Act 2006** [**15.3.6-15.3.8**] and/or **Charities Acts** [**15.2.5.2, 15.2.5.3**], and from common law trustee duties [**15.6.4**]. Regulators such as the Homes and Communities Agency, funders or purchasers of services may require or expect compliance with a code of conduct. The organisation's governing document may include conflict of interest rules. And even where there is no external or constitutional obligation, there may be a personal or organisational desire to comply with the highest standards of best practice.

15.2.4.1 Overlapping duties

With all these potential duties relating to conflict of interest, it is not surprising that there can be overlaps and sometimes conflicts between them, and compliance with one set of duties does not necessarily mean compliance with another.

A typical charitable company, for example, may have provisions in its governing document allowing trustees to be paid for services provided to the company, or may be allowed to make such payments under the **Charities Act 2006** [**16.3.2**]. However, even full compliance with constitutional or Charities Act requirements will not fulfil all of the requirements of company law, which require service contracts with company directors to be kept as part of the company's statutory registers and to be available for inspection or copying by company members [**18.5.7**], and in some circumstances may require the contract to be approved by the company members [**16.3.2**].

Similarly, compliance with company law and even authorisation by company members may still be a breach of a trustee duty, for example if the transaction is one which requires Charity Commission consent.

15.2.4.2 Different duties in different situations

Under company law there is a duty to avoid conflict of interest situations (**situational conflicts**) [**15.3.8**], conflicts arising from transactions between the organisation and a governing body member or connected person (**transactional conflicts**) [**15.3.6**], and conflicts arising from receiving benefits from third parties [**15.3.7**]. However some conflicts can be allowed under the governing document, or can be approved by the unconflicted directors or by company members.

Under charity law there are general rules on conflict of interest [**15.6.4**], but with separate statutory requirements when disposing of charity land to a governing body member or connected person [**61.12.2**], or paying a governing body member or connected person for services provided to the charity [**16.3**]. Governing body members of charitable companies must comply with their duties both as company directors and charity trustees.

When dealing with conflicts of interest it is essential to be aware of the full range of obligations and to ensure compliance with all that apply.

15.2.4.3 Conflict of interest policies and registers

It is good practice for every organisation to set out in a code of conduct or policy how conflicts are managed. This may cover:

- the range of conflicts of interest covered by the policy, perhaps giving examples of each and clarifying that it covers conflict of loyalties as well as financial benefit;
- the legal and other external rules applying to the organisation;
- provisions in the governing document relating to conflict of interest;
- the concept of connected person [**15.2.5**] and whether it differs for different types of conflict of interest;
- the organisation's rules for declaring and recording conflicts of interest at the time of election or appointment to the governing body, and regularly reviewing and updating the declarations;
- the organisation's rules for declaring conflicts of interest when a relevant issue is first discussed, or as soon as the governing body member becomes aware that there is or might be a conflict of interest;
- situations where Charity Commission consent must be sought;
- action required after a declaration of a conflict of interest;
- action required if someone believes a conflict of interest has not been declared.

Sample conflict of interest policies, declaration forms and registers of interests are available on the websites of the National Council for Voluntary Organisations [see end of **chapter 1**] and the Institute of Chartered Secretaries and Administrators [see end of chapter]. These should be adapted to meet the organisation's requirements as a charity and/or company and under its own governing document.

15.2.4.4   Responses to conflict of interest

Policies typically require three levels of response after declaration of a conflict of interest. For a minor conflict, the governing body member should not take part in the decision making process or in discussions relating to it. For a more serious conflict, the governing body member may be required to withdraw from the meeting while the issue is being discussed or decided. For very serious or persistent conflicts of interest, resignation from the governing body – or withdrawal for a period – may be appropriate. Other steps such as confidentiality undertakings may also be appropriate. It is vital that a policy meets not only good practice, with a view to protecting the organisation's reputation, but also the technical requirements that apply.

It is essential to minute the declaration of interest, the steps taken and, where necessary, the approval of the governing body, by formal resolution if required. Where other authorisation is required, for example from the company members [**15.3.8**], a funder, the Charity Commission or another regulator, the fact that this has been obtained should also be minuted.

A policy will often, particularly for companies and/or charities, have to be accompanied by provision in the governing document [**15.3.8.4**].

15.2.4.5   Disinterested quorum

When making decisions, there should be a **disinterested quorum**. A disinterested quorum means that without the member(s) who have a conflict of interest, there are still enough governing body members to form a valid quorum, If there is not a disinterested quorum, the meeting is inquorate in relation to that decision, and a decision cannot be made. If a person who has a conflict of interest does take part in the decision, their vote cannot be not counted.

In some situations, so many governing body members have a conflict of interest that it is not possible to achieve a disinterested quorum. An example is a community nursery where all or most of the governing body are parents with children at the nursery, who stand to gain or lose financially from a decision about fees.

If there are problems in creating disinterested quorums, it may be possible to amend the governing document to allow interested (conflicted) persons to be included in the quorum in some circumstances. For a charity, such amendment would require Charity Commission consent if it allows governing body members who would benefit to participate in decisions, but consent is not required if the amendment is to allow those with a conflict of loyalties [**15.2.3**] to take part.

If the governing document of a charity does not allow conflicted persons to be included in the quorum but without them there is not a quorum, the conflicted governing body members should contact the Charity Commission, who will generally authorise them to take part in the decision provided they act in the interests of the beneficiaries as a whole rather than in their own personal interest. The Commission may also recommend restructuring the governing body so there can be a disinterested quorum in this type of situation.

If the organisation is not charitable, governing body members should take specialist advice about the validity of decisions made in this situation.

These issues are discussed in the Charity Commission's CC24 *Users on board* and *A guide to conflicts of interest for charity trustees*.

15.2.5   Connected persons

The rules on financial gain apply to persons **connected with** governing body members in the same way as to governing body members themselves.

Unfortunately there is no standard definition of what constitutes a **connected person**. Different statutory definitions apply in relation to the duties of company directors [**15.2.5.1**], the duties of charity trustees in relation to remuneration and benefits [**15.2.5.2**], and the duties of charity trustees in land transactions [**15.2.5.3**]. Yet different definitions may be used under trust law [**15.6.4**] or the organisation's governing document [**7.4.9**, **7.4.10**], and the concept of a person 'who shares a common purse' is also used [**15.2.5.4**].

A voluntary organisation may wish to adopt a wider definition of connected person than is legally required. For example, the Companies Act definition treats a director as being connected with a corporate body only if the share or voting control is equivalent to 20% of the total of that organisation. Governing documents of voluntary organisations generally treat people as connected even if they hold a much smaller share, typically more than 1% of the voting rights.

The wide range of potentially connected persons will be difficult to deal with in practice. To ensure comprehensive disclosure, the governing body member would have to list every possible connected person in a register of interests [**15.2.4.3**], and ask all such persons to notify him or her if they become aware of a transaction or arrangement that may cause any risk of any sort of conflict.

15.2.5.1 Connected persons: company law

For the purposes of company law, the following are treated as connected with a company director:

- any members of a director's family, which includes the director's spouse, civil partner or any other person with whom the director lives as a partner in an enduring family relationship (this does not include a grandparent, grandchild, sister, brother, aunt, uncle, nephew or niece); the director's parents, children or stepchildren; and any children or stepchildren aged 18 or over of the director's spouse, civil partner or other partner;
- a body corporate if the director, or the director and any connected person together, directly or indirectly own 20% or more of the nominal value of the share capital, or directly or indirectly control more than 20% of the votes at any general meeting;
- a director acting as trustee of a trust, where the director or connected person is a beneficiary of the trust, or where the trust powers may be exercised for the benefit of the director or connected person (but this does not apply where the trust is for the purposes of an employee share scheme or pension scheme);
- a person acting in his or her capacity as a business partner of the director or a person connected to the director;
- a firm or other body which is a legal person [**3.1.1**] in which the director or a connected person is a partner. *Companies Act 2006 ss.252-255, sch.1*

The Companies Act makes it clear that the rules for some transactions apply not only to directors but also to connected persons. Other parts of the Act refer to transactions in which the director has 'a direct or indirect interest', without explicitly mentioning connected persons. Good practice would be to treat these rules as if they apply to connected persons as well as the director.

15.2.5.2 Connected persons: remuneration of charity trustees

For the rules governing remuneration and the provision of benefits to charity trustees and persons connected with them, a connected person is:

- the trustee's spouse, civil partner, or person living with the trustee as if a spouse or civil partner;
- the trustee's child (including stepchild or illegitimate child), parent, grandchild, grandparent, brother or sister, or the spouse or civil partner of any of these;
- a person carrying on business in partnership with the trustee or with any person listed above;
- an institution controlled by any person falling within any of the above ('control' means that the person can ensure that the organisation does what he or she wishes, which could include a charity's trading company if the charity or a person nominated by the charity is its sole member);
- an institution controlled by two or more persons listed above;
- a body corporate in which any connected person, or two or more connected persons, hold a substantial interest, defined as one-fifth (20%) or more of the share capital or the voting rights. *Charities Act 1993 ss.73A,73B(5), sch.5 para.2-4, amended by Charities Act 2006 s.36, sch.8 para.178*

15.2.5.3 Connected persons: disposal of charity land

Special rules [**61.12.2**] apply where a charity's land (including a lease) is to be sold, leased or otherwise disposed of to a **connected person**, or to a trustee for or nominee of a connected person. For this purpose the definition of connected person is wider than above, and includes:

- a trustee of the charity, or a holding or custodian trustee [**20.4**] for it;
- anyone who has given any land to the charity;
- a child (including stepchild or illegitimate child), parent, grandchild, grandparent, brother or sister of any trustee or donor of land;
- an officer or agent [**14.1**, **20.5**] or an employee of the charity;
- a spouse, civil partner or co-habitee of any person listed above;
- a person carrying on business in partnership with any of the above;
- an institution controlled [**15.2.5.2**] by any person falling within any of the above;
- an institution controlled by two or more persons listed above;
- a body corporate in which any connected person, or two or more connected persons, hold one-fifth or more of the share capital or the voting rights.

Charities Act 1993 s.36(2), sch.5, amended by Charities Act 2006 sch.8 para.178

15.2.5.4 Common purses

Trust and charity law have always been clear that the rules against personal benefit extend to indirect benefit, and use the concepts of 'sharing a common purse' or 'common interest'. Spouses or partners, dependent children and business partners, for example, are all likely to be seen as sharing a common purse.

15.2.5.5 Governing document

The governing document may prohibit some or all payments or benefits not only to members of the governing body, but also to individuals, trusts or other bodies connected to or associated with them. If the organisation is a company or charity and the provisions in the governing document are different from company and/or charity law, the more strict requirement – the requirement that catches the largest number of people – applies in every case. So if a charity's constitution defines a connected person as a company in which a trustee owns more than 1% of the share capital, the constitutional definition would take precedence over the charity law definition of owning more than 20% of the share capital.

15.3 DUTIES OF COMPANY DIRECTORS

The **Companies Act 2006** introduced statutory **general duties** for company directors. These replace the common law **fiduciary duties** [**15.4.1**] that previously applied, but interpretation of the statutory rules will be based on the previous case law. *Companies Act 2006 ss.171-177,182*

Directors of charitable companies and community interest companies have additional duties [**15.6**, **15.3.9**], and in all companies the duties of directors change radically if the company is or will become insolvent [**24.2.3**].

The inter-relation of the general duties of company directors, special duties for charitable and community interest companies, radically different duties in insolvent companies, constitutional provisions and in some cases requirements of regulators, funders or purchasers of services means that the situation can be very complex and legal advice may need to be sought.

Many directors of companies are also members of the company [**12.4.1**]. Their duties as directors do not extend to their role as a company member.

15.3.1 Duty to act within powers

A director must act in accordance with the company's articles (and for companies formed before 1 October 2009, the memorandum) of association, and only use powers for the purposes for which they were conferred. *Companies Act 2006 s.171*

15.3.2   Duty to promote the success of the company

A director must act in a way that he or she considers, in good faith, is most likely to promote the success of the company for the benefit of its members. In commercial companies this means for the benefit of the shareholders. Where the company is set up with the purpose of benefiting people other than or in addition to its members, as most voluntary sector companies are, a director must instead act in good faith in a way most likely to promote the achievement of that purpose.

Companies Act 2006 s.172

In promoting the company's success, the directors must take into account the likely long-term consequences of their decisions; the interests of employees; the need to foster relationships with suppliers, clients and others; the impact of the company's operations on the community and environment; the desirability of maintaining a reputation for high standards of conduct; and where promoting the benefit of the members, the need to act fairly between members of the company. Minutes and other records of directors' decisions should make clear that these factors have, where appropriate, been considered.

If the company is insolvent, the directors' duty ceases to be to the company and is to its creditors (the people to whom it owes money) [**24.2.3**].   *Companies Act 2006 s.172(3); Insolvency Act 1986 s.214*

15.3.3   Duty to exercise independent judgment

A director must exercise independent judgment, but in doing so can act in a way authorised by the company's articles or memorandum, or in accordance with an agreement that restricts the directors' discretion but has been properly entered into by the company. An example of such an agreement might be a funding agreement which obliges the company to undertake, or not to undertake, certain other kinds of activity.   *Companies Act 2006 s.173*

The duty to exercise independent judgment means that a director should not make decisions based on the instructions or direction of a third party. A director who is appointed to the governing body by another body [**13.4.1**], for example a local authority, must act independently, and not as directed by the appointing body or as the director thinks the appointing body would want him or her to act.

15.3.4   Duty to exercise reasonable care, skill and diligence

A director must exercise reasonable care, skill and diligence. The standard required is that which would be expected to be exercised by a reasonably diligent person with the level of skill that might reasonably be expected of a person carrying out the functions carried out by that director.   *Companies Act 2006 s.174*

This applies an objective test, so a higher standard would be expected, for example, from the directors of a large complex company, than from a director of a small, straightforward company, and a director who acts as treasurer would be expected to exercise a higher level of financial skill than one who is not treasurer.

This objective definition of the required standard of competence, based on the nature of the company and the role fulfilled by the directors as a whole and each individual director, means that companies need to think carefully about the implications of appointing directors who are very inexperienced, have learning difficulties or for other reasons lack key knowledge or skills. Their inexperience or disability will not excuse failure to perform to the required level, so companies may need to provide training or other support to ensure all directors can act at a level appropriate to directors of such an organisation.

In addition to the statutory obligation, a director must also use the general knowledge, skill and experience that they actually have. This means, for example, that a director who is a financial specialist would be expected to use those skills, even though such skills would not be expected of other directors and even though the director is not the company's treasurer.

15.3.5   Conflict of interest duties of company directors

The statutory duties of company directors relating to conflict of interest (**Companies Act 2006** ss.175-177) distinguish between situations where:

- the conflict is **transactional**, arising from a **transaction or arrangement with the company** [**15.3.6**], for example where a director or connected person is or could be a supplier of goods or services to the company, or they rent property to or from the company;

- a director or connected person could, because of the director's role in the company, receive **benefits from a third party** [**15.3.7**], such as free gifts from a potential supplier;

- the conflict is **situational** [**15.3.8**]. This does not arise from a transaction with the company, but for example where the director has a **conflict of duties** between their role as a director and some other role or situation; or where information, property or opportunities arising from a person's role as a director are used by the director, a connected person or some other third party with whom the director is involved, for a purpose unrelated to the company itself.

These different types of conflict of interest are subject to varying statutory duties. Some of the duties apply differently to charitable and non-charitable companies, and some apply differently to public companies (plc's) than to private companies [**3.3.1**], which virtually all voluntary sector companies are. This book does not cover duties in public companies.

Directors' conflicts of interest – in particular conflicts of duties – have previously been dealt with less formally. But now they may need to be dealt with under procedures which are explicitly set out in the articles (and for companies formed before 1 October 2009, the memorandum) of association, or they may require approval through a resolution of the company members or directors [**15.3.6.3**, **15.3.8**]. For community interest companies, conflicts of interest must not breach the community benefit rules [**15.3.9**].

All company directors therefore need to fully understand the different types of conflict and the relevant requirements, and need to check the articles (and memorandum if applicable) to see if they contain specific provisions allowing or prohibiting particular conflicts of interest or procedures for dealing with them. Constitutional amendments are likely to be needed, and specialist advice should be sought to ensure the amendments are allowed and are appropriately worded. For charitable companies, Charity Commission consent will be required if the conflict of interest involves benefit to a director or connected person [**7.5.3**].

An example of a provision authorising a **transactional** conflict of interest would be one which allows payment to a trustee for services, rent or interest on a loan. An example of a provision allowing a **situational** conflict would be power for the board to approve a director who is also a governing body member or employee of another organisation. In a charitable company, adding provisions for transactional conflicts would generally need Charity Commission consent [**7.5.3**]; provisions for dealing with situational conflicts would not, unless they allow personal benefit for trustees.

15.3.6 Transactional conflicts

Where a director or connected person [**15.2.5.1**] has or might have an interest in a **transaction or arrangement** with the company, this must nearly always be declared to the other directors [**15.3.6.1**, **15.3.6.2**].

In a *non-charitable* company, some transactions or arrangements between the company and a director or connected person need to be authorised by the members of the company [**15.3.6.3**]. In a *charitable* company some transactions or arrangements with the company need consent from the Charity Commission followed by authorisation by the members of the company [**15.3.6.3**].

15.3.6.1 Declaration of proposed transaction or arrangement

A director who is in any way interested in a proposed transaction or arrangement with a company, whether directly or indirectly, for example through a connected person [**15.2.5.1**], must declare the full extent of that interest to the other directors. This can be done at a meeting of the directors or by notice in writing sent to the directors by post, by hand or electronically. The declaration must be minuted in the minutes of the next directors' meeting. *Companies Act 2006 ss.177,184*

As an alternative to notice of interest in a specific transaction, the director may give a general notice to the directors, stating the nature and extent of his or her interest in a specified body or the nature of his or her connection with a specified person. The declaration must be made before the company enters into a transaction or arrangement to which the conflict of interest applies. It must be given at a meeting of the directors, or the director must take reasonable steps to ensure it is read at the next meeting of the directors after it has been given. Once notice has been given, the director is treated as having an interest in any transaction with that person or body. One form of general notice is an entry in a register of directors' interests, provided the initial entries and updates are all brought to the attention of directors.   *Companies Act 2006 s.185*

If a declaration is or becomes inaccurate or incomplete, the director must make a new declaration.

It is not necessary to declare an interest where the director is not aware of the interest, or is not aware of the proposed transaction or arrangement; the other directors are already aware of the conflict of interest or ought reasonably to be aware of it; the interest is not likely to give rise to a conflict of interest; or it concerns terms of that director's service contract [**16.3.2**] which have already been considered by the directors or a sub-committee of directors.   *Companies Act 2006 s.177(5),(6)*

However, where a director is aware of an actual or potential interest it may be advisable to declare it even if there is not a statutory duty to do so.

15.3.6.2 Declaration of existing transaction or arrangement

There is a separate duty to declare existing transactions, for example where a director joins the board after the transaction has commenced. The declaration must be made as soon as reasonably practical.   *Companies Act 2006 s.182*

15.3.6.3 Transactions in a non-charitable company

Some transactions between the company and a director or person connected with a director [**15.2.5.1**] must be authorised by the company members. These include payments for loss of office [**16.3.2**]; giving a director a service contract for more than two years [**16.3.2**]; a director or connected person acquiring a substantial non-cash asset, such as property, from the company [**16.3.9**]; and loans, guarantees, quasi-loans or credit provided to directors or connected persons [**16.3.8**].   *Companies Act 2006 s.180(2)*

In a *non-charitable* company, a transaction or arrangement with a director or connected person which does not need authorisation by the company members must be disclosed to the company directors, but does not need to be authorised by them.   *Companies Act 2006 s.175(3) 6*

15.3.6.4 Transactions in a charitable company

The transactions requiring approval by company members in a non-charitable company [above] also require such approval in a *charitable* company. However, the members can authorise these only if the type of transaction or the particular transaction is allowed under the articles or memorandum, *and* the Charity Commission gives prior written consent for authorisation by the members.
Companies Act 2006 s.181(3); Charities Act 1993 ss.66,66A, replaced & inserted by Companies Act 2006 s.226

If a transaction or arrangement with a director or connected person does not need authorisation by the company members, it must be approved either by the company members or by the unconflicted directors. They can do this only if the transaction or arrangement is explicitly allowed either by the articles or memorandum, or by an order of the Charity Commission.   *Companies Act 2006 s.181(2)*

15.3.7 Duty not to accept benefits from third parties

Directors must not accept a benefit from a third party given because they are a director or because they do or do not do something as a director. Benefits that cannot reasonably be regarded as likely to give rise to a conflict of interest are not forbidden, for example a company director being taken out to lunch by the solicitors advising the director on an issue. The duty not to accept benefits continues after the person ceases to be a director, in respect of things done or not done while a director. *Companies Act 2006 ss.170(2)(b),176*

15.3.8 Situational conflicts of interest

Section 175 of the **Companies Act 2006** is headed 'duty to avoid conflicts of interest', and requires a director to avoid situations in which he or she has or might have a direct or indirect interest that actually or potentially conflicts with the interests of the company. It is important to recognise that this duty applies even if no actual conflict arises, if there is a situation which might give rise to a conflict, such as a director working for a funder of the organisation. *Companies Act 2006 ss.175,170(2)*

The s.175 duty applies particularly, but not exclusively, to the use or exploitation of any property, information or opportunity, regardless of whether the company itself could or would take advantage of that opportunity. This obligation continues after the person ceases to be a director in respect of exploitation of property, information or opportunities he or she became aware of while a director.

Examples of such conflicts of interest would be where a director learns something through the company and uses it to gain a financial advantage for himself or herself (a form of **indirect benefit, 15.2.2**); or where a director who is also a governing body member or employee of another organisation learns something through the company, such as a new source of funding, which is of interest to the second (a **conflict of duties, 15.2.3**).

15.3.8.1 S.175 and transactions with the company

Crucially, in *non-charitable* companies s.175 **does not apply** where a director or connected person enters into a transaction or arrangement with the company – even though this is what most people think of as the main type of conflict of interest. This type of conflict of interest is covered under other rules [**15.3.6**].

In *charitable* companies, s.175 **does apply** to transactions or arrangements with the company which are not authorised by the articles or memorandum [**15.3.6.4**].

15.3.8.2 Compliance with s.175

A director is not in breach of his or her duty under s.175 to avoid conflict of interest situations if:

- the director could not reasonably regard the situation as likely to give rise to a conflict, for example where he or she is a local authority councillor in an area where the company has never previously operated or even considered operating; *Companies Act 2006 s.175(4)(a)*
- there are provisions for dealing with the particular type of conflict of interest in the memorandum or articles of association (sometimes called **safe harbour** provisions), and these are complied with; *Companies Act 2006 s.180(4)*
- the conflict has been authorised, if allowed, by the company members or directors [**15.3.8.3, 15.3.8.4**]; or
- in a charitable company, the Charity Commission has made an order authorising a transaction or arrangement [**15.3.10**].

The rules requiring explicit authorisation for s.175 conflicts within the memorandum or articles and/or by the company members or directors do not apply to conflicts that existed before 1 October 2008. *Companies Act 2006 (Commencement No.5) Order 2007 [SI 2007/3495] sch.4 para.47(1),(2)*

15.3.8.3 Situational conflicts in non-charitable companies

In a *non-charitable* private company [**3.3.1**] *set up on or after 1 October 2008*, the directors can authorise a situational conflict of interest or conflict of duties provided that nothing in the articles (or for companies set up before 1 October 2009, the memorandum) invalidates such approval or explicitly says that such a conflict is not allowed. For example, if the articles say that a person who is a local authority councillor or officer in an area in which the company operates cannot be a director of the company, the directors cannot approve such a person becoming or remaining a director. *Companies Act 2006 s.175(5)*

188

In a *non-charitable* company *set up before 1 October 2008*, the directors can authorise a situational conflict of interest or duties only if the particular type of conflict of interest is explicitly allowed by the articles or memorandum, or the company members have passed a resolution [**19.7.4**] authorising the directors to approve such conflicts. This could be done by a special resolution amending the memorandum or articles, or an ordinary resolution.

Companies Act 2006
(Commencement No.5) Order 2007 [SI 2007/3495] sch.4 para.47

Authorisation by the directors must comply with procedural requirements [**15.3.8.5**].

15.3.8.4 Situational conflicts in charitable companies

In a *charitable* company, regardless of when it was set up, the directors may only authorise a situational conflict if the articles (or for companies set up before 1 October 2009, the memorandum) explicitly permit authorisation of that particular type of conflict, and the authorisation is given in accordance with those provisions. Unlike non-charitable companies [above], the members of the company cannot simply pass a resolution allowing particular types of conflicts.

Companies Act 2006 s.181(2)

15.3.8.5 Putting the right procedures in place

It is vital for *charitable* companies to amend their articles [**7.5.3**] to include power for conflicts to be dealt with by resolution under ss.175 and 181, including power for the directors to authorise persons to serve as directors even though they have a conflict of duties.

Non-charitable companies formed before 1 October 2008 may need to remove provisions in their memorandum or articles that would prevent the directors authorising conflicts under s.175. In non-charitable companies set up from 1 October 2008, the company members may simply pass a resolution [**19.7.4**] allowing the directors to make such authorisations.

Without these amendments or resolution, the directors will not have power to authorise persons with unavoidable conflicts of duties to serve on the governing body. It will be virtually impossible to create a governing body where no one has an actual or potential conflict of duties.

The directors' authorisation if allowed, or authorisation by the company members if the directors are not allowed, may be for a one-off situation, or for an ongoing situation such as a director of the company also being a director or employee of a subsidiary of the company or a director or employee of another organisation. The authorisation should be subject to suitable conditions such as confidentiality, and withdrawal from the meeting on each occasion when the matter which creates the conflict arises.

Any authorisation by the directors, whether in a charitable or non-charitable company, must be properly made at a quorate meeting, with the conflicted director(s) not counting towards the quorum. The conflicted director(s) must not take part in the decision – or if they do take part, their votes cannot be counted towards the majority needed for authorisation.

Companies Act 2006 s.175(6)

In both charitable and non-charitable companies a decision to authorise a conflict of interest under s.175 cannot be one which requires approval by the members of the company rather than by the directors [**15.3.6.3**].

15.3.9 Additional duties in community interest companies

Directors of community interest companies must comply not only with the duties of all company directors, but also with the community interest principles [**16.3.2**].

15.3.10 Variation of duties by Charity Commission order

The Charity Commission can make an order authorising an act by directors of a charitable company even though it involves a breach of the Companies Act statutory duties.

Charities Act 1993 s.26(5A), inserted by Companies Act 2006 s.181(4)

15.3.11 Consequences of breach of duty

A director who breaches any of the statutory duties may be required to account to the company for any profit or loss or may be unable to enforce the agreement with the company, or the transaction could be set aside by the court. In addition, failure to declare an interest in a transaction is an offence.

An existing company member may seek court consent to bring a **derivative action**, also called a **derivative claim**, on behalf of the company against one or more directors for an actual or proposed breach of duty [**12.10.1**].

15.4 DUTIES OF IPS DIRECTORS

As well as their specific duties under the governing document (the rules), industrial and provident society law and the general law, the courts have imposed on IPS directors two broad duties to their organisation: **fiduciary duty** and **duty of care**. Directors of charitable IPSs have additional duties as charity trustees [**15.6**].

A director in breach of fiduciary duty or duty of care may be sued by the society, or by one or more members of the society.

15.4.1 Fiduciary duty

Fiduciary means 'in good faith', from the Latin *fides* (trust, faith, trustworthiness). Fiduciary duty means that everything done by a director must be done in good faith *(bona fide)*, for the benefit of the organisation as a whole, and for a proper purpose.

In making decisions the directors must:

- act in the best interests of the society as a whole and all its members (in a non-charitable IPS) or all its beneficiaries (in an charitable IPS);
- not misuse the society's property;
- not misuse information for personal gain even after they have left the governing body; and
- not allow their personal interests or the interests of any other body, even one which appointed them as a director, to override the interests of the IPS.

This duty is to the society *as a whole*. Directors must not place the interests of any individual members, employees or beneficiaries, or any group of them, above the interests of the whole society.

This duty changes dramatically when a society is, or is becoming, insolvent. The primary duty immediately becomes to act in the best interests of its creditors (the persons to whom it owes money) and to minimise the potential loss to them [**24.2.3**].

Most directors of an IPS are also ordinary members of it. Their fiduciary duty does not extend to their role *as a member*. When voting as society members at a general meeting, directors may vote however they wish. *North-west Transportation Co Ltd v Beatty [1887] 12 AC 589*

15.4.1.1 Conflict of interest

Governing body members in industrial and provident societies have a duty to avoid conflicts of interest. There is no legal obligation to disclose a conflict of interest unless this is required by the governing document, but it is good practice to do so. If a conflict is not disclosed the society can void (invalidate) a contract with the director or recover from the director the amount paid on the contract.

15.4.1.2 Connected persons

IPS legislation does not define who is a connected person. For charitable IPSs, the Charities Act definitions should be used [**15.2.5.2**, **15.2.5.3**]. For non-charitable IPSs, good practice would be to follow the Companies Act definition [**15.2.5.1**]

15.4.2   Duty of care

Industrial and provident directors have a common law **duty of care** to the IPS. This means that they must act carefully and responsibly, exercising both the knowledge, skill and experience one would objectively expect from someone carrying out their functions, and a degree of skill that may reasonably be expected from a person of their knowledge and experience. A director who does not exercise an appropriate duty of care may be considered negligent, and may face civil claims or be prosecuted under criminal law.   *Re D'Jan of London Ltd [1993] BCC 646*

15.5   CHARITABLE INCORPORATED ORGANISATIONS

Governing body members in a charitable incorporated organisation (CIO) have duties as charity trustees [**15.6**], and a specific duty to exercise their powers and perform their functions in the way they decide, in good faith, would be the most likely to further the purposes of the CIO.   *Charities Act 1993 sch.5B para.9,*
to be inserted by Charities Act 2006 sch.7 [expected April 2010]

A CIO trustee has a duty to exercise such care and skill as is reasonable in the circumstances, taking into account any special knowledge or experience that he or she has or purports to have. Where a trustee is acting as a CIO trustee in the course of a business of profession, he or she has a duty to exercise the special knowledge or experience that would be expected of a person in that business or profession. At the time of writing (mid 2009), consultation had taken place on whether these duties could be altered under the CIO's constitution.
Charities Act 1993 sch.5B para.10, to be inserted by Charities Act 2006 sch.7 [expected April 2010]

A conflict of interest must be declared to the other trustees before a CIO trustee or connected person [**15.2.5.2**] can benefit from any transaction or arrangement with the CIO. At the time of writing, CIO regulations were expected to say that a CIO trustee must not accept benefits from third parties – including a CIO's trading company or other associated body – given because the person is a trustee or because of doing, or not doing, something as a trustee; and that a CIO trustee who would benefit personally, either directly or indirectly, from any transaction or arrangement which the CIO proposes to enter into must not take part in any decision whether to enter into the transaction or arrangement, and must not be counted as part of the quorum for the decision.   *Charities Act 1993 sch.5B para.11,*
to be inserted by Charities Act 2006 sch.7 [expected April 2010]

15.6   DUTIES OF TRUSTEES

Duties as trustees arise under both charity law and trust law. In considering these duties a distinction must be made between:

*   trust law duties and powers that apply only to trustees of organisations set up as trusts [**2.3**], whether charitable or non-charitable (referred to in this section as **trustees**);
*   trust law duties and powers, such as those under the **Trustee Act 2000** [**58.1**], that apply to trustees of all trusts, whether charitable or non-charitable, and to governing body members of charitable associations [**2.2**] and bodies established by royal charter (all referred to in this section as **trustees under the Trustee Act 2000**);
*   charity law duties that apply to governing body members of all charities, regardless of their legal structure and regardless of whether they are registered with the Charity Commission (referred to as **charity trustees**);
*   charity law duties that apply only to governing body members of charities registered with the Charity Commission (**trustees of registered charities**);
*   trust and/or charity law duties that apply to holding or custodian trustees [**20.4**] who hold property on behalf of trusts or charities;
*   trust and/or charity law duties that may arise in many other situations where one or more individuals or a corporate body holds property, money or other assets on behalf of another person or persons, even if there is nothing in writing saying that a trust has been created [see, for example, **48.2.1**].

Because all trustees have been entrusted with managing property or money for beneficiaries or for a charitable purpose, they have a **duty of trust**, the key elements of which are set out below. They will have overlapping duties if they are also company or industrial and provident society directors [**15.3**, **15.4**]. Failure to comply with the relevant trustee duties constitutes a breach of trust for which a trustee can be held personally liable.

Trustees need to meet often enough to exercise their duties properly. The Charity Commission recommends, in CC48 *Charities and meetings*, an absolute minimum of two meetings per year.

15.6.1   Initial duties

Before agreeing to become any type of trustee, the person must disclose any circumstances which might lead to a conflict between personal interest and duties as a trustee. It is good practice to record this in a register of interests which is regularly updated.   *Peyton v Robinson [1823] 25 RR 278*

After being appointed or elected, a trustee has a duty to:

- ensure he or she has been properly appointed or elected;
- understand the organisation's objects and the trustees' powers;
- become familiar with the governing document and other relevant documents;
- ascertain what assets the organisation has and that they are appropriately safeguarded;
- ensure that if necessary, property is properly vested in her or him [**20.4.5**];
- take reasonable steps to find out whether the organisation has been properly managed, and if necessary take steps to put it right. A trustee who does not do this could be held liable for the actions of previous trustees.

15.6.2   Duty to comply with governing document

All trustees, of any type, must act at all times strictly within the objects, powers, rules and administrative provisions set out in the governing document [**chapter 7**]. Action outside the governing document must be authorised by the Charity Commission (if the body is charitable) or the court. In some situations it may be possible to amend the governing document [**7.5**].

15.6.3   Duty to act in the best interests of beneficiaries

All trustees, of any type, must act at all times in the best interests of the trust or charity and all its beneficiaries, both current and future. Where a trustee has a **conflict of loyalties** or **conflict of duties** [**15.2.3**] and is torn between two (or more) different roles, this should be declared, and the decision as to how the conflict was dealt with should be minuted. Trustees who have a conflict of loyalties must make decisions without regard for their own interests and views, and without regard for the views of any individual or body which appointed them. A trustee who does not feel able to comply with this requirement should not take part in the decision.   *Report of the Charity Commissioners 1991, para.41-43*

A local authority or other corporate body which serves as a charity trustee must act in the best interests of the charity, not in accordance with its own policy, as must a person appointed by such a body to serve as a trustee. Guidance is available from the Charity Commission [see end of **chapter 1**] in RR7 *The independence of charities from the state* and OG 56 B2 *Local authorities and trustees*.

15.6.4   Duty to avoid conflict of interest

All trustees have an obligation to avoid conflict of interest [**15.2**] in relation to themselves and persons connected with them [**15.2.5**]. If a trustee's personal interest is likely to conflict with that of the trust or charity this must be disclosed to the other trustees, and the trustee must not take part in any discussion or decision in which he or she has such a conflict. The Charity Commission's *Guide to conflicts of interest for charity trustees* explains conflicts of interest and loyalties and the steps that need to be taken.

15.6.5   Duty to safeguard assets

Under their duty to safeguard the organisation's assets, all trustees, of any type, must:

- ensure the trust or charity receives all sums due to it, for example grants, dividends, rate relief and recovered tax;
- invest prudently [**58.6**];
- take reasonable precautions to safeguard against fraud and dishonesty [**53.1.3**];
- insure its buildings and valuable assets [**23.6**];
- in general, not refuse money, property or other assets offered to a charity unless the governing document gives them the power to disclaim assets or the Charity Commission allows it [**48.3.2**].

Trustees under the **Trustee Act 2000** should make good use of the investment powers granted under that Act [**58.1.2**].

15.6.5.1   Duty to safeguard permanent endowment

One aspect of the duty to safeguard assets is the obligation to safeguard a charity's **permanent endowment** [**58.8.1**].

Charity trustees must ensure that money or property held as permanent endowment is not treated as expendable unless it is allowed to be spent [**58.8.2**]. It must be separately shown in the annual accounts as a capital fund [**54.2.6**], and must not be used, sold or disposed of without the consent of the Charity Commission except where such consent is not required [**24.3.3**, **24.9.1**].

15.6.6   Duty not to profit

Unless the governing document specifies otherwise, a trustee has a duty to serve gratuitously (without payment) and not to make any profit or receive any benefit from the trust unless this is authorised by statute, the governing document, the Charity Commission or the court [see **chapter 16** for more about payments and provision of benefits to trustees].

A trustee or connected person [**15.2.5.2**] who receives an unauthorised payment, profit or benefit could be required to return it to the trust or charity or, if it cannot be returned, the trustee could be required to repay the value.

Special rules apply when a charity sells land to or buys land from a trustee or connected person [**61.12.2**]. Other rules apply to registered social landlords.

15.6.7   Duty of care

A trustee must operate with the standard of care a prudent businessperson would have in managing her or his own affairs.   *Re Luckings Will Trust [1968] 1 WLR 866*

This does not mean that trustees must have detailed technical knowledge, but they must have a general awareness of financial and legal issues and must take proper professional advice when appropriate.

In appointing advisors, nominees and custodians, making investments, acquiring land, delegating to agents or others, or exercising other powers under the **Trustee Act 2000**, the standard required for trustees under the Act is higher [**58.1.2**]. They must exercise such care and skill as is reasonable in the circumstances, having particular regard to any special knowledge or experience the trustee has or holds himself or herself out as having. Where a trustee has special knowledge or skill, a higher level of care is required. Trustees acting in the course of their business or profession must exercise a duty of care in keeping with any special knowledge or experience that it is reasonable to expect of a person acting in the course of that kind of business or profession.   *Trustee Act 2000 s.1*

These duties of care relate only to the trustees' duty to the trust or charity and its beneficiaries. Trustees have other duties of care to employees, people who use its premises, its service users and many others. They may also have a specified duty of care under company, industrial and provident society or charitable incorporated organisation (CIO) law [**15.3.4**, **15.4.2**, **15.5**].

15.6.8 Duty to act personally

Trustees of any type must act personally unless delegation is allowed by statute or explicitly authorised in the governing document [**15.8**]. Failure to attend meetings or to participate in decisions about the trust could constitute a breach of the duty of care.

15.6.9 Duty to act collectively

In making decisions, trustees must act as a group. An individual trustee or a minority group of trustees may not make decisions or take action unless they are authorised to do so by the trustees as a body. This includes 'chair's action' or other decisions or actions by individual officers [**14.2.1**].

Trustees' decisions may be made by a majority vote unless the governing document specifies that they must be unanimous.

Provided the governing document allows delegation to committees [**15.8.2**] these may be set up. They must report to the trustees who are not on the committee at the earliest opportunity. If the governing document does not allow committees they may be set up, but can only make recommendations, not decisions.

15.6.10 Duty to keep accounts

All trustees have an obligation to keep proper financial records [**53.1.1**]. All charities must prepare annual accounts, have them examined or audited if this is required under the **Charities Act 1993** or other legislation or by funders or the governing document, and make them available to the public [**chapter 54**].

15.6.11 Duties when investing

When investing, all trustees must comply with the charity's governing document and any statutory requirements [**chapter 58**].

Trustees under the **Trustee Act 2000** must comply with the Act when exercising powers under it, including powers of investment [**58.1**]. They must exercise their statutory duty of care [**58.1.2**], and ensure investments are suitable. Proper advice must be sought before investing unless the trustees conclude that it is unnecessary or inappropriate to obtain such advice.   *Trustee Act 2000 ss.3-5*

15.6.12 Statutory duties

Charity trustees must ensure that the charity is registered if it is required to be [**8.1**], and that they and their charity comply with the Charities Acts and all legislation relevant to its work and activities.

15.7 DUTIES OF COMMITTEE MEMBERS OF AN ASSOCIATION

If an unincorporated association is set up exclusively for charitable purposes [**5.2**] and operates for the benefit of the public it is a charity. The members of its governing body are charity trustees and have all the duties of charity trustees, and are also trustees for the purposes of the **Trustee Act 2000** [**15.6**].

If it is set up for non-charitable purposes, the members of its governing body have fiduciary duties, a duty not to misuse powers and a duty of care comparable to the common law and case law duties of industrial and provident society directors [**15.4**]. Apart from this their duties are determined by their governing document.

15.8 DELEGATION

15.8.1 'A delegate may not delegate'

Governing body members act not on their own behalf, but in a company or industrial and provident society, on behalf of the company or IPS as a corporate body and its members; or in a membership association, on behalf of the members.

Thus governing body members in membership organisations, as persons to whom duties and powers have been delegated, are already delegates. As such they are subject to the basic principle *'delegatus non potest delegare'* – a person to whom any responsibility has been delegated may not delegate it further, unless this is explicitly authorised by statute or by whoever did the initial delegating.

It follows that a governing body in an incorporated body or association may delegate duties, powers and functions to committees, individual members of the governing body, employees or others only if they are allowed to do so by the governing document or statute, by the members in a membership organisation, or by the Charity Commission in a charity. It may be possible to alter the governing document [**7.5**] to allow delegation to allow delegation.

15.8.2 Delegation by trustees

Specific rules apply to trustees in charitable and non-charitable trusts and charitable associations. Like other governing body members, these trustees 'have no right to shift their duty on to other persons' and may delegate only if they have explicit authorisation to do so. Such authorisation may come from powers of delegation in the governing document [**7.4.15**], statute [**20.4**, **20.5**], or a Charity Commission scheme or order [**4.5.4**, **4.5.5**].

Turner v Corney [1841] 5 Beav 515;
Pilkington v Inland Revenue Commissioners [1964] AC 612

15.8.2.1 What can be delegated

Under the **Trustee Act 2000** [**20.4**, **20.5**], trustees of charitable associations and trusts may delegate carrying out decisions taken by the trustees; functions relating to investment and land management; functions relating to fundraising, other than carrying on a trade which is integral to the charity's primary purpose [**56.4.5**]; and other functions which may be (but at the time of writing had not been) set out in orders made by the home secretary. There are rules about who these functions can be delegated to.

Trustee Act 2000 s.11(3)

In relation to functions not covered by the **Trustee Act**, trustees of charitable trusts and associations may delegate to one trustee or to committees made up of trustees, provided all decisions are made by a majority of the trustee body. They may also authorise two or more trustees to sign deeds, contracts or other documents on behalf of all the trustees.

Re Whitely [1910] 1 Ch 600; Charities Act 1993 s.82

15.8.2.2 Delegation by an individual trustee

Unless it is prevented or restricted by the governing document, individual trustees in a charitable or non-charitable trust or charitable association have a statutory right to delegate virtually all of their powers, including their decision making power, by power of attorney. They can do this for up to 12 months.

Trustee Act 1925 s.25, amended by Trustee Delegation Act 1999 s.5

Under this procedure, the power of attorney must be worded as specified in the **Trustee Delegation Act 1999** s.5, and must be executed as a deed [**20.3**]. Before or within seven days after giving power of attorney, the trustee must give notice in writing to every other trustee and anyone with power to appoint trustees, setting out the date the power comes into effect, its duration, what is being delegated, who it is delegated to, and the reason for the delegation. The trustee remains personally liable for anything done, or not done, by the person to whom he or she has delegated.

Such delegation may be by a **lasting power of attorney** [**21.1.2**].

15.8.3 Effective delegation

When duties, powers or tasks are delegated to individual members of the governing body, committees whether permanent or short-term, outside professionals or employees, the governing body generally remains primarily responsible for decisions and actions taken by the delegates. The members of the governing body should:

- where applicable, ensure they comply with their statutory duty of care under the **Trustee Act 2000** [**58.1.2**];

- ensure all decisions about delegation are properly made and minuted;
- be clear whether what is being delegated is the right to *make decisions*, the right to *make recommendations* to the governing body, or the right to *take action* within the scope of decisions made by the governing body;
- ensure that the limits to the delegation are clear;
- exercise reasonable supervision over any individuals or groups acting on their behalf;
- ensure that committees have clear terms of reference and employees have up to date job descriptions;
- ensure that all decisions and actions are within policies and budgets approved by the governing body;
- require all decisions and actions to be fully and promptly reported to the governing body;
- retain the right to revoke the delegation.

Governing body members must also supervise any outsiders who are appointed to undertake specific functions on behalf of the governing body. Governing body members remain liable for any losses to the organisation arising from the acts of those persons unless the governing document provides otherwise or they have been appointed under the provisions of the **Trustee Act 2000 [20.5]**.

Any governing body, even one which does not have powers of delegation, can appoint individuals to collect information and make recommendations to the governing body, provided the final decision clearly rests with the governing body.

Although primary liability remains with the governing body, case law makes it clear that where a properly selected employee causes loss to the organisation, the members of the governing body are unlikely to be required to make good the loss.

15.9 POWERS OF THE GOVERNING BODY

Powers are what give the organisation, its members or its governing body the right to take certain actions in order to achieve the organisation's objects [**5.1** and **7.4.3-7.4.8**]. Powers must generally be explicitly granted in statute or the governing document, although some may be implied. The first requirement for governing body members is therefore to read the governing document and understand the powers outlined there and who has the right to exercise them.

Most governing documents in membership organisations give the governing body power to manage the organisation on behalf of the members. But most governing documents limit this power by saying that certain actions must be done by the organisation's members. Where it is not clear whether a specific power rests with the membership as a whole or with the governing body, legal advice may be needed to clarify the situation.

The governing body operates *as a body*. Individual governing body members – including the chairperson – can act on its behalf only if they have been explicitly authorised to do so by the governing document or by a decision of the governing body or the organisation's members. An unauthorised action taken by an individual is *ultra vires* unless it is subsequently properly ratified.

Resources: DUTIES AND POWERS OF THE GOVERNING BODY

See end of **chapter 1**.

Institute of Chartered Secretaries and Administrators: www.icsa.org.uk, 020 7580 4741, info@icsa.co.uk.

Statute law. www.opsi.gov.uk and www.statutelaw.gov.uk.

Much but not all case law. www.bailii.org.

Updates cross-referenced to this book. www.rclh.co.uk.

Chapter 16
RESTRICTIONS ON PAYMENTS AND BENEFITS

16.1 RESTRICTIONS ON PAYMENTS AND BENEFITS

Common law and in some cases statute law and an organisation's governing document dictate what sort of payments can be made or benefits provided to members of an organisation or its governing body. The rules may cover:

- **reimbursement** for out of pocket expenses;
- **remuneration** for services provided to the organisation;
- **salary** or wages as an employee of the organisation;
- **payment** for goods provided to an organisation, rent on property, interest on a loan or any other transaction from or to the organisation;
- **dividends** on profits earned by an organisation with shareholders;
- being a user of the organisation's **services** or activities or receiving a benefit, such as a scholarship or accommodation, as a beneficiary of the organisation;
- getting **preferential treatment** or benefiting in other ways;
- benefiting indirectly through a closely linked person or company, or a **connected person** being remunerated by or benefiting from the organisation;
- benefiting from **information** obtained as a member of the governing body.

Some payments which are called 'reimbursement for expenses' are in fact remuneration and must be treated as such [**16.1.4.2, 16.3.1**].

16.1.1 Initial considerations

In some circumstances payments or benefits are explicitly allowed; in others they are prohibited; in others they are allowed only to certain people, and/or if certain criteria are met or authorisation obtained. It is important to be aware of the relevant provisions of each organisation's governing document, as well as the requirements of charity, company, community interest company and/or industrial and provident society law if applicable.

Even where a payment or benefit is permissible under charity, company or IPS law and/or the governing document, it is still subject to rules governing the management of conflict of interest, will need to be declared and may need to be approved [**15.2**, **15.3.5**, **15.4.1**, **15.6.4**, **15.6.6**].

For charities, if a payment or benefit is outside what is allowed by the governing document or the provisions of charity law [**16.3.2.2**], the Charity Commission may make an order [**4.5.4**] authorising the payment.

As well as the legal issues, reputational issues may arise in making payments to governing body members or others connected with the organisation.

16.1.2 Payments and benefits to connected persons

Most applicable company and charity law rules apply not only to governing body members, but to persons connected with them [**15.2.5**]. Unfortunately, company and charity law define **connected person** differently – and even within charity law there are different definitions for different purposes. The governing document, funders/purchasers of services, or the organisation's policies may then add even more connected persons to the statutory definitions. It is essential to understand which rules apply in which circumstances.

Both charity and company law require disclosure of transactions with governing body members and connected persons in annual reports [**54.2.8**, **54.3.6**]. For other organisations where it is not a statutory requirement, it is good practice to ensure full disclosure of transactions with any person with any connection with a member of the governing body. Key tools in this process will be codes of conduct, registers of interests, and declaration of interests at meetings [**15.2.4**].

16.1.3 Documentation for expenses

Vouchers (receipts, mileage records or other documentation) should always be provided by anyone claiming expenses unless it is genuinely impossible to do so. These should be adequate to show that the expenditure was genuinely incurred, necessary and properly authorised. Minutes should be kept of all decisions authorising reimbursement, especially for unusual expenses.

16.1.4 Tax, national insurance and employment rights

16.1.4.1 Genuine reimbursement only

Where a member of the organisation or its governing body receives no payment other than allowed reimbursement, the rules on tax and similar issues are generally the same as for volunteers [**39.2**]. Reimbursement for genuine expenditure necessary for the work is not subject to income tax or national insurance, should not create an entitlement to minimum wage or other employment rights, and should not affect eligibility for state benefits.

16.1.4.2 Payments other than genuine reimbursement

Some payments which are called 'expenses' are actually taxable income and may be **remuneration** rather than reimbursement. Anyone who is remunerated by an organisation, receives reimbursement which is not allowed free of tax by HM Revenue and Customs (HMRC), or receives other taxable income may be liable to income tax through PAYE [**30.4**] or self assessment [**38.3.1**], and may be entitled to minimum wage [**30.2.1**] and other employment rights. Some state benefits, may be affected by remuneration or other taxable income [**39.11**].

16.2   MEMBERS OF THE ORGANISATION

The governing documents of most membership organisations – including companies, industrial and provident societies, charitable incorporated organisations and unincorporated associations – contain restrictions or prohibitions on the distribution of profits, surplus or other assets to members of the organisation. Such restrictions may also be imposed by charity law, or the law relating to community interest companies or certain industrial and provident societies.

For charitable companies, prior Charity Commission consent is required for any amendment to the company's governing document to allow payment or other benefit to company members or persons connected with them [**15.2.5**].

Charities Act 1993 s.64, amended by Charities Act 2006 s.31

16.2.1   Reimbursement of expenses

Ordinary members of a membership organisation – those who are not members of the governing body – do not have a statutory right to be reimbursed for expenses incurred on behalf of the organisation, but neither is there any prohibition on it. If the governing document prohibits payments to members, any reimbursement must be limited to genuine out of pocket expenditure.

16.2.2   Distribution of surplus or profit

16.2.2.1   Charities

A charitable membership organisation cannot distribute or pay its profits or surplus to its members, but this does not prevent members receiving charitable benefits whose costs are covered by the profit or surplus. For example a charitable nursery with parents as members can use its surplus to reduce fees, thus providing a benefit for the members, but could not pay the cash to its members. More information is in Charity Commission CC24 *Users on board: Beneficiaries who become trustees* and CC11 *Trustee expenses and payments*.

16.2.2.2   Community interest companies

A community interest company registered as a company limited by shares may pay dividends to its members (shareholders). Its governing document may allow dividend payments only to organisations which are prohibited from distributing their assets, or to any shareholder but with the dividends subject to a cap set by the CIC regulator. Information about CIC dividends is available from the CIC regulator [see end of **chapter 1**].

16.2.2.3   Prescribed community benefit societies

Prescribed community benefit industrial and provident societies [**3.5.2**], have a constitutional prohibition on the distribution of assets and must use them for the purposes of the organisation.

16.2.2.4   Other non-charities

The governing document of many non-charitable organisations prohibits distribution or payment of surplus or profit to members. Where there are no such restrictions, a non-charitable organisation which is not a CIC or prescribed community benefit society may distribute its assets among its members or in any other way agreed by the members or the governing body. This is subject to any agreement with funders or others for the use, return or disposal of funds or other assets.

16.2.3   Payment for goods or services and provision of benefits

Ordinary members of an organisation who are not on its governing body may be paid for goods or services provided to the organisation or receive benefits from it, unless this is prohibited by the governing document. If the member is on the governing body, the rules on payments for governing body members [**16.3**] apply.

16.3   GOVERNING BODY MEMBERS

The rules on benefits and payments to members of governing bodies and persons connected with them [**15.2.5**] arise from overlapping sources. Such sources always include the organisation's governing document, and may also include the law relating to trusts, charities, community interest companies, other companies, and/or industrial and provident societies. Further rules may arise from obligations imposed by regulators such as the Homes and Communities Agency; the terms of gifts, grants or contracts; or internal rules or codes of conduct. It is vital that all the applicable requirements are considered before providing any payment or benefit to a governing body member, especially where there are conflicts or overlaps between the different rules.

Most of the rules relate to **conflict of interest** [**15.2**]. These must be understood and carefully followed before any payment or benefit is provided to a governing body member or **connected person** [**16.1.2**].

One of the basic principles of trust law which applies to all charities is that charity trustees or persons connected with them must not profit or benefit unless this is explicitly allowed under the terms of the governing document or statute law, or authorised in some other way [**15.6.6**], generally by the Charity Commission. These rules are explained in more detail in CC11 *Trustee expenses and payments*, available from the Commission. The Commission takes unauthorised benefits very seriously.   *Re French Protestant Hospital [1951] 1 All ER 938; Charities Act 1993 s.64*

Even where payments or benefits are permitted, the governing body must consider whether they are prudent and advantageous to the organisation, and whether there are risks of VAT issues or reputational, governance or management problems, for example if some people are paid and others are not.

The minutes should show the steps taken to comply with the rules in the governing document, statutory requirements under company, charity or other law, or the requirements in any code of conduct. Typically these require that the person concerned declares their interest in the decision, is not present for the discussion and does not take part in the decision [**15.2.4**].

A governing body member or connected person who receives an improper payment or benefit may have to repay to the organisation all the money received or any element of profit in it, or the value of non-financial benefits.

A company or charity which makes any payment, including reimbursement of expenses, or provides any material benefit to its governing body members may need to disclose these in the notes to its annual accounts [**54.2.8**, **54.3.6**]. Even where there is no statutory obligation to disclose this, it is good practice to do so.

16.3.1   Reimbursement of expenses

Reimbursement, where allowed, can be only for expenditure actually incurred by the person in carrying out duties for the organisation. Expenditure which was not actually incurred ('The bus fare would have been £2 but I got a lift') or loss of income ('I had to take unpaid time off work in order to attend this committee meeting, so am out of pocket') are not covered by the reimbursement rules. Such payments come under the rules on remuneration [**16.3.2**, **16.3.3**].

16.3.1.1   Unincorporated charities

Trustees of all trusts and charitable associations, as well as holding or custodian trustees [**20.4**], have a statutory right to be reimbursed for expenses genuinely incurred in serving as a trustee and for other costs properly incurred in administering the organisation, unless this is prevented by the governing document. Expenditure which has not been authorised by the trustees cannot be reimbursed unless it is subsequently approved by them.   *Trustee Act 2000 s.31*

16.3.1.2   Non-charitable associations

Governing body members in non-charitable associations do not have a right to reimbursement unless it is explicit in the governing document or has been approved by the members of the organisation.

16.3.1.3 Companies

The articles of association (or memorandum, for companies formed before 1 October 2009) do not need to authorise repayment of genuine expenses necessarily incurred by a company governing body member in connection with the company's business, but it is commonly included.

There is a statutory right for a company to make a loan to a company director to cover expenses incurred, or to be incurred, in carrying out duties for the company. *Companies Act 2006 s.204*

Where the costs incurred by the governing body member are for defending proceedings relating to the company, the governing document can and generally does provide for an indemnity [**22.7.8**]. The company may also, under strict conditions, make loans to a governing body member to cover the cost of defending proceedings or seeking relief from liability. *Companies Act 2006 ss.205,206*

16.3.1.4 Charitable incorporated organisations

Governing body members of charitable incorporated organisations (CIOs) have a statutory right to be reimbursed for expenses they incur in carrying out their duties. *Charities Act 1993 sch.5B para.12, to be inserted by Charities Act 2006 sch.7 [expected April 2010]*

16.3.1.5 Industrial and provident societies

The rules of an industrial and provident society must provide for the right of governing body members to be reimbursed for expenses. *Industrial & Provident Societies Act 1965 sch.1*

16.3.2 Remuneration for services not as a governing body member or employee

Where an organisation is allowed to make payments to its governing body members for work done for the organisation, different rules are likely to apply to payment for serving as a member of the governing body [**16.3.3**], serving as an employee [**16.4**], or providing services in other situations [this section].

16.3.2.1 Governing document

Governing documents often contain provisions allowing payments to governing body members in specified professions, such as accountants and solicitors, for professional services to the organisation. These provisions generally apply only to specific 'professional' work, not work related to running the organisation.

Some governing documents may include wider provision, allowing a member of the governing body or connected person to be paid for any services provided to the organisation, but not for serving as a trustee or employee. This is often subject to safeguards, such as no more than a specified proportion of the governing body members receiving such payment at any one time or during any one year.

16.3.2.2 Trusts and charitable associations

Trustees in charitable and non-charitable trusts and in charitable associations, including holding or custodian trustees [**20.4**], who are solicitors may hire their business partner(s) to undertake professional work for the trust, and the partner may then be paid. It must be clear that the partner, not the firm, is being hired, and any payment from the charity must be to the partner and not to the firm. *Clack v Carlon [1861] 30 LJ Ch 639; Re Gates [1933] Ch 913*

16.3.2.3 All charities

Guidance on remuneration to charity trustees is set out in Charity Commission booklet CC11 *Trustee expenses and payments* [see end of **chapter 1**].

Under the **Charities Act 2006**, a charity trustee or person connected with a trustee (a **relevant person**, **15.2.5**) can be remunerated for services provided to the charity – but not for services as a trustee or as an employee – provided:

- nothing in the governing document expressly forbids such payment;
- the trustees have considered the Charity Commission's guidance on trustee payments;

- the trustees (excluding the trustee who would be paid or is connected to the person or business who would be paid) are satisfied that it is in the best interest of the charity, and agree the amount or a maximum amount to be paid;

- the amount or maximum payment is reasonable and set out in an agreement; and

- only a minority of the trustees are at any time entitled – either directly or through connected persons – to remuneration under such agreements or other arrangements. *Charities Act 1993 ss.73A-73C, inserted by Charities Act 2006 ss.36,37*

The relevant trustees are disqualified from acting as a trustee in relation to decisions or other matters about the agreement. The Charity Commission can require the trustee or connected person to repay remuneration or the value of any benefit in kind where this disqualification rule has not been followed.

The rules on declaring conflicts of interest [**15.6.4**] must be followed, and charitable companies must follow the rules for transactions with directors [**16.3.2.5**].

16.3.2.4 Charitable incorporated organisations

Charitable incorporated organisations are subject to the rules relating to charities [**16.3.2.3**].

16.3.2.5 Companies

The governing document of *non-charitable* companies, including community interest companies, generally allows directors to be paid for services provided to the company. Such payments must comply with the rules on transactions with company directors [**15.3.6**] but do not generally need authorisation by the company directors or members unless the contract is for more than two years.

Governing documents of *charitable* companies traditionally prohibited such payments, but with Charity Commission consent can be amended [**7.5.3**] to take advantage of the Charities Act 2006 provisions on paying governing body members for services other than as a governing body member or employee [**16.3.2.3**]. Payments must be approved by the directors under the Companies Act provisions for charitable companies [**15.3.6**] or procedures in the governing document, and must comply with the rules for all charities using these provisions [**16.3.2.3**].

In all companies the rules on payments to directors also apply to connected persons [**15.2.5**], and the directors must comply with the rules on conflict of interest [**15.3.5**]. In a community interest company, any payment to a director must be reasonable [**16.3.2.6**].

If company directors are paid for their work for the company – whether as directors, employees or in any other capacity – a copy of their service contract or a memorandum setting out the terms of their remuneration must be kept and must be open to company members [**18.5.7**].

A resolution by the company members is required if a company wants to give a director a contract of employment or contract to provide services for two years or more, which cannot be terminated by the company by giving notice or can be terminated only in specific circumstances. Approval by company members is also required for any payment to compensate a director or connected person for loss of their position as a director or any other paid position with the company, including a transfer of undertaking [**29.7**], unless such payment is no more than £200. Members of charitable companies may approve these transactions only if they are allowed by the governing document *and* approved by the Charity Commission.
Companies Act 2006 ss.188,215-222; Charities Act 1993 ss.66,66A, inserted by Companies Act 2006 s.226

16.3.2.6 Community interest companies

A community interest company's governing document will say that any decision to pay a director for services to the CIC must be approved by the CIC's members or the directors. If there is no provision for payment in the governing document, advice should be sought from the CIC regulator [see end of **chapter 1**].

All payments to CIC directors must comply with the **community interest test** and the **asset lock** [**3.4**]. Unreasonably high payments are unlikely to comply, and could be challenged by the CIC regulator or the CIC's members.

16.3.2.7   Industrial and provident societies

Industrial and provident society rules will include any restrictions on payments to governing body members. Charitable IPSs must comply with the rules for charities [**16.3.2.3**] even if they are not registered with the Charity Commission.

16.3.2.8   Non-charitable associations

Non-charitable associations must comply with any restrictions in their governing document. If payments to governing body members are prohibited, the organisation may be able to amend its governing document to allow it [**7.5.1**].

16.3.3   Payment for serving as a governing body member

16.3.3.1   Non-charities

For non-charities, the rules on payment for serving as governing body members are the same as payment for providing other types of services to the organisation [**16.3.2.5-16.3.2.8**].

16.3.3.2   New charities

New charities may be registered with the power to pay trustees for serving as trustees, provided the governing document limits the remuneration to a reasonable amount. The charity's founders will need to convince the Charity Commission that there is good reason for including this in the governing document.

16.3.3.3   Existing charities

An existing charity which does not have an explicit power in the governing document to pay trustees for serving as trustees cannot do so, nor is this covered by the Charities Act provisions on paying trustees for services [**16.3.2.3**]. To pay trustees for serving as trustees, the charity must get Charity Commission authorisation. When deciding whether to allow this, the Commission considers the size and complexity of the charity, whether appropriate measures exist to manage the conflict of interest, whether the trustees need specialist skills not available through staff or external advisors, the existence of objective methods for fixing proper remuneration, and whether people are excluded from trusteeship because of their economic circumstances.

Charitable companies with power to pay governing body members must comply with the company law rules on authorisation by the company directors and/or members and keeping copies of service contracts [**16.3.2.5**].

16.3.4   Payment from an associated body

Charity trustees who are also members of the governing body of a subsidiary non-charitable company [**51.5.1**] and are paid a fee as directors of that company may keep the fee if the governing document *of the charity* explicitly allows them to. If it does not, they may apply to the Charity Commission for authorisation to keep the fee, or must pay it to the charity. Consent to keep the fee is likely to be given only if evidence is given that from the charity's point of view it is necessary that the trustees should be directors of the subsidiary, they should be paid for their services in that capacity, the level of pay is reasonable for the services they actually provide, and the work cannot be done by someone who is not a trustee.

Payment for other services from a subsidiary to a trustee of a parent charity would be likely to violate the rule against indirect benefit for trustees. The Charity Commission's advice should be sought before any such payment is made.

16.3.5   Payment for goods

A charity must not purchase goods from a charity trustee, a holding or custodian trustee for the charity, a business or person connected with a trustee [**15.2.5**] or a business in which a trustee owns shares unless the governing document or the Charity Commission authorises such transactions, or the goods are incidental to the provision of permitted services [**16.3.2**].

In a company, whether charitable or non-charitable, purchases from company directors or connected persons must comply with company law rules [**16.3.2.5**].

Organisations which are neither charities nor companies are not subject to restrictions on purchasing goods from governing body members or persons connected with them unless these are included in the governing document.

16.3.6 Purchases by governing body members

Some governing documents impose, for purchases of goods or services **by** governing body members from the organisation, the same rules as for purchases of goods or services by the organisation **from** a governing body member. Even where this is not the case, the rules on conflict of interest [**15.3.5**, **15.6.4**] apply.

Discounts and preferential treatment should not be offered or given to governing body members or connected persons [**15.2.5**].

16.3.7 Rent

A charity trustee, holding or custodian trustee or connected person [**15.2.5**] may be paid rent by their charity only if the governing document or Charity Commission authorises this. The rent must be 'reasonable'. If there is any doubt about what is reasonable, the governing body should take and record independent valuation advice.

The payment of rent to company directors and connected persons is subject to the rules on conflict of interest [**15.3.5**] and transactions with the company [**15.3.6**]. Independent valuation advice should be obtained.

Organisations which are neither charities nor companies are not subject to restrictions on paying rent to governing body members or persons connected with them unless these are included in the governing document.

16.3.8 Loans

16.3.8.1 Loans to the organisation

There is no restriction on a governing body member making an interest-free loan to their organisation, but rules apply to loans on which interest must be paid.

In charities, interest on a loan may be paid to a trustee or connected person [**15.2.5**] only if this is authorised by the governing document or the Charity Commission. Governing documents which allow payment of interest to governing body members usually specify the maximum level of the interest. If the amount is specified by reference to a rate at a bank which is now defunct, the comparable business rate at its successor bank should be used. The Bank of England (020 7601 4878, enquiries@bankofengland.co.uk) can advise. If the charity is a company, the rules on directors' transactions with the company apply [**15.3.6**].

Non-charitable companies may pay interest on a loan to a director or connected person if the Companies Act rules on transactions with directors [**15.3.6**] are complied with, and there is no prohibition in the governing document. If the organisation is a community interest company, the rules on reasonableness and the asset lock must not be breached [**16.3.2.6**].

All details of the loan arrangement should be put in writing at the time the loan is made.

16.3.8.2 Loans from the organisation

A charity which is not a company may make a loan to a governing body member only if it is authorised by the governing document or the Charity Commission.

A company can generally make loans or quasi-loans (a loan that someone other than the borrower agrees to repay) to directors of the company or its holding company only if this is allowed by its governing document. Loans to a director over a total of £10,000, or over £50,000 if the loan is to enable the director to cover expenses properly incurred for the purposes of the company or for performing her or his duties as a director, must be approved by the company members.

Companies Act 2006 ss.197-214

In a *charitable* company, any loan to a director or connected person that does not require company members' approval must be authorised by the governing document or Charity Commission. A loan that requires members' approval must be authorised by both the governing document and the Charity Commission.

Charities Act 1993 ss.66-66A, inserted by Companies Act 2006 s.226

Members' approval is not required for a loan to enable a director to defend proceedings relating to alleged negligence, default, breach of duty or breach of trust. This allows companies with properly worded governing documents to assist directors in defending themselves in these circumstances.   *Companies Act 2006 ss.189,190*

16.3.9   Land and assets

When a company director or person connected with a director [15.2.5] acquires land or substantial non-cash assets from a company, or when a company acquires them from a director or connected person, the transaction must be approved by the company members. Substantial in this context means the asset's value exceeds 10% of the asset value of the company and is more than £5,000, or exceeds £100,000. These provisions are buttressed by complex further provisions and advice should be sought.   *Companies Act 2006 ss.190,191*

Special provisions also apply when a charity, regardless of whether it is a company or not, is selling land or giving a tenancy or lease to a trustee of the charity or to a person connected with a trustee [61.12].   *Charities Act 1993 s.36*

A charity which wishes to purchase land or other assets from a trustee or former trustee will generally be prevented from doing so by the rules against trustee benefit, and should take advice from the Charity Commission.

16.3.10   Other benefits

Charity trustees are not permitted to benefit from their charity in any other way, for example living in charity property, unless it is authorised by the governing document, statute or the Charity Commission.

In community interest companies, directors may not use other benefits as a way of circumventing the asset lock [3.4].

16.3.11   Small gifts

In principle the same rules apply to small thank you, get well and similar gifts for a charity's trustees, former trustees or persons connected with them: a charity's funds should not be used to purchase them. In practice Charity Commission consent is not required for a token of appreciation worth less than £25. If gifts are worth more than that, a collection could be taken so well-wishers, rather than the charity, pay the extra. Alternatively the Commission's operational guidance (on its website) should be consulted or advice should be sought from the Commission.

16.3.12   Rules for registered social landlords

For registered social landlords (RSLs), additional rules govern the circumstances under which employment, a tenancy, a grant, or purchase of goods or services can be entered into with a current or former member of the governing body, an employee, or a person connected with a governing body member or employee. Organisations which are not themselves RSLs but which work closely with them may be required by the RSL to observe these rules. Information about these rules is available from the Homes and Communities Agency.

16.4   GOVERNING BODY MEMBERS AS EMPLOYEES (AND VICE VERSA)

Where employees are allowed to be governing body members, they become subject to the same duties and disclosure of conflict of interest rules as other governing body members [15.2, 15.3.5, 15.6.4]. Similarly a governing body member who is likely to become employed by the organisation, is applying or might apply for a job – or who is connected with someone who might do so – should disclose the interest and should not (and in some cases must not) take part in discussions or decisions about the job or terms of employment.

Even where governing body members or connected persons can be employees, or *vice versa*, great care should be taken with the conflict of interest and reputational issues that are likely to arise. Legal advice is advisable.

16.4.1   Charities

Employees are prohibited from being members of a charity's governing body unless the governing document provides otherwise or the Charity Commission authorises it. Charity trustees cannot resign in order to receive a benefit from their charity, so even though the trustee has resigned or will resign prior to an appointment, the charity must get an order [**4.5.4**] from the Charity Commission authorising the employment.

The Charity Commission will register new charities with constitutional provisions allowing employees to be trustees, provided the governing document contains appropriate provisions to manage the conflicts of interest that inevitably arises. It is likely, for example, to prohibit the employee trustees from taking part in any discussions or decisions relating to their terms of employment. Before registering the charity, the Commission will want to know why employees should be trustees. They will be especially concerned if employees make up more than a small minority of the governing body.

For an existing charity whose governing document does not allow employees to serve as trustees, the Commission will not allow the governing document to be altered unless there is a very strong reason to do so. Their website contains operational guidance on the issues they consider.

Employee trustees, like all trustees, are under a duty to act in the best interests of the charity as a whole and its beneficiaries [**15.6.3**], even if this is in conflict with their best interest as an individual or employee.

16.4.2   Non-charities

In non-charitable organisations, the governing document often prohibits employees from serving on the governing body. It may be possible to amend the governing document [**7.5**].

16.4.3   Companies

Company directors – regardless of whether the company is or is not charitable – are subject to disclosure and conflict of interest rules if they are paid by the company [**15.3.5**, **15.3.6**]. Copies of their contracts must be kept as part of the company's statutory records [**18.5.7**], and special rules apply to the approval of contracts for more than two years or if it is terminated [**16.3.2.5**].

16.4.4   Connected persons

Charity Commission advice must be sought before any charity employs a person connected with a trustee [**15.2.5**], or appoints or elects a trustee connected with an employee, unless the governing document allows trustees to be employees.

Persons connected with company directors [**15.2.5**] are subject to the same rules as directors [**15.3.5**].

16.4.5   Employees of other organisations

There are no prohibitions on employees of other organisations being on a governing body, although **conflict of duties** (also called **conflict of loyalties** or **duality of interest**) should – and in companies must – be treated in the same way as conflict of interest [**15.2.3**, **15.3.8**, **15.6.4**].

Where Organisation A allows an employee to sit on the governing body of Organisation B during work time, and B makes a payment to A to compensate for the loss of its employee's time, this creates an indirect benefit for the individual – because B is in effect making a payment towards the individual's salary, even though the payment is going to A rather than directly to the individual. The individual has a conflict of interest which must be dealt with in organisation B in the same way as any other conflict of interest [**15.3.5**, **15.6.4**].

If Organisation A – the individual's employer – is a charity, it must be satisfied that paying its employee's usual salary during the time spent with another organisation is within its own objects or powers, even if the salary is being reimbursed by B.

B's payment towards the salary may have implications for VAT [**57.13.1**] or trading [**56.4**].

16.5   SERVICE USERS / BENEFICIARIES

Strictly speaking, the rules against charity trustee benefits prevent a trustee receiving any benefits from the charity unless this is authorised by the governing document or Charity Commission [**15.6.6**] . But this is inconsistent with the reality of many charities where users of the charity's services serve on the governing body, or charities such as community associations where all members, including its governing body members, are eligible to use the association's facilities.

Guidance on user involvement in charities – including involvement as governing body members – while staying within trust and charity law is set out in Charity Commission booklet CC24 *Users on board: Beneficiaries who become trustees*, available from the Commission [see end of **chapter 1**].

16.5.1   The legal position

In any organisation, whether charitable or non-charitable:
- if the governing document states that members of the governing body may (or must) be users of the organisation's services, or that they may (or must) be members of an organisation whose members are entitled to use services, then beneficiaries/users may be members of the governing body;
- if the governing document excludes beneficiaries/users from the governing body, they cannot be members of the governing body.

If the governing document of a *non-charitable* organisation does not say anything one way or the other, beneficiaries/users may be members of the governing body.

If the governing document of a *charitable* organisation does not say anything one way or the other, there is no problem with a governing body member receiving a general benefit available to large numbers of people (such as using a community association's facilities). But Charity Commission advice should be sought before electing or appointing as a member of the governing body a person who is receiving a benefit specific to them such as housing, a grant or scholarship, or providing such a charitable benefit to an existing governing body member.

It may be possible to alter the governing document [**7.5**] but Charity Commission advice should be sought before making any alteration allowing beneficiaries or service users to serve as governing body members in a charity.

Material benefits provided to governing body members in a charity may have to be disclosed in the notes to the annual accounts [**54.2.8**].

16.5.2   Avoiding conflict of interest

Where beneficiaries/users serve on a charity's governing body, the rules on disclosing conflict of interest, not taking part in discussions or decisions where there is a conflict of interest, and acting always in the best interest of the charity and all its beneficiaries must be carefully followed [**15.2.3**, **15.6.3**]. They must not use their position to gain an advantage for themselves or connected persons [**15.2.5**]. In practice, this means:
- a governing body member must not take part in any discussion or decision relating to benefits specific to her or him or a connected person, such as selection for a holiday;

- there is probably no significant conflict of interest in taking part in discussions or decisions about services or activities which are equally available to all, or very large numbers, of the organisation's users (for example an advice line or a school);

- everything between is a grey area in which governing body members need to exercise common sense, remembering their overriding duties to avoid conflict of interest and to act not in their personal interest or the interest of a particular group or faction, but in the best interests of the beneficiaries as a whole;

- all decisions about which beneficiaries or users should be chosen for a grant, service or activity must be scrupulously fair and must not give any unfair advantage to a member of the governing body or connected person;

- decisions must be properly minuted, and if they involve a benefit to a specific member of the governing body or connected person should make clear that he or she was not involved in the discussion or decision.

If in doubt – especially where a benefit of substantial value is to be given to a member of the governing body or connected person – the Charity Commission should be consulted or legal advice taken.

16.5.2.1 When everyone has a conflict of interest

Sometimes all or a majority of governing body members would stand to gain or lose from a decision, for example in a community nursery where the parents who make up the governing body have to decide whether to raise fees [**15.2.4**]. They could not all withdraw, because there would then be no one to make the decision. If the organisation is charitable the governing body members should contact the Charity Commission, who will authorise them to take part in the decision on a one-off basis or by amending the governing document to allow this, and/or will recommend amending the governing document so there are enough governing body members who can form a disinterested quorum. A non-charity which does not have enough governing body members to form a disinterested quorum should take legal advice.

Resources: RESTRICTIONS ON PAYMENTS AND BENEFITS

See end of **chapter 1**.

Statute law. www.opsi.gov.uk and www.statutelaw.gov.uk.

Much but not all case law. www.bailii.org.

Updates cross-referenced to this book. www.rclh.co.uk.

Chapter 17

THE REGISTERED OFFICE AND OTHER PREMISES

For sources of further information see end of chapter 1.

17.1   COMPANIES

All companies must have a **registered office**. Certain information must be displayed there, and at other premises where a company carries out its activities.

17.1.1   Domicile

A company's **domicile** is the country (England and Wales, Wales on its own, Scotland or Northern Ireland) where its registered office must be, as stated in the articles of association (or memorandum, if incorporated before 1 October 2009).

A company whose domicile is England and Wales and whose registered office is in Wales can pass a special resolution [**19.7.4**] to change its domicile to Wales, and a company whose domicile is Wales can pass a special resolution to change its domicile to England and Wales. Apart from this, domicile cannot be changed.

Companies Act 2006 s.88(2),(3)

A company whose domicile is Wales is a **Welsh company** and is able to submit its company documents in Welsh.

17.1.2   Registered office and inspection place

A company must have a **registered office** at all times. This is the official address, where official company correspondence and legal documents are sent.

Companies Act 2006 s.86

The registered office can be any address even if the company does not occupy the premises (for example, the company's solicitor's address), or a box number at the company's premises. It cannot be a box number at the post office or at other premises which are not occupied by the company.

If the registered office is not the company's usual office, there should be clear arrangements to ensure any papers delivered to the registered office quickly reach the people who need to see them. A claim form (writ) or other legal notice runs from the date it is served at the registered office, not the date the directors become aware of it, and judgment can usually be entered against the company if it fails to respond to a claim form within the specified time limit.

The address of the first registered office is notified to Companies House when the company is registered [**1.5.5**]. As soon as the company is registered its name must be displayed at the office [**17.1.3**] and must be on certain documents [**18.1.1**].

In the past, nearly all of a company's records that had to be open to the public [**18.5.1**] had to be kept at the registered office. From 1 October 2009 these records may be kept at the registered office and/or another place in the company's country of domicile [**17.1.1**].   *Companies (Company Records) Regulations 2008 [SI 2008/3006]*

A place other than the registered office at which records which must be open to the public are kept is an **inspection place**, also called the **single alternative inspection place** (**SAIL**). Companies House must be notified on form **AD02** of the SAIL's address, and on **AD03** of the records kept there.

The address of the registered office, any inspection place and the company records held at those locations must be provided in writing, within five working days, to any person the company deals with in the course of business who asks for the information.   *Companies (Trading Disclosures) Regulations 2008 [SI 2008/495] regs.1(2)(c),9*

17.1.3   Name at premises

A company's full registered name must be displayed at its registered office and any inspection place [above], unless the company has been dormant [**54.3.10**] at all times since it was set up. The name must be outside the premises or visible from the outside during business hours, and must be positioned so it can be easily seen by any visitor to the location. The name must also be displayed at any other location where the company operates, unless the location is used primarily as living accommodation.   *Companies (Trading Disclosures) Regulations 2008 [SI 2008/495] regs.3-5*

If a **business name** (a day to day name different from the registered name) is displayed, it must be clear which is the registered name.

17.1.4   Changing the registered office or inspection place

A company's registered office can be changed at any time by a resolution of the directors, unless the articles say it must be done by the members. The registered office must remain in the country of domicile [**17.1.1**]. Companies House must be notified on form **AD01** within 14 days of the decision. The change of address takes effect as soon as it is registered by Companies House, but for 14 days after registration, legal documents may be delivered to the previous registered address as well as the new one.   *Companies Act 2006 s.87*

If the company directors or members resolve to change the address of the inspection place [**17.1.2**], Companies House must be notified on form **AD02**. If the records are to revert from an inspection place to the registered office, form **AD04** is used to notify Companies House.

When the registered office or inspection place is changed the name must be displayed at the new location [**17.1.3**]; paper and electronic documents must be changed [**18.1.1**]; and the name must be removed from premises no longer used by the company. As well as notifying Companies House, other regulatory or registration bodies must also be informed of any change of registered office.

17.2   INDUSTRIAL AND PROVIDENT SOCIETIES

17.2.1   Registered office

An industrial and provident society must have a registered office in its area of registration. The address of the registered office must be included in the IPS's rules.   *Industrial & Provident Societies Act 1965 s.1(1), sch.1 para.3*

If the registered office is not the society's usual place of business, there should be clear arrangements to get all official communications delivered to the registered office to the relevant people immediately.

The registers of members and officers [**18.6**] must be kept at the registered office, and a copy of the most recent balance sheet and auditors' report must be on public display there [**54.4.2**].   *IPSA 1965 ss.40,44(1)*

17.2.2 Name on premises

The IPS's full registered name must be painted or affixed on the outside of the registered office and at each place where the society operates. *Industrial & Provident Societies Act 1965 s.5(6)*

The provisions relating to IPSs which use a trading or operating name for their day to day work are the same as for companies [**17.1.3**].

17.2.3 Changing the office

An IPS can change its registered address by using the amendment procedure in its rules. The change must be notified to Mutual Societies Registration. Registration and regulatory bodies must be notified of the change. *IPSA 1965 s.10(2)*

17.3 TRUSTS AND UNINCORPORATED ASSOCIATIONS

Trusts and unincorporated associations do not have a registered office, and are not required to put their name on any premises they use unless they are required to disclose their charitable status [**17.4.2**].

17.4 CHARITIES

17.4.1 Address or principal office

Before registering a charity the Charity Commission must be satisfied that the trustees intend it to be governed by the laws of England and Wales [**4.4.5**].

Charitable companies and industrial and provident societies must have a registered office [**17.1.2**, **17.2.1**], and a charitable incorporated organisation (CIO) must have a **principal office** in England or Wales. Charitable trusts or associations do not need to have a registered or principal office. All they need is a correspondent's address, which must be kept current with the Commission.

17.4.2 Status at premises

Charitable status does not, in itself, require a name or other information to be shown on premises. But if a registered charity with annual income over £10,000 displays a notice at any premises encouraging people to donate money or goods to or purchase goods from the charity, the notice must state that the organisation is a registered charity [**18.1.5**]. *Charities Act 1993 s.5(1),(2)*

When the charitable incorporated organisation structure becomes available (expected April 2010), regulations may set out requirements for disclosure of CIO status at its principal office and other premises where it operates, and may also set out rules relating to disclosure of names other than the registered name.

17.4.3 Changing address

Any change in the charity's address as shown in the register of charities, or in the address of the correspondent named in the annual return, must be notified to the Charity Commission. *Charities Act 1993 s.3(7)(b)*

Resources: THE REGISTERED OFFICE AND OTHER PREMISES

See end of **chapter 1**.

Statute law. www.opsi.gov.uk and www.statutelaw.gov.uk.

Much but not all case law. www.bailii.org.

Updates cross-referenced to this book. www.rclh.co.uk.

Chapter 18

COMMUNICATION AND PAPERWORK

For sources of further information see end of chapter 1.

18.1 PUBLICATION OF NAME AND STATUS

For companies, industrial and provident societies and charities, it is an offence to issue documents which do not include specified details, or to authorise documents to be issued without them. Failure to comply with these rules may not only result in fines, but may also expose a person signing a cheque or ordering goods or services to personal liability if the organisation refuses to honour the cheque or pay for what has been ordered. The safest course is to include the details on every publication, document, letter, compliments slip, outgoing email, fax and website.

18.1.1 Companies

For companies, the obligation to include the details on paper and electronic documents arises as soon as the certificate of incorporation [**1.5.8**] is received. The company's name on the documents must be exactly as shown on the certificate of incorporation, except that capitalisation can be ignored.

The company directors, the company secretary if there is one, senior managers and the company itself can be fined if the company fails to comply with the disclosure requirements relating to documents [below] or premises [**17.1.3**].

Companies (Trading Disclosures) Regulations 2008 [SI 2008/495] reg.10

18.1.1.1 Name, status, number, registered office and charitable status

The company's **full registered name**, as on the certificate of incorporation; its **registration number**; its **domicile** (the part of the UK in which it is registered, **17.1.1**); the address of its **registered office** [**17.1.2**]; for a company which does not use *limited* or the equivalent as part of its name [**6.4.5**] the fact that it is a limited company; and for a community interest company which is not a public company [**3.4**] the fact that it is a limited company must be shown on all:

- **business letters**, including **outgoing emails** and **faxes**;
- the company's **website**;
- **forms** used to order goods, services or money.

Companies (Trading Disclosures) Regulations 2008 [SI 2008/495] regs.6,7

If another address is included as well as the registered office, it must be clear which is the registered office.

A charitable company must include a statement of charitable status [**18.1.5.4**] if its name does not contain the words *charity* or *charitable*.   *Charities Act 1993 s.68*

There are no rules governing what must be on compliments slips, but they could become business letters so it is best always to include the details.

18.1.1.2 Registered name and charitable status

The company's **full registered name** – but not domicile, registration number or registered office – and the fact that it is a charity if its name does not include *charity*, *charitable* or the Welsh equivalents must be shown on:

- all its notices (for example, notice of meetings) and other official publications;
- cheques and endorsements (cheques signed over to a third party);
- invoices and receipts issued by the company;
- promissory notes (unconditional promises to pay);
- bills of exchange (a cheque or other written authorisation where the company authorises someone else, such as a bank, to pay money to a third party);
- letters of credit (agreements to provide credit);
- applications for licences to carry on a trade or activity;
- conveyances (deeds transferring property);
- all other business correspondence and documentation.

Companies (Trading Disclosures) Regulations 2008 [SI 2008/495] reg.6; Charities Act 1993 ss.67,68

18.1.1.3 Business names

If a day to day **business name** (sometimes called a **trading** or **operating name**) [**6.5.1**] is also included on any of the documents listed above, it must be clear which is the registered name. If an address other than the registered address is included, it must be clear which is the registered address.

18.1.1.4 Names of directors

The names of directors do not have to be published on its stationery or electronic documents. But if the names of some directors are included on a paper or electronic business letter (except within the text of the letter or as a signatory) the names of *all* directors and shadow directors [**13.1.3**] must be listed.

Companies (Trading Disclosures) Regulations 2008 [SI 2008/495] reg.8

If the honorary officers (president, chairperson, treasurer etc), company secretary or senior staff are not directors, their names can be on a business letter. But if they are directors – as some of them are likely to be – their names cannot be on, even if they are identified as chairperson etc rather than as a director, unless all the other directors are included as well.

The usual practice is not to include directors' names, so the headed paper does not have to be reprinted or changed every time there is a change of directors.

18.1.1.5 Other registration details

An organisation registered for VAT must include its name, address, VAT registration number and certain other information on invoices and receipts which it issues [**57.3**]. Some other registrations [**1.9**] may need to be disclosed on headed paper and other documents.

Any obligation to disclose information on headed paper or business letters should be assumed to include documents sent electronically, including faxes and emails.

18.1.1.6 Winding up, or heading towards it

When a company is being wound up [**24.3.1**], whether voluntarily or by the court, every invoice, order for goods or services, business letter or order form – whether hard copy, electronic or any other form – and its websites must include a statement that it is being wound up. *Companies (Registrar, Languages & Trading Disclosures) Regulations 2006 [SI 2006/3429] reg.7(1)*

When a company is in administrative receivership or receivership, a moratorium is in force for it or it is in administration [**24.5**], a statement to this effect must be included on all of these documents. *Companies (Trading Disclosures) (Insolvency) Regulations 2008 [SI 2008/1897]*

18.1.2 Industrial and provident societies

An industrial and provident society must put its full name on all business letters, notices, advertisements and other official publications, bills of exchange, promissory notes, endorsements, cheques, orders for money or goods, bills, invoices, receipts and letters of credit [see **18.1.1.2** for definitions]. *Industrial & Provident Societies Act 1965 s.5(6)*

Where the name of a charitable IPS does not include the word *charity* or *charitable* or the Welsh equivalents, the fact that it is a charity must be stated on these documents, and in any conveyances (deeds transferring property). *IPSA 1965 s.5A, inserted by Co-operatives & Community Benefit Societies Act 2003 s.2*

All business letters, orders and invoices must also include the address of the registered office, registration number, and 'Registered in England and Wales' or 'Registered in Scotland'.

If a day to day business name [**6.5.1**] is included it must be clear which is the registered name. If an address other than the registered address is included it must be clear which is the registered address.

An IPS registered for VAT or registered with some other bodies may need to include those details [**18.1.1.5**].

It is advisable to follow the same rules for emails and faxes.

18.1.3 Charitable incorporated organisations

When the structure becomes available (expected April 2010) charitable incorporated organisations will need to include their full registered name on all business letters; notices, for example for general meetings, and other official publications; cheques, orders for money or goods, bills of exchange, promissory notes and endorsements [see **18.1.1.2** for definitions]; conveyances; bills, invoices, receipts and letters of credit. *Charities Act 1993 s.69C, to be inserted by Charities Act 2006 sch.7 para.1 [expected April 2010]*

If the CIO's name does not include *charitable incorporated organisation*, *CIO* or the Welsh equivalents, the documents must state that the organisation is a CIO.

CIOs should assume that the above rules apply to documents sent by fax or email or in any other form.

A CIO registered for VAT or registered with some other bodies may need to include those details [**18.1.1.5**].

18.1.4 Trusts and unincorporated associations

There are no legal requirements for publishing the name or address of a non-charitable trust or unincorporated association, but clearly it is sensible for the name to be on all its business and official documents. Charitable trusts and associations must comply with charity requirements [**18.1.5**].

A trust or association registered for VAT or registered with some other bodies may need to include those details [**18.1.1.5**].

18.1.5 Registered charities

18.1.5.1 Statement on business documents

All charities registered with the Charity Commission with annual income of more than £10,000 in their last financial year must include a statement of registered charity status in the specified form [**18.1.5.4**] on cheques, invoices, receipts, bills and orders for money or goods, bills of exchange, promissory notes, endorsements and letters of credit [see **18.1.1.2** for definitions]. *Charities Act 1993 s.5*

Charitable trusts and associations with income over £10,000 do not have to put the statement on business letters. But it is good practice to put it on headed paper, compliments slips and emails as these may be used for orders, receipts etc.

A charitable company with income of any amount whose name does not include *charity*, *charitable* or the Welsh equivalent must include the statement on all its letters, the documents listed above, and any conveyances (deeds transferring property). A similar rule is likely to apply when industrial and provident societies and other formerly exempt charities become registered with the Charity Commission [**8.1.2**]. *Charities Act 1993 s.68(1)*

Separate rules apply to charitable incorporated organisations [**18.1.3**].

18.1.5.2 Statement on fundraising documents

The statement of charitable status must also be included on written or printed documents, notices or advertisements which are intended to persuade the reader to give or pay money, goods or property to the charity. *Charities Act 1993 s.5(1),(2)*

Examples of materials on which the statement must appear include:
- a leaflet or email message asking people to donate goods for a jumble sale;
- a recycling container outside a local supermarket, for materials the charity is collecting to raise money;
- a poster or newspaper advertisement for a concert where admission will be charged or a collection will be taken;
- an article in the charity's newsletter about a fundraising event;
- a letter, email message or webpage asking for donations;
- an order form, on paper or electronic, for goods sold by the charity;
- a list of services provided by the charity, if a charge is made for them.

If in doubt, include the statement.

18.1.5.3 Statement not required

An unincorporated association or trust which is registered as a charity but had income of £10,000 or less in its last financial year does not have to include the statement on any documents, but it is good practice to do so.

Excepted charities which are not voluntarily registered [**8.1.3**] and exempt charities [**8.1.2**] must not use the statement, but may say 'Excepted charity' or 'Exempt charity' or if they are recognised as charitable by HM Revenue and Customs can indicate this.

18.1.5.4 Form of the statement

The statement must be 'a registered charity', 'registered as a charity', 'registered charity number [or no.] 1234567', 'registered with the Charity Commission', or *Elusen cofrestredig*. The latter is acceptable only where the document on which it appears is wholly in Welsh. The statement may be in any language but must be in English as well, unless the document and statement are wholly in Welsh.
Charities Act 1993 s.5(2),(2A)

18.1.5.5 Charities operating in Scotland or Northern Ireland

Charities operating in Scotland or Northern Ireland must comply with the relevant rules when operating in those areas.

English and Welsh charities operating in Scotland and registered with the Office of the Scottish Charities Regulator (OSCR) may refer to themselves in Scotland as a 'charity', 'charitable body', 'registered charity' or 'charity registered in Scotland'. If they are not required to register with OSCR, they may refer to themselves as a charity, but must make clear that they are established under the law of England and Wales, for example, 'a charity registered with the Charity Commission' or, for charities exempted or excepted from registration with the Charity Commission 'recognised by HM Revenue and Customs as a charity and established in England and Wales'. Similar rules will apply to charities registered in Northern Ireland but operating in Scotland. *Charities & Trustee Investment (Scotland) Act 2005 ss.13,14*

The terms 'Scottish charity' and 'registered Scottish charity' can be used only by charities established in Scotland or managed or controlled wholly or mainly in or from Scotland, and registered with OSCR.

Every charity registered with OSCR must include its name as entered in the Scottish charity register, any other name by which it is commonly known, its registration number, and if its name does not include *charity* or *charitable* the fact that it is a charity, on business letters and emails; advertisements, notices and official publications; any document which solicits (asks for) money or other property for the benefit of the charity; bills of exchange (but not cheques), promissory notes, endorsements [see **18.1.1.2** for definitions] and orders for money or goods; bills, invoices, receipts and letters of credit; educational or campaign documentation; conveyances for land; and contractual documentation. *Charities References in Documents (Scotland) Regulations 2007 [Scottish SI 2007/203]*

For charities newly registered with OSCR, the disclosure rules apply to documents issued or signed by the charity from six months after the registration date.

Charities registered with the Charity Commission for Northern Ireland must state that they are registered on any notice, advertisement or other document which solicits money or other property for the benefit of the charity; and on bills of exchange, promissory notes, endorsements [see **18.1.1.2** for definitions], cheques, orders for money or goods, bills, invoices, receipts and letters of credit. At the time of writing (mid 2009) the rules for charities based in England and Wales or Scotland and operating in Northern Ireland had not been published. *Charities Act (Northern Ireland) 2008 s.19*

18.2 NOTICE AND OTHER COMMUNICATIONS IN NON-COMPANIES

Detailed statutory rules apply to communication between a company and its members [**18.3**]. For other organisations, rules for communications from the organisation (such as notice of meetings or annual accounts) or to the organisation (such as applications for membership, nominations, proxy votes) are generally set out in the governing document.

18.2.1 Electronic communications

18.2.1.1 Unincorporated associations and trusts

Unincorporated organisations must comply with any rules in the governing document about the form in which notice and other communications must be given to the organisation's members and others entitled to receive them, and the way it must be delivered. If the governing document specifies how notice is to be given, other methods (including electronic) cannot be used unless the governing document is amended to allow them [**7.5**].

Where electronic communications are allowed, procedures must always be put in place for members who do not wish to receive the organisation's official communications in this way.

18.2.1.2 Incorporated organisations other than companies

At the time of writing (mid 2009) the statutory rules on communications to and from charitable incorporated organisations (CIOs) had not been finalised, but were expected to be similar to the rules for companies [**18.3**].

At the time of writing the government intended to remove statutory obstacles to industrial and provident societies communicating electronically with their members, statutory authorities and other IPSs.

18.3   COMMUNICATIONS TO AND FROM A COMPANY

The statutory **company communications provisions** cover communications sent *to* a company, in schedule 4 of the **Companies Act 2006**, and those sent *by* a company, in schedule 5. Communications between companies must comply with schedule 5. The provisions also apply to communications to and from company directors, acting on behalf of the organisation.   *Companies Act 2006 ss.1143-1148*

The rules apply to information or documents sent *to* the company by its members, debenture holders or others who are required under statute or the governing document to communicate with the company; and information or documents sent *by* the company that must under statute or the governing document be sent to its members, debenture holders or others. The rules do not apply to information where there is no statutory or constitutional duty to send it.

18.3.1   Deemed delivery

A communication is deemed to have been received by the intended recipient:

- 48 hours after it is posted, if it is sent by post to an address in the UK and the company can show it was properly addressed, prepaid and posted;
- 48 hours after it is sent, if it is sent by email, fax or other electronic means and the company can show it was properly addressed;
- when the material is first made available on a website or, if later, when the recipient receives (or is deemed to have received) notice of the fact that it is available on the website.   *Companies Act 2006 s.1147*

No part of Saturday, Sunday, Christmas, Good Friday or a bank holiday is counted as part of the 48 hours. So, for example, information posted or emailed at 11am Friday (assuming Friday is not a bank holiday) is deemed to have been received at 11am Tuesday, or at 11am Wednesday if the Monday is a bank holiday.   *Companies Act 2006 s.1173(1)*

The statutory time periods for deemed delivery do not apply for communications sent by a company to its members if a different period is specified in the company's articles. For communications sent to holders of debentures, a different period may be specified in the instrument constituting debentures. And for communications sent by the company which are not sent to recipients in their capacity as members or debenture holders, a different period may be specified in any agreement between the company and the intended recipient.

18.3.2   Authentication

Information sent or supplied to a company on paper is sufficiently **authenticated** if it is signed by the person it is from. For information sent to it electronically, the company can decide what sort of confirmation of identity it requires. If the company does not do this, an electronic document is sufficiently authenticated if it contains or is accompanied by a statement of the sender's identity, and the company has no reason to doubt the truth of the statement.   *Companies Act 2006 s.1146*

18.3.3   Communications on paper

A document or information in hard copy can be supplied by hand or by post *to* a company by its members or others who have a statutory or constitutional duty or right to communicate with it. It can be supplied at the organisation's registered office or at an address specified by the company or the Companies Act for the purpose.   *Companies Act 2006 sch.4 para.3-4*

Hard copy communications *by* a company to members or others with whom it has a statutory or constitutional duty or right to communicate can be supplied by hand or post to an address provided by the recipient for this purpose, to a company at its registered office, to a member of the company at the address in the register of members, to a member of the governing body at the address in the register of directors, to an address authorised by statute for the supply of the document or information, or if none of the above is available, to the intended recipient's last address known to the company. *Companies Act 2006 sch.5 para.3,4*

18.3.4 Electronic communications

Electronic communications include email, fax, CDs or other electronic media, or any other communication which is sent and received electronically. Special rules apply to websites [**18.3.5**]. *Companies Act 2006 s.1168*

18.3.4.1 Consent to receive electronic communications

Where company members or others are communicating with a company for a statutory or constitutional purpose (for example applying for membership or submitting a proxy), the document or information may be provided electronically *to* the company only if the company has agreed, in general or in the specific circumstance, that it may be provided in that form, or if the Companies Acts specifies that the company is deemed to have agreed to electronic communications. *Companies Act 2006 sch.4 para.6; sch.5 para.6*

For electronic communications sent *by* a company for a statutory or constitutional purpose (for example notice of general meetings), to an individual or an organisation which is not a company, the company must obtain individual written consent from each intended recipient to receive information this way, either in general or in specific circumstances. If an intended recipient does not give consent, the company may not send information to that recipient electronically. If the intended recipient is a company, information may be sent electronically if that company has agreed to receive it in that form, or is deemed to have agreed by a provision in the Companies Acts. *Companies Act 2006 sch.5 para.6*

The concept of **deemed agreement** [**18.3.6.1**] – tacit agreement by failing to respond to the company's request for consent – does not apply. To send communications electronically, the company must receive explicit consent from each recipient, and the consent must be for each purpose or for some or all purposes generally. The only exception is where the recipient is a company and is deemed by the Companies Acts to have agreed to receive electronic communications.

18.3.4.2 Address

Electronic communications supplied electronically can only be sent to an electronic address (email address, fax number etc) specified for the purpose by the company (if sent *to* the company) or by the intended recipient (if sent *by* the company), or deemed by the Companies Acts to have been so specified.

The Companies Act does not require communications *to* a company to come from an email address, fax etc specified by the sender. Some companies may want to specify, as part of their authentication rules [**18.3.2**], that electronic communications can only be sent from an address that has been notified to the company, but this could cause problems where members or others use multiple email addresses.

If the information is in electronic form but is delivered by hand or post (for example on a CD), it can only be delivered by hand to the recipient, or supplied to an address to which it could validly be sent if it were in hard copy [**18.3.3**]. *Companies Act 2006 sch.4 para.7, sch.5 para.7*

18.3.4.3 Right to hard copy

A company member or debenture holder who receives information sent electronically *by* the company has a right to be sent hard copy on request. This must be sent within 21 days, and no additional charge can be made. *Companies Act 2006 s.1145*

18.3.5 Other formats

Information can be sent by a company member etc *to* a company in a format that is neither in hard copy nor electronic form if the company agrees, and can be sent *by* a company to a member or other person in such format if the intended recipient agrees. An example is a visually impaired company member who agrees to receive notices orally. *Companies Act 2006 sch.4 para.8, sch.5 para.15*

18.3.6 Providing information on a website

Notice of meetings, annual accounts and information which a company has a statutory or constitutional obligation to provide can be provided via its website only if the intended recipient has agreed and has not revoked the agreement, or can be **deemed** to have agreed, to receive information this way. *Companies Act 2006 sch.5 para.9*

18.3.6.1 Deemed agreement

The rules relating to **deemed agreement** are complex and must be carefully followed. It is advisable to take legal advice the first time a request for consent is sent out, to ensure it includes all the necessary information.

A company member is deemed to have agreed to receive information via website if *all* of the following apply:

- the articles say that information can be provided on a website, or the company members have passed a resolution allowing it generally or for specific types of information;
- the company has asked each member to agree that the company may provide documents or information generally, or the specific documents or information in question, to him, her or it by means of a website;
- the request to the member explicitly states that if the company does not receive a response within 28 days beginning with the date on which the company's request was sent, the member will be deemed to have given consent;
- the request was not sent to the member within 12 months of a previous request relating to the same or similar documents or information; and
- the company does not receive a negative response from the member within the 28 day period.

The effect of this is that if a member does not want to receive information via website, they must respond within 28 days. But if they are willing to receive information this way, they do not have to respond to the request. By not responding, they will be deemed to have agreed.

Similar rules apply for providing information via website to debenture holders.
Companies Act 2006 sch.5 para.10,11

18.3.6.2 Governing document authorisation

Companies can use a website to communicate with members and others to whom official information must be sent only if this is authorised by the articles or by an ordinary resolution of the members. But constitutional provision or a resolution does not in itself give a right to communicate by website to all members; the company can do this only if the particular member has given agreement or deemed consent.

18.3.6.3 Accessibility

Official information on a company website must be in a form that enables text to be read and illustrations to be seen with the naked eye. This includes with spectacles etc. *Companies Act 2006 sch.5 para.12*

18.3.6.4 Notification and availability

When official information is placed on an company website, the company must notify the member, debenture holder or other intended recipient and must provide details of what is on the website, where it is and how to access it. Notice may be given by post, by hand or electronically, but if it is done electronically the appropriate consents must have been received from the member [**18.3.4.1**].
Companies Act 2006 sch.5 para.13,14

The information must be available on the website for the period specified in the Companies Act or other relevant legislation, or if there is no such period, for 28 days beginning with the date on which the notification is sent to the person in question or, if later, beginning with the date on which the information first appears on the website.

18.4   RECORD KEEPING

All organisations should, as a minimum, keep adequate minutes, membership lists, service user records and financial records for their own purposes. But for most organisations there are also legal requirements about what must be kept and for how long. These are summarised below.

As well as needing to be kept for legal reasons, the organisation's documents are historical records, and should be kept as a record of the organisation's development and achievements. In particular copies should be kept of minutes of members' and governing body meetings, and annual accounts and reports. It is also sensible to keep publicity materials and other items which could be useful in future for people studying or writing about the organisation.

Unless the law specifies otherwise, most records can be kept electronically. Because of the risk of corruption or obsolescence, records which must by law be kept should be kept in at least two formats, and anything kept on computer must be protected from tampering and should be regularly backed up, with the backup kept off site. From time to time material should be transferred to new media (CDs do not last forever) and if necessary, converted into a more up to date or more widely supported format. Even where there is no statutory obligation to retain records, these procedures are good practice for all archive material.

If records are stored off the premises it is essential to keep a record of where they are – and to keep records of where this record is!

18.4.1   Access to records

The normal rule on minutes is that anyone who is entitled to attend the meeting must be allowed access to the minutes of that meeting.

For other records, the organisation's governing document may say who has access to minutes and other documents. Company law sets out very specifically who has access to the company's statutory records [**18.5**], and charity, company and industrial and provident society law gives a right to annual reports and accounts. Data protection law has strict rules about who has access to personal data about individuals [**43.3**]. But if neither the governing document nor statute law says anything about access, the organisation decides who can see what.

Each organisation should develop appropriate confidentiality procedures [**43.1**] in relation to sensitive information about individuals, and in relation to the organisation and its work. Minutes of governing body meetings, for example, may be commercially sensitive if they contain information about the organisation's financial position and its fundraising plans, contract bids or grant applications.

All rules on access to information must comply with the **Data Protection Act** [**43.3**], **Human Rights Act** [**64.3**] and **Freedom of Information Act** [**43.2**]. For companies, industrial and provident societies and charities, the public has a right of access to certain information [**18.5.1.3**, **18.6.1**, **18.10.2**], and it may be an offence not to provide it. This overrides the Data Protection Act and other restrictions such as copyright.

18.4.2   How long to keep records

Set out below are **retention periods** for financial, employment, charity and company records which are likely to be held by voluntary organisations. Some periods are set by legislation and the records *must* be kept. Others *should* be kept to ensure the organisation has the necessary information during the period covered by the **Limitation Act 1980** (the **statute of limitations**). For other records it is a matter of what is sensible and appropriate for the organisation.

The **Data Protection Act** does not specify how long personal data must or may be kept. The data protection principles [**43.3.3**] say data may not be held longer than is necessary for the purposes for which it is held – but the organisation can decide what those purposes are and how long is necessary.

In most cases it will be sensible to retain records for a significant period beyond any legal minimum, to ensure they are available for any unexpected legal purpose, or if a service user returns to the organisation, or as part of the organisation's historical archives. The organisation's data retention policy should be clear what should be kept, why it is being kept and for how long, and should be linked to the data protection policy on retention of information about individuals.

Where records must be kept for a specified period – either by law, or because funders or the organisation itself have said they should be – the files, boxes, CDs or other media, or computer files in which they are kept should be clearly labelled 'Keep until [date]'. Information stored electronically should be regularly transferred so it does not become unusable.

18.4.2.1 Not very long

Information which is clearly out of date, such as old postal or email addresses, should not be kept unless there is a specific reason to do so (for example, if a service user's previous address might need to be known for some reason).

Other information that should be kept only for a short time includes, for example, details of people who have ordered free publications or have made initial enquiries but not followed them up, unless there is good reason for keeping their details and they have been told this will be done.

18.4.2.2 Six months to one year

Claims for discrimination generally have to be brought within three months but in some cases the time limit can be extended, so **application forms** and short-listing and selection notes for unsuccessful job candidates should be kept for at least seven months, and it may be sensible to keep them for a year. The successful candidate's application form, references and other pre-employment checks become part of her or his personnel record [**18.4.2.8**].

In most cases Criminal Records Bureau disclosure certificates must not be kept for longer than six months. After that, only a record of the fact that a disclosure was obtained should be kept on the personnel file [**41.4.1**]. Organisations registered with Ofsted, the Care Quality Commission or similar regulatory bodies may need to keep CRB disclosure certificates and other pre-employment checks until the next inspection. If in doubt, guidance should be sought from the regulator.

18.4.2.3 Two years

Records showing that the **working time** regulations are being complied with must be kept for at least two years [**31.1.4**].

18.4.2.4 Three years or more

Claims by adults for **negligence** and **personal injury** must generally be brought within three years of the event which gave rise to the injury or when it was realised that an injury had been suffered. Relevant documentation should be kept for at least three years, but may need to be kept much longer. A child may bring a claim any time up to his or her 21st birthday, so an appropriate retention period will be needed.

The organisation's **accident book** [**40.9.3**] must be kept for three years from the date of the last entry.

There is no specified period for keeping correspondence about **donations**, but it is generally advisable to keep it for three years. Documentation relating to funds for restricted purposes should usually be kept until the funds have been spent and accounted for, in case there are any problems or the organisation needs to ask the donor(s) for consent to use the donation for another purpose [**48.2.3**].

18.4.2.5 Three years, but keep for six

Pay records relating to statutory sickness, maternity, paternity and adoption pay, student loan repayments and tax credits must be kept for at least three years from the end of the tax period to which they apply. HM Revenue and Customs recommends that **PAYE documentation** and correspondence with HMRC about PAYE is also kept for three years. But because HMRC can bring a claim in relation to PAYE or minimum wage for up to six years after the end of the relevant tax period, and an employee can bring a claim for breach of contract for up to six years after the act which gave rise to the breach, these records should be kept for at least six years from the end of the tax year to which they apply.

Under company law private companies, including charitable and community interest companies, must keep their **accounting records** [**18.4.2.8**] for at least three years from the end of the financial year to which they apply. But because tax law requires accounting records to be kept for six years from the end of the financial year, they should be kept for the longer period.   *Companies Act 2006 ss.386-388*

18.4.2.6 Four years or longer

Business Link, the government's advice service for small businesses, says that documents relating to **government grants** must generally be kept for four years from receipt of the grant, and that no documents should be destroyed while the grant is still being received. For all grants it is sensible for the recipient to confirm with the funder how long paperwork relating to the grant should be kept.

18.4.2.7 Five years

Records of tests of equipment, substances and processes carried out under the **Control of Substances Hazardous to Health Regulations** [**40.6.7**] must be kept for five years from the date of the test. Records of exposure to **asbestos** [**40.7.1**] and other harmful substances must be kept for five years from the last entry in the records, unless they relate to identifiable individuals, in which case they must be kept for 40 years.

Organisations required to carry out **customer due diligence** [**53.6**] under the **Money Laundering Regulations** must keep the records for five years from the end of the business relationship or occasional transaction.

18.4.2.8 Six years

Any organisation which is or might be subject to corporation tax on its profits or income tax on its income [**56.2**] must keep its **accounting records** for six years from the end of the financial year to which they apply.

All charities, other than charitable companies [**18.4.2.5**], must keep their accounting records for six years. Unlike most of the charity accounting regulations, this also applies to exempt charities.   *Charities Act 1993 ss.41,46*

At least one copy of each year's annual accounts and report should be kept indefinitely, as an historical record.

If the organisation is registered for VAT, **VAT records** must be kept for six years from the end of the financial year. HM Revenue and Customs may agree to them being kept for a shorter period if it is genuinely impractical to retain them.

Most charities must keep **gift aid records** [**50.2.2**] for six years after the accounting period to which the tax claim relates. For charitable trusts, the retention period is similar but is calculated differently.

Contracts and agreements such as licences, loan agreements and contracts with suppliers can generally be enforced for six years from the act which gave rise to a breach or the end of the contract, so should be kept for six years after the contract ends. Contracts made as deeds [**20.3**] should be kept for 12 years.

Although most employment claims must be brought within a much shorter period, claims for breach of contract can be brought in the courts up to six years after the act which gave rise to the claim. **Personnel records**, including references and other checks made before or during employment and records relating to leave, absence, performance, training and disciplinary matters, should therefore be kept for at least six years after the employment has ended. Some records, such as those required under the Care Standards Act, may need to be kept for longer periods [**18.4.2.13**].

Payroll records, including records of overtime and bonuses, records of pension deductions, expense accounts and records, and details of redundancy and other termination payments must be kept for six years from the end of the tax year to which they apply.   *Taxes Management Act 1970*

For employees entitled to benefits under a **retirement benefits** scheme, records must be kept for six years from the end of the scheme year in which a notifiable event occurs, for example if an employee is retired due to incapacity.

18.4.2.9   10 years

Documentation relating to the purchase or sale of **major goods or capital items** should be kept for at least 10 years, because claims for defects can in some cases be made during this period.

Limitation Act 1980 s.11A,
inserted by Consumer Protection Act 1987 sch.1 para.1

Documentation for electronic and electrical equipment, even small items like mobile phones, may need to be kept longer [**18.4.2.13**].

Minutes of the meetings of company members and company directors must be kept for at least 10 years [**18.5.8**], but it is generally sensible to keep them throughout the life of the company and beyond.

Names cannot be removed from the **register of company members** [**18.5.2**] until at least 10 years after the person has ceased to be a member.

An agreement with a **trade union** should be kept for 10 years after it ends.

18.4.2.10   12 years

Documents relating to **property**, such as leases, title deeds, searches and planning permission, should be kept for 12 years after the organisation's interest in the property ends. Even when a lease is assigned, relevant documents or copies should be kept for 12 years from the lease's expiry date.

Other contracts and agreements should also be kept for 12 years after they have ended if they were made as **deeds** [**20.3**] rather than as simple contracts. **Deeds of covenant** [**50.2.6**] should be kept for 12 years after they have ceased to apply.

An employer's group health or personal accident **policies** should be kept for at least 12 years after the policies end.

18.4.2.11   15 years

Some information about workers in **children's homes** must be retained for 15 years. Details are available from Ofsted.

18.4.2.12   40 years or longer

Individuals' medical records required under **hazardous substances** regulations – COSHH [**40.6.7**], lead, and asbestos – must be kept for 40 years. Medical records required under the ionising radiation regulations must be kept for 50 years or until the person reaches age 75, whichever is later.

18.4.2.13   Variable

General **correspondence** and information, whether on paper or electronic, which does not have any legal implications should be kept for as long as it may be needed or relevant. Organisations should have guidelines on how long such information is kept, to ensure essential documents are not destroyed or deleted while also ensuring the organisation does not become overwhelmed with stored communications.

Many employees are entitled to 13 weeks' **parental leave** [**32.7**], to be taken within five years of the child's birth or adoption, or by the child's 18th birthday if the child is disabled. Records should be kept at least for that long, and if requested must be provided to the employee's next employer.

Criminal Records Bureau and other checks for work regulated under the **Care Standards Act** must be kept for varying periods, depending on the nature of the work. Details are available from the Care Quality Commission and Ofsted [**41.4**].

Documents showing an employee's right to work in the UK should be kept for at least two years after the employee stops working for the employer [**29.5.1**].

Except for medical records relating to specific substances [**18.4.2.12**], there is no requirement to keep employees' **medical records**, medical examinations etc for a specified period. Together with related documents such as accident and absence records, they should be kept at least as long as personnel records [**18.4.2.8**], and some commentators suggest keeping them for at least 30 years, in particular where there is a risk of a claim for a long-term or delayed health problem arising from the employment.

Anyone other than a private household who purchased **electronic or electrical equipment** (computers, televisions, mobile phones, printers etc) before 13 August 2005 is responsible for paying for its proper removal and disposal [**63.12.6**]. Records for equipment purchased by organisations after that date should be kept throughout the life of the equipment, to show that the distributor – rather than the purchaser – is responsible for its disposal.

18.4.2.14 Indefinitely

Where an employer has a statutory duty to consult with employees, employee representatives or trade union representatives, the **consultation records** should be kept indefinitely.

Under the **Pensions Act 1995** s.49 and subsequent regulations, most occupational pension scheme records have to be kept indefinitely, including trust deeds and rules, minutes of meetings of the pension trustees, contribution records, actuarial records, insurance and investment records, and annual accounts. Details of pension recipients have to be kept for 12 years after the person's benefit ends.

Organisations which provide other types of pension – not through an occupational pension scheme – should consult the pension provider about the records which must be kept and how long they must be retained.

It is recommended that **investment certificates** and the organisation's **register of fixed assets** (buildings etc) be kept indefinitely.

A company's **statutory registers** [**18.5**] must be kept throughout the life of the company, and beyond [**18.5.1.5**].

It is sensible to keep at least one copy of annual accounts and reports indefinitely as a record of the organisation's history and achievements.

18.4.3 When the organisation winds up

When an organisation is being wound up the final governing body members are responsible for ensuring its records are kept for the periods specified above, or such other periods as are required by statute or under the organisation's governing document. The retention of documents is important for all organisations, but in particular for unincorporated organisations, where the members of the governing body may be held personally liable even if the organisation no longer exists.

Decisions need to be made about who is to take responsibility for keeping the records, and where they are to be kept. Everyone involved in the final stages of the organisation should be given a detailed list of where the records will be, in the hope that someone will know where they are when and if they are needed. If it is not feasible to keep everything that should be kept, decisions need to be made about what to keep. These decisions should be recorded, and a record should be kept of what has been discarded. Most documents can be scanned and kept electronically but legal advice should be taken before doing this.

For a company dissolved before 1 October 2009 all of its statutory records [**18.5**], including minutes, statutory registers and accounting records, should be kept for at least two years and may need to be kept for 20 years; for companies wound up after that date records should be kept for six years or possibly longer [**18.5.1.5**].

If a charity is wound up, its financial records must be kept for at least six years unless the Charity Commission agrees they can destroyed or otherwise disposed of earlier. The Commission must be notified where the records are kept.

Charities Act 1993 ss.41,46

18.5   COMPANY RECORDS

18.5.1   The statutory records

Company law defines a number of **statutory records** and sets out the information which must be kept, the form, how it is updated, whether Companies House needs to be notified of changes, where the information may be kept, how long it must be kept, who has access to it and who has the right to a copy of it.

As with other aspects of company law, there are penalties for not maintaining these records, not keeping them up to date or persistently failing to notify Companies House of changes where this is required. For example, if a company does not keep registers of company members and directors or does not allow members of the public to see them, the company and every one its officers can be fined – although in practice such fines are rarely levied.

Information about the requirement to file information with Companies House is available from Companies House [see end of **chapter 1**]. Much information can be filed electronically.

The rules relating to company records apply to all companies, including community interest companies. Some additional rules, not covered in this book, apply to companies limited by shares rather than by guarantee. Charitable companies must comply with charity law [**18.10**] as well as company law.

18.5.1.1   Format

Pre-printed combined registers are available from legal stationers, but these registers are generally designed for companies with shareholders, so some sections are not relevant for companies limited by guarantee.

There is no need to buy a pre-printed register. Ordinary paper or a bound book with blank pages can be used. Alternatively the statutory records may be kept in electronic form, but must be capable of being printed.   *Companies Act 2006 ss.1135,1138*

All statutory records, whether on paper or kept electronically, must be kept in a form which cannot be altered without proper authority, and which makes it as easy as possible to discover falsification.

Data in the registers must comply with the **Data Protection Act 1998** [**43.3**], but the rights of access under the Companies Acts [**18.5.1.3**] override data protection rules.

18.5.1.2   What must be kept, and where

Companies limited by guarantee, including community interest companies limited by guarantee, must keep the following records:
- register of members [**18.5.2**];
- if there are more than 50 members and the register is not alphabetical, an alphabetical index of members [**18.5.3**];
- a register of directors (members of the governing body) [**18.5.4**];
- a register of directors' residential addresses [**18.5.5**];
- a register of secretaries, if there is or ever has been a secretary [**18.5.6**];
- if directors are paid for any work they do for the company, their contracts with the company [**18.5.7**];
- minutes books for general meetings, records of written resolutions and minutes of meetings and resolutions of the directors [**18.5.8**];
- accounting records [**18.5.10**];
- a register of charges (mortgages etc) and a copy of every charge [**18.5.11**].

There are slightly different requirements for companies with only one member, and considerably more requirements for companies limited by shares.

Most statutory records must be kept at the registered office, but some can be kept at an alternative **inspection place** [**17.1.2**]. There can only be one alternative inspection place, so all records which are not kept at the registered office must be at one other place. The inspection place must be notified to Companies House.

Companies (Company Records) Regulations 2008 [SI 2008/3006]

18.5.1.3   Access

Documents which must be open to inspection by company members and/or the public must be available for inspection for at least two hours between 9am and 5pm on working days, provided the person who wants to inspect them has given at least 10 days notice. The notice is reduced to two days during the notice period for a general meeting, the time while a written resolution is being considered, or when a liquidator, administrator, receiver or manager of the company's property has been appointed.   *Companies (Company Records) Regulations 2008 [SI 2008/3006] reg.4*

Where the company has a right to charge a fee to people inspecting its records, the maximum is £3.50 per hour or part thereof (as at 1/8/09). People who have the right to inspect the documents also have a right to make a copy of it, but the company does not have to assist them in this.   *Companies (Fees for Inspection of Company Records) Regulations 2008 [SI 2008/3007]*

18.5.1.4   Copies

Where the company has an obligation to provide a copy of information from the registers and has a right to charge for this, the maximum fee (as at 1/8/09) is £1 for each of the first five entries; £30 for the next 95 entries or part thereof, £30 for the next 900 entries or part, £30 for the next 99,000 entries or part, and £30 for the remainder of the entries in the register or part. A lower fee may be charged, or none. For company records that are not registers, the fee is 10p per 500 words or part thereof copied. As well as the above fees, the company may make a reasonable charge for delivering the copy.   *Companies (Fees for Inspection & Copying of Company Records) Regulations 2007 [SI 2007/2612] regs.3,4*

Where information is requested in hard copy, it must be provided in that format. Where it is requested in electronic format the company does not have to provide it electronically if it is only kept in hard copy. Nor does the company have to provide information in any order, structure or form different from how it is kept.
Companies (Company Records) Regulations 2008 [SI 2008/3006] regs.7-9

18.5.1.5   How long the records must be kept

Some statutory records need only be kept for a specified period; others must be kept throughout the life of the company and beyond.

For companies dissolved [24.1.5] before 1 October 2009, the records should be kept for at least two years afterwards, as a court may declare the dissolution void (invalid). If a company was struck off the register [24.4] the records should be kept for 20 years, because the company can be reinstated to the register during that period.   *Companies Act 2006 (Commencement No 8, Transitional Provisions & Savings) Order 2008 [SI 2008/2860] sch.2 para.89,91*

For companies dissolved on or after 1 October 2009, application can be made within six years for the company to be restored to the register, so records should be kept for at least that period. But an application for restoration can be made at any time to bring a claim for personal injury against the company, so it may be sensible to keep some records, plus documents relating to personal injury (public liability) insurance, for a longer period [18.4.2.4]. Records on exposure to health hazards already have to be kept for 40 years or longer [18.4.2.12].
Companies Act 2006 ss.1024,1029,1030

18.5.2   Register of members

Membership [12.4.1] gives the right to vote and therefore to control the company, so the records of who is and is not a member must be kept accurate and up to date. This vital task is very widely neglected.

What must be kept. For a company limited by guarantee the register of members must contain the name and address of every company member, the date of becoming a member (the date the name is entered in the register after the member has been properly admitted under the provisions in the articles of association), the date of ceasing to be a member, and the class of membership if the company has different types of membership.   *Companies Act 2006 s.113*

If the company has only one member (for example, a trading company wholly owned by a charity), the register must state this and give the date on which the company became a single member company.

Form. In a bound or unbound book, or electronically provided it can be printed out. *Companies Act 2006 ss.1134,1135,1138*

Updates. Must be kept up to date with all changes to members' details, details of new members and the date of resigning or otherwise ceasing to be a member.

The names of former company members cannot be removed from the register until 10 years after they ceased to be a member. Prior to 6 April 2008, the time limit was 20 years. *Companies Act 2006 s.121*

Notification. A company limited by guarantee does not need to notify Companies House who its members are, or changes in the membership.

Where it must be kept. At the registered office or **inspection place [17.1.2]**.
CA 2006 s.114; Companies (Company Records) Regulations 2008 [SI 2008/3006]

How long it must be kept. Throughout the life of the company and beyond [**18.5.1.5**].

Access. Must be open to company members free of charge, and to the public for which a fee can be charged [**18.5.1.3**]. *Companies Act 2006 s.116*

Prior to 1 October 2007 a company could close the register for up to 30 days in each year. This provision was repealed by the **Companies Act 2006**.

Any member of the public has a right to inspect the register of members and be provided with a copy some or all of the register. But anyone exercising this right must provide their name and address, the purpose for which the information will be used, and, if the access is sought on behalf of others or the information will be disclosed to anyone else, similar details for them. The company can apply to the high court if it thinks the information is not going to be used for a proper purpose. An organisation considering this step should take advice about whether the purpose is one that can reasonably be challenged. *Companies Act 2006 ss.116-120*

Copies. Any person is entitled to a copy of the register of members or any part of it, within five days of their request being received, unless the company applies to the court for permission not to comply with the request [above]. A fee may be charged [**18.5.1.4**]. *Companies Act 2006 ss.116-120*

18.5.3   Index to register of members

What must be kept. If there are more than 50 members and the register is not alphabetical, an alphabetical index must be kept indicating where to find each member's name in the register (the page number, or the date under which it is listed). *Companies Act 2006 s.115*

Form; how long it must be kept; access. As for the register of members.

Updates. Must be updated within 14 days of a name being added to the register or any details being changed.

Where it must be kept. In the same place as the register of members.

Copies. No statutory obligation for the company to provide a copy of any information in the index, but anyone can copy it themselves unless the company has successfully applied to the court not to allow access.

18.5.4   Register of directors

What must be kept. The register of directors [see **13.1.3** for who is a director] must contain for each director:

- full name, with forenames in full unless the person is a peer or an individual usually known by a title, in which case the title can be used instead of or in addition to forename and/or surname;
- any former name or names by which the person was known for business purposes [but see **18.5.4.1** for exceptions];
- a service address [**18.5.4.2**];
- nationality;
- date of birth;
- business occupation (if any);

- if the director is a corporate body, its corporate name, registered or principal office, the type of corporate body and its registration number;
- the date elected or appointed as a director and ceasing to be a director.

Companies Act 2006 ss.163,164

Prior to 1 October 2009, details of the directors' other directorships had to be included in the register of directors. These no longer need to be included, but it is advisable for them to be disclosed in a register of interests [**15.2.4**, **15.3.5**].

It can be helpful to have spaces on the register, next to 'date appointed' and 'date left post', for 'date Companies House notified'.

Form. As for the register of members [**18.5.2**].

Updates. Must be kept up to date.

Notification. Companies House must be notified within 14 days of the appointment or election of a director (form **AP01** if the director is an individual, **AP02** if the director is a corporate body); the retirement, resignation, death or removal of a director (**TM01**); or any change in a director's name, service address, residential address, or other particulars entered in the register (**CH01** for individual director, **CH02** for corporate director). The forms can be downloaded from the Companies House website [see end of **chapter 1**]. *Companies Act 2006 ss.162-167*

Where the register must be kept. At the registered office or **inspection place** [**17.1.2**]. *Companies (Company Records) Regulations 2008 [SI 2008/3006]*

How long it must be kept. Throughout the life of the company and beyond [**18.5.1.5**]. The names of former directors cannot be removed.

Access. Must be open to members free of charge, and to the public for which a fee may be charged [**18.5.1.3**].

Copies. No statutory obligation on the company to provide a copy of information from the register of directors, but anyone may copy information directly from the register or obtain it from Companies House.

Availability via Companies House. Details of current company directors can be inspected at Companies House, or for a small fee can be purchased online via the Companies House website [see end of **chapter 1**].

18.5.4.1 Former names

A previous name does not need to be included if it was never used for business purposes, or if it was used for business purposes but changed or stopped being used before the person reached the age of 16, has not been used for the past 20 years, or was used before taking a title by a peer or other person usually known by a British title. *Companies Act 2006 s.163(3),(4)*

18.5.4.2 Service addresses

From 1 October 2009 the registers of directors and secretaries must show a **service address** – an address where Companies House correspondence may be sent to the director and legal documents may be served on him or her. It can be the director's or secretary's residential address, the company's registered office, or any other address where documents can be physically delivered and an acknowledgement of delivery can be obtained. *Companies Act 2006 s.163(1)(b); Companies Act 2006 (Annual Return & Service Addresses) Regulations 2008 [SI 2008/3000] reg.10*

Directors who prior to 1 October 2009 had to give a residential address but who now want to use a different service address should notify Companies House of their new service address and their usual residential address on form **CH01**. A secretary can submit a new service address on form **CH03**. The company must then enter the appropriate addresses in the registers.

18.5.5 Register of directors' residential addresses

From 1 October 2009, all companies must keep a confidential **register of directors' residential addresses** which includes the director's usual residential address, or a statement that the director's usual residential address is the same as the service address in the register of directors. *Companies Act 2006 s.165*

Updates. Must be kept up to date.

Notification. Companies House must be notified on form **CH01** within 14 days of any change in a director's service address or usual residential address. A change of service address must be accompanied by either a notice of any resulting change in the company's register of directors' residential addresses, or a statement that no such change is required. *Companies Act 2006 s.167(3)*

Where the register must be kept. Only at the registered office, and carefully protected against unauthorised access.

How long it must be kept. Throughout the life of the company and beyond [**18.5.1.5**].

Access. Unless it is used as service address, a director's or former director's usual residential address is **protected information** and can be used or disclosed by the company only to communicate with the director, to provide information to the registrar of companies as required under the Companies Acts, when disclosure is required under an order of the court, or when the director has given the company consent to use the address for a particular purpose. It is an offence to use it for any other purpose. Anyone using the information for company purposes must be made aware that it is protected and must not be used or disclosed inappropriately. *Companies Act 2006 ss.240,241*

Availability via Companies House. Provided protected information is submitted on the appropriate part of form **IN01** for the first directors, **AP01** for new directors or **CH01** when a director's details are changed, Companies House will not make it available to the public, can use it only for the purpose of communicating with the director, and can disclose it only to specified public authorities or credit reference agencies or under court order. A director, or the company acting on behalf of a director, may apply to Companies House to stop them disclosing the residential address to credit reference agencies. *Companies Act 2006 ss.242-244;*
Companies (Disclosure of Address) Regulations 2009 [SI 2009/214] regs.2-8

The registrar of companies can put the residential address on the public record if the director does not reply to documents sent to that address that require a reply within a specified period, or if there is evidence that documents sent to the service address are not being brought to the attention of the director.
Companies Act 2006 s.245

An individual whose residential address was placed on the public record at Companies House between 1 January 2003 and 30 September 2009 may apply to Companies House not to have that address made public. *Companies Act 2006 s.1088;*
Companies (Disclosure of Address) Regulations 2009 [SI 2009/214] regs.9-13

18.5.6 Register of secretaries

What must be kept. If there is or ever has been a company secretary, there must be a register of secretaries which must include:

- the name of each secretary [**14.3**] or all the names of joint secretaries;
- any former name or names by which the person was known for business purposes [see **18.5.4.1** for exceptions];
- a service address [**18.5.4.2**];
- date appointed and date of ceasing to be secretary. *Companies Act 2006 ss.275-277*

A secretary does not have to provide a residential address and if they do, there are no provisions under the **Companies Act 2006** for it not to be disclosed. However a secretary whose residential address was on the public register prior to 1 October 2009 can apply to Companies House in the same way as a company director for it not to be made public [**18.5.5**].

Form; updates; notification; where it must be kept; how long it must be kept; access; copies; availability via Companies House. As for the register of directors [**18.5.4**].

18.5.7 Directors' service contracts

What must be kept. Contracts of employment and other contracts under which a director or shadow director [**13.1.3**] agrees to provide services, as a director or in any other capacity, to the company or a subsidiary, plus any contracts with a third party under which the director will provide services to the company or a subsidiary. If the contract is not in writing, a memorandum setting out the terms of the contract must be kept. For charitable companies, agreements with trustees or connected persons must be in writing [**16.3.2**]. *Companies Act 2006 ss.227,228*

Updates. If a contract is changed the new version must also be kept.

Where they must be kept. At the registered office or **inspection place** [**18.5.1.2**]. All service contracts must be kept together.

How long they must be kept. At least one year from the expiry or termination of the contract.

Access. Open to company members free of charge [**18.5.1.3**].

Copies. Any company member must be provided with a copy of the contract or memorandum, within seven days of their request. A fee may be charged [**18.5.1.4**]. *Companies Act 2006 s.229*

18.5.8 Directors' indemnities

What must be kept. Copy of directors' and officers' insurance [**23.10**] or any other provisions for indemnifying directors. *Companies Act 2006 s.237*

Updates, where they must be kept, how long they must be kept, access, copies. As for directors' service contracts [**18.5.7**]. *Companies Act 2006 s.238*

18.5.9 Minutes books and records of resolutions

What must be kept. Minutes books containing an **authenticated** copy of the minutes of all general meetings [**19.11**], written resolutions by the company members [**19.10.2**], and meetings of the directors (governing body) [**19.12.7**].
Companies Act 2006 ss.248,249,355-358

Minutes are authenticated if they are signed by the person chairing that meeting or the next meeting. Resolutions are confirmed if they are signed by a director or the company secretary.

The articles of association generally require minutes of sub-committees to be kept as well. Even if this is not required, it is good practice.

Under the **Companies Act 1985** minutes of managers' (senior staff) meetings also had to be kept. This requirement is not in the **Companies Act 2006**, but it is good practice.

Form. Kept in a way which makes it as difficult as possible for anyone to alter them, and which makes it possible to detect falsification. *Companies Act 2006 s.1138*

Updates. Any alteration to the minutes (for example, to make a correction agreed at the next meeting) should be dated and initialled by the chairperson or secretary.

Where they must be kept. Minutes books of general meetings and records of written resolutions must be kept at the registered office or **inspection place** [**18.5.1.2**]. Minutes of directors' meetings may be kept anywhere convenient.

How long they must be kept. Minutes of general meetings, records of written resolutions and minutes of directors' meetings must be kept for at least 10 years. It is good practice to keep them throughout the life of the company, and beyond [**18.5.1.5**]. *Companies Act 2006 ss.248(2),355(2)*

Access. Minutes of general meetings and records of written resolutions must be open to company members free of charge [**18.5.1.3**]. Minutes of directors' meetings do not have to be open to anyone other than the directors and auditors.

Copies. Any company member is entitled to a copy of all or part of the minutes of any general meeting, within 14 days of asking for it. The company may charge a fee. There is no statutory obligation to provide anyone, other than the directors or auditors, with a copy of minutes of directors' meetings.

18.5.10   Accounting records

What must be kept. Accounting records must include up to date details of income, expenditure, assets and liabilities. If the company deals in goods, the records must also include an annual stock check.   *Companies Act 2006 ss.386,387*

Where they may be kept. Anywhere agreed by the directors.

How long they must be kept. Must be kept for three years and should generally be kept for at least six years [**18.4.2.5**].   *Companies Act 2006 s.388(4)*

Access. Open at all times to the company's officers [**14.1.1**] and its auditors.
Companies Act 2006 ss.388(1),499(1)

Copies. The company's officers and employees must provide its auditors with any information and explanations the auditors consider necessary for the performance of their duties [**55.2.1**]. Apart from this there is no statutory obligation on the company to provide copies of the accounting records to anyone, including the company's officers, but the officers may copy information from the records.

18.5.11   Register of charges and copies of charges

What must be kept. A **charge** is a mortgage or other loan, including floating charges, secured on the company's assets [**61.11**, **59.5**]. The register must be up to date, and must include date of the charge, a description of the instrument (if any) creating or evidencing the charge, names of the parties, details of the property secured by the charge, and amount of the charge.   *Companies Act 2006 s.876;*
Companies (Particulars of Company Charges) Regulations 2008 [SI 2008/2996]

When the charge is vacated (paid off) the entry should be crossed through or there should be space for the date vacated. It is sensible to have columns for the dates Companies House was notified of the creation and vacation of the charge.

In addition to the register, the company must also keep a copy of every charge.
Companies Act 2006 s.875

Information about registration of charges and mortgages is in Companies House GP3 *Life of a company: Event driven requirements*.

Form. As for register of members [**18.5.2**].

Notification. Notice of a charge or mortgage being created must be given to Companies House, with a £13 fee (as at 1/8/09), within 21 days on form **MG01**. Failure to do this is an offence, and the charge will be largely ineffective.
Companies Act 2006 ss.860-874

If **debentures** [**59.5.2**] are issued this must be notified to Companies House on form **MG07** or **MG08**.

Any repayment, in full or in part, or any other change must be notified on the relevant forms.

Where they must be kept. At the company's registered office or **inspection place** [**18.5.1.2**].

How long they must be kept. The **Companies Act 2006** does not specify how long records of charges should be kept but the normal rules about keeping property records and deeds for 12 years from the end of the company's interest in them [**18.4.2.10**] should be followed.

Access. Open to company members and to creditors (people to whom the company owes money) free of charge, and to the public for which a fee may be charged [**18.5.1.3**].

Copies. There is no obligation to provide copies.

Availability via Companies House. Details of charges can be inspected at Companies House, or can be purchased online via the Companies House website [see end of **chapter 1**].

18.5.12   Register of directors' interests in shares and debentures

From April 2007 the **Companies Act 2006** repealed the duty to keep a register of directors' interests in the shares or debentures [**59.5.2**] of the company, its parent company, its subsidiary company, or another subsidiary of the same parent company.

18.5.13 Register of holders of debentures

What may be kept. There is no obligation to keep a register of holders of the company's debentures [**59.5.2**], but if the company issues debentures and such a register is kept, it must comply with statutory requirements. Few voluntary organisations have debentures. *Companies Act 2006 ss.743-748*

Form. As for register of members [**18.5.2**].

Where it must be kept. At the registered office or **inspection place** [**18.5.1.2**].

How long it must be kept. Not specified but any liability arising from making, deleting or failing to make an entry in the register is not enforceable after 10 years. *Companies Act 2006 s.748*

Access. Open to holders of the company's debentures and shares free of charge, and to others for which a fee may be charged [**18.5.1.3**]. The company can apply to the court if it believes that the reason for requesting access is not a proper purpose. The register may be closed for up to 30 days each year if this is authorised in the company's articles of association, the debentures or the trust deed for the issue of the debentures. *Companies Act 2006 ss.744-746*

Copies. Holders of debentures have a right to a copy of any entry in the register, unless the company applies to the court on the basis that the copy is not sought for a proper purpose. A fee may be charged [**18.5.1.4**].

18.5.14 Register of sealings

What may be kept. A register of sealings is a list of documents the company has signed under seal [**20.1.3**]. Companies no longer need to have a seal, and even if they have one there is no obligation to keep a record of when it is used. If a register is not kept it is good practice to keep a record in minutes of the directors' meetings of when the seal's use is authorised and when it has been used.

18.6 INDUSTRIAL AND PROVIDENT SOCIETY RECORDS

One of the advantages of an industrial and provident society is that the record keeping is less onerous than for companies, with fewer statutory requirements.

Registers must be kept permanently. For details of how long to keep financial and employee records, see **18.4.2**. *Industrial & Provident Societies Act 1965 s.44*

18.6.1 Register of members

The register of members of an industrial and provident society must be up to date and must include each member's name and address, date registered as a member, date when ceased to be a member, the number of shares held by the member and the amount paid or agreed to be considered as paid on them, and other property such as loans or deposits held by each member.

The register must be kept at the registered office. If it is not in a bound book, there must be precautions against falsification.

Members and people with an interest in the society's funds have a right to see basic information for all members (name, address, date of joining or ceasing to be a member) but they have no right to see any financial entries (relating to shares and other property) except their own. So a duplicate register with only the 'public' information must be compiled, or the original register must be produced in such a way that it can be shown with only the 'public' information revealed. *Industrial & Provident Societies Act 1965 ss.44(3),46(1)*

An IPS's rules may say that officers have the right to inspect financial entries, or that the members can pass a resolution authorising any person(s) to do so. A person who is not an officer or authorised by a resolution may inspect financial entries only with the written consent of the person whose entry it is. *IPSA 1965 s.46(2)*

The IPS's auditors and registration authorities have the right to inspect the whole register at any reasonable time, and to see all documents relating to the IPS's affairs.
Industrial & Provident Societies Act 1965 s.44(4);
Friendly & Industrial & Provident Societies Act 1968 s.9(5)

If asked to do so by at least 10 members who have been members for at least one year, the registration authority can appoint an auditor to inspect the records and report on the society's affairs.
IPSA 1965 s.47

18.6.2 Register of officers

The register of officers covers committee members/directors, secretaries and treasurers and must include name, address, date of becoming an officer and date of ceasing to be an officer. It must be kept at the registered office, and if not in a bound book must be in a format which minimises the risk of falsification.
Industrial & Provident Societies Act 1965 s.44

Mutual Societies Registration must be notified in the annual return [**54.4.2**] of changes in committee members.

The register of officers must be open in the same way as the register of members to members, people with an interest in the IPS's funds, the IPS's auditor, the registration authority, and any auditor appointed by the registration authority.

18.6.3 Accounting records

The society must keep proper financial records showing its transactions, assets and liabilities. Members have no statutory right to see the financial records, but they do have a right to see their own financial details.
Industrial & Provident
Societies Act 1965 ss.45, 46

In addition, the rules may allow for members to see the financial records and/or for officers to see individual members' financial details, or the members may pass a resolution allowing someone to see individual details [**18.6.1**].

The most recent audited balance sheet [**54.4.2**] must be conspicuously displayed at the society's registered office.
IPSA 1965 s.40

18.6.4 Charges on assets

All charges on the society's assets must be notified to Mutual Societies Registration on form **AI** within 21 days along with a certified copy of the document creating the charge. The charge may be inspected by the public, but a register of charges does not have to be kept.
Industrial & Provident Societies Act 1967 s.1

If the charge is not notified within 21 days, or if there is an error in the registration of the charge, an application must be made to allow late registration or to amend the error.

18.7 CHARITABLE INCORPORATED ORGANISATIONS

At the time of writing (mid 2009) regulations on the paperwork requirements for charitable incorporated organisations (CIOs) had not been finalised. They will be similar to the rules for companies [**18.5**] but there are likely to be some significant differences. The final rules for the registers and other paperwork requirements will be available from the Charity Commission.

18.8 TRUSTS

Trustees in bodies set up as trusts must ensure the following are kept safely:
- the deed, declaration of trust, will or other instrument which set up the trust;
- deeds of appointment of new trustees, if under the terms of the governing document they are appointed by deed rather than by election;
- deeds for vesting assets in the trustees [**20.4.5**];
- details of retirement or death of trustees;

- financial records as required for tax, VAT and charity purposes;
- minutes of meetings of the trustees and their committees.

Charity requirements [**18.10**] apply to charitable trusts.

Members of the public have a right to some information about charitable trusts [**18.10.2**], but have no right to know anything about a private trust.

18.9 UNINCORPORATED ASSOCIATIONS

There is no statutory requirement for a non-charitable unincorporated association to keep any registers of members or committee members, or even to keep minutes. But it is good practice to keep such records, and they may be required by the association's governing document or funders.

If the association is charitable, the requirements of charity law apply [**18.10**].

It is implicitly the treasurer's duty to keep financial records and the secretary's duty to keep records of members and committee members and minutes of meetings, but the association's governing document, members or governing body may assign these duties to anyone.

For how long to keep records see **18.4.2**. For the organisation's purely internal records, such as minutes and records of members, the governing document may specify how long they must be kept. Otherwise, they should be kept indefinitely.

Unless the governing document specifies otherwise, the records may be kept anywhere reasonable and the association may decide for itself who may see the records. Generally the lists of members, officers and governing body members and minutes of general meetings should be open to members of the association. Minutes of meetings of the governing body should be open to members of the governing body. The governing document might say that they must also be open to all members of the association, or a general meeting or meeting of the governing body might agree that they should be open to all members.

Members of the public do not have a statutory right to know anything about the association unless it is charitable [below].

18.10 CHARITIES

All charities must keep accurate and up to date records of income, expenditure, assets and liabilities and the records required for their particular legal structure. Records must be retained for at least six years. For details of how long to keep other financial and employee records, see **18.4.2**.   *Charities Act 1993 s.41*

18.10.1 Notification to Charity Commission

In order to keep the register of charities up to date, the Charity Commission must be notified in writing of the following changes in registered charities:
- change in the name of the charity;
- change to the charity's objects, powers, or any other provision in the governing document affecting the charity's use of its income or property;
- change in type of governing document;
- change of correspondent (the Commission's contact person in the charity), address or other information held in the register.

The register is updated when the above information is provided, and annually through the Charity Commission's annual information update or annual return [**54.2.10**].

Registered charities with annual income over £25,000 (and other charities if requested to do so by the Commission) must file their annual accounts and report with the Commission [**54.2.9**]. The content of the report depends on the charity's income and on whether it is unincorporated or incorporated.

18.10.2   Access to information

Members of the public may consult the register of charities at Charity Commission offices [see end of **chapter 1**], or may request from the Commission details of charities, their objects, gross annual income and expenditure, and correspondent's name and address. Charity annual reports held by the Commission are also available. Extracts from the register, compliance information, full annual reports and other details are on the Commission website.   *Charities Act 1993 ss.3(8),47(1)*

The Commission publishes, with each charity's entry on the website, the names of the charity's trustees, but not their addresses. Where a trustee is at risk of personal danger if their name is publicised, the trustee can apply to the Commission for a dispensation from having their name included in the charity's annual report and the register of charities, and on the Commission's website.

All charities, even those which are not registered with the Commission, must provide a copy of their most recent annual accounts and report within two months to any member of the public who asks for it [**54.2.14**]. The public does not have a statutory right to any other information about charities.

Resources: COMMUNICATION AND PAPERWORK

See end of **chapter 1**.

Statute law. www.opsi.gov.uk and www.statutelaw.gov.uk.

Much but not all case law. www.bailii.org.

Updates cross-referenced to this book. www.rclh.co.uk.

Chapter 19

MEETINGS, RESOLUTIONS AND DECISION MAKING

19.1   MEETINGS AND THE LAW

Meetings of an organisation's members, governing body and committees are governed by:

- the organisation's **governing document** and its standing orders or other rules relating to its meetings;
- for companies, **company law** [throughout this chapter];
- for industrial and provident societies, legislation relating to notice [**19.3.1.3, 19.3.4.1**] and resolutions [**19.7.5**];
- for charitable trusts and associations, legislation relating to notice [**19.3.1.4, 19.3.3.3**];
- **common law** relating to **private meetings**, if the governing document, and legislation if relevant, are silent about a matter. Different rules apply to **public meetings** [**47.7.2**].

236

Decisions made at a meeting which is not properly convened or conducted are not valid. Basic good practice for all meetings – not just in charities – is set out in the Charity Commission's CC48 *Charities and meetings*, free from the Commission.

19.1.1 Validity of meetings

A meeting is valid only if it is **properly convened**, **legally constituted** and **properly held**. These requirements have been defined in common law. Decisions made at an invalid meeting may be subsequently ratified at a valid meeting – but if not ratified could, if challenged, be held to be invalid.

Re Sick & Funeral Society of St John's Sunday School, Golcar [1973] Ch 51

19.1.1.1 Properly convened

To be properly convened:

- the meeting must be called by a body or individuals having the right to do so under the governing document or statute;
- a general meeting (meeting of the organisation's members) must be convened in the interests of the organisation as a whole, not in the interests of a particular individual or group of members;
- a general meeting must not be convened at an unreasonable time or place;
- in choosing the time and place there must not be any deliberate intention of excluding certain members by making it impossible or very difficult for them to attend;
- notice must be sent to everyone entitled to receive it [**19.3.1**]; and
- the notice must give all legally required information [**19.3.6**].

19.1.1.2 Legally constituted

To be legally constituted:

- there must be a properly appointed chairperson for the meeting [**19.5.1**];
- a quorum must be present when the meeting starts and, if required, throughout the meeting [**19.6**];
- for companies, the provisions of the Companies Acts relating to meetings must be complied with;
- for other types of organisation, such as industrial and provident societies or charitable incorporated organisations, any statutory provisions relating to their meetings must be complied with; and
- the provisions of the governing document must be complied with.

19.1.1.3 Properly held

For a meeting to be properly held:

- if those attending are not all in the same room, they must all be able to see and hear each other through audio-visual links, unless the governing document allows meetings where members cannot all see and hear each other;

Byng v London Life Assurance Ltd [1989] 2 WLR 738, 1 All ER 560

- for companies, decision making and voting must follow the procedures set out in the Companies Acts [**19.7.4**];
- decision making and voting must follow the procedures set out in the organisation's governing document; and
- the chairperson must ensure 'the sense of the meeting is ascertained' on all matters under discussion, in other words that resolutions and issues are clearly presented and members who want to give their views are enabled to do so;

National Dwellings Society v Sykes [1894] 3 Ch 159,162

- the chairperson must not refuse to allow relevant amendments to resolutions, unless amendments at the meeting are prevented by statute or the governing document;   *Henderson v Bank of Australasia [1890] 45 ChD 330*
- the meeting must be held fairly, people must have a right to be heard on matters which affect them individually, and other principles of natural justice [see, for example, **12.8.5**] must be followed.

237

19.1.2 Decisions without attending meetings

19.1.2.1 Written resolutions, postal and electronic voting

Company members have a statutory right to make most decisions by written resolution [**19.10.2**], and do not have to hold any general meetings unless the articles require this, the members require it, or a director or auditor is going to be removed before the end of their term of office [**19.2.2.1**].

Organisations which are not companies may make decisions without a meeting by using written resolutions [**19.10.1**] or postal or electronic voting [**19.8.4**] only if this is explicitly allowed by the governing document.

19.1.2.2 Telephone and electronic meetings

Provided all participants can see and hear each other [**19.1.1.3**], any organisation can hold meetings by video conference or electronic media unless the governing document prohibits this. Only if the governing document explicitly allows can meetings can be held via telephone, the internet, instant messaging or other methods where participants can communicate but not see and hear each other.

If the governing document does not allow meetings or decisions by telephone or electronic media, an in principle decision made in this way may be ratified at a subsequent valid meeting, or it may be possible to ratify it by written resolution [**19.1.2.1**, **19.10**].   *Re Associated Color Laboratories Ltd [1970] 12 DLR (3d) 338, 73 WWR 566*

Community Network [see end of chapter] can provide advice on telephone meetings and suitable governing document amendments.

The rules relating to notice, quorum, chairing, minutes etc for meetings held by telephone or electronic media are the same as for meetings in person.

19.1.2.3 Appointing a proxy

Members unable to attend a general meeting may be able to appoint a **proxy** to attend on their behalf. Company members have a statutory right to appoint a proxy to attend, speak and vote on their behalf at a company meeting [**19.8.3.2**]. In non-companies, an eligible member can appoint a proxy if the governing document allows [**19.8.3**]. In a non-company a proxy has a right to attend and vote, but can speak at the meeting only if the governing document explicitly allows.

19.1.3 Company law versus the articles

Because company law contains many provisions relating to decision making and a company's articles of association may also be very detailed, it can sometimes be difficult to know which provision takes precedence. In general:

- if neither company law nor the articles say anything about a particular point (for example, about procedures for chairing meetings) the company's standing orders or internal rules prevail, or if there are none, common law;
- if company law has provision and the articles do not, company law prevails;
- if the articles say something and company law does not, the articles prevail;
- if company law and the articles both say the same thing, there's no problem;
- if company law is different from the articles, the articles generally take priority but for some issues (for example, the obligation to allow proxy voting or to allow written resolutions on company law matters) company law prevails. The most significant of these provisions are explained in this chapter.

19.1.4 Conflicts of interest

It is good practice for participants in any meeting to declare any relevant **conflict of interest** at the start of the meeting or when an issue starts to be discussed, even if the conflict has already been disclosed through a **register of conflicts of interest** [**15.2.4**]. However the legal position distinguishes between meetings of the members of an organisation, and meetings of the governing body.

Governing body members normally have a legal duty to act in the best interest of the organisation, and in many cases must declare conflicts of interest [**15.3.5**,

15.6.4]. But ordinary members of an organisation – including governing body members, when taking part in a general meeting – are in most cases entitled, unless the governing document says otherwise, to act and vote in their own interest.

The exception is charitable incorporated organisations, where ordinary members of the CIO, like governing body members, have a statutory obligation to act in the interest of the CIO, and must therefore declare conflicts of interest [**12.4.2**].

19.2 GENERAL MEETINGS

Companies, industrial and provident societies, charitable incorporated organisations and most associations are two-tier structures which have **members of the organisation**, and a separate **governing body** which is responsible for managing the organisation on behalf of the members. A **general meeting** is a meeting of the members of the organisation. In small organisations the same people may occupy both tiers, but the two tiers are constitutionally and legally separate and must act separately.

Company law includes detailed provisions for most aspects of company meetings, but the meetings of other membership organisations are governed primarily by their governing document and common law. A governing document may include detailed provisions for notice [**19.3**], quorum [**19.6**], decision making [**19.7**], minutes [**19.11**] and other matters, and these must be carefully followed.

Where there is neither statutory provision nor specific provision in the governing document, the organisation may have standing orders or other rules. If not, the common law applies.

19.2.1 Annual general meetings

Under common law there is no requirement for a membership organisation to hold an annual general meeting, but the requirement is generally included in the governing document. The governing document should include the rules for notice, quorum, chairing, business at the meeting, and adjournment.

19.2.1.1 Companies

Unless required under the articles of association, private companies (which virtually all voluntary sector and community interest companies are) are not required to hold an annual general meeting or any other general meetings. There are statutory provisions for circulating the annual accounts and reports [**54.3.8**], and the decisions normally taken at an AGM can be made at an ordinary general meeting [**19.2.2.1**] or by written resolution [**19.10.2**].

Where a company whose articles require an AGM had in place on 30 September 2007 an elective resolution [**19.7.4.6**] not to hold AGMs, the company can continue not to hold them and in due course should amend its articles to remove the requirement.

Most voluntary sector companies with a membership wider than the directors are likely to want to hold AGMs, and some funders may require or expect it. But where there is no particular need for an AGM, companies may wish to amend their articles [**7.5.3**] to remove the requirement, and make alternative arrangements for the election of directors and other business which the articles specify for the AGM.

Where the articles require an AGM, any provisions about when the first AGM must be held, the maximum time between AGMs, notice period, quorum etc must be followed. If the articles do not say anything, the company law rules for general meetings apply [**19.2.2.1**].

If there is no requirement for an AGM the directors may choose to hold one, or company members may require one to be called [**19.2.2.2**]. This would generally just be called a **general meeting** rather than an AGM. The company law rules for general meetings must be followed [**19.2.2.1**].

19.2.1.2 Ordinary business at a company AGM

Where a company's articles require an AGM, they are likely to list the business which must be transacted. This generally includes the **ordinary business** of presentation and consideration of the accounts, balance sheet, directors' report and auditor's report (if one is required) for the previous year [**54.3.8**]; election of directors [**13.4.2**]; if required, appointment of independent examiner or auditor(s) [**55.3.3**]; and setting the remuneration of the auditor [**55.3.4**] or authorising the directors to set it.

If the articles do not say that this business must be transacted at the AGM or another general meeting, it does not have to be done at a meeting. The annual accounts and reports may simply be sent or provided to all company members and others entitled to receive them [**54.3.8**], directors remain in post until they are removed or replaced under the procedures in the articles, and the company law provisions on renewal of the auditor's term apply [**55.3.3**].

19.2.1.3 Special business at a company AGM

Where the articles require an AGM and specify the ordinary business, other business may also be included, or the AGM may be closed and a general meeting (which may in the articles be called an extraordinary general meeting or EGM) may be convened for the other business. Anything which is not ordinary business would be **special business** and depending on what is being proposed, requires an ordinary or special resolution [**19.7.4**].

19.2.1.4 Charitable incorporated organisations

The constitution of a charitable incorporated organisation must include provision for an annual general meeting of the CIO's members. At the time of writing (mid 2009) detailed regulations had not been finalised. *Charities Act 1993 sch.5B para.13(3), to be inserted by Charities Act 2006 sch.7 para.2 [expected April 2010];*

19.2.2 General meetings other than the AGM

General meetings other than the AGM are called **general**, **ordinary**, **extraordinary** or **special** meetings. There is usually no significance in what they are called. The governing document usually sets out any requirement for how often general meetings must be held; the procedure for calling a general meeting; the procedure, if any, for a minimum number or percentage of members to require (**requisition**) the secretary or governing body to call a general meeting; who is entitled to attend and vote at general meetings; and others entitled to receive notice of general meetings.

Statutory provisions apply to companies, and similar provisions may apply to charitable incorporated organisations (CIOs). Where statutory provisions are different from those in the governing document it is not always clear which takes precedence, and legal advice may be necessary.

19.2.2.1 Company general meetings

Any meeting of the company members which is not defined in the notice of the meeting as an AGM is under company law a **general meeting**. In the articles it may be called an **extraordinary general meeting** (**EGM**) or similar name.

Unless the articles require it, private companies are not obliged to hold general meetings, except to remove a director or auditor before the end of their term of office [**13.5.6**, **55.3.6**] or if the members of the company require it [below].

The directors may call a general meeting at any time, provided they give proper notice [**19.3**] and comply with any provisions in the articles, and must call any general meetings required by the articles of association. *Companies Act 2006 s.302*

19.2.2.2 Company members' right to require a general meeting

Company members holding at least 10% of the voting rights have a right to require (**requisition**) the directors to call a general meeting. If more than 12 months has elapsed since the last general meeting, it may be possible in some situations for this to be done by only 5% of the members. *Companies Act 2006 s.303*

If the organisation has only individual members and/or organisational members with one vote each this will be 10% (or 5%) of the members, but this will not be the case if some members have more than one vote.

The request must state the general nature of the business to be dealt with at the meeting, and may include the text of any resolution proposed for the meeting. Within 21 days of receiving it, the directors must send out notice of a general meeting. Where the request includes a proposed resolution, the text must be included in the notice. Depending on the resolution the period of notice is the same as for a general meeting or for a special resolution at a general meeting [**19.3.4.1**]. The general meeting date cannot be more than 28 days after the notice date. *Companies Act 2006 s.304*

If the directors do not send out notice of a general meeting within the 21 day period, those who requested it (or those representing more than half their total voting rights) may call a general meeting. The company must reimburse them for any reasonable expenses incurred in calling the meeting. *Companies Act 2006 s.305*

19.2.3   Preparing for a general meeting

General meetings are normally called by the governing body, who direct the secretary or company secretary (if there is one) and/or others to undertake the necessary preparation. In all organisations – not only companies – this involves ensuring:

- all rules relating to notice for the meeting are complied with [**19.3**];
- a suitable venue is booked for the meeting, and all necessary special provisions (disability access, interpreters, crèche etc) are arranged;
- accurate lists exist of members, auditors, debenture holders (if applicable) and others who under the governing document or statute must be invited to general meetings;
- lists are drawn up of any others who will be invited (funders, patrons etc);
- if the annual accounts, report of the auditor or independent examiner (if any) and report of the governing body are going to be presented, that they are completed, approved, signed as required, printed and circulated [**chapter 54**];
- if legislation or the governing document requires the accounts to be approved by the governing body and presented at the meeting, the originals of the signed accounts and report are available at the meeting, or if the governing document requires the accounts to be approved at the general meeting, originals are available to be signed at the meeting;
- notice and all necessary documentation is sent out as required, including the text of any resolutions;
- for all companies, and for other organisations where the governing document allows proxy voting, a statement is included informing the members of their right to appoint a proxy [**19.8.3**] and the necessary forms are produced;
- if the governing document allows postal or electronic voting [**19.8.4**], the necessary statement and forms are included;
- arrangements are made for attendance sheets and for proof of authority for representatives of members which are themselves organisations;
- arrangements are made for voting, for example voting cards, ballots for elections and/or voting slips if a poll [**19.8.2**] is expected;
- postal or electronic votes are totalled before the meeting, and proxy votes if the proxy has been given to the chairperson rather than to an individual who will attend the meeting;
- the governing document and any standing orders relating to general meetings are read and understood by the chairperson and secretary, and will be available at the meeting in case they need to be referred to;
- the meeting is run according to the governing document, standing orders, any applicable legislation, and common law;
- the meeting is properly minuted [**19.11**];
- all necessary changes are made to registers (lists) of governing body members and other registers after the meeting [**18.5-18.9**];

241

- if applicable, all necessary information and forms are sent to Companies House within the required period, which is usually 14 or 15 days after the general meeting, and/or are sent to the Charity Commission or other regulators.

19.3   NOTICE

Common law applies unless there are specific provisions in legislation or the governing document.

19.3.1   Entitlement to notice

19.3.1.1   Common law and the governing document

Notice must be given to everyone entitled to attend the meeting and to others entitled, under statute or the governing document, to receive notice.

John v Rees [1970] Ch 345,402

Unless legislation [below] or the governing document says otherwise, the organisation is not obliged to give notice:

- to a member who is too ill to attend;   *Young v Ladies' Imperial Club [1920] 2 KB 523*
- to a member who is too far away to attend; or   *Smyth v Darley [1849] 2 HL Cas 789*
- if all members entitled to attend are present and agree to a meeting being held without notice.   *Re Express Engineering Works [1920] 1 Ch 466*

Unless they are too ill or too far away to attend, notice must be given to members who have said they are unable to attend.   *Re Portuguese Consolidated Copper Mines [1889] 42 ChD 160*

It is the member's responsibility to ensure the organisation has a correct address if notices are sent, or might be sent, by post.

19.3.1.2   Companies

Notice of a company's general meetings must be given or sent to all company members and directors [see **13.1.3** for who is a director], unless the articles provide otherwise, and to the company's auditors, if any.   *Companies Act 2006 ss.310,502(2)*

Unless the articles provide otherwise notice must be given even if members are too ill or too far away to attend or have said they cannot attend.

19.3.1.3   Industrial and provident societies

In an industrial and provident society, notice of general meetings and all information sent to members about general meetings must also be sent to the society's auditor or auditors.   *Friendly & Industrial & Provident Societies Act 1968 s.9(7)*

19.3.1.4   Charitable trusts and associations

It is not necessary to give notice to a member of a charitable trust or association if the charity does not have a UK address for him or her.   *Charities Act 1993 s.81*

19.3.2   Non-receipt of notice

Under common law, a meeting is invalid unless notice is given to every person entitled to receive it [**19.3.1**]. Governing documents therefore nearly always provide that accidental failure to give notice or non-receipt of notice does not invalidate the meeting, and company law also includes this provision in relation to most general meetings and resolutions. But deliberately 'forgetting' or neglecting to give notice makes the meeting invalid.   *Companies Act 2006 s.313*

19.3.3   How notice is given

19.3.3.1   Common law and the governing document

For non-companies with nothing in the governing document about how notice is given, the governing body decides but the method(s) chosen must be reasonable. What is 'reasonable' depends on the circumstances. It might be reasonable, for example, for notice to be given verbally, displayed at the organisation's premises,

advertised in the organisation's newsletter or on its website, advertised on posters, given by hand to each member, or sent by post, fax, email or other electronic means. Failure to give reasonable notice could invalidate decisions made at the meeting.   *Labouchere v Earl of Wharncliffe [1879] 13 ChD 346,352;*
Young v Ladies' Imperial Club [1920] 2 KB 523

If important decisions about the organisation or the rights of members will be considered at the meeting, notice should be given individually to each member instead of being given publicly.   *Re GKN Sports & Social Club [1982] 1 WLR 774, 2 All ER 855*

19.3.3.2   Companies

Provided the legal requirements are complied with, notice of a company general meeting may be given in hard copy, electronically or on a website, or a combination of these methods. Company law specifies the addresses (postal or electronic) to which communications can be sent or delivered, when they are deemed to have been delivered, and how communications can be authenticated [**18.3**].

If given electronically or on a website the rules relating to electronic communications [**18.3.4**, **18.3.6**] must be strictly followed. In particular:

- notice can be given by email, fax, posting a CD or similar electronic means only if the member has explicitly agreed to receive notice (of this particular meeting, or all general meetings) by this method;

- notice can be given via a website only if this is allowed under the articles or by a resolution of the members, *and* the particular member has either explicitly agreed to receive notice by this method or can be treated as having given **deemed agreement** [**18.3.6**];

- where a member has received notice electronically or via a website they can still request a hard copy, and this must be provided free of charge.
Companies Act 2006 s.308, sch.4,5

When a company puts a notice of a meeting on a website, this must be notified to each member who has agreed (or been deemed to have agreed) to receive notice via the website. This notification may be done by post, by hand or electronically, but if it is done electronically the appropriate consent to receive notices electronically must have been received from each member notified in this way. This notification must state that the notice relates to a general meeting; give the place, date and time of the meeting; give the website address; give the place on the website where the notice may be accessed; and explain how the notice (including any documents or information forming part of the notice) may be accessed.
Companies Act 2006 s.309(2), sch.5 para.13

The notice itself must be available on the website throughout the notice period until the end of the meeting in question.   *Companies Act 2006 s.309(3)*

Guidance on electronic communications with company members is available from the Institute of Chartered Secretaries and Administrators [see end of chapter].

19.3.3.3   Charitable trusts and associations

Notice of meetings of a charitable trust or association may be sent by post and is deemed to be given 'by the time at which the letter containing it would be delivered in the ordinary course of post' [**19.3.5**]. Other forms of notice may be permitted by common law or the governing document [**19.3.1.1**].   *Charities Act 1993 s.81*

19.3.3.4   Charitable incorporated organisations

The regulations for charitable incorporated organisations, which at the time of writing had not been finalised, will allow for electronic communication between the CIO and its members. The rules are likely to be similar to those for companies [**19.3.3.2**]. Details will be available from the Charity Commission.

19.3.4   Period of notice

If neither statute nor the governing document specifies a period of notice, the governing body decides the period, which must be 'reasonable' for an organisation of that type. There is no default position in common law, but the company law requirement of 14 days for general meetings could be used as a guide [**19.3.4.1**].

19.3.4.1 Companies

The statutory period of notice for all general meetings of private companies (which the vast majority of voluntary sector companies are) is 14 days, unless the articles of association require longer. Companies whose articles require a longer notice period may wish to amend them [**7.5.3**]. *Companies Act 2006 s.307(1),(3)*

Members holding not less than 90% of the total voting rights of the company (or a higher percentage, not exceeding 95%, if specified in the articles) may agree to shorter notice. *Companies Act 2006 s.307(6)*

The consent to a shorter period of notice does not have to be in writing, but it would be sensible to get written consent. The consent may be given either before or at the meeting. But if consent is not sought until the meeting and the required number of members do not agree, the meeting cannot be held.

19.3.4.2 Industrial and provident societies

In general industrial and provident society legislation does not set out a period of notice, but it must be included in each society's rules. The exception is when an auditor is being removed or is not being reappointed [**55.5**]. In this situation the society must be given notice at least 28 days before the meeting and must then give notice to members and the retiring auditor with the notice of the meeting, or 14 days before the meeting. *Friendly & Industrial & Provident Societies Act 1968 ss.5(1)(a),6*

19.3.5 Clear days

Unless otherwise defined by statute or in the governing document, any period of notice referred to in the governing document means **clear days**. *Re Railway Sleepers Supply Company [1885] 29 ChD 204*

Under common law clear days do not include the day on which the meeting is to be held, and the day on which the notice is handed to someone or left at their address, or the days on which it is posted, is in the post and is assumed to be delivered. A governing document may specify how many days a notice is assumed to be in the post. If it does not, company law [**18.3.1**] could be used as a guide.

Company law defines clear days in the same way, and also specifies when a communication – whether sent through the post or electronically – is deemed to have been delivered [**18.3.1**]. *Companies Act 2006 s.360*

19.3.6 Contents of notice

Under common law a notice for a general meeting must contain the date, time and place of the meeting; type of meeting (annual general, extraordinary general etc); a clear indication of the business to be transacted, especially special business [below], with any decisions to be made set out clearly enough to enable members to know what is being considered; date of the notice; and signature of the person calling, or authorised to call, the meeting.

If one meeting is to be held immediately after another, the time may be given as 'at the conclusion of the XXX meeting'.

Routine matters are **ordinary business**. **Special business** may be defined in the governing document, or if not defined, includes matters such as amending the governing document or expelling a member. Ordinary and special business should not be confused with ordinary and special **resolutions** [**19.7.4**].

Unless required under legislation or the governing document, there is no obligation under common law to include in the notice the exact details of business or to give the full text of resolutions. However, it is good practice to do so. *Betts & Co Ltd v MacNaughton [1910] Ch 430*

The notice usually includes the agenda, showing the order in which the items of business will be taken. Unless a majority at the meeting agrees otherwise, the items must be considered in the order they are listed on the agenda. *John v Rees [1970] Ch 345,378*

Matters which are not included in the notice cannot be considered at the meeting unless they are minor and unimportant and are included under an 'any other business' item on the agenda. *Young v Ladies' Imperial Club [1920] 2 KB 523*

19.3.6.1   Companies

The notice of a company general meeting must contain the date (including year), time and place of the meeting; the exact wording of any special resolution [**19.7.4.1**], and a statement that the resolution is special; the general nature of other business, including the exact wording or a general explanation of ordinary resolutions [**19.7.4.4**]; a statement that every member has a right under the **Companies Act 2006** s.324 to appoint a proxy, who does not have to be a member of the company, to attend, speak and vote instead of the member [**19.8.3.2**]; the deadline for returning proxy forms, which must not be more than 48 hours (as defined in the Act) before the meeting; statements properly provided by members [**19.3.7**] about any matter to be dealt with at the meeting.

Companies Act 2006 ss.283(6),311,315, 325, 326

The notice should also contain details of how to obtain a proxy form, if they are not sent out with the notice.

Failure to include the statement that any member may appoint a proxy is an offence but does not invalidate the meeting.   *Companies Act 2006 s.325*

A resolution which is not covered by the 'general nature of other business' as given in the notice cannot be passed at the meeting. However members may, after the formal business has been completed, discuss matters which are not included in the notice. They may not make decisions, but the discussions and recommendations may be taken into account by directors when they later make decisions.

19.3.7   Company members' statements

Members representing 5% of a company's voting rights may require the company to circulate a statement of not more than 1,000 words about a resolution or other business to be dealt with at any general meeting.   *Companies Act 2006 ss.314-317*

The statement may be in hard copy or electronic form, must be authenticated [**18.3.2**], and must be delivered to the company at least one week before the meeting at which it is to be proposed. It must then be circulated, insofar as possible, in the same way and at the same time as the notice of the meeting, or as soon as reasonably practicable after notice has been given. Where statements are delivered to the company at the last minute, the company will need to have procedures to circulate them very quickly, either electronically to members who have agreed to receive company communications this way [**18.3.4**], or by first class post.

The company or any other person may apply to the court if they believe the right to require a statement to be circulated is being abused.

Unless the company members have previously agreed otherwise, circulation of members' statements is at the expense of the members who requested the circulation. If the members have not agreed to pay for the distribution, the members requesting it must provide to the company, no later than one week before the meeting to which it applies, a reasonable sum to cover distribution costs. If this is not provided, the company does not have to circulate the statement.

19.4   POSTPONEMENT OR CANCELLATION

Postponement is delaying a meeting after notice has been given, but before the meeting has begun. It is different from **adjournment** [**19.9**], which is stopping a meeting after it has started with the intention of continuing it at another time.

Unless the governing document explicitly allows, a meeting for which notice has been properly given may not be postponed or cancelled. The meeting must technically be opened and then be properly adjourned.   *Smith v Paringa Mines [1906] 2 Ch 193*

19.5   CHAIRING MEETINGS
19.5.1   Appointment of chairperson

If a chairperson has been elected or appointed under the governing document but is not present, or is unable or unwilling to chair, the deputy or vice-chair chairs, if one has been chosen under the rules in the governing document. If there is no deputy or vice-chair or they are not at the meeting, the meeting must elect someone to chair the meeting. The governing document may specify how this is done.

Under common law, where the governing document does not specify how the chairperson is to be chosen, the members present at a meeting may elect any member present to chair the meeting. For companies, if the articles do not specify who chairs general meetings, any member at the meeting may be elected to chair.

Companies Act 2006 s.319

19.5.2   Chairperson's duties

The person chairing the meeting has a duty to:

- ensure that he or she has been properly appointed as chair;
- act in the interests of the organisation as a whole;
- ensure in a company that the Companies Acts are followed, or in other types of organisation that any statutory requirements are complied with;
- ensure that the requirements and procedures in the governing document and standing orders are followed;
- ensure that the meeting has been properly convened [**19.1.1.1**] and proper notice [**19.3**] has been given;
- ensure that the rules relating to quorum [**19.6**] are followed;
- take the business in the order set out in the notice of the meeting or the agenda, unless a majority of members present agree to a change in the order;
- ensure that no business is transacted unless it is within the scope of the notice which has been given;
- ensure that speakers keep their remarks to the business under discussion;
- clearly state resolutions, ensure that voting or other decision making is properly carried out, ensure that only people authorised to vote take part in decisions, and declare the results of decisions [**19.8.5.4**];
- organise a poll (counted vote) if one is demanded [**19.8.2**];
- keep order;
- adjourn the meeting properly, if adjournment is necessary [**19.9**];
- ensure that the meeting is minuted and any decisions recorded [**19.11**];
- ensure that there is a clear end to the meeting.

The person chairing the meeting has the right to insist that a disorderly or abusive person leaves the meeting [**47.7.1**], and to call the police if necessary.

19.6   QUORUM

A meeting may not transact business (vote or make decisions in any other way) unless it is **quorate**. A **quorum** is the minimum number of members with voting rights who have to be present. Unless the governing document or legislation specifies otherwise, the quorum for a general meeting is a majority of the members and may not be less than two.   *Ellis v Hooper [1859] 28 LJ Ex 1; Sharp v Dawes [1876] 2 QBD 26; Re Sanitary Carbon Co [1877] WN 223*

In organisations which are not companies the quorum includes only members present in person, unless the governing document states that the quorum also includes members represented by proxies [**19.8.3**].

In a company, unless the articles of association require otherwise, the quorum for a general meeting is two members personally present or represented by proxies. However the two persons present cannot both be representatives of the same corporate member, nor can they both be proxies appointed by the same member. A quorum of one is valid for a company's general meeting if it is a private company with only one member [**12.4.1**].   *Companies Act 2006 s.318*

If a meeting is inquorate, it must be **adjourned** [**19.9**]. The governing document may include rules for adjournment in this situation. Although an inquorate meeting cannot make any decisions, after adjournment the members may discuss issues and make recommendations. Decisions can then be made at a quorate adjourned meeting or, if allowed, by written resolution [**19.10**], or recommendations may be taken into account when the directors subsequently make decisions.

If the governing document or legislation prohibits some members from participating in certain decisions – for example, if they have a conflict of interest [**15.2**] – they are not part of the quorum for that part of the meeting. If there are not enough disinterested (unconflicted) members to form a quorum, that issue cannot be decided [**15.2.4**].   *Yuill v Greymouth Point Elizabeth Railway & Coal Company Ltd [1904] 1 Ch 32*

19.6.1   Members leaving during meeting

If the meeting starts with a quorum but some members subsequently leave and the number falls below the quorum, generally no further decisions can be made and the meeting must be adjourned.   *Re Romford Canal Co [1883] 24 ChD 85*

If, however, the governing document specifies that a quorum needs to be present 'when the meeting proceeds to business' (or words to that effect), the quorum needs to be present only at the start of the meeting. Decisions are valid even if they are taken after numbers fall below the quorum.   *Re Hartley Baird Ltd [1954] 1 Ch 143*

If the meeting must be quorate throughout and a person deliberately leaves in order to make it inquorate, that member would be unlikely to be able to claim successfully that decisions made after his or her departure were invalid.

Ball v Pearsall [1987] 10 NSWLR 700

19.7   MOTIONS AND RESOLUTIONS

Many voluntary organisations do not go through a formal process of motions, resolutions, amendments and voting at meetings. But even where an organisation operates in general by **consensus** [**19.8**], some decisions – such as those required under the governing document, by statute or by external bodies such as a bank when changing signatories – should be made through a formal motion and vote.

A **motion** is any matter of business requiring a decision. A motion is **moved** or **proposed**, is **seconded** if this is required, is put to the **vote**, and if it is agreed becomes a **resolution**. But the terms proposal, motion and resolution are often used interchangeably.

A motion must be proposed as required by the governing document or by standing orders or other rules governing the meeting [**7.4.25**]. Unless required by the governing document or rules, there is no need for any motion to be seconded.

Once a motion has been proposed, it can be withdrawn only if the meeting agrees.

19.7.1   Amendments

An **amendment** is a proposal to change a motion. Prior notice of an amendment must be given if required by the governing document or other rules; otherwise an amendment may be proposed at any time before a vote is taken on the motion.

If prior notice of the motion has been given, the amendment cannot create a situation where a substantively different matter is being voted on. For company special resolutions [**19.7.4.1**], generally the only amendments that should be made are to correct typographical or grammatical errors.

If the governing document or standing orders do not specify the procedure for amendments, the chairperson decides whether to accept an amendment, whether to allow amendments to an amendment, and whether to call a vote on each amendment separately and then put the revised motion to the meeting, or to wait and vote on all the amendments (and amendments to amendments) together. In this case they are voted on in the order in which they affect the motion, not the order in which they were proposed. The agreed amendments are then incorporated into the original motion, and the new version is put to the vote.

Amendments are always voted on before the original motion. The motion which is put to the meeting after all the agreed amendments have been incorporated into it is called a **substantive motion**.

19.7.2 Dropped motions

A motion is **dropped**, is **withdrawn** or **fails** if a seconder is required by the governing document or other rules and no one seconds it, or if the person who proposed the motion withdraws it and the meeting agrees to this withdrawal. A proposed amendment may be withdrawn only if the meeting agrees.

A motion is **shelved**, **deferred** or **not put** if the meeting decides through a procedural motion [below] not to vote on it.

19.7.3 Procedural motions

Formal or **procedural** motions regulate the business of a meeting, but are not directly concerned with the content of the business. A **dilatory motion** is a procedural motion which is misused, for example to call a vote before adequate time has been given to discussion. A chairperson has the right to reject a procedural motion if it appears to have been proposed for a dilatory purpose.

The main procedural motions are:

- **That the question now be put**, proposed after adequate discussion, or sometimes as a way of curtailing discussion prematurely. In the latter case the chairperson has to decide whether to allow it to be voted on. This motion is called a **closure**. If approved, the original motion is voted on; if not approved, discussion on the original motion continues.

- **That the meeting proceed to next business**, to move on without voting on the motion. If approved, the motion is **shelved** and the meeting moves to its next business; if not approved, the original discussion continues.

- **That the question not now be put** (called a **previous question**). If this is agreed, the original motion is shelved and the meeting moves to its next business. If not approved, the original motion is immediately voted on, without further discussion.

- **That the meeting postpone consideration of the matter** until later in the meeting or until a subsequent meeting, usually because of inadequate information at present. If approved, discussion is **postponed**; if not approved, discussion continues.

- **That the debate be adjourned**, which has the same effect as postponement. Usually postponement is used before discussion starts on a motion, and adjournment after discussion has started.

- **That the recommendation be referred back to committee**, to require further work to be done or information to be provided by the committee which proposed the motion. If approved, discussion is **curtailed**; if not approved, discussion continues.

- **That the meeting be adjourned**, to close the meeting and re-open it at another time [**19.9**].

19.7.4 Company resolutions

A company resolution which is not passed properly is invalid, so it is important to understand different resolutions and how they are passed either at a general meeting or by written resolution. GP3 *Life of a company: Event driven requirements* from Companies House [see end of chapter] has a section on resolutions.

19.7.4.1 Special resolutions

A **special resolution** must have at least 75% of the votes cast, or more if it relates to an **entrenched provision** [**19.7.4.3**]. If passed at a general meeting it requires at least 14 clear days' notice [**19.3.5**] or longer if required by the articles of association. If passed as a written resolution it must comply with the relevant rules [**19.10.2**].   *Companies Act 2006 ss.283,307*

In companies limited by guarantee a special resolution is required:

- to amend the articles of association or the objects clause [**7.5.3**];

Companies Act 2006 ss.21,31

- to change the name of the company [**6.7.1**], unless the articles specify that it can be changed without a special resolution;   *Companies Act 2006 ss.77-79*

- for a company whose registered office must be in England or Wales to change its domicile to Wales only, or for a company whose registered office must be in Wales to change it to England or Wales [**17.1.1**]; *Companies Act 2006 s.88*
- in some situations, to wind up the company [**24.4.3**, **24.5.3**];
- for any other decisions where the articles of association or statute specifically require a special resolution.

Charitable companies must obtain prior written consent from the Charity Commission for a change of objects and some changes to the articles. Similar consent provisions apply to charities registered in Scotland and Northern Ireland.
Charities Act 1993 s.64, amended by Charities Act 2006 s.31; Companies Act 2006 ss.21,31

After notice of a special resolution has been given, the only changes allowed at the meeting are very minor ones which do not alter the substance.

19.7.4.2   Notification to Companies House

Special resolutions must be notified to Companies House within 15 days of being passed. The notification should be headed with the company name and number and should start:

> At a general meeting of the above-named company, duly convened and held at [address] on the [...] day of [month] [year], the following special resolution(s) was/were duly passed.

If the resolution has been passed in writing rather than at a meeting [**19.10.2**], the notification should start:

> The following special resolution(s) was/were duly agreed by being signed by the appropriate percentage of the members under the provisions of the Companies Act 2006 s.288.

The resolution(s) should then be set out in full, and the notification should be signed and dated by the company secretary (if there is one) or a director. Some amendments, for example to change the name or objects, must be accompanied by a Companies House form.

A special resolution to change a company's name [**6.7.1**] takes effect only after it has been notified to Companies House and a revised certificate of incorporation has been issued; a change to the objects [**7.5.3**] takes effect only after it has been registered at Companies House. *Companies Act 2006 ss.80,81,631*

19.7.4.3   Entrenched provisions

The articles may state that amendment or repeal of certain **entrenched provisions** [**7.5.3**] requires more than 75% of the votes cast. The procedure is the same as for a special resolution, but with the higher vote. Companies House must be notified on form **CC03** that the resolution relates to an entrenched provision and the entrenched criteria for amendment or repeal have been met.

19.7.4.4   Ordinary resolutions

Unless company law or the articles of association specify that something must be passed by a special resolution, an ordinary resolution will suffice. This requires 14 days' notice or, if longer, the notice required under the articles, and needs a simple majority (more than half the votes) unless the articles say it needs more.

A company member may propose an amendment to an ordinary resolution without advance notice, but only if it does not substantively alter its nature and create a situation where a different matter is being voted on. The amendment must also not impose any new or different obligations on the company. Amendment procedures are dealt with in the articles or under common law [**19.7.1**].

19.7.4.5   Ordinary resolutions with special notice

Some ordinary resolutions require **special notice** to be given to the company. These are not the same as special resolutions [**19.7.4.1**]. Resolutions requiring special notice are to remove a director [**13.5.6**], to appoint a director at the same meeting to replace one who has been removed, to appoint as auditor anyone other than the current auditor, or to remove an auditor before the end of their term of office [**55.3.6**]. *Companies Act 2006 s.168,511,515*

To ensure the director or auditor can present their case, resolutions to remove them before the end of their term of office must be dealt with at a general meeting. The written resolution procedure cannot be used. The general meeting may be called by the directors or requisitioned by the company members [**19.2.2.2**].

Companies Act 2006 s.288(2)

When special notice is required, a member's (or the directors') notice of intention to propose the resolution must be given to the company at least 28 days before the meeting. If possible, the company must give notice of the resolution to members at the same time and in the same way as the usual notice is given [**19.3**], or if it is not possible to give notice in the same way, notice must be given at least 14 days before the meeting by advertising in an appropriate newspaper or, if the articles allow, in any other appropriate way.

Companies Act 2006 s.312

If the directors call a general meeting to take place less than 28 days after the special notice has been given to the company, the resolution must be considered at that general meeting.

Companies Act 2006 s.312(4)

19.7.4.6 Elective resolutions

Under the **Companies Act 1985** private companies could by elective resolution dispense with certain requirements of the Act, such as holding an AGM or presenting the annual accounts and report to a general meeting. The elective resolution provisions were repealed by the **Companies Act 2006**, because the same provisions can be brought into force by amending the articles. Organisations which relied on elective resolutions should amend their articles accordingly.

Revocation of elective resolutions, if required, is by ordinary resolution [**19.7.4.4**].

19.7.4.7 Resolutions as part of the company constitution

Some resolutions form part of the **company constitution** [**7.1.1**]. This includes all special resolutions, as well as some other agreements affecting the articles. Such resolutions or agreements must be attached to all copies of the articles unless they have already been incorporated into the articles.

Companies Act 2006 s.36

19.7.5 Industrial and provident society resolutions

In general, industrial and provident society law does not say anything about the form of resolutions or the majority required to pass them, leaving it to each society's rules. The main exceptions are when a society amalgamates with another society or a company, transfers its business to another society or a company, or converts into a company [**10.5.1, 11.5.6**].

For a resolution to amalgamate or transfer business, a **special resolution** is required with two-thirds of votes cast in person or, if the rules allow, by proxy at a general meeting. This must be followed by confirmation by a majority of votes cast at a second general meeting held between two weeks and one month after the first.

Industrial & Provident Societies Act 1965 ss.50, 51

For a special resolution to convert to a company, at least half of the society's members eligible to vote must vote at the first meeting either in person or, if the rules allow, by proxy. The resolution must be carried by a three-quarters majority. The rules for the second meeting are the same as for an amalgamation or transfer.

IPSA 1965 s.52, amended by IPSA 2002 s.1

A copy of the resolution, signed by the chairperson of the second meeting and the secretary, must be sent to Mutual Societies Registration within 14 days of the second meeting. The resolution does not take effect until it is registered.

Dissolution of an IPS [**24.6**] requires the written consent of at least three-quarters of the members.

IPSA 1965 s.55(b)

19.8 VOTING PROCEDURES

In many voluntary organisations formal voting is relatively uncommon, and the emphasis is on reaching a **consensus** decision with which everyone agrees, or agrees to accept even if they do not fully agree with it. However, where a decision is required under statute or the governing document or has legal or financial implications, there should be a vote – even if the vote comes at the end of a discussion in which consensus has been reached – unless the governing document allows for decisions to be made by consensus. Without a vote and an announcement of the result, it could subsequently be claimed that the decision had not been properly made. The people who count votes are **scrutineers** or **tellers**.

Methods of voting are:

- by **show of hands** [**19.8.1**];
- by **voice**, saying 'aye' and 'nay' or 'yes' and 'no', but this is imprecise and should be used only if there is a very clear majority;
- a **poll**, which is a counted vote [**19.8.2**];
- a **ballot**, where secrecy is important or where voting is being done by post or electronically [**19.8.4**] or as a written resolution [**19.10**];
- by **division**, as in Parliament, where members physically move into an area to show how they are voting.

Elections can be organised by Electoral Reform Services [see end of chapter].

19.8.1 Show of hands

19.8.1.1 Common law and the governing document

The common law method of voting is by show of hands. This should generally be used unless the governing document specifies otherwise.

Where members may be entitled to more than one vote, the governing document needs to be read carefully to determine whether they have these multiple votes on a show of hands, or only one vote.

If voting by proxy [**19.8.3**] is allowed in an organisation which is not a company, the governing document should be clear whether only members present may vote on a show of hands, or whether proxies may vote as well. If proxies are able to vote, it should be clear whether they have only one vote on a show of hands, regardless of how many proxies they hold, or have multiple votes if they hold multiple proxies. Special rules apply to proxy voting at company meetings [**19.8.3.2**].

For a show of hands, members are sometimes given a voting card to ensure that every hand raised actually represents a person entitled to vote. This may be particularly important if people present are entitled to multiple votes on a show of hands, or if a number of people who do not have voting rights are present.

Unless the governing document specifies otherwise, the person chairing the meeting has a right to vote. He or she may be entitled to a second or casting vote in case of a tie [**19.8.5.2**].   *Nell v Longbottom [1894] 1 QB 767,771*

19.8.1.2 Company law

Unless the articles of association require otherwise or a poll is demanded, decisions at company meetings are made on a show of hands. On a show of hands each member present has one vote, even if they would be entitled to multiple votes on a poll. Each proxy [**19.8.3.2**] present is also entitled to one vote, even if they have been appointed as a proxy by several members. But where a proxy has been instructed by one or more members to vote in favour of a resolution and by other member(s) to vote against, the proxy has one vote for and one vote against. Where members or proxies have multiple votes, it is best to use a poll [below].

Companies Act 2006 ss.282(2),285; Companies (Shareholders' Rights) Regulations 2009 [SI 2009/1632] reg.3

The chair may or may not have a second or casting vote in case of a tie [**19.8.5.3**].

19.8.2 Poll

19.8.2.1 Common law and the governing document

A **poll** is a counted vote. It is sometimes a simple head-count, but usually each person's vote is recorded on a voting slip or by signing a voting list. There is a common law right for any member to demand a poll, but the governing document may remove or restrict this right.   *R v Wimbledon Local Board [1882] 8 QBD 459*

In a non-company, proxies [**19.8.3**] may vote in a poll unless the governing document specifies otherwise. In a company a proxy can always vote in a poll.

Situations in which a poll may be ordered by the chair or demanded by any member include:

- the vote on a show of hands is too close to be accurate without a better count or a written record of the vote;
- people present as proxies are not permitted to vote on a show of hands but could vote on a poll;
- members or proxies entitled to multiple votes can have only one vote on a show of hands, but want an opportunity to cast all their votes; or
- people want an adjourned poll so others can vote on the matter.

Unless the governing document specifies otherwise:

- the chairperson may decide to take the vote by poll without first having a vote by show of hands;
- if a vote by show of hands is taken, any demand for a poll must be made immediately, otherwise the vote stands;
- the original vote (by show of hands) ceases to have effect as soon as the poll is demanded;
- a poll, once demanded, must be taken, and should be taken immediately if possible;
- if it is not practicable to take the poll immediately, the chair may adjourn the meeting to allow the poll to take place at another time;
- if the poll is not taken immediately, members who were not present for the original show of hands have a right to vote in the poll;
- the demand for a poll does not stop a meeting from carrying on with its other business.

19.8.2.2 Company law

Company members have a statutory right to demand a poll on any matter except the election of a person to chair a meeting and the adjournment of a meeting. A proxy [**19.8.3.2**] can take part in a demand for a poll.   *Companies Act 2006 ss.321(1),329*

Rules for calling a poll are set out in the articles of association, and generally allow the chair, or a small number of members present at the meeting, to call for a poll. A provision in the articles is void (invalid) if it requires a poll to be demanded by more than five members who have the right to vote, or by members with more than 10% of the total voting rights of all members who have the right to vote at the meeting.   *Companies Act 2006 s.321(2)*

When voting on a poll, a member entitled to more than one vote does not need to cast all the votes the same way.   *Companies Act 2006 s.322*

19.8.3 Voting by proxy

19.8.3.1 Common law and the governing document

A **proxy** is a person appointed to represent a member who cannot attend a meeting. The term 'proxy' also refers to the form or document used for the purpose of making the appointment [see **19.8.3.4** for a sample form].

In common law there is no right to appoint a proxy, so proxies may be appointed only if the governing document or legislation gives the right to do so, and their voting rights depend on the wording of the governing document or statute.
Harben v Phillips [1883] 23 ChD 14

19.8.3.2 Company law

From 1 October 2007 every company member has the right to appoint a proxy or in some cases proxies to attend, speak and vote on their behalf, even if the articles of association expressly forbid it. Every company must include a statement in every notice calling a general meeting informing the members of their right to appoint a proxy or, if applicable, proxies [**19.3.6.1**].   *Companies Act 2006 ss.324,325*

The articles may prescribe the format and the deadline for delivering the proxy form. The deadline cannot be more than 48 hours before the meeting (excluding all of Saturday, Sunday, Christmas, Good Friday and bank holidays). Forms can be submitted electronically if the company allows this and the requirements for authentication are met [**18.3.2**]. *Companies Act 2006 ss.327(2)(a),1173(1)*

A proxy may be revoked at any time up to the beginning of the meeting, unless the articles specify an earlier cut-off point. This cannot be more than 48 hours (as defined above) before the meeting. Special rules apply for the appointment and revocation of proxies for a poll. *Companies Act 2006 s.330*

A proxy is entitled to exercise all the votes to which he or she is entitled. So a person who is proxy for several members may vote on behalf of all of them, and a person who is a member in her or his own right and is also proxy for another member or members has two or more votes. However, on a show of hands a proxy can exercise only one vote, or possibly two [**19.8.1.2**]. A poll should therefore be called so proxies can exercise all their votes [**19.8.2.2**].

19.8.3.3 Charitable incorporated organisations

At the time of writing (mid 2009) it was not expected that members of charitable incorporated organisations (CIOs) would have a statutory right to appoint a proxy, but they would be allowed to include it in their constitution. The Charity Commission's model clause for an association model CIO [**1.4**] is likely to be less burdensome than for company proxies.

19.8.3.4 Example of a proxy form

The sample proxy form below is intended for a company, but can be adapted for other types of organisation where the governing document allows proxies. If the section in italics on the form is not included, it is an **ordinary form** which simply gives the proxy the right to vote on behalf of the member. If the section in italics is included, it is a **two-way form** which instructs the proxy how to vote – either for or against a resolution or resolutions, or abstaining. If a two-way form is filled in but the member does not instruct the proxy one way or the other, the proxy can decide how to vote. This is called a **special proxy**.

[NAME OF COMPANY]

I/We _____ of [address] _____ being a member of [name of company] appoint

(see note 1) the chairperson of the meeting /
_____ of _____

as my/our proxy to attend, speak and vote for me/us and on my/our behalf at the [Annual] General Meeting of the company to be held at [place] on [date] and at any adjournment thereof.

My/our votes are to be cast on the resolutions below as indicated with an X.

RESOLUTION	*FOR*	*AGAINST*	*ABSTAIN*
That [text of resolution]	____	____	____
That [text of resolution]	____	____	____

Where no voting instruction is given, the proxy may vote or abstain from voting on any resolution as he or she may think fit.

Signature

Dated this _____ day of _____ 20___

NOTES

1. If you wish you may delete the words 'the chairperson of the meeting' and insert the name and address of your own choice of proxy. Please initial such alteration. The proxy does not have to be a member of the company.

2. [Include this note only if the company has organisations as members.] Where the member is an organisation, this form must be executed under its seal or signed by a person who has been duly authorised by the governing body of the member organisation.

3. This document may be returned to the company by post or by hand to [address], by fax to [fax number], or as an email attachment to [email address]. [Delete any which do not apply, or add other options as appropriate.]

4. This proxy form must reach the company's registered office not less than 48 hours before the time fixed for the meeting. Saturday, Sunday, Christmas, Good Friday and bank holidays are not included in the 48 hours. A late proxy cannot be treated as valid.

5. If this proxy form is executed under a power of attorney or other authority such power of attorney or other authority must be lodged with the company along with the proxy form.

If the organisation is not a company:

- the word 'company' must be replaced by 'organisation', 'society' etc;
- 'attend, speak and vote' must be changed to 'attend and vote', unless the organisation's governing document allows proxies to speak as well as vote;
- note 3 must allow for electronic delivery only if the governing document (or statute law, for example for charitable incorporated organisations) allows this;
- the deadline in note 4 must comply with the governing document.

19.8.4   Postal and electronic voting

A **postal voting** procedure may be used alongside, or instead of, voting in person and proxy voting, but only if the governing document explicitly allows it. With a postal vote, the member fills in a ballot and returns it to the organisation by post or hand, or by fax or as an email attachment if the governing document allows.

In a company, members can submit votes electronically (by fax, email etc) if postal voting is allowed under the articles and the vote is authenticated [**18.3.2**],.

19.8.5   Counting the votes

On a show of hands, votes are counted of individual members present and entitled to vote, duly authorised representatives of organisational members [**12.2.5**] present and entitled to vote, and proxies present and entitled to vote under company law or, for non-companies, under the governing document. Votes cast by post or electronically are counted only if the governing document specifically states they are included in a show of hands.

Where a poll [**19.8.2**] is taken or the vote is by ballot, all votes validly cast must be counted.

19.8.5.1   Majorities and percentages

Careful attention needs to be given to the governing document and, for companies, company law when counting votes.

A **simple majority** means more than half the votes. It is not necessarily the same as having the highest number of votes (**first past the post**). If, for example, 20 members vote and Ali gets seven votes, Ben gets five and Carol gets eight, Carol is elected on a highest number of votes basis, but not if the governing document requires a majority. However, elections are generally run on a first past the post basis, so the person(s) with the most votes win.

Some organisations use a **single transferable vote process**, where votes are transferred to the person's second choice, third choice etc until there is a clear majority. This can be done only if the governing document specifically allows. Information is available from the Electoral Reform Society [see end of chapter].

A resolution requiring 'at least 75% of the votes cast' or 'a three-quarters majority' would need 15 votes out of 20; a resolution requiring 'more than three-quarters of the votes cast' or 'more than 75%' would need 16.

However, it may not be so straightforward. A careful analysis of the governing document and statute law may be necessary to determine whether the required total is based on:

- the number of **members present and voting** (the default position for meetings of organisations which are not companies, unless the governing document specifies otherwise);
- the number of members **present and entitled to vote**;
- the total number of **members eligible to vote** [for example, for written resolutions by a company, **19.10.2.3**]; or

- the number of **votes cast** (the default position for company meetings, and non-companies where proxies or postal voting are allowed).

Knowles v Zoological Society of London [1959] WLR 823

Abstentions do not need to be counted or announced, but it may be appropriate to do so where there is a significant number of abstainers, or where the outcome of the vote requires a majority of members present and entitled to vote.

19.8.5.2 Equality of votes: Non-companies

The governing document should set out what happens in case of an **equality of votes** (a **tie vote**). Often the procedure is for the person chairing the meeting to have a **casting vote**, but this must be explicit in the governing document. There is no obligation to use a casting vote. *Nell v Longbottom [1894] 1 QB 767,771*

If the chairperson is entitled to vote in his or her own right, the casting vote is a **second vote**.

If there is no provision for the chair to have a casting vote or if the chair does not use it, a poll may be called [**19.8.2**] which might result in the tie being broken, or the motion is not passed because it does not have the necessary majority.

19.8.5.3 Equality of votes: Companies

In the past, company articles of association generally allowed the person chairing a general meeting to have a second or casting vote. However the **Companies Act 2006** prevents a company resolution from being passed with such a vote in any company registered on or after 1 October 2007. A chair who is a company member can, however, vote in his or her own right in the same way as other members.

Companies Act 2006 ss.281,282

In a company registered before 1 October 2007, the chair is entitled to a second or casting vote if the articles included this provision on 30 September 2007. If the articles did not include it at this point, they cannot be amended to include it, unless they had been amended before this date in order to comply with the new law by removing the right to a casting vote. *Companies Act 2006 (Commencement No.5) Order 2007 [SI 2007/3495] sch.5 para.2*

19.8.5.4 Announcing the result

The number of votes cast for and/or against does not have to be announced, but for anything requiring more than a simple majority it is good practice to say it has been passed by the required majority. This avoids any doubt in future. The vote as announced by the chairperson should be minuted [**19.11.1.2**].

A motion agreed by everyone who is entitled to vote is carried **unanimously**. A motion agreed by everyone who votes on it – but with some people abstaining – is carried ***nem con*** (*nemine contradicente*, 'with no votes cast against').

19.9 ADJOURNMENT

Adjournment means extending a meeting to another time in order to deal with unfinished business. A meeting may be adjourned by agreement of a majority of the members present and voting. Alternatively it may be adjourned by the person chairing the meeting:

- in situations where the governing document explicitly gives the chairperson power to adjourn;
- if it has to be adjourned to take a poll [**19.8.2**]; *R v D'Oyly [1840] 12 A&E 159*
- if the chair is unable to keep order after making genuine attempts to do so, and the members will not pass a resolution to adjourn; *John v Rees [1970] Ch 345*
- if a quorum is not present [**19.6**]; or
- if practical circumstances make it impossible to consider a resolution to adjourn, for example a breakdown of electricity in a meeting held at night.

Byng v London Life Assurance Ltd [1989] 2 WLR 738, 1 All ER 560

If the governing document says that the chairperson *may* adjourn a meeting if asked to do so by a majority of the members present he or she is not obliged to do so. If it says that the chairperson *shall* adjourn the meeting there is an obligation to do so.   *Salisbury Gold Mining Co v Hathorn & others [1897] AC 298*

An adjourned meeting is a continuation of the original meeting. Under common law, resolutions passed at the adjourned meeting take effect as from the date of the original meeting unless the governing document specifies otherwise. This does not apply to companies, where a resolution passed at an adjourned meeting is valid from the date on which it was actually passed, not the date of the original meeting.   *Jackson v Hamlyn & others [1953] 1 Ch 577, 1 All ER 887; Companies Act 2006 s.332*

Notice of an adjourned meeting needs to be given only if required by the governing document, the original meeting was adjourned *sine die* (without fixing a date and time for the new meeting), or new business is to be considered at the adjourned meeting.   *R v Grimshaw [1847] 10 QB 747*

Even if notice does not legally have to be given, it is usually good practice to notify members of the date and time of the new meeting.

A proxy [**19.8.3**] appointed for the original meeting may take part in the adjourned meeting unless the proxy has been revoked in the meantime, or the member votes in person at the adjourned meeting. Under common law a proxy form submitted between the original and adjourned meetings is not valid for the adjourned meeting, but company law allows proxies to be appointed for the adjourned meeting.   *Jackson v Hamlyn & others [1953] 1 Ch 577; Companies Act 2006 s.327(2)*

19.10 WRITTEN RESOLUTIONS

19.10.1 Common law and the governing document

Except in companies [**19.10.2**], written resolutions are valid only if the governing document allows members' decisions to be made in this way. Where they are allowed, unless the governing document indicates otherwise:

- the members can sign separate sheets (rather than all having to sign the same sheet), provided every sheet contains a full copy of the resolution;
- the resolution must be agreed by 100% of the members entitled to vote on it.

Unless the governing document or the resolution itself specifies otherwise, a written resolution comes into effect when the final signature is received. The signed sheets should be kept in the minutes book.

19.10.2 Company written resolutions

Members of private companies (which virtually all voluntary sector companies are) may pass nearly all resolutions in writing, without a meeting, even if the articles of association prohibit written resolutions. The only exceptions are resolutions to remove a director or auditor before the end of their term of office [**13.5.6**, **55.3.6**], which must always be dealt with at a general meeting.

Companies Act 2006 ss.288,300

If written resolutions are prohibited by the articles, it may be sensible to amend them to avoid confusion [**7.5.3**].

A **written resolution** may be proposed by the directors or by the members of the company. If the resolution is a **special resolution** [**19.7.4.1**], this must be indicated on the notice.

19.10.2.1 Circulating the resolution

A written resolution must be circulated to every company member in the same way as notice of meetings [**18.3**].

Insofar as possible the resolution must be circulated at the same time to everyone entitled to vote. The **circulation date** is the date it is first circulated, and no one can become entitled to vote on the resolution after the first copy of it has been circulated (so if the first copy is posted or emailed at 3pm on 14 October, a person who is admitted to company membership at 4pm that day is not entitled to vote).

Every copy of the resolution must be accompanied by a statement informing the member how to agree to the resolution, and the date by which the resolution must be passed if it is not to lapse. This date must be 28 days beginning with the circulation date, unless the company's articles specify otherwise for this type of resolution. A signature after the period is not valid. If the resolution is on a website, it must remain on the site from the circulation date until the date it would lapse.
Companies Act 2006 ss.289-291,297,299

19.10.2.2 Resolutions proposed by members

If requested to do so by 5% of the company members, or by a lower percentage if allowed by the articles of association, the company must circulate a written resolution proposed by the members, and if requested a statement of up to 1,000 words by the members. Unless the company resolves that it will cover the costs of circulation, it is obliged to circulate the resolution and statement only if the members requesting it deposit or pay to the company an amount sufficient to cover the costs of circulation.

The company or any other person who claims to be aggrieved can apply to the court if it believes members are abusing the right to request a resolution.
Companies Act 2006 ss.292-295

19.10.2.3 Approving the resolution

Written resolutions are allowed even if the articles say they are not. To be passed as a written resolution, a resolution which would be a special resolution if passed at a meeting [**19.7.4.1**] must be agreed by 75% or more of the members entitled to vote (not 75% of those who actually vote). Ordinary resolutions [**19.7.4.4**] must be agreed by a simple majority (more than 50%) of the members entitled to vote.
Companies Act 2006 ss.282(2),283(2)

However, at the time of writing (mid 2009), guidance from the Department for Business, Innovation and Skills was that if the articles require a larger majority or unanimity for a written resolution, the provisions in the articles apply. For the avoidance of doubt, it may be sensible to comply with the higher requirements until it is clarified whether these or the Companies Act rules apply, or to amend the articles [**7.5.3**] so they match the Companies Act requirements.

To agree to a written resolution, the company member or someone acting on behalf of the member must provide to the company an authenticated document [**18.3.2**] identifying the resolution and indicating agreement to it. Once given, agreement cannot be rescinded.

Agreement may be sent in hard copy or, if the company has provided a fax number, email address or other electronic address, by that method.

The resolution is passed when the required majority is reached. If the majority is not reached by the date on which the resolution lapses [**19.10.2.1**], the resolution is not passed.
Companies Act 2006 ss.296,297

A written resolution which would require notification to Companies House if it had been passed at a meeting [**19.7.4.2**] must be notified to Companies House in the usual way. Instead of giving the date and place of a meeting the notification should state that the resolution was passed under the provisions of the **Companies Act 2006**.

After being passed the resolution must be signed by the company secretary or a director and must be kept in the same way and for the same period as minutes of general meetings [**18.5.9**].
Companies Act 2006 ss.355,356

A written special resolution or other resolution affecting the company constitution [**19.7.4.7**] must be treated in the same way as if it were passed at a general meeting.

19.11 MINUTES

Minutes are a written record of the business carried out at meetings. Their purpose is to provide a record, both for current use and for historical purposes, of decisions and actions.

19.11.1 Content

19.11.1.1 What the minutes should include

For any meeting, the minutes should include:

- name of the organisation;
- description of the meeting (annual general meeting, meeting of the board of trustees, meeting of the finance sub-committee etc);
- date, including the year, of the meeting;
- place of the meeting;
- list of members present (for large general meetings it is sufficient to indicate the number of members present, but the sign-in sheet or other record of the members attending should be kept with the minutes in the minutes book);
- list of others 'in attendance' (optional for large meetings);
- who chaired and took the minutes (optional, but helpful if issues need to be checked later);
- apologies for absence (optional);
- corrections, if any, to the minutes of the previous meeting;
- acceptance and signing of the (corrected, if necessary) minutes of the previous meeting;
- matters arising from the previous minutes not covered elsewhere;
- a separate minute for each item covered at this meeting (see below);
- date, time and place of the next meeting (optional).

19.11.1.2 What each minute should include

The minute for each item must include any decision reached by the meeting, including a decision not to make one. It may also include:

- important points raised in the discussion;
- details of any document, report or advice relied on in reaching a decision;
- action required to implement the decision, who will take the action and any deadlines for the action.

For a general meeting or for legal business, each minute should also include:

- full text of every motion [**19.7**];
- names of proposer and seconder, if any;
- full text of any amendments;
- result of the vote on each amendment and the motion, as announced by the person chairing the meeting.

If the minutes are written by hand, any errors should be crossed through and visibly corrected, with all corrections initialled.

19.11.2 Minutes books

The official copy of the minutes should be written or permanently glued into a bound book, or kept in a ring binder with each page serially numbered and signed or initialled by the person who signs the minutes. Minutes can be kept electronically but there must be adequate protection against falsification and against the technology becoming obsolete or corrupted, and they must be able to be printed.

Where resolutions are passed without a meeting, for example as written resolutions [**19.10**], records of the resolutions must be kept in the same way as minutes.

For non-companies, minutes books should be kept for as long as the organisation exists. For companies they must be kept for at least 10 years after the date of the meeting or resolution, but it is good practice to keep them at least for as long as the company exists, as a record of the organisation's past. *Companies Act 2006 s.355*

19.11.3 Approval and signature

If the minutes are written directly into a minutes book, they may be read out at the end of the meeting and signed by the person chairing the meeting. More frequently draft minutes are distributed before the next meeting, and at that meeting are approved and signed.

The minutes do not have to be read out unless required by the governing document or standing orders. Even if reading out is required, the minutes may be **taken as read** at the meeting if they have been distributed beforehand.

Approval indicates that the minutes are an accurate record of the meeting. If they are not accurate, a motion to alter them is put to the meeting. Only the people who were at the original meeting should approve the minutes or vote on whether to alter them, because only they can know whether the minutes are accurate. The full text of the alteration should be included in the minutes of this current meeting, and should also be written by hand into the minutes of the previous meeting and be initialled before those minutes are signed.

19.11.3.1 Minutes as evidence

Under common law, once the minutes are signed they are *prima facie* evidence of the proceedings at that meeting (accepted as accurate but can be rebutted). Some governing documents contain a clause saying that signed minutes are conclusive proof of the proceedings. This means they cannot be rebutted unless they were signed fraudulently or in bad faith.   *Kerr v Mottram [1940] Ch 657*

Under company law, minutes of a general or directors' meeting signed by the person who chaired the meeting or the next meeting are evidence of the proceedings at the meeting. A written resolution properly passed [**19.10.2**] and signed by the company secretary or a director is evidence of the resolution.   *Companies Act 2006 ss.249,356*

Rules similar to those for companies are likely to apply to meetings of a charitable incorporated organisation's members and trustees.

19.12 MEETINGS OF THE GOVERNING BODY

Common law principles [throughout this chapter] apply to meetings of governing bodies. In addition, the governing document generally includes some rules for these meetings. If it does not, or if additional rules need to be agreed:

- in an unincorporated association, the committee members agree rules for their meetings;   *Cassell v Inglis [1916] 2 Ch 211,222*

- in a trust, the trustees agree the rules for their meetings;

- in a company, the articles of association may provide that rules for meetings of the directors are agreed by the directors but if not, such rules would have to be agreed by the company members;

- in an industrial and provident society or charitable incorporated organisation, the governing document sets out how rules for governing body meetings are decided.

The rules may be agreed on a one-off basis, but usually they are fixed as standing orders [**7.4.25**]. They generally cover frequency of meetings, notice, quorum, chairing, voting and minutes. Standing orders or other rules can expand on but not override anything in the governing document.

19.12.1 Frequency

Unless the governing document or standing orders specify otherwise, governing body members may meet as frequently or infrequently as they like. They must, however, meet often enough in a company to fulfil their duties under the Companies Acts, and in a charity to fulfil their duties as charity trustees [**chapter 15**]. The Charity Commission recommends at least two meetings per year but active organisations will need more.

Governing body members are not obliged to attend all meetings, but they have a duty to attend when they are 'reasonably able to do so', and the governing document may say that they are or may be removed from office if they do not attend for a specified period [**13.3.1**].   *Re City Equitable Fire Insurance Co Ltd [1925] Ch 407*

A governing body member who does not take part in the organisation over an extended period could be held to be in breach of his or her duty to the organisation [**chapter 15**]. If a company becomes insolvent, a director who has consistently failed to attend governing body meetings could be disqualified from being a company director. *Dorchester Finance Co Ltd v Stebbing [1989] BCLC 498*

19.12.2 Notice

Unless the governing document or standing orders specify otherwise, governing body meetings are generally called by the chairperson or, in a company, the company secretary if there is one. In a company any director may call a governing body meeting (unless prevented from doing so by the articles of association), and the company secretary must call one if asked to do so by a director.

Unless the governing document specifies otherwise:

- reasonable notice needs to be given for governing body meetings, indicating when and where the meeting is to be held;

- notice does not have to be in writing;

- notice must be given to all members of the governing body, even if they have said they cannot attend; *Re Portuguese Consolidated Copper Mines [1889] 42 ChD 160*

- notice does not have to be given if the governing body meets regularly at the same time and place. *Compagnie de Mayville v Whitley [1896] 1 Ch 788*

In charitable trusts and associations, notice of meetings of the governing body does not have to be given if the charity does not have a UK address for the governing body member. For other types of organisation, notice should be sent to all governing body members unless the governing document specifies otherwise.

Charities Act 1993 s.81(3)

19.12.2.1 Agenda

Unless required by the governing document, there is no legal requirement to notify governing body members beforehand of the agenda or purpose of any governing body meeting, but it is good practice to do so.

19.12.2.2 Meetings without notice

If all the members of a governing body are together and they all agree, they can hold a meeting there and then, without any notice, and can agree any resolution provided they are unanimous. The resolution should be recorded in the minutes book or be included in the minutes of the next meeting. *Re Bonelli's Telegraph Co [1871] 12 Eq 246*

19.12.3 Chairing

If the governing document does not specify how the governing body chairperson is appointed, the members may elect one of their number to take that role. The duties arise from common law [**19.5.2**].

19.12.4 Quorum

Unless the governing document specifies otherwise, the quorum for a meeting of the governing body is:

- in an unincorporated association, all the members of the governing body; *Brown v Andrew [1849] 18 LJ QB 153*

- in a charitable trust, a majority of the trustees; *Re Whitely [1910] 1 Ch 600*

- in a company, a majority of the directors. *York Tramways v Willows [1882] 8 QBD 685*

If a company's articles empower the directors to set a quorum but do not say what the quorum is if it is not set, the default is 'the number of directors who usually act at meetings'. *Re Regents Canal Iron Co [1867] WN 79*

If a governing body member cannot attend a meeting it may be possible in some situations to appoint an alternate [**13.4.3**] who counts towards the quorum. If a significant number of members are unable to attend, decisions can be made without a meeting [**19.12.6**] if the governing document allows.

If the total number of governing body members falls below the quorum, decisions made by the remaining members will not be valid. They should operate only to fill vacancies (if the governing document gives them the right to appoint governing body members) or, in a membership organisation, to call a general meeting of the organisation's members. If the organisation is a charity and is in a position where it cannot make the governing body quorate, the remaining trustees or the charity's members can ask the Charity Commission to appoint trustees [**13.4.1**]

19.12.4.1 Disinterested quorum

For governing body meetings in companies and charities the quorum in relation to each issue must be **disinterested**, and in general cannot include a member who has a conflict of interest or serious conflict of loyalties in relation to a contract, transaction or decision under discussion [**15.3.5**, **15.6.4**]. This includes where a connected person [**15.2.5**] has a conflict of interest. In organisations which are neither companies nor charities, the governing document may include a similar rule.

The rules on disinterested quorum may mean that a meeting is quorate for some decisions but not others. The chair and/or secretary should monitor to ensure the meeting is quorate for each decision. The minutes should show that persons with a conflict of interest or conflict of loyalties did not take part in relevant decisions or discussions. In some cases, it may not be possible to make a decision [**15.2.4**].

19.12.5 Decision making

Unless the governing document specifies otherwise, decisions at governing body meetings are made by a majority of votes, and the chairperson does not have a casting vote in case of a tie. The company rules preventing a chairperson from having a second or casting vote [**19.8.5.2**] apply only to decisions by company members, not company directors, so a provision in the articles that gives a second or casting vote to the person chairing a meeting of the governing body is valid.

19.12.6 Decisions without a meeting

The **Companies Act 2006** allows virtually all decisions of company members to be made by written resolution [**19.10.2**], but there is no statutory right for company directors to make decisions in this way. Provision for written resolutions by directors should therefore be included in the articles of association.

Companies whose articles do not include provision for the governing body to make decisions without a meeting, and governing bodies in organisations which are not companies, may make decisions in writing provided the resolution is agreed by all the governing body members entitled to vote on the matter [**19.10.1**]. *Re Bonelli's Telegraph Co [1871] 12 Eq 246*

The rules on email, internet, telephone or video conference meetings are the same as for general meetings [**19.1.2.2**]. Unless everyone can see and hear each other, decisions made by such means are not valid unless the governing document allows. Decisions made by such means should be ratified by a written resolution (if allowed) or at a valid meeting.

19.12.7 Minutes

Proper records must be kept for all meetings of and resolutions by a company's governing body [**19.11**], and this is also likely to be a statutory requirement for charitable incorporated organisations (CIOs). *Companies Act 2006 s.248*

In other organisations, minutes of governing body meetings must be kept if this is required by the governing document or standing orders. Even where there is no statutory or constitutional obligation to keep minutes, it would be extremely poor practice not to. Minutes should be approved and signed in the same way as for general meetings [**19.11.3**].

The **Companies Act 2006** requires governing body minutes to be kept at the registered office or any convenient place, and to be open to the company's directors and auditors [**18.5.9**]. For organisations which are not companies, minutes of governing body meetings do not have to be kept in a specified location or be open to anyone other than members of the governing body and the organisation's auditors or independent examiner, unless this is specified in the governing document.

19.13 COMMITTEES AND SUB-COMMITTEES

Decisions may be delegated to committees if the governing document allows or there is a statutory right to delegate [**14.6**, **15.8**]. In general if the main body is called a board, council etc the delegated body will be called a **committee**, but if the main body is called a management committee, executive committee or any other type of committee, the delegated body is called a **sub-committee**.

In general, committees set up by the members of the organisation or by the governing body must comply with the same requirements for meetings as the body which set them up. So unless specified otherwise in the governing document, a committee set up by the governing body has to follow the same procedures as the governing body, and one set up by the organisation's members has to follow the procedures for general meetings.

Unless specified otherwise in the governing document, standing orders, the terms of reference for the committee [**14.6.1**] or the minute of the meeting which established the committee, the following rules apply:

- the common law relating to meetings [throughout this chapter] applies to committee meetings;
- the members of the committee may decide how often to meet;
- the provisions applying to notice for governing body meetings [**19.12.2**] apply to committee meetings;
- the quorum is all the members of the committee;

Re Liverpool Household Stores Association [1890] 59 LJ Ch 616

- the chairperson does not have a casting vote [**19.8.5.2**].

Minutes must be kept if required by the governing document, standing orders, the committee's terms of reference, or the resolution under which the committee was set up. Even if they are not required, it is poor practice not to keep minutes.

Resources: MEETINGS, RESOLUTIONS AND DECISION MAKING

Charity meetings. Charity Commission, www.charitycommission.gov.uk, 0845 300 0218, email via website.

Company meetings and resolutions. Companies House, www.companieshouse.gov.uk, 0303 1234 500, enquiries@companieshouse.gov.uk.

Institute of Chartered Secretaries and Administrators, www.icsa.org.uk, 020 7580 4741, info@icsa.org.uk.

Elections. Electoral Reform Services, www.electoralreform.co.uk, 020 8365 8909, enquiries@electoralreform.co.uk.

Electoral Reform Society, www.electoral-reform.org.uk, 020 7928 1622, ers@electoral-reform.org.uk.

Telephone meetings. Community Network, www.community-network.org, 020 7923 5250, enquiries@community-network.org.

Statute law. www.opsi.gov.uk and www.statutelaw.gov.uk.

Much but not all case law. www.bailii.org.

Updates cross-referenced to this book. www.rclh.co.uk.

Chapter 20
ASSETS AND AGENCY

For sources of further information see end of chapter.

20.1   LEGAL OBLIGATIONS

Legally enforceable obligations are those which the courts will enforce. They include contracts and other legally binding **agreements**, and obligations which are imposed by the **common law** or **statute**. People responsible for the organisation and its activities must be aware of the organisation's legal obligations and the potential liabilities if the obligations are not met.

20.1.1   Agreements

The main types of enforceable agreement are:

- **contract**: a binding agreement between two or more parties, involving consideration [**21.1**];

- **deed**: a binding agreement, not necessarily involving an exchange of consideration, which takes its validity from formalities [**20.3**];

- **trust**: a binding arrangement where assets given by one party are held on trust for beneficiaries or charitable purposes [**20.2**].

Even a signed agreement is generally not legally enforceable if no contract, deed or trust is created. For example if a funder agrees in writing to make a grant but does not do so, the agreement is enforceable through the courts only if it was in the form of a contract, which grants generally are not [**52.1**], or a deed, or if the funder was under a statutory or other legal obligation to make the payment.

20.1.2   Common law and statutory obligations

Many statutes contain obligations which can be enforced through the civil courts [**64.1**]. An employer, for example, has a **statutory duty** to provide a safe workplace for its employees [**40.2.1**]. If it fails to do so, the Health and Safety Executive may bring an action against the employer, and/or any employee may sue the employer for breach of statutory duty. For more about statutory duties, see **22.3**.

Numerous other obligations are imposed by the common law [**64.2.1**], most notably in **tort** [**22.6**]. An example is the **duty of care**, under which everyone has to take reasonable care where it is reasonably foreseeable that negligence – a lack of care – could cause personal injury or damage.

263

20.1.3   Execution of documents

Some documents, to be legally binding, must be **executed**. This applies in particular to deeds [**20.3**], and to contracts relating to real estate.

To be validly executed by an individual, the document needs to be signed by the individual making it, with the signature witnessed by one person, with the witness's name and address beside the signature. The witness's occupation should be included but is often omitted.

For organisations, the nature of the execution depends on the organisation's legal structure. There may also be provisions in the organisation's governing document; where these are different from the statutory requirements, advice should be taken about which applies.

Guarantees [**22.5.3**] must always be in writing but do not have to be executed. Simple contracts, that are not contracts for real estate or guarantees, do not legally have to be signed, but signatures reduce the risk of dispute about the terms.

Electronic signatures are acceptable in some circumstances, but advice should be taken before using these.   *Electronic Signatures Regulations 2002 [SI 2002/318]; Mercury Tax Group Ltd & another, R (on the application of) v HM Revenue & Customs & others [2008] EWHC 2721 (Admin)*

20.1.3.1   Companies

Company documents are executed by being signed by two directors, or by the company secretary and a director. Provided it is not prohibited by the articles of association, they can also be signed by a single director in the presence of a witness, who must also sign.   *Companies Act 2006 s.44*

If a document is being signed on behalf of two companies that share a director or secretary, that director or secretary may sign on behalf of both parties, but must sign separately for each party – it is not sufficient to sign the document only once.

Alternatively if the company has a **seal** – a stamping device that meets the requirements of company law – the document can be executed by having the seal impressed on the document or on a red wafer stuck to it. The articles of association may require the document to be signed by at least one director or other authorised person to show the use of the seal is authorised.   *Companies Act 2006 s.44,45*

Contracts can be entered into under the company seal, or by any person authorised to do so by the directors.   *Companies Act 2006 s.43*

20.1.3.2   Charitable incorporated organisations

At the time of writing (mid 2009) it was expected that documents will be executed by a charitable incorporated organisation (CIO) by having the CIO's seal affixed to it, or by being signed by two trustees, or where the CIO has only one trustee, by being signed by that trustee. Contracts will be entered into under the CIO's seal or by any person authorised to enter into the contract.

20.1.3.3   Industrial and provident societies

Documents are executed by an industrial and provident society by being sealed with the IPS's seal, or by being signed by the secretary and a committee member or by two committee members.   *Industrial & Provident Societies Act 1965 s.29C, inserted by Co-operatives & Community Benefit Societies Act 2003 s.5*

20.1.3.4   Charitable trusts and association

Documents executed by a charitable trust or association must be signed by all the trustees, unless they have passed a general or specific resolution authorising two or more trustees to sign on their behalf. Each signature must be witnessed by a non-signatory, in the same way as for execution of documents by individuals [**20.1.3**].   *Charities Act 1993 s.82*

20.1.3.5   Non-charitable trusts and associations

For private trusts and non-charitable associations, documents are executed, unless the governing document indicates otherwise, by being signed by at least one person authorised by the governing body, with the signature witnessed.

20.2   TRUSTS

Obligations under **trust law** arise where a trust [**2.3.4**] is created by deed or under the terms of a will, or where a trust would be assumed by the courts to exist, even if one has not been formally created [**48.2.1**]. Those holding or controlling the trust's assets are **trustees**, and have certain duties and powers [**15.6**, **58.1**]. Any use of the assets for purposes or beneficiaries other than those intended is a **breach of trust** [**48.2**], as is any action which contravenes trust law or, in a charity, charity law.

The beneficiaries are entitled to the benefit of the trust (have a **beneficial interest**) even though they are not a party to the formal arrangement between the donor (settlor) and trustees. In a private trust, any beneficiary may sue to enforce its rights. In a public or charitable trust the individual beneficiaries generally cannot sue to enforce their rights, but the attorney general or Charity Commission may bring a claim on their behalf. A donor may sue if its donated assets are not used as intended.

20.3   DEEDS

A document which has been properly drawn up and **executed** [**20.1.3**] as a deed is enforceable even though there may be no trust or contract. Deeds are used for a variety of reasons, such as where no contract is created but there is a need for the agreement to be legally enforceable; to create or record the terms of a trust; or to record certain other important events such as a change of name, appointment of a trustee or the grant of a property right. In some cases, such as leases for more than three years, the law requires a deed.

Deeds are also used to create a long-lasting obligation, because under the **Limitation Act 1980** obligations in a contract are generally enforceable only for six years, but those in a deed are usually enforceable for at least 12 years.

A **supplemental deed** adds to or amends an existing deed. It is executed in the same way as an ordinary deed.

20.3.1   Wording of the deed

A deed must make clear that it is intended as a deed, and that it has been executed and delivered [below]. It often starts '*This deed* is made the ___ day of [month and year]', thus making clear that it is intended to be a deed. This may be followed by **recitals**, a short statement of why the deed is being created. These often start with 'whereas'. The detailed **operative provisions** follow.

The deed includes wording such as 'Executed and delivered on the date inserted above' or 'Executed and delivered by the parties on the date inserted above', if there are two or more parties. It ends with signatures or an organisation's seal.

20.3.2   Execution and delivery

Deeds no longer need to be **under seal**, with sealing wax or a red wafer (sticker). Now, to be valid, a deed must make clear it is intended to be a deed, and be executed as appropriate for the organisation's legal structure [**20.1.3**].
Companies Act 2006 s.46; Industrial & Provident Societies Act 1965 s.29C(4); Charities Act 1993 s.82

A deed is not valid until it is **delivered**. It does not physically have to be given to the person to whom the promise in the deed is made, but there must be some indication that the person now intends to be bound by it. The term 'executed and delivered' or 'signed and delivered' and a signature are adequate to show this.

A deed which is intended to take effect only on the occurrence of an event is delivered as an **escrow**, and comes into effect as a deed only if the event on which it is conditional occurs.

If these formalities are observed, the promise made in the deed is legally enforceable, but if the wording or execution is not right it may not be enforceable.
Law of Property (Miscellaneous Provisions) Act 1989 s.1

20.4 OWNERSHIP OF ASSETS

Assets – money, equipment, investments, land etc – can be owned only by **legal persons** [3.1.1]. These are **natural persons** (human beings), and **corporate persons** (incorporated bodies). Companies, industrial and provident societies, charitable incorporated organisations, and charitable trusts or associations which have incorporated their trustee body [2.4] can own assets in their own right, but for unincorporated associations and trusts the situation is more complex.

20.4.1 How unincorporated bodies hold assets

An unincorporated association or trust is not a legal person [2.2.4]. It may 'own' assets in the sense of having the **beneficial right** to them or a **beneficial interest** in them, the right to use and benefit from them. But the **legal title** must be held on its behalf by one or more **legal persons**.

20.4.1.1 Investments, leases, land and buildings

If an unincorporated trust or association purchases or is given investments, land or buildings, or enters into a lease, it should either:

- if it is a charity, incorporate its governing body so the governing body can hold the property as a corporate body, even though the organisation itself remains unincorporated [2.4];

- **vest** [20.4.5] ownership in all of the members of the governing body;

- vest ownership in one or more **nominees** – a legal person or persons, often referred to as **holding trustees** [20.4.4] or a **custodian trustee** [20.4.2], who hold assets on behalf of the members of the governing body; or

- become incorporated [**chapter 3**] so it is no longer unincorporated.

For a non-charitable association, an alternative is for the investments, leases, land or buildings to be held by all the members under terms set out in the governing document (a form of contract) or under another contractual agreement among the members. Legal advice should be taken before setting up this arrangement.

Any rules in the governing document specifying how assets are held must be strictly followed. In most cases, legal advice is advisable.

20.4.1.2 Other assets

Physical assets other than land and investments may be held by the members of the governing body of an unincorporated organisation without needing to be formally vested in them. They can be transferred by **delivery**, which simply involves handing them over, rather than having to be formally transferred.

A case in 2000 confirmed that intangible assets such as intellectual property rights and goodwill [44.1] are held by the members of an unincorporated association, subject to the contract they enter into when they join the association. This contract is created by the constitution [7.1.2], as well as any other explicit or implicit contractual obligations between the member and the association.

Artistic Upholstery Ltd v Art Forma (Furniture Ltd) [2000] FSR 311

20.4.2 Custodian trustees

A **custodian trustee** is a corporate body (or in the case of the treasury solicitor, the public trustee and the official custodian for charities, an individual) authorised under the **Public Trustee Act 1906** to hold investments or land on behalf of others. A custodian trustee generally makes a charge for holding assets.

20.4.2.1 Trust corporations

Trust corporations may hold land and/or investments. They include:

- corporate bodies appointed by the Charity Commission as charity trustees or custodian trustees; *Charities Act 1993 s.35*

- banks, local authorities or other corporate bodies defined as trust corporations and authorised to act as custodian trustees by the **Public Trustee Act 1906** and the **Trustee (Custodian Trustee) Rules 1975** *[SI 1975/1189]*;

- corporate bodies prescribed as trust corporations by the lord chancellor.

20.4.2.2   Official custodian for charities and public trustee

The **official custodian for charities** [4.5.3] is a Charity Commission official who holds land, but generally not investments, on behalf of unincorporated charities. If a charity has investments as well as land, these generally have to be held in another way. There is no charge for having land held by the official custodian. Details are available from the Charity Commission.   *Charities Act 1993 ss.21-23*

The **public trustee** is a government official who holds investments and land on behalf of individuals, private trusts and non-charitable bodies, but not charities.

20.4.3   Custodians

A custodian does not 'own' assets in the same way as a custodian trustee [above] or a holding trustee [below], but undertakes the safe custody of assets or of documents or records concerning the assets. For trusts, charitable associations and other bodies covered by the **Trustee Act 2000**, the rules on use of custodians are the same as for nominees [58.1].   *Trustee Act 2000 ss.17-23*

A custodian cannot be appointed by an organisation which has a custodian trustee, or in relation to any assets held by the official custodian for charities.

20.4.4   Holding trustees or nominees

Holding trustees, increasingly called **nominees**, can hold legal title to land, investments or other assets for the benefit of the beneficiaries (in a charity) or for the members of the association (in a non-charity). Legal advice should be sought before appointing holding trustees or nominees to hold land.

Being a holding trustee is not the same as being a trustee of a trust [13.1.6] or a charity trustee [13.1.7] – although the same person may hold both roles. Charity trustees are responsible for managing the charity (often called, in this context, **managing trustees**). Nominees hold assets on behalf of the managing trustees, but have no say in the management of the charity or the assets they hold.

20.4.4.1   Nominees for trusts and charitable associations

Unless the governing document specifies otherwise, a nominee or custodian for a trust, charitable unincorporated association or other organisation subject to the provisions of the **Trustee Act 2000** must be two or more trustees of the trust, to act as joint nominees or joint custodians; one of the trustees, if that trustee is a trust corporation [20.4.2.1]; a corporate body controlled by the trustees; or an individual or corporate body whose business consists of or includes acting as a nominee or custodian.   *Trustee Act 2000 s.19*

In appointing a nominee or custodian under these provisions, trustees must exercise their statutory duty of care [15.6.7, 58.1.2]. Appointments must be in writing and be reviewed regularly. Unless the organisation is an exempt charity [8.1.2], the trustees of all charitable organisations must comply with Charity Commission guidance.   *Trustee Act 2000 ss.16-22*

If the governing document allows, an individual or corporate body which does not meet the Trustee Act requirements may be appointed as a holding trustee. For individuals, a minimum of three is usually required. There is no maximum.

20.4.4.2   Nominees for non-charitable associations

Provided the governing document allows, any individual or corporate body may be a holding trustee or nominee for a non-charitable association. The maximum number of holding trustees for land is four.   *Trustee Act 1925 s.34*

20.4.4.3   Nominee companies

Nominee companies are set up for the purpose of holding property, and are most frequently used by investment managers to hold stocks and shares they are managing. As a nominee the company holds the title to the property, but the organisation is beneficial owner [20.4.1]. Nominee companies typically hold shares owned by many owners, although it is possible to create a nominee company to hold the investments or land of only one organisation.

20.4.5   Vesting in trustees, nominees and custodians

The process of passing the legal ownership of investments or land to a new trustee, a nominee or a custodian is called **vesting**. Vesting must take place whenever a new trustee, nominee or custodian is appointed.

Where nominees (holding trustees or a custodian trustee) are to be appointed, the organisation's governing document may specify who they are to be. If it does not, the governing body can choose, provided that they comply with the requirements of the **Trustee Act 2000** [**20.4.4**] and exercise their statutory duty of care [**58.1.2**]. The appointments must be in writing. The Charity Commission's CC42 *Appointing nominees and custodians* explains the process.

20.4.5.1   Deed of appointment

If detailed provisions for appointing nominees (holding trustees and/or a custodian trustee) and the terms on which they hold property are not set out in the organisation's governing document, a **trust deed** should be drawn up. Even if this is not done the nominees have the responsibilities of trustees, but these will not be as clear or as easily managed.

If the organisation's governing document does not set out the procedure for removing and replacing nominees, this should be set out in the trust deed. A **supplemental deed** will need to be drawn up to appoint new nominees.

20.4.5.2   Holding property for non-charitable associations

Assets [**2.3.5**] cannot be held in trust for the purposes of a non-charitable association, so must be held for the benefit of identifiable members. If the property is held 'for the members of the association', that would apply only to the members at the time the trust is established, and not future members. Therefore the wording which should be used is 'for the members for the time being of the association'. **For the time being** means at any given point in time.

20.4.6   Powers, duties and liabilities

As nominees, holding and custodian trustees hold assets on behalf of the organisation, must carry out the wishes of the organisation unless doing so would be unlawful or in breach of trust, and do not have any management powers in relation to the organisation or to the property they hold.

A nominee or custodian may enter into an agreement to act as an **agent** [**20.5**] of the organisation, buying and selling investments or signing leases as directed by the organisation and subject to the control of the organisation. But they cannot do this without such agreement.

20.4.6.1   Liability of nominees

If a *custodian* trustee undertakes an act which is unlawful or in breach of trust, full legal liability rests with the governing body which authorised the act.

If *holding* trustees undertake such an act they, rather than the governing body which authorised the act, are liable – even if the holding trustees have acted at the bidding of the governing body. It is therefore especially important for holding trustees to be fully aware of the purposes for which the property is held, and any conditions attached to the property. If instructed to carry out an act which is in breach of those trusts, the holding trustees should refuse to do so.

20.4.6.2   Appointments under the Trustee Act 2000

Governing body members are not liable for the defaults of nominees or custodians appointed under the provisions of the **Trustee Act 2000**, provided the trustees exercised their statutory duty of care [**15.6.7**, **58.1.2**] in entering into arrangements with the nominee or custodian, keeping the arrangements under review, and intervening if necessary.   *Trustee Act 2000 s.23*

20.4.7   Delegation by trustees

Specific rules on delegation apply to trustees in charitable and non-charitable trusts and charitable associations [**15.8.2**].

20.4.7.1   Statutory power to delegate

Unless specifically excluded under the governing document, trustees under the **Trustee Act 2000** [**15.6**] have statutory power to appoint nominees and custodians to hold property [**20.4**], unless the governing document already provides for property to be held only by a custodian trustee or the official custodian for charities; and to appoint agents [**20.5.1**]. In appointing nominees or custodians or delegating to agents, trustees must exercise a duty of care as defined by statute [**15.6.7**]. *Trustee Act 2000 ss.11,16-27*

A **nominee** in this context holds land, investments or money on behalf of the trustees in its own name, but has no powers of management. Nominees are often referred to as **holding trustees** or **custodian trustees** [**20.4.4**].

A **custodian** looks after records, documents of title etc on behalf of the trustees. A custodian has no powers in relation to the assets.

Holding and custodian trustees are generally appointed to eliminate the need to transfer the title to trust property when trustees change. This facilitates the sale and purchase of shares and similar assets. Custodians are appointed to reduce the risk of loss of documents.

An **agent** is someone to whom functions are delegated [**20.5**]. The **Trustee Act 2000** allows delegation only of specific functions, and only to certain persons [**20.4.4.1**].

Charities also have a statutory power to appoint custodian trustees (a form of nominee), and to have land held by the official custodian for charities [**4.5.3**].

20.4.7.2   Liability for acts of agents, nominees and custodians

Trustees are not liable for any losses arising from actions and functions delegated to an agent, nominee or custodian appointed under **Trustee Act 2000** powers, provided the trustees exercise all aspects of their statutory duty of care [**15.6.7**, **58.1.2**]. *Trustee Act 2000 ss.1, 22*

For other issues around liability for acts of agents see **20.5.6**.

20.5   AGENCY

Agency exists when one person or group (the **principal**) authorises another (the **agent**) to act on their behalf. Unlike the relationship with a holding or custodian trustee, which is based on a trust, the agency/principal relationship is based on contract [**21.1**]. An agent may enter into contracts and do other acts which bind the principal.

No particular formalities are required to appoint an agent, except that if the agent is to execute deeds [**20.3.2**], he or she must be appointed by deed (a **power of attorney**); or if the agent is appointed under the provisions of the **Trustee Act 2000** [**20.4.7**], the appointment must be in writing.

20.5.1   Agents appointed under the Trustee Act 2000

The only persons who can be appointed as agents to exercise powers under the **Trustee Act 2000** are a person or body properly appointed as a nominee or custodian, or one or more trustees. If two or more persons are appointed as agents for a particular function, they must act jointly. *Trustee Act 2000 s.12*

The **Trustee Act 2000** says that beneficiaries cannot be appointed as agents, even if they are trustees. The Charity Commission's view is that this provision does not apply to charitable trusts. The reasoning is that in this context charities technically do not have beneficiaries, because they are established for charitable *purposes* rather than for the beneficiaries. *Trustee Act 2000 s.12(3)*

Agents may be appointed to undertake a wide range of activities, such as discretionary investment of the trustees' funds. Agents with asset management functions (property or investments) must be appointed in writing and operate within a written policy statement. *Trustee Act 2000 s.15*

20.5.2   The creation of agency

The appointment of an agent under the provisions of the **Trustee Act 2000** must always be in writing and is therefore always express (explicit). In other situations, agency can arise without explicit authorisation.

20.5.2.1   Express appointment

The appointment of an agent is **express** (explicit) where the parties agree that one party will become the other's agent. The agent's authority may be general, or may be limited to a specific transaction or types of transactions. The principal must be certain that all limitations are carefully set out; otherwise the principal may be bound by acts of the agent which are outside what the principal intended.

20.5.2.2   Apparent and usual authority

Once the principal has indicated that someone is their agent – for example, an employer authorising an employee to enter into contracts or undertake other binding actions – the principal will be bound by those actions. This applies even if a contract exceeds the agent's authority, unless the party with whom the contract was made was aware that the agent was acting outside his or her authority.

20.5.2.3   Implied authority

In certain situations, including some which might not be immediately recognised as contractual, the law **implies** that one party is authorised to act as another's agent. For example company directors are agents for the company, and the governing body members of an unincorporated association are agents for the members of the association.

20.5.2.4   Ostensible authority

Even where a person does not have authority to enter into contracts, a court might say that the other party was reasonable in assuming that the person did have such authority – for example assuming that an employee with the title director of publications has the right to enter into a contract with an author or publisher. This is called **ostensible authority**.

20.5.2.5   Agencies of necessity

In certain very limited circumstances, for example where a person is looking after the goods of another and it is necessary to protect them from damage, the person taking the protective steps may under the law of agency be able to recover the costs from the owner or principal.

20.5.3   Payments to agents

Whether the agent is entitled to a commission or other payment depends entirely on what has been agreed between the principal and agent. There is no presumption that an agent is entitled to be paid.

20.5.4   What can be delegated to agents

A governing body can delegate decision making powers only if this is allowed in its governing document, by statute, or (for charities without such powers) by the Charity Commission. Governing body members of most organisations have statutory power to delegate certain functions, providing they act in accordance with their statutory duty of care and other requirements imposed by the relevant legislation. Staff can delegate only if authorised to do so.

20.5.5   Duties of an agent

An agent must act with care and skill, avoid conflicts of interest and duty, not take bribes or make secret profits, and must indemnify (compensate) the principal for any losses incurred by the principal because of the agent's negligence or acting outside its authority.

20.5.6   Liability for contracts made by an agent

If when making a contract on behalf of the principal the agent names the principal, the agent generally has no rights under the contract. However in some cases an agent could have rights as a third party under the **Contracts (Rights of Third Parties) Act 1999 [21.1.5]**.

Generally a principal is liable only for the acts of a properly authorised agent. If an unauthorised person enters into a contract, or if an agent enters into an unauthorised contract, the principal may take on the liability by ratifying the contract. But if the principal does not do this. the agent may be held liable to the person they contracted with, or if the principal is held liable under the contract, the agent will be liable to the principal.

If the agent did not have authority and knew it, the agent may be liable to be sued for the tort [**22.6.1**] of **deceit**.

20.5.6.1   Liability for contracts made by employees

A third party dealing with an employee is entitled to assume that the employee is authorised to act on behalf of the employer. A contract, even a very onerous one, entered into by an employee nearly always binds the employer. The only situation where it might not is where the employee did not have authority to enter into it and the third party actually knew, or ought reasonably to have known, that the employee had no such authority.

20.5.7   Ending an agency arrangement

An agency arrangement is a contract and can be ended by anything that will bring a contract to an end [**21.6**].

An agency arrangement may also end if either the principal or agent becomes unable to manage his or her own affairs. This terminates any informal agency or agency under a normal power of attorney, but an **enduring power of attorney** registered with the Court of Protection or a **lasting power of attorney [21.1.2]** continues despite the person's mental illness or other incapacity.

Mental Capacity Act 2005; Lasting Powers of Attorney, Enduring Powers of Attorney & Public Guardian Regulations 2007 [SI 2007/1253]

The death or bankruptcy of the principal terminates an agency arrangement. Inconsistent conduct, such as disposal by the principal of goods the agent has been asked to sell, may terminate the agency.

The principal (or where the principal has died, the person dealing with his or her affairs) should ensure that any third party likely to deal with the agent knows the agency arrangement has ended.

An arrangement for an agent to negotiate the sale of goods on behalf of a principal is a **commercial agency agreement**. Termination for any reason – even for the agent's breach – may give the agent a right to substantial compensation, so legal advice should be sought before terminating or not renewing such arrangements.

Commercial Agents (Council Directive) Regulations 1993 [SI 1993/3053]; Lonsdale (t/a Lonsdale Agencies) v Howard & Hallam Ltd [2007] UKHL 32

Resources: ASSETS AND AGENCY

Statute law. www.opsi.gov.uk and www.statutelaw.gov.uk.

Much but not all case law. www.bailii.org.

Updates cross-referenced to this book. www.rclh.co.uk.

Chapter 21
CONTRACTS AND CONTRACT LAW

For sources of further information see end of chapter.

21.1 CONTRACTS

If an agreement meets the criteria to be a contract, it is enforceable as a contract in the courts. In most cases there is no need for a document, and if there is one there is generally no need for it to be signed.

21.1.1 Elements of a contract

For a valid contract there must be at least two parties with **capacity** to enter into a contract [**21.1.2**], who **intend** to create a legally binding relationship. An **offer** must be made and accepted, there must be sufficient **certainty** about what has been agreed [**21.1.1.3**], and there must be **consideration** [**21.1.1.5**].

21.1.1.1 Offer

For a contract to be made there must be **offer** and **acceptance**. An offer may be quite straightforward – 'I offer you £10 in exchange for that book' – or it may be inferred from behaviour, as the person stands silently at the till with the book in her hand and offers £10 to the sales assistant. An offer generally may be withdrawn at any time before it is accepted.

Some situations in which there may appear to be an offer are actually an **invitation to treat**, which is a step prior to an offer. When goods are displayed on a bookshop's shelves, the offer is not made until the purchaser takes a book to the till, and acceptance comes when the cashier agrees the sale.

Other examples of an invitation to treat are property put up for sale at an auction, where the offer is made by a potential purchaser, and acceptance comes on the fall of the auctioneer's hammer; a house put up for sale, where the informal offer precedes the offer made in the formal contract and acceptance comes on 'exchange'; and an invitation to bid for work, where offers are made by those who bid for the work, and the purchaser might accept one of the offers. Some bid arrangements bind the offeror; others leave the bid open for a specified period.

21.1.1.2 Acceptance

Acceptance must be clear and unqualified. If it is ambiguous ('it sounds OK, but I'll have to check with the board') there is no acceptance.

Acceptance must be distinguished from **counter offer**. In acceptance, the **offeror** makes the offer, and the **offeree** accepts the offer unconditionally. With a counter offer, the offeree accepts the offer but seeks to change it, perhaps by changing the price, the specification of the goods or services to be provided, or other terms. The offeree thus becomes the offeror, and the original offeror becomes the offeree and has to decide whether to accept this counter offer.

A common difficulty arises where one party offers goods or services on its **standard terms of supply**, and the other party then orders them but on its **standard terms of purchase**. In this situation it may be very difficult to determine whether agreement has been reached, and if so on which set of terms.

Complex rules govern when acceptance takes place, particularly if it is undertaken by post or electronically. If this is an issue, legal advice should be sought.

21.1.1.3 Certainty

An offer and acceptance give rise to a contract only if there is sufficient **certainty** as to what has been agreed. If key terms are not agreed – who the parties are, what is to be provided and when, what is to be paid or given in return – there is generally no contract, although in some cases uncertainty may be resolved by looking at normal usage or custom in that trade or occupation.

21.1.1.4 Conditional contracts

Although the acceptance must be unconditional, the offer may make clear that the contract comes into being only if certain conditions are met. This may be the occurrence of an event, for example a charity agreeing to provide services *when it has purchased a property in the area*, or may be more subjective, such as an offer of employment *subject to receipt of references satisfactory to the employer*.

Even where the words are clear, it may be unclear whether the condition being met is the formal confirmation of a contract already in existence, or whether there is no contract until the condition is met. In the first example above, the contract is in place, but does not come into effect until the charity purchases a suitable property. In the second example the contract is not created until satisfactory references are received – but if the employer allows the person to start work before this, the courts are likely to say that a contract is in place [**26.2.1**].

21.1.1.5 Consideration

A contract is created only if **consideration** – goods, services, money or something else of material value – is given or promised in exchange for what is offered. Consideration may be something of value to the recipient, but can also be something which causes the giver to suffer a detriment.

Some key points relevant to consideration are:

- it need not be given immediately, so a promise to do or provide something in future is valid consideration;
- something given in the past, even five minutes ago, cannot be used as consideration for a contract which is being entered into now;
- the amount of the consideration is irrelevant, so a contract may be created by agreeing to pay a nominal amount such as a peppercorn or £1 in return for a very substantial benefit, or by paying 'pocket money' to a volunteer [**39.4**];

- the consideration must come from the other party or parties to the contract. Consideration from a third party cannot support a contract between the other two parties, although in some situations a third party can sue on a contract he or she is not party to [**21.1.5**]. Contracts may involve more than two parties if each provides something to and receives something from the others.

21.1.1.6   Contractual intention

Even where an agreement is made and there is consideration, the courts will not enforce it as a contract unless it is clear, or can be implied (assumed) from the circumstances, that the parties **intended** the agreement to be a binding contract.

The courts nearly always imply that arrangements of a business nature, where one party is paid or receives something of value in return for providing goods or services to another, are intended to be legally binding. This applies even if the agreement is made verbally and one party subsequently wants to treat the agreement as not binding because of a change of circumstance.

Bear Stearns Bank plc v Forum Global Equity Ltd [2007] EWHC 1576 (Comm)

Agreements which might not be enforced by the courts include:

- where the parties have agreed that an agreement is **binding in honour only** or have made another clearly expressed intention that it not be enforceable;
- **family or social agreements**, because the parties do not generally intend to create a legal relationship (but if they make clear that they do intend this, the agreement will be enforceable);
- **heads of terms**, where the parties have agreed the main headings or issues but have not yet completed detailed negotiations;
- **letters of intent**, where one party or both has said they intend to enter into a contract, but have not yet agreed the terms;
- **subject to contract** agreements or a **memorandum of agreement**, where the parties set out an agreement between them which may or may not be contractual, depending on whether it meets the criteria for contracts [**21.1.1**];
- where the maker of the agreement merely states its **current policy or intentions**, effectively reserving the right to change its intention.

If goods, services or money have already been provided by one party and accepted by the other, or of the terms have been agreed with sufficient certainty to create a contract, a court might well enforce 'subject to contract' agreements, heads of terms, letters of intent and similar arrangements as a contract.

Diamond Build Ltd v Clapham Park Homes Ltd [2008] EWHC 1439 (TCC)

Other agreements which might not be enforced by the courts include:

- where the agreement gives one party complete or disproportionate freedom to vary the terms, because this would be an unfair contract [**21.2.7**];
- collective agreements [**36.3.4**] between employers and employees or between employers and trade unions, which are presumed not to be legally binding unless expressly stated to the contrary.

21.1.1.7   Contracts with and without signatures

The vast majority of contracts do not have to be in writing, and if in writing do not have to be signed. Statute law creates a limited number of exceptions, for example contracts for the sale of an interest in land must generally be in writing, and some consumer credit agreements are not enforceable unless certain formalities are complied with.   *Consumer Credit Act 1974, amended by Consumer Credit Act 2006*

Employers are obliged to provide a written **statement of employment particulars** to virtually all employees [**26.7**], but a contract of employment may exist even if nothing is put in writing [**26.2**].

If a contract is to be signed the persons signing must be authorised to do so, although in many cases the contract will be valid even if the signatories are not properly authorised [**20.5.2**].

In some cases signatures sent by email, fax or other electronic means are acceptable but advice should be taken.   *Electronic Signatures Regulations 2002 [SI 2002/318];*
Mercury Tax Group Ltd & another, R (on the application of) v HM Commissioners
of Revenue & Customs & others [2008] EWHC 2721 (Admin)

Where there is no need for a signature a valid contract can be entered into with a simple email, even if the email does not include the name of the person sending it. To avoid inadvertent creation of a contract it may be sensible to include a statement in email footers that a contract cannot be entered into by email unless it is accompanied or confirmed by a valid purchase order (or whatever).

21.1.2 Capacity to contract

For a contract to arise the parties must have **contractual capacity**, which means they must be legally capable of entering into a contract.

21.1.2.1 Minors

Generally contracts by a person under the age of 18 are valid. But if the contract is to purchase goods or services, the contract is enforceable in the courts only if it is for **necessaries**. This includes contracts for obvious necessities – shelter, food, clothing – as well as for services such as education, medical care and legal advice, and for any goods or services 'which are appropriate for that person'.

From the other side, a minor who enters into a contract of employment or to *provide* goods or services is bound by the contract if it is as a whole for his or her benefit (a **beneficial contract of employment**), but is not bound by a contract which is as a whole oppressive or unfair.

A contract with a minor which is not valid under the above provisions may be **voidable**. It binds both parties, but the minor can **repudiate** (disclaim) it before or within a reasonable time after reaching age 18.

If a contract is neither valid nor voidable the adult or other party will be bound, but the minor will not. However, the minor becomes bound if he or she ratifies (confirms) the contract after becoming 18.

To avoid the risk of an invalid or voidable contract, an organisation should not allow a minor to enter into a contract on its behalf.

21.1.2.2 Mental incapacity

A contract with a person who does not have sufficient mental capacity is voidable (can be invalidated) by that person if the other party knew of the person's condition when the contract was entered into. To void the contract, it would have to be shown that the mentally incapacitated person did not sufficiently understand the transaction. Different levels of understanding are necessary for different transactions, and detailed advice is required in this area.

The property or affairs of some people who do not have full mental capacity are under the control of the court, and the person is not legally able to enter into agreements about those matters.   *Mental Capacity Act 2005*

If a person made an **enduring power of attorney** before 1 October 2007 which is registered with the court of protection, or a **lasting power of attorney** since then, the person named as attorney can act on their behalf. There are two types of lasting power of attorney, one relating to property and financial affairs and the other to personal welfare.   *Lasting Powers of Attorney, Enduring Powers of Attorney & Public Guardian Regulations 2007 [SI 2007/1253]*

If the subject matter of the contract is not covered under a lasting or enduring power of attorney and the person is considered not to be capable of managing his or her own affairs, an order of the court of protection may be necessary.

21.1.2.3 Contracts under the influence of drink or drugs

If a person entering into a contract is so incapacitated by alcohol or other substances as to be incapable of understanding the transaction and the other party knows this, the contract is voidable by the person who was incapable. Or when no longer incapacitated, he or she can ratify it to make it binding.

21.1.3 Contracts by an organisation

Just as individuals must have capacity to contract, so must organisations. A voluntary organisation should contract only if:

- the contract is within its constitutional objects [**7.4.2**];
- the organisation (as a company, industrial and provident society or charitable incorporated organisation) or the governing body (in a trust or unincorporated association) has the power to enter into such a contract [**7.4.3**]; and
- the individuals who negotiate, agree and/or sign the contract on behalf of the organisation are authorised to do so, by statute or charity law, the governing document, other agreed rules, their job or role description, or a decision of the governing body or other appropriate body [**20.5.2**].

A person who enters into a contract which does not meet these criteria could be held liable to the organisation for the contract. The other party to the contract will generally be able to enforce the contract, either against the organisation or against the individual(s) who authorised or entered into it.

21.1.4 Joint and several liability

If two or more individuals or organisations together promise to do or pay something under a contract, their liability may be **joint**, or **joint and several.**

Normally if two parties make a promise that they will together deliver money, goods or a service to someone else, the liability is **joint**. Joint contracted parties make one promise binding all of them, and each is liable for its share of the total.

If the liability is to be **joint and several**, this must be explicit within the contract. The parties make one promise binding all of them, and each also makes a separate promise binding her or him alone. This does not entitle the person receiving the promise to obtain more than was originally promised by all together, but that person may seek to obtain it from any one (or more) of the parties.

Where two or more individuals or organisations agree to provide goods or services on a joint and several basis, each is potentially liable to provide the full amount – even if they have an agreement between themselves that one will, for example, provide 75% and the other 25%.

In unincorporated organisations, the members of the governing body have joint and several liability for the organisation's debts and other contractual obligations [**22.2.3**].

21.1.5 Privity of contract and third party rights

Before 11 May 2000, only the parties to a contract gained rights under the contract. If, for example, a contract between two parties specified that goods or services were to be provided to a third party and this was not done, the contract had to be enforced by the contracting party rather than by the third party. This rule was known as **privity of contract**.

The rule is different for contracts entered into on or after 11 May 2000. Where a contract clearly intends a benefit for a third party – by mentioning the third party by name, or by describing the third party or parties as members of a particular class (group) – the contract may explicitly give that party the right to enforce the contract. Even where such right is not explicit, the third party has a right to enforce the contract unless the contract explicitly excludes this.

Contracts (Rights of Third Parties) Act 1999

An example is where a care organisation enters into a contract with the local authority to provide services to named individuals, or to a class of individuals. If those services are not provided, the local authority can sue the organisation under the contract, and the individual as a third party could sue the organisation for failure to provide services to which he or she was contractually entitled.

Other exceptions to the basic rule on privity of contract include:

- if two parties enter into a contract with one another as a result of a representation made by a third party, a **collateral contract** may be created where the third party becomes liable even though they are not a party to the contract;
- third parties can very occasionally use trust law [**2.3**] to obtain a benefit intended for them under a contract.

21.2 CONTRACT TERMS

A vast body of contract law exists in relation to the terms of contracts. Where the terms are unusual or problematic or there is a dispute between the parties, it is important to take legal advice. Detailed rules govern how the courts ascertain terms of a disputed contract.

21.2.1 Terms agreed verbally

In a dispute about a **verbal** or **oral contract**, the court will look at what the expressed words meant. If the agreement has been put in writing the court will generally look at **verbal evidence** only if the written terms do not cover everything that was agreed verbally. If they cover everything but are (or are alleged to be) at variance with what was agreed verbally, the courts will not generally look at any verbal agreements.

Organisations which receive assurances prior to signing a written contract should therefore ensure those promises are written into the contract. This is particularly important if there is an **entire agreement** clause in the contract, stating that the contract contains everything agreed by the parties.

21.2.2 Terms implied by the court

Occasionally, terms omitted from a contract may be **implied** into it. One way this is done is by applying the **officious bystander** test, where the court imagines a person eager to give their view overhearing the contract being made. If the bystander asks 'Would X be a term of this contract?' and both parties to the contract would reply 'Yes, of course', the court will imply the term into the contract.

Terms may also be implied into a contract because of the conduct of the parties in similar contracts or arising from custom and practice.

21.2.2.1 Duty to cooperate

The purchaser and supplier have an implied **duty to cooperate** in contracts for the supply of computer systems and possibly similar contracts. This means that the purchaser should clearly state its needs, the supplier should be clear if these needs cannot or might not be able to be met and should inform the purchaser of suitable alternatives, and the purchaser should be willing to adapt working practices to the new system.   *Anglo Group plc v Winther Brown & Co Limited & another [2000] EWHC 127 (TCC)*

21.2.3 Terms implied by statute

21.2.3.1 Consumer contracts

The original stance of the law on contracts was *caveat emptor* – 'let the buyer beware'. It was up to buyers to inspect the goods or to specify in detail what they required. The seller had no duty to disclose any fault.

Purchasers now have some protection under statute, particularly where they are **consumers** (individuals who are acting for purposes outside their trade, business or profession). Consumer contracts for goods, for example, automatically include the following terms, unless they are explicitly and lawfully excluded [**21.2.7**]: that the vendor owns the goods, that goods sold by description or sample will correspond with the description or sample, and where the goods are sold in the course of business, they are of a satisfactory quality.   *Sale of Goods Act 1979 ss.12-15*

Similar terms are implied in hire purchase agreements and contracts for the supply of services.   *Supply of Goods & Services Act 1982; Supply of Goods (Implied Terms) Act 1973 ss.8-11*

Goods which become defective within six months of purchase are assumed to have been defective when sold. In most cases the purchaser can choose whether to receive a repair or replacement, or if neither is reasonable, a reduction in purchase price or rescission of the contract with a refund [**21.6.5**].   *Sale & Supply of Goods to Consumers Regulations 2002 [SI 2002/3045]*

Information about consumer contracts is available from Consumer Direct and the Office of Fair Trading [see end of chapter]. At the time of writing (mid 2009) the government had proposed consolidating and enhancing consumer law.

21.2.3.2 Unfair and aggressive trading

In selling to consumers, misleading actions, misleading omissions and aggressive sales and marketing practices are prohibited and in most cases are a criminal offence. A practice is misleading if it contains false or deceptive information or does not include essential information such as full price including tax and delivery, and 'causes or is likely to cause the average consumer to take a transactional decision he would not have taken otherwise'. Aggressive trading includes refusing to end a home visit when asked to do so. Guidance is available from the Office of Fair Trading [see end of chapter].   *Consumer Protection from Unfair Trading Regulations 2008 [SI 2008/1277]*

Advertising which misleads **traders** is also prohibited. A trader is anyone acting for purposes relating to their trade, craft, business or profession, or acting in the name of or on behalf of a trader.   *Business Protection from Misleading Marketing Regulations 2008 [SI 2008/1276]*

For more about advertising and marketing see **43.4** and **45.2**.

21.2.3.3 Distance contracts and online contracting

Specific data protection, telecommunications and distance selling rules apply to distance marketing and sales [**43.4**] and the contracts that are created.

Where a contract for goods or services is agreed without face to face contact (by telephone, internet, post, catalogue, email, fax or media advertising) the customer must be made fully aware of key contractual issues, including the supplier's name, description of the goods or services, price inclusive of VAT, any delivery costs, the costs (if any) of using the distance communication, arrangements for payment, the period for which the offer or price is valid, the minimum length of any contract, and information about the right to cancel. The information must be given verbally, or must be included in catalogues, websites, advertisements or similar material. If not given in writing these details must be confirmed 'in good time' in writing or other **durable medium**, which includes email.   *Consumer Protection (Distance Selling) Regulations 2000 [SI 2000/2334]*

Unless agreed otherwise, the goods or services must be delivered within 30 days. The consumer in most cases has the right to cancel the distance contract within seven working days, and any advance payment must be returned within 30 days.

Businesses, including voluntary organisations, which trade online must provide their contact details; specified information about any advertisements, promotional offers or competitions; details of the process by which the contract will be concluded; and an acknowledgement of receipt of the order without undue delay, sent electronically.   *Electronic Commerce (EC Directive) Regulations 2002 [SI 2002/2013]*

Guidance on distance selling is available from the Office of Fair Trading [see end of chapter]. At the time of writing (mid 2009) the government had consulted on proposals to standardise distance selling rules across the EU.

21.2.3.4 Doorstep contracts

Consumers have a seven-day period in which to cancel a contract for goods or services worth more than £35 entered into during a sales visit to their home or place of work. This right applies regardless of whether the visit is unsolicited or has been requested by the consumer. Salespersons must inform consumers in writing about this right to cancel and must provide other information, and the seven days runs from when the customer is notified of the right to cancel.   *Cancellation of Contracts made in a Consumer's Home or Place of Work Regulations 2008 [SI 2008/1816]*

21.2.3.5 Interest on late payments

All businesses, voluntary organisations and public sector bodies have a right to charge interest on amounts due on commercial contracts made with other businesses or the public sector. This is a statutory right, and does not need to be explicitly included in the contract.   *Late Payment of Commercial Debts (Interest) Act 1998, amended by Late Payment of Commercial Debts Regulations 2002 [SI 2002/1674]*

Interest can be charged from the payment date specified in the contract or, if no date is specified, from 30 days after invoice date or delivery of the goods or services, whichever is later.

The maximum that can be charged under these provisions is the Bank of England official dealing rate (called **reference rate**) plus 8%. The reference rate on 30 June is used for interest which starts to run between 1 July and 31 December, and the rate on 31 December is used for interest which starts to run between 1 January and 30 June.

Once statutory interest begins to run, the supplier is also entitled to charge a fixed sum as compensation for the costs involved in collecting the debt. The fixed sum is £40 for a debt less than £1,000, £70 for a debt of at least £1,000 but less than £10,000, or £100 for a debt of £10,000 or more. Details of the statutory provisions, Bank of England reference rates and how to calculate interest are on the **Better Payments Practice Campaign** website [see end of chapter].

The statutory provisions do not apply if the contract contains different provisions. But if those provisions are unfair or excessive, they can be struck out by the court and the statutory provisions will apply.

21.2.4 Cross-border contracts

An organisation which purchases or supplies goods or services outside the UK should be clear about **jurisdiction** (which country's law applies to the contract), and when purchasing or supplying within the European Union must ensure the contract does not breach EU rules on exclusions and limitations [**21.2.7**]. Legal advice is likely to be necessary for contracts outside the EU, and may also be necessary for contracts within the EU.

At the time of writing (mid 2009) new EU rules, called **Rome I**, were expected to come into effect on 17 December 2009 harmonising the way contract disputes are handled in EU member states. *Law applicable to contractual obligations [EC 593/2008]*

Non-contractual obligations, such as negligence and other torts [**22.6**], are covered under EU rules called **Rome II**, which came into effect on 11 January 2009. In general the jurisdiction will depend on the law of the country where the damage occurs or is likely to occur, but there are exceptions to this. *Law Applicable to Non-contractual Obligations (England & Wales & Northern Ireland) Regulations 2008 [SI 2008/2986]*

21.2.5 Standard contracts

A **standard contract** is one whose terms apply to all of the provider's dealings of that nature, rather than being individually negotiated with the purchaser of the goods or services [**21.3.1**]. These terms may be set out in a document, be displayed on the wall of premises where the goods are sold or on a website, or be referred to as being available for inspection elsewhere.

The basic rule is that a party who agrees to a contract is bound by all the terms even if they did not fully understand them, or if they read them and thought they meant something else. Terms may also be implied on the basis that all the prior contracts were subject to them, and while they were not specifically referred to in this case it is to be implied that they applied here.

21.2.6 Guarantees, indemnities and performance bonds

Entering into a contract to provide or purchase goods or services always involves a risk of non-performance. Where the risk is perceived as significant, the contract may require security or surety in the form of a **guarantee**, **indemnity** or **performance bond**.

Anyone asked to provide a guarantee or indemnity, or taking out a performance bond, should take specialist advice.

21.2.6.1 Guarantees and indemnities

Where a party to a contract wants protection against the other party not meeting its contractual obligations, it may require a **guarantee** – a promise by a third party, who does not have an interest in the contract, to meet the debts or obligations of the defaulting party. Leases frequently require a guarantor [**62.2.3**]. A guarantee must always be in writing.

Less commonly, a contract may be supported by an **indemnity**, where a party promises to compensate one of the contractual parties for loss or damage. An example is an indemnity to compensate for losses arising if a service is not delivered on time. An indemnity may be separate from the main contract, and does not necessarily have to be in writing. Indemnities are sometimes provided by commercial third parties such as insurance companies.

An indemnity of this sort should not be confused with an indemnity clause [**21.2.6.3**].

It is not always straightforward to distinguish between a guarantee and an indemnity, but they are dealt with differently in law, and it is important to understand the differences. If, for example, an arrangement is a guarantee but is not in writing, it will not be enforceable – but if it is an indemnity it may be enforceable even if it is not in writing.   *Pitts & others v Jones [2007] EWCA Civ 1301*

21.2.6.2 Performance bonds

Where there is concern about possible non-completion of a project or other failures, such as failure to deliver a service on time or to specification, a party to the contract may require the other party to provide a **performance bond**. These are provided by insurance companies or banks.

Performance bonds will generally have significant cost, but the level of security is likely to be much greater, in particular if there is any risk that the party which gives a guarantee or indemnity could become insolvent, or could face insolvency if required to meet the guarantee or indemnity.

Everyone should be aware of the limits of a performance bond. Generally a guarantee or indemnity lasts for as long as the contracting party is liable, which could be for up to 12 years, and is potentially for an unlimited amount – although both the time period and the amount can be limited within the terms of the guarantee or indemnity. Performance bonds, on the other hand, will normally be for a relatively short period – typically up to 12 months after completion of the contract – and the amount will nearly always be fixed.

21.2.6.3 Indemnity clauses

An **indemnity clause** in a contract seeks to substantially widen one party's liability for breach of contract. The remedy for breach of contract is normally only damages, and what will be paid is limited in a number of ways [**21.7.2**]. An indemnity clause increases the other contractual party's liability beyond the narrower liability it would face under the normal rules for the award of damages.

An example is a contract between a local authority and voluntary organisation for the provision of services, where the organisation must indemnify the local authority for any loss it incurs if the organisation does not provide the required services – even though much of the compensation it might seek would not be available in a normal breach of contract claim.

Advice should be taken before agreeing an indemnity clause.

21.2.7 Exclusions and unfair terms

Providers of goods or services often seek to protect themselves by drawing up detailed terms which exclude certain liabilities – for example by reducing the length of the limitation period, imposing a cap on liability, or excluding or limiting liability for **consequential loss** arising from failure to provide the agreed goods or services. But both the courts and statute law are increasingly hostile to unfair terms and exclusions in standard and other contracts, particularly where the purchaser is a consumer [**21.2.3.1**]. For example:

- the courts strictly interpret clauses in the agreement against the person who drew up the agreement and will give the narrowest application, so any doubt will be resolved in favour of the other party;
- liability for negligently causing death or injury cannot be excluded [**22.7.5**];
- liability cannot be excluded for loss or damage to a consumer due to negligence in the manufacture or distribution of goods;
- guarantees cannot be used to restrict consumers' rights;

- terms implied by statute [**21.2.3**] cannot be excluded for consumers, and may only be excluded in other contracts if it is reasonable;
- other clauses in written standard terms or where the purchaser is a consumer are allowed only if they are reasonable;
- liability for breach of the contract cannot be excluded;
- entitlement to perform the contract in a substantially different way from that originally agreed is not binding even if it is included in written standard terms.   *Unfair Contract Terms Act 1977 ss.2-7*

The implications for voluntary organisations are:

- if the organisation provides goods or services to consumers in the course of a business under unfair terms, the consumer is not bound by the unfair terms;
- the rules apply, but to a considerably lesser extent, where the organisation is not acting in the course of a business when it makes the contract;
- in certain circumstances the members of the governing body of a trust or unincorporated association might be consumers and be protected if they enter into a contract which includes unfair terms.   *Unfair Terms in Consumer Contracts Regulations 1999 [SI 1999/2083]*

21.2.8   Misrepresentation

A purchaser who enters into a contract because of a **representation** (a statement about the goods, services or terms of the contract) which has been made to them, whether verbally or in writing, has considerable common law rights if that representation turns out to be wrong. But some representations, such as non-specific sales talk designed to encourage purchase, or statements of law or opinion, do not generally give rise to these rights.

If the representation was unambiguous and material to the contract and the purchaser relied on it, the purchaser may be able to rescind the contract [**21.6.5**], or the court may relieve the purchaser of the obligation to complete the contract or may award damages to the purchaser [**21.7.2**]. Misrepresentation may also give rise to rights outside the contractual relationship through the law of tort [**22.6**].

A person who makes a misrepresentation is liable, even if it is not made fraudulently, unless they can prove they had reasonable grounds to believe and did believe that the facts represented were true.   *Misrepresentation Act 1967 s.2(1)*

Rights arising from misrepresentation are considerably reduced if the contract includes a clear **non-reliance** or **entire agreement** clause, saying that the parties have not relied on any representations other than those in the contract.

21.2.9   Disclosure of information

There is generally no duty on a supplier to tell purchasers that there is a defect in the goods or a problem with the services. However, a supplier must disclose where goods have a hidden or latent defect which later causes injury; where a representation is technically true, but misleading; and generally, where a representation has been made but then circumstances change and it is rendered untrue. Disclosure is also required where the parties have a special relationship, for example where one relies on the other's expertise such as an organisation relying on their bank manager's financial advice; or where there is a fiduciary relationship, for example where one party may have a position of undue influence over another [**21.2.10.4**].   *Hedley Byrne & Co Ltd v Heller & Partners Limited [1963] UKHL 4*

For certain contracts, such as insurance, there is a positive duty on both or all parties to disclose all information that might be of importance [**23.3.3**].

21.2.10   Unenforceable contracts

Some agreements may meet all the criteria for being contracts, but will not be enforced by the courts.

21.2.10.1   Contracts 'tainted by illegality'

The courts will not enforce contracts to commit a crime, or where goods sold are to be used for an illegal purpose, or to indemnify others against liability for unlawful acts, for example a contract to pay an employee's fine if the employee is caught speeding while delivering for the organisation.

Contracts to deliberately commit a civil wrong such as avoiding tax in a contract of employment are generally not enforceable. But the contract is enforceable if neither party realised that the wrong was being done.

21.2.10.2 Contracts contrary to public policy

Contracts considered to be contrary to public policy will not be enforced by the courts, for example contracts which promote sexual immorality, interfere with the course of justice, seek to deprive the courts of jurisdiction, or are in **restraint of trade**. A contract which includes a covenant (promise) by employees that they will not compete with their employer after they leave a job [**26.8.2**] may be in restraint of trade, with the covenant enforceable only insofar as it is reasonable.

21.2.10.3 Contracts that damage competition

Agreements that might distort competition, such as two organisations agreeing not to compete for certain contracts, may be unenforceable and may be a **cartel offence**, punishable by a substantial fine. Even communication between potential rival suppliers or tenderers could be construed as **bid rigging** [**52.3.2**].

Competition Act 1998; Enterprise Act 2002 ss.188-190

Basic information is available from the Office of Fair Trading [see end of chapter], but this area of law is extremely complex. Further specialist advice is likely to be needed before taking part in any discussions, even informally, with actual or potential competitors or entering into any non-competition arrangement.

21.2.10.4 Duress and undue influence

Pressuring a person to enter into a contract, through threats of violence or any other threat which is legally wrong, may render the contract invalid. Difficult issues arise as to the boundary between **duress** and normal commercial pressure. **Undue influence** short of duress may also invalidate a contract, particularly where a special relationship exists between the parties, such as parent/child, doctor/patient, solicitor/client, and trustee/beneficiary.

21.3 CONTRACTS TO PURCHASE GOODS OR SERVICES

Voluntary organisations should seek to ensure that all contracts for goods and services they purchase are on advantageous terms. Many suppliers, if pressed, are prepared to offer a discount, especially to regular customers or charities. For the clauses which might be included in a contract to purchase services, see **38.4.2**.

21.3.1 Creating standard terms of purchase

An organisation which regularly purchases goods or services in commercial quantities should develop its own **terms of purchase** and specify that they apply in each contract with a supplier. Legal advice should be sought before drawing up standard terms.

If a supplier seeks to supply on its own terms, considerable confusion may arise as to whose terms apply. If possible the organisation should get the supplier to sign and return a copy of the organisation's conditions to indicate their agreement to them. If there is a regular relationship it may not be necessary to do this each time a supply is purchased.

21.3.2 Finance and hire purchase agreements

Hire purchase or finance agreements are often particularly complex and onerous. Faced with a complex agreement, an organisation should carefully consider the terms and seek to negotiate improvements where necessary, or consider going or threatening to go to another supplier who provides a plain English contract or less onerous terms. Especially where substantial sums are involved, it may be advisable to obtain professional advice.

The legislative protection available in this area is largely designed to assist individual consumers [**21.2.3.1**], and may not cover voluntary organisations.

21.3.2.1   Advice on contracts

Organisations frequently seek advice on contract terms from the person they are dealing with, which may be unwise. Standard terms often exclude any representations which are not actually written into the contract, and some go even further and provide that the person making the representation should be treated as the agent of the purchaser and not the agent of the seller. If advice is needed, it should be sought from the local authority's consumer rights unit, an independent consumer rights organisation, or a solicitor.

21.3.3   Large-scale purchases

EU **public procurement** rules may apply where an organisation making a large purchase of goods, services or works receives more than 50% of its funding from a **purchasing authority** (central government, a local authority or a government agency) or from the national lottery, and more than 50% of the organisation's governing body is appointed by the government, a government agency, local authorities etc.

Where the rules apply, the organisation is a **contracting authority** and must generally advertise the contract throughout the EU in a specified manner and then follow a specified regime to select the party with whom they will contract. If the organisation fails to follow these procedures, an aggrieved third party may make a complaint to the European Commission or bring a claim in the UK courts.

For the EU procurement thresholds and more about the process, see **52.2.1**. The Office of Government Commerce [see end of chapter] can provide details.

21.4   CONTRACTS TO SUPPLY GOODS OR SERVICES

A voluntary organisation may be involved in contracts for the supply of goods or services to a wide variety of parties, including individuals, other voluntary organisations, and institutional purchasers such as local authorities. Contracts to provide services and goods are covered in **chapter 52**. Where the organisation is involved in substantial or routine provision of goods or services, consideration should be given to developing standard terms [**21.2.5**].

21.5   TRANSFERRING OR VARYING A CONTRACT

21.5.1   Transferring a contract

Assignment means transferring the benefit of a contract to someone who was not a party to the original contract, for example when an organisation incorporates [**10.1.2**] or merges [**11.5.2**] and passes the benefit of a contract to the successor organisation. Assignment may take place under a contract or by deed [**20.3**]. It does not normally require the consent of the other party.

If a party wishes to transfer obligations (as well as benefits) under a contract it is necessary to **novate** the contract. This requires the original parties to the contract and the **transferee** (the person to whom the contract is being transferred) to enter into a new contract, in which the parties accept that the obligations will be discharged by the transferee. It is only possible to novate a contract if all parties agree. If they do not, the original contract remains in place.

Certain contractual rights are not assignable. These include contracts of employment, unless they are transferred as part of a transfer of an undertaking [**29.7**] or specifically allow transfer to another employer; contracts where assignment is prohibited by provisions within the contract; or where assignment is prevented by statute, such as some pension rights.

21.5.2 Varying a contract

A contract may be varied (changed):

- where there is **accord and satisfaction** [below], with consideration;
- by **deed** [**20.3**], in which case no consideration is needed;
- where **estoppel** applies [**21.5.2.2**]. In this situation no consideration is given but the variation must be negative only (an agreement not to enforce an existing obligation).

21.5.2.1 Accord and satisfaction

A variation other than by deed or estoppel must involve **accord** (agreement) and **satisfaction** (consideration). Some new consideration [**21.1.1.5**], however nominal, will be needed.

If neither party has yet started its part of the contract, consideration is provided by mutual release. But if one or both parties have started performing their part of the contract, additional consideration must be provided. If an existing staff member, for example, agrees to accept a restrictive covenant [**26.8.2**] in her or his contract of employment, the agreement is not binding unless the employer provides a payment or other consideration when the staff member agrees the change.

The consideration may be nominal, such as £1, but without it the variation is not binding and the original contract can be enforced.

21.5.2.2 Estoppel

Estoppel occurs when one party to a contract (A) agrees not to enforce a contract condition, in a way that benefits B and disadvantages A, but without A receiving any consideration from B. If A then tries to enforce the original contract, they will be **estopped** (prevented) from enforcing it.

An example is a tenant whose premises are flooded, where the landlord (A) agrees to accept half the normal rent while the flood damage is being made good. The landlord cannot then change its mind and claim full rent for the period of repairs.

21.6 ENDING CONTRACTUAL OBLIGATIONS

The obligations which are created when a contract comes into existence continue to bind the parties until the contract is ended by performance; is discharged by agreement, breach, frustration or rescission [below]; is repudiated by an individual who did not have capacity to contract [**21.1.2**]; ceases to be enforceable because too much time has passed [**21.7.9**]; or the obligation is estopped [**21.5.2.2**].

21.6.1 Performance

The vast majority of contracts end by **performance**: fulfilling the terms of the contract by one party providing the required goods or services and the other paying for them.

21.6.2 Discharge by agreement

If the contract is not fulfilled the parties may agree that it is **discharged** (completed by something different from what was originally agreed). This may involve agreeing to end the contract completely, to replace it with a new contract, or to vary the existing contract [**21.5.2**]. The discharge must involve accord and satisfaction [**21.5.2.1**] unless it is done under a deed [**20.3**] or estoppel [**21.5.2.2**].

21.6.2.1 Forbearance

If the change in the arrangements is not formalised by a deed or by accord and satisfaction, the party to whom a right is owed may simply choose not to enforce the right. Generally such **forbearance** does not legally discharge the contract, and the party is able to change its mind and enforce its right unless it is estopped.

21.6.3 Frustration

The parties may be released from their obligations under a contract if an unforeseeable event makes its fulfilment illegal or impossible. Examples include destruction of the subject matter of the contract, for example a work of art which was to have been exhibited being destroyed in a fire; the death or incapacity of an individual due to provide services; or where the means of performing the contract can no longer be undertaken, for example because of war or a disaster.

Sums due but not paid cease to become due, and sums already paid are recoverable. But the court may allow a party who has incurred costs or expenses to recover these or obtain sums in respect of them.   *Law Reform (Frustrated Contracts) Act 1943 s.1*

21.6.4 Force majeure

The court may or may not find that an event such as a strike, riot, explosion or hurricane frustrates a contract. Many contracts therefore include a *force majeure* clause which allows the contract not to be fulfilled at all if a specified unforeseen event occurs, or not to be fulfilled for the duration of the event. *Force majeure* is not defined in English law, so its application depends entirely on the wording of the contract. If an unforeseen event occurs and there is no *force majeure* clause, the doctrine of frustration [above] may apply.

21.6.5 Rescission

A contract based on a misrepresentation [**21.2.8**] may be **rescinded** (set aside) by the party who was misled or by the court. **Rescission** is also possible for certain unfair contracts, or where a fundamental term has been breached [below].

21.6.6 Discharge by breach

In certain circumstances where there has been a breach [**21.7**], the wronged party may choose to treat the contract as **discharged** (ended) by the breach. Unless otherwise agreed, the wronged party is entitled to damages [**21.7.2**].

21.6.6.1 Repudiation

Repudiation occurs when one party shows an intention no longer to be bound by the contract, for example where an employer treats an employee so badly that the employee is entitled to believe that the employer has repudiated the contract [**34.2.9**]. It is generally very difficult to ascertain whether one breach is enough to constitute repudiation, and there is considerable case law on the subject.

21.6.6.2 Condition precedent

In some contracts, one party must do something before the other party has any liability. Thus if one party agrees to pay for a service monthly in arrears, the liability to pay does not arise until that service has been received for a month. If less than a month of service is provided the **condition precedent** has not been met and no liability will arise.

21.6.6.3 Breach of fundamental term

The law recognises two types of contractual terms: **conditions**, which are key terms, and **warranties**, which are minor terms. The breach of a warranty generally only gives the injured party a right to monetary compensation (**damages**). Breach of a condition gives the right to **rescind** (terminate) the contract as well as the right to damages. Distinguishing between conditions and warranties can be difficult and depends on each particular contract.

21.6.6.4 Late delivery

Generally the timing of performance under a contract is not critical and is not treated as fundamental. Therefore late delivery of a service or goods does not in itself usually constitute a failure to perform a contract.

Where the contract makes clear that time is to be **of the essence**, failure to perform on time may constitute a breach of the contract, thus giving the injured party rights either for breach of a condition or for breach of a warranty.

Where there is a delay, the injured party may be able to make time of the essence by warning the defaulting party.

21.7 REMEDIES FOR BREACH OF CONTRACT

Non-performance means not doing what is required under a contract. **Defective performance** means providing what is required, but not to the required timing, quantity, quality or standard. Non-performance or defective performance generally constitutes a **breach of contract**.

All breaches of contract, unless otherwise agreed, entitle the wronged party to damages [**21.7.2**]. In addition, some breaches entitle the wronged party to treat the contract as discharged by the breach [**21.6.6**] or to an order of the court that the contract be performed [**21.7.6**].

A breach of contract is a civil wrong, entitling action to be taken in the civil courts. In limited circumstances it may also be a criminal offence, for example harassing a residential tenant who has a contractual right to quiet enjoyment.

Complex rules govern rights in breach of contract cases. Legal advice is required if there is any likelihood that a contractual dispute will end up before the courts.

21.7.1 Alternatives to court action

Methods other than court proceedings should always be considered when there is a contractual problem. Depending on the circumstances, these may include:
- the wronged party agreeing to discharge the contract by accepting the defective performance [**21.6.2**];
- forfeiting any deposit;
- appealing to a higher level in the other party's organisation or firm;
- using mediation or arbitration to resolve the dispute [**65.2**];
- involving other clients or customers of the supplier;
- involving the professional or trade association of the supplier;
- if the contract involves a public sector body, using the Compact as the basis for discussions [**48.4.1**];
- involving the local authority's consumer protection department;
- involving the media or local or national politicians;
- where one exists, involving the ombudsman or regulator for that type of work.

Practical solutions are usually the best. A workable solution at an early stage may well be better than a slightly better solution after many weeks or months of discussions, letters, meetings and disagreements. A careful analysis of whether a contract dispute is worth pursuing may prevent much wasted time and energy.

21.7.2 Damages

Breach of a legally enforceable contract gives rise to a right to **damages**, unless this right is specifically excluded. The wronged party must show that some sort of loss occurred, and the loss arose directly from the breach of the contract.

The purpose of damages is to put the wronged party, insofar as possible, in the position it would have been in if the contract had been performed. Complex rules govern the level of damages. In most contract cases damages are **compensation**, rather than a penalty. **Punitive** or **exemplary damages** may be awarded in some court cases [**65.4.7**], but generally not in contract cases.

21.7.2.1 General damages

General damages are those which both parties could reasonably have anticipated would occur if either party had failed to honour their part of the contract.

In the classic case, a miller gave a carrier a broken mill shaft to be delivered for repair. The carrier was slow, and because the miller did not have a spare shaft he was unable to work during the period of delay. The carrier did not know that the miller did not have a spare, and so could not have anticipated that the miller would not be able to work. The carrier was therefore held to be liable only for damages for being slow, not for the additional loss of profit suffered by the miller.

Hadley & another v Baxendale & others [1854] EWHC Exch J70

21.7.2.2 Special damages

Special damages are direct losses incurred by the wronged party. If, for example, a badly installed tank bursts, the purchaser will be entitled to general damages to compensate for the inconvenience. If the purchaser has to hire a dehumidifier and replace all the carpets, those costs would be the special damages.

21.7.2.3 Mitigation

Where there is a breach of contract, the wronged party cannot sit still and allow damages to build up. They must take steps to try to **mitigate** (minimise) the loss, and avoid any steps which might increase the loss. An employee who is alleging unfair or wrongful dismissal, for example, has a duty to mitigate the loss by looking for a new job [**37.4.2**]. If this is not done, damages will be reduced.

21.7.2.4 Damages for injured feelings or reputation

The courts have for a long time resisted awarding damages for hurt feelings or damaged reputations arising from breach of contract. However, in certain limited circumstances such awards may be made.

21.7.3 Liquidated damages, penalties and indemnities

A contract may contain a clause providing that late delivery will require the defaulting party to make a fixed payment. A fixed payment which is based on a genuine estimate of the amount of loss is referred to as **liquidated damages**, and is enforceable. Although such a clause is often colloquially called a **penalty clause**, the courts will not enforce a pre-quantified payment if it is a penalty whose object is to force performance or penalise the party in default by making them pay an extravagantly large sum.

Damages are limited by a range of rules. Increasingly, a party to a contract circumvents these limitations by putting an **indemnity clause** [**21.2.6.3**] in the contract, saying that all losses suffered by this party as a result of breach will be recoverable, even if the normal laws governing damages would not cover the expense or loss. Indemnity clauses can have serious implications, and legal advice should be sought before agreeing to them. Insurance may be needed to cover possible liability arising from such a clause.

21.7.4 Deposits and part payments

A **deposit** is a sum paid by a purchaser as a guarantee that he or she will fulfil the contract by paying the remaining amount. A purchaser who defaults by not paying the remaining amount is generally unable to recover the deposit, unless the forfeited deposit is so large as to amount to a penalty [**21.7.3**]. Where the contract is with a consumer [**21.2.3.1**] rather than a business, the consumer has even stronger protection against unfair penalties or forfeiture of deposit.

Unfair Terms in Consumer Contracts Regulations 1999 [SI 1999/2083]

Part payment is not made as a guarantee, but is simply a partial payment of the purchase price. A purchaser who defaults may recover the amount paid, minus any damages awarded to the person to whom the part payment was made.

21.7.5 Restitution

Where one party pays money for goods or a service and there is a total failure to provide what has been purchased, the court will order the payment to be returned. This is called **restitution**. Where there is only a partial failure, for example a builder who only half finishes a job, there is no right to restitution. The wronged party will, however, have a right to claim damages.

21.7.6   Specific performance

Specific performance is an order from the court that the party in breach must fulfil its obligations under the contract. The court will generally make this award only if damages are an insufficient remedy. Specific performance is unlikely to be awarded where:

- the goods or service are readily available elsewhere, so there is no particular need for them to be provided under this contract;
- specific performance would give rise to unfairness, for example where the purchaser paid only a nominal price;
- the wronged party has acted in an unfair way, but perhaps short of giving rise to any counterclaim by the party in breach;
- specific performance is impossible, for example where the vendor does not own the goods which they failed to deliver;
- the contract requires a service to be provided personally [**25.1**], for example under a contract of employment;
- specific performance would require constant supervision by the court.

21.7.7   Injunctions and stop now orders

An **injunction** is a negative or **restraining** order. Where an injunction is to prevent future breaches, the court is generally willing to grant it. If it relates to a past act, for example to undo something already done by the defaulting party, the court will look at the balance of convenience. The injunction is unlikely to be granted if the disadvantage suffered by the party in breach, in having to undo the act, heavily outweighs the advantage to be gained by the wronged party.

Consumers and consumer protection bodies can apply to the court for a **stop now order**, a form of injunction covering the sale of goods, consumer contracts, distance selling, misleading advertising and similar matters. Some of these matters are now criminal offences under consumer protection law [**21.2.3.2**].

21.7.8   Declaration

The parties to a contract may seek a **declaration** from the court, for example to clarify a disputed contractual term.

21.7.9   Extinction of remedies

The wronged party may delay so long in bringing action for breach that its right to do so is **extinguished**. The rights contained within the contract itself are not lost, merely the right to bring a case in the courts to enforce those rights.

The **limitation period** is three years for personal injury claims, six years for damages and other remedies arising from breach of contract, and 12 years if the contract was made under seal (as a deed) [**20.3**]. Complex rules govern the date from which the start of the period runs. *Limitation Act 1980*

Resources: CONTRACTS AND CONTRACT LAW

Consumer advice. Consumer Direct, www.consumerdirect.gov.uk, 08454 04 05 06, email via website.

Fair contracts, competition. Office of Fair Trading, www.oft.gov.uk, 08457 22 44 99, enquiries@oft.gsi.gov.uk.

Late payment of commercial debts. Better Payments Practice Campaign, www.payontime.co.uk.

Public procurement. Office of Government Commerce, www.ogc.gov.uk/procurement.asp, 0845 000 4999, servicedesk@ogc.gsi.gov.uk.

Statute law. www.opsi.gov.uk and www.statutelaw.gov.uk.

Much but not all case law. www.bailii.org.

Updates cross-referenced to this book. www.rclh.co.uk.

Chapter 22
RISK AND LIABILITY

For sources of further information see end of chapter.

22.1   RISK ASSESSMENT AND MANAGEMENT

In the same way that an organisation carries out ongoing health and safety risk assessments [**40.3**], it should also undertake regular legal, financial and security risk assessments. It should also assess risks related to information, the organisation's activities and services, computers and other equipment, reputation, staff, the external environment, and any other risks. Risk assessments should:

- look systematically at the activities carried out and services provided by the organisation;
- look at the systems and procedures used (or not) in carrying out the work;
- identify key risks;
- help the people involved in managing the organisation and undertaking its activities and services agree what level of risk is acceptable;
- assess adequacy of controls and gaps in the ways work is carried out;
- recommend changes to help reduce risk or mitigate impact.

Risk management is not about avoiding risk. It is about identifying risks, deciding what level of risk is acceptable, and taking steps to reduce risks or minimise negative impact if they do happen. It is about creating a risk management culture in which people are **risk aware**, but not **risk averse**.

Risk assessment can be developed through internal audit processes [**22.1.2**], but to be truly effective it needs the input of paid staff, volunteers and governing body members, and possibly service users or others affected by the organisation.

Risk assessments are necessary to comply with charity trustees' duty to consider major risks and establish systems and procedures to mitigate them [**22.1.3**].

22.1.1 Carrying out a risk assessment

A risk assessment looks at causes of risk, what can go wrong, how likely it is to happen, how serious it would be if it did happen, what is already being done to reduce the likelihood of it happening or to minimise the negative impact if it does happen, what else could or should be done, and an action plan.

Any risk assessment, especially when done for the first time, is likely to identify many areas of concern. Some can be dealt with immediately with little outlay of time or money. Others are more complex, and governing body members or managers may feel overwhelmed by all that needs doing. A simple technique for prioritising is to rate probability and impact for each area of risk, along the following lines, and multiply them to give an indication of what should be prioritised:

- **Probability**: 1=very unlikely, 2=unlikely, 3=possible, 4=likely, 5=highly likely
- **Impact**: 1=insignificant, 2=fairly serious, 3=serious, 4=very serious, 5=major disaster

Information about how to identify, assess and manage risk is available in *Charities and risk management* from the Charity Commission and *Living with risk: Risk management and insurance advice for the voluntary and community sector*, free from the Association of British Insurers [see end of chapter].

The Charity Commission suggests that risk be looked at under the headings of **governance and management**, **operational risk**, **financial risks**, **environmental and external factors**, and **compliance risk** (law and regulation).

22.1.2 Risk management and action plans

The risk assessments should lead to action programmes which include deadlines and named responsibility for implementing changes, regular reports by senior management to the governing body on the action programme and new areas of risk, and regular reports on internal controls and their adequacy. The process of reporting on controls and their adequacy is sometimes called **internal audit**.

Risk assessments should be repeated whenever there is a change in activities, services, premises or equipment. Most risk assessments should be done at least annually but for some types of work or equipment might need to be done much more frequently, while every two or three years may be enough for areas which are intrinsically low risk and have not changed. Where circumstances change suddenly, an on the spot risk assessment may be necessary.

Risk management is not about avoiding risk completely; this is impossible. Rather, it is about being aware of risks, judging their significance, avoiding or reducing them if possible, and putting sensible plans (and where appropriate, insurance) in place in case risk becomes reality. The aim is to keep risk at a level with which the organisation is comfortable, so that if things do go wrong – as, inevitably, they sometimes will – the impact can be managed effectively.

22.1.3 The risk mitigation statement

Trustees of charities which are required to have a full audit [**54.2.7**], must state in the notes to the accounts whether they have considered major risks to the charity, and put in place systems and procedures to mitigate (reduce) those risks. It is good practice for smaller charities to include the statement as well. Major risks and the risk mitigation measures should be summarised.

Guidance on how to record the required details in the report is available from the Charity Commission. The risk assessment must look not only at financial risks, but at the full range of risks outlined in this chapter.

22.1.4 Business continuity

Business continuity, **disaster recovery** or **contingency planning** involve putting in place procedures to enable the organisation to continue operating even after serious or catastrophic events such as flood, fire, burglary, complete collapse of the computer system, all key staff off ill or a major scandal.

Business **continuity management** does not start when the crisis happens. It starts long before, by identifying the organisation's most critical functions, putting in place systems to ensure those functions could continue, documenting the systems, keeping key documents such as leases and insurance policies as well as up to date copies of essential information (including the continuity plan) off the premises but easily accessible, and regularly reviewing the plan.

The **Business Continuity Institute** and **Charity Disaster Recovery Network** [see end of chapter] have information about continuity planning and free checklists.

22.2 NATURE OF LIABILITY

Liability means being held legally responsible for actions taken and for **defaults** (actions not taken) or **errors and omissions**. A corporate body, the members of a membership organisation, members of the governing body, employees, volunteers, agents (persons acting on behalf of an organisation) and persons saying they are acting on behalf of an organisation when they are not authorised to do so may all be held liable in various ways.

The prospect of liability is frightening, but must be kept in perspective. It generally becomes an issue only if the organisation breaks the law, cannot pay what it owes, or faces an uninsured loss. Few organisations ever get into such difficulty, and the likelihood of an individual facing personal liability is very small indeed.

22.2.1 Sources of liability

Liability might arise because a corporate body, a governing body, employees, volunteers or persons acting on behalf of the organisation or its governing body act:

- in breach of **criminal law** [**22.3**];
- in breach of **statutory duty** [**22.3**];
- in breach of **covenants** or other property rights or duties [**60.7**];
- in breach of **trust** [**22.4**], creating a liability to the organisation, its members, or third parties to whom a duty of trust or fiduciary duty is owed;
- in breach of **contract** [**22.5**], creating a liability to the other party or parties or to third parties who benefit from the contract;
- in breach of duties in an **insolvency** [**24.2.4**]; or
- in a way which causes a **tort** (a civil wrong against a person, such as negligence, libel or trespass) to be committed [**22.6**].

Who is liable in any situation will depend on whether the organisation is incorporated or unincorporated; on who authorised an action or contract, carried out an action or entered into a contract, and whether they were authorised to do so; or who did not do something they had a duty to do.

22.2.2 Personal liability

The term **personal liability** is used here to mean situations where a member of the governing body, an employee or other individual associated with the organisation:

- has to use personal funds to meet the organisation's obligations;
- has to make good losses caused to the organisation because of his or her actions;
- has to repay to the organisation any personal profit from an unauthorised contract or transaction; or
- is held responsible in law for offences caused by or on behalf of the organisation.

Individuals held financially liable for the organisation's obligations may be entitled to be indemnified (compensated) by the organisation, the members of the governing body or the members of the organisation [**22.7.8**]. In some situations a governing body member may apply to the court or Charity Commission for relief from personal liability [**22.7.7**], or they may be covered by insurance [**23.10**].

291

22.2.2.1 Liability in incorporated organisations

Members of companies, charitable incorporated organisations (CIOs) and industrial and provident societies have **limited liability** in virtually all situations [**22.7.1.1**]. The liability of the members of a company limited by guarantee is limited to the amount – usually £1 – which they promise to contribute if the company is wound up with outstanding debts [**24.2.4**]. In a CIO, there may or may not be a guarantee; if there is none, the CIO's members have no liability for its debts. In a company limited by shares or an IPS, members' liability is limited to the amount unpaid on their shares.

All other liabilities rest with the company, CIO or IPS itself, or in some situations with its officers (governing body members, the company secretary if there is one, and sometimes senior management).

22.2.2.2 Liability in unincorporated associations and trusts

In unincorporated organisations liability normally rests with the members of the governing body, although in some situations members of the organisation who are not on the governing body could be liable [**22.3.3.4**].

Where a charitable association or trust has incorporated its governing body [**2.4**], the members of the governing body still have personal liability.

22.2.3 Joint and several liability

Where the members of an organisation or its governing body are held liable for the organisation's financial obligations, the liability is **joint and several** [**21.1.4**], so each could be held liable for all or any part of the obligation.

If two or more persons are held liable for the same loss or damage arising from tort [**22.6**] or breach of contract [**22.5**], but only some of them are sued, those who are sued are entitled to recover a contribution from the other liable persons. The court decides what each person's contribution should be, based on their responsibility for the loss or damage. *Civil Liability (Contribution) Act 1978 ss.1,2*

22.2.4 Liability for the acts of others

The general rule of liability is that persons are liable for their own acts. But there are many situations where a person might be held liable instead of, or in addition to, the person who committed the act:

- if a person (an agent) who is authorised to act on behalf of someone else (the principal) enters into a contract on behalf of the principal, the principal is liable for the contract [**20.5.5**];
- if an employee is negligent or commits another tort the employee is liable, but the employer has **vicarious liability** and may also be held liable for the acts of the employee [**22.6.4**];
- trustees may be held liable for losses caused by persons acting on their behalf but not properly supervised by them [**15.8.2**].

Statute law frequently makes one party liable for the acts of another. Employers, for example, may be liable for unlawful discrimination by their employees or by customers, service users etc [**28.1.8**]. This is a civil matter. Statute law may also impose criminal liability on a person who authorised or allowed a criminal act, even if someone else actually committed the act.

22.2.4.1 Liability for acts of 'rogue trustees'

In general, governing body members are not liable for unauthorised acts by other members of the governing body. However an employment tribunal found that a local authority, as an employer, was liable for the unauthorised acts of a councillor which led to an employee resigning and claiming constructive dismissal [**34.2.9**]. The case illustrates the importance of being absolutely clear about who is authorised to speak for, make decisions or take action on behalf of the organisation and its governing body, and ensuring they do not overstep their authority. *Moores v Bude Stratton Town Council [2000] UKEAT 313 99 2703*

22.3 CRIMINAL OFFENCES AND BREACH OF STATUTORY DUTY

22.3.1 What they are

Liability for **criminal offences** arises from offences against persons, property or the public interest. Action is generally brought by the state, rather than by individuals, and the person(s) responsible may be fined or imprisoned.

22.3.1.1 Statutory duties

The state also imposes many **statutory duties**, for example in relation to duties to employees [**26.4-26.6**], health and safety [**chapter 40**], the supply of food and drink [**40.10.1**, **47.2**, **47.5**], and use of land [**63.5**]. Many statutory duties – such as the duty to send in company accounts and reports on time, or to put a charity's status on all its financial documents – are offences where failure to act (**default**) may be punishable by fines, or in some cases imprisonment.

Many other statutory duties can be enforced by the courts, but default is not in itself punishable. Examples include the duty to register a charity or to provide itemised pay statements to employees. A person ordered by the court to put right the default who does not do so may be found to be in **contempt of court**. Contempt is a civil wrong but may be punished by a fine or imprisonment.

22.3.1.2 Corporate manslaughter

In the past, a corporate body such as a company could not be found guilty of manslaughter unless it could be shown that one or more directors was a **controlling mind** of the company or in relation to the act which led to the death. A company could be fined for breach of health and safety law, but not for manslaughter. Now **corporate manslaughter** (corporate homicide in Scotland) has been redefined to cover death caused by overall management failure by senior management. This allows an incorporated body to be charged and face an unlimited fine.

Corporate Manslaughter & Corporate Homicide Act 2007 s.1(3)

Individual senior managers or governing body members can be prosecuted for manslaughter only if they were personally grossly negligent. They cannot be prosecuted because of failings on the part of the company.

An unincorporated organisation is not covered by the Act unless it is a partnership, trade union or employers' association which is also an employer.

CMCHA 2007 s.1(2)

22.3.2 Reducing the risk of liability

To reduce the risk of statutory duties not being fulfilled or offences taking place, members of the governing body should:

- carry out reviews, provide training and put documentation in place to ensure there are people (governing body members, employees, volunteers, professional advisors) aware of the full range of the organisation's legal obligations;

- put proper procedures in place and ensure adequate monitoring of staff and others, especially those who have access to money, children, vulnerable adults or dangerous equipment or are in other situations where unlawful or dangerous acts are most likely to occur;

- in a company, charitable incorporated organisation (CIO) or industrial and provident society, ensure they receive proper financial reports clearly setting out the organisation's financial position so that they are not at risk of continuing to operate while the organisation is, or is becoming, insolvent.

22.3.3 Who is liable

A person who commits a criminal act or breach of statutory duty is liable. The person may be a corporate body or an individual.

An employer has **vicarious liability** [**22.6.4**] for a breach of statutory duty by an employee, and in some cases may have vicarious liability for criminal offences by employees committed in the course of work. A funding body could possibly be held liable for breach of health and safety law by an organisation it funds, if the funder has sufficient control over the funded project or activity [**40.2.5**].

22.3.3.1 Corporate body

Under common law [**64.2.1**], corporate bodies were not generally held liable for criminal acts, on the basis that they could not be hanged or imprisoned. Now it is increasingly common for corporate bodies to be fined for criminal acts, as well as for breaches of statutory duty by the organisation itself or by its governing body or employees, such as breaches of health and safety or data protection law.

22.3.3.2 Governing body

Members of a governing body are personally liable for their own criminal acts as individuals or as a body. They may also be held vicariously liable for acts committed by employees in the course of their work [**22.6.4**] and in some cases for acts committed by third parties [**28.1.8**], and may be held liable for acts by other members of the governing body if it can be shown that they authorised the action and/or were negligent in allowing it to take place [**22.2.4.1**].

Authorising or assisting a criminal act or a breach of statutory duty, or allowing premises to be used for a crime, may also be an offence. Particular care must be taken to ensure premises are not used for drug related offences [**63.5.5**].

In trusts and unincorporated associations, the members of the governing body are responsible for ensuring that statutory obligations are met.

In incorporated organisations it is the organisation itself which is responsible and is generally liable if obligations are not met, but governing body members may be held personally liable for some defaults of the organisation, such as:

- failure to operate PAYE [**30.4.3**];
- failure to comply with health and safety legislation [**chapter 40**] and other statutory duties;
- failure to comply with many duties arising from the organisation's status as a company, industrial and provident society or charitable incorporated organisation, such as the duty to submit annual accounts to the regulatory body;
- allowing the organisation to continue operating when it is, or is inevitably going to become, insolvent, or deceiving creditors or others when a company is or is becoming insolvent [**24.2.4**];
- failure to comply with some Charities Act requirements, in particular where an offence is committed with the 'consent or connivance … or … neglect' of governing body members or others. *Charities Act 1993 s.95*

22.3.3.3 Industrial and provident society directors

In industrial and provident societies, every offence committed under the **Industrial and Provident Societies Act 1965** or the **Friendly and Industrial and Provident Societies Act 1968** is considered to have been committed by any officer who under the governing document is responsible for fulfilling that duty. If no such officer is named, every member of the governing body is considered liable unless it can be proved that he or she did not know the offence was being committed, or attempted to prevent it. *Industrial & Provident Societies Act 1965 s.62*

22.3.3.4 Ordinary members

In a company, charitable incorporated organisation or IPS, the ordinary members (those who are not officers or governing body members) are not liable for criminal acts or breaches of statutory duty committed by the organisation, its governing body or other members unless they authorised the acts or took part in them.

In unincorporated membership organisations, where the members *are* the organisation, the ordinary members could be held liable for criminal acts and breaches of statutory duty committed by the organisation, its governing body or other members, including breach of health and safety and similar duties. *R v RL & another [2008] EWCA Crim 1970*

22.3.3.5 Individuals

Individuals are always liable for their own criminal actions, regardless of whether they do it as an individual or as an employee, volunteer, governing body member or in any other capacity.

22.3.4 What happens

A breach of statutory duty or a criminal offence may lead to a penalty, fine or imprisonment. It may also give rise to a civil claim for tort [**22.6**].

Insurance cannot cover penalties or fines, but it is possible to take out insurance to cover legal costs arising from a successful defence in criminal cases and breach of statutory duty [**23.9.3**, **23.10.1**], and to cover civil claims [**chapter 23**].

22.3.4.1 Civil enforcement

If an act which should have been done (for example, submitting charity accounts) has not been done, a court may order it to be done. Failure to comply with the ruling can lead to penalties for contempt of court.

22.3.4.2 Criminal penalties

On conviction for a criminal offence a corporate body may be fined, members of a governing body may be fined or imprisoned, and/or other individuals who carried out the act, authorised it or allowed it to happen may be fined or imprisoned.

For some statutory breaches a penalty is automatic without any need for a court case. An example is failure to submit company annual accounts on time [**54.3.8**].

22.3.4.3 Relief from liability

A company director, company secretary, charity trustee, senior employee of a company or charity, or auditor/independent examiner may be relieved of personal liability [**22.7.7**].

22.4 BREACH OF TRUST / FIDUCIARY DUTY

22.4.1 What it is

Breach of trust or **breach of fiduciary duty** (duty to act in good faith) occurs when a person in a position of trust breaks that trust. In organisations, the members of the governing body have a duty of trust and fiduciary duty to the organisation, its members and its beneficiaries [**15.3-15.6**]. Breach of trust or breach of fiduciary duty may arise where some or all governing body members:

- allow money or property to be used for purposes for which it was not intended or are not allowed under the governing document or charity law;
- cause a loss to the organisation through mismanagement, failure to show a proper duty of care [**15.3.4**, **15.6.7**] or failure to take professional advice;
- steal money or property from the organisation (which is a criminal offence as well as a breach of trust);
- make a personal profit or gain a benefit from the organisation when not allowed to do so [**15.2**];
- misuse information obtained through their position as a trustee or governing body member.

22.4.2 Reducing the risk of liability

Breaches of trust or fiduciary duty are unlikely if governing body members:

- act honestly and reasonably;
- act within the terms of the governing document and the authority delegated to them;
- obtain proper information and advice when making any decision with financial or legal implications;
- declare any conflict of interest and act accordingly [**15.3.5**, **15.6.4**];
- understand and comply with the rules on remuneration, profit or gain for governing body members and persons connected with them [**chapter 16**];
- in charities, get formal advice from the Charity Commission if there is any doubt about whether an act could be in breach of trust [**22.7.3**].

22.4.3   Who is liable

22.4.3.1   Trustees

Potential liability for breach of trust rests with:

- all charity trustees (anyone on the governing body of a charitable organisation, regardless of whether it is registered with the Charity Commission);

- trustees in non-charitable trusts;

- nominees (holding trustees and custodian trustees) and custodians [20.4], if they act outside the terms of their agreement with the organisation for which they are holding assets;

- holding trustees [20.4.4], if they do anything in breach of trust, even if it is authorised by the organisation for which they are holding assets;

- anyone who holds money or property on trust for someone else or for charitable purposes (for example someone who says they are raising money for one or more individuals, named charities or a charitable purposes).

Trustees may be held liable for losses arising from the acts of agents (persons authorised to act on their behalf) unless they can show that they have exercised their proper duty of care in appointing and supervising the agents [15.8.2].

If more than one trustee is liable the liability is joint and several [21.1.4]. Each trustee is liable for up to the full amount of the loss even if some of them were more involved in the breach than the others.   *Attorney General v Wilson [1840] 47 RR 173*

A trustee is not liable for breach by a former trustee, but if he or she becomes aware of the breach there is an obligation to take action as quickly as possible to recover the loss to the organisation.   *Harvey v Olliver [1887] 57 LT 239*

A trustee who retires remains liable for breaches which he or she committed, as does the estate of a trustee who dies. A trustee who retires or resigns knowing that a breach of trust is likely to take place could be liable along with those who actually commit the breach. A trustee who leaves the organisation in these circumstances should put his or her concerns in writing to the other trustees (and the Charity Commission, if the organisation is charitable), and could apply to be relieved of liability [22.4.4.3].   *Head v Gould [1898] 2 Ch 250*

22.4.3.2   Company and IPS directors, CIO trustees

Limited liability does not protect against liability for breach of fiduciary duty or breach of trust. Potential liability rests with directors of all companies and industrial and provident societies, whether charitable or non-charitable, and with trustees of charitable incorporated organisations.

The required standard of care is lower in a non-charitable company or IPS than in a charitable one [15.3.4, 15.6.7]. However, in all companies – whether charitable or non-charitable – the duties are now statutory [15.3] rather than solely based on case law. Any company member may seek to bring a **derivative claim** [12.10.1], on behalf of the company, against one or more directors for failure to comply with their statutory duties as directors.   *Companies Act 2006 ss.260-264*

22.4.3.3   Non-charitable associations

There appears to be no English case law relating specifically to the fiduciary duties of governing body members in non-charitable associations, but it is reasonable to assume they are similar to those for directors of non-charitable companies.

22.4.4   What happens

22.4.4.1   Reinstatement of losses

If an organisation suffers loss due to breach of trust or fiduciary duty, the liable persons could be required by the organisation, the other members of the governing body, the Charity Commission or the court to repay, with interest:

- any losses to the organisation because the person did not show a proper standard of care [15.3.4, 15.6.7], for example where the governing body did not take advice before investing or put procedures in place to prevent fraud;

- any losses arising to the organisation because the person acted outside his or her powers or outside the organisation's objects or powers, or in ways which were not properly authorised;

- in trusts and charitable associations, any losses arising from the actions of agents acting on their behalf, but not if the agent was properly appointed and supervised by the trustees [**15.8.2**].   *Trustee Act 2000 s.23*

Trustee indemnity insurance [**23.10**] cannot cover any action which the trustees knew was wrong or did in 'reckless disregard' of whether it was wrong, so it is not likely to cover any of the above situations.

A company can take out **directors' and officers' insurance** to indemnify company directors, the secretary and senior managers [**23.10**].

22.4.4.2 Reinstatement of profit or gain

Even if the organisation has not suffered any loss, the person could be required to repay to the organisation any profit or gain, or the value of any non-monetary benefits, which were not allowed or properly authorised [**chapter 16**] or in which a conflict of interest was not properly disclosed and acted upon [**15.3.5**, **15.6.4**].

22.4.4.3 Relief from liability

Charity trustees may apply to the Charity Commission or court to be relieved from liability for breach of trust, and company directors may apply to the court to be relieved from liability for breach of fiduciary duty [**22.7.7**].

22.5 BREACH OF CONTRACT

22.5.1 What it is

An organisation's liability under **contract** typically arises if the organisation cannot or does not pay sums due under a contract or provide goods or services it has committed itself to provide, the goods or services provided do not meet the standards specified in the contract or required or implied by statute [**21.7.3**], or the company breaches the conditions of the contract.

22.5.2 Reducing the risk of liability

To reduce the risk of liability arising from contracts:
- no contract should be authorised unless it is reasonably certain the organisation will be able to meet its contractual obligations;

- no one should enter into a contract or other agreement on behalf of any organisation unless they have explicit authorisation to do so;

- anyone entering into a contract should make clear they are doing so on behalf of the organisation (in an incorporated body) or its governing body (in an unincorporated organisation);

- legal advice should be taken about the possibility of limiting or excluding liability under the contract [**22.7.5**];

- members of an unincorporated organisation should not enter into any arrangement to pay later unless they have adequate resources in hand, or credit arrangements are available and authorised by the governing document;

- everyone involved with the contract should understand contract law and what the contract requires, and the effects of not meeting the requirements.

22.5.3 Who is liable

In breach of contract situations, the distinctions between incorporated and unincorporated organisations become highly significant.

22.5.3.1 Incorporated organisations

In an incorporated organisation (a company, charitable incorporated organisation or industrial and provident society) the organisation as a corporate body enters into contracts. Those who agree the contract – the governing body, or persons with delegated authority such as committees, officers or employees – act as **agents** of the organisation and as such are not a party to the contract [**20.5**].

However, the members of the governing body or the person(s) who agreed a contract could be held personally liable if the contract is *ultra vires* (outside the organisation's objects or powers) [**5.8**] or outside their authority to agree it [**20.5.5**].

There is also a risk of liability if a member of the governing body makes a negligent mis-statement in a way which indicates that he or she is accepting personal responsibility for the statement. *Williams & another v Natural Life Health Foods Ltd & another [1996] EWCA Civ 1110*

22.5.3.2 Disqualified company directors and CIO trustees

A person who serves as a company director while disqualified [**13.3.3**] may be held liable for all of the company's debts incurred while he or she was a director. At the time of writing (mid 2009) it was expected that the same or similar rules would apply to trustees of charitable incorporated organisations.

Company Directors Disqualification Act 1986 s.15

22.5.3.3 Governing body members during insolvency

A director, secretary or senior employer who allows a company or industrial and provident society to continue operating or to operate fraudulently while it is, or is becoming, insolvent may be held liable for all debts incurred during this period [**24.2.4**, **24.10.5**]. The same or similar rules are likely to apply to trustees of charitable incorporated organisations (CIOs).

22.5.3.4 Persons acting for not-yet-incorporated bodies

If an organisation is in process of registering as a company, any contracts, deeds or other obligations will be with the person(s) who entered into them on behalf of the organisation, rather than with the company – even if the organisation becomes incorporated before the contract takes effect. *Companies Act 2006 s.51*

The court might apply similar rules to pre-incorporation agreements on behalf of an industrial and provident society or charitable incorporated organisation.

22.5.3.5 Principals in unincorporated associations

An unincorporated association, not having a legal identity of its own [**2.2.1**], cannot enter into contracts as an organisation. Only individuals or incorporated bodies can enter into the association's contracts, only those parties to the contract can be held liable and their liability is **unlimited**.

The determination of who is liable may be complex and illustrates the importance of making clear decisions and keeping clear minutes or records of decisions and delegation of authority. This is especially important when entering into any long-term financial commitments, or when entering into agreements which commit the association to providing goods or services. The key issues are who made the decision to enter into the contract, and who actually entered into the contract by making a verbal agreement or signing a written agreement.

Primary liability rests with the **principals** (the individuals who authorise an action), but they may have a right to be indemnified by the association or its members [**22.7.7**]. Depending on the situation the principals might be:

- all the members, if the decision is taken in a general meeting;
- all the members of the governing body, if they make the decision or explicitly delegate decision making authority;
- one or more members of the organisation, governing body members, officers or employees, if they rather than the members as a whole or the governing body as a whole make the decision to enter into the contract;
- individuals, if they enter into a contract without authority from the members or the governing body, or enter into a contract which goes beyond what they are authorised to do.

The law in this area is not clear, but the general view is that members of an association's governing body are normally the principals.

A principal entering into a contract on behalf of other principals (for example, the treasurer acting on behalf of all the governing body members) must make clear that he or she is entering into it 'for and on behalf of the association'. If this is not made clear, the person entering into the contract could be held solely liable.

A person who is not a principal and who enters into a contract with proper authority to do so is an **agent**, and is generally not liable for the contract [**20.5.5**]. For example, if the governing body decides to enter into a contract and an officer or employee then signs it, that person is the agent of the governing body.

An agent who enters into an unauthorised contract is generally personally liable, and the contract does not bind the principal(s). But the principals could be held liable if they ratify the contract, or ratify it by implication by using goods which have been ordered without authorisation. *Delauney v Strickland [1818] 2 Stark 416*

No one in an unincorporated association has the right to commit the association to spending more money than it has, so the association cannot borrow money or purchase anything on credit unless authorisation to do so is explicitly given in the governing document or by the members. *Cockrell v Aucompte [1857] 2 CBNS 440*

If such authorisation is given by the members, only those who authorise it can be held liable if the association subsequently cannot repay the borrowing or meet its financial obligations. However, such authorisation may be implied if the members have previously known about contracts on credit and allowed them to go ahead. *Todd v Emly [1841] 7 M&W 427; Harper v Granville-Smith [1891] 7 TLR 284*

Contracts involving ongoing obligations, such as leases and contracts of employment, may be entered into even if the association may not have sufficient funds to pay them into the distant future, provided the governing document authorises such transactions. It is wise to ensure the contract contains a termination clause which allows the organisation to end the agreement.

Principals who leave an association remain liable for their contracts, and after death liability passes to their estate. **Novation [21.5.1]** enables a principal to transfer his or her contractual obligations to another member of the organisation or governing body member, but only if the that person and the other party to the contract agree.

Where the principal has the benefit (rather than the liability) of a contract, for example where money is owed to the association under a contract entered into by the principal, the contract can be **assigned** to a new principal [**21.5.1**]. This does not require the consent of the other party to the contract.

The risks of unlimited liability are reduced if the governing document contains a clause limiting the liability of the association's members and/or governing body members [**22.7.4**], or if liability can be limited within the contract [**22.7.5**].

22.5.3.6 Trustees

A body established as a trust is unincorporated and therefore cannot enter into contracts in its own right. All contracts are entered into by one or more trustees or others authorised to act on their behalf, and those considered to be principals [above] will be held liable for claims arising from the contract.

Unless a contract is transferred to new trustees by novation or assignment [**21.10.1**], a trustee retains the right to enforce the contract and remains liable for it even after retiring. When a trustee dies, liability passes to her or his personal representatives. As with unincorporated associations, it may be possible for the trustees to limit their contractual liability [**22.7.4, 22.7.5**].

22.5.3.7 Members of incorporated trustee bodies

To make it easier for charitable trusts and associations to enter into contracts, it is possible to incorporate the trustee body [**2.4**]. This gives the trustees corporate personality and enables them to enter into contracts as a corporate body, rather than as individual trustees. It does not, however, limit the liability of the trustees, so they remain fully liable as individuals in the same way as in any unincorporated association or trust.

22.5.3.8 Guarantors

Any person who gives a **personal guarantee** [21.2.6] for any transaction – bank overdraft, loan, credit account with a supplier etc – is personally liable if the organisation defaults. The guarantor will be entitled to indemnification from the organisation, but that is not much use if the organisation has no assets.

22.5.4 What happens

If contractual obligations are not met, the organisation (if it is a corporate body) or the individuals liable for the contract (in an unincorporated organisation) may be sued. If the organisation is unincorporated the suit may be brought against one or more members of the governing body, or if the other party wishes to claim against a larger group a **representative action** may be started, where a number of individuals are sued as representatives of a larger group.

A number of remedies are available through the courts, including **damages** (money compensation) and **specific performance** (ordering the organisation to provide the goods or services) [see **21.12** for more about breach of contract, and **chapter 65** for dispute resolution procedures].

It is possible to take out insurance to cover damages awarded by the court [**23.5.8**]. If damages are not covered by insurance and are more than the organisation can pay, the organisation becomes insolvent (if it is a corporate body) or the individuals who have been sued are personally liable (in an unincorporated organisation). The individuals may be entitled to be indemnified by the organisation [**22.7.7**] and/or a contribution from other principals [**22.2.3**]. The right to be indemnified by the organisation is meaningless if the organisation has no assets.

If individuals who are held liable do not pay damages awarded by the court, the judgment may be enforced by seizure of possessions or a **garnishee order**, where the court orders sums to be deducted from wages. Individuals with insufficient assets to meet the financial obligations could be personally bankrupted.

22.6 TORT

22.6.1 What it is

Tort comes from the French *tort*, 'wrong', and refers to an injury, loss or damage caused to a person through acts such as negligence, nuisance, defamation or trespass. A tort is a civil wrong [**64.2.1**], where action is brought by persons rather than the state. An act which causes a tort is **tortious** or **wrongful**. In some cases such as assault the tort may also be a criminal offence.

For most torts there must be either intention to commit the act (as in trespass or defamation) or negligence. But there are some acts for which there is **strict liability**, where the person is liable simply by committing the act, even without intention or negligence. Some of the more common torts are set out below.

22.6.1.1 Negligence

Negligence occurs when a person who has a **duty of care** towards another person does not take reasonable care, and the other person suffers injury, loss or damage as a result. For example:

- employers have a duty of care to employees, to provide competent staff and a safe workplace and work systems; *English v Wilsons & Clyde Coal Co Ltd [1937] UKHL 2*
- occupiers of land have a duty to take reasonable care to ensure that premises are safe for visitors and people exercising the 'right to roam' over land, and even have a duty of care to trespassers [**63.5**]. Even where a potential danger is signposted to the public, liability can still arise if the occupier knows that warnings are being ignored, or if children are involved.

Negligence may occur in various aspects of a voluntary organisation's work, for example an injury caused by sports which are not properly supervised or where proper equipment is not provided, or loss suffered as a result of giving inaccurate advice. In general, the higher the risk, the greater the level of care required.

22.6.1.2   Harassment

Harassment is a tort and criminal offence. The term is not defined in the **Protection from Harassment Act 1997**, but includes causing alarm or distress, by verbal or other means, on at least two occasions [**40.5.3**]. Harassment, using a different definition, is also a tort under anti-discrimination legislation [**28.1.6**].

22.6.1.3   Trespass

Trespass involves assaulting a person, which is also a criminal offence; entering or remaining on land without authorisation, which is also a criminal offence in some circumstances [**63.5.3**]; or interfering with another person's goods.

22.6.1.4   Passing off

Passing off [**44.5**] occurs where a supplier of goods or services makes a **misrepresentation** to actual or potential customers or clients about the source of those goods or services, and another supplier is damaged as a result. An example is an organisation seeking care contracts and using a name which causes it to be confused with another organisation offering similar services.

22.6.1.5   Defamation

Defamation [**45.3**] involves publishing material which lowers the public's view of a person. **Libel** is published in a permanent form; **slander** is transient, usually oral. A claim of slander requires the person to have been damaged in some way, but libel does not require this and can be a crime as well as a tort.

22.6.1.6   Nuisance

Public nuisance is a crime, and may be a tort if it causes special damage to a person. Noise nuisance, for example, is both a tort and a criminal offence [**63.12.5**]. **Private nuisance** is only a tort and is usually something which interferes with a person's enjoyment of their land, such as blocking light [**60.7.2**].

22.6.2   Reducing the risk of liability

The risk of tortious acts occurring can be reduced if:
- risk awareness, risk assessment and risk management are seen as an essential part of the organisation's activities, rather than as a burden or afterthought;
- everyone involved in the organisation's activities understands relevant aspects of the law and their duty of care;
- governing body members are properly recruited and trained;
- the governing body is clear about what can and cannot be delegated to staff or others, and are aware of the obligation to exercise proper supervision;
- employees, volunteers and contractors are properly recruited, trained and supervised;
- there are clear rules for situations when an employee or volunteer must get authority from a superior;
- anyone making a statement or representation makes clear that they are making it on behalf of the organisation, and are not taking personal responsibility for the statement;
- proper records are kept of all incidents involving personal injury, violence, trespass, damage to people's property etc;
- the organisation has a clear procedure for dealing with complaints and keeping records of action taken.

22.6.3   Who is liable

Liability may arise for the acts of employees, volunteers, contractors, governing body members, ordinary members, service users and others involved with the organisation. It is important to be clear about who could be held liable in these situations.

22.6.3.1 Incorporated organisations

Corporate bodies can commit torts and be sued in the same way as individuals. Governing body members are not personally liable for a tort committed by an incorporated body unless they directed or authorised the tort (collectively or as an individual), or it occurred because of the governing body member's negligence.

Performing Right Society Limited v Ciryl Theatrical Syndicate Ltd [1924] 1 KB 1

22.6.3.2 Governing body

Members of a governing body are liable for their own torts, those of the governing body, and those of the organisation or others, which they authorise or allow to happen. They can also be liable for torts of their employees and sometimes others, even if they did not authorise them [**22.6.4**].

Liability in tort is similar to liability in contract [**22.5.3**]. In incorporated organisations with limited liability, any claim for damages is generally against the organisation. However, even in a limited liability organisation, members of the governing body could be held personally liable if they authorise a tort. If a successful claim is brought against an incorporated body which is not insured and does not have sufficient assets to meet the claim, the organisation becomes insolvent.

In unincorporated associations or trusts, one or more named individuals would be sued. If they have to pay damages to the other party and the organisation does not have insurance to indemnify them they may be entitled to be indemnified by the organisation (provided the organisation has sufficient assets to do this), its members and/or the other persons who authorised or committed the tort [**22.7.8**].

Members of an unincorporated association are generally unable to bring a claim for personal injury against the governing body, on the basis that governing body members do not have a duty of care to the organisation's members [**22.6.3.4**]. However, in a case in 1998 it was held that a club committee did have a duty of care to its members, and had to compensate a member who was injured as a result of breach of that duty. *Melhuish v Clifford & others (1998) EWHC (QB) 18 Aug 1998 (unreported)*

22.6.3.3 Holding trustees

If an unincorporated association's property is held by holding trustees [**20.4.4**] they could possibly be held liable, for example for claims arising under the **Occupier's Liability Acts** [**63.5**] if they, rather than the governing body members or all the members of the association, are considered to be the occupiers of the land.

22.6.3.4 Ordinary members

Ordinary members of an unincorporated association may all be liable in tort if they all authorised or are all carrying on the activity which causes the injury, loss, damage, nuisance or defamation. They could also be liable if only some of the members are carrying on the activity, but all the members are in overall control of it; or if all the members, rather than the governing body or holding trustees, are considered to be the occupiers of premises or the employer.

An individual member or a group of members could be found liable in tort if they are specifically responsible for an activity or for the safety of premises and are in breach of their duty of care. *Prole v Allen [1950] 1 All ER 476*

The members of an unincorporated association do not have a general duty of care towards each other, beyond that owed between strangers, although there are exceptions [**22.6.3.2**]. So in general, a member of an unincorporated association cannot claim against other members unless it can be shown that the member had a specific responsibility, for example for keeping the premises in a fit state, or knew of a danger and failed to warn the other members. *Prole v Allen [above]*

22.6.4 Vicarious liability

22.6.4.1 Vicarious liability for tortious acts of employees

In general, persons are liable only for their own tortious acts and those they authorise. But employers have **vicarious liability** for the torts of their employees, even if the employer did not authorise or order the employee's act and even if the employer did not know about it.

Vicarious liability does not depend upon any fault on the part of the employer. All that must be proved is that the person committing the act is an employee of the employer, the act occurred during the course of the employee's employment, there is a 'sufficiently close' connection between the act and the employment, and the act committed by the employee is one which entitles the person who has been injured to bring court proceedings.

Considerable legal argument has gone into defining whether an act occurs 'in the course of employment'. For example, in one case an employer was found liable for damage caused when the employee had broken company rules by smoking while delivering petrol, and had started a fire. But in another case an employee had broken the rules by picking up a hitch-hiker, and the employer was found not liable for injuries sustained by the hitch-hiker in an accident.   *Century Insurance Co Ltd v Northern Ireland Road Transport Board [1942] UKHL 2; Twine v Bean's Express Limited [1946] 62 TLR 458*

An employer may be liable for an employee's act either directly, or through the employer's negligence. For example, an employer who hired a porter who had custody of keys to flats, without checking to discover that the porter had a long criminal record, was found liable for the subsequent thefts.   *Nahhas v Pier House (Cheyne Walk) Management [1984] 270 EG 328*

There is no statutory obligation for the employer to insure against most claims from third parties, but it is wise to do so [**23.5**]. Some insurance may be required by registration bodies such as Ofsted, or by funders.

22.6.4.2   Vicarious liability for breach of statutory duty

An employer can be held vicariously liable not only for an employee's breach of a common law duty such as negligence, but also for an employee's breach of a statutory duty unless the statutory provision explicitly excludes such liability.

Where a case involves discrimination, an employee will be taken to have been discriminatory in the course of employment – and the employer will be vicariously liable – if the employee would not have been in a position to discriminate but for the fact of his or her employment [**28.1.6**]. So, for example, an employer can be liable for an employee's discriminatory act at an office party even away from the work premises. The employer's only defence is that they took all reasonable steps to prevent or stop the discriminatory actions.

Under the **Protection from Harassment Act 1997** an employer can be held liable for harassment by its employees, provided there is a sufficiently close connection with employment [**40.5.3**]. The statutory defence in discrimination cases (that they took all reasonable steps to prevent harassment) is not available. The only way an employer is not liable is by proving that there is no connection between the alleged harassment and the activity of their employment.
Majrowski v Guy's & St Thomas' NHS Trust [2006] UKHL 34

22.6.4.3   Injury to other employees

Vicarious liability covers not only injuries or losses caused to third parties, but also those caused to **fellow parties** (other employees of the same employer). An employer must take out **employers' liability insurance** [**23.4.1**] to insure against claims by fellow employees, covering situations where one employee causes injury to another and the injured employee successfully sues the employer.

22.6.4.4   Liability for acts of volunteers

In general employers have vicarious liability only for the acts of employees. But there could be vicarious liability for the acts of volunteers if the 'volunteer' is in fact an employee [**39.4**], or if the court feels that the relationship between the organisation and the volunteer is sufficient to justify a liability being imposed.

Even if the organisation is not vicariously liable, it might be possible for a claim to be brought against the organisation for its own liability in, for example, not properly training or supervising the volunteer.

22.6.4.5   Liability for acts of secondees

Unlike volunteers, secondees are employees [**25.5.4**]. Vicarious liability generally rests with the organisation which controlled the secondee at the time of the negligent act, but it might not be clear whether this was the seconding organisation, or if the secondee is a temporary deemed employee of the organisation to which he or she was seconded [below]. Where the seconding and receiving organisations have joint control of the employee, there can be joint liability.

Viasystems (Tyneside) Ltd v Thermal Transfers (Northern) Ltd [2005] EWCA Civ 1151

22.6.4.6 Liability for acts of temporary deemed employees

An employer may have vicarious liability for acts by a **temporary deemed employee**. This could be an agency temp, secondee or other person who is not legally an employee of the employer, but over whom the employer exercises practical control. *Hawley v Luminar Leisure & others [2006] EWCA Civ 18*

22.6.4.7 Liability for acts of contractors

Employers or other principals are not generally liable for torts by independent contractors, including self employed people carrying out work for an employer. But they could be held liable in some situations [**38.4.3**], for example if they were negligent in hiring that contractor.

In one case, a hospital hired a contractor to run a 'splat wall' (where participants don a velcro suit, then trampoline against a velcro wall) at a fundraising event. A woman was injured due to the contractor's negligence, but a court held that the hospital also owed a duty to the injured party, to check whether the contractor held public liability insurance – which the hospital had done. The court also held that the duty did not extend to actually examining the policy – which had expired four days before the injury. *Gwilliam v West Hertfordshire Hospitals [2002] EWCA Civ 1041*

The case illustrates the importance of taking care to hire proper contractors, being satisfied as to a contractor's competence, and confirming that the contractor holds appropriate insurance cover – perhaps even insurance that indemnifies the organisation for claims arising from the contractor's negligence. But the case also illustrates that there are limits to how much checking an organisation needs to do before hiring a contractor.

Where work is contracted or sub-contracted, there can be dual vicarious liability in the same way as in a secondment [**22.6.4.5**].

22.6.4.8 Liability for acts of third parties

In situations where an organisation's service users, customers or other third parties harass an employee racially, sexually or in any other unlawful way, the employer may be held liable for that harassment if it did not take reasonable steps to reduce the likelihood of the harassment occurring [**28.1.6**].

22.6.5 What happens

The award in tort is **damages** for the loss, injury, damage or nuisance caused. and in some situations an **injunction** may be granted [**65.4.7**]. A judgment against a corporate body or individual is enforced in the same way as for contracts [**22.5.4**].

22.6.5.1 Claims against employers

Both the employee and the employer are liable for a tortious act by an employee [**22.6.4**]. Both may be sued, but because the employer normally has greater resources and is more likely to be covered by insurance, the injured party is more likely to sue the employer. If the claim is successful and is not covered by the employer's insurance, the employer may then seek to recover from the employee the losses which have been caused to the employer.

22.6.5.2 Contributory negligence

Where there is a successful claim, the person at fault may be able to show that the injured person's own negligence or actions contributed to his or her injury. In rare cases it might be shown that the claimant consented to the risk of injury, for example by deliberately breaching well known safety procedures.

Damages awarded to a claimant may be reduced to such extent as the court thinks just and equitable, having regard to the claimant's share in the responsibility for the injury.   *Law Reform (Contributory Negligence) Act 1945 s.1*

22.6.5.3   Reduced liability for 'desirable activities'

If an organisation or individual is negligent or in breach of a statutory duty (such as health and safety) and as a result a person is injured, the court can consider whether the steps needed to comply with duty of care or the statutory duty might have prevented a 'desirable activity' from being undertaken at all or in a particular way, or might discourage people from carrying out a desirable activity.

Compensation Act 2006 s.1

An intention of this legislation was to make it easier to recruit volunteers, by enabling volunteers and volunteer-involving organisations to argue in their defence that it is better to provide activities even with volunteers who are perhaps not fully trained, than not to provide them at all. However, many organisations argued that if an organisation with volunteers is seen as having a reduced duty of care, people might be less willing to use the organisation's services.

22.7   PROTECTING AGAINST LIABILITY

The best way to protect against a liability is not to incur it in the first place. But where liability might arise, various types of protection may be available.

22.7.1   Incorporation

Where an unincorporated organisation's potential liabilities are or could be more than its assets, the possibility of limiting personal liability by becoming a company, charitable incorporated organisation (CIO) or industrial and provident society should be considered [**3.1.3**].

If the organisation does not itself wish to incorporate it may in some situations be able to limit liability by setting up a separate company. The company could, for example, take on a potentially risky contract to provide services. It could then sub-contract provision of the services to the original unincorporated organisation, on contractual terms which specifically limit the unincorporated organisation's liability [**22.7.5**]. Legal advice should be taken before including such terms in a contract.

22.7.1.1   Liabilities of governing body members

Incorporation does not protect the governing body members of a company, charitable incorporated organisation or IPS from all liability. Those remaining include:

- fines or penalties for their own, or in some cases the organisation's, criminal acts or breach of statutory duty [**22.3**];
- personal liability where they direct or authorise a tort (a civil wrong, see **22.6**) or breach of statute;
- liability to the organisation for their own breach of trust or fiduciary duty [**22.4**], or breach which they knowingly allow to happen;
- liability if they enter into *ultra vires* or unauthorised contracts [**5.8**];
- liability for a company's debts while serving as a company director while disqualified [**22.5.3.2**] (this may also apply to CIO trustees);
- liability for the organisation's debts if it operates while insolvent or while becoming insolvent, or seeks to defraud creditors while it is becoming insolvent [**24.2.4, 24.10.5**].

Trustee indemnity (or liability) insurance or directors' and officers' insurance can cover some of these, but not all [**23.10**].

22.7.2   Insurance

Insurances are covered in detail in **chapter 23**.

22.7.3 Charity Commission advice

A charity trustee uncertain about whether an action could be a breach of trust may seek advice from the Charity Commission. Trustees who reveal all material facts and then act in accordance with advice given by the Commission under the provisions of the **Charities Act 1993** s.29 will not be held liable for any breach of trust arising from such action. But this does not protect from other forms of liability arising from the action. *Charities Act 1993 s.29, amended by Charities Act 2006 s.24*

22.7.4 Limitation of liability under the governing document

The governing document of an unincorporated association may contain a clause saying that ordinary members (those who are not members of the governing body) are not liable for the organisation's debts or actions. This does not protect them if they are a member of the association's governing body, are a principal to a contract [**22.5.3.5**], enter into an unauthorised contract, or are liable for criminal or tortious acts. *Overton v Hewett [1886] 3 TLR 246*

Similarly the governing document of a trust may include a **trustee exemption clause** limiting the liability of trustees for losses caused to the charity by, for example, poor investment performance. The extent to which trustees can limit their liability in relation to negligence may be limited, if for example they are acting professionally, and in charitable trusts such a clause would require the trustees to have acted in good faith. *Armitage v Nurse & others [1997] EWCA Civ 1279*

22.7.5 Contractual limitation of liability

It is possible – and highly desirable – for unincorporated associations and trusts to include in contracts a clause limiting the liability of its members or the members of its governing body to the extent of the assets of the organisation. *DeVries v Corner [1865] 13 LT 636; Warborough Investments v Berry [2003] EWHC 3153*

Such a clause might say, for example,

> The personal liability of the person(s) signing this contract on behalf of ABC, any member of the governing body of ABC and any other person held liable under this contract shall be limited to the amount of the net assets of ABC available to meet such claim.

Many parties to contracts are unwilling to include such a clause, but a friendly landlord might, or a local authority or other body purchasing services from an unincorporated organisation.

22.7.6 Exclusion of liability

Liability may in some circumstances be limited by an **exclusion of liability** or **disclaimer** notice or clause. This might be on display, printed on documents such as admission or cloakroom tickets, or included in a contract [above], licence or lease, or on a website. Legal advice should be sought before attempting to exclude liability in this way, as the law restricts the effectiveness of exclusion clauses [**21.7.6**].

Simply saying that the organisation is not liable, for example for incorrect advice, will not necessarily provide protection, and does not absolve the organisation of its obligation to take reasonable steps to ensure information and advice is accurate and up to date.

Liability for death or personal injury cannot be excluded.

Unfair Contract Terms Act 1977 s.2

22.7.7 Relief from liability

A company director, company secretary or senior employee who is or may be liable because of negligence, default or any breach of duty may apply to the court for relief from personal liability on the basis of having acted honestly and reasonably. An application may be made to the court even if a claim has not been brought. *Companies Act 2006 s.1157*

If the court or Charity Commission finds that a member of the governing body of a charity, its auditor or independent examiner is or may be liable for breach of trust, it may relieve the person of some or all personal liability for that breach if the person acted honestly and reasonably and 'ought fairly to be excused'.

Trustee Act 1925 s.61; Charities Act 1993 ss.73D-E, inserted by Charities Act 2006 s.38

If an organisation is neither a company nor a charity, there is no statutory provision for governing body members to apply to the court for relief from liability.

22.7.8   Indemnity

To **indemnify** means to compensate for a loss suffered. Persons involved with voluntary organisations may have a statutory and/or common law right to be indemnified, or may be entitled to indemnity under the governing document. But the right to be indemnified by an organisation is not worth anything if the organisation does not have sufficient assets or insurance cover to do so.

If it is not possible to be indemnified from the organisation's funds and a governing body member – or anyone else connected with the organisation – has been held liable for a disproportionate amount in a situation where there is joint and several liability, he or she is entitled to a contribution from the others [**22.2.3**].

It is not possible to be indemnified for fines or penalties, or to be indemnified by an organisation in situations where the person is liable to the organisation itself, for example for breach of trust or fiduciary duty [**22.4**].

22.7.8.1   Statutory rights: trustees

A trustee of a trust or charitable association is entitled to be reimbursed out of trust funds for expenses and liabilities properly incurred on behalf of the trust, if he or she acted with proper authority and with due care. Some liabilities may be covered by trustee indemnity insurance [**23.10**]   *Trustee Act 2000 s.31*

22.7.8.2   Statutory rights: companies

Companies are allowed – but not required – to indemnify directors, the company secretary, senior employees or auditors in respect of proceedings bought by third parties and applications for relief from liability [**22.7.7**].

The indemnity can cover a loan to fund legal costs and the payment of those costs if the defence is successful, and can also cover the legal and financial costs of an adverse judgment. The company may purchase insurance to cover these indemnities [**23.10.1**]. But neither the indemnity nor insurance can cover the costs of an unsuccessful criminal defence, criminal penalties, penalties imposed by regulatory bodies, or an unsuccessful application for relief from liability.

The indemnity can be paid as costs are incurred, rather than waiting until the end of the case. If the individual's defence is unsuccessful, the indemnity has to be repaid to the company.   *Companies Act 2006 ss.232-234*

If the governing document restricts the range of indemnity that can be provided, it should be updated to include the current broader range. For charities, such a change requires the Charity Commission's consent [**16.3.10**].

22.7.8.3   Common law rights

A member of the governing body of a non-charitable association or an ordinary member of any association who is successfully sued by a third party is entitled to be indemnified by the association for damages and costs only if he or she was sued as a representative of all the members, or he or she was carrying out activities for, and with the approval of, the association and its members.

Egger v Viscount Chelmsford [1964] 3 All ER 406,413

This right to be indemnified extends only to the assets of the association. If the association does not have adequate funds, there is no right to be indemnified by the ordinary members of the association unless this is explicit in the governing document [below].

If some or all of the members of the governing body are liable for a contract, any member who pays more than a proper share is entitled to a contribution from the other liable governing body members. Similarly if some or all of the members of an unincorporated association are liable for a contract, any member who pays

more than a proper share is entitled to a contribution from the other liable members.
Earl Mountcashell v Barber [1853] 14 CB 53; Boulter v Peplow [1850] 9 CB 493

22.7.8.4 Governing document

The statutory and common law rights to indemnity may be extended if the governing document includes a clause indemnifying governing body members, or ordinary members of an association, from the organisation's funds for liabilities properly incurred in managing the organisation [**7.4.22**]. Such a clause would generally prohibit the person from being indemnified if he or she had acted outside the objects or powers as set out in the governing document, without proper authority, or without proper duty of care to the organisation. It cannot allow a person to be indemnified if he or she has acted criminally.

The right to indemnity in an unincorporated association may be further extended if the governing document includes a clause entitling members of the governing body, or ordinary members of the association, to be indemnified by the organisation's *members* if they are successfully sued for an act properly undertaken on behalf of the members, and if the association does not have sufficient assets to indemnify them.

This reduces the liability of the member who can claim from the other members – but it increases the liability of all the other members, making them liable even where they are not a principal to a contract or have not authorised or taken part in a tort. Legal advice should be taken before putting into a governing document any clause giving members of an association the right to be indemnified by other members.

Without such a clause, individual members who are sued have no right to be indemnified by the other members of the association.

If an unincorporated association has property which is held by holding trustees [**20.4.4**], the association's governing document or the deed of trust setting out the relationship between the association's members and the holding trustees should include provision for indemnifying the holding trustees from the association's funds for losses they incur.

22.7.8.5 Indemnity insurance

Companies have a statutory right to purchase **directors' and officers' (D&O) insurance** [**23.10**] against some liabilities for their directors, and to fund their directors' expenditure in defending some types of legal proceedings. Most charities have a right to purchase **D&O** or **trustee indemnity insurance** [**23.10**], unless this is prohibited by their governing document. The governing document can be amended with Charity Commission consent.

Resources: RISK AND LIABILITY

Insurance. See end of **chapter 23**.

Risk assessment and management. Association of British Insurers: www.abi.org.uk, 020 7600 3333, info@abi.org.uk.

Business Continuity Institute: www.thebci.org, 0870 603 8783, bci@thebci.org.

Cabinet Office preparing for emergencies website: www.preparingforemergencies.gov.uk, 020 7276 1234.

Charity Commission, www.charitycommission.gov.uk, 0845 300 0218, email via website.

Charity Disaster Recovery Network: www.cdrn.co.uk, 0845 1303 845.

Institute of Risk Management: www.theirm.org, 020 7709 9808, enquiries@theirm.org.

Vicarious liability in charities. Charity Commission [above].

Statute law. www.opsi.gov.uk and www.statutelaw.gov.uk.

Much but not all case law. www.bailii.org.

Updates cross-referenced to this book. www.rclh.co.uk.

Chapter 23

INSURANCE

For sources of further information see end of chapter.

23.1   THINKING ABOUT INSURANCE

Insurance products are an important method of managing risks and should always be considered as part of a governing body's review of risk control generally. Business Link [see end of chapter] provides useful advice and guidance, and the Charity Commission's CC49 *Charities and insurance* sets out which insurances are mandatory or advisable for charities.

But insurance is only one way to deal with potential liabilities. Other ways are covered in **22.7** and **21.7.6**.

23.1.1   Obtaining insurance

Insurance policies are not standard and the names of insurance products are not used consistently, so two identically titled policies may offer significantly different cover. To ensure they obtain insurance appropriate to their needs, organisations should consider taking advice from their solicitor or a qualified insurance broker (also called insurance intermediaries).

The FSA register, on the Financial Services Authority website [see end of chapter], can be used to check whether a broker is registered with the FSA, and geographical lists of registered brokers are available from the British Insurance Brokers' Association [see end of chapter]. A good broker should identify relevant insurable risks, explain the types of insurance and cover available, prevent duplication of cover, advise on best value, obtain competitive premium quotes from a range of insurers, and provide assistance when claims have to be made.

Details of brokers who specialise in insurance for voluntary organisations may be available from organisations such as the National Council for Voluntary Organisations and Wales Council for Voluntary Action, voluntary sector umbrella bodies and local councils for voluntary service. NCVO, WCVA and umbrella or support organisations may themselves offer policies specifically for voluntary organisations, at better rates than are available on the commercial market.

23.1.2 Regulation of insurance

Any organisation which arranges any insurance in the name of another person, introduces them to a broker, or assists with proposal or claim forms 'by way of business' for some economic benefit, may need to register with the Financial Services Authority [**1.9.3**]. Any organisation which does more than simply take out insurance for itself should consider obtaining advice on its position.

23.1.3 Allocating responsibility

A named post holder – typically the treasurer, chief executive or senior employee, or head of finance – should have explicit responsibility for insurances. This includes identifying the organisation's insurance requirements; ensuring decisions about insurance are properly made by the governing body or by a committee or employee with delegated authority to make such decisions; taking out the insurance; notifying insurers of all changes material to the policy, including new activities, services, equipment or premises; ensuring policies are renewed and premiums are paid on time; keeping the governing body informed about insurance matters; and notifying claims within policy time limits.

The organisation's procedures for dealing with insurance should allow decisions to be made quickly when necessary.

23.1.3.1 Annual review

Insurance should be reviewed regularly by the governing body. At least once a year it should be an agenda item, with a full written report which includes details of risks covered under each policy, and level of cover; exceptions (risks not covered); excess (the amount the organisation has to pay on each claim); cost of each policy; and current or potential developments in the organisation's activities, premises, equipment etc which might indicate the need for increased levels of cover or extended areas of cover. The review should include copies of the insurers' confirmation of payment of the most recent premium for each policy.

The review provides an opportunity for governing body members to confirm that full disclosure [**23.3.3**] has been made to the insurer.

23.1.3.2 Related matters

The governing body should also:
- ensure the organisation is identifying and managing risk appropriately [**22.1**];
- ensure the organisation complies with all legal requirements which could affect insurance, for example in relation to health and safety;
- allocate clear responsibility for dealing with emergencies such as fire, theft or violence, and ensure procedures are in place to minimise risks to people and property;
- ensure copies of insurance policies and other key documents, such as the register of assets [**23.6.2**], are kept off the premises.

23.2 POWER TO INSURE

As with any action taken by an organisation, taking out insurance requires that the organisation has the power to do so.

23.2.1 Statutory power

Where there is a statutory duty to insure, all organisations have power to do so. Every employer has a statutory duty to take out **employers' liability insurance** [**23.4.1**], and vehicles used on the road must be covered by **third party insurance** [**23.8.1**]. Insurance may also be required for some registrations and licences. **Public liability insurance**, for example, is likely to be a requirement for obtaining a premises licence [**47.2**], or for working with children.

Trustees of trusts and charitable associations have statutory power to insure any buildings or contents against loss or damage, and in most cases have statutory power to purchase trustee indemnity insurance [**23.10**]. *Trustee Act 1925 ss.19,20, amended by Trustee Act 2000 s.34*

A company is permitted to insure its officers (directors, company secretary and senior management) and their auditors against personal liability arising from their actions – or inaction – as officers or auditors [**23.10**]. A charitable company may do so unless its governing document prohibits this. It may amend the governing document to allow this only with the prior consent of the Charity Commission [**23.2.3**]. *Charities Act 1993 s.73F, inserted by Charities Act 2006 s.39*

23.2.2 Implied power

The Charity Commission's view is that trustees of charities should insure charity property for its full value. Because trustees have a duty to safeguard the charity [**15.6.5**], they could in some circumstances be held to be in breach of trust if they do not insure appropriately.

The Charity Commission allows charity funds to be used for insurance to cover buildings, either as a freeholder or tenant [**23.6.1**], contents [**23.6.2**], public liability [**23.5.1**], the organisation's vehicles [**23.8**], and additional premiums payable by employees or volunteers for using their own vehicle for the organisation's work [**23.8.1.1**]. Unless the power to take out other insurances is included in the governing document, charities need specific advice or consent to do so [below].

23.2.3 Advice or consent

The Charity Commission's CC49 *Charities and insurance* states that charities may take out insurances for which there is no statutory power or power in the governing document only if the charity's circumstances make it necessary or prudent, paying the premiums will not affect the charity's charitable work, and the trustees are advised by their legal or other independent financial advisors to have such insurance. Even within this framework, some insurances – in particular trustee indemnity or directors' and officers' insurance – may require explicit consent [**23.10**].

23.2.4 Governing document

The governing document may contain power 'to effect such insurances as the governing body thinks fit' or a similar wording [**7.4.4, 7.4.21**], or a catch-all power 'to do all such other lawful things as are necessary for the achievement of the objects' [**7.4.3**]. These general wordings give non-charities the power to take out any insurances, but do not give charities power to take out insurances requiring advice or Charity Commission consent [above].

A non-charity whose governing document does not contain an insurance power or general power should seek legal advice before taking out any insurance except those where there is a statutory duty or power to insure [**23.2.1**].

23.3 TAKING OUT INSURANCE

A company, industrial and provident society, charitable incorporated organisation or incorporated governing body [**2.4**] takes out insurance in its own name. Technically an unincorporated association or trust cannot take out insurance in its own name, and some insurers may require any insurance to be held in the names of one or more individual members of the governing body acting as representatives of the other governing body members. If the members in whose name the insurance is held cease to be on the governing body, new people should be appointed to hold the insurance and the insurer should be notified. The policy must clearly cover (indemnify) all potentially liable parties, not just those in whose name the insurance is held.

23.3.1 Premiums and renewal

Insurance costs are driven by a global market and can change significantly from year to year. The effective purchasing of insurance requires an understanding of the significant details of the cover offered, and a comparison of competing prices. Insurers may have periods of discounted premiums to build their share of the market for a particular type of insurance.

Where risks are non-standard, the quality of the information provided by the organisation about how it manages risks may affect the way a risk is assessed by an insurer and hence the premium quoted.

Under an Association of British Insurers and British Insurance Brokers' Association code of practice, providers of employer's or public liability insurance are expected to provide at least 21 days notice of renewal terms or of their intention not to renew the policy.

23.3.2 Basis of insurance

The organisation must be clear how the payment of any claim would be calculated under the policy. The payment may be, for example, on a **new for old** basis, an **indemnity** basis (paying out the current value of what has been lost), or for a **fixed amount** which is paid out if an event occurs, regardless of the actual loss.

23.3.2.1 Subrogation

If an organisation suffers loss, it may have a right to recover that loss from the person who caused it. If the organisation instead receives payment from an insurer for its loss, the insurer then has the right to recover the amount it has paid out from the person who caused the loss. The insurer's right of recovery is **subrogated** to (substituted for) the organisation's right of recovery.

23.3.2.2 Average clauses

Most commercial insurance policies contain **average clauses**, which reduce the insurer's liability to pay the full amount of a partial loss. For example if a building having a reinstatement cost of £1 million is only insured for £600,000 (60% of the reinstatement cost) and is completely destroyed, the insurer's maximum liability is clearly only £600,000. But if the building suffers damage worth £200,000, the insurer would still pay only 60% of the loss, i.e. £120,000.

Regular revaluation of the assets or risk insured is vital. Some policies contain inflation clauses, but this should not mean that revaluation is neglected. Where a property is subject to a preservation or conservation order or is listed, the need for accurate valuation on a reinstatement basis is even greater.

Building valuations frequently exclude VAT when quoting reinstatement figures. Leaving out this VAT from the amount for which buildings are insured [**23.6.1**] could leave the organisation seriously under-insured. It is essential that any irrecoverable VAT is included in the policy sums.

Where values or costs have gone down, revaluation may mean that the level of cover can be reduced.

23.3.3 Duties of good faith and disclosure

Insurance policies are contracts of **the utmost good faith**. This means that any **material fact** or **material change** likely to affect the insurer's decision to insure or the level of premium charged must be disclosed to the insurer. Failure to do so can invalidate the policy. Because of this, some leases include obligations on tenants to disclose any such factors to the landlord, and employment contracts or policies may require employees to disclose to the employer.

The obligation to disclose covers a very wide range of factors likely to affect the risk of whatever is insured against. For example, various insurances might be invalidated by failure to disclose earlier claims, a previous refusal or imposition of specific conditions on insurance, the appointment of a new employee who has a criminal conviction, the non-standard construction of a building, sharing premises with another organisation or premises being open to the public, or non-occupation of premises.

The organisation is obliged to disclose not only what it is actually aware of, but also what reasonable enquiry would have revealed. This means that procedures should be put in place to discover whether new employees, volunteers or members of the governing body are aware of any matters about themselves which should be disclosed. For more about how to find out about these matters see disqualification of governing body members [**13.3**], and checks on employees and others [**41.4**].

Proposal forms are usually comprehensive, but the fact that the form does not ask about a particular matter does not relieve the organisation of the need to disclose.

The duty exists at the date of the start of the policy, so if further facts become known between completing the proposal form and acceptance by the insurer, these must be disclosed. A further duty of disclosure arises on each renewal.

Disclosure of matters seen by insurers as positive, such as installing a burglar alarm, may result in a lower premium.

23.3.4 Policy terms

The full policy should be obtained and checked, and all relevant staff and governing body members should be made aware of policy requirements. Particular concerns are likely to be:

- **conditions** to be complied with, such as reporting loss to insurers and police within a defined period;
- **warranties** (factual conditions which the organisation promises are true, as a condition of cover), because a breach of warranty may be sufficient to invalidate the policy entirely even if the breach is unrelated to the cause of the loss;
- **exclusion** of particular risks or circumstances, such as more than £50 cash kept on the premises, cash not in a locked safe overnight, lack of proper door or window locks;
- whether there is an **excess** (the organisation's obligation to meet the first part of the claim);
- **limitation**, such as no more than three claims in any period;
- **endorsements** (additions to or exceptions from cover).

23.3.4.1 International risks

If an organisation might suffer losses or incur liabilities abroad, these risks should be set out clearly in the application for the relevant policy.

23.3.4.2 Age exclusions

Some insurances which cover employees and/or volunteers in case of sickness, injury or death or for negligence in carrying out certain duties may offer cover only up to age 60, 65 or 70, or may not cover them under age 16 or 18. It is essential to check all policies for any age exclusions, and to extend the policy to cover staff in higher or lower age groups. Volunteering England [see end of chapter] may have details of insurers who provide cover for younger or older volunteers.

23.3.5 Claims

The duty of good faith applies to all aspects of insurance, including claims. Any attempt to inflate the claim artificially or withhold information might invalidate the entire claim. Insurers share information among themselves, and may refer fraudulent claims to the police.

Conditions in the policy must be strictly adhered to. Brokers may assist, but for very large or potentially contested claims, legal advice or the assistance of a professional claims adjuster may be needed. Where the claim involves potential liability to employees or third parties, the organisation must not admit any liability and must generally leave all negotiation to the insurer.

It is generally necessary to report to the insurer all incidents relevant to the policy, even if a claim is not made.

23.3.6 Complaints

The Association of British Insurers [see end of chapter] and Financial Ombudsman Service deal with complaints which cannot be resolved with the insurer.

23.4 INSURANCES RELATING TO WORKERS

23.4.1 Employers' liability

Every employer has a statutory duty to insure all staff, and may be fined £2,500 for each day it does not have **employers' liability insurance** (also called **employers' liability compulsory insurance**). The Health and Safety Executive [see end of **chapter 40**] has a useful guide.   *Employers' Liability (Compulsory Insurance)*
Act 1969; Employers' Liability (Compulsory Insurance) Regulations 1998 [SI 1998/2573]

The insurance must cover the organisation (or, in unincorporated organisations, the members of the governing body or others considered for legal purposes to be the employer) for claims of up to £5 million for each incident leading to illness, injury or death arising out of and in the course of the employee's work, where the employer was in breach of a statutory duty to the employee or can be shown to have been negligent. In practice, most employers' liability policies have an upper limit of £10 million. Higher cover may be appropriate in some situations.

The premium is based on the number of employees and the type of work they do.

The employer must prominently display, within 30 days of the policy being renewed, a copy of the current certificate of insurance at all of its premises where employees work, or make it available electronically and tell all employees where it can be viewed. Failure to do this can lead to a significant fine.   *Employers' Liability*
(Compulsory Insurance) (Amendment) Regulations 2008 [SI 2008/1765]

23.4.1.1 Who must be covered

Employers' liability insurance is required for all employees, including temporary, part-time and casual employees, employees who work off site or at home, and apprentices. Some trainees, especially on government schemes, and some contractors or self employed people are considered to be employees for this purpose, and the employer must ensure they are covered by the employers' liability insurance. Organisations which provide work for people serving community service orders may be obliged to cover them under the policy as well.

There is no obligation to take out employers' liability insurance for other trainees or volunteers, but it is good practice to extend it to include them, because a court could in some circumstances deem them to be 'employees' for these purposes. Where injury to trainees, volunteers, members of the governing body and self employed people is not covered under employers' liability, it may be appropriate to cover it under a public liability policy [**23.5.1**].

There is no statutory requirement to cover employees who are based abroad, but employers should consider taking out other insurances to cover injury, illness or death. If the employee is a UK resident working under a UK contract of employment, insurance should be taken out in the UK as any action would almost certainly be raised in a UK court. Cover may also, depending on local legislation, be required or advisable in the country where the work is being done.

23.4.1.2 What is not covered

Employers' liability insurance covers only illness, injury or death caused by the employer's negligence or breach of duty (normally breach of health and safety law). It does not cover situations where the employer has shown the required standard of care [**40.2.5**]. It covers only injury to the person, not to the person's clothing, property or other objects. If the employer wants to cover these risks, separate insurance is needed [**23.4.3, 23.6.2.2**].

23.4.2 Employer's legal costs

Employers' **legal costs** or **legal expenses** insurance [**23.9.3**] is sometimes called **employers' protection** or **employers' indemnity insurance**. This is not the same as employers' liability insurance [above], and is not legally required. Typically it covers the employer's legal costs for claims of unfair dismissal, wrongful dismissal, breach of the contract of employment, or unlawful discrimination. It generally also covers employment tribunal awards.

23.4.3 Health care, sickness, accident and death

An organisation may choose to provide life insurance, sickness and/or accident cover, health care or permanent health cover as a benefit for employees or volunteers. This may cover illness, injury or death only if it is caused in the course of work, or regardless of how it is caused and whether it is linked to work.

An employer is obliged to provide these only if they are promised in an employee's contract of employment. Most of these insurances are treated by HM Revenue and Customs as a benefit in kind and are taxable [**30.4.9**]. If the insurance pays an income to the employee, the organisation should make clear whether this is intended to cover all or some of its sick pay obligations [**31.6, 27.5.2**].

Some insurances provide a long-term income to an employee who becomes too ill or injured to work [below]. Legal advice should be obtained before taking out any such insurance, because it may have the unforeseen consequence of making it very difficult to dismiss an employee who is receiving, or is about to start receiving, payments under the policy [**34.6.1**].

Because these insurances provide a benefit to the individual covered (or his or her estate), they should not be provided for anyone who is, or is connected with [**15.2.5**], a member of a charity's governing body unless the governing document explicitly allows governing body members to receive such benefit or consent has been obtained from the Charity Commission.

23.4.3.1 Types of insurance

Health care insurance provides for private health care in addition to, or instead of, NHS care, and may also cover employees' families. It does not pay any additional income to the insured person.

Permanent health or **income protection insurance** pays an ongoing income, generally monthly, to an employee who is unable to work for an extended period due to illness or disability. Sometimes the policy is narrowly defined to cover only permanent incapacity for any sort of work. 'Permanent' insurance means that unlike the other insurances, it cannot be cancelled or changed by the insurer if the insured person's health changes, although the premium may be increased.

Critical illness insurance pays a fixed sum and/or an ongoing income if the employee is diagnosed as having a defined disease such as cancer or heart disease.

Sickness insurance is similar but does not have to involve a critical illness.

Personal accident insurance covers injuries or death arising from an accident. The insurance generally provides a lump sum at the time of injury, and/or a weekly or monthly income for a fixed period.

Life insurance or **death in service insurance** pays a fixed sum and/ or an ongoing income to the employee's spouse or civil partner, or sometimes other partner or dependant, if the employee dies while employed.

23.4.4 Key workers

Key worker insurance provides payment to the organisation to help cover the cost of replacement staff if a key worker dies or is unable to work.

23.4.5   Travel

If employees or volunteers travel outside the UK on behalf of the organisation, it is good practice for the organisation to take out **travel insurance** to cover their medical expenses, emergency travel costs, repatriation, and compensation in case of death or serious injury. The organisation may also want to insure their baggage, personal effects and money.

Travel insurance should also be considered for people who travel on behalf of the organisation within the UK. Such insurance usually applies only where the travel involves a minimum number of nights' accommodation and/or pre-booked flights.

Advice should be sought from the Charity Commission before taking out travel insurance for governing body members or connected persons [**15.2.5**].

23.5   INSURANCE FOR CLAIMS BY THIRD PARTIES

23.5.1   Public liability

Most situations in which a third party or member of the public suffers injury or loss can be insured against. Organisations need to consider potential risks, and decide which are worth insuring against.

Public liability, **personal injury** (PI) or **third party insurance** protects the organisation (or the members or governing body members of an unincorporated organisation) from claims by members of the public for death, illness, injury, or loss of or damage to property caused through the negligence of the organisation or someone working for it. It is generally linked to premises, or to specific activities such as a lunch club, sports activities, a festival or open day. It does not cover liability arising from professional services [**23.5.3**], products manufactured or supplied by the organisation [**23.5.4**], and some other specific liabilities.

'Public' generally includes users/beneficiaries, visitors to the organisation's premises (and sometimes even trespassers), passers-by, and anyone other than employees with whom the organisation comes into contact. Volunteers, trainees and members of the organisation need special attention [**23.5.1.2**, **23.5.1.3**].

Many funders and registration bodies require organisations to have public liability insurance. Even where it is not required, every organisation which occupies premises or organises activities should have it.

Public liability insurance is often combined with employers' liability insurance, buildings insurance and/or contents insurance. Minimum cover is typically £2 million for any one incident, but may be much higher if the organisation's activities could cause serious injury or damage. The premium depends on the nature and scale of risk. Public liability insurance is generally renewed annually but it is possible to it take out for an event or activity of a few weeks, days or even hours.

To have a valid claim, the claimant must be able to show that he or she suffered injury or loss, and that this was caused by the organisation or its worker(s) acting negligently, not taking reasonable care, or breaching another duty.

23.5.1.1   Limitation of liability

Liability for damage to or loss of property, for example in car parks and cloakrooms, may be excluded or limited by putting up a disclaimer notice [**22.7.6**]. To be effective the notices must satisfy certain conditions, and legal advice should be obtained as to their wording and effectiveness. Liability for personal injury or death can never be limited or excluded.

23.5.1.2   Volunteers, trainees etc

If volunteers, trainees and members of the governing body are not explicitly included under employers' liability insurance [**23.4.1**], they should be explicitly included in its public liability insurance.

As well as themselves becoming ill or injured as a result of the organisation's negligence, a volunteer or trainee might cause injury or property damage to a user of the organisation or to someone else. The organisation's public liability [**23.5.1**] or professional indemnity [**23.5.3**] insurance should clearly include liability for injury or damage caused by volunteers and others who are not employees but who carry out work on behalf of the organisation.

In some situations a volunteer or other person could be sued as an individual for damage or injury caused to a third party. The organisation's public liability or professional indemnity insurance should indemnify (compensate) volunteers or trainees who have such claims brought against them.

23.5.1.3 Members

In some situations one or more members of an unincorporated association could be held liable for injury or damage to another member [**22.6.3**]. A membership association should therefore ensure that its public liability policy includes **member to member insurance** to cover this.

23.5.1.4 Contractors

The organisation should ensure that contractors and self employed people it hires have, if appropriate, their own public liability insurance to cover them for injury or damage to the organisation's staff or property or members of the public, and/or professional liability insurance [**22.6.4**]. If the contractor does not have appropriate insurance it raises potentially serious questions about their standing. In some cases the contract may require the organisation to arrange its own cover.

In many cases it will also be appropriate for the organisation to require the contractor's insurance to indemnify it for any claims brought against it because of the contractor's negligence or failure to comply with statutory duties.

23.5.2 Special activities

Special events or **special activities insurance** should be arranged for activities or events which are not covered by the organisation's usual public liability policy, or for organisations which do not have public liability insurance.

Insurance for equipment, materials and valuable items at the event or in transit to or from it [**23.6.2.3**], and pluvius (rain), non-appearance or cancellation insurance [**23.9.2**] should also be considered. Organisations have a duty to check that service providers have public liability insurance, particularly where there is an identifiable risk of injury to participants [**22.6.4**].

23.5.3 Professional liability

Professional liability, **professional indemnity**, **errors and omissions** or **malpractice insurance** covers the organisation (or, in an unincorporated organisation, the members of the governing body) for claims arising from loss or injury caused by services provided negligently or without reasonable care. Such loss might arise, for example, from care or treatment which causes illness, injury or death; incorrect welfare benefits advice which leads to a claimant not getting benefits to which he or she is entitled; or misleading information about tenants' rights which leads to a tenant being evicted.

It does not matter whether the service, information or advice is provided free of charge or for a fee, or if information or advice is given on a telephone or internet helpline or on a website rather than in writing or face to face. Where information or advice is passed on beyond the original recipient, further individuals may have claims if in the circumstances they would be reasonably entitled to rely upon it.

Professional liability cover is often included as part of trustee indemnity insurance [**23.10.1**]. Professional liability insurance or trustee indemnity insurance often covers defamation [**23.5.5**], inadvertent breach of copyright [**23.5.6**], inadvertent breach of confidentiality [**23.5.7**] and/or loss of documents or data [**23.6.5**]. It is important to check that the organisation is not double-insured for these or other risks.

In some situations some liability may be excluded by drawing a disclaimer notice to the client's attention [**22.7.6**]. Liability for personal injury or death cannot be excluded.

23.5.4   Product liability

Product liability arises from illness, injury, death or damage to property caused by a defect in a product, even if there is no negligence. **Product liability insurance** covers organisations which manufacture, sell or supply goods against claims arising from product defects. In some situations an organisation which allows its trademarked logo to be used on a product could be held liable for losses arising from defects in the product, so product liability insurance may be advisable.

23.5.5   Defamation

If the organisation publishes in any media (including electronic), if staff or others representing it send emails outside the organisation, or if people representing it speak in public situations, it is advisable to have insurance to cover claims for defamation [**45.3**]. This may be included as part of professional or trustee indemnity or other insurances.

23.5.6   Breach of copyright

If the organisation produces publications, advertisements, videos or other materials, including electronically, it may want to insure against claims for inadvertent breach of copyright or other intellectual property rights [**chapter 44**]. This may be included with other insurances.

23.5.7   Breach of confidentiality

If a worker, user/beneficiary or other person can show that he or she has been damaged because the organisation or someone working for it disclosed information which should have been kept confidential, he or she could bring a claim against the organisation (or, in an unincorporated organisation, the members of its governing body). Insurance is available to cover inadvertent breach of confidentiality and/or breach of **Data Protection Act** duties [**43.3**].

23.5.8   Breach of contract

If an organisation is obliged to provide goods or services under contract and is unable to do so, it may be liable to the other party for any loss suffered by that party as a result [**22.5**].

An organisation cannot insure against its own deliberate default on a contract. However it can take out **consequential loss insurance** [**23.9.1**] to cover situations where a contract cannot be performed because of some act beyond its control, such as flood or fire. An alternative is to include a *force majeure* clause in the contract saying the organisation will not be liable if it cannot provide the service because of specified circumstances beyond its control [**21.11.4**, **22.7.5**].

A form of insurance bond, sometimes called a **performance bond**, is sometimes used to protect against failure to complete a contract (such as building works) or to deliver services satisfactorily [**21.2.6**]. They may also be used instead of or in addition to insurance for some aspects of events [**23.9.2**].

23.5.9   Debts to third parties

An organisation cannot insure in a conventional way against its inability to pay money it owes, because the insurer would in effect be guaranteeing its debts.

23.6   PROTECTING THE ORGANISATION'S ASSETS

Many insurances are available to protect the organisation from loss or damage to its premises and possessions.

If property belongs to the organisation itself, there is no statutory obligation to insure it. However all charity trustees have a duty to safeguard the charity's assets [**15.6.5**], and the Charity Commission considers that failure to insure buildings and valuable contents could constitute a breach of trust [**22.4**].

If property used by the organisation belongs to someone else – for example premises rented from a landlord, a photocopier leased from a photocopier company, paintings lent by the local art gallery or a local artist, a laptop computer belonging to an employee or volunteer – it is essential to be clear who is responsible for insuring it against loss, damage and theft. If an asset is being used as security for a loan, the lender will almost certainly require it to be insured.

Insuring property for less than the true value could invalidate the insurance or lead to only partial recovery on a claim [**23.3.2.2**]. The amount insured should be regularly reviewed, even if the policy contains provision for inflation increases.

All policies should be carefully checked for exclusions. Many do not cover, for example, damage caused by riots, explosion or impact of vehicles, and none automatically cover damage caused by terrorism [**23.6.1.4**]. The implications of these exclusions should be carefully considered, for example where a tenant has a full repairing lease [**62.2.4**] and could be obliged to make good the damage.

23.6.1 Buildings

Usually the freeholder takes out **buildings insurance** but in some cases, particularly with long leases, the responsibility may be shifted to the tenant [**62.2.6**]. The insurance covers damage to the structure, and may also cover damage to its grounds and items such as fences.

Buildings insurance may include damage arising from:

- fire only (which may include lightning and some explosions);
- fire and special perils, which includes named perils such as storms, flood, earthquakes, aircraft, riots, terrorism and malicious damage; or
- all risks, which covers all causes except those which are explicitly excluded. Exclusions might include subsidence, defective design etc.

Buildings cover does not always include the land, roads, pavements, bridges, culverts etc which could be damaged, by flood for example. Consideration should be given to their inclusion.

As well as insuring the premises, the organisation should consider other costs it might incur if its building is unusable, and possibly take out consequential loss insurance [**23.9.1**].

23.6.1.1 Basis of insurance

Buildings insurance should normally be on a full **reinstatement** basis, including cover for site clearance, professional fees and any special additional costs because, for example, the building is on a difficult site for rebuilding or has important historical detail. For an old or obsolete building the freeholder or other owner may insure for a lesser **first loss** value, in order to reduce outgoings. This is generally not advisable and in some situations, such as buildings subject to listing or a conservation order, it is inappropriate.

If a building is held on mortgage the bank or other mortgagor generally requires it to be insured for its full rebuilding cost.

If the organisation is unable to reclaim VAT [**57.1**], the sum insured should include all VAT which the organisation would have to pay. Building valuations might or might not include VAT, so it is important to check them before setting the amount to be insured [**23.3.2.2**].

23.6.1.2 Insurance by a landlord

If the organisation rents and the landlord is responsible for insuring the premises, the organisation must:

- check that its fittings and fixtures [**60.7.8**] are covered (or the organisation should insure them under its own policy);
- ensure the policy covers the value of any improvements made by the organisation (or the organisation can insure this itself);
- check that the policy covers rental losses, so the organisation is not responsible for paying rent while the building is unusable, and that the period is suffi-

cient to allow rebuilding (and/or take out its own insurance to cover the rent it would have to pay while the premises are being repaired or rebuilt);

- ensure a full range of risks are covered, and either arrange or get the landlord to arrange cover for omitted risks;
- monitor the extent of cover and any excess (first part of any claim which will not be paid by the insurer) during the period of the lease;
- consider what additional costs the organisation might have if the building was damaged, and take out additional insurance as appropriate [**23.9.1**].

The links between lease provisions and insurance arrangements should be carefully considered. For example if the building is damaged the lease may allow the landlord to terminate the lease and keep all the insurance money, thus depriving the organisation of the value of improvements it has made. The easiest way to protect the organisation's improvements to leased property is to include them in the organisation's own policy. Or if the improvements are covered by the landlord's policy, the organisation's interest should be noted in the landlord's policy.

The lease should also provide that if the landlord fails to reinstate the premises, the liability to pay rent ceases.

Organisations which are themselves landlords should consider the same issues, and should generally ensure they are covered for two or three years' loss of rent (or more, if necessary) while the building is being reinstated after damage.

23.6.1.3 Building works

Where building works or renovations are being undertaken, the organisation should ensure that the contractor is insured for public liability [**23.5.1.4**], and for non-completion of the work if, for example, the contractor goes out of business. This is called a **performance bond** [**21.2.6**]. The organisation should also ensure that the actual works are covered against loss or damage, through **contractor's all risks cover**. Some contracts may require this insurance to be arranged by the organisation or jointly by the organisation and contractor.

23.6.1.4 Terrorism

For non-domestic premises, cover for damage to or loss of buildings or contents or consequential loss caused by terrorist attacks is not automatically included in insurance policies and must be purchased as an additional peril.

Insurers are allowed to provide terrorism cover only up to a certain amount. Organisations which need higher cover must take out insurance through Pool Re (a government-backed insurance pool) or an alternative scheme. There are subtle but important differences in the definition of terrorism used in policies and the Pool Re arrangements. These make specialist insurance advice essential.

23.6.1.5 Glass

Plate glass windows are frequently excluded from the landlord's obligation to insure. If this is the case, the tenant will need to take out separate cover. This may also cover sanitary ware, sinks and similar items.

23.6.1.6 Engineering

Boilers, lifts, lifting equipment, air conditioning and similar electrical or mechanical equipment can be insured against breakdown and some damage. Unless the equipment has been decommissioned and is out of use, the cover is valid only if the equipment is regularly inspected as required by statute [**40.7**].

23.6.2 Contents

Contents insurance generally covers loss of and damage to movable items in the building, and usually in the grounds: equipment, machinery, furnishings and stock or supplies. Some **fixtures and fittings** [**60.7.8**] such as wall lamps, built-in display cases or fitted carpets might not fit easily into either a buildings policy or a contents policy, and advice should be taken from the insurer or broker to be sure such items are covered.

Specific items such as bicycles, computers, anything with a value of more than a defined amount, cash, food in freezers, other food, documents [**23.6.5**] and data stored on computer or disk may need separate extensions within the policy.

Some contents policies cover accidental damage; others do not. If it is an **all risks** policy or has an extension for theft, it generally covers theft of contents by persons other than staff, governing body members and others in a position of trust in relation to the organisation. Cover for theft by them needs separate **fidelity insurance [23.6.3.1]**.

The risks covered by the policy need to be carefully examined along with any exclusions and limitations. Cover against theft, especially, is increasingly qualified by requirements for alarms, specific locks and other safeguards. These apply especially to cover for cash or equipment such as computers and sound systems.

It is normally sensible for contents insurance to be on a **new for old** or **reinstatement** basis [**23.3.2**]. If the organisation is prepared to replace its lost or damaged equipment with second-hand items or is willing to cover the additional cost of new items, the insurance may be on an **indemnity** basis, with the value adjusted to allow for wear and tear and depreciation. If the organisation cannot reclaim VAT it should include VAT when working out the value of contents.

To ensure that all items are covered and to make it easier to claim in case of theft or damage, an up to date **inventory** or **register of assets** should be kept off the premises, listing all furniture, equipment and other items. It should show when items were obtained, the purchase price (or value, if received as a gift), serial number or other identifying data, whether the equipment is security marked and/or registered with the police, and any other relevant information.

23.6.2.1 Computers

Rather than including computers as part of the standard contents policy, it may be appropriate to take out a separate policy to cover repair or replacement of the computer, regardless of how the damage or loss was caused; the cost of replacing software, reinstating data etc if information is erased or corrupted; and/or consequential loss [**23.9.1**] if the organisation could suffer financial loss as a result of having to operate without the computer.

If the loss is caused by breakdown, the insurance cover generally operates only if a manufacturer's guarantee or a maintenance and servicing agreement was in force at the time of the breakdown.

23.6.2.2 Property of workers, users and members

Contents insurance covers equipment, goods etc belonging to the organisation. Additional cover will normally be needed if the insurance is to cover personal property belonging to employees, volunteers, members, users of services or facilities, or visitors to the premises. It is especially important to be clear about this if people bring valuable equipment onto the premises.

23.6.2.3 Items off the premises

Many contents policies cover items in transit or when away from the premises for limited periods, but some do not. Even if items are covered in transit, they may not be covered if the vehicle they are in is unattended, or if they are visible in the vehicle. The organisation should consider the need for more extensive cover, for example if staff take equipment home or off site.

23.6.3 Money

The organisation should arrange insurance against loss or theft of money if it receives substantial amounts of cash or cheques; it keeps substantial cash, cheques or unused postage stamps on its premises or elsewhere; or individuals carry large amounts of money to or from the bank or anywhere else.

A money policy is subject to strict limitations and may cover only theft by third parties, not by staff or governing body members. Some policies provide cover for theft of money by employees, where the loss is discovered within a specified period (generally three to seven days). Such cover can be extended to volunteers.

23.6.3.1   Fidelity

Fidelity or **fidelity guarantee insurance** covers the organisation for theft by, or dishonesty of, employees, volunteers, governing body members and/or others who handle money or valuable equipment for the organisation. The Charity Commission recommends that charities take out this cover if its financial advisors or insurance brokers advise it.

It is important to check the policy details carefully, since cover may be dependent upon safeguards such as the organisation obtaining a certain number of references, asking whether the person has any unspent convictions [**41.8**] for offences involving deception, theft, fraud or dishonesty, or undertaking a criminal record check [**41.4**]. Before arranging such insurance, the insurer may investigate the individuals covered and the organisation's financial procedures.

When new individuals take on financial or similar responsibilities, they must be added to the policy unless the policy is explicitly 'all employees', 'all employees, volunteers and trustees', or whatever is appropriate.

23.6.4   Money owed to the organisation

Where the organisation sells goods or provides services on credit, **credit insurance** may be available to cover purchasers' failure to pay in some circumstances.

23.6.5   Documents and data

It is possible to take out insurance to cover costs arising from loss of documents or information. This is often included as part of another cover. Insurance to cover loss of computer data may be included as part of a separate computer insurance policy, and will require safe storage of backups.

23.7   HIRING PREMISES

An organisation which hires out its premises should make absolutely clear, in writing, who is responsible for insuring against damage to the building, damage to or theft of contents, and public liability while all or part of the premises are in use. It may be possible to arrange extensions as required with the organisation's insurer, and to include the cost of these as part of the booking fee.

If the party hiring the premises is required to arrange its own cover, the organisation should have procedures to confirm that this has been done and to have its name included as joint insured. Such arrangements impose considerable administrative burden on the organisation.

Similarly an organisation which hires premises from someone else should be clear about its potential liability in case of damage, theft or injury to the public while it is using the premises.

23.8   VEHICLES

An organisation which operates its own vehicles or vehicles owned by others, or whose employees or volunteers use their own or other people's vehicles for work purposes, must ensure that they are properly insured. The Community Transport Association [see end of chapter] can provide information on insurances for vehicles and drivers.

Exclusions should be carefully examined. In particular, many policies do not cover use by drivers under 25 unless they are individually named in the policy, and policies held by employees or volunteers may not cover use for business purposes [**23.8.1.1**].

All relevant information, including medical conditions and driving convictions of anyone who might drive the organisation's vehicles, must be disclosed to the insurer, and the information must be kept up to date.

23.8.1 Third party

No vehicle can be used on a road unless it is insured for injury to or death of passengers and third parties, and damage to the property of passengers and third parties. It is an offence for the owner or keeper of a vehicle to use it, or allow it to be used, without this insurance. There is no obligation for the insurance to cover injury or death of the vehicle owner or driver, or damage to their property.

Road Traffic Act 1988 s.143

Third party insurance also covers vehicle accidents on private property, and some legal expenses arising from vehicle accidents. It may also cover injury or damage caused by passengers or by trailers or caravans being towed by the vehicle.

23.8.1.1 Employees and volunteers using their own vehicles

Most insurance for private vehicles covers **social, domestic and pleasure use**, but not **business use**. 'Business use' means using the vehicle for the purposes of any employment, for example driving to work related meetings, delivering the organisation's goods, or transporting clients. Journeys between home and the employee's usual place of work are generally 'domestic' rather than business use, but some insurers may charge an extra premium for regular commuting.

Most insurers treat work as an unpaid volunteer as social, domestic and pleasure use, but some define it as business use. 'Unpaid volunteer' means receiving no more than reimbursement of genuine out of pocket expenses, with mileage reimbursed at no more than the HM Revenue and Customs approved rate [**39.3.1**]. Volunteering England [see end of chapter] can provide information.

Employees, volunteers, trainees and others who use their cars for business use must inform their insurer that they are using the car for work purposes, and ensure the insurer amends the policy to cover this use, or provides written confirmation that such amendment is not required.

An organisation which fails to warn employees about the need to check insurance for business use could be found to be negligent if a vehicle which turns out to be uninsured is involved in an accident while being used for the organisation's work. Organisations should check at least annually that those who use their own vehicles are appropriately insured and still hold a valid driving licence, and should have procedures requiring drivers to inform them of any change to their vehicle, insurance or driving licence.

An organisation might want to ask its insurer to arrange **motor contingency insurance**. If this can be arranged, it provides third party cover for the organisation in case employees' or volunteers' own insurance has lapsed or is invalid.

If employees or volunteers use their cars only occasionally for the organisation, for example for one-off events, the organisation may be able to arrange **occasional business use** cover for all such drivers. The insurer should be approached in good time, in case insurance cannot be arranged and the employees and volunteers each have to arrange their own insurance.

23.8.2 Insuring the vehicle

Third party insurance does not cover damage to the user's own vehicle. **Third party, fire and theft insurance** adds to the basic third party policy additional protection if the vehicle is stolen or damaged by fire. Theft insurance may cover not only the vehicle but also items which form part of the vehicle and its equipment, such as the radio or toolbox. It may also cover theft of other items left in the car, but generally only if they are locked in the boot or otherwise out of sight.

Comprehensive insurance covers third party, fire, theft and a range of other risks such as collision (damage to the car caused by the driver), windscreen breakage, and theft of items left in the car.

23.8.3 Charging for journeys

Vehicle insurance policies generally exclude any use of the vehicle for **hire or reward**. But this exclusion may not apply to users of cars holding up to eight passengers who charge passengers only enough to cover the cost of each journey.

HM Revenue and Customs guidelines on allowable reimbursement for vehicle use by employees and volunteers [**30.4.10**] are generally used to determine the allowable mileage rate for journeys, but the owner or keeper of the vehicle should confirm this with the insurer. If an organisation charges for use of its vehicles an amount greater than what is allowed by the insurer, or if employees or volunteers use their own cars to carry passengers and charge them more than this, the vehicles will need to have additional insurance for hire or reward use.

Even where hire or reward insurance is not required, the organisation, employee or volunteer is obliged to notify the insurer that passengers are being charged.

Organisations operating minibuses (seating nine to 16 passengers) and larger buses should contact the Community Transport Association [see end of chapter] for advice about insurance and driver licensing.

23.8.4 Driving abroad

UK insurance provides the minimum legally required third party insurance throughout the EU, but any additional insurance, such as fire and theft, must be specially arranged through the insurer. The **green card**, issued by insurance companies to show that the vehicle has EU third party insurance, is not legally required so long as the policy is available.

Detailed information about driving abroad or taking a car abroad is available from insurers and motoring organisations. Organisations which provide transport services (minibuses, dial a ride etc) should contact the Community Transport Association [see end of chapter].

23.9 LOSS TO THE ORGANISATION

An organisation may itself suffer various types of loss which it may want to insure against.

23.9.1 Consequential loss or business interruption

If flood, fire or other disaster prevents an income generating body from operating for a period, it may suffer significant loss of income. Even small localised damage, such as a flooded basement or a fire near a desk, may have a significant impact if it destroys vital records or equipment.

Such losses can be covered under **business interruption**, **loss of business** or **consequential loss insurance**. These provide a guaranteed income until the organisation is able to restart the income generating activity. The insurance might cover loss of profit, the additional costs of carrying on work at different premises, or amounts due if work required under a grant or contract cannot be performed as required.

Organisations which do not carry out trading or income generation should insure on an **additional expenses** basis, to take account of rent for alternative accommodation, one-off costs to make the premises suitable, reprinting stationery and similar costs.

In all cases it is crucial to allow for an adequate indemnity period. For some premises the standard period of 12 months may not be adequate for repairs or rebuilding, or may not allow enough time for the organisation's trading or operating position to be restored. If the indemnity period is set at two or three years, the sum insured should reflect the revenue or additional expenses for that period.

To prevent the organisation becoming completely immobilised by a fire, theft or other loss it is crucial to keep duplicates or backups of crucial records off site and to have a **business continuity plan** [**22.1.4**].

23.9.2 Failure of events

An organisation may suffer financial loss or loss of reputation if a public event is cancelled or is unsuccessful, by having financial obligations which it has to meet anyway and/or because it does not receive the income it anticipated. Some of these losses can be insured against, but a careful decision has to be made about whether the risk justifies the cost.

Cancellation insurance covers the organisation's financial obligations or loss of income if an event is cancelled for reasons beyond its control. Cancellation due to lack of support is not covered.

Non-appearance insurance covers loss of money or reputation as a result of a speaker or other key person not appearing.

Pluvius insurance (Latin, 'rain'), covers losses suffered because an event is wholly or partly stopped by rain. It is important to be clear about how much rain has to fall and where it will be measured. Cover is less expensive if the insurance is taken out well before the event.

23.9.3 Legal costs

Legal costs or **legal expenses insurance** covers the solicitors' and other costs incurred in specified court proceedings or employment tribunal claims. Some policies also cover damages which the organisation is ordered to pay, for example damages awarded to employees. It is essential to be clear about whether the insurance covers only legal expenses (solicitor etc costs), or covers damages as well.

Insurance cannot cover penalties or fines arising from criminal acts or breach of a statutory duty.

Policies may be linked to an advice line which provides initial advice on issues which may give rise to a claim. The insurance may require such advice not only to be taken but also to be followed. This may limit the organisation's freedom to choose its own advisors or resolve matters in the way it wishes, which some organisations may find unacceptably restrictive.

23.9.4 Charity protection

Charity protection or **trust** (not trustee) **indemnity insurance** protects a charity from losses to the charity caused by one or more members of the governing body and not recoverable from the individuals involved. It is generally included in trustee indemnity insurance [below].

23.10 TRUSTEE INDEMNITY AND DIRECTORS' AND OFFICERS' INSURANCE

The potential liabilities faced by members of the governing body and ordinary members of organisations are covered in **chapter 22**. These liabilities might be to third parties (for example through the organisation's or their own breach of contract, negligence or breach of duty) or to the organisation itself (for example for using its funds for purposes for which they should not have been used). Cover is available for some situations where charity trustees or directors and officers of companies or industrial and provident societies may be held personally liable.

Charity trustees may use charitable funds to purchase **trustee indemnity insurance** if they believe it is in the best interests of the charity to do so, even if it is not authorised by the governing document. Charity Commission consent is required if the governing document explicitly prohibits the use of the charity's funds for this purpose. If the trustees as a body do not take out this insurance, individual trustees can arrange and pay for their own insurance privately if they wish. *Charities Act 1993 ss.73D-F, inserted by Charities Act 2006 ss.38,39*

Directors' and officers' insurance (D&O) is a similar insurance for company and industrial and provident society directors. Companies have a statutory right to purchase this. *Companies Act 2006 ss.234-237*

Non-charitable IPSs can take out D&O insurance if the governing document allows. A charitable IPS may do so only if its rules contain explicit power to do so. Consent is required from Mutual Societies Registration in the Financial Services Authority to include such power. When IPSs cease to be exempt charities [**8.1.2**] such consent will have to come from the Charity Commission.

Details of trustee indemnity or directors' and officers' insurance must be disclosed in a company and/or charity annual report [**54.2.8**, **54.3.6**].

Governing body members often believe, incorrectly, that this insurance will protect them against all personal liability. This is not the case. The insurance is not necessarily appropriate for all organisations, and in many cases is taken out primarily to reassure and encourage people to join the governing body.

23.10.1 What is covered

When a governing body member causes a loss to the organisation because of breach of trust or breach of duty as a trustee or company director [**22.4**], the governing body member normally has to make good the loss to the organisation. Trustee indemnity or D&O insurance covers some of these liabilities.

For many governing body members, the main value of the insurance is that it covers legal defence costs, which can be substantial even if no wrongdoing is subsequently proved.

The insurance generally provides a range of other cover, such as professional indemnity, fidelity, loss of documents, breach of copyright, and/or breach of confidentiality. It may in some cases cover some liability arising from breach of contract. All policies are different, so it is important to check what is and is not covered and to be sure that the organisation is not paying twice for the same cover under two different policies.

23.10.2 What is not covered

Trustee indemnity or directors' and officers' insurance cannot cover:

- penalties for breach of statutory duty, or fines;
- liability arising from any act which the person knew was fraudulent or dishonest;
- the cost of unsuccessfully defending a criminal prosecution for dishonesty or wilful misconduct;
- in a company, charitable incorporated organisation or industrial and provident society, liability arising from fraudulent trading, where the director or trustee deceived creditors [**24.2.4**];
- in any charity, any act which the trustee knew was in breach of trust, or committed in reckless disregard of whether it was in breach of trust. This includes liabilities to the charity resulting from conduct which the trustee knew or ought to have known was not in the best interest of the charity.

The insurance generally cannot cover losses arising from the trustees' or directors' failure to insure the organisation's assets, where such failure is a breach of trust [**22.4**].

If the act which gives rise to the liability is not covered under the insurance, the governing body member will be obliged to indemnify the organisation for its losses and will not be entitled to be indemnified under the insurance.

Claims may arise from an allegation that a governing body member has acted beyond their powers, particularly in making arrangements with or promises to employees (such as the promise of a payout to a departing employee). It is likely to be worth seeking specific confirmation of the policy coverage in respect of this.

When a company, charitable incorporated organisation or industrial and provident society is being wound up, the liquidator can require member(s) of the governing body to contribute to a company's assets because of **wrongful trading** [**24.2.4**]. Directors' and officers' or trustee indemnity insurance will generally cover this. However some case law suggests that a liquidator may be legally an officer of the organisation. In this situation the insurance will not generally pay out, as it will not make a payment from one officer (the governing body member) to another (the liquidator). Incorporated organisations should ensure that D&O or trustee indemnity insurance explicitly covers claims by the liquidator in cases of wrongful trading.   *Re Home Treat Ltd [1991] BCLC 705*

Resources: LIABILITY AND INSURANCE

Liability and insurance. CC49 *Charities and insurance*: Charity Commission, www.charitycommission.gov.uk, 0845 300 0218, email via website.

Association of British Insurers: www.abi.org.uk, 020 7600 3333, info@abi.org.uk.

Business Link: www.businesslink.gov.uk, 0845 600 9 006.

Financial Services Authority: www.moneymadeclear.fsa.gov.uk.

Brokers. British Insurance Brokers' Association: www.biba.org.uk, 0901 814 0015, enquiries@biba.org.uk.

Names of insurers for voluntary organisations. National Council for Voluntary Organisations: www.ncvo-vol.org.uk, 0800 2 798 798, helpdesk@askncvo.org.uk.

Wales Council for Voluntary Action: www.wcva.org.uk, 0800 2888 329, help@wcva.org.uk.

Umbrella organisations, councils for voluntary service etc.

Sports activities. Central Council of Physical Recreation: www.ccpr.org.uk, 020 7854 8500, info@ccpr.org.uk.

Vehicles and drivers. Community Transport Association: www.communitytransport.com, 0845 130 6195, advice@ctauk.org .

Volunteers. Volunteering England: www.volunteering.org.uk, 0800 028 3304, volunteering@volunteeringengland.org.

Statute law. www.opsi.gov.uk and www.statutelaw.gov.uk.

Much but not all case law. www.bailii.org.

Updates cross-referenced to this book. www.rclh.co.uk.

Chapter 24

FINANCIAL DIFFICULTIES AND WINDING UP

For sources of further information see end of chapter.

24.1 CLOSURE OF AN ORGANISATION

How an organisation ends depends on whether it is incorporated or unincorporated, and whether it is solvent (able to pay its debts) or insolvent. The terms **winding up**, **dissolution** and **liquidation** are in practice used interchangeably to describe the process, but have different meanings legally.

Even where the organisation is solvent, specialist advice may be advisable to ensure all liabilities are met, assets are disposed of in accordance with the governing document, and it is wound up properly.

Where insolvency is a realistic possibility – or an inevitability – **professional advice is essential**. The Charity Commission's CC12 *Managing financial difficulties and insolvency in charities* outlines some of the issues and applies for the most part to non-charities as well, but is not a substitute for proper advice.

24.1.1 Pension scheme deficit

An organisation which operates its own occupational pension scheme [**30.6.4**] or is a member of a **multi-employer occupational pension scheme** such as, for example, the Pensions Trust could be affected by **pension scheme deficit** if it winds up for any reason. If the organisation has not contributed enough to the pension scheme, it could become liable to pay to the scheme an amount adequate to cover its full pension liability [**30.6.5**].

Any organisation which operates or is a member of an occupational pension scheme should take advice from its pension provider, accountant and legal advisor before taking any steps towards winding up – regardless of the reason for the winding up, and even if the organisation is solvent.

24.1.2 Transfer of employees

Where an organisation is subject to bankruptcy or insolvency proceedings [**24.5**] under the control of an insolvency practitioner whose intention is to liquidate (sell) the organisation's assets without the work being continued, employees do not transfer under the transfer of undertakings (TUPE) regulations [**29.7**] when the relevant assets are sold. But if the intention is that the purchaser of the assets will continue the work, relevant employees may transfer under TUPE [**29.7.1**]. *Transfer of Undertakings (Protection of Employment) Regulations 2006 [SI 2006/264] reg.8(7); Oakland v Wellswood (Yorkshire) Ltd [2008] UKEAT 0395 08 0511*

24.1.3 Winding up

Winding up is the process of ceasing to operate: stopping activities and services, dismissing staff, closing premises, paying the bills, terminating contracts, dealing with liabilities, and distributing any remaining assets. The rules for dealing with payment of debts when an organisation is wound up are explained below [**24.10**].

When a solvent organisation is wound up, it is likely that some assets will remain after payment of all debts and the costs of winding up. These assets may be distributed only as set out in the dissolution clause in the governing document [**7.4.27**]. The most usual requirement is that they must be given to one or more organisations which have similar objects and prohibit their profits from being distributed to at least the same extent as the dissolved organisation. The decision as to how the assets should be distributed may be left to the members of the organisation or to the governing body. In some cases third parties must be consulted. Alternatively, the governing document may name a specific organisation or organisations to which the assets must be given.

Clubs and some other non-charitable organisations may be allowed to distribute surplus assets to their members [**24.8.1**].

24.1.4 Liquidation

Liquidation is a formal process governed by the **Insolvency Act 1986** as amended. Liquidation involves selling or disposing of the assets of a company, charitable incorporated organisation or industrial and provident society and dealing with the liabilities, which includes distributing money released from the sale of assets among those entitled [**24.10.4**]. Liquidation can occur when the organisation is **solvent** or **insolvent,** and either under a court order (**compulsory liquidation**) or without (**voluntary liquidation**).

Where a formal liquidation is not necessary, the governing body ensures financial liabilities are met, contracts are terminated and any remaining assets are distributed as specified in the governing document.

24.1.4.1 Insolvency practitioners

Licensed **insolvency practitioners** are individuals, usually accountants or solicitors, licensed under the **Insolvency Act 1986** ss.390-393 to carry out activities such as administration and liquidation of companies and industrial and provident societies. Although called insolvency practitioners, they also deal with liquidations of solvent organisations.

Any accountant or solicitor may advise on liquidation, but only a minority of accountants and a very small minority of solicitors are insolvency practitioners, and of those only a very small number have experience of voluntary sector insolvency. Costs for liquidation vary widely, and quotes – along with information about their previous experience working with voluntary sector organisations – should if possible be obtained from more than one potential liquidator before selecting one.

24.1.4.2 Official receiver

The **official receiver** is a civil servant in the Insolvency Service, appointed by the court to deal with liquidations. The official receiver also deals with bankruptcies, where an individual is insolvent and made bankrupt by the court as a result.

The official receiver should not be confused with a **receiver and manager** (now usually called an **interim manager**) appointed by the Charity Commission to manage a charity whose assets are at risk because of mismanagement [**4.5.10**].

24.1.5 Dissolution

Dissolution is the final stage in ending the organisation, when it ceases to exist. Companies, charitable incorporated organisations and industrial and provident societies come into being by registration, and cease to exist only when they are formally dissolved and removed from the relevant register.

Unincorporated trusts and associations may dissolve themselves using the procedure in their governing document [see **24.8** and **24.9.3** for what happens if there is no procedure]. If the organisation is a registered charity, the Charity Commission must be notified that it has been dissolved.

24.1.5.1 Dissolution without winding up

An organisation may be dissolved without being liquidated or wound up, for example if its assets, liabilities and work are all transferred to another organisation, or if two organisations are dissolved and merge to form a new organisation [**11.5**].

24.1.5.2 Between liquidation and dissolution

An incorporated body which is being liquidated, but has not yet been dissolved, is still in existence and can still receive legacies. This has implications where the company is insolvent, and the legacy therefore becomes available to meet the company's debts [**50.6.1**]. *Re ARMS (Multiple Sclerosis Research) Ltd; Alleyne v Attorney General & another [1997] 2 All ER 679*

24.1.6 Checklist for winding up

Among the issues that need to be considered when winding up are:

- who within the governing body and staff will oversee the legal and financial arrangements and who will support staff and others affected by the closure;
- provisions in the governing document for winding up [**7.4.27**], and in particular which decisions need to be made by members of the organisation rather than by the governing body, and any rules on disposition of assets remaining after all liabilities have been met;
- notifying the organisation's accountant, auditor and solicitor at an early stage, in particular if there is any possibility that the organisation may be insolvent;
- whether the organisation is legally solvent or insolvent [**24.2**];
- whether the organisation will be formally liquidated, in which case the insolvency practitioner, rather than the governing body or members of the organisation, oversees the process and determines what happens with the assets;
- the organisation's assets, liabilities and cashflow projections for the winding up period, and whether there are outstanding or hidden liabilities [**24.10.3**];
- terms of grants, service agreements or contracts, and in particular whether any money is likely to have to be paid back for failure to complete the work or whether anything funded with a capital grant will need to be returned;
- whether the organisation is incorporated (in which case the Insolvency Act or other statutory procedures apply) or unincorporated (in which case winding up is governed only by the governing document);
- whether the organisation holds any permanent endowment [**24.3.3**, **24.9.1**];
- if the organisation owns property, how long it is likely to take to sell or transfer it;
- terms of leases or licences, in particular provisions for break clause, notice or assignment, and any obligations which could require time or money, such as a repairing clause [**62.2.4**];

- whether the organisation's work is being transferred, in which case TUPE almost certainly applies to the transfer of employees [**29.7**], or is stopping;
- the number of redundancies, and employees' redundancy entitlements including consultation rights [**35.2**] and redundancy pay [**35.7**];
- employees' statutory or contractual entitlement to notice [**34.3**];
- implications for service users – what arrangements need to be made to transfer them or recommend alternatives;
- transfer or disposal of equipment;
- confidentiality and data protection issues in the transfer, including safekeeping and/or disposal of information [**chapter 43**];
- assignment of copyright and other rights to the organisation's intellectual property [**chapter 44**];
- deciding whether any insurances need to remain in place after closure, and cancelling other insurances;
- notifying all suppliers and ensuring all accounts are properly closed;
- notifying all customers, beneficiaries and other stakeholders;
- drawing up proper final accounts, getting them approved as required, and submitting them to regulators and registration bodies;
- deregistering as a charity and company, and ending other registrations [**1.9**].

This list is only an overview. In reality, many more decisions and actions will be required.

24.2 SOLVENCY AND INSOLVENCY

An organisation does not become insolvent when it runs out of money. It is likely to have become insolvent much earlier, at the point when it became clear that there was no realistic hope of financial survival.

24.2.1 Tests for insolvency

Two 'tests' – the **cashflow test** and the **balance sheet test** – are used to determine if an organisation is, or is likely to become, insolvent. If an organisation fails on either, it needs to take urgent advice from an accountant or solicitor.

24.2.1.1 Cashflow test

An organisation fails the **going concern** or **cashflow test** if it cannot pay its debts when they fall due, or this is likely to occur within the foreseeable future. 'Foreseeable' depends on the organisation and the situation, but is generally the next 12 months.

Under what is sometimes known as the **legal action test**, an organisation will fail the cashflow test where legal action has been brought against it in one of the following ways:

- a creditor (a person to whom money is owed) for more than £750 has demanded the amount due, often by the creditor serving on the organisation a **statutory demand**, and the organisation has not paid within three weeks or made satisfactory arrangements to pay;
- the high court, when dealing with a winding up petition by a creditor, is satisfied that the organisation is unable to pay its debts as they fall due; or
- the organisation has not paid a creditor after being ordered by a court to do so.

Insolvency Act 1986 s.123(1)

24.2.1.2 Balance sheet test

An organisation fails the **balance sheet test** if the value of its total assets is less than its total liabilities, taking into account current and contingent liabilities and sometimes also prospective liabilities. *Insolvency Act 1986 s.123(2)*

Current liabilities are due now (generally defined as within the next 12 months). **Contingent liabilities** are those which will arise only if a specific event does or does not happen, such as redundancy payments. **Prospective li-**

abilities are those which the organisation knows it will have, such as a loan due for repayment in two years' time.

The liabilities included in the balance sheet test depend on assumptions about the organisation. If the governing body can reasonably assume that the organisation will be able to continue operating into the foreseeable future, it can do its balance sheet test on a **going concern basis**, and does not need to include liabilities contingent on winding up (redundancy payments, pension fund deficit, winding up costs, etc). But if this assumption cannot reasonably be made, the test must be on a **break-up basis**, including all the liabilities contingent on winding up.

An organisation which passes the balance sheet test (has assets worth more than liabilities) but cannot pay its debts when they are due will not generally be considered insolvent if it can borrow against the value of its assets, sell the assets and use the money to pay the debts, or arrange to pay creditors later.

24.2.1.3 Technical insolvency

If an organisation is able to pay its debts as they fall due but fails the balance sheet test, it is sometimes said to be **technically insolvent**. An organisation in this situation should seek advice.

24.2.2 Insecure funding

Many voluntary organisations have virtually no assets and are wholly dependent on external bodies for their funding. There is often a period towards the end of the financial year when the organisation has no guarantee of funding for the next year, and has inadequate reserves to operate beyond the end of the financial year.

If an incorporated body could find itself at the beginning of the financial year (or any other time) without sufficient funds to meet its liabilities, it should strictly speaking take advice from an insolvency practitioner [**24.1.4.1**], who might well advise winding up. Similarly, if there is any risk that an unincorporated organisation could find itself unable to pay its bills, it really should start winding up in order to reduce the risk of personal liability for governing body members.

But if these steps were taken every time an organisation with inadequate reserves faced financial uncertainty, many viable organisations would close each year. Unfortunately, not taking the steps puts governing body members at risk of personal liability [**24.2.4.1**] in unincorporated organisations, and could also put them at risk even in incorporated bodies [**24.2.4.2**]. There is no easy solution.

The risks inherent in this situation emphasise the importance of incorporation to reduce the risk of personal liability [**3.1.1**], building up enough reserves to ensure the organisation would be able to meet all its liabilities on winding up, not becoming over-dependent on a small number of funding sources, and educating funders to make decisions in good time.

24.2.2.1 Precautionary redundancy notices

An organisation facing closure if funding is not forthcoming should take steps to reduce its liabilities. This may include issuing **precautionary notice of redundancy** [**35.4.1**], which provides a framework for collective and/or individual consultation [**35.2**] to take place before dismissal notices are issued, and reduces the risk of the employer being held liable for a **protective award** [**35.2.2**] for failure to carry out collective consultation if 20 or more employees may be redundant.

Advice needs to be taken and a balance needs to be struck between prudence and realism. If the organisation has to wind up, having given employees precautionary notice or actual notice of dismissal will reduce its liabilities. But if funds are forthcoming and the organisation can be rescued, employees who have been issued notice of dismissal can compel the organisation to make them redundant, thus making the organisation liable for statutory and contractual redundancy pay [**35.7.1**]. And even if employees do not demand to be made redundant, the issuing of redundancy notices is likely to have been disruptive and demoralising.

24.2.3 Action when facing possible insolvency

Once there is a reasonable probability that the organisation is or will become insolvent, certain steps are obligatory or advisable. Action at this point could make the difference between governing body members being personally liable or not.

24.2.3.1 Companies, CIOs and IPSs

When a company or industrial and provident society is in this situation, its highest priority in law is to safeguard the interests of its **creditors** – the people to whom it already owes money. It must take advice as a matter of utmost urgency from its accountant or solicitor, and is likely to have to call in an insolvency practitioner [**24.1.4.1**]. The same rules are likely to apply to charitable incorporated organisations (CIOs).
Insolvency Act 1986 s.214

The organisation should do everything possible to collect all sums owing to it, and should not pay into any account which is overdrawn. The organisation should not make any payments to one creditor in preference to others, and should ensure that creditors who fall into the same class [**24.10.4**] will be treated equally.

If the directors/trustees know, or should know, that they cannot avoid liquidation, they should not make or authorise any expenditure without taking advice. Continuing to operate could constitute **wrongful** or **fraudulent trading** [**24.2.4.2**], or give rise to a claim of **preference** [**24.10.4**].

24.2.3.2 Trusts and associations

Trusts and associations do not have the same legal duty to safeguard the interests of creditors – but they should do so, because the creditors may sue individuals involved in the organisation [**24.2.4.1**]. The organisation would be very foolish indeed to continue incurring debt, and should take advice as a matter of utmost urgency from an accountant or solicitor.

24.2.4 Personal liability

It is a very serious matter to continue operating while the organisation could become or is already insolvent. Doing so exposes members of the governing body and in some cases other individuals – even if they have limited liability – to the risk of personal liability for the organisation's debts. To reduce this risk it is essential that governing body members receive proper financial information, understand it, monitor reserves in relation to liabilities, and take appropriate action if they believe there is any risk of the organisation becoming insolvent.

24.2.4.1 Insolvency in unincorporated associations and trusts

Anyone to whom money is owed by an unincorporated association or trust may be able to bring a claim against:

- any member or members of the current governing body;
- anyone who has been on the governing body at any time since the contract or other arrangement on which the money is due was put in place [**22.5.3**];
- in some rare situations, any ordinary member of the organisation (not a member of the governing body); and/or
- anyone who signed a contract, ordered goods or entered into an agreement without being properly authorised by the governing body to do so [**20.5.5**].

A person who has to pay more than a fair share of the organisation's debts is entitled to a contribution from other members of the governing body, but this involves taking further legal action.
Civil Liability (Contribution) Act 1978

Many governing documents provide for members of the governing body to be indemnified (compensated) by the organisation if they suffer any loss as a result of their position. But this is of no use if the organisation has insufficient assets.

The governing document may say that governing body members have a right to be indemnified by the organisation's members (rather than by the organisation itself) if they suffer any loss. In this situation the governing body members could bring a claim against any or all of the organisation's members.

Even without this clause in the governing document, an association's members could be liable for its debts if the decisions which led to the insolvency were taken by the members in a general meeting rather than by the governing body.

Any individual against whom legal action is taken could be personally bankrupted, and should take independent legal advice.

24.2.4.2   Insolvency of incorporated bodies

In a company, charitable incorporated organisation or industrial and provident society the ordinary members have **limited liability** in the event of the organisation becoming insolvent. In a company limited by guarantee or CIO their maximum liability is the amount of the guarantee set out in the articles of association or CIO constitution [**12.4.1**, **12.4.2**]. In a company limited by shares or IPS the maximum is the amount unpaid on their shares.

In general the officers (members of the governing body, the company secretary if there is one or IPS secretary, and in some cases senior management) are protected from personal liability if the organisation becomes insolvent. But they may, individually or as a group, lose the protection of limited liability if the organisation goes into insolvent liquidation and they have allowed it to continue operating while they knew or reasonably should have known that it was, or was inevitably going to become, insolvent. This is known as **wrongful trading**, and the liquidator can bring a claim against some or all officers requiring them to contribute to the company's assets.   *Insolvency Act 1986 s.214*

An example of how these provisions operate in practice can be seen from a situation where the governing body genuinely and reasonably believes the organisation will receive enough funding to keep it solvent. If they do not receive the funding and the organisation becomes insolvent, the liquidator would be unlikely to claim against the officers – provided they had taken action to wind up the company as soon as it became clear they were not going to receive the funding. If the directors continued operating even after this had become clear, they could be held personally liable.   *Robin v Gunner & another [2004] EWHC 316 (Ch)*

Fraudulent trading occurs when an officer or employee of a company or IPS deliberately seeks to defraud any creditor while the organisation is or is becoming insolvent, or at any other time. This is a criminal offence under the **Companies Act** and a civil offence under the **Insolvency Act**, so the individual(s) can be fined or imprisoned as well as being required by the court to contribute to the organisation's assets. It is also likely to be a criminal offence for CIOs.
                                    Companies Act 2006 s.993; Insolvency Act 1986 s.213

Company, CIO or IPS officers may also be held personally liable if they have entered a contract or taken other legal action without being authorised to do so [**20.5.5**], have acted in breach of trust or in breach of fiduciary duty [**22.4**], or have acted dishonestly or fraudulently.

The company, CIO or IPS may be able to insure against some of these liabilities through directors' and officers' or trustee indemnity insurance [**23.10**]. Company directors may be able to apply to the court for relief from liability, and CIO trustees may be able to apply to the Charity Commission or court [**22.7.7**].

Company directors of an insolvent company who have acted in a way which makes them unfit to manage a company may be disqualified from serving as a director of any company or being involved with setting up or managing any company [**13.3.3**]. At the time of writing (mid 2009) these rules did not apply to IPS directors, but were expected to be extended to apply to them [**13.3.4**]. It was unclear whether similar rules would apply to CIO trustees.

24.2.4.3   Insolvency of a charity

In all charitable organisations, even those with limited liability, the members of the governing body may be found to be in **breach of trust** if they have not acted prudently, for example if they did not receive proper financial information, meet regularly, take and act on proper financial advice, or make decisions properly. In these situations the Charity Commission could require the trustees to repay to the charity any losses incurred by the charity [**22.4**].

Trustee indemnity insurance [**23.10**] provides some protection against this, but cannot cover situations where the trustees knowingly acted in breach of trust, or acted in reckless disregard as to whether something was in breach of trust.

A trustee may apply to the Charity Commission or court for relief from some or all liability for breach of trust [**22.7.7**].

24.3 WINDING UP A COMPANY

A company can cease to exist only in the following ways:

- it ceases to operate and applies to the registrar of companies for a **voluntary striking off** from the register of companies [**24.4.1**];
- it consistently fails to comply with company legislation, and is **struck off** by the registrar [**24.4.2**];
- it is solvent and there is a **members' voluntary liquidation** [**24.4.3**];
- it winds up voluntarily through a **creditors' voluntary liquidation** when it is, or is about to become, insolvent [**24.5.3**];
- it is insolvent, action is brought against it by its creditors and there is a **compulsory liquidation** by the court [**24.5.4**]; or
- the attorney general takes proceedings to cancel the registration of a company which has been registered with illegal objects.

Liquidation procedures are outlined in Companies House leaflet GBW1, and procedures for striking off, dissolution and restoration in GP4. Both are available from Companies House [see end of chapter]. Further information regarding liquidation is available from the Insolvency Service [see end of chapter].

As soon as a decision to wind up is made, however informally, the organisation should notify its accountant, auditor and solicitor. Advice may be needed on the most appropriate type of winding up, and on the procedures. Failure to follow the procedures is in many cases an offence.

A company may be merged or amalgamated with or taken over by another company, without being wound up, if the high court agrees. Legal advice is necessary.

24.3.1 Disclosure when winding up

When a company is being wound up, whether voluntarily or by the court, or is in administration or administrative receivership or a moratorium is in force for it, a statement to this effect must be included on all of its websites and on many documents issued by or on behalf of the company [**18.1.1.6**].

24.3.2 Alternatives to liquidation

Liquidating a company is a complex procedure involving a liquidator [**24.4.3**] and costing thousands of pounds. If the company is solvent, alternatives are voluntary striking off [**24.4.1**] or making the company dormant [**54.3.10**]. If the company is insolvent, a company voluntary arrangement [**24.5.1**] or administration order [**24.5.2**] may be possible.

24.3.3 Incorporated bodies with permanent endowment

Permanent endowment [**58.8.1**] is money held on condition that it cannot be spent (so only the interest or dividends it earns can be spent), property held on condition that it cannot be sold, or property held on condition that if it is sold, the proceeds from the sale cannot be spent. Incorporated charitable bodies cannot hold permanent endowment, so it is generally held by a separate unincorporated trust, called a **special trust** [**9.2.3**], linked to the incorporated body.

If the incorporated body is wound up, the special trust is dealt with in the same way as for an unincorporated charity with permanent endowment [**24.9.1**]. The permanent endowment is not available to meet the incorporated body's debts.

24.4   SOLVENT COMPANIES

24.4.1   Voluntary striking off

The **voluntary striking off** procedure enables a company which is not insolvent and has not operated in the previous three months to apply to be struck off the register and dissolved. The procedure contains safeguards to protect members, creditors (current, contingent and prospective [**24.2.1.2**]), employees and others involved with the company, by requiring the company to send to all of these the same form that is sent to Companies House and giving them the opportunity to object to the striking off. *Companies Act 2006 ss.681,1003*

A detailed summary of who can apply to have a company struck off, the circumstances in which an application can be made and how to apply is in GBW2 from Companies House [see end of chapter].

This is a useful and inexpensive way to close a company which is solvent and is no longer required. If it may be required in future, it may be more sensible to put it into dormancy [**54.3.10**].

A company struck off before 1 October 2009 can be restored to the register within 20 years of dissolution, for example if a creditor claims the former company owes it money and should not have been struck off. A company struck off on or after 1 October 2009 can be restored to the register within six years. *Companies Act 2006 s.688; Companies Act 2006 (Commencement No.8, Transitional Provisions) & Savings Order 2008 [SI 2008/2860] sch.2 para.89,91*

24.4.2   Striking off by registrar

A company may be **struck off** by the registrar and dissolved if it appears that it is defunct. This could happen if the company persistently does not send in annual returns and accounts to Companies House, or if post sent by Companies House to the registered address is returned undelivered. *Companies Act 2006 s.1000*

Assets of a company struck off by the registrar are ***bona vacantia*** (belong to the Crown). They can be recovered by applying to the court for the company to be reinstated, but legal advice is needed and the process is costly. *Companies Act 2006 ss.1012,1034*

24.4.3   Members' voluntary liquidation

If a company is solvent and the members want to end it, but the voluntary striking off procedure [**24.4.1**] is not appropriate, the members must pass a special resolution [see **19.7.4** for procedure] for the company to be wound up voluntarily. The liquidation process is explained in GBW1, available from Companies House [see end of chapter]. *Insolvency Act 1986 s.84*

In rare cases, the articles of association may say that the company is to be dissolved at a particular time, or after a particular event occurs. In this case, if the company is solvent, an ordinary resolution [**19.7.4**] is adequate for voluntary winding up. *Insolvency Act 1986 s.84(1)(a)*

The above resolutions lead to a **member's voluntary liquidation**. The process starts with a majority of the directors (or both of them if there are only two) making a **declaration of solvency**, confirming that they believe the company will be able to pay its debts, plus interest, in full within a specified period which cannot be more than 12 months from the start of the winding up. In practice the period specified is invariably the full 12 months. This statement cannot be made more than five weeks before the resolution of voluntary winding up is passed.

Voluntary liquidation usually starts as soon as the resolution of voluntary winding up is passed. A liquidator is appointed, and the company ceases to operate except as far as is required to wind up. However it continues to exist as a company until it is dissolved.

The disadvantage of a members' voluntary liquidation over a voluntary striking off is that it costs more. The advantages are that the company cannot generally be restored to the register, and the process is managed by a liquidator who is appointed by the company at a **liquidation meeting**. In addition, if an unexpected liability arises that makes the company insolvent, the voluntary liquidation can relatively easily be converted into insolvent liquidation.

If at any time during the winding up the liquidator believes the company will not be able to pay its debts in full within the period specified in the declaration of solvency, the liquidator must take steps to convert the winding up into a creditors' voluntary liquidation [**24.5.3**].

24.5   INSOLVENT COMPANIES

If a company already is or is about to become insolvent, a company voluntary arrangement or administration order may be an alternative to winding up. Basic guidance on liquidation and insolvency is in GBW1, available from Companies House [see end of chapter], but ***specialist advice should be taken at the earliest opportunity.***

When a company is being wound up, is in administrative receivership, receivership or administration, or a moratorium is in force for it, a statement to this effect must be included on certain documents and all its websites [**18.1.1**].

24.5.1   Company voluntary arrangements

In a **company voluntary arrangement** (CVA) the company directors make a proposal to the company's members and creditors (persons to whom money is owed) for a **composition** in satisfaction of its debts or a **scheme of arrangement** of its affairs. A CVA cannot be proposed by creditors or the company's members/shareholders.   *Insolvency Act 1986 ss.1-7B, as amended by Insolvency Act 2000*

A CVA must be administered by a licensed insolvency practitioner, from whom advice should be sought at an early stage [**24.1.4.1**].

The basic purpose of a CVA is that a company can, by reaching an agreement with its creditors, avoid liquidation or administration [**24.5.2**]. The proposal must satisfy creditors that a better financial result will be achieved for them than through liquidation or administration.

24.5.1.1   Moratorium

Small companies [**54.3.2**] can obtain from the court a **moratorium** of up to 28 days, which can in some circumstances be extended, to give directors time to put together proposals for a CVA. During the moratorium the company's creditors cannot bring action against the company. At the time of writing (mid 2009), the government was consulting on whether a moratorium should also be available to medium and large companies.   *Insolvency Act 1986 s.1A, inserted by Insolvency Act 2000 s.1*

24.5.2   Administration

Administration is a procedure which places a company under the control of an insolvency practitioner and the protection of the court. The aims of administration, in order of priority, are to rescue the company as a going concern or where that is not possible, to achieve a better result for creditors than a winding up; and a realisation of property to make distributions to one or more secured or preferential creditors [**24.10.4**].   *Insolvency Act 1986 sch.B1, inserted by Enterprise Act 2002 s.8*

An administration order can be sought from the court by the company, its directors or a creditor. But in most cases an out of court procedure, which entitles the directors of the company or the company's floating charge holders [**24.10.4.4**] to appoint an administrator, can be used. Special rules apply where a company is in liquidation, or is subject to a company voluntary arrangement [**24.5.1**].

A company in administration is protected from having a winding up petition issued against it. Except with permission of the administrator or the court, no steps may be taken to enforce security over the company's property and no legal proceedings may be brought or continued against the company.

The administrator has wide powers and duties, and in general becomes responsible for managing the company's affairs. His or her objective is to act quickly, efficiently and in the best interests of the company and creditors as a whole.

24.5.3 Creditors' voluntary liquidation

A **creditors' voluntary liquidation** takes place where a declaration of solvency [**24.4.3**] has not been made. Despite what it is called, it does not start with the creditors, but with the company members passing a special resolution [**19.7.4**] saying the company cannot continue operating because of its liabilities and that it is advisable to wind up.

From this point, the interests of creditors are paramount and the directors cannot carry out any of their powers unless approved by the court. The only exceptions are that the directors can summon a meeting or meetings of creditors and prepare a statement of affairs in a prescribed form; dispose of perishable goods and other goods whose value would be reduced unless immediately disposed of; and take steps to protect the company's assets, through expenditure directed solely to winding up the organisation (for example to collect money owing to it) or necessary to prevent loss (for example maintaining insurance policies). In rare cases the liquidator may allow the directors to retain more of their powers.

At the creditors' meetings the creditors have their say as to the appointment of a liquidator. After the liquidator is appointed, creditors' meetings will vote on resolutions proposed by the liquidator for distribution of the company's assets. These resolutions are passed if they are approved by the majority in value of claims against the company.

Even though the creditors do not start the liquidation process, they can and almost invariably do assert control. However, the decisions about distribution of assets are subject to statutory and common law provisions which establish certain preferential creditors who are entitled to priority over other creditors [**24.10.4**].

The general aim of the creditors' voluntary winding up is to realise assets and ensure that as much money as possible is made available for those entitled to it. Once that has been done, the life of the company is brought to an end.

Insolvency Act 1986 s.84(1)(c)

24.5.4 Compulsory liquidation

The high court and in some cases county courts may wind up a company in a variety of situations, including where the company is unable to pay its debts [**24.2.1**]; the company members pass a special resolution [**19.7.4**] asking to be wound up by the court; it is just and equitable that the company be wound up; the company does not operate in the year after incorporation, or suspends operation for a year; or an automatic moratorium for a small company [**24.5.1.1**] comes to an end and no approved voluntary arrangement is in effect.

These and other grounds on which a petition for the compulsory winding up of a company may be presented to the court are set out in the **Insolvency Act**.

Insolvency Act 1986 s.122(1)

Issuing or threatening to issue a petition is a classic way for a creditor to seek to enforce a debt. But a petition for winding up may also be presented to the court by the company, all the company directors, any contributory (generally a current shareholder), a liquidator, the secretary of state for business, Innovation and skills, or the official receiver [**24.1.4.2**].

Insolvency Act 1986 s.124

If the petition is accepted, the court makes the winding up order and appoints the official receiver or an insolvency practitioner as liquidator. The process is then broadly similar to the process in a creditors' voluntary winding up but is completely under the jurisdiction of the court.

The presentation of a winding up petition can have a dramatic effect on a company. If a winding up order is made, it takes effect from the date the winding up petition was presented to the court, rendering void any transactions relating to the company's property from that date. A winding up order also means that the powers of the directors cease and are assumed by the liquidator, and the company's employees are dismissed.

24.6   INDUSTRIAL AND PROVIDENT SOCIETIES

A solvent industrial and provident society may be wound up by an **instrument of dissolution** signed by at least 75% of the society's members. A county court may set aside an instrument of dissolution if a member of the society or any other person having an interest in or claim on its funds petitions the court within three months.

Industrial & Provident Societies Act 1965 ss.55(b),58

Alternatively most IPSs may amalgamate with, or undertake a transfer of engagements to, another IPS or company [**11.5.6**].

An insolvent society is wound up and dissolved in the same way as a company under the **Insolvency Act 1986** [**24.5**]. But the procedures for administration orders and voluntary arrangements are available only to limited companies or their foreign equivalents, and cannot be used for IPSs.

IPSA 1965 s.55(a);
Insolvency Act 1986 (Amendment) Regulations 2005 [SI 2005/879]

As with companies, there is a strict order for the payment of debts [**24.10.4**]. At the time of writing (mid 2009) the **Company Directors Disqualification Act 1986** [**13.3.3**] did not apply to IPSs, but was expected to be extended to them.

24.7   CHARITABLE INCORPORATED ORGANISATIONS

At the time of writing (mid 2009), the procedures for winding up, insolvency and dissolution of charitable incorporated organisations (CIOs) had not been finalised. It was proposed that insolvent CIOs would be wound up in the same way as companies [**24.5**],. For solvent CIOs there would be **voluntary dissolution** requested by the trustees, or **administrative dissolution** where the Charity Commission believes a CIO is no longer in operation, or in certain other situations. Up to date information is available from the Charity Commission [see end of chapter].

24.8   NON-CHARITABLE ASSOCIATIONS

A non-charitable association must comply with any provisions for dissolution in its governing document. If there are none, the organisation may be dissolved if all the members agree (**acquiescence**). Alternatively there may be **spontaneous dissolution** if the organisation has become inactive and it no longer has any assets, contracts or anything else that would indicate a continuing existence. Or the high court may, on application, wind up the organisation.

Notification should be given to members, employees, creditors (persons to whom money is owed), funders, and bodies such as HM Revenue and Customs.

If the association is insolvent, the members of the governing body or in some cases the ordinary members could be held liable for its debts [**24.10.5**].

24.8.1   Distribution of assets

If an unincorporated non-charitable organisation is solvent and has assets remaining after paying its debts, the distribution of the assets must comply with any provisions in the governing document.

Donations or legacies received for charitable purposes or the very few types of non-charitable purposes for which a trust can exist [**2.3.4**] are held on a **constructive trust** [**48.2.1**]. They must be used only for the purposes for which they were given, or be transferred to an organisation with relevant objects.

Other assets of non-charitable associations are held on contract for the members. In the absence of any provision in the governing document for their distribution, they are assumed to belong to the members at the time of dissolution, but not former members. Members are entitled to equal shares unless some classes of members have different constitutional rights [**12.2**]. The distribution is subject to income tax. Members dissatisfied with the distribution may apply to the high court.

Brown v Dale [1878] 9 ChD 78; Re St Andrew's Allotment Association [1969] 1 WLR 229; Abbatt v Treasury Solicitor [1969] 1 WLR 561,569; Re Sick & Funeral Society of St John's Sunday School, Golcar [1973] Ch 51

If an association has no members, its property is **bona vacantia** (belongs to the Crown). If it has only one surviving member and there is no constitutional provision for distribution of its assets, the property may be *bona vacantia* or belong to the member.

Re Brighton Cycling & Angling Club Trusts (1956) The Times 7 Mar 1956;
Hanchett-Stamford v HM Attorney-General & others [2008] EWHC 330 (Ch)

24.9 CHARITABLE TRUSTS AND ASSOCIATIONS

The process for dissolving a charitable trust or association depends on whether it is solvent or insolvent, whether its governing document contains a procedure for dissolution, and whether it holds any **permanent endowment**.

When any charity is dissolved or ceases to operate, the trustees must notify the Charity Commission. Failure to notify the Commission could lead to its making enquiries about what has happened to the charity and its assets, with the possibility of action against the former trustees if the assets have been wrongly applied. The charity's financial records must be kept for at least six years unless the Commission says they can be destroyed.

Charities Act 1993 s.3B(3), inserted by
Charities Act 2006 s.9; Charities Act 1993 s.41(4)

24.9.1 Unincorporated charities with permanent endowment

A charitable trust or association which has permanent endowment [**24.3.3**] generally cannot distribute that endowment, and thus cannot legally be dissolved. The Charity Commission must generally be consulted, and may suggest that the charity be amalgamated with another charity with the same or similar objects [**11.5.4**] or amend its objects to allow for the use of its assets [**5.7.2**].

There is an exception for some charitable trusts and associations which are not exempt charities [**8.1.2**]. If the charity's gross income in the last financial year was not more than £1,000, the market value of the permanent endowment is not more than £10,000, or (regardless of income or market value) the permanent endowment was given by more than one person or institution and for more than one common purpose, the trustees of an unincorporated charity may pass a resolution to spend the permanent endowment for the purposes for which it was originally given. Once the permanent endowment has been used for its stated purposes, the organisation can wind up in the usual way.

Charities Act 1993 ss.74-74B,
amended & inserted by ChA 2006 s.40

Trustees of other charities – with annual income over £1,000, permanent endowment with a market value over £10,000, and the permanent endowment donated by a single individual or institution, or by two or more individuals or institutions for a common purpose – may in some circumstances spend their endowment and wind up the charity. The decision to do so must be made by the trustees and must then be notified to and approved by the Charity Commission, which may require the trustees to publicise the resolution or provide additional information. Information about the procedure is available from the Commission.

Charities Act 1993 ss.75-75B, amended & inserted by Charities Act 2006 s.43

Comprehensive guidance is in CC44 *Small charities: Transfer of property, alteration of trusts, expenditure of capital*, available from the Commission [see end of chapter].

24.9.2 Dissolution procedure

If a charitable association or trust does not have permanent endowment and its governing document contains a dissolution procedure, the charity must follow this. Any assets must be distributed as specified, and the trustees must notify the Charity Commission and provide the required information. The Commission has a 'fast track' procedure for charities with annual income under £20,000.

24.9.3 No dissolution procedure

If a charitable association of trust does not have permanent endowment and the governing document does not include provision for dissolution, it may be able to use the procedure below if its annual income less than £10,000. If the procedure is not applicable it may be able to amend the governing document to include a dissolution procedure [**7.5.1**], or must contact the Charity Commission. There is a 'fast track' procedure for charities between £10,000 and £20,000.

24.9.3.1   Small charities

Where an unincorporated charity does not have permanent endowment, and there is no dissolution procedure, the trustees may pass a resolution by a two-thirds majority to transfer the assets to one or more charities which have substantially similar purposes. To do this:

- the charity's gross income in the last financial year must be less than £10,000;
- it must not hold **designated land** (land held on condition that it can be used only for the purposes or any particular purposes of the charity); and
- the trustees must be satisfied that it is expedient in furthering the interests in which they hold the property to make the transfer.

The trustees must send a copy of the resolution to the Commission with a statement of their reasons for having passed it. The Commission may require the trustees to give public notice of the resolution, to take account of any representations by interested parties made within 28 days of the public notice, and/or to provide additional information or explanation.

The resolution takes effect after 60 days, or a longer period if the Commission requires public notice or information or if it objects to the resolution on procedural grounds.   *Charities Act 1993 ss.74-74A, amended & inserted by Charities Act 2006 s.40*

Transfers can also be made where a charity has permanent endowment but there are stricter rules, for example that the purposes of the transferee charity must be substantially similar to all the purposes of the transferor charity.

Charities Act 1993 s.74B, inserted by Charities Act 2006 s.40

24.10   PAYMENT OF DEBTS

Strict rules govern the use of a company's or industrial and provident society's funds after a decision has been made to wind up the organisation, or after it has become clear that such a decision will have to be made. These rules are designed to protect creditors, and apply even if the company or IPS is solvent. The same rules are expected to apply to charitable incorporated organisations when the structure becomes available (expected April 2010).

The rules do not apply to unincorporated organisations, but if the organisation is insolvent the members of the governing body will generally be advised to follow similar rules.

24.10.1   Solvent companies, CIOs and IPSs

A solvent company or industrial and provident society that is being wound up under a members' voluntary liquidation [**24.4.3**] is not allowed to operate or make any expenditure after the liquidation meeting, even if it is solvent, unless this is authorised by the liquidator. The liquidator will oversee the disposition of the organisation's assets and the fulfilment of its financial obligations, and must approve all expenditure.

These restrictions do not apply to other forms of solvent winding up in a company or IPS, and at the time of writing (mid 2009) were not expected to apply to solvent charitable incorporated organisations.

24.10.2   Solvent trusts and associations

If an unincorporated association or trust is solvent, the governing body may decide how and when to pay off its bills and fulfil its other financial obligations during the winding up. If any money or property remains after all the organisation's liabilities have been met, it may be used or distributed only as specified in the organisation's governing document [**24.8.1**, **24.9**].

24.10.3   Hidden liabilities

Before dissolving an organisation, careful thought should be given to whether there are any potential claims against it. If its assets are completely used or are transferred to another organisation and a claim later emerges, the members of the governing body of the original organisation will have no funds to meet the claim. If assets are transferred, it is sensible for the transferring organisation to require an indemnity for any future claim. This should be done as a deed [**20.3**].

24.10.4   Priority of payment

When an insolvent company or industrial and provident society is wound up, its financial affairs must be settled in a statutory **order of payment** as defined in the insolvency legislation. The process is supervised by the liquidator, and no payment can be made to anyone without his or her approval. At the time of writing (mid 2009), similar rules were expected to apply to insolvent charitable incorporated organisations.

The liquidator will gather details of all creditors, then calculate what proportion of those debts can be paid. Very often the liquidator will only have funds available to pay a small percentage of each debt, known as a **dividend**.

If the company, CIO or IPS does anything with the intention of putting one or more creditors in a better position at insolvency, this **preference** can be set aside by the court if it took place while the organisation was unable to pay its debts, or in the six months before insolvency, or in the two years before insolvency if the preference was to a connected person [**15.2.5**]. Before the **Enterprise Act 2002** this was known as **fraudulent preference**, but is now simply called **preference** and can be challenged by an administrator or liquidator making an application to the court. *Insolvency Act 1986 ss.239,240*

The order of entitlement is:

- permanent endowment [**24.3.3**];
- assets subject to fixed charges [**24.10.4.1**];
- the expenses of winding up [**24.10.4.2**];
- preferential debts [**24.10.4.3**];
- assets subject to floating charges, after deduction of the prescribed part, if applicable [**24.10.4.4**], and subject to payment of the expenses of winding up;
- unsecured creditors [**24.10.4.4**];
- the members (shareholders) in a company limited by shares or an IPS, who usually receive nothing in relation to their shareholdings.

24.10.4.1   Secured creditors with fixed charge

The organisation's obligations must first be met to **secured creditors** with a fixed charge, such as a debenture or mortgage, on specific property [**59.5**].

A **secured creditor** with a fixed charge recovers their debt outside of the liquidation process, by taking possession of the property subject to the charge, selling it and recovering the money owed from the proceeds of sale. If after the sale of that security there is any surplus left, the secured creditor pays that to the liquidator. If the sale of the security is not enough to cover the full amount owed to the creditor, they claim the remainder as an unsecured creditor [**24.10.4.4**].

24.10.4.2   Winding up costs

The costs and expenses of the winding up, including remuneration of the liquidator, get first priority from those assets which are not subject to a fixed charge [**59.5**]. The costs and expenses are payable as of right out of floating charge assets [**59.5.2**] in certain circumstances. *Insolvency Act 1986 ss.115,175(2); s.176ZA, inserted by Companies Act 2006 s.1282*

24.10.4.3   Preferential debts

The categories of preferential debts rank equally and must all be paid in full before any other debts can be paid. If they cannot all be paid in full, they are paid in equal proportions. *Insolvency Act 1986 s.175, sch.6, amended by Enterprise Act 2002 s.251*

Preferential debts are:

- remuneration of employees for the preceding four months, to a maximum of £800 (as at 1/8/09);
- full holiday pay due to employees;
- payments due as contributions to occupational pension schemes and state scheme premiums;
- money owed that has been lent to the company to enable it to pay its employees during the preceding four months.

Payments to employees are subject to national minimum wage [**30.2**] even if the employer is insolvent. The preferential debt payment to an employee may not on its own be enough to meet the minimum wage obligation, but with the payment from the national insurance fund [**24.10.6.1**] should be enough.

24.10.4.4 Secured creditors with floating charge

Next to be paid are holders of a **floating charge** [**59.5.2**] over some or all of the organisation's assets. A floating charge is not linked to a specific asset.

A **prescribed part** is ringfenced for payment to unsecured creditors before any distribution is made to holders of floating charges created after 15 September 2003. *Insolvency Act 1986 s.176A, inserted by Enterprise Act 2002 s.252*

24.10.4.5 Unsecured creditors and shareholders

After payment of the winding up costs, secured creditors and preferential debts, any remaining funds and the **prescribed part** [**24.10.4.4**] are divided by the liquidator among the unsecured creditors:

- tax, national insurance contributions and VAT due to HM Revenue and Customs;
- trade creditors or suppliers;
- non-domestic rates;
- the unsecured portion of fixed charge debts;
- salary and other pay due to employees above the amount classed as a preferential debt [**24.10.4.3**], plus redundancy and pay in lieu of notice claims which always rank as unsecured;
- everything else the organisation owes.

If anything remains, it must be distributed according to the dissolution clause in the governing document. If there is no such provision in a non-charitable organisation, any remaining assets are normally distributed to the members [**24.8.1**].

24.10.5 Insolvent trusts and associations

Unincorporated organisations are not covered by the order of preference rules [**24.10.4**], because the members of the governing body are liable for the full amount of the organisation's debts. However, unincorporated organisations are likely to be advised to pay their debts in this order, and if claims are brought against individual members of the governing body or others held liable for the organisation's debts, the claims should be paid in this order.

24.10.6 Payments to employees

In looking at the rights of employees in an insolvency, a distinction must be drawn between:

- what the employee is entitled to under **statute**;
- what the employee is entitled to under his or her **contract of employment**;
- how much of the entitlements can be claimed from the **national insurance fund**, which the employee may therefore be able to rely on getting;
- if the employer is a company, charitable incorporated organisation or industrial and provident society, how much of the employee's entitlement becomes a **preferential debt** [**24.10.4.3**] and therefore ranks above most other debts when the organisation's assets are being liquidated;

- how much of the employee's entitlement is an **unsecured debt** [**24.10.4.4**].

If the employer is a company, CIO or IPS, the employee will receive the full amount of preferential debt only if the organisation has sufficient assets, and is very unlikely to receive the full amount of unsecured debt.

If the employer is an unincorporated association or trust, the employee will receive anything beyond what can be claimed from the national insurance fund only if the organisation has sufficient assets, or if the employee sues one or more members of the governing body.

If an employer fails to consult over redundancies and the tribunal makes a **protective award** [**35.2.2**], this cannot be recovered from the assets if the award is made after the liquidation.

Day v Haine [2007] EWHC 2691 (Ch)

24.10.6.1 Claiming from the national insurance fund

The **national insurance fund** is run by the Insolvency Service Redundancy Payments Office (part of the Department for Business, Innovation and Skills) and is intended to ensure that employees get at least some of what they are entitled to if their employer is insolvent. However, it only covers situations where the employer is a company or a limited liability partnership [**3.6**], and not (at the time of writing), other types of incorporated body such as industrial and provident societies or charitable incorporated organisations. It also covers situations where the employer is an individual, but not where it is an unincorporated association or trust.

Employment Rights Act 1996 ss.166-170,182-190

The RPO pays claims relating to wages/salary, holiday pay, unpaid pension contributions and notice pay, as set out below. In addition, HM Revenue and Customs pays claims for statutory maternity, paternity, adoption and sick pay.

When an eligible employer becomes insolvent, the liquidator or (if there is no liquidator) the employee claims from the RPO, which then recovers as much as it can of the amount it has paid from the assets of the organisation.

Occasionally the RPO makes a payment to employees of an insolvent unincorporated organisation, and then seeks to recover the amount from the organisation or the individual members of the governing body. But there is no statutory entitlement for employees of unincorporated bodies to be paid by the RPO.

24.10.6.2 Pay

Where an employer becomes insolvent its employees are entitled to full pay until notice of redundancy is given or up to the date the employer became insolvent. Pay for the four months until the date of insolvency, to a maximum of £800 (as at 1/8/09), is a preferential debt. The remainder is an unsecured debt. For employees of eligible employers, up to a maximum of eight weeks, subject to a maximum of £380 per week (as at 1/10/09), can be claimed from the NI fund.

24.10.6.3 Holiday pay

Employees are entitled to holiday pay accrued to the date of insolvency, with the daily rate worked out as 1/7th of weekly pay or 1/365th of annual pay. The full entitlement is a preferential debt. For employees of eligible employers, holiday pay accrued in the 12 months to the date of insolvency up to a maximum of six weeks, subject to a maximum £380 p.w. (as at 1/10/09), can be claimed from the NI fund.

24.10.6.4 Pension contributions

Employees are entitled to contractual pension contribution entitlement accrued to the date of insolvency. Some contributions owing by the employer to an occupational pension scheme (not a personal pension scheme) are preferential; the remainder are unsecured.

For employees of eligible employers, contributions which have been deducted from the pay of the employee during the 12 months ending on the day before the employer became insolvent but which have not been paid into the pension scheme, can be claimed from the NI fund. So also can whichever is the lesser of:

- the balance of the employer's contributions relating to the 12 months ending on the day before the employer became insolvent; or
- the amount certified by an actuary as necessary for the scheme to meet its liability on dissolution for payment of benefits to the employees;
- an amount equal to 10% of the total pay of the employee concerned for the 12 months ending on the day before the employer became insolvent.

24.10.6.5   Pay during notice period

Employees are entitled to pay during the statutory or contractual period of notice [**34.3**], whichever is longer, or pay in lieu of notice. This is an unsecured debt.

For employees of eligible employers, one week's pay after one calendar month of service, rising to one week's pay per year of service up to a maximum of 12 weeks, can be claimed from the NI fund. This is subject to a maximum of £380 per week (as at 1/10/09).

Entitlement to pay in lieu of notice is subject to the employee's duty to mitigate the loss [**37.5.1**], and any payment from the NI fund will generally be based on the assumption that the employee has at least claimed jobseeker's allowance.

24.10.6.6   Redundancy pay

For employees of eligible employers, the full statutory redundancy payment [**35.7.1**] is an unsecured debt but can be claimed from the NI fund. Contractual redundancy pay is an unsecured debt and cannot be claimed from the NI fund.

24.10.6.7   Other

Anything else owed to an employee is an unsecured debt. Any basic award made for unfair dismissal [**37.4.2**], and a reasonable repayment of any fee or premium paid by an apprentice or articled clerk can be claimed from the NI fund.

Resources: FINANCIAL DIFFICULTIES AND WINDING UP

Your organisation's accountant, auditor and/or solicitor.

Charities. Charity Commission: www.charity-commission.gov.uk 0845 300 0218, email via website.

Companies. Companies House: www.companieshouse.gov.uk, 0303 1234 500, enquiries@companieshouse.gov.uk.

Industrial and provident societies. Financial Services Authority Mutual Societies Registration: www.fsa.gov.uk (at the time of writing, access is via Doing business with the FSA / Small firms / Mutual societies), 020 7066 8002, mutual.societies@fsa.gov.uk.

Insolvency. Insolvency Service: www.insolvency.gov.uk, 0845 602 9848, email via website.

Redundancy. ACAS, BIS, Business Link, CIPD, Directgov, PEACe, TUC: see end of **chapter 25**.

Redundancy Payments Office: www.insolvency.gov.uk, 0845 145 0004.

Redundancy and insolvency: A guide for employees. From the Insolvency Service [above].

Your rights if your employer is insolvent. www.direct.gov.uk.

Statute law. www.opsi.gov.uk and www.statutelaw.gov.uk.

Much but not all case law. www.bailii.org.

Updates cross-referenced to this book. www.rclh.co.uk.

Any organisation depends on people to carry out its work. Part III is about how the law governs an organisation's relationships with those people: its employees, volunteers, other staff and independent contractors.

Chapter 25

EMPLOYEES AND OTHER WORKERS

For sources of further information see end of chapter.

25.1   EMPLOYEES AND OTHERS

When an individual carries out work for an organisation, the legal relationship between them depends on whether there is:

- a **contract of employment** (also called a **contract of service**), creating a relationship of **employment** [**25.1.1**];

- a **contract for services**, creating a **self employment** relationship [**25.1.3**];

- another type of contract, perhaps creating a **worker** relationship [**25.1.2**]; or

- no contract, as for example in the case of most (but not all) volunteers [**39.4**].

'**Contract**' in this context does not depend on whether there is a document called a contract, or even whether there is a document. The existence of a contract depends not on paperwork but on the nature of the relationship between the individual and the organisation, and in particular on whether the individual receives money or something else of value in return for doing the work [**21.1.1**].

Organisations need to be absolutely clear which category each relationship falls into. Where the individual receives or is going to receive *any* payment (other than a volunteer receiving only reimbursement of genuine out of pocket expenditure), there should be an appropriate written contract setting out the details of the relationship. This applies not only to long-term staff, but also to temporary or casual workers. **Chapter 27** contains a model contract for employees, and **38.4.2** outlines points to be included in a contract with a self employed person.

In many cases a written contract should also be provided where a person does not receive pay but receives something else of value, such as accommodation, in return for work.

The nature of the relationship determines how employment and employment related legislation affect the parties. This includes:

- **employment legislation** which sets out the statutory rights available only to employees, such as redundancy pay, maternity and paternity pay, a minimum period of notice and the right not to be unfairly dismissed;

- other employment legislation, which sets out rights such as minimum wage and working time rights which are available not only to employees but also to a wider category of workers;

- **employment related legislation** such as health and safety [**40.2**] and equal opportunities [**chapter 28**], which in each case sets out who is covered by the legislation;

- **tax and national insurance rules**, which define the 'employees' for whom the employer must operate PAYE [**30.4**]. The definition of employee for tax purposes is much wider than the definition of employee for the purposes of employment rights.

If the nature of the relationship is not clear, the organisation and individual can agree what they would like the legal relationship between them to be. However, neither this agreement nor the way the parties operate is decisive. Only a court or tribunal, after considering all the circumstances, can determine the legal nature of the relationship.

Information about employment status and employment rights is available from the Department for Business, Innovation and Skills, Business Link, ACAS, the Trades Union Congress and the Chartered Institute of Personnel and Development, and specifically for voluntary organisations from PEACe at London Voluntary Service Council [see end of chapter].

25.1.1   Employees

Employment law defines an **employee** as an individual who has entered into or works under a **contract of employment**, and defines a contract of employment as a **contract of service or apprenticeship.**   *Employment Rights Act 1996 s 230*

Individuals working under a contract of employment have employment and employment related rights. Contracts of employment are explained in **chapter 26**, and **chapter 27** contains an annotated model contract.

The employer must operate PAYE if the employee's earnings are above the thresholds for tax and national insurance [**30.4.4, 30.4.6**].

25.1.2   Workers

In legal terms a **worker** is defined as an individual who works under a contract of employment [**26.1**], or works under any other contract where he or she has to perform work or services personally for the other party to the contract, except where the individual is carrying out a business or profession and the other party is a customer or client of that business.   *Employment Rights Act 1996 s.230(3)*

The contract may be written, oral, or implied from the circumstances.

Workers' rights thus apply not only to employees but also to casual workers [**25.3.2**], freelance workers who do not run their own business as a self employed person, and in some cases volunteers who are paid or receive something else of value [**39.4.1**]. Agency workers [**25.5.2**] are entitled to some workers' rights.

A person who can sub-contract the work or employ someone else to do it (and thus does not have to perform it personally), and/or is genuinely self employed [**38.1.1**] and doing the work for a customer or client, is generally not a worker.

25.1.2.1   Rights of workers

Workers' rights include **minimum wage** [**30.2**], **working time rights** [**31.1**], **part-time workers' rights** [**26.4.2**], and the **right to be accompanied** at disciplinary and grievance hearings [**33.1.1**]. All **equal opportunities** rights apply not only to workers as defined above, but also to self employed people [**28.1.2**].

25.1.2.2   Minimum wage

For the purposes of **national minimum wage** [**30.2**], the definition of worker also includes **home workers**, even though they may not be obliged to perform the work personally; **agency workers**, even though the contract is normally between the worker and the agency rather than between the worker and the body for whom the work is done [**25.5.2**]; and **voluntary workers** if they receive anything other than allowed reimbursement, subsistence, training and accommodation [**39.4.3**]. *National Minimum Wage Act 1998 ss.34,35,44*

25.1.3 Contractors and self employed workers

A **contractor** is taken on to provide a service, and has a **contract for services**. A contractor may be:

- an individual undertaking work through their own business on a **self employed** basis [**38.1**];
- an individual who is not doing the work through their business but is not an employee for the purposes of the work – for example, a person providing carpentry or training, but not running a business as a carpenter or trainer;
- two or more persons undertaking work jointly as a formal or informal **partnership** or an **unincorporated association** [**2.1**]; or
- a **corporate body** (company, industrial and provident society, charitable incorporated organisation or limited liability partnership).

Some of the differences between employees or workers and contractors are:

- an employee or worker must provide his or her services personally, but a contractor – unless the contract specifies otherwise – can sub-contract the work or employ someone to do the work;
- contractors have a business relationship with their client;
- contractors generally have control of the manner in which they work;
- contractors generally provide the equipment or facilities necessary to carry out their work;
- contractors generally carry the risk of work not being done on time, and have to bear the cost of putting right inadequate work;
- contractors do not have employment rights or the rights of workers, except for equal opportunities rights;
- an employer must insure against claims by its employees who become ill or injured as a result of the employer's negligence or breach of a statutory duty [**23.4.1**], but does not have to insure against claims by its contractors;
- an employer usually has **vicarious liability** for its employees' acts within employment [**22.6.4**], but is not generally liable for the acts of contractors;
- an employer generally owes a higher duty of care to its employees than to its contractors [**40.2.1**];
- an employer must operate PAYE and pay employer's national insurance for employees and workers, but contractors are generally responsible for dealing with their own tax and NI [**30.4**].

25.1.3.1 Employment and self employment

Tax law and employment law define employment and self employment differently, so a person could be an employee for tax purposes but not for the purposes of employment rights, or *vice versa*. These criteria are explained in **chapter 38**.

The organisation should be satisfied that anyone hired on a self employed, freelance or consultancy basis meets the criteria for being genuinely self employed, for the purposes of both tax and employment law, in relation to the particular piece of work. Serious difficulties can arise for both the individual and the employer if a person who is legally an employee is treated as self employed.

25.2 PART-TIME WORKERS

Part-time employees or workers are those defined *by the employer* (not by statute) as working less than full time. Full-time workers are those who are paid wholly or in part by reference to the time they work, and are considered by the employer to work full-time. Part-time workers are those who are paid wholly or in part by reference to the time they work, and are *not* identified by the employer as full-time.

Part-time Workers (Prevention of Less Favourable Treatment) Regulations 2000 [SI 2000/1551] reg.2

Unless they are genuinely self employed [**38.2.2**] part-timers are employees or workers for the purposes of employment and equal opportunities legislation, and have the same statutory rights as full-time staff (*pro rata* if applicable). They are also generally entitled to the same contractual rights, *pro rata*, as comparable full-time staff working for the same employer [**26.4.2**].

The earnings of part-time employees and workers are subject to tax and national insurance under PAYE in the same way as full-time employees [**30.4.1**].

25.2.1 Job sharers

The term **job sharer** has no meaning in law. In legal terms **job sharers** who divide the work between them are part-time employees [above].

25.2.2 Sessional workers

The term **sessional worker** has no meaning in law and is usually used to refer to a person who works 'sessions' on a regular basis or when needed. Depending on the circumstances a sessional worker may be a part-time employee [**25.2**], a casual worker [**25.3.2**], employed by someone else [**25.5.4**] or supplied by an employment agency [**25.5.2**], or meet the tests for genuine self employment [**38.2.2**].

25.2.3 Zero hours contracts

With a **zero hours contract** there are no fixed hours, but the employer agrees to offer work to the person and the person has to do it if it is offered unless there is a genuine reason to refuse, such as being ill or on holiday leave. Even if no work is given to the person, there is a continuing employment relationship and the person has the same employment rights as any other employee. This is different from casual workers [**25.3.2**].

Where rights such as sickness or maternity pay are dependent on how much an employee earns, the legislation provides for earnings to be averaged over a specified number of weeks to determine eligibility.

Legal advice should be taken before offering a zero hours contract.

25.3 NON-PERMANENT WORKERS

25.3.1 Fixed-term and temporary employees

Fixed-term employees are contracted to work for a fixed period, or to complete a specified task, or until a specified event does or does not occur, such as a person returning from maternity leave or funding not being obtained. The employee is treated as dismissed at the end of the period, when the event occurs or on completion of the task. 'Fixed-term' also applies to **temporary employees**, who are employed on a basis which is not intended to be permanent, but do not have a fixed ending date.

The employer must inform fixed-term employees that their employment is not intended to be permanent. Unless it is made explicit that a contract of employment is temporary, fixed-term, or for completion of a specific task, it is assumed to be open-ended or continuing.

Unless they are genuinely self employed [**38.2.2**] or are supplied by an employment agency [**25.5.2**], fixed-term employees have the same statutory employment rights, including dismissal and redundancy rights, as permanent employees [**26.4.3**]. In terms of contractual entitlements, fixed-term employees have the right not to be treated less favourably than comparable permanent employees of the same employer doing similar work, unless the less favourable treatment is objectively justified [**26.4.3**].

Where a person has four years' continuous employment after one or more renewals of a fixed-term contract, the contract automatically becomes permanent unless the employer can show an objective reason for keeping it on a fixed-`term basis. *Fixed-term Employees (Prevention of Less Favourable Treatment) Regulations 2002 [SI 2002/2034] reg.8.*

25.3.2 Casual workers

A **casual worker** is employed on one or more occasions, with no obligation on the employer to offer work or on the worker to accept it, or for the employer to provide any work. If work is offered and accepted there is a contract, but only to provide work for the specified day, session or period. There is no ongoing **mutuality of obligation** – and therefore no contract of employment [**26.2.3**].

Casuals have the rights of workers [**26.4.1**] – including part-time rights if working less than full time – but do not have the full range of employment rights.

25.3.2.1 Casual or employee?

Much case law concerns casuals who have sought to show that they are employees and therefore entitled to claim unfair dismissal or other rights of employees. Case decisions are inconsistent on whether and when a series of apparently casual contracts becomes an ongoing contract of employment, and legal advice should be sought before hiring anyone on a series of casual contracts.

Even very part-time work, if it is regular, can create an ongoing contract of employment. For example a person who was contracted to work 5.5 hours on alternate Fridays was held to be an employee, because there was an ongoing obligation on both the employer and employee. *Colley v Corkindale [1995] ICR 965 EAT*

In another case a tutor carried out work for a local authority. The local authority was not under any obligation to offer pupils, and there was no obligation on the tutor to accept, but the tutor worked for 10 years apart from periods totalling 14 months when there were no pupils. The courts decided that there was sufficient mutuality of obligation to create a contract of employment, within which the periods of non-work were a 'temporary cessation of work'. *Cornwall County Council v Prater [2006] EWCA Civ 102*

In a case where a television network was obliged to offer a reporter at least 100 days' work per year and the reporter could accept or refuse the work, the employment appeal tribunal said that mutuality could be implied into the agreement because the reporter had an implied obligation to accept or refuse the work 'in good faith'. *ABC News Intercontinental Inc v Gizbert [2006] UKEAT 0160 06 2108*

25.3.2.2 Keeping casual workers casual

Organisations which do not want casual workers to be legally employees should make clear in a written contract that work will be offered on an 'as required' basis, that there is no obligation on the part of the organisation to offer any work, and that the worker is free to refuse any offer of work. It is essential to keep meticulous records for casuals, and to monitor for 'drift' into part-time employment.

25.3.2.3 Tax status of casuals

A casual is treated as an employee for the purposes of tax and national insurance, and they must be put through the PAYE system [**30.4**].

25.3.2.4 'Cash in hand' pay for casuals

Cash in hand is where a person is paid without deduction of tax or national insurance, and sometimes without even entering the payment in the accounts. This is very poor practice and is likely to be unlawful. The organisation will be in breach of its obligation to operate PAYE [**30.4**], and if it does not enter the payment in its accounts, it will be in breach of its duty to maintain proper financial records [**53.1.1**]. If the person is on state benefits and is not declaring the income, the organisation may be colluding with benefit fraud. If the person is from abroad and is not entitled to work in the UK, the organisation can face a penalty for employing a person illegally and the individual can jeopardise their right to remain in the UK [**29.5**].

25.3.3 Bank or pool staff

Bank staff who are on an organisation's books and are offered work if it is available may be employees on a zero hours contract [**25.2.3**] or casual workers who are not employees [**25.3.2.1**], or may be employees if they are regularly offered work and accept it. The key issue is whether there is mutuality of obligation, with the organisation obliged to offer work and the worker obliged to accept it.

25.4 EMPLOYEES ON JOINT CONTRACTS

Joint employment by two organisations – for example a charity and its trading company – can avoid the restrictions on employment businesses [**25.5.3**] and the VAT charge which might arise where one organisation provides an employee to another and charges for his or her work [**57.13.1**]. However, difficult issues can arise concerning:

- which employer controls allocation of time;
- what happens if one employer is dissatisfied with the employee's work;
- how liability for salary, sick pay, maternity pay etc is calculated;
- whether dismissal by one employer results in dismissal by the other (and the implications for a potential unfair dismissal claim, if there is no fair reason for dismissal by the second employer);
- what happens if one employer becomes insolvent, in particular whether the other employer is liable for the failed employer's obligations to the employee.

Careful drafting of both contracts is necessary to avoid these problems.

25.5 WORKERS SUPPLIED BY SOMEONE ELSE

It is not uncommon for a voluntary organisation to use workers provided by agencies or other organisations. The workers may be supplied by:

- an **employment agency** [**25.5.2**] which provides a **recruitment service**, being paid a fee to match employers and potential employees, with the worker becoming employed by the employer;
- an employment agency which supplies staff on a **temporary** basis and pays the workers;
- an **employment business** [**25.5.3**] which itself is an employer, employing people and supplying them to another person to be used in their business or organisation;
- an employer which continues to pay the worker's salary but 'lends' the worker to another organisation, as a **secondee** [**25.5.4**].

25.5.1 Obligations of employment agencies and businesses

Statutory rules for employment agencies and businesses include:

- employment agencies and businesses must provide certain information to the hirer (**end user**) before providing services, including whether they are acting in the capacity of an employment agency or employment business, details of the fees payable and, in the case of an employment business, details of the procedure to be followed if a worker introduced or supplied to the organisation proves to be unsatisfactory;
- agencies placing actors, models and extras cannot charge upfront fees before they find them work;
- employment businesses cannot withhold workers' pay simply because they cannot produce an authenticated timesheet;
- agencies must obtain information on any health and safety risks known to the employer, and the steps taken to prevent or control those risks;
- there are limits on the time during which a 'temp to perm' fee can be charged when a worker placed as a temp takes up permanent employment with that employer. *Conduct of Employment Agencies & Employment Business Regulations 2003 [2003/3319]*

Details of these and other statutory requirements are available from the Department for Business, Innovation and Skills [see end of chapter].

Contractual issues can arise with agencies supplying or introducing staff, and professional advice should be considered.

25.5.2 Employment status of agency workers

The legal provisions which regulate employment agencies and employment businesses do not govern whether an individual provided by an employment agency on a temporary basis (an **agency worker**, more often referred to as an **agency temp**) is employed, and if so by whom. This is determined by case law.

Generally an employment agency which supplies an agency worker has a contract with the organisation which will use the worker (the **end user**), and with the worker. In some circumstances the contract between the agency and worker could be a contract of employment, but generally is not because the agency does not normally have the control necessary in an employment relationship and there is a lack of mutuality of obligation. There is generally no contract between the end user and the worker.

This was confirmed by a court of appeal decision in February 2008, which made clear that a contract between the end user and worker should be implied only in exceptional circumstances, where the relationships were not adequately covered in the contract between the agency and end user and between the agency and worker. The court said that the mere fact that the person has been an agency worker with the end user for an extended period does not create a contract between the worker and end user. *James v London Borough of Greenwich [2008] EWCA Civ 35*

Agency workers have the statutory rights of workers [**26.4.1**]. When the EU **directive on temporary agency work** is implemented (by 5 December 2011) they will after 12 weeks with the same end user be entitled to some of the same contractual rights as if they had been directly hired by the employer [**26.4.4**].

25.5.3 Employment businesses

Where a body which is not an employment agency provides a worker, it is an **employment business** if the receiving organisation pays the providing organisation, and the providing organisation then pays the worker. The worker has a contract of employment with the providing organisation, but there could also be a contract of employment with the receiving organisation if it exercises control over the worker and there is mutuality of obligation.

An employment business is different from **secondment** [below], where the receiving organisation does not pay the providing organisation. It is also different from an arrangement where an organisation is clearly the employer and simply arranges for another body to operate PAYE on its behalf.

Where staff are supplied, the providing organisation is carrying out a service which is subject to VAT, and may have to register for VAT and charge VAT to the receiving organisation [**57.13.1**].

25.5.4 Secondees

A **secondee** is an employee who is lent to another organisation while the first employer continues to pay his or her salary. The providing organisation is generally – but not always – considered to be the employer. Legal advice should be taken to ensure that the rights and obligations of all parties are clear, especially in relation to VAT [**57.13.1**], intellectual property rights [**chapter 44**], supervision and control, discipline, and terminating the arrangement. These arrangements should be set out in a written agreement, and should be regularly monitored to ensure they remain appropriate.

If a secondee causes loss or injury, the organisation or employer which has control over the actions of the secondee is generally held to be vicariously liable [**22.6.4**]. This organisation should ensure its insurances cover the secondee and his or her actions [**23.4**, **23.5**].

25.6 POSSIBLY WORKERS OR EMPLOYEES

People working for an organisation may or may not be working under a contract, and that contract may or may not be a contract of employment. It may be difficult to determine which rights do and do not apply in some situations, and specialist advice may be needed.

Employer's liability insurance [**23.4.1**] is unlikely to cover non-employees, so the organisation should ensure it is protected for claims by non-employees arising from its negligence.

A person who is not an employee or worker for the purposes of employment and employment related legislation may still be considered an employee for the purposes of tax and national insurance, in which case the employer will have to operate PAYE [**30.4**]. Conversely, a person could be an employee for the purposes of employment law, but not for PAYE.

25.6.1   Apprentices and trainees

The terms **trainee** and **apprentice** are used in many ways and advice will often be needed to determine eligibility for employment rights in any particular situation.

Trainees who carry out work for the employer as part of their traineeship are generally entitled to employment rights, while students and others on **work placement** are generally not employees and are entitled only to limited rights [**26.4.7**]. A trainee who takes on additional tasks for the employer, perhaps for additional payment, may be both a trainee and employee. Someone called an **intern** may be a volunteer, trainee, student on work placement or employee, depending on the specific arrangements.

Traditionally, a **contract of apprenticeship** is between an apprentice who agrees to 'serve his master' and the employer who agrees to teach the apprentice. The contract is for a fixed period or until specified qualifications are achieved. Traditionally contracts of apprenticeship did not create an employment relationship, but the **Employment Rights Act 1996** defined them as contracts of employment, entitling the apprentice to most statutory employment rights [**26.4.7**].

Employment Rights Act 1996 s.230(2)

So-called **modern apprenticeships** – government-sponsored **apprenticeships** and **advanced apprenticeships** – and **national traineeships** are generally three-way relationships, where an employer provides work experience and a college or other training provider provides the training element under an individual learning plan. Apprenticeships under these programmes generally involve a contract of employment between the employer and apprentice, and the apprentice is entitled to most employment rights [**26.4.7**]. In 2009 a **National Apprenticeship Service** was set up to promote apprenticeships.

25.6.2   Volunteers

For tax and national insurance purposes, volunteers who are paid anything more than reimbursement of genuine expenses are treated as employees [**39.3**]. This applies even if the payment is called an honorarium, sessional fee, pocket money or even 'expenses' (if it is not genuine reimbursement).

For employment law purposes, volunteers who receive no reward or payment other than genuine reimbursement are normally not employees or 'workers' because no contract is created between the individual and organisation. However, in some situations a contract could be created, entitling the so-called volunteer to employment or workers' rights [**39.4**].

25.6.3   Office holders

Office holders are distinguished from employees because their rights and duties are defined by the office they hold, rather than by a contract of employment. Examples include company directors and company secretaries [**14.1.1**, **14.3**], whose duties are defined by company law and the company's articles of association, trade union officials, police constables, judges and justices of the peace.

A person may be both an office holder and an employee. A company director, for example, may be paid under a contract of employment with the company [**18.5.7**]. In this situation one role can be terminated without losing the other.

25.6.4   Clergy

In the past, **ministers of religion** (which include clergy of all denominations, even if not called ministers) were treated by the courts as appointed to a holy office, rather than being employed by the church or religious body. The courts now hold that if the relationship between church and minister has the characteristics of a contract of employment in terms of rights and obligations, these cannot be ignored simply because the duties are of a religious or pastoral nature. The courts have found that a minister was a 'worker' for the purposes of the sex discrimination legislation, and another was entitled to claim unfair dismissal. The same principles would be likely to be applied to claims for other equal opportunities or employment rights.   *Percy v Church of Scotland Board of National Mission [2005] UKHL 73;*
New Testament Church of God v Rev Stewart [2007] EWCA Civ 1004

In due course statutory employment rights may be extended to ministers of religion, although the court of appeal said in the unfair dismissal case above that it would be wrong to impose a contract of employment on a church whose religious dogma is opposed to a contractual relationship with its minister.

25.6.5   Overseas workers and workers from abroad

Issues around the employment status and rights of British workers who work overseas, or in some cases workers from abroad who work in the UK, are complex [**26.11**], and specialist legal advice should be sought.

Resources: EMPLOYMENT RIGHTS

ACAS: www.acas.org.uk, 08457 47 47 47.

Business Link: www.businesslink.gov.uk.

Chartered Institute of Personnel and Development: www.cipd.co.uk, 020 8612 6200, email via website.

Department for Business, Innovation & Skills: www.bis.gov.uk, 020 7215 5000, email via website.

Directgov: www.direct.gov.uk.

National Apprenticeship Service: www.apprenticeships.org.uk, email via website.

PEACe (Personnel Employment Advice and Conciliation Service): www.lvsc.org.uk, 020 7700 8147, peace@lvsc.org.uk. Only serves voluntary organisations in London, but its website is available to anyone.

Trades Union Congress: www.tuc.org.uk, 0870 600 4 882, info@tuc.org.uk.

Statute law. www.opsi.gov.uk and www.statutelaw.gov.uk.

Much but not all case law. www.bailii.org.

Updates cross-referenced to this book. www.rclh.co.uk.

Chapter 26

RIGHTS, DUTIES AND THE CONTRACT OF EMPLOYMENT

For sources of further information see end of chapter 25.

26.1 THE CONTRACT OF EMPLOYMENT

Employing staff brings the organisation into one of the most complex and litigated areas of law. It also creates clear conflicts of interest, and governing body members or others who agree contracts or are responsible for managing staff must ensure they obtain independent advice. It is not appropriate to act solely on the basis of information and advice provided by staff or trade unions.

The environment within which contracts of employment operate is not static, and contracts should be reviewed at least every 18-24 months to ensure they reflect not only current law, but also current best practice.

Confusion often arises because 'contract of employment' has various meanings:

- the **contractual relationship** between the employer and employee, which exists as soon as an offer of employment is made and accepted, even if this is only oral;

- all the **terms and conditions** which govern that relationship, which may be **express** (explicit) or **implied** (assumed);

- the written **statement of employment particulars**, which by law must be given to all employees whose employment lasts a month or more; and
- the **written terms and conditions of employment**, which generally include everything required in the statement of employment particulars and replace the statement, and also include additional terms and conditions.

The statement of particulars or the terms and conditions are often called the contract, but the actual contract is wider than any document, and encompasses rights and duties which are not written but are implied by law [**26.3.3**].

Information about contracts of employment is available from the Department for Business, Innovation and Skills, Business Link, ACAS, CIPD, the Trades Union Congress and PEACe [see end of **chapter 25**]. Trade unions representing voluntary sector employees [see end of **chapter 36**] can also advise.

26.1.1 Other types of contract

Other types of agreement have different legal consequences from contracts of employment. These include contracts with people legally defined as **workers** who are not employees but have some employment rights, such as casual workers [**25.1.2**]; contracts with people who are self employed [**38.1**]; and arrangements with volunteers, which may or may not be contractual [**39.4.1**].

26.2 CREATING THE CONTRACT OF EMPLOYMENT

The relationship between the employer and employee exhibits the key elements necessary in law to make a contract [**21.1.1**]: clear **agreement** between the employer and employee, with pay or other **consideration** in return for work, and with the **intention** of being legally bound. It is a **contract of employment** rather than any other type of contract because it gives the employer 'control' of the employee's work, there is mutuality of obligation, and it requires the person to provide work personally rather than being able to sub-contract it [**25.1.2**].

26.2.1 Agreement

In all contracts, agreement is reached through a process of **offer and acceptance**. This may be done formally in writing or by an informal oral exchange, or may even be inferred from conduct. The contract comes into being as soon as there is an agreement, even if it is oral.

26.2.1.1 Offer and acceptance

When a potential employee applies for a job this is generally not the offer, more an enquiry about the possibility of an offer.

Following the selection process [**29.3**], the employer makes the offer. If the employer's offer is **unconditional**, the contract exists as soon as the future employee accepts it unconditionally.

The offer may be **conditional** on acceptance within a time limit, or upon one or more events such as passing a medical examination or receiving satisfactory references [**29.6**]. If the employer makes the conditions clear, no contract is created until the conditions are met or the employer allows the employee to start working. If the employer does not make clear that the offer is conditional, a contract is created as soon as the employee accepts. The employee may then be able to claim for damages if the employer seeks to renege on the contract, for example because of an unsatisfactory reference.

Even if employment is made conditional on completion of a satisfactory **probationary period**, the contract of employment exists from the point when the offer of work is first made and accepted. The implications of a probationary period will depend on what, if anything, the contract says [**27.1.6**, **29.4**].

The employee can accept the offer orally, in writing, or simply by turning up and starting work. If sent through the post, the employee's acceptance is treated as being made as soon as it is posted unless the employer states otherwise.

26.2.1.2 Withdrawal of offer

The employer may withdraw the offer if it is not accepted within a specified time limit or if the employer has a change of heart before the offer is accepted. A withdrawal becomes effective when it reaches the potential employee. Once the offer has been accepted, withdrawal by the employer constitutes breach of contract.

26.2.1.3 Counter offer

The employee may accept the offer only exactly as made. If the employee seeks to accept the offer but on a condition, for example that the paid holiday is longer than specified by the employer, this is a **counter offer** by the employee. It is then open to the employer to accept or refuse this counter offer.

It is important for the employer to respond if an employee attaches an unacceptable condition to the acceptance. If employment commences without clarification and there is later a dispute, the courts might rule that the employee's condition has been incorporated into the contract.

26.2.1.4 Redeployment

An important exception to the need for acceptance to be unconditional arises when an existing employee is being made redundant but is offered the chance to try a different job within the organisation [**35.6**]. The employee can in effect conditionally accept by taking the new job for a trial period before deciding whether to accept that job or opt for redundancy.

26.2.2 Intention to create a legal relationship of employment

For a contract to exist, both parties must **intend** the agreement between them to be legally binding [**21.1.1**]. There is a presumption that the relationship is intended to be legally binding and that a contract of employment exists if the worker is paid or remunerated in other ways for doing work, and thus receives **consideration** [**26.2.3**]; there is **mutuality of obligation**, with the employer obliged to provide work and the worker obliged to do it; the employee's work is controlled by the employer; and there is an obligation for the employee to provide work personally.

Although the relationship as a whole is a binding contract, either side may specify matters which they do not intend to form part of the contract. For example, an employer may say that when pressure of work allows, it is their practice to give sabbaticals to staff. It may need very careful analysis to ascertain whether an obligation binding on the employer has been created or whether the decision to grant a sabbatical is within the employer's discretion. Legal advice should always be taken when drawing up contracts of employment, to avoid creating contractual obligations that the employer does not want to create.

26.2.3 Consideration

Consideration is anything of material value. In a contract of employment both sides provide consideration – the employer generally in the form of a salary or wage, the employee by doing work. If consideration is not provided by both parties, there cannot be a contract.

Consideration does not need to be monetary. It may consist of meals, luncheon vouchers, accommodation, a car, training, membership of the organisation, preferential rates for the organisation's goods or services, or anything else of value.

26.2.4 Certainty

In order to create a contract, the agreed terms must be clear and certain [**21.1.1**]. If they are too vague there is no contract. However the court seeks to prevent contracts failing because of an uncertainty about the terms, by implying terms or otherwise filling the gap [**26.3.4**].

Many contracts contain terms which specify that a particular point is to be 'as agreed' between the employer and an employee. Such an agreement to agree creates no certainty and cannot itself be enforced. It should therefore be avoided.

26.2.5   Capacity to contract

A contract with a person under the age of 18 or who is mentally incapacitated may in some situations be voidable (can be invalidated) by that person [**21.1.2**].

26.3   CONTRACT TERMS

When a contract of employment comes into existence its terms may be **express**, **imposed** by statute, **implied**, or **incorporated** by reference to another document or source.

26.3.1   Express terms

Express terms are explicitly expressed, orally or in writing. They include the statement of employment particulars [**26.7**] and, if provided, a more comprehensive written contract, as well as terms agreed orally or in correspondence.

Under the **Unfair Contract Terms Act 1977**, some types of contractual term are unenforceable, or are enforceable only if they are reasonable. But this Act has been held not to apply to employment contracts, because an employee does not 'deal as a consumer'.   *Unfair Contract Terms Act 1977; Commerzbank AG v Keen [2006] EWCA Civ 1536*

26.3.2   Imposed terms

Many contract terms are **imposed** by statute, for example the right to minimum wage and minimum period of notice. Imposed terms can be excluded from the contract only in the rare situations where the legislation specifically allows this.
Employment Rights Act 1996 s.203

26.3.3   Mutual duties implied into the contract

Within every employer-employee relationship there are core duties on both parties which are **implied** into the contract. Some of these duties arise from statute, and others from common law. Breach of these duties may, if sufficiently serious, justify immediate termination of the contract [**34.2.9**, **34.2.10**].

26.3.3.1   Employers' duties

Employers have a duty:

- to pay wages, although in some cases the contract only gives the employee the *opportunity* to earn wages [**25.2.3**];
- to provide work, or perhaps more accurately, not to withhold work unreasonably when there is work available to be done;
- to comply with statutory obligations;
- to reimburse costs or expenses incurred by an employee in carrying out the employer's requirements [**30.4.9**];
- to provide a safe system of work, selecting proper staff and providing safe and adequate materials and equipment [**40.2.1**];
- not to order the employee to do something illegal or dangerous or carry on a dishonest activity;   *Malik v Bank of Credit & Commerce International SA [1997] UKHL 23*
- to maintain a relationship of trust and confidence with the employee, which generally can be characterised by behaving in a reasonable and fair way towards the employee.

26.3.3.2   Employees' duties

Employees' duties include:

- to be available, ready and willing to work;
- to maintain the trust and confidence of the employer;
- to provide services personally to the employer [**25.1.2**];
- to cooperate with the employer;
- to accept the 'control' of the employer and carry out reasonable instructions;
- to take reasonable care in carrying out the job;

- to display proper competence in carrying out the job;
- to adapt, after training if necessary, to new ways of work;
- to be loyal and give honest and faithful service;
- to pass on to the employer the copyright or other rights for work produced in the course of employment [**44.2.3**];
- not to obtain secret profits or compete with the employer;
- to tell the employer of any information relevant to the employment which comes into his or her possession;
- to treat the confidential information or trade secrets of the employer as secret [**43.1.5**], although if the employer is acting unlawfully there is a duty to bring this to the attention of the employer, and if the employer is acting unlawfully or against the public interest there may also be a 'just cause' defence and protection under the whistleblowing legislation in making this public [**33.5**].

26.3.4 Other implied terms

A contract normally has implied in it all the mutual duties which characterise the employee-employer relationship [**26.3.3**]. If the mutual duties, the express terms or those imposed by statute do not deal with all the issues, a tribunal or court will, in case of dispute, seek to establish what has been impliedly agreed between the parties. A number of methods are used for this.

26.3.4.1 Implied by custom

Where there are well known, reasonable, and clear **customs and practice** which generally apply to this particular type of contract, it is assumed in the absence of evidence of a contrary intent that these apply to the contract in question.

26.3.4.2 The officious bystander test

A term will be implied if it is obvious that the parties would have intended it. 'Obvious' is defined by imagining an officious bystander asking the parties, when the contract was made, what they intended. 'Do you intend for paid bank holidays to be additional to statutory or contractual annual leave?' the nosey bystander would have asked. If the employer and employee would both have said 'Of course', the court will imply that term into the contract.

26.3.4.3 Implied by conduct

If both parties operate the contract in a way which shows that they agreed upon a particular issue, for example the office opens at 9.00 and closes at 5.00 and the employee attends during that period, the court will imply a term that the hours of work are 9.00 to 5.00.

26.3.4.4 Characteristic terms

A court may imply a term simply because such a term is typical or characteristic, reasonable and necessary. For example when a written contract provided that the employee was entitled to sick pay but did not specify for how long, the court implied a term that sick pay would not continue forever but only for a reasonable period.
Howman & Son v Blyth [1983] IRLR 139, ICR 446 EAT

26.3.4.5 Exceptional circumstances

While an employer cannot generally require an employee to undertake work that is not included in the contract, there is an implied term that in exceptional circumstances, the employee will do such work temporarily if it is suitable and is not disadvantageous in terms of benefits or status.
Millbrook Furnishing Industries Ltd v McIntosh [1981] IRLR 309

26.3.5 Incorporated terms

Incorporated terms exist when the parties have agreed that they will accept a separate source for contractual terms. A staff handbook [**26.8**] is an example, but depending on how the contract is worded this may simply be regarded as guidance as to how the contract is to be carried out rather than part of the contract itself. Other examples of incorporated terms are staff salaries linked to scales determined externally, or agreeing to be bound by a collective agreement [**36.3.4**].

Some incorporated terms must be included in the statement of employment particulars [**26.7.3**], but for others the statement may refer to other documents.

If the terms of a collective agreement between an employer and trade union are incorporated within a contract of employment, those terms continue to apply to the contract even if the employer withdraws and is no longer a party to the agreement.

The terms also continue to apply if the employment is transferred to another employer [**29.7.7**]. At the time of writing (mid 2009) the employer is also bound by subsequent changes under the collective agreement, even though it not a party to those changes. It was not clear whether this decision would be appealed, so up to date advice should be sought. *Transfer of Undertakings (Protection of Employment) Regulations 2006 [SI 2006/246] reg.4; Whent & others v T Cartledge Ltd [1996] UKEAT 39 96 1612; Alemo-Herron & others v Parkwood Leisure Limited [2009] UKEAT 0456 08 ZT*

26.4 STATUTORY RIGHTS NOT DEPENDENT ON LENGTH OF SERVICE

All employees have a wide range of statutory rights, some of which are also available to 'workers' [**25.1.2**] who are not classed as employees. Every employment right imposes a corresponding duty on the employer.

Employment rights are covered in detail in **chapters 25-37**, but the most important are listed here. Statutory rights are available regardless of the number of hours worked per week, and so are available even to employees or workers who work a very low number of hours per week, and those on zero hours contracts [**25.2.3**] even if the employer provides no work. *Employment Rights Act 1996 s.210(4)*

26.4.1 Rights of employees and other workers

Many rights apply from the first day of employment, and in some cases even before a contract comes into being (for example, the right not to be discriminated against in selection for employment).

26.4.1.1 Right not to be discriminated against

Anyone working under a contract of employment or a contract to provide services personally has the right not to be treated less favourably in recruitment or any aspect of employment, except in very specific circumstances where it is allowed, on the basis of **racial group** (race, colour, ethnic origin, national origin or nationality) [**28.2**]; **sex**, pregnancy, gender reassignment, or being married or in a civil partnership [**28.3**]; **disability** [**28.7**]; **sexual orientation** [**28.5**]; **religion or other belief** [**28.4**]; or **age** [**28.6**]. There is a right not to be dismissed for any reason connected with any of these.

Unlike most other workers' rights, discrimination legislation protects not only employees and 'workers' [**25.1.2**] but also self employed people. These rights may in some situations also apply to volunteers [**39.4.3**].

Ex-offenders have the right not to disclose spent convictions and not to have them taken into account [**29.6.3**], except in specific situations where they must be disclosed [**41.8.2**] or taken into account [**chapter 42**].

26.4.1.2 Rights related to pay

All employees and workers [**25.1.2**] including casual and agency workers, have a statutory right:

- if they are at least 16 years old, to be paid no less than the **national minimum wage** [**30.2**];
- to receive an **itemised pay statement** [**30.1.3**];
- not to have **unauthorised deductions** made from pay [**30.1.4**];
- for men and women to receive equal pay for work of equal value [**28.8**].

Employees – but not other workers – have the right:

- in general, to receive **statutory sick pay** [**31.6.1**];
- to be a **preferential creditor** for at least some of the money they are owed if the employer becomes insolvent [**24.10.8**].

26.4.1.3 Trade union and employee representatives' rights

All employees have a statutory right:

- to belong, or not to belong, to a **trade union**, to take part in trade union activities, and not to suffer a detriment or be unfairly dismissed because of trade union membership or activities [**36.4.1**];
- to seek **recognition** for a trade union [**36.3.3**];
- to have reasonable time off, with or without pay, to take part in **activities of a union** recognised by the employer [**36.4.2**];
- to take reasonable time off, with pay, to carry out **duties as an official of a trade union** recognised by the employer or as a **union learning representative** [**36.4.3**];
- to take reasonable time off, with pay, to act as an **employee representative** for redundancies, business transfers, and statutory information and consultation [**36.1**];
- not to be dismissed or suffer a detriment for taking part in **protected industrial action** [**36.6.1**].

26.4.1.4 Health and safety rights

Employees, apprentices and trainees have a statutory right:

- to work in a **healthy, safe environment** [**40.2.1**];
- to take reasonable time off, with pay, to serve as a **health and safety representative** [**40.2.8**];
- not to be victimised or unfairly dismissed because of action taken to prevent or put right health and safety risks [**40.2.2**].

Virtually all employees and other workers [**25.1.2**], including casual and agency workers, have the right:

- not to be required to work more than **48 hours per week** on average [**31.2**];
- to paid **annual leave** [**31.4**];
- not to be required to work more than a maximum number of hours without daily and weekly **rest periods** [**31.3**].

26.4.1.5 Other rights

All employees – but not other workers – have a statutory right:

- to take reasonable time off, with or without pay, for **public duties** [**31.7**];
- to take reasonable time off, with or without pay, to deal with emergencies relating to **dependants** [**32.8**];
- to take reasonable time off, with pay, to serve as a trustee of the employer's **occupational pension scheme** [**30.6.4**];
- to be paid **damages** if they are injured or become ill as a result of their employer's negligence or breach of duty [**23.4.1**];
- not to be penalised for disclosing in good faith and honest belief **information about alleged wrongdoing** by the employer [**33.5**];
- to have dismissals, disciplinary action and grievances dealt with through appropriate procedures [**33.1, 33.2**];
- to be offered any **suitable alternative employment** if being made redundant [**35.6**];
- to have most of their contractual rights protected if the undertaking in which they are employed is transferred to another employer [**29.7**];
- not to be subject to detriment, dismissed or selected for redundancy because they have claimed a **statutory employment right**.

Employees and other workers [**25.1.2**], including casual and agency workers, have a statutory **right to be accompanied** in hearings under a disciplinary or grievance procedure [**33.1.1**].

Everyone working for an organisation has **data protection** rights [**43.3**].

Shop workers have a right **not to work on Sundays** [**31.2.6**].

26.4.2 Rights of part-time workers

Part-time workers [**25.2**] are entitled to the same statutory rights as full-time workers. They are also entitled to the same contractual rights *pro rata*, provided that there is a **comparator** – a full-time worker doing the same or broadly similar work for the same employer – and there is no objective reason for the employer to treat the part-timer less favourably than the comparable full-timer.

Part-time Workers (Prevention of Less Favourable Treatment) Regulations 2000 [SI 2000/1551]

Part-time rights apply not only to employees, but to virtually anyone working under a contract [**25.1.2**], including casuals and agency workers. People who are genuinely self employed [**38.2.2**] are not protected by part-time workers' rights.

A part-time worker may ask the employer, in writing, for an explanation for being treated less favourably than a comparator, and the employer must provide this in writing within 21 days of the request.   *Part-Time Workers Regs 2000 reg.6*

Where full-time workers who work overtime receive an enhanced rate of pay, part-timers do not become eligible for this higher rate until they have worked at least as many hours as the comparable full-timer.

Dismissal is automatically unfair [**34.7.1**] if it is for a reason connected with the regulations.

26.4.2.1 Comparators

A comparator must normally be doing the same or comparable work for the same employer at the same establishment. However if there is no comparator at an establishment, a comparator at a different establishment of the same employer can be used. Workers of an associated employer, such as a charity's trading company, cannot be considered.

There is no statutory definition of 'establishment'. There are case law definitions, but they relate to collective redundancies [**35.2.2**].

Workers who have worked full-time and become part-time can be their own comparator if they continue to work for the same employer but for fewer hours, even if the new or varied contract is of a different type or the work is different, or if after an absence of less than 12 months, the worker returns to the same job or a job at the same level but at a lower number of hours.   *Part-time Workers (Prevention of Less Favourable Treatment) Regulations 2000 [SI 2000/1551] regs.3,4*

26.4.3 Rights of fixed-term employees

Fixed-term employees [**25.3.1**] have the same statutory employment protection as permanent employees, except that a statement of employment particulars [**26.7**] does not have to be given to an employee whose employment is expected to last or has lasted less than one month.

In terms of contractual entitlements, fixed-term employees have the right not to be treated less favourably than comparable permanent employees of the same employer doing similar work, unless the less favourable treatment is objectively justified. In determining whether they have been less favourably treated, the tribunal scrutinises contracts on a term by term basis, rather than looking at the overall package.   *Fixed-term Employees (Prevention of Less Favourable Treatment) Regulations 2002 [SI 2002/2034] reg.3*

A European court of justice decision in 2008 confirmed that the rights of fixed-term employees extend to pension rights. Employers which do not provide comparable pension rights and cannot justify this should seek legal advice.

Impact v Minister for Agriculture & Food (Ireland) [2008] EUECJ C-268/06

Dismissal is automatically unfair [**34.7.1**] if it is for any reason connected with the fixed-term regulations.   *Fixed-term Employees Regs 2002 reg.6*

26.4.3.1 Comparators

For fixed-term employees, a comparable employee must be a permanent employee employed by the same employer at the same establishment [**26.4.2.1**] to do the same or broadly similar work, taking into account – where relevant – whether they have a similar level of qualification or skill. If there is no comparator at the same establishment, a comparator at a different establishment of the same employer can be used.
Fixed-term Employees (Prevention of Less Favourable Treatment) Regulations 2002 [SI 2002/2034] reg.2

A fixed-term employee has the right to request in writing a statement from the employer setting out the reasons for any treatment. The statement must be provided within 21 days of the request.
Fixed-term Employees Regs 2002 reg.5

26.4.3.2 Dismissal at the end of the fixed term

Non-renewal of a fixed-term contract constitutes a dismissal for the purposes of redundancy pay and unfair dismissal. Fixed-term employees who have worked for the statutory qualifying period therefore have the right to claim unfair dismissal [**34.7.2**] or redundancy pay [**35.7.1**] if their contract is not renewed – even though it was clear right from the beginning that the contract would terminate at that point. To avoid a claim of unfair dismissal there must therefore be a fair reason for dismissal [**34.6**] – which will usually be redundancy – and fair procedures must be followed [**34.5.2**].

Fixed-term employees have the right to be notified of any suitable vacancy when their employment is coming to an end. Failure to offer a suitable vacancy could, if the employee has worked for at least one year, lead to a claim of unfair dismissal.

26.4.4 Rights of agency workers

At the time of writing (mid 2009) agency temps were not employees of either the agency or the end user, but had statutory rights specifically as agency workers [**25.5.1**], and some workers' rights including minimum wage [**30.2**], working time rights [**31.1**], and equal opportunities and health and safety rights.

The EU **directive on temporary agency work** will, when implemented in the UK, entitle agency temps to the same basic statutory and contractual employment rights as if they had been directly hired by the employer. These will include pay, holiday, working time, rest periods and maternity leave, but not sick pay or occupational pension rights. They will also be entitled to equal access to collective facilities such as canteens, childcare facilities and transport services.
EU Directive on Temporary Agency Work 2008/104/EC

The directive provides for agency workers to be entitled to these rights from day one, but in the UK entitlement will not start until the temp has worked for the employer for 12 weeks (except where there is already entitlement to relevant statutory rights from day one). The directive has to be implemented by 5 December 2011.

26.4.5 Maternity rights

All pregnant women and new or breastfeeding mothers have the right:

- to paid time off for **ante-natal care** [**32.2.1**];

- to be offered **alternative employment** while pregnant or breastfeeding if their work puts them or their baby at risk [**40.3.2**], or to be suspended on full pay if alternative work is not available [**32.2.10**];

- to **ordinary** and **additional maternity leave**, with maintenance of all terms and conditions of employment apart from remuneration [**32.2.4**];

- to **return to the same job** on the same pay and conditions after ordinary or additional maternity leave unless a redundancy situation has arisen [**32.2.4**], or if the same job is not available after additional maternity leave, to be offered suitable alternative work;

- not to be dismissed or made redundant for reasons connected with pregnancy, and the right to a written statement of reasons for dismissal or redundancy while pregnant or during ordinary or additional maternity leave [**34.1.1**].

Mothers, fathers, persons with parental responsibility, spouses, partners, civil partners and adopters also have employment rights as parents, but at the time of writing (mid 2009) these required 26 weeks' or one year's continuous service [**26.5**].

26.4.6 Rights of young workers

Young employees (under age 18) and in some cases other young workers [**25.1.2**] have specific rights:

- some young employees have the right to **paid time off for study** [**31.8.2**];
- young people are not allowed to do certain types of work [**40.6.1**];
- there are limits on the **times** that young people can work [**31.5**];
- young employees and other young workers, including casuals, have the right to more frequent and/or longer **rest breaks** and rest periods [**31.5**], and if they are of school age, to at least one two-week break during school holidays;
- young employees, trainees and apprentices must be given increased protection under **health and safety** legislation [**40.3.2**].

From 2013, young people between minimum school leaving age [**31.5**] and 17 who do not have the equivalent of at least two GCSEs will have to be in full-time education or training, be receiving training under a contract of apprenticeship [**25.6.1**], or be receiving training as part of full-time employment. The age limit will increase to 18 from 2015.   *Education & Skills Act 2008 ss.2,3*

26.4.7 Rights of apprentices and trainees

The terms **trainee**, **intern** and **apprentice** are used in many ways [**25.6.1**] and advice may be needed to determine eligibility for employment rights in any particular situation.

Trainees who carry out work for an employer as part of their traineeship are generally entitled to employment rights. Their contract (which may be called a **training contract**) may include explicit provision for termination if the trainee does not satisfactorily complete the training, or if the employer does not have a suitable employment position at the end of the traineeship.

Students and others on **work placement** are generally not employees and are not entitled to the full range of employment rights, but health and safety law and the working time regulations [**31.1**] apply. An **intern** may be a trainee, work placement, employee or volunteer, with rights dependent on their situation.

Traditional **contracts of apprenticeship** [**25.6.1**] where the apprentice 'serves his master' and learns from the master are contracts of employment, entitling the apprentice to most statutory employment rights. There are special rules regarding national minimum wage [**30.2.1**].   *Employment Rights Act 1996 s.230(2)*

A traditional apprenticeship cannot generally be terminated even for misconduct or by giving notice, and apprentices cannot be made redundant except where the redundancy arises from a fundamental change to the employer's business.

Wallace v C A Roofing Services Ltd [1996] IRLR 435 QBD;
Whitely v Marton Electical Ltd [2002] UKEAT 0841 01 2611

Government-sponsored **apprenticeships**, **advanced apprenticeships** and **national traineeships** usually involve the apprentice, the employer and a college or other training provider in a three-way relationship [**25.6.1**]. Apprentices under these programmes must be paid at least £95 per week (as at 1/8/09). They are generally entitled to most employment rights and the right not to be dismissed during the apprenticeship unless the contract explicitly allows for termination on the basis of redundancy or misconduct.   *Flett v Matheson [2006] EWCA Civ 53*

26.4.8 Rights of ex-employees

In general a claim for breach of an employment right cannot be made for an event that takes place after employment ended. But the right not to be discriminated against or victimised can extend beyond the employment relationship, for example if an employer refuses to give a reference to a person who previously brought a discrimination claim against the employer or made a protected disclosure under the whistleblowing legislation [**33.5**].   *Woodward v Abbey National Plc [2006] EWCA Civ 822*

26.5 STATUTORY RIGHTS REQUIRING CONTINUOUS EMPLOYMENT

Some statutory rights are available only to employees who have completed a minimum period of **continuous employment** (also called **continuity of service** or **continuous service**) with the same or an associated employer.

26.5.1 Continuity periods

26.5.1.1 One month

A qualifying period of one calendar month applies to employees' right to:

- a written **statement of employment particulars** [**26.7**];
- **pay during medical suspension** [**30.1.11**], and the right not to be dismissed during medical suspension [**34.7.1**];
- if on wages, a **guarantee payment** for days when contracted to work but no work is available [**30.1.9**];
- statutory **notice of termination** of employment [**34.3.1**].

26.5.1.2 26 weeks

Provided they have worked for at least 26 weeks up to and including the 15th week before the expected week of childbirth:

- mothers have the right to 39 weeks **statutory maternity pay** (SMP), which at the time of writing was expected to increase to 52 weeks in 2010 [**32.2.6**];
- fathers, partners (male or female) or civil partners of a woman have the right to two weeks **paid ordinary paternity leave**, and are expected to be entitled, from 2010, to up to 26 weeks **additional paternity leave**, and up to 26 weeks **additional statutory paternity pay** [**32.3**].

Provided they have worked for at least 26 weeks ending with the week in which they are notified by an approved adoption agency of being matched with a child:

- an employee who is adopting as a single person, or one person (either male or female) in a couple which is adopting, is entitled to 26 weeks **ordinary adoption leave** immediately followed by 26 weeks **additional adoption leave** [**32.4.1**], with the same rights to return to work as for maternity leave [**26.4.5**]; and is entitled to 39 weeks **statutory adoption pay** (SAP), which is expected to increase to 52 weeks in 2010 [**32.4.2**];
- the other person (whether male or female) in a couple which is adopting is entitled to **paternity leave (adoption)** and **paternity pay (adoption)** [**32.4.3**] in the same way as ordinary paternity leave and pay.

Provided they have at least 26 weeks' continuous employment, the right to request **flexible working** is available to:

- parents, guardians and their partners of children under 17, or under 18 if the child is disabled [**32.5**];
- carers of persons aged 18 and over [**32.6**].

At the time of writing (mid 2009) it was expected that employees with at least 26 weeks' continuous employment would get the right to request **time off for training** [**31.8.2**].

26.5.1.3 One year

Employees have the right, after a qualifying period of one year:

- to **parental leave**, which may be paid or unpaid [**32.7**];
- to claim **unfair dismissal** if dismissed without a fair reason [**34.6, 34.8**] or without a fair procedure (in some cases no qualifying period is required);
- to receive a written **statement of reasons for dismissal** within 14 days of asking for it, if dismissed or if a fixed-term contract is not renewed [**34.1.1**].

An employee may have specific rights if an employer, in trying to avoid the employee reaching the one-year mark, dismisses without giving the required statutory notice [**34.3.1**, **34.8**].

26.5.1.4 Two years

Employees have the right, after two years' continuous service:

- to a **statutory redundancy payment** [**35.7.1**];
- to take **time off to look for work** if being made redundant [**35.5**].

26.5.2 Determining continuous employment

Continuity might arise from **one continuous contract**, from **a series of continuous contracts** with the same or an associated employer without any break of one week or more between contracts, or under **transfer of undertakings** provisions [**29.7.1**].

Even if no hours are worked during a week, an individual can have continuous employment if, during the week, the relationship is governed by a contract of employment such as a **zero hours contract** [**25.2.3**].

The period of continuity starts on the first day of the contract. This could be prior to the first day on which the employee arrives for work, for example if the contract starts on 1 June but this is a Saturday and the employee does not actually start work until the Monday.   *Employment Rights Act 1996 s.211*

26.5.2.1 Breaks in employment

Normally, if an employee ceases to be employed for a week or more and is then rehired by the same employer, this breaks the continuous employment and there is no continuity with the previous employment. But there are a number of exceptions, including:

- when an employee whose contract was terminated while away due to sickness is re-engaged within 26 weeks of the contract being terminated;
- when an employee is on maternity, paternity or adoption leave;
- when work ceases temporarily;
- absence from work which by arrangement or custom does not break continuity, such as a sabbatical.   *Employment Rights Act 1996 s.212*

Extended breaks, such as long sabbaticals, career breaks or breaks to look after children, should be offered only after taking legal advice. Unless carefully worded, it could be unclear whether continuity of employment is or is not preserved during the break.

During some breaks in a contract continuity is not broken, but the date of commencement of continuous employment is brought forward by the number of days involved in the absence:

- if the reason for the work ceasing temporarily is a strike or lockout (but if the employee is dismissed during a strike and then rehired, this does break the continuity of employment);
- absence on military service.

Continuity is not broken if the employee is dismissed but subsequently re-employed as a result of an appeal against dismissal, or following a successful arbitration by ACAS [**37.1.2**], or an order of reinstatement following a successful unfair dismissal claim [**37.4.1**].   *Employment Rights Act 1996 s.213*

26.5.2.2 Continuity for redundancy purposes

Certain weeks of employment spent overseas do not count for redundancy purposes but continuity is nevertheless preserved. There are special provisions for continuity where a person who has received a redundancy payment is subsequently re-engaged.   *Employment Rights Act 1996 ss.214,215*

26.5.2.3 Change in employer

Employment with a new employer is continuous if:

- all or part of the previous employer's work is transferred to or taken over by the new employer [**29.7**];
- the new employer is associated with the previous employer, for example is a company in the same group [**29.7.8**]; or
- in an unincorporated organisation, there is a change in the governing body members or other persons who are technically the employer.

Affleck & another v Newcastle Mind & others [1999] UKEAT 537 98 1003

26.6   RIGHTS DEPENDENT ON NUMBER OF WORKERS

Certain employment rights (and employer duties) apply only if the employer has a minimum number of employees or, in some cases, a minimum number of employees and workers together.

As soon as there are **five employees**, the employer must:

- have a **written health and safety policy** and a **written health and safety risk assessment** [**40.2.6**, **40.3**] (all other health and safety requirements apply as soon as there is even one employee);
- offer access to **stakeholder pensions** [**30.6.8**], unless other pension provision is offered or the employees do not earn enough to be counted in the total.

An employer with **21 or more employees** must in some situations formally **recognise a trade union** [**36.3.3**].

Employers with **50 or more employees** in the UK (averaged over the previous 12 months) must:

- **inform and consult** their employees about matters affecting the organisation's future, if employees have requested an information and consultation agreement [**36.2.1**];
- give paid time off for employees to serve as information and consultation representatives or **works council representatives** [**36.1**];
- give paid time off for employees to serve as representatives for the employer's **occupational pension scheme** [**30.6.4**].

26.7   STATEMENT OF PARTICULARS

26.7.1   Section 1 statement

Within two months of an employee starting work, or sooner if he or she is to work abroad, the employer must provide a **written statement of initial employment particulars** covering the major terms of employment if the employee will work for one month or more. If an employee works for more than one month but leaves before two months, a statement must still be given. The statement is sometimes called the **section 1 statement** because it is required under the **Employment Rights Act 1996** s.1.   *Employment Rights Act 1996 ss.1(1), 2(5),(6), 198*

If full terms and conditions [**chapter 27**] are provided containing all the required information, a separate statement is not necessary.

It is good practice to give two copies of the statement to the employee when the offer of employment is made and accepted, or before the employee starts work, or as soon as he or she starts. The employee should sign and return one copy and keep one. However, the statement is valid even if it is not signed by either the employer or employee.

26.7.2   Statement not provided

An employee can ask an employment tribunal to make a declaration if the employer has not given a written statement or has given only an incomplete statement, or if there is a dispute about the accuracy of the terms in the statement provided. A claim for failure to provide a written statement may be made by an employee who has been employed for more than two months, or within three months after the date of termination of employment.

The tribunal's job is merely to ensure that terms are accurately set down. It cannot interpret what the terms actually mean.

The tribunal has no power to make any monetary award or to change any of the terms, even if it feels they are unfair. It can, however, in limited circumstances change the statement or fill in omissions. For example, where the employer and employee have orally agreed a particular term but this was wrongly stated in the written statement, the tribunal has power to alter the incorrect particulars.

The tribunal can also fill in gaps if required particulars have been left out. In doing this, it looks first at what was actually agreed. If this cannot be ascertained, the tribunal will see whether it can be implied from the other terms or from how the contract was operated in practice.

Where an employee wins certain claims against an employer – for example for unfair dismissal, discrimination or breach of contract – and the employer had not provided a statement of particulars at the time the proceedings started, the tribunal must award the employee two weeks' pay and may award four weeks' pay, even if it makes no other award. *Employment Act 2002 s.38*

26.7.3   Required particulars

The statement or a full contract containing the required particulars may be issued in instalments so long as all the instalments are issued within the two month period. If there is nothing to be entered for a particular, this must be stated. *Employment Rights Act 1996 ss.1(2), 2(1)*

An outline contract, including all required particulars with details of each, is in **chapter 27**.

26.7.3.1   Single document

The following information must be included in a single document:
- full name of employer and employee;
- date when this employment began, and date when continuous employment [**26.5.2**] began;
- amount of wages or salary, pay scale or method of calculating pay, any other benefits (payments in kind etc), and the intervals at which the employee is paid [**27.3**];
- hours of work, with terms and conditions relating to normal working hours [**27.2.4-27.2.6**];
- entitlement to holidays and holiday pay [**27.4**];
- job title or a brief description of the work of the employee;
- place of work or, if the employee is going to be working in several places, details of that and the address of the employer [**27.2.7**];
- details of who an employee dissatisfied with a disciplinary or dismissal decision relating to him or her or who has a grievance should apply to, and the process for making such application. *Employment Rights Act 1996 ss.1-3, as amended*

26.7.3.2   Single or separate documents

The following may be included in the above document, or in separate documents:
- for employment which is not intended to be permanent, the period for which it is expected to continue or the date on which fixed-term employment is to end [**27.2.2**];
- details of any collective agreements [**27.12.3**];
- if an employee is going to be required to work outside the UK for more than one month, details of the period, the currency in which pay will be made outside the UK, any additional pay or benefits, and terms and conditions relating to returning to the UK [**27.2.3**]. *Employment Rights Act 1996 s.1*

26.7.3.3   Reasonably accessible documents

The following information may be included in the written statement or a written contract of employment, or the statement may include reference to another documents (such as a staff handbook) or documents which are reasonably accessible to the employee:

- period of notice to terminate employment [**27.6.2**] – for this, there can be reference to the statutory provision or a collective agreement, if these are reasonably accessible;
- incapacity for work due to sickness or injury, including sick pay or lack of it [**27.5.1, 27.5.2**];
- pension details or the lack of pension, including whether there is a contracting out certificate in force [**27.3.4**];
- details of any disciplinary rules, and procedures for taking disciplinary and dismissal decisions relating to the employee [**27.7**]. *Employment Rights Act 1996 ss.1-3*

26.7.4 Changes in the particulars

If there is any change in the particulars a new statement must be given in writing to every employee affected by the change within one month after the change, or sooner if the employee is to go abroad. Particulars which have not changed do not need to be repeated in the new statement, but there needs to be a reference back to the previous statement, with a note that these particulars have not changed. The changes must be in a single document, not in instalments.

Employment Rights Act 1996 s.4

If the change is one for which reference could be made in the statement of particulars to another document, the notification of change can also make reference to another document.

Notification must be given within one month but it is not necessary to issue new particulars if the only change is that the employer has changed its name, but is still the same employer; or that there is a new employer, with no effect on the employee's continuity of employment [**29.7**]. In this case, the notice must state when the employee's period of continuous service began. *ERA 1996 s.4(6),(8)*

26.8 CONTRACTUAL RIGHTS AND OBLIGATIONS

Only the statement of employment particulars has to be given to employees. But employees may be entitled to a wide range of additional **contractual rights** such as enhanced (more than the statutory minimum) parental, sickness or redundancy rights, or may be subject to contractual **obligations**, such as an obligation to inform the employer of any other employment they undertake.

These contractual terms could be made reasonably available to the employee in the course of work, or be agreed orally or in some other way with the employee. Where there is no dispute about additional terms, they are binding even if they are not in writing or not signed by the employer or employee.

But to avoid subsequent disputes and court cases, it is good practice for the full terms to be set out in a **written contract of employment** or **statement of terms and conditions of employment**. This should include everything required in the statement of employment particulars, plus other terms which the employer wants to form part of the contract. Some of the most common contractual rights and obligations are set out in **chapter 27**.

26.8.1 Discretionary benefits

Some rights included in the contract may be **discretionary**, such as compassionate leave or sabbaticals [**27.5.5**] or a performance bonus [**30.1.6**]. The contract should make clear that these benefits are non-contractual and are at the discretion of the employer. Where a discretionary benefit is always or virtually always granted, it may become a contractual right.

Great care must be taken when making decisions about discretionary benefits, to ensure decisions are made consistently and not on the basis of discriminatory criteria. There is an implied expectation [**26.3.4**] that discretion will be exercised honestly and in good faith, and not arbitrarily, capriciously or unreasonably.

Abu Dhabi National Tanker Company v Product Star Shipping Ltd [1993] 1 Lloyds LR 397

26.8.2   Restrictive covenants

Employees have an implied duty not to make secret profits or compete with the employer during employment [**26.3.3.2**]. The use of **restrictive covenants** which seek to limit competitive behaviour after employment [for example **27.6.5**] is growing as organisations move increasingly into the contract culture. It is important to consider whether there are some areas of work which need this protection, but such covenants must do no more than protect the employer's legitimate interests, and must be reasonable in what they cover and how long they last. Legal advice should always be sought before including them.

Where a restrictive covenant might be held to be unreasonable but the employer wants to restrict the employee's right to take other work after leaving this employment, the contract might allow for **garden leave** where the person stays on the payroll but remains at home and is not allowed to work for anyone else [for example **27.6.2.3**].

26.8.3   Enforcing the contract

Most disputes involving contracts of employment are resolved through informal discussion and negotiation. If a dispute cannot be resolved in this way, an employee can bring a grievance against the employer [**33.4**] and if necessary take legal action through an employment tribunal, the county court or high court.

An employer can take disciplinary action and, if the matter is serious, ultimately dismiss the employee and/or bring a legal case against the employee. A court will not order an employee to perform the terms of the contract, but may restrain a breach of contract (prevent the employee from continuing the breach).

Procedures for dealing with employment disputes are covered in **chapter 37**.

26.9   CHANGING THE CONTRACT

If any requirement forms part of the contract, the usual rules on varying contracts apply [**21.5.2**]. The employer can generally vary it only if the employee consents, or the employer is willing to vary it unilaterally [**26.9.3**] and take the risk of claims for breach of contract and unfair dismissal. All employment contracts are governed by implied duties to maintain relationships of trust and confidence [**26.3.3**], so variation should be undertaken only after taking legal advice.

If a change affects an item in the statement of particulars [**26.7.3**], affected employees must be given at least one month's notice in writing. Special rules govern changes to contracts following a TUPE transfer of staff [**29.7.6**].

26.9.1   Changes not requiring consent

Some changes can occur without needing the employee's consent:

*   contract terms **imposed** by statute are automatically changed when the legislation changes [**26.3.2**];
*   terms dependent on an external agreement or other source **incorporated** into the contract change when that agreement changes [**26.3.4.5**];
*   some contracts include **express** (explicit) clauses allowing the employer to make changes without consent, for example a mobility clause requiring the employee to work at any location, a flexibility clause requiring the employee to do 'any work reasonably requested by the employer', or a variation clause allowing the employer 'to make reasonable changes in the contract'.

Advice may be needed when drafting express clauses and before implementing them. A flexibility clause, for example, can be exercised only if it is reasonable to do so. An employer who needs to make employees redundant [**35.1.2**] could face difficulties if there is a mobility clause allowing employees to work at other locations, and employees attempt to argue that they are not redundant. A variation clause allowing unspecified changes could be void (invalid) because it is not clear enough, or because it risks undermining the implied duty of mutual trust and confidence [**26.3.3**].   *Land Securities Trillium Ltd v J Thornley [2005] UKEAT 0603 04 2806*

26.9.2 Changes with consent

Any contractual provision, except those which are imposed by statute and cannot be altered unless the statute is changed, can be changed with the agreement of the employee and employer. Any change requires additional consideration [**21.5.2**]. Where the change brings mutual benefit – such as longer hours provided to the employer and more pay provided to the employee – there is clear consideration for the new contract. Where the change is detrimental to the employee, such as a reduction in sick pay, a compensating change favourable to the employee is often made, or a small payment may be considered. If there is no consideration a contract change is not enforceable, for example where a restrictive covenant [**26.8.2**] preventing the employee from taking other work is added to the contract, without the employee receiving any consideration.

The agreement to vary a contract does not have to be in writing. However, the change must be put in writing if it affects the statement of particulars [**26.7.4**], and it is good practice to put all changes in writing.

Where contractual changes are offered as part of a package, employees cannot 'cherry pick' which ones they will accept. Unless the employer agrees otherwise, agreement has to be for all the changes or none. For example in a case where the employer wanted to standardise contracts, it offered employees reduced working hours with higher hourly pay, but lunch hour would cease to be paid. The employees lost their case when they said they had accepted reduced hours and higher pay but not the unpaid lunch hour, and complained because they were not being paid for it.　　*North Lanarkshire Council v Cowan [2008] UKEAT S 0028 07*

The nature of any work inevitably changes. It is good practice to review contracts at least every 18-24 months to ensure they reflect legal and organisational changes and best practice, and to update them by mutual consent if necessary. Even if the contracts are not formally updated, an employee and employer may be considered to have agreed tacitly to a change if they have gone along with a change in work practices.

26.9.3 Changes imposed by employers

In some situations employers may feel they need to impose changes without the employee's consent. This may go smoothly but can have potentially very serious implications, and should not be done without legal advice.

26.9.3.1 Acquiescence by employee

One way to vary a contract unilaterally is for the employer simply to operate as if the new terms were agreed and in place. If the employee goes along with the change without protesting against it, the change may be seen by the courts as part of the contract – or it may not, which means this approach can be risky.

An employee who accepts the new terms, however unwillingly, but then refuses to work under them is in breach of contract.　　*Robinson v Tescom Corporation [2008] UKEAT 0567 07 0303*

26.9.3.2 'Stand and sue'

An employee who explicitly rejects the new terms but continues to work has the right to claim damages at any time in the next six years. For example if the imposed change is a reduction in paid leave, an employee who works under protest can at any time in the next six years sue for damages for **breach of contract** [**37.5.2**] for the unpaid amounts. This is called the **stand and sue** option.

Employees will not necessarily win their breach of contact claim. In a case in 2007 the court of appeal ruled that an employer was not in breach of contract by imposing reduced allowances for car users, because the employer had given 'proper notice' to employees and the change was 'appropriate to the employees' duties'.　　*Wetherill & others v Birmingham City Council [2007] EWCA Civ 599*

26.9.3.3 Refusal to work

An employee who rejects the new terms and refuses to work may be allowed to continue working under the old terms, in which case the employer has impliedly agreed that the old contract remains in place. Alternatively the employer may take disciplinary action and dismiss the employee, and run the risk that the employee will claim wrongful dismissal [**34.4.1**] and/or unfair dismissal [**34.5**].

26.9.3.4   Resignation by employee

If the change is serious enough, the employee may treat it as a **repudiation** of the contract by the employer, resign, and bring a claim of unfair or wrongful **constructive dismissal** [**34.2.9**].

26.9.3.5   Dismissing the employee and offering a new contract

Another option could be to seek to change the contract by terminating the old contract, and offering a contract on new terms.

The employee will have no claim for **wrongful dismissal** [**34.4.1**] provided the required notice is given [**34.3.1**, **34.3.2**] and the employer goes through the necessary consultation process if more than 20 employees are involved [**35.2.2**].

An employee who has worked for the one year qualifying period may be able to claim **unfair dismissal** [**34.7.2**]. Employers must therefore be able to show that they had a potentially fair reason for dismissal [**34.5.1**], and that they acted fairly. An employment tribunal will look at whether dismissal procedures were properly followed, and in particular at whether the employee was consulted by being told what changes were proposed and why, was given time to consider the changes, and had the opportunity to make representations.

Where employees have refused to accept a new contract but employers acted fairly, the tribunals have found in a number of cases that the dismissal was necessary for 'some other substantial reason' [**34.5.1**], such as a business reorganisation, and was therefore not unfair.   *Kerry Foods Ltd v Lynch [2005] UKEAT 0032 05 2005*

This is a very complex area and should not be done without specialist legal advice.

26.10   STAFF HANDBOOK AND POLICIES

Staff handbooks bring together guidance for employees on a variety of issues. A handbook might include detailed policies, operating procedures, guidance on how to deal with problems within the job, documents referred to in the statement of particulars, and details relating to the contract of employment.

All but the very smallest employers should aim to provide all employees with the following policies and procedures as a bare minimum, either as part of the staff handbook or as separate documents:

- disciplinary and grievance procedures [**33.2.2**], which have to be provided as part of the statement of particulars;
- health and safety policy and any guidelines or procedures [**40.2.6**];
- equal opportunities policy and procedures [**28.1.10**];
- whistleblowing policy [**33.5**];
- key operational guidance, such as data protection [**43.3**], confidentiality [**43.1.3**], and acceptable use of email and internet [**43.5**];
- where applicable, policies on safeguarding children and vulnerable adults [**41.1.2**] and other policies relating to specific activities or service users.

26.10.1   Contractual or not?

Unintended consequences can arise if it is not clear whether some or all of the handbook or a particular policy document forms part of the contract of employment. So the handbook should clearly state whether it contains contractual terms, and if so which terms are contractual and which are not.

If the contract or statement of particulars refers to the handbook, it should state whether the entire handbook, or only part of it, is incorporated into the contract. Similarly, every relevant policy document should state whether it forms part of the contract. If something in the handbook forms part of the contract, any changes are subject to the rules on varying a contract [**26.8**].

Even where the handbook is not explicitly part of the contract, it may have legal consequences. If, for example, it sets out safety procedures and makes clear that breach of these will be gross misconduct, and all employees were made aware of this, this will be taken into account in any subsequent tribunal hearing.

26.11   OVERSEAS WORKERS AND WORKERS FROM ABROAD

Specialist legal advice is generally needed when taking on employees to work overseas.

26.11.1   Employment rights

Employment tribunals in England and Wales can hear only cases where the employee resides or the employer carries on business in England and Wales. There are comparable rules for tribunals in Scotland.   *Employment Tribunals (Constitution & Rules of Procedure) Regulations 2004 [SI 2004/1861] reg.19*

26.11.1.1   Statement of particulars and the contract of employment

Where an employee is to work overseas the statement of employment particulars [**26.7**] may need to include information specifically about the overseas posting, and a worker who is going abroad within the first two months of employment must be given the statement before they go [**26.7**]. The contract should make clear that the law of England (which in this context includes Wales) will apply.

26.11.1.2   Territorial jurisdiction

Since 1999 most statutory employment rights have not been subject to any statutory **territorial jurisdiction** – the geographic area within which the right applies. It has been left to the courts to determine which rights are or are not available to employees of British companies working overseas for their employers. The courts base their decisions on the principle that a contract of employment should generally be governed by the law of the country where the employee usually carries out the work, or if the employee does not usually carry out the work in one country, the contract should be governed by the law of the country where the employer is situated. However if the circumstances as a whole indicate that the contract is more closely connected with the law of another country, then that country's law should apply.   *Contracts (Applicable Law) Act 1990 sch.1 art.6(2)*

26.11.1.3   Expatriates working overseas for a British company

The case law in relation to a British employee working overseas for a British company is unclear and complex, and specialist legal advice should be sought.

The most significant cases are **Serco Ltd v Lawson** and **Botham v Ministry of Defence**, both of which considered the right to claim unfair dismissal. Their basic principle is that expatriate British employees working overseas are unlikely to be able to claim unfair dismissal unless they are working for an employer based in Great Britain, and the employee is either:

- posted abroad by for the purposes of the employer's business in Great Britain (rather than for a business that the employer is carrying out overseas); or
- operating within what is in effect a British enclave in a foreign country (in these cases, British military bases in Germany and on Ascension Island); or
- working in a similar situation where there are 'equally strong connections with Great Britain and British employment law'.   *Serco Ltd v Lawson, & Botham v Ministry of Defence [2006] UKHL 3*

Although these cases related to the right to claim unfair dismissal, the principles have since been applied to other statutory rights.

26.11.1.4   Peripatetic employees

Another case heard at the same time as Serco and Botham [above] considered whether **peripatetic employees** – those who work at various locations overseas or even, in the case of airline pilots, primarily in the air – are entitled to claim unfair dismissal. The key issue here, the House of Lords said, is whether the employee is working in Great Britain at the time of the dismissal, which in the case of peripatetic employees is likely to mean based primarily in Great Britain.

Crofts & others v Veta Limited & others [2006] UKHL 3

26.11.1.5 Workers from abroad in the UK

Workers from abroad who are working in the UK, even temporarily, have the same rights as UK workers. For rules on entitlement to work in the UK, see **29.5**.

26.11.1.6 British employers operating in the EU

EU nationals working in the EU for a UK-based organisation are unlikely to meet the tests set out in Serco v Lawson [**26.11.1.1**]. They are however likely to be entitled to UK statutory rights which derive directly from EU directives (such as working time rights, see **31.1**), but not rights which are based solely on UK law (such as unfair dismissal and unfair deduction from wages). *Bleuse v MBT Transport Ltd & another [2007] UKEAT 0339 07 2112*

26.11.1.7 EU employees temporarily working in another EU state

Workers who normally work in one EU member state and are posted for a limited period to another EU state must be given at least the minimum employment rights available in the state where they are temporarily working, even if these are more advantageous than the statutory rights in their home country. This applies to maximum work periods, minimum rest periods, minimum paid annual holidays, minimum rates of pay, rights of agency workers, health and safety rights, non-discrimination provisions, and protective rights for pregnant women and new mothers, children and young people. *Posting of Workers Directive [96/71/EC]*

UK employment legislation covers everyone employed in the UK, regardless of where they are from. But British employers who temporarily send employees to other EU member states must ensure those employees receive at least the minimum entitlements in those states.

26.11.1.8 Transfer of undertaking outside the UK

The rules on transfers of undertakings [**29.7**] apply where the transferred entity (a business or part of a business) was situated in the UK immediately before the transfer. The regulations do not place a geographic limit on where the undertaking is based after the transfer. The TUPE rules can therefore apply to a transfer from the UK to another country. *Holis Metal Industries Ltd v GMB & another [2007] UKEAT 0171 07 1212*

26.11.2 Equal opportunities rights

Equal opportunities legislation [**chapter 28**] is clearer. The Sex Discrimination Act and Equal Pay Act apply to all employment unless it is wholly outside Great Britain. The employment provisions of the Race Relations and Disability Discrimination Acts, and the employment equality regulations on religion and belief, sexual orientation and age, apply if employment is 'at an establishment in Great Britain,' defined as the employee working:

- wholly or partly in Great Britain; or
- wholly outside Great Britain, and the employer has a place of business in Great Britain, the work is for the purposes of that business, and the employee is ordinarily resident in Great Britain at the time of applying for or being offered employment or at any time during the employment.

Resources: RIGHTS, DUTIES AND THE CONTRACT OF EMPLOYMENT

ACAS, BIS, Business Link, CIPD, Directgov, National Apprenticeships Service, PEACe, TUC: see end of **chapter 25**.

Equalities and Human Rights Commission: see end of **chapter 28**.

Statute law. www.opsi.gov.uk and www.statutelaw.gov.uk.

Much but not all case law. www.bailii.org.

Updates cross-referenced to this book. www.rclh.co.uk.

Chapter 27

MODEL CONTRACT OF EMPLOYMENT

For sources of further information see end of chapter 25.

The model contract below (with the text in this font) indicates what must be included in the statement of employment particulars [**26.7**] and whether it has to be in a single document or can be in or refer to separate documents. It also includes optional matters which might be included in the contract, but do not have to be.

The commentary, indented and in this font, **must not be included**.

As with all models, this must be carefully reviewed before use, to ensure it is up to date and appropriate for the organisation. Legal advice is likely to be needed.

27.1   INTRODUCTION

This contract sets out the main terms and conditions under which you are employed by [Organisation] (the Employer) and includes all particulars required by the **Employment Rights Act 1996**.

> *Comment:* Unless indicated otherwise, all statute references in this chapter are to the **Employment Rights Act 1996**.
>
> Like any model, this model contract should be used with care and generally only after legal advice. For existing employees, changes can normally be made only with consent [**26.9**].
>
> This model can be adapted for part-time or fixed-term employees. Unless there is objective justification for different treatment, part-time workers must receive the same rights *pro rata* as comparable full-timers [**26.4.2**], and fixed-term employees must receive the same rights as comparable permanent workers [**26.4.3**].
>
> This model must not be used for people who are hired on a self employed basis [**38.1**] or for volunteers [**39.5**].
>
> Much of the information in this contract must be given to virtually all employees as part of the **statement of particulars** [**26.7**]. If all the information required in the statement is included in the contract, a separate statement does not have to be given.   *Employment Rights Act 1996 s.1*
>
> Employment law changes constantly, and the organisation's employment practices may also change over time. To ensure that contracts reflect these changes, it is vital to have an experienced solicitor review them regularly.

This contract is conditional on references, [medical check, Criminal Records Bureau disclosure, etc] satisfactory to the Employer being obtained.

> *Comment:* If the contract is given and/or the person is allowed to start work before satisfactory references or other checks have been obtained, this sentence must be included to ensure the employer has the right to terminate if the documentation is not received or is not acceptable.

27.1.1   Name and address of employer

Name and address of Employer: _____

> *Comment:* The full name of the employer [**29.1**] must be included in the statement of particulars single document [**26.7.3**]. The employer's address must be given if it is not shown later as the place where the employee will work.   *Employment Rights Act 1996 ss.1(3)(a), 2(4)*
>
> Thought should be given to how to refer to the employer in the contract. If the contract says that notice (for annual leave etc) must be given 'to the Employer', it may not be clear who it is to be given to. If the contract says notice is to be given to the manager, chairperson etc this is clearer, but may become inappropriate if the organisation's management structure changes. It is generally easiest to refer to 'the Employer' throughout, and attach a memorandum indicating who the appropriate person is. It may be appropriate to give an alternative in case the named person is not available.

You may also be required to work for subsidiaries or other organisations associated with the Employer.

> *Comment:* This sentence should be included if the organisation has, or may create, subsidiary bodies or is or may become part of a charity group or company group [**9.4**].

27.1.2   Name of employee

Name and address of Employee: _____

> *Comment:* The full name of the employee must be included in the statement of particulars single document. The employee's address does not have to be included but usually is.   *Employment Rights Act 1996 ss.1(3)(a), 2(4)*

27.1.3   Job title

Job title: _____

> *Comment:* The job title, with a brief description of the job if this is not apparent from the job title, must be included in the statement of particulars single document..   *Employment Rights Act 1996 ss.1(4)(f), 2(4)*

Reporting to: _____

The Employer reserves the right to change this reporting line at any time to meet the needs of the Employer.

Your duties are set out in your job description which [forms / does not form] part of this contract. These are the normal duties which the Employer requires from you at the date of your appointment. However it is necessary for all staff to be flexible, and all employees will be required from time to time to perform other duties appropriate to the grade and nature of your job as may be required by the Employer for the efficient running of the organisation.

> *Comment:* It is not advisable to include a detailed job description in the contract or to have it form part of the contract, as any variation would then require the consent of the employee [**26.9**].

27.1.4   Part-time employees

Part-time employees are entitled to all benefits and rights under the terms of this contract, on a *pro rata* basis.

> *Comment:* Unless different treatment can be objectively justified, part-time employees must have the same contractual rights, *pro rata*, as a comparable full-time employee [**26.4.2**].

27.1.5   Right to work in the UK

By accepting this contract you confirm that you are entitled to work in the United Kingdom without any additional consents or approvals, and you agree to notify the employer immediately if you cease to be so entitled during your employment.

> *Comment:* Even with this clause, the employer is obliged to check and keep a copy of specified documents to confirm the employee is entitled to work in the UK [**29.5.1**].

27.1.6   Probationary period

This post is subject to a probationary period of _____ [weeks / months], which may be extended by the Employer. Subject to satisfactory completion of the probationary period, you will be confirmed in post. During the probationary period, employment may be terminated by either party by one week's notice in writing.

> *Comment:* There is no obligation to include a **probationary period**. Even with a probationary period, the contract comes into effect at the start of employment, not when the employee is confirmed in post. During the probationary period the employee has all statutory rights, including the right to receive a statement of employment particulars within the first two months [**26.7**], and all contractual rights unless the contract explicitly states otherwise.
>
> The contract may say that the employer does not need to follow its disciplinary procedure [**33.3**] to dismiss during the probationary period, or may allow for a simplified procedure. If there is a risk of a claim for discrimination or unfair dismissal, the organisation should follow its disciplinary procedure even during the probationary period.

27.2   DURATION, TIME AND PLACE OF WORK

27.2.1   Period of continuous employment

This employment begins on [date] and is not continuous with any previous employment.

or

This employment begins on [date] and is continuous with your previous employment, which began on [date].

or

This employment begins on [date] and is continuous with your previous employment with [name of previous employer, if employment was with an associated employer], which began on [date].

> **Comment:** The starting date for the employee's period of **continuous employment** [**26.5.2**] must be included in the statement of particulars single document. This is very important, because significant employment rights depend on the length of the period. *Employment Rights Act 1996 ss.1(3)(c), 2(4)*
>
> Employment begins (or began) when the contract starts, which is not necessarily the first day of work. For example if the offer letter says the contract starts on 1 June but it is a Saturday and the person does not start work until Monday, the date of commencement is 1 June.
>
> For new employees this clause should say that the contract is not continuous with any previous employment. For current employees who are starting a new post within the organisation or with a subsidiary or associated organisation, the start date for continuous employment will be the date they started working within the group as a whole.
>
> Where employees are transferred from another employer under TUPE provisions [**29.7**], a new contract is not normally issued because terms and conditions are carried over to the new employer. Where an employee transfers but not under TUPE, previous service may in some circumstances be recognised. If so, this should be specified.
>
> If an employee's contract is terminated for more than a week and the employee is then rehired by the same employer, there is normally no continuity with the previous employment. But there are a number of exceptions [**26.5.2**].

27.2.2 Fixed-term contract

This is a fixed-term contract. Unless previously terminated, your employment will end on [date]

or

on completion of [task]

or

[when specified event occurs or does not occur].

> **Comment:** If the contract is for a **fixed term** [**25.3.1**] this clause must be included in the statement of particulars single document, the letter of appointment or another document given to the employee. The clause must not be included if the contract is intended to be indefinite (open-ended). *Employment Rights Act 1996 s.1(4)(g)*
>
> Fixed-term contracts need to be worded very carefully, as they can expose the employer to large claims for wrongful dismissal [**34.4.1**]. The phrase 'unless previously terminated' should be included, as it allows termination by giving notice before the contract would otherwise end.
>
> Even though a fixed-term contract specifies when it will end, non-renewal at the end of the term constitutes a dismissal and, if the work itself is ending, a redundancy. The usual procedure for redundancy [**chapter 35**] must be followed.
>
> Where a person has been engaged for four or more years on one or more consecutive fixed-term contracts, the contract generally becomes permanent when it is next renewed [**25.3.1**].

27.2.3 Work outside the UK

[Details as required]

> **Comment:** This clause should be included only if the employee is to work outside the UK for more than one month. The statement of particulars single document or another document given to the employee

must include the period of work outside the UK, the currency in which payment will be made, any additional payment or benefits arising from the work outside the UK, and any terms or conditions relating to returning to the UK. The information must be given before the employee leaves the UK. For more about overseas workers see **25.6.5** and **26.11**.

Employment Rights Act 1996 s.1(4)(k)

27.2.4 Normal hours of work

Your normal hours are ____ a.m. to ____ p.m. Monday to Friday.

or

You are normally required to work ____ hours per week excluding meal breaks.

or

You are normally required to work _____ hours per week excluding meal breaks. The Employer operates a flexitime system with core hours from _____ a.m. to _____ p.m. from Monday to Friday. You are expected to work _____ hours per day (excluding meals) during core hours, and to agree the remaining hours with the employer.

The Employer may vary the normal hours by giving you at least two weeks notice in writing, provided there is no increase or decrease in the hours of work per week

> ***Comment:*** The hours of work and the terms and conditions relating to normal working hours must be included in the statement of particulars single document. Employees cannot be required to work more than 48 hours per week, averaged over 17 weeks, unless they have opted out of the 48-hour limit [**27.2.6**]. *Employment Rights Act 1996 ss.1(4)(c), 2(4)*
>
> If **flexitime** operates, the core hours (if any) and the procedure for arranging hours of work should be stated.
>
> If hours vary from week to week, this must be stated, for example 'The number of hours per week will vary between 10 and 25.' If hours vary, the contract should state how and when the employee will be notified.
>
> Some contracts now operate on the basis of monthly or annual (also called **annualised**) hours, rather than weekly.

You will have a meal break of one hour per day, which is not working time and is not paid. Your meal break will be arranged with the Employer to ensure there is adequate attendance of staff throughout the day.

> ***Comment:*** The contract should state whether the hours of work include meal breaks, and whether meal breaks are paid or unpaid.
>
> Every employee who works more than six hours must be given a break of at least 20 minutes during the working day [**31.3.1**]. This need not be paid.

These are the normal hours of work required. The nature of the work is such that employees may be required from time to time to work outside these hours. In these circumstances as much notice as possible will be given to employees and as much effort as possible will be made to fit in with the wishes and other commitments of employees. It must be recognised however that on occasion, in the interest of [clients / service users / the effective operation of the organisation], such requirements may arise at short notice.

> ***Comment:*** This clause does not have to be included. Even if it is included, employees can be asked or required to work different hours only if the change is reasonable or is clearly necessary, for example in a genuine emergency.

27.2.5 Overtime arrangements

[For example] There is no payment for overtime and you are not expected to work more than [35] hours per week. When more than [35] hours are worked, the additional hours should be taken as time off in lieu (TOIL) within one month. TOIL not taken within one month can be carried forward only with the written agreement of the Employer. TOIL must be authorised in advance by [your manager]. If regular overtime working seems necessary, this should be discussed as a matter of urgency with [your manager].

or

You may be required to work overtime not exceeding [10] hours in any week and not exceeding in total [20] hours in any calendar month. The additional hours should be taken as time off in lieu (TOIL) within one month *[then add the TOIL details as set out above]*.

or

You are expected to work a minimum of [35] hours per week plus such additional hours as are needed to meet the organisation's objectives [or the clients' needs, or whatever]. There is no payment for overtime and time off in lieu is not normally given.

or

Overtime is paid at the rate of £_____ per hour. No overtime will be paid unless the overtime work has been authorised in advance in writing by [your manager].

> **Comment:** If overtime is or might be required, the arrangements for the overtime and for overtime pay (if any) must be included in the statement of particulars single document. *Employment Rights Act 1996 s.1(4)(c)*
>
> The above clauses are examples. The clause used should make clear whether overtime working is essential, whether it must be authorised beforehand and if so by whom, whether there is any limit on the amount of overtime which can be required or can be worked, and the rules for accruing and taking time off in lieu.
>
> Unless the contract specifies it, there is no implied duty on an employee to work overtime, even when it is really necessary.
>
> Most employees cannot be required to work more than an average 48 hours per week in total unless they have signed an opt-out agreement [**27.2.6**]. Employers have a duty to make reasonable enquiries about whether an employee has other work which could take them over the 48 hours [**27.8.1**].
>
> The statement of particulars single document should state whether overtime is paid, and if so at what rate. The law makes no presumption as to the level of overtime pay, or whether there are special payments for evenings, weekends or holidays. Where overtime attracts a special rate of pay, part-time workers do not have a statutory entitlement to this until they have worked as many hours as their full-time comparator [**26.4.2**].
>
> If overtime is not paid, the contract should state whether **time off in lieu** (TOIL) is given, and if so how much overtime can be accumulated, whether TOIL has to be taken within a fixed period, and whether arrangements have to be made with a manager before taking TOIL.
>
> Overtime where the person works 'voluntarily', with no pay and no right to TOIL, could count legally as working hours. Such unpaid overtime could bring pay below minimum wage level [**30.2**], bring a part-time worker's pay below that of a full-time comparator [**26.4.2**] and/or take the worker over the 48-hour working time limit [**31.2.1**].
>
> If overtime pay or TOIL is to be given, the employer should consider how overtime working is to be recorded and verified. The employer should also be aware of its duty of care to ensure that employees do not suffer risks to their health as a result of overwork [**40.5.1**].

27.2.6 Limitation of working week

Unless and until you give three months' notice in writing revoking this clause, the limitation of the working week to 48 hours under the Working Time Regulations 1998 will not apply.

> **Comment:** Employees can be required to work more than 48 hours per week only if this is included in the contract or they have agreed in writing to do so [**31.2.3**]. Even where it is in the contract or a written agreement, employees always have a statutory right to revoke their agreement on seven days' notice or such longer notice as is required by the employer, up to three months. The UK could in future be required by the EU to repeal the provisions allowing employees to work more than 48 hours a week, so the current situation should be checked before including the clause above.

27.2.7   Place of work

Your place of work will be

_____ or such other place as the Employer may require

or

_____ or such other place within ____ miles of this location as the Employer may require

or

_____ or such other place within [specified geographic area] as the Employer may require.

> *Comment:* Place of work, or an indication that the employee is required or allowed to work in more than one place, must be included in the statement of particulars single document.   *Employment Rights Act 1996 ss.1(4)(h), 2(4)*

27.2.7.1   Mobility clause

> *Comment:* A clause that requires or allows employees to work at a place other than the one specified in the contract is a **mobility clause**. Even where the contract provides for a move, the employer must behave reasonably in asking the employee to work at a different place, and must give reasonable notice of the move.
>
> Legal advice should be sought before requiring employees to move house or work at any distance from where they were originally hired to work, because the transfer could constitute a redundancy [**35.1.2**] entitling the employee to redundancy rights.
>
> If the contract does not include a mobility clause, an employee who is required to work at a different location may be entitled to resign and claim constructive dismissal [**34.2.9**]. But if work is no longer available at the original location, work at the new location could constitute suitable alternative employment, and an employee who unreasonably refuses could lose entitlement to a redundancy payment [**35.1.2**].

27.2.7.2   Home working

> *Comment:* If the employee is required or permitted to work from home this must be specified [see **63.9** for issues on working at home]. If the employee must or might work from home additional clauses should be included covering issues such as the employer's right to conduct health and safety assessments; the employee's obligation to comply with the employer's data protection, confidentiality and other relevant policies while working at home; insurance; and the employer's right to recover its property and all paper and electronic documents produced by or provided to the employee in the course of employment. The contract should require equipment provided by the employer and information belonging to the employer to be stored securely and to be transported securely between home and the employer's premises. Legal advice should be sought about the clauses to be included.

27.2.8   Accommodation

[Details]

> *Comment:* If the employee is or could be required to reside in accommodation provided by the employer (usually called **tied** or **live-in accommodation**), this should be indicated in the contract of employment. There should be a separate agreement for occupation of the accommodation. This may be a **service occupancy** where the employee lives in the accommodation rent-free in return or part-return for working for the employer, or a **service tenancy** where the employee pays rent to the employer. Legal advice should be sought for drawing up the agreement, and on the tax [**30.4.9**] and minimum wage [**30.2**] implications of providing accommodation.

27.3 REMUNERATION AND PENSIONS

27.3.1 Starting salary

£_____ per _____.

or

You will start at point ____ on the _____ scale, for which the salary is currently £_____ per _____.

> **Comment:** The amount of salary or wages, pay scale or method of calculating pay, and any other benefits such as payments in kind must be included in the statement of particulars single document [see **30.1** for more on salary]. For workers aged 16 or over, pay cannot be less than the national minimum wage [**30.2**].   *Employment Rights Act 1996 ss.1(4)(a), 2(4)*
>
> If salary is linked to an externally negotiated scale, this must be stated. The governing body should think carefully before committing the organisation to an external pay scale over which it has no control.

27.3.2 Pay period

[For example] You will be paid monthly in arrears on the _____th of the month or, if it falls on a weekend or public holiday, on the working day before.

> **Comment:** The interval at which the employee is paid must be included in the statement of particulars single document.   *ERA 1996 ss.1(4)(b), 2(4)*
>
> Examples are 'weekly on Fridays', 'monthly on the last Thursday in each month', 'monthly on the 15th of each month or on the working day before if the 15th is not a working day, half in advance'.
>
> If payment is or may be made direct into the employee's bank account, this should be stated.

27.3.3 Annual increases

> **Comment:** Unless salary is linked to an externally negotiated agreement which includes annual increases [**27.3.1**], there is no requirement to include arrangements for increases. The employer should not commit itself to automatic increases unless it is confident it will have adequate funds now and in future.
>
> Any length of service increase awarded after the first five years of employment must be justifiable under age discrimination law [**28.6.2**].

27.3.3.1 Based on annual review

Your salary will be reviewed annually, with any increase payable from [1 April] or such other date as decided by the Employer. The Employer is under no obligation to award an increase following a salary review, and the amount of any increase is at the discretion of the Employer.

27.3.3.2 Based on salary scale increments

[For example] Provided you have been in post for at least six months, you will go up one point on the salary scale on [1 April] each year until you reach the ceiling for your post, which is at point _____.

or

You will go up one point on the salary scale each year on the anniversary of your starting the post, until you reach the ceiling for the post which is at point _____.

or

Provided you have satisfactorily completed the annual appraisal carried out by the Employer, you will go up one point on the salary scale each year on the anniversary of your starting the post, until you reach the ceiling for the post which is at point _____.

27.3.4 Pension

[If the employer is exempt from having to provide a stakeholder pension scheme and does not provide any other pension provision] The Employer does not provide or contribute to a pension scheme and there is no contracting-out certificate in force.

or

[If the employer has a stakeholder pension scheme but does not contribute to it] The Employer has created stakeholder pension arrangements with [name of company and contact details]. The Employer does not make a contribution to such pension and there is no contracting-out certificate in force.

or

[If the employer has a stakeholder pension scheme and contributes to it] The Employer has created stakeholder pension arrangements with [name of company and contact details]. The Employer makes a contribution of _____% of your salary to such pension [after you have been employed for ___ months]. There [is / is not] a contracting-out certificate in force in relation to the state second pension.

or

[If the employer contributes, or is willing to contribute, to an appropriate personal pension] The Employer contributes _____% of your salary to a personal pension scheme, details of which will be provided separately. There [is / is not] a contracting-out certificate in force in relation to the state second pension.

or

[If the employer will contribute to a personal pension only if the employee also does] The Employer will match your contribution to its personal pension scheme, to a maximum of _____% of your salary. Details of the pension scheme will be provided separately. There [is / is not] a contracting-out certificate in force in relation to the state second pension.

or

[If the employer has an occupational pension scheme] The Employer provides a pension scheme with [name of institution] and will make a contribution to the scheme of _____% of your salary [after you have been employed for _____ months]. The scheme [is / is not] a contracted out scheme. Full details of the scheme are available from/in _____.

or

[as the paragraph above, plus] You are not obliged to join this scheme, and if you request it the Employer will contribute an equivalent amount to a personal pension scheme of your choice.

and, if any sort of pension provision is provided

The Employer is entitled at any time to terminate the scheme, reduce its contribution or replace the existing scheme as it deems fit.

> **Comment:** The pension arrangements (or lack of them) must be included in the statement of particulars single document, or the statement must refer to another document. If the employer operates a pension scheme, the statement or other document must indicate whether it is contracted out of the state scheme [**30.6.3**]. *Employment Rights Act 1996 ss.1(4)(d)(iii), 2,6*
>
> Unless the employer is exempt from the obligation to provide access to a stakeholder pension [**30.6.8**], employees must be given details of the stakeholder pension provider. There is no obligation for the employer to make a contribution to a stakeholder pension.
>
> It is recommended that the employer reserves the right to change or terminate the pension. Even with this, the employer must consult with employees about any changes to contractual pension entitlements.
>
> See **30.6** for more on pensions.

27.3.5 Deductions

The Employer may deduct from your salary or other sums due to you an amount to cover losses sustained in relation to property or money of the Employer or of any client, customer, visitor or other employee during the course of your employment caused through your carelessness, negligence or recklessness or through breach of the Employer's rules or any dishonesty on your part.

[Contracts for employees in charity shops and other retail outlets must add] Where the Employer makes a deduction due to a cash shortage or stock deficiency, the total amount will not be more than 1/10th of the gross amount payable to you for that day.

The Employer may also deduct from salary or other sums due to you a day's or part day's pay for each day or part day of unauthorised absence. Unauthorised absence is failing to appear for work at the appropriate time unless absence is due to genuine sickness or injury which has been notified to the Employer in accordance with this contract, or leave for which prior permission has been granted, or genuine reasons outside your control which are acceptable to the Employer.

The Employer may also deduct the amount of any accidental overpayment to you, and/or the amount of any loan made to you for any purpose, and/or any other amount due to the Employer under any agreement with you.

The Employer will notify you in writing of the details of any such deduction, and will provide you with copies of any supporting documents reasonably requested in connection with the deduction.

> **Comment:** There is no obligation to include a deductions clause in the statement of particulars. However an employer is prevented from making deductions except in limited circumstances [**30.1.4**], unless the contract allows. A deduction which is not authorised by statute or the contract may be made only if the employee has given written consent to the deduction before the act to which the deduction applies took place.
> *Employment Rights Act 1996 ss.13,14*
>
> Statutory rules apply to deductions from shop workers' wages.
> *Employment Rights Act 1996 s.18*
>
> If an employer makes a deduction which is not authorised by statute, the contract or prior consent of the employee – for example, to recover a loan or to recover a loss caused by the employee – it cannot then attempt to recover that money by going to court or in any other way. In addition, the employee may be able to bring a breach of contract claim.

27.4   HOLIDAY ENTITLEMENT

27.4.1   Public holidays

Full-time employees are entitled to a paid holiday on all public holidays, in addition to their annual leave entitlement. Part-time employees are entitled to paid time off for each public holiday, calculated as one-fifth of their normal weekly working hours. [If the time off is not taken on the public holiday, it must be taken in the week in which the public holiday occurs or in the week immediately before or after.]

> *or*

You may be required to work on public holidays. If so you will be entitled to take equivalent paid time off. [Such time off must be taken in the week in which the public holiday occurs or in the week immediately before or after.]

> *or*

All employees are entitled to time off on all public holidays, as part of their annual leave entitlement as specified below. If the time off is not taken on the public holiday, it may be taken at any time as part of annual leave.

> **Comment:** There is no statutory requirement to give time off on public holidays [**31.4.2**]. But if leave is given for public holidays, the statement of particulars single document must include details of how they are treated. See **31.4.2.2** for how to calculate bank holiday entitlement for part-time workers. *Employment Rights Act 1996 ss.1(4)(d)(i), 2(4)*

27.4.2   Annual leave

27.4.2.1   Entitlement

Full-time employees are entitled to _____ days holiday on full pay for each completed leave year, and *pro rata* for each partial leave year. [After _____ years, leave entitlement increases to _____ days and thereafter by one additional day for each year of service to a maximum of _____ days at the end of your fourth year of employment.]

Part-time employees are entitled to _____ weeks holiday on full pay for each completed leave year, and *pro rata* for each partial leave year. For these purposes a 'week' is the number of hours worked in a normal working week, or if this is not regular, the average number of hours worked in the 12-week period before the leave year starts. [After _____ years, leave entitlement increases by one-fifth of your normal working week for each year of service, to a maximum of _____ days total at the end of your fourth year of employment.]

Annual leave entitlement [includes / is in addition to] paid time off for public holidays.

Annual leave cannot normally be taken during the first three months of employment.

> ***Comment:*** The statement of particulars single document must include details of annual leave entitlement, plus sufficiently detailed particulars to enable any accrued holiday pay due on termination of employment to be calculated. If additional holiday leave is available but without pay or with reduced pay, this must be stated in the statement. The statement must make clear whether public holidays are included as part of the holiday entitlement, or are additional to it.   *Employment Rights Act 1996 ss.1(4)(d)(i), 2(4)*

> From 1 April 2009 all full-time workers have a statutory entitlement to a minimum of 28 days paid annual leave (5.6 weeks equivalent for part-time workers). This statutory annual leave may include public holidays, or be in addition to public holidays. See **31.4** for issues in calculating annual leave if public holidays are or are not included as part of it.

> During the first five years of employment with the same or an associated employer, annual leave can be increased without contravening the age discrimination regulations [**28.6.2**]. If the employee has more than five years' service, such increments should be awarded only if they can be objectively justified.

The rules in the Working Time Regulations 1998 concerning notification of holidays and refusal of holidays will not apply to this employment. All leave dates must be arranged with and agreed by the employer.

The employer reserves the right to make any working day falling between Christmas and New Year's Day a compulsory holiday, to be taken from your annual leave entitlement.

> ***Comment:*** The contract should state whether holiday leave has to be agreed by anyone, whether a minimum notice of intention to take it has to be given, and whether there are any periods when annual leave must or must not be taken. The **Working Time Regulations 1998** include provisions for notice of intention to take leave and counter notice by the employer [**31.4.6**] but these provisions can be excluded in the contract.

27.4.2.2   The leave year

The leave year is from 1 January to 31 December [*or* 1 April to 31 March, or whatever].

The first [20 days/4 weeks, or as applicable for part-time workers] of your entitlement to statutory annual leave cannot be carried forward into a new leave year. The remaining [8 days/1.6 weeks, or as applicable] can be carried forward if the Employer's written consent to do so is obtained before the end of the leave year.

> ***Comment:*** The **Working Time Regulations 1998** prohibit the first 20 days/four weeks of statutory annual leave from being carried forward [**31.4.3**]. The remainder can be carried forward if this is allowed under the contract of employment, a collective agreement which forms part of the contract, or a workforce agreement [**31.1.2**].

[Where you are entitled to additional contractual leave, you may carry forward some or all of the contractual entitlement, but only if the Employer's written consent to do so is obtained before the end of the leave year. If such consent is not obtained any contractual leave not taken by the end of leave year is forfeited.

or

A maximum of ___ days of your contractual entitlement can be carried forward to the next leave year. Any additional contractual leave entitlement not taken by the end of the leave year is forfeited.]

27.4.2.3   Accrued leave at the end of employment

On being given notice of termination of employment or giving notice of resigning, you will at the Employer's discretion be paid for annual leave entitlement accrued but not taken, or may be obliged by the Employer to take the remaining leave.

> ***Comment:*** After a worker gives notice of leaving or the employer gives notice of dismissal, the employer may want to be able to require the employee to continue working, in order to complete vital tasks. Conversely, it may be better to be able to require the employee to take any unused leave during this period.

If at the end of your employment you are entitled to be paid for any accrued leave not taken, the amount of payment will be calculated on the basis that each day of paid holiday is equal to 1/260th of your annual salary for full-time employees; for part-time employees it is calculated on a *pro rata* basis.

Where termination of employment is for gross misconduct or follows your resignation in breach of contract, such accrued but untaken holiday will be based on your minimum holiday entitlement under the Working Time Regulations only, and not on your contractual entitlement. For these purposes any paid holiday that has been taken by you, including any paid holiday on public holidays, will be deemed first to be statutory paid holiday.

If you have taken more holiday than your accrued entitlement at the date of termination of employment, the Employer will be entitled to deduct the appropriate amount, calculated at 1/260th of your annual salary for full-time employees or on a *pro rata* basis for part-time employees, from your final pay.

> **Comment:** The Working Time Regulations allow a deduction to be made for excess statutory leave taken [**31.4.4**]. The contract should allow deduction for excess contractual leave (leave taken above the statutory minimum).

27.5   OTHER LEAVE AND ENTITLEMENTS
27.5.1   Absence due to sickness or injury

You confirm to the Employer that you are in good health and not suffering from any medical condition, disease, illness (whether physical or mental) or other problem which could affect your capacity to carry out your work for the Employer, or that you have previously disclosed these to the Employer in writing. You agree that should you start to suffer from such you will immediately notify the Employer.

If you are absent due to sickness or injury you must report this to the Employer as soon as possible on the first day of absence, with an indication of the likely period of absence or a doctor's certificate.

> **Comment:** Details about entitlement to sick leave, sick pay, notification procedures and certification must be included in the statement of particulars single document, or there must be reference to another reasonably accessible document where the employee can get this information.
> *Employment Rights Act 1996 ss.1(4)(d)(ii), 2(2), 6*

By the end of the [fourth] day's absence you must provide a self certification note, available from the Employer or your GP. For any period of [one week] or more a doctor's certificate must be provided.

> **Comment:** Employers are required to keep records of absence. HM Revenue and Customs has produced an optional self certification form **SC2**, employee's statement of sickness, to assist employers. There is no obligation to require SC2 or a doctor's certificate, but without it an organisation which can recover statutory sick pay [**31.6.1**] from HMRC may not have adequate evidence that the employee was entitled to it.
>
> The employer may require self certification or a doctor's certificate after a shorter or longer period than indicated in the clause above.

Provided that you comply with the notification procedures the Employer will provide sick pay as set out below.

If you are ill or injured during a holiday and provide a medical certificate, the period covered by the certificate will be classed as sick leave rather than holiday leave.

> **Comment:** This clause is optional.

During any period of sick leave [lasting one month or more] you will accrue only statutory annual leave under the Working Time Regulations, and not contractual annual leave.

> **Comment:** This clause is optional. The employer may want to include it if the employee is entitled to contractual annual leave [**27.4.2.1**].

The Employer may, if concerned about your health, require you to have a medical examination by [the Employer's doctor / a doctor appointed by the Employer] and/or may require you to arrange for your own doctor to provide a full report. The Employer will meet any costs incurred in this.

> ***Comment:*** This clause is optional, but an employee cannot be required to undergo a medical examination (or other tests, such as drug or alcohol checks) unless the contract allows the employer to require this.
>
> Employers must take reasonable steps to adapt jobs or find alternative work for employees who are unable to work because of disability, which could include long-term sickness [**28.7.1**]. Employers who unjustifiably fail to take such steps could be liable for unlawful discrimination.

27.5.2   Sick pay

Provided that you comply with the notification procedures set out above, the Employer will provide sick pay as set out below.

[Statutory sick pay only] During absence due to sickness or injury you will receive statutory sick pay to which you are entitled. Your qualifying days in respect of statutory sick pay are Monday to Friday [or days the employee usually works] or such other days as are agreed in writing by the Employer.

> ***Comment:*** Employers are required to pay **statutory sick pay** (SSP) to employees who are entitled to it and have complied with the statutory rules, and may be able to recover some of it from HM Revenue and Customs [**31.6.1**]. If only SSP is to be paid there is no need to include this in the statement of particulars, but doing so makes clear that there is no further sick pay entitlement. Most voluntary sector employers offer more than SSP, and the statement should include details of this.
>
> SSP is payable only in respect of qualifying days [**31.6.1**], but these do not have to be included in the contract.

or

[SSP plus contractual sick pay] During absence due to sickness or injury you will receive statutory sick pay for which you are eligible, plus additional sick pay of up to the following amounts to bring your total pay to the following maximums:

[for example]

During your first [three] months of employment: no entitlement to contractual sick pay;

Thereafter, during your first [two] years of employment: up to [two] weeks' full pay during any 12-month period;

During your [third] year of employment: up to [three] weeks' full pay and [three] weeks' half pay during any 12-month period;

Thereafter you will be entitled to up to [five] weeks' full pay and [five] weeks' half pay during any 12-month period.

If you are ill for longer than these periods you are entitled only to statutory sick pay, although the Employer may at its discretion make additional sickness payments.

> ***Comment:*** There is no statutory requirement to pay employees more than SSP, so this clause is optional. However, most employers pay at least some additional (contractual) sick pay. The amounts suggested here are only examples, and the provision not to pay contractual sick pay in the first three (or whatever) months is also optional.
>
> For most employers it is no longer possible to recover statutory sick pay from the government [**31.6.1**], so before making any commitment to contractual sick pay, the employer should ensure it can afford to pay both the statutory and contractual elements of sick pay as well as meet the cost of any temporary staff to replace the person who is ill.
>
> The level of contractual sick pay can be increased during the first five years of employment without breaching the age discrimination regulations [**28.6.2**], but an increase requiring five years' service or more must be justifiable.
>
> If a contract says nothing about sick pay entitlement, a court would try to infer from other sources what had been agreed. In the complete absence of any such evidence, the court may assume that salary was payable 'for a reasonable period' during sickness or injury.

[SSP plus discretionary sick pay] During absence due to sickness or injury you will receive statutory sick pay for which you are eligible. At the Employer's discretion, you may also be paid addi-

tional sick pay of up to the following amounts to bring your total pay to the following maximums:

[Then as follows under 'Contractual sick pay', above]

> **Comment:** Even where the contract says that a payment is discretionary, a contractual entitlement may arise if it is, in fact, paid in practice.

It is your responsibility to obtain any state benefits you are entitled to and to inform your employer of your entitlement. Such entitlements will be deducted from contractual sick pay.

For calculating sick pay a 12-month period commences 12 months before the date when the period of absence due to sickness began.

> *or*

For sick pay purposes a year runs from 1 January to 31 December [or whatever]. Sick leave entitlement will be worked out pro rata from the beginning of this contract until next [31 December].

> **Comment:** It may be administratively easier to have everyone on the same sick leave year, which would generally be the same as the annual leave year [**27.4.2.2**]. However it is fairer to use a rolling year, based always on the previous 12 months.

Contractual sick pay may be terminated, suspended or deducted if you fail to follow the notification procedure, or if your absence or continued absence is due to your taking a clearly unwarranted risk, even in your own time; abusing alcohol or drugs or other substance abuse; breach of health and safety law or health and safety rules in the course of your work; or being involved in conduct prejudicial to your recovery. You will be given the opportunity to comment on any such proposal prior to it being implemented.

> **Comment:** This clause is optional.

Where you receive sick pay for any period because of any injury caused to you by a third party which gives you a right to recover damages or compensation from that third party, the amount of such sick pay shall be a loan to you by the Employer, repayable from damages or compensation you receive. You are required to inform the Employer of any such damages or compensation.

> **Comment:** This clause enables the employee to include the sick pay in any damages claim, for example after a car accident. If the employee is awarded damages, the employer can then seek reimbursement from the employee.

27.5.3   Parental and carers' rights

You are entitled to the following in accordance with legislation in force at the time: maternity, paternity and adoption leave and pay; parental leave; leave to deal with dependant emergencies; the right of parents and carers to request flexible working; and such other statutory employment rights as are available to parents, carers and families.

> **Comment:** There is no need to include this in the statement of particulars or contract, but doing so makes clear that the employee is entitled only to statutory provision. If the employer wants to give additional contractual entitlements – such as enhanced maternity, paternity or adoption pay or leave, parental leave or dependants leave – these should be clearly set out in the contract. Legal advice may be necessary to ensure the contractual and statutory entitlements dovetail with each other, are consistent, and do not breach sex discrimination or other equal opportunities legislation.

27.5.4   Time off for public duties

You will be allowed time off work for public duties in accordance with employment legislation in force at the time. [This time off is paid. You are required to claim all attendance allowances and loss of earning payments as may be possible in the circumstances, and to remit them to the Employer to offset your salary costs.]

> **Comment:** Time off for public duties does not have to be paid [**31.7**], so nothing needs to be included in the contract. If the employer is going to pay, the employee should be required to claim all allowances etc so these can be offset against salary. The employer may want to include a limit on the amount of paid time off, for example adding 'for a maxi-

mum of 12 days [or whatever] in any 12-month period' at the end of the first sentence in brackets, and making clear that if additional time off is allowed it will be on an unpaid basis and the employee will be able to keep any attendance allowance or loss of earnings payments.

27.5.5 Other contractual or discretionary benefits

Comment: Only benefits which the employer intends to be contractual should be included in the contract of employment, and it should be clear whether they are **entitlements** or **at the employer's discretion**. Rather than being included in the contract, discretionary benefits can be included in non-contractual policies or the staff handbook [**26.10**].

27.5.5.1 Special leave

[For example] Leave on a paid or unpaid basis may be granted in urgent or special personal circumstances. Leave of up to _____ working days may be granted by [your line manager, the chief executive or the chairperson], and if more than _____ days, whether paid or unpaid, must be confirmed by _____. Special leave if granted is on a case by case basis and does not create a precedent.

Comment: There is no statutory requirement to provide special leave (sometimes called **compassionate** or **discretionary leave**). But some contracts set out an entitlement and approval procedure for this, and may include a safeguard that any leave of more than a certain amount needs to be confirmed by someone higher in the organisation. It is important to be clear how special leave fits in with leave to deal with dependant emergencies [**32.8**].

27.5.5.2 Study or training leave

[For example] Requests for study leave or time off for training on a paid or unpaid basis will be dealt with, where applicable, in accordance with any statutory right to request time off for training. Where the statutory right does not apply, requests will be dealt with in the same way as special leave.

Comment: There is no statutory obligation to allow study leave except for some 16 and 17-year-olds [**31.8.2**]. At the time of writing (mid 2009), the government had proposed giving employees a statutory right to request time off for training [**31.8.2**]. Some employers consider it good practice to offer study or training leave even without a statutory obligation. The employer should have clear guidelines about this, for example whether the studies must be work related, whether leave is paid or unpaid, maximum leave, any contribution by the employer towards the cost of the course or books, and whether the employer will require repayment of some or all contributions towards the costs and/or salary for paid leave if the employee leaves within a specified period.

27.5.5.3 Sabbatical leave

[For example] After _____ years continuous employment you may apply for up to _____ months unpaid sabbatical leave. The application must be made at least six months before the intended start date. Any decision to grant such leave is at the discretion of the Employer, whose primary consideration will be whether your work can be covered in your absence.

If sabbatical leave is granted you will have the right to return to the same or a substantially similar post on the same terms and conditions as if the employment had been continuous, with no loss of rights.

Comment: A small number of employers allow all staff, or senior staff, to take time off after an extended period of service (such as five or seven years). Before offering even an unpaid sabbatical, the employer should consider the potential costs of recruiting, training and supporting a replacement worker during the sabbatical. Unless the organisation has and expects to maintain substantial reserves, it should be wary of making contractual commitments such as this. Most organisations will not find it wise to include such a provision.

> If the right to request a sabbatical is linked to length of service of more than five years it must be justifiable, for example for the retention or motivation of staff [**28.6.2**].

27.6 TERMINATION OF EMPLOYMENT

27.6.1 Retirement

Your employment will automatically terminate when you reach age [65]. You have the right to ask to continue working after retirement age.

or

The employer does not have a mandatory retirement age but may require you to retire at any time after you reach age 65. You have the right to ask to continue working.

> *Comment:* Employers are not obliged to set a retirement age, but at the time of writing (mid 2009) it was not unlawful to do so [**28.6.1**] provided it is the same for men and women. An employee could not be required to retire below age 65 unless this is objectively justified, and there is a statutory right for all employees facing retirement to ask to continue working [**28.6**]. [See **34.2.8** for more about retirement.]

27.6.2 Termination by notice

27.6.2.1 Notice by employer

Except for dismissal for gross misconduct where dismissal may be without notice, the minimum notice of termination of employment to which you are entitled is:

In your first month of employment: no notice;

then in the first two years of continuous employment: one week's notice;

after two years of continuous employment, two weeks' notice;

then one additional week for each completed year of employment, to a maximum of 12 weeks' notice after 12 years of continuous employment.

Notice will be in writing.

> *Comment:* The notice required to be given by the employer and employee to terminate the contract must be given in the statement of particulars, or the statement may refer the employee to the law or to a collective agreement provided the employee has reasonable access to it.
> *Employment Rights Act 1996 ss.1(4)(e), 2(3), 6*

> The clause above sets out the statutory minimum notice to which all employees are entitled [**34.3.1**]. An employer can agree in the contract to give longer notice, but not less. *Employment Rights Act 1996 s.86(1)*

> Although the statutory minimum notice periods cannot be reduced in the contract, there is nothing to stop either party from waiving its right to notice on any occasion. *Employment Rights Act 1996 s.86(3)*

> Note that there is a contradiction between this notice clause, which sets out the statutory minimum, and the probationary period clause above [**27.1.6**], which commits the employer to giving (and requires from the employee) more than the statutory minimum in the first month. If a probationary period clause is included, the notice required should be consistent with the notice clause.

The Employer reserves the right to make a payment in lieu of notice should it so wish. Any payment in lieu of notice will be an amount equal to your salary for the period, less an amount equal to income tax and national insurance normally deductible.

> *Comment:* There is no obligation to include provision for **pay in lieu of notice** (PILON). In some situations where there is a PILON clause the employer may be entitled to pay a reduced amount if the employee obtains other employment during the notice period; in other situations the employer must pay the full amount even if the employee gets other work [**34.3.7**]. The amount paid by the employer is subject to tax and national insurance in the usual way.

Technically PILON cannot be given unless the contract allows, but in practice it is often done [**34.3.7**]. If a PILON clause is not included but the employer makes a payment in lieu of notice, this is technically damages for breach of contract [**21.7.2**]. Damages are not generally taxable so may be paid without deduction of tax or national insurance, but HM Revenue and Customs closely scrutinises such payments and legal advice should be sought.

In the case of gross misconduct you may be dismissed without notice and without pay in lieu of notice.

> *Comment:* This clause allows the employer to dismiss without notice (summary dismissal) in very serious cases [**33.3.10**].

27.6.2.2 Notice by employee

The notice you are required to give is:

In your first month of employment: none;

thereafter, one week's notice.

Notice must be in writing.

> *Comment:* This clause sets out the legal minimum notice which employees are required to give [**34.3.1**]. *Employment Rights Act 1996 s.86(2)*
>
> Virtually all employers require longer notice. Many employees are required to give the same notice as they are entitled to receive.

27.6.2.3 Work during the notice period

Regardless of whether you or the Employer give notice, the Employer reserves the right to require you to remain away from work for some or all of the notice period, and/or to take any accrued leave owing to you [**27.4.2.3**]. Where the Employer exercises this right, you will be required to comply with any conditions relating to your work laid down by the Employer. While on full pay during such time you may not undertake any employment or any work on your own behalf without the Employer's prior written permission.

> *Comment:* This clause should be included if there could be situations where the employer would prefer that the employee not come in to work during the notice period, or does not wish the employee to work during the notice period for another employer that is in competition with the employer.

27.6.3 Redundancy

In the event of being made redundant you will be entitled to such payment and other rights as the relevant statutes in force at the time require.

> *Comment:* If only the minimum statutory provisions apply [**35.7.1**], there is no need to include anything about redundancy in the contract. If the employer wishes to give contractual redundancy payments which are more generous than the statutory provision, or to give contractual redundancy payments to employees who are not covered by the statutory provision, this should be included. Details can be included in a redundancy policy or staff handbook.
>
> Some voluntary organisations have very generous contractual redundancy pay. This is good for the employees, but could create serious difficulties for the organisation if it cannot meet its contractual obligations.
>
> See **chapter 35** for more about redundancy.

27.6.4 Recovery of training costs

Where the Employer has paid training costs for you of more than £_____ during the [12 month / 24 month] period prior to the date that you cease your employment, you [must / may be at the Employer's discretion required to] repay to the Employer a proportion of the training costs calculated as follows: [*for example*] one-half of the cost of the training if you leave during the training or within six months of finishing it; and one-quarter of the cost if you leave from six to 24 months from the end of the training.

Comment: This is optional. If it is included, it must be consistent with any provisions on study leave and time off for training [**27.5.5.2**]. Where lengthy or costly courses are paid for by the employer, the organisation may wish to enter into a more detailed agreement.

27.6.5 Consequences of termination

Upon termination of this contract you must:

(a) On the request of the Employer resign, without claim for compensation, from all offices held by you in the Employer [or any subsidiary, associated or affiliated organisation ('the Group')]. If you fail to do so, the Employer is authorised to appoint any person to sign all required documents and take any required action on your behalf to give effect to your resignation;

(b) Immediately deliver to the Employer, or as it may direct, all books, documents, papers, correspondence, lists, records, materials and other property (on whatever media and wherever located) of or relating to the work of the Employer [or the Group] or its contacts which may then be in your possession or under your control, together with all copies and extracts from them;

(c) Delete any information relating to the work of the Employer [or the Group] stored on any magnetic or optical disk or memory and all materials derived from such sources which is in your possession or under your control outside the Employer's premises;

(d) Not at any time after termination of employment represent yourself as being in any way connected with the work of the Employer [or the Group];

(e) Not for a period of one year thereafter either on your own account or for any other person, firm or company transact business with, solicit, accept orders, interfere with or endeavour to entice away from the Group to engage in business of the nature carried on by the Employer during the 12 months preceding termination, any person, firm or company which is, or at any time during such period has been, a customer or client of or in the habit of dealing with the Group;

(f) For a period of one year thereafter neither solicit, entice nor procure any employee to leave the employment of the Group who is or, during the preceding 90 days was, an employee of the Employer or the Group.

> *Comment:* None of these clauses is required, but voluntary organisations are increasingly aware of the need to protect their information and intellectual property when an employee leaves.
>
> Clauses such as (e) and (f) are **restrictive covenants** limiting competitive behaviour after termination of employment [**26.8.2**].

27.7 DISCIPLINE AND GRIEVANCE
27.7.1 Disciplinary and grievance procedures

You are subject to the Employer's disciplinary and grievance procedures, which are attached to this contract but do not form part of it.

If you wish to appeal against a disciplinary or dismissal decision you may apply in writing to [position] in accordance with the Employer's disciplinary procedure.

If you wish to raise a grievance, you may apply in writing to [position] in accordance to the Employer's grievance procedure.

The person to whom you must apply to raise a grievance or appeal against a disciplinary or dismissal decision may be changed at any time by the Employer giving notice to you in writing.

> *Comment:* The statement of particulars must identify to whom and how a complaint about a disciplinary decision or any decision to dismiss an employee should be made, and with whom a grievance should be raised. In addition it must include any disciplinary rules and details of any disciplinary procedures, or must refer to another document which is reasonably accessible to employees.
>
> If the disciplinary and grievance procedures form part of the contract, the rules governing variation of contract apply [**26.9**]. It is better to have them as a separate document which is explicitly not part of the contract [**33.1.2**].
>
> See **chapter 33** for more about disciplinary and grievance matters.

27.7.2   Suspension

The Employer may suspend you while carrying out a disciplinary investigation into any alleged act or default. Such suspension will be for so long as appropriate, and depending on the circumstances may be on full or reduced pay or without pay.

> *Comment:* There is no obligation to include this in the contract. But unless the contract contains a provision allowing suspension, such action may be in breach of contract. Hence even if the disciplinary procedure is excluded from the contract for the reasons stated above, the right to suspend should be included in the contract.
>
> Similarly if you wish to include disciplinary suspension, demotion or transfer as a disciplinary penalty after a disciplinary hearing, the contract must include specific provision. Even with contractual provision, the necessary disciplinary procedures must be followed [**33.3**].

27.8   DISCLOSURES

27.8.1   Outside remuneration connected with your employment

If you receive any outside remuneration for work undertaken on behalf of the Employer or arising directly from your employment by the Employer (for example, fees for a speaking engagement or an article), you are required to disclose and pay these to the Employer.

> *Comment:* There is no obligation to include anything about outside remuneration, but doing so avoids doubt if employees receive outside fees for work directly connected with their employment.

27.8.2   Paid work

You must devote your full time and attention to your employment and are therefore not allowed to undertake any other paid work while employed by the Employer.

> *or*

You must inform the Employer in writing before taking up any other paid [or unpaid] work, and must keep the Employer informed of the nature and hours of any such work. Where the Employer reasonably believes your total working hours exceed or may exceed an average of 48 hours per week, the Employer will ask you to opt out of the 48-hour limit imposed by the Working Time Regulations unless you have already opted out [**27.2.6**].

> *or*

You must notify the Employer in writing on each Monday of the number of hours (if any) worked for any other employer or on a self employed or any other paid basis in the previous week.

> *and, if desired*

Where the Employer reasonably believes that such employment is having or will have an adverse effect on the Employer or your health or your ability to undertake this job, the Employer may require you to cease such employment or reduce the hours worked.

> *Comment:* Requiring an employee to inform the employer of outside work is good practice because the **Working Time Regulations 1998** put a duty on employers to ensure an employee does not work more than an average of 48 hours per week in all employments [**31.2.1**], unless the person has opted out in each of the employments.

27.8.3   Conflict of interest

You must disclose to the Employer any direct or indirect relationship that you or any close relative have with any customer, client or beneficiary of the Employer, or any direct or indirect interest held by you in a company, firm, organisation, agency or other body which carries on a business or operations the same as or similar to those of the Employer.

If you or a close relative has any direct or indirect interest in any company, firm, organisation, agency or other body which may enter into a contract with the Employer, this interest must be disclosed to the Employer as soon as you become aware of it.

> *Comment:* Although there is a common law duty to give honest and faithful service and to pass on information relevant to the employment

[**26.3.4**], there is generally no statutory obligation for an employee to declare conflicts of interest to the employer. If the organisation does work in which conflicts of interest might be significant, a clause such as this may be appropriate.

If the organisation is a company and/or charity and the employee or a person connected with the employee is a company director and/or charity trustee, there is an obligation to disclose conflicts of interest [**15.2**].

27.8.4 Inducements

If at any time you are offered any gift or consideration as an inducement to influence a contract or obtain preferential treatment for any customer, client or beneficiary of the Employer, or if any suggestion of this type is made to you, you must report it immediately to the Employer.

> *Comment:* There is no obligation to include this but in some situations it may be appropriate.

27.8.5 Relationships within work

If you or a close relative enters into a close personal relationship with an employee of the Employer or a member of the Employer's [management committee / board], you are required to disclose this to the Employer. Depending on the circumstances the Employer may need to inform the Charity Commission and/or may change lines of accountability.

> *Comment:* There is no obligation to include a '**love contract**' such as this, but it may be sensible to avoid the risk of favouritism (or allegations), and to avoid a situation where a person connected with a charity trustee is being paid by the organisation without this being authorised by the governing document or the Charity Commission [**16.4.4**].

27.9 TRADE UNION MEMBERSHIP

You may join any trade union of your choice.

> *Comment:* For more about trade union membership see **36.4.1**.

27.10 THE EMPLOYER'S POLICIES

> *Comment:* It is important to be clear whether policies are contractual or non-contractual. If they are contractual, they can be changed only with the consent of every employee to whom they apply. Even if the policy itself is non-contractual, there can be a contractual obligation to comply with it – as in many of the clauses below.

27.10.1 Competition

During your employment and for the six months afterwards you must not, directly or indirectly, engage in or undertake any work which is or is intended to be in competition with the Employer. This includes work undertaken on your own account, or as a partner, or as an agent, employee, officer, director, consultant or shareholder of any company or other entity, as a member of any firm, or in any other way.

> *Comment:* This clause is a **restrictive covenant** [**26.8.2**], limiting what the employee can do after termination of employment. Legal advice should always be sought before including restrictive covenants.
>
> Note that this clause overlaps with, but is different from, clause (e) in **27.6.5**. It is important to ensure internal consistency within a contract, and between contractual and non-contractual provisions.

27.10.2 Personal data

For the purposes of the Data Protection Act 1998 you give your consent to the holding and processing of personal data provided by you to the Employer for all purposes relating to the performance of your employment. This includes administering and maintaining HR records; paying and reviewing salary and other remuneration and benefits; providing and administering benefits including, if relevant, pension or insurance; undertaking performance and fitness appraisals and reviews; maintaining sickness and other absence records; providing references and information to future employers, and if necessary, HM Revenue and Customs and governmental and quasi-governmental bodies for social security and other purposes; providing information to organisations with whom we may work in partnership, merge or transfer an undertaking; and transferring information concerning you to a country or territory outside the European Economic Area.

The employer's data protection and confidentiality policies, with which you must comply, are in the staff handbook and do not form part of this contract.

27.10.2.1 Sensitive personal data

From time to time it may be necessary to process sensitive personal data, for example about your health. By signing this contract you agree that the Employer may retain and process sensitive personal data about you as the needs of the Employer require, both inside and outside the European Economic Area.

> *Comment:* The **Data Protection Act 1998** requires explicit consent to store or process sensitive personal data, which includes information about racial or ethnic background, health, disability, religious belief, trade union membership, marital status or criminal convictions [**43.3**].

27.10.3 Confidentiality

You must not at any time during your employment or after the termination of your employment disclose any confidential information arising out of your employment, unless such disclosure is authorised under the Employer's policies on data protection and confidential information, or is protected under the Public Interest Disclosure Act. Confidential information includes any information (whether or not recorded in documentary form, or stored on any magnetic or optical disk or memory) which is not in the public domain relating to the business, products, affairs and finance of the Employer for the time being confidential to the Employer and trade secrets including, without limitation, technical data and knowhow relating to the business of the Employer or any of its business contacts.

> *Comment:* If the organisation does not have a data protection and confidentiality policies, replace the words from 'under' to 'information' with 'by the Employer'. For more about confidentiality see **43.1**, and for more about whistleblowing see **33.5**.

27.10.4 Use of email, internet and telephones

If you are provided with access to telephones, computers and electronic communication devices, these are intended for business use and you must comply with the Employer's policy on their use. The policy is in the staff handbook and does not form part of this contract. The Employer reserves the right to monitor email, telephone, internet and other communications in accordance with the policy, and your signature on this contract indicates your consent.

> *Comment:* For more about employees' right to privacy, the employer's right to monitor communications, and acceptable use policies for computers and electronic communications see **43.1.4** and **43.5**.

27.10.5 Intellectual property rights

Copyright, database rights, registered and unregistered design rights, patents and any other intellectual property rights in any materials in any medium produced by you during the course of your employment belong to the Employer. You must return all such materials and any copies in your possession to the Employer on request.

You must, at the Employer's request and cost during the employment and thereafter, if required, take all steps as may be necessary or desirable to substantiate the Employer's rights in respect of any such work.

> *Comment:* There is no need to include this in a contract, because copyright material, designs, databases and inventions created during employment belong to the employer [**44.2.3**]. But a clause like this provides additional clarity and protection for the employer.

27.10.6 Health and safety

The health and safety of all employees and of visitors to the Employer's premises are an important consideration. You have a legal duty to take care of your own health and safety and that of others who may be affected by what you do or do not do. The Employer's health and safety policy, with which you must comply, is in the staff handbook and does not form part of this contract.

> *Comment:* This is a statutory obligation for all employees, but it does not hurt to remind them. For more about health and safety, see **chapter 40**.

27.10.7 Smoking

Smoking is not allowed anywhere in the Employer's buildings, grounds and vehicles, except in designated outdoor smoking areas. For the Employer's rules about smoking in other vehicles or premises such as clients' homes, see the smoking policy with which you must comply but which does not form part of this contract.

> *Comment:* There is no obligation to include anything about smoking but the organisation may wish to do so. See **40.4.2** for more about smoking at work.

27.10.8 Equal opportunities

Every employee must act at all times in accordance with equal opportunities legislation and the Employer's equal opportunities policies and codes of practice. These are in the staff handbook and do not form part of this contract.

> *Comment:* As with health and safety, some employees may need reminding. For more about equal opportunities, see **chapter 28**.

27.10.9 Media

Communication with the press, television or radio, or via blogs, social networking sites or other media, must be authorised by the Employer if it is in any way connected with your employment or is likely to contain reference to the Employer. The Employer's media policy, with which you must comply, is in the staff handbook but does not form part of this contract.

> *Comment:* The organisation may wish to include a clause such as this.

27.11 EMPLOYEE BENEFITS

> *Comment:* The following clauses relate to financial matters other than salary and pension, and to 'perks'. Some of these benefits may be subject to tax and national insurance.

27.11.1 Removal expenses

The Employer will contribute £_____ towards your removal expenses to take up this post.

> *Comment:* There is no obligation to pay relocation expenses. If payment for removal expenses meets certain requirements and is less than £8,000 (as at 1/8/09), it is not subject to tax or national insurance [**30.4.9**].

27.11.2 Reimbursement of expenses

Out of pocket expenses and agreed travel and subsistence costs will be reimbursed in accordance with the Employer's financial procedures. These do not form part of this contract.

> *Comment:* There is no need to include anything about reimbursement of expenses, since employees have a right to be reimbursed for essential or authorised expenditure. Some reimbursements may be subject to tax [**30.4.9**].

27.11.3 Car use

Use of your own vehicle for authorised work purposes will be reimbursed at a mileage rate set out in the Employer's financial procedures. Mileage records must be kept and must be submitted in accordance with the Employer's procedures.

> *Comment:* There is no obligation to include this, but if the employee might use a privately owned vehicle it is good practice to set out the

rules in a handbook, or possibly in the contract. Reimbursement at more than the rate allowed by tax law is subject to tax [**30.4.10**]. Staff who use their own vehicles must be aware of the need to inform their insurer that the vehicle is being used for work purposes [**23.8**]. If a car comes with the job, this should be reflected in a clause in the contract.

27.11.4 Use of facilities

Use of the employer's facilities or equipment for personal use is not permitted without prior written consent from the Employer.

> **Comment:** There is no need to include this but the organisation may want to. It is generally preferable to include matters like this in the staff handbook, where they can be easily revised, rather than in the contract.

27.11.5 Gratuities

You are not allowed to accept gratuities, money or non-monetary gifts from clients or users of the Employer's services. If such gratuities or gifts are given to you without your prior knowledge, they must be given to the Employer.

or

You are not allowed to accept money from clients, customers or users of the Employer's services, nor may you accept a non-monetary gift with a value of more than £___. If money or such a gift is given to you without your prior knowledge, it must be given to the Employer. You may keep a non-monetary gift with a value under £_____ provided you report it in writing to the employer.

> **Comment:** There is no need to include this in the contract. Rules such as these are generally better in a staff handbook, where they can be more easily changed.

27.12 THE CONTRACT ITSELF
27.12.1 Transfer and secondment

The Employer is entitled to assign its rights under this agreement to any subsidiary or associated employer, or any body with which it may be merged or which may succeed it, on giving you written notice of its intention to this effect. It may also require you to work for another organisation, while remaining employed by the Employer.

> **Comment:** This clause gives the employer the right to transfer the employee's contract to an associated organisation such as a trading subsidiary, a new organisation set up to undertake a specific project etc. It also allows the employer to require the employee to work for any organisation on a seconded basis. Both transfer and secondment raise significant issues [**29.7, 25.5.4**].

27.12.2 Variation

The Employer reserves the right to make reasonable changes to any of your terms and conditions of employment. You will be notified in writing of minor changes of detail, and any such change takes effect from the date of the notice or such other date as specified in the notice. More significant changes will be made only after consultation, and with at least one month's written notice.

> **Comment:** A clause such as this can be very useful in enabling the employer to make minor or relatively minor changes to the contract. Even with this provision, the employer should be very cautious about making changes without the employee's consent [**26.9.3**], and if in any doubt should seek legal advice.

27.12.3 Collective agreements

This contract is affected by the terms of a collective agreement between [trade union or unions] and [employer or other party to the agreement].

or

This contract is not covered by any collective agreement.

> *Comment:* If any collective agreement [**36.3.4**] directly affects the terms of employment it must be referred to in the statement of particulars. If the employer is not a party, the names of the parties to the agreement must be included. A collective agreement might or might not be contractual.
>
> *Employment Rights Act 1996 s.1(4)(j)*

27.12.4 Rights of third parties

This contract does not purport, and is not intended, to confer any benefit on any third party pursuant to the Contracts (Rights of Third Parties) Act 1999.

> *Comment:* For more about rights of third parties under a contract, see **21.1.5**.

27.12.5 Governing law and jurisdiction

This agreement shall be governed by and construed in accordance with the law of England and Wales [or Scotland]. Each party irrevocably agrees to submit to the exclusive jurisdiction of the courts of England and Wales [or Scotland] over any claim or matter arising under or in connection with this agreement.

> *Comment:* Specifying that the contract is subject to the English (which includes Welsh) or Scottish courts will provide some certainty as to the approach that would be taken. If, as a matter of fact, a non-UK national is employed outside the UK it is doubtful that UK courts would accept jurisdiction [**26.11**].

Signatures

Signed: [Name]

For and on behalf of [Employer]

[Date]

I have read, understood and accept the above terms and conditions of employment.

Signed: [Employee]

[Date]

> *Comment:* A written statement of employment particulars [**26.7**] or broader written contract does not need to be signed by either the employer or employee. However signatures are proof that the employee has received the statement of particulars, and for a broader contract signatures show that each side has accepted the terms as set out.

Resources: MODEL CONTRACT OF EMPLOYMENT

ACAS, BIS, Business Link, CIPD, Directgov, PEACe, TUC: see end of **chapter 25**.

Statute law. www.opsi.gov.uk and www.statutelaw.gov.uk.

Much but not all case law. www.bailii.org.

Updates cross-referenced to this book. www.rclh.co.uk.

Chapter 28
EQUAL OPPORTUNITIES IN EMPLOYMENT

For sources of further information see end of chapter.

28.1 UNLAWFUL DISCRIMINATION

Unlawful **discrimination** involves treating people less favourably because they are members of a particular group or have a particular characteristic. Discrimination may be **direct [28.1.3]** or **indirect [28.1.4]**, or may take the form of **victimisation [28.1.5]** or **harassment [28.1.6]**.

The legislation covers all stages of employment: recruitment and selection, conditions of employment, benefits, transfer or promotion, dismissal, and in some situations acts by the employer after employment has ended [**28.1.2**].

In very specific circumstances [**28.1.7**], employers are allowed to treat one group more favourably, and therefore other groups less favourably.

Good practice is promoted through guidance and codes of practice issued by the **Equality and Human Rights Commission** [see end of chapter]. Failure to comply with the codes is not unlawful, but is taken into account in discrimination cases. The EHRC also has investigatory and enforcement powers. Equality legislation is developed by the **Government Equalities Office** [see end of chapter].

28.1.1 Discriminatory grounds

Discrimination is unlawful only if it is on a **prohibited ground**. These are also referred to as equality **strands**, and under the **Equality Act [28.1.12]** are likely to be called **protected characteristics**. Prohibited grounds are:

- **racial group** or **racial grounds**, defined as race, ethnic origin, national origin, colour or nationality [**28.2**];
- **sex**, being **married** or in a **civil partnership**, **gender reassignment**, **pregnancy** or **maternity** [**28.3**];
- **religion**, **religious belief**, **philosophical belief** or lack of belief [**28.4**];
- **sexual orientation** [**28.5**];
- **age** [**28.6**];
- having a **disability**, as defined under the legislation [**28.7.1**].

Other aspects of anti-discrimination legislation apply to **equal pay** [**28.8**], **part-time** workers [**26.4.2**], **fixed-term** employees [**26.4.3**] people with a spent **criminal conviction** [**41.8**], and belonging or not belonging to a **trade union** or taking part in trade union activities [**36.4.1**].

Equality legislation not only prohibits unlawful discrimination, but in some cases requires public sector bodies to eliminate discrimination and promote equality of opportunity in the exercise of public functions [**42.2**]. At the time of writing (mid 2009) these **equality duties** covered race, sex and disability, but the **Equality Act** [**28.1.12**] was expected to extend them to cover gender reassignment, religion/belief, sexual orientation and age, and possibly socio-economic inequality.

28.1.1.1 Discrimination on the basis of perceived characteristics

Legislation covers discrimination on the basis of the person's **perceived** as well as their actual age or sexual orientation. So it is as unlawful to discriminate against a heterosexual woman who is perceived as being lesbian, as it is to discriminate against a lesbian. *Employment Equality (Age) Regulations 2006 [2006/1031] reg.3(3)(b); Equality Act (Sexual Orientation) Regulations 2007 [2007/1263] reg.3(2)*

At the time of writing (mid 2009) there was no legislation or case law making it unlawful to discriminate on the basis of perceived racial group, sex, religion or disability. However, the **Equality Act** [**28.1.12**] was expected to extend discrimination on the basis of perceived characteristics to these strands.

28.1.1.2 Discrimination where the person does not have the characteristic

The age, sex and disability legislation say that discrimination can occur only against a worker who has the relevant characteristic. But for race, religion/belief and sexual orientation, the legislation states that discrimination occurs 'on grounds of' the relevant characteristic, without requiring the worker who has been discriminated against to have that characteristic. This wording could, for example, enable a white employee who has been required to carry out racist instructions or listen to racist comments by colleagues to claim direct discrimination or harassment. *Wethersfield Ltd (trading as Van & Truck Rentals) v Sargent [1999] IRLR 94 CA*

28.1.1.3 Discrimination by association

Similarly, in relation to race, religion/belief and sexual orientation where the worker is not required to have the relevant characteristic in order to claim discrimination, the courts have said it is unlawful to discriminate on the basis of a worker's association with persons with that characteristic. This includes, for example, discriminating against a white person who has a black partner. **Discrimination by association** is sometimes called **associative discrimination**.

In a decision in 2008 the European court of justice ruled that it is unlawful to directly discriminate against or harass a non-disabled worker because of their association with a disabled person – in this case, a non-disabled mother looking after her disabled child. Following this decision, the employment tribunal confirmed that all relevant sections of the **Disability Discrimination Act 1995** should be read as applying not only to a disabled person but also to a person associated with a disabled person. *Coleman v Attridge Law & Steve Law [2008] EUECJ C-303/06; Coleman v EBR Attridge Law LLP & Steve Law (2008) London South ET 2302745/2005*

The same principle is likely to apply to religion/belief, age and sexual orientation, which all come under the same EU Directive. At the time of writing (mid 2009) the **Equality Act** [**28.1.12**] was expected to make discrimination by association because of any of the protected characteristics unlawful.

28.1.2 Who is protected

Discrimination legislation protects all employees whether full or part time, permanent or temporary, as well as applicants for jobs [**chapter 29**], casual workers [**25.3.2**], workers supplied by an agency or by another person, self employed workers, and anyone else who is contracted to provide work personally to the employer. The legislation covers individuals in vocational training, and in some situations might also apply to volunteers [**39.4.3**].

Protection may in some cases apply to discriminatory acts by the employer even after employment has ended. For example, if an employer refuses to give a reference to a person who has brought a discrimination claim against the employer, this may constitute victimisation [**29.6.1**].

Workers are protected by discrimination legislation if they work at an establishment in Great Britain, and work wholly or partly in Great Britain. In some situations they may be protected if they work wholly outside Great Britain [**26.11.2**].

28.1.3 Direct discrimination

Direct discrimination involves treating someone less favourably, on discriminatory grounds, than a person who does not have that characteristic is or would be treated in the same or a similar situation, where such treatment is not a proportionate means of achieving a legitimate aim. For something to be **proportionate** it must be an **appropriate and necessary** way of achieving something legitimately necessary for the work, by falling within the genuine occupational requirement or other provisions allowing such discrimination [**28.1.7**].

28.1.4 Indirect discrimination

Indirect discrimination in general involves use of a **provision, criterion, or practice** which is not a proportionate means of achieving a legitimate aim, and which is applied to everyone equally but has the effect of putting people of a particular group at a disadvantage because they disproportionately cannot comply with it. An example is a requirement to be able to speak a specific language, which puts people of other ethnic or national groups at a disadvantage, but which may be proportionate and therefore lawful if the work involves communication with speakers of that language who may not know English, and the employer does not have other employees who could communicate with those people.

At the time of writing (mid 2009) a different definition of indirect discrimination was used for some aspects of race discrimination [**28.2.2**], but this was expected to be standardised in the **Equality Act** [**28.1.12**]. Also at the time of writing disability discrimination law had the concept of disability related discrimination but this was possibly going to be replaced with indirect discrimination [**28.7.3**].

28.1.5 Victimisation

Victimisation involves treating a worker less favourably than he or she would otherwise be because the worker has brought a discrimination claim against the employer or another worker, given evidence or information in connection with proceedings brought by someone else against the employer or another worker, or taken other action under discrimination law. These are called **protected acts**. Victimisation can also occur when an employer treats a worker less favourably because of the worker's threat to undertake a protected act, or a suspicion by the employer that the worker intends to do any of them.   *Sex Discrimination Act 1975 s.4;*
Race Relations Act 1976 s.2; Disability Discrimination Act 1995 s.55; Employment Equality (Religion or Belief)
Regulations 2003 [SI 2003/1660] reg.4; Employment Equality (Sexual Orientation) Regulations 2003
[SI 2003/1661] reg.4; Employment Equality (Age) Regulations 2006 [SI 2006/1031] reg.4

Workers are not protected against victimisation if they if they make false allegations or provide false information or evidence, or if they do not act in good faith.

28.1.6 Harassment

Harassment occurs where an employer subjects a worker – or allows a worker to be subjected – to unwanted conduct on the grounds of race, ethnic or national origin, disability, religion or belief, sexual orientation or age, which has the purpose or effect of violating that worker's dignity or creating an intimidating, hostile, degrading, humiliating or offensive environment for that worker. For sexual harassment and harassment on the basis of sex, see **28.1.6.1**.

Race Relations Act 1976 s.3A, inserted by RRA 1976 (Amendment) Regulations 2003 [SI 2003/1626] reg.5;
Disability Discrimination Act 1995 s.3B, inserted by DDA 1995 (Amendment) Regulations 2003 [SI 2003/1673]
regs.3,4; Employment Equality (Religion or Belief) Regulations 2003 [SI 2003/1660] reg.5;
Employment Equality (Sexual Orientation) Regulations 2003 [SI 2003/1661] reg.5;
Employment Equality (Age) Regulations 2006 [SI 2006/1031] reg.6

At the time of writing (mid 2009) harassment on the basis of colour or nationality was not explicitly covered under the 2003 amendments to the **Race Relations Act 1976 [28.2]**, so a person claiming harassment on those grounds would have to show direct discrimination, or would have to claim harassment on the basis of race or ethnic or national origin. This discrepancy was expected to be remedied in the **Equality Act [28.1.12]**.

Examples of behaviour which could constitute harassment include unwanted physical contact, offensive comments or emails that are 'intended to be a joke', isolating a person and not including them in conversation or events, unwelcome remarks about a person's dress or appearance, shouting at staff, insulting or constantly criticising staff, and setting impossible deadlines or standards.

Harassment may be based on the characteristics of a person or group with whom the worker associates [**28.1.1.2**] – even where direct discrimination by association does not apply. Harassment by association could occur, for example, where a worker is mocked for having a relationship with a younger or older person.

Treating a person who does not have the characteristic as if he or she did – for example a case where a man known to be heterosexual was called 'faggot' and subjected to homophobic 'banter' because he lived in Brighton and had gone to boarding school – can be harassment.   *English v Thomas Sanderson Ltd [2008] EWCA Civ 1421*

Unless they can show they took reasonably practicable steps to prevent it happening, employers are liable for harassment carried out by workers in the course of their employment and could also be liable for harassment by customers, service users or other third parties [**28.1.6.1, 28.1.8**].

As well as being an offence under the equality legislation, harassment may also be a criminal offence under the **Protection from Harassment Act 1997** [**40.5.3**] or the **Racial and Religious Hatred Act 2006** [**47.9.2**], or may constitute bullying under health and safety legislation [**40.5.3**].

28.1.6.1   Sexual harassment

The definition of harassment on grounds of sex, including **sexual harassment**, is wider than for the other strands. Such harassment occurs when a person:

- engages in unwanted conduct that is related to the sex of the person claiming harassment (A) or the sex of another person, which has the purpose or effect of violating A's dignity or creating an intimidating, hostile, degrading, humiliating or offensive environment for A;

- engages in any form of unwanted verbal, non-verbal or physical conduct of a sexual nature that has the same purpose or effect as above for A; or

- because of A's rejection of or submission to such unwanted conduct, treats A less favourably than if A had not rejected or submitted to such conduct.

Sex Discrimination Act 1975 s.4A, inserted by Employment Equality (Sex Discrimination) Regulations 2005
[SI 2005/2467] reg.5 & amended by SDA 1975 (Amendment) Regulations 2008 [SI 2008/656] reg.3

An example is a case where the use of pornography on a workplace computer by male employees in the presence of a female colleague gave rise to a claim for sexual harassment, even though the woman was not shown the pornographic images and did not make a complaint at the time about the pornography. Because the male employees' behaviour had undermined the woman's dignity at work, the burden of proof shifted to the employer [**28.9.1**] to disprove that she had suffered any harassment.   *Moonsar v Fiveways Express Transport Ltd [2004] UKEAT 0476 04 2709*

Harassment on grounds of **gender reassignment** occurs if a person who intends to undergo, is undergoing or has undergone gender reassignment is subject to harassment as defined in the first and third bullet points above.

Harassment on grounds of pregnancy, maternity leave, or civil partnership is not explicitly covered under the amendments to the Sex Discrimination Act, so a person harassed on those grounds would have to show direct discrimination.

An employer may be liable for acts of sexual harassment by third parties where harassment is known to have occurred on at least two previous occasions, unless the employer has taken reasonably practical steps to avoid it. *Sex Discrimination Act 1975 (Amendment) Regulations 2008 [SI 2008/656] reg.4*

28.1.6.2   Cards and parties

It is not unlawful for holiday, birthday, valentine's day and similar cards to be exchanged at work – but unwanted cards or gifts, especially those which are sexually suggestive or offensive or are rude about age, could constitute harassment. So also could cards which assume everyone celebrates Christmas as a Christian religious festival. Employers should be sensible about whether an explicit policy is required, or common sense is enough. If a worker claims harassment, the tribunal will look at all the circumstances, and in particular the claimant's perception.

Where there is a work culture of celebrating holidays or birthdays, engagements, births and similar personal events, either in the workplace or informally during a lunch break or after work, it is important to ensure these are sensitive to individuals, and that some workers are not excluded because of age, religion, sexual orientation or similar factors. Even where such events are held away from the workplace, the employer could be liable for discrimination or harassment if the event can be shown to be work related.

28.1.6.3   Overheard comments

Overheard comments, even if they do not directly apply to a worker, can be discriminatory. In one case where a Maltese worker overheard her supervisor saying she would vote for a particular candidate who 'would get rid of the foreigners', both the employer and a supervisor were found guilty of racial discrimination. The tribunal found that this and similar remarks showed that the supervisor had a 'substantial dislike of foreigners'. *Ruby Schembri v HSBC & D Jones (2006) Watford ET*

28.1.7   When direct or indirect discrimination is allowed

In some situations it may be lawful to recruit, train, transfer, promote or dismiss a person specifically because he or she is of a particular group, provide preferential access to training for people of a particular group, or encourage people of a particular group to apply for some types of work. Unless such discrimination is permitted under genuine occupational requirement, positive action or other explicit provisions, it is unlawful.

28.1.7.1   Genuine occupational requirement

Where being of a particular racial group, religion, sex, sexual orientation or age group, or holding a particular religious or other belief, can be shown to be a **genuine occupational requirement** (GOR) or in some situations a **genuine and determining occupational requirement** for a particular position, it is not unlawful for an employer to treat other groups less favourably. At the time of writing (mid 2009) a genuine occupational requirement was still referred to as a **genuine occupational qualification** (GOQ) in some of the legislation, but the definitions were expected to be standardised in the **Equality Act [28.1.12]**.

Disability legislation does not include provision for GORs.

GOR/GOQ posts must be defined as such right from the beginning [**29.2**]. This a complex area and legal advice should be sought from an experienced solicitor or the Equality and Human Rights Commission before advertising a post as a GOR/GOQ job, or defining a post as GOR/GOQ in relation to transfer, promotion, training or dismissal. The EHRC cannot give 'exemption', but can advise on whether a job is likely to fall within the exemptions. The fact that such advice has been requested (and acted or not acted on) is taken into account if a claim is subsequently brought that it was unlawful to define the post as a GOR/GOQ job.

For more about GORs/GOQs in specific situations, see the sections in this chapter on the various equality strands.

28.1.7.2 Positive action in training and encouragement to apply

Equal opportunities legislation contains very limited provision for some **positive action** by employers and training providers, allowing them to provide access to training for groups which have traditionally been excluded from certain types of work, in order to give them a better chance of competing for or being promoted to such work. Employers can also encourage people from particular groups to apply for some types of work. But although they have been given preferential access to training and/or encouraged to apply for jobs, people from these groups cannot – under these positive action provisions – be treated preferentially when they apply for work or promotion or are being considered for promotion or transfer.

For race and sex discrimination, the right to undertake positive action is based on the relevant group(s) being **under-represented** in the employer's workforce as a whole, or at a particular level or for a particular type of work. For age, sexual orientation, and religion/belief, the right to undertake positive action is based on the employer's belief that the action will help to **compensate for disadvantage** in employment suffered by the group. The disability legislation does not include positive action provisions, but includes a much more wide-ranging obligation to make reasonable adjustments to enable a disabled person to work [**28.7.3.2**].

For more about positive action in specific situations, see the sections below on specific equality strands.

28.1.7.3 Positive action with two equally qualified candidates

At the time of writing (mid 2009), the government had proposed that the **Equality Act [28.1.12]** would allow employers to use a protected characteristic as a factor in selection or promotion, but only where two candidates are equally qualified and the particular group is under-represented in the employer's workforce or at that level or type of job. These provisions would not allow use of these criteria to select a less well qualified person, and the employer could not have a general policy of using these provisions in every case.

28.1.7.4 Positive discrimination

Positive action is not the same as **positive discrimination**, where employers are allowed or even required to hire people from particular groups to meet quotas or 'to balance the staff team'. Positive discrimination is unlawful, and must not be confused with the positive action [see above].

28.1.7.5 Equality duties

Public bodies have a statutory duty to promote equality of opportunity [**42.2**]. Contracts or grant aid conditions with voluntary sector bodies are likely to require the voluntary organisation to comply with this **equality duty**.

28.1.8 Acts by workers and third parties

It is unlawful to instruct, induce, or attempt to instruct or induce a person to do any act which is contrary to anti-discrimination legislation.

28.1.8.1 Liability of employer

Even where there is no encouragement to act unlawfully, an employer has **vicarious liability [22.6.4]** for discriminatory acts by its workers carried out in the course of employment, unless the employer can show that it took all reasonably practicable steps to prevent the acts. An employer can also in some circumstances be liable for acts by clients, contractors and other third parties – for example where a client uses racially abusive language to a worker.

Gravell v London Borough of Bexley [2007] UKEAT 0587 06 0203

In these cases much depends on the tribunal's view of whether the act occurred 'in the course of employment', and whether the employer could have prevented the action. Reasonable steps include providing diversity awareness training; ensuring equal opportunities policies reflect changes in the law; making clear that discriminatory comments, behaviour, 'jokes' and harassment are unacceptable whether made by employees, contractors, clients, visitors or anyone else; encouraging a positive approach to adapting premises, work and services to make them more accessible to people with disabilities and people from other cultures; and monitoring the organisation's procedures and taking appropriate action if it appears that unlawful discrimination is or may be occurring.

Another aspect of vicarious liability arises where an employer becomes liable for discrimination by an agent [**20.5**] acting on its behalf. In one case, for example, a training organisation placed a trainee surveyor with a firm of chartered surveyors for her training. When the trainee became pregnant the surveying firm dismissed her, and the training organisation was held to be liable for discrimination by the surveying firm which was acting on its behalf in providing training.

Lana v Positive Action Training in Housing (London) Ltd [2001] UKEAT 245 00 1503

28.1.8.2 Liability of worker who discriminates

In situations of vicarious liability the worker can bring a claim against both the employer and the worker or agent who carried out the discrimination. Even if the employer is found to have taken reasonably practicable steps to prevent the act and is therefore not liable, the worker or agent can be held liable.

Yeboah v Crofton [2002] EWCA Civ 794

28.1.9 Advertising and publicity

It is unlawful to publish or cause to be published advertisements which indicate, or could reasonably be interpreted as indicating, an intention to discriminate unlawfully. Use of terms such as 'waitress', 'postman', 'stewardess', 'youthful' or 'mature' are assumed to indicate an intention to discriminate, unless the advertisement clearly indicates otherwise.

Claims about discriminatory advertising must generally be brought by the Equality and Human Rights Commission rather than by an individual. However, following a European court of justice decision in 2008, the **Race Relations Act 1976** was amended to allow a claim to be brought by an individual who is deterred from applying for a job because of an advertisement which is discriminatory on the basis of race.

Race Relations Act 1976 s.1(1A)(b), amended by RRA (Amendment) Regulations 2008 [SI 2008/3008]

28.1.10 Equal opportunities policies

Many voluntary organisations have equal opportunities policies which commit the organisation to going beyond the minimum required by the law. Where such policies form part of the contract of employment or other contract, they may give an enforceable right not to be discriminated against in relation to matters referred to in the policy. The right not to be discriminated against on the basis of class or caste is not, for example, part of UK law, but if it forms part of a contractual policy, a person treated less favourably, victimised, harassed or dismissed because of their class or caste could bring a breach of contract claim against the employer.

Guidance on developing an equal opportunities policy is available from ACAS and PEACe [see end of **chapter 25**].

28.1.11 Human rights and discrimination

Article 14 of the **European convention on human rights [64.3]**, brought into UK law by the **Human Rights Act 1998**, provides that the rights guaranteed by the Convention must be enjoyed without discrimination on any grounds. This is not a freestanding right not to be discriminated against, because the discrimination must be in relation to a Convention right.

The protections under article 14 are very broad, covering political or other opinion, language, religion, social origin, association with a national minority, property, birth or other status, as well as sex, race, colour and national origin. 'Other status' is likely to include disability, sexual orientation, age and marital status.

Only public authorities and other bodies carrying out public functions are directly bound by the Human Rights Act, but article 14 has an impact on all employment related matters, because all UK legislation must be interpreted compatibly with Convention rights.

28.1.12 Equality Act

At the time of writing (mid 2009) the government was committed to an **Equality Act** to consolidate, simplify and modernise discrimination law, and extend some of the protections. In particular it was expected to harmonise the definitions of indirect discrimination [**28.1.4**]; provide protection against discrimination by association [**28.1.1.3**]; bring equal pay [**28.8**] within the Act; simplify the definition of disability and the justification tests in disability discrimination law [**28.7**]; extend age discrimination protection to the provision of goods, services and facilities [**42.8**]; and extend the equality duties [**42.2**] to cover all equality strands.

It was also proposed that employers could use a protected characteristic as a factor in choosing between equally well qualified candidates [**28.1.7.3**]; that a person directly discriminated against because of a combination of two protected characteristics could bring a **dual discrimination** claim; and that employment tribunals would be able to make wider recommendations in discrimination cases, requiring an employer to take specific steps in relation to all or part of the workforce rather than just in relation to the worker who made the complaint.

The proposed timetable was for the equality bill to be passed in spring 2010 and for its provisions to start being implemented in October 2010.

28.2 RACE DISCRIMINATION

Race discrimination covers discrimination on the basis of **race, colour, nationality** (including citizenship), **ethnic origin** or **national origin**. Since 2003, slightly different rules apply to discrimination on the basis of race, ethnic origin and national origin than to discrimination on the basis of colour and nationality. The rules were expected to be standardised in the **Equality Act** [**28.1.12**].

Race Relations Act 1976 ss.3(1),78(1)

The Race Relations Act does not define the various racial grounds, but case law defines an **ethnic group** as 'a segment of the population distinguished from others by a combination of shared customs, beliefs, traditions and characteristics derived from a common or presumed common past, even if not drawn from what in biological terms is a common racial stock'.   *Mandla (Sewa Singh) v Dowell Lee [1982] UKHL 7*

National origin is not limited to nationality in the legal sense of the citizenship a person acquires at birth, but can be based on communal origins. English, Scots and Welsh are different national origins.   *BBC Scotland v Souster [2000] ScotCS 308*

For victimisation and harassment on racial grounds, see **28.1.5** and **28.1.6**.

28.2.1 Direct discrimination

Direct race discrimination [**28.1.3**] involves treating someone less favourably on racial grounds, where such treatment is not explicitly allowed under the provisions for genuine occupational requirement, positive action or employment in a private household, or under immigration law.

28.2.1.1 Workers from outside the EU

Although the **Race Relations Act 1976** makes it unlawful to treat a person less favourably on the basis of nationality or citizenship, it is not unlawful to refuse to hire someone who is not entitled to work in the UK. Most workers who are not from the European Economic Area (the European Union plus Iceland, Liechtenstein, Norway) or Switzerland require permission to work in the UK, and employers have a duty to confirm that anyone they hire has the right to work here. The procedures used to confirm right to work in the UK should be carried out in ways which are not discriminatory [**29.5.1**].

Under the points based system introduced in 2008, most people who are not from the EEA or Switzerland must be sponsored to work in the UK [**29.5.3**]

28.2.1.2 Genuine occupational requirement: race, ethnic or national origin

Being of a particular race, ethnic origin or national origin can used as a factor in employment, training, promoting or transferring a person to a job or dismissal if it is a **genuine and determining occupational requirement** [**28.1.7.1**] for the work or the context in which it is carried out, and it is proportionate [**28.1.3**] to apply the requirement. *Race Relations Act 1976 s.4A, inserted by RRA 1976 (Amendment) Regulations 2003 [SI 2003/1626] reg.7*

Where it is important that the employee understands the cultural and religious background of the people with whom he or she is working, it is accepted that those services may be most effectively provided by a person of the relevant racial group. But posts which are largely managerial or administrative do not generally fall within the provision. *Tottenham Green Under Fives Centre v Marshall [1989] IRLR 147; London Borough of Lambeth v Commission for Racial Equality [1990] IRLR 231*

28.2.1.3 Genuine occupational qualification: colour and nationality

At the time of writing (mid 2009), colour and nationality could be used as a factor in recruiting or selecting a person for a job, or promoting or transferring a person to a job, providing training for the job or dismissal:

- for reasons of authenticity in drama or entertainment (for example, portraying a black person); *Race Relations Act 1976 s.5(2)(a)*

- for work as an artist's or photographic model, in order to achieve authenticity; *RRA 1976 s.5(2)(b)*

- for reasons of authenticity in a restaurant or other place where food or drink is served (for example, in a Chinese restaurant); or *RRA 1976 s.5(2)(c)*

- where the job holder will provide persons of a racial group with personal services promoting their welfare, and these services can most effectively be provided by a person of that colour or nationality. *RRA 1976 s.5(2)(d)*

A post can be filled under s.5(2)(d) only if the employee is going to be primarily involved in face to face or other direct contact with the members of the defined racial group. If challenged, the employer must show the services are most effectively provided by a person of a particular colour or nationality. Because of the overlaps between race and colour, and between ethnic origin, national origin and nationality, it is safer to rely on the GOR provisions [**28.2.1.2**].

28.2.1.4 Employment in a private household

Employment for the purposes of a private household is generally exempt from the Race Relations Act, but discrimination against contract workers hired to work in a private household is unlawful. Victimisation on the basis of race, ethnic origin or national origin of anyone hired to work in a private household is also unlawful. *Race Relations Act 1976 s.4(3), amended by RRA 1976 (Amendment) Regulations 2003 [SI 2003/1626] reg.6(2)(b)*

28.2.1.5 Positive action by employers

Positive action [**28.1.7.2**] can be undertaken in favour of a particular racial group in order to provide access to training and to encourage members of that group to take advantage of opportunities for doing particular work, provided that in the previous 12 months there were no persons of that racial group doing that type of work at that establishment, or the proportion of persons of that racial group doing that work was small in comparison to everyone employed there or in comparison to the population of the area from which the employer normally recruits for work at that establishment. *Race Relations Act 1976 s.38*

In addition to training which can be provided by employers, training can in some situations be provided by others for one racial group [**42.3.2**].

The **Equality Act** [**28.1.12**] may allow preference to be given on the basis of racial group when choosing between two equally well qualified candidates, where people of that group are under-represented in the workforce or that type of work.

28.2.2 Indirect discrimination

For discrimination on the basis of race, ethnic origin and national origin, the standard definition of indirect discrimination [**28.1.4**] applies. *Race Relations Act 1976 s.1A, inserted by Race Relations Act 1976 (Amendment) Regulations 2003 [SI 2003/1626] reg.3*

In relation to nationality or colour, the definition of indirect discrimination is slightly different and involves a **requirement or condition** (rather than a provision, criterion, or practice) which the employer cannot show to be **justifiable** (rather than proportionate), and which is applied to everyone equally but has the effect of putting people of a particular group at a disadvantage because they disproportionately cannot comply with it. The **Equality Act [28.1.12]** was expected to replace this definition with the standard definition. *Race Relations Act 1976 s.1(1)(b)*

28.3 SEX DISCRIMINATION

Sex discrimination covers not only **sex**, but also being **married** or in a **civil partnership**, **pregnancy**, **maternity leave**, or intending to undergo, undergoing, or having undergone **gender reassignment**. *Sex Discrimination Act 1975 ss.1-3A*

For victimisation and harassment on grounds of sex, see **28.1.5** and **28.1.6**.

28.3.1 Civil partners

Civil partners are entitled to the same statutory and contractual rights and benefits as married staff. This covers contractual benefits such as pensions and private health care, as well as informal or extra benefits such as time off to get married. *Civil Partnership Act 2004*

Rights that are available only to married employees and civil partners do not need to be made available to partners who are not married or in a civil partnership. *Employment Equality (Sexual Orientation) Regulations 2003 [SI 2003/1661] reg.25*

Employees have no legal duty to notify their employer that they have entered a civil partnership or got married, but some may want to do so in order to claim relevant employment benefits. Employers should maintain confidentiality where employees want it, so that assumptions are not made about a person's sexual orientation by an unwanted disclosure about their marital/civil partnership status.

28.3.2 Direct discrimination

Direct sex discrimination **[28.1.3]** involves treating someone less favourably on one of the grounds covered under the sex discrimination legislation, unless such treatment is allowed due to pregnancy and maternity leave, or under genuine occupational qualification, positive action or other exceptions.

28.3.2.1 During pregnancy and maternity leave

Less favourable treatment on the grounds of pregnancy and maternity leave is direct sex discrimination. Women have the right not to be subjected to any detriment for a reason due to their pregnancy, childbirth or maternity leave, and dismissal on the basis of pregnancy or childbirth is automatically unfair **[32.1.3]**. *Sex Discrimination Act 1975 s.3A; Maternity & Parental Leave etc Regulations 1999 [SI 1999/3312] reg.19*

Special treatment for women in relation to pregnancy and childbirth does not constitute unlawful sex discrimination against men. *SDA 1975 s.2(2)*

28.3.2.2 Genuine occupational qualification

Depending on the circumstances, being of a particular sex can be a **genuine occupational qualification [28.1.7.1]**:

- if the job requires a man or woman to undertake it for physiological reasons (other than strength), for example for authenticity for a part in a dramatic performance; *Sex Discrimination Act 1975 s.7(2)(a)*
- for decency or privacy, for example in situations involving physical contact, people in a state of undress or people using sanitary facilities; *SDA 1975 s.7(2)(b)*
- the job involves living or working in a private home and it would be inappropriate for a man to be in close physical or social contact with a woman, or *vice versa*; *SDA 1975 s.7(2)(ba)*
- the employee must live on premises provided by the employer, and it is unreasonable to expect the employer to provide separate facilities for the sexes (for example, on an oil rig); *SDA 1975 s.7(2)(c)*
- the job is within a institution such as a hospital and it is reasonable that it should not be held by a person of a particular sex; *SDA 1975 s.7(2)(d)*

- it is likely that the job will have to be undertaken outside the UK in a country whose customs or laws would make it difficult for it to be properly undertaken by a person of a particular sex; *Sex Discrimination Act 1975 s.7(2)(g)*

- the job is one of two to be held by a married couple or a couple in a civil partnership; or *SDA1975 s.7(2)(h)*

- statutory restrictions apply.

The provision which is most used by voluntary organisations allows an employer to recruit a person of a particular sex because:

- the worker provides individuals with personal services promoting their welfare or education or similar services, and those services can most effectively be provided by a person of that sex. *SDA 1975 s.7(2)(e)*

At the time of writing (mid 2009) the **Equality Act [28.1.12]** was expected to replace GOQ with **genuine occupational requirements [28.1.7.1]**.

28.3.2.3 Other exceptions

Other exceptions under the **Sex Discrimination Act 1975** cover gender reassignment [**28.3.3**], situations where communal accommodation is provided, ministers of religion, and sports and competitions.

28.3.2.4 Positive action by employers

Positive action [28.1.7.2] can be undertaken to give access to training for women or men and to encourage either women or men to take advantage of opportunities for doing particular work, provided that in the previous 12 months there were no persons of that sex doing that type of work at that establishment, or the proportion of persons of that sex doing that work at that establishment was small in comparison to everyone employed there or in comparison to the population of the area from which the employer normally recruits for work at that establishment. *Sex Discrimination Act 1975 s.48*

Training can also in some situations be provided by others for one sex [**42.4.1**].

At the time of writing (mid 2009) it was proposed that the **Equality Act [28.1.12]** would allow preference to be given on the basis of sex where there are two equally well qualified candidates and one sex is under-represented in the employer's workforce or for that type of work.

28.3.3 Trans people

The term **trans people** is sometimes used to refer to transvestites, transgender people and transsexuals. These terms were not, at the time of writing, legally defined. Trans refers to the gender of the individual, and is therefore different from sexual orientation [**28.5**] which is about who the individual is attracted to.

Transvestism refers to people who regularly or occasionally dress as the opposite gender, without necessarily identifying with that gender. **Transgender** may be used to refer to people who are living fully in a gender other than the one with which they were registered at birth; they may or may not have undergone surgery. **Transsexual** may be used to refer to a person who identifies with another gender but is not yet living fully in it. In practice transgender and transsexual are used interchangeably.

At the time of writing (mid 2009) there was no legislation prohibiting discrimination against transvestites, although it could potentially be covered under sex discrimination legislation if, for example, a cross-dressing man could show he is treated less favourably than a cross-dressing woman would be.

Nor was there any legislation protecting transsexuals or transgender people in general, but they have employment rights in relation to gender reassignment [below], and if they have a gender recognition certificate [**28.3.3.2**] are protected under sex discrimination legislation in their acquired gender. It was expected that the **Equality Act [28.1.12]** would extend some protection to transsexuals.

Information about trans equality is available from **Press for Change** [see end of chapter].

411

28.3.3.1 Gender reassignment

Direct discrimination on the basis of a person intending to undergo, undergoing or having undergone gender reassignment is unlawful in employment and vocational training unless there is a genuine occupation qualification for the work to be done by a man or by a woman [**28.3.2.2**], and in addition one of the following **supplementary genuine occupational qualifications** applies:

- the job involves performing intimate physical searches required by statute;
- the job involves working or living in a private home, and there might reasonably be objections to a person intending to undergo, undergoing or having undergone gender reassignment having the likely level of physical or social contact with, or knowledge of intimate details of, a person living in the home;
- it is impracticable for the worker to live elsewhere than in premises provided by the employer, and the only available premises are such that reasonable objection could be taken, for the purpose of preserving decency and privacy, to the worker sharing accommodation and facilities with either sex while intending to undergo or undergoing gender reassignment, and in addition it is not reasonable to expect the employer to equip those premises with suitable accommodation or make alternative arrangements; or
- the worker provides vulnerable individuals with personal services promoting their welfare or similar personal services, and in the reasonable view of the employer those services cannot be effectively provided by a person while that person is intending to undergo or undergoing gender reassignment.

Sex Discrimination Act 1975 ss.7A,7B, inserted by Sex Discrimination
(Gender Reassignment) Regulations 1999 [SI 1999/1102] reg.4

At the time of writing (mid 2009) it was expected that the **Equality Act** [**28.1.12**] would extend indirect discrimination to cover gender reassignment.

28.3.3.2 Transitioning to a new gender

Where a worker is transitioning into their new gender – with or without intending to undertake surgery – the employer should sensitively discuss arrangements with them. This could include, for example, who needs to be told and when the worker will do this; use of single sex facilities; whether and when the worker intends to change their name; and how much time off they might need for medical treatment such as hormone therapy and surgery and the likely timescale for this.

28.3.3.3 Gender recognition

Persons who have undergone gender reassignment, and others who have taken decisive steps towards living fully and permanently in a gender which was not the one they were registered with at birth, can apply for a **gender recognition certificate**. This entitles them to the rights and responsibilities of their new gender, including a new birth certificate, the right to marry a person of the opposite sex, and a pension in accordance with their new gender from the point when they begin to live with their acquired gender. *Gender Recognition Act 2004*

It is an offence for an employer to disclose information about an individual applying for or having a gender recognition certificate, unless the individual cannot be identified by the disclosure or has given consent. Such information is also sensitive personal data under the **Data Protection Act 1998** [**43.3.1**].

28.3.4 Indirect discrimination

The test for cases of indirect sex discrimination is the standard test [**28.1.4**].

Sex Discrimination Act 1975 s.1(2)(b), inserted by Employment Equality
(Sex Discrimination) Regulations 2005 [SI 2005/2467]

Examples of indirect discrimination include a requirement to work certain shift patterns which more women are unable to comply with compared to men; making part-time employees redundant before full-time employees, because more women than men work part-time; and a **dress code** which requires men to wear a shirt and tie but does not require women to dress in a similarly 'smart' way, or requires women to dress smartly but allows men to dress casually.

28.4   RELIGION OR BELIEF

The **religion or belief** regulations cover religion, religious or philosophical belief, and lack of belief. *Employment Equality (Religion or Belief) Regulations 2003 [SI 2003/1660] reg.2(1), amended by Equality Act 2006 s.77(1)*

The 2003 regulations referred to 'similar philosophical belief', but the Equality Act 2006 amendment removed 'similar'. Factors taken into account when considering what constitutes a belief include whether there is collective worship, a clear belief system, or a profound belief which is more than an opinion, has 'sufficient cogency, seriousness, cohesion and importance and is worthy of respect in a democratic society'.   *McClintock v Department of Constitutional Affairs [2007] UKEAT 0223 07 3110*

The definition could encompass cults, and could be interpreted by the courts as including beliefs such as pacifism or strong beliefs about climate change and the environment.

For victimisation and harassment on grounds of religion or belief, see **28.1.5** and **28.1.6**.

28.4.1   Direct discrimination

Direct discrimination [**28.1.3**] occurs where a person is treated less favourably in any aspect of employment on the grounds of religion or belief, and such treatment is not allowed under the genuine occupational requirement or positive action provisions.   *Employment Equality (Religion or Belief) Regulations 2003 [SI 2003/1660] reg.3(1)(a)*

28.4.1.1   Genuine occupational requirement

For organisations which have an ethos based on religion or belief, there are exemptions where being of a particular religion or belief is a **genuine occupational requirement** [**28.1.7.1**] for recruitment, promotion or transfer to a post, training for a post or dismissal from it. In organisations which do not have an ethos based on religious or similar belief, religion or belief can be used as a factor only if it is a **genuine and determining occupational requirement**.

Religion/Belief Regs 2003 reg.7

Under the GOR provisions a Muslim community centre, for example, might be able to specify that a community worker must be Muslim, even if some or most of the employee's work would be with non-Muslims. But a secular (non-faith based) community centre would be able to advertise for a Muslim community worker only if being of this faith is a genuine **and determining** requirement, with a substantial proportion of the employee's work being with Muslims and being of a type that requires the employee to be Muslim.

Even the Muslim community centre would be unlikely to be able to specify that its bookkeeper has to be Muslim. However, it might be able to say that the bookkeeper has to be willing to work in an organisation with an Islamic ethos, and/or that the bookkeeper has to be able to speak Arabic or another relevant language – but only if these requirements are justifiable and proportionate, and thus do not constitute indirect discrimination [**28.1.4**].

Religious organisations are also allowed, in some situations, to discriminate on the basis of sexual orientation [**28.5.1.1**].

28.4.1.2   Faith schools

Foundation or voluntary schools with a religious character are allowed to give preference in the appointment, promotion or remuneration of teachers or headteachers to people with religious beliefs in accordance with those of the school, or who attend worship in accordance with those beliefs, or who give or are willing to give religious education at the school in accordance with those beliefs. In appointing or terminating employment of a teacher, conduct incompatible with the religion may be taken into account.   *Independent Schools (Employment of Teachers in Schools with a Religious Character) Regulations 2003 [SI 2003/2037]*

28.4.1.3   Positive action by employers

Positive action provisions [**28.1.7.2**] allow people of a particular religion or belief to be given preferential access to training or to be encouraged to apply for particular work, where the employer reasonably believes that such treatment would prevent or compensate for disadvantages linked to religion or belief suffered by persons doing or likely to take up that type of work.

Employment Equality (Religion or Belief) Regulations 2003 [SI 2003/1660] reg.29

At the time of writing (mid 2009) it was proposed that the **Equality Act** [**28.1.12**] would allow preference to be given on the basis of religion or belief when choosing between equally well qualified candidates, where people of one religion are under-represented in the employer's workforce or in that type of work.

28.4.2 Indirect discrimination

The standard test for indirect discrimination [**28.1.4**] applies.

Employment Equality (Religion or Belief) Regulations 2003 [SI 2003/1660] reg.3(1)(b)

Examples of indirect discrimination are requiring staff, including church-going Christians, to work on Sundays; requiring female staff, including strictly observant Muslim or orthodox Jewish women, to wear a short-sleeved uniform which exposes their arms; not allowing any men, including Sikhs, to wear caps or other head coverings; and holding job interviews or important meetings on religious holidays. These requirements are unlawful unless the employer offers alternatives for members of the relevant religious group, or can show that the requirement is necessary and appropriate.

28.4.3 Religious holidays and observance

Employers are not obliged to provide prayer rooms or facilities for religious observance, but if asked to do so should consider the request seriously. Failure to comply with the request, unless there is a legitimate and proportionate reason, could constitute indirect religious discrimination.

Similarly employers are not obliged to provide paid time off for religious holidays, even Christmas and Easter, unless there is a contractual entitlement. However, employers should allow employees who wish to do so to take paid annual leave for religious observance, and should seriously consider requests for unpaid leave. Failure to allow time off for observance, without having a legitimate and proportionate reason, is likely to constitute direct or indirect religious discrimination.

During Ramadan, a month-long observance when Muslims fast from dawn until dusk, and other holidays when people of specific religious groups are required to fast, an employer might consider allowing several short breaks during the day rather than an extended lunch hour, and allowing flexible hours so workers can leave early to break the fast.

28.4.3.1 Cards and parties linked to religious holidays

The law does not prohibit *different* treatment unless it is *less favourable*. So if an employer wants to send employees cards at Christmas, it is not unlawful to send cards with a religious theme to employees known (not assumed) to be practising Christians, and non-religious cards saying 'Happy holidays' to others, or sending cards as appropriate at Eid, Rosh Hashanah, Diwali, Chinese new year or other festivals. Where the employer does not know an employee's beliefs, it is likely to be preferable to send non-religious cards.

The law does not prevent workplace or work related Christmas parties, and does not prevent Christmas cards or decorations being displayed. In any event most such decorations and events are now more secular than religious. Where the decorations or events are explicitly religious, care should be taken not to create an environment which is intimidating or offensive to people of other beliefs or none. Non-alcoholic drinks should be available (this is important not only for people whose religious beliefs forbid alcohol, but also for recovering alcoholics and people who will be driving), and if alcohol is given as a raffle or similar prize an alternative should be available. With many Christmas parties, the issue is not so much potential religious discrimination as the risk of sexual harassment [**28.1.6.1**], or the employer being held liable for racist, sexist, homophobic and other comments or behaviour by inebriated workers [**28.1.8.1**].

28.5 SEXUAL ORIENTATION

The **sexual orientation** regulations cover an orientation towards people of the same sex, the opposite sex, or both the same sex and the opposite sex (bisexuality). The regulations do not cover transvestism [**28.3.3**], or sexual practices such as sado-masochism. *Employment Equality (Sexual Orientation) Regulations 2003 [SI 2003/1661] reg.2(1)*

For victimisation and harassment on grounds of sexual orientation, see **28.1.5** and **28.1.6**.

Information about good practice in relation to sexual orientation is available from **Stonewall** [see end of chapter].

28.5.1 Direct discrimination

Direct discrimination [**28.1.3**] is where a person is treated less favourably in any aspect of employment on the grounds of sexual orientation, unless this is allowed under the genuine occupational requirement or positive action provisions, or the special rules on employment for the purposes of an organised religion.

Employment Equality (Sexual Orientation) Regulations 2003 [SI 2003/1661] reg.3(1)(a)

28.5.1.1 Genuine occupational requirement

Sexual orientation can be used as a factor in recruitment, transfer, promotion, training or dismissal only if it is a **genuine and determining occupational requirement** [**28.1.7.1**]. An example would be a requiring counsellors for gay and lesbian teenagers to themselves be gay or lesbian. *Sexual Orientation Regs 2003 reg.7*

If the counsellor has to be lesbian or has to be a gay man, the relevant provisions of the Sex Discrimination Act [**28.3.2.2**] would also have to apply.

28.5.1.2 Employment for purposes of an organised religion

Discrimination on the basis of sexual orientation is also allowed in 'employment for the purposes of an organised religion', in order to comply with the doctrines of the religion or to avoid conflicting with the strongly held religious convictions of a significant number of the religion's followers. *Sexual Orientation Regs 2003 reg.7(3)*

28.5.1.3 Positive action by employers

The **positive action** [**28.1.7.2**] provisions are the comparable to those for religion and belief [**28.4.1.3**]. *Sexual Orientation Regs 2003 reg.26*

At the time of writing (mid 2009) it was proposed that the **Equality Act** [**28.1.12**] would allow preference to be given to a person known to be gay, lesbian or bisexual when choosing between two equally well qualified candidates, where gays, lesbians or bisexuals are under-represented in the employer's workforce.

28.5.2 Indirect discrimination

The standard criteria for **indirect discrimination** [**28.1.4**] apply.

Employment Equality (Sexual Orientation) Regulations 2003 [SI 2003/1661] reg.3(1)(b)

Unlawful indirect discrimination could include publicising jobs only or primarily in publications aimed at gay men and lesbians, as these are less likely to be read by heterosexuals; or making clear explicitly or in subtle ways that same-sex partners are not welcome at the organisation's events or social functions.

28.6 AGE

An **age group** is defined as 'a group of persons defined by reference to age, whether by reference to a particular age or range of ages'.

Employment Equality (Age) Regulations 2006 [SI 2006/1031] reg.3(3)

The legislation law allows length of service and other age related criteria to be used as factors in recruitment, promotion or rewarding workers only if this can be objectively justified. Justification for using age or age related criteria could include fixing a minimum age to qualify for certain benefits, in order to recruit or retain older people; fixing a maximum age for recruitment or promotion based on the training requirements of the post or the need for a reasonable period of employment before retirement; or encouraging and rewarding loyalty.

For victimisation and harassment on grounds of age, see **28.1.5** and **28.1.6**.

Information about good practice in relation to age is available from Business Link and the **Employers Forum on Age** [see end of chapter].

28.6.1 Direct discrimination

The definition of **direct age discrimination [28.1.3]** is the same as for the other strands. Direct discrimination is unlawful unless it is allowed and can be justified by the employer. *Employment Equality (Age) Regulations 2006 [SI 2006/1031] reg.(3)(1)(a)*

28.6.1.1 Genuine occupational requirement

An employer is allowed discriminate if possessing a characteristic related to a particular age group is a **genuine and determining occupational requirement [28.1.7.1]**. This is unlikely to apply to many situations except perhaps acting jobs and models. An organisation tempted to use age as a factor in recruiting should be able to show, if challenged, that the discrimination is both necessary and proportionate. *Employment Equality (Age) Regulations 2006 [SI 2006/1031] reg.8*

28.6.1.2 Retirement

Where a job applicant is already over the default retirement age (65, at the time of writing) or the employer's normal retirement age (whichever is higher), or will reach that age within six months of their application, it is not unlawful to treat them less favourably on the basis of age [**34.2.8**]. At the time of writing (mid 2009) this was being challenged by Heyday, an organisation linked to Age Concern, and in addition the government had said that it would review the default retirement age in 2010. *Employment Equality (Age) Regulations 2006 [SI 2006/1031] reg.7;*
Age Concern England (Incorporated Trustees of the National Council on Ageing) v Secretary of State
for Business, Enterprise & Regulatory Reform [2009] EUECJ C-388/07

Specific rules define when a dismissal is and is not regarded as being for reasons of retirement, impose a statutory process for informing the employee, and allow employees to ask to continue working [**34.2.8**]. If a dismissal is not legally a retirement it is likely to be unlawful age discrimination and an unfair dismissal.
Employment Rights Act 1996 ss.98ZA-98ZF, inserted by Age Regs 2006 sch.8 para.23

28.6.1.3 Pension schemes

Age related rules in occupational pension schemes and in employer contributions to personal pension schemes are generally unlawful, but there are a number of exemptions. *Employment Equality (Age) Regulations 2006 [SI 2006/1031] sch.2, amended by*
Employment Equality (Age) (Amendment No.2) Regulations 2006 [SI 2006/2931]

28.6.1.4 National minimum wage

National minimum wage (NMW) is based on age [**30.2**]. Employers who pay more than NMW and base their pay structure on the NMW pay brackets can pay less to workers aged 16-17 and 18-21 than to workers doing comparable work who are over 21. But employers who do not base their pay structure for that type of work on the NMW age brackets cannot pay less on the basis of age, unless this is objectively justified. *Employment Equality (Age) Regulations 2006 [SI 2006/1031] reg.31*

28.6.1.5 Redundancy payments

Statutory redundancy pay continues to be calculated on the basis of number of years' employment in different age brackets. For **enhanced redundancy pay** (redundancy payments to employees who are not entitled to statutory redundancy pay, or payments at more than the statutory minimum), age or length of service can be taken into consideration provided the age brackets are the same as for the statutory scheme. For redundancy payment schemes based on age or length of service that do not mirror the statutory scheme, the employer needs to show objective justification. *Employment Equality (Age) Regulations 2006 [SI 2006/1031] reg.33*

For more about statutory and enhanced redundancy pay, see **35.7**.

28.6.1.6   Positive action

The **positive action** [**28.1.7.2**] provisions in relation to age are similar to those for religion/belief and sexual orientation, allowing preferential access to training and encouragement to take advantage of opportunities for doing particular work in order to prevent or compensate for disadvantage experienced by some age groups. Positive action could be used, for example, where a particular age group is under-represented in jobs of a particular type or within that employer's work-force.   *Employment Equality (Age) Regulations 2006 [SI 2006/1031] reg.29*

As with other forms of positive action, age could not at the time of writing (mid 2009) be used as a factor in selection. But it was proposed that the **Equality Act** [**28.1.12**] would allow preference to be given, when choosing between two equally well qualified candidates, to a candidate in an age group under-represented in the employer's workforce.

28.6.2   Indirect discrimination

The standard definition of **indirect discrimination** [**28.1.4**] applies. Anything based on length of experience or service is potentially indirect age discrimination, because younger workers are less likely than older workers to meet the requirements. Redundancy criteria based on length of service or 'last in first out', for example, are likely to be unlawful unless the employer can show they are objectively justifiable [**35.3.2**].   *Employment Equality (Age) Regulations 2006 [SI 2006/1031] reg.3(1)(b)*

28.6.2.1   Benefits based on length of service

Pay rises and other employment benefits linked to length of service are allowed where the worker has five years or less service with the same or an associated employer. When benefits are awarded on the basis of length of service to a worker who has more than five years of service, the employer must be able to justify the pay rise or benefit as fulfilling a business need for the employer. This could include rewarding experience or loyalty, or increasing the motivation or some or all workers.   *Employment Equality (Age) Regulations 2006 [SI 2006/1031] reg.32*

28.6.3   Young workers

Children cannot be employed before their 13th birthday. From 13 to school leaving age, limits on working hours [**31.5.1**] and types of work [**40.6.1**] are enforced by the local authority education department. Workers under 18 have specific protection under the working time [**31.5.2**] and health and safety law [**40.3.2**].

These rules apply to paid work (including work for their family), but do not apply to unpaid voluntary work. However, good practice would generally be to stick to the limits even when the young person is volunteering.

Before a person under school-leaving age can be employed, the local education authority must grant a permit to the employer.

Employer's liability insurance [**23.4.1**] should be checked to ensure it covers young employees and volunteers.

A person under 18 is bound by a contract of employment only if it is on the whole for her or his benefit [**21.1.2**].

28.7   DISABILITY AND LONG-TERM SICKNESS

Disability discrimination has some similarities with the other equality strands, but is also significantly different:

- rather than direct and indirect discrimination [**28.1.4**], there is at the time of writing (mid 2009) **direct disability discrimination** [**28.7.2**], **disability related discrimination** [**28.7.3**], and discrimination arising from the employer's **failure to make reasonable adjustments** [**28.7.3.2**];
- unlike the other strands where the definitions of race, sex, religion/belief, sexual orientation and age are relatively straightforward, the definition of disabil-

ity is complex, based at the time of writing on statutory descriptions of 'normal day to day activities' and extensive case law;

- all other equality strands are 'mirrored': everyone has a race, colour, nationality, national origin or ethnic origin; everyone has a sex; everyone has a religion or philosophical beliefs or a lack of them; everyone has a sexual orientation; everyone has an age – so anyone can bring a claim for discrimination under those strands. But the disability legislation applies only to disabled people. There is no 'mirror' – no corresponding provision – for non-disabled people.

For victimisation and harassment on grounds of disability, see **28.1.5** and **28.1.6**.

28.7.1 Definition of disability

Disability is defined as a physical (including sensory) or mental impairment which has a substantial and long-term adverse effect on a person's ability to carry out at least one normal day to day activity linked to mobility; manual dexterity; continence; ability to lift, carry or move everyday objects; speech, hearing or eyesight; memory; ability to concentrate, learn or understand; or perception of the risk of physical dangers. Mental impairment includes mental illness (even if not clinically well recognised) and learning disability. At the time of writing (mid 2009) it was expected that this list of capacities would be repealed by the **Equality Act [28.1.12]**. *Disability Discrimination Act 1995 s.1, sch.1 para.4; DDA 2005 s.18(2)*

An effect is long-term if it has lasted or is likely to last for at least one year, and/or is likely to last for the rest of the person's life if this is likely to be less than a year. If an impairment ceases to have a substantial adverse effect or the effect is intermittent, it is treated as continuing to have the effect if the effect could well recur. *DDA 1995 sch.1 para.2; SCA Packaging Ltd v Boyle (Northern Ireland) [2009] UKHL 37*

HIV infection, multiple sclerosis and cancer are defined as disabilities from the point of diagnosis. Other progressive conditions are not classed as a disability until they have a substantial adverse effect. *DDA 1995 s.6A, inserted by DDA 2005 s.18(3)*

A person who is registered with the local authority as blind or partially sighted, or is certified as blind or partially sighted by a consultant ophthalmologist, is deemed to be disabled for the purposes of the DDA. They do not have to show that the condition has a substantial adverse effect their normal day to day activities. *Disability Discrimination (Blind & Partially Sighted Persons) Regulations 2003 [SI 2003/712]*

An impairment which would have a substantial effect but does not because it is being treated or corrected (for example medically controlled epilepsy, or limb loss corrected with a prosthesis) is classed as a disability. This does not apply to sight impairments corrected with spectacles or contact lenses. *DDA 1995 sch.1 para 6*

A serious disfigurement, such as a birthmark or burns injury, is classed as a disability even if it does not have a substantial adverse effect. *DDA 1995 sch.1 para.3*

An addiction to or dependency on alcohol, nicotine or any other substance is not a disability, unless it is a result of a drug being medically prescribed. However a condition caused by the addiction, such as liver disease or depression, could be a disability. *Disability Discrimination (Meaning of Disability) Regulations 1996 [SI 1996/1455] reg.3*

A tendency to set fires, steal or physically or sexually abuse other people, exhibitionism and voyeurism are not disabilities. *Disability Discrimination (Meaning of Disability) Regulations 1996 [SI 1996/1455]reg.4*

Among the many conditions that have been held to be disabilities, provided they have or would without medication have a serious adverse effect, are depression, diabetes, and dyslexia.

28.7.1.1 Discrimination against able-bodied people

The legislation prohibits discrimination on the basis of disability, but does not say anything about discrimination against able-bodied people. So it is not unlawful for an employer to give preference to a disabled person, or to disabled people in general, in recruitment and selection or in other aspects of employment. However the organisation's funders or its own equal opportunities policy may require posts to be openly advertised and appointment to be made solely on the basis of merit, and this would prevent this type of positive discrimination.

It is discriminatory to favour people with a specific type or types of disability, for example to give preference to people with a visual impairment, because this is then direct discrimination against people with other disabilities.

28.7.2 Direct discrimination

Direct disability discrimination occurs where an employer treats a disabled person, on the grounds of the person's disability, less favourably than it would treat a person without that disability whose relevant circumstances, including abilities, are the same as or not materially different from those of the disabled person. Direct disability discrimination also occurs when a person is treated less favourably because of their **association** with a disabled person – for example, where the parent of a disabled child is treated less favourably than the parent of a non-disabled child would be [**28.1.1.3**]. *Disability Discrimination Act 1995 s.3A, inserted by Disability Discrimination Act 1995 (Amendment) Regulations 2003 [SI 2003/1673] reg.4*

An example of direct discrimination is a case where an employee returned to work after having lost her sight due to a stroke, and was dismissed on the basis of generalised and stereotypical assumptions regarding her lack of sight, without meeting her, seeking her input or referring to a medical report.

Tudor v Spen Corner Veterinary Centre & Tschimmel (2006) ET 2404211/05

28.7.2.1 Supported employment

It is lawful to provide **supported employment** only to people with a particular disability. *Disability Discrimination Act 1995 s.18C (originally DDA 1995 s.10)*

28.7.3 Disability related discrimination

Disability related discrimination occurs where, for a reason which relates to a person's disability, an employer treats the person less favourably than a person to whom the reason does not apply is or would be treated, and the employer cannot show that the different treatment is justified. *Disability Discrimination Act 1995 s. 3A(1), inserted by DDA 19955 (Amendment) Regulations 2003 [SI 2003/1673] reg.4*

An example is dismissal on the basis of long-term sickness absence caused by a disability. An employer who dismisses because of the *absence* (rather than because of the disability itself) is dismissing for a disability related reason.

28.7.3.1 Justification

An employee who brings a claim of disability related discrimination must show that he or she has been treated less favourably for a disability related reason. The employer is then liable unless it can show that the treatment was justified by being both material in the circumstances and substantial. *Disability Discrimination Act 1995 s. 3A(3), inserted by DDA 1995 (Amendment) Regs 2003 reg.4*

'Material' means a reasonably strong connection between the reason and the circumstances of the individual case, and 'substantial' means it is more than minor or trivial. In addition, the reason given by the employer has to be reasonable.

Jones v Post Office [2001] EWCA Civ 558; Williams v J Walter Thompson Group Ltd [2005] EWCA Civ 133

28.7.3.2 Comparators

Traditionally, an employer was held to have discriminated unlawfully if an employee was treated less favourably for a disability related reason which would not have applied to a non-disabled person. So dismissal of a disabled person for long-term absence, for example, would be unlawful because a person without the disability would not have been absent, and would therefore not have been dismissed.

Clark v TDG Ltd (t/a Novacold) [1999] EWCA Civ 1091

This approach was overturned in 2008, in a decision which means the correct comparator in the above case would be a person without the disability who is absent for the same period – regardless of the reason. Under this approach, it is more difficult for the worker to claim disability related discrimination. But there is still an obligation for the employer to make reasonable adjustments to enable the worker to continue working [**28.7.4**], and a dismissal will be unfair unless the employer can show the employee is incapable of doing the work [**34.6.1**].

London Borough of Lewisham v Malcolm [2008] UKHL 43

At the time of writing (mid 2009) the government was consulting on whether, in light of the Malcolm decision, the **Equality Act [28.1.12]** should replace disability related discrimination with indirect discrimination [**28.1.4**] and should provide that an employer cannot objectively justify indirect discrimination if it has failed to make reasonable adjustments.

28.7.4 Reasonable adjustments

A third form of disability discrimination arises from an employer's failure to make reasonable adjustments where a provision, criterion, or practice operated by or on behalf of the employer, or any physical feature of the premises occupied by the employer, places the disabled person at a substantial disadvantage compared with people who are not disabled. There is no 'justification' defence; the employer's only defence is that it was not reasonable to make the adjustment.

Disability Discrimination Act 1995 ss.3A(6), 4A, inserted by DDA 1995 (Amendment) Regs 2003 regs.4,5

Employers also have a duty to make reasonable adjustments in relation to individuals on work placement. This is defined as 'practical work experience undertaken for a limited period for the purposes of a person's vocational training'.

DDA 1995 ss.14C,14D, inserted by DDA 1995 (Amendment) Regs 2003 reg.13

The duty to make reasonable adjustments does not apply if an employer does not know and could not reasonably be expected to know that a person is disabled and is likely to be substantially disadvantaged. The code of practice on disability discrimination and case law make clear that employers should do all they can to find out whether a person has a disability [**28.7.6**]. *DDA 1995 s.4A(3), inserted by DDA 1995 (Amendment) Regs 2003 reg.5; Eastern & Coastal Kent PCT v Grey [2009] UKEAT 0454 08 2301*

In determining what is a reasonable adjustment, factors taken into account include the effectiveness of the adjustment in preventing a disadvantage, how practical it is, the financial and other costs, the size and financial position of the employer and the nature of its activities, and the availability of financial or other assistance [**28.7.4.3**]. *DDA 1995 s.18B(1), inserted by DDA 1995 (Amendment) Regs 2003 reg.17*

The legislation gives as examples: making adjustments to premises; allocating some of the disabled person's duties to another person; altering the person's hours; assigning the person to a different place of work; allowing the person to be absent for rehabilitation, assessment or treatment; providing training or mentoring for the disabled person or any other person; acquiring or modifying equipment; modifying instructions or reference manuals; modifying procedures for testing or assessment; providing a reader or interpreter; or providing supervision or other support. *DDA 1995 s.18B(2), inserted by DDA 1995 (Amendment) Regs 2003 reg.17*

28.7.4.1 Redeployment

Another adjustment involves transferring a disabled person to fill an existing vacancy. Case law has confirmed that where an employee becomes disabled and is unable to do their job, it is a reasonable adjustment to create a new post or redeploy them to another job, even if they are not the best candidate for the job or there has not been a competitive recruitment process. This is permissible because it is not unlawful to treat a disabled person more favourably than a person without that disability is treated [**28.7.1.1**]. *Archibald v Fife Council [2004] HL 32*

Giving priority for such work to other employees, even those threatened with redundancy [**35.6**], could constitute disability discrimination.

28.7.4.2 Sick pay during disability related sick leave

In a case in 2004, the court of appeal said that the duty to make reasonable adjustments includes a duty to consider paying employees who are legally disabled while they are on sick leave, even if they are contractually entitled only to reduced pay or statutory sick pay. But in subsequent cases the courts said that the purpose of a reasonable adjustment is to enable a disabled person to continue working or return to work. Only in rare cases would it be a reasonable adjustment for an employer to continue paying full salary or sick pay after the employee's entitlement to sick pay had ended, since this would be a disincentive to return to work. *Nottinghamshire County Council v Meikle [2004] EWCA Civ 859; O'Hanlon v HM Revenue & Customs [2007] EWCA Civ 283*

28.7.4.3   Funding for adjustments

Funding may be available through the **Access to Work** programme to enable a disabled person to apply for work, do the work or remain in work. The funding could contribute towards the costs of equipment, adaptations to premises, support workers, communicators for job interviews, travel costs if the person cannot use public transport, and other adjustments. Details are available through the disability employment advisor at the local Jobcentre Plus.

28.7.5   Disability, health and safety, and fire safety

Health and safety or fire safety cannot be used as justification for direct discrimination, and can be used as justification for disability related discrimination only if it is reasonable to do so. It cannot be used as a reason for not making reasonable adjustments, unless it is reasonable for the employer not to make the adjustment.

By working with individual disabled workers and with organisations of or for disabled people, employers can in most situations adapt premises, equipment or systems so they are safe for disabled people (and everyone else), thus complying with both health and safety/fire safety law and the duty to make reasonable adjustments for a disabled person. The Health and Safety Executive [see end of chapter] has guidance on carrying out risk assessments in relation to disabled people.

If it is genuinely not reasonable for the employer to make adjustments that will both meet the needs of the disabled person and comply with health and safety and/or fire safety requirements, health and safety and fire safety obligations override DDA obligations.

28.7.6   Good practice for disability and long-term illness

It is good practice to have procedures:

- to ensure the organisation asks enough to ascertain whether job applicants or employees may have a disability which could affect their ability to carry out the job as defined, and whether they may need adjustments in order to be able to apply for the job, do the work or carry on working [**28.7.3.2**];
- to ensure that information about an individual's health is understood to be sensitive data under the **Data Protection Act 1998** [**43.3.1**] and is disclosed only to those people who have a need to know, and that no one is told without the individual being informed that this will happen;
- to ensure procedures are in place and known to all staff, and equipment is available, for dealing with potential health risks to persons who are or may be ill or disabled (for example fits or asthma attacks);
- to offer suitable alternative work, if available, to employees who are unable to carry on with their usual work [**28.7.4.1**].

Employers have a duty to be aware that workers who have frequent or long-term sickness absences may be, or become, legally classed as disabled and therefore have rights under the DDA. Employers are expected to take reasonable steps to determine the nature of the illness, and if appropriate to consider adjustments.

It may be possible to dismiss an employee who is genuinely incapable of carrying out the required work if the work cannot be adapted and there is no other suitable work available. Legal advice should be taken before doing this [**34.6.1**].

An employee cannot be required to have a medical examination unless this is specified in the contract of employment [**27.5.1**]. Dismissal for refusing to have a test or medical examination could be unfair dismissal, and forcing a person to have a test where this is not required by the contract could lead to a claim for constructive dismissal [**34.2.9**].

28.8   EQUAL PAY AND CONDITIONS

Every employee's contract of employment is considered to include an equality clause, giving contractual equality for like work to that of an employee of the other sex. **Like work** means the work is of the same or a broadly similar nature, or a job evaluation study has rated it as being equivalent, or the work is of equal value in requiring comparable effort, skill and decision making.   *Equal Pay Act 1970 s.1*

The equality clause applies not just to pay but to all contractual terms of employment – such as entitlement to holidays, bonuses, travel concessions, pensions and redundancy pay.

The Equal Pay Act applies not only to employees but also to apprentices, others working under a contract, and people undertaking work on a self employed basis. Its intention – not achieved after nearly 40 years – was to bring women's pay and other conditions up to the levels of men's, but it applies to men as well as women. Men cannot, however, claim contractual benefits relating to special treatment of women in relation to pregnancy and childbirth.

Unequal pay or conditions between a man and a woman doing comparable work are not unlawful if the difference is genuinely due to a **material factor other than sex**. An example would be a man and a woman doing the same work or work of equal value for the same employer, one in the southeast and one in the northeast, with the difference in their pay attributable to the different salary levels in those areas.

Where the material factor is not in itself discriminatory on the basis of sex – such as the geographic differentials – the employer does not have to provide objective justification for differences in pay and conditions. But where the material factor is or could be indirectly discriminatory [28.1.4] on the basis of sex, the employer must show that the difference is necessary and proportionate. An example would be a job which requires the worker to be available at short notice being paid more than the same type of job but where there is no requirement to be available at short notice. 'Needing to be available at short notice' could justify higher pay – but could be discriminatory because more women than men have childcare or caring responsibilities that make it difficult for them to work at short notice.

Experience has been held to be a material factor in relation to equal pay claims, but since October 2006 pay differentials based on experience could, except in the first five years of service, be discriminatory on grounds of age [28.6.2.1] unless they can be justified.

28.8.1   Comparators

For most discrimination, it is enough to show that a hypothetical person of the other sex, another racial group etc *would have been* treated differently. To claim equal pay, however, there must generally be an *actual* **comparator**. This person:

- must be of the other sex;
- must be employed by the same employer or an associated employer (two companies where one is controlled by the other, or two companies controlled by the same third person or company);
- must generally be employed at the same establishment (or must be employed at another establishment owned by the same or an associated employer, with common terms and conditions applied at the two establishments); and
- must be doing work which is like (the same or broadly similar), or rated as equivalent, or of equal value.   *Equal Pay Act 1970 s.1(6)*

A predecessor can be a comparator, but only the predecessor's actual terms and conditions at the time of termination can be used – not what would have happened if the predecessor had continued to be employed. A successor cannot be a comparator.   *Walton Centre for Neurology & Neuro Science v Bewley [2008] UKEAT 0564 07 2305*

Despite the Equal Pay Act requirement that there be an actual comparator, the European court of justice has said that a claim could instead in some situations be based on statistical data showing that more women than men (or more men than women) are adversely affected by an aspect of pay or conditions.

Allonby v Accrington & Rossendale College & others [2004] EUECJ C-256/01

28.9 REDRESS

Employers should have clear procedures for employees to raise concerns about any form of discrimination. This should be done through the normal grievance procedure [**33.4**], but given the sensitive nature of the issues it may be sensible to create a more private grievance procedure for the initial complaint.

ACAS has a conciliation procedure [**37.2.2**] for individual cases. Either the employee or employer may call in ACAS at any time.

If the case is unresolved, the Equality and Human Rights Commission [see end of chapter] has powers to investigate complaints, issue unlawful act notices, and institute legal proceedings. Alternatively, an individual may take the case to an employment tribunal [see **chapter 37** for procedure, time limits and awards].

28.9.1 Burden of proof

Under the **burden of proof** rules in the original race, sex and disability discrimination legislation, the complainant/worker had to show that they had been treated less favourably than someone else had been or would have been, and that the reason for the less favourable treatment was their race, sex or disability. If the employer claimed there was some other reason for the less favourable treatment, the worker had to show that the reason was indeed race, sex or disability.

Now, for virtually all forms of discrimination, there is a **reverse burden of proof**. The worker still has to show that they have been less favourably treated and that they believe this to have been on the basis of their race, sex, disability, religion/belief, sexual orientation or age – but their complaint is upheld unless the employer proves it did not commit or permit the act. So the burden is initially on the complainant to make their case, but once this case has been established the employer has the burden of proving that it did not act unlawfully.

At the time of writing (mid 2009) the former approach – with the burden of proof fully on the worker – still applied to discrimination on grounds of colour or nationality under the **Race Relations Act 1976** [**28.2**], and a case in 2007 found that it also still applied to claims of victimisation under the Race Relations Act [**28.1.5**]. These anomalies were expected to be remedied by the Equality Act [**28.1.12**].
Oyarce v Cheshire County Council [2007] UKEAT 0557 06 1306

Resources: EQUAL OPPORTUNITIES

All equality strands. Equality and Human Rights Commission: www.equalityhumanrights.com; 0845 604 6610 England, 0845 604 8810 Wales, info@equalityhumanrights.com.

Government Equalities Office: www.equalities.gov.uk, 020 7944 0601, enquiries@geo.gsi.gov.uk.

Equal opportunities in employment: ACAS, BIS, Business Link, CIPD, Directgov, PEACe, TUC: see end of **chapter 25**.

Access to Work (support for disabled workers). www.jobcentreplus.gov.uk and local Jobcentre Plus.

Age. Employers Forum on Age: www.efa.org.uk, 0845 456 2495, efa@efa.org.uk.

Disability access. Centre for Accessible Environments: www.cae.org.uk, 020 7840 0125, info@cae.org.uk.

Risk assessment for disabled (and all other) **workers.** Health and Safety Executive: www.hse.gov.uk, 0845 345 0055, hse.infoline@natbrit.com.

Sexual orientation. Stonewall: www.stonewall.org.uk, 08000 50 20 20, info@stonewall.org.uk.

Trans equality. Press for Change, www.pfc.org.uk.

Young workers. Children's Legal Centre: www.childrenslegalcentre.com, 0845 120 2948, clc@essex.ac.uk.

Statute law. www.opsi.gov.uk and www.statutelaw.gov.uk.

Much but not all case law. www.bailii.org.

Updates cross-referenced to this book. www.rclh.co.uk.

Chapter 29
TAKING ON NEW EMPLOYEES

For sources of further information see end of chapter.

29.1   DEFINING THE EMPLOYER

Before hiring a new employee, it is essential to clarify who the employer is. If the organisation is **incorporated** as a company, charitable incorporated organisation or industrial and provident society [see **chapter 3**], or if it is a charitable trust or association which has **incorporated its trustee body** [**2.4**], it is able to enter into contracts, including contracts of employment, in its own right. The employer is the company, CIO, IPS or trustee body itself.

If the organisation is an **unincorporated association** or a **charitable trust** and has not incorporated its trustee body, the members of the governing body [**13.1**] are legally the employer. This is the case even though the organisation itself is generally named as the employer in the statement of employment particulars or written contract [**27.1.1**].
Affleck & another v Newcastle Mind & others
[1999] UKEAT 537 98 1003

If an employee is employed by one body and then lent or seconded to another [**25.5.4**], it must be made clear – ideally in a formal **secondment agreement** – who is legally the employer and who is responsible for managing the employee.

Sometimes an employee is shared between two associated organisations, such as a charity and its trading subsidiary. A decision needs to be made as to whether one organisation employs the worker and charges the other for a share of salary and other costs, in which case VAT may need to be charged on payments between the organisations [**57.13.1**]; the employee is the joint employee of both [**25.4**]; or the employee is separately employed on a part-time basis by each organisation.

Regardless of how the person is employed, salary and other costs must be apportioned in a way that ensures that a charity's funds and other resources are not used for purposes that are not charitable [**51.5.3**].

A person hired on a self employed basis must genuinely meet the criteria for self employment in relation both to employment law and tax [**38.2**].

29.2 THE RECRUITMENT PROCESS

An employer should always be able to show, if challenged, that neither direct nor indirect discrimination [**28.1.3**, **28.1.4**] took place during recruitment, and that it made reasonable adjustments to enable a disabled person to apply for the job and to do it if hired [**28.7.4**]. To do this, the whole recruitment process should be organised consistently, with proper records kept at each step.

The organisation must consider whether any of its employees are currently being made redundant, or if there is a likelihood of this. If those at risk of redundancy could be suitable for the new post, or could with training be suitable, they must be offered the new job on a permanent or trial basis [**35.6**]. If more than one suitable person is being made redundant, they are all entitled to apply for the post before it is openly advertised.

29.2.1 Job description

There is no statutory obligation to draw up a **job description**. However, it is difficult to recruit successfully if the employer is not clear about the work to be done, and it can be difficult to monitor work and deal with unsatisfactory performance where there has been no agreement about what was supposed to be done and to what standards. Even for new posts where it is unclear what the work will eventually involve, a job description should be drawn up for the initial months, with an indication of when and how it will be reviewed and revised.

A job description should reflect the need for flexibility.

The statement of employment particulars [**26.7**] (or written contract containing the required particulars) which must be given to virtually all employees must contain a clear job title or a brief job description. It is not advisable to include a detailed job description in the statement of particulars or contract, as this means it becomes part of the contract and could be difficult to change. The job description itself should indicate that it is not part of the contract.

29.2.2 Person specification

A **person specification** lists the key skills, knowledge, experience or personal characteristics (such as being able to work collaboratively, or to work on one's own) needed for the job. In general it is good practice to include only **essential** criteria, but sometimes it may be appropriate to include **desirable** criteria as well. It should be clear whether applicants must meet each criterion now, or whether that skill, knowledge or qualification can be gained on the job.

All criteria should be justifiable in terms of the duties in the job description. Great care should be taken to ensure that no person specification requirement has the effect of discriminating unjustifiably against any group covered by equal opportunities legislation – even if any such discrimination is unintentional [**28.1**].

To avoid age discrimination, the emphasis should be on **competencies** rather than **length of service**. Unless there is a legal or other genuine requirement for a person to have done the work for a specified period, the focus should be on what the person needs to be able to do rather than how long they have done it. If a specified period of experience is required it should be less than five years [**28.6.2**].

There is no statutory requirement for a person specification. However, if there is no record of the key criteria and how individual candidates matched these, it could be difficult to demonstrate that shortlisting and selection were conducted in a non-discriminatory way.

29.2.3 Advertising

There is no statutory obligation to advertise jobs, but recruiting only through informal networks may give rise to indirect discrimination [28.1.4].

Unless the advertisement clearly indicates otherwise, terms which imply that the job is open only to non-disabled people, or people of a particular racial group, sex, sexual orientation, religion/belief or age group are likely to be discriminatory [28.1.9]. This includes terms such as foreman, girl Friday, mature or youthful.

To avoid allegations of indirect discrimination, advertisements should be placed in publications which are read by all sectors of the community, and notices of vacancies should be widely circulated. If vacancies are widely advertised, they can also be advertised in publications intended primarily for particular groups.

Jobs advertised on websites should also be advertised in print publications, as at the time of writing people of certain age groups use the internet less than other groups, so website-only publicity could be discriminatory on grounds of age.

29.2.3.1 GOR/GOQ jobs

If it is a **genuine occupational requirement** (GOR) or **genuine occupational qualification** (GOQ) [28.1.7] to be of a particular racial group, sex, religion/belief, sexual orientation or age group, this must be specified in the advertisement and notices of the vacancy, with a statement that the post is exempt and the section of the relevant legislation which applies.

It is lawful to place advertisements for GOR/GOQ posts in publications targeted specifically at the group(s) for which the post is intended.

29.2.3.2 Giving preference to disabled people

It is not unlawful to give preference to disabled applicants, for example to say that all disabled applicants who meet the person specification will be shortlisted, provided that all disabilities are treated equally. It is also not unlawful to say that only disabled applicants will be considered for a post [28.7]. If the organisation is going to do this it should be stated in the advertisement and person specification.

29.2.4 Enquiries and application

It is important to have guidelines for dealing with enquiries, to ensure that unlawful discrimination does not occur at this stage. It should be clear that the organisation will take reasonable steps to adapt initial information and the application process for a person with a disability, if requested to do so [29.2.6].

There is no statutory obligation to provide an **application form**, but if there is one it should ask only for information relevant to the post. Questions relating to racial group, sex, marital/civil partnership status, religion/belief, sexual orientation or age should be asked only if being of a particular group is a genuine occupational requirement or genuine occupational qualification [28.1.7].

29.2.4.1 Bias-free applications

While nothing can be completely bias free, some organisations seek to reduce the risk of discrimination by using a process in which the applicant is identified by a code number and provides information on separate forms.

- **Competencies**. This is the main form, on which applicants are encouraged to focus on what they have done and can do in relation to the skills, knowledge and experience required for the post, rather than on job titles or how long they did a particular job. Shortlisters and interviewers see only this form.

- **Adjustments for a disabled applicant.** This asks whether the applicant has a disability and would need the employer to make any special arrangements if they are shortlisted or offered the post. This form is not seen until after the initial shortlisting. If the applicant is shortlisted, the relevant person in the organisation looks at this form and makes adjustments as necessary for the next stage – interview, testing and/or practical exercise. Interviewers or testers are provided with information about the disability only to the extent required to enable them to adapt the process.

- **Personal details.** This form covers name, address, date of birth, educational history, work history including dates, references, eligibility to work in the UK [**29.4**], and any questions about criminal record [**29.6.3**]. This is not seen by anyone involved in selection until after the interviewers have made their choice. It is then used to corroborate information provided on the competencies form, and as the basis for criminal records, medical and other checks.
- **Monitoring** [below]. This should always be anonymised and used for statistical purposes only. It should not be used in any way linked to the individual.

Where the post involves work with children, vulnerable adults, money or valuable property, some of the information on the personal details form may need to be checked at an earlier stage, but ideally this should be done by someone who will not be involved in shortlisting or interview.

The Employers Forum on Age [see end of **chapter 28**] has a template for a bias-free form.

29.2.5 Monitoring

There is in general no statutory obligation to monitor information relating to job applicants, although public bodies need to do so as part of their equality duties [**42.2**], and many funders require it. Even if it is not required, monitoring helps employers assess whether they have been effective in attracting applications from a broad cross-section of the community, and whether reasonable numbers from various groups were shortlisted.

Because there is no statutory obligation to undertake monitoring, applicants cannot be required to provide monitoring data and should not be rejected on the basis that they did not do so.

Much of the information collected as part of monitoring is sensitive data under the **Data Protection Act 1998** [**43.3.1**], and should be kept in an anonymised form which cannot be linked to any individual. If the information is used in any way for selection decisions or in relation to individuals or can be linked to identifiable individuals, it must comply with data protection requirements.

29.2.6 Adjustments for disabled people

Employers must make reasonable adjustments to the recruitment or selection process, in order to remove or reduce any substantial disadvantage faced by a disabled person who has applied or wishes to apply for a post [**28.7.4**]. There is no duty to make such adjustments if the employer did not know or could not reasonably have known that the person had a disability, but the employer does have a duty to take reasonable steps to find out. *Disability Discrimination Act 1995 ss.3A(6), 4A, inserted by DDA 1995 (Amendment) Regs 2003 regs.4,5*

The easiest way to find out is usually to ask at enquiry stage whether the applicant would need any adjustments to enable them to apply, and to ask at application stage whether they would need adjustments to take part in the selection process or do the job as advertised. It is acceptable to ask as part of the application process whether there are any factors which could affect the applicant's ability to do the job as described, and to ask what adaptations might be required.

29.3 THE SELECTION PROCESS

An employer should be able to show that the shortlisting process, interviews, any tests, presentations or practical exercises, and the selection decision itself were based on relevant criteria which did not discriminate unlawfully on the basis of racial group, sex, religion/belief, sexual orientation, disability or age.

A complaint of discrimination must generally be made within three months of the date of the act being complained about, but the employment tribunal can hear a complaint made later than this if it would be just and equitable to do so [**37.3.2**]. An employer should keep documentation relating to the recruitment process for at least six months, and preferably for one year.

29.3.1   Shortlisting and interview

There is no statutory requirement to record the criteria used for shortlisting and interview and how candidates were assessed, but it is sensible to do so. The person specification provides a useful checklist for this purpose.

Interviewers must not create an impression of discrimination by asking inappropriate questions, for example asking whether candidates have children and what provision they would make during school holidays. If the job requires the person to be able to work during school holidays, the job description and person specification should make this clear and there is no need for the question to be asked.

There is no statutory obligation to ask all candidates the same questions, or to ask them all in the same way. The intention should be to elicit comparable information, so candidates can be fairly compared. Especially where a candidate has not understood the question or is struggling to reply, it is sensible to rephrase the question or ask the candidate to clarify or expand on their response.

29.3.2   Tests

Tests and exercises can be effective in assessing candidates' knowledge and skills, but great care should be taken to ensure they actually assess what they are supposed to, and to ensure the people evaluating them have clear criteria and know how to carry out and assess the test. If an applicant has a disability, the employer must consider reasonable adjustments to the test, and must ensure the criteria for passing the test do not unjustifiably put the disabled person at a disadvantage.

Tests must not involve unjustifiable questions or tasks which have the effect of unlawful discrimination. Questions which assume knowledge of British history, for example, may indirectly discriminate against people who are not British – and will therefore be permissible only if the job requires knowledge of British history.

29.3.3   Selection

Written records of the reasons for selection decisions do not have to be kept, but without such records it can be difficult for an employer to show that it has not discriminated unlawfully in reaching its decision.

Candidates do not have to be told why they were not selected. If they are told, great care should be taken, because if a candidate later makes a complaint of discrimination anything said about the reason for non-selection could be significant.

29.3.4   Offer of employment

An **offer of employment** and its **acceptance** may be oral or in writing [**26.2**]. Putting it in writing reduces the risk of misunderstanding.

If the offer is conditional upon satisfactory references, a criminal record check, a medical test, evidence of the right to work in the UK, or any other condition, this must be clear and explicit. If this is not made clear and the offer of employment is subsequently withdrawn, this could constitute breach of contract and the employer could become liable for damages for wrongful dismissal [below].

An offer subject to satisfactory completion of a probationary period generally creates a contract from day one [**26.2**], subject to any special conditions, such as shorter notice, specified as applying during the probationary period [**29.4.1**].

Unless the offer of employment sets out all the key conditions of employment, there is a risk that any issue omitted by the employer could later be contested by the employee. It is therefore advisable to send with the offer a written contract or statement of employment particulars [**26.7, chapter 27**], even though this generally can be provided at any time in the two months after the person starts work.

29.3.4.1   Pre-employment dismissal

If an unconditional offer of employment is made and accepted and is subsequently withdrawn, the individual will be able to bring a claim for wrongful dismissal [**34.4.1**] even if he or she has not yet started work.   *Sarker v South Tees Acute Hospitals NHS Trust [1997] UKEAT 493 96 2503*

The person may also be able to claim unfair dismissal if the reason is one which does not require one year's employment [**34.7.1**], and/or discrimination [**28.1.1**].

29.3.5 Misrepresentation

Misrepresentations [**21.2.8**] made prior to the creation of the contract may give rise to a right to claim damages. If a misrepresentation is sufficiently serious and has been incorporated into the terms of the contract, the wronged party may be entitled to terminate the contract without notice [**34.2.9**, **34.2.10**].

To guard against the possibility of misrepresenting its position, the employer should put all relevant information in writing. It should also reduce the risk of a potential employee's misrepresentation by, for example, ensuring all questions in application forms and other documents are unambiguous, requiring documentary proof of key qualifications, and making enquiries of previous employers.

29.4 PROBATIONARY PERIOD

There is no obligation to have a probationary period, but many employers do – and many mistakenly believe that merely saying that there is one gives them the right to summarily dismiss the employee during or at the end of the period.

29.4.1 Contract conditional on satisfactory probationary period

Even if there is a probationary period, for the purposes of employment rights the contract of employment comes into effect when the offer of work is unconditionally made and accepted [**26.2.1**]; the period of continuous employment [**26.5.2**] begins when the contract specifies or (if earlier) when the employee actually start work; and the employer must give a written statement of particulars within two months of their starting [**26.7**]. The employee has full statutory rights during the probationary period, and all contractual rights unless the contract explicitly says that these rights do not apply.

If the probationary period ends successfully the employer does not 'confirm the contract', but in effect confirms that the contract which is already in existence will not be terminated. If the probationary period is not successful, the employee is dismissed according to the terms of the contract or by being given the statutory period of notice, which is one week, after the first month of employment [**34.3.1**].

29.4.2 Dismissal during or at the end of the period

The most common contractual differences during a probationary period are that the employer or employee can terminate employment without giving the full contractual notice, and the full disciplinary procedure does not have to be followed.

If shorter notice is allowed, the amount should be specified in the contract. If the probationary period is more than one month, the notice required must not be less than one week, as this is the statutory minimum [**34.3.1**].

Unless the contract says otherwise, the contractual disciplinary procedure [**33.1.2**] applies during the probationary period. Dismissals should comply with the ACAS code of practice on disciplinary matters [**33.2.1**].

29.4.3 Extending a probationary period

A probationary period can be extended only if the contract explicitly allows this, and any extension must be made before the period has expired.

Przybyiska v Modus Telecom Ltd [2007] UKEAT 0566 06 0602

29.5 WORKERS FROM OUTSIDE THE UK

An employer who hires employees who are not entitled to work in the UK can face an on the spot penalty of up to £2,000 per worker or a court-ordered penalty of up to £10,000 per worker, and in addition can face criminal penalties of an unlimited fine and up to two years in prison. So it is important for everyone involved in recruitment to understand the rules and know how to comply with them without discriminating unlawfully. Information is available from the UK Border Agency [see end of chapter]. Separate rules apply to volunteers [**39.6**].

29.5.1 Checking entitlement to work

If it turns out that an employee is not entitled to work in the UK, it is a statutory 'excuse' for the employer to show that it saw the original and kept a copy of a **specified document** or documents before the person started working, and for employees hired on or after 29 February 2008, has carried out annual checks on employees who have restrictions on their right to work in the UK.   *Immigration, Asylum & Nationality Act 2006 s.15; Immigration (Restrictions on Employment) Order 2007 [SI 2007/3290]*

At the time of writing (mid 2009) it was expected that legislation would be introduced allowing information about immigration restrictions to be included, if an employer requests it, on a criminal record check [**41.4.1**].

29.5.1.1 Pre-employment checks

To have a statutory excuse, the employer must, before hiring the person, see and keep a copy of one document or a combination from either **list A** (for individuals not subject to immigration control or with no restrictions on their stay in the UK) or **list B** (where leave to enter or remain in the UK is time limited). The list of documents is different for employees who started work before 29 February 2008.

- **List A (single document)**: UK passport; a passport, biometric immigration document or travel document showing the person has the right of abode or right to remain in the UK for an indefinite period; a passport or national identity card showing the person is an EEA [**29.5.1.5**] or Swiss national; or a residence permit issued by the UK to an EEA or Swiss national.

- **List A (combination)**: an official document giving a permanent national insurance number (P45 or P60 from the previous employer, or letter from a government department); plus a UK birth, adoption or naturalisation certificate or certain documents from the Home Office or Border Agency (UKBA) which indicate the person is allowed to stay in the UK indefinitely.

- **List B (single document)**: a passport, biometric immigration document, identity card or travel document showing the person has the right to stay in the UK and an unrestricted right do the type of work in question; or a residence card or document issued by the Home Office or UKBA to a family member of an EEA or Swiss national.

- **List B (combination)**: a work permit issued by the Home Office or UKBA; plus a passport, other travel document or identity card showing the person can remain in the UK and take the employment in question or a letter from the Home Office or UKBA confirming the same; such a letter or immigration status document, plus an official document giving a permanent national insurance number; or an application registration card or certificate of application (less than six months old) issued by the Home Office or UKBA stating that the holder is permitted to take employment, with evidence of verification by the UKBA employer checking service.

To avoid a claim of racial discrimination, all potential applicants should be treated the same. Procedures should comply with the guidance for employers on the avoidance of unlawful discrimination, available from the Border Agency [see end of chapter]. It is acceptable to ask on an application form whether the applicant needs permission to work in the UK, and to ask for the relevant documentation at any stage in the recruitment process.

Once the employer has established that an applicant is from outside the EEA [**29.5.1.5**], it is not unlawful racial discrimination to require that person to provide evidence of their right to work in the UK – even though persons from outside the EEA are thus being treated less favourably than those from within the EEA.

Olatokun v IKON Office Solutions [2004] UKEAT 0074 04 1005

The employer should be satisfied that the document appears to be one of the specified documents, appears to be an original, and appears to relate to the person, and must take all reasonable steps to check the validity of the document. The Border Agency helpline advises on the acceptability of documents.

29.5.1.2   What to keep and how long to keep it

For a passport or other travel document, the employer must keep copies of the front cover, and any pages containing the holder's personal details, date of expiry, and information indicating the holder is entitled to enter or remain in the UK and undertake the work in question. For other documents, the employer must keep a copy of the entire document. In all cases the copy must be in a format which cannot subsequently be altered. *Immigration (Restrictions on Employment) Order 2007 [SI 2007/3290]*

Unless the document is a P45 part 2, the employer should photocopy it and immediately return the original to the individual. The copy should be kept for at least two years after the person ceases to be employed by the employer. A P45 part 2 must be kept for at least three years, for tax purposes [**18.4.2**].

29.5.1.3   Annual checks

Where a document or documents in list B [**29.5.1.1**] are provided, the employer has a statutory excuse only for 12 months from the date the person provided the documents. It is therefore necessary for the employer to obtain, check and keep copies of the documents again before 12 months has elapsed.

29.5.1.4   Applications for renewal

An employee who applies for renewal of their right to work before their existing permission expires can continue working until their application is decided. To have evidence that the employee can continue working, the employer should obtain from the employee a copy of their application.

If the employee's application is rejected, it would be unlawful for the employer to continue employing them, and dismissal will be fair on the basis of being in breach of a statutory restriction [**34.6.4**].

Where the employee's status is unclear and the employer is genuinely concerned about continuing to employ them, a dismissal may be fair on the basis of 'some other substantial reason' [**34.6.5**]. A proper investigation should be held and the necessary disciplinary procedure followed [**33.3**]. *Klusova v London Borough of Hounslow [2007] EWCA Civ 1127*

29.5.1.5   Transfers under TUPE

An employer transferring employees under the **Transfer of Undertakings (Protection of Employment) Regulations** [**29.7.1.1**] , where those employees are sponsored under the points based immigration system [**29.5.3**], must notify the UK Border Agency within 28 days of the transfer.

If the receiving organisation (the **transferee**) is a licensed sponsor, it must also notify UKBA within 28 days of the transfer. If the transferee is not licensed, it must apply to become licensed within 28 days. Failure to do this will mean that the employee is no longer working legally in the UK, which could have serious implications for both the employee and transferee employer.

As part of the transfer process, the transferee should ensure that the transferor carried out pre-employment [**29.5.1.1**] and annual checks [**29.5.1.3**]. The transferee is also obliged to carry out new checks within 28 days. However, at the time of writing (mid 2009) it was unclear whether the criteria to be used were those in force when the employee was originally hired, or the criteria in force at the time of transfer. Transferees should contact UKBA [see end of chapter] for advice.

29.5.2   EEA nationals

The European Economic Area is made up of the European Union plus Iceland, Liechtenstein and Norway. EEA nationals and their family members have the right to work, study or set up in business in the UK.

These rights are unrestricted for nationals of Austria, Belgium, Cyprus, Denmark, Finland, France, Germany, Gibraltar, Greece, Iceland, the Republic of Ireland, Italy, Liechtenstein, Luxembourg, Malta, the Netherlands, Norway, Portugal, Spain and Sweden. Switzerland is not part of the EEA but Swiss nationals have the same rights.

29.5.2.1 Worker registration scheme

Nationals of the Czech Republic, Estonia, Hungary, Latvia, Lithuania, Poland, Slovakia and Slovenia who wish to work for an employer in the UK for more than one month must register with the Border Agency's **worker registration scheme** before or within one month of starting work. The employer has to carry out the usual pre-employment check [**29.5.1.1**], and any person from one of these countries who is not already registered should be advised to register immediately and provide a copy of their application to the employer.   *Accession (Immigration & Worker Registration) Regulations 2004 [SI 2004/706]*

The employer must check within one month of the person starting work that he or she has applied to register with the scheme. Provided the employer has kept a copy of the application form, the worker can continue to be hired until the Border Agency makes a decision about registration. Once the person is registered a copy of their registration certificate is sent to the employer and must be kept. If registration is refused, the employer is notified and must immediately dismiss the worker. It is an offence for an employer not to comply with these rules.

A person who has been employed by the same employer and registered under this scheme for 12 months can apply for a residence permit confirming their right to live and work in the EEA.

The worker registration scheme will end on 30 April 2011.

29.5.2.2 Bulgarian and Romanian nationals

Many but not all workers from Bulgaria or Romania have to apply for an **accession worker card**, and in some cases the employer must also apply for a work permit. Those who do not need an accession worker card or work permit can apply for a **registration certificate** to show they have the right to work in the UK. It is unlawful to hire a Bulgarian or Romanian national who needs an accession worker card and does not have one.   *Accession (Immigration & Worker Authorisation) Regulations 2006 [SI 2006/3317]*

29.5.3 Non-EEA nationals

Information about entitlement to work in the UK is available from the UK Border Agency [see end of chapter]. For people from outside the EEA or Switzerland, any restrictions on their right to work in the UK (or the lack of restrictions) will be shown in their passport or other travel document. Permission to work will be shown in their passport or travel document, a work permit or similar document. The employer must see, check and keep a copy of these documents before hiring the person, and in some cases must carry out the checks annually [**29.5.1**].

29.5.3.1 Commonwealth citizens and people with indefinite leave to remain

People with indefinite leave to remain in the UK, Commonwealth citizens with right of abode, and some Commonwealth citizens with a grandparent born in the UK are entitled to live and work in the UK without needing to get any consent. Their passport or travel document will show that they have right of abode or indefinite leave to remain, or that there is no time limit on their stay in the UK.

29.5.3.2 The points based system

Since 29 February 2008 a five-tier **points based system** (PBS) has been introduced for workers from outside the EEA and Switzerland. The points are based on workers' skills, and are intended to assess aptitude, experience and age, as well as the need for those skills in the UK economy, English language ability, prospective earnings, and funds available for maintenance. Admission under each tier is based on different criteria, and involves different rights and conditions.

Information is available from the UK Border Agency. A calculator on the website enables potential applicants to assess their points before applying.

Individuals given the right to work in the UK before the relevant PBS provisions came into effect can continue to be employed until their permission ends. The employer should keep a record of such permission, and ensure it becomes a licensed sponsor [**29.5.3.4**] and issues a certificate of sponsorship in enough time for the employee to apply for extension of the appropriate points based visa.

29.5.3.3 Tier 1: Highly skilled workers

The former highly skilled migrant programme and similar schemes were replaced in early 2008 by four **tier 1** categories: **general highly skilled migrants** (for people who are looking for highly skilled employment, or some people who are self employed or setting up a business in the UK), **investors**, **entrepreneurs**, and **post-study work**. 'Highly skilled' includes people such as doctors, scientists and engineers. The post-study category allows graduates of UK universities from outside the EEA to remain in the UK for two years after graduation, in order to obtain a work or business related visa.

Applicants under tier 1 must score at least 95 points but do not need a job offer in order to apply, and their permission to work is not linked to a particular job or type of work.

Dependants of workers admitted under tier 1 are allowed to work in the UK. A person admitted under tier 1 can switch to tier 2 or 4 while in the UK.

29.5.3.4 Licensed sponsors

Applicants in tiers 2-5 must have a **certificate of sponsorship** or **confirmation of acceptance for studies** from a **licensed sponsor** before applying to come to the UK or for permission to stay. A licensed sponsor is an employer or educational institution registered on the Border Agency's **sponsorship register** to sponsor workers, trainees or students in a specific tier or tiers. A licence is valid for four years from the date of registration or from when applications start being taken from workers or students in that tier.

At the time of writing (1/8/09) the licence application fee is generally £1,000, but is £400 for charities as defined under the Charities Acts and comparable legislation in Scotland and Northern Ireland, companies defined as small under the **Companies Act 2006 [54.3.2]**, and organisations which are neither charities nor companies but employ no more than 50 employees.

Sponsors are rated as A or B (a transitional rating), based on their experience and policies in sponsoring migrant workers. The applicant is given a specified number of points based on the sponsor's rating.

Sponsors must comply with **sponsorship duties** on record keeping, reporting, compliance, cooperation with the Border Agency, and duties specific to each tier.

29.5.3.5 Tier 2: Skilled workers

Tier 2 came into effect on 27 November 2008, replacing the work permit regime for skilled workers. 'Skilled' includes workers such as administrators, teachers and nurses. This tier covers:

- **tier 2 general shortage occupations**, as identified by the Migration Advisory Committee;
- **tier 2 general** jobs that have passed the **resident labour market test**, where the employer can show it advertised the vacancy through Jobcentre Plus and could not fill the post from within the UK;
- **intra-company transfers**, where a skilled non-EEA employee who has been working overseas for the employer for at least six months, can be transferred to work for the employer in the UK;
- **ministers of religion** and other religious workers coming to the UK for more than two years to carry out preaching, pastoral duties or missionary work within a religious organisation, or to work in a religious order within a community which involves a permanent commitment, such as a monastery or convent;
- individuals switching from a **post-study** category under tier 1;
- elite **sportspersons** and coaches.

At the time of writing (mid 2009), the government had proposed removing tier 2 general and intra-company transfers from this list.

In order to offer tier 2 employment, the employer must be licensed as a **sponsor** [**29.5.3.4**] and must provide a certificate of sponsorship to the applicant.

With the certificate the individual can then apply for a visa and is assessed on the basis of points. Points for tier 2 are based on proficiency in English, prospective earnings, and having enough savings to cover their costs and those of any dependants for the first month or having confirmation that they will be maintained and accommodated by their employer for the first month.

Tier 2 visas are issued for up to three years plus one month, and can be extended for up to two years. A migrant under tier 2 can then apply for citizenship, or make a new application under the points based scheme. A person admitted under tier 2 can switch to tier 1 or 4 while in the UK, provided they meet the requirements for that tier.

At the time of writing (mid 2009), dependants of workers admitted under tier 2 were allowed to work in the UK, but the government had proposed restricting this right. The employer must maintain up to date contact details for sponsored employees. If an employee who has been granted a visa under tier 2 does not take up the job or is absent without authorisation for 10 days, the employer must report this to the Border Agency. The employer must also report termination of the employment for any reason, any significant changes to the sponsored individual (such as a change of job or salary, but not a change to job title only or annual salary increase), and details of any third party who assisted in the recruitment.

29.5.3.6 Tier 3: Low skilled workers to fill temporary labour shortages

Tier 3 is available for limited numbers of low skilled workers who are needed to fill temporary or seasonal labour shortages in the UK. Dependants are not entitled to accompany workers admitted under tier 3, and tier 3 workers cannot change to another tier while in the UK.

29.5.3.7 Tier 4: Students

Since March 2009 students from outside the EEA or Switzerland are admitted to the UK under **tier 4**. They must have a certificate of acceptance for studies from an educational institution licensed as a sponsor [**29.5.3.4**], be able to show they can financially support themselves and any dependants without taking paid work, and supply their fingerprints.

Sponsors must keep copies of the passports of sponsored students, keep up to date contact details for them, and inform the Border Agency if a student does not enrol on their course, is absent without authorisation or stops their studies.

Dependants can accompany students admitted under this tier, and can work provided the student's permission to stay in the UK is for 12 months or more. A person admitted under tier 4 can change to tier 1 or 2 if they are eligible.

Students can work in the UK for unlimited hours during vacations, and a maximum of 20 hours per week during term. They must fill in **form OSS1**, available from Jobcentre Plus. The work must not involve engaging in business, being self employed or providing services as a professional sportsperson or entertainer.

29.5.3.8 Tier 5: Youth mobility and temporary workers

Tier 5 came into effect on 27 November 2008, replacing working holidaymaker, gap year and similar schemes. It covers:
- **creative and sporting workers**, coming to the UK to work or perform as sportspersons, entertainers or creative artists for up to 12 months;
- **charity workers**, coming to the UK to do unpaid voluntary work for a charity for up to 12 months [**39.6.1**];
- **religious workers** who do not meet the criteria for entry under tier 2 [**29.5.3.5**] and are coming to the UK for up to 24 months;
- **government authorised exchange schemes**;
- **youth mobility scheme**, for people aged 18 to 31 from Australia, Canada, Japan and New Zealand, coming to the UK for up to 24 months;
- workers carrying out work covered under **international agreements** such as the General Agreement on Trade in Services and similar agreements, and employees of overseas governments and international organisations.

To apply, the individual must have a sponsor [**29.5.3.4**] and certificate of sponsorship. Points are awarded based on their sponsorship and their available funds for maintenance. For youth mobility schemes the individual's national government is the sponsor, and for government exchange schemes the sponsor is always an overarching body which manages the exchange scheme, rather than an individual organisation. The length of stay and rules for extension vary depending on the category within tier 5.

British overseas citizens, British overseas territories citizens and British nationals (overseas) can also apply under the youth mobility scheme, and do not need a sponsor.

Dependants can be admitted and can work provided the worker's permission to stay in the UK is for 12 months or more. A person admitted under tier 5 cannot switch to another tier, and in most cases cannot switch to another tier 5 category.

29.5.3.9 Visitors visas

New rules were introduced from 27 November 2008 for a range of visas for short-term visitors to the UK. In most cases the maximum stay is six months.

A **business visitors visa** covers attending conferences, negotiating or signing agreements and contracts, undertaking fact-finding missions, checking details or goods, conducting site visits or carrying out promotional activities. Roles such as representing overseas news media, or acting as an academic visitor or visiting professor are also covered.

Sportspersons and support staff coming for specific sporting events, and amateur sportspersons joining UK amateur teams for up to six months can apply for a **sports visitors visa**.

Entertainer visitors visas are available for professional entertainers coming to the UK to take part in music competitions, a charity show, or a show where they will receive no fee; amateur entertainers coming to the UK for a specific engagement; and professional and amateur entertainers taking part in a 'permit free festival' such as the Edinburgh Festival.

Student visitors are admitted for up to six months to undertake study at an organisation on the Department for Business, Innovation and Skills' register of education and training providers. They and their dependants may not engage in any paid work while in the UK, and the period cannot be extended.

29.5.4 Refugees and asylum seekers

A **refugee** is a person who has sought asylum because of a well founded fear of persecution in their own country, and has been granted the right to live in the UK for an initial period of five years. Refugees and their dependants have the right to work in the UK.

An **asylum seeker** has applied for refugee status and is waiting for their case to be decided. Asylum seekers and their dependants cannot take paid work but there is a concession under which they can do unpaid voluntary work [**39.6.2**]. An asylum seeker who has not received an initial decision after 12 months can apply for permission to work. If granted, permission applies only to the asylum seeker.

Asylum seekers who have been refused refugee status but would be at risk of serious harm if they returned to their home country may be given **humanitarian protection** or **discretionary leave**. The asylum seeker and their dependants can work while in the UK on this basis.

Where a person applies for an extension to humanitarian protection or discretionary leave, their leave is automatically extended while their application is being considered. All rights, including any right to work or study, are also extended. Employees may be unwilling to give employers a copy of their application for extension as it often contains sensitive and confidential information regarding their application for asylum. Employers should therefore accept as proof of the asylum seeker's right to work or continue working a copy of their old status document, and a letter from their solicitor confirming that an application was submitted before the leave expired.

Information about the rights of refugees, asylum seekers and those given humanitarian protection is available from the Refugee Council [see end of chapter].

29.6 PRE-EMPLOYMENT CHECKS

While some employers are satisfied with information provided by candidates about their experience and background, most require additional information in the form of references, medical checks, criminal record checks and/or confirmation of qualifications. In some cases, there is a statutory obligation to carry out these checks, or funders require it.

If employment is explicitly made conditional on receipt of satisfactory references or checks, it may be terminated if these are not received or are unsatisfactory. It is the employer's decision whether they are satisfactory. An employee who has worked for at least one month is entitled to a statutory period of notice [**34.3.1**].

29.6.1 References

29.6.1.1 Duty of former employer to employee

There is normally no obligation on a former employer to provide a reference, unless it is required as part of a dismissal settlement [**37.2**], or failure to provide it could constitute victimisation, or there is a contractual or statutory obligation to provide a reference.

If a reference is provided, the employer giving it has a duty of care to the employee, and must:

- exercise reasonable skill and care, and ensure the reference is true and accurate (although it does not have to be comprehensive); *Spring v Guardian Assurance plc & others [1994] UKHL 7*
- be fair, and ensure it does not give a misleading impression; *Bartholomew v London Borough of Hackney & another [1998] EWCA Civ 1604*
- ensure it does not include complaints against a worker unless the worker is aware of them; and *TSB Bank plc v Harris [1999] UKEAT 1145 97 0112*
- ensure that a reference does not allude to an employee's misconduct if the employer has not carried out an investigation and does not have reasonable grounds for believing the misconduct has occurred. *Cox v Sun Alliance Life Ltd [2001] EWCA Civ 649*

An employee who is not hired or suffers other loss because a reference does not meet the above criteria may claim damages from the employer.

Failure to provide a reference to an employee who has brought, or threatened to bring, a discrimination or whistleblowing claim may constitute victimisation [**28.1.5, 33.5**]. An employer who usually provides references should be careful not to be seen to be discriminating against a former employee, if it does not provide a reference and this is inconsistent treatment.

Information defined as sensitive personal data under the **Data Protection Act 1998** [**43.3.1**] should not be disclosed unless the employee has given explicit consent.

29.6.1.2 Duty of former employer to prospective employer

The employer providing the reference also owes a duty of care to the prospective employer. If, as a result of an inaccurate or negligent reference, the new employer hires an unsuitable worker and suffers loss, the employer who provided the reference could be held liable.

29.6.1.3 Duties of new employer

If the offer of employment is conditional on satisfactory references, it is up to the potential employer to decide whether a reference is or is not acceptable.
Wishart v National Association of Citizens Advice Bureaux [1990] ICR 794, IRLR 393

Some employers ask for written references; others prefer the telephone. For practical and equal opportunities reasons it is a good idea to make a list of questions to ask and to keep a written record of points raised in telephone references, especially if the reference is unsatisfactory.

It is not sensible to accept, without further investigation, written references submitted by a potential employee or a very anodyne reference provided by a former employer, since the provision of such references is frequently a term of settlement for a contested dismissal.

Employees or potential employees generally have the right to see references received about them (including notes of telephone conversations) if, as is likely, the references are kept in a manner which makes them personal data under the **Data Protection Act 1998** [**43.3.1**]. However they do not have the right to see a reference if:

- the recipient (the new employer) has made clear to the referee and data subject (the employee) that the reference will be kept confidential;
- the referee has given the reference in confidence;
- reasonable efforts have been made to seek consent but the referee has withheld it, and such withholding of consent is reasonable;
- the referee cannot be contacted and it is reasonable for the recipient not to show the reference to the data subject; or
- the reference contains information about another person who has not consented to it being disclosed, and the information cannot be removed or made anonymous. However, the recipient may have a duty to show the reference to the data subject even without consent, for example if the information about the other person is already known or is innocuous.

29.6.2 Medical checks

An employer does not have to undertake a medical check on prospective or existing workers unless it is required by specific regulations, such as the obligation to offer a free health assessment before assigning work that makes a person a night worker [**40.3.2**]. A medical check should be required as part of the recruitment process only if it is necessary for the prospective job. Particular reference should be made to the guidance about workers' health information in the information commissioner's employment practices code [see end of chapter].

A medical test cannot be carried out if the employee refuses it. An employer generally can dismiss or refuse to employ a person who refuses to have a medical check, but only if there is a statutory requirement for a medical test or if a medical test is explicitly a condition of employment.

Failure to hire a person for medical reasons could in some situations constitute unlawful disability discrimination [**28.7**].

29.6.2.1 Medical records

An employer can ask for a report from an employee's doctor only if the employee gives consent. The employee has the right to see a copy of the doctor's report before it is sent to the employer, query items in the report, and have her or his objection appended to the report if the doctor does not change the report.

Access to Medical Reports Act 1988

The organisation should have proper procedures for keeping medical and other personal information strictly confidential [**43.1.3**].

29.6.3 Criminal record checks and other safeguards

Some but not all employers have access to individuals' criminal records through the Criminal Records Bureau, and employers who work with children or vulnerable adults have access to further information through the Independent Safeguarding Authority. Some employers have a statutory obligation to carry out these checks, others are advised to do so, and others may be able to do so if their internal policies or procedures require it. For more information see **chapter 41**.

29.7   TRANSFER OF UNDERTAKINGS

An organisation which is taking on work previously done by another employer, or is transferring any of its work to another employer, needs to consider whether it is affected by **TUPE** – the **Transfer of Undertakings (Protection of Employment) Regulations 2006** *[SI 2006/246]*. Basic information is available from the Department for Business, Innovation and Skills [see end of chapter]. But this area is particularly complex, can have significant legal and cost implications and changes constantly, so **it is vital to seek legal advice** at a very early stage.

29.7.1   Effect of the regulations

TUPE applies when an **economic entity** is transferred from one employer (the **transferor**) to another (the **transferee**), or when a **service provision change** takes place from one service provider (transferor) to another (transferee). These are all referred to as **relevant transfers [29.7.2]**.

29.7.1.1   Transfer of rights and liabilities

Employees and apprentices employed by the transferor immediately before the transfer are automatically transferred to the transferee, on the same terms (apart from occupational pension rights in some cases) and with continuity of employment preserved.

Transfer of Undertakings (Protection of Employment) Regulations 2006 [SI 2006/246] regs.3,4

The regulations transfer not only the contracts of employment, but also all rights, powers and duties in connection with the contract. These include the right to any unpaid wages due to the employee while employed by the transferor, and any liability for compensation for unfair dismissal where a former employee was dismissed by the transferor.

Where the transfer is between two private (non-public sector) employers, any claim for personal injury against the transferor transfers to the transferee, as does the indemnity provided by the transferor's employers' liability insurance **[23.4.1]**. Where the transfer is from a public sector body to a private employer, the transferor and transferee are jointly liable for personal injury claims against the transferor.

TUPE 2006 reg.17

Along with the details of all outstanding or potential employment related claims against the transferor **[29.7.3.1**, the transferee should also obtain details of any relevant insurance held by the transferor. Legal advice must be sought about the implications for the transferee.

Criminal liability, for example arising from non-compliance with health and safety law, does not transfer and remains with the transferor.   *TUPE 2006 reg.4(6)*

29.7.1.2   Insolvent transferor

Where the transferor is subject to insolvency proceedings at the time of the transfer, certain liabilities do not transfer to the transferee if they are covered under the national insurance fund scheme **[24.10.8]**. These are unpaid statutory redundancy pay, pay arrears, payment in lieu of notice, holiday pay, and any basic award for unfair dismissal. Any other payments due to employees transfer to the transferee.   *Transfer of Undertakings (Protection of Employment) Regulations 2006 [SI 2006/246] reg.8*

Where it could help the transferring undertaking or business or part of it to survive, changes in terms and conditions that would not normally be allowed may be able to be agreed with trade union representatives or elected employee representatives. Such changes cannot be agreed with individual employees.   *TUPE 2006 reg.9*

When a business is subject to insolvency procedures **[24.5.2]**, the liquidator often dismisses employees as a way of making it more attractive to a potential purchaser, even if the intention is for the work to continue. If the transfer to a purchaser would be a relevant transfer **[29.7.2]**, the dismissals are covered by TUPE and are likely to be unfair unless they are for an economic, technical or organisational reason entailing changes in the workforce **[29.7.5]** – even if there is no potential purchaser at the time of the dismissal. If the work is not intended to continue after the liquidation, the dismissal may be fair **[24.1.2]**.

Cab Automotive Ltd v Blake & others [2008] UKEAT 0298 07 1202

29.7.2   Relevant transfers

A **relevant transfer** may be a business transfer [**29.7.2.1**] or a service provision change [**29.7.2.2**]. The two categories are not mutually exclusive and some transfers, such as outsourcing of a service, may meet both definitions. TUPE applies to public and private (non-public sector) undertakings, including charities and other voluntary organisations.   *Transfer of Undertakings (Protection of Employment) Regulations 2006 [SI 2006/246] reg.3(1)*

29.7.2.1   Business transfer

A **business transfer** occurs when there is a transfer of an **economic entity** – an undertaking, business, or part of an undertaking or business – from one employer to another. There must have been a stable economic entity before the transfer, and the entity must retain its identity after the transfer.

An economic entity is 'an **organised grouping** of resources' which is situated in the UK immediately before the transfer. It may be a whole organisation or a recognisable and identifiable part, such as a branch, department or group of workers. Although it is called an organised grouping, even a single person can be an economic entity.   *TUPE 2006 reg.3(2)*

An organised grouping exists only where there is an individual employee or team of employees 'essentially dedicated' to carrying out the activities that will be transferred, even if the employees do not work exclusively on those activities.

29.7.2.2   Service provision change

Service provision changes concern relationships between contractors and the clients who hire their services. Changes to these contracts can take place when a service previously undertaken by the client is awarded to a contractor (**contracting out** or **outsourcing**), when a contract is assigned to a new contractor on subsequent retendering, or when the service is taken back in-house (**contracting in** or **insourcing**).   *TUPE 2006 reg.3(1)(b)*

Even if the transferee provides the service in a slightly different way from the transferor, the transfer is covered by TUPE if it is fundamentally or essentially the same.   *Metropolitan Resources Ltd v Churchill Dulwich Ltd & others [2009] UKEAT 0286 08 2406*

A service provision change does not occur where the contract is wholly or mainly for the supply of goods for the client's use. It also does not occur where a client engages a contractor on a one-off, short-term basis, such as a contract to provide security staff for a specific event.   *TUPE 2006 reg.3(3)*

Where one service is transferred to two or more transferees, it is necessary to look at it in the same way as a business transfer [**29.7.2.1**]: identifying the activities carried out as part of the service (similar to identifying an economic entity), identifying whether there is an organised grouping of employees carrying out the activities, and determining which employees are carrying out each activity. Depending on the exact details of the transfer, a tribunal might find that some employees transfer to one of the new transferees and some to the other, or that the transferee which takes the greater part of the activities must take all of them. Or it may not be a TUPE transfer, if the service is so broken up that it is impossible to identify which part of the service (and therefore which employees) went to each transferee.   *Kimberley Group Housing Ltd v Hambley [2008] UKEAT 0488 07 2504; Thomas-James & others v Cornwall County Council & others (2008) ET 1701021-22, 28 Mar 2008 (unreported)*

29.7.2.3   Transfers outside the UK

TUPE applies only if the transferring economic entity is situated in the UK immediately before the transfer. It may also, in some situations, apply where the transferee – the new contractor – is outside the UK and the intention is for the transferred work to take place there. This could have implications where, for example, an international charity based in the UK wants to transfer some or all of its operations abroad.   *Holis Metal Industries Ltd v GMB & another [2007] UKEAT 0171 07 1212*

29.7.2.4   Voluntary sector transfers

Situations where a voluntary organisation could be involved in a TUPE transfer include:

- receiving a grant, service agreement or contract for work previously done by another organisation or by a department, team or individual in that organisation;

- taking on a project or other piece of work previously run by another organisation;

- when a new (independent) organisation is set up to take on a project or piece of work previously done by another body;

- two organisations merging, or one taking over the other, or an unincorporated organisation incorporating;

- purchasing, receiving or renting property used for an undertaking, and continuing the undertaking.

In these and similar situations it is essential to take specialist advice to determine whether TUPE does or does not apply and the implications.

29.7.2.5   Transfers not covered

A change in control (for example through change of trustees in an unincorporated association or trust) or a change in ownership (for example through a sale of a majority shareholding) is not generally a transfer, because there is no change in the employer – merely a change in the control or ownership of the employer.

An administrative reorganisation of public authorities or the transfer of functions between public authorities is not covered by TUPE, but transfers out of the public sector can be covered.

The sale of assets only, without any of the connected activity or business, is generally not a transfer, nor is the sale of assets as part of a liquidation where it is not intended that the work will continue [**24.1.2**].

29.7.3   Information and consultation rights

Both the transferor and transferee have an obligation to inform and consult all employees who will be affected by the transfer – not just those who will be or might be transferred. Recognised trade union(s) [**36.3.3**], representatives elected by the employees for other purposes [**36.1**] but authorised to act on their behalf in relation to the transfer, or representatives elected under TUPE regulation 14 must be informed of when the transfer is to take place and the reasons for it, the legal, social and economic implications for affected employees, and whether either employer intends to **take measures** in relation to affected employees. 'Measures' would include redundancies, changes to terms and conditions, or changes to job roles.   *Transfer of Undertakings (Protection of Employment) Regulations 2006 [SI 2006/246] regs.13,14*

The information has to be given 'long enough before a relevant transfer to enable consultations to take place', and consultation must begin 'in good time'. Where special circumstances make this impractical, the employer must take all steps that are reasonably practicable in the circumstances.   *TUPE 2006 reg.13(2),(9)*

If either the transferor or transferee fails to consult as required, the tribunal can award up to 13 weeks' actual pay per employee. The transferor and transferee are jointly and severally liable for any such compensation – so it is crucial that each employer ensures that the other is consulting properly.   *TUPE 2006 reg.15*

29.7.3.1   Employee liability information

The transferor must provide the transferee with specified information about transferring employees at least 14 days before the transfer. The information must be provided in writing or in another readily accessible form.   *TUPE 2006 reg.11*

This **employee liability information** includes the identity and age of each transferring employee; details as included in the employee's particulars of employment [**26.7.1**]; details of any disciplinary action taken against the employee or grievance raised by the employee in the previous two years, which was covered by the ACAS code [**33.2.1**]; details of any court or tribunal case, claim or action brought by the employee against the transferor in the last two years or which the transferor has reasonable grounds to believe the employee may bring; and details of any collective agreements applicable to the transferring employee.

If the transferor fails to provide this information or the information is inaccurate, the transferee may bring a claim against the transferor within three months of the date of the transfer. Any award made by the employment tribunal is likely to be at least £500 per affected employee, and could be considerably more.

Because this information is required by law, its disclosure is permitted under data protection law. The information commissioner's [see end of **chapter 43**] guidance on disclosure in TUPE situations makes clear that information must be accurate, up to date and secure, and can only be used for the purpose of assessing potential liabilities linked to the transfer. Information which is outside the scope of TUPE – for example to potential bidders for the sale of business – should be anonymous, or be disclosed only with the consent of the relevant employees.

29.7.4   Right to object to transfer

An employee has the right to object to being transferred or being employed by the new employer. This prevents that employee's transfer, and terminates the contract of employment. The employee must give proper notice [**34.3**], and will not have the right to claim unfair dismissal or redundancy against either the transferor or transferee.   *Transfer of Undertakings (Protection of Employment) Regulations 2006*
[SI 2006/246] reg.4(7),(8)

Where the identity of the transferee is withheld until after the transfer has taken place, an objection is valid if it is made as soon as the employee finds out who their new employer will be.   *New ISG Ltd v Vernon & others [2007] EWHC 2665 (Ch)*

29.7.5   Dismissal connected with a transfer

A dismissal, including a constructive dismissal [**31.2.9**], by either the transferor or transferee is automatically unfair [**34.7.1**] if it is because of the transfer or a reason connected with the transfer. But if the employer can establish that the dismissal is because of changes in the workforce arising from an economic, technical or organisational (**ETO**) reason or factors which are not connected with the transfer, it will have a defence against a claim of unfair dismissal.

The phrase 'changes in the workforce' has been interpreted by the courts as meaning a change in the number of employees or in the work done. This is a particularly complex area of law, and specialist advice should always be obtained.

Even where there is a fair or potentially fair reason for the dismissal, the employer must follow a fair dismissal procedure [**34.5.2**] and give notice as required by statute or under the contract [**34.3**].

The original employer's liability to the dismissed employee transfers with the undertaking, so if the claim cannot be brought against the old employer it will be brought against the new one.   *Transfer of Undertakings (Protection of Employment) Regulations 2006*
[SI 2006/246] reg.7; Litster v Forth Dry Dock & Engineering Co Ltd [1988] UKHL 10

29.7.6   Variation of contract

Prior to the 2006 regulations, only contractual changes unrelated to the transfer were allowed before or after a transfer. Now the transferor or transferee can also make changes to terms and conditions that are connected to the transfer, provided the sole or main reason is changes arising from an economic, technical or organisational (ETO) reason [**29.7.5**]. This provision allows harmonisation of terms and conditions of employment between existing and transferred employees, but only if there is an ETO reason. The availability of an ETO reason is likely to be limited, and legal advice should always be sought.   *Transfer of Undertakings (Protection of Employment) Regulations 2006 [SI.] reg.4(4)*

29.7.6.1   Changes beneficial to employee

Even wider scope for changes arises from a case which held that the **European acquired rights directive** *[2001/23/EC]]*, which TUPE implements in the UK, is not intended to protect employers, and that there is nothing to stop an employee enforcing new contractual terms that are more favourable to him or her. This could include, for example, an employer wanting to increase an employee's salary, holiday entitlement or other benefits to bring them in line with other employees.
Regent Security Services Ltd v Power [2007] EWCA Civ 1188

The decision in this case held that where some contractual changes are favourable to the employee and some are not, the employee can choose to enforce only the beneficial terms – thus having the advantage of whichever terms are most favourable, regardless of whether they are in the new or old contract.

In any case, legal advice should always be sought if seeking to harmonise or vary terms and conditions of employment connected in any way with a TUPE transfer.

29.7.6.2 Changes detrimental to employee

If an employee suffers or would suffer 'material detriment' because the transfer involves a substantial change in working conditions, the employee can resign and claim wrongful and/or unfair constructive dismissal [**34.2.9**, **34.4.1**] unless the transfer is caused by the insolvency of the transferor. *Transfer of Undertakings (Protection of Employment) Regulations 2006 [SI 2006/246] reg.4(9),(10)*

29.7.7 Employees' rights after transfer

Once the transfer has been completed, the contract of employment between the employee and the previous employer is deemed to have been made with the transferee employer, with automatic continuity of all rights and contractual terms except, in most cases, those relating to occupational pension schemes. The new employer does not have to provide new written particulars of employment [**26.7**], but does have to notify the employee of the identity of the new employer.
Transfer of Undertakings (Protection of Employment) Regulations 2006 [SI 2006/246] reg.4(1)

29.7.7.1 Occupational pension scheme rights

Specialist pensions advice should always be obtained where occupational pension scheme rights exist – both in relation to the rights of transferred employees, and in relation to exit debt if the transferor is ceasing to exist or could find itself with no employees in its pension scheme [**30.6.5**].

Where the original employer contributes to an employee's *personal* pension plan or a stakeholder pension, these rights and liabilities transfer. However in relation to *occupational* pension schemes, the rights and liabilities do not transfer if they are related to old age, invalidity or survivors' benefits. Other rights under an occupational pension scheme, such as enhanced redundancy entitlement [**35.7.2**] or early retirement benefits, do transfer. *Transfer of Undertakings (Protection of Employment) Regulations 2006 [SI 2006/246] reg.10*

Although most occupational pension scheme rights do not transfer, the transferee must establish a minimum level of pension provision for transferred employees who were entitled to participate in the scheme. This requires matching employee contributions, up to 6% of salary, to a final salary, money purchase or stakeholder scheme [see **30.6** for definitions]. Different rules apply where the transferor is a public sector body [**29.7.7.4**]. *Pensions Act 2004 ss.257,258; Transfer of Employment (Pension Protection) Regulations 2005 [SI 2005/649]*

29.7.7.2 Trade union recognition

If the transferred undertaking retains a separate identity, any recognition of an independent trade union [**36.3.3**] by the transferor is transferred to the new employer. But if the transferred undertaking is merged into the transferee's business and loses its identity, union recognition is not transferred. *Transfer of Undertakings (Protection of Employment) Regulations 2006 [SI 2006/246] reg.6*

29.7.7.3 Collective agreements

Any relevant **collective agreements** [**36.3.4**] between the transferor employer and a trade union or unions are automatically transferred to the new employer. This means, for example, that transferred staff continue to be entitled to pay rises negotiated under such an agreement before the transfer, or arising after the transfer as a result of national agreements. *Transfer of Undertakings (Protection of Employment) Regulations 2006 [SI 2006/246] reg.5*

If the terms of a collective agreement between an employer and trade union are incorporated within a contract of employment, those terms continue to apply to the contract after the employment is transferred to another employer. At the time of writing (mid 2009) the employer is also bound by subsequent changes under the collective agreement, even though it not a party to those changes. It was not clear whether this decision would be appealed, so up to date advice should be sought. *Transfer of Undertakings (Protection of Employment) Regulations 2006 [SI 2006/246] reg.4; Whent & others v T Cartledge Ltd [1996] UKEAT 39 96 1612; Alemo-Herron & others v Parkwood Leisure Limited [2009] UKEAT 0456 08 ZT*

29.7.7.4 Public sector contracts

As well as TUPE, Cabinet Office rules referred to as **TUPE Plus** apply to transfers from the public sector to the private (non-public) sector.

The Cabinet Office statement of practice on staff transfers requires transferees to provide pensions to transferring employees that are broadly comparable to their public sector pension. Transferees cannot reduce pension provision to the minimum levels required under TUPE [**29.7.7.1**].

Workers employed by the transferee after a transfer are not generally covered by TUPE. But where work is contracted out from a public sector employer to a private (non-public sector) employer, employees who join the transferee to work on the public sector contract after the contract has been awarded must be offered terms and conditions which are, overall, no less favourable than those of employees who have transferred from the public sector body. The public sector body must monitor compliance through its best practice reviews.

These provisions are in the code of practice on workforce matters in local authority service contracts, published in ODPM (Office of the Deputy Prime Minister) circular 03/2003, and the code of practice in workforce matters in public sector service contracts, published by the Cabinet Office in March 2005.

29.7.7.5 Health service transfers to social enterprises

In his 'next steps review' of the National Health Service in mid-2008, Lord Darzi proposed that NHS workers who set up social enterprises to provide health services should be able to remain in the NHS pension scheme.

29.7.8 Transfers between associated employers

For the purposes of employment legislation, two employers are treated as associated if one is a company which is directly or indirectly controlled by the other or if both are companies which are controlled by the same third party [see **9.4.1** for more about company groups and control]. *Employment Rights Act 1996 s.231*

In common usage, **associated employers** also refers to other similar relationships, for example where an organisation which is not a company is controlled by another organisation.

For the purposes of TUPE, transfers between associated employers are treated in the same way as other transfers between employers.

Resources: TAKING ON NEW EMPLOYEES

Employment rights and good practice, including recruitment and TUPE. ACAS, BIS, Business Link, CIPD, Directgov, PEACe, TUC: see end of **chapter 25**.

Equal opportunities. See end of **chapter 28**.

References and other checks. Criminal Records Bureau: www.crb.gov.uk, general enquiries 0870 90 90 811, email via website.

Independent Safeguarding Authority: www.isa-gov.org.uk, 0300 123 1111, scheme.info@homeoffice.gsi.gov.uk.

Information Commissioner's Office: www.ico.gov.uk, 08456 30 60 60, email via website.

Workers from abroad. Border Agency: www.ukba.homeoffice.gov.uk, employer's helpline 0845 010 6677.

UK Visas: www.ukvisas.gov.uk.

Joint Council for the Welfare of Immigrants: www.jcwi.org.uk, 020 7251 8708, info@jcwi.org.uk.

Refugee Council: www.refugeecouncil.org.uk. For details of advice lines see website or ring 020 7346 6700.

Statute law. www.opsi.gov.uk and www.statutelaw.gov.uk.

Much but not all case law. www.bailii.org.

Updates cross-referenced to this book. www.rclh.co.uk.

Chapter 30
PAY AND PENSIONS

For sources of further information see end of chapter.

30.1 PAYMENT OF SALARIES AND WAGES

Traditionally **wages** are paid on an hourly, daily, piecework or similar rate, and a **salary** is a fixed weekly, monthly or annual rate regardless of the amount of work. **Remuneration** refers to any payment for work. These terms are used interchangeably, and under employment law **wages** means 'any sums payable to the worker in connection with his employment'. *Employment Rights Act 1996 s.27(1)*

30.1.1 What counts as pay

For most employment law and tax purposes, pay includes:
- any fee, bonus, commission or other payment in connection with the worker's employment, even if it is not covered by the contract of employment;
- holiday pay [**31.4.5**], statutory sick pay [**31.6.1**], maternity, paternity and adoption pay [**32.2.6**, **32.3.2**, **32.4.2**], and guarantee payments [**30.1.9**];
- pay for time off as allowed under statute for public duties [**31.7.1**] or trade union duties [**36.4.2**];
- pay while suspended on maternity or medical grounds [**30.1.11**];
- pay in lieu of notice, where paid under a contractual provision [**30.1.12**];

- luncheon vouchers, gift vouchers and other vouchers with a fixed monetary value which can be exchanged for money, goods and/or services;
- reimbursement for expenses not incurred solely for work;
- some benefits such as accommodation, use of a company car etc.

Employment Rights Act 1996 s.27(1),(5)

The following are not classed as wages for employment law purposes, but may be subject to tax:

- pensions;
- redundancy payments [**30.4.15**, **35.7**];
- a lump sum payment on retirement [**30.4.15**];
- compensation for loss of office;
- payment in kind other than vouchers or tokens with a fixed monetary value;
- tips or gratuities paid directly to the worker by a third party [**30.4.13**].

Employment Rights Act 1996 s.27(2)

The following are not classed as wages for the purposes of employment law, and in general are not taxable:

- reimbursement for genuine out of pocket expenses incurred solely for work purposes;
- a loan or advance on wages from the employer [**30.4.2.1**].   *ERA 1996 s.27(2)*

A different definition of pay applies for minimum wage [**30.2.2**].

30.1.2 Rate of pay

Subject to the obligation to pay at least the national minimum wage [**30.2.1**], the employer is free to choose how much to offer for any job (except where salaries are governed by statute or an employer has negotiated pay levels with a trade union). However once the rate of pay and any provision for increments have been set, they can generally be changed only with the consent of the employee [**26.9**].

Men and women must be paid the same for like work or work of equal value [**28.8**], and in most cases part-time and comparable full-time workers, and fixed-term and comparable permanent employees, must be paid the same for comparable work [**26.4.2**, **26.4.3**].

There is no statutory obligation to give cost of living increases, annual increments or any other pay rises. Before making a contractual commitment to regular pay rises – especially if they will be linked to an external scale or an indicator such as the retail price index over which the organisation has no control – the organisation should be very confident it will have adequate funds to meet its commitments for as long as that person is employed.

Increments based on length of service do not breach age discrimination rules during the first five years of employment, but after five years they are discriminatory unless there is a legitimate business reason for the increment [**28.6.2**].

If increments or bonuses are linked to performance or satisfactory appraisals this is often called **performance related pay** [**30.1.6**], and where they are related to profit it is called **profit related pay** [**30.1.7**].

30.1.3 Itemised pay statements

All employees and workers [**25.1.2**] must be given an **itemised pay statement** at or before the time of payment showing:

- gross amount of wages (full amount before any deductions);
- amounts deducted for tax and national insurance;
- for deductions of a fixed amount, the details and amount of each deduction, or if a separate standing statement of deductions has been made, the total figure for fixed deductions;
- for variable deductions, the amount and purpose of each;
- the net amount payable (after all deductions);
- where different parts of the net payment are paid in different ways, the amount and method of each part payment.   *Employment Rights Act 1996 s.8*

If a **standing statement of fixed deductions** is given, it must be given to the worker in writing at or before the time of the payment when the deductions are made. It must include, for each deduction, the amount, the intervals at which it is made and the purpose. A new statement of fixed deductions must be issued at least once every 12 months. If any detail is changed, the employer must give written notice of the change, or must issue a new statement of fixed deductions which then remains valid for 12 months. *Employment Rights Act 1996 s.9*

If an itemised pay statement or statement of fixed deductions is not given at or before the time of payment, or is given but does not include all required information, the employee can be awarded the amount of all unnotified deductions in the 13 weeks before the claim was brought. *Employment Rights Act 1996 ss.11,12*

30.1.4 Deductions from pay

An employer may not make any deduction from wages paid to an employee or worker [**25.1.2**, **30.1.1**] unless:

- it is required or authorised by virtue of a statutory provision (for example income tax, national insurance, repayment of student loan, or court order);
- the worker has been overpaid wages or expenses (but there are exceptions to this; see **30.1.4.1**);
- the worker has taken part in a strike or other industrial action [**36.6**];
- the deduction is authorised by the worker's contract [**27.3.5**];
- the worker agreed to the deduction in writing before the act which gave rise to the deduction [**30.1.4.2**];
- a court or tribunal has ordered the worker to pay the employer, and the worker has given prior written agreement to the amount being deducted; or
- the contract authorises the employer to make a deduction and pay it over to a third party, or the worker has authorised this in writing (for example for payroll giving or trade union subscriptions). *Employment Rights Act 1996 ss.13-16*

30.1.4.1 Overpayments

If the employer overpays wages or expenses because of an **error of fact**, it may claim the overpayment back from the worker or deduct it from a future payment. Errors of fact include, for example, adding up incorrectly, making a payment to the wrong person, or paying for hours which an hourly paid worker did not work.

If the employer overpays because of an **error in interpreting the law** – for example, failing to operate PAYE properly – the overpayment can be deducted or claimed back only if the worker agrees.

Even where deduction for overpayment is allowed the courts may prevent recovery, so legal advice is advisable before making a deduction. *Sunderland Polytechnic v Evans [1993] UKEAT 334 92 1102; Avon County Council v Howlett [1983] 1 All ER 1073 CA*

30.1.4.2 Contractual or prior consent

Unless a deduction is authorised by statute or is to recover an overpayment, it may be made only if it is explicitly authorised by the written contract or a written agreement. The agreement must have been made prior both to the deduction and the circumstances which gave rise to the deduction. Thus if a worker receives a loan from the employer or causes the employer a loss and then signs an agreement for the loan or loss to be recovered by deductions from salary, the agreement is not valid. The employer can recover the amount only by taking legal action against the worker, or by the worker making the payment voluntarily.

30.1.4.3 Disciplinary penalties

A deduction can be made for disciplinary matters only if the disciplinary proceeding is being held by virtue of a statutory provision (for example the police whose disciplinary processes are governed by statute), or if the right to make the deduction is explicit in the contract. *Employment Rights Act 1996 s.14(2)*

This means that unless the contract allows [**27.3.5**], an employer cannot make a deduction even for unauthorised absence (although workers paid wages only for hours worked do not have to be paid if they do not work). Unless the contract allows, deductions cannot be made because work was not done properly, or to cover damage to the employer's property, or because the worker took money from the employer or his or her till was 'short', or for any other reason unless it relates to disciplinary proceedings held by virtue of a statutory provision.

Even during a disciplinary investigation, a worker can be suspended without pay or on reduced pay only if the contract allows [**27.7.2**] or the suspension is linked to a disciplinary proceeding held by virtue of a statutory provision.

For workers in retail employment, even if deductions are allowed they cannot generally be more than 10% of the gross wages payable to the worker for the day when the shortage occurred.   *Employment Rights Act 1996 ss.17-22*

30.1.4.4 Recovering costs of training

Employers often want to recover training costs where a staff member leaves shortly after completion of expensive training, does not return after paid sabbatical leave, or is similarly perceived as indebted to the employer. Contractual provision or prior consent to recover in these circumstances is enforceable only if the amount is a genuine pre-estimate of the loss or damage the employer will suffer. If it more than this, the courts will not enforce it.

30.1.4.5 Trade union subscriptions

Deductions for trade union subscriptions (**check-off**) can be made only if the employee has authorised the deduction in writing, and has not withdrawn the authorisation [**36.4.2**]. The employee has the right to withdraw authorisation at any time provided the employer is given enough notice, in writing, to ensure the deduction is not made.   *Trade Union & Labour Relations (Consolidation) Act 1992 s.68*

30.1.5 'Weekly pay' and 'normal hours'

When the amount of a statutory payment or benefit depends on the level of **weekly pay**:

- if pay does not vary according to the amount of work done, weekly pay is the amount due under the contract of employment;
- if pay varies according to the amount of work done, number of hours worked or commission earned, weekly pay is the average for the previous 12 weeks.
                    Employment Rights Act 1996 ss.221-228

If hours vary from week to week, weeks in which the employee earned nothing from the employer do not count in the calculation. Instead, previous weeks in which there were earnings are included, to bring the total number of weeks in the calculation up to 12.

Different rules apply to normal hours and weekly pay for the purposes of minimum wage [**30.2.2**] and working time rights [**31.2.2**], and there is a statutory definition of weekly pay for the purpose of redundancy payments [**35.7.1**].

30.1.6 Performance related pay

Performance related pay is additional pay if an individual's, team's or organisation's work reaches agreed standards or targets. Charities and other organisations can give a contractual or discretionary right to performance related pay. Great care must be taken to ensure performance assessment is fair and does not indirectly discriminate on the basis of sex, racial group, disability, religion or other belief, or age, or working part-time or on a fixed-term contract.

Performance related pay is subject to tax and national insurance.

30.1.7 Profit related pay

Profit related pay is similar to performance related pay but in for-profit businesses is based on the business's profits, or the profits earned by an individual or team. It is subject to tax and national insurance in the usual way.

30.1.8 Cash in hand

Cash in hand refers to the practice of paying cash to workers without deducting tax and/or national insurance, sometimes without keeping proper records of the workers' name, address and national insurance number, and sometimes without declaring the payments as required to HM Revenue and Customs (HMRC).

Unless the worker is genuinely self employed in relation to this work [**38.2.2**], it is the employer's obligation to operate PAYE, deduct tax and national insurance contributions (NICs) if required and account for them to HMRC. If this is not done the employer could be required to pay to HMRC the tax and NICs which should have been deducted, and will be able to recover this from the worker only if he or she agrees [**30.1.4.1**]. There may also be penalties for late payment.

If the worker's income is under the NI threshold *and* he or she has no other taxable income, tax and NICs do not need to be deducted. The only valid way the employer can confirm that the worker has no other taxable income is by getting the worker to complete form P46 [**30.4.4**].

Even where the worker is earning less than the NI threshold and has completed a P46 to say he or she has no other taxable income, the employer must keep proper records of payments made to the worker. If the worker is paid more than £100 total during the tax year, this must be notified to HMRC at the end of the year.

30.1.8.1 Cash in hand and tax evasion

Tax evasion is a statutory offence, and anyone who does not pay tax on taxable income or colludes with non-payment is liable to up to seven years' imprisonment and an unlimited fine. Organisations which pay cash in hand should be aware of the risk to the organisation for failure to operate PAYE and for colluding with tax evasion, and the risk to the worker for tax evasion and possibly also for benefits fraud if the worker is receiving state benefits.
Finance Act 2000 s.144

HMRC's **tax evasion hotline** is open seven days a week on 0800 788 887 for anyone who wants to report, in confidence, tax evasion.

30.1.9 Guarantee payments

Employees who have worked more than one month and who are on wages rather than a fixed salary are entitled to **guarantee payments** for days when they are contractually obliged to work, but the employer provides no work because there is not enough work or for any other reason affecting the normal working of the employer's business.
Employment Rights Act 1996 ss.28,29

In any three month period, guarantee payments are payable only for the number of days the employee normally works per week. They are paid at the statutory daily rate set each year in the **Employment Rights (Increase of Limits) Order** (£21.50 as at 1/8/09) or at the employee's usual daily rate, whichever is lower.
Employment Rights Act 1996 ss.30,31

If an employer reduces hours or pay to less than 50% for at least four consecutive weeks, or for six or more weeks within a period of 13 weeks, an employee who has worked more than two years may be able to claim redundancy pay [**35.7.1**].
Employment Rights Act 1996 ss.147,148

30.1.10 Pay when employee cannot get to work

Employees have an implied duty [**26.3.3**] to be available for work, but severe weather conditions, transport strikes or other events outside the employee's control may prevent employees getting to their place of work. Employers are not obliged to pay an employee who is not at work, but the employer and employee should try to find way to enable the employee to work. This could include, for example, using alternative transport, working from home or at another location that is more accessible, making up the time later, or taking paid annual leave.

30.1.11 Pay during medical and maternity suspension

After one month's employment most employees are entitled to be paid their normal wages for up to 26 weeks while suspended on medical grounds for reasons covered by the **Control of Lead at Work Regulations 1980** *[SI 1980/1248]*, **Ionising Radiations Regulations 1999** *[SI 1999/3232]* or **Control of Substances Hazardous to Health Regulations 1988** *[SI 1988/1657]*. Workers on a fixed-term contract for three months or less become entitled to pay during medical suspension only if they are continuously employed for more than three months.

Employment Rights Act 1996 ss.64,65

A woman is entitled to full pay if health and safety regulations prohibit her from doing her normal work because of pregnancy, childbirth or breastfeeding, and no suitable alternative work is available [**32.2.10**].   *Employment Rights Act 1996 ss.66-68*

30.1.12 Pay during notice period

During the notice period [**34.3.6**], regardless of whether the notice of termination has been given by the employer or employee, the employee is entitled to full pay. This applies even if there is no contractual entitlement to pay, for example an employee on sick leave who has used all of his or her sick pay entitlement.

30.1.13 Discretionary payments

Many voluntary sector employers offer staff more generous arrangements than their contract provides for, such as additional paid sick leave, paid sabbaticals or paid compassionate leave. Even where the organisation makes clear that these extra benefits are non-contractual and are entirely at the employer's discretion, a court may still find the employer in breach of contract if the discretion is exercised in a way which is irrational or perverse. Legal advice should be taken before saying no to a discretionary payment.   *Clark v Nomura International plc [2000] IRLR 766*

30.2 MINIMUM WAGE

Virtually all employees and workers are entitled to **national minimum wage** (NMW), which is set annually in the **National Minimum Wage Regulations 1999 (Amendment) Regulations** and goes up on 1 October each year. The current rates are available from the Department for Business, Innovation and Skills and the national **minimum wage helpline** (0845 600 0678).

From 1 October 2009 the rates are £5.80 for workers over age 21, £4.83 for those aged 18 to 21, and £3.57 for those over school leaving age but not yet 18. Age discrimination legislation explicitly allows these age differentials [**28.6.1**]. At the time of writing (mid 2009) the government was considering whether 21-year-olds should be entitled to the adult rate from 1 October 2010.   *National Minimum Wage Regulations 1999 (Amendment) Regulations 2009 [SI 2009/1902]*

30.2.1 Entitlement

A 'worker' is anyone who works under a contract of employment [**26.1**] or apprenticeship, or who works under a contract where they have to do the work personally (cannot sub-contract it) unless they are working for someone who is a client or customer of their own business.   *National Minimum Wage Act 1998 s.54*

The contract does not have to be in writing. In practice this means that almost everyone who is paid for work is entitled to minimum wage, unless they are genuinely self employed and are carrying out the work as part of their self employment. Minimum wage must be paid to home workers, pieceworkers and commission workers, to workers from overseas who are working in the UK, and to workers who usually work in the UK but are temporarily working outside the UK.

The following are not entitled to minimum wage:

- workers under school leaving age [**31.5**];

- apprentices on specified government apprenticeship schemes, who are under the age of 19 or are in the first 12 months of the apprenticeship (but most apprentices must get a minimum rate of pay – not the same as minimum wage – of at least £95 per week, as at 1/8/09);

- workers participating in schemes funded by the government or European Social Fund to provide training, work experience or temporary work or to assist them in seeking or obtaining work;

- during the first six weeks when a worker who has been participating in such a government or ESF scheme is employed for a work trial period under government sponsored arrangements;
- participants in specified European Community programmes;
- students undertaking higher education or further education courses, who are on work experience of up to one year required for the course;
- some people who have been homeless or living in a hostel for homeless people, and are now working in a scheme for homeless people and are receiving accommodation and other benefits, which may include money, from the scheme;

National Minimum Wage Regulations 1999 [SI 1999/584] reg.12, as amended

- workers who live in a household as part of a family which is not their family and share the household work, such as au pairs, companions and nannies;

NMW Regs 1999 reg.2(2)

- residential members of religious communities which are – or have been established by – charities, but not if the communities are independent schools or provide further or higher education;

National Minimum Wage Act 1998 s.44A,
inserted by Employment Relations Act 1999 s.22

- jobs done under informal arrangements between friends or neighbours;
- most volunteers and voluntary workers [**39.4.3**];
- people who are genuinely self employed and are carrying out work as part of that self employment.

30.2.2 What counts as pay

'Pay' is defined differently for the purposes of minimum wage than for other employment law purposes [**30.1.1**] or for tax [**30.4.2**]. When calculating minimum wage, the following count as pay:

- gross pay, before deduction of tax, national insurance and most other authorised deductions [**30.1.4**];
- repayments made by the worker to the employer, for example where a worker repays the employer for a season ticket loan, rather than the employer deducting the repayment from the worker's pay;
- special allowances, for example for working in dangerous conditions, working unsocial hours, working in a particular area (such as London weighting), being on call – but only if these allowances are consolidated into standard pay;
- payments as part of an incentive, merit or performance related pay scheme;
- bonuses.

30.2.2.1 Accommodation offset

Where the employer provides accommodation to the worker for which the worker does not have to pay (either directly or through deduction from wages), an amount called the **accommodation offset** counts as pay for the purposes of minimum wage. Changes are made annually or bi-annually in the **National Minimum Wage Regulations 1999 (Amendment) Regulations**. Details are available from the national minimum wage helpline [see end of chapter]. From 1 October 2009 the offset is £4.51 per day (£31.57 per week). *National Minimum Wage Regulations 1999 [SI 1999/584] regs.30(d),36,37*

The accommodation offset includes provision for heat, light etc. A further deduction from wages cannot be made for these if it would bring the worker's pay to below minimum wage level. *Leisure Employment Services v HM Revenue & Customs [2007] EWCA Civ 92*

30.2.2.2 What does not count

The following do not count towards minimum wage pay:

- a loan or advance on wages (but it counts when it is repaid to the employer, either directly by the worker or by deduction from wages);
- the employer's contribution to pension schemes;
- redundancy payment or lump sum on retirement;
- rewards under a staff suggestions scheme;

- tips, gratuities and service charges that are paid directly to the worker by the customer, are pooled before being distributed to workers through a tronc, or (from 1 October 2009) are paid through the payroll;
- a premium (additional payment) above the worker's basic rate pay, for working overtime, or at particular times (such as bank holidays), or on particular duties (such as shift working or on call working) – although in 2009 it was ruled that an on call sleep-in payment does count as pay;   *Smith v Oxfordshire Learning Disability NHS Trust [2009] UKEAT 0176 09 2406*
- special allowances [**30.2.2**] that are not consolidated into standard pay;
- a premium above the employer's normal hourly rate for a particular type of work, for working nights or at weekends;
- reimbursements or allowances for clothing, travel, subsistence and other expenditure incurred for work;
- payments made by the worker for expenditure necessary for work but not reimbursed by the employer;
- payments by the worker for tools, equipment, uniforms and other items necessary for the work and purchased from the employer;
- the value of accommodation above the offset [**30.2.2.1**];
- the value of benefits in kind, such as meals, luncheon vouchers, fuel, a car or use of a car, assistance with removals, medical insurance, etc.
  National Minimum Wage Regulations 1999 [SI 1999/584] regs.9,34-36

Although the above do not count towards pay for the purposes of minimum wage, some of them do count for employment law and/or tax purposes [**30.1.1**, **30.4.2**].

30.2.2.3 Pay reference period

The **pay reference period** is the worker's actual pay period, to a maximum of one calendar month. For daily paid workers the pay reference period is one day, for weekly paid workers one week, for monthly paid workers one month, and for workers paid less frequently it is one month. Specific rules apply where money earned in one reference period is not paid to the worker until the next period, or where the worker receives an annual bonus.   *NMW Regs 1999 reg.10*

30.2.3 Hours of work

The hours for which minimum wage must be paid depend on whether the worker is paid for time work, salaried hours work, output work or unmeasured work.

30.2.3.1 Time work

Time work is where a worker is paid according to the number of hours worked. The hours may be fixed or variable, and include:

- time when the person is required to be at work (either as basic work hours or overtime) and is at work, including training at or away from the place of work;
- time when the worker is at work but cannot work, for example because equipment has broken down;
- time on **standby** or **on call** at or near the place of work (but not time on standby or on call at home – and specific rules apply where sleeping facilities are provided for while the person is on standby or on call, see **30.2.3.5**);
- time walking or travelling in connection with work during normal working hours or the normal range of hours, including lunch and tea breaks on board the train, bus, plane etc (but not travel between home and work);
- time waiting for a train, or changing trains or other form of transport (but not lunch or tea breaks while waiting for transport).
  National Minimum Wage Regulations 1999 [SI 1999/584] regs.3,7,15,20

Minimum wage must be paid for all time work hours.

Lunch and other rest breaks, periods when the worker is absent from work or is on holiday, sick leave or maternity, paternity or adoption leave, or absence while engaged in industrial action do not count as 'hours' for minimum wage purposes – even if, for example, the person works during their lunch break. Any pay received for these periods is not counted as minimum wage pay.

'Hours' for the purpose of minimum wage are calculated differently than 'working time' for the working time regulations [**31.2.1**].

30.2.3.2   Salaried hours work

Salaried hours work is where a worker is entitled under his or her contract to an annual salary, is required to work a basic minimum number of hours in a year (which may be expressed in weekly terms, for example 35 hours per week), and is paid in equal instalments (usually monthly or weekly, but it could be fortnightly, bi-monthly or whatever).   *National Minimum Wage Regulations 1999 [SI 1999/584] regs.4,16,21-23*

Work is considered to be salaried if the basic payment is the same each time, apart from variations resulting from a performance bonus, a pay increase, pay for working overtime, or the worker leaving partway through the pay period.

Salaried hours workers include those who work only part of the year, such as school staff, but receive equal payments through the whole year.

The hours for which minimum wage is payable are calculated in the same way as for time workers [**30.2.3.1**], except that hours of absence, such as rest breaks, lunch breaks, holidays, sickness absence and maternity, paternity or adoption leave are payable if they form part of the worker's basic minimum hours under the contract. So if a person is required to work 35 hours per week including lunch breaks, time at lunch is counted as work hours. If the person is required to work 35 hours excluding lunch breaks, the lunch break does not count as work hours and minimum wage is not payable for it, even if the person works through the lunch period (unless the employer counts this as overtime and makes an additional payment for it).

Time when the worker is on reduced pay or no pay due to sick leave, maternity, paternity or adoption leave or other long-term leave does not count as hours for minimum wage, nor does time when the worker is engaged in industrial action.

30.2.3.3   Output work

Output work is paid according to the quantity of items produced or made, or the number of sales or deals made by the worker. It is usually called **piecework** or **commission work**.

Output work may be **home work** – defined under minimum wage law as work which does not have to be done at the employer's place of work, and where the worker does not have to do the work personally.   *National Minimum Wage Act 1998 s.35*

For output work the employer must either pay at least minimum wage for the number of hours actually worked, or must agree a **mean hourly output rate** based on how many **subject pieces** (pieces of work) an average worker can produce in an hour. The number of hours to be paid is then based on the number of pieces produced, divided by the mean hourly output rate. For each hour, the worker must be paid minimum wage plus 20%. This ensures that workers who are slightly slower than average still receive minimum wage.
National Minimum Wage Regulations 1999 [SI 1999/584] regs.5,17,24-26A,
amended by NMW Regulations 1999 (Amendment) Regulations 2004 [SI 2004/1161] reg.2

Strict rules govern how the mean hourly output rate is set and the information that the employer has to provide to output workers.

30.2.3.4   Unmeasured work

Unmeasured work is work which is not time work, salaried hours work or output work. It includes work where certain tasks must be done but there are no specified hours or times when they must be done. The employer requires the worker to work when needed or when work is available. The employer can either pay minimum wage for every hour worked, or come to a **daily average** number of hours. If there is a daily average, it must be in a written agreement.
National Minimum Wage Regulations 1999 [SI 1999/584] regs.6,18,27-29

Unmeasured work for minimum wage is different from unmeasured time for the purposes of the working time regulations [**31.2.1**].

30.2.3.5   Time when sleeping

Where a worker is provided with living accommodation or sleeping facilities at or near work and is required to be available all or some time **on call** or **standby**, there is a statutory right to minimum wage for the hours the person is 'awake for the purpose of working'. This has been interpreted as meaning the person is actually working, or is required to be on call or standby and is awake. Minimum wage is not payable when the worker is sleeping.   *National Minimum Wage Regulations 1999 [SI 1999/584] 1999 regs.15(1), 16(1), as amended; Hughes v Jones & another (t/a Graylyns Residential Home) [2008] UKEAT 0159 08 0310*

In some situations it may be possible to write the contract in a way that on call or standby time is unmeasured work, and is covered by a daily average agreement. In this case the employer would only be obliged to pay minimum wage only for the agreed daily average hours.

Even if minimum wage is not payable for hours when a person is sleeping or not working, the hours may still be working time for the purposes of the working time regulations [**31.2.1**].

30.2.4   Records

Employers must keep adequate records to show that workers are being paid at least minimum wage. For workers clearly paid over minimum wage there is no need to keep extra records. Where a worker is paid at or not much above minimum wage, detailed records of hours worked, overtime and time off should be kept, adequate for the employer to show that minimum wage has in fact been paid. Details of any mean hourly output rate [**30.2.3.3**] must be kept.

Records must be kept for at least three years after the end of the pay reference period following the pay period that the records cover. However it is advisable to keep records for at least six years.   *National Minimum Wage Regulations 1999 [SI 1999/584] reg.38*

30.2.5   Enforcement

A worker who believes he or she is not being paid the minimum wage has a right to see the employer's minimum wage records. The request must be in writing, and the employer must produce the records within 14 days of the request, or within such time as is agreed with the worker. The worker has a right to be accompanied by another person when inspecting the records, and has a right to make a copy of the records.   *National Minimum Wage Act 1998 s.10*

A worker who is denied access to records or is not being paid the minimum wage can bring a claim in the employment tribunal or court. The worker can be awarded an amount to bring payments up to minimum wage (backdated up to six years), or where access to records is denied, can be awarded up to 80 times the minimum wage.   *NMWA1998 ss.11,17, amended by Employment Act 2008 s.8*

Rather than going to a tribunal or court, a worker or former worker can inform the enforcement agency, HM Revenue and Customs. HMRC can issue an enforcement notice, requiring the employer to pay minimum wage for each named worker or ex-worker, backdated for up to six years, plus a penalty of 50% of the minimum wage to be paid (with a maximum penalty of £5,000). If the backdated minimum wage and half the penalty are paid within 14 days of the enforcement notice, the remainder of the penalty is waived.   *NMWA 1998 ss.19-19H, inserted by Employment Act 2008 s.9*

In addition there are six criminal offences, each punishable by an unlimited fine: refusal or wilful neglect to pay the minimum wage, failing to keep minimum wage records, keeping false records, producing false records or information, intentionally obstructing an enforcement officer, and refusing or neglecting to give information to an enforcement officer.   *NMWA 1998 ss.31-33, amended by Employment Act 2008 s.11*

A worker who is dismissed or victimised because of seeking to enforce his or her right to minimum wage, or is dismissed because he or she is becoming eligible for minimum wage (or for a higher rate), can bring a claim of unfair dismissal or victimisation.   *NMWA 1998 ss.23-25*

30.3   WORKERS ON STATE BENEFITS

Workers on state benefits such as jobseeker's allowance, income support, employment and support allowance, and incapacity benefit may have restrictions on the number of hours of paid work each week, and on the maximum they can earn (the **earnings disregard**, or earnings from **permitted work**).

For some benefits the earnings disregard is very low (£5 or £20 per week), so with the minimum wage requirement this means very little paid work per week. People receiving incapacity benefit or employment support allowance may be able to earn up to £92 per week (as at 1/8/09) from permitted work [**39.11.5**].

There is no restriction on earnings for people receiving state pensions, but income is taxed.

The fact that a state benefit claimant or pensioner is allowed to have earnings does not mean that the earnings are exempt from other rules. The worker must be paid the minimum wage [**30.2**], and if their income is more than the relevant thresholds tax must be paid [**30.4.4**], and national insurance if the person is not a pensioner [**30.4.6.1**].

The claimant must notify the Department for Work and Pensions of all work, even if unpaid [**39.11.1**].

Housing benefit (or **local housing allowance** for tenants in the private rented sector) and **council tax benefit** are affected by earnings and the local authority needs to be notified of any change in circumstances.

Information about working while claiming benefits and how much can be earned should be sought from the Directgov or Department for Work and Pensions websites [see end of chapter] or from the local Jobcentre Plus.

30.4   PAYE

Every employer, even if it has only one part-time employee, must register with HM Revenue and Customs and operate the **pay as you earn** (PAYE) scheme in respect of all workers to whom it applies. Proposed changes in rates and allowances for income tax and national insurance are announced in the government's pre-budget in November and confirmed in the budget in March.

Operating PAYE incorrectly or failing to operate it can lead to interest and late payment penalties, so it is sensible to undertake a regular review of PAYE arrangements with the organisation's auditor or other financial advisor. Errors in tax returns or documents sent to HMRC should be reported promptly, which will reduce the risk of a penalty from HMRC. Deliberate failure to operate PAYE in order to avoid paying tax can lead to fines and imprisonment [**30.1.8.1**].

This book does not cover PAYE, income tax and national insurance in detail. HMRC [see end of chapter] has helplines and a comprehensive website.

The Scottish parliament has powers to charge different rates of income tax, so employers with staff working in Scotland may need to take advice.

30.4.1   People covered by PAYE

PAYE applies to every individual paid by an organisation in return for work, even one who might not normally be thought of as an employee, unless the individual:

- is recognised by HMRC as self employed in relation to the work [**38.3**];
- does not have a P45, will work for the employer for less than one week during the tax year and will earn less than the national insurance lower earnings threshold for that week [**30.4.6.1**]; or
- earns less than the lower earnings limit [**30.4.6.1**] from this employer, and has no other taxable earnings.

30.4.1.1   Students

Tax does not need to be deducted from wages of full-time students who work only during the summer, winter and Easter holidays, provided the student completes

form **P38(S)** and their earnings do not exceed the earnings threshold [**30.4.6.1**]..
If they work during term or their holiday earnings exceed the threshold, they
should fill in a **P46** [**30.4.3.1**]. Even if they work only during holidays and their
overall earnings are below the threshold, NI contributions may be payable.

30.4.2   What counts as pay

PAYE covers wages or salary as well as commissions and bonuses, one-off or lump
sum payments, sick pay, maternity, paternity and adoption pay, holiday pay, tips
collected by the employer and distributed to employees [**30.4.13**], some payments
on termination of employment [**30.4.15**], and other money payments. PAYE may
also cover 'perks' and other non-money benefits, such as accommodation or personal use of a company car [**30.4.10**], and LETS or other time credits [**30.4.14**].

Although national insurance and income tax are both collected under PAYE, they
are covered by different legislation. Some income is subject to tax but not NI,
some is subject to NI but not tax, and some is not subject to 'ordinary' NI but is
subject to class 1A or class 1B contributions [**30.4.6.3**]. Some aspects of tax and
NI are being brought into line with each other, but some differences will remain.

Special rules apply to employees who ordinarily live in the UK but work abroad,
and to people from outside the UK who work in the UK. Rules specific to any
workers in these categories should be checked with HMRC.

30.4.2.1   Loans to employees and advances on wages

If a loan from an employer to an employee is in the form of an advance on wages,
the full amount of pay before deduction of the advance is taxable when the employer recovers the advance.

An employer cannot make a deduction from wages to recover a loan or advance
unless the right to make this type of deduction is explicit in the contract of employment, or the employee has given consent to the deduction before receiving
the loan or advance [**30.1.4.2**].

Any loan by a charity should be reasonable and for a good reason, such as enabling the employee to buy a season ticket.

30.4.3   Employers' duties

The employer has a duty to register for PAYE, operate it and keep all legally required PAYE records. Comprehensive information is available on the HMRC
website and through its helplines [see end of chapter].

The employer must deduct tax and national insurance contributions (NICs) from
workers' wages, and send them, along with an additional amount for employer's
NICs, to HMRC – usually monthly but for small employers quarterly.

If this is not done the employer could be held liable for all tax and NICs which
should have been deducted and paid to HMRC, plus employer's NICs. The tax
and NICs owed will be worked out on a 'grossed up' basis that will make them
much higher than if they had been paid when they should have been, and in addition the employer will be liable for interest plus penalties for late payment.

When workers for whom PAYE has been operated leave work they must be given
form **P45** showing taxable income during the tax year, tax deducted and their tax
code. The worker must then give this to their next employer, or to Jobcentre Plus
if they are claiming benefits.

Most forms can be filed and payments made electronically, and HMRC is introducing compulsory electronic filing for some forms.

30.4.3.1   New employees

When a person first does paid work for an organisation, the employee must give
the employer a form **P45** showing taxable income and tax paid so far in the tax
year and their tax code. If the employee does not have a P45, the employer must
provide a form **P46**, on which the employee indicates whether he or she has any
other paid work. From the P45 or P46, the employer knows which tax code to use,
and how much tax to deduct.

A P45 must be submitted by the employer to HMRC. Depending on how much the employee will earn, the employer may need to submit or keep a P46.

If the employee has only this one source of earned income, the employer does not have to deduct tax unless the employee earns more than their personal allowance [**30.4.4**]. But if the employee has other employments as well, the allowance will be given at only one place of employment, or will be divided by the tax office between them. An employer might have to deduct tax even from earnings of as little as £1 per week, if the employee's allowance is all being used elsewhere.

The same applies if the person has taxable income from a source other than employment, and all or part of the personal allowance is set against that income. This particularly applies to pensioners, whose personal allowance is set against their taxable pension income.

If a new employee does not provide a P45 and does not complete P46, the employer must complete section 1 of a P46 and submit it to HMRC, and until hearing back from HMRC must tax the person at **basic rate** (BR) [**30.4.4**].

30.4.3.2 At the end of the tax year

The **tax year** runs from 6 April to 5 April. At the end of each tax year the employer must complete and submit an **annual return** (**P35**) to HMRC by 19 May, with a **P14** for each employee. Each person employed as of 5 April must be given, by 31 May, form **P60** showing their total taxable income during the tax year, how much tax and national insurance was deducted and their tax code.

The value of benefits provided to employees and expenses paid to them may need to be itemised by the employer on form **P11D** or **P9D** [**30.4.7**] and submitted to HMRC by 6 July unless the employer has a dispensation from having to file them [**30.4.7.1**] or has entered into a PAYE settlement agreement [**30.4.7.2**]. The same information must be provided to the employee by 6 July.

30.4.4 Income tax allowances and codes

The rate at which income tax is paid depends on the amount of **taxable income** (income from all sources which is subject to tax, minus tax allowances and tax reliefs). The law is in the **Income Tax (Earnings and Pensions) Act 2003**.

Everyone who receives taxable income is entitled to receive a certain amount free of tax. The **personal allowance** changes each year, and for tax year 2009-10 is £6,475 (£125 per week, £540 per month) for a person under 65. £9,490 from age 65-74 and £9,640 for age 75 and over. An individual's actual tax allowance may be more or less than this. For example, if they owe money to HMRC their personal allowance will be reduced, or if they are married or blind their allowance will be higher.

At the time of writing (mid 2009) it was expected that from 6 April 2010 the personal allowance would be reduced by £1 for every £2 of income over £100,000.

A **tax code** represents an employee's total allowances and enables the employer to work out tax on earnings above the allowances. Adding '5' to the end shows that employee's allowance – so tax code 647 means an allowance of £6,475.

The **tax bands** for 2009-10 are 20% **basic rate** on taxable income up to £37,400, and 40% **higher rate** on taxable income over £37,400. A 50% **additional rate** on income over £150,000 was expected to start on 6 April 2010.

It is the employee's obligation to notify the tax office of any changes which might affect the tax code, or to notify the employer and the employer notifies the tax office. Even if an employer knows an employee is entitled to additional allowances, the tax code must not be changed until the employee or employer notifies the tax office of the change and HMRC issues a new tax code.

30.4.5 Tax reliefs and credits

Individuals may be entitled to tax reliefs and/or tax credits. With **tax reliefs**, tax does not have to be paid on the income, or tax which has been paid is rebated in some way. With **tax credits**, HMRC provides a payment to eligible people.

30.4.5.1   No tax deducted by employer

Some tax reliefs are dealt with by the employer deducting the amount from the employee's earnings before working out how much tax is payable on earnings. Tax reliefs handled like this include payments to occupational pension schemes [**30.6.3.1**], and payments to charities under a payroll giving scheme [**50.4**].

30.4.5.2   Tax relief at source

Tax relief is available on some life insurance premiums and premiums for some types of medical insurance for people over 60, and pension contributions up to a specified limit. These reliefs are dealt with by the insurance or pension company.

30.4.5.3   Tax relief claimed by taxpayer

Some reliefs are obtained only if the employee claims them through **self assessment**. These include tax relief on some loans, maintenance payments, some work related expenses [**30.4.9.3**], some vocational training, and additional tax relief for higher rate taxpayers on pension contributions and on donations made to charities under gift aid [**50.2.2**]. Relief is usually given by an adjustment to the employee's tax code.

30.4.5.4   Tax credits

Working tax credit (for people who work at least 16 hours per week, on either an employed or self employed basis, and are on a low income) and **child tax credit** (for couples or lone parents who may or may not be in work, who are on a low income and have responsibility for a child or young person) are paid by HMRC direct to the recipient's bank account so do not involve the employer. A person on WTC whose hours fall below 16 per week must notify HMRC within one month of the reduction in hours and may need to claim jobseeker's allowance or income support. The **tax credits helpline** is 0845 300 3900.

30.4.6   National insurance

Employers are required to deduct employees' **class 1 national insurance contributions** (NICs) and pay them to HMRC, along with an employer's contribution towards each employee's NI. NI applies to employees aged between 16 and state pension age (at the time of writing 60 for women and 65 for men, but to be equalised upwards to 65 for women from 2010 to 2020). Information is available from the HMRC website and national insurance helplines [see end of chapter].

To be entitled to a state pension, employees have to have paid NI contributions for a qualifying period [**30.5.1**]. Self employed people pay **class 2** and **class 4** national insurance. Some other state benefits, such as jobseeker's allowance, also require payment for a qualifying period. Details are available from Directgov and the Department for Work and Pensions [see end of chapter].

30.4.6.1   Limits and thresholds

Statutory sick, maternity, paternity and adoption pay are available only to employees who earn at least the NI **lower earnings limit** (£95 per week, £412 per month in tax year 2009-10). **NI contributions** become payable when earnings reach the **earnings threshold** (£110 per week, £476 per month, £5,715 per year for each employment in tax year 2009-10). There are two earnings thresholds – the **primary threshold** for employee's NICs and **secondary threshold** for employer's NICs – but in 2009-10 they are the same.

If an employee earns between the LEL and the earnings threshold no national insurance is payable, but the employer must inform HMRC on a form **P46** [**30.4.3.1**], keep a record of the employee's earnings on form **P11** or a similar record, and report the earnings to HMRC at the end of the year on **P14**.

The **upper accruals point** is £770 per week (£3,337 per month, £40,040 per year) in tax year 2009-10. Employees who are members of contracted-out occupational pension schemes [**30.6.4.2**], and their employers, pay reduced rate NICs [**30.6.3.2**] up to the upper accruals point, and full NICs between the upper accruals point and the upper earning limit.

When earnings reach the **upper earnings limit** (£844 per week, £3,656 per month, £43,875 per year in tax year 2009-10), employees' NICs go down to 1%. There is no upper earnings limit at which employers' NICs are reduced.

If an employee has more than one employment with earnings above the primary threshold, NICs are payable in each. But employees who believe they will pay the full employees' NICs, up to the upper earnings limit, during the year can apply to HMRC on form **CA2700** to have their NICs reduced at one of the employers. Form CA2700 only lasts for one tax year so the employee must apply each year.

30.4.6.2   Class 1 contributions

Employees' class 1 NICs are also called **primary NICs**, and **employers' class 1 NICs** are called **secondary NICs**.

People over state pension age (60 for women and 65 for men at the time of writing, but to be equalised to 65 between 2010 and 2020) do not pay employees' NICs, but must show the employer a passport or birth certificate as proof of age, or give the employer a **CA4140** or **CF384** issued by HMRC. Employers' NICs have to be paid for pensioners at the same rate as for other employees.

Married women and widows used to be able to pay reduced liability class 1 contributions. This is no longer possible, but a woman who had reduced liability on 5 April 1978 is entitled to keep it unless her circumstances change. Employers' NICs have to be paid for women with reduced liability at the same rate as for other employees.

For employees in a contracted-out occupational pension scheme [**30.6.4.2**] both employees' and employers' NICs are reduced, but the difference between the reduced and full amounts must be contributed to the pension scheme.

30.4.6.3   Class 1A and 1B contributions

Class 1A NICs must be paid by employers who provide employees with company cars, fuel or other benefits which are available for the employees' private use.

Where the employer has entered into a **PAYE settlement agreement** for the payment of tax [**30.4.7.2**], employer's NICs on expenses payments or benefits covered by the agreement are **class 1B NICs**.

Class 1A and 1B NICs are not paid through the payroll. They are declared as part of the employer's annual return at the end of the tax year and are paid by the employer at that time.

30.4.7   Form P11D and P9D

Unless it has a dispensation [**30.4.7.1**], the employer must notify HMRC by 6 July on form **P11D** of most reimbursements for expenses and other benefits to:

- employees who earn £8,500 or more per year, including the expenses and the value of the benefits (this includes employees who join during the year and would have earned at least £8,500 if they had worked for the whole year);
- all company directors [**13.1.3**], including employees who are also company directors, and in organisations which are not companies, all members of the governing body [**13.1**]. But this normally does not apply to unpaid directors/ governing body members of charities and other voluntary organisations.

Where a P11D is required, it must include details of reimbursements or benefits even if they are not subject to tax or national insurance.

Form **P9D** is used for taxable reimbursements or benefits totalling more than £25 reimbursed to employees who earn less than £8,500 per year and are not company directors or governing body members. Non-taxable reimbursements and benefits do not have to be included.

The information on the P11D or P9D must also be provided to the employee by 6 July, and the employee must notify it to HMRC on a self assessment tax return. If HMRC does not provide a self assessment return, the employee must ask for one.

If the benefits or reimbursements listed on the P11D or P9D are taxable, HMRC will issue a revised tax code so tax can be deducted from future payments to the individual, or if the person is not an employee HMRC will tax them through self assessment. If reimbursements are not taxable (because they meet the criteria set out in **30.4.9.1**), the employee should indicate this on his or her tax return.

30.4.7.1 Dispensation

If the only entries on the P11D would be reimbursement of expenses genuinely incurred wholly to carry out the organisation's work, the employer can obtain **dispensation** from having to submit the forms by using form **P11DX** to contact HMRC. There is no need for a dispensation from P9D, because this does not have to be filled in if the only reimbursements or benefits are free of tax.

Although employers with a dispensation do not have to send details of expenses payments to HMRC, it must provide the details to employees by 6 July. It should be made clear to employees that these payments are covered by the employer's dispensation and do not have to be disclosed by the employee on a tax return.

30.4.7.2 PAYE settlement agreement

To avoid the employer having to fill in P11D and P9D and notify the employee of small-scale or occasional taxable expenses payments and benefits, and the employee then having to declare them on a tax return and pay tax on them, the employer can make a **PAYE settlement agreement**. This is a formal contract between the employer and HMRC under which the employer – not the employee – pays the tax and/or national insurance due on payments and benefits. NI contributions paid through a PAYE settlement agreement are **class 1B [30.4.6.3]**.

30.4.8 Student loan repayments

Where an ex-student started higher education after August 1998 and still owes a student loan, **student loan repayments** are made by deduction from pay once the student is earning at least £15,000 per year (tax year 2009-10). The employer must not make deductions until receiving a notice to start student loan deductions (form **SL1**) from HMRC, or receiving from the employee a P45 with a Y in the 'continue student loans' box. Deductions must be entered on the P11, and are paid to HMRC along with tax and national insurance.

The employer must continue the deductions until a stop notification is received from HMRC. When an employee for whom student loan deductions are being made leaves, the employer must enter Y in the student loans box on the P45.

30.4.9 Tax and NI treatment of expenses and benefits

If an employee pays for work related expenses, the tax and national insurance treatment depends on whether the employer reimburses the employee or the employee remains out of pocket. The rules on expenses, benefits and 'perks' received by employees are complex, and are different for expenses incurred or benefits received by employees, volunteers [**39.2.1**] or self employed workers.

Some of the most common reimbursements and benefits are explained here, but it is essential that employers check the HMRC expenses and benefits guide for *every* type of reimbursement made or benefit provided to employees.

Even the same benefit may be treated differently in different circumstances. Office equipment provided for home use, for example, is free of tax and NI and does not have to be included on P11D [**30.4.7**] if it is intended solely for business use and there is no significant private use. But if it is not provided solely for business or there is significant private use, it must be listed on P11D and is subject to class 1A national insurance.

30.4.9.1 Reimbursement by employer

An employer's **reimbursement** of an employee's out of pocket expenditure is not classed as wages or remuneration and is not subject to tax or national insurance, provided that the expenditure was genuine (was actually incurred), it was necessary for the work, and reimbursement for this type of expenditure is legally allowed to be paid free of tax and national insurance.

Most other reimbursement is subject to tax and/or NI. However there are some exceptions to the rule that expenditure must have been incurred and be necessary for the work. For example **incidental overnight expenses** (also called **personal incidental expenses),** such as newspapers and laundry while an employee is on a business trip or attending work related training involving an overnight stay, are free of tax and NICs if the employer pays the employee no more than £5 per night for stays in the UK and £10 for stays abroad (tax year 2009-10). If the employer pays more than this, the full amount (not just the excess above £5/£10) must be entered on form P11D [**30.4.7**] and is subject to class 1 NICs.

Similarly employees who by agreement with their employer work at home can be paid up to £3 per week (tax year 2009-10) **homeworking allowance** free of tax and NI to cover **household expenses** such as electricity. Home workers who are paid more than this for expenses must provide evidence of the costs incurred.

30.4.9.2   Scale rate payments

Where expenses are incurred relatively often and it is difficult to get receipts, the employer can agree **scale rate payments** with HMRC. These are payments of a fixed amount, intended to cover no more than the average cost of routine expenses, as evidenced by a sampling exercise carried out by the employer. Examples include the cost of cleaning uniforms, or household expenses where employees can show that on average they spend more than £3 per week, or the cost of routine travel for work purposes. A scale rate payment can be paid to employees only if they have actually incurred expenditure or, in the case of household expenses, have actually worked at home. They must be entered on form P11D.

From 6 April 2009 HMRC has agreed **benchmark scale rates** which can be used for meal allowances when an employee is away from their normal place of work for a day or part of a day, without the employer having to carry out a sampling exercise. These are £5 when an employee leaves home before 6am and this is earlier than usual; £5 when the employee is away from home or the normal place of work for at least five hours; £10 when the employee is away from home or the normal place of work for at least 10 hours and buys two meals; and £15 when the employee works later than usual, until later than 8pm, and buys a meal they would ordinarily have at home. The employer has to indicate on form **P11DX** [**30.4.7.1**] that it intends to reimburse at these rates (or lower).

Similarly HMRC has agreed that employees who incur travel and subsistence costs when travelling outside the UK can be reimbursed at (or below) the Foreign and Commonwealth Office benchmark rates for travel in that country, and the payment does not have to be covered by a dispensation or be reported on a **P11D**.

An employer can reimburse more than the benchmark rates if higher scale rates are agreed with HMRC, or the employee provides receipts.

A scale rate payment is not the same as a **round sum allowance**, which is made to employees regardless of whether they incur any expenditure (for example a weekly payment to cover travel even if the employee did not incur any travel costs that week). Round sum allowances are subject to tax and NI through PAYE.

30.4.9.3   Expenses not reimbursed by employer

If the employer does not reimburse for any or all expenses, the employee may be entitled to **tax relief**. For some expenditure, such as on tools or special clothing, this might be in the form of a **flat rate deduction** from tax agreed between HMRC and the relevant trade union. If a flat rate deduction has not been agreed, the employee can recover the amount spent only by claiming relief on a self assessment tax return. Tax relief is available for non-reimbursed expenditure on:

- buying and maintaining tools and special work clothes which are not provided by the employer and are used only for work;
- travel expenses necessary to do the job (but not travel to and from the usual place of work);
- other necessary expenses incurred wholly and exclusively in doing the work;
- a portion of council tax, rates, water charges, rent, mortgage repayments and insurance, where the employee carries out 'substantive duties' at home be-

cause they cannot be done at the employer's premises, or are such that the employee has to live too far to drive to the employer's premises every day;

- wear and tear on a car provided at the employee's own expense to do the job;
- some fees which must be paid by an employee to carry on a profession;
- fees or subscriptions to some professional bodies and societies, listed in HMRC 'List 3', where membership is a statutory requirement for the employment, or the activities of the body are directly relevant to the employment.

30.4.9.4   Relocation expenses

Payment for relocation expenses of up to £8,000 (tax year 2009-10) is not subject to tax or national insurance and does not have to be included on form P11D [**30.4.7**] provided the move is necessary to enable the employee to take up a new job (for the same or a different employer) or to carry on the same job at a new location, the employee's current home is not within reasonable travelling distance of the new workplace, and the reimbursed costs are covered by this exemption.

30.4.9.5   Beneficial loans

A **beneficial loan** is one provided by an employer to an employee on an interest-free or reduced interest basis, for example to purchase a season ticket. Tax is due on the interest that the employee is assumed to have saved by not having to obtain the loan from a bank or other lender. The interest on which the tax is due is based on the **official rate of interest**, set each year by HMRC.

30.4.9.6   Benefits and 'perks'

'Perks' and benefits which may be taxable or subject to national insurance include accommodation, travel season tickets, luncheon vouchers worth more than 15p per day, medical insurance or medical care, gifts or meals unless the value is trivial, gifts from clients and virtually everything else which has a money value.

Childcare [**30.4.12**] and reimbursement for use of the employee's own vehicle [**30.4.10**] may (or may not) be free of tax and national insurance.

Some benefits and perks which have been exempted from tax and national insurance include:

- general welfare counselling provided by the employer;
- pensions advice to the value of £150 per employee per year provided by an outside consultant or agency, so long as the advice is available to all employees rather than just some;
- breakfast, other meals or refreshments provided to employees who cycle to work on days designated by the employer as **cycle to work days**;
- late night taxis journeys, but only in very specific circumstances and only to a maximum of 60 journeys per employee per year;
- accommodation services and supplies used in the performance of duties away from the employer's premises.

The expenses and benefits guide on the HMRC website should be checked in relation to these and all other benefits provided to employees.

30.4.9.7   'Trivial' benefits

Strictly speaking, everything provided by an employer to an employee is subject to tax (and in some cases national insurance) unless there is an explicit statutory provision or an **extra-statutory concession** by HMRC saying it is not. This includes so-called gifts from the employer. However in practice the employer's tax office may be willing to agree that small gifts or perks, such as birthday flowers or a box of chocolates, may be treated as **trivial** and be excluded from tax. HMRC guidance for its staff does not give a monetary definition of trivial but says each case will be decided on its merits, using a common sense approach.

Benefits (even if minor) given as a reward, for example for good performance, cash gifts and vouchers are **not treated as trivial** and are subject to tax. Benefits which are contractual are unlikely to be treated as trivial.

30.4.10 Cars and driving

Reimbursing employees for use of their own cars, or allowing them to use a work vehicle for private use, has tax and national insurance implications which must be considered by the employee and employer. Details are available from HMRC.

30.4.10.1 Business use of private vehicles

Employees' use of their private vehicles to carry out an organisation's work is called **business use**, even if the organisation is not a business. The **approved mileage allowance payment** (AMAP) is the maximum which can be reimbursed for employees' use of their own vehicles free of tax and national insurance and without having to be included on P11D or P9D [**30.4.7**].

The AMAPs for cars and vans (tax year 2009-10) are 40p per mile for the first 10,000 miles of reimbursed business use and 25p for each additional business mile. For motorcycles the AMAP is 24p per mile and for bicycles 20p per miles.

An employer can pay less than the AMAP, or nothing at all. In these situations the employee may then be able to claim tax relief, called **mileage allowance relief**, on the amount which has not been reimbursed [**30.4.9.3**].

If an employee is reimbursed more than the AMAP, the excess must be entered on form P9D or P11D and is subject to class 1 national insurance. Reimbursement for travel between home and the usual place of work, even at or below the AMAP, is subject to tax and class 1 NI.

An employer who reimburses employees for business use of their cars can choose to pay an additional 5p per mile **passenger payment** for each employee who travels as a passenger in the car on a business journey. This additional amount is paid to the employee and is free of tax and national insurance.

Employees who use a private vehicle for work must notify their insurer [**22.8**].

30.4.10.2 Use of company cars for private motoring

If the employer provides an employee or a member or his or her family or household with a car which can also be used for private motoring, this must be reported to HMRC on form **P46(Car)** . Details must be included on P11D or P9D [**30.4.7**] and class 1A national insurance is payable at a **scale charge** (also called **car benefit charge**). Accessories added after the car was registered increase the car's value, and therefore the car benefit, in the year they are added and each additional year, unless they have been added solely for use by a disabled person.

30.4.10.3 Fuel

The value of fuel provided free of charge by an employer for an employee's private use is subject to class 1A national insurance as a **car fuel benefit charge**. If the organisation is VAT registered it must account for VAT on the fuel. Where the employee is reimbursed for fuel, rather than being directly provided with it, the reimbursement is subject to tax and class 1 national insurance.

30.4.10.4 Transport for disabled workers

Where a disabled person is provided with a vehicle for travel to and from work or receives some or all of the journey costs, there is no tax or NI on the amount received or the value of the vehicle and it does not have to be entered on P11D.

30.4.10.5 Cash in lieu of car

A cash alternative to a car is subject to tax and national insurance in the same way as any payment to an employee.

30.4.11 Cycle to work

Under the government's **cycle to work scheme** an employer can purchase bicycles and related safety equipment for employees who will use it 'mainly' for work purposes or for travel between home and work. The employer leases it to the employee for between one and three years, deducting the lease fee from the employee's salary, then sells it to the employee for a nominal amount at the end of the period. Provided the scheme's rules are followed there is no tax or national insurance on the employee's payments to the employer. Information is available from HMRC, and from **Cyclescheme** or **Booost** [see end of chapter].

30.4.12 Childcare

There is no tax or national insurance on **childcare** or the value of the subsidy for childcare at a free or subsidised workplace childcare facility, provided by the employer on its own or jointly with others.

For childcare where the employer directly contracts with and pays the fees to a nursery, playscheme, childminder or nanny, or for childcare vouchers provided by the employer which the employee uses to pay for childcare, there is no tax or national insurance on the first £55 (tax year 2009-10) per parent per week. Any payment or voucher above this amount must be entered on form P11D or P9D [**30.4.7**] and is subject to class 1A national insurance [**30.4.6.3**].

The childcare used, whether contracted by the employer or employee and even if it is provided by a relative or nanny, must be registered with Ofsted [**41.3.1**].

If the employer reimburses the employee for childcare or pays a higher salary to cover the cost of childcare, the payment is subject to tax and national insurance through the payroll. Where the reimbursement is to cover the costs of childcare while the employee is away from home on business travel, the payment is not subject to tax or NI but must be entered on form P11D.

Parents who work at least 16 hours per week and receive working tax credit [**30.4.5.4**] may be entitled to a tax credit for up to 80% of childcare costs. HM Revenue and Customs has guidance on its website to help parents decide whether it is more advantageous for the employer to pay for childcare (either directly or through vouchers) or for the employee to receive a cash alternative from the employer, pay for the childcare directly, and receive a tax credit towards the costs.

30.4.13 Tips and gratuities

If the employer collects a compulsory service charge and some or all of it is distributed to workers, this must be itemised on the workers' pay slip [**30.1.3**] and the employer deducts tax and national insurance contributions in the usual way. This applies regardless of whether the service charge is distributed by the employer or through a **tronc** (a system for pooling tips or service charges and then sharing them out).

Tips or voluntary service charges paid by credit card, or collected by workers and then given to the employer or a troncmaster for distribution, may be subject to tax and NI when they are distributed to workers, or only tax – depending on who distributes them and how decisions about their distribution are made. The employer must notify HMRC as soon as it becomes aware that a tronc is operating.

If workers collect and keep their own tips, there is no NI on the tips but the workers must pay their own tax on them through self assessment.

30.4.14 Time credits

Organisations which are part of a **local exchange trading scheme** (LETS), or **time bank** which provides credits in exchange for work may decide to pay wholly or partly in these credits. Note that this type of **time bank** (two words) is different from a **timebank** (one word), intended to promote volunteering.

Where LETS or time credits are used by an employer as an alternative to payment there are clearly implications for minimum wage [**30.2**], and it could affect the worker's entitlement to welfare benefits [**30.3**]. In addition the credits may be treated by HMRC as income, and the person who earns them may have to pay tax and national insurance on their value. Any organisation considering using LETS or other non-money schemes as a form of payment for work done for the organisation should seek advice from their PAYE office.

For individuals involved in LETS and time bank schemes in a personal capacity the credits are normally not subject to tax or national insurance, but could be if the person is providing services which are his or her occupation or profession, or goods which he or she would normally sell. For scheme members who receive state benefits, the Department for Work and Pensions' guidance on time exchange says that time credits do not affect state benefits. At the time of writing this does not apply to LETS credits, and they must be declared to the Department for Work and Pensions.

30.4.15 Pay on termination of employment

Contractual pay in lieu of notice is subject to tax and national insurance in the usual way, even if the contract says that the payment is discretionary. **Non-contractual pay in lieu of notice** may be treated as damages rather than pay and may be paid without deduction of tax and NI [**34.3.7**].

Statutory redundancy pay is not subject to tax or NI. **Contractual redundancy pay** is subject to tax and NI, but HMRC may agree to exempt payments up to £30,000 [**35.7.3**]. There is no tax or NI on a discretionary payment (one which there is no contractual obligation to make) of money and/or non-cash benefits, such as a car, of up to £30,000 total.

Payments which appear to be non-contractual but are given as a matter of course may in fact be contractual, and tax advice should be sought before making them.

Other termination payments, for example on retirement or death, may be taxable unless they are linked to a pension or an employer-financed retirement benefits scheme. Tax advice should be sought before making any such payment.

30.4.16 Construction industry scheme

An organisation which spends more than £1 million per year, averaged over three years, on construction work is called a **contractor** and must comply with special tax provisions. Construction work includes the development of new buildings, and the repair and maintenance of existing buildings. Most charities are exempt from this **construction industry scheme**, but non-charitable subsidiaries are not. Details of the scheme are available from HMRC [see end of chapter].

Income Tax (Construction Industry Scheme) Regulations 2005 [SI 2005/2045]

A contractor must check whether construction sub-contractors are registered with HM Revenue and Customs; pay sub-contractors gross (without deducting tax or national insurance) or with tax deducted at the standard rate, depending on the type of registration; deduct tax at a higher rate from payments made to unregistered sub-contractors; and make a monthly return to HMRC which includes a declaration that the tax status of all sub-contractors has been verified.

An organisation with a substantial construction programme under the £1 million annual average threshold should monitor all building work, for example redecorating its existing premises, in case this takes it into the 'contractor' category.

30.5 STATE PENSIONS

Information about state pensions and contributions to them is available from HM Revenue and Customs, Business Link and the Directgov website [see end of chapter].

30.5.1 Basic state pensions

The **basic state pension** is a paid at a flat rate, not based on the amount earned. People of **state pension age** are entitled to the basic state pension if they (or for married women, their husband) have paid sufficient national insurance contributions (NICs). At the time of writing (mid 2009) the requirement to qualify for a full pension is 39 years' NICs for women and 44 years for men.

Where a person has paid some but not the full number of years' NICs, their pension is reduced. People who will not have paid NICs for the full 39 or 44 years can make a one off payment to top up for up to six additional years. Those who will reach pension age between 6 April 2008 and 5 April 2015, and already have 20 qualifying years, can top up for a further six years. *Pensions Act 2008 s.135*

At the time of writing state pension age is 60 for women and 65 for men, but is being equalised at 65 between 2010 and 2020. From 6 April 2010:

- women born between 6 April 1950 and 5 April 1955 will become eligible for state pension at between 60 and 65; and those born after 5 April 1955 become eligible at 65;

- for women and men born between 6 April 1959 and 5 April 1978 state pension age will be gradually increased between 2024 and 2046 to 68, and people born after 5 April 1978 will have a state pension age of 68;   *Pensions Act 2007 sch.3*;

- the number of qualifying years will be reduced to 30, and national insurance credits will be treated in the same way as paid contributions;

- the basic pension will be linked to earnings rather than inflation, which should lead to faster increases in the amount of pensions;

- from 2012 a new form of workplace pension, called a **personal account** [**30.6.9**], will be introduced.   *Pensions Act 2007*

Pensions for people who reach state pension age before 6 April 2010 will be called **category A retirement pensions**, and for those who reach pension age on or after 6 April 2010 **category B retirement pensions**.

30.5.2 Additional state pensions

30.5.2.1 State earnings related pension (SERPS)

Employees who paid class 1 national insurance contributions (NICs) [**30.4.6.2**] for some or all of the period from April 1978 to April 2002 are entitled to a **state earnings related pension** (SERPS), also called **additional pension**.

30.5.2.2 State second pension (S2P)

From 6 April 2002 SERPS was replaced by the **state second pension** (S2P). This provides a second tier pension for employees who pay class 1 national insurance contributions, and those whose income is between the NI lower earnings level and the earnings threshold [**30.4.6.1**] and who therefore do not pay NICs.

Certain carers and those entitled to employment and support allowance, incapacity benefit or severe disablement allowance are deemed to have earnings equal to the earnings threshold, and will build up eligibility for S2P.

It is possible to contract out of S2P if the employee has an appropriate personal pension [**30.6.3.2**] or is a member of an occupational pension scheme [**30.6.4.2**].

From around 2030 S2P will become flat rate rather than being linked to earnings. The government hopes that long before then, employees will be members of an occupational pension scheme or the national pensions savings scheme [**30.6.9**], or will have personal pensions.

30.6 OCCUPATIONAL AND PERSONAL PENSIONS

At the time of writing (mid 2009) there is no obligation for employees to participate in any pension scheme other than state pensions [**30.5**], and employers are not under any statutory obligation to contribute to a non-state pension scheme.

At the time of writing, possible pension arrangements are:

- the employee relies solely on the **basic state pension** [**30.5.1**], plus **SERPS** [**30.5.2.1**] and/or **state second pension** (S2P) [**30.5.2.2**];

- the employee stays in S2P, but tops up with a **personal pension** [**30.6.6**] or **stakeholder pension** [**30.6.8**], with the employer possibly making a contribution to the pension;

- the employee contracts out of S2P and takes out an **appropriate personal pension** (sometimes called a **rebate only pension**) or stakeholder pension, under which HM Revenue and Customs rebates to the pension plan part of the employee's and employer's national insurance contributions;

- the employer organises a **group pension plan** [**30.6.7**], with a number of individual and/or appropriate personal pensions with the same pension provider;

- the employer provides an **occupational pension scheme** [**30.6.4**], which the employer decides is either additional to S2P or contracted out of S2P.

Information about occupational and personal pensions is available from the **Pensions Regulator** and the **Pensions Advisory Service** [see end of chapter]. It is also provided by solicitors, accountants and financial advisors, some of whom are tied to particular companies or products and cannot provide independent advice.

30.6.1 Consultation with employees

Employers with 50 or more employees must consult pension scheme members and potential members before making any **listed changes**, as defined in the regulations, to occupational or personal pension provision. The scheme trustees must also consult the members and potential members.
Occupational & Personal Pension Schemes (Consultation by Employers & Miscellaneous Amendment) Regulations 2006 [SI 2006/349]

Even where there are fewer than 50 employees, employers are obliged under contract law to consult employees about such changes, and in some circumstances to obtain their consent [**26.9**].

30.6.2 Pensions and equality

Occupational pension schemes with different pension ages for men and women contravene the requirement for men and women to receive **equal pay** for work of equal value [**28.8**], so men and women must be allowed to take their pension at the same age.
Barber v Guardian Royal Exchange Assurance Group [1990] EUECJ R-262/88

Occupational pensions or employers' pension contributions can be offered to employees who are **married** or in a **civil partnership**, without also being offered to employees who are single. They cannot be offered only to married employees without also being offered to those who are civil partners.
Employment Equality (Sexual Orientation) Regulations 2003 [SI 2003/1661] reg.25

Age discrimination in occupational pension schemes and employer contributions to personal pensions is generally unlawful, but there are some exemptions.
Employment Equality (Age) Regulations 2006 [SI 2006/1031] sch.2, amended by Employment Equality (Age) (Amendment No.2) Regulations 2006 [SI 2006/2931]

Employers who operate occupational pension schemes or make any other pension provision must provide it to **part-time workers** on the same basis as full-timers who are engaged in broadly similar work, unless there is an objectively justified reason for not doing so.
Part-time Workers (Prevention of Less Favourable Treatment) Regulations 2000 [SI 2000/1551]

Fixed-term employees must be offered either the same pension entitlements as comparable permanent employees, or equivalent benefits such as higher pay to take account of the pension contribution the employer would make for a permanent employee, unless there is an objectively justified reason for not doing so.
Fixed-term Employees (Prevention of Less Favourable Treatment) Regulations 2002 [SI 2002/2034] reg.3

It is unlawful to treat **disabled people** less favourably in the provision of pensions, including any provision for permanent health insurance or early retirement, even if the costs are higher than for comparable provision for non-disabled people.
Disability Discrimination Act 1995 s.68(1), amended by DDA 2005 s.11; DDA 1995 ss.4G-4K, inserted by DDA 1995 (Pensions) Regulations 2003 [2003/2770]

30.6.3 Tax, national insurance and pension contributions

All occupational pension schemes must be registered with HM Revenue and Customs. Employer contributions are not subject to income tax as a benefit to the employee. For the employer, both employee and employer contributions are allowable deductions for income tax and corporation tax purposes, and there is no capital gains tax on the disposal of scheme investments.

30.6.3.1 Tax relief on pension contributions

Contributions are made to pension plans net of tax (after tax has been deducted). The pension provider recovers from HM Revenue and Customs the basic rate tax which the employee has paid on her or his contribution, and applies this to the employee's pension fund. A taxpayer who pays higher rate tax [**30.4.4**] can recover the additional tax through self assessment.

In tax year 2009-10, tax relief is available on an individual's total occupational, personal and/or stakeholder pension contributions to a maximum of £3,600 per year or 100% of the employee's salary, whichever is higher. For non-taxpayers, the maximum is £3,600.

The annual tax-relievable maximum that can be added to an individual's pension by the individual and employer combined is £245,000 (£255,000 in tax year 2010-11), with a maximum lifetime allowance for tax relievable contributions of £1.75 million (£1.8 million in 2010-11). From 6 April 2011, tax relief on pension contributions will be reduced for employees whose annual income of £150,000 or over.

30.6.3.2 National insurance and contributions

For many pensions the employee can **contract out**, giving up the right to state second pension (S2P). For occupational pension schemes the employer and employee pay reduced national insurance contributions [**30.6.4.2**]. For **appropriate personal pensions** and for stakeholder pensions the employee and employer pay full NICs, with HM Revenue and Customs contributing the difference between the reduced and full rates (the **NI rebate**) to the employee's pension plan.

30.6.4 Occupational pension schemes

Occupational pension schemes, sometimes called **employers'** or **company pension schemes**, are offered by employers for the benefit of employees and former employees. They are regulated by the Pensions Regulator.

Special rules apply when an employee with occupational pension scheme rights is transferred to another employer under the **Transfer of Undertakings (Protection of Employment) Regulations** (TUPE) [**29.7.7**]. Specialist advice must be taken in this situation (and for TUPE transfers in general).

Where members of the **Local Government Pension Scheme** are transferred to the private sector (including the voluntary sector) as a result of privatisation or contracting out of public sector services, the new employer may apply to LGPS for admitted body status. If the employer is admitted, relevant employees are able to remain in LGPS. Some National Health Service employees who are transferred out of the NHS may be able to remain in the NHS pension scheme [**29.7.7**].

30.6.4.1 Final salary or money purchase

An occupational pension scheme may be:

- **salary related** (also called **defined benefit** or **final salary**), giving a pension based on the employee's salary at or near retirement and how long he or she was a member of the scheme;
- **money purchase**((**defined contribution**), where contributions paid into the scheme are invested and on retirement are used to buy a pension, so the amount depends on the value of the investment and the cost of purchasing an **annuity** (to provide a regular pension) at the time of retirement; or
- **mixed benefit** schemes which combine elements of both defined benefit and defined contribution schemes.

30.6.4.2 Contracted in or out

With a **contracted-in** occupational scheme the employee remains within the state second pension [**30.5.2.2**], while taking out a separate pension through the occupational scheme. The employer might or might not contribute to this. Both the employee and employer pay full national insurance contributions.

With a **contracted-out** occupational scheme, the employee gives up the right to state second pension from the date of contracting out, and the employer and employee pay reduced national insurance contributions. Special rules apply to the amount the employer contributes to the occupational scheme.

30.6.4.3 Contributory or non-contributory

For occupational schemes the employer sets the contribution, if any, to be made by the employee. If the employee is required to contribute, it is a **contributory** occupational pension scheme. If the employee does not have to contribute, the scheme is **non-contributory**.

30.6.4.4 Additional voluntary contributions

An employee who wants to contribute more than the specified amount to an occupational scheme may pay **additional voluntary contributions** (AVC) linked to the occupational pension scheme, take out a **free-standing additional voluntary contributions** (FSAVC) plan with any insurance company, or (subject to rules about maximum levels) contribute to a **stakeholder pension [30.6.8]**.

30.6.4.5 Trustee knowledge and understanding

At least one-third of the trustees of an occupational pension scheme must be nominated by the scheme members. All trustees, not just those nominated by members, have a statutory duty to have appropriate knowledge and understanding in respect of law relating to pensions and trusts, and must be conversant with the scheme documentation. The Pensions Regulator's codes of practice for trustees provide practical guidance. *Pensions Act 2004 ss.241,247*

Most schemes with fewer than 12 members all of whom are trustees, and certain other schemes, are exempt from the one-third rule and the rules on trustee knowledge and understanding. However, trustees would be foolish to administer even a small scheme without appropriate knowledge. *Occupational Pension Schemes (Trustees' Knowledge & Understanding) Regulations 2006 [SI 2006/686]; Occupational Pension Schemes (Member-nominated Trustees & Directors) Regulations 2006 [SI 2006/714]*

30.6.4.6 Issues in occupational schemes

An occupational pension scheme may be expensive to administer, so a scheme for an individual employer is likely to be suitable only if at least 100 employees join. This problem can be overcome by joining a multi-employer scheme [**30.6.4.7**].

Employees who move to another employer cannot continue contributing to an occupational scheme unless the new employer is also a member. The options will be to leave contributions in the scheme; or if they have at least three months' qualifying service, to have a cash sum transferred to the new employer's occupational scheme or to a personal pension plan [**30.6.6**] or to get a refund of their contributions. *Occupational Pension Schemes (Early Leavers) Regulations 2006 [SI 2006/33]*

To ensure pension obligations under a salary related scheme can be met until the last surviving scheme member ceases to draw their pension, the employer may be obliged to make very large contributions to the scheme well into the future. This commitment should be taken on only after taking detailed legal and financial advice. With the aim of removing any existing **pension deficit** and avoiding future deficit, employers who provide these schemes must meet a **statutory funding objective**, agree with pension trustees a statement of funding principles and a schedule of contributions that is consistent with the statement, and if necessary agree a recovery plan to ensure the pension meets the funding objective within a specified period. Organisations with such schemes also need to take regular advice about steps needed to ensure they manage any pension deficit. Detailed advice will also be needed about how their potential liability is shown on their balance sheet [**54.2.6, 54.3.5**]. *Pensions Act 2004 ss.221-227*

The employer must also pay a levy to the **pension protection fund**, which provides protection for employees whose employers have become insolvent with insufficient pension funds. *Pensions Act 2004 ss.127-131*

30.6.4.7 Multi-employer schemes

Some voluntary organisations may provide access for their staff to an occupational pension scheme run by a local authority, an umbrella voluntary sector body such as the National Housing Federation or a similar body, or schemes such as those run by the **Pensions Trust** for charity and not-for-profit sector employees (www.thepensionstrust.org.uk, 0845 123 6660). If an employee moves to a new employer who is also a scheme member, the employee can stay within the scheme.

30.6.5   Pension scheme exit debt

Complex rules apply if an organisation which is a member of a multi-employer occupational pension scheme has a **cessation event**. This is when the employer becomes insolvent, withdraws from the scheme for any reason, or does not have any employees who are members or eligible to be members of the scheme. Withdrawal might occur because the organisation is ceasing to operate, but it could also occur when it is winding up its current structure in order to merge with another organisation [**11.5.3**] or to incorporate [**chapter 10**].

Pensions Act 1995 s.75, amended by Occupational Pension Schemes (Employer Debt) Regulations 2005
[SI 2005/678]; OPS (Employer Debt etc) (Amendment) Regulations 2005 [SI 2005/2224],
amended by OPS (Employer Debt & Miscellaneous Amendments) Regulations 2008 [SI 2008/731]

An organisation which has not paid enough to the scheme to cover its full pension liability now and in future could find that this debt **crystallises** and it is required to pay the full amount immediately to the pension scheme.

However where the cessation event is that there are no more members in the scheme, there is a 12-month grace period during which time the employee will presumably try to get at least one employee to join.

For other cessation events – such as an incorporation where the organisation's employees are going to remain in the pension scheme under the new organisation to which they are being transferred – the pension provider and employer can make a **withdrawal agreement** under which the employer pays an amount based on how much has already been paid into the scheme. The employer puts in place a **guarantor**, agreed by the pension provider, who will if required pay the remainder of the potential debt.

For 'ongoing organisations with low levels of liquidity such as charities', the Pensions Regulator can agree with the pension provider an **approved withdrawal arrangement**, under which the employer can pay a lower amount. When the cessation event is a winding up to incorporate or merge, the guarantor will presumably be the new incorporated or merged organisation.

Any organisation which is a member of an occupational pension scheme should take advice from its pension provider, accountant and legal advisor before taking any steps that could lead to a cessation event.

30.6.6   Personal pension plans

Any employee can take out a **personal pension plan** with an insurer or other provider. All personal pension plans are **defined contribution** (money purchase), providing benefits based on the amount of money in the fund at retirement and the cost of buying an annuity at the time of retirement [**30.6.4.1**].

Some employers contribute a fixed percentage of the employee's salary to a personal pension, or a fixed percentage up to a maximum amount. This may be a contractual benefit, or discretionary on the part of the employer.

Personal pension plans are not linked to a particular employment, and can be maintained regardless of changes during the person's working life. But a future employer which has its own occupational pension scheme or group personal pension plan might not be willing to contribute to an individual plan.

30.6.7   Group personal pension plans

A **group personal pension plan** is not an occupational pension scheme, but is a personal pension plan [**30.6.6**] arranged by the employer for a group of employees. Because a number of staff join the same plan, administrative costs are reduced and more of the contribution can be invested towards the pension. The employer may be able to negotiate a return of some or all of the commission, which can also be used to enhance benefits.

30.6.8   Stakeholder pensions

Stakeholder pensions are low cost **defined contribution [30.6.4.1]** schemes intended primarily for employees earning between £9,000 and £18,000 per year. They are also open to people who are in paid work but not as employees, those who are not earning but can afford to make contributions, and as an additional pension to employees who are members of occupational pension scheme. The Pensions Regulator [see end of chapter] provides information about stakeholder pensions and pension providers.   *Welfare Reform & Pensions Act 1999 ss.1-3;*
Stakeholder Pension Schemes Regulations 2000 [SI 2000/1403]

All employers, unless exempt [**30.6.8.1**], are required to designate a stakeholder scheme, provide specified information about it to all relevant employees [**30.6.8.3**], and offer access to relevant employees. They must also provide a facility to deduct contributions from employees' pay for the stakeholder scheme.

The employer does not have to contribute to a stakeholder pension scheme, or can make contributions dependent on the employee also contributing.

30.6.8.1   Exempt employers

An employer is exempt from having to provide access to a stakeholder scheme if it has fewer than five employees, or it has five or more employees but none has earned more than the national insurance lower earnings limit [**30.4.6.1**] in any week in the previous three months.

An employer is also exempt if it has an occupational pension scheme [**30.6.4**] which all employees, except those who are under 18 or within five years of retirement age, are entitled to join within 12 months of starting work; or if all employees have the right to receive employer contributions to a group personal pension plan [**30.6.7**], the contributions are at least 3% of each employee's basic pay, the employer offers a payroll deduction facility for the employees' contributions, and the pension plan imposes no charges when an employee leaves the scheme or ceases to pay contributions.   *Stakeholder Pension Schemes Regulations 2000 [SI 2000/1403] reg.22,*
amended by Stakeholder Pension Schemes (Amendment) (No.2) Regulations 2001 [SI 2001/934] reg.14

30.6.8.2   Relevant employees

Unless the employer is exempt, access to a stakeholder pension must be offered to every employee who is not eligible to join an existing occupational pension scheme [**30.6.4**] and is not contractually entitled to an employer's contribution of at least 3% of basic pay to a personal pension plan; has been continuously employed for more than three months; and has had earnings at or above the NI lower earnings limit [**30.4.6.1**] for three consecutive months. The only exception is an employee who is not eligible to make contributions because of a restriction imposed by HM Revenue and Customs.   *Stakeholder Regs 2000 reg.23,*
amended by Stakeholder Regs 2001 reg.15

Apart from some government employees, stakeholder pension contributors must be resident in the UK.

30.6.8.3   Designating a scheme

All employers, except those who are exempt, must consult relevant employees and designate a registered stakeholder pension scheme. An employer who ceases to be exempt has three months to comply. The employer can consult relevant employees (or all employees) in any appropriate way. There are penalties of up to £50,000 for failure to designate or operate a stakeholder pension scheme.

Registered schemes are listed on the Pensions Regulator's website [see end of chapter], but the organisation should seek independent financial advice before choosing one. Some scheme providers can set up payroll deduction facilities as part of their service, which may be helpful for small organisations. The employer can, if it wishes, designate more than one scheme.

The employer must then provide employees and organisations representing them with basic information about the scheme [**27.3.4**], offer payroll deductions from employees' earnings, pay the deductions to the scheme provider, maintain records of deductions and payments, and check from time to time that the scheme is still registered with the Pensions Regulator.

Employees can choose to join a different scheme, in which case they will have to make their own payment arrangements unless the employer agrees to make deductions for that scheme. Employees can also choose not to join any scheme, and can change their mind at any time.

30.6.9 Personal accounts

At the time of writing (mid 2009), it was expected that the **national pensions savings scheme** would be set up by the Personal Accounts Delivery Authority by October 2012, with enrolments phased in over two years.

Every **jobholder** aged from 22 to state pension age, whose earnings are between £5,035 and £33,540 (set at 2006-07 values) per year and who is not in an employer's occupational pension scheme [**30.6.4**] or qualifying group pension plan, will be automatically enrolled in the scheme and get a **personal account** unless they opt out. Jobholders with earnings less than the qualifying amount, or aged 16 to 21 or above state pension age, can opt in to the scheme. A jobholder is anyone working under a contract of employment [**26.1**], including temporary employees. *Pensions Act 2008 ss.3,8,9*

It was expected that jobholders in the scheme would have to contribute a minimum 4% of their salary, matched by 1% tax relief and a minimum 3% from the employer. The employer's contribution would be phased in, at 1% in 2012, 2% in 2013 and 3% in 2014. There will be an annual contribution limit of £3,600 (set at 2005 values).

It will be unlawful for an employer to encourage or force jobholders to opt out of the automatic enrolment scheme or a qualifying occupational or personal pension scheme, to offer inducements to do so, or to subject a jobholder to a detriment for joining or not joining a scheme. A dismissal connected with a person joining or not joining a scheme is automatically unfair [**34.7.1**]. *Pensions Act 2008 ss.55-57*

When personal accounts become available, employers will no longer be obliged to provide access to a stakeholder pension [**30.6.8**].

Information about the scheme is available from the Department for Work and Pensions [see end of chapter].

Resources: PAY AND PENSIONS

General information about pay & pensions. ACAS, BIS, Business Link, CIPD, Directgov, PEACe, TUC: see end of **chapter 25**.

Minimum wage. National minimum wage helpline: nmw@hmrc.gov.uk, 0845 6000 678.

State benefits. Department for Work and Pensions: www.dwp.gov.uk, list of helplines on website.

Tax & national insurance. HM Revenue & Customs: www.hmrc.gov.uk.
New employer's helpline: 0845 60 70 143.
Employer's helpline: 08457 143 143.
Tax credits helpline: 0845 300 3900.
For other helplines see list on HMRC website.

Cycle to work scheme. Cyclescheme: www.cyclescheme.co.uk, 01225 448 933, otherqueries@cyclescheme.co.uk.

Booost: www.booost.uk.com, info@booost.uk.com.

LETS & time credits. LETSlink UK: www.letslinkuk.org, 020 7607 7852, admin@letslinkuk.net.

Time Banks UK: www.timebanks.co.uk, 01452 541439, info@timebanks.co.uk.

Occupational, personal & stakeholder pensions. Pensions Regulator: www.thepensionsregulator.gov.uk, 0870 606 3636, customersupport@thepensionsregulator.gov.uk.

Pensions Advisory Service: www.pensionsadvisoryservice.org.uk, 08456 012 923, enquiries@pensionsadvisoryservice.org.uk.

State pensions. Business Link and Directgov: see end of **chapter 25**..

Statute law. www.opsi.gov.uk and www.statutelaw.gov.uk.

Much but not all case law. www.bailii.org.

Updates cross-referenced to this book. www.rclh.co.uk.

Chapter 31

WORKING TIME, TIME OFF AND LEAVE

*For sources of further information see end of chapter. For payment and leave rights for parents, carers and others with dependants, see **chapter 32**. For rights of trade union and employee representatives, see **chapter 36**.*

31.1   WORKING TIME RIGHTS

Rights related to working time are granted in the **Working Time Regulations 1998** and other legislation. The main provisions of the regulations, which are intended to protect the health and safety of employees and other workers, are:

- a limit of 48 hours on average weekly working time [**31.2.1**], although at the time of writing (mid 2009) employees can agree to work longer;
- a limit of eight hours average normal daily working time, with some exceptions, for night workers [**31.2.4**];
- compulsory health assessments for all night workers [**40.3.2**];
- daily rest breaks [**31.3.1**] and daily and weekly rest periods [**31.3.2**];
- 5.6 weeks paid annual leave [**31.4.2.1**].

Working Time Regulations 1998 [SI 1998/1833], as amended

Some of the rights include **flexibilities**, under which the rights can be changed or even excluded. Other rights are absolute and there is no flexibility.

Basic information about working time rights is available from the Department for Business, Innovation and Skills, ACAS, Business Link and the Trades Union Congress [see end of chapter]. The Health and Safety Executive [see end of chapter] or local authority environmental health department can deal with questions relating to the weekly and night working time limits and health assessments.

31.1.1   Who is covered

Working time rights apply to all workers [**25.1.2**]. This includes all employees, whether full-time, part-time, sessional, temporary or fixed-term, as well as most others who are paid or receive consideration (something of value) for their work. Unpaid trainees are also entitled to working time rights. For agency workers the obligations generally fall on the party which actually pays the worker.

Working Time Regulations 1998 [SI 1998/1833] regs.36,42

The rights do not apply to people who are genuinely self employed [**38.2**] and working for customers or clients of their own business, or to volunteers who are not working under a contract [**39.4**]. Some rights apply differently to workers who are above the minimum school leaving age but under 18, and the hours of school-age workers are subject to separate legislation [**31.5**].

31.1.2   Collective and workforce agreements

Some working time rights can be adapted through agreements with individual workers, a **collective agreement** [**36.3.4**] between an independent trade union or unions and the employer, or, where there is no collective agreement or mechanism for setting terms and conditions by collective agreement, a **workforce agreement**.   *Working Time Regulations 1998 [SI 1998/1833] reg.23*

A workforce agreement can apply to all the relevant members of the workforce or only a particular group, and may be agreed by the relevant workers or by workers' representatives. The agreement must be in writing for a specified period of not more than five years, and must be signed by the workers' representatives or, if the employer has 20 or fewer workers, by the representatives or by a majority of workers employed by the employer.   *WT Regs 1998 sch.1*

31.1.3   Enforcement

Regulations relating to weekly and night working limits and health assessments are enforced by the Health and Safety Executive [see end of chapter], and those relating to time off, rest breaks and annual leave through employment tribunals.

All workers are protected against detriment for asserting any rights related to the working time regulations. Any dismissal connected with asserting these rights is automatically unfair [**34.7.1**], with no qualifying period.

31.1.4   Record keeping

Adequate records must be kept to show that no worker is working more than 48 hours unless they have opted out from the 48-hour limit [**31.2.2**], that the night work limits [**31.2.4**] are being complied with, and the working time rules for workers under 18 [**31.5.2.1**] are being followed. These records must be kept for at least two years.   *Working Time Regulations 1998 [SI 1998/1833] reg.9*

31.2   HOURS OF WORK

Employers must take all reasonable steps to ensure that workers are not required to work more than an average of 48 hours for each seven-day period, unless they have signed an opt-out [**31.2.3**].   *Working Time Regulations 1998 [SI 1998/1833] reg.4*

31.2.1   Working time

Working time is time when a person is working, is at the employer's disposal, and is carrying out the worker's activities or duties.   *WT Regs 1998 reg.2*

This includes, for example, business lunches, travel time where travel is required as part of the work (but not routine travel between home and work), time worked at home where the employer has agreed beforehand that the work may or must be done at home, training directly related to the worker's job, and time spent working abroad, if the worker works for an employer who is based in the UK. Where there is doubt about what counts as working time, workers (or their representatives) and the employer can agree this.

Working time does not include rest breaks when no work is done, time spent travelling outside normal working time, day release courses, and training that is not job related.

31.2.1.1 On call time

Time when a worker is required to be at a place of work specified by the employer is working time, even if they are sleeping or doing something other than carrying out their duties. This includes sleep-in staff and others who have to be on or in the near vicinity of the employer's premises even when not working, and workers who are provided with living accommodation in order to be on call. Time when workers are on call but are away from the workplace, and thus free to pursue leisure activities, is not working time. *Landeshauptstadt Kiel v Jaeger [2003] EUECJ C-151/02*

EU proposals in 2008 that on call time should be divided into **active** (when carrying out work for the employer) and **inactive**, and that inactive on call time should not count as working hours, were not agreed.

Time when on call but sleeping is **not** working time for the purposes of minimum wage [**30.2.3**].

31.2.1.2 Unmeasured time

The 48-hour limit does not apply to **unmeasured time**, where a worker's time is not measured or predetermined, or where it can be determined by the worker. This applies only to managing executives and others with autonomous decision-making powers, family workers, and workers officiating at religious ceremonies.
Working Time Regulations 1998 [SI 1998/1833] reg.20

31.2.1.3 Voluntary overtime

Another aspect of unmeasured time is where a worker is required or expected to work a stated number of hours or is required to complete a stated amount of work, but voluntarily (or under pressure) works additional hours.

In this case all the hours required by the employer – either explicitly, or implicitly where there would be a likely detriment if the worker did not do the extra hours – count towards working time. Voluntary hours where the worker genuinely works of their own free will, are not counted. *Working Time Regulations 1999 [SI 1999/3372]*

It is good practice for the employer to state explicitly that additional hours are not required and are worked voluntarily. The employer then has a duty to ensure that the work it requires can be done within the obligatory hours. A worker cannot be required to work 'voluntary' hours, and cannot be dismissed or subjected to a detriment for refusing to do so.

Alternatively the worker and employer can agree that the worker will opt out of the 48 hour limit [**31.2.3**]. In this situation, it does not matter whether working time is measured or unmeasured.

31.2.2 Average weekly hours

The **reference period** for computing average weekly working time is generally 17 weeks. Exceptions are where the worker has worked less than 17 weeks, in which case the reference period is the number of weeks they have worked; where a different reference period of up to 52 weeks has been agreed in a collective or workforce agreement [**31.1.2**]; or where the regulations specify that the reference period can be extended to 26 weeks. This includes situations where the work is done at a significant distance from the worker's home so it is advantageous to work longer hours for a short period, to get it done more quickly; where the work is carried out 24 hours a day, as in residential institutions; where there is a foreseeable surge in activity, such as seasonal work; or where the work is affected by an unusual and unforeseeable event. *Working Time Regulations 1998 [SI 1998/1833] regs.4,21*

If a worker has taken statutory annual leave [**31.4.2.1**] or statutory maternity, paternity, adoption or sick leave during the reference period, those days are not included the reference period. Instead, the days the person works immediately after the reference period are counted as part of the period, up to the total number of days' leave during the period. So if a person took five days sick leave during the reference period, the first five days they work after the period count as part of that reference period.

Where a person has worked more than 48 hours per week average during part of a reference period, they are entitled to reduce their hours to bring the total for the period down to 48 hours. *Barber & others v RJB Mining (UK) Ltd [1999] IRLR 308*

31.2.2.1 Record keeping

The employer must keep adequate records to show that workers are not working more than 48 hours per week on average. Where the person's weekly hours are well under 48 and they have no other work, there may be no need to keep detailed records. But if they have not opted out [**31.2.3**] and their hours are close to 48, or if they have other work which counts towards the 48 hours, the employer may need to keep detailed records and monitor working time quite closely.

31.2.2.2 Workers with more than one job

The 48-hour limit applies to the total number of hours worked, so a person who averages 24 hours in one job and 25 in another is exceeding the limit. Each employer has a duty to ensure that workers do not exceed the 48-hour total. This may involve requiring workers to inform the employer if they are doing other work and the average number of hours in that work [**27.8.2**], or each employer may be able to protect itself by asking the worker to sign an opt out agreement [**31.2.3**].

31.2.3 Opt out agreements

An individual worker may agree at any time to opt out of the 48-hour limit, but cannot be forced to do so. The agreement must be in the contract of employment [**27.2.6**] or in another written form. The worker can cancel the agreement at any time by giving at least seven days' notice, or such longer notice period – which can be up to three months – as has been specified in the written agreement. *Working Time Regulations 1998 [SI 1998/1833] reg.5*

The employer must keep records of who has opted out, but does not need to keep detailed records of the hours worked. An opt out agreement covers only the 48-hour limit. It cannot cover other working time rights. *Working Time Regulations 1999 [SI 1999/3372]*

31.2.4 Night work limits

Employers must take all reasonable steps to ensure that the normal hours of work for night workers are not more than eight hours, including overtime, in each 24-hour period, averaged over the reference period [**31.2.2**]. *Working Time Regulations 1998 [SI 1998/1833] reg.6; WT (Amendment) Regulations 2002 [SI 2002/2138] reg.7*

Night time means 11pm to 6am. Another period can be agreed in a collective or workforce agreement [**31.1.2**] or a binding agreement between the employer and an individual worker or workers, provided the agreed period is at least seven hours and includes midnight to 5am. Night workers are any workers whose daily working time includes at least three hours of night time on most of the days they work, or on a proportion of days as agreed in a collective or workforce agreement, or sufficiently often that working such hours is 'normal' for them. *WT Regs 1998 reg.2(1)*

The eight-hour average is not an eight-hour limit. For example, a worker aged 18 or over is allowed to work six days in a week. If their normal night hours are four shifts of 12 hours, they normally have 48 hours of night work per week. 48 hours divided by six days is eight, so they are still within the eight-hour average despite working 12 hours on each shift.

Workers aged under 18 can work at night only in specific circumstances [**31.5**].

All night workers must be offered a free health assessment before they start working nights and on a regular basis, usually annually, while they are working nights [**40.3.2**]. In some situations, night workers may have the right to be transferred to work which is not at night. Employers must keep the assessments as part of their working time records [**31.2.4**].

31.2.4.1 Special hazards

There is an absolute (not average) limit of eight hours per 24 where night work involves special hazards or heavy physical or mental strain. Such work must be identified in a collective or workforce agreement [**31.1.2**] or through a health and safety risk assessment [**40.3.2**].   *Working Time Regulations 1998 [SI 1998/1833] reg.6(7)*

31.2.4.2 Exceptions and compensatory rest

The night work limits do not apply where the worker's time is unmeasured [**31.2.1.2**]; the worker has to work at a significant distance from home, and chooses to work longer hours over fewer days to complete the work more quickly; the worker constantly has to work in different places, making it difficult to work to a set pattern; the work involves security or surveillance to protect property or individuals; the work requires 24-hour staffing, such as hospitals, residential institutions and media; there are busy peak periods, for example over the summer; or there is an emergency or other unforeseeable situation.   *Working Time Regulations 1998 [SI 1998/1833] regs.20, 21*

In these situations – apart from where working time is unmeasured – workers are entitled to **compensatory rest** equal to the rest time they have missed. Total rest weekly time must be at least 90 hours for workers aged 18 or over [**31.3.2**]. Workers under 18 are entitled to more [**31.5**].   *WT Regs 1998 reg.24*

31.2.5 Flexible and annualised hours

Parents of children under 17 or disabled children under 18, and carers of adults have the right to request **flexible working** [**32.5**]. Even where there is no statutory duty for the employer to consider requests for flexible working, it is generally considered good practice to do so as it may help to retain experienced workers.

Flexible working may include working fewer or different hours, allowing **flexitime**, defining the work requirement in terms of monthly or annual hours rather than weekly, working in a different location, or other adaptations to the work pattern that suit both employee and employer.

Flexitime is where, on a contractual or discretionary basis, an employer allows employees to choose their own hours of work. It must be clear whether the time is completely flexible, or there are **core hours** that the person must work.

Some employers, rather than requiring employees to work a specified number of hours per week, require a specified number of hours per month or per year (**annualised hours**). As with ordinary flexitime, it is essential to be clear whether specified times or hours must be worked each workday or week or month, and how annual leave is accrued.

31.2.6 Sunday working

31.2.6.1 Shop workers

Apart from those who are employed to work only on Sundays, shop workers cannot be required to work on Sundays, and have the right not to be dismissed or subject to any detriment for refusing to work on Sundays. The rights are enforced through the employment tribunal.   *Employment Rights Act 1996 ss.36-43*

Where the contract does not require Sunday working, a shop worker who agrees must sign an **opt in agreement**. Where the contract requires Sunday working the shop worker may give the employer a signed and dated **opt out notice**. The opt out does not come into effect until three months after its date. During the notice period the worker must work Sundays if required to do so, and cannot be dismissed or subject to any detriment because of having given an opt out notice.

31.2.6.2 Non-shop workers

Non-shop workers can be required to work on Sundays unless their contract says otherwise. However if an employee asks not to work on Sunday (or any other day) for religious reasons, and the employer unjustifiably refuses, this could constitute religious discrimination [**28.4**].

31.3 REST

31.3.1 Rest breaks

Workers aged 18 and over are entitled to an uninterrupted 20-minute break when the actual (not average) working day is more than six hours. This has to be during the working day, not at the beginning or end, and should be away from the workstation if the worker has one. The break may be paid or unpaid. The entitlement to a rest break may be modified or excluded (removed) by a collective or workforce agreement [**31.1.2**]. The same exceptions and compensatory rest rules apply as to night work [**31.2.4.2**].   *Working Time Regulations 1998 [SI 1998/1833] reg.12*

Workers under age 18 are entitled to longer breaks [**31.5**].

The employer has to ensure workers can take the break and must encourage them to do so, but does not have to make them take it.   *Commission of the European Communities v United Kingdom [2006] EUECJ C-484/04*

Additional breaks may be necessary for health and safety reasons, for example if a worker is engaged in monotonous tasks or computer work [**40.6.2**]. The employer may make these breaks obligatory.

31.3.2 Rest periods

Workers aged 18 and over are entitled to a **daily rest period** of 11 consecutive hours between each working day, and a **weekly rest period** of 24 consecutive hours in each seven-day period, or two 24-hour periods in each 14-day period. Workers under age 18 are entitled to longer rest periods [**31.5**]. The weekly rest period is additional to statutory annual leave entitlement [**31.4.2.1**].   *Working Time Regulations 1998 [SI 1998/1833] regs.10,11*

The rules relating to daily and/or weekly rest periods may be changed or excluded by a workforce or collective agreement [**31.1.2**]. The same exceptions and rules relating to compensatory rest apply as for night work [**31.2.4.2**].

31.3.2.1 Shift workers

The 11-hour daily rest does not apply where a worker changes shifts and it is not possible to take the full 11 hours before the new shift pattern starts, or where a worker's hours are split up over the day and it is not possible to have a break of 11 consecutive hours, for example a cleaner who works mornings and evenings. Such workers are entitled to compensatory rest [**31.2.4.2**].   *WT Regs 1998 reg.22*

31.4 ANNUAL LEAVE AND BANK HOLIDAYS

All workers are entitled to **statutory annual leave**. If the contract provides for more than this, the extra entitlement is **contractual** leave. Employers may need to review contracts with employees and other eligible workers [**25.1.2**] to ensure contractual provision complies with the statutory requirements.

Special rules apply to workers under age 18 [**31.5**].

31.4.1 Record keeping

There is no statutory obligation for the employer to keep annual leave records, but they should be kept for management and personnel purposes, and to be able to show that the employees are taking at least their statutory minimum leave.

31.4.2 Leave entitlement

31.4.2.1 Statutory annual leave

From 1 April 2009 all workers [**25.1.2**] are entitled to 5.6 weeks paid statutory annual leave (28 days for a person who works five days per week). The maximum is 28 days – so a person who works three days a week is entitled to 5.6 x 3 = 16.8 days, but a person who works six days a week is only entitled to 5.6 x 5 = 28 days, not 5.6 x 6.   *Working Time Regulations 1998 [SI 1998/1833] reg.13A, inserted by Working Time (Amendment) Regulations 2007 [SI 2007/2079] reg.2*

Where a worker is contractually entitled to paid time off for bank holidays, these count towards the statutory entitlement unless the contract says they are additional to annual leave [**31.4.2.2**].

Where the normal working week is a specified number of days per week, the statutory annual leave entitlement is 5.6 times that number of days. For part-time workers or where the normal working week is a specified number of hours, it may be easier to specify the annual leave entitlement as 5.6 times the number of weekly hours rather than days. The employer is allowed to round up statutory holiday entitlement to full days, but cannot round down.

Business Link and ACAS [see end of chapter] have guidance on working out entitlement for people who work more or less than five days a week, annualised hours, irregular hours or on a casual basis.

31.4.2.2 Bank holidays

There is no statutory entitlement to bank holidays, but time off equivalent to the eight bank holidays was added in 2007 and 2009 to the original 20 days' statutory annual leave entitlement. These additional days do not have to be given on the actual bank holidays.

At the time of writing (mid 2009) the government was considering adding another bank holiday as a workers' memorial day. This could lead to the statutory annual leave entitlement being increased to 29 days (5.8 weeks).

31.4.2.3 Contractual annual leave and bank holidays

Most voluntary sector employers give contractual entitlement to annual leave and bank holidays. Where there is contractual entitlement to bank holidays, the contract should make clear whether bank holidays are included as part of statutory (or, if greater, contractual) annual leave, or are additional to the statutory or contractual entitlement. The contract should also make clear whether there is any requirement or right to work on bank holidays, and if so any arrangements for ordinary or enhanced time off in lieu [**27.4.1**] or overtime pay.

Contracts need to be carefully reviewed to ensure workers are getting at least the statutory minimum. For example a contract giving four weeks annual leave including bank holidays would not meet the statutory requirement.

Where the contract says employees are entitled to 'statutory annual leave plus bank holidays' this is, from 1 April 2009, 28+8 days (rather than 20+8 or 24+8 days as it might have been when the contract was agreed). This may be more than the employer wishes to give as paid leave, and advice should be taken about amending the contracts. This would require employee consent [**26.9.2**].

31.4.2.4 Part-time workers and bank holidays

Four bank holidays are always on Monday, so where part-time workers are entitled to time off on bank holidays in addition to their annual leave entitlement, those who normally work Mondays will get more days off than those who do not. There is no law requiring all part-time employees to have the same entitlements as each other, but if there are full-time employees who normally work Mondays and get time off for bank holidays, part-time workers who do not work Mondays would be disadvantaged in relation to them. This could be unlawful discrimination on grounds of part-time working [**26.4.2**].

To avoid such discrimination, employers should give all part-time workers comparable time off for bank holidays, regardless of which days of the week they work [see **27.4.1** for a contract clause].

31.4.3 Leave year

The leave year is usually specified in the contract of employment or a collective or workplace agreement [**31.1.2**], or may be agreed between workers and the employer. In the absence of agreement, each leave year for the purposes of statutory annual leave starts on 1 October if the worker started work with the employer on or before 1 October 1998, or on the date the worker started work with the employer if this is after 1 October 1998. *Working Time Regulations 1998 [SI 1998/1833] reg.13(3)*

31.4.3.1   Compulsory leave

The employer can require a worker to take all or part of their **statutory** leave entitlement at specified times, for example on bank holidays or during a Christmas or summer shutdown. The employer must give notice in advance, either by specifying the leave date(s) or period(s) in the contract of employment, or by giving notice of at least twice the period of leave to be taken. For example if the employer is requiring the worker to take one day off, two days' notice must be given. The notice period can be changed through collective or workplace agreements or contractual arrangements [**31.1.2**].   *Working Time Regulations 1998 [SI 1998/1833] reg.15*

The employer can require **contractual** leave to be taken at specific times if the contract allows for this.

31.4.3.2   Carry over

In each leave year, the first four weeks (20 days, for a worker working a five-day week) of **statutory** annual leave are available only for the leave year to which they apply. Untaken leave cannot be carried over into the next leave year, nor is the employee entitled to payment in lieu of leave not taken.
Working Time Regulations 1998 [SI 1998/1833] reg.13

The additional 1.6 weeks (eight days, for a worker working a five-day week) can be carried over only if allowed by the contract of employment, a collective agreement forming part of the contract, or workplace agreement [**31.1.2**].
WT Regs 1998 reg.13A(7), inserted by WT (Amendment) Regulations 2007 [SI 2007/2079] reg.2

However, where a worker is prevented by sickness from taking statutory annual leave during the leave year, it can be carried over to the next year, or in some situations the worker may be entitled to pay in lieu of leave not taken [**31.4.7.1**].

Contractual leave can be carried over or be replaced by pay if the contract allows or the employer and employee agree.

31.4.4   Starting or leaving during the leave year

ACAS and Business Link [see end of chapter] have guidance on calculating statutory entitlement for workers who start or leave during the leave year.

31.4.4.1   Starting during the leave year

Where a worker starts during the leave year, entitlement to **statutory** annual leave is accrued at the beginning of each month, at the rate of 1/12th of the annual entitlement per month. Entitlement to **contractual** annual leave is accrued as specified in the contract.   *Working Time Regulations 1998 [SI 1998/1833] reg.15A, inserted by Working Time (Amendment) Regulations 2001 [SI 2001/3256] reg.4*

31.4.4.2   Leave accrued but not taken when a worker leaves

Where a worker leaves during a leave year, entitlement is proportionate. A worker who leaves during the year is entitled to pay in lieu for **statutory** annual leave not taken, even if dismissed for gross misconduct.   *WT Regs 1998 reg.14*

Pay entitlement for statutory annual leave not taken is worked out as the annual salary divided by the number of working days in the year. For an employee on a five-day week, working days would be worked out as 365 days, minus 104 weekend days, minus 28 days statutory annual leave, minus eight bank holidays if the employee is entitled to them in addition to statutory annual leave.
Leisure Leagues UK Ltd v Maconnachie [2002] UKEAT 940 01 1403

Entitlement to pay in lieu for **contractual** leave not taken depends on the contract. If the contract does not specify how such pay is to be calculated, the formula above should be used, but with annual contractual leave entitlement subtracted from the number of working days.

31.4.4.3   Too much leave taken

Where a worker leaves during the leave year and has already taken more statutory annual leave than he or she is entitled to for that portion of the year, a collective or workforce agreement [**31.1.2**] or the contract of employment may require the worker to 'pay back' the additional time. The agreement or contract may specify that this will be done by working for the relevant amount of time, and/or repaying the employer the value of the additional time taken.

Working Time Regulations 1998 [SI 1998/1833] reg.14(4)

If neither a relevant agreement nor the contract of employment allows the employer to recover payment for annual leave taken but not yet accrued, the employer will not be able to do so.   *Hill v Chapell [2002] UKEAT 1250 01 2003*

Even where an agreement or the contract allows the employer to recover payment for annual leave taken but not accrued, the employer can do this by deduction from pay only if the contract explicitly allows for such a deduction [**30.1.4**].

31.4.5   Holiday pay

For the purposes of statutory annual leave, a week's holiday pay is:

* for a worker with regular hours, pay for the number of hours specified in the contract of employment (excluding overtime, unless the contract requires a minimum amount of overtime to be worked);

* for a worker with variable hours, the average hourly rate of pay multiplied by the average of their normal weekly working hours over the previous 12 weeks;

* for a worker who does not have normal working hours, the average weekly pay received over the previous 12 weeks, excluding weeks with no pay.

31.4.5.1   Pay in lieu of annual leave

Statutory annual leave cannot generally be replaced by pay or extra pay in lieu of leave, except where a worker leaves or is dismissed during the leave year and has not taken all of the leave accrued during the year [**31.4.4**]. Entitlement to pay in lieu of **contractual** leave not taken will depend on provisions in the contract.

31.4.5.2   Rolled up holiday pay

Rolled up holiday pay is where pay for annual leave is included with weekly or monthly pay, rather than being paid while the worker is actually on leave. It is often used where employees work only part of the year, for example only during term time. The **contractual** element of holiday pay, if any, can be rolled up if the contract allows. The **statutory** element of annual leave pay cannot be rolled up, and must be paid while the employee is actually on annual leave.

Robinson-Steele v R D Retail Services Ltd [2006] EUECJ C-257/04

31.4.6   Notice of annual leave

Unless specified otherwise in contracts of employment or a collective or workplace agreement [**31.1.2**], the worker can choose when to take **statutory** annual leave but must give the employer notice of at least twice the amount of leave to be taken – so one day's leave requires two days' notice, three weeks' leave requires six weeks' notice etc. The employer can agree to leave with shorter notice.

Working Time Regulations 1998 [SI 1998/1833] reg.15

The employer can refuse to allow a worker to take the leave requested. Such refusal is called a **counter notice** and must be given within a period equivalent to the period of leave. So if the worker requests one day's leave, a refusal must be given within one day of the worker giving notice; if the worker requests three weeks' leave, a refusal must be given within three weeks of the request.

Alternatively an employer can exclude the worker's right to specify holiday dates for statutory annual leave. This is normally done in the contract of employment, but can be done in a collective or workplace agreement or other binding agreement with the worker. The worker then does not have a right to specify dates, so the employer can simply refuse without having to give counter notice.

For **contractual** leave, the contract should set out the notice that has to be given, and any right of the employer to not to grant leave at the requested time.

31.4.7   Annual leave during long-term absence

The situation with regard to annual leave entitlement during long-term sick leave can be complex, and legal advice should generally be sought. Similar issues may arise in relation to other long-term absence, such as a sabbatical [**31.8.6**].

For accrual of annual leave entitlement during maternity, paternity or adoption leave, see **32.2.4**.

31.4.7.1 Statutory annual leave and sickness absence

The European court of justice ruled in 2009 that **statutory annual leave** [**31.4.2.1**] accrues during sick leave, even if the worker is off for the entire leave year, and even if they are receiving only statutory sick pay or no pay.

The ECJ said that a person who is on sick leave for the entire leave year accrues entitlement to statutory annual leave. Each EU member state can decide whether the leave must be 'taken' during the leave year (with the worker being paid at the end of the leave year for statutory annual leave, even though they are on sick leave), and/or whether the leave can be carried over to the next leave year. At the time of writing (mid 2009), this had not been clarified in the UK and legal advice should be sought.   *Stringer & others v HM Revenue & Customs [2008] EUECJ C-520/06*

Workers who are not paid for annual leave or allowed to carry it forward could be entitled to make a claim not only under the Working Time Regulations but also for unlawful deduction from wages [**30.1.4**].   *Revenue & Customs v Stringer & others [2009] UKHL 31*

The ECJ decision also said a worker who is absent for only part of the leave year but is prevented by sickness from taking their leave during the year is entitled to carry untaken leave forward to the next leave year.

On termination of employment, a worker is entitled to be paid in lieu of accrued statutory annual leave that has not been taken due to sickness absence.

31.4.7.2 Contractual annual leave and sickness absence

Contractual annual leave continues to accrue during sick leave and other long-term leave unless the contract says it does not. Employers may wish to consider revising future contracts to say that contractual annual leave does not accrue during sickness absence or other absence of more than a certain period.

31.5 WORKERS UNDER AGE 18

Specific rules on working time and breaks apply for **school-age workers** (from 13 to **minimum school leaving age**, MSLA), and for **young workers** between MSLA and their 18th birthday. MSLA is the last Friday in June in the academic year in which the young person turns 16.

Health and safety law requires special risk assessments for employees, workers and work experience placements who are under 18 [**40.3.2**], there are restrictions on the types of work they can do [**40.6.1**], and where the worker is under MSLA the employer may have to obtain a work permit from the local authority. Some employment rights are different for under-18s [**26.4.6**].

Some of the rules on school-age and young workers do not apply to young volunteers [**39.4**]. But as the rules are intended to protect children and young people, good practice is generally to apply the rules to young volunteers.

31.5.1 Under minimum school leaving age

31.5.1.1 Hours of work

For **school-age workers**, 13- and 14-year-olds cannot work more than five hours on Saturdays and on weekdays when they are not required to attend school. Young people from 15 to minimum school leaving age cannot work more than eight hours. On Sundays the maximum is two hours for all workers from 13 to school leaving age.   *Children & Young Person's Act 1933 s.18, amended by Children (Protection at Work) Regulations 1998 [SI 1998/276] reg.2*

School-age workers cannot work before 7am or after 7pm on any day. On a day when they are required to attend school, they cannot work during school hours (9.30am-4.30pm, including the lunch break), and cannot work for more than one hour before school starts or more than two hours total. They cannot work more than a total of 12 hours during a week when they are required to attend school.

During school holidays, the maximum 13- and 14-year-olds can work is 25 hours per week. For 15- and 16-year-olds the maximum is 35 hours.

31.5.1.2 Rest breaks and annual leave

Workers between 13 and school leaving age who work more than four hours in any day must have a one-hour rest break. All workers of this age must have each year at least two consecutive weeks' leave during school holidays. *Children & Young Persons Act 1933 s.18(1), inserted by Children (Protection at Work) Regulations 1998 [SI 1998/276] reg.2*

31.5.2 School leaving age to 18

31.5.2.1 Hours of work

For **young workers** between minimum school leaving age and their 18th birthday, there is an absolute (not average) limit of eight hours' work in any day and 40 hours in any week. All employments are added together for these limits. There is an exception where working more than the limits is necessary to maintain continuity of service or production or there is a surge in demand, no adult is available to do the work, and the worker's education or training is not adversely affected. *Working Time Regulations 1998 [SI 1998/1833] regs.5A,27A, inserted by Working Time (Amendment) Regulations 2002 [SI 2002/3128] regs.6,17*

Young workers are not allowed to work during the **restricted period**, which is between 10pm and 6am, or between 11pm and 7am if their contract provides for them to work after 10pm. There are exceptions for work in hospitals or similar workplaces, and for work connected with cultural, artistic, sporting or advertising activities. Further exceptions allow working during the restricted period – but not between midnight and 4am – in certain businesses such as retail trading or bakeries, where work during these hours is necessary to maintain continuity of service or production or there is a surge in demand, no adult is available to do the work, and the worker's education or training is not adversely affected. *WT Regs 1998 regs.2,6A,27A, amended/inserted by WT (Amendment) Regulations 2002 [SI 2002/3128] regs.3,8,17*

31.5.2.2 Rest breaks and leave

Young workers are entitled to a 30-minute rest break when daily working time is more than 4½ hours. If the worker is employed by more than one employer, their total working time for that day is considered when determining whether they are entitled to a rest break. *Working Time Regulations 1998 [SI 1998/1833] reg.12(4),(5)*

Young workers are entitled to a 12-hour rest period in each 24-hour period they work. The 12 hours do not have to be consecutive if periods of work are split up over the day or are short. In addition they entitled to 48 hours' weekly rest in each seven-day period, which cannot be averaged over a fortnight. In some situations, a young worker's weekly rest entitlement can be reduced to 36 hours. *WT Regs 1988 reg.10(2),(3),11*

A young worker's right to daily and weekly rest can be changed or excluded only if there are unusual or unforeseeable circumstances beyond the employer's control, the work to be done by the young worker is temporary and must be done immediately, and there is no adult worker available to do the work. Equivalent time off must be given in the following three weeks. *WT Regs 1998 reg.27*

Annual leave entitlement for young workers is the same as for adults [**31.4.2.1**].

31.5.2.3 Time off for study or training

Employees aged 16 and 17 who are not in full-time secondary or further education and who left school with few or no qualifications must be given reasonable paid **time off for study or training** (TfST). Paid time off must also be given to 18-year-olds who want to complete study or training they began at 16 or 17. *Employment Rights Act 1996 s.63A, inserted by Teaching & Higher Education Act 1998 s.32 & amended by Right to Time Off for Study or Training Regulations 2001 [SI 2001/2801]*

Employers must cover the cost of wages, but government funding is available to help cover the cost of the study or training, and for support costs such as books, equipment, travel or childcare expenses. Information is available from the Department for Children, Schools and Families [end of chapter].

From 2013, many young people between minimum school leaving age and their 17th birthday (18th from 2015) will have to be in full-time education or training, an apprenticeship, or full-time employment which includes training [**26.4.6**].

31.6   SICK LEAVE AND PAY

There is no statutory entitlement to sick leave, so an employer can decide how much to offer in the contract of employment or on a discretionary basis. During sick leave employees are likely to be entitled to **statutory sick pay** [**31.6.1**], and the employer may offer additional contractual sick pay.

Workers on long-term sick leave are entitled to fully paid statutory annual leave even though they are not at work and are not being paid, or are being paid only SSP [**31.4.7**]. During long-term sick leave workers are entitled to contractual sick pay unless the contract says otherwise.

As well as issues around sick pay, employers need to be aware of the duty to make **reasonable adjustments** to enable the worker to continue working [**28.7.4**] if the sickness is or could be a disability under the **Disability Discrimination Act 1995** [**28.7.1**], and issues around dismissing a worker during long-term sick leave or while they are receiving sick pay or benefits under employer-provided permanent health insurance [**34.6.1**].

31.6.1   Statutory sick pay

Most employees and agency workers are entitled to 28 weeks of **statutory sick pay** (SSP) from their employer in each **period of incapacity for work** (PIW) due to illness or injury.

Where the employer pays in any tax month SSP that is more than 13% of the employer's and employees' combined class 1 national insurance contributions [**30.4**] for that month, the SSP can be recovered from HMRC through the **percentage threshold scheme**. If SSP is 13% or less of class 1 NICs for the month, the SSP cannot be recovered.

Employees who are not entitled to SSP must be given form **SSP1**, with which they can claim employment and support allowance at the local Jobcentre Plus.

Information about eligibility, qualifying days, PIWs, SSP rate, recovery from HMRC, linking periods (where one PIW follows within a specified period of another), and what happens when an employee who is still ill is no longer eligible for SSP, is available from HM Revenue and Customs [see end of chapter].

31.6.1.1   SSP during the statutory maternity leave period

A woman cannot receive statutory sick pay during the period she is entitled to statutory maternity pay, even if she has returned to work and is no longer receiving SMP, or even if the sickness is not related to pregnancy or childbirth [**32.2.8**]. She receives SMP instead.

31.6.2   Contractual sick pay

Most voluntary sector employers also give **contractual sick pay**. SSP and incapacity related benefits are assumed to count towards contractual entitlement, but some organisations specify that contractual entitlement is in addition to state benefits. For example, entitlement to half pay would be made up of SSP plus additional pay to bring the total to half pay. This is different from an entitlement to 'SSP or state incapacity related benefits plus half pay'. The statement of particulars or written contract [**26.7, 27.5.2**] must specify sick pay entitlement.

Where the employee receives incapacity benefit or employment and support allowance through the Department for Work and Pensions rather than SSP through the employer, the employee should be contractually required to report this to the employer so the amount can be deducted from any contractual sick pay. Such deduction can be made only if the contract allows for it [**27.5.2**].

31.6.3 Sickness records

Employers must keep records of all periods of sickness lasting four or more consecutive days, even if these are not work days. HMRC's form **SSP2** may be used but does not have to be. SSP records must be kept for at least three years.

The SSP regulations do not specify what proof of incapacity to work must be kept. But the employer needs to be able to prove to HMRC or the Department for Work and Pensions, if required, that every person to whom SSP was paid was genuinely unable to work. It is sensible, but is not legally required, to require employees to provide an employee's statement of sickness (form **SC2**) for any absence lasting four to seven days, and a medical certificate for an absence of more than a week. At the time of writing (mid 2009) it was expected that from spring 2010 medical certificates ('sick notes') would be replaced with **fit notes** emphasising what workers can do and what would enable them to return to work, rather than signing them off as ill for a defined period.

Absence and medical documentation can help ensure the employer has adequate records for personnel purposes, can help the employer determine whether the employee may be entitled to the protection of the **Disability Discrimination Act [28.7]**, and can serve as evidence if the employer has to take disciplinary action [**33.3**] or dismiss for lack of capability through ill health [**34.6.1**].

Sickness records constitute sensitive personal data and must comply with the relevant provisions of the **Data Protection Act [43.3.1]**.

31.6.4 Long-term sickness absence

Where ill health or injury results in frequent or long-term absence from work or makes it difficult for the employee to do the work, the employer should discuss the situation with the employee and take reasonable steps to adapt the work so the employee can do it. This could include, for example, changing the nature of the work or the hours or place of work, or providing training or equipment.

Where there are persistent periods of short absence caused by sickness there may be an underlying medical disorder, and appropriate medical advice should be sought. With long-term absence or short absences caused by a long-term condition, the employer should take reasonable steps to find out the true medical position, generally by obtaining a medical report [**29.6.2**].

If the condition constitutes a disability under the **Disability Discrimination Act 1995 [28.7.1]**, the employer has a statutory duty to make reasonable adjustments to the job or provide suitable alternative work [**28.7.4**].

The National Institute for Health and Clinical Excellence (NICE) [see end of chapter] has guidance, including a checklist, on dealing with long-term sickness absence (which it defines as lasting four weeks or more) or a number of absences each lasting less than four weeks.

31.7 TIME OFF FOR PUBLIC SERVICE

31.7.1 Public duties

Employees have a statutory right to time off, which may be paid or unpaid, for public duties. This right covers duties as a justice of the peace, or as a member of a local authority, relevant health body, relevant education body (including school governing bodies), statutory tribunal, prison independent monitoring board or visiting committee, national park authority, police authority, water customer consultation panel, or the Environment Agency.   *Employment Rights Act 1996 s.50, as amended*

At the time of writing (mid 2009) the Department for Communities and Local Government had consulted on whether the right to time off should be extended to members of probation boards, court boards, youth offender panels and probation trust boards; lay advisors for multi-agency public protection arrangements; and co-opted overview and scrutiny committee members. CLG was also looking at whether board members of registered social landlords, and tenant management and arm's length management organisations should be included.

Under this right, the employer must give reasonable time off to attend meetings of the body and its committees, or to perform duties approved by the body. The time off must be reasonable for the duties involved and the employer's needs. Disputes are settled by the employment tribunal.

The employer may give a right to pay for such time off [**27.5.4**] contractually or on a discretionary case by case basis, or require the time to be unpaid. If the employer gives paid time off it may want to limit the number of paid hours or days.

The employer and employee should be clear what happens to attendance allowances and other payments received by the employee from the outside body. Good practice is to have a contractual requirement for these to be reported to the employer, with provision for the employer to deduct the amount from wages due to the employee for the period.

31.7.2 Jury service

There is no statutory right to time off for jury service, but an employer's failure to allow an employee time off could be contempt of court.

It is unlawful to subject employees to a detriment because they have been called for or been absent on jury service. 'Detriment' in this context does not include failure to pay wages while the employee is on jury service, unless there is a contractual entitlement to pay. *Employment Rights Act 1996 s.43M,. inserted by Employment Relations Act 2004 s.40(1),(2)*

Where an employee's absence on jury service could cause substantial harm to the organisation, the employer should explain this to the employee and require the employee to apply to be excused from jury service or have it deferred. Dismissal because an employee has been called for or been absent on jury service is automatically unfair, but not if the employer has required the employee to apply for excusal or deferral and the employee has refused or failed to do so. *Employment Rights Act 1996 s.108(3), inserted by Employment Relations Act 2004 s.40(4),(6)*

31.7.3 Military service

Where an employee who is a member of the reserve forces is called up for service, the employer is entitled to financial awards to cover costs including recruiting and training a replacement, and retraining the reservist when he or she returns to work. *Reserve Forces (Call-out & Recall) (Financial Assistance) Regulations 2005 [SI 2005/859] regs.6,7*

Where the organisation would be seriously harmed by the employee's absence, the employer can apply, within seven days of the employee being served with a call-up notice, for the notice to be deferred or revoked. Details of how to apply are included in a letter for employers included with the employee's call-up papers, and are also publicised in the media at times of mobilisation. *Reserve Forces (Call-out & Recall) (Exemptions Etc) Regulations 1997 [SI 1997/307]*

Regardless of the length of military service, reservists who apply to return to work must be offered the same occupation on terms and conditions no less favourable than they would be entitled to if they had not done military service. If this is not reasonable and practicable, the reservist must be offered 'the most favourable occupation and on the most favourable terms and conditions which are reasonable and practicable'. *Reserve Forces (Safeguard of Employment) Act 1985 s.1*

Employees who are re-employed after military service have a **protected period** of employment of between 13 and 52 weeks depending on long the person was employed by the employer prior to call-up. During this period they can be dismissed only if it becomes unreasonable or impractical for the employer to continue to employ them on the same terms. *Reserve Forces (Safeguard of Employment) Act 1985 s.7*

Information is available from **SaBRE** [see end of chapter].

31.7.4 Volunteering

There is no statutory obligation to provide time off, paid or unpaid, to enable employees to volunteer, unless it is to carry out a specified public duty [**31.7.1**]. At the time of writing (mid 2009) the Department for Communities and Local Government had consulted on ways to encourage participation in voluntary sector boards, but did not intend to give a statutory right to time off for this.

Some employers organise volunteering opportunities, such as a team spending a weekend decorating a community centre. Issues such as health and safety and insurance must be carefully considered, and the employer must ensure that opportunities to participate do not have the effect of discriminating unlawfully against some employees [28.1.4].

31.8   OTHER TYPES OF TIME OFF AND LEAVE

Other types of time off or leave may be available to some or all workers on a statutory, contractual or **discretionary** basis.

Where a contractual right to leave is available to some employees but not others, this could lead to claims of indirect discrimination [28.1.4] if the people entitled to it are disproportionately of one protected group [28.1.1] compared with staff who are not entitled. Similarly, a policy which leaves decisions about time off or leave to the discretion of management could lead to discrimination claims, if people in one protected group are allowed to have time off and others are not.

Staff leave policies should make clear, where applicable, who makes the decision about whether leave can be taken, the duration, and whether it will be paid or unpaid. For long-term leave such as career breaks, legal implications about continuity of employment and similar issues must be considered [31.8.6].

31.8.1   Duties as a trade union or employee representative

There is a statutory entitlement to time off for trade union duties [36.4.2] and certain other duties as a representative of a trade union or an elected employee representative [36.4.3].

31.8.2   Study and training

Except for 16 and 17 year olds [31.5.2.3], there is no statutory right to time off for study or training.

However, at the time of writing (mid 2009), the government had proposed a new statutory right, expected to come into force in 2010, allowing employees to request time off for training that would benefit them and the employer. It was proposed that this new right, called **time to train**, would be similar to the right to request flexible working [32.5], that the time off would not have to be paid if the training is 'off the job' (as opposed to on the job), and that employers would not be obliged to contribute to the cost of the training. The right would only apply to employees with more than 26 weeks' continuous service with the employer.

31.8.3   Fertility treatment

If an employee undergoing fertility treatment has a medical certificate saying she is unfit for work, she is entitled to statutory and contractual sick leave and pay in the same way as for sickness [31.6]. In the absence of a medical certificate, she is entitled to sick leave and pay only if the contract includes provision for this, or if the employer offers her paid or unpaid sick leave on a discretionary basis.

If sick leave or leave specifically for fertility treatment is not available, the employee will have to take the time off as annual leave, or the employer may allow compassionate [31.8.5] or discretionary leave on a paid or unpaid basis.

Women who are undergoing IVF but have not yet had an egg or eggs implanted do not have the same employment rights as pregnant women [28.3]. However, dismissal related to her IVF treatment or being treated less favourably for a reason connected with IVF treatment is discriminatory on the basis of sex, because only women undergo the treatment.   *Mayr v Backerei und Konditorei Gerhard Flockner OHG*
[2008] EUECJ C-506/06

At the time of writing (mid 2009) it was unclear whether the woman gains protection under the EU pregnant workers directive as soon as the eggs are implanted, or only when she becomes pregnant. But in the above case, the European court of justice said a woman undergoing IVF should be treated as pregnant at 'the earliest possible date'.

31.8.4 Elective and cosmetic surgery

Where an employee chooses to have surgery or medical treatment for personal rather than medical reasons, the same rules on sick leave and sick pay apply as for fertility treatment [**31.8.3**].

It is important to distinguish between cosmetic surgery for personal reasons, and plastic surgery required for medical reasons or to correct a disfigurement as defined under the **Disability Discrimination Act 1995** [**28.7.1**]. It could be a breach of the DDA to refuse to allow paid time off for medically required plastic surgery or surgery for a disfigurement [**28.7.4**].

31.8.5 Compassionate leave

There is no statutory right to time off for bereavement or similar situations, but if the situation involves a person dependent on the employee, the employee may be entitled to the statutory **leave for dependant emergencies** [**32.8**]. In other cases, the contract may include provision for **compassionate leave** on a paid or unpaid basis, or the employer may allow discretionary leave. The contract or the organisation's policies must be clear about who can authorise compassionate leave, and who can decide whether it is paid, unpaid or a combination.

31.8.6 Sabbaticals and career breaks

A sabbatical, career break or 'grown up gap year' is a break from work, usually for at least three months, offered to employees who have worked for a specified period. If the qualifying period is more than five years, these breaks could be age discriminatory unless they fulfil a legitimate business need [**28.0.2**].

Career breaks are often offered only to senior managers, which could lead to claims of indirect discrimination [**31.8**].

A career break policy should make clear the qualifying period, the maximum duration of the break, whether all or some of the break is paid and the rate of pay, what happens with employee benefits such as pensions or a company car, whether the employee has the right to return to the same job on the same terms and conditions or whether there are circumstances where it might be a different job or different conditions, and how much notice has to be given if the employee decides not to return.

Legal advice will be needed about whether the employee's contract remains in place during the break, or the employee resigns with a legally binding promise of re-engagement at the end of the break. Advice is also needed on how to protect statutory rights dependent on length of service [**26.4**].

Resources: WORKING TIME, TIME OFF AND LEAVE

ACAS, BIS, Business Link, CIPD, Directgov, PEACe, TUC: see end of **chapter 25**.

Children and young people as workers. Local authority education department.

Children's Legal Centre: www.childrenslegalcentre.com, 01206 872466, clc@essex.ac.uk.

Department for Children, Schools and Families: www.dcsf.gov.uk, 0870 000 2288, info@dcsf.gsi.gov.uk.

Reservists. SaBRE: www.sabre.mod.uk, 0800 389 5459, email via website.

Sickness absence. National Institute for Health & Clinical Excellence: www.nice.org.uk, 0845 003 7780, nice@nice.org.uk.

Statutory sick pay. HM Revenue & Customs: www.hmrc.gov.uk, 08457 143 143, email via website.

Time off for public duties. Department for Communities and Local Government: www.communities.gov.uk, 020 7944 4400, contactus@communities.gov.uk.

Working time. Health and Safety Executive: www.hse.gov.uk, 0845 345 0055, hse.infoline@natbrit.com.

Statute law. www.opsi.gov.uk and www.statutelaw.gov.uk.

Much but not all case law. www.bailii.org.

Updates cross-referenced to this book. www.rclh.co.uk.

Chapter 32
RIGHTS OF PARENTS AND CARERS

32.1 STATUTORY RIGHTS

Information about statutory maternity, paternity and adoption pay is available from HM Revenue and Customs, and about parents' and carers' other statutory rights from the Department for Business, Innovation and Skills, Business Link, ACAS and the Trades Union Congress [see end of chapter].

32.1.1 Eligibility

Only employees [**25.1.1**] are entitled to the statutory rights of parents and carers. This includes part-time, fixed-term, temporary and sessional employees, but does not include others who are legally defined as 'workers' [**25.1.2**].

32.1.2 Statutory v contractual rights

Statutory rights do not need to be set out in the contract of employment, and if they are included, advice should be taken to ensure they are summarised accurately. Rather than summarising the rights, it is generally better just to say the employee is entitled to statutory rights in force at the time [**27.5.3**].

Many voluntary sector employers have **contractual** provisions for parents and carers which are different from the statutory rights. These do need to be clearly set out in the contract. Where contractual and statutory provisions differ, the employee may take advantage of whichever is more favourable to him or her.

32.1.3   Detriment and dismissal

It is unlawful to subject an employee to a detriment and is automatically unfair [**34.7.1**] to dismiss them because they have taken or sought to take maternity, paternity, adoption, parental or dependants' leave, or have requested the right to work flexibly, or because the employee is or would become entitled to maternity, paternity or adoption pay.

If the detriment or dismissal relates to pregnancy or childbirth, it is automatically sex discrimination on the basis of pregnancy [**28.3**]. It can also be sex discrimination to treat a man less favourably than a woman would be treated, for example to deny flexible working to a male parent or carer when it would be given to a woman in the same or a comparable situation.

The detriment does not have to be deliberate. In a case where an employer did not notify a woman on maternity leave about a job vacancy, the employment appeal tribunal found that the woman had suffered a detriment and therefore sex discrimination – even though she might not have had the necessary experience to apply for the job. This case illustrates the importance of thinking very widely about what could constitute a detriment or pregnancy discrimination.

Visa International Service Association v Paul [2003] UKEAT 0097 02 2005

32.1.3.1   Right to written reasons for dismissal

An employee who is dismissed for any reason or made redundant while pregnant, on maternity leave or on adoption leave must be given a written notice of the reasons for dismissal. The same will apply to additional paternity leave [**32.3.3**] when it becomes available.

Employment Rights Act 1996 s.92(4),(4A), amended by Employment Act 2002 sch 7 para 31

32.1.3.2   Dismissal related to pregnancy, childbirth or adoption

Dismissal solely or mainly because of pregnancy or adoption is nearly always automatically unfair [**34.7.1**]. An exception is if it is not reasonably practicable for the employee to return to their old job after additional maternity or adoption leave for a reason other than redundancy, and they have been offered another suitable job and refused it [**32.2.4.10**].

A dismissal during pregnancy is not unfair if the employer did not know, and had no reason to believe, the employee was pregnant.

Ramdoolar v Bycity Ltd [2004] UKEAT 0236 04 3007

An employee can be dismissed during pregnancy or maternity/adoption leave if the reason is, and can be shown to be, totally unconnected with the pregnancy or adoption. Similarly, the employee can be made redundant if this is unconnected with the pregnancy or adoption and there was no suitable alternative work on terms and conditions that were not substantially less favourable to the employee. To avoid the risk of an unfair dismissal and/or sex discrimination claim, legal advice should always be taken before dismissing or making an employee redundant while they are pregnant or on maternity or adoption leave.

Even if a dismissal takes place several months after the pregnancy, maternity leave or adoption leave ended, it can be unfair if the reason is related to the pregnancy or adoption, for example dismissal because of absence or incapability arising from post-natal depression. Legal advice should be taken before dismissing, or undertaking disciplinary action which could lead to dismissal, in this situation.

Similar rules are likely to apply to employees on additional paternity leave [**32.3.3**] when this becomes available.

32.2   MATERNITY ENTITLEMENTS

It is important to be clear about the distinction between **statutory** and **contractual** rights, and not to confuse them.

32.2.1   Time off for ante-natal appointments

All pregnant women have a statutory right to paid time off for ante-natal care attended on the advice of a registered medical practitioner, midwife or nurse registered as a health visitor. This includes medical appointments, relaxation classes, parentcraft classes and other recognised care. *Employment Rights Act 1996 ss.55,56*

Except in the case of the first medical appointment, an employer who requests it must be shown a certificate from the doctor, midwife or nurse confirming the pregnancy, and/or an appointment card or other evidence of the appointment.

The right to time off for ante-natal care does not include time off for fertility treatment [**31.8.3**].

Fathers or partners are not entitled to time off for ante-natal appointments, but it is good practice for employers to allow them to take paid time off or to make up the time. The employer can ask for evidence of the appointment.

32.2.2 Dates for statutory maternity leave and pay

Statutory maternity provisions involve a number of different dates, and both the employer and employee must know what needs to be done, and when.

32.2.2.1 Dates based on EWC

Eligibility dates are based on the **expected week of childbirth** (**EWC** – sometimes still called **expected week of confinement**). For these purposes a week always starts at midnight between Saturday and Sunday. The main dates are:

- end of the 16th week before EWC (24th week of pregnancy): a stillbirth after the end of this week gives the woman full maternity entitlement (a live birth gives full entitlement at any time);
- into the 15th week before EWC (25th week of pregnancy): qualifying date for entitlement to statutory maternity pay [**32.2.6**];
- end of the 15th week before EWC: date by which employee must notify employer that she is pregnant, EWC and when she intends to start maternity leave [**32.2.4.1**];
- last payday before the end of the 15th week before EWC: end of the eight-week reference period for determining average weekly earnings, for statutory maternity pay [**32.2.6.3**];
- at least four weeks (28 days) before the woman intends to start maternity leave: date by which the employee must notify employer of when she intends to start maternity leave, if different from the date given above;
- beginning of the 11th week before EWC (29th week of pregnancy): the earliest that the woman can start statutory maternity leave and maternity pay unless the baby is born earlier;
- beginning of the fourth week before EWC (36th week of pregnancy): maternity leave automatically starts if the woman is absent for one day or more for a pregnancy related reason.

32.2.2.2 Dates based on the date of birth

Ordinary maternity leave always starts, if it has not already, on the day after the birth. The compulsory maternity leave period [**32.2.3**] starts the day after the birth.

32.2.2.3 Dates based on start of maternity leave

The latest that a woman can return from ordinary maternity leave [**32.2.4**] is the first day after 26 weeks of maternity leave, unless the baby was born less than two weeks before. The latest date that a woman can return from additional maternity leave is the first day after 52 weeks of maternity leave.

32.2.2.4 Qualifying period

There is no qualifying period for entitlement to ordinary and additional maternity leave. But to be entitled to statutory maternity pay [**32.2.6**], the employee must have at least 26 weeks of continuous employment [**26.5**] up to the end of the 15th week before the expected week of childbirth.

32.2.3 Compulsory maternity leave

The **compulsory maternity leave** period is the two weeks after the date of the birth (four weeks for factory workers), during which a woman is not allowed to return to work and is not allowed to carry out any work for the employer, even from home. It is an offence for an employer to require an employee to work during the compulsory leave period.

Maternity & Parental Leave etc Regulations 1999
[SI 1999/3312] reg.8; Public Health Act 1936 s.205

32.2.4 Statutory maternity leave

There are two types of **statutory maternity leave**: ordinary maternity leave (OML) and additional maternity leave (AML). There is no qualifying period of employment, and all pregnant employees are entitled to both. **Ordinary maternity leave** is 26 weeks from the day it began, or until two weeks after the birth if this is later than the 26 weeks. **Additional maternity leave** (AML) lasts for 26 weeks from the end of ordinary maternity leave.

Maternity & Parental Leave etc
Regulations 1999 [SI 1999/3312] regs.6(3),7 amended by MPL (Amendment) Regulations 2002 [SI 2002/2789]
reg.8(a),(b), & MPL etc & Paternity & Adoption Leave (Amendment) Regulations 2008 [SI 2008/1966] regs.4-7

32.2.4.1 Notice of pregnancy and leave

No later than the end of the 15th week before the expected week of childbirth, or as soon as reasonably practicable thereafter, the woman must notify the employer that she is pregnant, the expected week of childbirth, and the date she intends to start her ordinary maternity leave. The proposed start date cannot be earlier than the beginning of the 11th week before the EWC. The employer may, but does not have to, require this notice to be in writing. The employer must require the woman to provide written confirmation of the EWC (form **Mat B1**) from a registered medical practitioner or midwife to prove eligibility for statutory maternity pay [**32.2.6.1**], and may ask for it even if the woman is not eligible for SMP.

MPL Regs 1999 reg.4(1),(2), amended by MPL Regs 2002 reg.5(a)

The woman can change the date she intends to start ordinary maternity leave by giving the employer notice, in writing if required, at least 28 days before the date that is being changed or the new date, whichever is earlier. If 28 days' notice is not possible, notice must be given as soon as reasonably practicable.

MPL Regs 2002 reg.5(b)

32.2.4.2 Start of leave

Ordinary maternity leave starts on the start date notified by the employee to the employer [above], or the day after the date of the birth if it has not already started by then, or the day after the woman is absent for one day for a pregnancy related reason after the beginning of the fourth week before the EWC.

MPL Regs 1999 reg.6, amended by MPL Regs 2002 reg.7

Where OML starts on a date other than the one notified to the employer, the employee must notify the employer as soon as reasonably practicable that she has given birth or been absent for a pregnancy related reason. A woman who fails to notify the employer loses her entitlement to statutory maternity leave.

MPL Regs 1999 reg.4(3),(4), amended by MPL Regs 2002 reg.5(d),(e)

32.2.4.3 Notification of end of leave period

When an employer is notified that an employee intends to take ordinary maternity leave or that OML has started because of the birth or a pregnancy related absence, the employer must give the employee notice of when her additional maternity leave period will end. This notice must be given within 28 days of the employer receiving the employee's notice. If the employee gave notice of when she intended to start OML but then changed that date, the employer's notice of when AML will end must be given within 28 days of the OML period starting.

MPL Regs 1999 reg.7(6), inserted by MPL Regs 2002 reg.8(c) & amended by MPL etc
& Paternity & Adoption Leave (Amendment) Regulations 2006 [SI 2006/2014] reg.7

32.2.4.4 Rights during maternity leave

All **statutory** rights continue during ordinary and additional maternity leave, other than the right to receive wages or salary. **Contractual** rights and obligations also continue – including, for example, health insurance, private use of a company car or mobile phone, gym membership, non-cash vouchers such as childcare vouchers which can only be used by the employee, or accrual of annual leave entitlement above the statutory entitlement [**31.4.2**]. Benefits provided *solely* for business use, such as a fuel card provided only for business use, do not have to be continued during maternity leave. Seniority rights continue during maternity leave.   *Employment Rights Act 1996 s.71, amended by Maternity & Paternity Leave (Amendment) Regulations 2002 [SI 2002/2789] reg.9; MPL etc Regulations 1999 [SI 1999/3312] reg.17, amended by MPL Regs etc & Paternity & Adoption Leave (Amendment) Regulations 2008 [SI 2008/1966] reg.4*

At the time of writing (mid 2009), guidance from HM Revenue and Customs was that only non-cash contractual benefits – such as those listed in the paragraph above – continue during maternity leave. However, the guidance was not legally binding and there was considerable legal disagreement about whether cash benefits also had to continue during maternity leave. An employer who wishes to stop any benefits when a woman starts maternity leave should take advice.

32.2.4.5   Pension rights during maternity leave

An employee who is receiving statutory or contractual maternity pay must continue to pay contributions to occupational pension schemes, personal and stakeholder pensions [**30.6**], based on the actual maternity pay received.

For occupational pensions, and for personal pensions where the employer normally contributes, the employer must continue to contribute based on the pay the employee would have received if she were not on maternity leave, including any pay increases. The employer may be obliged to pay contributions during the entire maternity leave period even if there is no maternity pay [**32.2.4.4**].
Social Security Act 1989 sch.5 para.5

At the time of writing (mid 2009), guidance from the Department for Business, Innovation and Skills was that employers have to make pension contributions only while the woman is receiving maternity pay. As with the HMRC guidance [above] this was not legally binding and there was legal uncertainty about this, so advice should be taken before stopping employer pension contributions.

Some occupational schemes, and all personal pensions, allow employees to make up contributions missed during unpaid leave. Some employers have contractual provisions under which they make up contributions if the employee remains employed or in an occupational scheme for a specified period after maternity leave.

The Pensions Advisory Service [see end of chapter] provides detailed information on pension rights during maternity leave.

32.2.4.6   Salary sacrifice schemes

Schemes where an employee gives up part of her salary in return for other benefits – most commonly childcare vouchers – can have an impact on the amount of maternity pay during the first six weeks [**32.2.6.3**].

The vouchers (or whatever salary has been sacrificed for) are non-cash benefits and must continue throughout maternity leave, even if the woman is not receiving any maternity pay and therefore has no salary to sacrifice. Guidance on salary sacrifice is available from HM Revenue and Customs [see end of chapter].

32.2.4.7   Accruing annual leave during maternity leave

Statutory and contractual annual leave [**31.4.2**] accrues during ordinary and additional maternity leave. At the time of writing (mid 2009) it was unclear whether the European court of justice decision [**31.4.7**] on carrying forward statutory annual leave that cannot be taken because an employee is on long-term sick leave will also apply to employees who are on maternity leave. In addition, where a woman has been unable to take her statutory annual leave in the appropriate year due to maternity leave, a refusal to allow her to take this leave on her return may amount to unlawful discrimination. Advice should be taken before denying statutory or contractual annual leave to an employee in this situation.

32.2.4.8   Keeping in touch during maternity leave

During maternity leave an employee may, if she and the employer agree, work for the employer for up to 10 **keeping in touch** (KIT) **days** without affecting her right to statutory maternity leave or pay. A KIT day could be used to carry out work, attend meetings or training, or any other purpose under her contract of employment. *Maternity & Parental Leave etc Regulations 1999 [SI 1999/3312] reg.12A, inserted by MPL Regs etc & Paternity & Adoption Leave (Amendment) Regulations 2006 [SI 2006/2014] reg.9*

The employer does not have to offer KIT days, and if offered the employee does not have to accept them. It is unlawful for the employer to subject the employee to a detriment if she takes part or refuses to take part in a KIT day, and a dismissal on this basis is automatically unfair. KIT days do not extend the maternity leave period, and cannot be taken during the two weeks after the birth.

Even if only part of a day involves work or training etc for the employer, it counts as a full day for KIT purposes. The regulations do not indicate how much the employee should be paid for KIT days, but government guidance is that she is entitled to be paid as under her contract of employment. The employer must ensure that she is not paid less than a man, or a woman who is not on maternity leave, would be paid for comparable work [**28.8**]. To avoid the risk of an equal pay or discrimination claim, it is advisable to pay the employee for a full day even if she only works for part of the day. HMRC guidance is that appropriate pension contributions should be made where an employee is paid for a KIT day.

Employers and employees have a statutory right to make reasonable contact with each other during maternity leave, for example to discuss returning to work. The employer and employee should agree beforehand what sort of contact the employee wants, for example whether she wants to be notified of workplace changes or training opportunities. *MPL Regs 1999 reg.12A(4), inserted by MPL & PAL Regs 2006 reg.9*

32.2.4.9 Notice of return

An employee who intends to return to work at the end of the additional maternity leave (AML) period as notified by the employer [**32.2.4.3**] does not need to notify the employer of her intention to return, although it is good practice to do so.

If she wants to return earlier than the end of AML, she must give the employer eight weeks' notice, calculated backwards from the proposed return date. Having given this notice, she can subsequently change it, provided there is at least eight weeks' notice of the new return date. The employer can agree to accept less than eight weeks' notice. *Maternity & Parental Leave etc Regulations 1999 [SI 1999/3312] reg.11, amended by MPL Regs etc & Paternity & Adoption Leave (Amendment) Regulations 2006 [SI 2006/2014] reg.8*

If the employee returns to work before the end of AML without giving eight weeks' notice, the employer can require her to remain away from work for eight weeks or until the end of AML, whichever is sooner. If the woman insists on returning to work, the employer does not have to pay her until the notice period or AML would have ended.

The employee does not physically have to return at the end of AML if she has notified the employer that she will be taking another leave to which she is entitled, such as parental leave, sick leave or annual leave, immediately after AML.

An employee who decides not to return must resign in the usual way [**34.3**]. Her contract may require her to return some or all contractual (but not statutory) maternity pay if she does not return or stay for a specified period [**32.2.7**].

Even if a woman gives notice early on in her maternity leave that she does not intend to return at the end of it, she continues to accrue annual leave [**32.2.4.7**], and remains entitled to pension contributions [**32.2.4.5**] and other contractual benefits until the employment actually ends.

32.2.4.10 Rights on return after maternity leave

After ordinary or additional maternity leave the woman has the right to return to the same job on the same pay and conditions as when she left, unless a redundancy situation has arisen [**32.1.3.2**]. If after AML there is a reason other than redundancy why the employer cannot offer the same job, she must be offered another job which is suitable and appropriate for her. If during leave she would have become entitled to an automatic pay increment or any other new rights during the time she was away, she is entitled to them as if she had never been on leave. *MPL Regs 1999 reg.18, amended by MPL (Amendment) Regulations 2002 [SI 2002/2789] reg.12*

32.2.4.11 Part-time working on return

There is no statutory right to work part-time. But any employee with childcare or carer responsibilities can request reduced hours or other flexible work arrangements, and the employer can refuse the request only if there is a legitimate business reason for doing so [**32.5**, **32.6**]. If an employer refuses, without objective justification, to allow a woman to reduce her hours, the woman may be able to bring a claim of pregnancy discrimination or sex discrimination.

32.2.4.12 Extending leave

An employee who extends ordinary maternity leave with four weeks or less parental leave [**32.7**], then returns to work without taking any additional maternity leave, has the same rights on return as if she had returned immediately after OML. An employee who extends OML with more than four weeks' parental leave, or extends AML, has the same rights as if she had returned after AML [**32.2.4.10**]. *Maternity & Parental Leave etc Regulations 1999 [SI 1999/3312] reg.18, amended by MPL (Amendment) Regulations 2002 [SI 2002/2789] reg.12*

Taking annual leave or sick leave at the end of OML or AML does not affect the employee's rights.

If the woman is unable to return at the end of AML because of sickness, the employer's usual sick leave rules apply [**31.6**]. But because of the possibility of a sex discrimination claim [**28.3**], legal advice should be sought before dismissing for sickness in these circumstances. There is no entitlement to statutory sick pay while she is or could be receiving statutory maternity pay [**32.2.8**].

32.2.5 Contractual maternity leave

Now that all new mothers are entitled to one year's maternity leave, few employers give additional entitlement. Where it is given, all statutory rights continue but it is important to be clear which contractual rights do and do not continue.

32.2.6 Statutory maternity pay

Most pregnant employees are entitled to **statutory maternity pay** (SMP) via their employer. Those who are not are normally entitled to **maternity allowance** via Jobcentre Plus. Information about SMP is available from HM Revenue and Customs [see end of chapter], and about maternity allowance from the Department for Work and Pensions.

If an employer has a contractual obligation to pay more than statutory entitlements, SMP or maternity allowance makes up part of this payment. Only the SMP part of the payment can be recovered from HMRC [**32.2.6.4**].

32.2.6.1 Eligibility for SMP

The qualifying week for SMP is the 15th week before the expected week of childbirth (EWC). A week runs from Sunday to Saturday. To be eligible for SMP, a pregnant woman must:

- have continuous employment [**26.5**] of at least 26 weeks continuing into the qualifying week;
- have average weekly earnings of not less than the national insurance lower earnings limit [**30.4.6**] for the **reference period**, the eight weeks up to and including the qualifying week;
- still be pregnant at the beginning of the 11th week before the EWC, or have had the baby by then;
- provide form **Mat B1** or similar confirmation of pregnancy from a registered medical practitioner or midwife;
- comply with the statutory requirements for notifying her employer of her pregnancy and the date she intends to start ordinary maternity leave [**32.2.4.1**]; and
- not be working for the employer.

'Must not be working for the employer' means that the woman must:

- be on leave, even if the leave is for sickness or another reason unconnected with the pregnancy, except as allowed on a KIT day [**32.2.4.8**];

- have resigned after the beginning of the qualifying week for a reason wholly or partly connected with her pregnancy; or

- have been dismissed by the employer or had her employment terminated without her consent, for example by redundancy, after the beginning of the 15th week before the EWC. *Contributions & Benefits Act 1992 s.164(2), amended by Statutory Maternity Pay (General) (Modification & Amendment) Regulations 2000 [SI 2000/2883]*

Provided she meets all the necessary requirements, the woman is entitled to statutory maternity pay from the employer even if she gives notice that she does not intend to return to work. If she is not entitled to SMP she should be given form **SMP1** so she can claim maternity allowance from Jobcentre Plus.

32.2.6.2 SMP period

SMP cannot start until the beginning of the 11th week before the expected week of childbirth unless the baby is born before then. If the woman wants to continue working past the 11th week, SMP can be postponed until the birth. Maternity leave and the SMP period automatically start on the day after the birth, or on the day after any day she is absent from work for a pregnancy related reason during the four weeks before the expected week of childbirth [**32.2.4.2**].

SMP is payable for 39 weeks. At the time of writing (mid 2009) the government was committed to extending SMP to 52 weeks, but no date had been set.

SMP is payable only for weeks when the woman does no work at all for the **liable employer**, unless the work is on a KIT day [**32.2.4.8**]. If the woman works for another employer before the birth, the liable employer remains liable for her SMP. If she works for another employer after the birth, the liable employer's liability for SMP ends. If she returns to work, for either the liable employer or another employer, before the end of the SMP period, she no longer receives SMP (unless the return is only for a KIT day for the liable employer).

SMP remains payable even if the child is stillborn or dies after birth.

32.2.6.3 SMP amount

SMP is paid at the **higher rate** for the first six weeks of maternity leave, then the **lower rate** for the remaining 33 weeks. The higher rate is 90% of the woman's normal weekly earnings during the **reference period**, the eight weeks up to and including the last payday before the end of the 15th week before the expected week of childbirth. The lower rate is a flat rate set each year by the government (available from HM Revenue and Customs) or 90% of the woman's normal weekly earnings during the reference period, whichever is lower.

Where an employee receives non-cash benefits such as childcare vouchers, gym membership or a car and gives up part of salary in return (a **salary sacrifice scheme**) this can affect her SMP entitlement, because her salary is lower than it would otherwise have been. HM Revenue and Customs has detailed guidance on the impact of salary sacrifices on maternity entitlement.

If a pay increase is awarded at any time from the beginning of the reference period to the end of maternity leave, the employee's normal weekly earnings must be recalculated and any SMP arrears must be paid to her. For most women this will mean that earnings related SMP (90% of average earnings) will have to be recalculated. *Statutory Maternity Pay (General) Regulations 1986 [SI 1986/1960] reg.21, amended by the SMP (General) (Amendment) Regulations 2005 [SI 2005/729] reg.3*

SMP is subject to tax and national insurance in the usual way. It can be paid in a lump sum, but this could create problems if the woman becomes ineligible for SMP, for example because of working for another employer after the birth.

32.2.6.4 Recovering SMP

The employer can recover SMP from HMRC by deducting the relevant amount from its PAYE payments. If the employer would have difficulties paying SMP, it can ask HMRC for funding in advance.

The amount which can be recovered is generally 92% of the gross (pre-tax and NI) SMP paid to the employee (tax year 2009-10). However an employer can claim 104.5% of the SMP if it qualifies for **small employer's relief** (SER). SER is available if the employer paid, or was liable to pay, £45,000 or less (tax year 2009-10) gross class 1 national insurance contributions [**30.4.6**] in the previous tax year. Class 1A and 1B contributions do not count towards this total. The 104.5% allows small employers to recover not only all of SMP, but also some of the employer's class 1 national insurance on the payment.

32.2.6.5   Record keeping

The employer must keep form **Mat B1** or other evidence of pregnancy, copies of form **SMP1** given to employees who are not eligible for SMP, and **SMP2** or a comparable record showing the date the SMP period began, all SMP payments made, and the reason for any week during the period of entitlement to SMP when an SMP payment was not made. SMP payments are recorded on the employee's P11 deductions working sheet and other PAYE records.

32.2.7   Contractual maternity pay

An employer may provide contractual maternity pay higher than statutory maternity pay and/or for a longer period, but cannot recover the additional amounts from HMRC.

If the employee does not return to work after maternity leave, the employer cannot require her to return any SMP. The employee can, however, be required to return some or all contractual maternity pay, provided this is explicit in the contract of employment. The contract might, for example, require her to return all or some contractual maternity pay if she does not return to work, or does not return for a minimum period. Any such minimum period must be reasonable.

Boyle & others v Equal Opportunities Commission [1998] EUECJ C-411/96

32.2.8   Sick pay during and after maternity leave

Provided the employee meets the requirements for statutory sick pay [**31.6.1**], it is payable in the normal way while she is pregnant but not on maternity leave. Once she is on maternity leave, both statutory and contractual sick pay are remuneration and are therefore not payable while she is on leave.

Department for Work & Pensions v Sutcliffe [2007] UKEAT 0319 07

An employee cannot receive SSP if on the first day of the period of incapacity for work (PIW) she is within the period of entitlement to statutory maternity pay (39 weeks at the time of writing, possibly to be increased to 52 weeks). This applies even if she has returned to work during this period, or if the sickness is completely unrelated to pregnancy or childbirth. She reverts to receiving SMP or maternity allowance, and can then be reconsidered for SSP if she is still ill when the SMP period ends.

Where the employee is long-term ill and entitled to higher contractual sick pay than maternity pay, or where her entitlement to SMP has ended, it may in some circumstances be advantageous to her to come off maternity leave by giving eight weeks' notice of intention to return to work [**32.2.4.9**], and then take sick leave.

32.2.9   Breastfeeding

A woman who is breastfeeding must inform the employer in writing, usually before returning to work after maternity leave. Employers must carry out a risk assessment to ensure her work does not pose a risk to her or her baby while she is breastfeeding [**40.3.2**], and must provide rest facilities for pregnant and breastfeeding women [**40.4.1**].

There is no statutory obligation to provide facilities for breastfeeding or expressing milk, but good practice is to provide a private, clean environment where the woman can express milk, facilities for sterilising and storing bottles, and a clean, secure refrigerator for storing expressed milk. If the woman wants to breastfeed at work and it is appropriate for her to do so, the employer should if possible provide a clean, private space for this (not the toilets).

32.2.10 Maternity suspension

A woman is entitled to maternity suspension if her work poses a health risk to her or her baby while she is pregnant, after she has given birth or while she is breastfeeding [**40.3.2**], and no suitable alternative work is available. She is entitled to full pay and continuation of all her employment rights if she is suspended on these grounds. If she turns down an offer of suitable alternative work she remains employed and keeps her employment rights, but is not entitled to be paid during the period of suspension.   *Employment Rights Act 1996 ss.66-70*

32.3 PATERNITY AND PARTNER ENTITLEMENTS

Although called paternity leave and pay, these entitlements are available to partners, including women, who are not the father of the child. Information is available from BIS, ACAS and the Trades Union Congress, and about pay entitlements from HM Revenue and Customs [see end of chapter for all details].

32.3.1 Ordinary paternity leave

Eligible fathers and partners are entitled to two weeks' **ordinary paternity leave** (OPL), also called **paternity leave (birth)**. To be eligible for OPL the employee must be the child's father and have responsibility for the child's upbringing, or if not the child's father must be the spouse, partner or civil partner of the child's mother and must have the main responsibility (apart from any responsibility of the mother) for the child's upbringing. The father or partner must have 26 weeks' continuous employment [**26.5**] with the employer by the end of the 15th week before the expected week of childbirth, and must have average weekly earnings of at least the national insurance lower earnings limit [**30.4.6**]. The father or partner applies for OPL on form **SC3**.

Paternity & Adoption Leave Regulations 2002 [SI 2002/2788] regs.4-7,12-14

OPL can be taken only as a one-week block or a two-week block. It cannot be taken as two separate weeks, or as separate days. The leave must be completed within eight weeks (56 days) of the birth.

32.3.2 Statutory paternity pay

Fathers and partners on OPL are entitled to **statutory paternity pay** (SPP), paid at a weekly rate set by the government each year (available from HM Revenue and Customs) or 90% of the employee's average weekly earnings, whichever is lower. Average earnings are calculated in the same way as for statutory maternity pay [**32.2.6.3**], as is recovery from HMRC [**32.2.6.4**]. Fathers or partners who are not entitled to SPP may be entitled to income support from the Department for Work and Pensions during the OPL period.   *Statutory Paternity Pay & Statutory Adoption Pay (General) Regulations 2002 [SI 2002/2822]*

32.3.3 Additional paternity leave

At the time of writing (mid 2009) it was expected that if statutory maternity pay entitlement is extended from 39 to 52 weeks [**32.2.6.2**], a new right to up to 26 weeks' **additional paternity leave** (APL) would be introduced.

Employment Rights Act 1996 s.80AA, inserted by Work & Families Act 2006 s.3

The government had proposed that:

* APL will be available only if the mother has been working and is entitled to statutory maternity pay or maternity allowance [**32.2.6.1**];
* to be eligible for APL the father or partner will have to have been entitled to ordinary paternity leave with the same employer and still be employed by that employer when APL starts;
* APL will not be able to start until 20 weeks from the date of the child's birth, unless the mother dies during or shortly after childbirth;
* APL will be able to be taken only if the mother returns to work before the end of her additional maternity leave (AML) [**32.2.4**] – so both parents cannot be off at the same time, except for the two weeks' ordinary paternity leave within the eight weeks after the birth;

- the father or partner will have to give eight weeks' notice of intention to take APL, coinciding with the mother's notice of intention to return to work [**32.2.4.9**];
- there will be able to be a gap between the mother returning to work and the father or partner starting APL;
- APL will have to be taken in a single block, and will end when the mother's AML would have ended. So if the mother takes some of her 26 weeks' AML, the father's or partner's entitlement will be reduced by the amount of AML the mother has taken, and cannot last beyond the end of the AML period.

It was proposed that the father's or partner's employer will not have to check with the mother's employer that she has returned to work, but HM Revenue and Customs will carry out random checks to identify and prevent fraud. There was still no clear proposal about what should happen if one or both parents change their mind and in particular if the employer cannot accommodate the change.

32.3.3.1 Keeping in touch days

At the time of writing it was proposed that fathers or partners on additional paternity leave would be entitled to 10 **keeping in touch** days [**32.2.4.8**].

32.3.3.2 Rights on return from APL

It was proposed that fathers or partners on additional paternity leave would have the right to return to the same job on the same terms and conditions as if they had not been absent, unless a redundancy situation has arisen. This is the same right as women have when returning from ordinary maternity leave [**32.2.4.10**].

32.3.4 Additional statutory paternity pay

At the time of writing (mid 2009) it had been proposed that the father or partner would be entitled to **additional statutory paternity pay** (ASPP) at the flat rate or 90% of average earnings, whichever is less, if the mother has not used her full entitlement to statutory maternity pay (SMP). Average earnings will be calculated in the same way as for SMP [**32.2.6.3**], but based on the father's or partner's earnings. ASPP will be payable only for as long as SMP would have continued, and will be recoverable from HMRC in the same way as SMP [**32.2.6.4**].

32.3.5 Dismissal during paternity leave

Dismissal during paternity leave for any reason connected with the leave is automatically unfair [**34.7.1**]. When additional paternity leave becomes available, an employee dismissed or made redundant while on APL will almost certainly have to be given written notice of the reason for dismissal.

Employment Rights Act 1996 s.92(4),(4A)

32.4 ADOPTION ENTITLEMENTS

An employee who adopts as a single person, or one person in a couple who adopts, is entitled to **adoption leave** and **adoption pay** equivalent to maternity leave and pay. In an adopting couple, the other adopter (who may be male or female) is entitled to **paternity leave (adoption)** and **paternity pay (adoption)** . Information about leave entitlements is available from BIS, ACAS and the Trades Union Congress, and about pay entitlements from HM Revenue and Customs [see end of chapter for all details].

32.4.1 Ordinary and additional adoption leave

To qualify for adoption leave, an employee must be newly matched with a child for adoption by an adoption agency, and have worked continuously for their employer [**26.5**] for 26 weeks ending with the week in which they are notified of being matched with a child for adoption or a child entering the UK from abroad for adoption. Where a couple adopts, they can decide which one takes adoption leave.

Paternity & Adoption Leave Regulations 2002 [SI 2002/2788] reg.15

The employee is entitled to 26 weeks' **ordinary adoption leave** (OAL), followed immediately by 26 weeks' **additional adoption leave** (AAL). The rules on notifying the employer of intention to take leave, keeping in touch days, giving notice of intention to return to work before the end of the AAL period, and rights on return are the same as for maternity leave [**32.2.4**].   *Paternity & Adoption Leave Regulations 2002 [SI 2002/2788] regs.16-27, reg.21A inserted & reg.25 amended by Maternity & Parental Leave etc & the PAL (Amendment) Regulations 2006 [SI 2006/2014] regs.14,15*

32.4.2   Statutory adoption pay

Statutory adoption pay (SAP) is payable for 39 weeks in the same way as statutory maternity pay [**32.2.6**], and is recoverable from HM Revenue and Customs in the same way. At the time of writing (mid 2009) the government's intention was to extend SAP to 52 weeks, but no date had been set.
Statutory Paternity Pay & Statutory Adoption Pay (General) Regulations 2002 [SI 2002/2822], as amended

32.4.3   Paternity leave and pay (adoption)

If a couple is adopting, the person who does not take adoption leave is entitled to **paternity leave (adoption)** and **statutory paternity pay (adoption)** on the same basis as paternity leave and pay (birth). If the paternity leave entitlements are extended, the adoption equivalents will also be extended.   *PAL Regs 2002 regs.8-14; SPP & SAP Regs 2002; Employment Rights Act 1996 s.80B, inserted by Work & Families Act 2006 s.4*

32.4.4   Dismissal during adoption leave

Dismissal during any adoption leave is automatically unfair [**34.7.1**] if it is for any reason connected with the adoption or taking adoption leave. An employee dismissed or made redundant while on ordinary or additional adoption leave must be given written reasons for the dismissal.   *Employment Rights Act 1996 s.92(4),(4A)*

32.5   FLEXIBLE WORKING TO CARE FOR CHILDREN

Parents of children aged under 17 (or under 18 if the child is disabled) and their partners have a statutory right to request flexible working arrangements to care for the child.   *Flexible Working (Eligibility, Complaints & Remedies) (Amendment) Regulations 2009 [SI 2009/595]*

Flexible working might include, for example, a reduction in hours of work; a change in times of work, including compressed hours (working fewer but longer days), flexitime, term-time or shift working, or staggered or annualised hours [**31.2.5**]; or a change in the place of work, for example home working.

To be eligible the employee must have or expect to have parental responsibility for the child; must be the child's mother, father, adopter, guardian, special guardian, foster parent or private foster carer or hold a residence order in respect of the child, or must be the spouse, partner or civil partner of that person; and must have been continuously employed [**26.5**] by the employer for at least 26 weeks at the time the request is made.   *Flexible Working (Eligibility, Complaints & Remedies) Regulations 2002 [SI 2002/3236] reg.3, amended by FW (EC&R) (Amendment) (No.2) Regulations 2007 [SI 2007/2286] reg.4*

The request is for a **variation of contract** [**26.9.2**], and if made will change the contract permanently, unless the employer and employee agree otherwise as part of their flexible working agreement. The new work pattern continues, rather than reverting to the original work pattern, even when the child is old enough that the parent is no longer eligible to request flexible working.

To be valid the request must be in writing and must include specified details, and only one application can be made in any 12-month period. An employer who agrees the request must notify the employee within 28 days of the application. An employer who does not agree the request must arrange a meeting with the employee, to take place within 28 days of the application. The application can be refused only if the employer considers that there would be a burden of additional costs, a detrimental effect on ability to meet customer demand or on quality or performance, an inability to recruit additional staff, an insufficiency of work during the periods the employee proposes to work, or proposed structural changes.
Flexible Working (Procedural Requirements) Regulations 2002 [SI 2002/3207]

There are penalties only if the employer refuses the application and does not hold the meeting with the employee, or if the employer does not give a legally acceptable reason for refusal. There are no penalties if the employer unreasonably refuses a request. However a sex discrimination claim could potentially be brought by a woman who is unjustifiably refused a flexible arrangement, or a man who is treated less favourably than a woman would be.

Detailed information about the procedure is available from BIS, ACAS and the Trades Union Congress [see end of chapter]. The BIS website has forms for requesting flexible working or responding to a request.

32.6 FLEXIBLE WORKING TO CARE FOR ADULTS

Carers of adults have the same right to request flexible working as parents [**32.5**], with the same eligibility and procedural requirements. The cared-for person must be aged 18 or over and must be the spouse, partner, civil partner or a relative of the employee, or be living at the same address as the employee. A relative is a parent, guardian, parent in law, adult child, adopted adult child, son or daughter in law, sibling, half-sibling, brother or sister in law, aunt, uncle, grandparent, step-relative or adoptive relative.   *Flexible Working (Eligibility, Complaints & Remedies) Regulations 2002 [SI 2002/3236] reg.3B, inserted by FW (EC&R) (Amendment) Regulations 2006 [SI 2006/3314] reg.5*

'Caring for a person' is not defined in the regulations, and employees are not required to demonstrate the level of care or show that they are the only person who could provide it. In general employees are unlikely to request a change of contract unless their caring responsibilities are regular and fairly substantial.

32.7 PARENTAL LEAVE

Parental leave is an unpaid leave to care for children, available to parents up to the child's fifth birthday (or 18th if the child is disabled), or within five years of the child being placed with the family for adoption (or until the adopted child's 18th birthday, if this is earlier).   *Maternity & Parental Leave etc Regulations 1999 [SI 1999/3312] regs.14,15; reg.14A, inserted by MPL (Amendment) Regulations 2001 [SI 2001/4010] regs.4,5*

The total leave is 13 weeks, or 18 weeks if the child is entitled to disability living allowance. The leave is available for each parent and each child, so if a couple has three non-disabled children under five or within five years of being adopted, the mother and father are each entitled to 39 weeks leave (3 x 13 weeks).

It is unlawful to dismiss an employee or subject her or him to a detriment for reasons related to parental leave.   *MPL Regs 1999 regs.19,20, as amended*

32.7.1 Eligibility

Only mothers, fathers named on the birth certificate, adoptive parents and others with parental responsibility under the **Children Act 1989** s.3 are entitled to parental leave. Others who want to take parental leave must make a consent order under the Children Act or apply to the courts for a parental responsibility order. An employer can use a workforce or collective agreement [**31.1.2**] to ease this requirement and allow employees to take parental leave without a parental responsibility or consent order.   *Maternity & Parental Leave etc Regulations 1999 [SI 1999/3312] reg.13, amended by MPL Regs 2001 reg.3*

Entitlement to parental leave does not start until the employee has one year's continuous employment [**26.5**].

Requests for parental leave do not have to be in writing, but it is sensible for the employer to require this. Parental leave is a right to take time off to look after a child; using it for any other purpose may be a disciplinary matter.

There is no statutory obligation to keep parental leave records. But the leave is cumulative and transfers between employments, so if an employee changes jobs the current employer is likely to be asked for details of leave taken. After changing employers, the employee must again build up one year's continuity before becoming entitled to the remaining leave.

32.7.1.1   A week's leave

Where the amount of time an employee is contractually required to work does not vary from week to week, a week's leave is that time. Where the time varies or the employee does not work every week, a week's leave is the weekly average the employee is required to work over a 52-week period.
Maternity & Parental Leave etc Regulations 1999 [SI 1999/3312] reg.14

32.7.2   Default provisions

Employers and employees can agree through a workforce or collective agreement [**31.1.2**] how parental leave should be taken. But in the absence of such agreement, default provisions apply. If a provision in a collective or workforce agreement is less favourable to employees than the relevant default provision, the default provision applies.
Maternity & Parental Leave etc Regulations 1999 [SI 1999/3312] reg.21,sch.1, sch.2 amended by MPL (Amendment) Regulations 2001 [SI 2001/4010] reg.6

32.7.2.1   Evidence of entitlement

Under the default provisions, the employer can require the worker to provide evidence of parental responsibility, the child's date of birth and/or placement for adoption, and if applicable the child's entitlement to disability living allowance.

32.7.2.2   Duration of leave

Under the default provisions, leave must be taken in blocks of one week, up to a maximum of four weeks' leave in a year for each child. If the leave is to care for a disabled child it can be taken in one-day blocks, or multiples of one day, again up to maximum of four weeks per year. A 'year' generally starts on the date the parent first became entitled to take leave for that child.

32.7.2.3   Notice and postponement

Under the default provisions, notice of intention to take leave must specify the start and finish dates and must be given at least 21 days before the start date. A father taking time off for the birth of a child must specify the expected week of childbirth and the amount of leave to be taken, and the notice must be given at least 21 days before the start of that week. Similarly an adoptive parent must specify the expected week of placement and the amount of leave to be taken, and must give notice at least 21 days before the start of the placement week.

The employer may postpone a request by up to six months, where the business cannot cope without the employee. No more than seven days after the request is given to the employer, the employer must give written notice of the reason for postponement and the start and finish dates when leave will be permitted.

Leave cannot be postponed where a father is taking it at the time of or immediately after the child's birth, or if an adoptive parent is taking it at the time of the child's placement for adoption.

Where the employer postpones leave under the default provisions and as a result the child passes its 5th (or 18th, where applicable) birthday, the employee remains entitled to the parental leave.
Maternity & Parental Leave etc Regulations 1999 [SI 1999/3312] reg.15(d)

32.7.3   Rights during leave and on return

An employee who takes parental leave for a period of four weeks or less is entitled to return to the same job. An employee who takes parental leave for more than four weeks is entitled to return to the same job or, if that is not reasonably practicable, to another job which is suitable and appropriate.

The employee remains employed during parental leave, with the same rights on return as at the end of additional maternity leave [**32.7.3**]. Occupational pension rights are an exception. Unless the contract or pension scheme specifies otherwise, occupational pension rights accrue only if the leave is paid.
MPL Regs 1999 regs.17-18A, amended by MPL (Amendment) Regulations 2002 [SI 2002/2789] reg.12

32.8   TIME OFF FOR DEPENDANTS

All employees, regardless of length of service, are entitled to reasonable time off to deal with unexpected or sudden situations relating to dependants, or to make necessary long-term arrangements for dealing with the situation.

Employment Rights Act 1996 s.57A,57B, inserted by Employment Relations Act 1999 sch.4 pt.2;

'Reasonable' and 'necessary' are not defined in the legislation, but 'necessary' depends on the nature of the incident, the relationship between the employee and dependant and whether anyone else is available to deal with the situation. 'Reasonable time off' depends on the employee's specific circumstances, but in most cases would not be more than a few hours or one or two days.

Qua v John Ford Morrison Solicitors [2003] UKEAT 884 01 1401

There is no right to pay during this leave. For salaried workers, the time will generally be paid. For daily or hourly paid employees, the contract may state that the leave is paid, or the employer may decide to pay on a case by case basis.

A dependant is a spouse, civil partner, parent, son or daughter, or anyone other than a tenant, lodger, boarder or live-in employee who lives with the employee. It could also be someone else, such as a more distant relative or neighbour, who 'reasonably relies' on the employee, for example a neighbour who has no one else to help make arrangements for them if they are ill or injured.

Examples of situations where time off could be taken include if a dependant gives birth or falls ill, or dealing with the death of a dependant, an unexpected breakdown of care arrangements, or an unexpected incident involving a dependant.

The right is intended to cover only unexpected situations. So if, for example, a child falls ill, this right gives the employee a day or two to take the child to the doctor and arrange childcare, but not several days off to look after the child. Similarly, this right gives to register a death and organise the funeral, but not a longer period to deal emotionally or practically with the bereavement.

Forster v Cartwright Black Solicitors [2004] UKEAT 0179 04 2506

In a case involving an employee who asked 10 days in advance for a day off when she knew her childminder would not be available and alternative childcare was not available, the employment appeal tribunal said that a situation had to be unexpected, but did not have to be sudden or an emergency.

Royal Bank of Scotland plc v Harrison [2008] UKEAT 0093 08 2706

There is no need for prior notice, but the employee must tell the employer, in writing or orally, the reason for the absence as soon as reasonably practical. The employee must also indicate the length of absence, unless this is impossible until the return to work.

An employee can bring an employment tribunal claim if the employer unreasonably refuses to allow time off, or has subjected the employee to detriment because of taking or seeking to take leave. A dismissal because the person has taken, or sought to take, justifiable time off is automatically unfair.

Where the employer gives a contractual right to compassionate, bereavement or similar leave and these are used for unexpected situations involving dependents, the provisions can be no less favourable than the statutory entitlement.

Resources: RIGHTS OF PARENTS AND CARERS

Maternity, paternity & adoption leave, flexible working, parental leave, leave for situations involving dependants. ACAS, BIS, Business Link, CIPD, Directgov, PEACe, TUC: see end of **chapter 25**.

Pension rights during leave. Pensions Advisory Service: www.pensionsadvisoryservice.org.uk, 08456 012 923, enquiries@pensionsadvisoryservice.org.uk.

Statutory maternity, paternity & adoption pay. HM Revenue & Customs: www.hmrc.gov.uk, 08457 143 143, email via website.

Statute law. www.opsi.gov.uk and www.statutelaw.gov.uk.

Much but not all case law. www.bailii.org.

Updates cross-referenced to this book. www.rclh.co.uk.

Chapter 33

DISCIPLINARY MATTERS, GRIEVANCES AND WHISTLEBLOWING

For sources of further information see end of chapter.

33.1 DISCIPLINE AND GRIEVANCE: LEGAL REQUIREMENTS

A **disciplinary** matter [**33.2**] involves an employer's dissatisfaction with an employee's ca[ability, performance or conduct. A **grievance** [**33.4**] relates to an employee's dissatisfaction with the employer, the work or another employee or employees.

Statutory procedures were in place for disciplinary matters, grievances and dismissals which started between October 2004 and 6 April 2009. These procedures have been abolished, and disciplinary and grievance matters arising since 6 April 2009 should generally comply with an ACAS code of practice [**33.2**].

Information about disciplinary action against an employee, or grievances raised by the employee, may need to be provided to a potential new employer as part of a transfer of employment under the TUPE regulations [**29.7.3**].

Whistleblowing [**33.5**] refers to raising an issue where an employee believes the employer or fellow employees are acting in a way which is unlawful, falls below proper standards, or is contrary to the organisation's purpose or policies. A whistleblowing allegation may be dealt with initially through the employer's grievance procedure, or through a separate whistleblowing procedure.

33.1.1 Right to be accompanied

Employees and others working under a contract [**25.1**], including casuals, agency workers, home workers, and freelances who are not genuinely self employed, have a statutory right to request, orally or in writing, to be accompanied at disciplinary or grievance meetings. The **companion** must be a full-time trade union official, a lay official certified by the union as having the necessary expertise, or a fellow worker chosen by the worker.

Employment Relations Act 1999 s.10,
amended by Employment Relations Act 2004 s.37; ERA 1999 s.13(4),(5)

A **disciplinary meeting** (called **disciplinary hearing** in the legislation) in this context is one that could result in the employer giving a formal warning to or taking some other action in relation to a worker, or confirming a warning already issued. A **grievance meeting** concerns the performance of a duty by an employer in relation to a worker.

Refusing to allow a worker to be accompanied could lead to an award by the employment tribunal of up to two weeks' pay (as at 1/10/09, maximum £380 per week). Subjecting the worker or companion to any detriment in relation to the right to be accompanied could also lead to a complaint to the tribunal.

The contract of employment or disciplinary and grievance procedures may allow a right to be accompanied at a wider range of meetings, and/or by other persons such as a friend or relative.

33.1.1.1 Postponement

If the chosen companion is not available, the worker can propose another date within five working days beginning with the first working day after the date set for the interview. Provided the requested date is reasonable, the employer must reschedule the meeting. 'Working day' excludes Saturdays, Sundays, Good Friday, Christmas and bank holidays.

Employment Relations Act 1999 s.10(4),(5)

33.1.1.2 Rights of the companion

A companion who is a fellow worker must be given reasonable time off to fulfil the responsibility. The companion has a right to address the meeting in order to present or sum up the worker's case, respond on the worker's behalf to any view expressed at the meeting, ask questions and confer with the worker, but does not have a right to answer questions on behalf of the worker, and cannot address the meeting if the worker does not want the companion to do so.

Employment Relations Act
1999 s.10(6), s.10(2B), inserted by Employment Relations Act 2004 s.37

33.1.1.3 Informal and investigatory meetings

There is no statutory right to be accompanied at informal discussions or meetings that are genuinely purely investigatory [**33.3.2.2**]. But if such a discussion or meeting could result in a warning, the worker must have a right to be accompanied. If necessary, the meeting should be stopped and reconvened after the worker has had an opportunity to request a companion.

33.1.1.4 Legal representation

There is no statutory right to be accompanied at a disciplinary or grievance meeting by a solicitor or other person acting in a legal capacity, and many contracts of employment explicitly state that such persons are not allowed as companions. However, the courts have ruled that where a disciplinary matter is so serious that the outcome 'might well irretrievably prejudice' the employee, failure to allow legal representation is a breach of the right to a fair hearing in article 6 of the European convention on human rights [**64.3.1**].

G, R (on the application of)
v the Governors of X School & another [2009] EWHC 504 (Admin);
Kulkarni v Milton Keynes Hospital NHS Foundation Trust & others [2009] EWCA Civ 789

Legal advise should therefore be taken before refusing to allow legal representation in cases which could lead to the employee being barred from work with children or vulnerable adults [**41.7.2**], being struck off a professional register and no longer being allowed to practice their profession, or a similar outcome.

33.1.2 Procedures and the contract

33.1.2.1 The statement of particulars

The principal **statement of employment particulars** [**26.7.3**] or the written contract must include details of any disciplinary rules applicable to the employee and procedures for taking disciplinary or dismissal decisions, or reference to a document which sets out these rules and procedures. It must also indicate who the employee should go to if dissatisfied with any disciplinary or dismissal decision relating to him or her, or to make a grievance relating to her or his employment. *Employment Rights Act 1996 s.3, amended by Employment Act 2002 s.35*

Any document referred to must be reasonably accessible to the employee in the course of employment, or in some other way.

The procedures contained or referred to in the statement do not need to cover health and safety matters, since these are governed by statute [**40.2**] or the employer's health and safety policy [**40.2.6**]. *Employment Rights Act 1996 s.3(2)*

There is no statutory obligation to have a whistleblowing procedure, since the basic rules are covered in the legislation [**33.5**], but it is good practice to do so.

33.1.2.2 Part of the contract or not?

Employees must be told how disciplinary and grievance matters are dealt with, but the procedure does not have to form part of the contract of employment.

From the employer's point of view, there are considerable advantages in making clear that the procedures are not contractual [**27.7.1**]. As an organisation grows or its management structure changes, it may need to amend its procedures. If the procedures are part of the contract, any change needs each employee's consent [**26.9.2**]. If the procedures are not part of the contract, reasonable changes can be made without consent, although the employer should consult trade union or employees' representatives before doing so.

More significantly, any dismissal always carries with it the risk of a claim for unfair dismissal [**34.5**]. With a contractual disciplinary procedure, the employer exposes itself to additional risks of a claim for breach of contract or wrongful dismissal [**34.4**] if it does not follow its procedure exactly as stated.

33.2 DISCIPLINE AND GRIEVANCE: GOOD PRACTICE

33.2.1 The ACAS code of practice

The **ACAS code of practice on disciplinary and grievance procedures** sets out the basic principles of good practice. The code itself, and guidance for complying with it, are available from ACAS [see end of chapter].

The code does not have force of law, and failure to comply with it is not in itself unlawful. However, an employer's unreasonable failure to comply with the code can be taken into account by the employment tribunal and can lead to an increase of up to 25% in any award made by the tribunal, and an employee's failure to comply can lead to a reduction of up to 25% in any award.
Trade Union & Labour Relations (Consolidation) Act 1992 s.207A, inserted by Employment Act 2008 s.3

The code's starting point is that disciplinary and grievance issues should, if possible, be dealt with through informal discussion or mediation [**37.1.2**]. Only if this is unsuccessful should formal procedures be used. These procedures should be specific, clear and in writing, and appropriate for the size and resources of the employer. If appropriate they should be agreed with union or employee representatives [**36.1**].

Under the code, the key elements in a fair and transparent procedure are:
- dealing with issues promptly;
- acting consistently;
- carrying out an investigation to establish the facts;
- informing the employee of the issue, and ensuring the employee can put his or her case before any decisions are made;
- ensuring the employee has the right to be accompanied [**33.1.1**];
- ensuring the employee has a right to appeal against any formal decision.

Written records should be kept of the outcome, the main reasons for the decision and any evidence, the date of action and any appeal, and subsequent actions and events. Without this information, the employer may not be able to protect itself against claims of discrimination [**chapter 28**] or unfair dismissal [**34.7**].

33.2.2 Developing appropriate procedures

It is not uncommon for organisations to develop procedures which are so detailed that they take a disproportionate amount of time – or so vague that vast time, effort and argument are put into working out what the procedure actually is. In avoiding these extremes, a balance has to be drawn between the need to be (and to be seen to be) fair, the organisation's resources, and the potential demands on managers' or governing body members' time.

The ACAS code of practice refers only to first and final warnings [**33.3.7**] for disciplinary matters. There is no need for verbal (oral) or intermediate warnings, or always to start with a first warning – for very serious matters, it is possible for a final warning to be given without a previous warning.

If the procedure includes requirements that there must always be verbal or intermediate warnings, or that a first or intermediate warning cannot be final, these provisions can be changed after consultation with employees or their representatives if the procedure is non-contractual. If it is contractual, any changes to the disciplinary procedure must be agreed by employees [**33.2.2.2**].

Model procedures are available from ACAS, and procedures specific to voluntary organisations from PEACe [see end of **chapter 25**].

33.2.2.1 Proceedings involving the senior staff member

Even where procedures are clear and workable, they are often unclear about the procedure when disciplinary action has to be taken against the chief executive or other senior staff member, or when this employee wants to bring a grievance. Attention should be given to this when drawing up the procedures.

33.2.2.2 Review

Procedures often turn out to be outdated or unworkable in practice, but even where there are no obvious problems, they should be reviewed periodically to be sure they are still appropriate for the organisation's management structure, and comply with any new statute or case law requirements.

Where procedures form part of the contract, changes generally require consent [**26.9.2**]. Where they are not part of the contract, amendments should be introduced on reasonable notice, and after consultation with staff representatives [**33.1.2.2**]. Advice should be taken before making any changes if a disciplinary or grievance proceeding has already started or is about to start.

33.2.3 Overlap between disciplinary and grievance procedures

Procedural difficulties sometimes arise if an employer starts disciplinary proceedings against an employee, and the employee simultaneously or subsequently raises a grievance against the employer or a fellow employee.

If the disciplinary and grievance matters are about separate issues, they should be dealt with in logical order, or it may be possible to deal with them simultaneously but in separate proceedings. If the matters are the same or overlapping, it may be possible to deal with them concurrently or to hold a combined meeting to deal with both matters. If this is not feasible, ACAS suggests that the disciplinary proceeding be temporarily suspended to deal with the grievance.

If a complex web develops with disciplinary action, grievances, appeals against disciplinary decisions and/or appeals against grievance decisions, legal advice should be taken to ensure that matters are dealt with properly and fairly.

33.3 DEALING WITH DISCIPLINARY ISSUES

A disciplinary procedures is a management tool, and should not be seen or treated as a judicial procedure focusing on fault and punishment. The intention should always be to identify what is going wrong and why, decide how to put it right, get it put right, and enable the employee and organisation to get on with their work.

A **disciplinary policy** sets out the organisation's general approach to disciplinary issues, and a **disciplinary procedure** sets out the steps to deal with the issues. The policy and procedure may be a single document.

The procedure might properly cover, for example:

- matters relating to **work performance**: quantity of work, quality of work, failure to do work or to meet targets or deadlines, which may be set out in a separate but linked **capability procedure**;
- matters relating to **conduct**: lateness, unauthorised personal use of the organisation's facilities, offensive behaviour;
- matters relating to long-term **absence**, persistent short-term absences, unauthorised absence, which may be set out in a separate **absence procedure**;
- **breach** of the organisation's policies, procedures and rules;
- matters relating to **health and safety**;
- matters relating to **bullying** and **harassment**, although these may be covered by a separate policy linked to the disciplinary policy [**40.5.3**].

A **disciplinary proceeding** is when the procedure is put into action – the investigation, meeting, decision, and appeal. **Disciplinary action** or a **disciplinary penalty** is what happens as a result of the proceeding. Disciplinary action may be a **warning** or ultimately dismissal.

The stages below comply with the ACAS code [**33.2**] but are more detailed.

33.3.1 Informal discussion

The intention of the ACAS code is that most workplace problems should be resolved informally. But even an informal discussion should not consist of vague 'get your act together' comments. As part of the discussion the employer should identify the problem or issue, hear the employee's views, and make clear the change required and the consequences of failure to improve. It is not necessary to keep a written record of informal discussions like this but it is sensible to do so.

33.3.2 Establishing the facts

Typically a disciplinary proceeding starts when an employee's line manager feels that informal discussions or normal management and supervision procedures are not having the desired effect, an incident of misconduct occurs, or the employer becomes aware of behaviour such as bullying or discrimination.

At this stage the manager should be thinking through the issues, and if appropriate discussing them with his or her manager. Ideally a person who is to hear the matter or a subsequent appeal should avoid being too closely involved, or involved at all, in this consultation or in the preparation of the case, but this may not be possible in a small organisation [**33.3.4.1**].

The purpose at this stage is to clarify what is known about the situation, and to consider the possible implications of starting a disciplinary proceeding. Attention should be given to:

- the nature of the problem and why it might be occurring;
- whether it could be occurring for reasons under the employer's control, for example the employee having been given inadequate information about rules;
- whether it is gross or very serious misconduct requiring very urgent action;
- whether the employee has been charged with or convicted of a criminal offence [**33.3.11**];
- the most appropriate person(s) to investigate, conduct the disciplinary meeting and make a decision on the issues;
- the steps necessary to investigate the matter fully;
- whether the matter can be fully investigated without the need to suspend the employee [**33.3.2.3**];
- the employee's length of service, overall record and whether there are any unexpired disciplinary warnings [**33.3.7**] or the employee has been subject to other disciplinary penalties [**33.3.8**];

- whether there are any special factors, for example if the situation is or could be perceived as constituting unlawful discrimination or detriment by the employer, or if the employee is a trade union lay official;
- whether there is a recognised trade union [**36.3.3**], and any procedural agreement or other agreement with the union which needs to be complied with;
- the overlap between the disciplinary procedure and other procedures, such as those concerning bullying, harassment [**40.5.3**] or child protection;
- whether dismissal is a possible outcome;
- the likelihood of a tribunal or court claim being brought;
- whether the organisation has insurance to cover employment claims [**23.4.2**], and if so whether advice must be taken from the insurer before starting any disciplinary proceeding, issuing a warning or taking other disciplinary action.

33.3.2.1 Legal advice

Unless the matter is very straightforward and is likely to be quickly and easily resolved, it is sensible to talk through with the organisation's legal advisors the issues and the procedure to be followed. Advice obtained at this stage can prevent mistakes which could lead to very large costs later.

It is also useful to get feedback from a solicitor or other unbiased third party on the relative seriousness of the issue. It is not always easy to maintain a sense of perspective, and treating an issue hastily or inappropriately could lead to claims for unfair and/or wrongful dismissal.

33.3.2.2 Investigatory meetings

The line manager or other person carrying out the investigation should investigate the matter by interviewing the employee and if appropriate other people, taking statements, and gathering documentation such as attendance records, performance records or supervision notes. 'Evidence' in this context means relevant information – it should not be seen as the sort of evidence collected by police.

The investigation should take place as soon as possible so memories are fresh. Legal advice may be necessary on how to undertake the investigation in the most effective way, and in ways which do not pre-judge the outcome.

A meeting with the employee which is purely investigatory is not a disciplinary meeting and should not be treated as such. But the employee should be made aware that the investigation could lead to a disciplinary proceeding being started.

33.3.2.3 Suspension during investigation

In some situations, such as alleged harassment or theft, the employer may not consider it appropriate for the employee to continue working during an investigation. But it is an implied term of a contract of employment that the employer will provide work [**26.3.3**], so an employee should be suspended only if there is provision for this in the contract of employment [**27.7.2**]. Any suspension must be on full pay unless the contract allows reduced or no pay during suspension during a disciplinary investigation.

Suspension should only be used if the employee is likely to impede a disciplinary investigation or commit further offences, and should not last too long. It should be made clear that the suspension is not a disciplinary penalty [**33.3.8**].

Gogay v Hertfordshire County Council [2000] EWCA Civ 228

33.3.2.4 Anonymity

A witness should be allowed to provide information anonymously only if the employer is satisfied that the witness has genuine grounds for fearing reprisal. The witness should provide a full statement to the employer – as if it were not going to be anonymous – which should then be edited by the employer to remove identifying details. The evidence should if possible be corroborated from other sources. The anonymised information should be provided to the employee facing the disciplinary charge before the disciplinary meeting [**33.3.3.1**], and the person conducting the meeting should interview the witness before the meeting, and if necessary after the meeting.

Linfood Cash & Carry Ltd v Thompson [1989] IRLR 235 EAT

Even if a witness can remain anonymous during the employer's disciplinary proceeding, continued anonymity may not be possible if the disciplined or dismissed employee subsequently brings a tribunal claim against the employer.

33.3.3 Informing the employee and arranging a meeting

If appropriate, the person who carried out the investigation should meet with the head of HR (if there is one), chief executive or chairperson to clarify the exact nature of the disciplinary complaint. If they decide there is a case, the employee should be informed in writing of the alleged problem and the possible consequences, and a meeting should be set up with the employee. The **disciplinary meeting** (sometimes called disciplinary interview or hearing) should be held promptly, but should give the employee reasonable time to prepare their case.

This letter should give enough detail about the disciplinary issue to enable the employee to prepare for the meeting; clearly state the date, time and place of the meeting; remind the employee of their right to be accompanied at the meeting [**33.1.1**], and indicate the possible outcome if the disciplinary meeting results in a finding that work or conduct is unsatisfactory. The letter might indicate that a first or final warning might be given, but must not give the impression that the matter has been pre-judged.

33.3.3.1 Disclosure

All evidence – statements from other people, and documents relied on – should be provided to the employee, in good time before the interview. If the employee asks for additional documents, these should be provided if they are relevant.

33.3.3.2 Postponement

In addition to the statutory right to postponement if the employee's chosen companion is not available [**33.1.1.1**], the employer may allow an employee to seek a postponement to prepare his or her case. In considering the request for postponement, the person dealing with the disciplinary matter needs to bear in mind the urgency and seriousness of the matter, and the need to deal with disciplinary matters quickly. This will normally result in agreeing to postpone, but seeking to keep the delay as short as reasonably possible.

33.3.4 The meeting

A disciplinary meeting should be treated as a serious meeting with a level of formality appropriate to the organisation and the situation, but it is not a trial and should not be treated as such.

At the meeting the employee should be told what has been alleged, even though this will have been set out in the letter giving notice of the meeting and the accompanying documents. The employer may call people to give evidence, or rely on written statements. If the employer asks people to make a statement at the interview, the employee should be given the opportunity to question each of them. Anonymous evidence should be used only in exceptional circumstances [**33.3.2.4**].

After the employer has set out all its information, the employee must be allowed to state his or her case. Only in very exceptional circumstances, such as the employee refusing to attend the interview [**33.3.4.4**], would it be fair to give a disciplinary penalty without hearing the employee's side of the story.

If a new fact which is part of the allegation emerges in the interview, the employee may request an adjournment to obtain a witness or additional material, or simply to consider his or her position. The employer should consider this request seriously. Similarly if the employer needs further investigation before a decision can be made, the meeting should be adjourned so that this can be looked into.

33.3.4.1 Impartiality

The staff or governing body members who hear and decide the case should be impartial, so the person who conducted the investigation should not hear the case at the disciplinary meeting, and a manager or governing body member who will hear any appeal should not be involved in the investigation or the disciplinary meeting.

In a small organisation this separation of the people involved in investigation, meeting and appeal may not be possible. In this case, the person(s) involved must make a genuine effort to be as unbiased as possible. Failure to act in an unbiased way could mean that the proceedings and any subsequent dismissal are unfair.

33.3.4.2   Record keeping

Records of disciplinary meetings should be notes, not minutes or a verbatim record, but they should be comprehensive and clear enough that they can be used in any appeal or tribunal claim made by the employee. In cases where a disciplinary meeting could lead to a final warning or dismissal, it is sensible for an experienced note taker who is not involved in the proceeding to be present. The notes should be written up immediately afterwards and should if possible be agreed by both the employer and employee. If the employee does not agree, their disagreement can be attached to the notes.

33.3.4.3   Tape recording disciplinary meetings

For long and difficult meetings it may be appropriate to tape record the proceedings, but not to transcribe the recording unless a dispute arises about the notes.

Neither the employer nor employee has a right to tape or video record disciplinary meetings, but neither is there any prohibition unless the contract or disciplinary procedure specifically says that proceedings cannot be recorded. If there is no prohibition and either party wants to record it, the reasons should be given and agreement should be negotiated. If the other party does not agree, the meeting should not be recorded.

In some situations, a recording made secretly at a disciplinary meeting or even at the discussions of the disciplinary panel outside the meeting could be admissible as evidence in employment tribunal proceedings. Legal advice should be sought before making secret recordings or attempting to use them as evidence.

Amwell View School v Dogherty [2006] UKEAT 0243 06 1509

33.3.4.4   Non-attendance or non-participation

If the employee does not attend the disciplinary meeting but has an excuse acceptable to the employer, the employer should reschedule the meeting. If the employee does not give a reason for non-attendance, gives an unacceptable reason or persistently misses rescheduled meetings, the employer may be justified in making a decision about a disciplinary penalty on the evidence available, even without hearing the employee's side.

A decision to proceed without hearing the employee should be made only if this is justifiable and reasonable, and if the employee was notified in advance that the meeting would proceed in his or her absence. If the employer's disciplinary procedure forms part of the contract of employment, a decision to proceed without hearing the employee may generally be made only if the procedure allows for this.

If an employee attends the meeting but refuses to speak, the employer may be entitled to make a decision based on evidence collected during its investigation and from other sources, provided the evidence is sufficiently indicative of guilt and there is no other explanation.   *Ali v Sovereign Buses (London) Ltd [2006] UKEAT 0274 06 2610*

33.3.5   Making a decision

Having heard and considered the evidence and the employee's response, the employer must come to a conclusion about what the facts were and what it believes actually happened. The employer should adjourn before making a decision.

The employer merely has to come to a reasonable decision. The evidence does not have to be of a standard that would be required in court, and the matter does not have to be proved beyond reasonable doubt; indeed, this may be impossible.

The interviewer(s) may decide that the case against the employee is not proved, that it is proved but no further action needs to be taken, or that it is proved and disciplinary action is appropriate.

33.3.6   Deciding the disciplinary action

Disciplinary action (also called a **disciplinary penalty** or sanction) is the action taken by the employer if it concludes, after the disciplinary meeting, that the employee's conduct or work was unsatisfactory. The usual actions are disciplinary warnings or ultimately dismissal, but other actions are also possible [**33.3.8**].

Factors in deciding the action should include:

- full background circumstances relating to the employee, in particular length of service, position and general behaviour;
- previous disciplinary proceedings, especially those of a similar nature, and any warnings which are still live [**33.3.7.1**];
- how the employer has dealt with similar disciplinary issues in the past (because the employer should behave consistently);
- whether the contract or any other document prescribes a defined penalty in this situation;
- any relevant reason, excuse or background circumstance.

The employer must believe (and believe that an employment tribunal would also believe) that the penalty is reasonable, taking all the factors into account.

If dismissal is decided on, notes should be made at the decision making stage specifically taking into account all these factors. These need to be communicated to the employee in the dismissal letter, for example 'In spite of your previous good performance record at [Organisation], we regard your actions and omissions in this case to be so negligent as to warrant dismissal because ...'

33.3.7   Warnings

A disciplinary warning is a notice given to an employee that their conduct or work is unsatisfactory. A warning must always be identified as such and should include:

- the type of misconduct or inadequate performance;
- the facts found;
- what changes or improvement are expected, any time period for such change or improvement, and if appropriate when and how it will be reviewed;
- the consequences of further misconduct or lack of improvement;
- any right of appeal and the timetable for the appeal [**33.3.12**];
- any disciplinary action in addition to the warning;
- the date after which the warning will be disregarded [**33.3.7.1**].

Some disciplinary procedures state or imply that whatever the nature of the offence, short of gross misconduct it must be dealt with through a series of warnings. But repeated verbal or written warnings are unlikely to be effective, and make it difficult and time-consuming for the employer to deal with disciplinary matters. The ACAS code refers only to first and final warnings, and recognises that the first occurrence of a serious matter may require a final warning without a first warning [**33.2.2**]. If the current disciplinary procedure requires more than this, the employer may wish to review and if possible change it [**33.2.2.2**].

If the procedure allows for verbal warnings and one is given, the employer should make a written record of what has been said and give a copy to the employee. Written warnings and records of verbal warnings should always be dated.

A final written warning must cover the same issues and must state clearly that if conduct or work remains unsatisfactory, the next step will or may be dismissal.

33.3.7.1   Expired warnings

At the time the warning is given, it must be clear when it will expire if work or performance improves and there is no further disciplinary problem. The duration of the warning will depend on the particular disciplinary matter and other background circumstances, but it is generally six months for a minor matter, and a year or more for more serious matters. For very serious offences such as dishonesty the warning may never expire. In this case the employer may wish to stipulate that the warning will only be taken into account if dismissal is contemplated at a later stage.

An expired warning should be disregarded when dealing with subsequent disciplinary matters. However, the misconduct which led to the warning – not the warning itself – can, if relevant, be taken into account when deciding the disciplinary penalty. For example when deciding whether to dismiss for a second incident of serious misconduct, it may not be unreasonable for the employer to take into account that misconduct serious enough to justify a warning had occurred, even if that warning has since expired. Legal advice should be taken before using such misconduct as a factor in dismissal.   *Airbus UK Ltd v MG Webb [2008] EWCA Civ 49*

Even after warnings have expired, it is sensible for the employer to keep summary records of disciplinary actions taken, warnings given and expiry dates. These summaries do not need to be kept in the individual employee's HR file.

33.3.8   Other disciplinary action

If there is explicit provision for it in the contract (and this is unusual for voluntary organisations), there may be other disciplinary penalties short of dismissal. This could include loss of pay, loss of the right to use the organisation's facilities for personal use, loss of the right to work paid overtime, suspension on reduced or no pay, a fine, disciplinary transfer, or demotion. None of these may be used unless the contract of employment explicitly allows it.

Even if such penalties are contractually allowed, the employee is likely to be able to claim constructive dismissal [**34.2.9**] if they are imposed inappropriately.

33.3.9   Dismissal

Dismissal is the ultimate disciplinary penalty and gives rise to vast numbers of employment tribunal and court claims, relating not only to the reasons for the dismissal, but also the procedure that has led to the dismissal [**34.2.5**]. If at any stage in the disciplinary proceeding it appears that dismissal may be an outcome, legal advice should be sought at that point.

An unfair procedure may give rise to a claim for unfair dismissal [**34.5**], and any failure to strictly comply with a contractual disciplinary procedure may give rise to a claim for wrongful dismissal [**34.4**]. If the procedure leading up to dismissal is unreasonable, the employee may be able to claim breach of the implied duty of trust and confidence [**26.3.3**], for which an unlimited award can be made.

In addition, any award to the employee may be increased by up to 25% if the employer unreasonably does not comply with the ACAS code of practice [**33.2**] – though the award may be decreased by up to 25% if the employee does not comply with the code.

The employee does not have to have worked any minimum period in order to claim wrongful dismissal, or unfair dismissal for one of the automatically unfair reasons. To claim unfair dismissal for other reasons, the employee has to have worked for a one year qualifying period [**26.5**].

Special reporting rules may apply when a person who has worked with children or vulnerable adults is dismissed for misconduct [**41.7.2**].

33.3.9.1   Dismissal with notice

Even if the employee has been warned that his or her actions could result in dismissal, notice must be given in the usual way [**34.3**]. Pay in lieu of notice can be given if the contract allows for this [**34.3.7**]. Pay for statutory annual leave [**31.4**] earned but not taken must always be given up to the date employment ends.

The notice of dismissal given to the employee after a disciplinary investigation and meeting should make clear whether the employee remains an employee until any appeal is heard, and if so on what terms, or ceases to be an employee at the end of the notice period and is reinstated if the appeal is successful. If the employee is reinstated, there will be no loss of continuity [**26.5.2**] or pay.

33.3.9.2 Summary dismissal

Summary dismissal is dismissal without notice or pay in lieu of notice. It should be used only in cases of gross misconduct [**33.3.10**], only after an investigation to substantiate the case against the employee, and generally only where the employee has been given a clear indication that action of that type may result in such dismissal. Dismissing an employee on the spot, without an investigation, is likely to be both unfair and wrongful.

33.3.9.3 Dismissal during probationary period

It is not uncommon, particularly where the disciplinary procedure is contractual, to include a clause in the contract stating that the procedure does not have to be followed during a probationary period [**27.1.6**, **29.4**]. Unless this is explicit in the contract, dismissal during the probationary period should follow the same procedure as for dismissal at any other time.

33.3.9.4 Settlement

Frequently at some stage of a disciplinary proceeding where dismissal is a possibility, the question of an agreed settlement arises. Settlement protects the employer from contractual claims which can be brought in the court, but in order to protect against claims in employment tribunals the settlement must follow strict guidelines [**37.2.2**].

33.3.10 Gross misconduct

Although the tribunals and courts have refused to define what constitutes **gross misconduct**, it is essentially an action so serious that it destroys the employer/ employee relationship of trust and confidence [**26.3.3**] and justifies immediate (summary) dismissal without warning and without notice [**34.2.10**].

Neary & Neary v Dean of Westminster [1999] IRLR 288

The contract or disciplinary procedure frequently lists key areas which the employer considers gross misconduct [**27.6.2**]. It should be clear that the list is not exhaustive, and that other behaviour can also be treated as gross misconduct.

The fact that the contract of employment, disciplinary procedure or other document lists particular behaviour as gross misconduct does not automatically mean that summary dismissal for such behaviour is fair. If the employee challenges the dismissal, the tribunal will look at whether the basic rule was fair, and whether it was fairly and reasonably applied in the particular circumstances. To avoid the risk of a finding of unfair dismissal, the employer should carry out an investigation, followed by the employee being allowed to provide his or her response before as impartial as possible an interviewer or panel. The employer should take the employee's previous conduct record into account.

33.3.11 Criminal offences and activities outside work

If an employee is charged with a criminal offence which could affect his or her work or the organisation's reputation, the organisation should take legal advice at an early stage.

If the offence was committed in the course of employment, the employer should deal with the matter giving rise to the charge through the normal disciplinary procedure or through the procedure for gross misconduct [**33.3.10**]. There is no need to wait for the outcome of criminal proceedings to start a disciplinary proceeding, and doing so may involve the employer in inordinate delay.

If the employee is charged with a criminal offence committed outside employment, the action to be taken should be based on his or her suitability for work.

The normal disciplinary procedure or procedure for gross misconduct should also be used, if appropriate, where an employee engages in activities which are not unlawful but are incompatible with the employee's work or could bring the employer into serious disrepute. An example might be a youth worker working with immigrant communities, who is photographed taking part in an anti-immigration demonstration.

33.3.11.1   Suspension

Even where an alleged offence is directly related to work or an activity is incompatible with an employee's work, the employee can be suspended on reduced pay or no pay during the organisation's own disciplinary investigation or as a disciplinary penalty only if the contract explicitly allows [**33.3.2.3, 33.3.8**].

If the police ask the employer not to investigate the matter until after the court case, a suspension, even on full pay, without carrying out a disciplinary investigation and meeting could breach the organisation's own procedures and the ACAS code. Advice should be taken in this situation.

33.3.11.2   Termination of employment

If the court bans the employee from undertaking work for the employer until the case is concluded, this may constitute **frustration [34.2.11]**, with the contract terminated because of an unforeseen event that makes it impossible for the contract to continue. The employer should seek legal advice before dismissing in this situation.   *Four Seasons Healthcare Ltd v Maughan [2004] UKEAT 0274 04 CK*

If an offence (or anything else) leads to a person being barred from working in a regulated activity with children or vulnerable adults [**41.7.1**], any such work must be stopped immediately. The person may, or in most cases must, be dismissed immediately [**34.6.4**], with no need for disciplinary proceeding or warning.

Depending on the nature of the offence and the sentence, conviction in the criminal court – whether for an action within or outside work – may frustrate the contract. But conviction on its own does not normally justify dismissal or other penalty by the employer unless the disciplinary procedure has been followed.

The employer does not have to form the view that the offence was committed. When an employee has pleaded guilty to an offence, or has been found guilty by the decision of a court or the verdict of a jury, it is reasonable for the employer to believe that the offence has been committed by the employee.
Peet v Nottinghamshire County Council [1992] EWCA Civ 1

Dismissal for an activity outside work which is not unlawful may be a fair dismissal 'for some other substantial reason' [**34.6.5**], provided a fair procedure was followed and the dismissal was reasonable in the circumstances.

33.3.12   Appeals

Appeals should always be allowed against a final warning, notice of dismissal or penalty. Many procedures also allow for appeal against a first warning.

When informing the employee of a warning or other disciplinary action, the employer should notify the employee of the right of appeal, and the appeal should be dealt with as quickly as possible. If possible the appeal should be heard by a different person or persons at a more senior level, although the courts and tribunals recognise that for small employers this may not be possible.

Legal advice should always be sought when dealing with an appeal against dismissal, or in any situation where an employee who has been disciplined might resign and claim constructive dismissal [**34.2.9**].

The nature of the appeal should be made clear. Some appeals do not review the finding of facts, only the penalty imposed after the finding of facts. Much more commonly, the appeal is a re-hearing so that all issues are again explored, and/or so procedural defects made at an earlier stage can be corrected.

There should generally be a time limit for an employee to lodge an appeal, so that the appeal does not arise many months after the initial disciplinary action. Five working days is generally appropriate, although the employer should still consider hearing an appeal that is lodged out of time. In such a case, the employer should seek legal advice on whether it is reasonable to time-out the appeal.

The disciplinary procedure or the notice of dismissal given to the employee should make clear whether the employee remains an employee until the appeal is heard, and if so on what terms, or ceases to be an employee. In the latter case, the employee would be reinstated if the appeal is successful, with no loss of pay or continuity of employment [**26.5.2**].

If the employee informs the employer of his or her wish to appeal and the employer does not follow an appeal procedure, any subsequent dismissal will be unfair. If either the employer or employee fails to comply with the procedure any compensation awarded by the employment tribunal may be increased or decreased according to which party is at fault.

For dismissals after 5 April 2009 an employee who believes he or she has a valid claim for wrongful and/or unfair dismissal may simply accept the dismissal and claim compensation, without appealing.

33.4 DEALING WITH GRIEVANCES

Grievance proceedings should, but do not necessarily have to, comply with the principles set out in the ACAS code of practice [**33.2**]. The stages below comply with the ACAS code but are more detailed.

An employee dissatisfied with the outcome of a grievance proceeding and appeal may be able to bring a claim in the employment tribunal, or may be able to resign and claim unfair constructive dismissal [**34.2.9**] on the basis of an unfair decision and/or an unfair process.

33.4.1 What constitutes a grievance?

Under the ACAS code, a **grievance** is a concern, problem or complaint that an employee or employees raise with their employer in writing. To avoid misunderstanding, it may be necessary for the employer to clarify whether the employee wants an issue raised in writing to be treated informally or as a grievance.

33.4.2 Related procedures

Employers may have separate policies under which employees can raise concerns about **bullying** and **harassment** [**40.5.3**]. **Health and safety** issues are generally raised under the health and safety policy [**40.2.6**], rather than as grievances.

Grievance procedures do not generally cover **whistleblowing** allegations [**33.5**] unless the employee wishes them to be treated as a grievance.

33.4.3 Good practice for grievances

The usual approach is to encourage employees initially to discuss the matter informally, if possible, with the person who is the cause of the grievance. If this is not possible or the outcome is unsatisfactory, the employee can take up the matter in writing with his or her line manager (or a specified person above, if the grievance concerns the manager).

At this stage a grievance should not go to the highest level, because this would not keep anyone available for the appeal stage. In a large(ish) organisation the highest level for most grievances is likely to be at head of human resources or chief executive level, unless the grievance involves very senior staff or is very serious. In a smaller organisation, the highest level may be the governing body, a human resources sub-committee, or a sub-committee set up specifically to hear an appeal.

A grievance procedure should follow the same basic principles as a disciplinary procedure [**33.3**], allowing employees to present their concerns and have them heard and dealt with in a fair, impartial manner. A model procedure is available from ACAS, and a procedure specifically for voluntary organisations from PEACe [see end of **chapter 25**].

As soon as reasonable after a grievance is raised, the employer should arrange a meeting at which the employee can explain the grievance and how they think it should be resolved. In most cases the employee has a statutory right to be accompanied by a trade union official or fellow employee at the meeting [**33.1.1**]. Even where there is no statutory right it is good practice to allow the employee to be accompanied, and to be accompanied by anyone, other than a lawyer.

The employer should decide what action, if any, to take as soon as reasonable after the meeting, and should inform the employee of the action and the employee's right to appeal. Any appeal should be heard promptly, and ideally by someone other than the person who dealt with the grievance.

Some procedures include very rigid timetables, but it is preferable for timing to be flexible. If the grievance procedure is part of the contract [**33.1.2.2**], a rigid timetable could give rise to a claim for breach of contract if the relevant person does not reply within the specified time.

Records of grievances raised and the employer's response or action and reasons should be retained. Copies of minutes or notes from grievance meetings should be given to the employee who raised the grievance.

33.5   WHISTLEBLOWING

In general it is a serious disciplinary matter for an employee to breach confidentiality by revealing information about the employer's activities. But where an employee reasonably believes disclosure would reveal or prevent malpractice or an unlawful act, there may be a **just cause** defence in disclosing the information. This is often referred to as **whistleblowing**.

In these situations the **Public Interest Disclosure Act 1998** protects employees and workers from victimisation or dismissal, provided they comply with the statutory procedures. There is no limit on the compensation that can be awarded to an employee who is unfairly dismissed or subject to detriment because of whistleblowing, and any dismissal is automatically unfair. Even after they have ceased working for the employer, employees and workers are protected from victimisation, with no time limit.   *Woodward v Abbey National plc [2006] EWCA Civ 822*

For the purposes of this Act, a 'worker' is defined more widely than usual [**25.1.2**] and includes a person who works under a contract of employment or other contract where he or she has to provide services personally, agency workers, home workers whose work is controlled by the employer, some trainees on work experience, and some NHS practitioners.   *Employment Rights Act 1996 s.43K,*
inserted by Public Interest Disclosure Act 1998 s.1

A whistleblowing **disclosure** is protected only if it falls into one of six categories and is made through a protected route. If the subject matter is not in one of the categories or a non-protected route is used, the employee or worker is not protected from victimisation or dismissal.

Organisations should develop a whistleblowing or disclosure procedure which encourages disclosure within the organisation as soon as staff become aware of potential problems. This may specify that disclosure should be made to a person or persons within the organisation, or to an external body which operates a hotline on behalf of the employer. Such disclosure enables corrective action to be taken, and reduces the risk of staff feeling the need to disclose information externally.

Information and advice on whistleblowing is available from **Public Concern at Work** and the **Campaign for Freedom of Information** [see end of chapter], and guidance on developing a disclosure policy is available from them, CIPD and the Institute of Chartered Secretaries and Administrators [see end of chapter].

33.5.1   What can be disclosed

For a disclosure to be protected, the employee or worker must reasonably believe that the disclosure tends to show that one or more of the following has happened anywhere in the world or is likely to happen: a criminal offence, failure to comply with any legal obligation, a miscarriage of justice, danger to an individual's health or safety, damage to the environment, or deliberate concealment of information tending to show any of these.   *Employment Rights Act 1996 s.43B(1),*
inserted by Public Interest Disclosure Act 1998 s.1

Even if the disclosure shows one or more of these, it is not protected if the worker commits an offence by making the disclosure (for example, contravenes the **Official Secrets Act**), or if legal professional privilege [**65.4.3**] applies.
ERA 1996 s.43B(3),(4), inserted by PIDA1998 s.1

33.5.2   Who it can be disclosed to

33.5.2.1   Employer, responsible person or legal advisor

A disclosure is protected if it is made to the employer; someone to whom the employer, under its disclosure policy, authorises disclosure to be made; a person other than the employer whom the employee or worker believes in good faith has a legal responsibility for the matter; or a minister of the Crown, where the employee or worker works for a government department or agency. It is also protected if made while obtaining legal advice. *Employment Rights Act 1996 ss.43C-43E, inserted by Public Interest Disclosure Act 1998 s.1*

33.5.2.2   Prescribed person

A disclosure is protected if it is made to a **prescribed person**, provided the employee or worker makes the disclosure in good faith, reasonably believes the information disclosed is substantially true, and reasonably believes the prescribed person is authorised to deal with such matters. *ERA 1996 s.43F, inserted by PIDA 1998 s.1*

Prescribed persons include the Charity Commission, HM Revenue and Customs, Health and Safety Executive, Environment Agency, bodies regulating health and social care work and work with children, and similar regulatory bodies. The police are not prescribed persons, but the Independent Police Complaints Commission is. *Public Interest Disclosure (Prescribed Persons) Order 1999 [SI 1999/1549], as amended*

33.5.2.3   Disclosure to others

A disclosure to others, for example an MP, the police or media, is protected only if the employee or worker makes the disclosure in good faith, reasonably believes the information disclosed is substantially true, does not make the disclosure for personal gain, and is acting reasonably, in all the circumstances of the case, in making the disclosure.

In addition, the worker making the disclosure must reasonably believe that he or she will be subject to detriment by the employer if disclosure is made to the employer or a prescribed person; the worker must reasonably believe it is likely that evidence relating to the matter will be concealed or destroyed if disclosure is made to the employer; or the employee or worker has already disclosed the information to the employer or a prescribed person, and appropriate action has not been taken. *Employment Rights Act 1996 s.43G(1),(2), inserted by Public Interest Disclosure Act 1998 s.1*

In deciding whether a disclosure to a person other than the employer or a prescribed person is protected, the tribunal considers the identity of the person to whom the disclosure is made, the seriousness of the matter, whether the matter is likely to continue or recur, whether the disclosure was made in breach of the employer's duty of confidentiality to another person, any action the employer or person to whom the disclosure was made has taken or should have taken as a result of a previous disclosure, and whether in making the disclosure the employee or worker complied with the employer's procedure for disclosure. *Employment Rights Act 1996 s.43G(3), inserted by Public Interest Disclosure Act 1998 s.1*

Resources: DISCIPLINARY MATTERS, GRIEVANCES AND WHISTLEBLOWING

Disciplinary and grievance procedures. ACAS, BIS, Business Link, CIPD, Directgov, PEACe, TUC: see end of chapter 25.

Whistleblowing. Campaign for Freedom of Information: www.cfoi.org.uk, 020 7831 7477, admin@cfoi.demon.co.uk.

Institute of Chartered Secretaries and Administrators: www.icsa.org.uk, 020 7580 4741, info@icsa.co.uk.

Public Concern at Work: www.pcaw.co.uk, 020 7404 6609, enquiries@pcaw.co.uk.

Statute law. www.opsi.gov.uk and www.statutelaw.gov.uk.

Much but not all case law. www.bailii.org.

Updates cross-referenced to this book. www.rclh.co.uk.

Chapter 34

TERMINATION OF EMPLOYMENT

*For sources of further information see end of **chapter 25**.*

34.1   GETTING IT RIGHT

In most cases, termination of the contract of employment is straightforward, with the employee giving notice. Occasionally a problem arises from an employee not giving proper notice, but far more frequent are problems arising from dismissals by the employer dismissing an employee without giving proper notice, or without following proper procedures or having a fair reason for the dismissal.

The resultant wrongful and unfair dismissal cases can be very damaging and expensive. Uninsured legal costs and a large award to an employee could cause the insolvent winding up of an incorporated organisation, or bankruptcy for governing body members in an unincorporated organisation. In addition, a hasty or badly planned dismissal can have long-lasting negative effects on morale within the organisation, its reputation and potentially its funding. It is therefore essential to take early legal advice when an employee might be or is being dismissed.

34.1.1   Statement of reasons for termination

All employees, regardless of length of service, must be given written notice of the reason for dismissal if they are dismissed while they are pregnant, or if their maternity or adoption leave period would be ended by the dismissal.

Employment Rights Act 1996 s.4; s.4A inserted by Employment Act 2002 sch.7 para.31

An employee with at least one year's continuous service [**26.5**], including an employee on a fixed-term contract which is not renewed, must be given a written statement of the reason(s) for the termination if they ask for it. The employer must provide this within 14 days of the request.

Employment Rights Act 1996 s.92(1)-(3), amended by Fixed-term Employees
(Prevention of Less Favourable Treatment) Regulations 2002 [SI 2002/2034] regs.18-20, sch.2 pt.1

If a statement is not provided or is untrue or inadequate, the employee may refer the matter to the employment tribunal. The tribunal may make a finding as to the reasons for the dismissal, and award two weeks' pay (maximum £380 per week, as at 1/10/09).   *Employment Rights Act 1996 s.93*

34.1.2 References and reporting

In general there is no legal obligation to provide a reference, but an employer who does so owes a duty of care to both the former employee and the new employer [**29.6.1**]. Failure to provide a reference for a worker who brought or threatened to bring a discrimination claim or who has made a whistleblowing disclosure could constitute victimisation [**28.1.5**, **33.5**].

Special reporting rules may apply when a person who has worked with children or vulnerable adults is dismissed for misconduct [**41.7.2**].

34.2 TERMINATION OF EMPLOYMENT

Normally an employment contract can only be lawfully terminated on notice as required by statute or under the contract [**34.3**]. An employer's failure to give notice as required constitutes **wrongful dismissal** [**34.4.1**]; an employee's failure to do so is **wrongful termination** [**34.4.3**].

34.2.1 Pre-employment termination

A contract of employment comes into existence when an offer of employment is unconditionally made and accepted [**26.2**]. Termination by the employer, even before the person has started working, could give rise to a claim for wrongful dismissal unless the required notice (with pay) is given. If the reason is connected with pregnancy, childbirth, trade union activities or anything else where dismissal is automatically unfair [**34.7.1**], the individual is entitled to claim unfair dismissal, and may also be able to bring a claim for discrimination.

Sarker v South Tees Acute Hospitals NHS Trust [1997] UKEAT 493 96 2503

34.2.2 Termination during or at end of probationary period

Many contracts specify a **probationary period** [**29.4**] during or at the end of which the employer or employee can terminate employment without giving the full notice required in the contract. The notice required to terminate the probationary period cannot be less than the statutory minimum [**34.3.1**].

During the probationary period the disciplinary procedure applies in the same way as for any other dismissal [**33.3**], unless the contract states otherwise.

34.2.3 Resignation

An employee may resign at any time by giving the notice required by her or his contract or by statute [**34.3**], whichever is longer. Leaving without giving the required notice could constitute **wrongful termination** [**34.4.3**].

Provided the employee gives the required notice, an employer cannot prevent an employee from resigning and cannot refuse to accept the resignation – unless the contract is for a fixed term and there is no provision for the employee to leave during the term [**34.2.6.1**],

34.2.3.1 Resignation in the heat of the moment

Where an employee is clearly angry or under stress and resigns in the heat of the moment, it may be sensible to allow a cooling-off period of one or two days before acting on the resignation. In exceptional circumstances, an employee who clearly might not have meant to resign could potentially claim unfair dismissal if it is not reasonable [**34.5.3**] for the employer to have treated the resignation as genuine without confirming it.   *Southern v Franks Charlesly [1981] IRLR 278*

34.2.3.2   Resignation as an alternative to dismissal

Employees are sometimes offered the opportunity to resign rather than go through a disciplinary proceeding and possibly (or probably) be dismissed. Unless such an offer can be shown to be a reasonable and proper way for the employer to act, the offer may be a breach of the employer's duty to maintain the employee's trust and confidence [**26.3.3**], and could lead to the employee resigning and claiming **constructive dismissal** [**34.2.9**] – even if the offer includes an attractive resignation package. Legal advice is essential before suggesting to any employee that they resign, or offering any inducement to resign. Any discussions about such a course of action should be **without prejudice** [**65.4.1**] , and any resignation should be subject to a **compromise agreement** [**37.2.2**].

34.2.4   Express dismissal

Dismissal, including dismissal after a disciplinary action, redundancy and the expiry of a fixed-term contract, occurs when the employer gives **notice** [**34.3**] to the employee. Proper notice according to the contract or statute, whichever is longer, must be given, unless misconduct is so serious that it justifies **summary dismissal** without notice [**33.3.10**]. Notice of dismissal must be given or sent individually to an employee, and must clearly indicate that it is a notice of dismissal and when the dismissal takes effect. If notice is given orally, it is sensible to confirm it in writing.

Dismissal without proper notice, or which in any other way contravenes the contract, is **wrongful dismissal** [**34.4.1**]. If either the reason or the process is unfair, it is an **unfair dismissal** [**34.5**].

Special care is needed when dealing with dismissals which could be seen as linked to racial group, sex, disability, religion or belief, sexual orientation, age, working part-time, trade union activity, or asserting a health and safety right or another statutory right, because the burden may be on the employer to show that the dismissal was not in fact for any of these reasons [**28.9.1**] and was thus not automatically unfair [**34.7.1**].

34.2.5   Dismissal following disciplinary action

Dismissal for a disciplinary (including capability) reason is an express dismissal [**34.2.4**], and must be based on a clear understanding of the ACAS code of practice on disciplinary and grievance procedures [**33.2.1**] and the organisation's disciplinary procedure [**33.3**]. Any award to the employee may be increased by up to 25% if the employer unreasonably does not comply with the ACAS code [**33.2**], and the award may be decreased by up to 25% if the employee does not comply.

To reduce the risk of legal claims, legal advice should be sought as soon as it appears that a disciplinary proceeding will or might end in dismissal. Failure to seek advice at this early stage may mean that the employer dismisses for a reason which is not justifiable and fair or uses a process which is not fair, which could lead to a claim for unfair dismissal [**34.5**]. Or the employer may not realise the importance of strictly following the disciplinary procedure if it is contractual [**33.1.2**], and may end up facing a claim for wrongful dismissal [**34.4.1**].

If the employer does not give at least one warning that dismissal may occur (except for summary dismissal for gross misconduct, **33.3.10**), the employer is likely to be held to have acted unreasonably and therefore unfairly. This could lead not only to a claim for unfair dismissal, but also for breach of the implied duty of trust and confidence [**26.3.3**], for which an unlimited award can be made.

Except in cases of summary dismissal, notice as required by statute or contract must be given.

The employee does not have to have worked any minimum period in order to claim wrongful dismissal, or unfair dismissal for an automatically unfair reason for which there is no qualifying period. To claim unfair dismissal for other reasons, the employee has to have worked for a one year qualifying period [**26.5**].

Special reporting rules may apply when a person who has worked with children or vulnerable adults is dismissed for misconduct [**41.7.2**].

34.2.6 Expiry of fixed-term contract

Non-renewal of a fixed-term contract [**25.3.1**] is an express dismissal [**34.2.4**]. An employee with the necessary period of continuous employment [**26.5**] is entitled to claim unfair dismissal unless there is a fair reason for dismissal (usually redundancy). If the reason is redundancy, an employee with two years' continuous service is entitled to a redundancy payment [**35.7.1**]. *Employment Rights Act 1996 ss.95,136, amended by Fixed-term Employees (Prevention of Less Favourable Treatment) Regulations 2002 [SI 2002/2034] regs.18-20, sch.2 pt.1*

34.2.6.1 Termination before expiry

A fixed-term contract should generally contain provisions allowing for termination by notice before it expires. The usual rules relating to fair dismissal [**34.5**] and termination by notice [**34.3**] apply.

If a fixed-term contract does not include provision for termination before expiry, termination by either side is a breach of contract. If the employer terminates, compensation will reflect what the employee would have earned for the remainder of the contract.

34.2.7 Dismissal during a TUPE transfer

Dismissals during a transfer of an undertaking [**29.7.5**] are generally automatically unfair, but an unfair dismissal claim may be made only if the employee has one year's continuous service with the transferring employer.

A dismissal by either the transferring or receiving employer may be fair if it is for an economic, technical or organisational (ETO) reason necessitating a change in the number or functions of staff – rather than being directly connected with the transfer – and a fair procedure is followed. In determining whether the procedure was fair, an employment tribunal will look at whether all statutory information and consultation requirements were complied with [**29.7.3**], particularly whether the employee was told what changes were proposed and why, was given time to consider the information and was given the opportunity to make representations.

This is a very complex area and specialist legal advice is essential.

34.2.8 Retirement

An employer may – but does not have to – set a **normal** (also called **mandatory**) **retirement age** at 65 or over. A retirement age below 65 has to be objectively justified. Where the employer has not set a retirement age, there is a national **default** (not compulsory) **retirement age** of 65 [**28.6.1**]. At the time of writing (mid 2009), default and mandatory retirement ages had been challenged and a final decision about their legality was awaited. The default retirement age will be reviewed in 2010. *Employment Equality (Age) Regulations 2006 [SI 2006/1031] reg.30*

34.2.8.1 Statutory retirement procedure

Retirement, even if it takes place at or after the normal or default retirement age, is unlawful age discrimination and an unfair dismissal unless the employer follows the **statutory retirement procedure**. *Employment Rights Act 1996 ss.98ZA-98ZF, inserted by Age Regs 2006 sch.8 para.23*

The statutory procedure requires the employer to give written notification to employees between six and 12 months before their intended retirement date, even if retirement provisions are included in the contract of employment or in a policy or procedure given to the employee. The notice must state that the employee has the right to ask to continue working beyond retirement age. *Age Regs 2006 sch.6*

An employee who wants to continue working must make the request at least three months before the retirement date, stating whether he or she wants the employment to continue indefinitely, or for a stated period or until a stated date.

The employer must consider the request, and either grant the request or meet with the employee within a reasonable time to discuss it. However there is no duty on the employer to grant the request, or to give a reason for not granting it.

The employee has a right to appeal if the employer does not grant the request, or allows the employee to continue working but for a shorter period than requested.

Where the employee is allowed to continue working for six months or more, the same notice procedure has to be gone through again.

A retirement dismissal is automatically unfair [**34.7**] if the employer has not given the employee the necessary notice at least six months before the intended retirement date, or if the dismissal takes effect while a 'duty to consider' procedure is still under way and the employer has not yet held the meeting with the employee or informed the employee of its decision, or if the employer has failed to consider the employee's appeal against a retirement decision.

34.2.8.2 Early retirement

An employer can require an employee to retire only on or after the normal or default retirement age. But an employee can choose to retire at any age, by giving notice in the usual way [**34.3**]. An employee who retires early will not become entitled to a state pension [**30.5**] until state pension age, but an occupational or personal pension [**30.6**] may include provision for the pension to start earlier.

An employer can provide life assurance cover to employees who retire early on grounds of ill health, but this must end when the employee reaches the employer's normal retirement age, or 65 if there is no normal retirement age.

Employment Equality (Age) Regulations 2006 [SI 2006/1031] reg.34

Termination of employment under a compromise agreement [**37.2.2**] is sometimes inaccurately called early retirement.

34.2.9 Repudiation by employer and constructive dismissal

Repudiation occurs when one party gives a clear indication that they no longer intend to be bound by a contract, by doing something fundamentally contrary to the contract. An employer may repudiate a contract by committing a serious breach of its obligations to an employee, including its duty of trust and confidence [**26.3.3**], or by committing a series of breaches until one is finally 'the final straw'. Repudiatory breaches may include, for example:

- dismissing without giving the required notice, unless summary dismissal is justified [**33.3.10**];
- requiring an employee to work in an unhealthy or unsafe situation;
- publicly reprimanding or arguing with the employee;
- failing to take reasonable steps to protect the employee from unlawful discrimination, victimisation or harassment, or from violence, abuse or bullying;
- demoting the employee without reason;
- varying the contract in a way which is detrimental to the employee, without the employee's agreement or without consultation, notice or a provision in the contract allowing this [**26.9**];
- any other action or series of actions which seriously undermines the employer/employee relationship.

An employee who resigns because of an action like this may allege **constructive dismissal**. The dismissal is 'constructed' out of the employer's behaviour, indicating an intention not to be bound by the contract. The employee may resign without giving notice, and may be entitled to claim constructive wrongful and/or unfair dismissal. However the employee must resign relatively quickly, or may lose the right to do so [**34.2.9.2**]. *Employment Rights Act 1996 s.95(1)(c)*

34.2.9.1 Acts by rogue trustees

An action, even if unauthorised, by an individual member of a governing body – a rogue trustee – could give rise to a claim for constructive dismissal if it provokes an employee into resigning [**22.2.4**]. To reduce this risk:

- members of the governing body and its sub-committees should be aware that they are not authorised to criticise employees' work except within the framework of the organisation's supervision, disciplinary and other procedures;
- an employee at the receiving end of such criticism, and other relevant employees, should be told clearly that the comments are not authorised, supported or endorsed by the employer, or where the comments may to some extent be supported, it should be clear that the rogue trustee's *actions* are not supported;
- the organisation's grievance procedure [**33.4**] should allow for employees to take action in this type of situation;
- governing body members who are aware of such comments should do what they can to prevent them or protect employees from them;
- the organisation should do, and be seen to do, everything in its power to control the behaviour of the governing body member.

In some situations, it may be appropriate to suspend or remove the person from the governing body [**13.5.4-13.5.6**] or its sub-committees.

34.2.9.2 Employee not treating action as repudiation

An employee may continue working despite the employer's action, waiting to see if things will improve and if not, resigning and claiming constructive dismissal later. But an employee who **affirms** the contract, by continuing to accept wages or other benefits or by delaying resigning, may lose the right to claim constructive dismissal if the delay is too long.

Continuing to work and resigning later is not possible where the employer summarily dismisses [**34.2.10**] without justification. The employee may well want to ignore the employer's repudiation and continue working, but his or her only remedies are to claim wrongful dismissal, and/or compensation or reinstatement for unfair dismissal.

34.2.10 Repudiation by employee and summary dismissal

Repudiation by an employee may occur if, for example, the employee commits an act which is **gross misconduct** [**33.3.10**] fundamentally undermining the employer/employee relationship. In this situation the employer may be justified in dismissing without notice or pay in lieu of notice, but it may be unfair [**34.5.2**] and/or wrongful [**34.4.1**] to dismiss without carrying out an investigation to confirm that the misconduct or breach of contract occurred.

34.2.11 Frustration

A contract is terminated by **frustration** [**21.6.3**] if something happens which makes it impossible for the contract to be carried out. The most obvious example is where the employee – or the employer, if an individual – dies, but frustration can also occur in other situations where the work cannot continue.

Imprisonment does not necessarily frustrate a contract, especially if the imprisonment is for a short time and is for a reason which does not affect the employee's suitability for the job. Legal advice should be taken before claiming frustration or dismissing an employee on the basis of imprisonment [**33.3.11**] or claiming frustration for any other reason.

A frustrated contract is terminated by action of law, rather than by a party to the contract. Generally there is no dismissal, and therefore no right to claim unfair dismissal, wrongful dismissal or a redundancy payment.

34.3 NOTICE

Unless employment is being terminated summarily [**33.3.10**] or by frustration [**34.2.11**], the employer or employee must give notice as required under the contract or statute. If there is a difference between statute and the contract, or between statute and what is implied, the longer period always applies.

Employment Rights Act 1996 s.86(3)

34.3.1 Statutory period of notice

In the first month of employment there is no statutory right for an employee or employer to be given notice. Thereafter, virtually all employees are entitled to the statutory minimum notice of:

- during the first two years of continuous employment [**26.5**], one week's notice;
- then one week's additional notice for every full year of continuous employment, to a maximum of 12 weeks' notice. *Employment Rights Act 1996 s.86(1)*

After the first month the statutory minimum which the employee must give to the employer is one week, regardless of length of employment. *ERA 1996 s.86(2)*

34.3.1.1 Employer giving short notice

Sometimes an employer tries to deprive the employee of employment rights by giving less notice than the employee is entitled to, so that the termination date falls before the expiry of the necessary qualifying period. In this case the **effective date of termination** [**34.8.1**] is postponed to the date on which notice would have expired if the employer had given notice as required by statute, but is not extended by the contractual notice period if this is longer than the statutory period. With the extension to comply with the statutory period, the employee may then have the necessary qualifying period to claim unfair dismissal. This provision does not apply to dismissal without notice for gross misconduct [**33.3.10**]. *Employment Rights Act 1996 ss.92(7),97(2)*

34.3.2 Contractual period of notice

Where the contractual notice period is different from the statutory period, the longer period applies. This means, for example, that contractual provision for one month's notice by an employer does not apply for employees who have worked five or more years, who under statute are entitled to five or more weeks' notice.

34.3.3 Implied period of notice

If the written contract does not specify the period of notice to be given by each party, the court may imply [**26.3.4**] a period longer than the statutory minimum. For example, it is generally implied that monthly paid employees are entitled to at least one month, even if their statutory entitlement is less than this.

The longer an employee has been employed and/or the more senior he or she is, the more likely it is that an extended period of notice will be implied. In the absence of an agreed notice period in the contract, the courts and tribunals have found that periods of six and even 12 months are appropriate for very senior members of staff.

Custom and practice in relation to notice periods in an industry or the accepted practice within an organisation may also give rise to an implied notice period.

34.3.4 Garden leave

Garden leave is where an employee, after the employer or the employee has given notice, is required not to come in to work during the notice period. The intention may be to protect the employer from a disgruntled employee, or to prevent the employee immediately starting to work for a competitor.

Garden leave can generally be required only if it is included in the contract [**27.6.2**], and only if it is reasonable in the specific situation. In rare situations, where there is clear evidence of wrongdoing by the employee, an employer may be able to impose garden leave even if there is no contractual provision. An example is where an employee hands in notice then deliberately collects confidential information to take to a competitor. *Symbian Ltd v Christensen [2000] EWCA Civ 517; Hutchings v Coinseed Ltd [1997] EWCA Civ 2736; SG & R Valuation Service Co v Boudrais & others [2008] EWHC 1340 (QB)*

The contract of employment remains in force during garden leave, so the employee must comply with any restrictions and is entitled to any contractual benefits such as a bonus. *Clark v Nomura International plc [2000] IRLR 766*

34.3.5 Waiving right to notice

Employers and employees have a statutory right to waive their right to notice, but cannot be required to do so. An employer may agree to accept less notice than an employee is contractually obliged to give, or an employee may agree to accept pay in lieu of notice [**34.3.7**]. *Employment Rights Act 1996 s.86(3)*

34.3.6 Pay during notice period

During the notice period, employees are generally entitled to full pay, even if they are on leave. But if the notice period required under the contract is at least one week longer than the statutory notice would be, the entitlement to full pay during the period of notice does not apply. Instead, the employee is entitled to their contractual entitlement during the period of notice – even if this is less than full pay. *Employment Rights Act 1996 ss.87(4),88*

This means that an employee entitled only to statutory notice when dismissed and statutory sick pay [**31.6.1**] while off sick and, is entitled to full pay if off sick during the notice period. But an employee entitled to contractual notice which is a week or more longer than statutory notice, is entitled only to SSP and contractual sick pay (if any) if off sick during the notice period. An employee in this situation who has exhausted their entitlement to SSP and contractual sick pay is not entitled to further pay during the notice period. *Burlo v Langley & another [2006] EWCA Civ 1778*

Pay for statutory annual leave [**31.4**] earned but not taken must always be given up to the date employment ends.

34.3.7 Pay in lieu of notice

Pay in lieu of notice means giving payment for the notice period, without allowing the employee to work through the period. Pay in lieu of notice is often referred to as a **PILON**. The tax and national insurance treatment of a PILON [**34.3.7.5**] depends on whether it is contractual, discretionary or non-contractual.

34.3.7.1 No contractual provision

Technically an employer may lawfully terminate a contract by giving pay in lieu of notice only if the contract provides for it or the employee agrees. However, if there is no contractual provision and the employer breaches the contract by giving pay in lieu, there is little point in the employee bringing a claim against the employer solely for its breach by paying in lieu. The remedy for dismissal without proper notice is payment of damages [**37.5.1**] for the employee's loss, generally the amount of salary the employee would have received in the notice period – so all that the employee would get by bringing a claim against the employer would be an amount equal to the PILON.

Because a PILON where there is no contractual provision is a breach of contract, it has the effect of releasing the employee from his or her contractual obligations such as non-competition and other restrictive covenants [**26.8.2**]. Advice should be taken about the potential implications of this.

34.3.7.2 Discretionary provision

Where the contract says the employee *may* be entitled to pay in lieu of notice or the employer *may* make such payment, this is a discretionary provision.

34.3.7.3 Non-payment of pay in lieu

Where there is discretionary provision or no contractual provision for pay in lieu, an employer who dismisses without notice generally makes a payment covering the full notice period. But if the employer does not pay for the full period and is subsequently sued by the employee, the employer may be able to argue that the employee had a duty to mitigate his or her losses [**21.7.2**] by seeking paid work during the notice period. The court or tribunal, in awarding the pay in lieu to the employee, may reduce the amount if the employee had other earnings during the notice period or did not take steps to mitigate loss by seeking other employment. *Cerberus Software Ltd v Rowley [2001] EWCA Civ 78*

34.3.7.4 Contractual provision

Where there is a contractual entitlement to pay in lieu, the employee is entitled to the full amount even if she or he goes immediately into a new job or does nothing to find work during what would have been the notice period.

34.3.7.5 Tax and national insurance on pay in lieu

General information on the tax treatment of PILONs is available from HM Revenue and Customs [see end of **chapter 30**], but specialist advice should be sought if any payment is to be made without deduction of tax and national insurance.

Where there is a **contractual** entitlement to a PILON, the pay is subject to tax and national insurance in the usual way.

Where a payment is made **without a contractual entitlement**, it is generally assumed to be payment as damages for breach of contract [**34.3.7.1**], and generally the first £30,000 should not be subject to tax or NI. But if the employer regularly makes non-contractual payments upon termination - referred to by HM Revenue and Customs as **auto-PILONs** – HMRC is likely to see it as an integral part of the employer-employee relationship and therefore subject to tax and NI. Specialist advice should be sought before making a payment in lieu of notice where there is no contractual provision for doing so.

A PILON made under a **discretionary** provision [**34.3.7.2**] is treated as contractual and is fully subject to tax and NI. However, the employer may choose not to exercise the discretion, and instead to dismiss without notice in breach of contract, and make a payment as damages for the breach. The first £30,000 of such a payment will be free of tax and NI, but HMRC may well say that the payment is not damages but is in fact a contractual PILON. Specialist advice should be sought before using this approach. *Cerberus Software Ltd v Rowley [2001] EWCA Civ 78*

Where a PILON is included as part of a **compromise agreement** [**37.2.2**], the tax position depends on whether the agreement comes into effect before the employment is terminated (in which case the PILON is taxable) or only on termination (in which case it may be treated as damages for breach of contract, depending on the circumstances, and therefore may not be taxable if it is under £30,000). Again, specialist advice is needed.

Although it may be difficult to enforce in practice, any agreement for a tax-free PILON should include a provision for the employee to indemnify the employer if the employer is held liable for tax.

34.3.8 Termination payments and benefits

As well as specific tax rules for pay in lieu of notice [above] and redundancy payments [**35.7.3**], there are complex rules on the tax treatment of other termination payments, bonuses and benefits [**30.4.15**]. These depend on whether the payment or benefit is – or is treated by HM Revenue and Customs as being – contractual, or is non-contractual, and on the total value of the payments and benefits.

34.4 WRONGFUL DISMISSAL AND TERMINATION

The principles applying to **wrongful dismissal** and **wrongful termination** arise out of the law of contract [**chapter 21**]. Like any contract, a contract of employment can be terminated only in accordance with the terms of that contract. If those terms are broken by the act or manner of termination, the employee has been wrongfully dismissed or has wrongfully terminated the contract.

34.4.1 Wrongful dismissal

Wrongful dismissal is not about the *reasons* for the dismissal and whether they were justified; it is solely about *procedure*. So a dismissal could be justified and fair, but could still be wrongful if the employer did not follow the appropriate steps or give the required notice.

The most common forms of wrongful dismissal are:

- prematurely ending a fixed-term contract [**25.3.1**] when the employee has not committed a breach which justifies this, or when the contract does not allow for termination before its expiry;
- dismissing without notice or with too short notice where there is no repudiation or contractual entitlement to dismiss summarily [**33.3.10**];
- dismissal without following the disciplinary procedure, where the procedure is part of the contract [**33.1.2**].

A claim for wrongful dismissal may be brought in either the civil courts [**65.4**] or the employment tribunal [**37.3**]. The award is generally damages for the amount of the employee's loss between the date of termination and the date the employer could lawfully have terminated [**37.5.1**].

Where wrongful dismissal has occurred, the employer and employee may seek to settle between themselves. A condition of such settlement is often that the employee will not bring a claim against the employer. A settlement preventing the employee from bringing **statutory** claims is enforceable only if it complies with strict rules [**37.2.2**]. A settlement under which the employee agrees not to bring **contractual** claims in court does not have to comply with any formalities, but to protect the employer it should be in writing and in a form prescribed by statute. Legal advice should be taken before entering into any such agreement.

34.4.2   Wrongful v unfair dismissal claims

From an employee's point of view, a claim of wrongful dismissal may in some situations be more advantageous than a claim of unfair dismissal because:

- there is no qualifying period of continuous employment [**26.5**], as there is for most unfair dismissal claims;
- the time limit for bringing a wrongful dismissal claim in the courts is six years, but in most cases only three months for unfair dismissal or for a wrongful dismissal claim in the tribunal;
- if the employee is highly paid and has a long period of notice or a fixed-term contract, a wrongful dismissal claim can be financially more advantageous than a claim for unfair dismissal, because if the claim is brought in the courts there is no upper limit to the amount which can be recovered as damages;
- compensatory damages for unfair dismissal may be substantially reduced because of an employee's contributory conduct [**37.4.2**], but there is no such reduction rule for damages for wrongful dismissal;
- damages for breaches leading up to the dismissal – rather than the dismissal itself – cannot be compensated as part of an unfair dismissal claim;
- financial assistance may be available for wrongful dismissal claims if they are brought in the court rather than in the employment tribunal;
- the employee can recover costs for a successful wrongful dismissal claim in the courts.

34.4.3   Wrongful termination by employee

Where an employee terminates wrongfully, usually by not giving the required notice, the employer has a right to claim damages. But except for very senior or valuable employees, an employer is unlikely to do anything about it.

Many contracts contain provisions that if an employee leaves without giving the required notice or refuses to work out the notice period, the employer is entitled to deduct from the final salary payment an amount equivalent to the number of days that the notice is short. This is based on the principle that the employee's breach of contract causes a financial loss to the employer. However such a clause may not be enforceable, because it is more of a penalty than a genuine pre-estimate of the employer's loss. In order to deduct lawfully there would have to be a contractual clause allowing such deduction, *and* the employer would have to be able to show that it actually suffered a loss equivalent to the deduction.

Giraud UK Ltd v Smith [2000] UKEAT 1105 99 2606

34.5 FAIR DISMISSAL

The principles of **fair** and **unfair dismissal** arise not from contract law, but from statutory employment protection legislation and case law. In most – but by no means all – situations the employee must have at least one year's continuous employment [**26.5**] in order to bring an unfair dismissal claim. Before taking any action which could conceivably give rise to a claim of unfair dismissal, even for employees with less than one year's service, an employer should seek legal advice.

34.5.1 Fair reasons

To be fair, a dismissal must arise from a fair reason. These are the **capability** or qualification of the employee [**34.6.1**], the employee's **conduct** [**34.6.2**], **redundancy** [**34.6.3, 35.1.1**], **statutory requirements** [**34.6.4**], **some other substantial reason** of a kind to justify the dismissal from that position [**34.6.5**], or **retirement** [**34.2.8**]. *Employment Rights Act 1996 s.98(1),(2), amended by Employment Equality (Age) Regulations 2006 [SI 2006/1031] sch.8 pt.1 para.22*

There must be a fair reason at the time of the dismissal. If an employer dismisses without good cause but subsequently discovers a good reason for the dismissal, the **after-discovered reason** cannot be used to justify the dismissal. It may, however, have the effect of reducing the compensation awarded, and if the employee is re-engaged after winning an unfair dismissal case, the after-discovered reason may become a legitimate reason to dismiss again. *Devis & Sons Ltd v Atkins [1977] UKHL 6; English v Martlet Estate Agents Ltd [2002] UKEAT 1030 01 1608*

34.5.2 Fair procedure

A dismissal is for disciplinary reasons may be for a fair reason – capability or conduct – but may be unfair if the employer does not achieve a reasonable standard of procedural fairness. The tribunal will look at matters such as the nature of warnings given, whether a proper investigation took place, and whether the employee was fully informed of the issues and evidence and had a genuine opportunity to put his or her case. Even where the dismissal is for misconduct and the employee has admitted the offence, it is still necessary to carry out an investigation. *Whitbread plc (t/a Whitbread Medway Inns) v Hall [2001] EWCA Civ 268*

This underlines the importance of properly conducting disciplinary proceedings [**33.3**] and giving, except in cases where summary dismissal is justified, at least one warning that dismissal might occur [**33.3.7**].

Dismissals for reasons of capability or conduct must in general comply with the ACAS code of practice on disciplinary and grievance procedures [**33.2.1**]. An employer's failure to follow the ACAS code without good reason could lead to a 25% increase in any tribunal award made to the employee, and an employee's failure to follow the code could lead to a 25% decrease in the award.

Specific rules apply for redundancy dismissals [**35.2**] and retirement [**34.2.8**].

34.5.3 Reasonable response

The employer must also be able to show that considering all the circumstances including its size and administrative resources, it acted reasonably in treating the cause of the dismissal as a sufficient reason for dismissal, dismissal was a **reasonable response**, and the dismissal was fair based on equity (the principles of fairness) and the merits of the case. *Employment Rights Act 1996 s.98(4)*

In assessing what is reasonable the tribunal does not substitute its own assessment for that of the employer. Provided the employer can show that its decision to dismiss was within a **band of reasonable responses**, that it acted reasonably, and that the procedure for the dismissal was fair and reasonable, the dismissal will be fair. *Post Office v Foley, & HSBC Bank Ltd v Madden [2000] EWCA Civ 3030*

34.6 FAIR REASONS FOR DISMISSAL

The legally fair reasons apply not only in the context of disciplinary dismissals (for capability or conduct), but also to dismissals for redundancy, retirement or because the employee is prevented by law from continuing the work. There is also a category of 'some other substantial reason', but this is not the general catch-all that some people think [**34.6.5**].

34.6.1 Capability or qualifications

Capability means skill, aptitude, health or other physical or mental qualities necessary to do the job, and **qualifications** means a relevant degree, diploma or other academic, technical or professional qualification. *Employment Rights Act 1996 s.98(3)*

One of the most frequent issues around capability involves absence or inability to carry out the work due to illness or injury [**34.6.1.1**]. Other reasons for dismissal under the 'capability' heading may be a lack of skill or ability, such as an inability to organise others or to provide the required quantity or quality of work. Capability is assessed in relation to the employer's needs, which may change over time.

If failure to achieve the necessary level of competence or the desired results stems from carelessness or negligence, it should be treated as a conduct issue.

In all cases, a disciplinary or capability procedure [**33.3**] must be followed, with an investigation, a meeting or meetings, warnings and target setting. Reviews with a reasonable opportunity to improve must be provided at each stage, with if applicable a clear indication that dismissal may follow if there is inadequate improvement.

34.6.1.1 Ill health

To dismiss fairly in a situation where ill health or injury results in frequent or long-term absence from work or makes it difficult for the employee to do the work, the employer must carry out a disciplinary or capability procedure [**33.3**], issue one or more warnings, and give an opportunity for the employee's health to improve. But well before this stage, the employer should be discussing the situation informally and formally with the employee, finding out about the employee's condition, and taking reasonable steps to adapt the work so the employee can do it [**31.6.4**]. This could include, for example, changing the nature of the work or the hours or place of work, or providing training or equipment.

If the condition constitutes a disability under the **Disability Discrimination Act 1995** [**28.7.1**], the employer has a statutory duty to make reasonable adjustments to the job or provide suitable alternative work [**28.7.4**]. Failure to do so may lead to a discrimination claim for less favourable treatment, failure to make reasonable adjustments, or unfair dismissal. The fact that the employer did not recognise the employee was disabled is unlikely to be a defence if it had been provided with – or should have sought – enough information to put it on notice. This is a complex area and legal advice should be sought before starting a disciplinary procedure arising from any condition which is or could legally be a disability, or dismissing anyone with such a condition.

34.6.1.2 Dismissal during sick leave

It is not necessary to wait until all statutory or contractual sick leave entitlement [**31.6**] is used before dismissing. However, dismissal on the basis of sickness during paid sick leave, where it appears that the employee is likely to be able to return before the sick leave period expires, is likely to be unfair. The length of sick leave and the impact of the absence on the employer are factors affecting whether it is reasonable to dismiss. *Coulson v Felixstowe Dock & Railway Co [1995] IRLR 11*

An employer who provides **permanent health insurance** [**23.4.3**] for employees should seek specialist advice before dismissing an employee covered by the insurance. These policies often provide that after an initial period of absence during which the employee receives sick pay from the organisation, the insurance starts to pay a sum as replacement of lost salary. Normally the policy provides that this payment will continue for as long as the person suffers illness or disability, if necessary until the age when the person would have retired. In a number of cases, courts have said that the existence of such insurance creates an implied term [**26.3.4**] in the contract that the employee will not be dismissed except for gross misconduct while receiving payments under the insurance. *Aspden v Webbs Poultry & Meat Group (Holdings) Ltd [1996] IRLR 521*

34.6.1.3 Incapability caused by employer

Where an employee's incapability is caused, at least in part, by the employer – for example, an employee off because of work related stress – this is a factor in deciding whether a dismissal is fair. In these situations the employer is obliged to 'go the extra mile' before dismissing, for example by making a particular effort to arrange alternative work or allowing longer sick leave than would ordinarily be allowed.

McAdie v Royal Bank of Scotland [2007] EWCA Civ 806

34.6.2 Conduct

A huge variety of conduct related reasons have been found to be fair, including poor timekeeping, absenteeism, failure to cooperate, breach of rules or guidelines, failure to obey an instruction, and violence or harassment inside the workplace or outside in relation to fellow employees. It is up to the employer to define what is or is not acceptable, but the definitions must be reasonable in the circumstances.

34.6.2.1 Criminal acts

Just as some criminal charges or convictions may not justify disciplinary action [**33.3.11**] and imprisonment does not necessarily bring the employment contract to an end [**34.2.11**], they may not justify dismissal. It is not enough for the employer simply to know that the police are taking action. The employer must make its own enquiries and come to its own conclusion that the offence was committed and that it has implications for the employment. The employer does not need to prove to itself that the employee is guilty before dismissing, merely to have reasonable grounds for believing that the employee is guilty. There is no need to wait for the outcome of any criminal prosecution and it is best not to do so, given that the employee will often have to be suspended on full pay in the meantime.

If the offence occurs outside the workplace, there must be some effect on the work – such as the likely impact on relationships with other employees, service users, funders or donors – for it to be a fair reason for dismissal.

34.6.3 Redundancy

A **redundancy** exists when the employer intends to stop carrying on the activity for which the employee is employed either totally or where the employee is employed, or when the need to carry out the work has ceased or diminished [see **chapter 35** for more about redundancy]. The dispute in redundancy situations is not generally about the reasonableness of the decision, but about whether the procedures used to select the individual were fair.

As well as investigating the fairness of the procedure, the tribunal is allowed to question whether any redundancy is a genuine redundancy, so it is important for an employer to have evidence about its financial situation, grant cuts or other reasons for closure or loss of the job.

Even in a redundancy situation, dismissal may be unfair if the person was selected for a reason which is automatically unfair [**34.7**], the employer failed to consult adequately before deciding to dismiss [**35.2**], the employer failed to consider alternative work [**35.6**], or the employer failed to use reasonable criteria for selecting those to be made redundant or the pool from which they would be chosen [**35.3**]. The employer can use any criteria it wants, but they must be fair and reasonable and must not have the effect of discriminating unlawfully.

As well as behaving reasonably, the employer must comply with statutory rules regarding consultation and notification [**35.2**].

34.6.4 Statutory requirements

This category of fair reasons for dismissal covers situations where the law prohibits an employee from continuing in the job. Such situations include, for example, a driver who has been disqualified from driving, or a care worker or childcare worker who has been barred from working in a regulated activity with children or vulnerable adults [**41.7**]. In these situations, the employer does not have to go through a disciplinary proceeding and give warnings before dismissing.

34.6.5　Some other substantial reason

Some other substantial reason (SOSR) is not a catch-all but may cover, for example, a reorganisation in the interests of organisational efficiency not fitting the criteria for redundancy, an employee's refusal to agree changes in the contract for which the employer can show that there is a substantial reason, the termination of a contract covering another employee's maternity leave, or an employee causing disharmony in the workplace. It is always safest to have legal advice when considering a SOSR dismissal.

34.6.5.1　Third party pressure to dismiss

Where a third party such as a funder or major customer demands that an employee be dismissed, it may be fair for as a SOSR dismissal. The employer must follow a fair procedure, ensure that dismissal is a reasonable response [**34.5.3**], and take into account the injustice to the employee. This involves considering the employee's work record, whether he or she could be given another role, how difficult he or she might find it to obtain alternative employment, and whether there is another way of satisfying the third party. If the employer has considered these issues, discussed them with the employee and feels there is no option but to dismiss, the dismissal may be fair. Legal advice should be sought before dismissing in these circumstances.　　*Greenwood v Whiteghyll Plastics Ltd [2007] UKEAT 0219 07 0608*

34.7　UNFAIR REASONS FOR DISMISSAL

In many cases where a claim may be brought for unfair dismissal, a claim may be brought for something else as well. A dismissal on the basis of the employee's religion, for example, is not only unfair dismissal, but also unlawful discrimination – and if proper notice is not given, it is also wrongful dismissal [**34.4.1**].

34.7.1　Automatically unfair

An unfair dismissal claim can be brought with no qualifying period [**26.5**] if a dismissal is solely or mainly for a reason defined in statute as **automatically unfair.** There is an exception to the rule that no qualifying period is needed, where the reason is linked to the transfer of an employee under TUPE [**34.7.1.6**].
　　Employment Rights Act 1996 ss.98B-105, as amended

34.7.1.1　No qualifying period: Discrimination

Dismissal is automatically unfair, with no qualifying period, if it is for a reason connected with:

- the employee's **race**, colour, ethnic group, national origin or nationality [**28.2**];
- **sex**, gender reassignment (transsexuality), marital status or civil partnership status [**28.3**]; ;
- virtually any reason connected with **pregnancy**, childbirth, maternity or maternity leave [**32.2**]
- claiming **equal pay** [**28.8**];
- **disability** [**28.7**];
- **religion** or belief [**28.4**];
- **sexual orientation** [**28.5**];
- **age** [**28.6**];
- an employer's failure to comply with the **statutory retirement procedure** [**34.2.8.1**];
- an employee bringing, or threatening to bring, a claim under the equality legislation for discrimination, victimisation or harassment, or supporting a person who has brought or threatened to bring such a claim.

34.7.1.2　No qualifying period: Pay and conditions

Dismissal is automatically unfair, with no qualifying period, if it is for a reason connected with:

- claiming **minimum wage [30.2]** or any other statutory right related to pay;
- taking, or seeking to take, ordinary or additional **adoption leave [32.4]**, **paternity leave** and (when it becomes available) additional **paternity leave [32.3]**, **parental leave [32.7]**, or leave to deal with **dependant emergencies [32.8]**;
- requesting **flexible working** as a parent **[32.5]** or carer **[32.6]**;
- claiming statutory rights as **part-time worker [26.4.2]** or **fixed-term employee [26.4.3]**;
- enforcing or seeking to enforce **working time** rights (48-hour week, rest breaks, rest periods, annual leave) **[31.2-31.4]**;
- a shop worker refusing or proposing to refuse to work on **Sundays** or on a particular Sunday **[31.2.6]**.

34.7.1.3 No qualifying period: Health and safety

Dismissal is automatically unfair, with no qualifying period, if it is for a reason connected with:

- serving or taking action as a **health and safety representative [40.2.8]**;
- bringing a **health or safety** danger to the employer's attention, refusing to work in an unsafe situation, or taking steps to protect him/herself or other people from danger **[chapter 40]**.

34.7.1.4 No qualifying period: Trade union and related rights

Dismissal is automatically unfair, with no qualifying period, if it is for a reason connected with:

- being, or proposing to become, a member of an independent **trade union**, not being a member of a union or refusing to join one **[36.4.1]**;
- taking steps in relation to **trade union recognition [36.3.3]**, or voting or proposing to vote in a ballot in connection with recognition;
- taking part or proposing to take part in **union activities** either in work time if permitted by the employer or outside work time **[36.4.2]**;
- taking part in **protected industrial action [36.6.1]**.

34.7.1.5 No qualifying period: Other unfair reasons

Dismissal is automatically unfair, with no qualifying period, if it is for a reason connected with:

- running for election or serving as an **employee representative** for the purposes of TUPE consultation **[29.7.3]**, redundancy consultation **[35.2]**, or the information and consultation regulations **[36.2.1]**;
- exercising or seeking to exercise the **right to be accompanied** at a disciplinary or grievance meeting **[33.1.1]** or a meeting to request flexible working **[32.5-32.6]** or the right to work beyond retirement age **[34.2.8]**, or accompanying or seeking to accompany a fellow worker to such a meeting;
- serving as a trustee of an occupational pension scheme **[30.6.4]**;
- being called for or serving on a jury **[31.7.2]**;
- in most cases, during the protected period after returning to work following military service **[31.7.3]**;
- making or threatening to make a protected whistleblowing disclosure **[33.5]**;
- claiming that the employer has infringed any other statutory employment right [see **26.4-26.7** for a list of these rights];
- bringing proceedings against the employer to enforce any statutory employment right.

34.7.1.6 Qualifying period: TUPE dismissal

In most situations, dismissal is automatically unfair if it is for any reason connected with a transfer under the Transfer of Undertaking Regulations (**TUPE**) **[34.2.7]**. But an unfair dismissal claim may be brought only if the employee has one year's continuous employment with the employer **[26.5]**.

34.7.2   Other unfair reasons

If a reason is not automatically unfair and is not a fair reason [**34.6**], it is an unfair reason. An employee who has worked for the employer for one year may bring a claim for unfair dismissal.

Dismissal while taking part in unofficial industrial action [**36.6.2**] is unfair but the employee cannot generally claim unfair dismissal.

34.8   ENTITLEMENT TO CLAIM UNFAIR DISMISSAL

An employee dismissed for a reason which is automatically unfair [**34.7**] has a right to bring a claim of unfair dismissal, with no qualifying period (apart from a TUPE dismissal). To bring a claim for a TUPE dismissal or other types of unfair dismissal, the employee must have at least one year's continuous employment [**26.5**] with the employer or an associated employer.

Application must generally be made to the employment tribunal [**37.3**] within three months of the **effective date of termination** [**34.8.1**]. In exceptional circumstances, the three-month deadline can be extended by the tribunal [**37.3.2**]. If the tribunal finds that the dismissal is not fair, it may award compensation [**37.4.2**] or in very rare cases require reinstatement or re-engagement [**37.4.1**].

Rather than go to tribunal, the employer and employee may agree a **settlement**. Usually a condition of settlement is that the employee gives up the right to take the case to tribunal. This condition is binding only if the settlement follows strict rules [**37.2.2**]. In any situation where the employer is settling by making a payment in addition to whatever is due to the employee, it is sensible to make payment dependent on the employee signing a **compromise agreement** [**37.2.2**].

34.8.1   Effective date of termination

The qualifying period and the time limit for bringing unfair and wrongful dismissal claims are based on the **effective date of termination** (EDT). For redundancy purposes this is called the **relevant date** [**35.7.1**].

34.8.1.1   Notice by employer

The basic rules for determining the effective date of termination are:

*   if the employee is dismissed with proper notice of dismissal [**34.3**] , the EDT is the date the notice period expires, regardless of whether the employee does or docs not work out the notice period;
*   if the employee is entitled to notice but is dismissed without proper notice, the EDT is the date the statutory notice period would have ended, regardless of whether the employee is or is not given payment in lieu of notice [**34.3.7**],;
*   if the employee is in the first month of employment and is thus not entitled to statutory notice, the EDT is the date specified as the last day of work or the date the dismissal is communicated to the employee, whichever is later;
*   if the employee is dismissed without notice for gross misconduct [**33.3.10**], the EDT is the date the dismissal is communicated to the employee;
*   the EDT of a fixed-term contract is the date the fixed term expires.

Employment Rights Act 1996 s.97, as amended

For a dismissal sent by post, the date it is communicated to the employee is when the employee actually receives and reads the letter, even if the letter says that dismissal is from the date the letter is written. It may be sensible to give notice to the employee orally, so it is clear that he or she has received the notice, and/or to send it recorded delivery.

McMaster v Manchester Airport plc [1997] UKEAT 149 97 2710;
Gisda Cyf v Barratt [2009] EWCA Civ 648

If the employer gives notice, and the employee then gives a shorter notice which takes effect earlier, the effective date of termination is the date on which the employer's notice would have taken effect.

Employment Rights Act 1996 s.95(2)

34.8.1.2   Notice by employee

An employee who resigns orally may state that it takes effect immediately or at the end of the notice period. Provided the resignation is clear, it cannot later be retracted unless there are special circumstances, such as clearly being in the heat of the moment, or if the employee had a mental impairment [**34.2.3.1**].

If an employee resigns by post without specifying when the resignation takes effect, the effective date of termination is likely to be taken to be the second day after a letter is posted first class.

For resignation by fax without a specified termination date, the effective date of termination is when the resignation is validly communicated by being sent to the employer, even if the employer does not read it until later. At the time of writing (mid 2009) there appears to be no case law on resignation by email or other electronic communication.   *Potter & others v R J Temple plc [2003] UKEAT 0478 03 1812*

If an employee resigns and claims **constructive dismissal [34.2.9]**, the effective date of termination [**34.8.1**] is the date of resignation, plus the statutory notice the employee would have been entitled to from the employer [**34.3.1**].

34.8.2   Qualifying employees

In general, only employees and apprentices have the right to claim unfair dismissal. Trainees, self employed people, non-employee 'workers' [**25.1.2**] and others who are not employees generally cannot bring a claim.

In the past, employees of a UK-based employer who worked outside the UK were not able to claim unfair dismissal, but they now may have this right [**26.11.1**].

34.8.3   Qualifying dismissal

To make a claim of unfair dismissal, the employee must have been dismissed. Dismissal normally occurs if the employer terminates the employee's contract of employment, usually by giving notice or dismissing with immediate effect although in some situations dismissal can be inferred from the circumstances; a fixed-term contract is not renewed; or the employee is entitled to terminate the contract because of the employer's conduct, and does so [**34.2.9**].

For the purposes of unfair dismissal, the employee is not considered to be dismissed if he or she is re-engaged before the dismissal takes effect or the employer offers to renew the contract of employment within four weeks of the dismissal.   *EBAC Ltd v Wymer [1996] 537 IRLB 3 EAT*

34.8.3.1   Termination by agreement

Unless it meets certain statutory requirements [**37.2.2**], any agreement between an employer and employee is invalid if it seeks to prevent the employee from exercising his or her right to make an application to the employment tribunal for any reason. An agreement, therefore, where an employer agrees to make a final payment to an employee, give a reference to an employee, or take other action on condition that the employee does not make a claim of unfair dismissal is invalid unless it is in the prescribed form.   *Employment Rights Act 1996 s.203, as amended*

34.8.4   Non-qualifying termination

A contract can come to an end without there being a dismissal which would give rise to a possible claim for unfair dismissal. This is the case, for example, when an employee resigns or the contract is **frustrated** [**34.2.11**].

Resources: TERMINATION OF EMPLOYMENT

ACAS, BIS, Business Link, CIPD, Directgov, PEACe, TUC: see end of **chapter 25**.

Statute law. www.opsi.gov.uk and www.statutelaw.gov.uk.

Much but not all case law. www.bailii.org.

Updates cross-referenced to this book. www.rclh.co.uk.

Chapter 35
REDUNDANCY

For sources of further information see end of chapter.

35.1 DEFINING REDUNDANCY

There are two statutory definitions of redundancy: one for the purposes of **fair dismissal** and **redundancy pay** [below], and a much wider definition for the purposes of **collective consultation [35.2.2.1]**.

Redundancy is highly regulated, and specialist advice should be sought at an early stage. Any failure to follow statutory or contractual requirements and a fair procedure may lead to unfair dismissal claims, or to discrimination claims in relation to selection for redundancy or failure to offer a suitable alternative job.

35.1.1 Definition for dismissal and redundancy pay

For the purposes of dismissal and redundancy pay, a redundancy dismissal is one which is attributable wholly or mainly to the fact that:

- the employer has ceased or intends to cease to carry on the business for the purposes for which the employee was employed;

- the employer has ceased or intends to cease to carry on the business in the place where the employee was employed; or

- the requirement of that business for employees to carry out work of a particular kind, or for employees to carry out work of a particular kind in the place where the employee was employed, has ceased or diminished or is expected to cease or diminish. *Employment Rights Act 1996 s.139(1)*

'Business' means any activity for which a person is employed, even if carried out by a charity or other voluntary organisation. The reduced need for the work may arise through lack of demand, lack of funding, or a decision by the organisation.

'Work of a particular kind' is 'work which is distinguished from other work of the same general kind by requiring special aptitudes, special skills or knowledge'.

Amos v Max-Arc Ltd [1973] ICR 46; IRLR 285

If a so-called redundancy does not meet the test for redundancy, the dismissal is not fair on the basis of redundancy, and an employee with the necessary continuity of employment may be able to make a claim of unfair dismissal **[34.7.2]** (unless the dismissal is fair on some other basis). In addition the employee will not be entitled to a redundancy payment **[35.7]**.

Even if the redundancy is genuine, the dismissal may be unfair if it is not carried out reasonably, for example if reasonable and fair criteria are not used to select the selection pool or the employees to be made redundant [**35.3**], or if collective redundancy consultation [**35.2.2**] is not carried out if required.

35.1.2 Specific situations

Redundancy requirements are complex, especially in situations such as those below where it is particularly important to take advice at an early stage.

35.1.2.1 Voluntary redundancy

Voluntary redundancy refers to a genuine redundancy situation where employees in the selection pool are invited to apply to be made redundant. This can be a useful way of avoiding compulsory redundancy, but there is a risk that those who volunteer may be those whom the employer would prefer to keep. Care needs to be taken to ensure the invitation to volunteer, and the criteria used for deciding which offers to accept, do not discriminate unlawfully.

If there is not a genuine redundancy situation, any 'voluntary redundancy' is a termination by agreement [**34.8.3**] and is likely to be unfair. The employer should put in place a valid agreement preventing the employee from bringing a claim against the employer [**37.2.2**].

35.1.2.2 Redundancy during maternity, adoption or paternity leave

A employee who is pregnant or on maternity [**32.2.4**] or adoption [**32.4.1**] leave, and who is at risk of redundancy, must be consulted in the same way as other employees. In being offered suitable alternative employment [**35.6**], this employee must be given priority over other employees who are being made redundant – even if this is economically disadvantageous for the employer, and even if the employee will not be able to start the new work until returning from leave. The same rules are likely to apply when additional paternity leave [**32.3.3**] becomes available.   *Maternity & Parental Leave Regulations 1999 [SI 1999/3312] reg.10; Paternity & Adoption Leave Regulations 2002 [SI 2002/2788] reg.23; Community Task Force v Rimmer [1986] IRLR 203 EAT;*

If no suitable alternative work is available, the employee can be made redundant even while on maternity or adoption leave.

35.1.2.3 'Bumping'

An employee (Worker A) whose post is redundant could be offered as suitable alternative employment a post held by Worker B, thus making B redundant instead. This is called **bumping**. Employers should consider whether bumping may be appropriate when proposing to dismiss an employee on grounds of redundancy, and legal advice should be sought if this might be relevant.   *Lionel Leventhal Ltd v North [2004] UKEAT 0265 04 2710*

35.1.2.4 Restructuring

If an **organisational restructuring** leads to a loss of jobs because there is no longer a need for so many employees to do the work, there is a redundancy situation. The employees who are potentially redundant must be offered suitable alternative work [**35.6**] if it is available. If there is no suitable alternative work, the employees are redundant.

A restructuring which does not lead to fewer jobs but needs employees to fill different roles may not create a redundancy situation. However, a similar process should be followed, involving consultation [**35.2**] and consideration of suitable alternative employment [**35.6**]. If the reason for a dismissal arising from a restructuring does not meet the statutory definition of redundancy, it may be a fair dismissal 'for some other substantial reason' [**34.6.5**].

35.1.2.5 Work at other locations

If the employee's contract of employment has a **mobility clause** [**27.2.7**], the employer can, if it is reasonable to do so, require the employee to move to another location. However, mobility clauses may constitute indirect sex discrimination [**28.1.4**], on the basis that more women than men cannot easily move location.

If one workplace closes or has insufficient work, the employee is redundant there. But if there is suitable alternative work at another site and the employee can be required to move there under the terms of his or her contract, is the employee genuinely redundant? In this situation the tribunal looks at the facts. In a case where an employee had worked at only one site, the court of appeal said there was a redundancy even though there was a mobility clause in the contract and work was available on another site.   *High Table Ltd v Horst & others [1997] EWCA Civ 2000*

A recent case suggests that an employer is entitled to invoke a contractual mobility clause in preference to following a redundancy procedure, but advice should be sought.   *Home Office v Evans & another [2007] EWCA Civ 1089*

Regardless of whether the contract contains a mobility clause, the offer of work at another location may be suitable alternative employment [**35.6**]. But if the location is so far away as to be unsuitable, the employee may be reasonable in declining an offer and should not lose redundancy pay entitlement.

35.2   CONSULTATION AND NOTIFICATION

An employer who proposes to make an employee or employees redundant must consult the individuals in the proposed redundancy selection pool [**35.3.1**]. Where 20 or more employees are potentially redundant, **collective consultation** may also be necessary [**35.2.2**]. The main aims of consultation are to explore alternatives to redundancy and whether alternative work is available.

To be fair, consultation must take place when proposals are at a formative stage, must be based on adequate information [**35.2.2.5**] with adequate time for response, and there must be genuine consideration of the response.

35.2.1   Individual consultation

There is no specific statutory obligation for an employer to consult individual employees prior to making them redundant, but case law has established that individual consultation is an essential part of a fair procedure and an employer's reasonable conduct [**34.5.2**]. Failure to consult may thus lead to a finding of unfair dismissal, unless the tribunal concludes that consultation would have been utterly futile. Failure to consult a worker who is on maternity leave or absent for a pregnancy related reason may be unlawful sex discrimination.   *Mugford v Midland Bank plc [1997] UKEAT 760 96 2301; McGuigan v T G Baynes & Sons [1998] UKEAT 1114 97 2411*

Consultation may be with each individual separately, with jointly in meetings, or a combination. As part of the consultation process, the employer should:

- explain the reason for the redundancies;
- explain the selection process, seek the employee's views on the selection criteria and give him or her an opportunity to explain any factors which may have resulted in potential selection for redundancy or the redundancy pool [**35.3**];
- explore with the employee ways of avoiding redundancy, such as retraining the employee for other work and making it clear that the employer will look for suitable alternative employment within the organisation [**35.6**]; and
- consider asking for volunteers for redundancy [**35.1.2.1**].

Consultation must not be used as a way of making employees decide who should be made redundant. This is an improper use of the consultation process.

Boulton & Paul Ltd v Arnold [1994] UKEAT 341 93 2305

35.2.2   Collective consultation

When an employer proposes to make 20 or more employees redundant within a 90-day period – using the definition of redundancy below – the employer has a duty to consult any independent trade union(s) recognised by the employer [**36.3.3**] or, where there is no recognised union, elected representatives of the employees likely to be affected by the redundancies [**36.1**]. If some but not all employees are represented by a recognised union, the employer must consult both the union(s) and representatives elected by the other employees.

Trade Union & Labour Relations (Consolidation) Act 1992 s.188, amended by Collective Redundancies & Transfer of Undertakings (Protection of Employment) (Amendment) Regulations 1999 [SI 1999/1925] reg.3

Consultation must be completed before any notice of dismissal is given. This is because the purpose of the consultation is to avoid or minimise redundancies, which realistically is unlikely to happen if notices have already been issued. Legal advice should be sought when dealing with notice of dismissal in collective redundancy situations, to ensure the consultation period provides enough time afterwards for the required notice [**34.3**].

Junk v Kuhnel [2005] EUECJ C-188/03

35.2.2.1   Definition of redundancy for collective consultation

In relation to the requirement to consult with recognised trade unions or elected employee representatives, redundancy is defined very widely, as any dismissal 'not related to the individual concerned or for a number of reasons all of which are not so related'. This covers most dismissals not directly related to an individual employee's competence, conduct or retirement.

Trade Union & Labour Relations (Consolidation) Act 1992 s.195, inserted by Trade Union Reform & Employment Rights Act 1993 s.34(5)

35.2.2.2   Counting the numbers

When determining whether 20 or more employees are to be made redundant, all employees who could be made redundant are included in the numbers, even if they are not entitled to redundancy pay or are volunteering for redundancy. Even where the employer is restructuring and proposes to offer alternative work – thus bringing the number of people actually being dismissed to below 20 – the duty to consult still applies if the proposed changes to the existing contracts are substantial.

Hardy v Tourism South East [2004] UKEAT 0631 04 2911;
Optare Group Ltd v Transport & General Workers Union [2007] UKEAT 0143 07 1007

The employees to be made redundant must be 'at one establishment'. This clearly means all working in the same place, but can also mean working in different locations. It can be difficult to determine what constitutes an 'establishment', and advice should be sought if this is an issue.

Barratt Developments (Bradford) Ltd v Union of Construction Allied Trades & Technicians [1978] ICR 319 EAT;
Rockfon A/S v Specialarbejderforbundet I Danmark [1995] EUECJ C-449/93

35.2.2.3   Period of consultation

The consultation must begin 'in good time', and must be completed before any redundancy notices are issued [**35.2.2**]. The minimum prescribed periods are 30 days before the first redundancy takes effect if between 20 and 99 employees are to be dismissed within a period of 90 days or less, and 90 days if 100 or more are being made redundant.

Trade Union & Labour Relations (Consolidation) Act 1992 s.188(1A), inserted by Collective Redundancies & Transfer of Undertakings (Protection of Employment) (Amendment) Regulations 1995 [SI 1995/2587] reg.3

If special circumstances make it impracticable to carry out the consultation as required, the employer must take all reasonable steps to comply to as great an extent as possible.

TULR(C)A 1992 s.188(7)

35.2.2.4   Purpose of the consultation

Consultation must be with representatives of all workers who may be affected, not only those under threat of redundancy, and must be undertaken by the employer 'with a view to reaching agreement' with the representatives. It must include ways of avoiding dismissals, reducing the number of employees to be dismissed, and easing the consequences of dismissals.

TULR(C)A 1992 s.188(2)

An employer is generally not required to consult on the reasons for redundancy, but where the redundancies arise from a proposed closure of the business, there is a duty to consult on the reasons for closure.

UK Coal Mining Ltd v National Union of Mineworkers (Northumberland Area) & another [2007] UKEAT 0397 06 2709

35.2.2.5   Provision of information

The employer must provide the union or employees' representatives in writing with the reason for the proposed dismissals, the number and description of workers proposed for redundancy, the total number of employees employed at the location, the proposed methods for selecting employees who may be dismissed and carrying out the dismissals, the period for the dismissals, and the proposed method of calculating any redundancy payments in addition to those required by statute.

TULR(C)A 1992 s.188(4), amended by Trade Union Reform & Employment Rights Act 1993 s.34(2)(a)

If employees have been invited to elect representatives but do not do so within a reasonable time, the employer must give the specified information to each affected employee. *Trade Union & Labour Relations (Consolidation) Act 1992 s.188(7B) inserted by Collective Redundancies & Transfer of Undertakings (Protection of Employment) (Amendment) Regulations 1999 [SI 1999/1925] reg.3(6)*

35.2.2.6   Protective awards

Failure to consult or provide information does not prevent an employer from making the redundancies, but the union or employees' representatives may make a complaint to the tribunal before the dismissals, or within three months after they have taken effect. The tribunal may make a **protective award** requiring the employer to pay each affected employee whatever the tribunal decides is just and equitable, up to a maximum of 90 days' pay.   *TULR(C)A 1992 ss.189-192, as amended*

The purpose of the award is primarily to provide a sanction for the employer's breach of its obligation to consult, rather than to compensate employees, so the seriousness of the default is the main consideration in calculating the amount. The starting point is the maximum 90 days' pay, which is reduced only if there are mitigating circumstances.   *Susie Radin Ltd v GMB & others [2004] EWCA Civ 180*

35.2.2.7   Official notification

An employer must notify the secretary of state for business, innovation and skills (BIS), through the Redundancy Payments Office [see end of chapter], if 20 or more employees are being made redundant in a 90-day period. This notice, by letter or on form **HR1**, must be given before any notice of dismissal is issued, and at least 30 days before the first dismissal takes effect if 20-99 employees are to be made redundant, or 90 days before if 100 or more employees are to be made redundant. If the period of notice specified in the contract of employment is longer than 30 or 90 days, the contractual period applies. The employer can be fined up to £5,000 for failure to give notice to BIS as required, and should also give a copy of the letter or HR1 to the employee representatives who will be consulted.
TULR(C)A 1992 s.193, amended by Collective Redundancies (Amendment) Regulations 2006 [SI 2006/2387]

35.2.3   Other obligations to consult

The contract of employment, contractual policies or a collective agreement with the union(s) may include specific requirements, such as consulting the recognised union(s) even if there are fewer than 20 redundancies. All provisions must be strictly followed. Failure to comply with contractual obligations could lead to claims for unfair and/or wrongful dismissal. The obligations under collective agreements may or may not be legally binding [**36.3.4**], but even if they are not binding, failure to comply with them could lead to a claim for unfair dismissal.

35.3   REDUNDANCY SELECTION

35.3.1   Selection pool

Unless all employees are to be dismissed, employers must ensure that the pool from which employees may be selected for redundancy is fairly defined. When considering whether the employer has acted reasonably, a tribunal may consider factors such as the extent to which other employees are doing the same or similar work, whether the jobs are interchangeable, contractual job descriptions, any agreement with unions as to the selection pool, and facts which may show that a pool was defined solely for the purpose of dismissing a particular employee. Failure to use the appropriate pool could make a redundancy dismissal unfair.

In general, an employer can decide which pool to use, provided the choice is reasonable. But the employment appeal tribunal has said it is unfair to limit the pool to employees in one division. This means that if a grant or contract for a piece of work ends with no further funding, it may not be a simple matter of making those employees the pool for redundancy. If other staff are doing the same or similar work, even in other teams or other parts of the organisation, those other staff may need to be included in the pool of employees to be considered for redundancy. Legal advice should be sought in this situation.
Kvaerner Oil & Gas Ltd v M G Parker & others [2003] UKEAT 0444 02 2801

35.3.2   Selection criteria

Employers must adopt fair and objective selection criteria that are suitable to the organisation. These might include attendance records, disciplinary records, skills, qualifications, performance and capability, and can be weighted as appropriate. Legal advice should be sought when drawing up selection criteria, to ensure they are objective and supported by evidence, and do not discriminate on the grounds of sex, race, disability, religion or belief, sexual orientation or age. Absence due to disability is usually disregarded in considering attendance records.

Any criterion based on length of service could be indirect age discrimination and should be justifiable as fulfilling a business need [**28.6.2**]. 'Last in first out' is lawful if it can be objectively justified – especially if it is used in a selection matrix with a number of other criteria.   *Rolls-Royce plc v Unite the Union [2009] EWCA Civ 387*

Employees in the selection pool are usually assessed by being marked against the criteria. An employer who fails to disclose details of an employee's own assessment if asked to do so, or does not allow the employee to contest the selection, may be in breach of its duty to consult [**35.2.1**]. Employees are not entitled to assessment details for other employees, although the employer must be able to show that the method of selection was fair in general terms, and was reasonably applied to the employee concerned.   *John Brown Engineering Ltd v Brown [1997] IRLR 90 EAT*

35.4   PERIOD OF NOTICE

An employee who is being made redundant is entitled to statutory or contractual notice, whichever is higher, in the usual way [**34.3**]. Individual notice must be given to each employee, so a general closure announcement is not adequate. An employee who is required to stop work before the end of the notice period – for example, if the employer closes – is entitled to pay in lieu of notice for that period.

35.4.1   Precautionary notice

An organisation approaching the end of a contract or funding cycle without knowing whether there will be replacement funding may need to undertake redundancy consultation [**35.2**] and give employees notice of redundancy, stating that they may be redundant if the funds are not forthcoming and there is no suitable alternative employment. This is often called a **precautionary** (or sometimes **protective**) **notice of redundancy**, and provides a framework within which the employer can start individual and, if necessary, collective consultation [**35.2**].

If the notice includes a dismissal date, such as 'You will be dismissed as of 31 March 2010 if funds are not available and there is no suitable alternative employment', it is a proper notice of dismissal. An employer who wishes to revoke a dismissal notice should obtain the employee's written consent.

Where notice of dismissal has been given, employees are entitled to serve a written **counter notice** that they wish to leave earlier and still claim redundancy pay [**35.7.1.4**].

35.5   RIGHT TO TIME OFF

An employee who has been given notice of dismissal due to redundancy and has the necessary qualifying period for redundancy pay [**35.7.1.2**] is entitled to reasonable time off with pay during working hours to look for another job or to make arrangements for training for future employment. There is no statutory amount of time an employee is entitled to take off.   *Employment Rights Act 1996 ss.52,53*

If the employer does not allow paid time off, the employee is entitled to be paid the amount he or she would have been entitled to if time off had been allowed, up to 40% of one week's pay. If the employer neither allows paid time off nor pays for the time not allowed, the employee may bring a complaint in the employment tribunal and may be awarded up to 40% of one week's pay.   *ERA ss.53(4),(5), 54(4)*

35.6 SUITABLE ALTERNATIVE EMPLOYMENT

The employer has a duty to offer suitable alternative work if any is available. If suitable work is offered and the employee accepts it, there is no redundancy and no break in continuity of employment [**26.5**] if the new contract starts as soon as the old contract ends or within four weeks of the termination. If suitable work is offered and the employee unreasonably refuses it, he or she loses the right to a statutory redundancy payment. An employer's failure to offer suitable alternative work makes the dismissal unfair. *Employment Rights Act 1996 s.141*

If alternative work is available, it must be offered to an employee at risk of redundancy even if he or she is not the best person for it. A competitive process is permissible only if two or more employees are being made redundant for whom the available work would be suitable, but there are not enough posts for both or all of them. Only the employees at risk of redundancy are entitled to apply.

Suitable alternative employment must automatically be given to a redundant employee who is pregnant or on maternity or adoption leave [**35.1.2.2**] – without the other redundant employees even being offered the opportunity to complete. The same is likely to apply when additional paternity leave becomes available.

The suitability of alternative work offered by the employer is judged objectively. Relevant factors include the nature of the work, its location and the contract conditions. *Employment Rights Act 1996 s.138(1),(2)*

35.6.1 Trial period

If the alternative employment differs in any significant way from the previous contract, the employee has a statutory right to a **trial period** of four weeks from the start of the new contract. This can be extended by agreement if additional time is needed for retraining for the new work. This agreement must be made before the employee starts the new work, must be in writing, and must specify the date on which the extended period ends and the conditions which will apply after the period. If the employee successfully completes the trial period there is no redundancy and no break in continuity. *Employment Rights Act 1996 s.138(2),(3),(6)*

An employee who resigns or is dismissed for a reason connected to the new employment (such as unsuitability) during or at the end of the trial period, whether standard or extended, is treated as having been made redundant under the previous contract and remains entitled to redundancy pay.

An employee who unreasonably terminates the new contract is deemed to have refused an offer of suitable work, and loses the right to redundancy pay. The refusal of alternative employment is judged subjectively, from the point of view of the employee. Personal factors such as needing to move house may be reasonable.

A resignation after the end of the trial period is an ordinary resignation, with no entitlement to redundancy pay.

35.7 REDUNDANCY PAYMENTS

In addition to entitlement to **statutory redundancy pay**, many voluntary sector employers provide for **non-statutory** (or **enhanced**) **redundancy pay**. This may top up the statutory entitlement, and/or give redundancy pay to employees who do not yet have the qualifying period for statutory entitlement. Enhanced redundancy pay may be contractual [**35.7.2.1**] or discretionary [**35.7.2.2**].

Regardless of whether they are entitled to any redundancy pay, all employees made redundant are entitled to payment of all wages owed up to the **relevant date** [**35.7.1.1**], holiday entitlement for untaken holiday leave (with the daily rate calculated as 1/7th of weekly pay or 1/365th of annual pay), and pay in lieu of notice if the employee has not been given the full notice required by statute or contract [**34.3**]. Special provisions apply if the employer is insolvent [**24.10.8**].

A redundant employee who starts a job with a new employer remains entitled to a statutory redundancy payment. Entitlement to enhanced redundancy pay depends on the contract of employment or the employer's policy.

35.7.1   Statutory redundancy pay

To qualify for statutory redundancy pay, the employee must have two years of continuous employment [**26.5.2**].

35.7.1.1   Relevant date

Statutory redundancy pay and the qualifying period are calculated up to the **relevant date**, and the six-month time limit for bringing a tribunal claim is calculated from this date. The relevant date is the date on which the notice of dismissal due to redundancy takes effect.   *Employment Rights Act 1996 ss.145,153, as amended*

35.7.1.2   Qualifying employees

Virtually all employees with the necessary continuous employment – including employees on fixed-term contracts which come to an end and are not renewed – are entitled to statutory redundancy pay. People who are 'workers' [**25.1.2**] but not employees are not entitled to statutory redundancy pay.

35.7.1.3   Dismissal after redundancy notice

An employee in a redundancy situation who is dismissed for misconduct which would qualify for summary dismissal [**33.3.10**] loses entitlement to statutory redundancy pay. This applies regardless of whether the employer dismisses summarily (without notice) or with notice. An employment tribunal may, if it considers it just and equitable, reinstate some or all of the redundancy pay entitlement.   *Employment Rights Act 1996 s.140(1),(3),(4)*

An employee who has already received notice of redundancy and is dismissed because of taking part in an unprotected industrial action [**36.6.2**] does not lose the right to statutory redundancy pay. However, the employer has the right to require the employee to make up the days lost by the industrial action, and if the employee refuses, the right to redundancy pay is lost.   *ERA 1996 s.140(2),(5)*

An employee dismissed for any other reason after receiving notice of redundancy remains entitled to statutory redundancy pay.

35.7.1.4   Resignation after redundancy notice

If an employee who has received notice of redundancy then gives **counter notice** that he or she is resigning before the redundancy notice expires but wants to claim statutory redundancy pay, the employer can require the employee to withdraw the resignation and work until the end of the redundancy notice. This notification must be in writing and must state that if the employee does not comply, the employer will contest the liability to make a statutory redundancy payment. An employee who then does not work out the notice is not entitled to redundancy pay unless the case is taken to employment tribunal and the tribunal orders payment.   *Employment Rights Act 1996 ss.136(4),142*

The employer may choose instead to accept the resignation and allow the employee to leave before the end of the notice period, with redundancy pay.

35.7.1.5   Calculation of redundancy pay

Statutory redundancy pay is calculated on the basis of:

- the employee's age at the relevant date [**35.7.1.1**];
- the number of years continuous employment [**26.5.2**], to a maximum of 20;
- within those 20 years (or fewer), the number of years aged under 22, aged 22-40, and aged 41 and above;
- the employee's current gross weekly pay or the statutory maximum (£380 for redundancies taking effect from 1/10/09), whichever is less. For employees with variable earnings, 'weekly pay' is the average pay in the 12 weeks before the relevant date.

To calculate statutory entitlement, the weekly pay is multiplied by 1.5 for each year of service at age 41 or over, 1.0 for each year of service between age 22 and 40, and 0.5 for each year of service below 22. The Business Link website [see end of **chapter 25**] contains a ready reckoner for working out entitlement.

Complex rules govern what is and is not included as pay. Specialist advice may be necessary if the employee earns less than the statutory maximum and it is necessary to work out the actual weekly pay. *Employment Rights Act 1996 ss.221-229,234*

If the employer has contributed to a pension scheme [**30.6**], a lump sum or pension payable under the scheme may be offset against redundancy pay. Details of this are on the BIS website [see end of **chapter 25**].

The employer must provide a written calculation of the entitlement. Failure to do so can result in a fine. *Employment Rights Act 1996 s.165*

35.7.2 Enhanced redundancy pay

Enhanced (non-statutory) **redundancy pay** must comply with age discrimination legislation [**28.6.1**]. The employer can use a weekly pay figure higher than the one used for statutory redundancy pay, and/or can multiply the total statutory entitlement or the total entitlement using the higher weekly pay amount, by any multiplier larger than 1.0. If the employer wants to increase redundancy pay above the statutory minimum using any other calculations, there must be an objective justification for doing so. To ensure enhanced redundancy payments are not at risk of breaching the age discrimination regulations, legal advice should be sought. *Employment Equality (Age) Regulations 2006 [SI 2006/1031] reg.33*

35.7.2.1 Contractual redundancy pay

Very generous contractual provision, such as one month's pay for every year or part-year of service, creates a potentially heavy financial burden if an employer has to make long-serving staff redundant. Failure to ensure that an unincorporated organisation has adequate assets to meet its redundancy obligations could mean that individual governing body members become personally liable [**22.5**].

Where a staff handbook refers to enhanced redundancy pay, this is assumed to be a contractual entitlement. *Keeley v Fosroc International Ltd [2006] EWCA Civ 1277*

35.7.2.2 Discretionary payment

Where there is no contractual obligation to pay more than statutory redundancy pay, a charity which is not a company may make a discretionary redundancy payment if it is doing so primarily in the interests of the charity and the payment is reasonable. But if it is making the payment primarily in the private interests of the redundant employee, it needs Charity Commission consent under the **Charities Act 1993** s.27. If in doubt, advice should be sought from the Commission.

In a company, whether charitable or non-charitable, the directors have a statutory duty to promote the success of the company, and in so doing to take into account the interests of the company's employees. They also have a statutory right, subject to procedural safeguards, to make payments to employees when all or part of the company is ceasing to operate or is being transferred to another body. These provisions can be used to authorise discretionary payments to employees of a company. *Companies Act 2006 s.172(1),247*

35.7.2.3 Discretionary payments becoming contractual

A discretionary payment may become impliedly contractual by custom and practice [**26.3.4**]. An employee who is not given a discretionary redundancy payment could claim breach of contract if other employees in a similar situation were given payments. If the employer wants to reduce the risk of this happening, the redundancy policy should make clear that enhanced payment is purely discretionary, and any payment should be accompanied by a statement that the employer is not to be regarded as being committed to making similar payments in future.

35.7.3 Tax and NI on redundancy pay

There is no income tax or national insurance on statutory redundancy pay. Nor is there any on contractual redundancy payments as long as the redundancy situation is genuine, the payment is compensation for loss of employment because of redundancy rather than payment for some other reason (for example, pay in lieu of notice or a payment in recognition for long service), and the combined total for the statutory and contractual redundancy payments is no more than £30,000. The portion of any redundancy payment over £30,000 is subject to income tax but not national insurance. *Income Tax (Earnings & Pensions) Act 2003 ss.309,401*

The tax treatment of discretionary payments depends on the nature of the payment, and specialist advice should be sought.

A statutory redundancy payment does not affect entitlement to jobseeker's allowance. Enhanced redundancy pay may affect entitlement to state benefits, and employees are advised to seek advice about this.

35.7.4 Non-payment of redundancy pay

35.7.4.1 Statutory redundancy pay

If the employer does not make a statutory redundancy payment to the employee within six months from the relevant date [**35.7.1.1**], the employee can either present a written claim for payment to the employer, or bring a claim for payment or unfair dismissal in an employment tribunal. Failure to do this may mean the employee loses entitlement to the payment, although in some situations the time limit for claiming redundancy pay may be extended for a further six months. *Employment Rights Act 1996 s.164*

If the employer is insolvent, the employee may be able to claim statutory redundancy pay and certain other amounts from the national insurance fund [**24.10.8**]. It may also be possible to claim from the NI fund where an employer is solvent but cannot or will not make a statutory redundancy payment.

35.7.4.2 Contractual redundancy pay

Remedies through the employment tribunal or national insurance fund do not apply to non-payment of contractual redundancy pay. If the employer is an incorporated body [**chapter 3**] and is solvent, an employee who wants to recover contractual redundancy pay sues the organisation in the courts; if the organisation is insolvent, the employee is treated as an unsecured creditor [**24.10.5**].

If the employer is an unincorporated organisation [**chapter 2**] the employee sues one or more members of the governing body. If the organisation is solvent any governing body members who are required to pay have a right to be indemnified (compensated) by the organisation. If the organisation is insolvent, the governing body members are personally liable for the debt to the employee [**22.5**].

35.8 MISUSE OF REDUNDANCY

An employer wishing to dismiss an employee without facing the real issue – usually inadequate performance or unacceptable conduct – may call the dismissal redundancy even though it does not meet the criteria for a genuine redundancy [**35.1.1**]. This approach risks the employee claiming unfair dismissal, with the employer unable to show that the dismissal was for a fair reason [**34.6**]. To prevent this, the employee should be required to enter into a formal settlement giving up the right to bring a claim against the employer [**37.2.2**].

Calling a dismissal a redundancy may preserve the employee's right to jobseeker's allowance, but could involve the organisation in making a fraudulent statement if the Department for Work and Pensions asks about reasons for the dismissal.

Resources: REDUNDANCY

ACAS, BIS, Business Link, CIPD, Directgov, PEACe, TUC: see end of **chapter 25**.

Redundancy payments helpline/Redundancy Payments Office: 0845 145 0004.

Statute law. www.opsi.gov.uk and www.statutelaw.gov.uk.

Much but not all case law. www.bailii.org.

Updates cross-referenced to this book. www.rclh.co.uk.

Chapter 36
EMPLOYER-EMPLOYEE RELATIONS

For sources of further information see end of chapter.

36.1   EMPLOYEE REPRESENTATIVES

For the purposes of consultation on redundancy [**35.2.2**], transfer of undertakings [**29.7.3**] and the information and consultation regulations [**36.2.1**], the employer must consult with representatives of any **recognised trade union** or unions [**36.3.3**] or, if there is no recognised union, with **elected employee representatives.** The procedures for electing employee representatives are set out in regulations. It is unlawful for an employer to dismiss or subject to detriment any employee for a reason connected with participating in an election for employee representatives or serving as an employee or trade union representative.

Trade Union & Labour Relations (Consolidation) Act 1992 s.188A, inserted by Collective Redundancies & Transfer of Undertakings (Protection of Employment) (Amendment) Regulations 1999 [SI 1999/1925] reg.4; Employment Rights Act 1996 ss.47,103, amended by 1999 Regs regs.12,13

For health and safety consultation [**40.2.8**], employers may consult with individual employees, trade union representatives or elected employee representatives.

Employee representatives have a statutory right to paid time off for duties during consultation on redundancy, transfer of undertakings, health and safety, and matters covered by the information and consultation regulations [**36.2.1**].

36.2   EMPLOYEE INVOLVEMENT

36.2.1   Information and consultation of employees

Under the **Information and Consultation of Employees Regulations 2004** (**ICE** or **TICER**), employers with 50 or more employees [**25.1.1**] have a statutory duty to inform and consult employees about specified matters. Where there is no recognised union [**36.3.3**] – and in some cases, even where there is – this must be done through elected employee representatives [**36.1**]. The consultation body is usually referred to as a **joint consultative committee** or **works council.** An employer who fails to inform or consult as required can be fined up to £75,000.

Information & Consultation of Employees Regulations 2004 [SI 2004/3426], as amended

The employer must inform employees (but does not have to consult) about recent and probable business developments and the economic situation, and must inform and consult about the situation, structure and development of employment within the organisation, including threats to employment. Where there could be substantial changes in how the work will be organised or in contractual relations, the employer must not only inform and consult, but must consult 'with a view to reaching agreement'.

But these obligations to inform and consult are triggered only if 10% of employees (minimum 15, maximum 2,500) request the employer to arrange for the election of employee representatives [**36.1**] and to negotiate an **information and consultation agreement**. The negotiation must be based on standard provisions, and if agreement is not reached within six months of the obligation being triggered, the Central Arbitration Committee [**36.3.3.2**] can impose the provisions. There is an exception for agreements negotiated before the regulations came into force, which did not necessarily have to comply with the default provisions.

Where an agreement covering all employees is in place, an obligation to renegotiate can be triggered by a request made by 40% of employees.

Information about the election of employee representatives and ICE agreements is available from ACAS and the Department for Business, Innovation and Skills [see end of **chapter 25**].

36.2.1.1   Transnational consultation

An employer based in the UK with more than 1,000 employees in the EU (of which there must be at least 150 employees in each of two EU member states) is a **community-scale undertaking** or **community-scale group of undertakings**. Such undertakings must set up transnational information and consultation arrangements if employees ask for this. This is usually through a **European works council** (EWC).

Transnational Information & Consultation of Employees Regulations 1999 [SI 1999/3323]

36.2.2   Duties of companies

As part of their statutory obligation to promote the success of the company [**15.3.2**], company directors must 'have regard to the interests of the company's employees'. This duty cannot be enforced by employees, because it is owed to the company rather than to the employees. *Companies Act 2006 s.172(1)*

A company with more than a weekly average of 250 employees in the UK must include in its annual report a statement of what has been done during the last year to maintain or develop arrangements to give employees regular information about matters concerning them, consult employees or their representatives on a regular basis, encourage involvement of employees in the company's performance, and make employees aware of the financial and economic factors affecting the company's performance.

Large & Medium-sized Companies & Groups (Accounts & Reports) Regulations 2008 [SI 2008/410] sch.7 pt.4

36.3   TRADE UNION RECOGNITION AND AGREEMENTS

Trade unions remain a primary channel for resolution of employer/employee matters, whether collective or individual. Information about unions is available from the **Trades Union Congress** [see end of chapter].

36.3.1   Staff associations or 'house unions'

In a **staff association** or **employees' association**, all the members work for one employer or a group of associated employers. A staff association can register as a trade union, but may not be able to be certified as an independent trade union [**36.3.2**]. These non-independent bodies are sometimes called **house unions**.

36.3.2   Independent trade unions

The **certification officer**, a government official, maintains a list of registered unions and if appropriate, certifies them as independent. A union may be certified as independent only if it is not dominated or controlled by an employer, group of employers or employers' association, and is not subject to interference by an employer, group of employers or employers' association, for example by an employer providing financial or material support. *Trade Union & Labour Relations (Consolidation) Act 1992 ss.5,6*

Most statutory trade union rights are available only to independent trade unions. An employer may make an informal or contractual agreement to give similar rights to a house union [**36.3.1**].

36.3.3 Recognised trade unions

If an employer agrees to negotiate with a trade union 'to any extent' for the purposes of collective bargaining, that union is considered to be **recognised** by the employer. Although recognition is often a matter of agreement between the employer and the union, a union has a statutory right to require recognition in some situations [**36.3.3.2**].

36.3.3.1 Voluntary recognition

Recognition may be negotiated between an employer and union(s), or may be implied from custom and practice. It does not have to be set out in an agreement, although it often is. An employer should seek advice before signing a recognition agreement. ACAS [see end of **chapter 25**] can work with employers and unions to achieve a **voluntary recognition agreement**. *Trade Union & Labour Relations (Consolidation) Act 1992 s.178(3)*

Recognition of this type is not permanent, and may be withdrawn by the employer at any time.

An employer might say that it has 'recognised' a union by according it courtesies and facilities such as a notice board or use of meeting rooms, allowing a union representative the right to speak on behalf of union members in disciplinary or grievance procedures, or consulting the union on various matters. This is not 'recognition', but simply acknowledgement. It does not confer the statutory rights which unions get when they are recognised by the employer as having the right to negotiate and strike a bargain with the employer.

36.3.3.2 Recognition through statutory procedure

Where voluntary recognition cannot be achieved, a union may require an employer with 21 or more employees or other workers [**25.1.2**] to enter into a legally binding agreement to recognise a union. The number includes workers for associated employers (where one organisation is controlled by another, or they are both controlled by a third). *TULR(C)A 1992 sch.A1, inserted by Employment Relations Act 1999 sch.1*

Details of the complex recognition procedures are available from the **Central Arbitration Committee** [see end of chapter] and in the statutory **code of practice on access and unfair practices during recognition and derecognition ballots**, available from the Department for Business, Innovation and Skills [see end of **chapter 25**].

Recognition is awarded by the CAC in relation to a **bargaining unit** if it is supported by a majority of bargaining unit workers voting in the ballot, and by at least 40% of the workers entitled to vote. The CAC may award recognition without a ballot if more than 50% of workers in the bargaining unit are members of the union(s) applying for recognition. Union recognition through the statutory procedure is legally binding and covers bargaining about pay, hours and holidays.

An employer which is approached for recognition should take early legal advice.

36.3.3.3 Recognition and transfer of undertaking

When an undertaking is transferred and retains a separate identity [**29.7.2**], the new employer must continue to recognise any union(s) recognised by the original employer. Having recognised the union, the new employer may then be free to change or withdraw from the recognition agreement. Different provisions apply where the original recognition was achieved under the statutory procedure. *Transfer of Undertakings (Protection of Employment) Regulations 2006 [SI 2006/246] reg.6*

36.3.4   Collective agreements

Collective agreements are negotiated between one or more independent union(s) and an employer or group of employers.   *Trade Union & Labour Relations (Consolidation) Act 1992 s.178*

They may be concerned primarily with the relationship between the union and the employer, or with the rights of individual employees. Either explicitly or by custom and practice, some or all the terms of the collective agreement may be incorporated [**26.3.5**] into individuals' contracts of employment. Different rules apply to collective agreements whereby employees agree not to take industrial action [**36.6.6**].

A collective agreement may codify certain rules under legislation, for example the employer's rules on parental leave where these differ from the statutory default procedures [**31.1.2**].

A collective agreement is legally binding on the parties only if it is in writing and indicates clearly that it is intended to be legally enforceable. If only part of the agreement is intended to be legally binding, this must be clearly stated.

TULR(C)A 1992 s.179

If an undertaking is transferred to a new employer, the provisions of the original employer's collective agreements that are in effect at the date of the transfer are transferred to the new employer. The new employer may be bound by subsequent changes to the agreement, even though it is not a party to those changes [**29.7.7**].

36.4   TRADE UNION RIGHTS

All workers have a right to belong or not belong to a union, and to take part in union activities at appropriate times. Trade union rights are buttressed by the **Human Rights Act 1998**, which implements article 11 of the **European convention on human rights**, protecting freedom of assembly and in particular the right to form trade unions. Information about trade union rights is available from the **Trades Union Congress** [see end of chapter].

Despite the general right to belong to a union, trade unions can have membership rules which in certain circumstances prohibit individuals who are or have been members of a particular political party from membership of the union.

Trade Union & Labour Relations (Consolidation) Act 1992 s.174, amended by Employment Act 2008 s.19

36.4.1   Trade union membership and activities

It is unlawful to refuse employment, dismiss, or subject a worker to a detriment because the person is or is not a member of a trade union, or has taken part in trade union activities. The detriment is unlawful regardless of whether it is because of an action taken by the employer, or failure by the employer to take an action. So-called 'blacklists', under which employers keep records of people who have taken part in trade union activities with a view to discriminating against them, are also unlawful.   *Trade Union & Labour Relations (Consolidation) Act 1992 ss.137,146, amended by Employment Relations Acts 1999 & 2004*

Advertisements are unlawful if they indicate or imply that employment is only available to union members or non-members, or that any membership related requirement will apply. Procedures where trade unions recommend people for employment are unlawful if they have the effect of discriminating against people who are not union members.   *TULR(C)A 1992 s.137(3),(4)*

Employment outside Great Britain is not covered.

36.4.1.1   Selection for employment

An applicant for a job may not be refused work on the basis of being, or not being, a member of a trade union; being unwilling to accept a requirement to join, leave or remain in a union; or being unwilling to accept a requirement to have union subscriptions deducted from wages.   *TULR(C)A 1992 s.137, s.146 amended by ERA 1999 sch.2*

An employer cannot run a **closed shop** where all workers must be members of a particular union or unions. However, an employer may ask or encourage job applicants to join the union. If they all agree, this has the effect of perpetuating the closed shop, but no one can be refused a job because they do not agree to join the union, nor can a worker be dismissed because he or she leaves the union.

36.4.1.2 Detriment

An employer cannot take any action or offer any inducement, or deliberately refrain from taking any action, in order to prevent a worker from joining a union or remaining in a union, compel a worker to join a union, penalise a worker or subject a worker to any detriment because he or she is a union member, prevent a worker from taking part in union activities at an appropriate time (outside the worker's working hours or at a time within working hours which has been agreed with the employer), or penalise a worker for taking part in union activities.

Trade Union & Labour Relations (Consolidation) Act 1992 s.146, amended by Employment Relations Acts 1999 & 2004

36.4.1.3 Dismissal on union grounds

An employee dismissed or made redundant on **union grounds** is automatically unfairly dismissed [**34.7.1**] unless the dismissal is because of participation in unprotected industrial action [**36.6.5**]. In addition to the usual remedy for unfair dismissal, the tribunal may require the employment to be continued, and may make an additional special award on top of the normal compensatory awards [**37.4.2**]. *TULR(C)A 1992 ss.152-166, amended by ERA 2004*

'Union grounds' means being, or not being, a union member; joining, or refusing to join, a union; or taking part or planning to take part in activities of an independent union at an appropriate time.

36.4.2 Rights of trade union members

Members of a trade union which is recognised by the employer either through a voluntary agreement or through the statutory procedure [**36.3.3**] have statutory rights. Members of unions which are not recognised by the employer have these rights only if the employer agrees to them informally or as part of the contract of employment.

36.4.2.1 Check-off

An employer is not obliged to deduct trade union subscriptions from union members' pay. But if an employer does operate **check-off**, strict rules apply to how the employer operates the procedure, and to the employee's consent, which must be given in writing at least every three years, and may be withdrawn at any time by notifying the employer in writing.

If the union has a political fund [**36.4.2.4**], the employer must not deduct the political fund contribution if the employee notifies the employer in writing that he or she is exempt from the obligation to contribute to the fund or has notified the union that he or she objects to contributing to the fund. *Trade Union & Labour Relations (Consolidation) Act 1992 ss.68,68A,86,87, as amended*

36.4.2.2 Paid time off for union duties

Officials of a recognised trade union have the right to paid time off to carry out duties connected with statutory consultation, collective bargaining and other matters agreed by the employer, and to attend industrial relations training. The amount of time allowed must be 'reasonable in all the circumstances'. The ACAS **code of practice on time off for union duties** describes what is 'reasonable'. *TULR(C)A 1992 ss.168,169, as amended*

Union learning representatives have a similar right to paid time off to assess learning and training needs, promote and arrange training, and provide information and advice about learning and training. *TULR(C)A 1992 s.168A, inserted by Employment Act 2002 s.43*

36.4.2.3 Time off for union activities

Members of a recognised trade union have a right to reasonable time off, which may be paid or unpaid, to take part in union activities. This does not include taking part in industrial action, whether protected [**36.6.1**] or not. *TULR(C)A 1992 s.170*

36.4.2.4   Objection to political fund

A trade union may use its funds for political purposes only if the funds are collected specifically for this and are kept in a separate **political fund**. A ballot on retention of the fund must be held every 10 years. A member has the right to object to making the contribution, and the union cannot then require the member to pay the contribution or subject the member to any discipline or detriment as a result of not paying.   *Trade Union & Labour Relations (Consolidation) Act 1992 ss.71-85*

36.4.3   Rights of trade unions

Trade unions recognised by an employer or group of employers [**36.3.3**] have certain statutory rights. The employer(s) may extend these rights to other unions or to a joint consultative committee or other representative body.

36.4.3.1   Collective bargaining

An employer is required to provide information to representatives of a recognised trade union if the union requests it for the purposes of **collective bargaining**. There is a general duty to provide all available information if its lack would impede the union's ability to negotiate, but there are a number of exceptions to this general duty, such as information obtained in confidence, information relating to specific individuals (unless the individual has authorised disclosure), or information which would cause 'substantial injury' to the employer.   *Trade Union & Labour Relations (Consolidation) Act 1992 ss.181,182*

The ACAS **code of practice on information disclosure**, available from ACAS [see end of **chapter 25**], sets out the information which should be disclosed.

36.4.3.2   Information and consultation

Trade unions recognised by the employer have a statutory right to be informed and consulted in relation to health and safety [**40.2.8**] and occupational pension schemes [**30.6.1**]. If employees are to be transferred to another employer or 20 or more employees are to be made redundant within a 90-day period, the employer must consult recognised union(s) or employee representatives [**29.7.3, 35.2.2**].

Trade unions recognised under the statutory procedure [**36.3.3.2**] have a right to be consulted by the employer at least every six months about the employer's staff training policy. Information to enable the union representatives to participate in the meeting must be provided by the employer at least two weeks before the meeting.   *TULR(C)A 1992 s.70B, inserted by Employment Relations Act 1999 s.5*

36.5   TRADE DISPUTES

A **trade dispute** is a dispute between an employer and workers or among workers, relating to terms and conditions of employment; physical conditions in which workers are required to work; engagement, non-engagement, termination or suspension of one or more workers; termination or suspension of the duties of one or more workers; allocation of work; disciplinary matters; a worker's membership or non-membership of a union; facilities for trade union officials; consultation and negotiation procedures; and/or recognition of a union.   *Trade Union & Labour Relations (Consolidation) Act 1992 s.218*

In a trade dispute or a dispute over union recognition, ACAS [end of **chapter 25**] may be approached by anyone to undertake **conciliation**, to enable the parties to reach a settlement, and/or **arbitration**, where arbitrator(s) or the Central Arbitration Committee devise a settlement which is binding on the parties.   *TULR(C)A ss.210-212*

36.6   INDUSTRIAL ACTION

Industrial action includes **strikes; action short of a strike** such as withdrawal of cooperation, refusing to undertake certain activities, overtime bans and working to rule; and **lock outs** where an employer stops workers from working.

36.6.1   Protected industrial action

It is lawful for a union or its officials or representatives to encourage people to take part in a strike or other industrial action only if the union has carried out a secret postal ballot complying with the relevant legislation among its relevant members, and the action has been agreed by the members. The employer must be notified of the ballot, must be informed of the result, and must be given details of the proposed action at least seven days before it starts. Industrial action, if approved, must start within four weeks of the ballot, but this can be extended for a further four weeks if the employer and union(s) agree, to allow more time for negotiation.   *Trade Union & Labour Relations (Consolidation) Act 1992 ss.226-234A, as amended*

The rules on ballots are set out in a **code of practice on industrial action ballots and notice to employers**, available from the Department for Business, Innovation and Skills [see end of **chapter 25**].

Industrial action approved through a proper ballot is **protected industrial action**. Dismissal primarily for a reason connected with participation in protected industrial action is automatically unfair [**36.6.5**], and the employee cannot be sued, for example for breach of contract or inducing breach of contract.
TULR(C)A 1992 s.219 as amended

Any member of the union has the right to require the union to conduct a ballot before it undertakes or continues industrial action.   *TULR(C)A 1992 s.62 as amended*

Unless industrial action is protected, participation in it may constitute breach of contract or inducement to breach of contract by the employees involved. To safeguard employees, industrial action should never be undertaken without getting proper advice from a trade union. Similarly, an employer or individual should take legal advice before taking any steps to stop industrial action. The Department for Business, Innovation and Skills [see end of **chapter 25**] publishes a guide for employers and employees on industrial action.

36.6.2   Unofficial action

If industrial action has not been approved by ballot or is subsequently repudiated by the union, it is **unofficial** or **unprotected industrial action**. The trade union is legally liable for unofficial action carried out by its members, unless it formally repudiates the action.   *Trade Union & Labour Relations (Consolidation) Act 1992 ss.20,21*

Participation in unofficial industrial action is generally a breach of contract by the employee, and there is generally no right to claim unfair dismissal for dismissal while taking part in an unofficial action [**36.6.5**].   *TULR(C)A 1992 s.237, as amended*

Any individual can apply to the high court to stop unauthorised or unlawful industrial action, if the individual can show that the industrial action would prevent or delay the supply of goods or services to him or her, or that the quality of the goods or services would be adversely affected.   *TULR(C)A 1992 s.235A, inserted by Trade Union Reform & Employment Rights Act 1993 s.22*

36.6.3   Peaceful picketing

Peaceful **picketing** is lawful provided it is at or near the place of work of the worker who is picketing and the worker's employer is a party to the dispute, or in the case of a trade union official taking part in a picket, it is at or near the place of work of a trade union member whom the official is representing or accompanying in a dispute with the worker's employer. The purpose must be to obtain or communicate information or persuade a person to work or not to work.
Trade Union & Labour Relations (Consolidation) Act 1992 ss.220,224

Picketing and other actions are unlawful if they try to make a person do or not do something unwillingly, or if they involve violence or harassment. *TULR(C)A 1992 s.241*

A code of practice sets a limit of six on the number of pickets at any entrance to a workplace. This restriction does not have statutory force, but it has been used as the basis for injunctions against mass pickets.

36.6.4   Deduction from wages

An employer has the right not to pay employees for days when they are engaged in industrial action, whether protected or not, and are not working. Where an employee is working to rule or taking other action short of a strike, the employer is entitled to deduct part of the wages or even full wages, if it has been made clear that part-performance of the contract is not acceptable. Advice should be taken about how to calculate the amount to be deducted.

36.6.5   Dismissal during industrial action

Dismissal is automatically unfair [**34.7.1**] if the principal reason is that the employee is taking or took part in protected industrial action [**36.6.1**], provided that the dismissal occurs:

- within the **protected period**, which is 12 weeks beginning with the first day of protected industrial action, plus an extension period equal to the number of days falling on or after the first day of the protected industrial action during the whole or part of which the employee is locked out by the employer;
- after the end of the 12-week period, where the employee had ceased to take part before the end of the period; or
- after the end of the period, where the employer had not taken reasonable procedural steps to resolve the dispute.   *Trade Union & Labour Relations (Consolidation) Act 1992 s.238A, inserted by Employment Relations Act 1999 sch.5, amended by Employment Rights Act 2004 ss.26-28*

There is a six-month limit for bringing an unfair dismissal claim for taking part in protected industrial action.   *TULR(C)A 1992 s.238*

Dismissal because an employee is taking or has taken part in an unofficial strike or other industrial action [**36.6.2**] is not a dismissal for a fair reason, but the employee loses the right to bring a claim of unfair dismissal. However, a claim can be brought if other employees who took part were not dismissed, or if another employee who was dismissed at the same time has been offered re-engagement within three months of dismissal. In this case, the time limit for bringing a claim is six months rather than three. A claim for unfair dismissal can also be brought if it can be shown that the principal reason for the dismissal was for a specified reason that is automatically unfair.   *TULR(C)A 1992 ss.237,238, as amended*

36.6.6   Collective agreements not to take industrial action

Some employers and trade unions have negotiated national **collective agreements** restricting employees' rights to strike or take industrial action. Most collective agreements between employers and trade unions are automatically incorporated into employees' contracts of employment [**26.3.5**]. But agreements limiting the right to strike or take industrial action are incorporated into individual contracts only if the trade union is independent [**36.3.2**], the agreement is in writing and states that it is incorporated into individual contracts, the agreement is reasonably accessible and available, and individual contracts explicitly or impliedly incorporate the terms.   *Trade Union & Labour Relations (Consolidation) Act 1992 s.180*

Resources: EMPLOYER-EMPLOYEE RELATIONS

Employment and trade union rights. ACAS, BIS, Business Link, CIPD, Directgov, PEACe, TUC: see end of **chapter 25**.

Trade union recognition and rights. Central Arbitration Committee: www.cac.gov.uk, 020 7904 2300, enquiries@cac.gov.uk.

Trades Union Congress: www.tuc.org.uk, 020 7636 4030, info@tuc.org.uk.

Voluntary sector trade unions. Unison: www.unison.org.uk, 0845 355 0845; email via website.

Unite: www.unitetheunion.org.uk, 0845 850 4242, email via website.

Statute law. www.opsi.gov.uk and www.statutelaw.gov.uk.

Much but not all case law. www.bailii.org.

Updates cross-referenced to this book. www.rclh.co.uk.

Chapter 37
EMPLOYMENT CLAIMS AND SETTLEMENT

For sources of further information see end of chapter.

37.1   ENFORCING EMPLOYMENT RIGHTS

Most statutory employment rights, such as rights relating to pay, unfair dismissal and discrimination, are enforced through **employment tribunals**. The main exceptions are health and safety, enforced by the Health and Safety Executive [**40.2.9**]; statutory sick pay [**31.6.1**] and statutory maternity, paternity and adoption pay [**32.2-32.4**] claims, enforced by HM Revenue and Customs; and minimum wage, enforced by either employment tribunals or HMRC [**30.2.5**].

Contractual employment rights are enforced through the courts, although some breach of contract claims can be brought instead in the tribunal [**37.5**].

Basic tribunal procedures are outlined here, and further information is available from Employment Tribunals [see end of chapter]. Court procedures are outlined in **65.4**. Tribunal and court proceedings may be complex and give rise to large awards, so experienced legal advice and representation are generally advisable at an early stage.

Employment related decisions made by the employment appeal tribunal, court of appeal, high court, House of Lords (supreme court from 1 October 2009), European court of justice and European court of human rights are available on the relevant website or at www.bailii.org. At the time of writing (mid 2009) employment tribunal decisions were expected to become available online.

37.1.1   Advice for employers and employees

ACAS, Business Link, Directgov and the Trades Union Congress [see end of **chapter 25**] provide basic information on all aspects of employment rights for, employers and employees. Detailed information and advice is available to employers and employees from ACAS and solicitors [**37.1.2**], and to employees from trade unions, citizens' advice bureaux, independent advice centres and law centres. Some CABx and advice centres also advise voluntary sector employers.

Organisations can insure against the cost of legal advice and employment related awards against them [**23.4.2**, **23.9.3**]. The insurer is likely to require the employer to follow its advice, which may limit the options available to employers.

37.1.1.1 Financial assistance

Employees on a low income may qualify for **legal aid** for advice from solicitors, through **Community Legal Advice** [see end of chapter]. Legal aid is not available for representation at employment tribunal proceedings in England and Wales, but is available for some tribunal cases in Scotland.

37.1.2 ACAS

The **Advisory, Conciliation and Arbitration Service** [see end of **chapter 25**], an independent body, provides information and advice on employment matters, undertakes enquiries into disputes or areas of employment, and helps achieve settlement in collective disputes and individual cases. Unlike tribunal hearings, ACAS procedures are confidential.

37.1.2.1 Mediation, conciliation and arbitration

To resolve disputes, ACAS provides mediation, conciliation and arbitration. **Mediation** is a voluntary process where an ACAS mediator helps the employer and employee(s) reach a solution. An agreement reached through mediation is not legally binding, but can be made binding as a **compromise agreement [37.2.2.2]** or through the involvement of an ACAS conciliator [**37.2.2.1**].

Conciliation is the same as mediation but is used where an the employee has brought or could bring an employment tribunal claim [**37.2.2.1**] against the employer. A conciliated settlement through ACAS is legally binding.

In unfair dismissal and some other cases, ACAS can provide **arbitration** as an alternative to the tribunal [**37.2.3**]. Unlike a conciliator, an arbitrator can seek evidence, call witnesses, and make decisions or awards.

37.2 SETTLEMENT

Given the costs and other problems raised by tribunal and court cases, the employer and employee should always consider attempting to reach a **settlement** by themselves or with the assistance of ACAS. This can be done before or after a claim has been made to the tribunal or court.

Care must be taken if a settlement is raised with a view of achieving the departure of an employee. The approach may give rise to a claim of constructive dismissal [**34.2.9**]. It is generally advisable for all settlement attempts to be conducted on a **without prejudice** basis [**65.4.1**].

37.2.1 Breach of contract

A claim for **breach of contract**, including wrongful dismissal [**34.4.1**], can be settled by the employer agreeing to make a payment or take other action such as re-engaging the employee, and the employee agreeing not to pursue the claim in the court or tribunal. There are no special formalities, but it is advisable for each side to take legal advice and for the agreement to be in writing.

37.2.2 Breach of employment legislation

Very strict rules apply to **settlement agreements** and **compromise agreements**, under which an employee agrees not to pursue a claim arising from the employer's breach of anti-discrimination or employment legislation, including unfair dismissal. Such settlements also frequently include provision for related issues such as contractual rights, confidentiality and references.

37.2.2.1 Settlement through ACAS

If either the employer or employee requests it, ACAS can help the parties reach a **conciliated settlement** or **settlement agreement** prior to a tribunal claim for discrimination or breach of employment legislation. If either party makes a complaint to the tribunal and the conciliation officer considers that there is a reasonable prospect of resolving the matter without having to go to tribunal, ACAS has a statutory obligation to seek a conciliated settlement.

A settlement through ACAS binds both parties. The employee cannot take matters covered in the settlement to tribunal or court, unless he or she was induced to enter into the settlement by a material and false statement by the employer. The employee can, however, take action on matters not covered in the settlement.

37.2.2.2 Compromise agreements

An agreement not arranged through ACAS is called a **compromise agreement**. A compromise agreement is valid only if it is in writing and:

- it relates to a particular complaint or complaints (not all possible complaints);
- the employee has received independent advice from a qualified lawyer, certified trade union official or certified advice worker on the agreement and its effect on his or her rights (at the time of writing the government had consulted on extending the range of permitted advisors);
- the employee's advisor is covered by professional negligence insurance or an indemnity against claims by the employee;
- the agreement identifies the advisor; and
- the agreement states the relevant Acts or regulations that contain conditions regulating compromise agreements, and confirms that those conditions are satisfied.

The agreement must be drafted carefully, and legal advice should be sought. It will not protect against a claim which is not specified in the agreement.

Employment Rights Act 1996 s.203(3-3B), amended by Employment Rights (Dispute Resolution)
Act 1998 ss.9,10, sch.1 para.24

37.2.2.3 Negotiated agreements by charities

In general, charities are allowed to make payments only if there is a contractual or statutory right or duty to do so. Other payments, including settlements and compromise agreements in employment disputes, are **ex gratia [53.3]** and may be made only if allowed by statute, the charity's governing document or the Charity Commission.

Companies, whether charitable or non-charitable, generally have wide general powers of management contained in their articles of association, and these are taken to include a power to compromise (enter into a negotiated agreement). For unincorporated charities, there are powers to compromise under the **Trustee Act 1925** s.15.

In these cases the Charity Commission will generally not need or wish to be involved, provided the charity trustees have taken professional advice and think that a particular settlement is in the best interests of the charity. An overly generous settlement which is not objectively justifiable could be *ultra vires* **[5.8]**.

Gibb v Maidstone & Tunbridge Wells NHS Trust [2009] EWHC 862 (QB)

For those few charities who find that they do not have power to enter into a compromise, it is possible to ask the Charity Commission to make an order **[4.5.4]** authorising a compromise. The Commission will need to be convinced that the proposed agreement is reasonable and it is expedient for the charity to pursue it.

Charities which are also housing associations must comply with additional rules.

The Trustee Act 1925 provisions for unincorporated charities do not apply to unincorporated non-charities. These organisations should take legal advice before entering into a negotiated agreement.

37.2.2.4 Non-binding agreement

If the employer signs an agreement or pays an employee to give up the right to claim in the employment tribunal, without complying with the compromise agreement rules, the agreement cannot be enforced by the employer. The employee retains the right to make or continue a claim, but any payment received from the employer may be taken into account in calculating entitlement to compensation.

37.2.3   Arbitration through ACAS

ACAS provides **arbitration** for straightforward unfair dismissal claims, or in relation to the right to request flexible working, as an alternative to employment tribunal hearings. Both the employer and employee must agree to arbitration. It is likely to be less expensive and less formal than tribunals, and unlike tribunal hearings is confidential. An arbitrator can call witnesses, decide a case and award compensation. Appeals are allowed only in very limited circumstances.

ACAS also provides arbitration in disputes between trade unions and employers [**36.5**].

37.3   TRIBUNAL PROCEEDINGS

Employment tribunal proceedings are governed by complex rules which can only be summarised here. The rules are set out in schedule 1 of the **Employment Tribunals (Constitution and Rules of Procedure) Regulations 2004** *[SI 2004/1861]*, as amended. **Employment Tribunals** [see end of chapter] provides detailed information, and it is generally sensible for both the employee and employer to seek legal advice at an early stage.

At the time of writing (mid 2009) the government had proposed a fast track system for straightforward monetary claims. The system will cover claims for unlawful deduction from wages [**30.1.4**], breach of contract [**37.5**], redundancy pay [**35.7.1**], holiday pay [**31.4.5**] and national minimum wage [**30.2**].

For equal pay complaints the procedure is different from the procedure for other employment tribunal claims, and cases are often very lengthy.

37.3.1   Questionnaire procedure

In discrimination and equal pay cases, a statutory questionnaire procedure enables the complainant to obtain information from the employer before making a claim. If the employer gives evasive or incorrect answers or does not respond to some parts of the questionnaire, this may in some cases be seen as evidence that the employer has discriminated unlawfully.

Similar inferences can be drawn if the employer does not reply or replies evasively to other questions, even if not asked under the statutory procedure.

Dattani v West Mercia Police [2005] UKEAT 0385 04 0702

37.3.2   Time limits

The time limit for submitting a claim to the employment tribunal is generally within three months of the action which gave rise to the claim, or three months after the effective date of termination [**34.8.1**]. For disputes over redundancy payments or unfair selection of employees for re-engagement after industrial action, the time limit is six months. An equal pay claim may be made at any time while the person is still doing the job to which the claim applies, or within six months of when she or he was last employed in that job, or later than six months if the employer deliberately concealed relevant facts.

The time limit may be extended for discrimination and some other cases, if it is just and equitable to do so. Very occasionally it may be extended in other cases, where it was not reasonably practical to make a claim within the specified period.

The time limit ends at midnight and is rigidly applied.

37.3.3   Claim

The employee (the **claimant**) makes a claim on **form ET1**, available from the Employment Tribunals website [see end of chapter]. The form is sent by post or electronically to the relevant tribunal, which sends a copy to the employer (the **respondent**) and invites a response on **form ET3** within 28 days.

Before or after submitting a response, the employer may ask the employee to clarify aspects of the complaint. If the employee fails to do so, the tribunal may order the employee to provide additional information. Similarly the employee can seek additional information relating to the employer's response.

However, the 28-day limit is very strict, and employers should not delay submitting an ET3 based on the information provided by the statement.

37.3.4   Conciliation / judicial mediation

Following a claim made to the employment tribunal, an ACAS conciliation officer is notified and contacts the parties with a view to effecting a binding settlement [**37.2.2.1**] through **conciliation**. If a settlement is reached, the details are recorded on **form COT3**. Alternatively, a binding settlement in the form of a compromise agreement may be reached independently by the parties [**37.2.2.2**].

37.3.5   Preparation

If settlement is not reached, either party may ask the other to provide additional information regarding the claim or response. Prior to the hearing, the employment tribunal issues directions concerning the exchange of documents both parties intend to rely on, the exchange of witness statements, and the parties agreeing a bundle which includes all relevant documents for use at the tribunal.

If one party believes the other has important relevant documents which have not been disclosed, it may apply to the tribunal for an **order for disclosure**, requiring the documents to be **revealed** (sent to the party who has requested them).

At least six bundles of documents should be prepared: for the party preparing the bundle and the other side, three for the tribunal, and one for the witnesses. The pages of the documents must all be numbered.

Normally witnesses attend tribunal proceedings voluntarily, but if a witness considered important by either party refuses to come, the party can ask the tribunal to order their presence.

37.3.6   Pre-hearing review

The tribunal may hold a **pre-hearing review**, a short hearing which generally makes a decision on any preliminary issues, for example whether there is an entitlement to bring a claim before the tribunal, or whether the employee has served a sufficient continuous period of employment [**26.5**] to qualify to proceed with the hearing. The review may deal with other procedural issues, such as ordering one party to produce documents or to provide further details of the claim.

The review also looks at the prospect of success. If the case looks hopeless, the tribunal may require the party bringing the case to pay a deposit of up to £500 as a condition of being allowed to proceed. Or the tribunal can **strike out**, at any stage in the proceedings, a claim or response (notice of appearance) on the grounds that the case has no real prospect of success.   *Employment Tribunals (Constitution & Rules of Procedure) Regulations 2004 [SI 2004/1861] regs.19,20*

37.3.7   Hearing

After the tribunal gives notice of the hearing, it may agree a postponement in order that any criminal case be dealt with first, or for some other reason such as the unavailability of important witnesses.

The parties may be unrepresented, or represented by solicitors, barristers, trade union or employers' body officials, or others. The case is heard by an **employment judge** on his or her own, or with two lay members – one with an employee background and one an employer background.

Apart from a few exceptional situations, the hearing is in public. At the hearing, the procedure is generally first to establish any preliminary questions, for example whether the employee was actually dismissed. If that is to be dealt with first, the employee begins. If that is accepted, the employer usually begins.

Anyone who has provided a witness statement is required to attend to be cross-examined. Evidence cannot be relied on unless contained in the witness statements, and great care should be taken to ensure they are comprehensive. Each witness statement should cross-refer to any relevant document in the bundle.

After the hearing, the tribunal makes its decision and sends it to both parties.

37.3.8 Appeal

An appeal against an employment tribunal decision must be made to the employment appeal tribunal (EAT) within 42 days of the date the decision is sent out by the tribunal office. The time limit ends at 4pm on the 42nd day, and is usually strictly applied.

An EAT can hear an appeal only if it is based on a point of law. After the EAT, a case may be appealed to the court of appeal and ultimately, if leave to appeal is given, to the supreme court. If the case concerns legislation derived from an EU directive, leave may be given to appeal to the European court of justice.

Some EAT cases can be conciliated by ACAS [**37.1.2**] if both parties agree. This may be appropriate if the employee is still employed by the employer, the case may be referred back to the tribunal, or the appeal is about a monetary award.

37.4 TRIBUNAL REMEDIES

Employment tribunals deal with a wide range of claims on employment related matters. In cases of unfair dismissal there are two remedies: reinstatement or re-engagement, and the payment of compensation. In other cases, the remedy is compensation or other payment. In rare cases, costs may be awarded [**37.4.7**].

37.4.1 Unfair dismissal: reinstatement and re-engagement

A **reinstatement order** requires the employer to treat the claimant as if he or she had not been dismissed. This is rarely made.

A **re-engagement order** requires the employer, a successor of the employer or an associated employer to offer the employee employment comparable to that from which he or she was dismissed. A reinstatement order re-creates the status quo, but a re-engagement creates a new contract between the parties.

Reinstatement and re-engagement orders are made only if the employee wants to return to work, and if it is practicable for the employer to take the employee back. If the employer refuses to comply without good reason, the tribunal may award compensation. The ceiling on the compensatory award [**37.4.2.2**] may be removed, and the tribunal may also make an additional award of between 26 and 52 weeks' pay. In calculating awards based on pay, the maximum weekly pay which is considered is £380 (as at 1/10/09).

37.4.2 Unfair dismissal: compensation

In most unfair dismissal cases the tribunal orders the employer to pay compensation in the form of a basic award and a compensatory award.

37.4.2.1 Basic award

The **basic award** is based on the employee's age, length of continuous employment [**26.5.2**], and gross weekly pay (to a maximum of £380 per week, for dismissals where the effective date of termination [**34.8.1**] is on or after 1 October 2009. It is calculated in the same way as a redundancy payment [**35.7.1**]. The maximum basic award is £11,400 (as at 1/10/09).

This basic award may be reduced if the tribunal thinks it is just and equitable, for example if the employee refuses unreasonably to take an offer of reinstatement, or if the employee's conduct before dismissal caused or contributed to the dismissal. Any statutory, contractual or discretionary redundancy payment [**35.7.1**, **35.7.2**] already made is deducted from the basic award. Incapacity benefit or employment and support allowance paid by the Department for Work and Pensions is also deducted, unless the contract allows for it to be paid in addition to normal salary during sickness [**31.6.2**]. *Employment Rights Act 1996 s.122, as amended*

If the employee has received jobseeker's allowance or income support, this does not lead to a reduction in the award. However, the DWP recovers the amount of the benefits from part of the award made by the employer.

37.4.2.2 Compensatory award

In addition to the basic award, the tribunal makes a **compensatory award** if it considers it just and equitable to compensate the employee for financial loss. The maximum is increased annually from 1 February, and is £66,200 as at 1/8/09.

The compensatory award is determined by a number of factors that are caused by or are a consequence of the dismissal, based on case law guidance. These are:

- **Immediate loss of wages**, calculated by looking at the loss the employee has suffered at the date of the hearing. This is generally the difference between the pay and other benefits the employee was receiving, including any increases that would have occurred, and any pay earned during the period up to the hearing. If the employee immediately obtained a new job at higher pay than the old job, there is no order under this head.

- **Future loss of wages**. If the employee is unlikely to get replacement employment immediately, or is likely only to obtain employment at lower pay, the tribunal estimates the likely future loss before the employee gets a job or receives pay at the old level. The award under this head is likely to be higher if the employee can show that jobs are difficult to get, either because of general economic circumstances or because of personal circumstances such as age.

- **Loss of protection**. An employee who finds new employment will not be entitled to protection from unfair dismissal or be able to claim redundancy pay until the necessary period of continuous employment has been accumulated [**34.8.2**, **35.7.1**]. A nominal sum, generally around £250, is awarded under this head to compensate for this lack of protection.

- **Loss of pension rights**. The government's actuarial department has produced guidelines to help tribunals assess this complex area. The amounts involved can be very high, especially in relation to final salary pensions [**30.6.4**].

- **Loss of fringe benefits**. The value of benefits such as car allowances, accommodation etc will be taken into account.

- **Expenses incurred in trying to mitigate loss** [**37.4.2.3**], such as journal subscriptions, fares to attend job interviews, or starting self employment.

Unlike in discrimination cases [**37.4.4**], personal injury, injury to feelings and aggravation cannot be taken into account in determining compensation for unfair dismissal. *Dunnachie v Kingston upon Hull City Council [2004] UKHL 36*

The tribunal may increase or decrease awards by up to 25% if the employer or employee does not comply with the ACAS code of practice [**33.2.1**].

37.4.2.3 Mitigation of loss

The tribunal has to assess whether the employee has taken reasonable steps to try to mitigate (reduce the level of) his or her loss by seeking replacement employment. If there is a failure or a partial failure to do this, the compensation may be reduced. *Employment Rights Act 1996 s.123*

Compensation may also be reduced where the conduct of the employee makes it reasonable and equitable to take this into account when assessing the employee's losses, or where the employee refused to use the employer's appeal procedure.

37.4.2.4 Procedural unfairness and Polkey reduction

Where a dismissal is unfair because the procedure was not fair [**34.5.2**], the tribunal considers what would have happened if a fair procedure had been followed. If the employer would have dismissed in any event, the court may reduce any compensatory award to reflect this. This is known as a **Polkey reduction** (or sometimes **Polkey deduction**). *Polkey v A E Dayton Services Ltd [1987] UKHL 8*

For example, an employee dismissed for misconduct without first being given the opportunity to give his or her version of events is likely to have been procedurally unfairly dismissed. However, the evidence might show that even if the employee had been give the opportunity, there would still be sufficient evidence of misconduct to have justified dismissal. In this situation, the compensatory award for unfair dismissal is likely to be reduced.

37.4.3 Redundancy

Unfair selection for redundancy is dealt with as an unfair dismissal claim [above].

If the employer does not pay statutory redundancy pay [**35.7.1**], the tribunal will order the payment to be made, and may also order compensation for financial losses arising from the non-payment of redundancy pay. *Employment Act 2008 s.7*

If an employer fails to consult the recognised trade union(s) or employee representatives as required, the tribunal makes a **protective award** requiring the employer to pay the redundant employees up to 90 days' pay [**35.2.2**].

If an employee who is under notice of redundancy is not given reasonable time off to look for work or to arrange training [**35.5**], the tribunal will make an award of up to 40% of one week's pay.

37.4.4 Discrimination

An employer may be ordered by the tribunal to pay a compensatory award [**37.4.2.2**] if it is shown that the employer discriminated on the basis of race, colour, ethnic or national origin, nationality, sex, gender reassignment, married or civil partnership status, pregnancy, disability, sexual orientation, religion or belief, age, part-time status, fixed-term status, or trade union membership or lack of it, or if dismissal was on any of these grounds, or if the employee was harassed or victimised on any of these grounds [**chapter 28**].

There is no ceiling to most of these awards, and they can take into account not only actual or potential money losses, but also personal injury (such as psychiatric illness caused by the discrimination) and **injury to feelings**. The injury to feelings element is normally between £500 and £25,000. Additional **aggravated damages** [**65.4.7**] may be added if the employer was malicious or heavy-handed.

The tribunal can hold both the employer and the individual who carried out the discrimination liable for the payment to the employee, and can apportion a percentage of blame to each of them. *Way & another v Crouch [2005] UKEAT 0614 04 0306*

The tribunal may also make an order declaring the rights of the parties, and make a recommendation of action to be taken to reduce the adverse effects of the discrimination. It is expected that the **Equality Act** [**28.1.12**] will enable tribunals to order employers to make changes affecting the workforce as a whole or part of the workforce, rather than only the employee who has brought the claim.

37.4.5 Equal pay and conditions

In equal pay claims [**28.8**], the tribunal may award arrears of pay and damages for non-cash benefits for up to six years before the date on which a claim was made to the tribunal. However, if the claim is based on jobs being rated as equivalent under a job evaluation scheme, the arrears can only be backdated to the date of the job evaluation study. Equal pay awards cannot take into account injury to feelings. *Equal Pay Act 1970 s.2AB, inserted by EPA 1970 (Amendment) Regulations 2003[SI 2003/1656] reg.5; Bainbridge v Redcar & Cleveland Borough Council [2007] UKEAT 0424 06 2303; Degnan & others v Redcar & Cleveland Borough Council [2005] EWCA Civ 726*

37.4.6 Other claims

For other employment related claims, the employer may be ordered:

- to pay arrears of minimum wage [**30.2.5**];
- to provide an itemised pay statement [**30.1.3**];
- to reimburse a worker for unlawful deductions from pay [**30.1.4**], and compensate the employee for financial loss arising from the deductions;
- to pay guarantee payments [**30.1.9**];
- to pay wages to an employee on medical or maternity suspension [**30.1.11**];
- to recompense the employee for time off to which he or she was statutorily entitled, but not allowed to take **31.1.3**];

- to provide a written statement of employment particulars [**26.7**];
- to take steps in relation to a disabled worker [**28.7.4**];
- to take other action or make other payments as necessary to ensure the employer meets its statutory obligations to the employee.

37.4.7   Costs

In the past, **costs awards** (requiring the employer or employee to contribute to the other's costs) in the tribunal were rare. They are now more frequent, because employment tribunals have a duty to consider awarding costs where the case had no reasonable prospect of success or where one of the parties or its representative has acted vexatiously, abusively, disruptively or unreasonably. The costs limit in this situation is £10,000.

Employment Tribunals (Constitution & Rules of Procedure) Regulations 2004 [SI 2004/1861] regs.38-41

When determining costs awards, tribunals are entitled to take into account the paying party's ability to pay.

ET Regs 2004 reg.41(2)

In addition, the tribunals are entitled to make **preparation time orders** in favour of parties who are not legally represented, and **wasted costs orders** against parties' representatives whether or not legally qualified, if they are acting for profit.

ET Regs 2004 regs.42-48

If a claimant persists with a claim after being ordered to pay a deposit at a pre-hearing review [**37.3.6**] and then loses, the deposit may be awarded as costs to the other party.

37.5   TRIBUNAL OR COURT: BREACH OF CONTRACT CLAIMS

Claims for breach of the contract of employment, including wrongful dismissal [**34.4.1**], can be brought in the high court [**65.4**]. This includes sums due under the contract, damages for breach, and counterclaims by employers against employees who bring breach of contract claims. A claim to the courts must be made within six years of the date of the act which gave rise to the claim.

Claims which arise or are outstanding at the termination of the employment – such as arrears of pay, accrued holiday pay or wrongful dismissal – can be brought instead in the employment tribunal. A breach of contract claim to the tribunal must be made within three months of the **effective date of termination [34.8.1]**, or if there is no EDT, within three months of the last day the employee worked. Any counterclaim by the employer must be made within six weeks of the employee's claim.

Some contract claims may only be brought in the court. These include claims where the employment has not terminated, and claims relating to living accommodation [**27.2.8**], intellectual property [**27.10.5**], restrictive covenants [**26.8.2**], obligations of confidentiality [**27.10.3**], and personal injury.

There is no qualifying period of employment [**26.5**] for breach of contract claims in either the tribunal or court.

The maximum award in the tribunal is £25,000. There is no limit in the courts, and the successful party is generally awarded legal costs. It is not allowed to go to the tribunal for the first £25,000 and the high court for an additional amount, so a high value breach of contract case should be brought in the high court.

Employment Tribunal Extension of Jurisdiction (England & Wales) Order 1994 [SI 1994/1623], as amended

37.5.1   Damages for wrongful dismissal

An employee who has been wrongfully dismissed [**34.4.1**] is generally entitled to damages covering financial loss between the date the employer actually terminated and the date the employer could lawfully have terminated. Thus if the employer could have terminated on three months' notice, damages are three months' wages plus other benefits such as bonuses. If the contract was for a fixed term of 18 months with no provision for termination before expiry and it was terminated wrongfully after eight months, damages would be 10 months' salary. In the tribunal (but not the high court) the award is limited to £25,000.

37.5.2   Suing on the contract

If an employer acts in a way which would entitle an employee to claim wrongful constructive dismissal [**34.2.9**], the employee may instead continue working and at any time in the next six years sue the employer for damages in the high court. In some situations the employee may be better off by doing this.

An example is where the employer wrongfully changes the employee's contract of employment, by reducing or removing entitlement to enhanced redundancy pay [**26.9.3**]. If the employee resigns and claims wrongful constructive dismissal, the damages would be limited to the period of notice he or she would have been entitled to, normally not more than 12 weeks. But an employee who carries on working, is later made redundant and sues the employer may be entitled to the difference between the old redundancy pay due and the new lower level actually paid.

37.5.3   Injunctions

Although the courts generally do not enforce contracts of employment by injunctions [**21.7.7**], they have in limited circumstances shown some willingness to force employees to honour post-termination obligations such as confidentiality [**27.10.3**] and not competing [**27.10.1**]. An injunction is available only through the high court, not the tribunal, and is a complex and expensive remedy.

37.5.4   Other breach of contract cases

A claim for breach of the contract of employment, other than a claim arising or outstanding at termination and dealt with in the employment tribunal, is dealt with in the high court in the same way as any other breach of contract case [**21.7, 65.4**]. In calculating the amount of damages, tax and national insurance will usually be deducted, along with any other money received by the employee such as payment in lieu of notice, compensation for unfair dismissal, non-contractual payments, and social security benefits covering what would have been the period of notice. Statutory and contractual redundancy payments are not deducted.

For a fixed-term contract [**25.3.1**] or where there is a very long period of notice, there may be a deduction to reflect **accelerated receipt** – the fact that the employee is receiving payment immediately, rather than having to wait for it.

37.5.4.1   Mitigation of loss

The employee has a duty to take reasonable steps to mitigate the loss, normally by seeking another job or perhaps becoming self employed. If another job is found, the salary from that job is deducted in calculating the damages. If the employee takes no steps to find another job, the earnings which might have been earned had those steps been taken will be estimated and deducted.

Where the claim is for the employer's failure to make a payment in lieu of notice specified in the contract, no deduction is made for other earnings or the employee's failure to mitigate. Where the claim is for the employer's failure to make a discretionary payment in lieu of notice, deduction may be made for failure to mitigate [**34.3.7**].

Resources: EMPLOYMENT CLAIMS AND SETTLEMENT

ACAS, BIS, Business Link, CIPD, Directgov, PEACe, TUC: see end of **chapter 25**.

Conciliation & settlement. ACAS, as above.

Employment tribunals. Employment Tribunals: www.employmenttribunals.gov.uk, 08457 959 775.

Legal aid. Community Legal Advice: www.communitylegaladvice.org.uk, 0845 345 4 345.

Statute law. www.opsi.gov.uk and www.statutelaw.gov.uk.

Much but not all case law. www.bailii.org.

Updates cross-referenced to this book. www.rclh.co.uk.

Chapter 38

SELF EMPLOYED AND OTHER CONTRACTORS

For sources of further information see end of chapter.

38.1   CONTRACTS FOR SERVICE

Businesses, organisations and self employed individuals who carry out work for others are **contractors**. If they in turn engage someone to do some or all of the work, that individual or body is a **sub-contractor**.

Contractors have a **contract for services** [25.1.3], which is usually in writing but does not have to be. The relationship between an organisation and its contractors is governed by contract law [**chapter 21**], regardless of whether the contractor is a self employed individual or a huge firm, and regardless of whether the contract is for a small piece of work or a major project.

38.1.1   Self employed individuals

In some cases it may be clear that an individual is self employed in relation to the work they are contracted to do, but in many cases it is less clear. In looking at the relationship, there are two separate issues:

- for the purposes of **tax and national insurance**: whether HM Revenue and Customs would treat the person as self employed for this work, and therefore taxed under self assessment rather than PAYE;

- for the purposes of **workers' and employment rights**: whether an employment tribunal or court would treat the person as self employed for this work, and therefore not entitled to rights as an employee or to most workers' rights.

Different **tests for self employment** are used to define self employment for tax purposes and for the purposes of employment law, so in some situations a person could be legally self employed for the purposes of tax but an employee or worker for the purposes of employment or workers' rights, or *vice versa*.

Massey v Crown Life Insurance Co [1977] EWCA Civ 12

38.2   EMPLOYMENT STATUS

Individuals who meet the tests for self employment [**38.2.2**] are not entitled to rights available only to employees, and are not entitled to most rights available to the wider group of people legally defined as 'workers' [**38.2.1.1**]. Conversely, if they do not meet the tests for self employment, they are likely to be entitled to rights as employees or workers. These rights are summarised in **chapter 26**.

38.2.1 The importance of the distinction

An employer who wrongly treats a person as self employed rather than as an employee or worker, regardless of whether this is deliberate or unintentional, could have claims brought against it by the individual for not providing workers' or employment rights such as maternity or paternity pay, and could face a claim for unfair dismissal if the contract is terminated without a fair reason [**34.6**].

38.2.1.1 Workers' rights

A **worker** [**25.1.2**] is a person who does not meet the legal criteria for working under a contract of employment [**25.1.1**], but is working under a contract where they have to provide their services personally, rather than being able to subcontract them. This includes, for example, casual workers [**25.3.2**]. Workers are entitled to some employment rights, including equal opportunities protection [**chapter 28**], minimum wage [**30.2**], paid holiday and other working time rights [**31.1**], part-time workers' rights [**26.4.2**] and the right to be accompanied at disciplinary and grievance hearings [**33.1.1**]. But workers are not entitled to the full range of employment rights.

Self employed individuals run their own business, carry out work for their clients, and do not necessarily have to perform the work personally [**25.1.3**]. Self employed individuals are entitled to equal opportunities protection, but not other rights of workers.

Freelance workers who do work for which they are not employees, but who do not run their own business, are workers rather than self employed.

The distinction between employee, freelance worker and self employed worker is not straightforward, and in some cases legal advice may be needed.

38.2.2 Tests for employment status

The main tests for self employment are outlined here, but they should be applied with caution. If in any doubt about whether an individual should be treated as an employee, a worker or self employed in relation to employment rights, the organisation should take legal advice. The individual's assurances that he or she is self employed, or the organisation's opinion of how the tests apply, are not enough.

38.2.2.1 The test of personal service

An employee must be personally involved in providing a service to the employer, but a self employed person does not necessarily have to undertake the work personally. So a very strong indication of self employment is that the person can appoint or sub-contract someone else to do the work. However, employment tribunals are increasingly finding that a limited or occasional right to delegate the work does not prevent a so-called self employed person from being an employee.

Nor does lack of a right to delegate mean that the person is not self employed, because in many cases genuinely self employed individuals are required to do the work themselves and do not have the right to sub-contract it.

38.2.2.2 The control test

Employment implies that the employer has the right to direct the employee, while self employed people generally have more choice about what they do, and how and when they do it. However, employees may exercise considerable control over their own work, while some genuinely self employed contractors may agree to follow detailed instructions. So the control test is not conclusive.

38.2.2.3 Integration test

Also called the **organisation test**, the **integration test** looks at whether the person's work is integrated into the core of what the organisation does or is an 'add-on', and the extent to which the person's role is integrated into the organisation's management structure. If the work is not integral and the person is not positioned within the management structure, the person may be self employed. But this test creates difficulties in defining what is and is not 'integral'.

38.2.2.4 Mutuality of obligation

In employment, the employer is obliged to provide work if it is available [**26.3.3**] and the employee has to do it. If the organisation has no obligation to provide work, and the person is free to take it or leave it when it is offered, the person is unlikely to be an employee for the purposes of employment law. He or she might be a casual or freelance worker [**25.3.2**], or self employed.

38.2.2.5 Documentation

Any documentation for the work will be closely examined, to see whether it contains terms typical of employment such as references to salary (rather than fee), arrangements for pay during holidays or sickness (which self employed workers do not generally receive), or dismissal (rather than termination of the contract). However, the documentation is not in itself conclusive, and a tribunal will look a the reality of the relationship between the parties.

38.2.2.6 VAT registration

If an individual is registered for VAT, this generally indicates that they are running their own business. But VAT registration is not, in itself, conclusive proof that the person is self employed in relation to a particular piece of work.

38.2.2.7 The independent business test

A fundamental test is whether the individual is genuinely in business on their own account, or is in fact part of the organisation to which the service is being provided. Individuals are more likely to be considered independent if they provide their own equipment and other resources, are in effect selling their services and expertise, invest their own capital in the business, and run financial risks and stand to gain or lose financially from the business.

A person who works for several different organisations and whose income is irregular is more likely to be considered independent than one who works most of the time for one organisation and is paid on a regular basis.

38.2.2.8 Intentions of the parties

If the results of the other tests are inconclusive, the intentions of the parties may be an important factor in clarifying whether the relationship between them is one of employment or of self employment.

38.2.2.9 The whole picture

No single test is conclusive, and in determining whether a person is self employed the employment tribunal or court will look at the whole picture.

An example is a part-time consultant orthodontist who held a series of annual contracts working three days a week for the Ministry of Defence. The advertisement for the post indicated it would be suitable for an independent contractor, and under the contract the consultant was responsible for her own tax, national insurance and negligence insurance, and could provide substitutes to do the work – all of which pointed to her being self employed.

But the advert used terminology such as salary and job share, and in practice the MoD arranged cover for her holidays and she worked as part of the MoD system – which pointed to her being an employee. The employment appeal tribunal held that because her terms were not confined to the contract, and taking into account the advertisement and the fact that she did not provide substitutes, she was an employee.   *Ministry of Defence HQ Defence Dental Service v Kettle [2007] UKEAT 0308 06 3101*

38.2.3 Non-tests

Working part-time – even very part-time – or as a job sharer has no bearing on whether a person is employed or self employed, nor does being employed on a temporary, fixed-term or casual basis [**25.3**].

A person who has many jobs or pieces of work, or works at home or at their own office is not necessarily self employed.

A person self defined or defined by others as 'self employed', 'freelance' or a 'consultant' is not necessarily self employed.

The fact that a person is self employed in one situation does not mean that they are self employed in all situations. An actor, for example, might be self employed as an actor, while being employed by a restaurant as a waiter.

The fact that a person is registered as self employed with HMRC, can prove that they have previously paid tax as a self employed person or are registered for VAT, does not provide a guarantee that the person can safely be treated as self employed for the purposes of employment rights.

38.3 TAX STATUS

Tax law distinguishes between:

- people who meet the HM Revenue and Customs tests for self employment [below], are registered with HMRC as self employed for tax purposes, and pay tax through **self assessment**;
- people treated as employees for tax purposes, who must be taxed under PAYE (this includes all employees, and the vast majority of workers [**25.1.2**]);
- individuals who do not meet the criteria for self employment, but have earnings or other income which does not have to be taxed under PAYE and is therefore taxed under self assessment.

Self employed individuals must register with HM Revenue and Customs within three months from the end of the month in which they start self employment. Failure to register may lead to a £100 penalty.

38.3.1 Tests for tax status

The criteria used by HM Revenue and Customs for determining tax and national insurance liability are similar to the tests for employment status [**38.2.2**], but are not quite the same and sometimes yield different results from the tests for employment status. The tax tests are available from HMRC [see end of chapter].

Before treating a person as self employed for the purposes of tax, it is essential to confirm that they will be self employed in relation to *this* work. A person doing the same type of work can be self employed in one capacity but employed in another, so the fact that the person is registered with HMRC as self employed does not necessarily mean that they can be treated as self employed for all their work.

HMRC has on its website an **employment status indicator** (ESI) which can be used to check whether individuals are self employed A copy of the result should be kept, because an organisation (called in this context an **engager**) can rely on the outcome of the ESI as evidence of the person's status for the purposes of tax and national insurance, provided the answers to the ESI questions are accurate, and the ESI has been filled in by the engager or their authorised representative. If it is filled in by the worker, the result is only indicative. The ESI cannot be used for workers providing services through an intermediary [**38.3.4**], company directors or agency workers.

38.3.2 PAYE

A person who is not genuinely self employed for the work they are contracted to do must be treated for tax purposes as an employee [**30.4**]. It is the employer's responsibility to ensure that PAYE is operated if it should be. If the organisation does not operate PAYE for the individual and HMRC finds that it should have, the organisation could be ordered to pay up to six years' income tax and national insurance contributions (NIC) on payments to the individual, plus interest and possibly penalties (which can be up to 100%) for late payment.

If an organisation fails to deduct tax and national insurance when it should but the individual has paid some or all of the tax and NI through self assessment, HMRC can make the employee, rather than the employer, liable for the amount which should have been deducted.   *Income Tax (Earnings & Pensions) Act 2003 ss.72E-72G, inserted by Income Tax (Pay As You Earn) (Amendment) Regulations 2008 [SI 2008/782] reg.7*

An organisation which has not deducted tax when it perhaps should have done should take advice from a solicitor or accountant with tax expertise. Drawing the matter to HMRC's attention may mean that it assesses the organisation for past failure to operate PAYE, but if the matter is ignored and HMRC discovers it in future, it may then assess for an even more substantial past failure.

38.3.3 Contracting with a business or organisation

Where an organisation appoints a firm – a partnership, cooperative or company – or a voluntary or not-for-profit organisation to undertake work on its behalf, the deduction of tax and national insurance is not generally an issue, because the organisation rather than an individual is being hired. However, the deduction of tax and NI may be an issue with some building contracts [**30.4.16**].

38.3.4 Contracting with an intermediary

Rules referred to as **IR35** apply to **personal service companies** (PSC) , where a self employed individual sets up a limited company or partnership and carries out work for clients through that body. If the individual undertakes so much work for a client that the relationship is, in effect, an employment relationship, the PSC is likely to have to operate PAYE for the individual.

Similar rules apply to work done by self employed individuals through a **managed service company** (MSC), where the individual is a shareholder in the company but does not exercise any control over it.

The rules on PSCs and MSCs do not affect organisations which enter into contracts with these bodies, because the organisation's relationship is with the PSC or MSC, rather than with the individual.

IR35 also does not affect individuals who work purely on a self employed basis, rather than through an intermediary company or partnership.

38.4 THE CONTRACT

As soon as one party offers to pay another in exchange for a service and the offer is accepted, a contract exists [**20.6.1**]. There is no obligation to put anything in writing, but it is sensible to have a written contract with all self employed individuals and other contractors. An organisation which regularly uses contractors should consider developing a suitable standard contract [**21.3.1**]. An organisation which is asked to sign a contract prepared by a contractor it should carefully consider the terms and if necessary take legal advice before signing.

38.4.1 Entering into the contract

Before hiring anyone on a self employed basis, the organisation should:

- consider whether the nature of the work, or the relationship between the organisation and individual, is such that an employment tribunal would say that the person is actually an employee or 'worker' and/or HMRC would say that PAYE should be operated;
- ask for confirmation, in writing, that the person is registered with HMRC as self employed for this type of work;
- ask for the person's tax office and reference number, and if in doubt, check with the tax office about whether it is permissible to treat the person as self employed for the work they are doing for the organisation.

If in doubt, it is generally safer to treat the person as an employee, even though this will have cost implications for employer's national insurance, statutory sick pay, holiday pay, and other statutory and contractual entitlements.

If the person is to be treated as self employed, ensure that an appropriate contract is signed by both parties, and review the health and safety, negligence and other risks arising from the relationship and ensure the individual and organisation have appropriate insurance cover.

38.4.2   Contract terms

There are no rules about what must be included in a contract with a self employed person or other contractor, or how long a contract should be. A good contract should include, as appropriate:

- the names of the parties;
- the nature of the work, either in general or in detail, perhaps with reference to another more detailed document which is attached;
- if the work involves unsupervised access to children or vulnerable adults, the obligation to provide a criminal record check [**41.4**].

Dates and deadlines

- The start date and if appropriate the finish date or deadline, and any deadlines between start and finish;
- how the contract may be terminated before the expiry of its term, and the notice which needs to be given by whichever side is ending it.

Fee

- The agreed fee and the basis on which it is made (for example per hour, per session or as a fixed fee for the job as a whole);
- whether the fee includes VAT, is exclusive of VAT or is not subject to VAT;
- if paid on an hourly or other open-ended basis, whether there is a maximum to the amount of time or money payable;
- any penalties or compensation if deadlines are not met;
- the circumstances, if any, when additional fees will be due (for example on publication of a second edition, or if rights to a publication are sold to another organisation);
- agreed expenses, how additional expenses are agreed, and the receipts or other documentation the contractor needs to provide.

Payment

- The intervals at which payment will be made;
- invoicing the organisation, and the period for payment;
- any interest on late payment [for the statutory right to charge interest on late payments even if it is not included in the contract, see **21.2.3**];
- if the contractor is an individual, the fact that they are responsible for all tax and national insurance on payments made to them and will indemnify the organisation for any liability in respect of tax and NI on those payments (the organisation still has to confirm that the person is indeed self employed, but this clause allows the organisation to recover tax and NI from the individual if necessary).

Nature of the work

- Where and how the work will be done;
- warranties that the contractor has the necessary skill and will take all reasonable care;
- the organisation's agreement to provide information, access to premises etc reasonably requested;
- issues around data protection and confidentiality of information;
- support or facilities to be provided by the organisation (for example typing, photocopying, telephone, access to library etc);
- obligation to indemnify the organisation if damage or loss is caused;
- what insurance, if any, the contractor is required to have and whether proof of insurance must be provided [**38.4.3**];
- agreement to comply with the organisation's equal opportunities, health and safety and other relevant policies.

Monitoring

- To whom the contractor reports, how often and in what form;
- if appropriate how and when the work will be reviewed, what happens if the brief has to be changed, what happens if the work is unsatisfactory, and how disputes about the work are to be handled;

- whether interim reports, drafts etc are required, and deadlines for these;
- provision, if any, for arbitration or other determination of disputes;
- procedure for terminating the work if there is a breach of contract and the matter cannot be resolved.

Rights and restrictions

- Whether the contractor will hold copyright, patent, design or other rights to any work produced, or whether the right(s) will be assigned to the organisation or will be held jointly [**chapter 44**];
- what rights, if any, the contractor has to use research data, written materials or other intellectual property for other purposes;
- any restrictions, for example not to do similar work for a competitor;
- if relevant who has the right to change the material for future use, what payments are made to the contractor for future use etc.

Completion and follow-up

- How the work will be assessed or evaluated on completion, and what happens if the organisation is dissatisfied with it;
- for consultancy type work, how and to whom recommendations will be submitted before a report is produced, and to whom the report is to be given;
- whether any follow-up is built into this contract, or whether follow-up, if any, is to be agreed later as a separate contract.

38.4.3   Liability and insurance

It is likely to be appropriate for the organisation to require the contractor to be insured for risks arising from its activities. This might include insurance covering public liability [**23.5.1**], professional indemnity [**23.5.3**], breach of copyright [**23.5.6**], defamation [**23.5.5**], breach of confidentiality [**23.5.7**], or whatever is appropriate for the work.

The organisation should check that all necessary insurance actually exists and adequately covers the possible risks. Where the contract extends over a long period, the organisation may wish to require proof of renewal.

The organisation is not normally liable for damage or loss caused by a contractor, but could be held liable where the organisation authorised the action which caused the loss or damage, it has a duty with strict liability [**22.6.1**, **40.2.5**], or it has not taken care to select a competent contractor.   *Pinn v Rew [1916] 32 TLR 451*

It may be appropriate to include in the contract provision for indemnity if the organisation suffers loss as a result of the contractor's activities. Where the risks are substantial, the organisation should require the contractor to take out insurance indemnifying (compensating) it.

The organisation must ensure that its own insurance covers risks arising from the work, and is not invalidated by, for example, the presence of a contractor or the fact that the work is being done by a contractor rather than an employee.

38.4.4   Terminating the contract

If one party is in breach of contract – for example if the contractor does not do the work as agreed or the organisation does not pay on time – the aggrieved party may take the other to court [**65.4**, **65.6**].

Resources: SELF EMPLOYED AND OTHER CONTRACTORS

ACAS, BIS, Business Link, Directgov, CIPD, PEACe, TUC: see end of **chapter 25**.

Tax and national insurance. HM Revenue and Customs: www.hmrc.gov.uk/selfemployed, 0845 915 4655.

Statute law. www.opsi.gov.uk and www.statutelaw.gov.uk.

Much but not all case law. www.bailii.org.

Updates cross-referenced to this book. www.rclh.co.uk.

Chapter 39
VOLUNTEERS

For sources of further information see end of chapter.

39.1   THE LEGAL POSITION OF VOLUNTEERS

At the time of writing (mid 2009) there is no general statutory definition of a volunteer, but for specific purposes the **National Minimum Wage Act 1998** refers to 'voluntary workers' [**39.4.3.1**], the **Job Seeker's Allowance Regulations 1996** and other legislation relating to state benefits refer to 'voluntary work' [**39.11.3**], and the **Police Act (Criminal Records) Regulations 2002** refers to 'volunteers' [**41.4.1**]. In relation to volunteers' possible entitlement to employment rights, case law is inconsistent but the decision in South East Sheffield CAB v Grayson [**39.4.2.3**] is the clearest starting point.

In common usage, volunteers are usually defined as people who give their time for some project or purpose, without being obliged to do so, and without pay other than reimbursement of genuine out of pocket expenses.

However, some people referred to by their organisations or themselves as volunteers do receive pay or other reward, and/or are obliged to carry out the work. The government, in particular, regularly proposes and sometimes implements schemes where 'volunteers' are paid, or where 'volunteering' is or borders on the compulsory, or where volunteering is rewarded – such as the 'fast track' citizenship for immigrants who are involved in volunteering [**39.6.3**].

570

39.1.1 Obligations of volunteers

All volunteers must comply with the law relating to the organisation's activities and services, for example, the law relating to health and safety [**chapter 40**], driving [**40.12**], work with children and vulnerable adults [**chapter 41**], equal opportunities in service delivery [**chapter 42**], confidentiality and data protection [**43.1, 43.3**], provision of food and drink [**40.10.1**], and fundraising [**chapters 48** and **49**]. When carrying out their work they have a duty of care [**22.6.1**] to the organisation, other workers, clients or service users, and members of the public with whom they come in contact.

Volunteers should also be required to comply with the organisation's internal policies, rules and guidelines if these are applicable to their work.

39.1.2 Rights of volunteers and duties of organisations

The legal rights of volunteers, and the corresponding duties of organisations, are often unclear, not least because the term 'volunteer' is used to describe a very wide range of people, some of whom may in fact be employees for the purposes of tax and national insurance and/or employment rights. In addition, both the EU and the UK are increasingly extending employment rights, including minimum wage, to a wider group of workers [**25.1.2**], which could include some volunteers.

These issues are particularly important where the volunteer is paid anything other than allowed reimbursement of expenses [**39.2.1**], receives anything else of value [**39.2.4**], or has a relationship with the organisation which is or could be seen as contractual [**39.4.2.1**]. In these situations, a so-called volunteer could be entitled to workers' rights or the full range of employment rights. In addition, their pay or the value of other benefits could be subject to tax, and depending on the circumstances the organisation would have to operate PAYE or the individual would have to declare it through self assessment.

Even where volunteers do not have workers' or employment rights:

- the organisation has a duty of care to them [**22.6.1**];
- if the organisation has employees it must comply with health and safety legislation [**chapter 40**], and it is good practice to do so even with no employees;
- data protection law [**43.3**] applies the same to volunteers as to anyone else;
- volunteers who are not legally employees own the copyright or other intellectual property rights to work they create for the organisation, unless the rights have been assigned to the organisation [**44.2.3**].

Unless the volunteer is legally an employee, there is no statutory obligation to take out insurance to cover situations where the volunteer becomes ill or is injured as a result of the organisation's negligence. But it is good practice to ensure they are covered under the organisation's employer's liability or public liability insurance [**39.9.1**].

Volunteers are not generally protected under the employment provisions of the equal opportunities legislation unless they are legally working under a contract, but may be protected under the service delivery provisions [**39.7**].

Volunteering England or Wales Council for Voluntary Action [see end of chapter] can provide basic information on legal aspects of volunteering. For complex matters it may be necessary to seek detailed advice from a solicitor or other advisor with specialist expertise in relation to volunteers.

39.1.3 Job substitution

Apart from asylum seekers [**39.6.2**], there is no statutory prohibition on **job substitution**– volunteers doing work that is or has been done by employees. But a volunteer receiving state benefits could be subject to the notional earnings rule [**39.11.2.5**], and if working under a contract [**39.4.2.2**] could be entitled to the same pay and conditions *pro rata* as a comparable full-time worker [**26.4.2**].

Particularly in the public sector, trade unions have agreements with some employers that volunteers will not be used for job substitution.

39.2 PAYMENTS AND PERKS TO VOLUNTEERS

Organisations are not obliged to make any reimbursements or other payments, or provide any benefits, to volunteers. But in looking at many rights and obligations in relation to volunteers, key issues are the nature of any payments or benefits provided to the volunteer, whether the organisation has created a relationship in which it is obliged to provide certain payments or benefits, and whether the individual is obliged to provide work in exchange for those payments or benefits.

In looking at payments and benefits, a distinction must be made between:

- allowed **reimbursement** of genuine out of pocket expenditure [below];
- additional payments which may be called reimbursement but are not;
- **remuneration**, which is payment or something else of value given in return for the work done by the volunteer;
- a one-off payment or gift given as a token of **thanks** to the volunteer;
- provision of **benefits** which are part of or necessary for the work, such as training or in some cases accommodation;
- provision of additional benefits or **perks**, such as a reduced fee for events, discounts in the organisation's shop, or training unrelated to the person's work.

39.2.1 Reimbursement of expenses

Reimbursement repays a person for expenditure which was genuinely incurred (the money was actually spent), was authorised by the organisation, was wholly for the organisation's work, was necessary for the work, and is properly documented [**39.2.1.1**].

Reimbursement which meets these criteria:

- is unlikely to be subject to tax or national insurance [**39.3**];
- should not affect volunteers on state benefits [**39.11**];
- is unlikely to be treated by the employment tribunal or court as consideration creating a contract [**39.4**] and entitling the volunteer to employment rights;
- can be made to governing body members of most organisations unless the governing document explicitly prohibits such payment, although there are some exceptions where the governing document must include explicit provision for this [**16.3.1**].

Even where reimbursement meets these criteria, it may not be allowed for asylum seekers who are volunteering [**39.6.2**].

39.2.1.1 Documentation

Volunteers should wherever reasonable provide receipts or other documentation to verify their expenditure. The organisation decides what it requires, but there should be enough information to show that the expenditure was incurred, was wholly for the organisation's work and was necessary for the work.

It is good practice to devise a claim form, with relevant documentation attached to the form. Where receipts are not available, for example telephone calls made from home, the volunteer should provide appropriate records or an explanation of how the amount was estimated, or a note should be made on the claim form indicating why there is no documentation.

39.2.2 'Paid volunteers'

Unless the person is on a training or return to work scheme which specifically allows payment tax-free, all payments apart from reimbursement of genuine expenses [**39.2.1**] are subject to tax and national insurance, could entitle the person to employment rights [**39.4**], could affect state benefits [**39.11**], could affect an asylum seeker's application to remain in the UK [**39.6.2**], and could be unlawful if paid to a member of the organisation's governing body [**16.3.1**]. This includes:

- anything called an 'expenses payment' or 'reimbursement' unless it complies with the rules for allowed reimbursements;
- any payment for the work, whether regular, one-off or sessional;

- anything called an allowance, 'pocket money' or similar;
- in many cases, something called an honorarium or thank you payment.

The amount is irrelevant, and even a token payment is treated in the same way as **remuneration** or **earnings**.

A person who receives such payment is sometimes called a **paid volunteer**, or in some legislation or government publications a **voluntary worker**. In some legislation even volunteers who are only reimbursed are called voluntary workers.

Some government-sponsored 'volunteering' schemes allow participants to be paid. These payments are subject to tax, national minimum wage and other employment rights unless the legislation which creates the scheme says they are not.

39.2.3 Honoraria and thank you payments

An honorarium is a payment which there is no contractual obligation to make. If a person is told that he or she will receive a payment, or if the payment is always made so the person expects to receive it, it is not an honorarium. It is a one-off payment and should be treated the same as other payments [**39.2.2**].

Provided that a one-off payment is given as a genuine thank you and is not given regularly, it may not be subject to tax. The organisation should take advice from its PAYE office or accountant before making such a payment. Even if a payment is not subject to tax, it may affect state benefits or an asylum seeker's application to remain in the UK, may be unlawful if paid to a member of the governing body, and the organisation may be restricted in its power to make the payment [**53.3**].

39.2.4 Benefits, perks and non-money gifts

Meals provided during unpaid volunteering are not subject to tax, are not unlawful if provided to governing body members, and should not affect volunteers who are asylum seekers or on state benefits.

Benefits with a financial value, such as protective clothing, training or supervision, can be provided if they are necessary for the volunteer's work.

Small perks which are not necessary for the work, such as reduced-price entry to the organisation's events or small discounts at the organisation's shop, small gifts such as flowers or chocolate, and occasional small-scale social events are not likely to be taxable, and should not affect state benefits. If made to a governing body member it could be an unlawful use of the organisation's funds [**16.3.11**], but in practice neither the Charity Commission nor the organisation's members would be likely to take action against the organisation. The provision or promise of such benefits could possibly be seen as consideration creating a contract [**39.4**], and thus have implications for employment rights.

Benefits or perks which are not necessary for the work and have a financial value, such as additional training or substantial discounts at the organisation's shops or for its events, could be subject to tax, could affect state benefits, could create an entitlement to employment rights, and if made to a member of a governing body could be an unlawful use of the organisation's funds. The organisation should take specialist advice before providing such benefits.

The provision of **accommodation** is complex and advice should be taken. If the volunteer must live there in order to carry out their duties, all or some the value of the accommodation may not be subject to tax. It will, however, affect some state benefits and could give an entitlement to minimum wage [**39.4.3.1**].

39.3 VOLUNTEERS, TAX AND NATIONAL INSURANCE

The reimbursements allowed tax-free by HM Revenue and Customs (HMRC) depend on whether the volunteer is **unpaid** (receives no payment other than reimbursement for allowed expenses) or **paid** (receives additional payment). Everyone, whether paid or unpaid, may be reimbursed tax-free for:

- actual expenditure incurred in the purchase of materials or services required to do the work (postage, photocopying etc);

- actual cost of specialist or protective clothing necessary for the work;
- actual cost of training, conferences, supervision etc necessary for the work, and directly related costs such as travel costs and accommodation or meals while attending such events.

Volunteers who receive only proper reimbursement – but not volunteers who receive additional payment – may be reimbursed tax-free for travel expenses or mileage between home and the place of volunteering. All volunteers, whether paid or not, may be reimbursed travel expenses or mileage to do the actual work.

HMRC generally allows volunteers who receive only proper reimbursement to be reimbursed tax-free for the actual costs of meals taken while volunteering and the actual cost of creche, childminding fees or other dependant care costs incurred in order to be available for voluntary work. For paid volunteers, these reimbursements are subject to tax and/or national insurance.

It is good practice for the organisation to have limits on the amount it will reimburse for meals, childminding and similar expenses.

39.3.1   Mileage

Reimbursement for mileage is tax-free if it is reimbursed at or below the HMRC **approved mileage allowance payments** (AMAP) rate, which is based on the total number of reimbursed miles for business use for the vehicle during the tax year. (Driving as a volunteer is classed as business use.) Volunteers must keep proper records showing journey details, mileage and purpose.

The allowances that can be reimbursed free of tax for cars and vans are (as at 1/8/09) 40p per mile for the first 10,000 business miles, and 25p per mile for additional miles. The per mile allowance for motorcycles is 25p and for bicycles 20p. If the volunteer can show that mileage costs were genuinely above these rates, HMRC will allow the additional amount to be paid free of tax and NI.

If the organisation reimburses at higher than the AMAP, the whole amount (not just the excess) is taxable and may have significant implications [**39.2.2, 39.10.4.1**]. If the organisation does not reimburse, or reimburses at less than the AMAP, volunteers may be able to set the expenditure against their taxable income. They should seek advice on this from their tax office.

39.3.2   Scale rate expenses

Organisations with large numbers of volunteers, where the paperwork involved in reimbursing actual expenditure would be disproportionately time consuming, may apply to the local HMRC inspector of taxes for permission to make **scale rate** [**30.4.9**] (also called **flat rate** or **lump sum**) expenses payments (such as '£7 per day to cover fares and lunch'). However, such consent is not granted very often. Without consent from HMRC, any such payment is subject to tax unless it can be shown that the volunteer spent at least that amount on the expenses.

Even where consent for scale rate payments is granted, it covers *only* the tax status of the payment. The payment could still have an impact on state benefits, employment rights, and/or rules on paying charity governing body members.

39.3.3   Tax

Volunteers who receive payments which are not proper reimbursement are generally treated for tax purposes in the same way as employees [**30.4**]. They must fill in form P46, and the organisation is likely to have to operate PAYE for any volunteer who receives more than the national insurance earnings threshold (£110 per week in tax year 2009-10) from the organisation, or pays tax on income from other sources and receives more than £1 per week from the organisation.

Where volunteers receive 'enhanced expenses', such as mileage at more than the HMRC approved rate, HMRC may allow this to be declared by the volunteer and taxed under self assessment, rather than through PAYE.

For more about income tax and national insurance see **30.4**. If the organisation is not registered for PAYE it should contact the HMRC new employer helpline [see end of **chapter 30**]. If it is already registered it should generally treat paid volunteers in the same way as new employees.

At the end of the tax year, the organisation must give all paid volunteers a record of what they have received as remuneration during the year, and may also need to provide a record of expenses payments on form P11D or P9D [**30.4.3**, **30.4.7**] and provide this information to HMRC.

39.3.4 National insurance

A paid volunteer who is paid more than the national insurance earnings threshold (£110 per week in tax year 2009-10) must pay employee's (class 1) NI contributions, and the organisation must pay employer's NICs [**30.4.6**].

39.3.5 Volunteers placed overseas

A volunteer who is normally resident in the UK and is placed overseas by a UK charity can receive tax-free travel to and from their placement, accommodation, insurance and a modest living allowance, and the charity can pay the volunteer's national insurance contributions while they are volunteering abroad. The charity should agree the level of living allowance with its PAYE office.

39.4 VOLUNTEERS AND EMPLOYMENT RIGHTS

Entitlement to workers' and employment rights depends on whether there is a **contract** between the individual and the organisation, and if so the nature of the contract. A contract may be written, verbal or implied (assumed from the nature of the relationship) [**21.1**].

At its simplest, a contract in this context is a relationship which involves **consideration** (payment or something else of material value) being provided in return for work; and the **intention** to create a legally binding relationship between the parties [**21.1.1**]. The courts and employment tribunals generally assume that if one party agrees to pay another for work, they intend the relationship to be legally binding. The parties do not have to state this explicitly.

If there is a contract it may be:

- a contract of employment [**25.1.1**], entitling the person to the full range of employment rights;
- another type of contract, for example for casual work, where the person is not entitled to all employment rights but is entitled to the more limited rights available to 'workers' [**25.1.2**]; or
- a contract with a self employed person, who in most cases is not entitled to workers' rights other than equal opportunities protection [**25.1.3**].

39.4.1 The range of relationships

The most likely relationships with so-called volunteers are:

- remuneration and/or benefits (including training) not necessary for the work, *plus* an obligation to do the work or a situation where the person does the work on a regular basis, probably creates a **contract of employment**, with entitlement to the same rights as any employee (see for example the Migrant Advisory Service case, **39.4.2.1**);
- remuneration and/or benefits not necessary for the work, *plus* one-off, occasional or non-regular work, probably creates a **contract**, with entitlement to workers' rights such as minimum wage (the Welcare case, **39.4.2.2**);
- benefits necessary for the work (such as training), *plus* a clear obligation to do the work in return for the benefit with a sanction or penalty if the work is not done, probably creates a **contract** or **contract of employment**, depending on the nature of the obligation, with entitlement to workers' or employment rights (the Relate case, **39.4.2.1**);
- any of the above *plus* an explicit statement that the parties do not intend the relationship to be contractual [**39.4.4**] may create a **non-contractual ar-**

rangement not entitling the person to workers' or employment rights, but this should not be relied on;

- only genuine reimbursement and/or training or other benefits necessary for the work, *plus* the person being free to stop volunteering whenever they want even if they have said they will commit to volunteering for a specified period, probably means there is **no contract**, therefore no entitlement to workers' or employment rights (the South East Sheffield CAB case, **39.4.2.3**).

Although the above outline illustrates the range of relationships, it does not mean that any particular relationship would or would not be defined by a court or tribunal as contractual. The tribunal cases described below illustrate the issues.

The fact that a tribunal or court finds that a contract has or has not been created does not affect, one way or the other, liability for tax and national insurance, because different criteria are used to determine employment status and tax status.

39.4.2   Tribunal decisions

Court or tribunal cases involving volunteers can give rise to confusing and sometimes contradictory decisions, as illustrated by the cases below. Any organisation faced with a claim or potential claim for employment rights by a volunteer should take advice from a specialist solicitor.

39.4.2.1   Volunteers held to have a contract of employment

A 'volunteer' office worker who received £25 per week (subsequently increased to £40) 'to cover expenses' was held to have a contract because she did not incur any costs for travel, meals or other expenditure, and received the payment even when she was on holiday. The payment was clearly for the work, rather than reimbursement. Because she worked regular hours each week in the organisation's office, the contract was held to be a contract of employment. The worker subsequently received £11,000 for unfair dismissal.   *Migrant Advisory Service v Chaudri [1998] UKEAT 1400 97 2807*

A contract does not have to involve payment. In one of the best-known cases, a counsellor was held to have a contract of employment, even though she did not receive any money payment, because:

- she was obliged to provide 600 hours of counselling after receiving training, or to repay the organisation if she left without good reason before providing the counselling;

- there was an expectation that after she had done a certain amount of counselling, she might be paid for future work;

- there was a long and formal written agreement, with detailed obligations on both parties;

- the agreement referred to the organisation as 'the employer'.
  Maria DeLourdes Armitage v Relate & others [1994] COIT 43538/94

This case illustrates the importance of looking at the entire relationship between the organisation and its volunteers. The phrasing and scope of any written agreements or internal procedures could be critical in showing an intention to create a binding relationship, especially where the organisation requires the person to work at specific times or for a specified period and imposes a sanction (in this case, having to repay the value of the training) if the volunteer does not do the work as agreed.

A 'volunteer' who is found to be working under a contract of employment is entitled to the full range of employment rights [**39.4.3**].

39.4.2.2   Volunteers held to have a contract

In one case a 'volunteer' was not required or expected to work regularly, but helped occasionally in a project to pack food and toiletries for refugees. When she attended she received a payment of £5 to £15, depending on the number of hours she worked. The tribunal held that she was working under a contract, but that it was not a contract of employment. A 'volunteer' in this type of arrangement would be entitled to workers' rights, but not the full range of employment rights [**39.4.3**].   *Elshami v Welcare Community Projects & Geta Leema [1998] COIT 6001977/1998*

39.4.2.3 Volunteers held not to have a contract

When a St John Ambulance volunteer claimed she was working under a contract because a condition of membership was that she do 30 hours of duties each year, the employment appeal tribunal held that this obligation was a condition of membership, not a contract to provide services.

Uttley v St John Ambulance & another
[1998] UKEAT 635 98 0109

Where an organisation offers to pay for the work done by a volunteer but the volunteer does not take up the offer, this does not create a contract with the volunteer. However, if the volunteer is receiving state benefits it could lead to them being treated for benefits purposes as if they are being paid [**39.11.2.5**].

Alexander v Romania at Heart Trading Co Ltd [1997] COIT 3102006/97

A requirement that volunteers comply with an organisation's policies and rules is not comparable to a requirement that they provide work. The latter may create a contract; the former does not.

Gradwell v Council for Voluntary Service Blackpool, Wyre
& Fylde [1997] COIT 2404314/97

The situation was clarified in 2003 and 2004, when two employment appeal tribunals said volunteers are unlikely to be working under a contract provided they:

- receive no payment other than reimbursement of genuine expenses [**39.2.1**];
- receive only training or other benefits that are necessary to do the work;
- do not receive perks or anything else that could be seen as consideration; and
- are not subject to sanctions if they decide not to work.

South East Sheffield Citizens Advice Bureau v Grayson [2003] UKEAT 0283 03 1711;
Melhuish v Redbridge Citizens Advice Bureau [2004] UKEAT 0130 04 2405

Volunteers who are not working under a contract are not protected under the employment provisions of the discrimination legislation, and are not entitled to workers' or employees' rights [below].

39.4.3 Rights of volunteers working under a contract

'Volunteers' who are working under a contract of employment are entitled to the full range of statutory employment rights, including parental and redundancy rights and the right to claim unfair dismissal [**26.4-26.7**]. Volunteers who are working under a contract which is not a contract of employment are 'workers' who do not have the full range of employment rights, but are entitled to protection under the employment provisions of equal opportunities legislation [**39.7**], national minimum wage [below], annual leave and other workers' rights [**26.4.1**].

39.4.3.1 National minimum wage

The **National Minimum Wage Act 1998** refers specifically to **voluntary workers**, who are working for a charity, voluntary organisation, associated fundraising body or a statutory body. Such voluntary workers are entitled to minimum wage unless, under the terms of their work, they are entitled to and actually receive:

- no money payments at all; or
- no money payments except reimbursement of genuine out of pocket expenses actually incurred in carrying out their duties or to enable them to perform their duties, or reasonably estimated to be or have been so incurred (but this cannot include accommodation expenses); and/or
- no money payments other than payment for subsistence (meals and living expenses, but not accommodation), provided that the work is done for a charity, voluntary organisation, associated fundraising body or statutory body *and* the voluntary worker has been placed with that body as a result of arrangements made by a charity acting in furtherance of its charitable objects (such as a CSV type placement);

and they are entitled to and actually receive:

- no benefits in kind at all; or
- no benefits in kind other than training provided with the sole or main purpose of improving the voluntary worker's performance of the work they have agreed to do; and/or

- no benefits in kind other than some or all subsistence (meals etc) and accommodation, as reasonable in relation to the work. *National Minimum Wage Act 1998 s.44, amended by Employment Act 2008 s.14*

This rule has the effect of entitling 'voluntary workers' to minimum wage if they receive, for example, training beyond what is necessary for their work, or if live-in voluntary workers are not on a CSV type placement and receive 'pocket money'. An organisation can set up a charity specifically to recruit voluntary workers and place them with itself or with other charities and voluntary organisations.

National minimum wage does not apply to residential members of most charitable religious communities who are paid for work by that community, but it does apply where the charitable religious community is an independent school or provides further or higher education. *NMWA 1998 s.44A, inserted by Employment Relations Act 1999 s.22*

39.4.4   Exclusion of contractual intention

If a person is obliged to work and receives remuneration or something else of value for the work, but the individual and organisation have explicitly stated that they do not intend their relationship to be legally binding, an employment tribunal or court *might* agree that a contract has not been created, and the person is thus not entitled to workers' and/or employees' rights.

The tribunal or court would look at the nature of the relationship, and whether it was reasonable for the parties to say that the relationship did not create a contract. Even if it is explicitly stated that the parties do not intend the relationship to be legally binding, the tribunal might find that in fact the 'volunteer' has a contract and is therefore entitled to employment rights.

An organisation which wishes to pay its volunteers or provide benefits without creating a contract should make clear in all relevant discussions, correspondence and the volunteer agreement, if there is one, that this is a voluntary relationship and is not intended to be legally binding. These statements will be taken into account if a volunteer subsequently claims employment rights, but will not be conclusive. Nor will such statements absolve the organisation from liabilities arising from its obligation to operate PAYE and/or to pay minimum wage if HM Revenue and Customs says that the organisation should have done.

Where a payment or provision of benefits is clearly in return for work, legal advice should be taken before stating that the relationship is not intended to be legally binding. Such a statement could be seen as an attempt to deprive workers or employees of their statutory rights, and is likely to be ineffective.

Employment Rights Act 1996 s.203; M & P Steelcraft Ltd v Ellis & another [2008] UKEAT 0536 07 2201

39.4.5   Unpaid volunteers

If a volunteer receives no money or anything else of value in return for work done for the organisation, there can be no contract, because the creation of a contract requires an exchange of consideration [**20.6.1**]. Where the volunteer receives no consideration, any agreement between the organisation and individual is unlikely to be a contract, and therefore unlikely to be legally binding on either party. There may be a moral obligation to comply with the terms of the agreement, but the obligation cannot be enforced in the courts and the person would not have workers' or employees' rights.

However, because of the possibility that something provided by the organisation, such as training or use of the organisation's facilities or even legitimate reimbursement, could be seen as consideration, any correspondence or agreement should make clear that this is a voluntary arrangement and is not intended to be legally binding [**39.4.4**].

It is very important to be aware that even a volunteer who receives no payment but receives something else of benefit from the organisation could in some situations be held to have a contract, as in the Relate case [**39.4.2.1**]. The minimum wage implications, in particular, could be very significant [**39.4.3.1**].

39.5   VOLUNTEER AGREEMENTS

There is no obligation to provide a volunteer agreement. It may be helpful, especially for long-term volunteers or those taking on a major task, to clarify the expectations for both parties, but for other volunteers such agreements may be seen as unduly formal or restrictive.

Where volunteers are given a letter or written agreement, it should:

- start with a statement that it sets out expectations and intentions, not binding obligations to offer work or to do it, and that the terms of the agreement are binding in honour only [**39.4.4**];

- state that neither party intends a contractual or employment relationship to be created, either now or in future;

- phrase time commitments in terms of hopes ('we hope you will stay with us for at least six months' rather than 'you must');

- make clear that payment will be made only for reimbursement of genuine, necessary, documented expenses [**39.2.1**];

- make clear that training, protective clothing etc will be provided to enable the person to carry out their voluntary duties, but the agreement should not offer benefits that are not necessary for the work;

- where benefits such as use of facilities are offered, make clear that these are discretionary and the organisation is not obliged to provide them;

- make clear that obligations to comply with the organisation's policies, such as equal opportunities, health and safety and confidentiality, are required for compliance with legal duties and for the proper performance of the organisation's work, rather than being obligations creating a contractual situation;

- avoid employment related terms such as contract, sick leave, annual leave, disciplinary procedure, promotion and dismissal;

- if there is any possibility at all that the volunteer could legally be an employee or worker [**25.1**], ensure that arrangements for dealing with unsatisfactory work or with situations where the volunteer is dissatisfied in any way – which in effect are disciplinary and grievance procedures – include the right to be accompanied [**33.1.1**], and if there is any possibility that the volunteer could be an employee, ensure these arrangements comply with the employer's disciplinary procedure. Volunteering England suggests using the term **problem solving procedures** instead of disciplinary and grievance procedures.

Volunteering England [see end of chapter] provides model volunteer agreements.

39.6   VOLUNTEERS FROM ABROAD

There is no restriction on nationals of European Economic Area countries (European Union [**29.5.2**] plus Iceland, Liechtenstein and Norway) and Switzerland volunteering in the UK. For nationals of other countries, advice is available from Volunteering England, Wales Council for Voluntary Action or the Border Agency [see end of chapter]. A person who is not entitled to work in the UK can be deported if they breach their entry restrictions, and an organisation which creates a contract of employment [**39.4.1**] with a so-called volunteer who is not entitled to work in the UK can be fined [**29.5.1**].

39.6.1   Non-EEA nationals

Nationals of non-EEA countries need to qualify under the points based system to take up employment or study in the UK [**29.5.3**]. Persons entitled to work or study in the UK under tiers 1-5 of the system, and their dependants, can volunteer, but persons admitted under a visitors visa [**29.5.3**] cannot volunteer.

39.6.1.1   Charity volunteering

Tier 5 of the points based immigration system includes provision for **charity workers**, who can do unpaid voluntary work in the UK for a charity for up to 12 months. To be admitted to the UK in this category:

- the volunteer must be sponsored by a registered charity;
- the volunteer's work must be directly related to the objects of the charity, and must not be primarily administrative, maintenance etc;
- the volunteer may receive only accommodation, meals and a living allowance as allowed under the minimum wage legislation [**39.4.3.1**];
- the volunteer cannot be in the UK for more than 12 months; and
- the volunteer may not apply for or take paid employment while in the UK.

Volunteering England [see end of chapter] can provide up to date information about immigration requirements for volunteers from outside the EEA.

39.6.1.2 Overseas students

Students from outside the EEA admitted under tier 4 of the points-based system [**29.5.3**] may undertake paid or voluntary work, and do not need consent for part-time or holiday work. Voluntary work is treated in the same way as employment, including the limit of 20 hours per week in term time unless the college agrees to more hours.

Short-term **student visitors** on a visitors visa [**29.5.3**] cannot volunteer.

39.6.2 Refugees and asylum seekers

There are no restrictions on volunteering, paid or unpaid, for **refugees** and people given **exceptional leave to remain** in the UK [**29.5.4**].

Asylum seekers cannot take up paid or unpaid employment while awaiting the outcome of their application for asylum or while they are appealing against a decision to refuse them asylum. But this prohibition does not apply to volunteering for a charity, voluntary organisation, or body that raises funds for a charity or voluntary organisation, provided the work is genuinely voluntary and is not job substitution (doing work that would ordinarily be done by a paid employee).

Asylum seekers can be provided with meals (or reimbursement for meals) while volunteering, and can be reimbursed for actual travel costs and normal volunteer expenses [**39.2.1**]. All reimbursements must be properly documented.

Advice should be taken before providing any other reimbursements or benefits, as these could jeopardise the asylum seeker's application for refugee status, and could also create a situation in which the organisation has unlawfully employed a person who is not entitled to work in the UK [**29.5.1**]. Volunteering England or Wales Council for Voluntary Action [see end of chapter] can provide advice.

39.6.3 Fast track citizenship

Immigrants who fulfil an **activity condition** by participating in 'prescribed activities' without pay may be able to gain UK citizenship in two years less than those who do not volunteer. At the time of writing (mid 2009) it was not yet clear when this provision would be introduced, what type of activities would be taken into account, how long the person would have to volunteer, and how their volunteering would be verified.

British Nationality Act 1981 sch.1 para.4B, inserted by Borders, Citizenship & Immigration Act 2009 s.41

39.7 EQUAL OPPORTUNITIES
39.7.1 Discrimination

The employment provisions of the equal opportunities legislation make it unlawful to discriminate – to treat someone less favourably – on the basis of race, colour, ethnic group, national origin, nationality, sex, gender reassignment (transsexuality), married status, disability, religion or other belief, sexual orientation or age, against an employee or most other people working under a contract [**chapter 28**]. They therefore apply if a volunteer has a contract with the organisation [**39.4**]. But even where (as will nearly always be the case) a volunteer is not working under a contract, organisations should not discriminate in recruiting, selecting or managing volunteers.

The employment provisions of the equal opportunities legislation apply to vocational training, and could thus possibly apply to volunteering which includes a training element.

In any case, it is unlawful to discriminate in provision of services [**chapter 42**], and providing opportunities for volunteering could in some situations be seen as providing a service.

If volunteers are paid for their work or receive payment in kind, they may be working under a contract and men and women should receive the same payments or benefits for work of equal value [**28.8**].

39.7.2 GORs and positive action

The legislation includes provision for recruiting people of a specific racial group, sex, religion or other belief, sexual orientation or age where it is a **genuine occupational requirement** (GOR) for the work [**28.1.7**], and for encouraging people of a specific group or groups to apply for work or specified positions [**28.1.7**]. Although the legislation does not apply to volunteers who are not working under a contract, it is good practice to operate within the legal framework.

39.7.3 Reasonable adjustments

The **Disability Discrimination Act 1995** requires employers to make **reasonable adjustments** to enable a disabled person to apply for employment, do the work, or continue working if they become disabled while they are an employee, Although the legislation does not apply to volunteers who are not working under a contract, good practice is to make volunteering accessible to disabled people, and to make reasonable adjustments to enable them to volunteer [**28.7.4**].

All organisations, even if they have no employees, must take reasonable steps to make premises, goods, services and facilities accessible or available to people with disabilities, and must not discriminate unjustifiably in service delivery against a person with a disability [**42.7.2**].

39.7.4 Age and volunteering

There is no minimum age limit for volunteering, but organisations which use under-18s as volunteers should consider their duty of care, insurance, good practice and relevant statutory restrictions [**39.10.2**].

Some organisations set an upper age limit for volunteers, and in some cases restrictions on some types of work are imposed by insurers [**39.9.3**]. It is not good practice to require a person who is capable of volunteering to stop doing so simply because they have reached a certain age. Each volunteer's capability needs to be monitored – regardless of age – and if appropriate their work or how they do it may need to be changed. If necessary the organisation can require a person to stop volunteering, but this should be done because of capability rather than age.

39.8 HEALTH AND SAFETY
39.8.1 Safety of volunteers

Health and safety legislation [**chapter 40**] may not apply to volunteers in exactly the same way as to employees [**40.2.1**], but it would be very poor practice to treat volunteers differently from employees. In any case:

- employers must provide a safe place of work for employees, which could be jeopardised if different standards are applied to volunteers;
- there is a statutory obligation for employers to protect the health and safety of the public, which in this context includes volunteers;
- health and safety risk assessments [**40.3**] must take into account risks not only to employees, but to others affected by the organisation's activities;
- all organisations, even those which are not employers, have a **duty of care** [**40.1.2**] to all volunteers, in particular to younger or older volunteers, volunteers with extra support needs, or volunteers who are vulnerable in some way.

All volunteers should know their rights and responsibilities in relation to health and safety, including their duty not put themselves or others at risk.

If a volunteer is injured due to the organisation's negligence, the volunteer may sue the organisation.

39.8.2 Safety of clients/service users

If a client, service user or member of the public is injured or suffers loss as a result of the organisation's or a volunteer's breach of health and safety duties, the organisation or individual(s) involved could be fined, and if there has been a breach of health and safety law or negligence, the organisation and/or volunteer may be sued by the injured person. In this situation, the organisation might be able to claim, under the **Compensation Act 2006**, that it is better to have provided the activity or service with volunteers who might not be fully trained, than not to have provided it at all [**22.6.5**]. This defence should not be relied upon.

39.9 INSURANCE

Organisations should consider the same insurance issues in relation to volunteers as for employees. Insurance is covered in **chapter 23**. Volunteering England has details of insurance brokers with experience of providing insurance for organisations which use volunteers.

39.9.1 Claims by volunteers

An organisation must take out **employer's liability insurance** to cover claims by employees if they become ill or are injured as a result of the employer's negligence or breach of a statutory duty [**23.4.1**]. There is no obligation to extend such insurance to cover volunteers, but it is good practice to do so. As an alternative, cover for volunteers can be included within an organisation's **public liability insurance** [**23.5.1**]. The employer's or public liability insurance policy should explicitly mention volunteers, otherwise they might not be covered.

The organisation may want to provide personal accident insurance [**23.4.3**], to cover injury or death arising from volunteering but not due to its negligence.

39.9.2 Claims against volunteers

Employers have **vicarious liability** for the negligent acts of their employees, and a claim for damage or loss caused by an employee is generally brought against the employer rather than the employee [**22.6.4**]. The legal position with regard to vicarious liability for acts of volunteers is unclear, and a claim could possibly be brought by a client or member of the public against a volunteer. The organisation should therefore ensure that its public liability insurance [**23.5.1**], professional indemnity insurance [**23.5.3**], product liability insurance [**23.5.4**] or other relevant insurance covers liabilities created by volunteers and indemnifies (compensates) them if a claim is successfully brought against them.

39.9.3 Age restrictions

Some insurers do not provide cover for volunteers over or under a specified age. It may be possible to negotiate extended cover, or the organisation may wish to consider changing its insurer. Volunteering England can provide information about insurers who provide cover for older and younger volunteers.

39.10 SPECIAL SITUATIONS

Information about the law as it relates to specific volunteering situations or specific types of volunteer is available from Volunteering England or Wales Council for Voluntary Action [see end of chapter]. Some of the more common situations are outlined here.

39.10.1   Work with children and vulnerable adults

The legislation on working with children and vulnerable adults applies to volunteers in the same way as to employees [**chapter 41**]. Volunteers are treated in the same way as employees for criminal record checks [**41.4.1**], except that the fee is waived for standard and enhanced level checks on volunteers, defined as 'a person who is engaged in any activity which involves spending time, unpaid (except for travelling and other approved out of pocket expenses), doing something which aims to benefit someone (individuals or groups) other than or in addition to close relatives'.   *Police Act 1997 (Criminal Records) Regulations 2002 [SI 2002/233] reg.2*

The rules on regulated and controlled activities, referral to the Independent Safeguarding Authority, and from November 2010 individuals' registration with the ISA and organisations checking the ISA website, are the same as for employees [**41.7**]. It is unlawful for a person who is barred from working with children or vulnerable adults [**41.7.1**] to work with that group, or for an organisation knowingly to offer such work to a barred person or allow them to continue doing the work.

Criminal record checks do not necessarily have to be carried out for all volunteers working with children or vulnerable adults [**41.6**], and even where they are carried out they are not a guarantee that the person is appropriate to work with those groups. Checks are not a substitute for good practice in recruitment, selection, induction, training, monitoring and supervision of volunteers, and there should be clear, effective procedures for clients or service users, employees or other volunteers to report concerns about a volunteer's behaviour.

39.10.2   Young people as volunteers

In general there are no restrictions on children and young people volunteering, but points to be aware of are:

- for potential volunteers under 16, it is sensible to get written consent from their parent or guardian;
- it is sensible to comply with the restrictions on employment of children and young people of school age [**40.6.1**];
- local authority consent may be required for young volunteers working in charity shops and other organisations that operate for profit [**40.6.1**];
- a person who regularly supervises or trains volunteers who are under 18 may have to have a criminal record check [**41.2**] and from November 2010, be registered with the Independent Safeguarding Authority [**41.7.3**];
- because of their immaturity and relative lack of experience, the organisation has a special duty of care to children and young people [**40.1.2**];
- the organisation should comply with health and safety requirements relating to young people at work [**40.3.2**];
- the organisation's insurance for volunteers [**39.9**] may need to be extended to cover volunteers who are under 18, and some insurers may not be willing to cover volunteers below 15 or 16;
- children under 16 cannot take part in house to house fundraising collections without an adult [**49.2.1**].

39.10.3   Volunteer fundraisers

A 'volunteer' fundraiser who receives payment other than genuine reimbursement [**39.2.1**], even if it is only just over £10 per day, and is not an employee of the organisation or its trading subsidiary must comply with the rules on **professional fundraisers** [**48.6.3**].

The Institute of Fundraising [see end of chapter] has a code of practice for volunteer fundraising. This distinguishes between volunteers acting **on behalf of** an organisation, where responsibility lies with the organisation, and volunteers acting independently **in aid of** an organisation, where responsibility remains with the volunteer.

39.10.4 Volunteer drivers

Information for and about volunteer drivers is available from Volunteering England, Wales Council for Voluntary Action, the Community Transport Association and the Royal Society for the Prevention of Accidents [see end of chapter]. Information should be sought regardless of whether volunteers are using their own vehicles or motorcycles, the organisation's, or vehicles provided by someone else.

39.10.4.1 Use of own vehicles: insurance

It is not generally necessary for volunteers to notify their insurer if they use their own vehicle or someone else's only for journeys between home and the usual place of volunteering. But the situation is different if the vehicle is used for the volunteering itself [see **23.8** for more about vehicle insurance].

Motor Conference, which represents 98% of insurers providing motor insurance in the UK, has given undertakings that motor insurance policies they provide covering social, domestic and pleasure or business use will cover driving carried out as a volunteer, even if the volunteer receives a mileage allowance – provided this is no more than the HM Revenue and Customs approved mileage allowance [**30.4.10**]. If the volunteer's insurer is a member of Motor Conference [see end of chapter], the organisation does not need to see written confirmation from the insurer that the insurance covers volunteer driving.

The organisation should, however, ask to see the volunteer's insurance policy, and confirm that the insurer has signed up to the undertakings. In addition, the volunteer should notify their insurer that they are using their vehicle for volunteer driving, because of the duty to provide all relevant information and in case their policy does not cover the intended driving. A form for a volunteer to notify their insurer is available from Volunteering England [see end of chapter]. Failure to inform the insurer may render the policy invalid.

If a volunteer receives anything more than a mileage allowance [**39.3.1**], the driving is likely to be classed as **hire and reward** and will not be covered by the insurance. Or if the so-called volunteer is paid for their work [**39.2.2**], the driving is likely to be classed as business use and will not be covered by social, domestic and pleasure policies.

Although the organisation cannot generally insure the vehicle (that is the responsibility of the vehicle's owner, keeper or driver), the organisation can provide a policy to protect volunteer drivers' no-claims discount or to pay any excess if they have an accident while driving for the organisation. Charity Commission consent should be sought before providing these insurances for members of a charity's governing body [**16.3.10**] or persons connected with them [**15.2.5**].

39.10.4.2 Documentation

To comply with its duty of care, the organisation should ask to see a valid driving licence (full, not provisional) and proof that the vehicle is insured for journeys made for voluntary work, is taxed and has an MoT certificate if required. Copies should be kept. It is good practice to ask to see these documents annually. In addition, the volunteer should be asked in writing about past and pending driving offences.

If mileage is to be reimbursed, the driver must keep a record of journeys [**39.3.1**]. The organisation may want to ask volunteers to sign a statement on the mileage claim form along the lines of 'I confirm that my vehicle remains insured for these journeys, is taxed and has a valid MoT if required, and that there have been no changes to my driving licence. I further confirm that I have declared all past driving offences, and that if I am charged with any driving offence I will immediately notify you of the charge and the outcome.'

39.10.4.3 The organisation's vehicles

If the organisation has its own vehicles, proper records must be kept of who is using the vehicles and for what purposes. All relevant requirements in relation to the vehicle, drivers and insurance must be complied with [**40.12**].

39.11   VOLUNTEERS AND STATE BENEFITS

Different state benefits have different rules, and especially when they change there may be problems of misinterpretation, or different benefits advisors may interpret the rules differently. The Department for Work and Pensions' *Guide to volunteering while on benefits* provides a useful summary, and detailed information is available from the Volunteering England and Wales Council for Voluntary Action [see end of chapter].

For all benefits, the legislation or the DWP defines **voluntary work** as work for an organisation whose activities are carried on otherwise than for profit, or work for someone other than a family member, where the claimant receives no payment other than reimbursement of reasonable expenses incurred in carrying out the volunteering. *See, for example, Jobseeker's Allowance Regulations 1996 [SI 1996/207] reg.4; Social Security (Incapacity for Work etc) Regulations 1996 [SI 1996/3207] reg.2(2)*

39.11.1   Notification

Before starting voluntary work, a claimant receiving jobseeker's allowance, income support, incapacity benefit or employment and support allowance must inform Jobcentre Plus, and a volunteer receiving housing benefit (local housing allowance for tenants in the private rented sector) or council tax benefit must notify the local authority. It is good practice for the organisation to remind volunteers that they are responsible for notifying the relevant agencies and for keeping receipts to show that any payments they receive are genuine reimbursements.

39.11.2   Reimbursement, payments and notional earnings

39.11.2.1   Unpaid and paid volunteering

In the sections below, '**unpaid**' means the volunteer receives no payment otherwise than reimbursement of genuine, reasonable expenses incurred in volunteering, and receives no benefits or perks other than those necessary to carry out the voluntary work or to do it better. '**Paid**' refers to 'volunteering' where the person receives payment beyond genuine reimbursement or benefits beyond what is necessary to do the work [**39.2.2**].

39.11.2.2   Allowed reimbursement and benefits

In general, the same reimbursement rules apply as for tax [**39.2.1**]. But there are differences, and advice should be sought if the situation is unclear. As an example of the confusions that can arise: both HM Revenue and Customs (for tax) and the Department for Work and Pensions (for volunteers on state benefits) traditionally allowed volunteers to be reimbursed for meals during volunteering. But in 2006 the DWP produced guidance saying that lunch reimbursement would count as earnings for volunteers on jobseeker's allowance and income support. After a campaign by volunteer-using organisations, DWP changed its mind – but it took more than two years until this was included in DWP's guidance for claimants.

Similarly, reimbursement of childcare expenses to allow a person to volunteer is generally allowed by the Department for Work and Pensions, and HM Revenue and Customs generally disregards it for tax purposes. But in 2007 the Department for Business, Innovation and Skills said it would be classed as income for the purposes of minimum wage [**39.4.3.1**]. Again this was successfully challenged, and the minimum wage legislation was amended to allow reimbursement not only for expenses necessary for the volunteering, but also reimbursement of expenses necessary to enable the person to volunteer [**39.4.3.1**].

These examples illustrate the complexity in knowing what can be reimbursed to volunteers on state benefits – as well as to any other volunteers – without having implications for the volunteer or the organisation.

39.11.2.3   Reimbursement in advance

Volunteers can be reimbursed for expenses in advance without it affecting their state benefits, provided they are required to supply receipts or other proof of expenditure and must return any unspent money. *Social Security Amendment (Volunteers) Regulations 2001 [SI 2001/2296]*

39.11.2.4 Earnings disregard and permitted work

Income related benefits such as jobseeker's allowance and income support are reduced if the claimant is paid more than the **earnings disregard** (as of 1/8/09, £5 per week for a single person, or £20 per week for a lone parent, carer, disabled person and certain other claimants). Genuine reimbursement [**39.11.2.2**] does not count towards this but scale rate or lump sum reimbursements do, even if authorised by HM Revenue and Customs for tax purposes [**39.3.2**].

Benefit is reduced pound for pound if the claimant earns more than the earnings disregard.

People who are receiving incapacity benefit can earn up to £20 per week doing **permitted work** , without it affecting their benefits, and in some cases may be able to earn £92 (as at 1/8/09) [**39.11.5**]. People who are earning in this way should not be referred to as volunteers; they are employees or workers [**25.1**].

Benefits in kind may also count against the earnings disregard and the permitted work limit.

Even though people who are receiving state benefits can receive income up to the earnings disregard or permitted work limit without it affecting their benefits, there may be other legal implications. The payment may create a contract entitling the person to minimum wage and other employment rights [**39.4.3**]; if paid to a member of the organisation's governing body it may be an unlawful payment [**16.3**]; and the individual will not be entitled to a free criminal record check [**39.10.1**]. The minimum wage rules mean that if minimum wage is £5.80 (as it is for the year starting 1 October 2009), the benefits of a person with a £20 earnings disregard or permitted work limit will be affected if they are paid for more than 3 hours 26 minutes.

Accommodation provided to volunteers who are receiving state benefits creates a particularly complex situation, and advice should be taken.

Volunteers receiving pension credit must declare any income above genuine reimbursements.

39.11.2.5 Notional earnings

Even where claimants are not paid anything other than allowed reimbursement [**39.2.1**], Jobcentre Plus or the local authority (for housing and council tax benefits) may treat them as having **notional earnings** (also called **notional income**) if they are doing their usual work or it would be reasonable for them to be paid. A 'volunteer' who is offered payment for the work but turns it down could also be treated as having notional earnings.

With notional earnings, claimants are treated as if they have been paid even though they have not been. Notional earnings are not generally assumed for voluntary work done for or organised through a charity or other voluntary organisation, local authority or health authority.

Social Security (Approved Work) Regulations 2000 [SI 2000/678] regs.2,8

39.11.3 Jobseeker's allowance

For unpaid volunteers receiving jobseeker's allowance (JSA), there is no restriction on volunteering provided they notify Jobcentre Plus of all voluntary work and income, are actively seeking work as agreed with the benefits advisor, are or can be available to work 40 hours per week, and are available as required to attend an interview or start work [below].

JSA is not generally payable for people volunteering abroad, even for a short period.

Volunteers receiving JSA must comply with the rules on notification, expenses and other payments [**39.11.1**, **39.11.2**]. It may be helpful for the organisation to provide a standard letter for volunteers to provide to Jobcentre Plus, saying that the volunteer will receive no payment other than reimbursement of genuine and reasonable out of pocket expenses, that the volunteer can be contacted via the organisation while volunteering if a job opportunity arises, and that the volunteer can be available on 48 hours' notice to attend a job interview or within a week to take up a job.

39.11.3.1 Availability

Most JSA claimants have to be immediately available to attend interview or start work, but if they are doing voluntary work, JSA rules allow 48 hours' notice of availability to attend interview and one week's notice to start a job. The rules also allow the claimant to be unavailable:

- for one period of up to two weeks in a calendar year while attending a residential workcamp in Great Britain run by a charity, other voluntary organisation or local authority, provided Jobcentre Plus has been notified beforehand;
- while working as a part-time lifeboat rescuer or firefighter;
- while working as a member of an organised group helping in an emergency, where there is serious risk to people's lives or health or to property of substantial value.   *Jobseeker's Allowance Regulations 1996 [SI 1996/207] reg.14*

39.11.4 Income support

Income support is not affected by unpaid voluntary work, provided Jobcentre Plus is notified of the volunteering and any income. The rules on notification, expenses and other payments [**39.11.1**, **39.11.2**] apply.

39.11.5 Incapacity and disability related benefits

A person receiving **incapacity benefit**, **severe disablement allowance**, income support on grounds of incapacity for work or disability or **employment and support allowance** (ESA) is allowed to volunteer, provided Jobcentre Plus is notified beforehand and all income is reported. There is no statutory limit to the number of hours for volunteering, but some benefits officers have questioned whether a person who consistently volunteers for more than 16 hours per week is actually unable to work.

Claimants on employment and support allowance who are assessed as able to work receive the **work related activity component** of the allowance. Those whose assessment indicates that it is not reasonable to require them to engage in work related activity receive the **support component**. Claimants receiving the work related activity component may be required to take part in activities to increase the likelihood of getting a job, which could include volunteering.
Welfare Reform Act 2007 ss.1-29 (pt.1)

39.11.5.1 Permitted work

Claimants on incapacity benefit, severe disablement allowance, income support on grounds of incapacity or disability or employment support allowance have a **permitted work lower limit** of £20 per week [**39.11.2.4**], but some can earn up to £92pw (as at 1/8/09) for a year for **permitted work**, or for more than a year as **supported permitted work**. At the time of writing (mid 2009) the government was considering a **community allowance** allowing claimants on incapacity benefit or ESA to do permitted work for more than a year in community organisations. People doing work which allows them to earn this higher limit are employees or workers [**25.1**] and should not be referred to as volunteers.

A doctor's approval is not required for permitted work, but Jobcentre Plus must be notified before starting the work and if the work changes. The rules on expenses and other payments apply [**39.11.2**].

39.11.5.2 Other sickness and disability related benefits

Statutory sick pay (from an employer) is not affected by volunteering, but the employer may question entitlement if the person is known to be volunteering.

Disability living allowance is not affected by volunteering unless the volunteering is overseas for more than six months.

Industrial injuries disablement benefit is not affected by paid or unpaid voluntary work, but the volunteering must be notified to the Jobcentre Plus office.

Industrial injuries reduced earnings allowance is not affected by unpaid voluntary work, but the person should check with Jobcentre Plus before receiving any payments other than genuine reimbursement.

Carer's allowance is not affected by unpaid voluntary work, unless it stops the volunteer caring for the disabled person for at least 35 hours per week. The Carer's Allowance Unit should be notified of the voluntary work. A person receiving carer's allowance cannot earn more than £95 per week (as at 1/8/09), and cannot do voluntary work abroad for more than four weeks.

39.11.6 Other benefits

Unpaid voluntary work does not affect eligibility for, or the amount of, **housing benefit**, **local housing allowance** or **council tax benefit**. Voluntary work and any income from it must be notified to the local authority, and will affect the amount if income other than genuine reimbursement is more than the earnings disregard [**39.11.2.4**].

Long-term volunteers living away from home can receive housing benefit, local housing allowance, council tax benefit or income support for housing costs in relation to that home for only 13 weeks.

Statutory maternity, paternity and **adoption pay** are not affected by volunteering. **Maternity allowance** is not affected by unpaid voluntary work, but is not payable for any day on which paid work is done.

39.11.7 Tax credits

Child tax credit and **working tax credit** should not be affected by unpaid volunteering.

39.11.8 Educational maintenance allowance

The **educational maintenance allowance** paid to some 16 to 19 year olds is not affected by volunteering.

39.11.9 Pensions

State retirement, **war disablement** and **war widow's pensions** are not affected by paid or unpaid voluntary work, and the pensions office does not have to be notified. Pension credit is not affected by unpaid voluntary work but could be affected by payment other than proper reimbursement, and could be stopped if the volunteering is overseas for more than four weeks at a time.

Resources: VOLUNTEERS

Volunteering England: www.volunteering.org.uk, 0800 028 3304, information@volunteeringengland.org.

Wales Council for Voluntary Action: www.wcva.org.uk, 0800 2888 329, help@wcva.org.uk.

Asylum seekers. Refugee Council: www.refugeecouncil.org.uk, 020 7346 6700.

State benefits. Jobcentre Plus: local office and www.jobcentreplus.gov.uk.

Department for Work and Pensions: www.dwp.gov.uk.

Directgov: www.direct.gov.uk.

Tax and national insurance. HM Revenue and Customs: local PAYE office; www.hmrc.gov.uk.

Volunteer drivers. Community Transport Association: www.communitytransport.com, 0845 130 6195, advice@ctauk.org.

Motor Conference: details available from Association of British Insurers: www.abi.org.uk, 020 7600 3333, motor@abi.org.uk.

Royal Society for the Prevention of Accidents (RoSPA): www.rospa.co.uk, 0121 248 2000, help@rospa.com.

Volunteers from overseas. UK Border Agency: www.ukba.homeoffice.gov.uk, 0870 606 7766.

Volunteer fundraisers. Institute of Fundraising: www.institute-of-fundraising.org.uk, 020 7840 1000, email via website.

Statute law. www.opsi.gov.uk and www.statutelaw.gov.uk.

Much but not all case law. www.bailii.org.

Updates cross-referenced to this book. www.rclh.co.uk.

Part IV covers the law as it affects services and activities which are common to most organisations, such as health and safety, equal opportunities, publications and campaigning. The law relating to services provided by specific types of organisation, such as community care, education or overseas development, is beyond the scope of this book.

Chapter 40

HEALTH AND SAFETY

For sources of further information see end of chapter.

40.1   HEALTH, SAFETY AND THE LAW

Health, safety and consumer protection are areas of law where very different legal duties overlap and where multiple liabilities may arise. If, for example, an employee is injured by faulty equipment:

- the employer may claim, both in breach of contract and in breach of statutory obligations, against the supplier for supplying faulty equipment;
- the Health and Safety Executive or local environmental health department may prosecute the employer for a breach of the **Health and Safety at Work etc Act 1974** or related regulations, leading to a fine or imprisonment, and may issue a prohibition or improvement notice [**40.2.9**];
- the employee may claim against the employer for breach of contract, negligence and/or breach of statutory duty.

Claims are frequently brought for both breach of statutory duty and negligence. A claim of **negligence** involves showing that the employer did not take reasonable care, but a breach of statutory duty may give rise to a **strict liability** [**40.2.5**] where the employer is liable even if negligence cannot be proved.

40.1.1　The statutory framework

The cornerstone of health and safety legislation is the **Health and Safety at Work etc Act 1974** and its detailed regulations, in particular the **Management of Health and Safety at Work Regulations 1999** *[SI 1999/3242]*. European Union **directives**, which member states must adopt into their national law, seek to harmonise provision for health and safety at work across the EU.

The **Health and Safety (Offences) Act 2008** increases the penalties available to the courts for breaches of the Health and Safety at Work Act.

Approved codes of practice (ACoP) provide guidance on implementation of health and safety law. A breach of a code cannot itself be prosecuted, but may form evidence of failure to achieve proper standards. As well as codes of practice, the Health and Safety Executive [see end of chapter] issues a great deal of information on practical steps for implementation.

The **Office, Shops and Railway Premises Act 1963** covers those premises. The **Factories Act 1961** covers any place, including out of doors, where people make goods or parts of goods, wash or fill bottles, sort or pack goods, or undertake printing or bookbinding. It does not apply if the goods are not to be sold.

Under the **Occupiers' Liability Act 1957**, persons with responsibility for premises must take reasonable care to ensure that anyone who is authorised or permitted to come onto the premises is safe while they are there, and the **Occupiers' Liability Act 1984** imposes a duty of care even to trespassers [**63.5**].

Organisations are affected by **consumer safety** legislation [**40.11**] both as purchasers and users of goods and services and as providers. A wide variety of legislation covers quality and safety of goods and services. Separate legislation covers food, transport, and public health.

An organisation can be charged with **corporate manslaughter** [**22.3.1**] where gross management failure is a cause of death. Governing body members can also be charged if directly implicated in a death.

40.1.2　Common law duties

In addition to their statutory duties, employers have a common law **duty of care** to protect the health and safety of employees. This is an implied part of the contract of employment [**26.3.4**]. Occupiers of land or premises have a common law duty to avoid risk of injury or death for anyone on the land or premises [**63.5**].

If an employer or person with responsibility for premises is in breach of this duty, a person who is injured or becomes ill (or the estate of a person who has died) has a right to make a claim for **negligence**. It is a legal obligation for all employers to have **employers' liability insurance** to cover claims by employees [**23.4.1**], and any organisation which has responsibility for premises or land used by non-employees or which provides services or activities for the public should have **public liability insurance** [**23.5.1**].

40.1.3　Registration

Until April 2009, every place where people were employed had to be registered with the local authority or the Health and Safety Executive. Offices, most shops and most factories no longer need to register, but those handling food or subject to other specific registration rules must still be registered.

40.2　HEALTH AND SAFETY AT WORK

The **Health and Safety at Work etc Act 1974** applies primarily to employers' obligations to employees. Some parts, but not all, cover employers' obligations to workers who are not classed as employees, and to visitors including volunteers, contractors, clients or users of the organisation and members of the public. It also covers the obligations of self employed people to themselves and to persons other than their employees, and obligations of persons who are not employers, but who have responsibility for non-domestic premises used by visitors.

The emphasis is on taking **reasonably practicable** steps to create safe workplaces and safe behaviour. In deciding what is reasonable and practical, the cost as well as the actual physical difficulties of providing safety arrangements can be taken into account. Ultimately the employment tribunal or court decides what is or is not reasonably practicable in any particular situation.

In 2007 the European court of justice confirmed that the obligation to protect health and safety only 'so far as is reasonably practicable' complies with the European Commission's framework directive on health and safety. This requires employers to take action 'to ensure the health and safety of workers in every aspect related to work'. *Commission v United Kingdom (Social policy) [2007] EUECJ C-127/05*

The standard of care required under health and safety law is the same for all organisations with employees, regardless of their nature or size, and prosecutions leading to fines or imprisonment can be brought against individual members of the governing body or others considered responsible for the breach.

40.2.1   Duties of employers

Employers have a duty to ensure, as far as is reasonably practicable, the health, safety, and welfare at work of their employees. This includes carrying out risk assessments [**40.3**] and taking all reasonable steps to:

- provide and maintain a working environment which is safe and without risks to health, and which has adequate facilities and arrangements for welfare at work;
- provide and maintain equipment and work systems which are safe and are not harmful to health;
- ensure safe use, handling, storage and transport of materials;
- provide appropriate information, training and supervision;
- keep the workplace, and the means of access and exit, safe and free of risk to health. *Health & Safety at Work etc Act 1974 s.2*

Employers have specific duties in relation to workers under the age of 18 [**40.3.2.2**, **40.3.2.3**, **40.6.1**], women who are pregnant or have recently given birth [**40.3.2.1**], and people who work at night [**40.3.2.4**].

The obligations are the same even if the employees are part-time, temporary, on a fixed-term contract, casual or sessional.

Workplace means any place where employees carry out work, which includes outdoors, clients' homes, employees' homes etc. Employers have no control over those environments, but have an obligation to take reasonably practicable steps to ensure safe systems and procedures.

Most employers must prepare a written health and safety policy and ensure employees are aware of it [**40.2.6**], produce written risk assessments [**40.3.1**], and consult safety representatives [**40.2.7**].

All goods supplied by one employer to another for use at work must, insofar as reasonably practicable, be safe for use in the workplace. If appropriate, information about health or safety risks and instructions about safe use must be supplied. *HSWA 1974 ss.5,6*

40.2.1.1   Health and safety poster and pocket card

Employers must make employees aware of general health and safety duties by displaying an approved poster or giving all employees an approved pocket card. These are available from HSE Books [see end of chapter]. New versions of the poster and card (to replace the previous leaflet) were published in April 2009, but the previous versions can be used until 5 April 2014, provided they are readable and the addresses of the enforcing agency and Employment Medical Advisory Service are up to date. This information is available from the HSE infoline [see end of chapter]. *Health & Safety Information for Employees (Amendment) Regulations 2009 [SI 2009/606]*

40.2.1.2   Duties to workers who are not employees and to the public

Employers must take reasonable steps to ensure that people who are not employees but who might be affected by their activities are not exposed to risks to their health or safety, and must provide information about health or safety risks. This includes trainees, people on work experience, volunteers, and self employed people and other contractors doing work for the employer [**40.2.1.4**]. *Health & Safety at Work Act 1974 s.3*

40.2.1.3   Duties to volunteers

The **Health and Safety at Work etc Act 1974** does not apply if an organisation has no employees. But organisations which are purely volunteer should nonetheless comply with the Act as much as they can, because the organisation has a duty of care [**40.1.2**] to everyone, and one way to comply with this is to comply with the legislation which sets out the basic standards of good practice. In any case, if volunteers receive pay or something else of value in return for their work they may in fact legally be employees [**39.4**], and the organisation may thus be obliged to comply with health and safety law.

40.2.1.4   Duties to self employed workers and other contractors

An employer has the same responsibilities to self employed workers or other contractors as it does to any member of the public. The employer must ensure they are safe, and must take reasonable steps to ensure they do not endanger the employer's employees. Regardless of whether they come regularly or only very occasionally, such as the annual visit of the auditor, they must be informed of hazards at the workplace and protective and preventative measures in force. *Management of Health & Safety at Work Regulations 1999 [SI 1999/2342] reg.12*

If appropriate, the employer must provide its own staff with training about how to maintain safety where there are workers who are not employees and may not be fully aware of the risks at work or the procedures for dealing with the risks.

The organisation should ensure that the contract makes clear the contractor's responsibility for their own health and safety and for that of the employer's employees, clients and members of the public with whom the contractor will be in contact, and others at the employer's premises. The insurance and indemnification position should be carefully considered [**38.4.3**].

A two-way flow of information should be established, with the contractor and employer informing each other of risks arising from their activities. The employer must also establish procedures to ensure that safety rules are maintained, and must take action if they are breached.

In some situations, a self employed person who is working under the control of an employer may be treated by the health and safety authorities as an employee for the purposes of health and safety legislation. *R v Associated Octel [1996] UKHL 1*

40.2.1.5   Duties to temporary and agency staff

People on fixed-term contracts, agency staff and other temporary workers must be given information about health and safety risks in the work they will be doing, the qualifications and skills they need to carry out the work safely, and any health surveillance [**40.3.3.1**] being provided. *Management of Health & Safety at Work Regulations 1999 [SI 1999/3242] reg.15*

Where staff are supplied by an employment agency or employment business (a business which places staff but is not an employment agency), the employment agency or business must obtain information on any health and safety risks known to the employer, and the steps taken to prevent or control those risks. *Conduct of Employment Agencies & Employment Business Regulations 2003 [SI 2003/3319]*

The employer must if appropriate provide its own staff with training about how to maintain safety where there are workers who are not employees and may not be fully aware of risks or the procedures for dealing with them.

40.2.2   Duties of employees

Individual employees must take reasonable care for their own health and safety while at work, and for the health and safety of others who might be affected by their acts. Employees must inform their employer of serious dangers or shortcomings in the health and safety arrangements, must operate equipment in accordance with proper instructions received, and must not interfere with or inappropriately use anything provided for health, safety or welfare purposes.

Health & Safety at Work etc Act 1974 ss.7,8;
Management of Health & Safety at Work Regulations 1999 [SI 1999/3242] reg.14

Employers who do not take appropriate action, including disciplinary action, if an employee operates equipment unsafely or works in an unsafe manner, will not be able to show that they have properly monitored and enforced safety procedures.

Employers can bring legal action against employees for breach of their health and safety duties.

Management of Health & Safety at Work & Fire Precautions
(Workplace) (Amendment) Regulations 2003 [SI 2003/2457]

40.2.2.1 Protection from victimisation

Employers must not victimise employees who complain or take reasonable action about health and safety. Employees, regardless of length of service, may bring a claim in an employment tribunal if they are dismissed, selected for redundancy or subjected to any other detriment because they:

- carry out, or propose to carry out, any activities which the employer has designated the employee to carry out in relation to health and safety at work;

- perform, or propose to perform, any functions as official or employer-acknowledged health and safety representative or safety committee member [**40.2.7**];

- bring to the employer's attention, by reasonable means and in the absence of a representative or committee with whom it would have been reasonably practicable to raise the matter, a concern about circumstances at work which the employee reasonably believes are harmful to health or safety;

- in the event of danger which the employee reasonably believes to be serious and imminent and which he or she could not be expected to avert, leaves or proposes to leave the workplace or any dangerous part of it, or refuses to return while the danger persists; or

- in circumstances of danger which the employee reasonably believes to be serious and imminent, takes or proposes to take appropriate steps to protect themselves or other persons from the danger. *Employment Rights Act 1996 s.100*

40.2.3 Duties of non-employees and the public

Everyone is prohibited from intentionally or recklessly interfering with anything provided in the interest of health, safety or welfare or using it inappropriately. This covers, for example, damaging a fire extinguisher or blocking a fire escape.

Health & Safety at Work etc Act 1974 s.8

40.2.4 Responsibility for premises

Anyone – even if not an employer – who is responsible for non-domestic premises where people who are not their employees work, visit or use the premises must take reasonable steps to ensure that the premises, the means of access or exit, equipment and materials are safe and free of risk to health or safety. Persons considered responsible for premises include anyone who is the owner or tenant of the premises, has responsibility for repairs, or has responsibility under a licence or tenancy for the health and safety of persons using the premises.

Health & Safety at Work etc Act 1974 s.4

40.2.5 Levels of liability

Liability for breach of health and safety falls into three broad categories:

- **absolute liability**: where it must simply be shown that the event or act occurred;

- **strict liability**: where it must be shown that the event or act occurred and was wrongful (contravened the Act or regulations);

- **normal liability**: where it must be shown that the event or act occurred and was wrongful, and that the employer or other person intended it to occur, was negligent, or was reckless as to whether it occurred.

Offences of **absolute liability** are very rare and there is no defence. An example is charging employees for required safety equipment. Even if steps were taken to prevent the breach, the simple fact that it occurred constitutes an offence.

Most health and safety duties are **strict liability**. Normally the only defence is that it was not reasonably practicable [**40.2.1**] to achieve a specific safety standard. *Health & Safety at Work etc Act 1974 s.40*

The employer or other person does not have to show that they did everything possible to prevent the problem or injury, but that they took reasonable steps to prevent foreseeable problems. A step may not be reasonable where there is a gross disproportion between the actual likelihood of risk and the cost in time, money and trouble in averting the risk.

40.2.5.1 Responsibilities of governing body members

Governing body members have collective responsibility for ensuring health and safety is properly implemented within the organisation. The Health and Safety Executive's guidance for company directors (which applies to all governing bodies, not just in companies) states that:

- the governing body should appoint one of its members to 'champion' health and safety issues;
- each board member should accept individual and collective responsibility;
- board members should keep up to date with relevant risk management issues;
- the board should review health and safety performance at least annually.

Governing body members can be held liable for breach of safety not only if they know about the situation which led to the breach, but also if they did not know but should have sought to find out whether the relevant safety procedures were in place. *R v P Limited & another [2007] EWCA Crim 1937*

40.2.5.2 Liability of funders

Where a body provides a grant or other funding and exercises some control over the recipient's activities, the funder could potentially be held liable for a breach of health and safety by the recipient.

40.2.6 Health and safety policies

All employers must have a **health and safety policy**, which must be in writing if five or more people are employed. It must include a general statement of policy, expressing a commitment to safety; organisational information, such as who is responsible for particular areas of health and safety; and arrangements for dealing with particular hazards. The details of hazards and measures to deal with them should be based on the **risk assessments** required under the **Management of Health and Safety at Work Regulations [40.3]**. *Health & Safety at Work etc Act 1974 s.2(3)*

A typical policy contains a general statement and details of the person(s) or postholder(s) responsible for overall implementation of the policy. The policy should generally be approved by the governing body, and must be signed and dated by the responsible person(s). It is advisable to review the policy annually, or whenever the organisation's activities change or it uses new premises.

The Health and Safety Executive [see end of chapter] produces guidance on policies and a sample policy statement.

40.2.7 Competent persons

Employers must appoint one or more **competent persons** to implement action required as a result of the risk assessments. *Management of Health & Safety at Work Regulations 1999 [SI 1999/3242] reg.7*

'Competent' is not defined in detail, but means having an appropriate balance of skills, knowledge and experience about the organisation's work, health and safety duties in general, and duties specific to the organisation and type of work. In small, relatively unhazardous environments, a person could probably be described as competent after reading relevant publications and attending a training course. For larger premises or where there are significant risks, considerable training may be necessary or the organisation may employ an outside specialist to carry out some of the functions required by the regulations.

40.2.8 Consultation with employees

Where there is a recognised trade union [**36.3.3**] at a workplace, a safety representative or representatives must be appointed and in some cases a safety committee established. Their duties are set out in the **Safety Representatives and Safety Committees Regulations 1977** *[SI 1977/500]*, an approved code of practice, and guidance notes issued by HSE. *Health & Safety at Work etc Act 1974 s.2(6)*

Where there is no recognised trade union, the employer must provide certain information about health and safety and consult employees about health and safety matters. This may be done directly, or through elected employee representatives.
Health & Safety (Consultation with Employees) Regulations 1996 [SI 1996/1513]

40.2.8.1 Trade union safety representatives

A recognised trade union has the right to appoint an employee as a **safety representative** to investigate accidents, hazards and reportable incidents, look into complaints, inspect the workplace and relevant documents, attend safety committee meetings, make recommendations for changes, and make representations to the employer on behalf of groups and individual employees.

Safety representatives have a right to reasonable paid time off to perform their functions and attend training. Like all employees, they are protected from victimisation because of their health and safety activities [**40.2.2.1**].

40.2.8.2 Safety committees

If at least two safety representatives request it, the employer must convene a **safety committee** within three months of the request. Before doing so, the employer must consult the trade union, but the employer can determine how often the committee meets, its composition and how the meetings are to be run.
Safety Representatives & Safety Committees Regulations 1977 [SI 1977/500] reg.9

40.2.8.3 Elected representatives

If employees are not represented by safety representatives appointed by a recognised trade union, the employer must consult each employee, or one or more employees elected as **representatives of employees' safety** (ROES). The regulations do not specify how the election should be held.
Health & Safety (Consultation with Employees) Regulations 1996 [SI 1996/1513]

Employers must consult in good time on any new work, procedures or equipment that could substantially affect employees' health and safety, and must consider points raised in the consultation.

ROES have similar rights to those of union safety representatives [**40.2.8.1**], but do not have the same rights to inspect the workplace or investigate accidents. The employer must provide reasonable facilities and training to enable ROES to carry out their duties, and ROES must be given paid time off in working time to stand as a candidate in an election and to perform their functions if elected.

ROES and individual employees are protected against victimisation or dismissal on the ground that they took part or intended to take part in consultation with their employer or in the election of a representative.

40.2.9 Implementation and enforcement

The **Health and Safety Executive** (HSE) is responsible for enforcing the Health and Safety at Work Act through a system of inspectors. It also carries out research, proposes regulations, and provides training and information.

The HSE shares its enforcement duties with **local authorities** and various government departments. Local authorities, through their environmental health departments, are generally responsible for enforcement in lower risk areas, including offices, warehouses, shops and leisure premises. The environmental health department will advise if they are not the appropriate enforcement agency.

Any agency or individual responsible for enforcing the Act has a right of access to premises, and when on the premises can question people, take copies of documents, demand facilities and assistance and take any steps necessary to investigate thoroughly.

If an inspector believes there is a contravention of health and safety legislation, or that there has been a contravention and a further one is likely, an **improvement notice** may be served. A **prohibition notice** is served if the inspector believes that an activity is likely to involve the risk of serious personal injury. Appeals are to the employment tribunal.

40.2.9.1 Criminal prosecution

Breach of the Act or its regulations may give rise to a criminal prosecution in the magistrates' courts, or in the crown court for a more serious matter. Not only the person breaking the particular section or regulation is liable, but also any other person whose act or default contributed to the breach. So if a breach occurs the employee who broke the regulation may be prosecuted; the members of the governing body and/or senior staff may be prosecuted, even if they were not aware of the specific breach; and if the employer is an incorporated body (a company, industrial and provident society or charitable incorporated organisation), the organisation may be prosecuted.

Health & Safety at Work etc Act 1974 ss.27,37;
sch.3A inserted by Health & Safety (Offences) Act 2008 sch.1

40.3 RISK ASSESSMENT AND MANAGEMENT
40.3.1 Five steps to risk assessment

The **Management of Health and Safety at Work Regulations 1999** *[SI 1999/3242]* provide the framework for risk assessments and related duties. All employers and self employed people are under a duty to identify and assess hazards to employees and others arising from their work.

The steps in a **health and safety risk assessment** are to:

- identify the **hazards** (dangers), which generally involves asking people involved in the organisation to identify hazards they perceive as affecting their activities, and take into account this and other information, identify what could go wrong (**risks**), and consider how likely the risks are to occur;
- decide who might be harmed and how, the type of injuries or illnesses which might occur, and how serious they might be;
- evaluate the risks, and decide whether existing precautions are adequate or whether more should be done;
- record the **significant findings** (only obligatory if five or more people are employed, but good practice for all organisations), and inform employees and others about them;
- review and revise when necessary, for example if there are significant changes in the work, there is an accident or near-miss, or a person returns to work after illness or injury that could affect or be affected by their work.

The report on the risk assessment must cover:

- the hazards and risks identified (what can happen, how likely it is to happen and how serious it is if does happen);
- the people at risk, including any special risks for new or expectant mothers, where there are women of a childbearing age;
- protective and preventative measures in place and to be taken;
- fire safety [**40.8**];
- procedures to deal with 'serious and imminent danger' (fire, attacks, etc) and the person(s) who would deal with them;
- any information received from other employers who share the premises, regarding risks from their activities.

Risk management should not be used to scare employees, create unnecessary paperwork, or amplify trivial risks. Nor should it be a bureaucratic or box-ticking exercise. It should be a common sense approach to creating a safe workplace.

The Health and Safety Executive [see end of chapter] has detailed information on risk assessment, including example assessments for specific types of work such as charity shops, village halls, food preparation and service, and office cleaning.

40.3.2   Risk assessment for specific workers

The law requires specific types of risk assessment to be carried out for pregnant women and new mothers, workers under the age of 18, and night workers. Special attention may also need to be given to risk assessments for disabled workers, and for people who work off site, including at home.

40.3.2.1   Pregnant women and new mothers

Where the workforce includes women of childbearing age and the work could involve risk to the health and safety of a pregnant woman, new mother or her baby, the risk assessment must take account of this risk. A new mother is one who has given birth within the previous six months or is breastfeeding.

Management of Health & Safety at Work Regulations 1999 [SI 1999/3242] reg.16

Employers must inform all employees of childbearing age of the found risks and actions taken to reduce these risks. If risk cannot be avoided by other means, the employer must make changes to the working conditions or hours of a new or expectant mother or offer suitable alternative work. If this is not possible, she must be suspended on full pay for as long as necessary to protect her health and safety or that of her child [**40.9.5**].

Employment Rights Act 1996 s.67

If she normally works at night and her doctor or midwife provides a certificate saying she should not continue to do so, the employer must offer alternative work which is not at night. If this is not possible, she must be suspended on full pay for the period covered by the certificate.

Failure to carry out a health and safety risk assessment in relation to a pregnant employee is not only a breach of health and safety law, but also direct discrimination under the **Sex Discrimination Act 1975** [**28.3.2**].

Hardman v Mallon (trading as Orchard Lodge Nursing Home) [2002] UKEAT 0360 01 2503

40.3.2.2   Young workers

Where an employee, potential employee, trainee or person on a work experience or similar programme is under the age of 18, the risk assessment must take account of their experience, maturity or awareness of risks; the nature of the work, the workplace, equipment, substances and processes; and the training provided or to be provided. The risk assessment must be carried out before they start work and they must be told of the risks and the safety measures in place. Where the potential worker is still of compulsory school age [**31.5.1**], the result of the risk assessment must be communicated to their parents or person with parental responsibility.

Management of Health & Safety at Work Regulations 1999 [SI 1999/3242] regs.3(5),10,19

Although there is no statutory duty to do so, such risk assessments should also be carried out for young volunteers.

There are restrictions on the amount and type of work that can be undertaken by a person of compulsory school age [**40.6.1**], and limits on working hours and night working for those above minimum school leaving age but below 18 [**31.5.2**].

40.3.2.3   Young night workers

Alongside the obligations to all young workers, is a further duty to offer workers between minimum school leaving age and 18 [**31.5.2**] a health and capacities assessment before they undertake any work between 10pm and 6am and at regular intervals while the night work continues. This is similar to a health assessment for adult night workers [below], but must also consider the worker's physique, maturity and experience, and must take into account the worker's competence to do the night work.

Working Time Regulations 1998 [SI 1998/1833] reg.7(2)

The obligation to offer a health and capacities assessment does not apply if the work is of an exceptional nature [**31.5.2**].

40.3.2.4   Health assessments for night workers

All night workers [**31.2.4**] must be offered a free health assessment before they start working nights. This must be offered on a regular basis, generally annually, while they continue to work nights. The worker is not obliged to take up the offer of the health assessment.

Working Time Regulations 1998 [SI 1998/1833] reg.7

The assessment can be made up of a straightforward screening questionnaire, and a medical examination if the employer has concerns about the worker's fitness for night work. The assessment should take into account statutory restrictions on working time [31.2] and the type of work that will be done, and must be linked to a risk assessment covering specific risks relating to night work.

The questionnaire should be drawn up and assessed by a suitably qualified health professional who understands how night working might affect health.

The employer can require a medical examination even if the worker has not completed a questionnaire or has not indicated a health condition on the questionnaire. The person who carries out the examination may produce a simple **fitness for work statement** which will be given to the employer, or clinical information which is confidential and can only be released to the employer with the worker's written consent.

If a qualified health professional advises that the worker has health problems which are caused or made worse by night work, the employer should if possible transfer the worker to work that is not night work.

Employers must take all reasonable steps to ensure that staff working night shifts do not work more than an average of eight hours in any 24-hour period [**31.2.4**].
Working Time Regulations 1998 [SI 1998/1833] reg.6

40.3.2.5 Disabled workers

There are no specific duties under health and safety law in relation to disabled workers, but a risk assessment should be carried out to identify hazards and the action needed to reduce risk. This should be directly linked to the employer's obligations under the **Disability Discrimination Act 1995** to make **reasonable adjustments** [**28.7.4**]. The HSE website [see end of chapter] has a section about health and safety for disabled people and their employers.

40.3.2.6 Work off the premises or at home

Risk assessments must be carried out for work done at other premises, out of doors, in service users' homes, or in workers' own homes. The assessment must take account not only of risks to the worker, but also risks caused to others on the premises. Where it is not possible to carry out assessments in relation to specific premises – for example where staff visit many clients' homes – the assessment should identify the range of risks.

40.3.3 Principles of prevention

The regulations set out **general principles of prevention** for deciding how to deal with risks. These include:
- try to avoid the risk altogether;
- evaluate risks which cannot be avoided;
- try to deal with the hazard itself (for example replace dangerous equipment, rather than put up a warning sign);
- adapt work procedures, equipment and workstations to the individual, paying particular attention to alleviating monotonous work;
- if technological changes make it possible for work to be done more safely, implement those changes;
- replace something dangerous with something less or non-dangerous;
- develop a coherent overall prevention policy;
- where possible, make changes that affect employees as a group rather than making individual changes;
- provide appropriate information and training to employees.

Management of Health & Safety at Work Regulations 1999 [SI 1999/3242] sch.4

40.3.3.1 Health surveillance

If a specific health risk has been identified, **health surveillance** may need to be maintained to see whether the risk is having an adverse effect on any staff member's health.
MHSW Regs 1999 reg.6

HSE guidance is that surveillance should be implemented if there is an identifiable disease or health condition relating to the work and it is possible to detect the disease or condition, it is reasonably likely that it may arise in the work conditions, and surveillance could help reduce the risks for the employee.

40.3.3.2 Emergencies

Specific procedures must be in place to deal with risks such as fires [**40.8**] and bomb threats which would pose a serious imminent danger. These procedures must be notified to all employees, and if there are five or more employees must be in writing.   *Management of Health & Safety at Work Regulations 1999 [SI 1999/3242] reg.8*

40.3.3.3 Particular individuals

The employer must not only set up safe procedures, but must also take into account the particular capabilities of those undertaking them, adjust the procedure to ensure they are effective, and provide training if particular skills need to be acquired. This could involve, for example, providing translations of safety procedures.   *MHSW Regs 1999 reg.13*

40.3.3.4 Shared premises

Where two or more employers share premises they have a duty to cooperate, exchange information and coordinate protective measures.   *MHSW Regs 1999 reg.11*

40.4 THE PHYSICAL ENVIRONMENT

Many detailed duties apply to the physical work environment. The matters covered below are not comprehensive, and organisations are advised to contact the local environmental health department, HSE information line or the local HSE office [see end of chapter] for information specific to their activities, services and premises. The **Centre for Accessible Environments** [see end of chapter] has guidance specifically relating to facilities for disabled people.

40.4.1 Workplace health, safety and welfare

All workplaces except domestic premises, means of transport, building sites and exploration and mineral extraction sites are covered by the **Workplace (Health, Safety and Welfare) Regulations 1992** *[SI 1992/3004]*. In general, **health** means protection from long-term injury or illness, **safety** means protection from immediate danger, and **welfare** means facilities for personal comfort at work.

40.4.1.1 Health

To minimise the risks to health there must be adequate **ventilation**, the **temperature** must be reasonable, and there must be room thermometers in enough rooms to be able to measure the temperature throughout the workplace.

There is no legal minimum or maximum indoor temperature, but the approved code of practice (ACoP) recommends a minimum of 16°C (61°F) for sedentary work and 13°C (55°F) for strenuous work. The ACoP does not give a recommended maximum. The Trades Union Congress recommends a maximum of 30°C (86°F), or 27°C (81°F) for those doing strenuous work. The British Safety Council recommends 25°C (77°F) maximum for sedentary workers, and the World Health Organisation recommends 24°C (75°F).

Other health requirements apply to **lighting**, which should be natural whenever possible; the **cleanliness** of floors, walls, ceilings, windows, furniture and fittings; and the amount of **space** per worker.

Workstations (the furniture or machinery where an individual works) must be appropriate for the individual and for the work, with equipment and materials within easy reach without requiring undue stretching or bending. If the work involves sitting, a suitable seat and, if necessary, footrest must be provided.

40.4.1.2 Safety

Premises must be in a good state of repair, with any defects put right or action taken to prevent injury. The regulations include specific requirements in relation to floors, staircases, doors and gates, transparent surfaces, glass, windows, skylights and ventilators. Emergency **lighting** must be provided if any person would be in danger were the normal lighting to fail.

Any area where there is a risk of a person falling or being injured by a falling object must be indicated and if appropriate fenced. Storage units must be appropriate for the items being stored and must not be overfilled, and stored items must be securely stacked and not stacked too high.

Machinery and other equipment must be kept in good working order and must not be used if it poses a threat to health or safety.

There must be enough space for workers to move about easily and safely, and pedestrians must not be endangered by vehicles on the premises.

40.4.1.3 Welfare

The regulations specify the requirements for toilets, basins, washing and changing facilities, and drinking water. There should be suitable facilities for **rest** and **eating** (for desk workers, the desk is sufficient), and rest facilities must be available for pregnant and nursing women. It is good practice to provide a private area where a nursing woman can express milk, and a refrigerator to store it.

Rest rooms and rest areas, if provided, must include adequate tables and seats with backs for the number of people likely to use them at any one time, as well as seating suitable and adequate for the number of disabled people at the workplace.

Parts of the workplace used or occupied directly by disabled people – including doors, passageways, stairs, showers, washbasins, lavatories and workstations – must be organised to take account of their needs. The Centre for Accessible Environments [see end of chapter] has guidance on facilities for disabled people.

Health & Safety (Miscellaneous Amendments) Regulations 2002 [SI 2002/2174]

40.4.2 Smoking

Virtually all enclosed and semi-enclosed public places, including workplaces, places of voluntary work and vehicles owned by the organisation, must be smoke-free. Employers must display the proper signage and are responsible for ensuring all staff, service users/customers and visitors are aware of the regulations. Smoking in non-smoking premises, permitting people to smoke in non-smoking premises, and failing to display the required no-smoking signs are all offences.

Smoke-free (Premises & Enforcement) Regulations 2006 [SI 2006/3368]; Smoke-free (Exemptions & Vehicles) Regulations 2007 [SI 2007/765]; Smoke-free (Signs) Regulations 2007 [SI 2007/923]
There are different regulations for Wales, Scotland and Northern Ireland.

40.4.2.1 Premises

Smoking rooms in workplaces and public places are generally not allowed. But provided certain conditions are met and they are formally designated as rooms in which smoking is allowed, smoking can be allowed in bedrooms in premises such as hostels and members' clubs, and in accommodation or smoking rooms used for people aged 18 or over in care homes, hospices or prisons.

Private premises must generally be smoke-free if any non-resident works at the premises or visits them for work purposes. There are exceptions where the work involves providing personal care for a resident or for certain other purposes.

Outdoor smoking shelters are allowed only if they are not substantially enclosed. **Substantially enclosed** premises are those which have a permanent or temporary roof or covering, (including covers such as canvas awnings), and any opening or openings in the walls or perimeter add up to less than half the total area of the walls or perimeter. Doors, windows and other openings that can be opened or shut do not count as openings.

Another exemption covers performers where the 'artistic integrity' of a performance requires the performer to smoke.

40.4.2.2   Vehicles

Vehicles used in the course of paid or voluntary work must be smoke-free if they are used by more than one person, unless it is a convertible car and the roof is open. There is an exception for vehicles used primarily for private purposes by the owner or by someone who has a general right to use it, rather than being able to use it only for specific journeys.

40.4.3   Noise

The level at which hearing protection must be available for workers is 80dB and the level at which workers are required to wear hearing protection is 85dB.

Control of Noise at Work Regulations 2005 [SI 2005/1643]

Employers must prioritise noise control measures in noisy industries such as construction, as well as in any situation where a worker is surrounded by intrusive noise for most of the working day, a worker has to raise their voice to be heard by someone only two metres away, or a worker uses noisy powered tools or machinery for more than 30 minutes a day.

40.5   THE EMOTIONAL ENVIRONMENT

Duty of care and health and safety duties are increasingly being applied not only to the physical environment, but also to stress and abuse within the workplace.

40.5.1   Stress and mental ill health

The Health and Safety Executive defines **stress** as 'the adverse reaction people have to excessive pressures or other types of demand placed upon them' and 'prolonged intensive pressure'.

The employer's duty of care and duty to provide a safe system of work include monitoring and minimising factors which may cause or exacerbate stress related illness such as anxiety, depression, heart disease, and back pain. The factors may be physical, such as excessive noise or overcrowding, or psychological such as overwork, bullying or fear of violence. Employers should work with their employees to develop the best ways to prevent and manage work related stress.

Failure to develop practices which acknowledge and seek to reduce foreseeable mental or physical illness caused by workplace stress may lead to legal action by employees, for negligence and/or failure to comply with health and safety duties.

In negligence cases, the courts use the 16 **Hatton principles** set out in a case in 2002 to assess whether psychiatric illness was **reasonably foreseeable**. These include:

- employers can usually assume an employee can tolerate the normal pressure of work, unless the employer knows of a particular problem or vulnerability;
- all occupations or jobs should be assessed on the same basis, and none should be seen as intrinsically harmful to mental health;
- employers are generally entitled to take at face value what they are told by their employees, unless the employer has good reason to believe otherwise;
- duty of care is triggered when a reasonable employer would realise that they should do something about the impending harm to health caused by the stress at work;
- breach of the employer's duty of care arises if the employer fails to take steps which are reasonable in the circumstances.   *Sutherland v Hatton [2002] EWCA Civ 76*

However, decisions in subsequent cases emphasised that these principles do not set out statutory duties, and every case must be dealt with on the basis of that particular employer's duty of care to its employees in general and to that particular employee. The courts have said, for example, that when an employee has had a work related psychiatric illness, the employer should be aware of potential vulnerability, should make 'sympathetic enquiries' about the employee's condition, and should make the work environment less stressful even if the employee does not ask for this.   *Hartman v South Essex Mental Health & Community Care NHS Trust [2005] EWCA Civ 6*

In another case, the court said that an employee should have been sent home pending urgent examination by the company's occupational health department, after she was promoted without being provided with adequate training, had explained to her manager her difficulties, regularly came into work late, and had said she did not know how long she would keep going before she would become ill.

Dickens v O2 plc [2008] EWCA Civ 114

Similarly, another case found that merely providing access to a counselling service is not, in itself, enough, if the employer does not take necessary steps to reduce stress such as reducing the employee's workload.

*Intel Incorporation (UK) Ltd
v Daw [2007] EWCA Civ 70*

40.5.1.1 Vicarious trauma

One of the Hatton principles [above] is that no occupation or job should be seen as intrinsically harmful to mental health. However, workers and employers should be aware of the possibility of **vicarious trauma**, where workers who are exposed to situations of extreme stress (for example, working with survivors of sexual abuse) can themselves develop traumatic symptoms.

40.5.2 Violence

The HSE definition of **violence** is 'any incident in which an employee is abused, threatened or assaulted in circumstances relating to their work'. An employer might define violence more broadly, to include bullying or harassment [**40.5.3**], nuisance phone calls or attacks on property. A workplace definition should make clear that it includes acts by fellow workers, management and members of the governing body, as well as by service users, customers and members of the public.

If violence poses a threat to the safety of workers or anyone else, the employer must do a risk assessment [**40.3**], take appropriate action to reduce the risks, and provide appropriate information and training to people who may be affected by the violence. An important part of risk management is to learn from any violent incident, and adapt procedures accordingly.

40.5.2.1 Physical restraint

Where employees or volunteers may have to deal with service users, customers or members of the public who may become violent, the organisation should have a clear policy on whether and under what circumstances physical restraint may be used, the type of restraint, and alternative methods of dealing with actual or threatened violence. People who may need to use physical restraint must understand the implications of engaging in action which could legally be assault.

Appropriate training must be provided, and detailed records should be kept whenever restraint is used. Incidents should be fully investigated, appropriate support should be offered to all those affected, and procedures should be amended to reflect lessons learned from the incident.

40.5.3 Bullying, harassment and victimisation

There is no statutory definition of **bullying** but it has been defined as 'offensive, intimidating, malicious, insulting or humiliating behaviour, abuse of power or authority, which attempts to undermine an individual or group of employees, and which may cause them to suffer stress'.

Under the **Protection from Harassment Act 1997**, **harassment** is not defined but includes alarming or causing a person distress, causing a person to think that violence will be used against them, or any other conduct where on at least two occasions 'a reasonable person ... would think the course of conduct amounted to harassment'.

Protection from Harassment Act 1997 ss.1-7

Under **equal opportunities** legislation [**28.1.6**], harassment is defined as unwanted conduct related to race, sex, disability, religion or other belief, sexual orientation or age, which has the purpose or effect of violating a person's dignity or creating an intimidating, hostile, degrading, humiliating or offensive environment for the person.

Employers have obligations under **health and safety law** to ensure employees' health is not jeopardised, including by bullying or harassment in the course of work. All organisations have a **duty of care** [40.1.2] not only to employees but to others, to prevent reasonably foreseeable illness or injury. Governing bodies or managers must take steps to prevent such action when they know or should know that it is happening and could cause physical or mental harm.

Organisational policies on bullying and harassment should state that bullying or harassment, whether isolated or systematic and whether physical, verbal or via electronic means such as emails, will be treated as a disciplinary offence. Managers must have the right to comment critically on people's work and their behaviour at work. But criticism becomes bullying or harassment when it focuses on the individual rather than on their work or behaviour, is destructive rather than constructive, and results in a person feeling threatened or compromised.

40.5.3.1 Remedies for harassment

A person who has suffered harassment has several remedies.

- If the harassment is discriminatory, the person who has suffered harassment can bring a **discrimination** claim in the employment tribunal against their employer and/or the perpetrator [**28.1.6**].

- A person who has suffered physical injury or illness or psychiatric illness, including stress or depression, because of the harassment can bring a **personal injury** claim against the organisation [**22.6.1**].

- Where an employer has not complied with its duties under health and safety legislation, an employee who has become ill or injured because of the harassment can bring a claim for **breach of statutory duties** [**40.2.9**].

- Because of the employer's duty to treat employees with respect [**26.3.3**], bullying or harassment could be a breach of contract, entitling the employee to resign and claim **constructive unfair dismissal** [**34.2.9**].

- **Harassment** under the **Protection from Harassment Act 1997** (PHA) is a criminal offence. In addition the harassed person can bring a civil claim against the perpetrator. The claimant only needs to show that they have suffered anxiety or distress, not that they have become ill or injured or that they have been discriminated against.

- If the harassment happens at work and is connected with employment, the harassed employee can also (or instead) bring a claim under the PHA against their employer. *Majrowski v Guy's & St Thomas' NHS Trust [2006] UKHL 34*

The claim periods are three months for discriminatory harassment, three years for personal injury and six years for PHA. Under discrimination legislation, an employer can show that they took all reasonable steps to prevent discriminatory harassment. This defence cannot be used for claims under the PHA; the employer's only defence is that there was no connection between the employment and the harassment.

40.5.4 Alcohol and drugs

Employers are in breach of their health and safety duties if they knowingly allow an employee under the influence of alcohol or drugs to continue working, where the employee's behaviour puts her/himself or others at risk. All organisations have similar duties, not only in relation to employees, under their duty of care.

Employees also have duties under health and safety law, not to put themselves or others at risk.

HSE and ACAS [see end of chapter] have guidance on alcohol and drug use at work and policy issues for different types of organisation.

40.6 SPECIFIC TYPES OF WORK

Health and safety and related law applies to a large number of specific types of work or work with specific equipment, such as manual handling, work at heights or work with food. Details are available from the Health and Safety Executive and specialist agencies such as the Food Standards Agency [see end of chapter]. For work with children and vulnerable adults, see **chapter 41**.

40.6.1   Young workers

Young people under the minimum school leaving age (MSLA – the last Friday in June in the academic year during which they turn 16) are referred to legally as **children**, and are subject to specific rules on employment if they 'assist in a trade or occupation carried on for profit', even if they receive 'no reward for their labour'. This definition is both wider than the normal definition of employment [**25.1**] – because it covers situations even where the child is not paid – but also narrower, because it covers only situations where the work is carried on for profit.   *Children's & Young Persons Acts 1933 s.30*

Under these rules, children under age 13 cannot be employed except for television, theatre, modelling or similar work. Children under the MSLA cannot be employed for any work which requires them to lift, carry or move heavy items which would be likely to cause injury. They cannot work in a kitchen, cinema or disco, and there are limitations on their employment in street trading, performances, sport, advertising and modelling.   *Children's & Young Persons Acts 1933 & 1963,*
amended by Children (Protection at Work) Regulations 1998 [SI 1998/276];
2000 [SI 2000/1333]; 2000 (No.2) [SI 2000/2548]

Before allowing anyone under minimum school leaving age to work in a for profit business, the employer must obtain an employment permit from the local authority. The authority's education welfare department or the Children's Legal Centre [see end of chapter] can advise. Some local authorities require permits for children working, even as volunteers, in charity shops, on the basis that charity shops operate for profit.

The restrictions on employment do not apply to charities and other not for profit [**1.1.1**] organisations, but these organisations should consider whether it is appropriate to allow young volunteers to carry out work they would not be allowed to do in a for profit organisation.

There are restrictions on the hours that anyone under the age of 18 can work [**31.5**], and special risk assessments must be carried before a person under 18 is employed [**40.3.2.2**]. For these purposes, 'employees' and 'workers' are defined in the usual way [**25.1**], and the restrictions do not apply to volunteers unless they are working under a contract [**39.4.1**]. However, it is not good practice to allow young volunteers to work during hours they would not be allowed to be employed, or to allow them to work without carrying out an appropriate risk assessment.

Employer's liability insurance [**23.4.1**] should be checked to ensure it covers all young employees, work experience placements and young volunteers.

40.6.2   Computers and display screens

The display screen regulations apply to all computer and microfiche screens, including laptop and similar computers if they are in prolonged use. The regulations set minimum requirements for the display screen, keyboard, software (easy to use, appropriate for the person), workstation desk, document holder if there is one, chair, and the workstation environment, including space, lighting, glare, noise, heat, radiation and humidity.   *Health & Safety (Display Screen*
Equipment) Regulations 1992 [SI 1992/2792]

In addition, employers should be aware of risks arising from workers using a laptop on trains or in hotels, including risks from poor posture, from carrying equipment and heavy papers, and from the possibility of attack.

Before anyone starts using display screen equipment, the employer must provide adequate health and safety training about the equipment, and must provide an eye test if requested to do so. Eye tests must be provided if requested at regular intervals thereafter, or when the person is experiencing visual difficulties. If spectacles or other corrective equipment are required specifically for the person to use a display screen, this must be provided by the employer. If the employee needs spectacles or a new prescription for other purposes, not just for display screen use, the employer is not required to provide them.

The employer must arrange work so a person using a display screen can take regular breaks. Every workstation must be risk-assessed, covering risks such as upper limb disorders (repetitive strain injury/RSI), stress and visual difficulties. HSE guidance acknowledges that it is still difficult to predict the likelihood of RSI and related injuries, and advises employers to encourage early reporting by users of any symptoms which may be related to display screen work. The risks of RSI are reduced if the worker does not have to sit in the same position for long periods, can take regular breaks, and can adjust the equipment and chair.

The regulations do not acknowledge a link between computer work and reproductive or pregnancy problems, so there is no statutory obligation for an employer to provide alternative work for pregnant women. There is, however, a duty to do a risk assessment and make appropriate changes to the job [**40.3.2.1**], and an employer might consider it good practice to offer alternative work if it is available.

40.6.3   Visits and adventure activities

Organisations arranging visits, adventure activities and similar events have a duty of care to group leaders and other staff whether paid or voluntary, participants, and members of the public. Leaders and other staff have a duty of care to participants and members of the public.

One person (or, for multi-organisation activities, one organisation) should have overall responsibility for all aspects of the activity, including safety, and should ensure that everyone contracted to provide goods or services complies with the required safety standards. This applies regardless of whether the activity is in the UK or overseas, and could include providers of transport, accommodation, catering, and the actual activities.

Risk assessments must be carried out for the overall event and specific aspects of it, and must be repeated if circumstances change. A river that was safe to cross in the morning may, for example, not be safe in the afternoon after heavy rains.

Especially for school and other educational visits, involving participants in aspects of the risk assessment can enhance their awareness of risks and risk management. The Department for Children, Schools and Families has guidance on its Teachernet website [see end of chapter]. Although intended primarily for school trips, the materials are useful for any similar activity with any age group.

For overseas activities, the British Standards Institute's BS 8848 (taken from the height of Mount Everest – 8848 metres) aims to reduce the risk of injury or illness. Details are available from BSI [see end of chapter].

Activities involving climbing and caving must comply with the work at height regulations.   *Work at Height (Amendment) Regulations 2007 [SI 2007/114]*

40.6.4   Work equipment and lifting equipment

Work equipment must be suitable for its use and must be used only for purposes for which it is intended. It must be kept in good repair, and where there is a health or safety risk must be used only by trained people. Instructions and information about the equipment must be easily available, and must be known not only to the people who use the equipment but also to managers and supervisors.
Provision & Use of Work Equipment Regulations 1998 [SI 1998/2306]

Traditionally, work equipment referred only to machinery and 'tools of the trade'. In a case involving a screw that flew out and injured a worker who was tightening a door closer, the screwdriver was clearly work equipment – but was the door closer? The House of Lords ruled that the door was used at work, and therefore the door closer, which enabled it to operate, was work equipment, This means that virtually all equipment used at work is covered by the regulations.
Spencer-Franks v Kellogg Brown & another [2008] UKHL 46

Under the regulations, an employer is liable for any equipment provided to or used by an employee. Non-employers are liable if they have control to any extent over equipment, the way it is used, or a person who uses it or supervises its use. But in a case in 2009, the House of Lords said that an employer is, like a non-employer, liable only if it has some level of control over the equipment.
Smith v Northamptonshire County Council [2009] UKHL 27

Lifting equipment and hoists must be strong and stable enough for each load, and must indicate safe load limits. Equipment intended to lift persons must be designed to prevent a person being crushed, trapped or struck or falling from the carrier, and must be inspected every six months unless it has been decommissioned and is out of use. *Lifting Operations & Lifting Equipment Regulations 1998 [SI 1998/2307]*

40.6.5 Personal protective equipment

Adequate and readily available protective clothing and equipment must be provided. The suitability of the equipment for its purpose and for the staff using it must be assessed, suitable training and information must be provided, and equipment and clothing must be properly stored and must be replaced as necessary. *Personal Protective Equipment at Work Regulations 1992 [SI 1992/2966]*

The regulations apply only to items used for health and safety reasons, such as raincoats, high visibility jackets, footwear, helmets, aprons and chef's hats. They do not cover uniforms or items which do not have a protective function.

The employer must take all reasonable steps to ensure protective equipment and clothing is used. Employees have a duty to use the equipment or clothing and to report any defect or loss to the employer.

The employer cannot charge employees for equipment or clothing required under these regulations. *Health & Safety at Work etc Act 1974 s.9*

40.6.6 Manual handling

Where people or large loads are being manually handled, employers and staff are generally aware of potential problems and good practice. But the manual handling rules apply just as much to office and catering situations where smaller loads might be involved, and other workplaces where items are carried, lifted, pushed or pulled, or where the work involves twisting or stretching. Potential hazards must be identified and avoided where possible, steps must be taken to reduce the risk of injury to the lowest reasonably practicable level, and information must be provided about the risks and safe handling. HSE has guidance on various types of manual handling, including home care work and other work involving lifting people. *Manual Handling Operations Regulations 1992 [SI 1992/2793]*

40.6.7 Hazardous substances

Harmful substances, including photocopier and printer toner, solvent based products such as glues and oil paints, and even hair dye and cleaning fluids are covered by regulations known as **COSHH**. The risk must be assessed (the manufacturer's hazard data sheet does not constitute a COSHH assessment), exposure to the substances must be prevented or limited, protective equipment must if appropriate be issued, appropriate information and training must be provided, health surveillance [**40.3.3.1**] and/or monitoring of **workplace exposure limits** (WEL) must be implemented if appropriate, and the safety procedures must be regularly monitored and updated. *Control of Substances Hazardous to Health Regulations 2002 [SI 2002/2677] & COSHH (Amendment) Regulations 2004 [SI 2004/3386]*

Records of tests of substances and processes carried out under COSHH must be kept for five years from the date of the test. Records of exposure must be kept for five years from the date of the last entry in the record, unless the tests relate to identifiable individuals, in which case the records must be kept for 40 years from the date of the last entry. *COSHH Regs 2002 regs.9(5),10(5)*

Potentially explosive substances, which include paints and solvents as well as petrol, are controlled by the **Dangerous Substances and Explosive Atmospheres Regulations 2002** *[SI 2002/2776]*, lead by the **Control of Lead Regulations 2002** *[SI 2002/2676]*, and substances which are dangerous to the environment by the **Health and Safety at Work etc Act 1974 (Application to Environmentally Hazardous Substances) Regulations 2002** *[SI 2002/282]*.

The regulations in 2002 introduced a requirement for employers, in certain circumstances, to draw up detailed procedures for dealing with accidents, incidents and emergencies that involve hazardous substances.

40.6.7.1   REACH

Any organisation which manufactures or imports more than one tonne of chemicals per year must comply with regulations on the registration, evaluation, authorisation and restriction of chemicals (REACH), which are coming into force in stages from 2008 to 2018. Information is available from the Health and Safety Executive [see end of chapter].   *REACH Enforcement Regulations 2008 [SI 2008/2852]*

40.7   PREMISES

Health and safety duties relating to premises are supplemented by building regulations, fire safety regulations and many other areas of law.

40.7.1   Asbestos

All **duty holders** (persons responsible for maintaining or repairing non-domestic properties or the communal parts of public properties, or with control of such premises) must carry out an assessment to determine whether asbestos is present on the premises, an ongoing review if the situation changes, and a risk assessment and management plan for asbestos on the premises.

Use of asbestos must be prevented or kept to the lowest risk possible, and at all times exposure must be kept below the maximum allowed control limit. Training is mandatory for anyone working with, or likely to be exposed to, asbestos at work.   *Control of Asbestos at Work Regulations 2006 [SI 2006/2739]*

40.7.2   Electricity and electrical equipment

Employers, employees and self employed people have an absolute obligation [**40.2.5**] to comply with the electricity regulations in all matters under their control.   *Electricity at Work Regulations 1989 [SI 1989/635]*

All electrical systems must be constructed, maintained and used in ways which prevent the risk of danger, and portable appliances such as kettles and computers need to be tested by a competent person. The Health and Safety Executive [end of chapter] advises that for most office electrical equipment, it is enough to do a visual check for obvious signs of damage and perhaps for a competent member of staff to carry out simple tests. For more complex equipment, HSE can advise on what needs to be tested and how often.

Electrical work in homes and out of doors must either be notified to the local authority's building control department or be carried out by a competent person registered with a building regulations part P self certification scheme. There is an exception for small DIY jobs such as replacing a socket outlet or light switch which is on an existing circuit and is not in a high-risk area such as a kitchen or bathroom, but it is recommended that if these are done on a DIY basis they are checked by a registered person. All electrical work, even DIY, must comply with electrical safety regulations.   *Building (Amendment) (No.3) Regulations 2004 [SI 2004/3210];*
Building & Approved Inspectors Regulations 2006 [SI 2006/652]

40.7.3   Gas

Landlords of all premises, whether domestic or non-domestic, must ensure that gas fittings and pipework are maintained in good condition. Every gas fitting and flue must be checked for safety by a person on the **Gas Safe Register** at not more than annual intervals, defects must be put right, inspection records must be maintained for at least two years, and the latest certificate must be issued to existing tenants and to any new tenants before they move in. Owners of gas fittings are responsible for having their own maintenance and service checks carried out. Information about gas safety is available from HSE [see end of chapter].
Gas Safety Management Regulations 1996 [SI 1996/551];
Gas Safety (Installation & Use) Regulations 1998 [SI 1998/2451]

40.7.4   Building construction

Anyone involved in commissioning building construction, including design and demolition, must ensure that only competent people are employed as CDM (**con-**

struction, design and management) coordinator, designer, principal contractor and contractor. Anyone working on construction under the control of another person must report anything they are aware of that might endanger health or safety.

Where the construction phase of a project, including design work or demolition, is likely to last more than 30 days or involve more than 500 person days of work, the client (the organisation paying for the work) must appoint a CDM coordinator and a principal contractor, and must take reasonable steps to ensure that the CDM coordinator, designers and contractors have proper health and safety arrangements in place. Guidance is available from HSE [see end of chapter].

Construction (Design & Management) Regulations 2007 [SI 2007/320]

40.7.5 Lifts

Occupiers of premises must ensure that all lifts are safe, properly maintained and inspected every six months, and that proper records are kept of maintenance and inspections.

Lifting Operations & Lifting Equipment Regulations 1998 [SI 1998/2307]

40.8 FIRE SAFETY

The **responsible person** – the employer, plus any person who has control over any part of the premises – must ensure fire safety. In non-domestic premises which are not workplaces, the person(s) in control of the premises are responsible. Where there is more than one responsible person, they must all take reasonable steps to work with each other. Responsibilities include:

- a general duty to ensure, so far as is reasonably practicable, the safety of employees;
- a general duty, in relation to non-employees, to take fire precautions that are reasonable in the circumstances to ensure that premises are safe;
- a duty to carry out a fire risk assessment.

Regulatory Reform (Fire Safety) Order 2005 [SI 2005/1541]

The risk assessment must give particular attention to those at special risk, such as people with disabilities, and must include consideration of any dangerous substances likely to be on the premises. The significant findings of the risk assessment must be in writing if there are five or more employees, but it is good practice to put it in writing even if there are fewer than five employees, or none. PEEPs – **personal emergency egress plans** – should be developed with workers, service users and others who regularly use the premises.

Risk assessment checklists and guidance on fire safety in specific types of premises are available from the Fire Protection Association and the Department for Communities and Local Government [see end of chapter].

Building work must comply with the revised part B (fire safety) of the building regulations, including a duty to ensure occupiers are aware of their building's fire protection measures so they can take these into account when carrying out fire risk assessments. *Building & Approved Inspectors (Amendment) (No. 2) Regulations 2006 [SI 2006/3318]*

40.8.1 Warnings and escape

Appropriate fire detection and warning systems, such as smoke detectors, electrical alarms or a shouted warning system must be in place. Adequate escape routes must be provided from all buildings, enabling people to turn away from the fire, wherever it may be in the building, and reach a protected staircase or exit.

All staircases and fire exits must be kept accessible and free from obstruction, and if locked or fastened they must be able to be easily and immediately opened. Special provision may be required for people with mobility difficulties or for premises used for public entertainment.

Fire exits must be clearly marked with signs complying with statutory requirements. If a fire exit is temporarily unusable, for example because of building works, all signs pointing to that exit should be removed.

Health & Safety (Safety Signs & Signals) Regulations 1996 [SI 1996/341]

40.8.2 Firefighting equipment

Fire extinguishers should be placed in positions where a person would not have to move more than 30m (slightly under 100ft) to reach them. They must be clearly marked with the type of extinguisher, the method of operation and the types of fire they can be used on. They should be checked every month, and inspected annually by a trained person.

Fire blankets can be used for small fires, including fires involving electrical equipment, oil or cooking fat. They can also be wrapped around a person whose clothing has caught fire.

40.8.3 Access

Designated fire access areas, dry riser mains and sprinklers must be kept clear. For buildings over 18m (59ft) in height, special access provisions are required.

40.9 INJURY AND ILLNESS

All workplaces should have adequate facilities and equipment for staff who become ill or injured at work.

40.9.1 First aid

There is no statutory obligation to provide first aid to anyone other than staff, but duty of care [40.1.2] means that facilities should also be available for others on the premises. Records must be kept whenever first aid is administered [40.9.3]. *Health & Safety (First-Aid) Regulations 1981 [SI 1981/917]*

40.9.1.1 First aiders

There is no statutory requirement to have trained **first aiders**, but a first aid risk assessment should identify whether they are needed, and if so, how many there should be. The Health and Safety Executive [see end of chapter] provides guidance on the recommended number of trained first aiders, based on the number of employees and the nature of the work. If the risks are low, one first aider may deal with up to 50 employees. In riskier situations, there should be more than one. First aiders must be able to leave their work in order to render help, and must have the physical capability to give that help.

If there are no first aiders, or to cover when there are none on duty, the workplace should have at least one **appointed person** to look after first aid boxes and rooms, and organise a first aid response, such as ringing for an ambulance. Appointed persons and others should not carry out first aid themselves unless they are trained to do so.

First aiders must hold a certificate from a first aid course approved by HSE. From 1 October 2009 two types of approved courses are available: three-day first aid at work (FAW), and for smaller, low-risk workplaces, emergency first aid at work (EFAW). Certificates for each are valid for three years, and annual update courses are available.

If the work is high risk and there are large number of employees, a first aid room should be provided.

40.9.1.2 First aid boxes

Clearly visible first aid boxes, marked with a white cross on a green background and containing items that have been highlighted in an assessment of first aid needs, must be maintained and must be accessible at all times. The Health and Safety Executive website [see end of chapter] provides general guidance on the contents.

The size and number of boxes depends on the number of staff. Employees who spend considerable time on the road or in isolated locations should be given portable kits.

40.9.2 RIDDOR

Employers, self employed people and anyone who controls work premises must report to the **Incident Contact Centre** [see end of chapter] or in some cases the local environmental health department serious injuries, near misses and illnesses caused by or at work to staff, service users, contractors, visitors or members of the public. These rules are called **RIDDOR**, from the name of the regulations.

Reporting of Injuries, Diseases & Dangerous Occurrences Regulations 1995 [SI 1995/3163]

Reportable events include:

- fatal incidents and death occurring within one year as a result of a reportable incident, even if the incident was not reported;
- accidents or incidents causing major injury;
- potentially dangerous occurrences which did not cause injury;
- injuries to an employee or self employed person causing more than three consecutive days' incapacity for work, even if the person is actually at work or if the days are weekend or other non-work days;
- injuries to members of the public or people not at work if they are taken from the scene of the incident to hospital;
- some work related diseases;
- any dangerous occurrence which could have resulted in a reportable injury, but did not.

In the case of death, a major injury or condition, or a dangerous occurrence, a report must be made immediately by the quickest means, usually telephone (0845 300 9923) or via www.riddor.gov.uk, with a written report on form **F2508** within 10 days of the incident. Over three-day injuries must be reported on form F2508 within 10 days of the incident. Diseases are reported on form **F2508A**. Additional reporting requirements apply if staff who are in contact with food have certain diseases.

A copy of the form must be sent to the organisation's insurers, and another copy kept indefinitely by the organisation.

Employers are encouraged not just to report incidents, but to investigate them and take steps to reduce the risk of recurrence. The Health and Safety Executive [see end of chapter] has guidance on investigating accidents.

40.9.3 Accident book

A record must be kept for at least three years of all accidents, dangerous occurrences and diseases, and incidents where first aid was administered. This record, called the **accident book** even though it covers more than accidents, must include the date and time of the occurrence, the full name and occupation of the injured person, the nature of the injury, where it happened, and the circumstances. For a reportable disease, the record must show the affected person's occupation, the date of diagnosis, and the name or nature of the disease. Where first aid is given, the record must also include the address of the person treated; the signature, name and address of the person making the entry; and the date of the entry.

It is good practice also to record, in the accident book or a separate incident book, minor accidents or incidents which were, or could have been, a danger to health or safety, such as an aggressive outburst.

Because data protection law requires personal data in accident books to be kept confidential, any book used since 1 January 2004 must have pages that can be removed and stored separately. Suitable books are available from HSE Books [see end of chapter].

40.9.4 Internal reporting

The organisation should establish procedures to ensure that notification is promptly given to the person's family or next of kin, the organisation's insurers, the safety representative(s) or safety committee [**40.2.8**], senior staff, head office and/or the relevant member of the governing body, and the person responsible for keeping personnel records.

40.9.5   Medical and maternity suspension

For certain work related illnesses caused by exposure to lead, ionising radiation and some other substances, employees must be suspended from the activity involving the exposure. Such suspension is generally on full pay [**30.1.11**].

Women who are pregnant, have recently given birth or are breastfeeding must be suspended with full pay if they undertake certain types of work and suitable alternative work is not available [**40.3.2.1**].

40.10   PUBLIC HEALTH

Public health regulations, enforced by the local authority's environmental health department, cover air quality, ventilation and pollution [**63.12.4**]; drainage; waste and rubbish disposal [**63.12.6**]; pests and vermin; food hygiene [**40.10.1**]; public entertainment [**chapter 47**]; and residential accommodation provided by the organisation for its staff, tenants, residents or visitors. Information is available from the local authority.

40.10.1   Food hygiene

An organisation involved in the production, supply or sale of food must comply with the **Food Safety Act 1990**, **Food Hygiene (England) Regulations 2006** *[SI 2006/0014]* or comparable regulations for other parts of the UK, and other regulations for specific types of food. They cover not only food prepared on the organisation's premises or bought in, but also food prepared at home for sale or distribution elsewhere. Although the regulations refer to food businesses, they also apply to organisations that do not charge for the food they provide.

Food safety procedures must be based on the principles of **hazard analysis critical control points** (HACCP). The organisation must ensure food is supplied or sold in a hygienic way, identify food safety hazards, and ensure safety controls are in place and are maintained and reviewed. Detailed information and guidance are available from the local authority's environmental health department and the Food Standards Agency [end of chapter].

40.10.1.1   Occasional provision of food

European Commission guidance makes clear that 'operations such as the occasional handling, preparation, storage and serving of food by private individuals at events such as church, school or village fairs' are not covered by the food hygiene regulations. However, even if the food hygiene regulations do not apply in this situation, individuals and the organisation still have a **duty of care** [**40.1.2**] to ensure food is safe, and may be subject to regulations which prohibit 'the placing of unsafe food on the market'. *General Food Regulations 2004 [SI 2004/3279]*

40.10.1.2   Registration

Organisations which produce or supply food on a regular basis – even if they do not charge for it, and even if 'regular' is only once a week – need to register with the local authority environmental health department.

Where premises are used by more than one organisation that produces or supplies food (for example a village hall where a community nursery provides food to children, and the local organisations for elderly people and Asian women provide food at their lunch clubs) each organisation that provides food must register. The premises do not have to be registered unless they also provide food.

If in doubt about registration, check with the local authority. Even the Food Standards Agency has said, 'There is a thin line between those very small, informal operations providing food on a regular basis who may be required to register with the local authority as a food operator, and those organising one-off events who do not.'

40.11   CONSUMER SAFETY

It is an offence to sell or in some cases provide goods to consumers – people acquiring them for private rather than business use – which do not comply with the relevant safety requirements. The regulations generally apply to new goods, and to the sale of secondhand goods 'in the course of business' or 'in the course of trade'. They also apply to products used by consumers in the course of a service, and products intended for businesses or professionals but which 'migrate' to the consumer market.   *General Product Safety Regulations 2005 [SI 2005/1803]*

If in any doubt at all about whether something needs to comply with the regulations, the organisation should check with the local authority's trading standards or consumer safety department – or not sell or provide the item.

The regulations do not apply to products supplied for repair or reconditioning before use, provided the supplier makes this clear to the person to whom the product is supplied. The regulations also do not apply to antiques.

There are two levels of duty. The higher duty applies to anyone considered to be a **producer** of the goods, which could include an organisation which does not actually produce the goods, but allows its logo or trademark to be placed on them. A lower duty applies to **distributors**.

Producers must be able to trace products, using identification or other reference marks. Distributors must keep records enabling them to trace unsafe products. Producers and distributors must notify enforcement agencies if they discover than any product they have sold or distributed is unsafe, and must also provide details of any action taken to counter the risk to consumers.

One of the most significant changes introduced by the 2005 regulations is an increased duty to be able to recall unsafe products. Organisations should ensure they are able to do this, and have insurance in place to cover the costs.

40.11.1   Sale of secondhand and donated goods

Although the sale of donated goods is not classed as trading for charity law and tax purposes [**56.3.2**], the fact that goods are donated is irrelevant for consumer safety purposes. Goods sold in charity shops are covered by consumer safety legislation, as well as goods sold at jumble sales or similar events which are held regularly and could be seen as constituting a business or trade. However, the Department for Business, Innovation and Skills' *General Product Safety Regulations 2005: Guidance for businesses, consumers and enforcement agencies* (August 2005) says that where goods are donated free of charge by members of the public, the organisation is not expected to keep documentation that would help trace the origin of products.

Even if one-off jumble sales and similar sales by a voluntary organisation are not regular enough to constitute a 'business', it is not sensible to sell or allow others to sell anything which could pose a risk to health or safety.

At a car boot sale, table top sale or similar sale, the person hiring the pitch is selling the goods and is responsible for ensuring the goods comply with the relevant legislation. The organisation hiring out the space might want to make it a condition that no secondhand electrical or gas appliances or dangerous toys are sold.

Where goods are sold at a car boot sale, fete or similar event by an organisation which is clearly commercial, the product safety regulations apply even if some or all of the profit will be donated to a charity or other voluntary organisation.

40.11.2   Providing goods free of charge

Products given away free as part of a commercial activity are generally covered by the regulations. But BIS guidance [above] says, 'voluntary organisations that exist solely to provide goods free of charge to the needy are probably not engaging in a commercial activity and are not therefore subject to the regulations'. The word 'solely' may be significant; many organisations which provide clothing, household goods and other items to people in need are not set up solely for this purpose. The word 'probably' is also significant. If in doubt, the local authority's trading standards or consumer safety department should be consulted.

40.11.3 Furniture and household goods

Many household goods may be sold only if they comply with safety requirements. In some cases, special labelling is required. Examples of items that should be sold only if the organisation can guarantee they comply with the rules include:

- new upholstered furniture and furnishings, including scatter cushions;

- secondhand upholstered furniture and furnishings if made since 1 January 1950 and being sold in the course of trade;

- nursery furniture which contains any upholstery (but changing mats, play mats, baby bouncers suspended from doorways, cot bumpers, bedclothes, and baby carriers and slings designed to be worn outdoors can be sold);

- baby car seats;

- new and secondhand electrical goods (but even if it does not comply with the regulations, it can be supplied as scrap or to a business which repairs and re-conditions electrical equipment);

- gas appliances, and oil heaters and lamps.

40.11.4 Toys

All new toys, including those which are handmade, must satisfy the applicable safety requirements, have a **CE marking** (likely to be replaced by **European norm EN** marking), and provide information about the manufacturer or importer. This requirement does not apply to secondhand toys, unless the toys were brought into the EU from a non-EU country and are subsequently being sold in the course of a business.

Handmade toys must be certified by the maker as complying with the relevant toy safety standard and must be labelled with the name and address of the individual, business or organisation who made it. Some toys must contain a warning or indication of precautions to be taken. Advice on the regulations and labelling is available from the local authority trading standards or consumer protection department.

40.12 TRANSPORT

Information and advice about all aspects of driver, vehicle and operator licensing, legislation, training and operations is available from the Community Transport Association [see end of chapter]. The Royal Society for the Prevention of Accidents [see end of chapter] produces a range of material on motoring safety, including guidance specifically for organisations with volunteer drivers.

40.12.1 Vehicle licensing and safety

An organisation which operates cars, vans, small buses (nine to 16 passengers), buses or coaches (more than 16 passengers) or other vehicles must ensure they meet all legal requirements and are roadworthy, and drivers are trained in their use and operation. Drivers must ensure that their vehicle complies with the full requirements of the **Road Vehicles (Construction and Use) Regulations 1986** [SI 1986/1078] and **Road Vehicles Lighting Regulations 1989** [SI 1989/1796], as amended. The organisation must ensure that maintenance systems are in place to ensure the roadworthiness of vehicles, including regular checks, defect reporting, safety inspections, servicing and MoTs.

40.12.1.1 Seatbelts and child restraints

All minibuses and coaches carrying three or more children on an organised trip must provide a forward facing seat with, as a minimum, a lap belt (lap and diagonal is preferable) for each child aged between three and 16. In minibuses or coaches first used on or after 1 October 2001, children may also be provided with approved rearward facing seats fitted with seat belts.

In a minibus with an unladen weight of 2,540kg or less, the driver is responsible for ensuring that seatbelts are worn by children aged under 14. At the time of writing (mid 2009), the Department for Transport had consulted on how to implement this requirement in heavier minibuses, buses and coaches. Passengers aged 14 or over are also required to wear seatbelts and must be informed of this verbally and/or by the display of specified pictograms adjacent to each seat, but the driver is not liable if they do not use seatbelts. *Motor Vehicles (Wearing of Seat Belts) (Amendment) Regulations 2006 [SI 2006/1892]*

In vehicles with up to eight passenger seats, a child under the age of 12 and under 135cm (just over 4ft 5in) must use a securely fitted baby or child seat, booster seat or booster cushion suitable for their weight. The driver is legally responsible for ensuring that all children under 14 are wearing a seat belt and/or a suitable restraint is used. Where the vehicle is provided by the organisation, or is the employee's or volunteer's own vehicle but is being used for work purposes, the organisation could also be held liable if it does not have and enforce a policy making clear that appropriate seatbelts or restraints must be used by children. *Seat Belts Regs 2006*

The only exception to the child restraint rules is for an 'unexpected necessity', when a child at least three years old can use an adult seat belt. A child under three years old must always be in a car seat, except in a registered taxi where they can travel unrestrained if no car seat is available.

40.12.1.2 Passenger carrying vehicles (PCVs)

In general, operators of vehicles with more than eight passenger seats must comply with **passenger carrying vehicle** (PCV) requirements, and drivers must be entitled to drive PCVs [**40.12.2.1**]. However, some voluntary organisations are entitled to a **section 19 permit** for small busses (nine to 16 passengers) or **section 22 community bus permit** for small or large busses (more than 16 passengers), allowing them to operate PCVs without complying with the full requirements. Information is available from Directgov and the Community Transport Association [see end of chapter]. *Transport Act 1985 ss.18 23, as amended; Section 19 Permit Regulations 2009 [SI 2009/365]; Community Bus Regulations 2009 [SI 2009/366]*

40.12.1.3 Local authority contracts

Organisations which provide transport under contract to local authorities must have their vehicles licensed as **private hire vehicles** (PHV), or must set up alternative licensing arrangements. The Community Transport Association [see end of chapter] can provide information on these. *Road Safety Act 2006 s.53*

40.12.2 Driver licensing and safety

Organisations have a duty of care to ensure the safety of employees, volunteers, passengers, other road users and pedestrians who may be affected by the organisation's activities. The HSE and the Department for Transport's Thinkroadsafety website [see end of chapter] can provide information, and the Royal Society for the Prevention of Accidents has guidance specifically for voluntary organisations on managing occupational road risk, with a draft policy.

Where a driver's licence is from a country outside the EU, DVLA or the Community Transport Association [see end of chapter] should be contacted for confirmation that it is valid for the type of vehicles operated by the organisation.

40.12.2.1 Driving a small bus

Ordinary driving licences (category B) cover vehicles with up to eight passenger seats. Drivers who passed their driving test before 1 January 1997 have a restricted D1 entitlement, which allows them to drive a small bus (nine to 16 passengers excluding the driver) provided they are 21 or over and the bus is not being used for 'hire and reward' (unless operating under a permit). When their licence expires, normally at age 70, a medical test must be passed to retain the D1 entitlement.

Drivers passing their driving test on or after 1 January 1997 receive a licence covering vehicles with up to eight passenger seats. In order to drive a small bus, drivers need to take a second test to gain a full D1 (PCV) entitlement unless all the following conditions are met:

- the vehicle is used for social purposes by a non-commercial body, and is not used for hire and reward (unless operating under a permit);

- the vehicle weighs no more than 3.5 tonnes fully loaded, or no more than 4.25 tonnes including any specialist equipment for carrying disabled passengers e.g. passenger lift, ramps, wheelchair and passenger restraints, etc;

- the driver is 21 or over, has held a car (category B) licence for at least two years, and is doing the driving on a voluntary basis; and

- if the driver is aged 70 or over, he or she passes a medical test when renewing their licence in order to retain their small bus entitlement.

Persons driving under this exemption must not receive any payment or consideration other than out of pocket expenses, cannot tow any size trailer, and can drive only in the UK.

Further information is available from the Community Transport Association, and in the DVLA's leaflet INF28 [see end of chapter].

40.12.2.2 Safety while driving

It is unlawful for a driver to hold a mobile phone while the car engine is on. The only exception is when the phone is used to call 999 or 112 in a genuine emergency when it is not safe or practical to stop. It is not prohibited to use a hands-free phone or to push buttons on a phone while it is in a cradle, or on the steering wheel or handlebars of a motorcycle. However, a driver using a hands-free phone or one in a cradle is still potentially subject to prosecution for failure to have proper control, or for dangerous driving if involved in an accident.

Road Vehicles (Construction & Use) (Amendment) (No.4) Regulations 2003 [SI 2003/2695]

The regulations apply to 'anyone who causes or permits any other person' to use a handheld phone while driving, so employers should have a clear policy that under no circumstances (except for calling 999 or 112) can an employee or volunteer use a mobile phone while driving as part of the organisation's work. Employers and colleagues should not ring staff members when they are known to be driving.

Resources: HEALTH AND SAFETY

Health and safety law and good practice. Health and Safety Executive: www.hse.gov.uk, 0845 345 0055, hse.infoline@natbrit.com. More comprehensive subscription service at www.hsedirect.com.

Health and Safety Books: www.hsebooks.co.uk, 01787 881165. Free publications from www.hse.gov.uk/pubns/index.htm.

Local H&S advice centres: details from Hazards Campaign, www.hazardscampaign.org.uk/direct/dirindex.htm, 0161 636 7557.

ACAS: www.acas.org.uk, 08457 47 47 47.

British Safety Council: www.britishsafetycouncil.co.uk, 020 8741 1231, mail@britsafe.org.

Health@Work: www.healthatworkcentre.org.uk, 0151 236 6608, info@healthatworkcentre.org.uk.

London Hazards Centre: www.lhc.org.uk, 020 7794 5999, mail@lhc.org.uk.

Royal Society for the Prevention of Accidents (RoSPA): www.rospa.co.uk, 0121 248 2000, help@rospa.com.

Trades Union Congress: www.tuc.org.uk, Know Your Rights line 0870 600 4882, info@tuc.org.uk.

Workplace Health Connect: www.workplacehealthconnect.co.uk, 0845 609 6006.

Health and safety and related training. British Safety Council [above].

Fire Protection Association [below].

Royal Society for the Prevention of Accidents [above].

Health and safety training specifically for voluntary organisations.

Local H&S advice centres [above].

Health@Work [above]

Accessible premises and facilities. Centre for Accessible Environments: www.cae.org.uk, 020 7840 0125, info@cae.org.uk.

Bullying. Andrea Adams Trust: www.andreaadamstrust.org, 01273 704900, mail@andreaadamstrust.org.

Children and young people as workers. Local authority education department.

Children's Legal Centre: www.childrenslegalcentre.com, 01206 872466, clc@essex.ac.uk.

Consumer and product safety. Local authority trading standards/consumer safety department.

Department for Business, Innovation and Skills: www.bis.gov.uk, 020 7215 0359, enquiries@bis.gsi.gov.uk.

Driving. Community Transport Association: www.communitytransport.com, 0845 130 6195, advice@ctauk.org.

Department for Transport: www.thinkroadsafety.gov.uk, 020 7944 8300, road.safety@dft.gsi.gov.uk.

Directgov: www.direct.gov.uk/en/motoring/index.htm.

Driver and Vehicle Licensing Agency: www.dvla.gov.uk, 0870 240 0009, drivers.dvla@gtnet.gov.uk.

Royal Society for the Prevention of Accidents (RoSPA) [above].

AA Risk Management Solutions: www.theaa.com, 0800 52 10 72, AARiskManagementSolutions@theAA.com.

Electricity. Local authority building control department.

Department for Communities and Local Government: www.communities.gov.uk, 020 7944 4400, contactus@communities.gov.uk

Fire. Local fire authority.

Department for Communities and Local Government [above].

Fire Protection Association: www.thefpa.co.uk, 01608 812500, fpa@thefpa.co.uk.

First aid. British Red Cross: www.redcross.org.uk, 08701 709 222, firstaid@redcross.org.uk.

St John Ambulance: www.sja.org.uk, 08700 10 49 50, info@sja.org.uk.

Health and Safety Executive: www.hse.gov.uk, 0845 345 0055, hse.infoline@natbrit.com.

Approved first aid training: local branches of the British Red Cross and St John Ambulance.

Food hygiene. Local authority environmental health department.

Food Standards Agency: www.food.gov.uk, 020 7276 8829, helpline@foodstandards.gsi.gov.uk.

Gas. Health and Safety Executive: www.hse.gov.uk, gas safety advice line 0800 300 363, hse.infoline@natbrit.com.

Gas Safe Register: www.gassaferegister.co.uk, 0800 408 5500, enquiries@gassaferegister.co.uk.

Personal safety. Police crime prevention unit.

Suzy Lamplugh Trust: www.suzylamplugh.org, 020 7091 0014, info@suzylamplugh.org.

RIDDOR: Incident Contact Centre: www.riddor.gov.uk, 0845 300 99 23, riddor@natbrit.com.

Smoking. Action on Smoking and Health: www.ash.org.uk, 020 7739 5902, enquiries@ash.org.uk.

Smokefree England: www.smokefreeengland.co.uk, 0800 169 169 7, email via website.

Smoking Ban Wales: www.smokingbanwales.co.uk, tobaccopolicybranch@wales.gsi.gov.uk.

Visits and adventure activities. Department for Children, Schools and Families: www.teachernet.gov.uk/wholeschool/healthandsafety/visits, 0870 000 2288, info@dcsf.gsi.gov.uk.

Statute law. www.opsi.gov.uk and www.statutelaw.gov.uk.

Much but not all case law. www.bailii.org.

Updates cross-referenced to this book. www.rclh.co.uk.

Chapter 41
SAFEGUARDING CHILDREN AND VULNERABLE ADULTS

For sources of further information see end of chapter.

41.1   LEGISLATION AND GOOD PRACTICE

Depending on the nature of the organisation and its work, there may be statutory requirements to register with a regulatory authority and/or for criminal records and other checks to be carried out on some or all paid staff and volunteers, and it may be unlawful to allow certain people to work with children (usually defined as under 18) or vulnerable adults.

The legislation is complex, overlapping, and subject to frequent changes, especially in 2009-2014 as the **Safeguarding Vulnerable Groups Act 2006** is phased in. Details of the rules for work with children should be sought from **Ofsted** and the local authority's children's services department, or for work with vulnerable adults from the **Care Quality Commission**, the **General Social Care Council** and the local authority's adult services department. Information about criminal record checks is available from the **Criminal Records Bureau**, and about vetting and barring from the **Independent Safeguarding Authority** [see end of chapter for all agencies].

As a matter of good practice, every organisation where it is relevant should appoint a member of the governing body and a staff member to oversee issues related to the safeguarding of children, young people and vulnerable adults. These safeguarding officers should ensure all governing body members and relevant staff, whether paid or unpaid, understand the legislative framework within which the organisation operates, and understand and comply with the organisation's safeguarding policies and procedures.

41.1.1 Relevant legislation

The **Rehabilitation of Offenders Act 1974** and related exception orders allow for certain convictions to become **spent** and not to be revealed after a specified period, but define certain types of work for which even spent convictions must be disclosed [**41.8**].

The **Children Act 1989** covers regulation of childminding and daycare for children [**41.3.1**].

The **Police Act 1997** and related regulations established the Criminal Records Bureau, and defined who is entitled to different levels of CRB disclosure [**41.4.1**].

The **Protection of Children Act 1999** requires childcare organisations to carry out CRB checks, and established the **POCA list** of people banned from working with children [**41.7.1**].

The **Care Standards Act 2000** and secondary legislation require registration of health and social care services and workers providing the services [**41.3.2, 41.3.3**], require organisations providing such services to carry out CRB and other checks on workers, and established the **POVA** (Protection of Vulnerable Adults) **list** of people banned from working with vulnerable adults [**41.7.1**].

The **Criminal Justice and Court Services Act 2000** defined the positions in childcare organisations for which CRB checks had to be carried out, and allowed judges to disqualify people from working with children.

The **Children Act 2004** creates an integrated approach to provision of services for children and young people through multi-agency **children's trusts** and **local safeguarding children boards**.

The **Childcare Act 2006** requires registration of childminders and others who provide similar care for children, and requires early years childminders to provide learning and development opportunities in line with the **early years foundation stage**.

The **Safeguarding Vulnerable Groups Act 2006** amends or repeals much of the above legislation, and introduces the **Independent Safeguarding Authority** scheme which is being phased in over several years starting in 2009 [**41.7**].

In addition, a wide range of education legislation covers work in schools and educational establishments.

41.1.1.1 Requirement, recommendation, good practice

The legislation in this field has been developed piecemeal, is often overlapping, and does not use consistent definitions even for a relatively straightforward word like 'child' – let alone for something as wide-ranging and potentially controversial as 'vulnerable adults' [**41.5**].

In addition, there is considerable confusion and misinformation about when criminal record checks are a statutory requirement, when they are recommended but not required, and when they may have to be carried out in order to avoid being in breach of the obligation not to employ or take on as a volunteer someone who is barred from working with children or vulnerable adults.

There is similar confusion about posts where it is unlawful to allow a particular person to work with children or vulnerable adults, and situations where the organisation has to make a decision about whether a person is unsuitable. Where a criminal record check reveals a previous conviction, for example, but the person is not barred from working with a group, the organisation can decide how to proceed – but may not have a clear idea of the criteria to use.

From 12 October 2009, the **vetting and barring** scheme [**41.7**] should start to clarify and simplify these matters, but because it is being phased in during 2009 and 2010 there may be two or three years when things remain unclear.

41.1.2 Good practice

The legal requirements are only one part of good practice in relation to work with children and vulnerable adults. A very large proportion of people involved in abuse and other unacceptable behaviour never come to the attention of the police. So a criminal record check is one tool in the toolkit of safe recruitment, but should never be used as a substitute for proper recruitment, selection, induction and supervision procedures for employees and volunteers, nor as a substitute for effective complaints procedures if any worker is acting in unsuitable ways.

Good procedures will not provide a guarantee against being found negligent if harm ever does come to a child or vulnerable adult, but being able to show that appropriate procedures were in place and were followed would be evidence that the organisation had complied with its duty of care [**21.6.1**].

Guidance on good practice and appropriate policies and procedures for work with children is available from Ofsted, the government's Every Child Matters website, the Safe Network, and London Voluntary Service Council [see end of chapter for contact details]. Organisations such as Voluntary Arts Network, Churches Child Protection Advisory Service and Child Protection in Sport Unit have guidance for specific sectors, which is usually more widely applicable than just that sector.

Guidance specifically on work with vulnerable adults is available from the Care Quality Commission and General Social Care Council. LVSC has some information specifically tailored to voluntary organisations.

41.2   PROTECTION OF YOUNG WORKERS

The child protection rules on criminal record and other checks apply not only to employees and volunteers who work with children and young people under the age of 18, but also to those who manage, train or directly supervise employees under the age of 16.

Other protections for young workers include restrictions on the types of work that young people of compulsory school age can be employed to do [**40.6.1**] and restrictions on the hours that anyone under the age of 18 can work [**31.5**]. Special risk assessments must be carried out before a person under 18 is employed [**40.3.2**]. These rules do not apply to volunteers, but organisations should consider whether it is appropriate to have young people carrying out work on an unpaid basis that would be unlawful if they were paid.

Employers' liability insurance [**23.4.1**] should be checked to ensure it covers all young employees, work experience placements and volunteers.

Further information is available from local authorities and the Children's Legal Centre [see end of chapter].

41.3   REGISTRATION FOR WORK WITH VULNERABLE GROUPS

Most organisations which work with children or vulnerable adults must register with and are regulated by Ofsted or the Care Quality Commission (or Care and Social Services Inspectorate Wales), and many staff must be registered with Ofsted or the General Social Care Council [see end of chapter for contact details].

41.3.1   Childminding and daycare

Childminding, full daycare, sessional care, crèches and out of school care are regulated by Ofsted if the care provider receives any type of payment, including payment in kind. **Childminding** is care for children on domestic premises provided by someone other than the child's parent, person with parental responsibility or foster carer. **Daycare** is on non-domestic premises.

Providers must be registered on the **early years register** if they provide childminding or daycare for the **early years foundation stage** (EYFS). Those providing childcare for children between EYFS and their eighth birthday are registered on **part A** of the **general childcare register** if they are obliged to register, or on **part B** if they are registering voluntarily.

Childcare Act 2006 ss.32-34,52,53; Childcare (General Childcare) Regulations 2008 [SI 2008/975]

The following are exempt from registering:

- nannies and other childminders who work only for one or two families in those families' own or each others' homes;
- childminders who care for a particular child for two hours or less per day;
- childminders (such as informal babysitters) who work only between 6pm and 2am;
- childcare in hotels, guesthouses and similar places if it is only between 6pm and 2am and the person does not care for more than two clients at a time;
- temporary childcare such as a creche or playscheme that is provided for two hours or less per day;
- temporary childcare that is provided for four hours or less per day, is offered on a day to day basis with no longer term commitment to clients, is available only for clients who intend to remain on the premises or in the immediate vicinity, is held on the premises for no more than 14 days in a year, and is notified in writing to Ofsted at least 14 days before the first day it is offered;
- some, but not all, activity-based provision (school study support or homework support, sport, performing arts, arts and crafts, and religious, cultural or language study) for children who are at least three years old;
- open access childcare (but not childminding) where a child who is older than the EYFS limit is allowed to leave the premises unaccompanied;
- home education arrangements;
- provision for children under three at maintained, special and independent schools, if the child will turn three before the end of their first term at the school. *Childcare (Exemption from Registration) Order 2008 [SI 2008/979]*

Anyone who is exempt from registering or provides care only for children aged eight to 18 can register voluntarily on **part B** of the general childcare register.
Childcare (Early Years & General Childcare Registers) (Common Provisions) Regulations 2008 [SI 2008/976] reg.3

41.3.2 Establishments and agencies for children

The **Care Standards Act 2000** covers virtually all work in children's homes, including schools where accommodation is provided for more than 295 days in a year, as well as work for residential family centres, agencies providing domiciliary care for children, fostering agencies, voluntary adoption agencies or adoption support agencies. *Care Standards Act 2000 ss.1-4, as amended*

These establishments and agencies must be registered with Ofsted, many staff must be registered with Ofsted or the General Social Care Council [see end of chapter], and for virtually all staff criminal record and other pre-employment checks must be carried out [**41.4.4**].

Foster parents are also covered under the Act.

41.3.3 Care work with vulnerable adults

For definitions of vulnerable adult, see **41.5**.

The **Care Standards Act 2000** covers work in independent hospitals, clinics and medical agencies; care homes which provide accommodation along with nursing and/or personal care; and work for a domiciliary care agency, nurses agency or adult placement scheme. These establishments and agencies must be registered with the **Care Quality Commission**, some staff must be registered with the **General Social Care Council**, and for virtually all staff, whether paid or voluntary, criminal records and other pre-employment checks must be carried out [**41.4.4**]. *Care Standards Act 2000 ss.1-4, as amended*

41.4 CRIMINAL RECORD AND OTHER CHECKS

Some employers must, and other employers may, obtain information about criminal records through the **Criminal Records Bureau** [**41.4.1**], and for certain types of work other checks are obligatory or advisable [**41.4.4**]. But checks are only one aspect of good practice, and are not a substitute for good recruitment, supervision and complaints procedures.

41.4.1 Criminal Records Bureau checks

Positions which are **exempt** (also called **excepted**) under the **Rehabilitation of Offenders Act 1974** [**41.8.2**] are eligible for **standard** or in most cases **enhanced disclosures** from the Criminal Records Bureau (CRB). As well as work with children and vulnerable adults, many other positions are exempt, such as security guards and solicitors. Information about CRB checks and exempt positions is available from the CRB [see end of chapter]. *Police Act 1997 ss.112-127 (pt.V)*

The fact that disclosures are available for a particular type of work does not necessarily mean that there is a statutory obligation to carry out a CRB check for that work. The obligation to carry out checks arises from other legislation, such as the **Care Standards Act 2000** [**41.4.4**] and legislation relating to the teaching profession.

Most organisations are not under a statutory obligation to carry out checks. But it is unlawful to offer paid or unpaid work in a **regulated activity** [**41.6**] to a person barred from working with children or vulnerable adults [**41.7.1**], and at the time of writing (mid 2009), the only way to find out if a person is barred is through a CRB check.

Similarly, the fact that CRB checks are available does not mean that all employers are entitled to carry them out. Checks are available only in relation to professions or positions specified in exception orders made under the Rehabilitation of Offenders Act 1974.

41.4.1.1 Standard and enhanced disclosures

A **standard disclosure**, also called a standard check, lists spent and unspent convictions [**41.8.1**], cautions, reprimands and warnings.

An **enhanced disclosure** is the highest level of disclosure. As well as the information included in a standard disclosure, it also includes other information from local police records, considered by the chief police officer to be relevant to the work to be carried out by the individual. *Police Act 1997 (Criminal Records) Regulations 2002 [SI 2002/233] reg.5A, inserted by PA 1997 (Criminal Records) (Amendment) Regulations 2006 [SI 2006/748]*

From 12 October 2009, all disclosures for regulated activities [**41.6**] with children and vulnerable adults are enhanced. If a person is barred from work with one or both of these groups [**41.7.1**], this is indicated, as applicable, in the disclosure.

41.4.1.2 Registered and umbrella bodies

Application for a disclosure is made to the Criminal Records Bureau jointly by the individual and a named representative of a body registered with the CRB. The only bodies which can register are those which involve professions or positions for which standard or enhanced checks are available, or **umbrella bodies**. Umbrella bodies can carry out checks on behalf of other organisations, but only in relation to professions and positions for which checks are available.

Registration with the CRB costs £300 (as at 1/7/09), plus £5 for each additional countersignatory (person able to sign applications on behalf of the registered body). Organisations can register only if they carry out at least 100 applications per year. To assist organisations which are not themselves registered, the CRB has a database of registered umbrella bodies.

41.4.1.3 Carrying out the check

An application for disclosure is filled in and signed by the individual, and signed by a countersignatory from the registered or umbrella body. The application must indicate the type of work for which the disclosure is being requested, as defined by the relevant Rehabilitation of Offenders Act exemption [**41.8.2**].

Applicants for relevant jobs or volunteer roles should be told that refusal to apply for a CRB check could mean that their application is not considered further or that they will be rejected for the work. A check should generally not be undertaken until all the other recruitment procedures have been carried out. If work is offered to the person, it should be clear that the offer is subject to a satisfactory CRB check.

The fee (as at 1/10/09) is £26 for a standard disclosure, £36 for an enhanced disclosure, and £6 for Adult First [**41.4.4**]. The fee is waived for checks on volunteers, defined as 'a person engaged in an activity which involves spending time, unpaid (except for travel and other approved out of pocket expenses), doing something which aims to benefit some third party other than or in addition to a close relative'.   *Police Act 1997 (Criminal Records) Regulations 2002 [SI 2002/233] reg.2*

For CRB purposes, students – even if they receive no monetary gain from the organisation – are considered paid employees rather than volunteers, if their volunteering may lead to a qualification. Information about specific situations is available from the CRB.

Umbrella bodies usually charge a fee to cover the cost of administration, even for checks on volunteers where the CRB fee itself is waived.

41.4.1.4   The disclosure

Any discrepancy between what the applicant says and what the criminal record reveals should be discussed with the applicant.

If the disclosure reveals a previous conviction, this does not necessarily mean the person is unsuitable. A person's suitability should be looked at as a whole, taking into account all available information including the nature of the offence and when it took place, whether the individual's circumstances have changed, and explanations offered by the individual. When individuals can register with the Independent Safeguarding Authority, starting on 26 July 2010, the ISA will assess the person's criminal record and determine whether they should be barred from working with children and vulnerable adults [**41.7.3**], but an organisation may feel that a person is not suitable even if he or she has not been barred. NACRO and the Apex Trust [see end chapter] have information on good practice in employing ex-offenders, and provide support for ex-offenders.

If an employer finds out about **spent** convictions these may be taken into account only if the position is exempt under the Rehabilitation of Offenders Act 1974 [**41.8.2**]. **Unspent** convictions can be taken into account for any work.

Information provided through a CRB disclosure or through the person revealing the information is sensitive personal data under the **Data Protection Act 1998** [**43.3.1**], and can be divulged only to someone who has a right to know it.

Where convictions are disclosed or the employer becomes aware of them, they are likely to have to be disclosed to insurers [**23.3.3**]. Failure to do so could invalidate some policies, although notification may not be required if the insurer is satisfied appropriate recruitment and safeguarding procedures are in place.

CRB checks only reveal information if a person has come to the attention of the police or has given cause for concern in other ways, so they should not be used as a substitute for good recruitment practice.

41.4.1.5   The CRB code of practice

Registered and umbrella bodies have access to particularly sensitive information, and must adhere to a CRB code of practice. This requires them to have written policies on the recruitment of ex-offenders; to store criminal record disclosures securely in lockable, non-portable storage containers such as filing cabinets; to dispose of disclosures once used; and to consider carefully the relevance of any convictions in assessing a person's suitability, so that those with convictions are not unfairly excluded from employment or volunteering opportunities.

A registered body can use the disclosure only for its own purposes, and cannot pass it on to anyone else. An umbrella body may pass the information only to the organisation on whose behalf it carried out the check, and must take reasonable steps to ensure that organisation complies with the code of practice. It is an offence to provide disclosure information to anyone who is not entitled to receive it.

If a relevant conviction has been disclosed, the organisation should draw up, with the individual, a risk assessment and risk management plan. This should, with the individual's consent, be kept in the individual's personnel file and the relevant details should be passed on to the person's supervisor or manager.

41.4.1.6 How long to keep disclosures

Most disclosures can be kept for only six months and must then be securely disposed of. When disposing of a disclosure the organisation should keep a record of the date and reference number of the disclosure (the top part of the form), to show that the check has been carried out.

If a regulatory body such as the Care Quality Commission or Ofsted requires original disclosure certificates – rather than records showing that the check has been carried out – the certificates may be kept only until the next inspection. The inspector who deals with the organisation can advise whether the actual certificates must be kept until the inspection.

41.4.1.7 Period of validity

There is no specified period of validity for a CRB check, as it indicates a person's criminal record on a specific date, and could change by the following day. Some organisations carry out a repeat check only if the person's work changes and there is a statutory requirement for a new check; other organisations require a repeat check after a specified period, even if the person's role has not changed. Each organisation needs to create a policy on how often it requires CRB checks, appropriate to its work and client groups.

For work with children and vulnerable adults, the Independent Safeguarding Authority will from 26 July 2010 provide ongoing monitoring and inform employers if a person who is registered with the ISA, in whom the employer has registered an interest, becomes barred [**41.7.3**]. But the ISA will notify the employer only about a barring decision. The employer can become aware of changes in the person's criminal record only by carrying out subsequent CRB checks.

41.4.1.8 CRB checks obtained for other purposes

The Criminal Records Bureau does not support **portability**, under which an organisation accepts a disclosure previously issued for a post in a different organisation. The CRB states that where a person changes jobs frequently, or needs a disclosure for two separate purposes at more or less the same time, an organisation may choose to use a previously issued disclosure – and it is free to do so – but the CRB does not support this. The organisation can obtain this disclosure only from the individual, not from the original organisation or umbrella body [**41.4.1.5**].

But from 12 October 2009 it is unlawful to hire an employee or take on a volunteer for regulated activity [**41.6.1**] if they are barred from working with children or vulnerable adults (as applicable), and until the ISA website becomes available [**41.7.5**], this information is only available through an up to date CRB check.

41.4.2 People not eligible for standard or enhanced checks

At the time of writing (mid 2009), only standard and enhanced disclosures are available through the Criminal Records Bureau. Where these are not available, the **Police Act 1997** provides a legislative framework for **basic disclosures**, available to all employers and covering only unspent convictions. But by mid 2009 this had still not been implemented, and it was not clear whether it would be.

In the absence of basic disclosures, an organisation may want to ask potential employees or volunteers about criminal convictions. Because the post is not eligible for standard or enhanced disclosures, the organisation will only be able to ask about **unspent** convictions [**41.8.3**].

Under the subject access provisions of the **Data Protection Act 1998** [**43.3.5**], individuals are entitled to obtain, via the local police, information about themselves held on the police national computer (PNC). Where a CRB check is not available, some organisations require individuals to obtain this information and provide it to the organisation – a process referred to as **enforced subject access**. Requiring a person to provide a police check which includes information about convictions or cautions is unlawful, because the record could reveal information that under the **Rehabilitation of Offenders** Act and the **Data Protection Act**, the organisation has no right to see. *Data Protection Act 1998 s.56*

624

41.4.3 Criminal records information from abroad

The Criminal Records Bureau has access only to information held by relevant authorities in the UK, so cannot provide information from foreign countries. The CRB has a webpage outlining how to obtain information from some countries. For other countries, information about how to obtain criminal records is available from the country's embassy or high commission (details from the Foreign and Commonwealth Office, www.fco.gov.uk, tel 020 7008 1500).

At the time of writing (mid 2009), work had begun on possible reciprocal arrangements with other countries. This is a complex area, because an offence in England may not be an offence in another country or *vice versa*, and some countries destroy records of offences committed by young adults.

41.4.4 Compulsory checks

There is a statutory obligation for employers to obtain certain information about all staff, paid and unpaid, in educational institutions, and in care homes, children's homes, health care organisations, residential family centres, voluntary adoption agencies, domiciliary care agencies and nurse agency staff. The rules are set out in regulations for each type of work, and are different for different types of provider and for different roles within each provider. Details are available from the Care Quality Commission, Ofsted and the General Social Care Council [see end of chapter]. Similar rules apply for other types of work with children.

For all of the above, the checks include not only criminal record checks, but also proof of identity, qualifications and previous employment, and being satisfied that the person is fit for the position they hold or are applying for. For new staff, checks must be carried out before the person starts work. In exceptional cases, a care worker may be allowed to start work in a care home, for a domiciliary care agency or as an adult placement carer on the basis of an **Adult First** check (known as POVAFirst until 12 October 2009).

For some posts (but not all), the organisation must obtain a birth certificate and current passport (if any), and a full employment history, with satisfactory written explanations of any gaps and verification (so far as reasonably practicable) of why previous employment involving work with children or vulnerable adults ended.

Where a person is employed by someone else, for example an agency worker or secondee , the receiving organisation must be satisfied that the employing organisation has obtained all relevant information. Agencies have a statutory duty not only to carry out criminal record checks on temps who work with children and vulnerable adults, but also to obtain copies of relevant qualifications and two references, and take all reasonable steps to confirm that an individual is not unsuitable for the work. If the agency discovers any new adverse information they must withdraw the temporary worker or, if the worker has been supplied on a permanent basis, inform the employer.

At the time of writing (mid 2009), it was expected that a new section 113CD in the **Police Act 1997** would allow employers to request that a criminal record check also include information about a person's immigration status and right to work in the UK [**29.5.1**].

41.5 DEFINITIONS OF CHILDREN AND VULNERABLE ADULTS

Under most legislation a **child** is defined as a person under the age of 18, although for some specific purposes it is defined as a person under the age of 16, or under school leaving age [**40.6.1**]. In relation to childminding and some other childcare services, **early years** provision ends on 31 August following a child's fifth birthday, and **later years** provision is from then until the child's eighth birthday. For some purposes the upper limit for later years provision is the child's 18th birthday. *Childcare (Early Years & General Childcare Registers) (Common Provisions)*
Regulations 2008 [SI 2008/976] reg.3

For the purposes of a standard Criminal Records Bureau check [**41.4.1**] a vulnerable adult is a person aged 18 or over who has a substantial learning or physical disability; a physical or mental illness or mental disorder, whether chronic or not, including an addiction to alcohol or drugs; or a significant reduction in physical or mental capacity.   *Rehabilitation of Offenders Act 1974 (Exceptions) Order 1975 [SI 1975/1023] sch.1 pt.4, amended by ROA 1974 (Exceptions) (Amendment) Order 2002 [SI 2002/441] reg.5(4)(f)*

For the purposes of an enhanced CRB check, the definition of vulnerable adult is a person who is 18 or over and:

* is dependent on others or needs assistance to perform basic physical functions, or is severely impaired in communicating with others, or is impaired in their ability to protect themselves from assault, abuse or neglect; and

* the dependency or impairment arises from a learning or physical disability, a physical or mental illness (whether chronic or not, and including an addiction to alcohol or drugs), or a reduction in physical or mental capacity; and

* the person is receiving accommodation and nursing or personal care in a nursing home; personal care or support to live independently in their own home; services provided by an independent hospital, clinic or medical agency or an NHS body; social care services, or any services in an establishment catering for a person with learning difficulties.   *Police Act 1997 (Criminal Records) Regulations 2002 [SI 2002/233] reg.5B, inserted by Police Act 1997 (Criminal Records) (Amendment) Regulations 2006 [SI 2006/748]*

The definitions for the purposes of criminal record checks, especially in relation to enhanced checks, may be amended from 12 October 2009 to take account of the definition of vulnerable adult under the **Safeguarding Vulnerable Groups Act 2006**. Under this Act, a vulnerable adult is a person aged 18 or over who:

* is in residential accommodation which includes nursing or other care;

* is in residential accommodation and is or has been a pupil at a residential special school;

* is in sheltered housing;

* receives domiciliary care because of his or her age, health or disability;

* receives any form of health care treatment, therapy or palliative care;

* receives welfare services (support, assistance, advice or counselling), including where its purpose is to develop or sustain the person's capacity to live independently; or

* receives any service or participates in any activity provided specifically for individuals who have any form of disability, have particular needs because of their age, or have a physical or mental condition of a type defined in regulations.   *Safeguarding Vulnerable Groups Act 2006 s.59; Safeguarding Vulnerable Groups Act 2006 (Miscellaneous Provisions) Regulations 2009 [SI 2009/1548] reg.2*

This list is not exhaustive, and s.59 also defines other people as vulnerable.

In *No Secrets: Guidance on developing and implementing multi-agency policies and procedures to protect vulnerable adults from abuse*, published in 2000, the Department of Health and Home Office defined a vulnerable adult as a person aged 18 or over 'who is or may be in need of community care services by reason of mental or other disability, age or illness; and who is or may be unable to take care of him or herself, or unable to protect him or herself against significant harm or exploitation'. At the time of writing (mid 2009) this guidance was being updated.

41.6   REGULATED AND CONTROLLED ACTIVITIES

From 12 October 2009, most work with children and vulnerable adults is **regulated** or **controlled**. For definitions of children and vulnerable adults, see **41.5**.

It is unlawful for a person who is **barred** from working with children or vulnerable adults [**41.7.1**] to work with them in a **regulated activity**, or for such work, whether paid or voluntary, to be knowingly offered to a person who is barred. Information about whether a person is barred is available via enhanced criminal record checks [**41.4.1.1**], and from November 2010 information about whether a person is registered with the Independent Safeguarding Authority will be available online to employers without having to carry out a CRB check [**41.7.5**].   *Safeguarding Vulnerable Groups Act 2006 ss.5-17, sch.4-6*

From 26 July 2010, individuals engaged in regulated activities will start being registered by the **Independent Safeguarding Authority** and will be **subject to monitoring** [**41.7.3**]. From November 2010 it will be unlawful for an organisation not to check the person's status before offering paid or voluntary work in a regulated activity.

A **controlled activity** [**41.6.2**] is one which is not regulated, but for which regulations may be made setting restrictions on who is allowed to do the work, provided they are appropriately supervised.

An activity is not regulated or controlled if it takes place within a family relationship, or within a friendship if there is no 'commercial consideration'. Regulations may (or may not) define what is meant by commercial consideration in this context. *Safeguarding Vulnerable Groups Act 2006 s.58*

The provisions as set out here apply only in England. Similar provisions apply in Wales under the **Safeguarding Vulnerable Groups Act 2006**, and in Scotland and Northern Ireland under comparable legislation.

41.6.1 Regulated activities

Regulated activities are those which involve contact with children or vulnerable adults frequently, intensively and/or overnight. A person who is barred from working with children or vulnerable adults cannot work or be offered work in a regulated activity. The Independent Safeguarding Authority's registration of individuals engaged in regulated activity begins on 26 July 2010 [**41.7.3**].

41.6.1.1 Regulated activities without a period condition

Regardless of the amount of time spent on them, the following are always regulated activities with children:

- early years childminding provided by a person who is required to be registered under the **Childcare Act 2006**, or later years childminding provided by a person who is required to be registered or is registered voluntarily [**41.3.1**];
- fostering, unless done without pay or directly arranged by the child's family;
- any work in an establishment or agency which provides treatment or therapy for children and is registered under the **Care Standards Act 2000**;
- being a trustee of a children's or vulnerable adults' charity [**41.6.1.4**], member of the governing body of an educational institution, or holding certain local authority and other positions. *Safeguarding Vulnerable Groups Act 2006 s.53, sch.4 para.1,4*

41.6.1.2 Regulated activities with a period condition

The following are regulated activities with children and/or vulnerable adults, if the same person, whether paid or unpaid, carries them out on three or more days in a 30-day period (the **period condition**):

- teaching, training, instruction, care or supervision of children or vulnerable adults, but not (in the case of children) if this is incidental to such activities being provided to people who are not children;
- advice or guidance provided wholly or mainly to children and relating to their physical, emotional or educational wellbeing;
- assistance, advice or guidance provided wholly or mainly for vulnerable adults;
- treatment or therapy provided for a child or vulnerable adult (but treatment is not regulated if the provision of treatment if not one of the main purposes of the activity);
- moderating internet chatrooms or similar electronic interactive communications likely to be used wholly or mainly by children or vulnerable adults;
- driving a vehicle being used solely for conveying children or vulnerable adults, and supervising or caring for the passengers (but it is not a regulated activity in all situations);
- any work in establishments which are mainly or exclusively for children, such as schools and children's hospitals or homes, and in childcare or day premises registered under the **Childcare Act 2006** or the **Children Act 1989**, if the person doing the work has the opportunity for contact with children;

- any work in care homes which are mainly or exclusively for vulnerable adults and are registered under the **Care Standards Act 2000**, if the person doing the work has the opportunity for contact with vulnerable adults;

- anything else defined in regulations, done on behalf of a vulnerable adult.

Safeguarding Vulnerable Groups Act 2006 sch.4 para.1(2),(14),2,3,7,10;
SVGA 2006 (Miscellaneous Provisions) Regulations 2009 [SI 2009/1548];
SVGA 2006 (Miscellaneous Provisions Order 2009 [SI 2009/1797] para.3(1),4;

Day to day management or supervision of a person carrying out the above activities is regulated.

Teaching, training, instruction, care, supervision, advice, guidance, treatment and therapy are not regulated if they are provided to a person aged 16 or 17 in the course of their employment or volunteering. *SVGA 2006 sch.4 para.2(2),(3)*

41.6.1.3 Night-time activities

Activities under the first four bullet points above (teaching, instruction, care and supervision; advice or guidance for children; assistance, advice or guidance for vulnerable adults; and treatment or therapy) are regulated if a person carries them out between 2 and 6am and has the opportunity for face to face contact with a child or vulnerable adult, even if this is not on three or more days in a 30-day period. *Safeguarding Vulnerable Groups Act 2006 sch.4 para.10*

41.6.1.4 Charity trustees

From 12 October 2009, being a trustee of a **children's** or **vulnerable adults' charity** is a regulated activity, and the rules on ISA registration and being barred apply [**41.6**]. A children's or vulnerable adults' charity is one whose workers are normally engaged in regulated activity relating to children or vulnerable adults. But if the work is incidental to the purposes for which the charity is set up, it is not a children's or vulnerable adults' charity and being a trustee is not a regulated activity. *Safeguarding Vulnerable Groups Act 2006 sch.4 para.4(4),(5)*

Trustees of children's and vulnerable adults' charities could not only be in breach of the **Safeguarding Children Act 2006** if they fail to carry out checks on new trustees, but also in breach of their duty of care to the charity and its beneficiaries [**15.6.7, 22.6.1**].

When a charity that will work with children or vulnerable adults seeks Charity Commission registration, the trustees must declare that they are not disqualified from acting as a trustee, and must indicate whether they are entitled or required to apply for a CRB disclosure [**41.4.1**] and if so whether this has been carried out. Details are available from the Charity Commission [see end of chapter].

The Charity Commission also asks charities working with children or vulnerable adults to confirm, when setting up the charity and in their annual returns, that they have a safeguarding policy in place.

41.6.2 Controlled activities

Controlled activities are activities – including ancillary work such as cleaning and administration – which are not regulated [**41.6.1**], are carried out by the same person on at least three days in any 30-day period, and are:

- in health care, treatment or therapy or in further education institutions, and provide opportunity for contact with children or access to their health records;

- educational or social services functions carried out for or on behalf of a local authority, and providing access to children's health, education or social services records;

- in health or social care, and involve access to vulnerable adults or their health or social care records. *Safeguarding Vulnerable Groups Act 2006 ss.21,22*

Regulations will set out whether some people are not permitted to work in a controlled activity, or may do so only if they are properly supervised. *SVGA 2006 s.23*

At the time of writing (mid 2009), there was no indication of when the provisions on controlled activities would be implemented. The Independent Safeguarding

Authority did not expect to start registering people in controlled activities until 2014 [**41.7.3**], but the restrictions could be in place before then.

41.7 VETTING AND BARRING

From 12 October 2009, virtually all legislation relating to suitability for work with children or vulnerable adults is consolidated in a **vetting and barring** scheme run by the **Independent Safeguarding Authority** (ISA), under provisions in the **Safeguarding Vulnerable Groups Act 2006** and related regulations. At the time of writing (mid 2009) most of these regulations were not yet available. Up to date information is available from the ISA and the Criminal Records Bureau [see end of chapter].

The ISA covers England and Wales, with similar provision in Scotland and Northern Ireland.

Under the original legislation, the organisation was going to be called the **Independent Barring Board**.

41.7.1 The children's and adults' barred lists

From 12 October 2009, the **children's barred list** integrates information from and replaces the **Protection of Children Act (POCA) list** of people considered unsuitable to work with children; **list 99**, of people banned from working in schools and further education institutions or restricted from certain types of work, or barred from working in education on medical grounds and for certain other reasons; and **disqualification** orders issued by the courts, banning a person from working with children. *Safeguarding Vulnerable Groups Act 2006 s.2*

The **adults' barred list** replaces the **Protection of Vulnerable Adults (POVA) list**, of people considered unsuitable to work with vulnerable adults.

Based on information in the old lists, the Independent Safeguarding Authority has made decisions about who should be barred from working with children and/or vulnerable adults, and has aligned the two lists.

The ISA's primary role is to make ongoing barring decisions on the basis of information provided by the Criminal Records Bureau, as well as on the basis of referrals from employers, regulatory bodies and some other bodies [**41.7.2**].

In some situations the ISA's decision is discretionary, but regulations prescribe which offences must result in automatic barring from working with children or vulnerable adults and how long a person who is barred has to wait before being able to ask for the bar to be removed. A person placed on a barred list will be able to make a representation to the ISA and the **care standards tribunal**, part of the first-tier tribunal [**64.7**], unless they have committed a serious offence.
Safeguarding Vulnerable Groups Act 2006 sch.3;
SVGA 2006 (Barring Procedure) Regulations 2008 [SI 2008/474];
SVGA 2006 (Prescribed Criteria & Miscellaneous Provisions) Regulations 2009 [SI 2009/37]

It is an offence for a person on the children's or adults' barred list to seek or carry out work with children or vulnerable adults (as applicable) in a **regulated activity** [**41.6.1**]. It is also an offence for or an employer knowingly to take on a person who is barred, for work with the relevant group. *SVGA 2006 ss.7,9*

The barred lists are accessed via enhanced criminal record checks, and from November 2010 information about whether a person is registered with the ISA will be available free of charge on the ISA website. At that time it will become unlawful to offer anyone work, paid or unpaid, in a regulated [**41.6.1**] activity without first checking the list.

41.7.2 Referral to the ISA

Organisations which provide regulated activities [**41.6**] have a statutory duty to refer to the Independent Safeguarding Authority anyone, whether paid or unpaid, they have dismissed or removed from work with children or vulnerable adults because the person has harmed, or might harm, a child or vulnerable adult. Resignation of a person in circumstances where they could have been dismissed or removed for this reason must also be reported. It is an offence to fail to provide information to the ISA without a reasonable excuse.

Safeguarding Vulnerable Groups Act 2006 ss.35-37

Other organisations which work with children or vulnerable adults but whose activities are not regulated may refer information to the ISA, but are not obliged to. Private employers (such as parents) and members of the public may also refer information to the ISA, but must do so through a statutory agency such as social services or the police.

The ISA will assess this information, along with information from the Criminal Records Bureau, and decide whether the referred person should be barred from working with children and/or vulnerable adults.

41.7.3 Vetting, registration and monitoring

From November 2010 no one will be able to start work or change jobs in a regulated activity [**41.6.1**], whether on a paid or unpaid basis, unless they are **subject to monitoring** by being registered with the Independent Safeguarding Agency. An exception for under-16s allows young people to undertake work experience without having to register with the ISA.   *Safeguarding Vulnerable Groups Act 2006 s.8*

Prior to that, from 26 July 2010, people starting work or changing jobs in a regulated activity will be able to register voluntarily.

From November 2010, people already working in regulated activities will have to apply for ISA registration if they want to start a new regulated activity, or are required to be registered as part of the phased-in process for existing workers. It is expected that all existing workers in regulated activities – starting with those who have never been CRB checked, or whose last CRB check was the longest time ago – will be registered by July 2014.   *Safeguarding Vulnerable Groups Act 2006 s.10(6)*

Registration for work in a controlled activity [**41.6.2**] is not expected to become compulsory until 2014.   *Safeguarding Vulnerable Groups Act 2006 s.23*

41.7.3.1 Applying for registration

The application for ISA registration is through the Criminal Records Bureau, and must be made by the individual through a CRB registered or umbrella body [**41.4.1.2**]. A one-off application fee (£64 as from 26/7/10, free for volunteers) is made up of £36 for an enhanced CRB disclosure [**41.4.1.1**], and £28 for the ISA application. The individual is responsible for payment, but an organisation can pay on behalf of the individual or can reimburse the individual.

An individual's registration is permanent, so there is no need to re-apply when changing jobs. If a volunteer who has received free registration subsequently changes to a paid job, the fee becomes payable.

41.7.3.2 Vetting

When a person applies to the CRB for ISA registration, the CRB provides the ISA with the person's criminal record, and the ISA uses this and other information to determine whether the person should be **registered** or **barred**.

Registration with the ISA signifies that the person is suitable to work with, as applicable, children or vulnerable adults – or perhaps more accurately, that the ISA has found no cause to bar the person from such work.

A **registered person** is subject to continuous monitoring by the ISA, through information provided by the CRB, other employers, social services and regulatory bodies. When new information becomes available that indicates a registered person might no longer be suitable to work with children or vulnerable adults, the ISA reviews its original decision and decides whether to bar the person.

41.7.4 Employer's interest in an individual

From 26 July 2010 an employer or organisation which uses volunteers can **subscribe** to the ISA, and register an interest in named employees and volunteers. The employer is notified if the ISA subsequently decides to bar the individual.

41.7.5   Online checking and CRB checks

From November 2010, organisations can check online whether an applicant for a job or volunteer role is registered with the ISA. Domestic employers can also check on nannies, private tutors, care workers etc.

The online check will indicate only whether the person is registered with the ISA – in other words, that they have been vetted and have not been barred. Non-registration may indicate either that the person has been barred, or that he or she has not applied for registration. Only an enhanced criminal record check [**41.4.1.1**] will indicate whether the person has been barred, and only an enhanced check combined with an application for ISA registration will enable a person who has not previously applied for registration to be vetted.

An online check is not, in itself, adequate where there is a statutory obligation for the organisation to carry out a criminal record check.

From November 2010 it is an offence, with a fine of up to £5,000, for an employer to employ someone, whether paid or unpaid, to work in a regulated activity with children or vulnerable adults who is not registered with the ISA, or to fail to check the system. *Safeguarding Vulnerable Groups Act 2006 ss.9-12*

41.8   REHABILITATION OF OFFENDERS

The **Rehabilitation of Offenders Act 1974** is a form of equal opportunities legislation, intended to reduce discrimination against ex-offenders who have not re-offended after completing their sentence. The Act:

- for most jobs, gives ex-offenders the right not to reveal convictions, even if asked, if these have become **spent** [**41.8.1**] after a rehabilitation period;

- for most jobs, makes it unlawful for an employer to dismiss an employee or refuse to employ a person because he or she has a spent conviction (but does not make it unlawful to dismiss or refuse to employ because of an **unspent** conviction);

- defines some jobs and occupations as **exempt** [**41.8.2**], where if asked the person must declare both spent and unspent convictions, and where the employer can refuse to employ the person or can dismiss him or her because of the conviction. *Rehabilitation of Offenders Act 1974 s.4*

Where convictions must be disclosed, this applies only if the person is asked. There is no obligation to reveal any information if not asked. However it is likely to be a negative factor if a person does not reveal a conviction which later shows up on a Criminal Records Bureau disclosure [**41.8.4**].

Advice about the Rehabilitation of Offenders Act, spent and unspent convictions, and exemption from not having to disclose spent convictions is available from the Criminal Records Bureau, Apex Trust, CIPD and NACRO [see end of chapter].

41.8.1   Rehabilitation periods

The heavier the sentence, the longer it takes for a conviction to be spent. **Rehabilitation periods** range from six months to 10 years, starting from the date of conviction. Suspended sentences are treated as if they were served, and sentences under the Armed Forces Acts are treated as above. The rehabilitation periods are halved if the offender was under 18 when convicted. *Rehabilitation of Offenders Act 1974 s.5, as amended*

The conviction does not become spent if the person is convicted of another offence during the rehabilitation period.

A sentence of more than 30 months' imprisonment or detention in a young offender institution can never become spent. An **unspent** conviction is one which is still within the rehabilitation period, or will never become spent.

The rehabilitation periods are treated as being the same for convictions abroad, if the offence would also be an offence in the UK.

41.8.2   Exemptions

There are a number of **exceptions** to a person's right not to reveal a spent conviction. These include the following, whether paid or voluntary:

- all workers carrying out a **regulated** or **controlled activity** with children or vulnerable adults [**41.6**];
- all workers in any establishment which has to be registered under the **Care Standards Act 2000** [**41.3.2**, **41.3.3**];
- barristers, solicitors, and chartered or certified accountants;
- posts involving access to persons receiving health services;
- medical practitioners and others in medical professions;
- signatories to applications for criminal records disclosures;
- applicants for licences under the **Licensing Act 2003** [**47.2**] and **Gambling Act 2005** [**49.6**, **49.8**].

Rehabilitation of Offenders Act 1974 (Exceptions) Order 1975 [SI 1975/1023] & subsequent orders

This list is not exhaustive. Full information is available from the Criminal Records Bureau [see end of chapter].

Applicants for, or workers already in, posts covered by the exemptions must, if asked, reveal all convictions, even those which are spent. The application form for jobs or volunteer roles covered by the exemptions should ask whether the applicant has any convictions, should include the statement, 'This post is exempt under the Rehabilitation of Offenders Act 1974 and you are required to reveal all convictions, even those which are spent, as well as cautions, reprimands and final warnings', and should make clear that the organisation will undertake a criminal records check [**41.4.1.1**]. A question requiring all convictions to be disclosed is an **exempted question**. It is good practice to indicate that a conviction does not necessarily disbar an applicant from consideration for the post.

Unless the person is barred from working with children or vulnerable adults [**41.7.1**] it is not unlawful to take on a person with a conviction for an exempt post, but it would be up to the employer to take reasonable steps to supervise the person's work. An organisation could be found to be negligent if the worker is involved in an offence while working for the organisation, and the organisation had not asked about convictions or done a criminal record check, or knew about a relevant conviction but had not taken reasonable steps to supervise the worker.

If a person is barred from working with children or vulnerable adults, it is an offence for them to apply for, take or continue working in such a position, and an offence for the organisation knowingly to offer such a position to them or allow them to continue working in it.

41.8.3   Work that is not exempt

At the time of writing (mid 2009), Criminal Records Bureau checks are available only for posts which are exempt [**41.8.2**]. For some other posts, such as those involving unsupervised access to money or expensive equipment or going into people's homes where there are no children or vulnerable adults, it may be appropriate to ask whether the applicant has any convictions, or any relevant convictions. The question should be followed by a statement that 'you are not required to reveal any convictions which are spent under the Rehabilitation of Offenders Act 1974'. As with exempt posts, it is good practice to indicate that a conviction does not necessarily disbar an applicant from consideration.

As with exempt posts, an employer could be considered negligent if the job involves risk to people or property, and information about relevant unspent convictions was not sought from the employee, or was not taken into account when offering paid or unpaid work.

When and if basic level CRB checks [**41.4.2**] become available, organisations will be able to carry out these checks for all employees and volunteers, even where the work is not exempt.

It is unlawful to ask or require individuals to obtain their records from the police and provide them to the organisation [**41.4.2**].

41.8.4   Undisclosed convictions

Unless a person is barred from working with children or vulnerable adults [**41.7.1**] or is specifically asked about convictions, he or she is under no obligation to disclose them. If an employer subsequently finds out about an unspent conviction (or a spent conviction, for an exempt post), disciplinary action or dismissal may – or may not – be justified. Legal advice should be sought before dismissing an employee, to ensure the dismissal is not unfair.

If the employee was asked during recruitment about convictions but failed to disclose an unspent conviction (or a spent conviction, for an exempt post), this could constitute **breach of contract**. The employer could be justified in dismissing the employee, but there is no obligation on the employer to do so unless the work involves access to children or vulnerable adults and the person has been barred from working with them. In other situations, if the employee has built up a good employment record with the employer, dismissal may not be necessary. The same basic principles apply to volunteers, except that volunteers are generally not working under a contract [**39.4**], so breach of contract is not an issue.

Unless the post is exempt, spent convictions are irrelevant, and if the organisation finds out about these they must not be taken into account.

Resources: SAFEGUARDING CHILDREN AND VULNERABLE ADULTS

Work with children. Local authority children's services.

Office for Standards in Education, Children's Services & Skills (Ofsted): www.ofsted.gov.uk, 08456 404040, enquiries@ofsted.gov.uk.

Child Protection in Sport Unit: www.thecpsu.org.uk, 0116 234 7278, cpsu@nspcc.org.uk.

Children's Legal Centre: www.childrenslegalcentre.com, 0845 120 2948, clc@essex.ac.uk.

Churches Child Protection Advisory Service: www.ccpas.co.uk, 0845 120 45 50, info@ccpas.co.uk.

Department for Children, Schools and Families: www.dcsf.gov.uk, 0870 000 2288, info@dcsf.gsi.gov.uk.

Every Child Matters: www.everychildmatters.gov.uk, 0870 000 2288, info@dcsf.gsi.gov.uk.

Fair Play for Children: www.fairplayforchildren.org, 0845 330 7635, fairplay@arunet.co.uk.

NSPCC: www.nspcc.org.uk, 0800 800 5000, help@nspcc.org.uk.

NSPCC safe communities toolkit. See NSPCC above.

Safe Network: www.safenetwork.org.uk, 0118 234 7217, info@safenetwork.org.uk.

Voluntary Arts Network: www.voluntaryarts.org, 029 20 395395, info@voluntaryarts.org.

Work with vulnerable adults. Local authority adult services.

Care Quality Commission: www.cqc.org.uk, 03000 616161, enquiries@cqc.org.uk.

Care and Social Services Inspectorate Wales: www.cssiw.org.uk, 01443 848450, cssiw@wales.gsi.gov.uk.

General Social Care Council: www.gscc.org.uk, 020 7397 5100, info@gscc.org.uk.

Action on Elder Abuse: www.elderabuse.org.uk, 0808 808 8141, info@elderabuse.org.uk.

Model policies or guidance specifically for voluntary organisations. Action in Rural Sussex: www.ruralsussex.org.uk, 01273 473422, info@ruralsussex.org.uk.

Charity Commission: www.charitycommission.gov.uk, 0845 300 0218, email via website.

PEACe (Personnel Employment Advice and Conciliation Service): www.lvsc.org.uk, 020 7700 8147, peace@lvsc.org.uk.

Criminal record & ISA checks. Criminal Records Bureau: www.crb.gov.uk, 0870 90 90 811, email via website.

Independent Safeguarding Authority: www.isa-gov.org.uk, 0300 123 1111, scheme.info@homeoffice.gsi.gov.uk.

Apex Trust: www.apextrust.com, 020 7638 5931, jobcheck@apextrust.com.

Chartered Institute of Personnel and Development: www.cipd.co.uk, 020 8612 6200, email via website.

NACRO: www.nacro.org.uk, 020 7840 7200.

Statute law. www.opsi.gov.uk and www.statutelaw.gov.uk.

Much but not all case law. www.bailii.org.

Updates cross-referenced to this book. www.rclh.co.uk.

Chapter 42

EQUAL OPPORTUNITIES: GOODS, SERVICES AND FACILITIES

For sources of further information see end of chapter 28.

42.1   THE LAW AND GOOD PRACTICE

At the time of writing (mid 2009), equal opportunities law covers discrimination in the provision of services on grounds of race, sex, religion or other belief, sexual orientation and disability. It does not cover age, but this was expected to be included in the **Equality Act [28.1.12]** during 2010.

The Equality Act will also replace all the different Acts and regulations covering equal opportunities in employment and service delivery. The process of consolidation and simplification should remove anomalies between the different equality strands, but may also remove or change some of the exceptions that have previously been allowed. Up to date advice is essential, especially when deciding to use an exception which allows discrimination against or in favour of a group.

When considering equal opportunities, it is important to distinguish between:

- **statutory requirements**, which must be complied with;
- **codes of practice** and guidance issued by the Equality and Human Rights Commission, where failure to comply may be taken into account if a discrimination case is brought against the organisation;
- requirements imposed by the organisation's **governing document**, which must be complied with unless legislation overrides them;
- requirements imposed by the organisation's **equal opportunities policy** or other policies, which can be changed by the governing body;
- requirements imposed by **third parties** such as funders or donors.

An organisation cannot be required, either by its governing document or policies or by third parties, to do anything which is unlawful.

Most equal opportunities legislation concentrates on employment [**chapter 28**]. This chapter looks at equal opportunities in relation to the goods, services, activities, education or training, facilities, premises and other benefits provided by the organisation. For ease of reference, the term **services** is used throughout this chapter to refer to anything provided by the organisation to its members, beneficiaries or members of the public.

Information about equal opportunities in service delivery is available from the Equality and Human Rights Commission [see end of **chapter 28**].

42.1.1 Forms of discrimination

The concepts of **direct** and **indirect discrimination**, **victimisation** and **harassment** generally apply to service delivery in the same way as to employment [**28.1.3-28.1.6**].

The rules on discriminatory advertising [**28.1.9**] apply in the same way as for employment. Where the law allows services to be provided only to specific groups, it is not unlawful to publicise them as being available only to those groups.

An organisation has **vicarious liability** [**28.1.8**] for discriminatory acts by employees in the course of their employment and for acts by agents acting on behalf of the organisation, and could also be liable for discriminatory acts by volunteers.

42.1.2 Discriminatory practices

Equal opportunities legislation is nearly always enforced by an individual bringing a claim against the service provider who has discriminated against them. But there is also provision for the Equality and Human Rights Commission to take action where no one has been a victim of a discriminatory practice, but a service provider adopts or maintains a practice that would be likely to result in unlawful discrimination. An example would be a community centre which hires out its premises for parties having a policy of not allowing Roma (Gypsies/Travellers) to book the premises – which is unlawful even if no Roma try to make a booking.

Race Relations Act 1976 s.28; Sex Discrimination Act 1975 s.29; Equality Act 2006 s.53 [in relation to religion/belief]; Equality Act (Sexual Orientation) Regulations 2007 [SI 2007/1263] reg.9

42.1.3 Equal opportunities and human rights

The **European convention on human rights**, implemented by the **Human Rights Act 1998**, includes a number of rights relevant to service delivery, including the right to private and family life (art.8), freedom of thought, conscience and religion (art.9), freedom of expression (art.10), and freedom of assembly (art.11) [**64.3.1**]. Article 14 prohibits these or any other Convention rights from being interfered with by discrimination. The definition of discrimination is extremely broad, and includes religion, property, birth or other status.

The Convention right not be discriminated against exists only in relation to other Convention rights. A claim for breach can be brought only against a public authority or body carrying out a public function [**64.3.2**]. This generally does not include voluntary sector organisations, but there are some exceptions.

42.2 EQUALITY DUTIES

Public authorities and other bodies which carry out public functions have statutory **equality duties** requiring them to take an active approach to eliminating certain forms of discrimination and promoting equality of opportunity. The equality duties apply not only to service delivery but also to employment [**chapter 28**] and everything the public authority does. They include a general duty ('to take an active approach...') as well as a number of specific duties.

The bodies to which the duties apply are set out in legislation, and include a small number of voluntary organisations whose work is defined in part by statute.

Where services are contracted out to a provider which is not itself a public body, the contractor – including voluntary organisations – must comply with the general equality duties. The specific equality duties do not apply to contractors, but compliance with relevant aspects of the duties, such as provision of monitoring data, is often made a condition of contracts or partnership arrangements with, or grant aid from, public authorities.

Information about the equality duties is available from the Equality and Human Rights Commission [see end of **chapter 28**].

42.2.1 Race equality duty

The **race equality duty** requires due regard for the need to eliminate unlawful discrimination and promote equality of opportunity and good race relations. It applies to bodies listed in the **Race Relations (Amendment) Act 2000** schedule 1A and subsequent **Race Relations Act 1976 (General Statutory Duties) Orders**. *Race Relations Act 1976 s.71, replaced by Race Relations (Amendment) Act 2000 s.2*

42.2.2 Gender equality duty

The **gender quality duty** applies to bodies listed in the **Sex Discrimination Act 1975 (Public Authorities) (Statutory Duties) Order 2006** *[SI 2006/2930]*. These bodies have a duty to show due regard for the need to eliminate unlawful discrimination and harassment on the basis of sex, and to promote equality of opportunity between men and women. *Sex Discrimination Act 1975 s.76A, inserted by Equality Act 2006 s.84*

42.2.3 Disability equality duty

Bodies defined as public authorities in the **Disability Discrimination Act 2005** schedule 1 and subsequent **Disability Discrimination (Public Authorities) (Statutory Duties) (Amendment) Regulations** must have regard to the need to eliminate unlawful discrimination, promote equality of opportunity between disabled people and other people, take account of disabilities even where this involves treating disabled people more favourably than other people [see **28.7** for why this is allowed], promote positive attitudes towards disabled people, and encourage participation by disabled people in public life. *Disability Discrimination Act 1995 s.49A, inserted by DDA 2005 s.3; Disability Discrimination (Public Authorities) (Statutory Duties) Regulations 2005 [SI 2005/2966]*

42.2.4 Other equality strands

At the time of writing (mid 2009), the **Equality Act [28.1.12]** was expected to create a single equality duty, extending the equality duties to age, sexual orientation, gender reassignment, and religion and belief. The basic principles will be the same as for race and sex.

42.3 RACIAL GROUP

Discrimination on the basis of **racial group** (race, colour, ethnic origin, national origin, nationality or citizenship) is generally unlawful. This applies regardless of whether the services are free or a charge is made. *Race Relations Act 1976 s.20,21*

Direct and **indirect discrimination** and **victimisation [28.1.3-28.1.5]** in provision of services is unlawful. **Harassment [28.1.6]** is unlawful in relation to race, ethnic origin and national origin. Harassment in relation to colour or nationality may be unlawful direct discrimination. *Race Relations Act 1976 ss.1,2; s.3A, inserted by Race Relations Act 1976 (Amendment) Regulations 2003 [2003/1626] reg.5*

42.3.1 Exceptions: membership

Associations and clubs (organisations with members) generally may not discriminate on the basis of racial group in choosing members or in providing services to their members. However, there are some exceptions.

42.3.1.1 Small clubs and associations

Clubs and associations with fewer than 25 members are allowed to use racial group as a factor in selecting members. This exception does not apply to trade unions [**42.3.1.3**] and professional organisations. *Race Relations Act 1976 s.25*

42.3.1.2 Cultural associations

Clubs and associations, regardless of size, are allowed to limit their membership and services to people of a specific racial group (not defined by reference to colour) if the main object of the organisation is to enable the benefits of membership to be enjoyed by people of that group.   *Race Relations Act 1976 s.26*

Other clubs and associations may not discriminate on the basis of racial group in providing services unless they are charities set up to provide services for that group, or can show that the group has a special need for the service [**42.3.2**].

42.3.1.3   Trade unions and professional associations

Trade unions and other organisations of workers, organisations of employees, or organisations whose members carry on a particular profession or trade for the purpose of which the organisation exists, may not discriminate on the basis of racial group in access to membership or the benefits of membership.   *RRA 1976 s.11*

Such organisations are, however, allowed to take **positive action [28.1.7]** to ensure that people from all racial groups are fully represented at various levels in the organisation. They are allowed to:

- encourage people of a particular racial group to join, if at any time in the previous 12 months there were no persons of that racial group as members, or the proportion of members of that racial group was small in relation to the number of people of that racial group who were eligible for membership;
- encourage people of a particular racial group to take advantage of opportunities to hold posts in the organisation or provide preferential access to training to help prepare them for such posts, if there are no people from that racial group or only a small proportion holding posts.   *Race Relations Act 1976 s.38(3)-(5)*

Racial group cannot, however, be used as a factor in selecting people for membership or for posts in the organisation.

There is no provision for other organisations to use these forms of positive action.

42.3.2   Exceptions: services

Although discrimination on the basis of racial group is generally unlawful, there are some situations where voluntary organisations may use racial group as a factor in providing access to services.

42.3.2.1   Charities

Charities may limit their services to a particular racial group if their governing document explicitly allows this, provided the group is not defined by reference to colour. If the governing document refers to colour, this must be disregarded and the charity's services are available regardless of colour.   *Race Relations Act 1976 s.34*

42.3.2.2   Special need

Charities and other organisations may restrict access to services or give priority to members of a specific racial group in order to meet their special needs in relation to education, training or welfare. This would apply where it can be shown that members of the group have a need which is different from, or is the same as but proportionately greater than, the needs of other racial groups.   *RRA 1976 s.35*

The special need cannot be based simply on people's preference to be with people of their own racial group.

Unless the organisation is confident that it could, if challenged, justify the provision of separate services or preferential access to services, it should take advice before designating services in this way.

42.3.2.3   Fostering and boarding out

Racial group can be used as a factor when making fostering or boarding out arrangements by which a person takes children, elderly people or people in need of a special degree of care and attention into his or her own home and treats them as if they were members of the family.   *Race Relations Act 1976 s.23(2)*

42.3.2.4   Training bodies

Providers of training may limit access to vocational training to people of a particular racial group, or encourage members of that racial group to take advantage of opportunities to do a particular type of work, if that group is under-represented in that type of work, compared to the proportion of people of that group in the population of Great Britain as a whole or the population of the area covered by the training provider. *Race Relations Act 1976 s.37(1)*

42.3.2.5 Education and training for people not resident in Great Britain

Colour or nationality/citizenship – but not race, ethnic origin or national origin – may be used as a factor in providing access to education, training and ancillary benefits for people who are not ordinarily resident in Great Britain. The provider of the education or training must reasonably believe that the person does not intend to remain in Great Britain after the course. Because of the overlap between colour and race, it is not advisable to use colour as a factor. *Race Relations Act 1976 s.36, amended by Race Relations Act 1976 (Amendment) Regulations 2003 [SI 2003/1626] reg.34*

For an explanation of why this provision applies only to colour and nationality and not to the other aspects of racial group, see **28.2**. This anomaly is likely to be removed under the Equality Act [**28.1.2**].

42.3.2.6 Sport and games

Discrimination on the basis of nationality, place of birth, or length of residence in any place is allowed when selecting a person or team to represent a country, place or area, or any related association, in any sport or game. *Race Relations Act 1976 s.39*

42.4 SEX

In general, no one may be denied access to goods, services, activities, education, facilities or premises (all referred to here as **services**) on the basis of sex, regardless of whether the services are provided for payment or free of charge. **Direct and indirect discrimination**, **victimisation** and **harassment [28.1.3-28.1.6]** are unlawful. *Sex Discrimination Act 1975 ss.1(3)(aa), 29-31,35 inserted by Sex Discrimination (Amendment of Legislation) Regulations 2008 [SI 2008/963] sch.1 para.1,4-6,8(d)*

Discrimination against a woman on the basis of pregnancy or because she has given birth within the previous 26 weeks is unlawful. At the time of writing (mid 2009) it was expected that this protection would be strengthened in the **Equality Act [28.1.12]**, and it would be made clear that breastfeeding is allowed in public places.

Where a service provider believes that the service would pose a risk to the health or safety or a pregnant woman or woman who has recently given birth, it is lawful to refuse to provide the service, or to offer or provide it only on conditions intended to remove or reduce the risk. However, this may be done only if the service provider operates an equivalent policy for people with other physical conditions, refusing to provide the service to them or imposing conditions on them for reasons of health and safety. *Sex Discrimination Act 1975 s.3B, inserted by SDA Regs 2008 sch.1 para.3*

It is unlawful to discriminate in the provision of services against a person who intends to undergo, is undergoing or has undergone gender reassignment. *Sex Discrimination Act 1975 s.2A inserted by Sex Discrimination (Gender Reassignment) Regulations 1999 [SI 1999/1102] reg.2 & amended by SDA Regs 2008 sch.1 para.2*

42.4.1 Exceptions

Although discrimination on the basis of sex is generally unlawful, there are some situations in which it is permissible to use sex as a factor in allowing access to membership or services.

42.4.1.1 Charities

A charity whose governing document restricts its beneficiaries to one sex may restrict the services it provides to that sex, if this is a proportionate means of achieving a legitimate aim [**28.1.3**], or it is for the purpose of preventing or compensating for a disadvantage linked to sex. *Sex Discrimination Act 1975 s. 43, amended by Sex Discrimination (Amendment of Legislation) Regulations 2008 [SI 2008/963] 2008 sch.1 para.11*

42.4.1.2 Membership organisations

The governing document of a not for profit organisation (unless the organisation was set up by statute) may restrict its membership, and the services it provides to members, to one sex if this is a proportionate means of achieving a legitimate aim [**28.1.3**], or is for the purpose of preventing or compensating for a disadvantage linked to sex. *Sex Discrimination Act 1975 s. 34, amended by Sex Discrimination (Amendment) of Legislation Regulations 2008 [SI 2008/963] 2008 sch.1 para.11*

42.4.1.3 Special care

Services provided at, or as part of, a hospital or an establishment for people requiring special care, supervision or attention can be limited to one sex. *Sex Discrimination Act 1975 ss.35(1),(1A), amended/inserted by SDA Regs 2008 sch.1 para.8*

42.4.1.4 Propriety and privacy

Services can be limited to one sex where it involves physical contact between the service user and another person, and the other person might reasonably object if the user were of the other sex. *SDA 1975 s.35(2)*

Services can also be limited to one sex where they are provided for, or are likely to be used by, two or more people at the same time, and the services are such that the presence of service users of one sex is likely to cause severe embarrassment to users of the other sex, or a user is likely to be undressed and might reasonably object to the presence of a user of the other sex. *Sex Discrimination Act 1975 s.35(1),(1C), amended inserted by SDA Regs 2008 sch.1 para.8*

Discrimination on the basis of gender reassignment is lawful only if it is a proportionate means of achieving a legitimate aim [**28.1.3**]. *Sex Discrimination Act 1975 s.35(2A), inserted by Sex Discrimination Act Regs 2008 sch.1 para.8(c)*

42.4.1.5 Communal accommodation

Residential accommodation may be limited to one sex if it includes dormitories or shared sleeping accommodation which, for reasons of decency or privacy, should be used by one sex only, or it should be used by one sex only because of the nature of the sanitary facilities serving the accommodation. Where other services are provided only to people using single-sex accommodation under this exemption, it is not unlawful to provide them as single-sex services. *Sex Discrimination Act 1975 s.46*

In providing access to residential accommodation, men and women must be treated as fairly and equitably as circumstances permit.

Discrimination in accommodation on the basis of gender reassignment is lawful only if it is a proportionate means of achieving a legitimate aim [**28.1.3**]. *Sex Discrimination Act 1975 s.46(4)(c), inserted by SDA Regs 2008 sch.1 para.14*

42.4.1.6 Education

Services may be limited to one sex in single-sex educational establishments and boarding accommodation. *Sex Discrimination Act 1975 s.26*

42.4.1.7 Training

Access to training for a particular type of work can be limited to one sex where it appears to the training provider that at any time in the previous 12 months there were no members of that sex, or a disproportionately small number, doing that work in Great Britain or in an area of Great Britain; or persons of one sex have special need of training because they have been carrying out domestic or family duties rather than being in full-time employment. *Sex Discrimination Act 1975 s.47*

42.4.1.8 Sport and games

Participation in sport, games or other competitive activities where strength, stamina or physique are important may lawfully be limited to men or women. Participation can be restricted on the basis of gender reassignment only if this is necessary to ensure fair competition or the safety of competitors at the event. *Sex Discrimination Act 1975 s.44, amended by SDA Regs 2008 sch.1 para.12*

42.4.1.9   Religious premises

Where religious doctrine requires facilities to be restricted to one sex or where a significant number of the followers of a religion would be offended if separate facilities were not provided, it is lawful to restrict facilities or services to one sex at a place used permanently or temporarily for the purposes of an organised religion.   *Sex Discrimination Act 1975 s.35(1),(1B), amended/inserted by Sex Discrimination (Amendment of Legislation) Regulations 2008 [SI 2008/963] 2008 sch.1 para.8*

42.4.1.10   Trade unions and professional organisations

Trade unions, other organisations of workers, employers' organisations and professional or trade associations may undertake **positive action [28.1.3]** if they have no or disproportionately few members of one sex, or if posts in the organisation are held by no or disproportionately few persons of one sex. The allowed positive action is encouraging persons of the under-represented sex to become members of the organisation or to take advantage of opportunities to hold posts in the organisation; and/or providing access to training for persons of one sex to enable them to take up posts in the organisation.   *Sex Discrimination Act 1975 ss.12,48(2),(3)*

Sex cannot, however, be used as a factor in actually selecting people for membership or for posts in the organisation.

There is no provision in the Sex Discrimination Act for this positive action to be taken by organisations other than trade unions and professional organisations.

42.5   RELIGION AND OTHER BELIEFS

It is generally unlawful to treat a person less favourably in the provision of goods, services, facilities, education and the use of premises (all referred to here as **services**) because of their religion or philosophical belief, including having no religion or belief. This includes discrimination on the basis of someone's actual religion/belief, the religion/belief they are thought to have, or the religion/belief of someone they are associated with. The law applies regardless of whether there is a charge for the services.   *Equality Act 2006 ss.44-46*

Direct discrimination, **indirect discrimination** and **victimisation** are unlawful. At the time of writing (mid 2009) there was no legislation specifically on **harassment** on the basis of religion/belief in the provision of services, but such harassment could constitute direct discrimination.

42.5.1   Exceptions

In some specific circumstances it is not unlawful to exclude, or give preference to, people of a particular religion or belief. Where there is any doubt about whether a restriction on the basis of religion/belief may fall within an exception, specialist advice should be sought.

42.5.1.1   Religious organisations

Restrictions on the provision of services (including membership restrictions) on the basis of religion or belief are permitted in certain circumstances by non-commercial religious or belief-based organisations, including those set up to practise or teach a particular religion or belief or to improve relations between different religions or beliefs. This only applies if the restrictions are imposed because of the purpose of the organisation or in order to avoid causing offence to people of that religion/belief on the grounds of that religion/belief.   *Equality Act 2006 s.57*

Examples include restricting participation in religious services, theological study groups, faith-based camps, or clubs, societies or social events run by the organisation, or restricting who can hire or live in the organisation's premises.

This exception does not apply where an organisation is acting under the terms of a contract with a public authority.

Religious organisations may also, in some circumstances, be allowed to discriminate on the basis of sexual orientation [**42.6.1.5**].

42.5.1.2	Charities

Where a charity's governing document restricts benefits to people of a particular religion or belief, the charity is permitted to limit its services accordingly. A charity set up to provide housing only to people of a particular religion or education only to people with a particular belief, for example, may do so.   *Equality Act 2006 s.58*

42.5.1.3	Education

Denominational schools and other schools recognised in law as having a religious character or religious ethos can use religion or belief as a factor when deciding admissions to the school or eligibility for access to benefits, services or facilities at the school.   *Equality Act 2006 ss.49,50*

Such schools and other educational institutions established to provide education about or within the framework of a specified religion or belief may limit, on the basis of religion or belief, the provision of services to people other than pupils, or the use or disposal of premises. Such restrictions are lawful only if they are on the grounds of the specified religion or belief, or are needed in order to avoid causing offence to people connected with the institution on the grounds of their religion or belief.   *Equality Act 2006 s.59*

An organisation established as a Muslim supplementary school or madrassa, for example, would be able to provide tuition only for Muslim pupils in accordance with its governing document as a charity [**42.5.1.2**]. But if it were to provide other services, such as a playgroup, welfare rights advice service or hiring out its premises, religion could be used as a factor only if there was a legitimate reason for doing so.

42.5.1.4	Special need for education, training and welfare

Another exception allows any organisation – even if it is not set up for religious or philosophical purposes – to provide services to meet special needs for education, training or welfare of people of a particular religion or belief. Separate provision may be lawful where, for example, it leads to better take-up of a service, or makes service delivery more effective.   *Equality Act 2006 s.61*

An example could be an advice centre having sessions specifically for the Sikh community, to encourage more Sikhs to use the service.

42.5.2	**Other types of belief**

The 2003 regulations on discrimination in employment on the basis of religion or belief referred to 'religious or *similar* philosophical belief' [**28.4**], but the **Equality Act 2006** s.44 replaced this with 'any religious or philosophical belief'. At the time of writing (mid 2009) it remained unclear how the courts will interpret 'any philosophical belief', and organisations need to be aware of this if they seek to limit access to services on the basis of a person's beliefs.

In particular, organisations may need to clarify their position on providing services to people whose beliefs are perceived as racist or otherwise unacceptable. This may include making it a requirement of membership that all members accept the organisation's commitment to equality of opportunity, and making clear that the organisation's services are open to everyone regardless of their *beliefs* but will not be available to anyone whose *actions* are racist, sexist or otherwise abusive while they are on the organisation's premises, taking part in the organisation's activities, or using the organisation's services or facilities.

42.6	**SEXUAL ORIENTATION**

It is generally unlawful to treat a person less favourably in the provision of goods, services, facilities, education and the use of premises (referred to here as **services**) because of their actual or perceived sexual orientation or their association with someone of a particular sexual orientation. Sexual orientation is defined as an orientation towards people of the same sex, the other sex, or both sexes.
    Equality Act 2006 s.81; Equality Act (Sexual Orientation) Regulations 2007 [SI 2007/1263] regs.3,4

Direct discrimination, **indirect discrimination** and **victimisation** are unlawful. At the time of writing (mid 2009) there is no legislation specifically on **harassment** on the basis of sexual orientation in the provision of services, but such harassment could constitute direct discrimination. The law applies regardless of whether there is a charge for the services.

42.6.1 Exceptions

In some circumstances it is not unlawful to exclude, or give preference to, people of a particular sexual orientation. Where there is any doubt about whether a restriction on the basis of sexual orientation is allowed, specialist advice should be sought.

42.6.1.1 Charities

Charities whose governing document allows them to provide services to people of a particular sexual orientation are permitted to do so. For example, a charity whose beneficiaries are people who are gay, lesbian, bisexual or questioning their sexuality are allowed to restrict their services to any or all of these groups.

Equality Act (Sexual Orientation) Regulations 2007 [SI 2007/1263] reg.18

42.6.1.2 Associations

An association (membership organisation) with fewer than 25 members may discriminate on the grounds of sexual orientation in admitting people to membership, or providing the association's services or other membership rights.

Sexual Orientation Regs 2007 reg.16

Associations with 25 or more members whose main object is to enable the benefits of membership to be enjoyed by people of a particular sexual orientation may exclude persons of other orientations. Advice should be sought before relying on this exception. *Sexual Orientation Regs 2007 reg. 17*

42.6.1.3 Education, training and welfare

Any organisation may provide services for people of a particular sexual orientation to meet their special needs for education, welfare or training. This could include, for example, counselling services specifically for gay men and lesbians where it is believed that this will lead to more gay men and lesbians using the service, and/or that this will enable the organisation to provide a more appropriate service. Note that if the service is going to be limited to gay men *or* lesbians, it must also comply with one of the exceptions for sex discrimination [**42.4.1**].

Sexual Orientation Regs 2007 reg.13

42.6.1.4 Living as a family

The sexual orientation regulations do not apply where arrangements are made for a child, elderly person or person needing special care to be taken into a private household and treated as if they are a member of the family. *Sexual Orientation Regs 2007 reg.6(1)*

42.6.1.5 Religious organisations

An exception applies to non-commercial organisations set up to practise, advance or teach the practice or principles of a religion or belief or to enable persons of a religion or belief to receive any benefit or take part in activities within the framework of that religion or belief. Under the exception, these organisations are allowed to restrict membership, participation in activities, provision of goods or services or the disposal of property on the basis of sexual orientation, but only if the restrictions are necessary to comply with the doctrine of the organisation or to avoid conflicting with the strongly held religious convictions of a significant number of the religion's followers. This provision does not apply to educational establishments or education authorities, or organisations funded by a public authority to provide the service. *Sexual Orientation Regs 2007 reg.14*

42.7 DISABILITY

The **Disability Discrimination Act 1995** not only makes it unlawful to discriminate against people with disabilities, but also requires providers of goods, services, facilities, education, transport, premises which are let out, and premises where services are provided to the public (collectively referred to here as **services**) to make reasonable adaptations to enable disabled people to use the services [**42.7.2**].

The provisions apply to all providers of services, regardless of whether services are provided for a charge or free. The definition of disability is the same as for the employment provisions of the Act [**28.7.1**].

Information about all DDA requirements is available from the Equality and Human Rights Commission [see end of **chapter 28**], at www.disability.gov.uk, and from many disability organisations. The EHRC's disability conciliation service can work with disabled people and service providers to help resolve problems. The Centre for Accessible Environments [see end of **chapter 28**] and some major disability organisations carry out access audits.

Direct discrimination [**28.1.3**] against a disabled person and failure to make reasonable adjustments [**42.7.1.3**] are unlawful, as is **victimisation** [**28.1.5**] of any person whether disabled or non-disabled.   *Disability Discrimination Act 1995 ss.19,20,55*

It is generally unlawful:

- to refuse to provide, or deliberately not to provide, a service to a disabled person which is provided or would be provided to other members of the public;
- to provide a service of a lower standard to a disabled person than would be provided to a non-disabled person;
- to make a service available to a disabled person on different terms than it would be provided to a non-disabled person.   *Disability Discrimination Act 1995 s.19*

In general it is not unlawful to refuse to provide a non-disabled person with a service which is provided to a disabled person, or to provide a service of a lower standard to a non-disabled person [**28.7**].

Harassment [**28.1.6**] of a disabled person is unlawful by organisations of workers or employers, trade and professional bodies, qualification bodies, and providers of practical work experience, vocational guidance or training, and employment services. At the time of writing (mid 2009) harassment in relation to other services provided to disabled people is not unlawful under the DDA, but could be unlawful under other legislation [**40.5.3**].   *Disability Discrimination Act 1995 ss.3B,13(3), 14A,14C,18D,21A, inserted by DDA 1995 (Amendment) Regulations 2003 [SI 2003/1673] regs.3,4,13,18,19*

42.7.1 Exceptions

There are limited exceptions under which it is lawful to treat a disabled person less favourably than a non-disabled person is or would be treated.

42.7.1.1 Justification for less favourable treatment

The non-discrimination provisions do not apply if the provider of services can show that providing a different service to a disabled person or refusing to provide a service is justified:

- for reasons of health or safety;
- because the disabled person is not capable of understanding or entering into a contract [**21.1.2**] or giving informed consent;
- because providing the service, or the same standard of service, to a disabled person or people would mean that the service could not be provided to other people; and/or
- because the costs of providing the service to a disabled person are higher, and therefore it is justified to charge a higher rate than is charged to non-disabled people. However, the costs of providing the service cannot take into account any costs incurred because of the duty to make reasonable adjustments [**42.7.1.3**].   *Disability Discrimination Act 1995 s.20(4)*

42.7.1.2   Supported employment

Organisations which provide supported employment may provide it for a specific group or groups of disabled people, even though this discriminates against people without that disability.   *Disability Discrimination Act 1995 s.18C, moved by DDA 1995 (Amendment) Regulations 2003[SI 2003/1673] reg.11*

42.7.1.3   Private clubs and associations

It is not unlawful for private clubs or associations with fewer than 25 members to discriminate against a disabled person in membership or services, or to discriminate against guests in relation to the services provided. This applies regardless of whether the organisation is incorporated or unincorporated, and whether it operates on a for profit or not for profit basis.   *Disability Discrimination Act 1995 ss.21F-21J, inserted by DDA 2005 s.12; Disability Discrimination (Private Clubs etc) Regulations 2005 [SI 2005/3258]*

Non-charitable voluntary sector associations or companies could in some circumstances be classed as 'private clubs' for the purposes of this legislation. A charitable organisation cannot be 'private' in this sense.

42.7.1.4   Charities

Charities set up to provide services to disabled people in general, or people with a specific disability, may limit membership and/or services to those people.

42.7.2   Adjustments to services and premises

Service providers must take reasonable steps to make their services available to disabled people. This includes, where it is reasonable:

- changing policies, procedures or practices which make it impossible or unreasonably difficult for disabled people to use a service;
- taking reasonable steps to remove, alter or provide reasonable means of avoiding physical features that make it impossible or unreasonably difficult for disabled people to use a service;
- providing a service by an alternative method, where physical barriers make it impossible or unreasonably difficult for disabled people to use the service;
- providing auxiliary aids and services to enable disabled people to use a service, such as information on audio tape or a sign language interpreter.

Disability Discrimination Act 1995 s.21

Unlike the duties in relation to employees [**28.7.4**], the duty to make reasonable adjustments in relation to access to services is a duty to disabled people in general. The service provider must therefore anticipate the needs of service users with different types of disability, and take reasonable steps to meet those needs.

Physical features include features arising from the design or construction of a building, approaches to or exits from the premises, any fixtures, fittings, furniture, equipment or materials in or on the premises, and any other physical element or quality of the land.   *Disability Discrimination (Service Providers & Public Authorities Carrying Out Functions) Regulations 2005 [SI 2005/2901] reg.9*

In relation to further and higher education and to employment services (provision of vocational guidance, vocational training or services to help people obtain or retain employment or to set up as self employed), the duty applies not only where policies, procedures or practices make access to the service **impossible or unreasonably difficult**, but also where they place disabled people at a **substantial disadvantage** in comparison with people who are not disabled.

DDA 1995 s.21A, inserted by DDA (Amendment) Regulations 2003 [SI 2003/1673] reg.19(1); DDA 1995 s.28T, inserted by DDA 1995 (Amendment) (Further & Higher Education) Regulations 2006 [SI 2006/1721] reg.8

42.7.2.1   Reasonable adjustments

'Reasonable' is not defined in the Act, and varies according to the type of services being provided, the nature of the service provider and its size and resources. In considering what is reasonable, factors which may be taken into account include whether the steps to be taken would be effective in making it easier for disabled people to access services, how practicable it is for the service provider to take the steps, and the disruption caused by taking the steps. The financial and other costs are also considered, along with the service provider's financial and other resources, the amount already spent on making adjustments, and the availability of financial or other assistance.

Reasonable adjustments need to be made not only to premises and physical features, but also to aspects of the organisation's work such as its signs, documents and websites.

42.7.2.2   Adjustments to premises

Compliance with the **Disability Discrimination Act** may require substantial physical alteration of buildings or grounds. It is important that the possible need for adaptations is considered when taking on new premises.

Where a lease requires the landlord's consent for such alterations, such consent must not be unreasonably withheld. Landlords have only 21 days to reply, after which they are deemed to be withholding their consent unreasonably and the matter may be referred to the county court. The landlord may make the consent subject to one or more reasonable conditions. *Disability Discrimination Act 1995 s.27, sch.4 pt.2; Disability Discrimination (Providers of Services) (Adjustment of Premises) Regulations 2001 [SI 2001/3253]*

If a landlord unreasonably withholds consent and an organisation goes ahead and makes changes to comply with its duties, the landlord can require reinstatement only if it could have been legally justified in refusing consent in the first place.

At the time of writing (mid 2009), it was expected that the **Equality Act [28.1.12]** would require landlords and managers of residential premises to make reasonable adjustments to communal areas to enable a disabled resident to use the premises. However, the resident could be required to pay for the adaptations.

42.7.2.3   Premises complying with Building Regulations part M

Part M of the **Building Regulations 2000** sets out rules on access to and use of new buildings, and for existing buildings when they are altered or undergo certain changes of use. *Building Regulations 2000[SI 2000/2531] sch.1 pt.M, amended by Building (Amendment) Regulations 2003 [SI 2003/2692] reg.2, sch.1*

Where a feature has been built or adapted within the previous 10 years to comply with part M, it is considered to comply with **Disability Discrimination Act** access requirements without having to be further altered or removed. *Disability Discrimination (Service Providers & Public Authorities Carrying Out Functions) Regulations 2005 [SI 2005/2901] reg.11(3), sch.1*

42.8   AGE

At the time of writing (mid 2009) there was no legislation making it unlawful to discriminate in general in the provision of goods, services and facilities on the basis of age. However it was expected that the **Equality Act [28.1.12]** would ban age discrimination against people aged 18 or over, except where age-based treatment is justified or beneficial. Beneficial services might include, for example, age based holidays and discounts for older people.

In the meantime, discrimination on the basis of age is unlawful by trade organisations, qualifications bodies, employment agencies and institutions of further and higher education, and by providers of vocational training or guidance, careers guidance, training facilities or practical work experience. *Employment Equality (Age) Regulations 2006 [SI 2006/1031] regs.18-23*

Resources: EQUAL OPPORTUNITIES: GOODS, SERVICES AND FACILITIES

See end of **chapter 28.**

Statute law. www.opsi.gov.uk and www.statutelaw.gov.uk.

Much but not all case law. www.bailii.org.

Updates cross-referenced to this book. www.rclh.co.uk.

Chapter 43

DATA PROTECTION AND USE OF INFORMATION

43.1 CONFIDENTIALITY, PRIVACY AND DISCLOSURE

If information is mismanaged, misused or treated carelessly, the consequences can be severe. Risk assessments and information security procedures should therefore be treated as seriously as health and safety [**22.1**, **43.1.6**], and should cover information about the organisation as well as about individuals.

43.1.1 Duties to maintain confidentiality

In considering the information to which an organisation has access, it is important to differentiate between information which:

- there is a legal duty to disclose to the relevant authorities;
- there is a legal obligation to treat as confidential, private and/or protected [below], and therefore disclosable to third parties only in limited circumstances;
- there is a legal duty to disclose to the person to whom it refers;
- the organisation chooses to treat as confidential and to limit disclosure; or
- can or must be made available to the public, such as annual accounts.

Legal obligations to maintain confidentiality may arise:

- under statute, including the **Data Protection Act 1998** [**43.3**] **Human Rights Act 1998** [**43.1.1.1**], **Freedom of Information Act 2000** [**43.2**], **Regulation of Investigatory Powers Act 2000** [**43.1.4**], and **Official Secrets Act 1989**;
- explicitly under a contract, where one or both parties agree not to disclose certain information or use it for other purposes;
- implicitly under a contract, for example in contracts of employment where it is implied [**26.3.3**] that the employee and employer will keep certain information confidential [**43.1.3**];

- through professional duties or other special relationships, as in the relationship between counsellors and their clients.

Confidentiality is not the same as secrecy. It is about establishing clear policies [**43.1.3**] and boundaries within which information may legitimately be shared on a **need to know** basis. Breach of a duty of confidentiality may give rise to a claim for damages, including damages caused by injured feelings, and orders preventing disclosure.

In some circumstances, an obligation or right to disclose information [**43.1.2**] may override a contractual or professional duty to maintain confidentiality.

43.1.1.1 Respect for private and family life

An organisation which is a public authority as defined by the **Human Rights Act 1998** s.6(3) [**64.3.2**] is obliged to respect individuals' private and family life, home and correspondence in its decisions and actions. In addition, all UK legislation must be interpreted in ways which uphold these rights – while balancing them against the Human Rights Act's right to freedom of expression.

At the time of writing (mid 2009), most voluntary organisations do not meet the definition of public authority so cannot have a claim under the HRA brought against them if they disclose information about individuals. But even where an organisation is not directly required to comply with the HRA, it may be required to do so under the terms of agreements or contracts with public sector bodies.

43.1.2 Disclosure of information

As well as the duties to maintain confidentiality and protect private information, there can also be a duty to disclose information. This may arise from:

- a common law duty of care, particularly in relation to children;
- a contractual obligation, for example where a local authority purchases services from an organisation and requires the organisation to provide certain information – but an organisation must be careful not to enter into agreements requiring it to disclose information that it does not have the right to disclose;
- statute, for example the obligation to report drug sales or use [**43.1.2.5**] or persons who harm or put at risk of harm children or vulnerable adults [**41.7.2**], the duty on organisations involved in some types of work to disclose under the **money laundering** regulations [**53.6.1**], and the duty on some bodies to disclose under the **Freedom of Information Act 2000** [**43.2**].

43.1.2.1 Issues around disclosure

Where there is a duty of confidentiality *and* a legal duty of disclosure (for example, a client disclosing to a counsellor that he or she is abusing a child), the person to whom the duty of confidentiality is owed should generally be informed of the duty of disclosure.

Where there is a duty of confidentiality *without* a legal duty of disclosure, disclosure without the consent of the person to whom the duty of confidentiality is owed could be a breach of confidentiality. Consent to disclose should be obtained, for example a counselling client agreeing that the counsellor can discuss him or her in supervision sessions.

Where the organisation has informed clients, service users or others that it has a policy of not disclosing information without the knowledge or consent of the individual, that policy will generally be binding. Confidentiality therefore should not be promised, or should be promised only with clear exceptions if legal obligations or the organisation's policies require, or might require, disclosure within the organisation or to an outside body.

It is always wise to document the reason for any disclosure that breaches confidentiality or is done without the agreement of the individual(s) concerned, and to ensure that it is properly authorised by an accountable senior member of the staff or governing body.

Insurance is available to cover claims for inadvertent breach of confidentiality [**23.5.7**].

43.1.2.2 Disclosure to parents or carers

For organisations which work with children, there is no legal obligation to disclose any information to parents, unless such obligation is included as part of the arrangement under which the organisation is doing the work. An exception is schools, where specific regulations give parents rights to information about their children. Where an organisation feels it is in a child's best interests to pass on information to a parent but is uncertain about the confidentiality implications, it should seek legal advice or advice from the local authority's child protection team.

For organisations working with adults, there is no legal obligation to pass information to the family or other carers.

A separate issue is the question of when parents or carers can request a disclosure on behalf of a child or adult who cannot exercise their rights on their own behalf. In this case, the organisation may have an obligation to disclose information to the parent or carer, but the person to whom the information is disclosed must be properly authorised and acting on behalf of the individual concerned.

'Properly authorised' in the case of children normally means the person with parental responsibility as set out in the Children Acts. Children are normally considered able to act on their own behalf in these matters from around the age of 12 [**43.3.4.6**]. In the case of adults, the person may be able to authorise another person such as a solicitor to act on their behalf, or may be able to appoint someone under a lasting power of attorney [**21.1.2**].

43.1.2.3 Disclosure of abuse

In relation to child abuse carried out by persons other than the organisation's staff, the duty of care to the child would generally override any duty of confidentiality to the abuser, and cases of actual or suspected abuse should be reported to the local authority's child protection team.

Abuse of adults, even if they are vulnerable, by persons other than the organisation's staff is not subject to a legal duty to disclose. If information is obtained subject to confidentiality, disclosure without the consent of the person who has disclosed the information and the abuser (if not the same person) could be a breach of confidentiality and breach of the Data Protection Act unless a person is at risk of serious imminent harm.

43.1.2.4 Disclosure of abuse by staff

Some organisations working with children and/or vulnerable adults are required to report to the **Independent Safeguarding Authority** any action by a staff member, inside or outside work, which harms or puts at risk a child or vulnerable adult [**41.7.2**]. Organisations which are not obliged to report have the right to do so, and may be required to do so by funders or their own policies. This rule applies to all staff, whether paid or unpaid, full- or part-time, permanent or temporary, and staff supplied by employment agencies or employment businesses.

43.1.2.5 Disclosure to police

Unless the police have a witness or search order, there is no general legal obligation to disclose information or allow access to the police, nor is there in general any obligation to pass on knowledge of a crime. However, it is a criminal offence deliberately to mislead the police, to receive a reward of any kind in return for not notifying the police about a criminal act, or not to notify the police about an act which could be construed as an act of terrorism [**46.6**] or as drug trafficking.

Failure to reveal information to the police about the sale, distribution, production or use of illegal drugs may be seen as evidence of unwillingness to take reasonable steps to prevent drug misuse [**63.5.5**].

Police with a search warrant can search for 'relevant evidence' to help in detection of crime. An organisation faced with police requests for legally confidential information should seek legal advice.

Even where there may not be a statutory duty to disclose unlawful acts, law-breaking should not be ignored or condoned. The organisation should have clear policies setting out what is not allowed on the premises or while taking part in the organisation's activities; what staff or others should do if they become aware of unlawful acts or acts which contravene the organisation's policies; sanctions for wrongdoing; situations in which the police must or may be notified and who is authorised to do so; record keeping procedures; and implications for staff and others of not complying with the organisation's policies and procedures.

Where a crime is committed against an organisation or the organisation becomes aware of a crime, factors to consider include:

- insurance policies will require notification to police before they will pay out;
- the responsibility of charity trustees to safeguard the charity's assets [**15.6.5**] should be considered before making any decision not to report a theft or similar act to the police;
- funders or supporters may react negatively if they discover that a criminal act known to the organisation has not been reported.

For disciplinary issues arising from criminal acts by employees see **33.3.11**, and for issues around dismissal see **34.6.2** and **34.6.5**.

43.1.2.6 Disclosure to courts and tribunals

Courts and tribunals have power to require disclosure of confidential information in some situations, but some information is **privileged** [**65.4.1**] and may not have to be revealed. Legal advice is necessary in this situation.

43.1.2.7 Whistleblowing

In general an employee must not breach confidentiality by revealing information about the employer's activities, or activities carried out by employees on behalf of the employer. But where disclosure would reveal or prevent malpractice or an unlawful act, the **Public Interest Disclosure Act 1998** may protect employees from victimisation or dismissal if they reveal such information [**33.5**].

43.1.3 Confidentiality policies

In addition to ensuring compliance with its legal duties, organisations generally want to protect a wide range of information from disclosure. A confidentiality policy can make clear to everyone involved:

- what information is held by the organisation, why it is held, how long it is held and how it is used;
- what is protected as personal data under the **Data Protection Act** [**43.3.1**], and what may not be covered under the Act but is considered confidential because the organisation and/or individuals involved believe it should be;
- who within the organisation has access to various types of information, and whether such access is automatic or needs to be authorised in each instance;
- who information can be disclosed to within the organisation;
- the circumstances, if any, under which information is disclosed to parties outside the organisation, and the procedure to authorise such disclosure;
- procedures for compliance with the **Data Protection Act 1998** [**43.3**] and, if applicable, the **Human Rights Act 1998** [**43.1.1.1**] and **Freedom of Information Act 2000** [**43.2**];
- links between the confidentiality policy and the whistleblowing policy [**33.5**] (note that a confidentiality policy, contract, or other agreement with a worker cannot prevent, or seek to prevent, the worker from making a disclosure which is protected under the **Public Interest Disclosure Act 1998**);
- penalties for breach of confidentiality.

43.1.3.1 Confidential information about individuals

Organisations which keep information about recognisable individuals must comply with the data protection principles [**43.3.3**], and most have to notify (register) under the **Data Protection Act** [**43.3.7**]. The confidentiality policy should cover issues such as:

- whether to allow individuals to limit the purposes for which their personal information is used;

- whether to obtain information from third parties, and if so whether and how to check it with the individual concerned;

- under what circumstances personal information can be passed on to third parties, how the person concerned is informed, and whether his or her consent is required and if so how it is obtained;

- who within the organisation has the right to know what about individuals, and in particular who has a right to know different types of confidential information and under what circumstances;

- whether to keep a record in the person's file of everyone to whom confidential information has been disclosed;

- the security measures to prevent loss of information or unauthorised disclosure, and the measures to deal with it if it occurs.

43.1.3.2 Confidential information about employees

Employers have an implied duty to maintain the employee's trust and confidence [**26.3.3**], which includes not inappropriately disclosing information about them. The duties of employers are clarified in the data protection code of practice on the use of personal data in employer/employee relationships, from the Information Commissioner's Office [see end of chapter].

The duty of confidentiality to employees does not extend to withholding information which there is a statutory obligation to disclose to the police or other authorities [**43.1.2**].

43.1.4 Monitoring staff communications

In general it is an offence to intercept telephone calls, email or other telecommunications. However, employers have wide powers to monitor and record such communications to or from staff, without the consent of either the staff member or the other party, where it is done to collect facts or evidence, ensure compliance with internal or external rules or regulations, monitor standards, ensure the effective operation of the employer's systems, for example by preventing computer viruses, prevent or detect crime, or investigate or detect unauthorised use of the organisation's computer or telephone systems.

Telecommunications (Lawful Business Practice) (Interception of Communications) Regulations 2000 [SI 2000/2699]

Communications can also be monitored, but not recorded, to find out whether they relate to the business, for example listening to voicemails in an employee's absence to find out whether they relate to the organisation's work. They can also be monitored but not recorded where the call is to or from a helpline which provides counselling or support free of charge (apart from the cost of the telephone call) and guarantees caller anonymity. All other helplines must inform callers that calls may be monitored.

Although the employer does not need to obtain explicit consent for permitted monitoring, it must make all reasonable efforts to inform employees, volunteers and other potential users of the system that such monitoring may be undertaken. This may be done by, for example, having a recorded message that calls may be monitored, including a message in emails saying that emails may be monitored, and including a clause in contracts of employment and volunteer agreements stating that calls, email and other telecommunications may be monitored [**27.10.4**].

In other situations it is an offence for the organisation to monitor telecommunications unless both the sender and recipient have given explicit consent or the organisation has reasonable grounds to believe they have done so, or the communication is made on a secure internal system within the organisation, such as a secure office intranet or a purely internal telephone system.

Regulation of Investigatory Powers Act 2000 ss.1,2

Any monitoring, whether of telecommunications or other communications, must not breach rights protected by the **Human Rights Act 1998** [**64.3.1**], and organisations should take legal advice before undertaking monitoring.

All information obtained through monitoring must comply with duties relating to confidential information [**43.1.3.1**, **43.1.3.2**]. If the information is subsequently stored or used, the processing must comply with data protection rules [**43.3**].

43.1.5   The employer's information and knowhow

Employees' disclosure or use of information gained during their employment is a complex area, and legal advice is likely to be necessary in case of dispute. An employer's right to take action to prevent a current or former employee disclosing or using information depends on the employee's job and the type of information involved, whether the person involved is still an employee, express terms of the contract of employment, whether it was made clear that the information was confidential, whether the information can be easily isolated from other information which the employee is free to use or disclose, and whether the information was available from other sources.

A court can grant an injunction restraining the employee, and anyone the employee has disclosed the information to, from making use of the information, and can grant damages to the employer for breach of contract.

43.1.5.1   Current employees

During employment, employees are bound by any express clauses in their contract imposing duties to keep information confidential, as well as the implied duty of confidentiality, which usually covers general information about the employer's business and **knowhow** (the employer's processes and procedures) and its **trade secrets** ; the duty to act honestly and in good faith; and the duty not to compete with the employer [**26.3.3**]. An employer therefore has quite extensive rights to prevent current employees disclosing or misusing information acquired from their employment.

Some judges define trade secrets narrowly to include only secret formulae and processes, but others define them as any information which, if disclosed, would be liable to cause real or significant damage to the organisation. This could include, for example, the names of customers or the contents of the next catalogue. Voluntary organisations' most valuable information may be about sources of funding, donors and ongoing research. If an issue could arise about whether this type of information could amount to a trade secret, legal advice should be sought.

43.1.5.2   Former employees

The restrictions after employment are generally less far-reaching. The employer may seek to include express clauses in the contract which restrict use, after the contract has terminated, of information acquired during the term of the contract, or restrict the employee's right to compete. Generally only clauses which restrict use of genuinely confidential information and trade secrets are enforceable [**27.6.5**]. Therefore one of the key issues in any case is what constitutes a trade secret of the employer, which may be defined narrowly or quite widely [**43.1.5.1**].

Former employees are also generally bound by a more limited implied duty of confidentiality, as well as the **Data Protection Act** [**43.3**], which makes it unlawful to access or use personal data without authorisation. They are also bound by the fact that all work covered by copyright or patent rights done by employees during the course of their employment belongs to the employer unless the employer has assigned the rights to the employee or someone else [**44.2.3**, **44.6.1**]; and the fact that employees are likely to infringe copyright if they seek to use reports, databases, computer programs or other material [**44.2**]. Apart from this, former employees are largely free to use information they carry away in their head.

In roles such as journalism where contacts are an important element in doing a job well, employees may be entitled to develop their own contact list separately from their employer's, which they could then take away. But if this list is held on the organisation's computer, the information belongs to the employer.

PennWell Publishing (UK) v Ornstein & others [2007] EWHC 1570 (QB)

43.1.6 Information security

Sensible steps to protect sensitive or confidential information include:

- a comprehensive confidentiality policy, clearly linked to other policies such as internet use [**43.5**], data protection [**43.3**], child/adult protection [**41.1.2**], whistleblowing [**33.5**], and a code of conduct for governing body members;

- including express confidentiality clauses in employee contracts [**27.10.3**, **27.10.4**] and in contracts with self employed and other contractors;

- ensuring that if the 'track changes' or 'reviewing' facility has been used in drafting documents, all changes have been cleared before the document is circulated so they do not remain accessible to recipients;

- restricting circulation of confidential material;

- where appropriate, disclosing confidential information to third parties only if they have signed confidentiality undertakings;

- marking documents and envelopes as confidential;

- using secure passwords and encryption to safeguard information that is transferred electronically, especially on devices vulnerable to loss or theft;

- having safe storage for confidential information;

- shredding documents before disposal;

- ensuring that electronic media, including hard disks, are securely wiped or securely destroyed before being disposed of, sold or given away;

- making it clear that data theft or misuse is as serious as any other theft or misuse of the organisation's property.

The Department for Business, Innovation and Skills [see end of chapter] has a range of information and good practice about information security.

43.2 FREEDOM OF INFORMATION

The **Freedom of Information Act 2000** (FOIA) provides a general right of access, although with significant exceptions, to information held by **public authorities** as defined in schedule 1 or designated under section 4 of the Act. In addition, a body may be designated as a public authority for the purposes of the FOIA if it appears to exercise functions of a public nature

Freedom of Information Act 2000 ss.1-5

The government consulted in 2008 on whether voluntary organisations and private companies should be designated as public authorities under the FOIA if they provide any service whose provision is a function of that authority. The government decided against this but said it would keep the issue under review, especially in relation to prisons, detention centres and care homes.

43.2.1 Right of access

Any person, even if not a UK resident or national, or body can apply to any public authority for information. A fee may be payable. In most cases the applicant must be told, within a specified period ranging from 20 to 60 days, whether the information requested is held by that authority (the **duty to confirm or deny** whether it holds information) and, if the information is held, to have it communicated to him or her. Where the authority does not reply or does not provide the information, the applicant may apply to the information tribunal. From January 2010 this tribunal is part of the general regulatory chamber in the first-tier tribunal [**64.7**]. *Freedom of Information Act 2000 ss.1,8-10*

Where an organisation which is not itself a public authority has provided information to the authority, for example as part of contract tender documents or monitoring of services, the authority may need to disclose that information in response to a FOIA request for information [**52.3.4**]. A case in Scotland in 2007 confirmed that even where a contractor to the public sector claims that information is commercially confidential (in this case, the details of a private finance initiative hospitals contract), the public body may still be obliged to make it public.

Docherty v Lothian NHS Board (2007) Scottish Information Commissioner 190/2007

In addition an organisation may be required, under grant or contract conditions, to comply with requests from a public authority for information which the authority is legally obliged to provide.

43.2.2   Publication schemes

Public authorities must publish and comply with schemes relating to the publication of information. These may be off the shelf schemes approved by the information commissioner or others, or may be drawn up by individual authorities and approved by the commissioner. Schemes must specify the classes of information the authority publishes, the manner of publication, and whether the information is available to the public free of charge or on payment. Material made available in accordance with a publication scheme is exempt from the right of access, so the authority does not have to respond to requests for it on an individual basis.

Freedom of Information Act 2000 ss.19,20

43.2.3   Exemptions

There are many exemptions to the right of access, where the authority does not have to confirm or deny whether it holds information and does not have to communicate the information. Exemptions apply, for example, to:

- information available to the public in other ways, for example under a publication scheme [above];
- information which could be prejudicial to national security, defence, international relations, or law enforcement;
- information defined as personal data under the **Data Protection Act** [**43.3.1**], although this may be overridden if there is a public interest justification for releasing the information;
- information obtained from a third party (rather than being generated by the public authority) whose disclosure would legally be a breach of confidence;
- information whose disclosure would prejudice the commercial interests of the public authority or any other purpose, unless it is in the public interest for the information to be disclosed;
- information held by government departments that relates to the formulation or development of government policy, or other information held by public bodies 'if, in the reasonable opinion of a qualified person, its disclosure would prejudice the effective conduct of public affairs'.   *Freedom of Information Act 2000 ss.21-44*

Information about the Act and its application to voluntary organisations is available from the Information Commissioner's Office, the Ministry of Justice and the Campaign for Freedom of Information [see end of chapter].

43.2.4   Environmental information regulations

Public bodies are also subject to the **Environmental Information Regulations** [**63.12.1**], which have provisions similar to those of the Freedom of Information Act.

43.3   DATA PROTECTION

The **Data Protection Act 1998** applies to **personal data** [**43.3.1**] about identifiable living individuals (**data subjects**). Organisations or individuals who hold personal data are **data controllers**. Most data controllers who hold personal data on computer must **notify** (register) under the Act [**43.3.7**]. All data controllers, even if they do not have to notify, must comply with the **data protection principles** [**43.3.3**] and other provisions of the Act.

The Data Protection Act is complex, and often requires the rights of different individuals to be balanced. Basic information is available from the Information Commissioner's Office [see end of chapter], but specialist advice should be sought if there is any doubt about how the Act applies, or individuals' rights to see and amend information held about them [**43.3.5**]. British standard BS 10012:2009 provides a framework for development of a system to manage personal data.

The main underlying purposes of the Data Protection Act are to prevent people from harm – for example if their information falls into the wrong hands, or if it is inaccurate, insufficient or in some other way deficient – and to allay concerns that many people have about privacy and the extent to which information can be used and passed on without their knowledge or consent.

43.3.1 Personal data

The **Data Protection Act** applies only to information that firstly is **personal**, about a living individual who can be identified, either directly or from other information held by or likely to be held by the data controller. This could include, for example, information identified by a code number, where the organisation has a list linking each number with a name. Secondly the information must be **data**, held or intended to be held on computer (including websites) or other electronic equipment with automatic retrieval, or in a **relevant filing system** – a paper-based record keeping system or other system (such as microfiche) structured in such a way that information about a particular individual can be readily located.

Data Protection Act 1998 s.1(1)

Personal data does not have to be written. It can include video, CCTV, photographic, audio, biometric and other non-text data.

The information commissioner [see end of chapter] produces guidance on what is and is not likely to be personal data under the Data Protection Act. But even with the guidance, it may be difficult to decide whether some information, especially if held on paper, falls under the legal definition of personal data. In terms of the confidentiality aspects of data protection, it is generally clear whether data protection rules should apply. The issue of whether something is or is not personal data may be more problematic where the individual seeks **subject access** [**43.3.5**] and the organisation is unclear what information needs to be provided. If this is an issue, specialist advice should be sought.

Durant v Financial Services Authority [2003] EWCA Civ 1746

43.3.1.1 Data protection v freedom of information

Personal data as defined under the **Data Protection Act** is in most cases exempt from the Freedom of Information Act, and generally cannot be disclosed by public authorities in responding to a request under the Freedom of Information Act [**43.2.3**]. The intention of this exemption is to protect individuals' privacy. This protection was undermined by the Durant case [above], which said that a document which merely mentions an individual is not personal data. This means it is not covered by the Data Protection Act and does not have to be disclosed to the individual if he or she makes a **subject access request** [**43.3.5**] – but it also means it *can* be disclosed if the information is held by a public authority and someone makes a relevant freedom of information request. Specialist advice should be sought if this becomes an issue.

The question of whether anonymised information can be personal data was tested in a case involving a FOI request for leukaemia statistics for an area of Scotland, held by the NHS Common Services Agency (CSA). Because the numbers were very low, it could be possible to identify the individuals involved even though their names were never used. The original decision was that the information was not personal data and could therefore be released under the FOIA. The House of Lords overturned this decision, saying that the information was personal data, and could therefore not be released under the FOIA unless it could be anonymised in such a way that individuals could not be identified.

Common Services Agency v Scottish Information Commissioner [2008] UKHL 47

There have also been cases where it was held by the information commissioner that personal data – details of the expenses of senior government officials – should be disclosed in the public interest.

43.3.2 Data controllers and data processors

Processing includes obtaining, recording, holding or carrying out any operation on information. Operations include organising, changing, retrieving, consulting, using, disclosing, erasing or destroying data.

A **data controller** is an organisation or individual who decides, either on its own or with others, how data is to be processed and the purposes for which it is used.

An organisation or individual who handles information on behalf of a data controller, but has no say in how the information is collected or used, is a **data processor**. Examples of data processors are payroll services, external fundraisers, or mailing houses.

The data controller must be satisfied that the data processor has adequate security [**43.3.3.1**], and must have a written contract setting out the data controller/data processor relationship and requiring the data processor to comply with its security obligations. *Data Protection Act 1998 sch.1 pt.II para.11*

43.3.2.1 Employees and volunteers

Employees who handle information on behalf of their employer are agents of the data controller, rather than being data processors. Although the Act does not explicitly mention volunteers, they are likely also to be agents if they are using the data under the direction and control of the data controller.

43.3.2.2 Joint activities

Where organisations undertake joint activities, share data or enter into partnerships with other bodies, it is essential to establish who is or are the data controller(s) and who, if anyone, is a data processor, and how their relationship is regulated [**43.3.4.3**].

43.3.2.3 Private use

The processing by an individual of personal data for his or her own personal, family or household affairs is, in effect, exempt from the **Data Protection Act**. This is what makes it permissible for families to photograph or video school activities in which their own children are taking part, for example [but see also **43.3.4.6**].

43.3.3 Data protection principles

All data controllers must comply with the eight **data protection principles**. The principles say that personal data must:

- be processed lawfully and fairly [**43.3.3.1**];
- be obtained only for one or more specified and lawful purposes, and not be processed in any manner incompatible with that purpose or those purposes;
- be adequate, relevant and not excessive in relation to the purpose(s) for which it is held;
- be accurate and, where necessary, be kept up to date;
- be held no longer than is necessary for the specified purpose(s);
- be processed in accordance with the rights of data subjects [**43.3.5**];
- be held securely, with appropriate technical and organisational measures to prevent unauthorised or unlawful processing of personal data, and to prevent accidental loss or destruction of, or damage to, personal data;
- not be transferred to a country outside the European Economic Area, unless that country ensures an adequate level of protection for data subjects in relation to the processing of personal data. *Data Protection Act 1998 sch.1*

43.3.3.1 Conditions for fair processing

In order for data to be fairly processed (obtained, stored, used and/or destroyed), the data subject must know who is collecting it, why they are collecting it, what they intend to do with it, and to whom it might be disclosed. The data controller may specify the purpose(s) directly to the data subject, or by notification to the information commissioner [**43.3.7**]. Even where the purpose has been notified to the information commissioner, it is good practice to inform the data subject unless it is obvious from the context in which the data is collected.

The processing must comply with the data protection principles [above]. It must also meet at least one of the following conditions. If it does not, the processing is automatically unfair.

- The data subject has given consent to the processing. This consent may be explicit, or may be implicit where the purpose is obvious, for example, a trainee at a training project providing information about his or her previous education and work experience.

- The processing is necessary to carry out a contract to which the data subject is a party – for example to buy goods or services from, or provide goods or services under contract to, the data subject – or for taking steps at the request of the data subject with a view to entering into a contract.

- The data controller needs to process the data in order to comply with a legal obligation, other than a contractual obligation.

- The processing is necessary to protect the vital interests of the data subject.

- The processing is necessary for the administration of justice or for government or other functions of a public nature.

- The processing is necessary for the legitimate interests of the data controller or of a third party to whom the information is disclosed. This condition is not valid where the processing or disclosure could prejudice the rights, freedoms or interests of the data subject.   *Data Protection Act 1998 sch.2*

43.3.3.2 Sensitive personal data

Further requirements apply to the processing of **sensitive personal data**, consisting of information relating to the data subject's racial or ethnic origin, political opinions, religious or similar beliefs, trade union membership, physical or mental health or condition or sexual life; the commission or alleged commission by the data subject of any offence; or any proceedings for any offence committed or allegedly committed by the data subject, the disposal of such proceedings or the court's sentence in any such proceedings.   *Data Protection Act 1998 s.2*

Before a data controller can process sensitive data, one of the conditions relating to all personal data [above] must be met. In some cases explicit consent from the data subject is required, but there are a number of exceptions such as where the information is being processed to comply with a legal requirement relating to employment, or to protect the vital interests of the data subject or another person where consent cannot reasonably be obtained, or where the information is used only for the purposes of equal opportunities monitoring. There are a number of other situations where sensitive information can be processed without explicit consent, but care should always be taken when using such information.
Data Protection (Processing of Sensitive Personal Data) Order 2000 [SI 2000/417]

43.3.3.3 How long information can be held

There is a pervasive myth that personal data has to be destroyed after a specified period. This is not the case, and relevant information can be kept as long as is reasonable for the purpose(s) for which it has been collected. The organisation's data protection policy should state how long different types of information must or may be kept. In drawing up a retention schedule, factors to consider include:

- legal requirements which set out a minimum period for which certain information must be held [**18.4.2**];

- information which should be held in case the organisation needs to bring, or has brought against it, legal action [**18.4.2**];

- other situations in which the information might be required, and it would matter that it was not available;

- wanting to keep information indefinitely for historical or research purposes, in which case safeguards have to be in place for information about individuals.

43.3.3.4 Disposal of information

All information containing confidential personal data, even if it is only a name or address, must be destroyed before being disposed of. Paper should be shredded. It is also possible to shred CDs, and advice should be taken about how to ensure information is completely removed from floppy disks, hard drives and other media. No computer should be passed on to anyone without ensuring the hard drive has been or will be completely wiped – simply deleting the data is not adequate.

43.3.3.5 Employment records

The information commissioner [see end of chapter] has issued a data protection code on employment records, covering recruitment and selection, employment records, monitoring at work, and information about workers' health. A summary is available for small organisations. Failure to comply with the code is taken into account in any claim involving alleged breach of data protection.

43.3.4 Provision or transfer of personal data

A data controller may provide personal data to third parties only if the disclosure is fair, is properly authorised, is compatible with a purpose for which the data is held, and falls within one of the conditions for fair processing [**43.3.3.1**]. In the case of sensitive personal data, explicit consent must have been obtained, or the disclosure must fall within one of the exemptions for sensitive personal data [**43.3.3.2**]. A disclosure may not be fair if the data subject was not aware that disclosure of that type might take place, and almost certainly is not fair if consent was sought but was withheld.

43.3.4.1 Exemptions allowing disclosure

The data controller may (but in most cases does not have to) disclose data, even if such disclosure is unfair or incompatible with the purpose, in order to assist the prevention or detection of crime, apprehension or prosecution of offenders, or assessment or collection of tax or duty. *Data Protection Act 1998 ss.27(3),(4),29(3)*

A statutory duty to disclose to the police or other authorities [**43.1.2**] or to make information available to the public, for example about a company's members [**18.5.2**] or directors [**18.5.4**], overrides most data protection duties.

43.3.4.2 Employee liability information

When all or part of an organisation's work is being transferred to another employer, the transferring employer has to provide specified details, called **employee liability information**, to the receiving organisation about the employees who will or may be transferred [**29.7**]. This disclosure is allowed under the Data Protection Act, but it should comply with the information commissioner's guidance on TUPE employee liability information [**29.7.3**].

43.3.4.3 Data sharing

Government departments and public bodies operating at the regional and local level are increasingly encouraged to share information, and voluntary organisations working alongside public bodies are affected by this. The information commissioner and the Ministry of Justice [see end of chapter] have set out the criteria which local authorities and other public bodies should use when considering whether to share information with other departments, authorities or agencies. Among the basic principles are that organisations should identify the benefits and risks, take reasonable steps to safeguard personal information, consider whether consent is needed, be transparent about what is being shared and why, ensure information is up to date and accurate, and ensure compliance with the **Data Protection Act** and other relevant legislation.

At the time of writing (mid 2009), legislation was expected which would lead to a code of practice on data sharing. Failure to comply with the code could be taken into account in legal proceedings.

Although intended primarily for public bodies, the guidance is applicable to voluntary organisations sharing information with each other as well.

It is good practice for organisations intending to share data on a regular basis to set up a data sharing protocol to ensure that all parties are working within the same or compatible data protection frameworks.

43.3.4.4 Off site working

Procedures must be put in place to ensure the safekeeping and proper use of personal data held by employees or volunteers who work at home or away from the organisation's premises, or where data is on laptops or other portable devices. All such data should be encrypted and securely password protected. This applies not only to data about individuals, but all information about the organisation.

43.3.4.5 Use of photographs and film

Photographs, videos and other media in which individuals can be identified can potentially be personal data [**43.3.1**], and any use of them must comply with the data protection principles. It is relatively straightforward to ensure that people in private settings, such as attending a training course, are aware that photographs are being taken and the purposes for which they will be used, and can opt out if they wish. For public or quasi public events, such as an organisation's summer festival, it may be possible to include a statement in advertisements or the programme that the event will be filmed and photographed for the organisation's fundraising and publicity purposes.

An exemption to the **Data Protection Act** allows photographs or film of individuals to be used for journalistic, artistic or literary purposes that are in the public interest. This allows, for example, use of crowd shots in newspapers or news programmes, even if individuals were not aware they were being photographed. However, the exemption is very limited, and organisations should not rely on it.

Data Protection Act 1998 s.32

Even where use of photographs and similar material is allowed, it is important to distinguish between current and archive material, especially in relation to children. People change their appearance, change their relationship with the organisation (or with the people they are with in the photograph) or die, so material more than a year or two old should generally be used only if it is appropriate to use archive material, and it should be made clear that the material is not current.

As well as potentially breaching data protection law, the European court of human rights has ruled that taking a photograph of a person without consent, even if the image is never published, could be a breach of the right to private life guaranteed under the European convention on human rights article 8 [**64.3.1**].

Reklos & Davourlis v Greece [2009] 1234/05 ECHR 200

43.3.4.6 Photographs or film of children

Images of children under 12 should not be used unless a parent or guardian knows they are being photographed, knows how the images will be used and gives consent. It is particularly important to ensure they know if the images will or might be used on a website.

Scottish law treats a young person as able to give consent at age 12 or older, but in England and Wales the person must be capable of understanding what he or she is being asked to consent to. This puts the obligation on the organisation which will use the images to decide whether to get consent from the young person or from a parent or guardian.

Although consent does not in most cases have to be explicit, it may be sensible to get it in writing.

43.3.4.7 Transfers outside the EEA

When data is transferred outside the UK, it should if possible be given the same level of protection – either by law or by contract – as it has within the UK.

Personal data can be transferred to countries within the European Economic Area (European Union plus Iceland, Liechtenstein and Norway), provided it complies with the rules for transfers within the UK.

Some countries outside the EEA are considered by the EU to have adequate safeguards. A list of these countries is available from the information commissioner. In the US there is a voluntary scheme under which organisations and businesses can commit themselves to the **safe harbor** privacy principles.

If a transfer does not fall within those safeguards, the data controller should:

- have in place **binding corporate rules**, legally binding internal rules approved by the information commissioner, about how transferred data will be protected within overseas parts of the same organisation;

- use model contracts with specified clauses agreed by the EU for the transfer of data to other organisations overseas;
- get explicit consent from the data subject for the transfer; or
- use a self assessment procedure to assess the risk and ensure appropriate procedures are in place.

Separate issues arise in relation to information about individuals placed on the organisation's website, which is available to viewers outside the EEA.

43.3.5 Individuals' right to data

With some exceptions, individuals have a **subject access right** to information about themselves, and a right to have the data corrected or deleted. A request must be made in writing by the data subject to the data controller. This can, but does not have to, be on a request form. The data controller may charge up to £10. The request must be answered within 40 calendar days of receiving the request.

Data Protection Act 1998 s.7

Where answering the request would involve the disclosure of information relating to another individual (including identifying a person as the source of the information), the data controller does not have to comply with the request unless the other individual has consented to the disclosure, or it is reasonable in all the circumstances to comply with the request without the consent of the other individual. Even if it is not possible to provide all the requested information to the data subject, the data controller must still provide as much of the information as it can without disclosing the identity of the other person – for example by leaving out names or other identifying details.

Data Protection Act 1998 s.7(4),(5)

The criteria used in determining whether it is reasonable to comply with a request for subject access without the consent of the other individual include any duty of confidentiality owed to the other individual (although the information commissioner has said that where information has been provided in a professional capacity, it is less likely that confidentiality can be invoked); any steps taken by the data controller to seek the consent of the other individual; whether the other individual is capable of giving consent; and any explicit refusal of consent by the other person.

Data Protection Act 1998 s.7(6)

43.3.5.1 Exceptions

Data subjects do not have access to data about themselves held only for the purposes of preparing statistics or carrying out research, where individuals cannot be identified in the final statistics or research.

Data Protection Act 1998 s.33(4)

In certain cases, public bodies in the fields of health, social work and education can withhold information if its disclosure would be likely to cause serious harm to the data subject or other individuals.

Data Protection (Subject Access Modification) (Health) Order 2000 [SI 2000/413]; Data Protection (Subject Access Modification) (Social Work) Order 2000 [SI 2000/415] & (Amendment) Order 2005 [2005/467]; Data Protection (Miscellaneous Subject Access Exemptions) Order 2000 [SI 2000/419] & (Amendment) Order 2000 [SI 2000/1865]

43.3.5.2 References

Under specific rules that apply to references relating to training, employment or providing a service, a person or organisation who *provides* a confidential reference does not have to disclose the reference to the individual. But a data controller who *receives* a reference may have to disclose it to the individual, even if it is marked confidential and even if the referee says they do not want it to be disclosed.

The information commissioner [see end of chapter] has issued guidance on the criteria for deciding whether to disclose a reference. These include whether the information is truly confidential or is already known to the individual, any explicit assurance of confidentiality given to the referee, any relevant reasons the referee gives for withholding consent, the potential or actual effect of the reference on the individual, the fact that a reference must be truthful and accurate and that without access to it the individual is not in a position to challenge its accuracy, that good employment practice suggests that an employee should have already been advised of any weakness, and any risk to the referee.

43.3.6   **Right to prevent use of data**

Individuals may prevent a data controller from using information about them in a number of ways. Where the data controller invites the data subject to give consent for data processing [**43.3.3.1**] or explicit consent for sensitive personal data [**43.3.3.2**], the individual can refuse to give this consent. There is an absolute right to prevent the use of personal data for direct marketing [**43.4.1**]. Individuals cannot be sent unsolicited direct marketing faxes [**43.4.1.3**], and have the right to opt out of unsolicited direct marketing telephone calls, emails or text messages [**43.4.1.2, 43.4.1.4**].

In addition, an individual can at any time prevent a data controller from using his or her personal data, where the use of that information would cause substantial and unwarranted damage or distress to himself or herself or to another person. The request must be in writing, and the data controller must reply within 21 days stating whether it intends to stop the data processing, and if not why not.

Data Protection Act 1998 s.10

Where significant decisions about an individual are made solely on the basis of automated processes, the individual can require the data controller not to make decisions about himself or herself solely on this basis. This includes, for example, automated employment selection processes and creditworthiness scoring.

Data Protection Act 1998 s.12

43.3.7   **Notification / registration**

Unless all information kept on computer is exempt [below], the organisation must **notify** the information commissioner, and must renew its registration every year. The procedure is quite straightforward. The annual fee (as at 1/10/09) is £35 for organisations which are not in 'tier 2'. An organisation is in tier 2 if its annual turnover is £25.9 million or more and it has 250 or more employees, and it is not a charity or a small occupational pension scheme. It is an offence not to notify if required to do so. *Data Protection (Notification & Notification Fees) (Amendment) Regulations 2000 [SI 2000/188] regs.7,7A, amended/inserted by (Amendment) Regulations 2009 [SI 2009/1677] reg.3*

The public register of data controllers is available on the Information Commissioner's Office website [see end of chapter], but inclusion on the register does not constitute any guarantee that data is being processed properly.

43.3.7.1   Exemptions from notification

An organisation does not have to notify (register) under the Data Protection Act if all of its information is within the following categories:

- it keeps data about prospective, current or past employees, workers [**25.1.2**] or volunteers, and uses it only for appointment, dismissal, pay, discipline, pensions, work management and other personnel purposes;

- it keeps data about past, current or prospective customers or suppliers, and uses the data only to keep accounts or keep records of sales and purchases in order to ensure that the appropriate payments or deliveries are made, and/or uses the data to advertise or market the organisation's business, activities, goods or services or to promote public relations in connection with the organisation's activities, goods or services; and/or

- the organisation is a non-profit body and the data is used only to establish or maintain membership of or support for the organisation, or to provide or administer activities for individuals who are members or have regular contact with the organisation. *DP Regs 2000 schedule paras.2-5*

In addition to meeting all of the above criteria if they are applicable, the organisation must not disclose the information to any third party unless it is for the relevant exempt purpose or the data subject has given consent to the disclosure. After the organisation's relationship with the individual has ended, the data must not be kept any longer than is necessary to carry out the relevant exempt purposes.

If the organisation uses the above data for any purposes which are not exempt, or keeps any other personal data, it is not exempt from notification.

It is permissible to notify voluntarily, even where it is not required. Where exemption is borderline, voluntary notification may be the simplest course of action.

43.3.8   Redress

An individual who has been harmed by a breach of data protection has the right to compensation, as well as having the information corrected or, if it is disputed, having their side of the story included. The individual also has the right to prevent a data controller from using data in a way that causes them serious harm.

If the data controller does not comply with these rights or the right of subject access [**43.3.5**], the individual can go to court to have them enforced.

Before taking legal action, anyone who has been adversely affected by a breach of data protection can ask the information commissioner to carry out an assessment as to whether a data controller is complying with the Act. This assessment is free, and the information commissioner must carry it out if requested to do so.

More generally, anyone may complain to the information commissioner about a breach of data protection. When carrying out an investigation, the commissioner has powers to obtain warrants to enter and search premises, serve information notices requiring information to be provided, and serve enforcement notices requiring action. Failure to comply with such notices is an offence.

A data subject or data controller may subsequently appeal to the information tribunal against the information commissioner's actions and, on questions of law, may make a further appeal to the high court. From January 2010 the information tribunal is part of the general regulatory chamber in the first-tier tribunal [**64.7.1**].

43.4   DIRECT MARKETING AND TELEMARKETING

The **Data Protection Act 1998**, telecommunications regulations [**43.4.1.2**], e-commerce regulations [**43.4.1.4**] and distance selling regulations [**21.2.3**, **49.3**] contain significant protections in relation to direct marketing.

As well as statutory rules, codes of practice are in place for advertising, sales and direct marketing [**45.2.1**], fundraising [**48.1**] and other aspects of marketing. Separate rules cover door to door and public marketing or fundraising [**49.2**].

43.4.1   Direct marketing

Direct marketing is defined as 'the communication (by whatever means) of any advertising or marketing material which is directed to particular individuals'. Activities defined by the information commissioner as marketing include fundraising and soliciting support, as well as more obvious direct marketing of goods and services, and may also include direct approaches to individuals to recruit them as volunteers. It covers approaches made by post, fax, telephone, email, SMS text message or any other method directed to a named individual.

Personal data cannot be used for direct marketing unless this purpose has been specified when the information was collected [**43.3.3.1**]. Even where this purpose was specified, an individual may at any time require the data controller to stop using, or not start using, his or her personal data for the purposes of direct marketing. As this is an absolute right, individuals should be given the right to opt out of receiving direct marketing materials, for example through a tick box on order forms or donation forms. Failure to offer this option may constitute unfair data processing.   *Data Protection Act 1998 s.11*

43.4.1.1   Direct marketing mail

As well as opting out of direct mail from specific organisations, individuals may choose to opt out completely from some or all types of direct mail through the **Mailing Preference Service** [see end of chapter]. MPS can also be used to stop mailings addressed to people who have died. **Baby MPS** allows parents who have suffered a miscarriage or bereavement of a baby in the first weeks of life to register their wish not to receive baby related mailings.

At the time of writing (mid 2009) the government had proposed an opt-in approach to direct mail, under which mailings could be sent to individuals only if they had signed up to a direct mail register. It had also proposed an opt-out system for unaddressed mail.

43.4.1.2 Direct marketing telephone calls

Individuals, organisations and businesses may opt out of receiving unsolicited direct marketing telephone calls on landlines or mobile phones by registering with the **Telephone Preference Service** [see end of chapter]. Registration of mobile phones stops unsolicited calls, but not text messages.

It is an offence for an organisation to make an unsolicited direct marketing call to anyone who has opted out through TPS – even if the number comes from the organisation's own database – unless the person being called has explicitly consented to receiving marketing calls from the caller. Information about how to suppress calls to registered numbers and how to obtain the TPS register on disk or other electronic media is on the TPS website.   *Privacy & Electronic Communications (EC Directive) Regulations 2003 [SI 2003/2426] regs.21.26; (Amendment) Regulations 2004 [SI 2004/1039]*

43.4.1.3 Direct marketing faxes

Businesses and organisations may opt out of receiving unsolicited faxes by registering with the **Fax Preference Service** [see end of chapter]. Individuals may be sent marketing faxes only if they have explicitly opted in to receiving them from that company or organisation. It is an offence to send an unsolicited direct marketing fax to any other residential phone number, even if it has not opted out, but individuals may opt out if they wish. Persons sending direct marketing faxes must check the numbers in the same way as for telemarketing calls [above].

Privacy Regs 2003 regs.20,25

43.4.1.4 Direct marketing email and text messages

Email addresses of recognisable individuals could be personal data under the Data Protection Act, so should not be used or passed on to third parties unless these purposes have been specified to the data subject.

Marketing emails must not disguise or conceal the identity of the sender, and must contain a valid email address. They may also, if the organisation is an incorporated body and/or a charity, need to contain other information [**18.1**].

Electronic Communications (EC Directive) Regulations 2002 [SI 2002/2013]

It is an offence to send spam – unsolicited emails, SMS text messages and other electronic marketing – from within the EU unless the person has explicitly opted in to receiving them. There is an exception for marketing similar products or services to existing customers, but even such customers must be provided with an opportunity to object when the data is initially collected and at any time subsequently. This rule applies to commercial relationships and does not apply where the individual is, for example, a member of or donor to an organisation.

Privacy & Electronic Communications (EC Directive) Regulations 2003 [SI 2003/2426] regs.22,23

In addition to a general opt-out statement on publicity, fundraising, membership and similar materials, organisations should use an opt-in statement along the lines of 'We may want to send you information about our work and products by email, text message, fax or other electronic media. Please tick here to give your consent for this.'

Any individual, whether a customer or not, can require a specific data controller in the UK to stop sending direct marketing emails, texts etc, and can make a complaint to the information commissioner if they do not. They can also register with the US-based **Email Preference Service** [see end of chapter], which might reduce the amount of unsolicited marketing material originating in the US and other non-EU countries.

As well as contravening data protection legislation, use of the internet to send unsolicited marketing material could be a breach of the sender's contract with their internet service provider (ISP).

43.4.1.5 Cookies

Regulations extend to the use of 'cookies' and similar tracking devices which store information about visitors to a website. Organisations with websites must provide information about the use of cookies and allow individuals to refuse them.

43.4.2   Sale or provision of lists

The sale or provision of lists, including lists of postal or email addresses, for direct marketing or any other purpose, or the compilation of personal data into directories for publication, is unlawful unless the person has been informed that the data will be used in this way and has been given a chance to opt out. The sale of lists also constitutes trading, and there may be implications for tax [**56.4.4**] and VAT [**57.8.2**].

43.5   TELEPHONE AND INTERNET USE POLICIES

It is good practice for organisations to draw up **acceptable use** policies or codes of practice on use of telephones, email, the internet and other electronic media by employees and volunteers. These should encourage responsible behaviour and good management practice and should safeguard staff privacy, while enabling employers to protect their legitimate interests.

Information about what should be included in acceptable use policies is available from ACAS and Out-law.com [below]. Out-law.com provides a free communications policy, covering email, internet, intranet, system security, working away from the organisation's own premises, monitoring of communications and data protection.

Where telephone calls are monitored, it is good practice for the organisation to provide separate lines (which may be payphones) for private use by staff, or to allow staff to use their own mobile phones.

To avoid disputes about whether employees and volunteers have been notified that communications will be monitored, it is good practice to have them sign the policy, or for a clause stating that communications will or may be monitored to be included in the contract of employment or volunteer agreement [**27.10.4**].

Resources: DATA PROTECTION AND USE OF INFORMATION

Data protection. Information Commissioner's Office: www.ico.gov.uk, 08456 30 60 60, notifications notification@ico.gsi.gov.uk, other emails via website.

Ministry of Justice: www.justice.gov.uk, 020 7210 8500, queries@justice.gsi.gov.uk.

Direct marketing. Direct Marketing Association: www.dma.org.uk, 020 7291 3300, info@dma.org.uk.

Email Preference Service: www.dmaconsumers.org/emps.html (based in the US).

Fax Preference Service: www.fpsonline.org.uk, 0845 070 0702, fps@dma.org.uk.

Mailing Preference Service: www.mpsonline.org.uk, 0845 703 4599, mps@dma.org.uk.

Telephone Preference Service: www.tpsonline.org.uk, 0845 070 0707; tps@dma.org.uk.

Freedom of information. Information Commissioner's Office and Ministry of Justice [above].

Campaign for Freedom of Information: www.cfoi.org.uk, 020 7831 7477, admin@cfoi.demon.co.uk.

Information policies. ACAS: www.acas.org.uk, 08457 47 47 47.

Department for Business, Innovation and Skills, www.bis.gov.uk, 020 7215 5000, enquiries@bis.gsi.gov.uk.

Out-law.com: www.out-law.com.

Statute law. www.opsi.gov.uk and www.statutelaw.gov.uk.

Much but not all case law. www.bailii.org.

Updates cross-referenced to this book. www.rclh.co.uk.

Chapter 44

INTELLECTUAL PROPERTY

For sources of further information see end of chapter.

44.1   INTELLECTUAL PROPERTY RIGHTS

Intellectual property (IP) refers to non-tangible assets such as names, goodwill and rights arising from the creation and invention of new products and creative works. Most intellectual property is protected by various legal rights, some of which arise automatically and some of which are effective only if registered.

Rights which exist without registration are copyright [**44.2**], database right [**44.2.10**], moral rights arising from copyright [**44.3**], the right to prevent others exploiting a reputation and goodwill [**44.5**], design right [**44.7**], and rights relating to confidential information [**44.8**]. Rights established through registration are registered trade marks [**44.4**], registered designs [**44.7**], and patents [**44.6**].

Like other property, intellectual property rights owned by an individual can be inherited. If they are owned by a charity, trustees who fail to protect the rights could be in breach of their duty to safeguard the charity's assets [**15.6.5**].

44.2   COPYRIGHT

Copyright gives the copyright owner the right to use or exploit the work, decide how it may be used or exploited by others, and prevent unauthorised persons from using it. It protects original literary, dramatic, musical and artistic works; sound recordings, films, broadcasts, and cable programmes; the typographical arrangement of published editions (what a publication looks like); and compilations of data that do not comply with the requirements for database right [**44.2.10**].

Copyright, Designs & Patents Act 1988 s.1

This covers most original written and artistic work, including articles, reports and books whether published or not, leaflets, fundraising materials, drawings, paintings, photographs, correspondence, music, dance, plays and theatrical productions, email and website design and content, and computer programs. It covers information on paper, film, videotape, audiotape, CD, DVD, websites, computer, computer disks and any other media.

Copyright does not generally protect the name of an organisation, but may protect the particular way the name is written or designed [**44.9**].

Copyright does not protect ideas or information [**44.8**]. Once they are written down, that version of the ideas or information becomes protected by copyright, but other people generally have the right to use those ideas or that information. (The copyright owners of this book can stop you from using the words as they are put together on this page, but cannot stop you from using the information on this page to write your own briefing on copyright.)

The person or persons who create a copyright work are referred to as its **author** or **creator**, regardless of the nature of the work or how many persons there are. The person who owns the actual work – for example a painting or a manuscript – is the **owner of the work**. The person who owns the copyright is the **copyright owner** [**44.2.3**], who may or may not be the author or owner of the work.

The **UK Intellectual Property Office** [see end of chapter] provides information on all aspects of copyright, including EU and international copyright. At the time of writing (mid 2009) the government had consulted on whether copyright law was too complex and should be reformed.

44.2.1 Creation

In the UK, copyright arises automatically as soon as a work is created and 'fixed' in some way, with no need for registration. An article, for example, is protected as soon as it is written on paper or computer, a drawing is protected as soon as it is drawn, a tune is protected as soon as it is recorded, and images on a website are protected as soon as they are created. If the copyright material is published, the form and appearance of the published edition or version may also be protected.

It is sensible to keep a record of the author and date of creation of any work produced for or by an organisation and regarded by it as a copyright work. Traditionally, authors recorded the creation of a work by posting a copy to themselves by registered post and leaving the envelope unopened, thus showing that the work was in existence at the date it was posted. This is not necessary, and it is usually enough to note on every draft of a work the date and author.

In some cases it may be appropriate to provide a copy of the material to a copyright registration service, which will issue a certificate showing the date on which the material was registered with them. If necessary, the service may provide evidence at court that the material was registered on a certain date.

44.2.2 Duration

The duration of copyright protection depends on the type of work and the date the work was first created. For literary, artistic, musical and dramatic works, copyright lasts until 70 years from the end of the calendar year in which the author dies. If the work is created by two or more people, it remains protected until the end of the calendar year 70 years after the death of the last surviving author.

The copyright in the published edition of the work lasts for 25 years. Even where the content of a work is out of copyright, a particular presentation of it may be protected. The duration for films is 70 years, and 50 years for sound recordings, broadcasts and cable programmes. The start date for the copyright period varies for each of these, but is based on when the work was created rather than on the death of the creator.   *Duration of Copyright & Rights in Performances Regulations 1995 [SI 1995/3297]*

At the time of writing (mid 2009), an EU-wide extension of the copyright period for sound recordings from 50 years to 70 years was being considered. The European Commission was also looking at whether the period for audiovisual materials should be extended to 70 years.

Works protected by copyright in the UK are also protected in countries which are members of the **Berne Convention** and the **Universal Copyright Convention**, but they should include the © symbol [**44.2.4**].

44.2.3   Ownership

The person who first creates a copyright work (the **author**) usually owns the copyright. If more than one person is involved each may own copyright in part, or they may jointly own copyright in the whole work.

The two important exceptions to the rule that the author owns copyright are where the work is produced by an employee [**44.2.3.1**], or the author assigns copyright to someone else [**44.2.3.4**].

Ownership of copyright must be distinguished from ownership of the work itself. Regardless of who owns the work, copyright remains with the author, his or her estate, or the person or company to whom the author has assigned copyright.

Ownership of copyright must also be distinguished from **moral rights** [**44.3**]. Authors may retain moral rights even if they no longer own the copyright.

44.2.3.1   Works produced by employees

Copyright in any work created by employees in the course of their employment belongs to the employer, unless there is an agreement to the contrary.

Copyright, Designs & Patents Act 1988 s.11(2)

To avoid uncertainty it is a good idea, but not essential, to include a clause in contracts of employment stating that copyright in everything done by the employee during the course of his or her employment belongs to the employer [**27.10.5**].

An employee who is working on a special project or a task which could arguably be outside the course of his or her employment should be asked to assign copyright to the employer [**44.2.3.4**].

44.2.3.2   Works produced by volunteers

Unless a volunteer is legally an employee [**39.4**], copyright in their work belongs to the volunteer rather than the organisation. Volunteers who produce copyright work should be asked to assign copyright to the organisation [**44.2.3.4**], or should agree a licence setting out the purposes for which it can be used [**44.11**].

44.2.3.3   Works produced by outside persons and agencies

Copyright in work done by self employed persons [**38.1**] and others who are not employees generally belongs to them, not to the organisation which commissions them and pays for the work. If the commissioning organisation wants to own the copyright or to share ownership with the author, this must be explicit in the contract for the work or a separate assignment of copyright. In the absence of such agreement, the courts will generally assume that the commissioning organisation has an exclusive licence [**44.11**] to use the work, but does not own the copyright.

Particular care should be taken when commissioning design of a website or logo, as the organisation's freedom to use the design may be limited if the designer owns the copyright to the work. An organisation should ensure that in such circumstances the designer assigns copyright to the organisation.

44.2.3.4   Assignment of copyright

To be legally binding, an assignment of copyright must be in the form of a contract [**21.1**] or deed [**20.3**], and must be signed by or on behalf of the assignor. In some situations the organisation may agree that the author(s) of the work will retain copyright, with the organisation granted a licence [**44.11**] to use the work.

Copyright, Designs & Patents Act 1988 s.90(3)

If an organisation does not secure copyright for a work, it will need the author's consent to use the work for any purpose other than what was explicitly agreed when the work was commissioned. In addition the organisation will not be able to stop the author from using the work for other purposes, and it will not be able to bring an action for copyright infringement if anyone else uses the work, because only the copyright owner can bring such action. These problems become particularly acute if the author cannot be traced or refuses to assign the copyright.

In situations where copyright is not assigned, the commissioning body may be able to assert a right to the copyright as a party to a joint venture.

44.2.4 Use of the copyright symbol

There is no legal requirement to use the © **symbol** to show a claim of copyright in the UK. If international protection is required, use of the symbol is obligatory for **Universal Copyright Convention** protection outside the UK.

Use of the symbol does not, in itself, prove ownership of copyright. However, the symbol followed by the name of the copyright owner and the year of copyright makes clear that copyright in the work is claimed, and should make it less likely that others will copy the work.

It also increases the likelihood that the copyright owner would be able to obtain damages from infringers, because it would be difficult for them to argue innocence if the work is marked with the symbol.

44.2.5 Breach of copyright

Copying, publishing, performing or using someone else's copyright material without permission is generally an infringement of their copyright. The copyright owner's legal remedies include an injunction against use of the material, an award of damages, or an account (award) of the profits made from the infringement. Infringement may also be a criminal offence if it involves commercial exploitation of copyright material.

Copyright, Designs & Patents Act 1988 ss.16-27,107-110,
amended by Intellectual Property (Enforcement etc) Regulations 2006 [SI 2006/1028]

44.2.6 Licensed use of copyright material

Permission to copy, publish or perform someone else's copyright material is generally referred to as a **licence**. Much material can be covered under various types of collective licence [below]. Where the organisation wants to use or copy material which is not covered by an exemption [**44.2.7**] or a collective licence, it is likely to need a specific licence [**44.11**].

At the time of writing (mid 2009), the European Commission had proposed EU-wide copyright licensing, in particular for online music, film and games.

44.2.6.1 Newspaper cuttings

Anyone can clip articles from a newspaper, but if the articles are photocopied, scanned, emailed or copied in any other way, even for internal management purposes, consent is required.

A licence is available from the **Newspaper Licensing Agency** [see end of chapter], covering photocopying and digital copying of articles from national, regional, local and foreign newspapers and some specialist publications.

Most voluntary organisations need a **basic business licence** which covers occasional copying of UK national newspapers. This can be extended to cover, if required, occasional copying of UK local and foreign newspapers, frequent copying, and/or digital copying. The basic business licence is issued free of charge to registered charities with up to five employees or with annual income below £250,000 (as at 1/8/09), and at a discount to larger registered charities. Organisations which have been copying material without a licence have to pay a one-off indemnity fee, calculated as a multiple of the current year fee, to cover past copying.

Even under the licence, copies may be made only for distribution to staff for internal management purposes. Copying for other purposes – for example, reproduction in a newsletter or on the organisation's website, or emailing to the organisation's members – must be licensed by the publisher of the newspaper.

44.2.6.2 Magazines, journals and books

Organisations which regularly copy from magazines, journals and books – whether print, online, or 'born digital' materials that are created digitally and may not even be capable of being printed – may obtain a copyright licence from the **Copyright Licensing Agency** [see end of chapter]. This eliminates the need to obtain consent each time material is copied. The licence also covers US digital publications. There is no provision for free or discounted licences for charities.

Under this licence, material can be photocopied, digitally copied or scanned, but there are detailed restrictions on the use or distribution of electronic copies.

44.2.6.3 Visual arts and photographs

Licences for use of visual art and photographs are available from **Design and Artists Copyright Society** [see end of chapter].

44.2.6.4 Music

A variety of licences may be required to perform copyright music and lyrics, or to play recorded music or videos/DVDs for anything other than personal use [**47.6**].

At the time of writing (mid 2009) the government was considering creating a **private right to copy** which would make it lawful for people to copy CDs etc onto a computer or MP3 player for their personal use. Even without legislation, some record labels explicitly allow such **format shifting**.

44.2.6.5 Broadcasts

Through a licensing scheme operated by the **Educational Recording Agency** [see end of chapter], educational establishments can record broadcasts. The licence does not cover Open University television programmes, which are subject to a separate licensing arrangement. *Copyright (Certification of Licensing Scheme for Educational Recording of Broadcasts) Order 2007 [SI 2007/0266], amended by 2008 Order [SI 2008/211]*

44.2.7 Use of copyright material without a licence

In limited circumstances, copyright material may be copied without a licence.

44.2.7.1 Educational use and 'fair dealing'

Fair dealing exceptions, where it is not necessary to get the copyright owner's permission to copy literary, dramatic or artistic works, include:

- making a single copy of a short extract of a published work for research for a non-commercial purpose, provided appropriate acknowledgement is given, or for private study for a non-commercial purpose;
- use of some copyright works for educational purposes, such as copying text or a film to prepare for teaching or for inclusion in an examination paper, or for performing a dramatic or musical work;
- single copies of short extracts made by librarians or archivists, provided the librarian or archivist is satisfied that the copies will be used solely for research or private study for a non-commercial purpose, and not for any other purpose. *Copyright, Designs & Patents Act 1988 ss.28-50; Copyright & Related Rights Regulations 2003 [SI 2003/2498]*

Prior to the 2003 regulations, single copies could be made for commercial research, but now even a single copy for commercial purposes requires a licence [**44.2.6.2**]. This has implications for trading companies, social enterprises or other organisations which operate commercially, as well as charities and other not for profit organisations which carry out research for a commercial purpose.

The legislation does not specify how much of a published work may be copied before the copying infringes copyright.

44.2.7.2 Review and criticism

For the purposes of criticism or review, the Society of Authors and the Publishers Association have indicated that in their view, permission is not needed to quote a single extract of less than 400 words from a prose work which has been made available to the public, or a series of extracts each less than 300 words and totalling no more than 800 words, provided the total quoted is not more than 25% of the work. Similar limits have been set for quotations from poetry. These are useful rules of thumb but do not have the force of law.

44.2.7.3 Copies for visually impaired people

Where a visually impaired person has a copy of a publication or a literary, dramatic, musical or artistic work which is not accessible to them because of their impairment, it is not a copyright infringement for a single accessible copy to be made for their use. Where the material exists only in inaccessible form, authorised bodies such as voluntary organisations and educational establishments can make multiple copies for use by visually impaired people. These exceptions to copyright law do not apply where making the accessible copy would involve recording a performance of music or would infringe database copyright [**44.2.10**].

Copyright (Visually Impaired Persons) Act 2002 [SI 2002/0033]

44.2.8 Computers and electronic media

Copyright law in relation to electronic information, especially on the internet and in relation to digitised media (**digital rights management**), is developing rapidly. Specialist legal advice may be needed, especially in relation to websites, computer programs and material created or held in digital format.

44.2.8.1 Computer programs

Computer programs or software are regarded as 'literary works' and are protected by copyright [**44.2**]. Running a program usually involves copying it, and converting a program into or between languages constitutes copying. To avoid breach of copyright, an organisation should have a licence from the manufacturer for each commercial computer program it uses.

Where anyone other than an employee designs programs or software for an organisation, the organisation should take legal advice to ensure copyright is assigned to it [**44.2.3.4**] or a comprehensive licence is drawn up allowing it to use and adapt the program or software [**44.11**].

44.2.8.2 Electronic and digitised media

Documents, designs and other creative work on computer, disk, CD, SMS text messaging or other electronic media are protected in the same way as any other work. The text of a document is copyright to the writer, and the way the document is designed is copyright to the person who designed it. If the work is created in the course of employment, the whole product is copyright to the employer [**44.2.3.1**]. Copying electronic or digitised documents without permission of the copyright owner is a breach of copyright unless it falls within a limited number of exceptions, such as compiling a backup copy of a computer program.

Copyright (Computer Programs) Regulations 1992 [SI 1992/3233]

44.2.8.3 Websites

The internet is not a copyright-free zone; indeed, its international nature means it may be subject to the laws of several countries. Websites are likely to be protected by copyright and unauthorised copying is likely to be infringement, although it may be unclear which country's laws would apply. Making an unauthorised link to another person's website may also be a breach of their copyright.

To reduce the risk of others using its copyright material, an organisation should make clear that its website as a whole and every page is copyright, that material may be downloaded and printed out for personal use but may not be reproduced or used in any other way without consent, and that other websites may not create links to the site without consent.

To reduce the risk of breaching copyright, an organisation should:

- ensure the designer of the website, if not an employee designing the website as part of their employment, has assigned copyright in the design to the organisation [**44.2.3.4**];
- ensure the organisation owns the copyright of all material included on the website, or has permission to reproduce it on the website;
- not create links to any other websites without their written consent;
- where links are created, make clear that the material on those sites belongs to those sites;

- have a policy on internet use by employees, volunteers and others [**43.5**], making clear that copyright material from the internet may not be downloaded or used without appropriate consent.

Information about individuals obtained over the internet, for example through membership forms or internet fundraising, must comply with data protection rules [**43.3**], and internet fundraising and marketing must comply with the relevant rules [**43.4**, **45.2.8**]. For registered charities, companies or industrial and provident societies, and organisations registered for VAT, the website should contain the same information as must be included on business stationery [**18.1**].

44.2.8.4 Email

Copyright in emails generally belongs to the author, but if they are created as part of employment it belongs to the employer. If emails are created during work time but not as part of employment, copyright could belong to either the employer or employee. Forwarding an email without consent is a breach of the author's copyright. An internet use policy should address these issues [**43.5**].

44.2.9 Creative Commons

The desire of some organisations to make their training materials, standard documents and other resources widely available on their websites or in other electronic formats does not fit comfortably with the restrictions of copyright law, the complexities of licensing, and the obligations to act for the success of the organisation or to safeguard the organisation's assets [**15.3.2**, **15.6.5**].

The **Creative Commons** scheme [see end of chapter] offers a useful framework for dealing with such issues. A Creative Commons licence permits users to download and distribute creative work freely. The copyright owner can choose to maintain certain rights granted to them by copyright law, such as the right to exploit works for commercial gain, to veto derivative works and/or to be credited each time their work is reproduced, but may give up such rights if they choose.

44.2.10 Databases

A **database** is a collection of independent works, data or other materials, arranged in a systematic or methodical way and individually accessible by electronic or other means. This includes directories, membership and similar lists, encyclopaedias, and other lists or collections of information, whether on paper, disk, CD, or any other medium.

Database **programs on computer** are protected under copyright law [**44.2.8.1**].

Database **content**, whether on electronic media or paper, is protected under copyright law if the structure, selection and arrangement involve sufficient skill and labour and are original enough to be 'an intellectual creation of the author'.

If database content does not meet the 'intellectual creation' test, but involves a substantial investment of financial, human or technical resources in obtaining or checking the data, it may have the lesser protection of **database right**. This prevents the unauthorised extraction (copying or other form of transfer) or reutilisation (distribution) of all or a substantial part of the data, or repeated use of even a small part of the data. **Fair dealing** exceptions allow copying of a small amount for non-commercial research or private study.

As with copyright, ownership rests with the person or persons who created the data, unless they are employees, in which case database right belongs to the employer. Protection under database right is initially for a period of 15 years from 1 January in the year after the database is first created or (if later) marketed. If the contents are updated in a way which amounts to a substantial new investment, a further 15 years of protection begins. *Copyright & Rights in Databases Regulations 1997*
[SI 1997/3032]

If the organisation would have had to collect and collate the data anyway – and therefore has not put substantial additional resources into creating the database itself – it may not even qualify for the protection of database right. An example might be an umbrella organisation which has to collect information about its member organisations in order to carry out its own work. It might have difficulty claiming that it has a database right in a directory of its members which it makes publicly available, unless it has made a substantial additional investment in creating that directory (as opposed to creating the data contained in the directory).

44.3 MORAL RIGHTS

In addition to protection of copyright works, the copyright legislation also provides for the creation of certain **moral rights**. These are:

* **paternity right**, which gives the author of a work the right to be identified as the author, but only if he or she specifically asserts this right [see the copyright page of this book for an example];

* the right not to be falsely described as the author of a work;

* the right of authors and film directors to object to certain deletions or adaptations being made to their works if the effect is derogatory;

* the right to object to the publication of photographs or films commissioned by an individual. *Copyright, Designs & Patents Act 1988 ss.77-95*

There are a number of exceptions, for example that employees who produce work in the course of their employment do not have paternity right or the right to object to derogatory treatment of their work.

Moral rights are not transferred when copyright is assigned, but persons who hold these rights may assign, waive, or give up their rights.

44.3.1 Performers' rights

Anyone performing live in public, broadcasting live or releasing a sound recording of their performance is able to assert **paternity right**, the right to be identified as the performer, and **integrity right**, the right to object to derogatory treatment of that performance. Performers must assert these rights in writing.
Performances (Moral Rights, etc) Regulations 2006 [SI 2006/0018]

The regulations cover the whole or any 'substantial' part of a performance and relate to all types of live performance and sound recordings of performances. However, protection does not cover audio-visual recordings of performances.

Organisations which produce, organise or promote a performance have specific duties under the regulations. These include, for example, a requirement to identify those involved in the performance except where specified exceptions apply.

44.4 REGISTERED TRADE MARKS

Trade mark registration is a relatively cheap and simple but under-used procedure, which can provide a useful deterrent against unauthorised use of the organisation's name, logo or slogans, and can also help with disputes where someone else uses the same or a confusingly similar mark as an internet domain name.

The term trade mark refers both to **trade marks** (for goods) and **service marks** (for services). Any word, sign or symbol – referred to as a **mark** – can be registered if it can be represented graphically (in words or illustration), and it is capable of distinguishing the applicant's goods or services from someone else's.
Trade Marks Act 1994 s.1(1)

Trade marks may consist of words, designs, letters, numerals, or the shape of goods or their packaging. They cover slogans, jingles and colours, and may even be granted for smells, sounds and gestures. To do this, the smell or sound would be described in words, and the gesture would be described in words or pictures.

There are some restrictions on what can be registered, including a restriction on purely descriptive words in common usage (such as 'The Cancer Helpline') unless the applicant can show that, through usage, it has built up a distinctive reputation linked to that name.

The marks most commonly registered by voluntary organisations are their name or names, abbreviations, slogans, logos, domain names, names of events, and marks which are a combination of one or more of these.

Information on trade mark registration is available from the UK Intellectual Property Office (UK IPO) [see end of chapter].

44.4.1 Registration classes

The **trade marks register** is divided into 34 classes of goods and 11 classes of services. Registration gives the owner the exclusive right to use the registered mark, but only in the registered class(es) of goods or services.

44.4.2 Conflicting marks

In the past, a trade mark could not be registered if it was already registered for the same class. But now an application is not automatically rejected if it is the same as or similar to another trade mark in the same class(es). Instead, the UK Intellectual Property Office sends a search report to the applicant, listing any marks which it considers to conflict with the applicant's. The applicant then has two months to decide whether to continue with the application, withdraw it, or restrict the scope so it does not conflict with another mark.

If the applicant proceeds, the UK IPO notifies the owners of conflicting UK trade marks and marks registered under the Madrid Protocol [**44.4.3**]. Owners of community (EU-wide) trade marks are contacted only if they have explicitly opted in for notification. If an owner of a conflicting mark opposes the application, the applicant can file a counter statement, and the UK IPO decides whether to accept or reject the application.

To reduce the risk of rejection, applicants should check the register for similar trade marks in the relevant classes before registering. This can be done by conducting a basic search on the UK IPO website, or using its expert search service, for which a fee is charged. Alternatively, from 1 October 2009 a **Right Start** application can be made for £100 for one class plus £25 for each additional class, and the UK IPO examines the applications and advises whether it meets the requirements for registration. If the application proceeds, the full registration fee – an additional £100, plus £25 for each additional class – is payable.

Owners of EU trade marks should opt in to ensure they are notified of any applications which could conflict with their own mark. This can be done via the uk IPO website.

44.4.3 Registration

The UK Intellectual Property Office provides official guidance on applications, or a solicitor, patent agent or trade marks agent can file applications on behalf of an organisation. Filing typically costs £900 to £1,500, which covers preparation and the application fee. The application fee (as at 1/10/09) for a single class is £200, or £170 if the application is filed electronically and all fees are paid in full at the time of filing. For each additional class the fee is £50. For an additional £300, the application is fast tracked and dealt with within 10 working days. There may be further fees if the application is opposed.

Trade mark registration is permanent, but lapses if a renewal fee (£200 for a single class and £50 for each additional class, as at 1/10/09) is not paid every 10 years. If a trade mark is not used in a five year period, it may be struck off the register.

A **community trade mark** covering all EU member states can be registered via the **Office for Harmonisation in the Internal Market** [see end of chapter].

Under the **Madrid system** for the international registration of trade marks, a UK national who has applied for or registered a trade mark in the UK can apply to the **World Intellectual Property Organisation** in Geneva [see end of chapter] to make simultaneous applications in any or all countries which are parties to the **Madrid agreement** or **Madrid protocol** (a total of 84, at 1/8/09).

44.4.3.1 Organisations with trading subsidiaries

A trade mark applicant should usually be the organisation which uses the mark. If the organisation has a separate trading subsidiary which uses the organisation's name in connection with the sale of certain goods, the application may be filed in the organisation's name with the trading subsidiary then licensed to use the mark [**44.11**], or the application could be filed in the name of the trading subsidiary with the parent organisation licensed to use it.

If there is any risk of the subsidiary becoming insolvent, it is advisable for the parent organisation to retain the rights and license the subsidiary, so there is no risk of the rights being lost in the insolvency.

44.4.4 Use of the registered and ™ symbols

The ® **symbol** does not have to be used for registered trade marks. If it is used, it may be used only for the class(es) for which the mark is registered. It is an offence to give the impression that something is registered when it is not, for example by using the symbol improperly. Anyone who prepares publications or is involved in trading should be made aware of the importance of proper use of the symbol, and should be clear which aspects of the organisation's work are and are not registered in relation to the trade mark.

The ™ **symbol** has no legal significance in the UK, but puts people on notice that the user of the mark regards it as their trade mark. The symbol may be used for marks which are not registered.

44.4.5 Use of trade marks

Registration of a trade mark stops others from registering the same mark in the same class, and from using the mark on goods or services in the class for which it is registered without the consent of the trade mark holder. Permission to use a mark should be recorded in writing in a licence [**44.11**].

Registration may also stop another party registering or using the mark in other classes, if the trade mark holder can prove confusion or bad faith. However, registration is often sufficient to prevent others from registering or using the same or a confusingly similar name.

An exception to the prohibition on using the mark in the same class is **comparative advertising** [**45.2.2**]. Use of a trade mark for this purpose is not infringement, provided there is no likelihood of confusion, the use is 'honest practice', and the use does not take unfair advantage of the trade mark or act detrimentally to the distinctive character or reputation of the mark.

Care needs to be taken when an organisation starts to provide new goods or services which are not in its registration class. Its trade mark will not be protected for the new activities, and if its trade mark is too similar to someone else's in that class, a claim could be brought against it for infringement of their trade mark.

44.4.6 Registration of domain names

As a name, a domain name cannot be protected by copyright, but the organisation's name, initials and/or domain name may be registerable as trade marks. In deciding whether a domain name is distinctive enough to be eligible for registration as a trade mark, suffixes such as .com and .co.uk are generally disregarded. A name prefixed with e– is treated as if it started with 'electronic', and a name prefixed with m– is treated as if it started with 'mobile'.

Even if an organisation has registered its domain name as a trade mark, this does not necessarily stop someone else from registering and using a domain name with the organisation's name or a very similar name. All relevant variants (.org, .org.uk, .com, .co.uk, .eu etc) should be registered as domain names, and should be renewed in good time so there is no possibility of registration lapsing.

With or without trade mark registration, it is possible to take legal action to assert the right to a domain name.

44.5   PASSING OFF

Passing off is using a name, domain name, logo, slogan, packaging etc which is the same as, or very similar to, someone else's in a way which deliberately or unintentionally causes loss of goodwill or financial loss to them. An action for passing off can be brought by the organisation which has suffered the loss, even if the name, slogan or other item which is being misused is not registered in any way, and even if the organisation is a charity or not for profit body rather than a business.   *The British Diabetic Association v The Diabetic Society [1996] EWCA Civ 839*

Generally a court grants protection against passing off only if the organisation can show it has an established reputation or goodwill in the name, slogan or whatever the other party is using to make its misrepresentation; and can show that the other party has deceived members of the public or trade in some way by means of the misrepresentation, or is likely to do so or enable someone else to do so. In addition the organisation has to show it has suffered or is likely to suffer damage or injury to its business, reputation or goodwill. The key test is whether the organisation has such a strong reputation in what it is seeking to protect that the other party's use of something similar would deceive or confuse members of the public.

An action for passing off is generally very expensive, because of the need to prepare detailed evidence proving the organisation's reputation and showing why the other party's actions are causing or are likely to cause damage or confusion. This is very different from an action for infringement of trade mark rights, where no damage or potential damage needs to be shown.

In particularly urgent cases, a court will sometimes grant an immediate (interlocutory) injunction to restrain the other party until the trial.

The remedies are an injunction, damages, and the defendant's profits from the passing off. Even when the action is successful, the organisation is unlikely to get all its costs paid by the other party.

44.6   PATENTS

Patents protect inventions by giving the owner a monopoly right to use the invention, and the right to prevent others using it. Patents generally protect scientific and industrial discoveries, such as manufacturing processes or chemical or biological products, but may also cover computer programs. Information about patents is available from the UK Intellectual Property Office [see end of chapter].

To be patentable, the invention must never have been made public in any way, anywhere in the world, before the date the patent application is filed. It is therefore essential that details of potential inventions are not disclosed to anyone, even by word of mouth, unless it is under conditions of strictest confidence, buttressed by a written confidentiality agreement.

Charities have a duty to safeguard the results of their research [**44.10**], so it is particularly important for them not to jeopardise their right to patent discoveries or inventions.

44.6.1   Ownership of patents

The person entitled to apply for a patent is generally the inventor or inventors, but there is a presumption that an employer owns the rights to any invention made by employees in the course of their normal duties or in the course of a project specifically assigned to the employee.   *Patents Act 1977 ss.39-43*

If the patent or invention is of outstanding benefit to the employer, the employee may be entitled to some personal benefit and can apply to the court or the Intellectual Property Office for compensation for his or her part in the invention.

For inventions by volunteers, self employed persons and others who are not employees, the rights of ownership rest with the inventor unless they have been assigned to the organisation [**44.2.3.4**].

44.6.2   Registration

Copies of patents and patent applications should be searched before any application for a patent is submitted. Information is available from the UK Intellectual Property Office [see end of chapter] on how to do this.

It usually costs at least £500 to register a patent, and much more if a patent agent is hired to handle the application. An application must be submitted to the UK IPO, or to the **European Patent Office** in Munich [see end of chapter] for a patent covering all EU countries. During the fairly lengthy procedure, the relevant office examines whether the invention described is patentable, and third parties can object to the application. If the application is approved, a further fee is payable.

44.6.3   Duration

A UK patent lasts for a maximum of 20 years from when the application was filed. The initial registration fee covers the first four years and after that an annual fee is payable. During the final five years, a court has power in some circumstances to compel the patent owner to grant a licence to third parties.

44.6.4   Use of patented inventions

The patent owner may license any person to exploit a patent [**44.11**]. If an unlicensed person uses a registered patent, the patent owner may bring court proceedings to obtain an injunction, and may also obtain damages or an account (award) of their profits.

44.7   DESIGN RIGHTS

Design rights protect the appearance of an object – its shape or surface pattern.

Unregistered design right protection arises automatically for an item whose design is original and not commonplace. It lasts for 15 years from the first recording of the design or 10 years from the first marketing of the item, whichever ends sooner.   *Copyright, Designs & Patents Act 1988 ss.213-264*

Design registration provides more protection, and is obtained from the UK Intellectual Property Office for designs which are new and have individual character. It lasts five years initially, then is renewable on five-year terms to a maximum of 25 years.   *Registered Designs Act 1949, amended by Registered Designs Regulations 2001*

An EU-wide **registered community design**, also initially for five years renewable to a maximum 25 years, is available through the Office for Harmonisation in the Internal Market [see end of chapter]. An EU-wide **unregistered design right** is automatic, lasts for three years from the date when the design was first made available or publicised to the public within the EU, and gives the copyright owner exclusive right to use the design.   *Regulation on community designs [EC 6/2002]*

44.8   IDEAS AND INFORMATION

Ideas are intellectual property, but cannot be protected while they are still in a person's head. Nor are they protected if they are communicated orally, unless they are covered by a confidentiality agreement. Once they are recorded on paper, computer or another medium they are protected by copyright [**44.2.1**], but others cannot be stopped from developing the ideas or using them in different ways.

As with ideas, there is no general law which protects rights in information and knowhow (processes and procedures). Once the information is written or recorded in another way, it is protected by copyright, and the way it is stored may be protected by copyright or under database right [**44.2.9**]. But the law will not stop someone from using the information, unless the information is by its nature confidential and it has been disclosed only in circumstances which imposed an obligation on the recipient to respect its confidentiality. This could include within the employment relationship [**43.1.6**], or where there is a contractual obligation to use information only for the purposes of the contract. In this case, unauthorised use is likely to be a breach of contract or a breach of the duty of confidentiality [**43.1.1**, **43.1.6**].

44.9   PROTECTING NAMES AND LOGOS

An organisation's name, logo and reputation are valuable assets which it should consider protecting. In terms of intellectual property rights, this includes preventing other organisations from using the same or a confusingly similar name or logo; preventing individuals or organisations from using the name without authorisation; and ensuring that when an organisation authorises use of its name or logo for commercial purposes, it is properly recompensed.

44.9.1   Stopping others from using a name or logo

The Charity Commission may require a charity, within a year of registration, to change its name if it is the same as, or too similar to, another charity's registered name [**6.8.2**], and Companies House may require a company or industrial and provident society to change its name within a year of registration if it is the same as or too similar to another company's or IPS's registered name [**6.8.1**].

Registration as a charity thus provides some protection against another registered charity using the name, and registration as a company or IPS provides some protection against another company or IPS using the name.

These registrations do not protect against any other type of organisation using the registered name, nor do they cover operating or trading names [**6.5**], logos etc, or protect against use of a name which is similar but not 'too similar'. This protection can be obtained only by registering the name, logo or other mark as a trade mark for the relevant class(es) of services or goods [**44.4**], bringing a passing off action if the name or other mark is used in a way which damages the organisation [**44.5**], or claiming copyright [**44.2.1**] not for the name itself (which cannot be copyright) but for the particular design of the name or for the logo.

As an alternative, it may be appropriate for the organisation to start using a new logo, use a different operating name [**6.5**] rather than the name which is being used by the other party, or even change its name [**6.7**]. This may seem like 'giving in', but may be preferable to ongoing confusion or an expensive and perhaps ultimately futile action for passing off.

Use of a name or logo by 'branches' which purport to be part of an organisation but are in fact not linked to it can be particularly problematic [**9.2.2**, **11.2**].

Use of another organisation's name as a domain name could be trade mark infringement if the name has been registered as a trade mark, or could be grounds for a passing off action [**44.5**]. There are a number of dispute resolution procedures under which domain name registries will force the transfer of a name which has been registered in bad faith.

44.9.2   Unauthorised use for fundraising

Often an organisation's name or logo is used not by another organisation, but by its own supporters – individuals, branches, other organisations or commercial bodies – who use the name to fundraise. This can become a problem if the persons undertaking the activity bring the organisation's name into disrepute, or undertake activities which the organisation does not approve of. Charitable institutions (charities and other 'good cause' organisations) can in this situation seek an injunction under the **Charities Act 1992** to stop the fundraising [**48.7**].

44.9.3   Goodwill in a company name

Any business or organisation – even if it is not a company – which has goodwill in a name can object to the company names adjudicator if a company is registered with a name which could cause confusion [**6.4.3**].

44.9.4 Commercial use

The Charity Commission advises charities to be wary of entering into arrangements where the charity's name is to be used by a commercial company in return for money, and advises trustees to have clear policies on companies it is prepared to work with [**48.6.4**]. Any such arrangements, including with a charity's own trading company [**51.6.1**] must be carefully considered by the trustees, be kept under review, and be in the charity's interest and on terms which are advantageous to the charity. The arrangements should be set out in a licence [**44.11**].

Unless the arrangements are with a trading company owned by the charity or other organisation whose name is being used, they must comply with Charities Act rules for commercial participators [**48.6.5**].

Advice must be taken about the tax and VAT implications of licensing a charity's name or logo [**56.4.14**, **57.11.1**], and should be taken about the organisation's potential liability for faulty goods [**23.5.4**] where a product is branded with the organisation's trademarked logo.

44.10 EXPLOITATION OF RESEARCH

Charities involved in research, whether as their main purpose or as incidental to their work, must ensure there is demonstrable public benefit in the research [**5.3**]. The trustees must consider how best to protect their intellectual property (IP) rights arising from the research, and take appropriate steps to ensure the charity benefits from any use of these rights.

Trustees have to consider these issues, but do not necessarily have to register or otherwise protect intellectual property rights. In some cases the trustees may feel that the charity's objects can be best achieved by making research results freely available, perhaps under a Creative Commons licence [**44.2.9**], even though this could result in a loss of income to the charity. This is acceptable, provided it can be justified within the trustees' obligation to act in the best interests of the charity and to safeguard its assets, including its intangible assets such as IP rights.

Where a charity funds someone to undertake research, it should retain the intellectual property rights for itself, or ensure that if the researcher or other owner of the rights exploits the rights commercially, the charity gets a proportionate share of the proceeds. This is likely to involve a complex licence or assignment of rights, and legal advice should be sought at an early stage in commissioning or funding the research.

44.11 LICENCES

The granting of a right to use someone else's intellectual property – regardless of whether the property is protected by copyright, by registration or in some other way – is called a **licence**. A licence may range from a short agreement allowing another body to use an organisation's name or logo for a specific one-off purpose or to reproduce a copyright illustration or article, to a hugely complex contract for exploitation of a valuable patent or software or to replicate an organisation's work through a franchise arrangement [**11.2.4**]. A licence does not have to be in writing, but to protect both parties, even simple licences should usually be in writing, and more complex licences or where the work is being used for the purposes of financial gain should always be in writing.

Unlike **assignment** [**44.2.3.4**], where the right itself is transferred, a licence gives only the right to use the work for a specified purpose and/or period. Ownership of the copyright or other right is not transferred.

44.11.1 What to include

All licences contain certain basic information, but for anything more than the simplest licence, legal advice should be sought to ensure the organisation's interests are protected (regardless of whether it owns the rights to the work, or is entering into an agreement to use work where the rights are owned by others). This is particularly important in relation to patented discoveries and inventions, software, and work which has involved or will involve substantial time and/or money.

At the very least, a licence should cover:

- who is granting the licence, and who is being given it;
- what intellectual property right(s) the licence covers;
- whether the licence is being granted on an **exclusive** or **non-exclusive** basis (whether the licensor is granting the licence only to the licensee, or may grant it to others as well);
- any restrictions on how the licensee can use the work;
- what payment, if any, the licensee must make, and whether it is in the form of a one-off fixed fee, an annual fixed fee, a royalty or other form of payment;
- the term (duration) of the licence;
- whether the licence can be terminated before the end of the term;
- which party is to deal with third party infringers;
- any requirements for confidentiality between the parties;
- any indemnities between the parties.

Trade mark licences usually allow the licensor to exercise quality control over the licensee's products or services, and licences for the use of a name or logo should allow for withdrawal of the right if the name or logo is used inappropriately.

Licences for trade marks and patents may be, but do not have to be, recorded at the Intellectual Property Office. There are advantages for the licensee if the licence is registered within six months of being granted.

44.11.2 Payments for intellectual property rights

Income received for intellectual property rights may be taxable, even for charities [**56.4.14**], and may be subject to VAT [**57.10.6**, **57.11.1**]. The tax and VAT treatment of payments for IP rights is quite complex for both charities and non-charitable organisations, and expert advice should be sought from a solicitor or accountant before entering into a licence.

44.11.3 Franchises

A franchise [**11.2.4**] is a complex licence where typically the franchisee receives the right to use the franchisor's name, advertising, goodwill, knowhow, products, services, methods of operating etc. Legal advice should be taken before entering into any franchise agreement.

Resources: INTELLECTUAL PROPERTY

Copyright, trade marks, patents, design rights. UK Intellectual Property Office: www.ipo.gov.uk, 0845 9 500 505, enquiries@ipo.gov.uk.

European Patent Office: www.epo.org, +49 89 23994636, email via website.

Office for Harmonisation in the Internal Market: oami.europa.eu [no www], +34 96 513 9100, information@oami.europa.eu.

World Intellectual Property Organisation: www.wipo.org, +41 22 338 9111, email via website.

Licences. Copyright Licensing Agency: www.cla.co.uk, 020 7400 3100, cla@cla.co.uk.

Creative Commons: www.creativecommons.org.uk, 020 7955 7655, info@creativecommons.org.uk.

Design and Artists Copyright Society: www.dacs.co.uk, 020 7336 8811, info@dacs.org.uk.

Educational Recording Agency: www.era.org.uk, 020 7837 3222, era@era.org.uk.

Newspaper Licensing Agency: www.nla.co.uk, 01892 525273, copy@nla.co.uk.

Research by charities. Charity Commission: www.charity-commission.gov.uk, 0870 333 0123, email via website.

Statute law. www.opsi.gov.uk and www.statutelaw.gov.uk.

Much but not all case law. www.bailii.org.

Updates cross-referenced to this book. www.rclh.co.uk.

Chapter 45

PUBLICATIONS, PUBLICITY AND THE INTERNET

For sources of further information see end of chapter.

45.1 PUBLICATIONS

When producing a publication of any size, from a leaflet to a huge tome, or setting up a website, or producing film, audio or video productions or advertising of any type, the following issues must be considered:

- who needs to give final approval to publications and other productions before they are produced or go 'live';
- who will own the copyright of the work [**44.2.3**];
- whether consent needs to be obtained from third parties for the use of copyright material or trade marks [**44.2.6, 44.2.7, 44.4.5**];
- for print publications, whether an international standard book number or serial number should be obtained [**45.1.1**];
- whether anything in the publication or production is or could be construed as being libellous [**45.3**], in particular dynamic content such as chatrooms or bulletin boards on websites;
- whether other liabilities could be created, for example through providing information or advice that could lead to a negligence claim [**22.6.1**];
- whether a publication or part of it could be, or come to be, treated as setting out the terms of a contract [**21.1.1**];
- if the organisation receives local authority funding for a publication or production, whether the material complies with the relevant rules [**45.2.6**];
- whether advertisements comply with the relevant aspects of the British code of advertising, sales promotion and direct marketing [**45.2.1**].

45.1.1 ISBN and ISSN

International standard book numbers (ISBN), **international standard serial numbers** (ISSN) for works published or updated more than once a year, and bar codes are used by publishers, distributors and booksellers to make the book trade more efficient, and have nothing to do with copyright. They are available free [see end of chapter]. Information about bar codes for books is provided when an ISBN is obtained. Information about bar codes for periodicals is available from the Periodical Publishers Association [see end of chapter].

It is a good idea to obtain an ISBN, ISSN or bar code for any publication which is likely to be sold through the book trade, but there is no obligation to do so.

45.1.2   Periodical registration

A newspaper or magazine which contains public news or commentary on the news must be registered with Companies House [see end of chapter] if it is published at intervals of 26 days or less, a charge is made for it or it is a free publication containing only or mostly advertisements, and the publisher is not a company incorporated under the Companies Acts.   *Newspaper Libel & Registration Act 1881*

Information is in booklet GPO3 from Companies House. Registration is on form **NLR1** with a registration fee of 50p (as at 1/8/09) with an annual return and filing fee of 25p or 50p each July.

45.1.3   Legal deposit libraries

Anyone who issues or distributes print publications, including items such as newsletters, pamphlets, and posters, to the public must send a copy to the legal deposit office at the British Library within one month of publication [see end of chapter]. The deposited publications form the national printed archive.

Legal Deposit Libraries Act 2003

Organisations wishing to send their publications to the other legal deposit libraries in Oxford, Cambridge, Edinburgh, Dublin and Aberystwyth should contact the Agency for the Legal Deposit Libraries [see end of chapter].

45.1.3.1   Non-print publications

At the time of writing (mid 2009), the British Library legal deposit office runs a voluntary deposit scheme for offline or handheld electronic publications (such as CD ROM), and also accepts online or pure electronic publications. Information is available from the British Library [see end of chapter].

The **Legal Deposit Libraries Act 2003** includes provisions which may make deposit of electronic publications a statutory requirement. At the time of writing (mid 2009) these had not been implemented.

45.2   PUBLICITY AND ADVERTISING

Publicity and marketing materials should comply with the **British code of advertising, sales promotion and direct marketing**. They may also be subject to rules on political publicity during elections [**46.5.1**], publicity by organisations funded by local authorities [**45.2.6**], and commercial participation in fundraising and promotions [**48.6.4**].

Publicity and similar materials, whether on paper or electronic, may need to include company details or VAT number [**18.1**]. An advertisement or other notice encouraging members of the public to donate to or purchase something from a registered charity must state that it is a registered charity [**18.1.5**].

45.2.1   The advertising, sales promotion and direct marketing code

The **British code of advertising, sales promotion and direct marketing**, also called the **CAP code**, was developed by the Committee of Advertising Practice and is available from and administered by the Advertising Standards Authority [see end of chapter]. It applies to charitable and voluntary organisations as well as to commercial businesses.

The basic principles are that advertisements, sales promotions and the promotional element of sponsorship arrangements should be legal, decent, honest and truthful; be prepared with a sense of responsibility to both consumers and society; respect the principles of fair competition generally accepted in business; and not bring advertising into disrepute.

The CAP copy advice team, based at the ASA, provides free and confidential pre-publication advice on the content of advertisements.

Various codes from the Institute of Fundraising, in particular the codes on distance fundraising and marketing [**49.3**], supplement the CAP code.

45.2.1.1 What is covered

The code covers:

- advertisements in UK newspapers, magazines, brochures, leaflets, circulars, mailings, fax transmissions, catalogues, follow-up literature, websites and other electronic and printed material;
- marketing databases containing consumers' personal information [**43.4**];
- posters and other promotional media in public places, cinema and video commercials, and advertisements in non-broadcast electronic media including on-line advertising in paid-for space, such as banner and pop-up advertisements;
- sales promotions and advertisement promotions.

It does not matter whether the publicity is about the organisation itself, issues dealt with by the organisation, or something sold, provided free of charge or organised by the organisation. Nor does it matter whether the organisation pays for the publicity, receives it free of charge, or receives it as part of a sponsorship or other arrangement.

The code does not cover broadcast commercials [**45.2.4**], press releases and other public relations material, or advertisements in foreign media. It does not apply to publicity on t-shirts, carrier bags, mugs etc, which is covered by trading standards legislation. Packages, wrappers, labels and tickets are not covered unless they advertise a sales promotion or are visible in an advertisement.

Specific rules apply to environmental claims, advertisements portraying children, advertisements or promotions directed at children, and distance selling (where the buyer and seller do not meet face to face).

45.2.1.2 Complaints

Complaints to the ASA are investigated and if upheld, the advertisement must be withdrawn. The code does not have the force of law, but if an advertiser refuses to comply with an ASA decision the ASA may refer the matter to the Office of Fair Trading, which can then seek an injunction from the court.

ASA decisions are widely publicised, and an organisation which has a case found against it often receives considerable adverse publicity.

45.2.2 Advertisements

Detailed rules in the code of advertising, sales promotion and direct marketing [**45.2.1**] set out specific procedures to help ensure compliance.

45.2.2.1 Truthfulness

Before submitting an advertisement for publication or putting it on a website, advertisers must hold evidence to prove all direct or implied claims which can be objectively substantiated. Opinions or one interpretation of evidence should not be presented as fact, but obvious untruths or exaggerations which are unlikely to mislead are allowed.

Composite case studies should be truthful in the general impression they create, and it should not be implied that a composite is one person's experience. If a model is used in a photograph this should be made clear if it is a relevant factor.

45.2.2.2 Comparative advertising

Advertisers should not unfairly attack or discredit other businesses or their products. Explicit or implicit comparisons with other businesses or products are allowed, provided the comparison is objective, is not misleading, does not create confusion between the advertiser and its competitor, and does not discredit or denigrate the competitor or its products. [See **44.4.5** for using other organisations' trade marks in comparative advertising, and **45.4** for comments made maliciously.]

Control of Misleading Advertisements Regulations 1988 [SI 1988/915] reg.4A,
inserted by Control of Misleading Advertisements (Amendment) Regulations 2000 [SI 2000/914] reg.5

45.2.2.3 Decency

Advertisements should not contain anything which would be likely to cause serious or widespread offence, and should not cause fear or distress unless there is a good reason for doing so. If fear or distress is likely to be aroused – such as in an advertisement for smoke detectors – it should not be disproportionate to the risk. Charities are given slightly more leeway than other advertisers in using shocking or distressing imagery to raise awareness, but must comply with the basic rules. Unsafe practices should not be shown unless they are promoting safety.

45.2.2.4 Privacy

Written consent should be obtained before portraying any person or a person's possessions or property in an advertisement, unless the portrayal is a general crowd scene, property in a general outdoor location, or a person who is the subject of a book or film being advertised.

Advertisers who do not have consent to portray entertainers, politicians and others who have a high public profile should not portray them in an offensive or adverse way, and should not claim or imply an endorsement where none exists. Portrayal of members of the royal family is generally not permitted.

45.2.3 Sales promotions

The sales promotion rules follow the same basic principles and general rules as for advertising. The rules are intended primarily to protect the public, but also apply to schemes where goods or services are offered on promotional terms to wholesalers and others who will sell or distribute them on, and to the promotional elements of sponsorship arrangements.

Promotions intended for or involving children under 16 should indicate whether an adult's consent is needed.

45.2.3.1 Promotions linked to charities and good causes

Special rules apply to promotions claiming that participation will benefit registered charities or other good causes, augmenting those required under the **Charities Acts 1992** and **2006** for commercial participation [**48.6.6**].

45.2.3.2 Sales terms

Claims or **representations** in any publication, including electronic, could be treated as a contract term or as a representation that induced a person to enter into a contract [**21.2.8**].

45.2.4 Broadcast advertisements

Broadcast advertisements are covered by the **radio advertising standards code** for licensed independent radio, and the **TV advertising standards code**, for terrestrial, satellite and cable independent television licensed by Ofcom.

Advertisements may be used to solicit donations (a **broadcast appeal**), to publicise an organisation and its work, to sell goods, or to publicise services, activities, events or facilities.

45.2.4.1 Charity advertising and appeals

Broadcast charity advertising is only acceptable from organisations which are recognised as charitable by the appropriate UK authority, or if based overseas have provided the broadcaster with evidence that they comply with relevant laws.

Non-charitable companies may promote the needs and objectives of charities provided they have the permission of the charity concerned, state whether any charity will benefit financially from the sale of goods, and state how any money donated to charity will be calculated.

Broadcast appeals by charities must not exaggerate the scale or nature of any social problem, be misleading about a charity's activities or how donations raised through a broadcast appeal will be used, or address any fundraising message specifically to children. At the time of writing (mid 2009), a broadcast appeal by a charity must not include comparisons with other charities, but the Broadcast Committee of Advertising Practice had recommended removing this ban.

Special rules apply when broadcast appeals are made by professional fundraisers or commercial participators [**48.6.6**, **48.6.7**].

45.2.5 Political publicity

45.2.5.1 Non-broadcast

Print and non-broadcast electronic advertising relating to political matters should comply with the code of advertising, sales promotion and direct marketing [**45.2.1**], and be legal, decent, truthful and honest. The identity and status of all political advertisers should be clear. If their address or other contact details are not generally available, they should be included in the advertisement.

45.2.5.2 Broadcast

Broadcast advertisements cannot be placed by or on behalf of any organisation whose objects are wholly or mainly of a political nature, nor can advertisements be directed towards any political end (which is widely defined) or be connected with an industrial dispute. The codes on radio and TV advertising contain guidance about these rules, and Ofcom is responsible for implementing them.

Communications Act 2003 s.321(2)

Even if a 'political' advertisement would be allowed under charity law [**46.4.2**], it cannot be broadcast if the organisation or the advertisement falls within the Communication Act's very broad definitions of 'objects of a political nature' and 'political ends'.

In a 1994 case involvement Amnesty International (British Section), the court suggested that 'wholly or mainly political' should be interpreted to mean at least 75%. *R v Radio Authority ex parte Bull & Wright [1996] EWCA Civ 1230*

At the time of writing (mid 2009), Animal Defenders International had challenged in the European court of human rights the UK's ban on broadcast political advertising, claiming that it is incompatible with freedom of expression under article 10 of the **European convention on human rights**.

45.2.6 Organisations funded by local authorities

Publicity issued by local authority funded voluntary organisations must comply with the government's code of recommended practice on local authority publicity, unless the organisation can prove that it raised the money for the publicity from a completely separate source, and shows the income and expenditure separately in its accounts. The code is available from the Department for Communities and Local Government [see end of chapter].

The primary requirement is for publicity about public issues and policies to be objective, balanced, informative and accurate. The definition of publicity is wide, and includes printed materials and advertisements, as well as badges, banners, t-shirts and similar items. It could also include campaigns, exhibitions, plays, conferences and any other public communication.

45.2.6.1 Party politics

Local authorities and, by extension, organisations funded by them cannot publish any material which wholly or partly appears to be designed to affect public support for a political party. *Local Government Act 1986 s.2*

Charities cannot in any case engage in such publicity [**46.4.2**], so this rule is unlikely to affect them. Local authority-funded non-charities which are involved in activities which could be construed as party political should be particularly careful when referring to politicians or political parties, or when commenting on controversial matters, or when using simplified publicity, such as a slogan. Particular care is needed before a local or general election [**46.5.1**].

45.2.7   Free distribution of printed material

A local authority, as **principal litter authority**, can designate public areas or roads in which leaflets and other free printed material cannot be distributed. Distribution includes handing out material, making it available to members of the public or putting it on vehicles, but does not include putting it inside a building or in a letter box. Distribution in a designated area is an offence.

The prohibition does not apply to material distributed by a charity, provided the material relates to or is intended for the benefit of the charity. It also does not apply to material distributed for political purposes or for the purposes of a religion or belief.   *Clean Neighbourhoods & Environment Act 2005 sch.3A*

An organisation planning to distribute material which is not clearly exempt should check with the local authority, and if necessary obtain consent.

45.2.8   Email, websites and other electronic communication

The rules that govern all publications apply just as strongly to emails and materials on the internet. In addition, it is an offence to send unsolicited commercial email (UCE/spam) or text messages to individuals, and special rules apply to the use of 'cookies' to track use of a website [**43.4.1**]. Organisational policies should prevent misuse, defamation, breach of copyright and other problems [**43.5**], and ensure that marketing complies with the distance selling regulations [**21.2.3**].

In particular, organisations should be aware that:

- moderators of websites likely to be used mainly by children must not be barred from working with children [**41.7**];

- websites must in general contain the same contact details and other information as would have to be included on printed materials [**18.1**];

- organisations could be held liable for defamatory, discriminatory or other unlawful material sent in emails, or posted on the organisation's website either by the organisation itself or through dynamic content such as discussion lists, chatrooms, blogs, social networking sites or wikis;

- organisations could be held liable not only in the UK but in each country where the material is downloaded, and could be held liable in another country for material which is lawful in the UK but unlawful there.

Organisations which allow other people to post information to their websites should take steps to control the risks. These include terms and conditions of use, regular monitoring of content, procedures to ensure unacceptable material is removed as soon as the organisation becomes aware of it, insurance, and possibly running the website through a separate company in order to isolate the risk.

45.3   DEFAMATION

For the purpose of **defamation** law, 'publication' refers to anything made public by disclosure to one or more third parties. This wide definition means that an organisation could find itself liable even if a defamatory comment is made only in a 'private' conversation, letter or email.

Emails and the internet pose potentially major risks of liability, because a defamatory comment can reach so many people so quickly and can leave the organisation exposed to claims not only in the UK, but in any other country where the material is downloaded. All organisations should have policies making clear that emails containing defamatory material must not be sent, even within the organisation, and must never be forwarded.

Defamation may be either **slander** [**45.3.2**], which covers a transitory occurrence such as a statement made orally or a gesture, or **libel**, if the comment is written or is recorded in any other permanent form such as video or on a website, or if it is broadcast or is made in the public performance of a play. Defamatory comments made in a speech are slanderous; if the speech is recorded in a transcript, tape or video or posted on the internet the comments become libellous.

Defamation claims must be brought within one year. To bring a claim for slander, a person must generally be able to prove actual damage. Proof of actual damage is not required to make libel actionable. *Defamation Act 1996 s.5*

Defamation insurance is available [**23.5.5**].

45.3.1 Defamatory comment

To be defamatory, a comment must:

- refer to an identifiable living person or corporate body, either by name or in a way by which people who know the person or corporate body would think that the comment referred to him, her or it;
- be published, which means it must be made, or be made available, to a third party (so a negative comment about a person made only to that person is not defamatory); and
- 'tend to lower the plaintiff [the person about whom the comment is made] in the estimation of right-thinking members of society generally, and in particular to cause him to be regarded with feelings of hatred, contempt, ridicule, fear and disesteem'. *Sim v Stretch [1936] 2 All ER 1237*

If A makes a defamatory comment about B to C, B can bring a claim against A. If C repeats the comment, B can bring a claim against both A and C.

If A makes a defamatory comment about B directly to B, and B then repeats it to C and C repeats it to D, this does not make either A or C liable for defamation—because B is considered to have consented to making the statement public.

A statement may be defamatory even if it does not directly defame a person or company, but contains **defamatory innuendo**.

45.3.1.1 Libel against a company

A House of Lords decision in 2006 confirmed that a trading company whose trading reputation is or could be damaged by a defamatory statement can bring a claim for libel. At the time of writing (mid 2009) it is unclear whether this applies to all organisations – including non-trading companies and charities – or only to trading companies. *Jameel & others v Wall Street Journal Europe Sprl [2006] UKHL 44*

45.3.2 Slander

For a statement to be slanderous, the person about whom it is made must generally be able to show that he or she has suffered damage which can be calculated in financial terms.

This requirement does not apply if a slanderous statement alleges or implies that the person committed an imprisonable offence, has a 'socially undesirable' disease or is unfit to carry on his or her occupation or profession, or if it implies that a woman has committed adultery or acted in an 'unchaste' way. In these situations, as in libel cases, there is no need for the person who is slandered to show that he or she has suffered damage as result of the slander.

45.3.3 Defences

Even if a comment has a defamatory effect, it is not unlawful if the person who made the comment can prove a defence.

45.3.3.1 Justification

Under the defence of **justification**, a defamatory comment is not unlawful if the person making the comment proves that it is true.

45.3.3.2 Privileged comment

Privileged comment means that a statement is not unlawful, even if it is defamatory, because it is justified on the basis of freedom of speech or protection of the public interest. Privilege may be **absolute** which means it always applies, or may be **qualified** which means it applies only if the statement is made without malice.

Absolute privilege applies to:

- statements made in the House of Commons or House of Lords, parliamentary papers of an official nature, and statements made by officers of state to one another as part of their official duties;

- statements relating to judicial proceedings made by judges, advocates, witnesses or jurors in the course of the proceedings;

- fair, accurate and contemporaneous reports, including reports in radio and television broadcasts, of public judicial proceedings in the UK, the European courts of justice and human rights, and United Nations criminal tribunals;

Defamation Act 1996 s.14

Absolute privilege also applies to communications between lawyers and their clients.

Qualified privilege applies to:

- fair and accurate reports, including broadcast, of public proceedings of a legislature, court, public inquiry, international organisation or international conference anywhere in the world; extracts from reports and papers published by a government, international organisation or international conference anywhere in the world; and extracts from any register or other document required by law to be open to public inspection;   *Defamation Act 1996 s.15; sch.1*

- statements made in pursuance of a legal, moral or social duty, where 'the great mass of right-thinking people' would consider it their duty under the circumstances to make the statement (for example reporting a suspected crime to the police or suspected child or elder abuse to social services);

Stuart v Bell [1891] 2 QB 341

- statements made to protect the public interest or the interests or reputation of the person making the statement.

Qualified privilege applies even where a statement is untrue or unprovable, provided it was made responsibly and in good faith.   *Loutchansky v Times Newspapers Ltd & others [2001] EWCA Civ 1805*

45.3.3.3   Fair comment

Opinions may be expressed, even if they have the effect of being defamatory, on matters of public interest and concern. This includes comments on public figures and on public works such as books and plays. This defence of **fair comment** does not apply where the opinion is expressed maliciously and/or the opinion is not based on any fact, or the facts on which the opinion is based are incorrect.

45.3.3.4   Offer to make amends

A formal **offer to make amends** by apology, correction and payment of compensation and costs, is a complete defence unless the person claiming defamation can show that the defendant knew that the publication was false and defamatory and knew that it referred to the claimant. If the offer to make amends is accepted, the court fixes the level of compensation.   *Defamation Act 1996 ss.2-4*

45.3.3.5   Responsibility for publication

Organisations are generally vicariously liable for the acts of employees [**22.6.4**], so libels in emails, websites or other publications produced by staff will generally create liability for the organisation.

A newsagent, library, website operator, internet service provider or similar body which distributes a libellous publication is potentially liable, but may be able to claim **innocent dissemination** if it can show that it did not know, and had no reason to believe, that what it did caused or contributed to the publication of a defamatory statement; it took reasonable care in relation to the publication; and it was not the author, editor or publisher of the statement.   *Defamation Act 1996 s.1*

45.3.3.6	Remedies for defamation

Defamation is a civil wrong – a tort – but unlike most torts, defamation cases are sometimes heard by juries. The remedies are injunctions to prevent repetition of the defamatory comment, and damages.

Newspapers and periodicals may be able to minimise damages by proving they were not malicious or grossly negligent in making the statement; proving they published a full apology at the earliest opportunity, or if the periodical appears less often than weekly, offered to publish it in another periodical chosen by the claimant; and paying a sum of money into the court. *Libel Act 1843 s.2*

45.3.4 Criminal libel and harassment

Libel (but not slander) may be a crime as well as a tort. A criminal libel case may be brought even if the defamed person is deceased, and even if the defamatory statement has not been made to a third party.

In some situations, defamatory oral or written attacks on an individual may constitute **harassment [22.6.1, 40.5.3]**. Indecent, offensive or threatening phone calls, letters, electronic communication or other articles may be **malicious communication.** *Malicious Communications Act 1988*

45.4 MALICIOUS FALSEHOOD

Although legitimate comparisons with someone else's goods or services are acceptable [**45.2.2.2**], negative comments cannot be made with malicious intent. If the person about whom the comment is made suffers loss as a result of a statement made maliciously, he or she can bring an action for **malicious** or **injurious falsehood**. Malicious falsehood is different from defamation in that:

- it applies only to comments about goods and/or services;
- the person about whom the comment was made must prove that it was made maliciously, and that actual loss was suffered as a result of the comment;
- the estate of a deceased person may be sued for malicious falsehood, but not for defamation;
- legal aid is available for cases of malicious falsehood, but not for defamation.

Resources: PUBLICATIONS, PUBLICITY AND THE INTERNET

Advertising, sales promotions and direct marketing. Advertising Standards Authority: www.asa.org.uk, 020 7492 2222, enquiries@asa.org.uk.

ISBN. UK ISBN Agency: www.nbdrs.com/isbn_agency.htm, 0870 777 8712, isbn@nielsenbookdata.co.uk.

ISSN. ISSN UK Centre: www.bl.uk/services/bibliographic/issn.html, 01937 546959, issn-uk@bl.uk.

Legal deposit libraries. Agency for the Legal Deposit Libraries: www.llgc.org.uk/aldl, 020 7388 5061, enquiries@aldl.ac.uk.

British Library legal deposit office: www.bl.uk/about/policies/legaldeposit.html, 01937 546268, legal-deposit-books@bl.uk or legal-deposit-serials@bl.uk.

Newspapers/periodicals. Companies House: www.companieshouse.gov.uk, 0870 333 36 36, enquiries@companies-house.gov.uk.

Periodical Publishers Association: www.ppa.co.uk, 020 7404 4166.

Publicity by organisations with local authority funding. Department for Communities and Local Government: www.communities.gov.uk, 020 7944 4400, contactus@communities.gov.uk.

Statute law. www.opsi.gov.uk and www.statutelaw.gov.uk.

Much but not all case law. www.bailii.org.

Updates cross-referenced to this book. www.rclh.co.uk.

Chapter 46

CAMPAIGNING AND POLITICAL ACTIVITIES

For sources of further information see end of chapter.

46.1 VOLUNTARY ORGANISATIONS AND CAMPAIGNING

Many people believe, erroneously, that voluntary organisations cannot engage in political activities. In fact, the voluntary sector has always been at the heart of political life in the UK, and charities are allowed to undertake political or campaigning activity provided it is within Charity Commission guidelines.

46.1.1 Defining 'political'

'Political' may be defined in a variety of ways, for example:

- party political, intended to affect support for a party or candidates;
- seeking to influence decisions and actions of government and public sector bodies at any level, from local to international;
- seeking to influence decisions and actions of any body which operates in the public arena, for example campaigning for a company which makes military equipment to convert to non-military production;
- seeking to influence any sort of change, even if it is purely individual, such as encouraging people to stop using plastic bags.

Different definitions of 'political' are used for different legal purposes. 'Political' advertising or publicity is defined differently, for example, in relation to print advertising in the Advertising Standards Authority's British code of advertising, sales promotion and direct marketing [**45.2.1**], broadcast advertising in the **Communications Act 2003** [**45.2.5**], publicity by local authority funded organisations in the **Local Government Act 1986** [**45.2.6**], and publicity during election campaigns in the **Representation of the People Act 1983** [**46.5**]. The Charity Commission uses a different definition [**46.4**], and the **Companies Act 2006** uses yet another [**46.3**]. In addition, a decision about whether an activity is 'political' may depend more on the views of the person describing it than on any legal definition of what is and is not political.

Even 'non-political' activities such as fundraising may be classed as political, and in particular could in some situations be legally defined as terrorism [**46.6.2**].

46.1.2   The law on campaigning

Voluntary organisations are affected not only by the rules specifically relating to political activities, but also by a range of other legal issues:

- the proposed activity must fall within the organisation's constitutional objects [**5.1**] and powers [**7.4.3**];
- the decision to undertake the activity must be properly made, and must be recorded in minutes or in some other appropriate way;
- funds raised specifically for the activity must be used only for it, and funds raised for other purposes cannot be used for this activity [**48.2**];
- the activity must not be in breach of any grant, contract or lease conditions;
- political advertising and publicity must in general comply with the requirement to be legal, honest, decent and truthful [**45.2.5**];
- local authority funding cannot be used for political publicity [**45.2.6**];
- in the run-up to an election, there are strict rules on political activities [**46.5**];
- no one may act in a way which is likely to incite racial or religious hatred, provoke violence or cause alarm [**47.9.2**];
- demonstrations and other public activities must comply with the relevant laws, and some require police permission [**47.7**];
- some activities may be defined as terrorism under the **Terrorism Act 2000**, as is any support for an organisation proscribed under that Act [**46.6**].

Information about the law relating to campaigning and political activities is available from **Liberty** [see end of chapter].

46.1.3   Human rights and campaigning

Articles 10 and 11 of the **European convention on human rights**, incorporated into UK law by the **Human Rights Act 1998**, guarantee the rights to freedom of expression and freedom of assembly and association [**64.3.1**]. But such rights are subject to limitations 'necessary in a democratic society', including national security, public safety, and the protection of the reputation or rights and freedoms of others. The Human Rights Act also provides a framework under which individuals and organisations can challenge public authorities [**64.3.2**] or organisations carrying out public functions.

Information about the Human Rights Act is available from Liberty and the British Institute of Human Rights [see end of chapter].

46.2   NON-CHARITABLE ORGANISATIONS

A non-charitable unincorporated association [**2.2**] or company [**3.3**] may be set up with explicitly political objects, unless it is a community amateur sports club (CASC) registered with HM Revenue and Customs [**1.8**] or a community interest company (CIC) [**3.4**].

Industrial and provident societies must be set up to carry on a trade, business or industry [**3.5**]. This is interpreted widely, but an organisation with purely or primarily political objects might not be able to register as an IPS.

Provided they remain within the law, within their objects and powers and within the requirements of funders and others, there are no external constraints on the political activities of non-charitable organisations which are not CASCs or CICs. However, funds received from a charity – whether as a grant, donation or membership fee – cannot be used in any way which breaches the rules on charity campaigning [**46.4**]. To prove they have not misused charitable funds, the non-charitable organisation may have to show these funds and what they have been spent on separately in their financial records and annual accounts. This is especially likely to apply where an organisation receives local authority funding [**45.2.6**].

The general rules on publicity and advertisements [**45.2**], as well as the specific rules on political publicity [**45.2.5**], must be followed.

46.3   POLITICAL DONATIONS AND EXPENDITURE BY COMPANIES

In general, a non-charitable company can make donations to a political party, other political organisation or independent election candidate, or incur political expenditure, only if this is authorised by the company's members. Such authorisation can be one-off, or can be for a period of not more than four years from the date the resolution is passed, up to an amount specified in the resolution.

Companies Act 2006 ss.362-368

A political organisation is one which carries on, or proposes to carry on, activities that could reasonably be regarded as intended to affect public support for a political party or an independent election candidate, or to influence voters in relation to any national or regional referendum held under the law of the UK or another EU member state.

Companies Act 2006 s.363

Authorisation by the company's members is not required for:

- the provision of meeting rooms or other facilities for a trade union (but donations to a trade union's political fund requires authorisation);
- membership subscriptions to a trade association;
- donations to all-party parliamentary groups;
- political donations if the total donations by the company and its subsidiaries in a 12-month period are not more than £5,000;   *Companies Act 2006 s.374-378*
- expenditure incurred in producing and disseminating news material intended to affect support for a political party, other political organisation or independent election candidate, by a company whose ordinary business includes producing and disseminating news.   *Companies (Political Expenditure Exemption) Order 2007 [SI 2007/2081]*

46.4   CHARITABLE ORGANISATIONS

Although charities cannot be set up for **political purposes**, they can undertake **campaigning** or **political activity** to achieve their charitable purposes. Indeed, the Charity Commission emphasises that 'campaigning, advocacy and political activity are all legitimate and valuable activities for charities to undertake', provided they further the charity's objects and are a reasonable use of its resources.

46.4.1   Political purposes

It is a basic principle of charity law that a charity cannot be established for political purposes [**5.3.6**]. Political objects or purposes include promoting the interests of a political party, or seeking to change or opposing change in the law or national or local policy in the UK or abroad.

Since a charity's objects must be exclusively charitable [**4.1**], an organisation which has one or more political objects cannot be registered or recognised as a charity. However, many objects once regarded as too political to be charitable are now recognised as charitable, such as the advancement of human rights or reconciliation, and the promotion of racial or religious harmony [**5.2.11**].

46.4.2   Campaigning and political activities

Charities can undertake campaigning or political activities, provided those activities are directly related to the achievement of their objects, are a reasonable way of achieving the objects, and there is no restriction on such activities in their governing document.

The Charity Commission's guidelines on acceptable activities are set out in CC9 *Speaking Out: Campaigning and political activity by charities*, available free from the Commission [see end of chapter]. Where there is doubt about whether an activity is permissible, advice should be sought from the charity's legal advisors or the Commission. If the charity cannot carry out the activity, it may be possible for it to be done by a non-charitable body associated with the charity [**9.5.2**], but the charity will not be able to fund it.

46.4.2.1 The distinction between campaigning and political activities

The Charity Commission makes a crucial distinction between **political activities** and **campaigning**. **Political activities** are defined as activities directed at securing or opposing any change in the law or in the policy or decisions of central government, local authorities or public bodies in the UK or abroad, or changes in the policies or decisions of international bodies such as the United Nations or European Union. Charity law imposes restrictions on political activities.

Campaigning is defined as activities intended to educate or involve the public or change attitudes or behaviour (for example, to make people aware of the impact of pollution, encourage people to drive less, or campaign for car manufacturers to produce fuel-efficient cars). There is no restriction on campaigning by charities, provided it is directly related to the achievement of the charity's objects. But campaigning for legislation that would require all cars to be fuel-efficient is a **political activity** and is covered by the rules.

46.4.2.2 General requirements

All activities undertaken by a charity must further its objects, so campaigning and political activity are not permitted on issues unrelated to the charity's objects. A charitable students union, for example, whose objects were in connection with its membership could not spend money campaigning against the Gulf War, nor could a students union campaign against withdrawal of free milk for schoolchildren since its objects did not involve the welfare of schoolchildren.

Webb v O'Doherty & others (1991) The Times 11 Feb 1991; Baldry v Feintuck [1972] 2 All ER 81

In addition, the activity must be a reasonable use of resources. The governing body has to believe that the campaign or political activity will further the charitable objects, and has to assess the effort or resources put into that activity against the likely benefit. This must be done not only when the activity is commenced but at regular intervals, to ensure the charity's resources are not being wasted in a fruitless campaign or political activity.

A charity does not need to have explicit powers to campaign in its governing document, but it cannot campaign if the governing document prevents such activities. For the avoidance of doubt, charities may wish to include an explicit power to campaign and carry out political activities as allowed under charity law.

Regardless of whether they are trying to change government policy or individual or corporate behaviour, charities must not base their campaigning on inadequate or distorted information. They must provide information which allows people to come to their own conclusion, rather than providing propaganda which does not allow people to make up their own mind.

All advertisements and promotions relating to the campaign or political activity must comply with the rules on advertising [**45.2**]. This can pose particular difficulties because the advertising rules – particularly in relation to broadcast advertisements – are far more restrictive than the charity law rules [**45.2.4**].

Campaigns and political activities should be explicitly covered in the charity's risk assessment and risk management strategies [**22.1**].

46.4.2.3 Limits on campaigning and political activity

Political activities cannot dominate the activities of the charity, except perhaps for a short period where the governing body believes it is in the interests of the charity to devote all or most of the charity's resources to the political activities.

For **campaigning** – seeking to raise awareness or to change individual or corporate behaviour – there is no limit on the time or resources that can be spent. An environmental charity, for example, can – if the governing body believes it is the best way to achieve the charity's objects – spend all its time campaigning for individuals, companies and other non-public bodies to act in ways which reduce pollution. But as soon as the charity starts campaigning for changes in the law or for public bodies to change the way they operate, the rules on political activities have to be taken into account.

46.4.3   Permitted political activities

Political activities – activities directly linked to changes in the law – can be undertaken by a charity provided their purpose is to achieve the charity's objects, they have some reasonable prospect of success, they are a reasonable way of achieving the objects, and they are not the charity's sole way of doing so (although they might, for a short period, be the charity's only or main activity). Acceptable political activity might include:

- entering into dialogue with politicians or government at any level;
- promoting and commenting on proposed legislation or policy changes;
- supporting or opposing changes in the law or public policy; making representations to government, MPs, local councillors etc; and seeking public support for its views;
- conducting research and telling voters how MPs or political parties have treated an issue or voted on it, as a way of enabling discussion and well founded argument to take place with politicians (rather than merely as a way of applying pressure on them);
- providing well reasoned and well founded material for its supporters to send to MPs and other politicians;
- presenting petitions to parliament or national or local government, provided each page states the purpose of the petition;
- commenting on broader public issues which relate to the charity's purposes or the way it delivers its services;
- seeking the support of MPs or local councillors on matters relating to its grants or contracts.

A charity may allow its premises to be used as a polling station, and may hire out its premises for MPs' or local councillors' surgeries or for meetings of non-charitable organisations, including political and campaigning bodies. All such lettings must be on a proper commercial basis.

A charity cannot support a political party, or seek to persuade members of the public to vote for or against a particular candidate or party. It may advocate a particular position even though a political party advocates the same position, but it must be clear that the charity's views are independent of the political party.

A charity may employ staff such as parliamentary officers to liaise with MPs and government or local authority officials. Their work must be focused on promoting discussion, rather than merely applying pressure.

46.4.3.1   Elections

A charity may, in the run-up to an election, prepare material which assesses and comments on the manifestos and other proposals of the parties as they relate to the charity's work, and may provide candidates with relevant material. Comments must be reasoned, balanced and well founded, and must not breach the restrictions imposed by electoral law [**46.5**].

46.4.3.2   European and international activities

Although the Charity Commission's guidelines refer to MPs and parliament, similar principles apply to political activities involving MEPs (members of the European parliament), the EU, foreign governments or the United Nations.

46.4.4   Demonstrations and direct action

Where a charity wishes to organise, promote or participate in a demonstration or direct action [**47.7**], the governing body must ensure the activity complies with the general rules on campaigning and political activities by charities, is properly planned with liaison with the relevant authorities, and is not planned in a way that will bring the charity or charities in general into disrepute. People involved with the demonstration should seek to ensure that it is at all times under the control of the charity or other organisers, is peaceful, and does not put the charity, its governing body, its members or those participating in the event at significant risk of having civil or criminal proceedings brought against them.

46.4.5 Affiliation to other bodies

The fact that an alliance or campaigning body is not charitable, or is charitable but includes non-charities among its members, does not preclude a charity from joining. But affiliation to a campaigning body or alliance cannot be used as a way of undertaking activities – whether charitable or non-charitable – which the charity itself cannot undertake.

Before joining any such body or alliance, the charity must ensure that it will advance the charity's purposes and that the charity's funds will not be used for activities which the charity itself could not undertake.

If an alliance or campaign starts to undertake activities which the charity would not be able to do, the charity will have to dissociate itself from these activities, and ensure that its name and any funds it has contributed are not used to support those activities.

46.4.6 Risks of non-compliance

Involvement in political activities which contravene Charity Commission guidelines could have serious consequences for the charity and its governing body.

46.4.6.1 Tax consequences

Tax reliefs for charities under s.505 of the **Income and Corporation Taxes Act 1988** [**56.4**] are available only if profits made or income received are used for charitable purposes. If funds are used for non-charitable purposes, such as improper political activities, tax relief will be lost and tax may become payable.

Because the governing body of a charitable organisation is supposed to act in a prudent manner to safeguard the funds of a charity [**15.6.5**], the members of the governing body could be personally liable to replace the funds lost as a result of unnecessary taxation.

46.4.6.2 Charity law consequences

The Charity Commission recognises that the borderline between appropriate and inappropriate political activity may be unclear. If it believes a charity has engaged in unacceptable political activity, it will investigate and seek explanations before taking any action.

The Commission's response will be influenced by the nature of the activity, how substantial it was, and whether the charity had previously been warned about such activity. Responses could include providing help and advice to prevent a recurrence of the problem, taking proceedings against the members of the governing body for repayment of the funds used for the improper political activity, taking proceedings in respect of any income lost to the charity because of unnecessary taxation [above], or seeking an injunction from the courts to prevent further activities of this nature.

In some cases, the Charity Commission may publish the results of its inquiry into a charity's political activities. This is useful in enabling other charities to ascertain the Commission's position, but it could have a substantial negative impact on the charity's funders and its public image. Even if the Commission finds that the activity was acceptable, the mere fact that a charity's name has been linked to an investigation may have a negative impact.

46.4.7 Avoiding problems

To avoid unnecessary difficulties around political activities by charities, all governing body members, ordinary members, employees and volunteers should be aware of what is and is not permissible for their charity.

It is advisable for each charity to draw up its own policy, applying the Commission guidelines to its own objects, and setting out procedures to be followed to ensure compliance. This can help ensure that governing bodies and staff neither adopt self censorship policies which are more restrictive than they need to be, nor recklessly leap into affiliations or activities which are not allowed.

In some cases it may be appropriate to set up a separate non-charitable political arm [**9.5.2**], or for the activities to be undertaken by a non-charitable members' support group or similar body. The charity will not be able to fund activities which it could not itself undertake.

There is nothing to stop the people involved in a charity from undertaking any activity in their personal capacity. But involvement in activity contrary to the charity's objects or which could bring the charity into disrepute could raise issues about continued employment [**33.3.11**] or involvement with the charity.

46.5   POLITICAL ACTIVITIES DURING ELECTIONS

Voluntary organisations and electoral law: Campaigning during a general election, free from the National Council for Voluntary Organisations [see end of chapter], gives a detailed introduction to the very strict requirements around political activities during the run-up to a parliamentary election. The same principles apply to local elections, and elections to the European parliament. The Charity Commission's *Charities and elections* [see end of chapter] has guidance specifically for charities.

The information below is based on electoral law.

46.5.1   Advertisements

Significant exceptions to the need to be 'truthful and honest' [**45.2.2**] apply to advertisements whose principal function is to influence opinion for or against a political party or electoral candidate contesting a UK, European parliamentary or local government election, or any matter before the electorate in a referendum. These advertisements do not have to comply with the requirements to be able to provide documentary evidence to prove all claims, to ensure comparisons are clear and fair, not to mislead, and not to attack or discredit others unfairly.

British code of advertising, sales promotion & direct marketing s.12

46.5.2   Authorisation of advertising and activities

While the rules on advertising content are eased during election campaigns, the rules on authorisation of advertising – and virtually all other campaigning related to the election – become much more strict. Organisations which engage in party political campaigning need to be careful not to breach these rules. The rules come into effect as soon as an election is called, and may also apply in the weeks before this if it is clear that an election will be called.

Charities cannot engage in party political campaigning, and many non-charities have restrictions in their governing documents and/or funding agreements.

46.5.2.1   Support for or against candidates

Expenditure may generally be incurred on presenting a candidate to the public, presenting information to the public about the candidate's views or backing for the candidate, or disparaging other candidates only if the expenditure is authorised in writing by the candidate's election agent.   *Representation of the People Act 1983 s.75*

This rule is strictly enforced, so publications or advertisements about candidate(s) or their views may generally be issued only with the prior consent of the election agent(s), and public meetings and public displays about one or more candidates or their views may be organised only with such consent. However, information about a candidate, his or her views and support for the candidate may be published in a newspaper or periodical or may be broadcast on radio or television without the agent's consent, provided it is not an advertisement.

Total expenditure of less than the permitted amount during the election period does not need consent, provided the expenditure is not incurred as part of a concerted plan of action involving one or more other persons. The permitted amount is £500 in respect of a candidate in a parliamentary election. For local government elections it is £50 plus 0.5p for every entry in the register of local government electors.   *Political Parties, Elections & Referendums Act 2000 s.131*

46.5.2.2   Public meetings

Expenditure on public meetings involving a candidate or candidates must be authorised in advance by the candidates' agents. Failure to obtain prior consent means the meeting cannot be held.   *Representation of the People Act 1983 s.75*

Charities often believe that if they invite one candidate to a public meeting during an election campaign, they have to invite all. This is not the case. Where reasonable they can invite only one or some candidates to present their views, provided the overall activities by the charity during the election period do not promote or favour one candidate or party. Charities may also take into account the risk of damage to their reputation if they invite certain candidates.

46.5.2.3   Transparency

Every event during an election period must clearly identify the election agent, and every publication in support of or against a candidate or party must include the name and address of the printer and publisher. All publications must also include the name and address of the printer, the promoter (the person who caused the material to be published), and the candidate or party on whose behalf the material is being published.   *Political Parties, Elections & Referendums Act 2000 s.143*

46.5.2.4   Support for or against a political party or issue

Limits apply to expenditure for or against a particular party or group of candidates, or for or against a particular issue where the issue is closely identified with a party or group of candidates, in national elections. The limits are £10,000 in England or £5,000 in Scotland, Wales or Northern Ireland during the election period. The value of expenditure in kind (property, services or facilities provided free of charge or at less than 90% of their market value) is included.   *Political Parties, Elections & Referendums Act 2000 ss.85-89,94(5)*

46.5.3   What voluntary organisations can do

During an election campaign, charities and other voluntary organisations may, without needing consent from an election agent and without falling foul of the rules on political activities by charities:

- publish information about the candidates or their views in their own newsletters or magazines, provided the periodical would have been published at that time as part of its normal cycle of publication, and provided that for charities, the information is objective and is not intended to affect support for or against a particular candidate or party;

- comment on aspects of the parties' manifestos and proposals which are relevant to their own objects, provided that if a charity does this the comment must be balanced and based on reasoned information;

- undertake political activities which are not related to the election of a particular candidate or party and make their views known to candidates and the public, including through the media, provided the activities are within the organisation's objects and powers, and for charities, they comply with the general rules on political activities [**46.4.2, 46.4.3**].

46.6   TERRORISM

Under the **Terrorism Act 2000**, terrorism is defined as the use or threat of action where:

- the action or threat of action is designed to influence the government or an international governmental organisation, or to intimidate the public or a section of the public;

- the action or threat of action is made for the purpose of advancing a political, religious or ideological cause; and

- the action involves serious violence against a person or serious damage to property, endangers a person's life other than that of the person committing the action, creates a serious risk to the health or safety of the public or a section of the public, or is designed to interfere seriously with or cause serious disruption to an electronic system. *Terrorism Act 2000 s.1*

This definition is very wide and potentially defines as 'terrorist' any individual or organisation, in the UK or abroad, who advocates violence or damage to property for a political, religious or ideological cause. This could include individuals or organisations campaigning against oppressive regimes or environmentally damaging practices.

46.6.1   Banned organisations

Some organisations based in the UK or elsewhere are **proscribed** by the home secretary. Any support for them – even wearing their emblem or helping to organise a meeting which will be addressed by one of their members – is an offence. A list of currently proscribed groups is on the Home Office website.

Terrorism Act 2000 ss.3,11-13, sch.2 as amended

46.6.2   Fundraising

Even where an organisation is not proscribed, it is an offence:

- to invite a person to provide money or property as a donation, loan or in any other way, where the fundraiser intends it to be used or has reasonable cause to believe it may be used for terrorist purposes; or
- to provide money or property as a donation, loan or in any other way, where the person providing the money or property knows or has reasonable cause to suspect that it will or may be used for the purposes of terrorism.

Terrorism Act 2000 ss.15,16

This could include, for example, fundraising in the UK for an organisation overseas that supports – even if it does not actually use – violence or property damage as a way of challenging a repressive regime.

Information about the implications of these rules is available from Liberty.

46.6.3   Charities and terrorism

In response to media and government concerns about charities being 'fronts' for terrorist organisations or as channels for transferring funds to such organisations, the Charity Commission has issued guidance for charities on reducing such risks, and for its staff on dealing with concerns or allegations of terrorist abuse. This is available on the Charity Commission website [below].

Charities which work in areas of conflict or have links with organisations in such areas may need to take advice about minimising risks to the charity's resources or reputation.

Resources: CAMPAIGNING AND POLITICAL ACTIVITIES

Liberty: www.yourrights.org.uk and www.liberty-human-rights.org.uk, 020 7403 3888, email via website.

Political activities and campaigning by charities. Charity Commission: www.charitycommission.gov.uk, 0845 300 0218, email via website.

Activities during election campaigns. Electoral Reform Society: www.electoral-reform.org.uk, 020 7928 1622, ers@electoral-reform.org.uk.

National Council for Voluntary Organisations: www.ncvo-vol.org.uk, 0800 2 798 798, helpdesk@askncvo.org.uk.

Freedom of expression and association. Liberty [above].

British Institute of Human Rights: www.bihr.org, 020 7848 1818, info@bihr.org.uk.

Statute law. www.opsi.gov.uk and www.statutelaw.gov.uk.

Much but not all case law. www.bailii.org.

Updates cross-referenced to this book. www.rclh.co.uk.

Chapter 47

PUBLIC EVENTS, ENTERTAINMENT AND LICENSING

For sources of further information see end of chapter.

47.1 THE LAW ON EVENTS AND ENTERTAINMENT

Any event which is open to the public and/or is held out of doors is likely to have to comply with a multitude of legal requirements – regardless of whether it is or is not publicly advertised, whether a charge is or is not made, whether it is open to all or only a section of the public, or if it is outdoors and open only to the organisation's members. Legal issues include:

- whether the event directly furthers the organisation's objects [**5.1**], or can be carried out as a fundraising activity [**56.4.6**];
- whether it is within the organisation's powers [**7.4.3**, **51.1.3**];
- VAT and other tax implications [**56.4.6**, **57.11.8**];
- whether to run the event through a trading company [**51.2**];
- whether a licence is required for the event or premises [**47.2**, **47.4**];
- use of copyright material [**44.2.6**, **47.4.2**, **47.6**];
- rules for bingo, gaming machines, lotteries etc [**49.6**, **49.8**];
- rules on the provision or sale of food and drink [**40.10.1**, **47.3**];
- restrictions in leases, property deeds or other premises agreements [**60.7.5**];
- fire regulations about the maximum number of people on premises;
- whether the police or other bodies need to be notified [**47.7**];
- the risk of creating a public nuisance [**22.6.1**] or too much noise [**63.12.5**];
- insurance [**23.5.1**, **23.9.2**].

47.1.1 Freedom of assembly and association

The **Human Rights Act 1998** guarantees the rights to freedom of assembly and association under article 11 of the **European convention on human rights** [**64.3.1**], but governments may limit these rights if necessary to maintain public safety or to prevent crime and disorder.

47.2 PREMISES LICENSED FOR ALCOHOL AND ENTERTAINMENT

A **premises licence** [**47.2.1**], **club premises certificate** [**47.2.4**] or **temporary event notice** [**47.2.3**] must be obtained before alcohol is sold on any premises or out of doors or is given to people who pay an admission fee or other indirect charge, or before regulated entertainment [**47.4**] takes place or late night refreshment [**47.5**] is provided.

General information about licensing is available from local authorities and the Department for Culture, Media and Sport. Information specifically about village halls, community centres and similar premises is available from ACRE and Community Matters [see end of chapter].

At the time of writing (mid 2009) the Department of Health had consulted on a mandatory code of practice on selling and marketing alcohol. Some rules may apply to licensed community premises, and up to date information should be sought.

47.2.1 Premises licence

A **premises licence** is granted by the local authority to a named person – including a 'legal person' [**3.1.1**] such as a company or other incorporated body – for specific premises. The licence may provide for the retail **sale of alcohol**, the supply of alcohol by or on behalf of a **club** to a member of the club, the provision of **regulated entertainment** [**47.4**], and/or the provision of **late night refreshment** [**47.5**].

Licensing Act 2003 s.1

A premises licence is most suitable for premises which are to be used regularly for the supply of alcohol and/or entertainment, and once granted is valid for the life of the business or organisation. A premises licence can be obtained on a time-limited basis, but this is unlikely to be of commercial benefit as it follows the same procedure as a permanent premises licence.

The extent to which each of the above activities is covered by the licence must be stated in the licence application. The application must include a floor plan of the premises and other general details, and must set out the terms of operation which will become the main conditions of the licence.

If the licence provides for the sale of alcohol, it must generally specify a **designated premises supervisor** (DPS), although in community premises the governing body as a whole can be responsible, rather than having a DPS. [**47.2.2**].

As well as applying to the licensing authority, a copy of the application must be sent to the police, the fire authority, the health and safety enforcement agency (generally the local authority's environmental health department, but could be the Health and Safety Executive), the local authority's child protection committee, the planning authority and the weights and measures/trading standards authority. Any interested party may make **representations**. If a representation is made, the licensing authority may choose to hold a hearing to decide the matter.

The application and annual fees for a premises licence vary according to the rateable value of the premises to be used for the licensable activities. The fee table for a premises licence is available from the relevant local authority. Failure to pay the annual fee may lead to its loss, so the fee date should be carefully diaried.

Licensing Act 2003 (Fees) Regulations 2005 [SI 2005/79] & (Amendment) Regulations 2005 [SI 2005/357]

Some alterations to a premises licence require an expensive **variation** process. but a simpler **minor variations** process is available for minor changes to the structure or layout of the premises, small adjustments to licensing hours, removal of irrelevant or unenforceable conditions, the addition of licensable activities (but not the supply of alcohol), and similar changes.

Legislative Reform (Minor Variations to Premises Licences & Club Premises Certificates) Order 2009 [SI 2009/1772]

Once a premises licence is obtained, the conditions need to be taken into account for any new building or alterations to the existing premises, because the licensing authority must be satisfied with the layout of the premises.

47.2.2 Designated premises supervisor and personal licences

Most premises where alcohol is supplied under a premises licence must have a **designated premises supervisor** (DPS), who has day to day responsibility for running the premises, but there is an exception for community premises [see below]. The DPS must hold a **personal licence** and is named in the premises licence. The premises licence itself need not be in the name of the DPS, but can be.

Only one person can act as a DPS at the licensed premises, regardless of how many people at those premises hold a personal licence. The DPS is therefore expected to spend a significant proportion of their time at the licensed premises, and should be contactable at all times.

Personal licences relate only to the sale or supply of alcohol under a premises licence, and are valid for 10 years. Applicants are subject to a criminal record check [**41.4.1**], and must hold an accredited personal licence qualification.
Licensing Act 2003 ss.15,111-135; Licensing Act 2003 (Personal Licences) Regulations 2005 [SI 2005/41]

From 1 August 2009, village halls, church halls and similar community premises can apply for removal of the requirement to have a DPS and to have all sales of alcohol authorised by a personal licence holder. Instead, the governing body as a whole takes on the responsibilities of a DPS, and must authorise the supply of alcohol.
Legislative Reform (Supervision of Alcohol Sales in Church & Village Halls etc) Order 2009 [SI 2009/1724]

47.2.3 Temporary event notices

A one-off event involving the sale of alcohol and/or public entertainment [**47.4**] which would normally need a premises licence can be held under a **temporary event notice** (TEN) at any premises or out of doors. A TEN might also be required for an event at a private home – such as a fundraising event – at which alcohol is to be sold or provided in return for a 'donation', or at which regulated entertainment [**47.4**] takes place.

A TEN event must not last longer than 96 hours, and the maximum number of people attending the event, including staff, must not exceed 499.
Licensing Act 2003 ss.98-110; Licensing Act 2003 (Permitted Temporary Activities) (Notices) Regulations 2005 [SI 2005/2918]

A temporary event notice may be used for unlicensed premises, and anyone aged 18 or over can apply, whether or not they hold a personal licence. The **premises user** (usually the event organiser) must serve the local authority and local police with the TEN at least 10 days before the event is due to start. Provided the police do not object, the event can go ahead and the local authority cannot impose any further conditions, limitations or restrictions. The notice fee is £21 (as at 1/8/09).

The same premises cannot be used more than 12 times or a total of 15 days in a calendar year starting from 1 January. A personal licence holder or their associate (including spouse, child or employee) is limited to 50 notices in a calendar year. A person who does not hold a personal licence and is not associated with a licence holder is limited to five notices in a calendar year.

47.2.4 Club premises certificate

With a **club premises certificate** from the local authority, a **qualifying members' club** may carry out licensable activities at their premises. These are the supply of alcohol by the club to members of the club, the retail sale of alcohol by the club to a guest of a member for consumption on the club premises, and the provision of regulated entertainment for members of the club and their guests.
Licensing Act 2003 s.70

A club holding a club premises certificate can supply alcohol without having a personal licence holder or a designated premises supervisor.

To qualify as a **club**, the club's rules must require an interval of at least two days between a person's nomination or application for membership and their becoming entitled to the privileges of membership, or if the rules allow a person to become a member without prior nomination or application, there must be an interval of at least two days between their becoming a member and becoming entitled to the privileges of membership. In addition the club must be established and conducted in good faith and must have at least 25 members.   *Licensing Act 2003 ss.62,63*

If the club wants to supply alcohol to members and guests, three additional conditions must be met: the club's purchase and supply of alcohol must be managed by a committee made up of elected members of the club, who must all be at least 18 years old; no person can receive any commission, percentage or similar payment deriving from the club's purchase of alcohol; and no person can derive any monetary benefit from the supply of alcohol to members or guests.   *Licensing Act 2003 s.64*

Similar rules apply to industrial and provident societies, registered friendly societies, and miners' welfare institutes.   *Licensing Act 2003 ss.65,66*

The rules introduced on 1 August 2009 on minor variations to premises licences [**47.2.1**] and allowing the governing body to carry out the duties of a designated premises supervisor and personal licence holders [**47.2.2**] apply to club premises.

47.3 OTHER RESTRICTIONS ON PROVISION OF ALCOHOL

Organisations which want to provide or sell alcohol need to ensure there are no restrictions in their governing document, lease or property deeds, and if they are charitable must consider charity law [below]. All organisations should also consider whether the provision or sale of alcohol might be considered objectionable by funders, supporters or the local community.

47.3.1 Alcohol sales and charitable status

The sale of alcohol cannot in itself be a charitable purpose, so it could jeopardise charitable status. To avoid this, the charity may arrange on an occasional basis for alcohol to be sold or supplied under a temporary event notice [**47.2.3**]; set up a separate members' club with a club premises certificate [**47.2.4**] or a trading company [**51.2**] with a premises licence [**47.2.1**]; or obtain a premises licence as a charity, but agree to restrictions so that charitable status is not jeopardised.

The Charity Commission regards sales of alcohol as 'ancillary', and therefore acceptable in terms of charitable status, provided that the provision or sale of alcohol is not expressly prohibited by the charity's governing document, lease or property deeds, and the area occupied by the bar and additional storage facilities does not substantially detract from the charitable use of the premises. The bar may be open only to people who are attending a charitable activity, either as participants or spectators. Further information is in Charity Commission booklet CC27 *Providing alcohol on charity premises*.

If a charity's governing document prohibits the provision or sale of alcohol, it may be possible to amend it [**7.5**].

47.3.2 Lease restrictions and restrictive covenants

Many leases and some freehold titles contain covenants [**60.7.5**] prohibiting or restricting the sale or provision of alcohol on the premises. Tenants and leaseholders in this situation who want to sell or provide alcohol must obtain consent from their landlord. Freeholders may either obtain consent from the owner of the land which has the benefit of the covenant, or may need to apply to a lands tribunal to have the covenant removed. The lands tribunal will in due course become part of the land, property and housing chamber in the first-tier tribunal [**64.7**].

47.4 REGULATED ENTERTAINMENT

The provision of **regulated entertainment** must be covered by a **premises licence**, **temporary event notice** (TEN) or **club premises certificate** [**47.2**]. This includes entertainment provided solely or partly for members of the public or to club members and their guests, regardless of whether a charge is made. It also includes private events, including fundraising events, at which a charge is made with the intention of making a profit.

Entertainment is regulated if it takes place in the presence of an audience of one or more persons, is not exempt [**47.4.1**] and is:

- a performance or rehearsal of a play (any dramatic piece, including improvisation, which consists of speech, singing or action and involves playing a role);
- an exhibition of a film or moving pictures;
- an indoor sporting event (a contest, exhibition or display of any sport in which physical skill is the predominant factor, or any physical recreation indulged in for competition or display);
- indoor or outdoor boxing or wrestling entertainment (the only regulated outdoor sports);
- a performance of dance and/or live music;
- any playing of recorded music, for example as an accompaniment to dancing.

Licensing Act 2003 sch.1 pt.1

A roofed building with spectators wholly inside the building is 'indoor'. A venue with a roof that can be opened or closed is not 'indoor' even if the roof is closed.

47.4.1   Exemptions

There are a number of general exemptions to the requirement for a premises licence, club premises certificate or TEN for the provision of regulated entertainment. However, if alcohol or late night refreshment is provided, a licence is still required for those activities. The main exemptions are:

- sacred or secular entertainment at **places of public religious worship**, but not including entertainment at an ancillary building (such as a church hall).
- entertainment for or incidental to **religious services or meetings**;
- **morris dancing** or any dancing of a similar nature, including the performance of unamplified live music as an integral part of such dancing;
- live or recorded **incidental music** such as background music in a supermarket, which is incidental to an activity which is not itself regulated;
- **garden fetes** or functions or events of a similar nature, if not being promoted or held for purposes of private gain;
- **film exhibitions** if the sole or main purpose of showing the film is to demonstrate a product, advertise goods or services, or provide information, education or instruction;
- **film showings** which are, or form part of, an exhibit for any purposes of a **museum or art gallery**;
- use of **television or radio** to simultaneously receive and play a programme broadcast by a service defined by the **Broadcasting Act 1990**, which includes most radio and TV programmes (but showing pre-recorded programmes requires a licence);
- **vehicles in motion**, where the entertainment takes place in a vehicle while it is not permanently or temporarily parked. *Licensing Act 2003 sch.1 pt.2*

At the time of writing (mid 2009), the government was considering a **low impact exemption** for venues with less than 100 capacity whose main business is not to put on live music, from needing a premises licence, TEN or club premises certificate to put on live music.

47.4.2   Use of copyright material

Regardless of whether a premises licence, temporary event notice or club premises certificate is required, the consent of the copyright owner(s) is needed if the work being performed is copyright [**44.2.6**]. Copyright works include music, plays, artistic works, film and video. For example, most videos are hired or sold only for domestic purposes, and may not be shown to an audience. A variety of copyright licenses may be needed if copyright music is being performed either live or recorded [**47.6**],including music in a play or a film.

47.5   LATE NIGHT REFRESHMENT

The supply of hot food or drink from premises, for consumption on or off those premises, between 11pm and 5am requires a premises licence or temporary event notice [**47.2**].

Licensing Act 2003 sch.2

Exemptions from the need for a licence include:

- hot food and drink supplied by a registered charity or a person authorised by them;
- hot drink from a vending machine where a member of the public inserts payment into the machine, and the drink is supplied directly to that person;
- hot food or drink supplied free of charge, where there has been no admission fee to the premises;
- hot food or drink supplied on a moving vehicle;
- hot food or drink supplied on or from premises licensed under certain other Acts, such as 'near beer' premises in London where some types of non-alcoholic beverages are sold.

A licence or TEN is not required for premises to which only the following persons and their guests are admitted and supplied with hot food or drink:

- guests of hotels, guest houses, lodging houses, hostels, caravan or camping sites and other overnight accommodation;
- members of recognised clubs;
- employees of a particular employer, for example, where refreshment is made available to employees whose shift patterns require them to be at the workplace between 11pm and 5am;
- persons engaged in a particular trade or who are members of a particular profession or follow a particular vocation.

47.6   PERFORMANCE OF COPYRIGHT MUSIC

A number of consents are required for performance of copyright music, whether live, recorded or broadcast. These licences are all separate, and having one does not remove the need for the others. Nor does being licensed – or exempt from being licensed – for regulated entertainment [**47.4**] give the right to use copyright material. At the time of writing (mid 2009) the UK Intellectual Property Office had consulted on music licensing, and the rules were expected to change.

Music licences are required for public events, and also for other public situations such as background music in shops and workplaces, street performances, processions, festivals, use of music in day centres or for dancing or keep-fit classes, or any other performance of live, recorded or broadcast music which is not within a purely domestic setting.

As well as obtaining licences, there may be a duty under the **Performances (Moral Rights) Regulations 2006** to identify those involved in the performance or recording [**44.3.1**]. For more about copyright in general, see **44.2**.

47.6.1   Performing right

A performing right licence from the **Performing Right Society** (PRS) [see end of chapter] applies to the copyright of the music and any lyrics. This licence provides royalties to composers and songwriters (or to whoever owns their copyright) and music publishers. Depending on the type of licence, it may cover live performance of music; public playing of recorded music on records, tapes, CDs or karaoke; jukeboxes; broadcasting music on radio, television or cable; and/or the right to play radio and television broadcasts or publicly show TV broadcasts which contain music. 'Publicly' includes at workplaces, for example playing CDs or the radio at work or having a TV available for staff or others.

The applicant for a PRS licence must be the owner or landlord of the premises on which the music will be played, not the organiser of the event. The fee depends on the extent of music usage, the type of premises being licensed and the capacity of the premises and/or average attendance at events. At the time of writing (mid

2009) there were special fees (**tariff CB**) for community premises run by voluntary organisations, but these were being reconsidered.

Except for universities, which have separate arrangements with PRS, the licensing of most musical performances (outside the curriculum) in schools and colleges of further education is administered on behalf of PRS by the Centre for Education and Finance Management [see end of chapter].

The licensing of most secular musical performances in churches and some church halls is administered on behalf of PRS by Christian Copyright Licensing International (CCLI) [see end of chapter]. CCLI also provides a range of licences to schools and churches for the reproduction of copyright music and lyrics for use in collective worship.

PRS does not licence live performance of all or part of musical shows, operas, ballets etc, the performance of specially written music for plays, or other dramatic or theatrical productions. These permissions must be obtained from the copyright owner, who is usually the publisher.

47.6.2 Recorded music, videos, DVDs

A different licence covers the copyright on the particular performance of the music which is recorded on a record, tape, CD or similar or is being broadcast on radio or TV, and is available from **Phonographic Performance Limited** (PPL) [see end of chapter]. For music on videos, the licence is from **Video Performance Limited** (VPL) at the same address. A PPL or VPL licence provides royalties to the performers on the particular recording, or to whoever owns the copyright on their performance.

At the time of writing (mid 2009) , charitable and other organisations concerned with the advancement of religion, education or social welfare do not have to obtain a PPL or VPL licence if there is no admission charge for the event at which the music is played, or if *all* the proceeds of any admission charge are applied for the purposes of the organisation. The same applies for events which are 'beneficial' to charitable and other similar organisations. PPL may interpret the 'all' strictly, and may not allow the exemption if any of the proceeds are used for any other purpose, such as room hire.

The government's music licensing review could result in withdrawal of the PPL exemptions, or extension of the exemptions to PRS licensing as well as PPL but limiting them to small charities, or other changes.

Community Matters [see end of chapter] has a joint licensing scheme with PPL for the use of sound recordings by some multi-purpose community organisations.

47.6.3 Record company

For use of records, CDs etc, another licence covers the copyright held by the sound recording manufacturer. It is available from the recording company.

47.6.4 Recording performances

The above licences give the right to play or perform music, but not the right to record the performance. Licences to record copyright music are provided by the **Mechanical Copyright Protection Society** (MCPS) [see end of chapter].

47.7 PUBLIC GATHERINGS

A **gathering** is public if it is held in a public place (including a road), or is held in a private place where the public or a section of the public are permitted, with or without payment, to attend.   *Public Order Act 1936 s.9*

A private place is one which the public have the right to enter only with the consent of the owner, occupier or lessee. It includes a public place hired for the occasion by the organiser of the gathering.

Depending on its nature and in some cases on its size, a public gathering may be a **public meeting** [47.7.2]; an **assembly**, which may or may not also be a meeting

[**47.7.3**]; a **festival** [**47.7.4**]; a **procession** or **march** [**47.7.5**], which may also be an assembly or meeting; or a **picket line** [**47.7.7**].

The local authority may have by-laws requiring it or the police to be notified of gatherings in public places.

Information about public gatherings is available from Liberty [see end of chapter]. The Home Office *Good practice safety guide for small events* and Health and Safety Executive *Event safety code* [see end of chapter] provide essential guidance. Before organising an event, it is essential to consider all aspects of insurance [**23.5**, **23.6**, **23.9.2**], and especially for large-scale events or events involving any risk to participants or the public, it is sensible to take legal advice beforehand.

All political events during the run-up to an election must comply with specific rules [**46.5**]. A charity involved at any time in a gathering of a political nature must comply with the rules on political activities by charities [**46.4**].

47.7.1 Admission, exclusion and problems

It is sensible to be aware of the possibility of problems at gatherings, and to have procedures for dealing with troublesome individuals or groups (either within the gathering or as bystanders), police intervention and similar matters.

For the responsibilities and rights of the person chairing a meeting, see **19.5.2**.

47.7.1.1 Public gatherings in a public place

The police may take action to prevent obstruction at a gathering in a public place. This may involve removing or arresting individuals or breaking up the gathering if a breach of the peace [**47.9**] occurs or is reasonably expected to occur, or arresting individuals for public disorder offences [**47.9**], breach of conditions imposed on a public event, and certain other offences.

Unless it is a rave [**47.7.4.1**], police do not have a right to stop a person travelling to a gathering simply because they believe a breach of the peace *might* occur.

Laporte, R (on the application of) v Gloucestershire Constabulary & others [2004] EWHC 253 (Admin) SJ 53

47.7.1.2 Public gatherings in a private place

Provided they do not discriminate unlawfully [**chapter 42**], the owners or managers of private premises do not have to make their premises available to anyone. The only exception is during election campaigns, when any candidate has the right to use a publicly owned hall for an election meeting, provided the meeting is open to the public and the intention is to discuss election issues.

The organisers of a public gathering in a private place may refuse admission to any person, provided this is not unlawfully discriminatory [**chapter 42**].

People who attend a public gathering in a private place, including a public place hired for the occasion, without paying an admission charge are admitted because the organiser grants them a licence to be there. They may be asked to leave at any time, with no reason. A person who refuses to leave becomes a **trespasser** and can be removed using reasonable force [**63.5.3**].

Where people pay an admission charge, the payment creates a contract. Unless they have contravened the conditions of admission, it is a **breach of contract** to ask them to leave, and an assault to remove them physically. If they have acted in a disorderly way or contravened the admission conditions, they may be asked to leave, and if they refuse they become a trespasser.

The police may enter a public gathering in a private place only if asked to do so by the occupiers of the premises or the organisers of the gathering, or if they have reason to believe that a **breach of the peace** [**47.9**] is being or is likely to be committed. They may help remove trespassers if asked to do so by the occupiers or organisers, and may arrest individuals for breach of the peace.

The organisers of the gathering must comply with all conditions in the hire agreement, lease or any other agreement for use of the premises.

47.7.1.3 Trespass by unknown persons

Where it is highly likely that trespass will occur but it is not known by whom, the premises owner may be able to get an injunction against unknown persons entering or remaining on the premises. *Hampshire Waste Services v Persons Unknown [2003] EWHC 1738*

47.7.2 Public meetings

In legal terms, a **public meeting** is a public gathering [**47.7**] held for the purpose of discussing or expressing views on matters of public interest. If it is held out of doors it is a **public assembly** even if there are only two people [**47.7.3**]. *Public Order Act 1936 s.9*

It is unlawful to disrupt or deliberately interrupt a public meeting or stop it from carrying on the business for which it was called, or to disrupt a meeting held as part of an election campaign. *Public Meeting Act 1908 s.1; Representation of the People Act 1983 s.97*

47.7.3 Public assemblies

A **public assembly** is a gathering of two or more people in a public place which is wholly or partly open to the air. It may be a public meeting [**47.7.2**] or another type of gathering. Some local authorities require notification of public assemblies. *Public Order Act 1986 s.16, amended by Anti-Social Behaviour Act 2003 s.57*

If there is evidence that public disorder or intimidation may occur, the police may impose conditions on location, number of participants or duration. *POA 1986 s.14*

The police may not ban an assembly unless it involves trespass. A **trespassatory assembly** is one which is to be held, or is being held, without the landowner's consent on land with no access or limited rights of access, and which is likely to cause serious disruption to the life of the community or is on a site of particular historical or archaeological interest. *POA 1986 s.14A*

Special permission is needed for assemblies in royal parks and in particular Hyde Park, and in Trafalgar Square [see end of chapter]. At the time of writing (mid 2009), separate rules apply for assemblies near Parliament [**47.7.6**].

47.7.4 Festivals, street parties, fetes etc

An outdoor festival, street party, fete or similar event open to the public must comply with the requirements for assemblies [above] as well as for licensing and copyright [**47.2, 47.6**], food hygiene [**40.10.1**], and all other relevant rules.

There may be important tax and VAT implications for running festivals, fetes and similar events as a way of raising funds [**chapters 56** and **57**]. Advice may need to be taken from an accountant or solicitor who specialises in charity matters.

47.7.4.1 Raves

A **rave** is an unlicensed gathering of 20 or more people at which amplified music is played at night. The police have power to stop people within five miles of a rave and direct them to turn back and to direct people to leave a rave. Vehicles and sound equipment can be seized, and anyone attending another unlicensed rave within 24 hours of being directed to leave the first one can be arrested. *Public Order Act 1986 ss.63-65, amended by Anti-Social Behaviour Act 2003 s.58*

47.7.5 Processions

The police must be given advance notice in writing of any proposal to hold a public **procession** or **march** intended to mark or commemorate an event, publicise a cause or campaign or demonstrate support for or opposition to the views or actions of a person or body of persons, unless the event is customarily held in the area. *Public Order Act 1986 s.11*

At least six clear days before the proposed date, a police station in the police area where the procession is intended to start must be notified of the proposed date, starting time, route, and name and address of at least one organiser. In exceptional circumstances notice may be hand delivered with less than six days' notice.

The purpose is to inform the police, not to seek their permission. The senior police officer may however impose conditions or in some cases apply to the court for a prohibition order. In exceptional circumstances the police may, with the consent of the home secretary in London or the local authority elsewhere, ban all or some marches in an area for up to three months.   *Public Order Act 1986 ss.12,13*

Information about processions and marches is available from Liberty [see end of chapter]. In London the police have a code of practice for marches. This is for guidance only, and is not legally binding.

47.7.6   Demonstrations near Parliament

A demonstration within the 'designated area' (approximately one kilometre in each direction from the Houses of Parliament) requires written notification to the metropolitan police commissioner at least six clear days before the event is due to start. Shorter notice is possible only if it was not reasonably practicable to give six days' notice, and in every case at least 24 hours' notice must be given.
Serious Organised Crime & Police Act 2005 ss.132-138

'Demonstration' is not defined but could be an assembly of two or more persons [**47.7.3**], or an event or static demonstration involving only one person. The police cannot refuse to allow the demonstration, but may impose conditions. These conditions may include not only number of participants, location and duration – as with any assembly – but also restrictions on noise and the size of banners, and any other conditions considered necessary. Loudspeakers and loudhailers are completely prohibited unless used by the police or other emergency services.

At the time of writing (mid 2009) the **constitutional renewal bill** was expected to repeal the rules on demonstrations near Parliament.

The rules on demonstrations do not apply to processions [**47.7.5**] near Parliament, for which six days' notice needs to be given anyway and for which there are different rules on the conditions that can be imposed.

Details and a map of the designated area are available from the Metropolitan Police public order branch [see end of chapter] or Charing Cross police station.

47.7.7   Picketing

Apart from the legislation on peaceful picketing by workers [**36.6.3**], picketing is not specifically allowed or prohibited. It could, however, constitute trespass, obstructing the highways, behaviour likely to cause a breach of the peace and/or public disorder, and if it involves two or more people is a public assembly [**47.7.3**].

47.8   LOUDSPEAKERS

Loudspeakers may be used only between 8am and 9pm. Notice as required under local by-laws must be given to the police, and other local by-laws must be complied with.   *Control of Pollution Act 1974 s.62*

47.9   PUBLIC DISORDER

Organisers of public events, especially large ones on contentious issues, should have contingency plans and ensure stewards are trained to deal with situations which might arise. For some activities, it may be appropriate to have independent legal observers present. Liberty [see end of chapter] can provide advice on this.

47.9.1   Breach of the peace and similar offences

Breach of the peace is a common law offence which occurs when harm is actually done or is likely to be done to a person, or in the person's presence to his or property, or when a person is in fear of being harmed or having his or her property harmed through an assault, affray, riot or other disturbance.
R v Howell [1981] 3 All ER 383

If a person of 'reasonable firmness' at the scene would fear for his or her safety there may be **affray**, where one or more persons use or threaten unlawful violence towards another person; **violent disorder**, where three or more are present and they use or threaten unlawful violence; or **riot**, where 12 or more people use or threaten unlawful violence for a common purpose. *Public Order Act 1986 ss.1-3*

47.9.2 Harassment and racial and religious hatred

Possession of racially inflammatory material, even without distributing it, is an offence. It is an offence to use threatening, abusive or insulting words or behaviour or to distribute or display threatening, abusive or insulting words or signs within the hearing or sight of a person likely to be caused **harassment** [**40.5.3**], alarm or distress, or if the words or signs are likely to stir up **racial hatred**, or with the intention to frighten someone, provoke violence or stir up racial hatred. It is also an offence to use words or behaviour, or to publish, display or distribute materials, which are threatening and are intended to stir up **religious hatred**.

Public Order Act 1986 ss.4-6,18,19,23; ss.29B,29C, inserted by Racial & Religious Hatred Act 2006

47.9.3 Aggravated trespass

Going onto outdoor land or into buildings without the consent of the landowner, and with the intention of disrupting or obstructing lawful activity or intimidating people to deter them from engaging in lawful activity, is **aggravated trespass**. This is an offence, unlike ordinary trespass which is a tort [**22.6.1**].

Criminal Justice & Public Order Act 1994 s.68, amended by Anti-Social Behaviour Act 2003 s.59

Resources: PUBLIC GATHERINGS, ENTERTAINMENT AND LICENSING

Licensing. Local authority licensing department.

Department for Culture, Media and Sport: www.culture.gov.uk, 020 7211 6000, enquiries@culture.gov.uk.

ACRE: www.acre.org.uk, 01285 653477, acre@acre.org.uk.

Community Matters: www.communitymatters.org.uk, 0845 847 4253, communitymatters@communitymatters.org.uk.

Music licensing. Performing Right Society (PRS) and Mechanical Copyright Protection Society (MCPS): www.prsformusic.com, 020 7580 5544, email via website.

Phonographic Performance Ltd (PPL): www.ppluk.com, 020 7534 1000, info@ppluk.com.

Video Performance Ltd (VPL): www.vpluk.com, 020 7534 1400, info@vpluk.com.

Centre for Education and Finance Management: www.ceduman.co.uk, 01494 473014, prs@cefm.co.uk.

Christian Copyright Licensing International (CCLI): www.ccli.co.uk, 01323 417711, email via website.

Public gatherings. Liberty: www.yourrights.org.uk and www.liberty-human-rights.org.uk, 020 7403 3888, email via website.

Health and Safety Executive: www.hse.gov.uk, 0845 345 0055, hse.infoline@natbrit.com.

Home Office: www.police.homeoffice.gov.uk, 020 7035 4848, public.enquiries@homeoffice.gsi.gov.uk.

Metropolitan Police public order branch (for demonstrations near Parliament): www.met.police.uk, 020 7230 9801/9805. Charing Cross police station 0300 123 1212.

Greater London Authority (for Trafalgar Square): www.london.gov.uk, 020 7983 4813, trafalgar.square@london.gov.uk.

Royal Parks (for Hyde Park and other royal parks): www.royalparks.org.uk, 020 7298 2000, hq@royalparks.gsi.gov.uk.

Statute law. www.opsi.gov.uk and www.statutelaw.gov.uk.

Much but not all case law. www.bailii.org.

Updates cross-referenced to this book. www.rclh.co.uk.

Part V covers the organisation's income from voluntary sources (donations, grants, fundraising and legacies) and from trading activities, including contracts and service agreements.

Chapter 48

FUNDING AND FUNDRAISING: GENERAL RULES

For sources of further information see end of chapter. Specific fundraising activities are covered in **chapter 49**.

48.1   FUNDRAISING AND THE LAW

This chapter covers general rules on fundraising; specific types of fundraising are covered in **chapter 49**. The term **funds** is used throughout to refer not only to money, but also to property of any sort donated to an organisation. This could include anything from jumble through to shares and land.

A voluntary organisation's efforts to bring in funds are subject to a wide range of legal requirements:

- charities, and in some cases a broader class of 'charitable institutions' [**48.6.1**], are subject to limits and controls on fundraising;

- charitable institutions are subject to specific controls if they pay even as little as £10.01 per day to a person to carry out fundraising [**48.6.3**], or if they are involved in a commercial venture where a business benefits from use of the charity's name [**48.6.4**];

- funds raised for a specific purpose may be used only for that purpose [**48.2**];

- many fundraising activities, such as public collections and lotteries, are regulated [**chapter 49**];

- particular issues may need to be considered when using volunteers [**39.10.3**] or consultants [**38.4.2**] to advise on or carry out fundraising;

- the organisation may have to pay tax on the income, or on any surplus or profit arising from the income [**chapter 56**];

- if payment is received for goods or services, the organisation may have to charge VAT to the purchaser [**chapter 57**];
- the sale of goods and services is affected by contract law [**chapter 21**], consumer protection law [**40.11**], and many other aspects of law;
- an organisation which sells goods or services through a trading subsidiary must ensure the relationship is properly handled [**chapter 51**].

Fundraising is not, in itself, a charitable activity. Charities which do not have a power to fundraise [**7.4.4**] should take advice before using resources in this way.

The **Institute of Fundraising** has codes of practice on many aspects of fundraising, and the **Fundraising Standards Board** is a self regulatory body for organisations that raise funds from the public, and suppliers providing fundraising services to the sector [see end of chapter]. Organisations which join the FRSB must comply with the Institute's codes of fundraising practice. If the voluntary self regulation scheme is not effective, the government can implement statutory control of fundraising.

Charities Act 2006 s.69

48.2 FUNDS RAISED FOR SPECIFIC PURPOSES

Funds (which in this context includes property of all types) given for a specific purpose must be used only for that purpose. Use of the funds for any other purpose may constitute fraud or deception, and/or be a breach of trust.

48.2.1 Trusts and constructive trusts

Trust law covers funds given to or raised by:
- an unincorporated association [**2.2**] or trust [**2.3**], whether charitable or non-charitable, for charitable purposes [**5.2.3**];
- a non-charitable association 'for the benefit of the members' [**2.2.4**];
- any third party, such as an individual or commercial body, if the funds are for charitable purposes or for the benefit of identifiable individuals such as victims of a disaster;
- a charitable company, under some circumstances, if the funds are to be used for a specific purpose.

Funds covered by trust law are subject to a **trust** between the donor, the persons responsible for the funds (the **trustees**), and the persons intended to benefit (the **beneficiaries**) [**2.3.1**].

Where funds are raised by a charitable trust or association, the members of the governing body are trustees for the funds. Where funds are raised by individuals or a non-charitable association, a **constructive trust** for those funds arises. A constructive trust is one which is not deliberately created [**2.3**], but is 'constructed' from the reality of the situation and the conduct of the fundraisers. A constructive trustee, like any other trustee, is obliged to use the funds only for the purposes for which they were raised, and is personally liable for their use.

48.2.1.1 Funds raised through charges for goods and services

The rules on breach of trust do not apply when goods or services are sold, charged for, or provided under a contract or most service agreements [**52.1.3**]. These situations are covered by contract law, not trust law. So long as the goods or services are provided as required, there is no obligation to use all the income to provide them. Some public sector purchasers may make it a contractual condition that any surplus is returned (**clawback**), but if this is not required, those funds may be used for any purpose within the organisation's objects or powers.

48.2.2 Non-charitable purposes

Apart from funds raised for identifiable individuals and a few other exceptions [**2.3.4**], trust law does not cover funds raised for non-charitable purposes. If funds are misused, the persons responsible may be liable for fraud or deception – but not breach of trust as well.

48.2.3   *cy près* uses for charitable funds

If funds (including property of any type) raised for a charity or for charitable purposes cannot be used as originally intended, because too much or too little was raised or because the purpose is no longer necessary or realistic, the original appeal is said to have **failed**. Guidance on dealing with funds raised through a failed appeal is in the Charity Commission's CC20 *Charities and fundraising*.

48.2.3.1   Solicitations with Charities Act 2006 statement

The **Charities Act 2006** allows funds raised in a failed appeal to be used for another purpose, but only if the request for donations (the **solicitation**) includes a statement that if the appeal fails from the outset, the donation will be used for similar charitable purposes unless the donor, at the time of making the donation, makes a **relevant declaration** . This declaration states that if the appeal fails from the outset, the donor wants the charity to give him or her the opportunity to request a refund.   *Charities Act 1993 ss.13-14A, amended & inserted by Charities Act 2006 ss.15-17*

If the appeal fails, the trustees holding the funds must contact all donors who have made a relevant declaration, asking if they want their money (or a sum equivalent to the value of donated property) back. If a donor cannot be contacted or does not reply within three months from the date of the letter, the Charity Commission will make a **scheme** [4.5.5] allowing the donation to be used *cy près* – for purposes that are within 'the spirit of the gift', and that take account of the social and economic circumstances at the time the change in purposes is made.
        Charities (Failed Appeals) Regulations 2008 [available from Charity Commission]

Relevant declarations must be kept for at least six years after the donation is used as originally planned, or a refund is sent under the above provisions, or the Charity Commission make a scheme for the donation to be used in another way.

48.2.3.2   Solicitations without the Charities Act 2006 statement

If the appeal fails and the original request for donations did not include the necessary statement, the charity must contact known donors, and ask if they would like a refund or will sign a disclaimer allowing their donation to be used for a different purpose. The charity must also try to locate other donors, through advertising in a specified way. Where donors disclaim a refund or cannot be identified, or if there are surplus funds, the Charity Commission makes a *cy près* scheme for use of the funds. The scheme allows for donors who were not originally located to claim their portion of the money or property up to six months after the scheme is made.   *Charities Act 1993 s.14; Charities (Failed Appeals) Regulations 2008*

Enquiries and advertisements are not required for the proceeds of cash collections made in collecting boxes or in similar ways, or for the proceeds of any lottery, competition, entertainment, sale or similar fundraising activity. These funds are conclusively presumed to belong to donors who cannot be identified, and will be covered by the Charity Commission scheme.   *Charities Act 1993 s.14(3)*

Where it would be unreasonable to make enquiries or advertise for donors, either because the amounts likely to be returned are very small or because so much time has elapsed since the money was raised, the court or Charity Commission may order that such property can be covered by the Commission's scheme. The Commission should be contacted about this procedure.   *Charities Act 1993 s.14(4)*

48.2.4   Alternative uses for non-charitable funds

The Charities Act rules on advertising and *cy près* schemes apply to all funds raised by charities, or raised by individuals and non-charities for charitable organisations or purposes. They do not apply to money or property raised by individuals and non-charities for non-charitable organisations or purposes, but the donor may take legal action if the funds are not used as the donor intended.

48.2.5   Fundraising for the public sector

In the past, the Charity Commission's view was that charities should not use their charitable resources to provide services that the state is obliged to provide, but could provide additional or top-up services. Its view now is that the law does not prevent charities from raising and using their own funds to provide services on behalf of public authorities, even if an authority has a legal duty to provide such a service [**5.3.1**]. Details are set out in CC37 *Charities and public service delivery*, available from the Commission [see end of chapter].

Where funds are being raised for equipment or buildings for a public sector body (or any non-charity), it is important to clarify with the recipient body in writing, before the fundraising starts, any conditions on the long-term use of the gift. Otherwise there is nothing to prevent the recipient from selling the equipment or building, or using them for unintended purposes.

48.3 GRANTS, DONATIONS AND GIFTS

A grant, donation or gift may be in the form of money, goods, other property, services, publicity or facilities. The key point is that the contribution is primarily a **gift**, the donor receives nothing more than a simple acknowledgement in return, and no contract [**21.1**] is created. The distinction between a grant or donation and a contract is often unclear [**52.1**], especially in relation to sponsorship [**56.3.3**] and local or health authority service level agreements [**52.1.3**]. Legal advice may be needed to clarify the position.

48.3.1 Enforceability of terms and conditions

Except where there is a statutory obligation for a public sector body to provide a grant (for example to students), grants and donations are given at the discretion of the donor or funder and can generally be stopped at any time – even if the promise of the grant or donation is made in writing. There may be a moral obligation on a funder or donor to provide what they have promised, but unless the promise has been made as a deed [**20.3**] or under a will, or the arrangement is actually contractual rather than a grant, the recipient's right to the grant or donation cannot be enforced in the courts. *Taylor v Dickens & another [1998] 3 FCR 455*

Even where the right to the grant or donation cannot be contested, it may be possible to challenge the way a donor made the decision to withdraw or stop a grant, if this did not follow the donor's or funder's own procedures or, in the case of public sector bodies, did not comply with the Compact [**48.4.1**].

48.3.1.1 Use for other purposes

Grants and donations may be given for purposes ranging from the very general ('to support the organisation's work') to the very specific. The purposes may be defined by the recipient organisation in its application or appeal, by the funder or donor, or jointly by the funder/donor and the recipient organisation.

Regardless of who defines the purpose, funds must be used only in that way unless the donor agrees otherwise. If they are used in any other way, the donor can take legal action to recover the money. Members of the governing body could be held personally liable to repay funds which have been misused [**22.4**].

48.3.1.2 Non-compliance with conditions

In addition to the terms specifying how a grant or donation is to be used and when it will be paid, there may be conditions setting out related requirements. These may range from the virtually non-existent ('to acknowledge receipt of this donation'), to many pages of small print. If the recipient does not comply with the conditions, the funder or donor may withdraw the funding, ask for its money to be returned, or in extreme cases take legal action against the organisation and the members of its governing body.

48.3.2 Refusing donations

A decision not to accept a donation, grant or other support offered to the organisation should be made only by the governing body, and only after careful consideration. Charity trustees must act in the best interests of the charity [**15.6.3**], and must be able to demonstrate clearly to the Charity Commission, if required to do so, how the best interests of the charity have been served in refusing a donation. Difficult issues may arise if what seems ethically or morally right is not necessarily in the organisation's financial interest.

A decision to **disclaim** (refuse) a gift can probably be justified if the aims or activities of the donor are contrary to the organisation's objects, acceptance could negatively affect support from other sources, conditions placed by the donor are unreasonable or contrary to the organisation's objectives, or the donation is the product of illegal activity.

In other situations, the issues are similar to those on ethical investment [**58.6.2**], and a refusal may be harder to justify as being in the best interests of the organisation and its beneficiaries. The guidance on unsolicited donations from the Institute of Fundraising [see end of chapter] may be helpful, and advice and if necessary consent should be sought from the Charity Commission.

48.3.2.1 Money laundering, terrorism, proceeds of crime and suspicious donations

Unscrupulous persons sometimes seek to use charities to 'launder' money – for example by making a loan in cash to a charity and requiring repayment by cheque, making a large donation to a charity and saying the charity can keep the interest but must return the donation, or making a donation on condition that it is passed on to a specified individual or organisation.

The Charity Commission encourages charities to be aware of these risks, and to put procedures in place for recognising and dealing with suspicious donations or loans. The Commission's guidance on charities and terrorism (OG96) says that donations or loans may be refused if the trustees have sought to find out more about a person unknown to them who makes or offers a large donation to the charity, and have not received satisfactory replies to their enquiries; a donation is conditional upon a particular organisation or individual being used to do work for the charity; or a donation or loan is offered in cash, with all or part of the money having to be returned to the donor after a specified period.

Charities concerned about any aspect of a donation or loan, especially if they wish to refuse it, should contact the Commission and may wish to contact the police.

48.4 GRANTS FROM PUBLIC SECTOR BODIES

The Treasury [see end of chapter] provides guidance on the law and good practice affecting public sector funding relationships with voluntary organisations.

48.4.1 The Compact

The **Compact**, local Compacts and Compact codes of practice set out good practice in relationships between the public and voluntary sectors. They are promoted and supported by the **Commission for the Compact**, **Compact Voice**, the **Compact Advocacy Programme** and the **Compact Mediation Scheme** [see end of chapter]. At the time of writing (mid 2009), the Commission for the Compact was consulting on a simplified version. In addition, there was discussion about whether breach of the Compact or its codes should be able to be taken into account in challenging decisions and actions by public bodies.

48.4.2 State aid rules

European Union rules on **state aid** are intended to prevent preferential public sector support which could distort competition within the EU. Where a recipient organisation is involved in an 'economically competitive' activity, some grants, subsidies, preferential loans or asset transfers at below market price from public sector bodies could fall within the rules. They cover any aid which:

- is from state resources (interpreted very widely, and including for example the national lottery or landfill tax credits);
- provides a benefit to some but not all undertakings of that type (an undertaking is defined as being active in a commercial market);

- distorts, or has the potential to distort, competition; and
- affects, or has the potential to affect, trade between EU member states.

An organisation operating only in one local area and very unlikely to attract service users or customers from another EU member state is unlikely to be affected by the rules. But organisations which charge for goods or services and actually operate in another EU member state, or could potentially attract customers or service users from there, should take advice from the Department for Business, Innovation and Skills state aid branch [see end of chapter] before accepting funds or assets from the public sector.

Even where aid appears to fall within the rules, it may be exempt. But if it is not exempt, the public sector body will need to seek consent from the European Commission to provide the aid. If it does not do so, and provides state aid unlawfully, the public sector body can be required – at any point in the following 10 years – to recover the funds from the recipient, plus interest at a punitive rate. Such recovery cannot take account of the effect on the recipient.

In December 2008 the state aid rules outlined above were eased to allow governments to provide grants and cheap loans to help undertakings weather the recession. These provisions were expected to last at least two years.

48.4.3 Grant cuts and decisions by public bodies

When a local authority substantially reduced two organisations' grants with only a few days' notice, the organisations sought judicial review [**64.1.1**]. The court found that the council had acted lawfully in making the cuts, but the council should have given notice in writing before a final decision was made, should have given organisations at risk of cuts reasonable opportunities to make representations to the council, and after the cuts were made, the appeal against them should have been heard by persons who were not involved in the original decision.

Haringey London Borough Council, R v [2000] All ER(D) 1583

Similar decisions about the need for public sector bodies to consult before cutting grants were made in Doody, R (on the application of) v Secretary of State for the Home Department *[1993] UKHL 8*, Coughlan and others, R (on the application of) v North and East Devon Health Authority *[1999] EWCA Civ 1871*, and Capenhurst and others, R (on the application of) v Leicester City Council *[2004] EWHC 2124*.

An organisation wishing to challenge a funding decision should initially use internal complaints procedures. To take further action, early advice and speed are essential. It may be appropriate to move on to judicial review [**64.1.1**], as in the cases above, or possibly a complaint to the Office of Government Commerce [see end of **chapter 52**] or the relevant ombudsman. The Compact [**48.4.1**] provides an essential starting point for any complaint. A judicial review must be brought within three months of a relevant decision.

It may also be possible to bring a discrimination claim for breach of a public sector body's duty to promote equality [**42.2**].

If EU procurement rules or the public contracts regulations [**52.2.1**] have been breached, it may be possible to make a challenge in the high court.

48.4.4 Clawback

In the past, public sector funding often included a requirement that any income earned as a result of a grant or contract had to be repaid to the public body. There was often also a requirement that if public sector funding was used to help purchase or refurbish a building, the organisation could not use the building as collateral for further loans and had to repay the proceeds if the building was sold.

The Treasury eased these **clawback** rules in 2005. Assets can now be used as collateral, and the public body can allow the organisation to keep income generated through a grant or contract or from the sale of an asset, provided the income will be used to achieve the same general outcomes as originally agreed.

Information about the clawback rules is available from the Development Trusts Association and Community Matters [see end of chapter].

48.5   CONDUIT FUNDING: RECEIVING AND PASSING ON FUNDS

Many funders and donors are able or willing to give funds only to registered charities. If they wish to support an organisation which has not yet completed the charity registration process or is excepted or exempt from registration [**8.1**], they may want to make the grant or donation to a registered charity (the **intermediary** charity), which in turn makes a grant to the recipient organisation. Receiving a grant or donation on behalf of another organisation is often called **conduit funding**. In effect, the intermediary allows the ultimate recipient to use its charity number to access funds that would not otherwise be available.

48.5.1   Legal issues

With a 'conduit' arrangement the donor fulfils its criterion of giving only to registered charities, the intermediary has provided a useful service, and the recipient has had access to charitable funds. But such arrangements are lawful only if:

- the original donor, if an organisation, makes its donation only for purposes which are properly charitable and are within its own objects and powers (so, for example, a funder prohibited from making grants to non-charities cannot get around this by using a charity to pass its grant on to a non-charity);

- the intermediary charity is satisfied about the legitimacy of the original donor and the recipient(s), maintains records of the checks carried out, and is satisfied that the arrangement is not being used for money laundering [**48.3.2.1**];

- the intermediary charity receives the donation only for purposes which are charitable and within its objects and powers;

- the intermediary passes on the funds for purposes which comply with the donor's wishes and are within its own objects and powers; and

- the recipient uses the money only for charitable purposes which comply with the wishes of both the original donor and the intermediary, and (if it is an organisation rather than an individual) are within its own objects and powers.

Breach of these rules may make the donation subject to tax [**56.4**] and could be a breach of trust [**48.2**] and/or *ultra vires* [**5.8**].

By acting as a conduit for funds, the intermediary becomes responsible for how those funds are used by the recipient. An intermediary which indiscriminately allows others to use its charity number and channels funds for organisations or individuals without proper procedures could find itself liable not only for breach of trust, but also for a recipient's misuse of the funds or even money laundering.

48.5.2   Internal guidelines

An intermediary should have clear written guidelines covering when it may be involved as a conduit, what checks must be carried out to ensure the arrangement is not being used for money laundering, the limits within which staff may authorise such arrangements without express authority from the governing body, the need for all authorisations to be reported to the next meeting of the governing body and to be minuted, and the need to monitor the recipient's use of funds. Guidelines and procedures should be regularly reviewed.

48.5.3   Funding agreement

The intermediary's rules should be reflected in a **funding agreement**. Because of the potential tax, charity law and other legal implications, it is sensible to have this reviewed by an experienced solicitor before issuing it to potential recipients. The agreement should be entered into prior to the recipient using the intermediary's name or charity number in any application for funding or publicity related to the funding.

The agreement should specify:

- that the intermediary's name and number can be used only in connection with the application or activity specified in the agreement;

- that all activities covered by the funding must be legally charitable and clearly fall within the intermediary's objects and powers;

- that the intermediary will be given copies of all applications and related documents either automatically or on request;
- that all grants or donations received under the arrangement must be initially paid to the intermediary;
- when the intermediary will pay the money on to the recipient, what triggers the payment, and that the intermediary has no obligation to make any payment if funds are not received from the original donor;
- who receives any interest earned during any period between the intermediary's receipt of funds and paying them on to the recipient;
- the intermediary's obligation to pay over to the recipient the tax recovered if the donor is an individual making the payment under gift aid [**50.2**];
- whether the intermediary makes any charge to the recipient for the use of its charity number and the related administration (such a charge may have implications for tax, see **56.4**, and VAT, see **57.10.10**);
- a warranty or promise by the recipient that the funds will be used only for charitable purposes, and only for purposes specified in its agreements with the original donor and with the intermediary;
- reporting arrangements from the recipient to the intermediary and the donor;
- any arrangements for the intermediary to monitor the accounts and relevant activities of the recipient, or to have access to such information on request;
- the intermediary's right to retain funds or return them to the original donor if the recipient does not comply with the agreement.

48.5.4 Financial procedures

To ensure there is no confusion about whose money it is and how it is to be used, the intermediary must have clear procedures for handling funds received on behalf of other organisations, including whether the money should be placed in a separate bank account; if the money is not kept in a separate bank account, how interest is calculated and recorded; how the release of funds is authorised; safeguards to ensure the intermediary does not use the funds for other purposes; and whether fidelity insurance [**23.6.3**] is needed to safeguard the funds.

The receipt of the funds will be included as part of the intermediary charity's annual income, and may put it into a higher income category where more detailed annual accounts or a full audit are required [**54.2.2**].

48.5.5 Fundraising by non-charities for a charity

In the situation described above, a registered charity allows its charitable status to be used to raise funds for an organisation which is not a registered charity. Similar procedures, adapted as appropriate, should be followed where a charity allows a non-charity to use its number to raise funds for the charity.

If the non-charity is a commercial body, such arrangements must comply with the rules on commercial participation [**48.6.4**] and the duty not to allow a charity's name to be used commercially unless this is beneficial to the charity [**44.9.3**].

48.6 PROFESSIONAL FUNDRAISERS AND COMMERCIAL PARTICIPATION

The **Charities Act 1992** part 2, as amended by the **Charities Act 2006**, and related regulations cover charitable institutions' use of **professional fundraisers**, arrangements with **commercial participators**, and other matters relating to fundraising. Information and advice are available from the Charity Commission, the Institute of Fundraising [see end of chapter] and specialist solicitors.

48.6.1 Charitable institutions

For the purposes of the fundraising regulations, a **charitable institution** is any body established for charitable [**5.2.3**], benevolent or philanthropic purposes.

Charities Act 1992 s.58(1)

Benevolent and **philanthropic** are not defined in statute, and case law is complex. In general the terms apply to purposes which are predominantly rather than exclusively charitable. The Big Lottery Fund, which supports only organisations established for charitable, benevolent or philanthropic purposes, defines benevolent and philanthropic as having 'the attributes of charity ... they must have nothing which is against the concept of charity, and they must act from a sense of altruism, for the public benefit and not for private or mutual benefit'.

It is good practice for all fundraising for good causes – even if the cause may not technically fall within the definition of philanthropic or benevolent – to comply with the Charities Act fundraising regulations.

When the **Charities Act 2006** rules on public charitable collections [**49.2.3**] come into effect, regulations or guidance may include definitions of benevolent and philanthropic.

48.6.2 Connected companies

For the purposes of the fundraising regulations, a **connected company** is one where one or more charitable institutions can exercise, or control the exercise of, all the voting rights at a general meeting of the company. *Charities Act 1992 s.58(5)*

Trading companies set up and controlled by charitable institutions are connected companies, but are not professional fundraisers [**48.6.3**] or commercial participators [**48.6.4**] when they are acting in relation to an organisation which controls them. Despite this, the Charity Commission's CC20 *Charities and fundraising* recommends that connected trading companies follow the rules for professional fundraisers and commercial participators even when acting for their parent body.

48.6.3 Professional fundraisers

Under the Charities Act 1992, a **professional fundraiser** is:
- an individual, partnership or corporate body who carries on a business for gain which is wholly or primarily engaged in soliciting money or other property for charitable, benevolent or philanthropic purposes (a **fundraising business**); or
- an individual or corporate body who is not working for a fundraising business as defined above, but who is being paid or rewarded for soliciting money or other property for a charitable institution and who is not explicitly excluded from the definition of professional fundraiser [below]. *Charities Act 1992 s.58(1)*

48.6.3.1 Who is not a professional fundraiser

The following are not professional fundraisers:
- a charitable institution or its connected company [**48.6.1**, **48.6.2**];
- a commercial participator [**48.6.4**];
- an employee or member of the governing body of the charitable institution for which funds are being raised or its connected company, provided the individual is raising funds in that capacity rather than in any other capacity;
- a collector for a public collection [**49.2**], unless he or she is the promoter of the collection;
- a person making a solicitation for a charitable institution or connected company as part of a radio or television broadcast;
- a person paid no more than £10 per day or £1,000 per year (excluding legitimate expenses) for soliciting funds for a charitable institution;
- a person who is paid no more than £1,000 in connection with soliciting funds for a particular fundraising venture. *Charities Act 1992 s.58(2),(3); Charities Acts 1992 & 1993 (Substitution of Sums) Order 2009 [SI 2009/508] art.3*

A volunteer fundraiser who is reimbursed for genuine out of pocket expenses [**39.2.1**] is not a professional fundraiser. But a so-called volunteer who is paid flat rate expenses which are more than genuine expenditure, or who is given an honorarium or any other payment, is a professional fundraiser if the payment is more than £10 per day, £1,000 per year or £1,000 per event above actual expenses.

Some persons who are not professional fundraisers have to make statements to donors similar to those made by professional fundraisers [**48.6.6.1**].

48.6.3.2 Grey areas

If in doubt about whether an individual, partnership or incorporated body falls within the statutory definition of professional fundraiser, it is essential to take advice from the Charity Commission, Institute of Fundraising or specialist solicitor, or to err on the side of caution and comply with the regulations.

48.6.3.3 Challenge events

A participant in a challenge event such as 'cycle through the Andes' [**49.5**] may be a professional fundraiser if he or she receives a tour or something else worth more than £1,000. Where the participant is a member of the governing body of the charity or connected to a governing body member [**15.2.5**], the implications of receiving the tour or other benefit must be considered in light of the governing body member's obligation not to benefit from the charity [**16.3.10**]. If there is any doubt about this, the participant should consult the Charity Commission as to whether its consent to participate is required.

48.6.3.4 Agents and fulfilment houses

Soliciting money or property may mean not only asking for it, but also receiving it as a result of a solicitation or processing responses to a promotion. So if, for example, a charitable institution has an agreement to pay a commercial business to receive donations from an appeal, crediting the donations temporarily to the business's account before they are paid over to the institution, the commercial business could be a professional fundraiser. The same may apply if a business is paid to send out information packs or to process catalogue sales. A business which undertakes this sort of work is called a **fulfilment house** and may well be classed as a professional fundraiser.

A fundraising business which telephones potential donors is a professional fundraiser, but so might be individuals or companies who answer calls from potential donors, if they tell callers anything about the charitable institution or its work, or if the money received goes initially into the fundraiser's account rather than direct to the charitable institution.

48.6.4 Commercial participators

A **commercial participator** is an individual, partnership or corporate body who carries on for gain a business other than a fundraising business [**48.6.3**], and who in the course of that business engages in a promotional venture (often called **cause related marketing**) to raise money for one or more charitable institutions [**48.6.1**].   *Charities Act 1992 s.58(1)*

The essence of commercial participation is that the commercial participator hopes customers will be more likely to choose a particular commercial product or service because they know some of the purchase price will be donated to a good cause.

Examples are donations to charities or other good causes of 5p for every tin of beans purchased, 50% of a restaurant's profits on world Aids day, £1 for each new account opened in July, 10p for each pack of Christmas cards, or a business agreeing to give £5,000 to a charity and publicising this to attract more customers.

A commercial participator's indication that a proportion or amount of money raised from a promotional venture will be given to one or more charitable institutions or will be applied for their benefit is a **representation**.

48.6.4.1 Who is not a commercial participator

A body involved in raising money for a charitable institution is not a commercial participator if:

- it is not a commercial business;
- it is a commercial business but is controlled by the institution for which it is raising funds [**48.6.2**];

- it is a commercial business but is not carrying on the promotion in the course of its normal business;

- it buys the goods from a charitable institution as a straightforward contractual transaction and then sells them on the same basis as any other goods, without representing that some of the profits will be donated to the charitable institution;

- the benefit to the charitable institution is not publicised in any way.

A connected company [**48.6.2**] is not a commercial participator when it is acting in relation to a charitable institution which controls it, but it may be a commercial participator when acting in relation to other charitable institutions.

A business which is not carries out a promotion to raise funds for charitable, benevolent or philanthropic purposes, rather than for charitable institutions, is not a commercial participator, but some similar rules apply [**48.6.6.5**].

48.6.4.2 Protecting the charity's name and reputation

A charity's name and reputation are valuable assets which must be protected. RS2 *Charities and commercial partners*, available from the Charity Commission, outlines the issues that need to be considered before entering into a commercial participation arrangement. The burden is on the charitable institution to ensure that the agreement is advantageous to the organisation and protects its reputation. This includes ensuring a sufficient price is obtained for the use of its name, being very specific about the purposes for which its name and logo can be used [**44.11**], ensuring the arrangements enhance (or do not detract from) the organisation's reputation, and minimising risk to the organisation.

The terms agreed with a commercial partner must be defined in detail, and must be reviewed regularly [**44.9.3**].

48.6.4.3 Tax and VAT

Licensing a commercial participator to use an organisation's name or logo is a trading transaction. The licence fee, and any fee received by the organisation to provide promotion, advertising or other services, may be subject to income or corporation tax [**56.4.14**] and/or VAT [**57.11**]. Specialist advice on the legal, tax and VAT implications should be sought before entering into any commercial participation arrangement.

48.6.5 Written agreements

A professional fundraiser or commercial participator must have a written agreement with the institution(s) for which it is raising funds. In many cases, the agreement will also involve the institution's trading subsidiary.   *Charities Act 1992*
s.59(1),(2)

The agreement must be signed by both (or all) parties. For the voluntary organisation, the signatory must be a member of the governing body or a person properly authorised by the governing body.

If there is no written agreement or a written agreement does not comply with the requirements, the professional fundraiser or commercial participator cannot enforce the agreement against the charitable institution without first getting a court order.

48.6.5.1 Professional fundraisers

An agreement between a charitable institution and a professional fundraiser must contain specified information, details of which are available from the Charity Commission. If more than one charitable institution is party to the agreement, the agreement must specify how the decision will be made about the proportion of money or property each will receive.   *Charitable Institutions (Fund-Raising)*
Regulations 1994 [SI 1994/3024] reg.2

48.6.5.2 Commercial participators

An agreement between a charitable institution and a commercial participator must include the information required for agreements with professional fundraisers, as well as specified information about the amount to be donated by the commercial participator to the charitable institution, or how the amount will be determined.   *Charitable Institutions (Fund-Raising) Regulations 1994 [SI 1994/3024] reg.3*

48.6.6   Statements to donors

Professional fundraisers and commercial participators raising money or soliciting property for one or more specific charitable institutions – or for a charitable, benevolent or philanthropic purpose rather than for a specific institution – must make a **solicitation statement** at the time, making clear their relationship with the organisation(s) for which they are fundraising. Guidance on the statements, including examples, is available from the Office of the Third Sector [see end of chapter].   *Charities Act 1992 s.60, amended by Charities Act 2006 s.67*

If the professional fundraiser or commercial participator approaches a potential donor or purchaser, the statement must accompany the solicitation or representation. Commercial participators selling goods may not need to put the statement on each item; a notice prominently displayed at the cash till may be adequate. If a public collection is organised by a professional fundraiser, the collectors must display the statement. If an individual or company is paid to organise a fundraising event, any publicity which asks for donations or indicates that a charitable institution will benefit must include the statement.

Failure to make the statement as required is an offence under the Charities Act 2006, and may also be a breach of trading standards requirements and the advertising code [**48.6.6.6**].

Additional information must be included if the statement is made as part of a radio or television broadcast with an announcement that payment can be made by credit or debit card [**48.6.7**], or if the solicitation or representation is made by telephone [**49.3.1**].

If funds are being raised for a registered charity which has total income of more than £10,000 per year, every written or printed notice encouraging people to give to the charity must state that the organisation is a registered charity [**18.1.5**].

48.6.6.1   Professional fundraisers

A professional fundraiser soliciting money or property for one or more specific organisations must include, as part of the solicitation, a statement clearly indicating the name(s) of the charitable institution(s), and if there is more than one, the proportion in which each is to benefit; and the method by which the fundraiser's remuneration in connection with the appeal is to be determined and the **notifiable amount** of the remuneration.   *Charities Act 1992 s.60(1),*
amended by Charities Act 2006 s.67(2)

The notifiable amount is the actual amount if this is known at the time the statement is made, or an estimated amount calculated as accurately as possible. If a percentage is used, it should be accompanied by a statement of the estimated amount.   *Charities Act 1992 s.60(3A), inserted by Charities Act 2006 s.67(5)*

If a professional fundraiser is soliciting funds for charitable, benevolent or philanthropic purposes ('for cancer research') rather than for a specific institution or institutions, the statement must indicate the fact that money or property is being solicited for those purposes rather than for a specific institution, how the decision will be made about how the proceeds will be divided among charitable institutions, and how the fundraiser's remuneration in connection with the appeal is to be determined and the notifiable amount of the remuneration.   *Charities Act 1992*
s.60(2), amended by Charities Act 2006 s.67(3)

48.6.6.2   Employees, officers and governing body members

A statement similar to a section 60 statement [above] must be made by anyone who is:

• an employee, officer or governing body member of a charitable institution, or an employee or officer of a company connected with a charitable institution;

• acting in that capacity as a collector for a street, house to house or public charitable collection [**49.2**];

- being paid as an employee, officer or governing body member and/or as a collector; and
- being paid more than £10 per day or £1,000 per year, or a lump sum of more than £1,000.

Unlike a section 60 statement, the statement only needs to say that the person is being paid as an employee, officer, governing body member or for acting as a collector. It does not have to include the amount of the remuneration.

Charities Act 1992 s.60A,60B, inserted by Charities Act 2006 s.68;
Charities Acts 1992 & 1993 (Substitution of Sums) Order 2009 [SI 2009/508] art.5

48.6.6.3 Fundraisers who are not professional fundraisers

Rules similar to those for professional fundraisers apply if a person is paid for carrying out a collection [**49.2**] but does not fall within the definition of a professional fundraiser [**48.6.3.1**] and is not an employee, officer or governing body member of the institution being collected for. This obligation does not apply if the person is paid no more than £10 per day, £1,000 per year, or £1,000 as a lump sum for acting as a collector for the charitable institution or institutions.

Charities Act 1992 s.60A,60B, inserted by Charities Act 2006 s.68

48.6.6.4 Commercial participators

A commercial participator raising money for a charitable institution must include as part of any representation a statement indicating the name(s) of the institution(s) concerned; if applicable, the proportion to be given to each institution; and the **notifiable amount** [**48.6.6.1**] of the sale price to be given to or applied for the benefit of the institutions, or the amount of the donation to be made by the commercial participator. *Charities Act 1992 s.60(3), amended by Charities Act 2006 s.67(4)*

The net amount which will be given to the organisation, after deduction of expenses and costs, should be stated. Examples are '3p for every item sold in June will be given to the Worthy Society, a registered charity', '10p per item sold will be given to the Worthy Society, with a minimum of £10,000', or '10% of the net profits on world Aids day will be donated to the Worthy Society'.

48.6.6.5 Commercial promotions for charitable purposes

Separate regulations apply to individuals, partnerships or corporate bodies which carry on a business for gain other than a fundraising business, and which raise money for charitable, benevolent or philanthropic purposes (rather than for a specific organisation or organisations, which would make them commercial participators).

These businesses are required to make a statement indicating the fact that the contributions raised are to be used for those purposes and not for a specific charitable institution, and must indicate how the decision will be made about which charitable institutions will receive the contributions.. From 1 October 2009 the rules on the notifiable amount are the same as for commercial participators [above]. *Charitable Institutions (Fund-Raising) Regulations 1994 [SI 1994/3024] reg.7, amended by*
Charitable Institutions (Fund-raising) (Amendment) Regulations 2009 [SI 2009/1060]

48.6.6.6 The advertising, sales promotion and direct marketing code

As well as complying with Charities Act requirements, promotions claiming that participation will benefit registered charities or good causes should comply with the British code of advertising, sales promotion and direct marketing [**45.2.1**].

In addition to the information that has to be provided by commercial participators, the code says that a promotion should also define the nature and objectives of the organisation which will benefit, if it is not a registered charity; not limit purchasers' or supporters' contributions, and ensure any extra money collected is given to the named charity or cause; provide to anyone who asks a current or final total of contributions; and take particular care when appealing to children.

48.6.7 Credit card fundraising

If a professional fundraiser makes a solicitation or a commercial participator makes a representation as part of a radio or television programme and there is an announcement that payment can be made by credit or debit card, donors who pay

721

more than £100 are entitled to give written notice within seven days of the broadcast saying they want their money refunded. An announcement to this effect must be made as part of the broadcast. *Charities Act 1992 ss.60(4),61(1), amended by Charities Acts 1992 & 1993 (Substitution of Sums) Order 2009 [SI 2009/508] art.6*

This right to a refund does not apply if the television or radio broadcast is made by the charity itself or a person speaking on its behalf, rather than by a professional fundraiser or commercial participator.

Similar rules apply where donations are made as a result of telephone fundraising or other fundraising that is not face to face [**49.3**].

48.6.8 Transfer of funds

Money raised by a professional fundraiser or commercial participator must be paid to the organisation's governing body, or into a bank or building society account in the name of the organisation or its governing body, as soon as reasonably practicable after its receipt or at any rate within 28 days or within the period agreed with the institution. *Charitable Institutions (Fund-Raising) Regulations 1994 [SI 1994/3024] reg.6(2)*

Money raised by a professional fundraiser should be transferred to the recipient organisation gross, before deduction of any fees or expenses.

Donated property must be kept securely and must be dealt with in accordance with the instructions of the organisation. If the property is sold or otherwise disposed of, the proceeds must be dealt with in the same way as money donations. *Charitable Institutions (Fund-Raising) Regulations 1994 [SI 1994/3024] reg.6(3)*

48.6.9 Fundraising records

A charitable institution which has an agreement with a professional fundraiser or commercial participator has a right to see all books, documents and other records relating to the agreement, on request and at all reasonable times. Records kept in non-legible form (for example, on computer or CD) must be made available on paper. *Charitable Institutions (Fund-Raising) Regulations 1994 [SI 1994/3024] reg.5*

48.7 UNAUTHORISED FUNDRAISING

It is not uncommon for individuals or commercial businesses to raise funds for good causes without informing the organisations for whom the funds are intended. Most of the time this is fine, but problems may arise when the fundraiser uses dubious methods, uses an organisation's name inappropriately, or does not hand over funds raised for the organisation.

48.7.1 Professional fundraisers and commercial participators

A charitable institution may take out an injunction to stop a professional fundraiser [**48.6.3**] or commercial participator [**48.6.4**] from raising money or property for it if there is no proper agreement with the institution, and if the court is satisfied that the contravention is likely to continue. *Charities Act 1992 s.59(3)*

Where there is a contract and a commercial participator or professional fundraiser uses inappropriate fundraising methods, they are (presumably) not fulfilling their contract with the organisation and the matter can be dealt with as breach of contract [**21.6**].

48.7.2 Unauthorised fundraising by others

A charitable institution may take steps to stop an individual or corporate body which is not a professional fundraiser or commercial participator from raising funds for it, if it objects to the methods being used for fundraising, feels that the individual or corporate body is not fit and proper to raise funds for it, or does not want to be associated with the particular promotional or fundraising venture. *Charities Act 1992 s.62*

The organisation must give notice that if the fundraising is not stopped immediately, an injunction will be sought under the **Charities Act 1992** s.62. The notice must specify the circumstances which gave rise to the serving of the notice, and the grounds on which the application for the injunction will be made. At least 28 days must elapse between giving the notice and applying for the injunction.

Charitable Institutions (Fund-Raising) Regulations 1994 [SI 1994/3024] reg.4

If the person stops the fundraising activity after receiving the notice, but starts the same or substantially the same activities within 12 months of the date of the notice, the organisation does not need to serve another notice or wait before seeking an injunction.

48.7.3   False statements about charitable status

It is an offence for a person soliciting money or other property to say that an organisation is a registered charity when in fact it is not. But it is a defence for the person to show that he or she believed on reasonable grounds that the organisation was a registered charity.

Charities Act 1992 s.63

48.7.4   Non-payment of funds raised

Any person who raises funds for a particular organisation or purpose is likely to be a constructive trustee [48.2.1] for those funds, and is obliged to give them only to the organisation for which they were raised or use them only for the purposes for which they were raised. Failure to do so, or taking a cut from a collection or appeal without telling donors that this would happen, is a breach of trust and may also be fraud or deception. Failure to pay over the funds is theft.

Resources: FUNDING AND FUNDRAISING: GENERAL RULES

Charity Commission: www.charity-commission.gov.uk, 0870 333 0123, email via website.

Fundraising Standards Board: www.frsb.org.uk, 0845 402 5442, info@frsb.org.uk.

Institute of Fundraising: www.institute-of-fundraising.org.uk, 020 7840 1000, email via website.

Office of the Third Sector: www.cabinetoffice.gov.uk/third_sector.aspx, 020 7276 6400, email via website.

Clawback rules. Community Matters: www.communitymatters.org.uk, 0845 847 4253, communitymatters@communitymatters.org.uk.

Development Trusts Association: www.dta.org.uk, 0845 458 8336, info@dta.org.uk.

Compact. Commission for the Compact: www.thecompact.org.uk, 0121 237 5900, info@thecompact.org.uk.

Compact Advocacy Programme: www.ncvo-vol.org.uk/compactadvocacy, phone and email as for Compact Voice.

Compact Mediation Scheme: www.cabinetoffice.gov.uk/third_sector.

Compact Voice *and* Local Compact Voice: www.compactvoice.org.uk; 020 7520 2453, compact@ncvo-vol.org.uk.

Public sector funding. Department for Business, Innovation & Skills state aid branch: www.bis.gov.uk, sapu@bis.gsi.gov.uk.

HM Treasury charity and third sector finance unit: www.hm-treasury.gov.uk, 020 7270 4558, public.enquiries@hm-treasury.gsi.gov.uk.

Statute law. www.opsi.gov.uk and www.statutelaw.gov.uk.

Much but not all case law. www.bailii.org.

Updates cross-referenced to this book. www.rclh.co.uk.

Chapter 49
FUNDRAISING ACTIVITIES

49.1   LEGAL ISSUES

Voluntary organisations undertake a vast range of fundraising activities, often without fully appreciating the legal implications [**48.1**]. In particular, the tax and VAT implications [**chapters 56** and **57**] must be fully understood, and attention must be given to licensing requirements [**47.2, 47.4, 47.6**].

General aspects of fundraising, including the rules on professional fundraisers and commercial participation, are covered in **chapter 48**. This chapter covers some specific activities; others are covered at various points in this book:

- advertising and commercials [**45.2**];
- appeals [**5.3.4**];
- running a bar [**47.2, 47.3**];
- fundraising events and entertainments [**47.4, 56.4.6, 57.11**];
- gift aid, legacies, and other forms of tax-effective giving [**chapter 50**];
- use of an organisation's name and logo [**44.9**];
- sponsorship [**56.3.3, 57.11.2**];
- sale of donated goods [**40.11, 56.3.2, 57.11.3**];
- trading activities, the sale of goods or services, and provision of services under contracts and service agreements [**21.2, 21.4, 40.11, chapters 51** and **52**].

The Institute of Fundraising [see end of chapter] has codes of practice on most types of fundraising, which should be followed as a matter of good practice. There are powers under the **Charities Act 2006** to further regulate fundraising if self regulation proves ineffective.

Charities Act 2006 s.69

49.2   PUBLIC COLLECTIONS

Until the **Charities Act 2006** provisions on public collections [**49.2.3**] are implemented in 2010 or later, the **House to House Collections Act 1939** and related regulations cover door to door collections [**49.2.1**], and the **Police, Factories etc (Miscellaneous Provisions) Act 1916** s.5 and related regulations cover street collections [**49.2.2**]. The 1939 and 1916 legislation was supposed to be replaced by part 3 of the **Charities Act 1992**, but this was never implemented, and was repealed by the Charities Act 2006.

The rules on collections apply not only to charities but to any public collection for a charitable, benevolent or philanthropic purpose [**48.6.1**]. In practice, it is safest to assume that all public collections by or for voluntary organisations or for 'good causes' are covered by the regulations.

The rules on professional fundraisers [**48.6.3**] are likely to apply if anyone is paid to carry out the collection, or if an employee, officer or paid governing body member is carrying out the collection.

49.2.1   House to house collections: the 1939 Act

For the purpose of the **House to House Collections Act 1939**, a house includes a place of business, so pub crawls and other fundraising activities involving going from one place to another are covered. The rules cover collection of money or other property, such as collecting goods for a jumble sale or the door to door sale of goods or services where some or all of the proceeds will be used for a charitable, benevolent or philanthropic purpose. The rules do not cover the collection of pledges such as gift aid declarations and direct debit forms.

49.2.1.1   Licensing

No later than the first of the month before the month when the collection will start, an application must be made for a licence. In the metropolitan police district the application is made to the commissioner of police; in the City of London, to the common council; and elsewhere, to the district or county council.

The time requirement may be waived if there is good reason for doing so. A licence may be granted for up to 12 months or in some cases for up to 18 months. If a licence is refused or revoked, any appeal must be lodged within 14 days.

House to House Collections Act 1939 s.2

If the collection is being taken for local purposes and is likely to be completed within a short period, a certificate may be granted exempting that collection from the need for a licence. *HTHCA 1939 s.1(4); House to House Collections Regulations 1947 [SI 1947/2662] reg.3, sch.1*

Some large national charities can apply to the Cabinet Office for exemption from having to register with each local authority. As a matter of courtesy, an exempt charity is expected to inform the relevant local licensing authorities about the dates of its collections. *HTHCA 1939 s.3*

49.2.1.2   The promoter and collectors

The **promoter** is the person to whom the licence is granted or who has been exempted from the need to obtain a licence. The promoter must ensure that the collection is carried out strictly in accordance with the licence or certificate and all legal requirements are met. Collectors must be over the age of 16 and be 'fit and proper persons'. *HTHC Regs 1947 regs.5,8*

49.2.1.3   Certificates and badges

All collectors must carry a certificate of authority in the prescribed form and wear an official badge, both signed by the collector. Certificates and badges are available from the Stationery Office [see end of chapter]. Charities registered with the Cabinet Office produce their own certificates and badges. *HTHC Regs 1947 regs.3,4*

Where collectors are paid or will receive a portion of the collection, they are likely to be required under the **Charities Act 1992** to make a statement telling donors that they are being paid and how much they will receive [**48.6.6**].

The promoter must keep the name and address of each collector to whom a certificate and badge have been given, along with the number of the collecting tin or receipt book given to them.   *House to House Collections Regulations 1947 [SI 1947/2662] reg.6(2)*

Collectors must return the certificate and badge to the promoter when the collection is completed or whenever required by the promoter, and the promoter must destroy them after the collection. It is an offence for a collector to display or use a badge or certificate which does not apply to the collection being taken, or which is designed to deceive.   *House to House Collections Act 1939 s.5, HTHC Regs 1947 regs.7,17*

49.2.1.4   The collection

Money may only be collected in a sealed tin or box which can be opened only by breaking the seal, and which is clearly marked with the purpose of the collection and an identification number; or if the minister for the Cabinet Office has given authorisation, in envelopes sealed by the donor; or if money is collected in any other way, by handing a receipt to the donor from a duplicate or counterfoil receipt book.   *HTHC Regs1947 regs.6(1),13*

The receipt book must be marked with the purpose of the collection and an identification number. Every receipt (with its counterfoil or duplicate) must be consecutively numbered and must include the number of the receipt book.

49.2.1.5   Counting up

Unless the collecting tins are delivered unopened to a bank, the money must be counted in the presence of the promoter and another responsible person. The amount and identification number of the tin must be entered on a list, which is then certified by the person making the examination. For an envelope collection, each envelope is treated as a collecting tin.   *HTHC Regs 1947 regs.12(1)-(3),13(2)*

Money accompanying a receipt book must be counted by the promoter and another responsible person, tallied with the receipt book, and entered on a list with the receipt book's identifying number.   *HTHC Regs 1947 reg.12(4)*

49.2.1.6   Returns

A return must be made to the licensing authority, listing all donations and expenditure incurred in connection with the collection, within one month of the expiry of the licence. Exempt national organisations must make an annual account to the Cabinet Office. If the organisation has to provide accounts for street collections, they can be combined if the licensing authority agrees.   *HTHC Regs 1947 reg.14*

The return must include the purpose of the collection, collectors' names and addresses and the amount collected by each, the total collected, costs of the collection, and how the profit was applied.

49.2.2   Street collections: the 1916 Act

Street collections are held 'to collect money or sell articles for charitable purposes' on a public road, pavement or footpath. They are covered by the **Police, Factories etc (Miscellaneous Provisions) Act 1916** s.5.

The licensing authority is the same as for house to house collections [**49.2.1.1**], but there is no obligation to license street collections, nor are there standard regulations. The **Charitable Collections (Transitional Provisions) Order 1974** *[SI 1974/140]* contains a model for local licensing authorities which choose to license street collections, but it is not obligatory and there are many variations.

The model rules state that collectors should not be paid. This has implications where the organisation is paying its collectors, or is paying a fundraising business which pays collectors. If collectors are being paid, it is important to ensure this does not contravene local licensing rules [**48.6.3**].

49.2.3   Public charitable collections: Charities Act 2006

Part 3 of the **Charities Act 2006** will, when implemented in 2010 or later, replace the rules on house to house and street collections with rules for **public charitable collections**. These will cover appeals in a public place (**public col-

lections) or by visits to homes or business premises (**door to door collections**), where all or part of the proceeds will be used for charitable, benevolent or philanthropic purposes [**48.6.1**]. Public places include roads, and public areas in stations, shopping precincts and similar premises. An **appeal** includes not only a request for donations, but also the sale of goods or services and the collection of pledges such as gift aid declarations and direct debits.

Charities Act 2006 ss.45-66
[expected 2010 or later]

The public collection rules do not cover appeals:

- in a place to which the public have access only if they make a payment or buy a ticket, or where they are allowed in only for the purpose of the collection;
- in the course of a public meeting;
- in a place of public worship, or in an enclosed graveyard, burial ground or other enclosed land next to a place of public worship;
- in a place where the occupier is the promoter of the collection and has given implicit or explicit consent for the public to have access; or
- in unattended collecting tins or other receptacles which are not in the possession or custody of a person acting as a collector.

Charities Act 2006 ss.45,46
[expected 2010 or later]

Failure to comply with any of the requirements is a criminal offence.

49.2.3.1 Public collections certificates and local authority permits

Unless a public collection is local and short-term [**49.2.3.2**], the **promoter** of a collection in a public place under the new rules must hold a **public collections certificate** (PCC) and a permit from the relevant local authority, and the promoter of a door to door collection (whether for money or goods) will require a PCC and notification to the local authority. Local authority permits can be refused, withdrawn or varied, with a right of appeal to a magistrate's court.

Charities Act 2006 ss.48-50,58-62 [expected 2010 or later]

PCCs will be valid for up to five years. In unincorporated charities, the certificate can be transferred from its holder(s) to another governing body member or members within the same charity. *Charities Act 2006 ss.51-57 [expected 2010 or later]*

The Charity Commission can refuse a PCC application if the amount likely to be used for charitable purposes would be inadequate in relation to the likely proceeds of the collection; the applicant or anyone else is likely to be paid an excessive amount in connection with the collection; or the applicant has been convicted of dishonesty or an offence relating to a public collection, has breached conditions in carrying out a previous public collection, or is not properly authorised by the organisation on whose behalf the collection is being promoted. An appeal against refusal or the attaching of conditions may be made to the charity tribunal.

The Charity Commission has powers to withdraw or suspend a PCC.

Regulations will set out the criteria for deciding whether a collection is local, the conduct of collections, certificates of authority, badges, and the minimum age of collectors. Information about consultations and the draft and final regulations is available from the Office of the Third Sector [see end of chapter].

Collections in privately owned places such as stations, airports and shopping precincts require the consent of the owner or landlord.

49.2.3.2 Local short-term collections

There will be an exemption for **local short term collections**, where the collection is local in nature and takes place within a prescribed period. Promoters of such collections do not need to hold a PCC or, for a public collection, a local authority permit. But they must notify the local authority of the proposed public or door to door collection, and the local authority can decide whether it is or is not local and short term. The local authority's decision can be appealed.

49.2.4 Face to face fundraising and prospecting

Face to face fundraising (sometimes called **chugging**) is where an individual is approached by a collector in a public place or door to door and is asked to sign a direct debit or standing order to donate to a charity or other good cause. An appeal for a direct debit or standing order is not covered by the rules on street collections [**49.2.2**] or house to house collections [**49.2.1**], but will be covered by the **Charities Act 2006** rules on public and door to door collections [**49.2.3**] when they come into effect. If the collectors are paid more than £10 per day or £1,000 per year the rules on professional fundraisers apply [**48.6.3**].

Face to face engagement (more often called **prospect gathering** or **prospecting**) is where members of the public are approached to provide their details, and are later asked to make a donation, take part in a campaign or become a volunteer. This does not directly involve soliciting donations, so is not covered by the rules on collections or professional fundraisers.

The Public Fundraising Regulatory Association [see end of chapter] is a self regulatory body for organisations and fundraising businesses involved in face to face fundraising and prospecting. PFRA and the Institute of Fundraising [see end of chapter] have codes which say that face to face prospect gatherers should comply with the same rules as face to face fundraisers.

49.2.5 No cold calling zones

Some neighbourhoods and communities have set up **no cold calling zones**, discouraging door to door sales and marketing. Every scheme is different and some cover door to door fundraising while others do not. It is sensible to check with the local authority's trading standards department whether a proposed fundraising area includes any cold calling zones. Calling at a home within a zone is not an offence, but the occupier could report the caller to trading standards or the police. Details are available from the Trading Standards Institute [see end of chapter].

49.2.6 Collections not covered by legislation

The rules on house to house, street or public collections do not apply where a collection or appeal takes place on private property (unless it is private property such as a railway station or shopping mall to which the public has access), or where a **static collection tin** or box is placed in a pub, office, shop or other private place. However, the general rules relating to fundraising apply [**48.2**]. Potential donors must be told what the collection is for and how the donations will be used, and any receptacle used for the collection must indicate the name of the organisation to which the donations will be given and, if applicable, the registered charity number, or the purposes for which the donations be used. The rules on professional fundraisers and commercial participators apply [**48.6**].

Every effort should be made to reduce the risk of theft or fraud. Collecting tins or boxes should (but in private places do not have to) be sealed and numbered. Static tins or boxes should be situated in a way that makes it very difficult for them to be stolen. Any place where a static tin is positioned should have a written agreement with the organisation for which they are collecting, and only an authorised representative of the organisation should be allowed to collect the tin.

The Institute of Fundraising [see end of chapter] has a code of practice on static collection points.

49.3 DISTANCE FUNDRAISING AND MARKETING

Distance fundraising and marketing include any situation where the fundraiser or seller does not meet face to face with the potential donor or purchaser, including direct mail, telephone, SMS text message, email and internet.

Organisations involved in distance fundraising must ensure they comply with relevant provisions of the **Data Protection Act 1998** [**43.3**], in particular the provisions on direct marketing [[**43.4**], telecommunications and e-commerce regulations [**43.4**] and distance selling regulations [**21.2.3**]. If relevant, they must also comply with Charities Act rules on professional fundraisers and commercial participators [**48.6**]. The Institute of Fundraising [see end of chapter] has codes of practice on various types of distance fundraising and marketing.

49.3.1 Telephone

Unsolicited direct marketing telephone calls cannot be made to an individual, organisation or business who has notified the organisation or has registered with the **Telephone Preference Service [43.4.1]** .

The Institute of Fundraising's code of practice on telephone fundraising should always be followed. This recommends that where possible a pre-call letter should be sent, and should include the option for the recipient to refuse a call.

For rules on gift aid declarations made by telephone, see **50.2.2**.

49.3.1.1 Professional fundraisers and commercial participators

All professional fundraisers and commercial participators [**48.6.3**, **48.6.4**] must give certain information to all potential donors, including those contacted by telephone [**48.6.6**] or by another oral method which is not a radio or television broadcast and is not made in the presence of the potential donor.

If a donor or purchaser contacted by telephone or similar method makes a commitment to give or pay more than £100 to the fundraiser or commercial participator, the donor or purchaser must within seven days of the payment being made be given a statement of their right to have the payment refunded. A payment is 'made' when the person gives authorisation for the payment on his or her debit or credit card, or when a payment made by post is posted, or when a payment made in person is actually made. *Charities Act 1992 ss.60(5),(6),61(2),(3), amended by Charities Acts 1992 & 1993 (Substitution of Sums) Order 2009 [SI 2009/508] art.6*

The fundraiser or commercial participator is entitled to deduct administrative expenses from the refund and to require the return of any goods already sent. There is no obligation to refund payment for services already provided at the time the notice was sent. *Charities Act 1992 s.61(4),(5)*

The refund provisions do not apply when the telephone call is made by the charitable institution itself, or by a person who is not a professional fundraiser or commercial participator, or by a professional fundraiser or commercial participator where the donation is made direct to the charitable institution. However, similar rules under the distance selling regulations apply in those circumstances [**21.2.3**].

49.3.2 Direct and electronic mail

Unsolicited direct mail, including fundraising materials, cannot be sent by post to an individual who has notified the organisation or has registered with the **Mailing Preference Service [43.4.1]**. Unsolicited direct marketing faxes cannot be sent to any individual, or to any business or organisation which has registered with the **Fax Preference Service [43.4.1]**.

Unsolicited commercial emails (UCE/spam) and SMS text messages can be sent to individuals only if they have explicitly agreed to receiving direct marketing emails or text messages from the organisation. It is an offence to send unsolicited emails or text messages to any person who has not agreed to receive them [**43.4.1**].

An individual can at any time require the organisation to stop sending unsolicited marketing, whether by post or electronically.

Electronic communications sent by companies must include the same details as on letters [**18.1.1**]. A registered charity with annual income over £10,000 must include its registered name and the fact that it is registered on all fundraising and marketing communications [**18.1.5**]. Other information, such as VAT number, may also need to be included [**18.1**].

Where goods or services are being sold, the distance selling regulations [**21.2.3**] apply. Direct mailings, whether by post or electronic, should comply with the British code of advertising, sales promotion and direct marketing [**45.2.1**] and the Institute of Fundraising code of practice on direct mail and electronic marketing.

49.3.2.1 Chain letters

Funds are sometimes raised by sending a letter or email asking recipients to contribute to an appeal and send the letter or email on to others. The Charity Commission discourages the use of chain letters because they can be difficult to stop and can give rise, when the appeal target has been met, to claims that the organisation is misleading the public. The Institute of Fundraising [see end of chapter] has guidance giving further reasons why chain letters should not be used.

If chain letters or emails are used to raise money for a charity or other organisation, they must comply with the rules for direct marketing [**49.3.2**].

49.3.3 Internet

Organisations undertaking internet fundraising or sales should comply with the law on distance selling [**21.2.3**] and good practice as it would apply to other forms of marketing and fundraising, and should obtain up to date legal advice.

In most cases the rules applying to disclosure of status, address, company and/or charity status and similar matters apply to websites in the same way as printed materials [**18.1**]. Even when the law is not clear about whether the same information has to be included on a website, it is good practice to do so.

For the rules on gift aid declarations made by internet, see **50.2.2**.

49.4 SALES

Sales of goods or services, whether through a shop or in other ways, must comply with rules on restrictions on trading [**51.1.3**], tax and VAT [**chapters 56** and **57**], professional fundraisers and commercial participation [**48.6**], and where appropriate the rules on distance selling [**21.2.3**]. Further issues arise where sales are carried out through a trading company [**chapter 51**].

49.4.1 Auctions and nearly new goods

Auctions can raise particularly complex issues:

- where the auction is carried out by a third party, that party will almost certainly be a professional fundraiser or commercial participator [**48.6**];
- if goods are donated to a charity but auctioned by a non-charity, including the charity's trading company, problems may arise around the charity transferring the goods to the non-charity, and the non-charity will have to pay tax on any proceeds that are not donated to the charity under gift aid [**51.7.3**, **56.2**];
- the sale is zero rated for VAT purposes only if the goods are donated to a charity and are sold by the charity or by an individual or organisation which donates *all* the profits from the sale to the charity under gift aid [**57.11.3**];
- even if the sale is zero rated it could, if carried out by the charity, take the charity over the threshold for VAT registration [**57.2.1**];
- if some of the profit goes to the donor of the goods, the sale will not meet the requirements for VAT zero rating, and may not be exempt from tax even if carried out by the charity [**56.3.2**];
- where auctioned goods or services have been donated, the charity may be able to recover gift aid if the purchaser makes a gift aid declaration [**50.2.2**];
- if the organisation has paid for the goods and/or has to pay the fundraiser or auctioneer, the auction may not raise enough to cover costs;
- descriptions of the goods must comply with the **Trade Descriptions Act 1968**;
- the organisation will need to take legal advice about the conditions of sale and the conduct of sealed bids, if used;
- if the auction is conducted by telephone, internet or any other method which is not face to face, the distance selling regulations apply [**21.2.3**];
- the organisation may want to take advice about whether it is reasonable to exclude or restrict liability for the quality and fitness of the goods being sold, since goods sold at auction are not consumer sales and are not covered by the **Sale of Goods Act 1979** and related regulations [**21.2.3**].

Legal advice will nearly always be needed when undertaking an auction. Similar issues may arise with sales of nearly new goods.

49.4.2   Car boot sales and temporary markets

An occasional car boot sale or temporary market does not require a licence if proceeds will be used solely or primarily for charitable, social, sporting or political purposes, or if there are fewer than five stalls, stands, vehicles or pitches from which goods are sold. In other situations a local authority licence is required. Even where the proceeds are for a charity or other good cause, a licence may be required if sales are held regularly.   *Local Government (Miscellaneous Provisions) Act 1982 s.37*

Care must be taken to ensure that such events are not used for the sale of pirated material, in breach of copyright or trade mark rights [**chapter 44**]. Consumer safety legislation may also apply [**40.11**]. If sales are held regularly, they may not qualify for tax relief [**56.4.7**] even if organised by a charity.

49.5   CHALLENGE EVENTS

A **challenge event** is where a person pays to take part in an organised event such as a parachute jump or mountain trek, and then raises sponsorship for a charity or other organisation, or where a person undertakes to raise a minimum amount in sponsorship and is then allowed to participate in the event. The event may be organised by a charity or other good-cause organisation, its trading subsidiary, or a third party.

Such events may be intrinsically risky, and raise complex issues around risk, insurance, liability, tax and VAT. These issues are covered in the Institute of Fundraising [see end of chapter] codes of practice for outdoor fundraising events in the UK and charity challenge events, both of which should be closely followed.

49.5.1   Risk and insurance

Before organising a challenge event, it is essential to undertake a thorough risk assessment and get advice about reducing risk and taking out appropriate insurances. Particular risks that need to be considered include:

- the suitability and fitness of participants;
- participants becoming injured or ill, either because of the organiser's negligence or for other reasons, and the availability of medical treatment especially for events in remote areas or overseas;
- problems arising from defective equipment or vehicles;
- problems related to accommodation and food;
- travel cancellations or delays;
- risks arising from extreme weather conditions, political unrest and crime targeted at tourists;
- worst case scenarios: death, kidnap, serious accident involving the group leaders or all participants;
- the organisation's or other bodies' failure to comply with contracts;
- the possibility of having to return payments to participants and/or sponsorship to donors if the event is cancelled or curtailed;
- participants not paying sponsorship income to the organisation;
- the overlap between insurances taken out by the organisation, the tour operator, and participants – who covers what, and whether there are any gaps.

An organisation which sells travel insurance connected with a challenge event (**connected travel insurance** or **CTI**) must be authorised by the Financial Services Authority or must be an appointed representative of an authorised person.

49.5.2   Transport and accommodation

An organiser of a challenge or similar event in effect becomes a package tour provider and must comply with the **Package Travel, Package Holidays and Package Tours Regulations 1992** *[SI 1992/3288]* as amended where an event – whether in the UK or abroad – lasts more than 24 hours and includes at least two of the following three components: transport (by any method), overnight accommodation, and/or other tourist services such as a tour guide. Specified information must be given in promotional material, before travel, and in a contract. Details are available from the Department for Business, Innovation and Skills.

For VAT purposes, the organisation is likely to be treated as within the tour operators' margin scheme (TOMS) [**57.11.9**].

If flights are provided, the organiser must be protected by an **air travel organiser's licence** (ATOL bond) or must act as an agent for an ATOL holder. This protects travellers if the organiser becomes insolvent. The Civil Aviation Authority has guidance for charities about what is involved and what needs to be included in initial advertisements and in the promotional material for the event.

49.5.3 Charity law

Under the **Charities Act 1992**, a person is likely to be a professional fundraiser [**48.6.3**] if he or she receives more than £10 per day, £1,000 per year or a lump sum of more than £1,000 to raise funds for a charitable institution.

The payment does not have to be in money. A person who receives a trip or event worth more than £1,000, in return for raising funds for the organisation, may be a professional fundraiser and need to comply with those rules. This could also apply where the participant initially pays for the event, but then receives a payment back from the organisation if he or she reaches a minimum sponsorship amount.

The organisation would have to have a fundraising agreement with the individual, and the individual would have to disclose information to donors about how much of the money raised actually goes to the charity or other organisation.

An organiser who is not a professional fundraiser may be a commercial participator [**48.6.4**] and if so must comply with similar rules.

49.6 LOTTERIES

The **Gambling Act 2005** regulates lotteries, and a number of other laws are relevant. Information is available from the Gambling Commission, the Department for Culture, Media and Sport, and the Lotteries Council [see end of chapter] and, for small society lotteries, the local authority. The Institute of Fundraising has a code of practice covering lotteries with either cash or non-cash prizes.

A **simple lottery** involves payment for an opportunity to win a prize wholly by chance. A **complex lottery** is where prizes are allocated by a series of processes of which the first relies wholly on chance but the later stages do not necessarily do so.
Gambling Act 2005 s.14

Payment includes money or other form of payment, but not the cost of ordinary postage or a normal telephone call to enter. If a person has a choice of paying to enter or of entering without payment by sending a letter or making a normal telephone call, it is a free draw [**49.7**] and is not regulated. *Gambling Act 2005 sch.2*

49.6.1 Raffles, draws and tombolas

A lottery with non-cash prizes is often called a **raffle**, **draw** or **tombola**. Even though these may not be thought of as lotteries, the same rules apply.

49.6.2 Lotteries and the law

A lottery is lawful only if it is an **incidental non-commercial lottery** [**49.6.3**], **private lottery** [**49.6.4**], **customer lottery** [**49.6.5**], **small society lottery** [**49.6.7**], **large society lottery** [**49.6.8**], **local authority lottery** or part of the National Lottery. Any other lottery is unlawful. A '100 club', for example, in which 100 people regularly pay a sum and draws are held, is legal only if it fits the specific requirements for a private or small society lottery.

Incidental non-commercial, private, customer and small society lotteries are **exempt lotteries**, because they are exempt from registering with the Gambling Commission. Small society lotteries, even though exempt from registering with the Gambling Commission, must register with the local authority.

Promoting a lottery includes arranging for tickets to be printed, advertising it, offering tickets for sale, or other activities involved in organising and publicising it. A lottery can be promoted only if it is an exempt lottery, or if it is a large lottery and the society or local authority running it has the relevant operating licence [**49.6.8.1**] and the promoter has a personal licence [**49.6.8.3**] if required.

Gambling Act 2005 ss.252,258

49.6.2.1   Age

Unlike other forms of gambling where the minimum age is 18, there is no minimum age for incidental non-commercial lotteries [**49.6.3**] and private lotteries [**49.6.4**]. This allows tickets to be sold to under-16s for tombolas and other lotteries at events held at schools and children's clubs.

For customer, small society or large lotteries, the minimum age for participation is 16. Promoters of these lotteries should ensure that tickets are not sold to or by anyone who is under 16, and should have procedures to reduce the likelihood of under-age involvement and to deal with it if it occurs. This may be a particular issue for lotteries whose tickets can be sold remotely, for example by internet.

49.6.2.2   Alcohol prizes

An exemption in the **Licensing Act 2003** allows alcohol prizes to be given in an incidental non-commercial lottery [**49.6.3**], provided that the alcohol is in a sealed container.   *Licensing Act 2003 s.175, amended by Gambling Act 2005 sch.16 para.20(2).*

There are no exemptions for other types of lottery, so alcohol prizes can be given only if the premises are licensed for the sale of alcohol, either by a premises licence, club premises certificate or a temporary event notice [**47.2**].

If lottery prizes include alcohol, tickets should not be sold to under 18s or alternative non-alcoholic prizes should be provided.

49.6.2.3   Charity law

If the lottery is organised by a registered charity whose annual income is more than £10,000, tickets and all publicity material must indicate that the organisation is a registered charity [**18.1.5**].

A person who organises or promotes a lottery may be a professional fundraiser or commercial participator [**48.6**], and if so must comply with the relevant rules.

Because of the charity law rules against a charity governing body member benefiting from the charity, a trustee should not take part in a lottery run by or for the charity. Even in non-charities, there may be reputational issues if governing body members or employees are allowed to participate and one of them wins.

49.6.2.4   Tax and VAT

Lottery tickets are not subject to VAT [**57.11.4**]. The proceeds of an incidental non-commercial lottery or small society lottery run by a charity, or a small society lottery run by a charity's trading company where the charity is the registered society, are not subject to income or corporation tax [**56.4.8**] if they are used solely for charitable purposes. The proceeds of large lotteries run by or for charities are not subject to tax provided the lottery is licensed by the Gambling Commission.

49.6.3   Incidental non-commercial lotteries

An **incidental non-commercial lottery** is one run as part of a non-commercial **connected event** such as a fundraising event. A **non-commercial event** is one where no part of the income is paid to the organisers or otherwise used for private gain. An incidental non-commercial lottery does not have to be for a 'good cause', does not have to be registered with the local authority or Gambling Commission and does not require an operating licence.   *Gambling Act 2005 sch.11 para.1,2*

In an incidental non-commercial lottery:

- tickets can be sold only at and during the connected event, and the winners must be announced during the event;
- no rollover is allowed;

- no more than £500 can be deducted from the proceeds for prizes and no more than £100 for the costs of organising the lottery, even if the prizes and organising expenses cost more than this;

- the proceeds of the connected event (after deducting its costs) and the proceeds of the lottery (after deducting no more than the allowed amount for prizes and the costs of organising the lottery) must be used for purposes other than private gain. *Gambling Act 2005 sch.11 para.3-7; Gambling Act 2005 (Incidental Non-commercial Lotteries) Regulations 2005 [SI 2007/2040]*

49.6.4 Private lotteries

A **private lottery** is limited to a specific group of participants and cannot be publicly advertised. It does not need to be registered with the local authority or Gambling Commission, but if run by an organisation must be authorised in writing by the governing body. A private lottery can be either a **private society lottery**, a **work lottery**, or a **residents' lottery**. *Gambling Act 2005 sch.11 para.9*

A **private society lottery** can be open only to members of one society – a membership organisation which is set up and conducted for purposes not connected with gambling – and other persons who are on premises used wholly or mainly for the society's administration or activities. Where a society has branches or sections, a private society lottery can be held only by and for a single branch or section. The promoters must all be members of the society. The lottery can be promoted for any of the society's purposes. *Gambling Act 2005 sch.11 para.10,13*

A **work lottery** can be open only to people who all work on the same premises, and the promoters must also work on the premises. 'Work' does not have to be remunerated, so a work lottery can be open to volunteers.

A **residents' lottery** can be open only to people who all live in a single set of premises, and must be promoted by a person or persons who live in the premises.

Work and residents' lotteries must be organised in a way that ensures no profits are made. *Gambling Act 2005 sch.11 para.11-13*

In a private lottery of any type:

- no advertisement of the lottery can be displayed or distributed except on the society's premises or where the persons for whom the lottery is promoted work or reside, and the advertisement must not be sent to any other premises;

- each ticket must be a document, and must include the names and addresses of the promoters, the ticket price, a description of the persons to whom the sale of tickets is restricted, and a statement that tickets are not transferable;

- tickets may only be sold by or on behalf of the promoters;

- there is no restriction on the price of tickets, but the price of every ticket must be the same (so no '5 for the price of 4' deals, or giving them away);

- the price must be paid to the promoters before the ticket can be given to the purchaser;

- there can be no rollover;

- tickets can be sent through the post;

- in a private society lottery the entire proceeds, after deducting only the cost of reasonable expenses, must be used for prizes, the purposes of the society, or both, and in a work or residents' lottery the entire proceeds, after deducting the cost of reasonable expenses, must be used for prizes. *Gambling Act 2005 sch.11 para.14-19*

49.6.5 Customer lotteries

A **customer lottery** does not have to be registered with the local authority or Gambling Commission. It can be promoted only by a person who occupies premises for business purposes, can be advertised only on the premises, and tickets can be sold or supplied only to people who are on the premises as customers of the promoter. The lottery must be organised in a way that ensures no profit is made.

All of the conditions are the same as for a work or residents' lottery [**49.6.4**]. In addition no prize can be worth more than £50, and the draw cannot take place within seven days of a previous draw in the same lottery or another customer lottery on the same business premises. *Gambling Act 2005 sch.11 para.20-29*

49.6.6   Society lotteries

A **society lottery** may be small [**49.6.7**] or large [**49.6.8**]. It must be promoted on behalf of a **non-commercial society**, defined as one which is established and conducted for charitable purposes, or for the purpose of enabling participation in or supporting sport, athletics or a cultural activity, or for any other non-commercial purpose other than that of private gain.   *Gambling Act 2005 s.19*

Only someone who is an officer (which in this context includes any full member of the governing body), employee or member of the society, or an external lottery manager [**49.6.9**] authorised by the society, can arrange for tickets for a small or large society lottery to be printed; arrange for promotional material to be printed, published or distributed; arrange for the lottery to be advertised; invite anyone to participate in the lottery; or sell or supply, or offer to sell or supply, tickets. It is an offence for anyone else to undertake any of these acts.   *Gambling Act 2005 s.252*

If a lottery is run by a charity's trading subsidiary, the subsidiary is an external lottery manager and must be registered with the Gambling Commission.

49.6.6.1   Social responsibility

Lottery promoters have a duty to take reasonable steps to reduce the risks of gambling for children and vulnerable people – which includes in this context people who are at risk of gambling too much. They should ensure information about how to gamble responsibly is easily available, along with information about sources of information and help for problem gambling. Information is available from Gamble Aware [see end of chapter].

49.6.7   Small society lotteries

A **small society lottery** must be registered with the local authority in the area where its principal office is, but does not have to be registered with the Gambling Commission. A lottery is a small society lottery if it is promoted wholly on behalf of a **non-commercial society** [**49.6.6**] for any of the society's purposes, and:

- its gross proceeds (income) are not expected to exceed £20,000;
- if it is part of a series of lotteries during a calendar year, the total proceeds of the series are expected to exceed or will not actually exceed £250,000;
- it does not take place in the three calendar years after the year in which the society held a large lottery.   *Gambling Act 2005 sch.11 para.30-32*

If the proceeds of the lottery at any time exceed £20,000, or the total proceeds of the society's lotteries in that year exceed £250,000, the lottery becomes a **large society lottery** [**49.6.8**].

49.6.7.1   Local authority registration

An organisation promoting a small society lottery must be registered with the local authority during the whole period the lottery is being promoted. The registration fee (as at 1/8/09) is £40, with an annual renewal fee of £20. The local authority may refuse an application for registration if it considers the applicant to be a commercial society, a person connected with the promotion has been convicted of a relevant offence or information provided with the application is false or misleading. Refusal or revocation of a licence can be appealed in the magistrate's court.   *Gambling Act 2005 sch.11 para.38,41-51*

The local authority will enter the applicant in a register, and notify both the applicant and the Gambling Commission of the registration.   *GambA 2005 sch.11 para.44*

Societies registered with the local authority must provide specified information within three months after the draw (or the last draw) took place.   *GambA 2005 s.39*

49.6.7.2   Tickets

The printing of lottery tickets is a specialist business, and advice about reputable printers should be sought from the local authority. In a small society lottery:

- no more than £20,000 worth of tickets can be offered for sale, or less if their sale would bring proceeds from sales to over £250,000 in this calendar year;

- a ticket must be a document, but can be sent electronically provided it is capable of being retained electronically or being printed out;
- tickets can be sold in vending machines, or remotely by telephone or internet;
- tickets can be sold in shops and kiosks or door to door, but not on the street (which includes passages through enclosed premises such as shopping malls);
- the ticket must include the name of the promoting society, the ticket price, the name and address of a society member chosen by the society as responsible for promoting the lottery or the name and address of the external lottery manager [**49.6.9**] if there is one; and either the date(s) of the draw or each draw, or information enabling the date(s) of the draw or each draw to be determined;
- there is no maximum price for tickets;
- the price paid for each ticket must be the same, and must be paid to the promoter before the ticket is given to the purchaser;
- no additional payment can be required for entry into the lottery.

49.6.7.3 Proceeds and prizes

In a small society lottery:

- at least 20% of the proceeds (income) of the lottery must be used for a purpose for which the society is conducted, and the remainder can be used for prizes and reasonable operating costs including external lottery manager fees;
- the maximum prize may not be more than £25,000, in money, money's worth or a combination;
- the lottery may include a rollover, provided that every affected rollover lottery is also a small society lottery promoted by the same society, and the maximum prize is not more than £25,000.   *Gambling Act 2005 sch.11 para.33-37*

The value of donated prizes is not included when calculating the 20% for the society's purposes and the maximum 80% for prizes and operating costs. However, it must be included in the return to the local authority.

49.6.8 Large society lotteries

A lottery promoted by a non-commercial society [**49.6.6**] is a **large society lottery** if the value of the tickets put on sale or actually sold is more than £20,000, or the total value of the lottery tickets put on sale or sold by the society in the year is more than £250,000, or the society held a large lottery in any of the three preceding calendar years.   *Gambling Act 2005 sch.11 para.31*

A large society lottery must be registered with the Gambling Commission [see end of chapter]. The Gambling Commission issues two types of licences for lottery operators: **operating licences** and **personal licences**. As well as these, the organisation will need a **premises licence** from the local authority [**47.2**], unless all the tickets are sold remotely.

49.6.8.1 Gambling Commission operating licences

Operating licences can be granted only to a non-commercial society [**49.6.6**], a local authority, or an external lottery manager [**49.6.9**].

A society which will manage and promote its own lotteries needs a **remote lottery operating (society) licence**, if any or all tickets are to be sold by telephone, internet, radio or television, or a **non-remote lottery operating (society) licence**, if tickets will be sold only non-remotely.

49.6.8.2 Small scale operators

For the purposes of personal licences [below], a **small scale operator** is a society which has no more than three people in **qualifying positions**, and each qualifying position is occupied by a **qualified person**.
                      Gambling Act 2005 (Definition of Small-scale Operator) Regulations 2006 [SI 2006/3266]

A qualifying position is one held by a person who has primary responsibility for managing or marketing the licensed activity (in this case, the organisation's lotteries), managing the information technology facilities used for the licensed activity, managing the organisation's financial affairs, or ensuring the organisation complies with the Gambling Act. A qualified person is one named on the operating licence as occupying such a position.

49.6.8.3   Gambling Commission personal licences

Unless it qualifies as a **small scale operator** [above], every organisation which runs a large lottery itself, rather than through an external lottery manager, must have at least one person who holds **management office** and who has a **personal management licence** (PML) from the Gambling Commission. This person is responsible for ensuring the lottery is properly run and complies with all regulatory requirements.   *Gambling Act 2005 s.80*

Management office means that in a company the person is a company director [**13.1.3**], and in an unincorporated organisation the person is a full member of the governing body [**13.1.5**, **13.1.6**]. The licence may authorise the holder to carry out certain functions in relation to the lotteries.

A large society lottery cannot be organised or publicised if no one holds a personal management licence. PML applications require enhanced criminal records checks [**41.4.1**] so cannot be obtained in a hurry.

A **personal functional licence** allows a person who does not hold management office to carry out certain functions in relation to the society's lotteries.

A small scale operator [above] which does not need anyone to have a PML should appoint a senior person to oversee the lottery and ensure regulatory compliance. This person does not have to be a member of the governing body. Details must be notified to the Gambling Commission on the application form for the operating licence [**49.6.8.1**], along with an enhanced criminal records check.

49.6.8.4   Tickets

The rules for large society lottery tickets are the same as for small society lotteries [**49.6.7.2**], except that the maximum value of tickets that can be offered for sale is £4 million for an individual lottery, or less if it would take the total sales for all lotteries in the calendar year over £10 million.   *Gambling Act 2005 (Variation of Monetary Limit) Order 2009 [SI 2009/207]*

Each ticket must include 'Licensed by the Gambling Commission, www.gamblingcommission.gov.uk'.

To reduce the risk of fraud, the Commission recommends that societies running large lotteries should not send unsolicited tickets to people who are not members of the society, or not send more than £20 worth of tickets to any address which is not an address of a member of the society. They should keep, for at least six months from the date of the draw, records of tickets distributed and not returned, with the address to which they were sent, total value and serial numbers.

49.6.8.5   Proceeds and prizes

In a large lottery:

- at least 20% of the proceeds (income) of the lottery must be used for a purpose for which the society is conducted, and the remainder can be used for prizes and reasonable operating costs including external lottery manager fees;
- the maximum prize may not be more than £25,000 or 10% of the proceeds, whichever is the greater, in money, money's worth or a combination (so if the full £4 million worth of tickets is sold, the maximum prize could be £400,000);
- the lottery may include a rollover, provided that every affected rollover lottery is also a large society lottery promoted by the same society, and the maximum prize is not more than £25,000 or 10% of the gross proceeds, whichever is the greater.   *Gambling Act 2005 sch.11 para.,33-35*

The value of donated prizes is not included when calculating the 20% for the society's purposes and the maximum 80% for prizes and operating costs. However, it must be included in the return to the Gambling Commission.

Returns and accounts must be provided as required to the Gambling Commission. Accounting records must be kept for at least three years from the date of the lottery to which they relate.

49.6.9   External lottery managers

An **external lottery manager** (ELM) is a person who is not an employee, officer or member of the society or local authority for whom the lottery is being promoted, and who will manage its lotteries on its behalf.   *Gambling Act 2005 s.257*

External lottery managers must have a non-remote **lottery operating (external lottery manager) licence** from the Gambling Commission, and a remote licence if they intend to sell tickets by telephone, internet or other remote means. If a charity's trading subsidiary organises its lotteries, it must register as an external lottery manager.

The organisation must check the Gambling Commission's website [see end of chapter] or take other steps to ensure the ELM has a valid operating licence.

The Gambling Commission advises organisations to ensure that any arrangement they enter into with an external lottery manager meets the organisation's requirements and provides safeguards against the poor results of a lottery or the financial failure of the lottery manager.

49.7   COMPETITIONS AND FREE PRIZE DRAWS

Competitions which involve skill, judgement or knowledge are not regulated under the **Gambling Act 2005**. The level of skill, knowledge or judgment required must be reasonably likely to prevent a significant proportion of people who wish to participate from doing so, or to prevent a significant proportion of people who participate from receiving a prize.   *Gambling Act 2005 s.14(5)*

If the competition requires a lower level of skill, knowledge or judgement, it is likely to be an illegal lottery, because a lottery – or the first stage in a multi-stage lottery – must be determined wholly by chance [**49.6**].

The level of skill, knowledge or judgement required must be appropriate to the likely participants – so a geography question in a competition for children, for example, would require a different level than in a competition in a specialist publication for geographers.

Competition prizes cannot be offered for predicting the result of a future event, or for predicting the result of an event which has already happened but where the result is not yet ascertained or not yet generally known. These are regulated as **betting** rather than competitions.

Free prize draws, where no payment is required to enter or where there is a choice of paying or entering without payment by ordinary post or by a normal rate telephone call, are not regulated. In the latter case, the system for allocating prizes must not distinguish between those who have paid to enter and those who have not.   *Gambling Act 2005 sch.2*

Provided the competition or prize draw is lawful, it is not subject to any specific legislation but should comply with the British codes of advertising, sales promotion and direct marketing [**45.2.1**].

Ticket sales for competitions are subject to VAT [**57.11.4**], and the proceeds are subject to tax [**56.4.8**].

49.8   GAMING

Gaming is playing any game of chance except for lotteries. Information about gaming and licensing is available from the Gambling Commission and the Department for Culture, Media and Sport [see end of chapter] and the local authority's licensing department. ACRE [see end of chapter] has information on how the rules apply to village halls and other community organisations.

Equal chance gaming is where the amount or value of prizes depends on the number of participants and/or the amount of money they stake. **Prize gaming** is where the prizes are set in advance, and do not depend on the number of participants.

Gaming occurs only if money or something else of value is staked on the outcome, or is received later in return for tokens. So there is no licensing requirement if bingo, cards or other games are played only for fun, with no money (or anything else which has a money value) changing hands.

For charities, occasional gaming as a means of fundraising does not jeopardise charitable status, and the proceeds are not subject to tax if they fall within the concession for fundraising activities and events [**56.4.6**]. Gaming which is not within the concession should be carried out through a trading company [**51.2**].

49.8.1 Clubs, miners' welfare institutes and licensed premises

Special rules apply to genuine **members' clubs**, established and conducted for the benefit of the members and which have at least 25 members, and **miners' welfare institutes**. To be classed as a members' club, a club cannot be established specifically for the purpose of gaming, unless it is a bridge club or whist club which does not provide facilities for any other type of non-machine gaming. Miners' welfare institutes are defined in the legislation.   *Gambling Act 2005 ss.266,268;*
Gambling Act 2005 (Gaming in Clubs) Regulations 2007 [SI 2007/1942]

49.8.1.1 Exempt gaming

Members' clubs and miners' welfare institutes can carry out **exempt gaming** without needing a permit, provided that:

- the gaming is equal chance, which includes bingo, bridge, and some types of poker [**49.8**];
- the participation fee is no more than £1 per day, except for whist or bridge clubs on days when no other type of gaming takes place, when the participation fee can be up to £18;
- stakes and prizes must comply with any relevant regulations (at the time of writing, the only regulations relate to stakes and prizes for poker);
- the club must not deduct anything from sums staked or won in the gaming;
- the gaming can only take place on one set of premises, so cannot be linked with games on other premises; and
- participants must have been members of the club or institute for at least 48 hours, or applied or been nominated for membership at least 48 hours before playing, or must be the genuine guest of a member or applicant for membership.   *Gambling Act 2005 ss.269,270; Gambling Act 2005 (Exempt Gaming*
in Clubs) Regulations 2007 [SI 2007/1944] regs.2-4

Similar rules apply for alcohol-licensed premises, except that the rule about membership does not apply, and no one under 18 years old can participate. There are rules about participation fees, stakes and prizes.   *Gambling Act 2005 ss.279,280;*
Gambling Act 2005 (Exempt Gaming in Alcohol-Licensed Premises) Regulations 2007 [SI 2007/1940]

49.8.1.2 Club gaming and machine permits

Members' clubs and miners' welfare institutes which want to carry out non-exempt gaming or have up to three **gaming machines** on premises must apply for a **club gaming permit** from the local authority. The same rules apply as for exempt gaming except that:

- there is no limit on maximum stakes or prizes for equal chance gaming;
- unequal chance games as set out in regulations are allowed (chemin de fer and pontoon);
- the public, and anyone under 18 years of age, must be excluded from any part of the premises where gaming is taking place; and
- the maximum daily admission charge is £20+VAT for bridge or whist clubs, and £3+VAT for any other permitted gaming.   *Gambling Act 2005 ss.271,272, sch.12;*
Gambling Act 2005 (Exempt Gaming in Clubs) Regulations 2007 [SI 2007/1944] reg.5

A **club machine permit**, also available from the local authority, allows up to three gaming machines but does not allow any other gaming. *GambA 2005 s.273, sch.12*

Gaming machines on alcohol licensed premises may be included in the premises licence or may require a separate **licensed premises gaming machine permit**.   *Gambling Act 2005 ss.262,263*

49.8.1.3   High turnover bingo

Where the total stakes or prizes for bingo games played in a club, miners' welfare institute or alcohol licensed premises in any seven-day period exceed £2,000, the organisation must apply for a **bingo operating licence** from the Gambling Commission [see end of chapter].

Gambling Act 2005 ss.275,281

49.8.2   Non-commercial gaming

Gaming at a **non-commercial event** [**49.6.3**] does not require a licence, provided that the money raised from the event and the profits from the gaming itself go to 'good causes' and are not used for private gain, and all players are told how money raised from the event and the gaming will be used. Reasonable expenses incurred in organising the event can be deducted from the profits, and money raised by persons other than the organiser do not count as proceeds from the event (for example, refreshments provided by an independent third party).

Gambling Act 2005 ss.297-301

The gaming can be equal chance or prize gaming [**49.8**]. For prize gaming there is no statutory limit on participation fees, stakes or prizes. For equal chance gaming the maximum participation fee is £8 per event, and this must allow entry to every game played at the event. The total amount or value of prizes or awards distributed for those games cannot exceed £600 per event.   *Gambling Act 2005 (Non-commercial Equal Chance Gaming) Regulations 2007 [SI 2007/2041] reg.3(2)-(3)*

A **race night**, where participants stake money on the outcome of recorded or virtual races, may be run as either equal chance or prize gaming in which case the rules above apply, or as an incidental non-commercial lottery [**49.6.3**]. A **casino night** can be run as prize gaming. ACRE and the Department for Culture, Media and Sport [see end of chapter] have information about these sorts of events.

If two or more equal chance gaming events are promoted by the same person on the same premises on the same day, the total participation fee for both or all events cannot exceed £8 and the total prizes cannot exceed £600. But if a series of events are held on different days, each one is treated separately. If people are entitled to attend the final event in the series only by virtue of having taken part in a previous event on a different day, the total value of prizes at the final event can be £900. *Gambling Act 2005 (Non-commercial Equal Chance Gaming) Regulations 2007 [SI 2007/2041] reg.3(4)-(6)*

Resources: FUNDRAISING ACTIVITIES

Charity Commission: www.charity-commission.gov.uk, 0870 333 0123, email via website.

Fundraising Standards Board: www.frsb.org.uk, 0845 402 5442, info@frsb.org.uk.

HM Revenue and Customs Charities: www.hmrc.gov.uk, 0845 302 0203, email via website.

Institute of Fundraising: www.institute-of-fundraising.org.uk, 020 7840 1000, email via website.

Collection badges & certificates. The Stationery Office: 01603 622211, customer.services@tso.co.uk.

Face to face fundraising. Public Fundraising Regulatory Association: www.pfra.org.uk, 020 7401 8452, info@pfra.org.uk.

Lotteries & gambling. Gambling Commission: www.gamblingcommission.gov.uk, 0121 230 6666, info@gamblingcommission.gov.uk.

Department for Culture, Media and Sport: www.culture.gov.uk, 020 7211 6200, enquiries@culture.gov.uk.

Lotteries Council: www.lotteriescouncil.org.uk.

Gamble Aware: www.gambleaware.org.uk, info@gambleaware.co.uk .

ACRE: www.acre.org.uk, 01285 653477, acre@acre.org.uk.

No cold calling zones. Trading Standards Institute: www.tsi.org.uk, 0845 608 9400, institute@tsi.org.uk.

Public collections. Office of the Third Sector: www.cabinetoffice.gov.uk/third_sector.aspx, 020 7276 6400, email via website.

Statute law. www.opsi.gov.uk and www.statutelaw.gov.uk.

Much but not all case law. www.bailii.org.

Updates cross-referenced to this book. www.rclh.co.uk.

Chapter 50
TAX-EFFECTIVE GIVING

For sources of further information see end of chapter.

50.1   TAX EFFECTIVENESS

All donations to charities and other voluntary organisations are **tax effective**, in the sense that the organisation is unlikely to have to pay income or corporation tax on them [**56.4-56.6**]. But donations to some organisations are even more tax effective, because the recipient body is able to recover the tax paid by the donor, or the donor is able to get tax relief on the income used for the donation. In general only charities can benefit from this type of tax-effective giving, but some arts bodies and sports clubs which are not charities are also eligible.

Tax-effective giving includes gift aid [**50.2**], payroll giving [**50.4**], gifts of shares and other assets [**50.5**], legacies [**50.6**] and some donations from businesses [**50.9**]. Different rules apply for each type of giving, and must be strictly followed.

Charity trustees have an obligation to maximise their charity's income [**15.6.5**]. This includes recovering tax whenever possible, so all charities should encourage individual donors to give through gift aid [**50.2**], and should ensure that gift aid declarations are sent to all donors who make eligible donations.

50.1.1   Charities in EU member states

At the time of writing (mid 2009), the rules on tax effectiveness apply only to donations to charities – and for some purposes community amateur sports clubs and some other organisations – based in the UK. But in January 2009 the European court of justice ruled that a donor in one EU member state should be eligible for tax relief on donations to a charity in another member state, provided that the donor can show that the recipient meets the requirements for charitable status in the donor's home country.   *Persche v Finanzamt Lüdenscheid [2009] EUECJ C-318/07*

At the time of writing it is unclear how or when the UK will implement this decision. In the meantime, information will be available from HM Revenue and Customs Charities [see end of chapter]. Until there is relevant legislation, individual donors who want to claim tax relief on donations to charities in other EU countries will have to challenge HMRC.

The ECJ has also ruled that charities based in one EU member state but with property in another should be eligible for tax reliefs in the country where the property is located [**56.4**]. This decision directly benefits charities, whereas the Persche decision benefits donors.

50.2 GIFT AID

Gift aid enables UK charities and certain other organisations to recover basic rate tax on donations of money received from individuals who pay UK income tax or capital gains tax, and gives businesses tax relief on such donations. Detailed information is available from HM Revenue and Customs Charities and the Institute of Fundraising [see end of chapter].

Income Tax Act 2007 ss.414-430;
Income & Corporation Taxes Act 1988 s.339, amended by Finance Act 2000 s.40

Gift aid may be used for donations to all UK charities even if they are not registered with the Charity Commission, Office of the Scottish Charity Regulator or Charity Commission for Northern Ireland. It may also be used for donations to community amateur sports clubs registered with HMRC [**1.8**], non-profit associations for scientific research or for the advancement of trade, and some national institutions.

A gift aid payment by an individual must be made from income which HMRC can confirm has had income tax and/or capital gains tax paid on it. Gift aid therefore cannot be used to pass on money collected from a number of unidentifiable individuals, for example in collecting tins. It also cannot be used for donations from one charity to another, or donations to a charity from a non-taxpayer such as a local authority or a person who does not pay UK tax (but see **50.1.1** in relation to donors who pay tax in another EU member state).

At the time of writing (mid 2009) the Treasury was considering changing gift aid to an **opt out** system, where all donations by individuals to charities and eligible organisations would be treated as gift aid donations unless the donor objected.

50.2.1 Gift aid as payment for benefits

A payment made under gift aid must be a donation. An individual or corporate donor cannot receive goods, membership services, or other services or benefits (including, for example, discounts on goods or services) in return unless these comply with the **donor benefit rules**. The maximum value of the benefits that a donor, or a person connected with the donor, can receive in return for his, her or its donations is:

- benefits worth up to 25% of the total gift aid donations (net of tax) in the tax year, if the total donations are £100 or less;
- benefits worth up to £25, if total donations are from £101 to £1,000;
- benefits worth up to 5% of the total donations, if total donations are from £1,001 to £10,000;
- benefits worth up to £500, if total donations are over £10,000.

Income Tax Act 2007 s.418, amended by Finance Act 2007 s.60;
Income & Corporation Taxes Act 1988 s.339, amended by Finance Act 2000 s.40; Finance Act 2006 s.58

If the donor receives benefits worth more than the allowed amount, the entire gift aid payment is treated as an ordinary donation and the charity is not able to recover tax on it.

A case in May 2005, where the Labrador Lifeline Trust was given 28 days to repay to the Inland Revenue £11,300 of mistakenly claimed gift aid, illustrates the importance of these rules. Rather than emphasising to people who were receiving a dog that a donation was purely voluntary and would help the charity's work, the impression was given that the 'donation' was a necessary requirement to receive a dog and was a payment for a service. The Revenue ruled that the charity was therefore not entitled to claim gift aid on those donations.

Even if a benefit is acceptable for gift aid purposes, there may be VAT implications [**57.11.1**].

50.2.1.1 Particular benefits

HMRC's detailed guidance on gift aid in specific situations, available on its website [see end of chapter], covers a range of situations where the donor or a person connected with the donor receives a benefit. The guidance includes membership subscriptions [**50.2.1.2**], educational school trips [**50.2.1.4**], educational trusts, sponsorship payments for adventure fundraising events, donations that attract a right of admission to some charity properties [**50.2.1.3**], admission to charity events, and payments for goods or services at a charity auction.

50.2.1.2 Membership subscriptions

Membership subscriptions are eligible for gift aid provided they do not give the member the right to use the charity's facilities or services, and any other benefits (such as newsletters or magazines) fall within the donor benefit limits [**50.2.1**].

50.2.1.3 Admissions to view property

The donor benefit rules do not apply to admission fees to view property that is open to the public and is preserved, maintained, kept or created by a charity as part of furthering its charitable purposes. Property includes buildings, grounds or other land, plants, animals, works of art (but not performances), artefacts, and property of a scientific nature.

To be eligible for gift aid, the donation must give the right of free admission to the donor, or the donor and members of his or her family, for a full year, or must give the right of reduced price admission for the first and every subsequent visit during a full year. Alternatively the donation can give the right of admission for a shorter period, such as a day or week, but in this case is eligible for gift aid only if the donation is at least 10% more than the public admission charge for that period.

Income Tax Act 2007 s.420

Free or reduced price admission provided to non-family guests of the donor, and the provision of anything other than admission, must comply with the donor benefit rules [**50.2.1**].

50.2.1.4 Educational school trips

Independent schools can charge for school trips, but non-independent schools cannot charge for trips held during school hours as part of the curriculum. They can, however, ask for a voluntary contribution towards the cost of the trip. Where a charitable school, or a charity associated with a state school, asks for such a contribution, it will be eligible for gift aid provided it is genuinely voluntary and does not affect whether a particular child can or cannot go, it is not refundable in any situation even if the trip is cancelled or the child does not go, and any benefit to the child (travel costs, travel insurance, food and drink, admission fees and similar costs) is within the gift aid benefit rules [**50.2.1**].

50.2.2 Donations from individuals

Individuals make gift aid donations net of tax, and the charity then recovers basic rate tax from HM Revenue and Customs. Tax can be recovered as soon as the charity receives the donation, provided the donor has:

- made a gift aid declaration [**50.2.2.1**] in writing or online covering the donation;
- made a gift aid declaration orally, and the charity has maintained an auditable record of the declaration and sent the donor a written statement of the oral declaration [**50.2.2.2**];
- made the donation under a deed of covenant that was in existence on 5 April 2000 [**50.2.6.2**]; or
- made the donation under a deed of covenant made on or after 6 April 2000 [**50.2.6.1**], and has also made a gift aid declaration covering the donation.

At the time of writing (mid 2009) the Treasury was considering removing the need for a declaration, and treating all donations to charities and other eligible organisations as gift aid unless the donor indicated otherwise.

50.2.2.1   Gift aid declarations

A gift aid declaration may be made in writing, electronically or orally. HMRC's sample declaration does not have to be used for written or electronic declarations, but if a declaration does not include all necessary information – including the dates of the tax year, and a note explaining that the donor must pay income tax or capital gains tax during the tax year at least equal to the tax the charity will reclaim on the donation(s) – HMRC may reject claims for tax recovery. Proposed alterations to HMRC's wording should therefore be cleared with HMRC.

Donations to Charities by Individuals (Appropriate Declarations) Regulations 2000 [SI 2000/2074], amended by Donations to Charities by Individuals (Appropriate Declarations) (Amendment) Regulations 2005 [SI 2005/2790]

There is no need for a signature or date on written or electronic declarations, but for practical reasons it is sensible for them to be dated.

50.2.2.2   Record of oral declaration

Where a declaration is made orally, in person or by telephone, the charity must either audio record it at the time it is made or send a **written statement** to the donor. The recording must be both audible and auditable, so must be kept in a way that enables it to be played back. If an appropriate recording is not made, the written statement must contain the same information as a written declaration [above], plus the date the donor made the oral declaration, the date the charity is sending the written statement to the donor, and the fact that the declaration will not take effect if the donor cancels it within 30 days of the charity sending the written statement. If the declaration was audio recorded at the time it was made, a written statement need not be sent to the donor unless HMRC requires it.

2000 Regulations, amended by 2005 Regulations

The donor does not have to sign or return the written statement. The charity can reclaim tax as soon as it sends the statement, without waiting until the 30-day cancellation period has ended.

50.2.2.3   Donations covered by a declaration

A declaration may be made at the same time as the donation, or before or after. It can cover a single donation to a charity, all donations made in the six tax years prior to the date of the declaration, and/or all future donations. All donations must be in money.

The actual period included in the six years prior to the declaration depends on the organisation's legal form [**50.2.3**]. The actual period does not have to be stated on the declaration.

Gift aid donations may include:

- donations made by named donors in collecting envelopes, provided each envelope includes the gift aid declaration or the donor has previously made an open-ended declaration to the charity;
- sponsorship, such as sponsoring someone to run a race, provided every copy of the sponsorship form includes the declaration and if it is in the form of a list, space for each sponsor to tick whether they want their donation to be gift aid;
- regular donations made through standing orders or direct debit;
- any other money donation which fulfils the gift aid criteria and is covered by a declaration.

A declaration which is not limited to a specific donation or limited in another way continues until it is cancelled by the donor.

50.2.2.4   Gift aid on donations of goods

Gift aid can only be claimed on donations of money, not on donations of goods. But donations of goods are eligible for gift aid if the donor remains owner of the goods until they are sold, the charity sells them on behalf of the donor, and the donor then donates all or part of the proceeds to the charity with a gift aid declaration. The rules are explained in HMRC Charities' detailed guidance on gift aid in specific situations, available on its website [see end of chapter], and include:

- the goods must remain the property of the donor until they are sold (note that there may be insurance issues here);

- it must be made clear to donors at the time the goods are given to the charity that they have the right to keep all or part of the proceeds from the sale;
- the goods must be allocated a unique reference number that allows them and the proceeds from their sale to be tracked through the entire process;
- after the sale the charity must contact the donor and offer to pay them the proceeds, and should allow at least 21 days for a reply;
- the charity must keep proper records of receiving the goods, their sale, their offer to pay the proceeds to the donor, and the donor's decision;
- if a gift aid declaration is completed before the sale, it cannot commit the donor to making a donation.

As well as detailed information from HMRC, guidance is also available from the Association of Charity Shops [see end of chapter]. It is crucial to get specialist advice on the potential VAT, tax and business rates implications of implementing the above procedures, because the potential loss of reliefs could outweigh the benefits of claiming gift aid.

At the time of writing (mid 2009) the Association of Charity Shops had asked the Treasury to consider a simpler procedure for small amounts of gift aid.

50.2.2.5   Writing off a loan

The writing off of a loan to a charity is not a payment of a sum of money, so cannot be classed as a gift aid payment. However, if the charity repays the loan, the lender can then donate that amount to the charity under the gift aid scheme, and the charity can recover tax on it.

50.2.2.6   Donations not covered by a declaration

The charity must have internal records enabling it to identify which donations are and are not covered by a declaration. When a donation is received that is not covered by a declaration, the charity should have procedures to ensure a declaration form is sent and the donor is asked, if he or she is a UK taxpayer, to complete it for the donation, and ideally for future donations.

The internal records must also ensure that declaration forms are not sent out in relation to payments made with CAF cheques, CAF vouchers or similar vouchers on which the Charities Aid Foundation or another charity has already claimed the tax. Tax must not be recovered on such donations.

50.2.2.7   Gift aid records

The charity must keep the actual declarations it receives and copies of the written statements it sends out, or a scanned copy of them; audio recordings of oral declarations, if a written statement was not sent to the donor; correspondence relating to declarations and gift aid donations, including changes of address notified to the charity; cancellations of declarations; and proper accounting records showing the donations received, the link to a gift aid declaration (through a code number or some other method), and tax recovered. Records do not have to be kept on paper.

A charity which does not keep adequate records could be required to pay back reclaimed tax, with interest, to HMRC, and could be liable to a penalty.

An association or incorporated body (company, industrial and provident society or charitable incorporated organisation) must keep gift aid records until six years after the end of the accounting period to which the tax claim relates.

A charitable trust must keep records until the later of:

- the 31 January which is 21 months after the end of the tax year to which the claim relates (so 31 January 2012, for records for a claim for 2009-10);
- one year after the tax claim is made, rounded to the end of the quarter (so records for a claim made on 25 May 2010 must be kept until 30 June 2011); or
- HMRC completing any gift aid or related audit it has started.

It is good practice for charitable trusts to keep records for at least six years.

Gift aid declarations which extend beyond the period covered by the tax reclaim must be kept, so they are available for the later periods.

50.2.3   Tax recovery

The charity can claim the tax as soon as it receives the money and a written, electronic or audio recorded oral declaration, or receives the money and a non-recorded oral declaration and sends out a written statement of the declaration [**50.2.2.2**]. Where payment is made by cheque or bank transfer, tax cannot be reclaimed until the cheque has cleared or the transferred funds have gone into the charity's bank account.

The rules and forms for tax recovery are available from HMRC Charities [see end of chapter]. From 1 April 2010, the deadline for reclaiming tax is:

- for associations and incorporated bodies, within four years from the end of the accounting period to which the claim relates;

- for charitable trusts, within three years of 31 January in the year following the end of the tax year to which the claim relates.

For claims made prior to 1 April 2010, the periods are two years longer (six years for associations and incorporated bodies, five years for trusts).

Claims involving transitional relief [**50.2.3.2**] must be made within two years from the end of the accounting period or tax year.

50.2.3.1   How tax is worked out

The amount of recoverable tax can be worked out by:

- dividing the current basic tax rate by (100 minus the basic tax rate);

- then multiplying this amount by the total amount of the gift aid donations.

For example:

- in a year when the basic tax rate is 20%, the charity receives donations totalling £5,000 that are covered by gift aid declarations;

- current tax rate 20, divided by (100 - 20) = 20/80;

- 20/80 multiplied by £5,000= £1,250 tax which can be recovered.

If the basic tax rate were reduced to 18%, the charity would only be able to recover £1,097.56 on £5,000 gift aid donations (18/82 x £5,000). If the tax rate went up to 22%, the charity would be able to recover £1,410.26 (22/78 x £5,000).

50.2.3.2   Transitional relief

The drop in basic rate income tax from 6 April 2008, from 22% to 20%, could have meant a reduction in the amount that charities could reclaim, from 28.2p for each £1 gift aid donation to 25p for each £1. In response to charities' concerns, the government introduced **transitional relief**, to enable charities to receive **gift aid supplement** on donations received during tax years 2008-09, 2009-10 and 2010-11. Charities reclaim tax at the basic rate for the year (20% in 2009-10), but the amount they actually receive is calculated at 2% more than the basic rate (22% in 2009-10).

Finance Act 2008 s.53, sch.19

50.2.3.3   Higher rate taxpayers

If a donor pays higher rate income tax (40% in 2009-10), the charity recovers tax at the basic rate and the donor is entitled to tax relief on the difference between the basic and higher rate. The donor claims this through his or her self assessment tax return. HMRC either gives credit against tax due from the individual, or adjusts the individual's PAYE code [**30.4.4**] to allow for the credit to be set against the tax due on earned income.

A donor, when filling in a self assessment tax return, can treat donations made since 5 April as if made in the previous tax year, and can include them on the tax return. This makes no difference to basic rate taxpayers, but enables higher rate taxpayers to recover their tax earlier. This arrangement affects only the donor's tax claim – not the recipient charity's.

Income Tax Act 2007 s.426

At the time of writing (mid 2009) the Treasury was considering whether to allow the charity – rather than the donor – to have the benefit of the higher rate tax, and was also considering the implications if additional rate tax [**30.4.4**] starts in April 2010.

50.2.3.4   Tax on restricted donations

Where a donation made under the gift aid scheme is limited to a specific purpose, it is a **restricted fund** [**48.2**] and must be used only for that purpose. At the time of writing (mid 2009) HMRC did not have a view on whether recovered tax also forms part of the restricted fund for gift aid purposes, but the Charities SORP 2005 [**54.2.3**] says that it forms part of the restricted fund unless the terms under which the donation was made indicate otherwise.

The organisation's systems should therefore allow the recovered tax to be allocated to the restricted fund, or donors should be informed before they donate that because of the administrative complexity, the recovered tax will be used for the charity's general purposes rather than the specific purpose.

50.2.4   Donors who do not pay enough tax

Donors who are not UK taxpayers, or do not pay enough income and/or capital gains tax to cover the tax recovered under gift aid, must not make a gift aid declaration. If they have a declaration in place but do not pay enough tax during the tax year, they should cancel their declaration. If this is not done and the charities to whom the donor has made gift aid donations recover more tax than the donor has paid, the donor becomes liable to repay the additional tax to HMRC.

50.2.5   Cancellation

A donor may cancel a gift aid declaration at any time. This does not have to be in writing, but to avoid problems the charity may ask for it to be put in writing.

If the cancellation is during the 30-day period after a written statement of an oral declaration is sent [**50.2.2.2**], the cancellation is retrospective and nullifies the declaration. If the charity has already recovered tax on the donation, it must repay the recovered tax to HMRC.

Cancellation of a written or electronic declaration, or an oral declaration more than 30 days after the written statement was sent, affects donations received by the charity on or after the date it is notified of the cancellation, or such other later date as the donor specifies.   *Donations to Charities by Individuals (Appropriate Declarations) Regulations 2000 [SI 2000/2074], amended by the 2005 Regulations [SI 2005/2790]*

50.2.6   Deeds of covenant

A **deed of covenant** is a promise in the form of a deed [**20.3**] to donate a stated amount to a charity. Tax on donations made under deeds of covenant is now recovered under gift aid. But because a deed of covenant is legally binding on the donor, charities may want to continue to encourage donors to make them, along with their gift aid declaration. For charities with a large donor base, covenants can provide virtually guaranteed income for an extended period, and covenants may be able to be used as security if the charity has to borrow.

50.2.6.1   Covenants made after 5 April 2000

A deed of covenant entered into after 5 April 2000 does not, on its own, allow the charity to recover the tax on the donations. For tax recovery, the deed of covenant (or any agreement) must be accompanied by a gift aid declaration [**50.2.2.1**].

There is no prescribed wording for a deed of covenant, and there is no minimum period. It can be a simple agreement to make a donation of a certain amount for a set number of months or years or indefinitely. To be binding, it must say that it is a deed, be signed in the presence of a witness, and say that it is 'delivered' [**20.3**]. If it does not meet these requirements it is not binding, and can be cancelled or ignored at any time by the donor.   *Law of Property (Miscellaneous Provisions) Act 1989 s.1*

50.2.6.2   Covenants in existence on 5 April 2000

For deeds of covenant made before 6 April 2000, tax is recovered under gift aid without any need for a gift aid declaration. The charity should ensure that a declaration is in place for other (non-covenanted) donations, and for any subsequent covenants. Covenants made before 6 April 2000 continue until they expire.

50.2.6.3   Termination

Because a deed of covenant is legally binding on the donor, it cannot be cancelled by the donor unless the deed allows this. Even if the donor ceases to pay tax and must cancel his or her gift aid declaration [**50.2.5**], the promise to make the donation remains in place until it expires.

However, a donor may ask the charity to release it from the covenant. A charity should do this only in exceptional circumstances, such as if the donor becomes unemployed or for another proper reason is unable to continue making payments. Releasing a donor, including a charity's trading company, from a covenant means giving up the security of a binding promise of continued payments, and this could contravene the trustees' duty to safeguard the charity's assets [**15.6.5**].

A release should be in writing and should be kept with the deed.

50.2.7   Donations from companies and partnerships

Gift aid donations from partnerships [**11.3**] – whether incorporated as a limited liability partnership, or unincorporated – are treated in the same way as donations from individuals. For an unincorporated partnership, the declaration may be made by one partner who is authorised to do so on behalf of all the partners, or each partner can make their own declaration. In LLPs one partner can make a declaration on behalf of the others.

Unlike individuals and partnerships, companies - including companies owned by the charity – make gift aid donations gross. The company donates the full amount to the charity, including tax, and claims tax relief when calculating its profits for corporation tax [**51.7.3**, **56.2.3**]. A gift aid declaration is not needed, as the charity does not recover anything from HMRC. *Income & Corporation Taxes Act 1988 s.339, amended by Finance Act 2000 s.40*

The same procedure applies to donations made under company deeds of covenant, regardless of when the covenant was made.

Charity trading subsidiaries have a nine-month period from the end of the financial year during which they can make the gift aid donation to the charity, but set it against their profits for the previous year [**51.7.3**].

A company which makes donations for charitable purposes, by whatever method, must list them in its annual report if the total value is more than £2,000 [**54.3.6**].

50.3   DONATING THROUGH SELF ASSESSMENT

Taxpayers who complete a self assessment tax return can nominate a charity to receive all or part of any repayment due to them. The charity must be registered with HM Revenue and Customs specifically for this scheme, and is allocated a reference code which the taxpayer must include on their self assessment return. Information about the scheme and the registration form for charities is available from HMRC Charities [see end of chapter]. *Income Tax Act 2007 s.429*

If the taxpayer is entitled to a repayment, HMRC pays the donation plus gift aid tax direct to the charity's bank account, without the donor having to make a gift aid declaration or the charity having to make a gift aid claim. Unlike ordinary gift aid, donations through self assessment can be made anonymously.

50.4   PAYROLL GIVING

The **payroll giving scheme** enables employees to make charitable gifts by deduction from their salary. It is different from gift aid because the charity cannot recover the tax paid by the donor. Instead, the deduction is made from the donor's gross pay before tax has been deducted – so the donor does not pay income tax on the money used for the donation. National insurance, however, remains payable on the full salary. *Income Tax (Earnings & Pensions) Act 2003 s.713; Charitable Deductions (Approved Schemes) Regulations 1986 [SI 1986/2211], as amended*

Donors under payroll giving cannot receive any benefits in return for their donation, and payroll giving cannot be used for payments covered by a deed of covenant or gift aid declaration.

An employer's payroll giving scheme must be approved by HM Revenue and Customs. At the employee's request, the employer deducts the amount from the employee's pre-tax salary and sends it to an approved **payroll giving agency**, which then sends it on, within 60 days, to the employee's charity of choice. The best known agency is Give As You Earn (GAYE), operated by the Charities Aid Foundation, but there are a number of other agencies run by individual charities or groups of charities. A list of these available from HMRC Charities [see end of chapter].

People receiving pensions through an occupational pension scheme can join the employer's payroll giving scheme if tax is deducted from the pension under PAYE.

50.5 GIFTS OF ASSETS

When an individual disposes of an asset which has increased in value, **capital gains tax** (CGT) may be payable on the gain (the increase in value) above the annual exemption (£10,100 in 2009-10).

Giving away an asset can be a disposal for CGT purposes, with the value of the gift assessed at its current open market value. This could mean that the donor is liable for CGT even though he or she has not been paid for the asset and thus does not have funds to pay the tax.

For tax on gains realised by organisations, see **56.2.5**.

50.5.1 Gifts to charities and certain other bodies

When an asset is donated to a charity or is sold to a charity at below market value, its value is assumed to be an amount which does not give rise to either a gain or a loss, so there is no capital gain and therefore no need for the donor to pay CGT. This also applies to gifts and sales below value to certain institutions listed in the **Inheritance Tax Act 1984 [50.6.2]**.   *Taxation of Chargeable Gains Act 1992 ss.257,258*

If the sale of the asset would make a loss, it may be advantageous for the donor to sell the asset to a third party, set the loss against tax liability, and donate the sale proceeds to the charity under gift aid. Before doing this, the rules on substantial donors need to be considered [**50.7**].

50.5.1.1 Gifts of shares, securities, land and buildings

In addition to relief from capital gains tax, there is also relief from income tax (for individuals) and corporation tax (for companies) on shares, securities and leasehold or freehold property donated to charities 'with no strings attached' or sold to them at less than market value. The tax relief is claimed by the donor, not the charity, and is in addition to the donor's relief from capital gains tax.
Income & Corporation Taxes Act 1988 ss.587B,587C as amended; Income Tax Act 2007 ss.431-446

To qualify, the shares or securities must be listed on a recognised stock exchange in the UK or elsewhere. Gifts of shares and securities can have particularly complex tax implications for both the donor and charity, and advice should be sought on maximising the benefits to both parties. This is particularly important if the substantial donor rules might apply [**50.7**].

In relation to real property the whole interest in the property must be given, the charity must agree to accept the property, and both parties should take advice to ensure the transaction complies with both tax law and charity law [[**50.7, 61.3.2**].

50.5.2 Gifts to non-charities

If an asset is given to a non-charity, the donor may have to pay capital gains tax. Specialist advice should be taken to ensure this is minimised.

50.6   LEGACIES AND LIFETIME GIFTS

A **legacy** or **bequest** is money or other assets left under the terms of a will. A **lifetime gift** or **lifetime legacy** is a gift of money or other assets made during the person's lifetime.

Inheritance tax is chargeable on the value of a person's estate at the date of death, plus, on a sliding scale, the value of gifts made during the seven years prior to death. There is no inheritance tax on bequests and gifts to a spouse, civil partner, charities and some other organisations [**50.6.2**], and on the first £325,000 (in 2009-10) of the remainder of the estate. Inheritance tax (40% in 2009-10) is payable on everything above this.

At the time of writing (mid 2009) there was pressure on the UK to extend inheritance tax relief to donations by UK taxpayers to charities in other EU countries [**50.1.1**].

50.6.1   Legacy fundraising

Legacies are an important source of income for both charities and non-charities, and many organisations undertake campaigns to encourage supporters to make wills and to leave a legacy to the organisation. Provided the organisation has adequate powers to undertake this sort of fundraising [**7.4.4**] there is no problem with a legacy campaign, but difficult issues arise if the organisation becomes too involved in the process of drafting wills. Involvement in, or funding of, the preparation of a will under which the organisation ultimately benefits may, unless handled very carefully, lead to a legal challenge on the basis of undue influence. There is also the risk of the organisation being sued for negligence if its advice does not meet professional standards.

Before undertaking a legacy campaign, the organisation should consider the Charity Commission's guidance *Paying for wills with charity funds* and the Institute of Fundraising legacy fundraising code of practice [see end of chapter].

The promise of a legacy is not legally binding [**48.3.1**], and an organisation has no recourse in law if a donor who has promised a legacy subsequently changes his or her will.

50.6.1.1   Legacies to an incorporated body

Where an incorporated body (company or industrial and provident society) is encouraging donors to leave a legacy, it may want to consider asking them to include a clause making clear that if the organisation becomes insolvent, the bequest cannot be used to meet the organisation's obligations to its creditors. This follows a ruling that until an insolvent company is dissolved, bequests and donations to the company can be passed on to creditors.   *Re ARMS (Multiple Sclerosis Research) Ltd: Alleyne v Attorney General & another [1997] 2 All ER 679*

At the time of writing (mid 2009), it was unclear how the above will apply to charitable incorporated organisations (CIOs).

50.6.1.2   Lifetime legacies

A **lifetime legacy** or **charitable remainder trust** is an arrangement – at the time of writing not available in the UK – where cash, shares or property are donated to a charity, but the donor is entitled to use the income derived from the asset, or the asset itself, during his or her lifetime. The donor receives capital gains tax relief at the time of the gift, and its value is not included in the donor's estate for the purposes of inheritance tax.

This arrangement is widely used in the United States, and at the time of writing (mid 2009) some organisations were campaigning for it to be made available in the UK.

50.6.2   Gifts to charities and certain other bodies

Gifts by an individual during his or her lifetime or on death are exempt from inheritance tax provided that they are to:

- organisations established for charitable purposes;

- designated institutions such as universities, museums, art galleries, the National Trust etc established for national purposes or public benefit;
- community amateur sports clubs registered with HM Revenue and Customs [**1.8**];
- local authorities, government departments or health service bodies;
- political parties; and/or
- registered social landlords (gifts of land only).

Inheritance Tax Act 1984 ss.23-26A, sch.3; Finance Act 2002 sch.18

In order to qualify for this relief, the following conditions must be met:

- the gift must be irrevocable;
- no one else may have an interest in the asset;
- there must be no limit on how long the asset can be held by the donor, or other limits on the donor's right to transfer the asset;
- any conditions required by the donor must be met within 12 months of the date of the transfer;
- if the asset is land or a building, the gift must not have conditions requiring the donor, the donor's spouse or a person connected with the donor to use the property rent free or at a rent below the market rate;
- the gift must be used only for charitable purposes or the purposes of the qualifying organisation; and
- if the will creates a new trust, the purposes must be wholly and exclusively charitable [**5.2.3**].

Bequests to existing charities and other qualifying organisations are exempt from inheritance tax. Straightforward money gifts are not likely to be complex, but charities and other qualifying organisations should use a solicitor to deal with any other bequests. For example, if an organisation is entitled to the residue of an estate and the executor sells the assets which make up the estate before passing the proceeds to the organisation, the gains could be subject to capital gains tax. But if the assets are passed to the charity or qualifying organisation which then sells them, capital gains tax would not be payable.

50.6.2.1   Legacies where the organisation no longer exists

Where a beneficiary charity ceases to exist as a result of a **relevant charity merger** and is entered in the Charity Commission's register of charity mergers [**11.5.4**] a legacy to the original charity will generally take effect as a gift to the new (merged) charity. However, a legacy may fail if the wording specifically provides that the organisation must be in existence at the time of the donor's death.

In other situations, a legacy may fail if the intended beneficiary no longer exists or if it has changed name or legal structure, and it is not absolutely clear that it is the intended beneficiary [**10.1.2.12**]. It is therefore good practice to inform known legators of any change in the organisation's name, legal structure and/or charity number. Where an organisation changes legal structure (for example, incorporates) or is involved in a merger which does not meet the criteria for a relevant charity merger, it may be advisable to retain the original charity as a shell, just to receive legacies [**10.1.4, 11.5.8**].

If a legacy clearly intended for a specific organisation fails, the property intended for the organisation becomes part of the deceased person's residual estate.

50.6.3   Gifts to other bodies

Bequests to organisations which do not qualify for inheritance tax exemption are subject to inheritance tax. The detailed terms of the will determine whether the estate of the deceased bears the tax and the organisation receives the full specified sum, or whether the tax is deducted from the sum before it is paid over to the organisation.

If an organisation which is not exempt from inheritance tax receives a gift from a living person who then dies within seven years, the value of the gift is added back into the donor's estate when calculating the estate's liability for inheritance tax.

The value added back is reduced on a sliding scale for each year the donor survived following the gift.

50.6.4 Changes and challenges

Some or all of the beneficiaries of a will may, within two years after the person's death, agree a **deed of variation** altering the way the estate is distributed. This may be done to maximise inheritance tax relief, or for other reasons. A charity can be party to a variation only if it can show that the variation is in the best interests of the charity.

50.6.4.1 Contested probate

Gifts in wills may be challenged in the courts by anyone, but this is most commonly done by relatives who feel they have not been provided for under the **Inheritance (Provision for Family and Dependants) Act 1975**, or by a charity or other party who believes the will is invalid or has not been properly administered. This gives rise to **contested probate**. Legal advice is essential.

50.6.4.2 Ex gratia payments

A charity occasionally feels that it has received a bequest which the donor may not actually have intended or which is unfair to the donor's dependants, and that it has a moral obligation to make an *ex gratia* **payment** to the donor's relatives or others, even if this is not in the charity's best interest. This may be done only with the consent of the Charity Commission under s.27 of the **Charities Act 1993 [53.3]**.

50.6.4.3 Disclaiming legacies

In some situations a charity may not want to accept a legacy, but it can refuse to accept it only if this is in the best interests of the charity [**48.3.2**] or the Charity Commission gives consent. An exception is Alcoholics Anonymous, which wished to have the right to disclaim legacies so that it could remain a self help organisation and did not want to have more assets than it needed for its day to day work. It succeeded in getting a private bill through Parliament allowing it to disclaim legacies. *Alcoholics Anonymous (Dispositions) Act 1986*

The Institute of Fundraising [see end of chapter] has a guidance note on the acceptance and refusal of donations.

50.7 SUBSTANTIAL DONORS

A person or business who makes donations to a charity or linked charities of £25,000 or more in a 12-month period or £150,000 in a six-year period is a **substantial donor** to that charity, and special rules apply. To come within these substantial donor rules, the donations must be eligible for tax relief. A donor is a substantial donor for every chargeable period (accounting year) in which the limits are exceeded and for the five subsequent chargeable periods.

Where a charity and substantial donor participate in certain transactions, tax exemption or tax relief is affected. The transactions are:

- unless they fall within allowed exemptions, payments by a charity to a substantial donor are treated as non-charitable expenditure, and are therefore not **qualifying expenditure** entitling the charity to relief from corporation or income tax [**56.4.3**];

- remuneration paid to a substantial donor is treated as non-charitable expenditure unless it is payment for services as a trustee and approved by the Charity Commission, other charity regulator or court;

- if the substantial donor receives value from a transaction with the charity and the transaction is of a type which would not be expected between independent parties, the charity is treated as having incurred an amount of non-charitable expenditure as decided by HM Revenue and Customs. *Income & Corporation Taxes Act 1988 ss.506A-506C, inserted by Finance Act 2006 s.54; Income Tax Act 2007 ss.549-557, amended by Substantial Donor Transactions (Variation of Threshold Limits) Regulations 2009 [SI 2009/1029]*

Transactions where the charity pays for goods or services or the donor provides financial assistance or sells or lets property to the charity are excluded from the rules, provided they are not part of a tax avoidance scheme and are no more beneficial to the charity than would be expected in an arm's length transaction. Similarly, services provided by the charity to the donor are excluded if the services arise from carrying out the primary purpose of the charity, and the donor receives them on terms no more beneficial than other beneficiaries.

A trading subsidiary or other company wholly owned by a charity is not treated as a substantial donor as a result of gifting its profits to the charity.

At the time of writing (mid 2009) HMRC had carried out several consultations on the substantial donor rules. This could lead to introduction of *de minimis* thresholds below which the rules do not apply, or even repeal of the rules.

50.8 PERSONAL CHARITIES

Individuals who want to make substantial donations to charities may find it appropriate to set up a personal charity, generally in the form of a charitable trust [**2.3**], with objects to support charitable work in general or to support particular charitable purposes.

In addition to the capital gains and inheritance tax advantages [**50.5**, **50.6**], the trust can be made the beneficiary of gift aid payments. The trust recovers the tax, and the trustees, who generally include the donor, can make a series of smaller donations from the trust's income. The whole of the income should generally be utilised in each year, unless it is being retained for a specific purpose [**58.8.3**].

Some trusts have as their main capital asset a large number of shares in the founder's company or a property asset. This arrangement may allow the donor to avoid capital gains tax or inheritance tax, while still being effectively able to control the company or asset which has been given. An example is a majority shareholder in a private company, who sets up a trust for charitable purposes with his or her shares. The donor and two other connected people – perhaps members of the donor's family – are named as trustees. The donor and other trustees control the charitable trust and also, through their control of the trust, the company. On the donor's death no inheritance tax is payable (because the shares have been donated to the charitable trust) but the donor's family retains control of the trust and company. Such arrangements are complex and require specialist legal advice.

50.9 GIFTS BY BUSINESSES

When a donation is made to a charity or community amateur sports club by an incorporated business (rather than a sole trader or unincorporated partnership), the company can set the donation against its pre-tax profits, so it does not have to pay corporation tax on the amount of the donation. The donor, rather than the recipient, receives the tax advantage. Similar rules apply for unincorporated businesses.

Gifts by a charity's trading company may be set against the previous year's profits if made within nine months from the end of the trading company's financial year [**50.2.7**].

Most other donations and gifts by a company or other business cannot be set against its income or profits, but there are a few exceptions.

A company which makes donations for charitable purposes, by whatever method, must list them in its annual report if the total value is more than £2,000 [**54.3.6**].

50.9.1 Benevolent gifts by traders

Businesses can get tax relief by setting donations to charities against their income or profits. This relief also applies to donations to non-charitable voluntary organisations, but only if the payment:

- is wholly and exclusively for the purposes of the business;

- is made for the benefit of an organisation established for educational, cultural, religious, recreational or benevolent purposes;
- is made to an organisation which is local in relation to the donor's business activities, and which is not restricted to persons connected with the donor;
- is not of a capital nature; and
- is reasonably small in relation to the scale of the donor's business.

Income Tax (Trading & Other Income) Act 2005 s.43; Corporation Tax Act 2009 s.1300

These payments are called **benevolent gifts by traders**. Typical examples are small annual subscriptions to organisations relating to the business's trade or professional vocation, such as a benevolent fund; small donations to local organisations which benefit the business's employees; and payments to sponsor a charitable or community activity, if the payment is made to advertise or publicise the business and is reasonable compared with the publicity involved. Despite being eligible for relief from corporation tax, sponsorship which explicitly benefits the donor may be subject to VAT [**57.11.2**] and may be taxable [**56.3.3**].

A business should not set any gifts against taxable profits without taking advice to ensure they comply with the requirements.

50.9.2 Gifts of assets

The gift of an asset from a company to a charity is treated for capital gains tax purposes in the same way as a gift by an individual [**50.5**], except that a company does not have an annual CGT exemption. The company does not have to pay tax on the disposal, but in general cannot set any loss relating to the asset against tax. Where the company gives shares, securities, land or buildings to a charity or sells them to a charity at less than market value, the value can be set against profits and thus reduce corporation tax [**50.5.1.1**].

50.9.3 Gifts of trading stock

A gift by a company or other incorporated body engaged in a trade or profession attracts tax relief for the company if the gift is made to a charity, community amateur sports club (CASC) or educational establishment (school, college or university), and consists of articles manufactured by, or of a type sold by, the company in the course of its trade. The donor must receive no benefit from the recipient related to the giving of the donation. *Income Tax (Trading & Other Income) Act 2005 ss.108,110; Corporation Tax Act 2009 ss.105,106*

If the business making the donation is a sole trader or unincorporated partnership, tax relief is available for gifts to charities, CASCs or educational establishments of articles manufactured by or of a type sold by the business.

50.9.4 Secondment of employees

A secondment is a temporary 'loan' of an employee to another organisation [**25.5.4**]. If the employee is seconded to a charity by a business (whether a company or other incorporated body, sole trader or partnership), the cost to the business is allowed as a deduction in calculating the profits of the business. 'Cost to the business' is the employee's salary and related costs. *Income Tax (Trading & Other Income) Act 2005 ss.70,71; Corporation Tax Act 2009 ss.70,71,1235*

The cost of a secondment to a non-charitable organisation cannot be deducted.

50.9.5 Donations by companies

Donations by a company to a political party or political organisation must be authorised by the company members [**46.3**]. This applies to donations to organisations which seek to influence support for a political party or influence voters in a referendum. It does not apply to donations to charities or to organisations simply seeking to promote public debate.

If donations to political organisations and/or charities total more than £2,000 during the financial year, they must be disclosed in the directors' annual report [**54.3.6**].

50.10   COMMUNITY INVESTMENT TAX RELIEF

Community investment tax relief (CITR) is a tax relief of up to 25% over five years for individuals and companies who invest in an accredited **community development finance institution.** CDFIs, in turn, invest in qualifying profit-distributing businesses, social enterprises and community projects in specified disadvantaged areas in the UK. Information about CITR and CDFIs is available from HM Revenue and Customs and the Community Development Finance Association [see end of chapter].

50.11   LANDFILL TAX CREDITS

Landfill tax is a tax paid by landfill site operators, based on the amount of waste which goes into their site. Through the Landfill Communities Fund, site operators are encouraged to make voluntary contributions, of up to 6% (as at 1/8/09) of their landfill tax bill, to approved community, social and environmental schemes. The site operator then receives 90% tax credit on the voluntary contribution.

Landfill Tax Regulations 1996 [SI 1996/1527], as amended

Charities and other organisations which are within 10 miles of a landfill site and meet certain criteria are eligible to receive contributions under this scheme if they are involved in land reclamation or restoration; anti-pollution, waste management, environmental protection and conservation activities; conservation or promotion of biological diversity; research and education on recycling, and development and promotion of products made from wastes; or development of markets for recycled waste.   *Landfill Tax (Amendment) Regulations 1999 [SI 1999/3270] & 2003 [SI 2003/2313]*

Organisations must be registered with Entrust, a private regulator set up by the government to oversee landfill tax credits. Information is available from HMRC and Entrust [below].

Resources: TAX-EFFECTIVE GIVING

Charity Commission: www.charity-commission.gov.uk, 0870 333 0123, email via website.

Fundraising Standards Board: www.frsb.org.uk, 0845 402 5442, info@frsb.org.uk.

HM Revenue and Customs Charities: www.hmrc.gov.uk, 0845 302 0203, email via website.

Institute of Fundraising: www.institute-of-fundraising.org.uk, 020 7840 1000, email via website.

Gift aid on donations of goods. Association of Charity Shops: www.charityshops.org.uk, 020 7255 4470, mail@charityshops.org.uk.

Community investment tax relief. HM Revenue and Customs: www.hmrc.gov.uk, 0845 010 9000, email via website.

Community Development Finance Association: www.cdfa.org.uk, 020 7430 0222, info@cdfa.org.uk.

Landfill tax credits. HM Revenue and Customs: as for community investment tax relief.

Entrust: www.entrust.org.uk, 0161 972 9900, information@entrust.org.uk.

Statute law. www.opsi.gov.uk and www.statutelaw.gov.uk.

Much but not all case law. www.bailii.org.

Updates cross-referenced to this book. www.rclh.co.uk.

Chapter 51
TRADING AND SOCIAL ENTERPRISE

51.1   VOLUNTARY ORGANISATIONS AND TRADING

Trading raises some of the most complex legal issues voluntary organisations will face. These involve the interaction of constitutional objects and powers, charity law, direct taxation law, VAT law, liability issues, and practical and management issues, and mistakes can be damaging. The time, financial investment, risks and liabilities involved in trading are frequently underestimated, and can lead to significant losses.

Charities should carefully consider the Charity Commission's CC35 *Trustees, trading and tax* before undertaking any trading or setting up a trading company.

51.1.1   Social enterprise

Trading by or on behalf of charities or for other social, community or environmental purposes is increasingly referred to as **social enterprise**. There is no statutory or agreed definition of social enterprise, **community business**, **community enterprise** or similar terms [**1.1.2**], but they all refer to bodies which receive all or most of their income through charging for goods or services – rather than being funded primarily through grants or donations – and which use all or most of their profits for charitable, community or environmental purposes rather than private gain.

'Social enterprise' is a concept, not a legal structure. A social enterprise may be an unincorporated or incorporated charity, or may be a non-charitable company limited by guarantee or industrial and provident society, a company limited by shares, a community interest company or a partnership.

51.1.2   The meaning of trading

For tax purposes, an organisation is likely to be **trading** if it receives payment in return for providing goods, services, facilities, publicity or other benefit.

Trading is subject to **corporation tax** (a tax on the profits of incorporated bodies or unincorporated associations) or **income tax** (a tax on the income of trusts). Much of the trading carried out by charities is **non-taxable trading**, such as **primary purpose trading** in direct furtherance of the charity's objects [**56.4.5**] or other trading which is exempt from tax [**56.4**]. Even if there is no tax on the profits or income, such activities are still trading.

Other trading carried out by charities is **taxable trading**, which must nearly always be carried out through a separate non-charitable entity, usually called a **trading subsidiary** or **trading company**.

The definition of trading for tax purposes, and the tax reliefs available for charities and in some cases for other organisations, are covered in **chapter 56**.

Especially in relation to sponsorship [**56.3.3**] and service agreements [**52.1**], it may be difficult to determine whether a relationship is trading and therefore potentially subject to tax, or whether it is a donation or grant and not subject to tax.

51.1.2.1   Trading, tax and VAT

VAT law [**chapter 57**] does not refer to trading, but to **business supplies** [**57.6.2**]. Business supplies may be exempt [**57.7**] or subject to VAT, and if subject to VAT it may be at zero rate, reduced rate or standard rate [**57.8**]. Tax law and VAT law are very different, with completely different rules:

- a trading activity carried out by a charity may be exempt from both tax and VAT, or subject to both tax and VAT, or exempt from tax but subject to VAT, or subject to tax but exempt from VAT;
- a trading activity carried out by a non-charity is relatively unlikely to be exempt from tax, but could be [**56.6**] – so the activity could be exempt from both tax and VAT, or subject to both tax and VAT, or exempt from tax but subject to VAT, or subject to tax but exempt from VAT;
- a trading activity might be exempt from VAT or zero rated when carried out by a charity but not when carried out by a non-charity – but some activities are exempt from VAT or zero rated regardless of who carries them out.

Generalisations such as 'we are a charity so we don't have to pay tax' or 'that activity is exempt from tax so it must be exempt from VAT as well' are *never* wise.

51.1.3   Restrictions on trading

There are no statutory restrictions on charities or other voluntary organisations carrying out any kind of lawful trading. However:

- a voluntary organisation may only carry out activities within its constitutional objects and powers or allowed by law [**51.1.3.1**];
- charitable status may be jeopardised if a charity undertakes too much trading which is not primary purpose trading [**56.4**];
- even where the trading is carried out by a charity, the profits will be subject to tax unless the trading is explicitly exempt from corporation or income tax and the profits are used exclusively for charitable purposes [**56.4.1**];
- a non-charity does not have to pay tax on any profits it donates to a charity under gift aid [**52.7**], but a charity cannot make a donation under gift aid so cannot avoid tax by 'donating' taxable profits to itself;
- if a charity trades in a way which means it has to pay tax, the trustees will generally be in breach of their duty to maximise the charity's assets [**15.6.5**].

In order to bypass the constitutional limitations on trading, avoid jeopardising charitable status, be able to recover tax and/or sometimes to take advantage of favourable VAT treatment, organisations often set up a separate **trading company** or **trading subsidiary** [**51.2**].

51.1.3.1 Restrictions in governing documents

Governing documents of charities and some non-charities may say that the organisation cannot undertake 'any permanent trading activities' or 'any substantial permanent trading activities' [7.4.4]. **Permanent** in this context means not only 'ongoing and long-term', but also regular or frequent. But even with such a restriction, a charity can:

- undertake permanent trading which is directly related to the charity's **primary purpose** or where the work is carried out primarily by the charity's beneficiaries as part of achieving the charity's objectives, and trading **ancillary** to its primary purpose [56.4.5];
- provide services explicitly allowed under constitutional objects or powers;
- sell **donated goods** [56.3.2];
- organise **fundraising events** which fall within HMRC extra-statutory concession (ESC) C4 [56.4.6];
- undertake fundraising or trading activities which are not within ESC C4, but fall within the exemption for **small-scale trading** [56.4.7].

If the governing document says that a charity cannot undertake 'any permanent trading activities *in furtherance of its objects*' or something similar, this may mean that it cannot undertake even primary purpose trading. In this situation advice should be sought from an experienced solicitor or the Charity Commission.

51.2 TRADING COMPANIES

Voluntary organisations may set up **trading companies** (also called **trading subsidiaries**) to carry out activities outside what they are allowed to do, or because they want to separate some activities from the work of the main organisation or keep the risk of liability separate. In some cases, there are VAT advantages in carrying out work through a non-charitable rather than charitable body.

In deciding whether to set up a trading company, governing body members need to ensure they get appropriate professional advice. Many organisations set up trading companies when they do not need to and there is no advantage in doing so, while others do not set up trading companies when they must or when it would be advantageous to do so.

51.2.1 When a trading company is not necessary

There are many situations where it is not necessary for a voluntary organisation – even a charity which is carrying out trading – to set up a trading company. However, the organisation may choose to set one up anyway in order to keep certain activities separate from the main organisation.

51.2.1.1 Charities

A trading company is not necessary if a charity is acting within its powers [51.1.3.1] and receives its income only from:

- genuine donations, grants and sponsorship which do not give any benefit to the donor other than simple acknowledgement [56.3];
- membership subscriptions entitling the member only to the right to attend general meetings, receive annual reports etc [56.3.5];
- the sale of donated goods [56.3.2].

Provided the charity has the necessary power to trade and all the trading income is used for its charitable purposes, a trading company is also not necessary for:

- trading activities directly related to its primary objects (primary purpose trading), ancillary (directly related) to primary purpose trading, or carried out mainly by the charity's beneficiaries [56.4.5];
- membership subscriptions entitling the member to activities or services within the charity's primary purpose [56.3.5];
- fundraising events covered by HMRC's extra-statutory concession C4 [56.4.6];

- small-scale fundraising and trading activities where the income does not exceed £5,000, or where it exceeds £5,000 but is not more than 25% of the charity's total incoming resources or £50,000 (whichever is lower) [**56.4.7**];
- lotteries and raffles [**56.4.8**];
- rents [**56.4.9**];
- dividends, bank interest and most other investment income [**56.4.11**];
- gains on the sale of assets [**56.4.16**].

The charity will not have to pay tax on any of these types of income, but it may need to charge VAT on some of the activities [**chapter 57**].

If there is any doubt about whether a charity has power to carry out trading in general or a particular type of trading, advice should be sought from a specialist solicitor or the Charity Commission.

51.2.1.2 Non-charities

For non-charities, there are generally no tax or VAT advantages in setting up a trading company. Indeed, a non-charitable voluntary organisation may want to do the opposite: to set up a charity to undertake its properly charitable activities [**9.4**], so that the charity can take advantage of tax or VAT exemptions.

Although there may be no tax advantages for a non-charity, it may still need to set up a trading company if the trading it wants to undertake is outside its objects or powers. Alternatively, it may be able to amend its governing document.

The profit from the activities carried out by a non-charitable voluntary organisation or its trading company will be subject to tax unless its income is in the form of donations, grants, sponsorship giving nothing other than simple acknowledgement to the sponsor, and/or membership subscriptions [**56.3**]; it is selling donated goods [**56.3.2**]; the profit arises from members in a membership organisation or club paying for goods or services in their capacity as members [**56.6.2**]; and/or it is running a fundraising event within extra-statutory concession C4 [**56.4.6**].

51.2.2 When a trading company may become necessary

Even if a trading company is not required at a particular point in time, the situation needs to be regularly monitored. A YMCA restaurant case from more than a century ago illustrates the risks. The restaurant, which was initially opened to provide meals to hostel residents who were the charity's beneficiaries, needed further income. It opened its doors to the public and was soon much more profitable. But it had moved from existing primarily to carry out the charity's purpose, to a mix of uses in which providing services to unconnected third parties predominated. The profits therefore became liable to tax. The trading should have been carried out by a trading company, which could have gained tax relief by donating its profits to the charity.   *Grove v Young Men's Christian Association [1903] 4 TC 613*

Existing activities should be regularly reviewed to ensure they can still be carried out within the charity. For all new developments or projects, consideration should be given to whether it is necessary to set up a trading company or there is a practical advantage in doing so. If trading starts out exempt from tax but becomes non-exempt, the charity may be taxed on up to six years' previous trading.

51.2.3 When a trading company is necessary

If a trading activity is outside an organisation's objects and powers as set out in its governing document, the organisation must set up a separate entity to carry out the activity. This is especially important for charities, whose trustees will be acting in breach of trust if they act outside the charity's objects or powers [**15.6.2**].

A charitable organisation carrying out trading which does not fall within what it is allowed to do [**51.2.1.1**] will have to pay tax on the profits or income from non-allowed trading. This would be a breach of the trustees' duties to act prudently, maximise the charity's income and not pay unnecessary tax [**15.6.5**], and they could be made personally liable to pay the tax or indemnify the charity for the tax it has paid. It could also jeopardise the charity's charitable status.

It is therefore nearly always necessary for a charity to set up a trading company when it is carrying out activities which are subject to tax. However, where the amount of tax that the charity would have to pay is so small that the cost of setting up and running a separate company would be disproportionate, the trustees may be able to justify carrying out the trading within the charity, even though the profit or income will be subject to tax.

51.3 SETTING UP A TRADING COMPANY

It is possible to buy an off the shelf company or register a new company within 24 hours [**1.5.1**], but it is more sensible to give a trading company careful thought beforehand and to set it up properly right from the beginning. For issues around setting up a company see **1.5**, and for setting up a subsidiary see **9.4** and **9.5**.

Charity trustees should consider the Charity Commission's guidance in CC35 *Charities, trustees and tax*, and take advice from experienced professionals.

51.3.1 Business planning

No trading company should be set up until there has been a proper and prudent consideration of its chances of success and the risk of failure. This generally involves the preparation of a full business plan setting out the company's commercial objectives and its financial projections. It should be prepared with, or at least commented on by, people with appropriate knowledge and professional expertise.

The business plan should be regularly reviewed and updated. It is a vital tool in ensuring the company achieves the aims set for it by the parent organisation, and is also part of the process by which the parent's governing body can demonstrate that it has acted appropriately and responsibly in deciding to set up the company.

51.3.2 Legal structure

It is generally important for trading bodies to have limited liability [**3.1.1**], so they are most commonly set up as a **company limited by shares** [**51.3.2.3**], or less frequently as a **company limited by guarantee** [**51.3.2.2**] or **industrial or provident society** [**51.3.2.1**]. For stand-alone trading companies – but not necessarily for trading subsidiaries set up by charities – a **community interest company** [**51.3.2.4**] limited by shares or guarantee may be appropriate.

The parent organisation usually owns all of the shares in a company (including a CIC) limited by shares or IPS, or controls all the votes in a company limited by guarantee. Other models are where a parent does not control a trading company but receives its profits, or where the trading company is the parent, with a subsidiary charity whose trustees are all or mostly appointed by the company [**9.5.2**].

51.3.2.1 Industrial and provident society

An industrial and provident society [**3.5**] must have at least three members (unlike a company, which needs only one) and is expensive to set up, so this structure is rarely chosen for trading companies.

51.3.2.2 Company limited by guarantee

The structure of non-charitable company limited by guarantee [**3.3.5**] is occasionally chosen for a trading company. The main advantage is that the structure can be more or less identical to the parent organisation, but with different objects and no restrictions on distributing surplus. The main disadvantage is that the trading company cannot raise money by issuing shares.

51.3.2.3 Company limited by shares

By far the most common choice for a trading company is a private company limited by shares [**3.3.6**]. A company can be formed with only one member so the parent organisation can be the sole member or, if the charity is unincorporated, can appoint one person as a member of the company. That company member holds one share and has power to appoint the directors.

The company is likely to have general trading objects allowing it to carry on any trade or business, and a general power to do anything incidental or conducive to this. The articles of association generally follow the Companies Act model articles [**1.5.3**] but should be adapted as appropriate, especially in relation to the company membership and the board of directors.

51.3.2.4 Community interest company

A community interest company (CIC) can be a company limited by guarantee or by shares [**3.4**]. A CIC is not charitable, but must use all or most of its profits and assets for the benefit of the community. This restriction may make it attractive as a stand-alone trading venture, because there is no risk of the profits or assets being used for private gain rather than for community or charitable purposes. It may be particularly appropriate where an organisation wants to be seen as a 'social enterprise' [**51.1.1**], although social enterprises do not have to be CICs.

For charities setting up a trading company, there is unlikely to be any particular advantage in setting up a CIC. In any company the charity – as sole member of the company, with power to appoint and remove the company directors – controls how the profits and assets are used, so there is unlikely to be a need for the restrictions on use of profit and assets imposed on CICs.

51.3.2.5 Partnership or sole trader

Very occasionally, short-term trading activity may be carried out by an individual operating as a sole trader, or by two or more individuals or corporate bodies acting as a partnership [**11.3**] who are authorised to trade to make a profit for the organisation. They are in effect undertaking the trading as agents for the parent organisation [**48.2.1**].

The lack of direct ownership by the parent organisation, potential tax complexities and the sole trader's or partners' potential unlimited liability mean that it is rarely advisable for an organisation to trade through a partnership or sole trader.

51.3.3 Joint ventures

Some trading activities are joint ventures between groups of voluntary organisations, or between a voluntary organisation and a commercial business, statutory body or individual [**11.3.2**]. A joint venture requires a specially prepared governing document, usually supplemented by a shareholders' or joint venture agreement. This sets out the terms of the venture, how control is exercised, how decisions are taken and, very importantly, how financial risk is apportioned and how the parties can withdraw. The agreement should be drawn up by a solicitor.

51.3.4 Accounting

Most charities and companies must consolidate their accounts with those of their subsidiaries [**54.2.2**, **54.3.2**]. It is essential to consult the parent organisation's accountants and solicitors before making any decisions about the preparation and presentation of the accounts of the parent organisation or trading company.

51.4 FUNDING THE TRADING COMPANY

The first really difficult decision in setting up a trading company is usually where the money will come from to fund it. This is by no means straightforward, even if the parent organisation is wealthy.

For the Charity Commission's guidance on funding of charity trading subsidiaries, see CC35 *Charities, trading and tax*.

51.4.1 Donations and grants

It may be possible to persuade individual supporters or outside bodies to make a grant or gift to the trading company to cover its start-up costs, but such funds are not readily come by.

The availability of grants specifically for 'social enterprises' [**51.1.1**] may in some circumstances make it advantageous to define and promote the trading company as a social enterprise, or even to set it up as a community interest company [**51.3.2.4**], which is more likely than an ordinary company to be perceived as a social enterprise. However, as with all funding, it is crucial not to turn the organisation into something it is not just because funding might be available.

51.4.2 Powers of parent body

The ability of the parent organisation to finance the trading company depends not only on how much money it has, but also on the powers in its governing document and legal limitations on the organisation's power to make loans and investments.

51.4.2.1 Non-charitable organisations

Non-charitable organisations can set up and fund a trading company provided they have power to do so under their governing document. If they do not have such power, the members may be able to approve the activity and expenditure anyway [**5.8**], or they may be able to amend the governing document [**7.5**].

If a members' club or association is considering financing the trading company from funds accumulated from members' subscriptions rather than from other income, it should take advice as to whether this threatens the tax-exempt status of the subscription income [**56.3.5**].

51.4.2.2 Charities

Charitable trusts and associations may invest in a trading company, provided the investment meets the requirements of the **Trustee Act 2000** [**58.1.2**]. Incorporated charities (whether companies, industrial and provident societies or charitable incorporated organisations) may invest in a trading company provided they have the appropriate investment powers.

51.4.3 Share capital

A common method of funding a trading company is by the parent organisation acquiring sufficient shares to provide the trading company with adequate capital, thus investing in the company in the same way as the parent body would with any other subsidiary. A number of difficult and somewhat contradictory issues arise when considering whether to use this **equity funding** approach.

51.4.3.1 Prudence and risk

A charity's trustees must consider whether they have the power to make such an investment [**58.1**]. Even where they have such power, they must take proper advice and make a proper decision about whether it is prudent to invest in a potentially risky trading venture [**58.3.1**].

If the trading company fails, shareholders are lowest in the list of priorities for payment. For this reason, the Charity Commission generally does not favour equity investment by a charity in a trading company, other than the minimal number of shares needed to form the company.

51.4.3.2 Tax exemption

Even if a charity has power to invest, and even if such investment can be shown to be prudent and not to put the charity's funds at risk, a further difficulty arises from potential loss of tax exemption on funds used for the investment.

Only **qualifying investments** are eligible for tax relief [**56.5.4**]. Investment in companies which are not listed on a recognised stock exchange is not explicitly authorised. Trading companies set up by a charity are unlikely to be listed on a stock exchange, but it is generally possible to obtain informal advice from HM Revenue and Customs that they will allow tax exemption on income used for investment in a charity's trading company under the provisions of schedule 20 of the **Income and Corporation Taxes Act 1988**. Before doing this they must be satisfied that the investment is made for the benefit of the charity, and not merely for the avoidance of tax. There is no provision for HMRC to give formal approval for such investment.

Income & Corporation Taxes Act 1988
sch.20 pt.1 para.9(1), as amended

Before giving even informal advice, HMRC will wish to see evidence of the arm's length nature of the transaction and the benefit expected to arise for the charity. This further emphasises the importance of appropriate business plans and professional advice prior to committing a charity's funds to a trading company.

51.4.4 Loans from commercial sources

Because of the high costs of such borrowing and the considerable difficulty in obtaining it, relatively few trading companies are funded by commercial lenders.

Another problem is that commercial lenders often require guarantees by the parent organisation. But if a guarantee is given by a parent charity for a loan to its trading company, funds given to the charity for its charitable purposes may be subject to tax and are potentially at risk, and the governing body which authorises such a guarantee is likely to be in breach of its duty to safeguard the charity's funds. Similar considerations apply to non-charitable organisations unless there is clear authority in the governing document for such a guarantee.

But without such a guarantee it is likely to be very difficult, especially when the company is starting, to borrow significant sums from outside sources. Or a lender may require guarantees from individuals, which puts them at risk [**59.5.3**].

In some situations, soft loans [**59.4.1**] with low interest rates, extended repayment terms and/or no need for a guarantor may be available to charities and other voluntary organisations, and possibly their trading companies.

51.4.5 Loans by a charity

The restrictions on equity investments by charities [**51.4.3**] also apply to loans by charities. To qualify for tax exemption a loan must be qualifying [**56.4.3**]. HMRC will give information advice about whether exemption will be allowed.

Loans must be very carefully structured in order to meet Charity Commission requirements. In particular, the usual issues of prudence apply [**58.1**]. The loan should be on full commercial terms, at a rate of interest appropriate to the nature of the loan and the risks involved, and where possible should be secured on assets owned by the trading company or by a third party guarantee or other security. The loan should be properly documented, with clear repayment provisions.

51.4.6 Retaining profit

The difficulties in obtaining start-up finance can also apply to **working capital**. For charities' trading companies, maximum tax efficiency is achieved by donating 100% of profits to the parent charity [**50.2.7**]. In the past, the donation had to be made by the end of the financial year, leaving the trading company with no working capital. Now the trading company can retain some or all of its profits as temporary working capital, then donate the profits to the charity at any time in the nine months after the end of the financial year, as new funds come in [**51.7.3**].

Even with the nine-month delay in having to donate the profits, the trading company may still not have enough funds to operate effectively. In this situation, the charity may allow the company to retain some profits to cover operating costs and finance future growth, even though the company must pay tax on the retained profits. Alternatively, provided it has power to do so and the rules on loans are followed [**51.4.5**], the charity may be able to lend the company funds to cover operating costs. Specialist advice may be needed to ensure the trading company does not have to pay tax where, with appropriate planning, this could be avoided.

51.5 MANAGING THE TRADING COMPANY

What starts out as a clear relationship between the parent organisation and its trading company may become unclear and fraught a few years down the line. Procedures should be put in place from the beginning to minimise the risk of this.

51.5.1   Ownership and control

Typically the trading company is a company limited by shares, **wholly owned** by the parent. This means that all of its issued shares are held by the parent organisation if the parent is incorporated, or holding trustees or nominees [**20.4.4**] appointed by the parent if it is unincorporated.

If shares in the subsidiary are held by nominees or holding trustees rather than by the parent organisation itself, a clear agreement must be drawn up to ensure the parent organisation retains control.

If the trading company is limited by guarantee rather than by shares, it is **wholly controlled** if the parent organisation or individuals appointed by it are the only members of the trading company, or the parent organisation has the right to appoint and remove all the members of the trading company's governing body.

Where the trading company is wholly owned or controlled, the parent body legally has final control. If the parent does not approve of decisions made by its representatives on the trading company's governing body it can appoint new representatives, or can use company law procedures to remove them from office [**13.5.6**].

51.5.1.1   Who can be a director?

The parent organisation can appoint anyone who is at least 16 years old, including members of its staff, to serve on the governing body of its trading company. It should be clear what happens to the appointment of staff if they stop working for the parent, and procedures should be in place to ensure that the company always has the minimum number of directors required under its governing document.

There is nothing to stop staff of the parent organisation from being paid an additional amount for their service as directors of the trading company, particularly if they are doing it in their own time, but only the trading company's funds – not the charity's – can be used for this.

The parent organisation can also appoint members of its own governing body as members of the trading company's governing body. If the parent organisation is a charity, its trustees can be paid for serving as directors of the trading company only if the charity's governing document or the Charity Commission permits this.

To ensure there are some directors who do not have a conflict of loyalties [**15.2.3**, **51.5.2**], it is advisable to have some governing body members of the trading company who are not directly linked to the parent organisation, and *vice versa*.

51.5.2   Maintaining the boundaries

Particularly where members of the governing body or staff of the parent organisation are also governing body members or staff of the trading company, dangerous confusions and conflicts of interest may arise. For example if a trading company is having financial difficulties, it may be in its best interests to get a loan from the parent – but is it in the parent's best interest to make the loan? The case of Wicksteed Village Trust, where over £1 million of charitable funds were lent to a subsidiary company, illustrates the risks. There was no formal loan agreement and no formal repayment plan, and the trading company had insufficient reserves to enable it to operate. A Charity Commission enquiry resulted in a 12-year repayment plan being put in place on commercial terms.

Charity Commissioners, Wicksteed Village Trust: Report of inquiry, April 2005

To keep clear boundaries between the parent organisation and trading company, the objectives and targets set in both organisations' business plans and any loan repayment plan should be closely monitored and regularly reviewed. Any issues or problems should be dealt with before they become serious. Agendas, meetings, minutes, financial records, correspondence and decision making of the two bodies should be kept completely separate.

Governing body members and staff of the trading company should have appropriate role descriptions, and where the same people are involved in both organisations the roles should be clearly separated. Conflict of interest rules in relation to both the parent and the trading company must be strictly followed [**15.2**].

The trading company's governing body should include some members, perhaps with commercial or legal expertise, who are not on the parent organisation's governing body, or better still, have no direct association with the parent. The presence of independent governing body members not only enhances recognition that the trading company is a legally separate organisation with potential conflicts of interest with the parent, but also brings in a wider range of experience.

51.5.3 Staffing issues

If the parent organisation's staff will or may be asked to work for the trading company, a suitable clause should be included in the contract of employment [**27.1**]. If there is no such clause, they should be consulted and their consent obtained for any changes in their terms of employment. Varying employees' contracts without their consent could be a breach of contract [**26.9.3**] or, if an employee resigns, could be treated as constructive dismissal giving rise to a claim for unfair dismissal [**34.2.9**]. If employees do not agree to work for the trading company, the organisation should take legal advice before proceeding.

It may be appropriate to include additional clauses in employment contracts for staff working with the trading company covering, for example, preservation of commercial secrets [**43.1.5, 27.10.3**], disclosure of personal interests [**27.8.3**], or non-competition during the period of employment and possibly for a reasonable period thereafter [**26.8.2**].

If a charity's staff work for the trading company, the charity will need to charge the company for their time and related costs [**51.6.3**]. This could potentially have VAT implications [**57.13.1**]. In some situations it may be advantageous for the parent and trading company to hire staff jointly [**51.6.3.1**], or for staff to be employed separately by the parent and the trading company [**51.6.3.2**].

51.5.4 Working relationships

Legally and financially the parent body and trading company must be clearly separated, but it is important to maintain close working links and good communication. In particular the activities of the two organisations should not be incompatible, and the trading company should not do anything which undermines the parent's objects or good name.

51.5.5 Management charges

In addition to recovering the costs of providing premises, staff and other resources [**51.6.3**], many parent organisations make a general charge to cover supervision and management of the trading company. Recovery of the actual costs (based on a proper estimate) is acceptable for tax purposes, but a management charge which includes any element of profit is likely to be taxable. Even if there is no profit element it could be subject to VAT [**51.6.4**].

An inflated management charge is sometimes made as a way of transferring the profits of the trading company to the charity. This is not a tax-effective way to transfer profits and could jeopardise the parent charity's tax exemptions.

51.5.6 Insurance

Because the trading company is legally a completely separate body, it is not covered by any of the parent organisation's insurances [**chapter 23**] unless this has been specifically agreed with the insurers.

51.5.7 Fundraising arrangements

The rules for professional fundraisers and commercial participators [**48.6**] do not apply to the relationship between charitable institutions and their wholly owned trading companies, or where such companies are jointly owned by two or more charitable institutions. The Charity Commission recommends that trading companies comply with the rules even though they do not need to, but there is considerable disagreement about whether this is best practice.

51.5.8   Separation of accounts and administration

At the time of writing (mid 2009), the Charity Commission says in CC35 *Trustees, trading and tax* that it has no objections to a parent charity and its trading company having a joint bank account in order to take advantage of better terms from the bank. However, this is not generally considered to be good practice.

Even if a parent organisation and trading company share a bank account, their financial decision making and records must be completely separate. All paperwork and records, especially minutes, contracts and other legal documentation, must make absolutely clear which organisation is involved with each transaction.

The two organisations must have separate cheques, headed paper, compliments slips etc, and different email headers and footers. It would be a serious breach for a parent organisation's governing body to allow itself to become liable for the debts of its trading company by making a decision at the wrong meeting, using the wrong headed paper or creating confusion in any other way.

51.5.9   Insolvency of trading company

Part of the reason for carrying out trading through a trading company is to protect the parent organisation if the trading activities fail. This protection can be badly undermined if clear separation is not maintained between the activities of the parent and trading company.

The arrangements between the organisations should always reflect the possibility of the trading company's insolvency [**chapter 24**], and make provision where possible to give the parent a preferred position. This may be done by, for example, securing loans by debentures or mortgages [**59.5**], or ensuring that assets revert to the parent if the trading company becomes insolvent.

Whatever the parent organisation's feelings about its moral obligations, it should not meet the debts of an insolvent trading company unless it obtains definitive legal advice that this is appropriate and lawful.

51.6   PAYMENT FOR SHARED RESOURCES

The parent organisation must take care – especially if it is charitable – not to allow its funds or resources to be used for activities of the trading company which are outside the parent's objects or powers.

All transactions between the two bodies should be on an arm's length basis and should be clearly documented. Even though the trading company's profits will be donated to the parent, the parent must make full charges to the company for shared resources and the company must pay for them. There may be VAT implications in making these charges [**51.6.4**].

Apart from anything else, commercial good sense requires that costs are properly apportioned. Otherwise it may not become apparent that the trading company is showing a profit only because the parent organisation is providing free staff time, premises and running costs. Furthermore, if a trading company becomes insolvent, a parent company which has proper records of the amounts it is owed may be able to recover those debts in the same way as other creditors.

51.6.1   Intellectual property

The parent body should carefully control the trading company's use of its **intellectual property** (IP) rights such as its name, logo, copyright, trade marks, patents, website, databases and research. A formal agreement [**44.11**] should ensure fair payment, especially if the parent is a charity. The agreement should control the manner in which the IP is used, contain provisions for reviewing and terminating the agreement, ensure VAT is properly charged for the rights if required [**57.8.2**], and avoid tax liability [**56.4.14**] for the parent on fees received for use of the rights. It must be clear that IP rights revert to the parent if the trading company becomes insolvent or is wound up for any reason.

51.6.2 Premises

A trading company may share premises with its parent organisation, subject to any constraints in the organisation's lease or other title documentation, mortgage or insurance restrictions, planning permissions, or other restrictions on use of the premises. The parent should recover at least the full costs of those premises, and in most cases a full market rent.

Rate relief may not be available for the portion of the building used for non-charitable purposes [**63.2.3**], so this will have to be recovered through the rent or borne by the trading company. The arrangement between the parent and trading company may be a lease or licence [**60.4**, **60.5**], with careful thought given to whether it is prudent to grant a secure lease [**60.4.5**].

51.6.3 Staff, equipment and overheads

The parent should create a legally binding agreement by which it can recharge the trading company at appropriate intervals for the costs of staff time, shared equipment, use of facilities and other overheads.

While it may be tempting to charge a mark-up on these services and make some profit for the parent, a parent which is a charity needs to think very carefully before doing this. The provision of such services is unlikely to be part of its primary purpose, and as non-primary purpose trading any profit could be subject to tax unless it falls within the exemption for small-scale trading [**56.4.7**].

The supply of staff, most photocopying and many other services may be subject to VAT, even if the parent body charges for them at cost with no mark-up [**57.13**].

51.6.3.1 Jointly hired staff

One way to avoid substantial recharges for staff time is for relevant staff to be hired by both the parent and trading company. This can be done by having a contract which states that both organisations are jointly the employer [**25.4**]. Simply putting into a job description or contract that the staff member is supposed to work for both organisations does not create a joint contract.

For staff who are properly jointly hired, the two organisations can have an arrangement whereby one organisation handles the payment of salaries, deduction of PAYE etc and then recovers these costs (and no more) from the other organisation. There is no VAT liability on the reimbursement of the salary costs between joint employers [**57.13.1**].

Joint contracts can raise many other issues, for example around what happens if one of the employers becomes insolvent, or if one employer but not the other wants to discipline or dismiss the worker, or ensuring time paid for by a charity is not used for non-charitable work. To ensure these issues are fully considered, legal advice should be taken before drawing up a joint contract of employment.

51.6.3.2 Separate contracts

Another way to avoid large recharges is for staff to have separate contracts with each organisation, with each employer paying the staff for its agreed hours and operating its own PAYE. This can help to clarify the separate roles and accountability of an employee who is working for both the parent and trading company, and can also make it easier to have a staff member on two separate salary scales if this is appropriate. However, there could be disadvantages for the employee in relation to pension provision.

51.6.4 VAT

A variety of complex issues arise around VAT and the relationship between the parent body and trading company. VAT is explained in **chapter 57**, but specialist advice is essential.

51.6.4.1 Avoiding VAT registration

Especially when a trading company is being charged for a portion of running costs and staff wages with linked national insurance and pension costs, the parent body can quickly reach the threshold where it has to register for VAT (as at 1/8/09, £68,000 in any 12-month period).

VAT registration may be advantageous, because it enables the organisation to recover some or all of the VAT it pays out [**57.1.1**]. But for parent organisations which do not want to register, it may be possible to avoid registration by reducing the amount charged by the parent to the trading company, for example by having the trading company make as many of its purchases as it can direct from an outside supplier rather than through the parent, having the trading company pay its share of bills direct to the supplier, and/or the parent and trading company hiring staff jointly [**51.6.3.1**] or on separate contracts [**51.6.3.2**].

51.6.4.2 Putting costs through trading company

Rather than putting all costs through the parent organisation and charging the trading company, it may be tempting to do the reverse: to put everything through the trading company, and have the company charge the parent for its use. This can be done, but:

- if the parent is a charity, it will be necessary to ensure that all amounts paid to the trading company can be properly regarded as being for charitable purposes only, and the trading company will have to donate its profits back to the parent by gift aid, to ensure no tax is paid unnecessarily on the sums paid by the charity to the company;

- the trading company may have to register for VAT and then charge VAT to the parent, which the parent will not be able to recover unless it is VAT-registered, and perhaps not even then [**57.9**];

- even if the trading company provides goods, services or staff free to the parent, it may have to charge VAT on the supply.

51.6.4.3 VAT group

If both the parent and trading company are registered for VAT, no VAT has to be charged on invoices between members of the same VAT group [**57.2.4**].

51.7 PROFIT SHEDDING

Profit shedding refers to the transfer of profits to another body for the purpose of reducing or eliminating the tax due on the profits.

51.7.1 Non-charitable parent

If the parent is not a charity, there is generally no tax advantage in transferring a trading company's profits to the parent. The best that the company can do is deduct from its taxable profits certain small donations to a parent organisation established for educational, cultural, religious, recreational or benevolent purposes, but only if these donations can be shown to benefit the business [**50.9.1**].

51.7.2 Management charges

An inflated or spurious management charge by the charity [**51.5.5**] should not be used as a way of transferring the trading company's profits to the parent. HM Revenue and Customs might not allow such a payment as a deduction from profits, so the trading company would have to pay tax on all or some of the amount – and in any case the charity could be liable for tax on any profit element in the charge, unless it falls within the exemption for small-scale trading [**56.4.7**].

51.7.3 Gift aid

Unlike individual gift aid, where the charity recovers from HM Revenue and Customs the tax paid by the donor, a business (including a trading company) donates the full amount to the charity, including tax, and claims tax relief when calculating its profits for corporation tax [**56.2.3**]. There is no need for the company to fill in a gift aid declaration or any form for the charity.

A gift aid donation must actually be transferred from the company to the charity; it cannot simply be shown in both sets of books.

Where a charity's trading subsidiary wishes to donate all of its profits to the charity, there can be a problem because the profits are generally not accurately known by the end of the financial year. If the company were to donate too little it would have to pay tax on the retained profits; if it were to donate too much it would not be able to recover the overpayment from the charity. To avoid these problems and the to help ensure the company has working capital [**51.4.6**], charity trading subsidiaries have a nine-month period from the end of the financial year during which they can make the gift aid donation to the charity, but set it against their profits for the previous year.   *Income & Corporation Taxes Act 1988 s.339(7AA), inserted by Finance Act 2000 s.40*

51.7.3.1 Gift aid and sale of donated goods

If a trading company sells donated goods, these sales are eligible for zero rate VAT, but only if the company donates 100% of its profits from the sale of the donated goods to a charity. Such sales may raise complex issues around who the goods were donated to and who is selling them [**57.11.3**].

51.7.3.2 Deeds of covenant

Where a trading company entered into a **deed of covenant** [**50.2.6**] before 1 April 2000, the deed remains binding but the donation is made under gift aid and must be made gross (including tax) rather than net of tax.

The Charity Commission's view is that the parent charity should not cancel such covenants, because the deed of covenant is a legally binding obligation which technically safeguards the charity's interests. Instead, the charity should accept a gift aid payment in lieu of the payment due under the deed.

There is no longer any tax advantage in entering into a deed of covenant.

51.7.3.3 Substantial donor rules

The rules in the **Finance Act 2006** relating to **substantial donors** [**50.7**] do not apply to a trading subsidiary in relation to its charitable parent.

51.7.4 Dividends

Payment by **dividends** does not allow recovery of tax, so a charity should allow its trading company to use dividends only if there is a specific reason for doing so and only after taking appropriate advice.

Where the parent organisation is non-charitable, dividends are the normal route for transferring funds from the trading company to the parent.

51.7.5 Capital gains

Unlike a charity, the trading company is fully liable for tax on capital gains arising from the sale or disposal of assets [**56.4.16**]. This can be avoided by transferring the gain to the charity as a gift aid donation, and/or having assets such as freehold property which may give rise to a capital gain owned by the charity, rather than the trading company.

Resources: TRADING AND SOCIAL ENTERPRISE

Tax and VAT on trading income. See end of **chapters 56** and **57**.

Trading by charities. Charity Commission: www.charitycommission.gov.uk, 0845 3000 0218, email via website.

Statute law. www.opsi.gov.uk and www.statutelaw.gov.uk.

Much but not all case law. www.bailii.org.

Updates cross-referenced to this book. www.rclh.co.uk.

Chapter 52

CONTRACTS AND SERVICE AGREEMENTS

For sources of further information see end of chapter.

52.1 CLARIFYING THE DIFFERENCE

Public sector bodies are increasingly contracting out services which they formerly provided. In separate but related developments, many public sector bodies which formerly provided grants for voluntary organisations are changing those grants to service agreements or contracts, and many voluntary organisations are sub-contracting work to other organisations.

There is much confusion about the distinction between grants, service (or service level) agreements and contracts, and the terms are used in a wide variety of ways. But what something *is* depends on the nature of the transaction, not on what it is called. Regardless of what it is called, if it meets the legal criteria for being a contract it is a contract, and if it does not meet the criteria it is not a contract.

To exacerbate the confusion, an arrangement has to be considered not only in terms of contract law, but also in relation to VAT [**57.6.3**] and whether it is a trading activity for the purposes of tax and charity law [**56.3.4**, **51.1.2**]. For example, a purchase/funding arrangement might be a contract under contract law but not be treated as a business supply for the purposes of VAT law – or it might not legally be a contract, but still be a business supply for VAT purposes.

52.1.1 Grants

The essence of a **grant** is that it is a donation or gift to support an organisation, service or activity, with the funder having no legal right to receive anything in return other than perhaps a simple acknowledgement, and reports on how the funds have been used [**48.3**]. This is different from a **contract** [**52.1.2**], where the organisation is paid to provide something *in exchange for* the payment.

770

A grant is given in trust [**48.2.1**], and if it is not used for the purposes for which it is given the funder can ask for it back, or can take legal action for breach of trust. Provided the grant has been properly used for the purposes for which it was given, the funder is unlikely to be able to require repayment or take legal action if the recipient does not comply with administrative requirements such as providing statistics – although without the statistics, it may be difficult for the organisation to show that the grant was used for the intended purposes.

A grant is by its nature **discretionary**, and may be changed or withdrawn at any time by the donor. (This does not apply to grants which a public body has a statutory obligation to provide, such as grants for students.) A donor may withdraw a grant, reduce it or pay it late, for any reason or none. The recipient organisation is unlikely to have any recourse in law, unless the grant or donation has been made as a deed [**20.3**], in which case it is enforceable by the recipient in the same way as a contract would be [**21.1**]; or in certain limited circumstances, a decision of a public body might be open to judicial review [**48.4.3**, **64.1.1**].

52.1.2 Contracts

A **contract** is a legally binding agreement between two or more parties [**chapter 21**]. An agreement is generally a contract if it involves **consideration**, with one party paying or providing something of value to the other in exchange for goods, services or something else of value; each party has accepted the other's offer; and the parties intend the agreement to be legally binding.

An arrangement where one party pays for something is virtually always treated by the courts as contractual. Even if the parties explicitly state that they do not intend it to be legally binding [**52.1.3.2**], the courts may find it to be binding and therefore a contract.

52.1.2.1 Legal enforceability

A contract can be enforced through the courts by either party [**21.7**]. If the provider of goods or services does not do what has been agreed, the purchaser can take action to require it to be done, terminate the contract and/or seek compensation for its losses. If the purchaser does not pay on time or fulfil its other obligations, the provider can take action to require payment and can seek compensation for losses suffered.

Legal action is, of course, the final step. The vast majority of contractual disputes are resolved by negotiation between the parties [**21.7.1**].

52.1.2.2 Tax and VAT

Grant income is not subject to tax [**56.3.4**], and goods and services provided under a grant are outside the scope of VAT [**57.1.3**].

An arrangement which involves payment received as consideration [**21.1.1**] is likely to be classed by HMRC as trading [**51.1.2**] and therefore potentially liable to tax, and is likely to be treated for VAT purposes as a business supply [**57.6.3**] and therefore potentially subject to VAT. However, different criteria are used for tax law, VAT law and contract law. A particular arrangement might be subject to tax and/or VAT but not be contractually binding, or could be contractually binding but not subject to tax and/or VAT because of the exemptions available for charities and some other voluntary organisations. It is essential to take specialist advice on these matters.

52.1.3 Service agreements

Terms such as **service agreement** and **service level agreement** (SLA) have no meaning in law, and are used in different ways by different purchasers or funders of voluntary sector services. It is essential to clarify what each person who uses the term means by it.

More importantly, all parties involved in a service agreement or SLA must be aware that the legal nature of an arrangement is not changed simply because of what it is called. The fact that 'service agreement' may sound less intimidating than 'contract' does not change the reality of what the arrangement is.

Some of the ways the terms 'service agreement' or 'service level agreement' are used are described below.

52.1.3.1   'Grant'

A service agreement or SLA may simply be a grant, perhaps with more detailed conditions of grant aid or a more detailed description of the service. It would be a matter for HMRC or the courts to decide in any particular case whether they perceive the agreement as a grant or as a payment for a service.

52.1.3.2   Non-binding agreement

A service agreement or SLA may clearly be an agreement to purchase services, but with an explicit statement that it is not intended to be legally binding. One of the key elements in creating a contract is the parties' intention to create a legally binding agreement [**21.1.1**], so if both parties have agreed that the arrangement will not be legally binding, it cannot generally be enforced in the courts. But in exceptional cases a court might agree to hear such a case, and could find that the agreement was in fact binding.

Even if the arrangement is not legally binding, it can be treated as trading for tax purposes and a business activity for VAT [**52.1.2.2**].

52.1.3.3   Dependent on process

Some purchasers say that after a formal process of competitive tendering [**52.2**] they award a contract, and if there is no formal competitive process they enter into a service agreement. But in relation to whether something is or is not contractual, the process by which an agreement is reached is irrelevant.

52.1.3.4   Internal agreement

An agreement between departments or units *within* an organisation cannot be a contract, because there is legally only one party (the main organisation). Where organisations are structured so that one budget-holding department or unit 'purchases' services from another, the agreements between departments are often called service agreements or SLAs.

52.1.4   The Compact

The Compact, local Compacts and Compact codes of practice [**48.4.1**] set out good practice in relationships between the public and voluntary sectors. Of particular importance in relation to contracts and service agreements are the *Compact code of funding and procurement*, and the Commission for the Compact's *Commissioning guidance* [see end of **chapter 48**].

The Compact for the Commission has said that EU procurement requirements [**52.2.1**] are not incompatible with the Compact, and that public sector purchasers should be able to comply with both EU rules and Compact principles.

The Compact and documents issued under it are not legally binding, but provide a framework for negotiations with a public body.

52.1.5   Human rights implications

Charitable and other independent care homes which provide accommodation plus nursing or personal care to individuals under local authority contracts are carrying out functions of a public nature and are thus public authorities as defined under the **Human Rights Act 1998** [**64.3.2**]. As a public authority, they are obliged to comply with the HRA.   *Health & Social Care Act 2008 s.145*

Where a public authority has a duty to ensure the provision of other services (not in care homes), a charity or other organisation providing that service under contract may or may not be carrying out a public function. This depends on the specific circumstances in each case.   *R v Leonard Cheshire Foundation & another [2002] EWCA Civ 366; Weaver, R (on the application of) v London & Quadrant Housing Trust [2008] EWHC 1377 (Admin)*

Even if an organisation is not defined as carrying out a public function, the public sector purchaser must comply with the HRA in all aspects of its work, and may seek to require any organisation providing services on its behalf or with its funding to do so as well. Voluntary organisations need to ensure they do not accept such obligations unless they are certain they can comply with them.

At the time of writing (mid 2009) the government was considering defining all charities as public authorities under the HRA.

52.2 ROUTES TO A CONTRACT

Competitive tendering (or just **tendering**) takes place when a purchaser invites bids from potential providers of goods or a service. Tendering may be **compulsory**, where European or national legislation requires a public sector body to invite competitive bids [**52.2.1**]; required under a public sector body's **standing orders** [**52.2.2**] or other rules; or **voluntary**, if the body is not required to invite competitive bids but decides to do so anyway.

For the tendering process, see **52.3**. Contracts may also be issued non-competitively [**52.2.2.2**], where the purchasing body's procedures allow this.

52.2.1 Public procurement

Contracting authorities must invite competitive bids from across the EU for a **public procurement** – a contract for supplies (goods), services and works of more than a specified value. The contract thresholds change every two years, and from 1 January 2008 range from £54,327 to £139,983 for services or supplies, and from £679,090 to £3,497,313 for works. Information about contracting authorities, public contracts and the public procurement thresholds is available from the **Office of Government Commerce** [see end of chapter].

Public Contracts Regulations 2006 [SI 2006/5]

Contracts below the relevant threshold are not covered by the procurement rules, nor are social welfare and health services (called **part B services**). However, these must comply with the principles underlying the rules [**52.2.2**].

A **contracting authority** is a government department, local authority, or other part of central or local government; or any organisation set up 'to meet needs in the general interest, not having an industrial or commercial nature', if the organisation is financed wholly or mainly by a contracting authority or if more than 50% of its governing body is appointed by a contracting authority.   *PC Regs 2006 reg.3*

This means that local authorities, health authorities, government agencies, NHS trusts and similar bodies must undertake a competitive tendering process for many large contracts. The same procedures could apply to voluntary organisations which fall into the definition of purchasing authority and enter into relevant contracts to purchase goods, services or works [**21.3.3**].

52.2.1.1 OJEU procedures

Contracts above the procurement thresholds must be advertised in the Official Journal of the EU (OJEU). The procurement process – usually called the **OJEU procedure** – may be:

- **open**, where anyone interested may tender for the contract;
- **restricted**, where those interested make an **expression of interest** and only those who are shortlisted (usually at least five) are invited to tender;
- **competitive dialogue**, where those who have been shortlisted enter into discussions with the purchaser to refine the requirements, and some or all of those bidders are invited to tender; or
- **negotiated**, where the purchaser selects one or more potential providers with whom to negotiate the contracts – in some cases without the contract needing to be advertised in OJEU.   *Public Contracts Regulations 2006 [SI 2006/5] regs.11-18*

52.2.1.2 Reserved contracts

Under EU procurement rules, a contracting authority may specify certain contracts as **reserved contracts**. Tendering for reserved contracts is open only to **supported factories, businesses** and **employment programmes**, where more than 50% of the workers are disabled people who by the nature or severity of their disability are unable to work in the open labour market. *Public Contracts Regulations 2006 [SI 2006/5] reg.7*

52.2.1.3 Framework agreements

EU procurement rules allow a contracting authority to enter into a **framework contract** with a number of suppliers, rather than entering into contracts with individual suppliers. Under this arrangement, the authority **calls off** supplies or services as required, and enters into specific contracts for those supplies or services. A framework contract cannot be for more than four years, but the called off contracts can be for a longer period. *Public Contracts Regulations 2006 [SI 2006/5] reg.19*

52.2.2 Standing orders and other rules

Contracts which are not subject to the public procurement rules may be subject to other statutory rules, for example on lettings or disposal of property. There may also be binding guidance, for example on the way funding issues are dealt with.

Even where there are no external rules, public sector bodies are subject to EU principles of non-discrimination, equal treatment, transparency and proportionality. Because of the need for transparency, open advertising may be necessary even for contracts that are below the relevant procurement threshold. A public sector body's rules are likely to be set out in their own **standing orders**, which typically require competitive tendering for contracts of more than a specified value.

Many public sector contracts that are below the OJEU thresholds are advertised on the Supply2gov website at www.supply2.gov.uk.

52.2.2.1 Select list tendering

Where public contract regulations or standing orders do not require contracts to be advertised openly, the purchaser may invite bids from potential contractors on a **select list** or **approved list**. These are contractors who have met the purchaser's criteria for inclusion on the list. This allows for competition, without the cost of open advertising.

52.2.2.2 Contracts issued without competition

For small contracts, public bodies may be able to issue contracts without putting the work out to tender or getting quotes from select list providers. This may give the provider considerable scope for negotiating the terms of the contract.

52.2.3 The best value framework

The **best value** framework requires local authorities and some other bodies to 'secure continuous improvement in the way in which its functions are exercised, having regard to a combination of economy, efficiency and effectiveness'. *Local Government Act 1999 pt.I, amended by Local Government & Public Involvement in Health Act 2007 sch.8*

Best value authorities must draw up annual performance plans setting out services to be provided, current standards and projected improvements. All services and activities must be reviewed against these projections, on a five-yearly basis.

Central government and the Audit Commission have wide powers to intervene, in order to monitor and if necessary take steps to ensure best value is achieved. Organisations involved in contracts, service agreements or grant funding from best value authorities must ensure they understand what the authority expects from them in terms of its annual plan, performance targets and reviews, and should consider how the need for competition may affect them in future.

52.2.4 Consortium bids

Especially for large or complex contracts, it may be tempting to set up a joint arrangement – which may be called a consortium, partnership, or anything similar – to apply for a contract. If this does not involve the creation of a separate legal entity, it runs the risk of creating an unincorporated **partnership** [11.3.1] and the partners could potentially be guilty of **bid rigging** [52.3.2.3]. An alternative is to set up a separate organisation to apply for contracts, but this brings its own complexities [**11.3.2**]. The Office of the Third Sector [see end of chapter] has guidance on consortia bids for contracts, but legal advice is essential.

52.3   THE TENDERING PROCESS

Tendering processes vary greatly in formality and flexibility, depending on the size and nature of the contract and the applicable regulations. Successful tendering depends on a very clear understanding of the particular tender requirements and the competition for each contract.

In most tenders, the bid constitutes a legally binding offer which can be accepted or refused within a time limit. This one-sidedly exposes the bidder to a potential obligation, while leaving the purchaser free to accept or refuse. This situation is exacerbated by the fact that the tender offer is generally on detailed contractual terms which are set by the purchaser and are heavily biased in its favour.

In some situations, the service specification and/or contract terms may be open to negotiation before, and sometimes after, acceptance of a bid. A bidder should do all it can to modify terms in its favour at an early stage, or if that is not possible, seek to agree that further negotiations can take place after the contract is awarded.

Some aspects of the tender process are explained here.

52.3.1   Specification

A **tender specification** describes the services, activities or goods which the purchaser wants to purchase. It is generally in two parts: the **service specification** sets out what is to be done or provided and similar matters relating directly to the service [**52.5.2**], and the **terms and conditions** set out the terms under which the service or goods are to be provided.

Usually the purchaser draws up the tender specification, sometimes after consultation with potential providers or service users. But sometimes the purchaser might place the onus on the bidders to specify the service and their terms. In this case the potential provider has to 'second guess' what the purchaser wants and what other bidders will offer. It is important to obtain the maximum possible information from the potential purchaser and other sources before proceeding.

The preparation of a service specification generally requires considerable time and research. To avoid it being misused by potential competitors, distribution should be limited. It is also not unknown for purchasers to ask potential providers to draw up specifications, then not to offer the contract to any of them but to re-advertise it using one of the provider's specifications as the purchasing body's own specification. Making clear that the specification is the copyright work of the bidding organisation [**44.2.3**] may reduce the risk of this happening.

52.3.2   Costing, pricing and full cost recovery

From the service and contract specifications, the service can be **costed**. Once the cost is known, a decision can be made about **pricing** – what to charge for the service [**52.5.5**]. There is more flexibility at the costing/pricing stage if the potential provider has itself prepared the service specification and can adapt it to fit a particular pricing structure.

52.3.2.1   Full cost recovery

Full cost recovery (FCR) means charging for services or goods at a rate which covers not only the direct costs, including the full costs of staff directly involved, but also a relevant portion of related costs such as premises, insurance, office costs, use of equipment, and costs related to management, governance, human resources, finance or similar support. Full cost recovery should also allow for future costs, such as redundancy pay [**52.5.6.2**] when the contract comes to an end.

Guidance on implementing full cost recovery is available from ACEVO and the Charity Finance Directors' Group [see end of chapter], and in documents published by HM Treasury and available on the 'public spending and reporting' section of their website [see end of chapter]. Costings which should be covered by contract fees are listed in *Improving financial relationships with the third sector: Guidance to funders and purchasers*, published by the Treasury in 2006.

52.3.2.2 Use of a charity's funds to subsidise public services

A charity can use its funds to provide or subsidise services that the public body has power (but not a statutory duty) to provide, and in many cases the funds can also be used to provide services that the public body has a statutory duty to provide [**5.3.5**]. Information is available in CC37 *Charities and public service delivery* from the Commission [see end of chapter].

52.3.2.3 Market rigging

It is a criminal offence for two or more parties to fix prices, divide up markets ('you run services in the north of the county, and we'll run them the south'), limit the supply of goods or services, or engage any other form of **bid rigging** or **market rigging**. To avoid potentially high fines, organisations should be very cautious about discussing prices or division of markets with any other potential supplier, or discussing potential bids for any contract – not just public sector contracts – with any other potential bidder, and should take legal advice before doing so.
Enterprise Act 2002 s.188

Information about these **cartel offences** is available from the Office of Fair Trading [see end of chapter].

52.3.2.4 State aid

EU restrictions on **state aid** [**48.4.2**] do not apply in situations where there is genuine competition for a contract. But where any element of subsidy or support is given to certain bidders or potential suppliers the rules could apply, and specialist advice must be taken. An organisation which receives illegal state aid could be required, for up to 10 years afterwards, to repay the funds to the public body.

52.3.3 Submitting the tender bid

If a tender specification indicates the form in which the bid is to be submitted, all instructions must be carefully followed. Deadlines are important and for competitive tendering cannot be stretched. Copies should be kept of everything.

Submitting the bid generally irrevocably commits the bidder, so it should be submitted only if all the implications have been fully considered and submission has been properly authorised. In some cases it may be possible to submit a conditional bid, for example 'conditional on TUPE [**52.5.6.1**] not applying', but otherwise a bid can be subject to further negotiation only if this is clearly agreed by both parties. Where changes are allowed, they should be agreed only after carefully reconsidering the implications for service delivery and cost.

52.3.4 Disclosure

The **Freedom of Information Act 2000** [**43.2**] requires public authorities, in certain circumstances, to disclose information they hold to anyone who makes an application. In the course of negotiating and entering into public sector funding arrangements, organisations will invariably disclose information to public authorities which could subsequently be disclosed. This could prejudice the organisation, since direct competitors would be given sensitive information relating to the tendering process. The potential implications of this should be considered when bidding for public sector contracts or applying for public sector grants.

During or after the contract term, the public body may be required to disclose information about the work carried out under the contract, and the organisation which has won the contract may thus be required to provide the necessary information to the public body.

The Freedom of Information Act does not apply directly to private and voluntary sector bodies carrying out contracts on behalf of public bodies, but the government is keeping this under review.

52.4 AGREEING THE CONTRACT

Before entering into a contract or service agreement, the governing body must understand the terms and conditions, as well as the implications of it being (or not being) legally enforceable. The agreement should be approved by the governing body or by a sub-committee, officer or staff member explicitly authorised to do so by the governing body. Only an authorised person should sign a contract, and it should be clear that they are signing on behalf of the organisation.

Legal advice will generally be necessary before entering into a service agreement or contract, at least until the organisation is accustomed to the process. Even where a contract or service agreement emanates from a previous grant funder with whom there is a relationship of trust, this should not lead to any less careful attention to detail. A checklist of key clauses and concerns can be very useful in reviewing contracts. The Charity Commission's CC37 *Charities and public service delivery* provides a useful starting point. Its guidance is suitable for non-charities as well as charities.

52.4.1 Power to contract

A contract may set out the powers under which the purchaser is acting, especially if it is a public sector body. If this is not included, the organisation should ensure the contract is within the purchaser's legal powers. Similarly the contract may set out the voluntary organisation's relevant constitutional objects and powers. Even if these are not specified, the organisation should enter only into agreements which are within its objects and powers [**7.4.3**].

To make clear that the organisation is acting as an independent service provider, the contract might include a clause stating that neither the organisation nor its employees are an agent or partner of the purchaser. This may help to ensure that the organisation will not be treated in law as an agent for the purchaser [**20.5**] or be held to have entered into a partnership arrangement [**11.3.1**].

52.4.2 Using model contracts

Model contracts for specific types of service are available from many umbrella or support organisations. It is always worth contacting a relevant organisation before entering into discussions about a contract or service agreement. As with all model contracts, care should be taken to ensure they are appropriate to each situation.

52.4.3 Drafts

Most contracts go through several drafts before they are finally signed. It can be helpful to ensure that each draft is dated and marked 'Draft' or 'Subject to contract', so it is easy to see which is the most recent version and so it cannot be taken as the final version. The most recent version should always be carefully scrutinised. Even an apparently minor change in wording or a typing mistake may have significant implications.

52.4.4 Annexes and schedules

Any document referred to in the contract and incorporated as part of it should generally be attached to the contract as an appendix, annex or schedule. A contract should never be agreed if the parties have not seen and agreed all the relevant annexes or other documents incorporated as part of the contract.

52.5 CONTENT OF A CONTRACT OR SERVICE AGREEMENT

There is no standard format for a contract, but set out below are some of the provisions commonly included in contracts and service agreements between public sector bodies and voluntary organisations, or between voluntary organisations contracting with each other. For more about contract terms in general, see **21.2**.

Where contract provisions are dictated by a purchaser and are manifestly unfair, it may be possible for a provider to complain to the Office of Fair Trading or under the Compact [**52.1.4**] that the contract terms are unfair [**21.2.7**]. An example is where the purchaser sets the terms and conditions and a maximum price it is willing to pay, and the price is unrealistically low.

52.5.1   Duration

The starting date and duration of the contract should be specified. The duration might be a specified period or ending date, or 'until terminated by either side in accordance with the terms of this agreement'.

Public sector bodies are not allowed to enter into contracts which 'fetter their discretion' (prevent them making free choices). They must retain the right to find other providers, so they must not commit themselves contractually for a longer period than is reasonable.

52.5.1.1   Rolling contracts

A contract for a specified period which contains provision to be extended (rolled over) at agreed intervals is called a **rolling contract**. A three-year contract, for example, might be rolled over for a further year after each satisfactory annual review, or might be rolled over for a further three years at the end of each three-year period. 'Rolling contract' may also refer to a contract which continues (rolls on) until one party terminates it. If a contract is to be 'rolling', it is essential to define within the contract what this is intended to mean.

52.5.2   Service specification

The service specification defines the service(s) to be provided and the required quantity and quality. It covers the nature of the service, who it is for, and quantity and quality criteria. The level of detail will depend on the nature and complexity of the service.

52.5.2.1   Service description

The service description should include the aims of the purchaser and the providing organisation; the name or description and general nature of the scheme, project or activity purchased under the agreement; what the service is expected to achieve (service objectives); and a description of the service. The service description should be detailed enough to make clear what is expected, but should generally avoid an over-rigid specification which does not allow for flexibility.

The organisation should commit itself only to what it knows it can deliver – not what it aspires to. Failure to comply with any aspect of the contract could lead to the provider not being paid for services already provided, having to return to the purchaser payments received in advance, and/or being required to compensate the purchaser for losses it has suffered because of the provider's failure to deliver the service as required.

52.5.2.2   Users/clients

It may be appropriate to define the people for whom the service is intended. This may include, for example, eligibility criteria, referral and acceptance procedures, whether the organisation can refuse to accept potential clients referred by the purchaser, how clients will be involved in decisions about services, how progress will be assessed, and procedures for discharge or onward referral to other services.

52.5.2.3   Outputs

Purchasers are increasingly unwilling to pay for a service without an indication of the quantity to be provided. These are sometimes called **output indicators**, and may be defined in terms of number of people, number of sessions or visits, opening hours or hours of availability. The providing organisation must be absolutely certain that it will be able to meet these obligations throughout the full period of the contract, especially during periods of staff holidays or other absence.

Where the quantity is given as a minimum, the contract should make clear what happens if more or less than the minimum is provided, and what happens if this is for reasons outside the provider's control.

Any contract requiring an open-ended service ('all clients referred by the purchaser' or 'all enquirers') needs careful scrutiny.

Particular attention should be given to terms such as 'every day' (does this mean 365/366 days a year, or only weekdays, or only weekdays which are not public holidays?) and 'during normal working hours' (whose normal working hours – the provider's or the purchaser's?).

If a new service is being started, adequate time and funding should be allowed for the start-up period.

52.5.2.4   Quality

Most contracts include **performance indicators** to assess the quality of service. While the organisation should aim for the highest standards, it should commit it-self within the contract only to what it knows it can provide. Where quality is to be monitored, the organisation should ensure that the monitoring processes are appropriate and transparent, and that it knows how the monitoring will be carried out, by whom, how often and against what standards.

52.5.2.5   Outcomes

Similarly, many contracts include **outcome indicators** to assess the impact or results achieved by the organisation's work. Particular care needs to be taken where outcomes are intangible ('increased confidence') or could be significantly affected by factors outside the organisation's control (an obligation to get clients into paid work, at a time when local businesses are declining). As with quality, organisations should commit themselves only to what they know they can achieve and assess, and should be especially wary of payments that are dependent on results over which the organisation may have little or no control.

52.5.2.6   Compliance with public sector duties

Public sector bodies are subject to many duties that do not directly apply to private or voluntary sector bodies, such as their duties to promote equality of opportunity [**42.2**], provide information under the **Freedom of Information Act** [**43.2**] and **Environmental Information Regulations** [**63.12.1**], and comply with the **Human Rights Act** [**64.3**]. Such obligations may be passed on to provider organisations through the contract. Organisations should not agree to comply with these obligations without understanding what is involved and what it could mean for them.

52.5.2.7   Compliance with the purchaser's policies

As well as being obliged to comply with a purchaser's statutory duties [above], the service specification may specify that the organisation must comply with specific policies required by the purchaser. Care should be taken before committing the organisation to complying with the purchaser's (or anyone else's) equal opportunities, data protection, child or adult protection or any other policies which could be changed in future without the organisation's agreement, and could increase the cost of delivering the service.

52.5.2.8   Management responsibilities

Depending on the nature of the service, it may be appropriate to specify:

- which decisions, if any, require consultation with the purchaser, and the procedures for such consultation and for resolving disputes;

- arrangements, if any, for a liaison group or other body to oversee or advise on services;

- whether the purchaser requires representation on the organisation's governing body or a committee overseeing the service, and a statement that such representative(s) shall not have voting rights, or shall not have voting rights on any matter relating to the contract;

- confidentiality of information and compliance with data protection rules, including provision for destruction or return of personal data at the end of the contract period [**43.1**, **43.3**];
- the organisation's right to make all decisions, other than those covered in the agreement, about eligibility for services, method of provision and management of the service.

52.5.2.9 Monitoring and evaluation

The contract might specify:

- how services will be assessed, how frequently and by whom;
- content and frequency of monitoring reports by the organisation;
- provision for inspections, surveys of users, meetings with users, and independent (external) assessment;
- the purchaser's right of access, if any, to the organisation's premises, services or information;
- procedures for negotiating changes in services due to changing needs or demand.

The purchaser has a right to require proof that services are being provided as required under the contract. Unless legislation or the contract specifies otherwise, it has no right to other information apart from charity and company annual reports [**54.2.9**, **54.3.8**].

The organisation should consider whether monitoring imposes unnecessary costs, is unnecessarily intrusive, interferes with service provision, or requires disclosures which are not allowed under the **Data Protection Act** [**43.3.4**] or other confidentiality obligations [**43.1.1**]. Disclosure issues may be particularly relevant where the purchaser is a potential competitor to provide the service, or where the purchaser demands identifying details for individual service users.

Monitoring and evaluation costs should be included in the price [**52.5.5.1**].

52.5.3 Sub-contracting

The contract may indicate whether the organisation is allowed to sub-contract some or all of the work. In some circumstances this might be a requirement, for example where a lead organisation is taking on a contract where some work will be undertaken by other organisations.

Where work is sub-contracted, the lead organisation remains responsible for the full contract, even for sub-contracted work, unless liability for sub-contracted work is explicitly excluded. The lead organisation should ensure it has appropriate contracts or other agreements with the bodies to which it is sub-contracting.

52.5.4 Enforcement by third parties

A contract which provides a benefit to a third party – such as a contract between an organisation and a local authority under which the organisation provides services to a client – can be enforced by that third party unless his or her third party rights are validly excluded [**21.1.5**]. The contract should make clear whether – as will be generally be the case – the rights of third parties are to be excluded.

52.5.5 Payment

The section on financial conditions may include some or all of the following points.

52.5.5.1 Price

The stated price should specify the fee basis. This may be, for example:

- **fixed fee**: an agreed sum;
- **actual cost basis**: often with a fixed maximum sum, and perhaps with any unspent funds clawed back [below];
- **block** or **volume fee**: an agreed sum for a minimum and/or maximum number of units (clients, hours, sessions etc);

- **unit** or **spot basis** : an agreed sum for each unit (client, hour, session etc);
- **cost plus** or **block plus basis**: a fixed sum, plus an extra fee for each unit or for each unit above the agreed minimum or maximum.

Particular care should be taken with actual cost pricing, to ensure agreement about what is included in the cost. With a contract, the organisation is being paid to provide a service and so long as it is provided, it should be of no concern to the purchaser how much (or how little) it actually costs to provide it. **Clawback** [**48.4.4**] is a relic of grant funding and should have no place in contract funding.

The contract should be clear about the period covered by the agreed fee, any provision for increases, and who meets extra costs arising because of variation due to legislative or regulatory change. The contract might specify whether a charge is to be made to users, and how the amount will be determined.

52.5.5.2 Provision for inflation

If the contract will or may last more than 12 months, the provider should have the right to increase fees on a fixed date. Providers need to ensure that any such **inflation clause** gives them a right to a measurable increase. A clause such as 'Fees will be increased on 1 April 2011 and in every subsequent year by the percentage agreed by the purchaser's social services committee' leaves all the discretion with the purchaser, and may lead to an impossibly low increase.

A specific index such as the retail price index (RPI) should be used only if it is appropriate and is likely to cover the provider's cost increases – if wages are increasing faster than prices, RPI will not do so. The contract should specify factors such as which month's figures are to be used, what happens if the index has gone down rather than up, and if RPI is used whether it is the 'all items' RPI or the RPI excluding mortgage or other payments.

52.5.5.3 Provision for increased needs of clients

The costs of providing some services can vary dramatically depending on the support needs of a service user. If, for example, a service user starts to need two care workers rather than one, costs can increase dramatically. Service providers need to reserve the right to increase fees in these cases. If purchasers will not agree to this sort of clause, or perhaps a range of fees across a band of needs, providers may need to review the service specification and reserve the right to stop providing services for people whose needs take them outside certain criteria.

Costs may also increase due to external factors. A war, for example, can lead to an increased number of asylum seekers moving to an area, which can put pressure on drop-in or advice services. Organisations need to be wary of contracts requiring them to provide services to everyone who demands them or to everyone referred by the purchasing body, with no provision for additional payment.

52.5.5.4 VAT

A quoted price is generally assumed to include any VAT which is payable, unless it explicitly says that VAT is not included [**57.6.3**, **57.10**]. It is therefore essential for the provider to include a statement in all contracts and service agreements saying all payments to be made under the agreement are exclusive of VAT.

If the organisation is registered for VAT and has to charge VAT on the service, this enables it to charge VAT at whatever the current rate is. If a VAT-inclusive fee had been specified and the VAT rate then goes up, the organisation cannot increase the amount for VAT.

If the organisation is not yet registered for VAT but will or may have to register in future and charge VAT on the service, this statement enables it to charge VAT when it registers. Without the statement, the quoted price would be assumed to include the VAT.

Even if the service is exempt from VAT [**57.7**], this clause allows the organisation to charge VAT if the service becomes subject to VAT.

Especially when changing from grant funding to service agreements or contracts, it is important to obtain specialist advice about the potential VAT implications.

52.5.5.5   Payment terms

A contract should specify:

- the frequency of payment (monthly, quarterly etc), and whether it will be made in advance, midway through the period or in arrears;
- when payment is due (for example 15 days before the start of the quarter, 28 days after date of invoice);
- whether payment is made automatically or only on submission of the provider's invoice;
- whether payment is contingent on the purchaser receiving monitoring or financial reports or other information from the organisation;
- whether interest will be charged on late payments and if so whether this is on contractual terms or in accordance with the **Late Payment of Commercial Debts (Interest) Act 1998 [21.2.3]**, which entitles providers to charge interest at a statutory rate and statutory compensation even if this is not specified in the contract;
- what happens if the organisation has been underpaid or overpaid.

Particular attention should be given to **cashflow**, especially where payment is in arrears, or is spread evenly across a period but the organisation will have substantial outlay at the start of the period or other peak times.

52.5.5.6   Financial monitoring and review

Provision for financial monitoring may be included as part of a contract. The organisation may be required to provide financial reports or accounts to the purchaser, and procedures may be included for reviewing and varying unforeseen financial costs.

52.5.6   Staffing

The contract may specify matters such as staff numbers and/or ratios, qualifications, procedures for criminal record checks, and provision for staff training and development. It may have provisions relating to use of agency and temporary staff, use of volunteers within the contract, and/or cover during holiday, sickness, maternity, paternity, adoption and other leave.

52.5.6.1   Transfer of undertaking

An organisation taking over a service previously provided by another body is likely to be affected by the **Transfer of Undertakings (Protection of Employees) Regulations** (TUPE) [29.7]. This is a very complex area and it is essential for the organisation to carry out appropriate due diligence [29.7.3] into any incoming workforce, and to seek independent legal advice (*not* from the local authority or other body from whom it is taking over the service) at a very early stage.

The organisation should ensure the fee it receives under the contract covers its liabilities if it is obliged to take on the employees who previously provided the service, and in particular to ensure that the fee will cover contractual pay increases and pension contributions, and potential redundancy pay.

52.5.6.2   Redundancy

Redundancies may arise during a contract if there is a reduction in the volume of services required, or at the end of a contract if the relevant staff do not transfer under TUPE to another provider. Any organisation entering into a contract (or any other funding arrangement) should ensure it budgets for potential redundancy costs.

Redundancy costs can be particularly high in relation to staff transferred to the organisation under TUPE, if they have several years' continuous service [26.5] and/or have a contractual entitlement to more than statutory redundancy pay. In the absence of any contractual agreement with the purchaser, all of these costs would fall on the service provider as the employer at the time of redundancy.

52.5.7 Premises, equipment and other support

The contract should specify any support to be provided by the purchaser: training, use of vehicles or equipment, vehicle maintenance, premises etc. If the purchaser is providing accommodation, the contract might include provisions about this, but it is nearly always better to have premises matters in a separate lease or licence [**chapter 62**].

If the contract provides for the purchaser to give premises, equipment or vehicles to the organisation or if the sum to be paid includes capital expenditure, the contract should clarify ownership of the items and any restrictions on their sale or disposal [**48.4.4**]. The EU state aid rules [**48.4.2**] may need to be considered.

52.5.8 Indemnity and insurance

The purchaser may require the organisation to indemnify (compensate) it for any claims, losses or expenses against it arising from the services provided by the organisation [**21.2.6**]. The organisation must look carefully at the extent of the indemnity clause and whether it is possible to insure its obligations, and must allow for the cost of such insurance.

A contract may specify that the organisation has to take out public liability [**23.5.1**], professional indemnity [**23.5.3**] and/or other insurances, including insurance to indemnify the purchaser. It is not uncommon for a purchaser to require proof that the insurances are in place and are renewed.

52.5.9 Information

The contract should contain a warranty that the purchaser has provided all the information it holds relevant to the delivery of the service, and will provide any further information as it becomes aware of it. This is especially important where the organisation is taking over a service previously provided by the purchaser.

52.5.10 Variation

Any contract may be varied (changed) if the parties agree, although in some situations further payment or other consideration may be necessary in order for the variation to be valid [**21.5.2**]. The contract might include provision for regular reviews at which the need for variation is discussed, or may include a procedure for agreeing changes. There is no obligation on either party to agree changes proposed in future, and lack of agreement will generally leave the old terms in place.

Providers should not agree clauses allowing the purchaser to make unilateral changes.

52.5.11 Disputes and breach of contract

If either side does not fulfil its contractual obligations, this is a breach of contract [**21.6.6**, **22.5**]. There may also be disputes as to how the contract is to take effect, particularly about price or other variation. Ultimately the injured party can take the other to court [**21.7**], but long before this happens the parties generally try to negotiate a settlement. The contract might include the procedure for such negotiation, and might also include provision for mediation or arbitration [**65.2**].

Where the organisation is unincorporated and the members of the governing body are therefore potentially personally liable for the organisation's financial obligations [**2.1**], it is important to try to include a clause limiting liability to the extent of the organisation's assets or to the extent of the organisation's insurance [**22.7.5**]. Legal advice should be sought about the wording of such a clause.

52.5.12 Termination

The contract is likely to include provision for either party to terminate the contract if the other is in serious breach, or a more general **break clause** allowing either party to terminate at any time or at specified times, for example after six months.

A break clause is often presented as advantageous to providers, on the basis that it allows them to withdraw from the contract. But it generally also allows the purchaser to withdraw. Serious consideration should be given to the implications of such a clause, including pension, TUPE and premises costs.

Some public sector bodies seek to include a clause allowing them to terminate for any breach of contract, rather than only a serious breach. Such a clause may not be enforceable where the contract is long-running, the organisation has made a substantial investment or taken on substantial obligations (such as a lease), and the breach was neither a serious breach nor an accumulation of less serious breaches that taken together constituted a very serious breach.

Rice (t/a The Garden Guardian) v Great Yarmouth Borough Council [2000] All ER (D) 902

52.5.13 Renewal and non-renewal

Unless the contract is for a time limited service, it may include procedures and the timetable for negotiating an extension or renewal. It is important to ensure that if the contract is not to be renewed, the organisation has adequate notice of this and adequate funds to cover wind-down or handover costs.

52.6 CONTRACTS WITH INDIVIDUALS

As well as its contracts with public sector and other bodies which are purchasing its services, a voluntary organisation may have agreements with individual clients, users or residents. If the individual is paying for the service, a contract exists and the same issues should be considered as with any other contract [above and **chapter 21**]. An individual who is not directly paying (or providing other consideration) for the service does not have a contract with the organisation. But if the organisation has a contract with a local authority or someone else to provide services to the individual, the individual may be able to enforce this contract unless the right to do so is explicitly excluded [**21.2.3**].

Legally binding contracts of this sort are different from arrangements colloquially called contracts and made with school pupils or service users as a way to demonstrate commitment to a particular relationship or process. Although such arrangements may be called contracts, they are generally not legally binding.

Resources: CONTRACTS AND SERVICE AGREEMENTS

Cartel offences. Office of Fair Trading: www.oft.gov.uk, 0800 085 1664, cartelshotline@oft.gsi.gov.uk.

Charities and public service delivery. Charity Commission: www.charitycommission.gov.uk, 0870 333 0123, email via website.

Compact. See end of **chapter 48**.

Full cost recovery. ACEVO: www.acevo.org.uk, 0845 345 8481, info@acevo.org.uk.

Charity Finance Directors' Group: www.cfdg.org.uk, 0845 345 3192, info@cfdg.org.uk.

Public sector contracts. ACEVO [above].

HM Treasury: www.hm-treasury.gov.uk, 020 7270 4558, email via website.

Improvement and Development Agency for Local Government: www.idea.gov.uk, 020 7296 6880, ihelp@idea.gov.uk.

Office of Government Commerce: www.ogc.gov.uk, 0845 000 4999, servicedesk@ogc.gsi.gov.uk.

Tax & VAT. See end of **chapters 56** and **57**.

Statute law. www.opsi.gov.uk and www.statutelaw.gov.uk.

Much but not all case law. www.bailii.org.

Updates cross-referenced to this book. www.rclh.co.uk.

Part VI provides an introduction to accounting, tax, VAT and other financial matters.

Chapter 53

FINANCIAL PROCEDURES AND SECURITY

53.1 FINANCIAL PROCEDURES

Putting proper financial procedures in place is not only good practice; it is a legal obligation arising from the duty of care that all governing body members have, the duty of charity trustees to protect their charity's assets [**15.6.5**], and from statutory requirements under charity, company and industrial and provident society legislation [**chapter 15**]. The procedures should ensure:

- financial risks are identified, assessed, appropriately managed and regularly reviewed [**53.1.2**];

- authority to authorise expenditure and payments is clearly delegated [**53.1.5**];

- all decisions about expenditure are made by people authorised to do so, and if appropriate are minuted or recorded in other ways;

- budgets and cashflow projections are prepared and monitored, and if necessary appropriate action is authorised and is taken to increase income and/or reduce expenditure;

- the organisation receives money due to it, claims all tax and rate reliefs to which it is entitled [**56.4**], and recovers tax where it is able to;

- salaries are properly calculated and PAYE is properly operated [**30.4**];

- payments to pension schemes are dealt with properly [**30.6**], and adequate provision is made for future pension liabilities [**30.6.4**, **30.6.5**];

- if required, the organisation registers for VAT and operates VAT [**57.2.1**];

- the organisation registers for income or corporation tax and if tax is due, meets its tax liabilities [**56.2**];

- cash, cheques, stock, equipment and valuables are protected [**53.1.7**, **53.1.8**];

- petty cash and bank accounts are operated properly [**53.1.6**];

- the organisation has policies on investments and reserves [**58.6**, **58.8.3**], complies with the policies, and reviews them regularly;
- all financial transactions are properly recorded, and the records are kept securely and safely [**53.1.1**];
- financial records are checked by at least one person who has not been involved in making the payment or writing up the records;
- the governing body, senior staff and others with responsibility for financial control receive regular financial reports;
- the financial records are checked or audited regularly – at least annually – by an appropriately qualified independent third party [**53.1.10**].

The Charity Commission's CC8 *Internal financial controls for charities* [see end of chapter] includes a basic checklist.

53.1.1   Financial records

All organisations must keep the financial records that are required by law, their governing document and funders. These records must be clear and comprehensive enough to explain the organisation's financial transactions, provide adequate information for financial planning and control, give an accurate picture of the organisation's financial position at any given time, and enable the members of the governing body to ensure the organisation's annual accounts comply with all relevant legislation, the governing document and funders' requirements.

For companies and charities, these are legal requirements. For industrial and provident societies the legislation is worded differently but the intention is similar.   *Companies Act 2006 s.386; Charities Act 1993 s.41;*
Friendly & Industrial & Provident Societies Act 1968 ss.1-2

For details of how long various types of financial records must be kept, see **18.4**.

Cross-referencing systems should enable easy correlation between the various records. The intention should always be to maintain an **audit trail** enabling each item of income or expenditure to be traced. An expenditure item, for example, should be traceable from the budget to the authorisation, to the purchase order, to confirmation that the goods have been received or the services provided, to the invoice, to the cheque or electronic payment, to the management accounts and the annual accounts. The accounting book entry for a gift aid donation must have a clear trail to the donor's gift aid declaration [**50.2.2**] and the tax recovery claim.

The purchase of equipment, and in some cases stock, should be logged in the relevant inventory with a cross reference to the purchase authorisation and payment.

Where grants or donations are received for a specific purpose, the financial records must indicate this clearly and must make it possible to show that the funds have been spent for this purpose [**48.2**].

Data should never be erased or removed from accounting records, whether on paper or computerised. Any correction should be added as a separate entry. If an entry is altered in paper accounts, it must be initialled by the person making the amendment. Computerised information should not be able to be altered or erased.

The records should be guarded against loss. An up to date backup of computerised information should always be kept, away from the premises. The accounting books should be kept separate from the supporting documentation, so that if the books are stolen or destroyed they can be reconstructed from the documentation.

53.1.2   Risk assessment and management

Financial and security risk assessments [**22.1**] look systematically at financial and related systems and procedures, identify key risks, assess adequacy of controls and gaps in the systems, and recommend changes to help reduce the risk of financial mismanagement or fraud. The starting points should be 'What could go wrong if we had incompetent or dishonest staff, volunteers, fundraisers, finance director, chief executive, treasurer, board members, investment advisors? What procedures can we put in place now, to ensure we have proper safeguards when and if we do have someone incompetent or dishonest in post?'

Financial risk assessment is often carried out as part of the **internal audit** process [**53.1.9**], but it should be undertaken even if the organisation does not have internal audit procedures in place.

In charities, this risk assessment is necessary to comply with the trustees' duty to consider major risks to the charity and establish systems to mitigate them [**22.1.3**]. Trustees of many charities must include in their annual report a statement of compliance with this duty [**54.2.8**].

53.1.3 Guarding against theft and fraud

A governing body which does not take proper precautions against loss, theft and fraud could be held to be negligent if assets go missing. The procedures should reduce the risk of loss, whether fraudulently or in error, and maximise the likelihood of it being discovered at a very early stage if it does happen.

Fraud is an intentional act involving the use of deception to make a gain for oneself or to cause loss or the risk of loss to another person. Fraud may occur through false representation (providing information dishonestly), failing to disclose information, or abuse of position. *Fraud Act 2006 ss.2-5*

Most fraud is financial or involves the theft of money or property, but it can also involve the theft of intellectual property [**44.1**], an employer's know-how [**43.1.5**], databases and other information, or individual or corporate identities [**53.2**].

About half of all fraud cases dealt with by the courts involve fraud by employees. Procedures to reduce staff fraud are outlined in *Tackling staff fraud*, available free on the website of fraud prevention service CIFAS [see end of chapter].

Fidelity insurance [**23.6.3**] can protect the organisation against theft or fraud by staff, governing body members and others within the organisation. The insurer may require evidence that anti-theft and anti-fraud procedures are in place.

53.1.3.1 Publication of signatures and bank account details

Annual reports and other documents published by the organisation on paper or electronically should not include signatures, because these can be scanned into other documents. Care should also be taken about having bank sort code and account numbers online, for example in a gift aid form. With signatures and bank details, fraudsters can write to the bank and arrange a payment or standing order from the charity to the fraudster. Where bank account details must be made public – as for gift aid direct debits, or for payments by bank transfer – it is recommended that a separate bank account, which can only receive income and from which no payments can be made, be set up to receive gift aid or BACS payments.

Annual accounts and reports and certain other documents submitted to regulatory authorities may need to be signed [**chapter 54**], and the signed documents may have to be published online. Companies House, the Charity Commission and other authorities are implementing procedures to reduce the risk of signatures and other information being used for identity theft [**53.2.1**].

Bank statements should always be carefully checked, to ensure all payments, especially those made electronically, were properly authorised by the organisation.

53.1.4 Segregation of duties

To minimise the risk of error or fraud, different stages of the financial process should be carried out by different people, and financial record keeping should be monitored and spot-checked by a manager or the treasurer. If the treasurer is the only person handling money, keeping records and preparing financial reports, another governing body member should monitor the records on a regular basis.

53.1.5 Authorisation of expenditure

Budgets should be approved by the governing body or an authorised sub-committee. It should be clear who can authorise expenditure within the budget; who (if anyone) can authorise expenditure outside budget; who monitors income and expenditure against the budget, to whom they have to report and how often; and who must take action if income is lower or expenditure higher than budgeted.

53.1.5.1 Reimbursement of expenses

Policies and procedures for reimbursing mileage and other expenses to employees and volunteers [**30.4.9**, **39.2.1**] should be clear. It is sensible to devise an expenses claim form, and to require receipts, mileage records or other documentation. Reimbursements should always be authorised in writing by someone other than the person who is receiving the money.

53.1.5.2 Payments to contractors and suppliers

A common form of fraud is creating a 'contractor' who is paid for services supposedly (but not actually) provided to the organisation, or an individual ordering goods for his or her personal use through the organisation's accounts. The likelihood of this being discovered is increased by having clear procedures for authorising expenditure, with another person monitoring the actual expenditure.

53.1.6 Bank accounts

Decisions to open, change or close bank accounts should be made only by the governing body, using the wording of the bank or building society mandate.

British Bankers Association guidelines require banks and building societies to check with the Charity Commission and, if appropriate, the charity concerned before opening an account in a charity's name. For all organisations, even if not charities, banks and building societies will verify the identity of at least two and usually all signatories.

The organisation's money should not be kept in anyone else's account. If it has to be kept there temporarily – perhaps because it has been collected as cash at an event – careful records must be kept and it must be paid over to the organisation as quickly as possible.

Proper procedures must be in place to keep records of telephone and electronic transactions. If money is transferred between accounts or between linked organisations, the transfers must be monitored and reconciled. Bank statements should be reconciled as soon as they are received with the accounting books, chequebook counterfoils, paying-in slips and direct debit and standing order records, and any discrepancies should be sorted out. Direct debits and standing orders to and from bank accounts, in particular, should be carefully scrutinised and any anomalies should be immediately investigated.

53.1.6.1 Signatories

Account signatories should be people currently involved in the organisation, so they are aware of authorisation procedures and the implications of the cheques or other documents they might sign.

As soon as a signatory leaves or no longer holds the relevant office – or before if appropriate – the signatories should be changed. Banks often require the outgoing signatory to confirm the change, to stop people from falsely telling the bank that they are new signatories. If it is not possible or appropriate for the outgoing signatory to do this, the reason should be explained to the bank.

The governing document may specify the signatories [**7.4.19**]. Some governing documents state that all signatories must be members of the governing body, but this can usually be amended [**7.5**].

Many organisations allow employees to sign cheques, but require cheques above a certain amount to be signed by at least one governing body member, and above a higher amount to be signed only by governing body members.

Cheques do not have to be signed by two people unless required by the governing document or internal procedures. But a governing body which allows cheques to be signed by only one person could be held to be negligent if that person misuses the cheques.

If cheque signatories are not available to sign cheques, the cheque should be made out and sent to them for signature. It has been found to be negligent for a company director – and, by implication, anyone else – to sign a blank cheque. This means that if the cheque is misused, the signatory could be personally liable to make good the loss to the organisation. The same holds for partially completed cheques, without the name or amount.   *Dorchester Finance Co Ltd v Stebbing [1989] BCLC 498*

A cheque should not be signed or a transaction authorised unless the signatory has seen the supporting documentation – an invoice if goods or services have already been provided, or an order form, order letter or pro forma invoice if they are being paid for in advance.

Payments to a signatory, or to a person, business or organisation connected with a signatory, should not be signed or authorised by that signatory. If it is unavoidable that they sign or authorise it, the transaction should be notified immediately to whoever is responsible for monitoring that level of transaction.

53.1.6.2 Electronic, telephone and automatic transactions

Procedures should ensure that non-cheque transactions, such as internet or telephone instructions, standing orders and direct debits, are properly authorised by the required number of signatories. Even if the bank will act on the instructions of one person, the organisation should have internal procedures requiring the transaction to be approved in the same way as if it were made by cheque.

Particular care must be taken in relation to passwords for telephone or internet banking, and PIN numbers for bank card transactions. These **must** be changed as soon as a person ceases to be a signatory, or ideally before.

53.1.7 Cash

The organisation should keep the minimum possible cash on the premises, ensure that it is covered under the organisation's contents insurance [**23.6.2**], and consider fidelity insurance [**23.6.3**]. **Petty cash** should be operated as an **imprest system**, under which a fixed amount or **float** is initially withdrawn from the bank and is put into the petty cash system, is used for cash payments, and when it reaches an agreed level is topped up to the agreed float amount.

If possible, all counting of cash should be witnessed and both people should sign a document verifying the amount. Incoming cash should be paid into the organisation's bank account as quickly as possible, and should not be directly used to pay for goods or services.

Especially in charity shops and other situations where a large amount of cash changes hands, precautions should be taken against theft and counterfeit notes. The police crime prevention unit can advise. Under health and safety law, appropriate precautions must be taken to protect staff who must carry cash in public or handle cash in other situations where they could be at risk of attack [**40.3**].

53.1.8 Equipment and stock

An up to date inventory (**register of assets**) should be kept of all equipment and other assets. For companies and charities, this is a legal requirement.
Companies Act 2006 s.386(3); Charities Act 1993 s.41

An organisation which sells goods should do a comprehensive stock check at least at the end of the financial year, and should check stock and keep other records as appropriate. For companies this is a legal requirement.   *Companies Act 2006 s.386(4)*

53.1.9 Internal audit

Internal audit is a process by which an authorised person or sub-committee monitors, assesses and reports to the governing body on the effectiveness of the organisation's financial systems and controls. The purpose is to look in detail at all procedures and ensure they are adequate to provide full and accurate financial information, keep money and other assets secure, and minimise the risk of fraud. The **financial risk assessment** identifies what can go wrong and what needs to happen to reduce the risk [**53.1.1**], and the **internal audit** confirms that those safeguards are in place and are working, and makes further suggestions.

The internal auditor or audit committee should not be directly involved in the organisation's financial processes or in carrying out the annual audit.

53.1.10 External examination or audit

The purpose of an external (usually annual) independent examination or audit is to inspect and verify the accounts [**54.2.7**, **54.3.7**]. Such checks are advisable even where they are not a statutory or constitutional requirement. However, an independent examination or audit reports only on the past. It does not predict cashflow problems (for which proper budgets and cashflow analyses are needed), nor will it prevent fraud (for which proper internal procedures are needed).

53.2 IDENTITY THEFT

Although the **customer due diligence** procedures required under the **Money Laundering Regulations** [**53.5.3**] can make it harder for identity thieves to use their new individual or corporate identities for fraud [**53.1.3**] or money laundering [**53.5**], it is by no means impossible. All financial or sensitive information should be stored securely, in locked filing cabinets or on password protected computers or encrypted media. On disposal, any material that contains a signature and/or any financial or personal details, account numbers, or anything else that could be used fraudulently should be shredded or disposed of securely.

53.2.1 Corporate identity theft

The requirement to file annual accounts and reports and other documents with the Charity Commission and Companies House, and the ease with which some of these documents can be obtained or downloaded, puts organisations at risk of their identity being stolen and misused.

53.2.1.1 Documents filed with Companies House

Documents filed with Companies House are available to any member of the public, and for only £1 (at the time of writing) anyone can purchase from the Companies House website a company annual return or other documents with the directors' signatures. Those signatures can then be fraudulently used to change the company's directors and registered office, and the company's name and amended address can be used to order goods or services on credit, based on the real company's creditworthiness. After the goods or services are received, the address may be changed back to the original – but even if it is not, the genuine company can end up being chased for the debt.

Companies House provides two services to reduce this type of corporate identity theft. The **Monitor** service notifies companies as soon as an email document is filed, which at least enables them to know if someone has filed a fraudulent form. Under **PROOF** (PROtected Online Filing), forms to change a company's address or directors' details can only be filed electronically with a secure password and from registered email addresses. Forms submitted on paper are not accepted.

53.2.1.2 Documents filed with the Charity Commission

Charity annual accounts and reports submitted to the Charity Commission no longer need to be signed, provided that the copy accurately shows the content of the original documents [**54.2.9**]. The accounts and reports are available on the Commission's website, but if they are submitted without signatures there will be no signatures on the website.

The Commission publishes on its website only the names of trustees, not their addresses [**18.10.2**]. The only address published on the website is a correspondent's address, which can be the charity's office or any other address.

53.2.2 Individual identity theft

The Home Office [see end of chapter] provides guidance for individuals on how to reduce the risk of their identity being stolen – and how to find out if it has been. Within organisations, stringent safeguards should be in place to protect individuals' details. It is not unknown for people to take temporary work (for which background checks might not be as rigorous as for a permanent post) in an accounts, payroll or human resources department, in which they have access to vast amounts of personal data that can be used to steal the identities of employees, service users, donors or others.

Until recently, company directors had to provide their residential address on annual returns and other documents filed at Companies House. From 1 October 2009 they can provide a service address rather than residential address [**18.5.4**]

53.3 EX GRATIA PAYMENTS

An *ex gratia* payment is one which the organisation feels morally obliged to make, even though it has no power or contractual obligation to do so and the payment cannot be justified as being in the interest of the organisation. An *ex gratia* payment might be made, for example, when an organisation receives, through an oversight or technicality, a legacy intended for another beneficiary.

53.3.1 Charitable organisations

A charity may make an *ex gratia* payment only with an order [**4.5.4**] from the Charity Commission, court or attorney general. The rules are explained in Charity Commission CC7 *Ex gratia payments by charities* [see end of chapter].

A payment which there is no legal obligation or power to make but is considered by the trustees to be in the interests of the charity is not technically an *ex gratia* payment, but still may be made only with a Charity Commission order. This could include, for example, a payment to show appreciation to a volunteer or employee for long service or for a particularly significant piece of work.

A payment made as a settlement to prevent a potential employment tribunal claim [**37.2**] is not an *ex gratia* payment. Provided such a payment is within the charity's powers and is reasonable, Charity Commission consent is not required.

If trustees are not clear whether they have power to make a payment, they should consult a solicitor or the Commission.

53.3.2 Non-charitable companies and IPSs

An *ex gratia* payment may be made by a non-charitable company (including a community interest company) or industrial and provident society only if it is genuine, reasonably incidental to carrying out the organisation's business, and made for the benefit and prosperity of the organisation. Although donations to charities might not fall strictly within these criteria, company and IPS donations to charities are regarded as permissible on the basis that they preserve goodwill.

Parke v Daily News [1962] Ch 927

In addition a company (but not an IPS) may make an *ex gratia* payment to current or past employees, if the company is ceasing operation or being transferred to another company. Prior to 1 October 2009, such a payment had to be authorised by the memorandum or articles of association or a resolution of the company members [**19.7.4**]. Since then, such a payment may be made by a resolution of the company members, or may be made by a resolution of the directors provided this is authorised by the articles of association and the payment is not for a director, former director or shadow director.

Companies Act 2006 s.247

53.3.3 Non-charitable associations

There are no external restrictions on the right of a non-charitable association to make an *ex gratia* payment. A decision to make such a payment should be properly made by the members of the association.

53.3.4 Tax on ex gratia payments

Ex gratia payments to individuals, including a cash payment or a non-cash gift on retirement, may be subject to tax and national insurance as individual income [**30.4.15**]. Advice should be taken before making such a payment or gift.

53.4 DONATIONS AND GRANTS TO INDIVIDUALS

In considering donations or grants to individuals, attention must be given to the consequences both for the donating organisation [**56.7.3**] and the recipient. One-off donations or grants by charities to individuals – for example, a grant to purchase essential furniture – are normally treated as donations with no tax consequences for the recipient. One-off donations or grants by non-charities, and regular payments by either charities or non-charities, are normally treated as income in the hands of the recipients, and the recipients may have to pay income tax if the payments plus their other taxable income exceed their personal allowance.

53.4.1 Payments to people receiving state benefits

Where a grant or other financial support is given to individuals receiving welfare benefits, thought may need to be given to the impact of such payments on their welfare benefit entitlement. In general, people receiving income-related benefits can receive regular charitable payments without it affecting their benefit, but this does not necessarily apply to all benefits. *Social Security (Miscellaneous Amendments No.4) Regulations 2006 [SI 2006/2378]*

Advice on this complex topic can be obtained from solicitors specialising in welfare benefits law and from organisations such as the Child Poverty Action Group.

53.4.2 Scholarships and bursaries

Unlike most regular payments to individuals, scholarships, bursaries etc are generally not taxed as income. However, if a company sets up an educational trust to provide scholarships for children of employees or if a scholarship is awarded for some other reason directly connected with another person's employment, the award is assessed as a benefit to the employee and he or she will be taxed on it. *Income Tax (Trading & Other Income) Act 2005 ss.776,215*

53.4.3 Research grants and prizes

The tax treatment of research grants depends on the circumstances, including the terms of the grant, the residence and employment status of the researcher and the country where the research is carried out. A research fellowship or other award payable over a period would be taxable income in the hands of the recipient, but the recipient would be able to deduct sums properly spent on travel, research books and other necessary expenditure to carry out the research.

53.5 PROCEEDS OF CRIME AND MONEY LAUNDERING

It is an offence for any individual or organisation to conceal, disguise, convert or transfer criminal property, or remove it from the UK; or to be involved in an arrangement which is known or suspected to involve another person acquiring, keeping, using or controlling criminal property; or to acquire, use or possess criminal property. Conspiracy or incitement do any of these things, or aiding or abetting them, is also an offence. *Proceeds of Crime Act 2002 ss.327-329, as amended*

Criminal property is property arising from conduct in the UK which is a criminal offence in the UK or, in many but not all cases, conduct anywhere in the world which would be an offence if it took place in the UK. There is no minimum level – so £2 stolen from a shop, £200 received through welfare benefit fraud or £20,000 from drug dealing are all criminal property, regardless of whether the offence took place in the UK or elsewhere. Knowing receipt of stolen goods is a crime and while there is in many cases no legal duty to report it, there is a clear moral or good practice duty to report it to the police or other authorities.

All **relevant persons** [**53.5.2**] must take steps to identify and prevent **money laundering**, which is the process of turning the proceeds of crime into 'innocent' money through a series of transactions which disguise where it came from. The rules on money laundering also apply to **terrorist financing**, as defined under the **Terrorism Act 2000** and similar legislation. *Terrorism Act 2000 ss.15-18; Money Laundering Regulations 2007 [SI 2007/2157] reg.2*

Organisations and individuals which are not 'relevant persons' may also be directly affected by the rules on money laundering and terrorist financing [**53.5.4**].

Information about money laundering is available from HM Revenue and Customs [see end of chapter], and for auditors, external accountants and tax advisors from the Consultative Committee of Accountancy Bodies [see end of chapter].

53.5.1 Disclosure of money laundering

It is unlawful for a person in the **regulated sector** [**53.5.2**] not to disclose money laundering. There are some exceptions, for example where the information is covered by professional legal privilege [**65.4.1**], or where a person who has received training on money laundering does not know or suspect that money laundering has occurred or will occur. *Proceeds of Crime Act 2002 s.330, as amended*

A disclosure which would be prohibited under other legislation, such as the **Data Protection Act 1998** [**43.3**], is **protected** under the money laundering regulations provided the information was obtained in the course of the discloser's trade, profession, business or employment; the information causes the discloser to know or suspect, or have reasonable grounds for knowing or suspecting, that a person is involved in money laundering; and the disclosure is made to a police officer, a Customs officer or a **nominated officer** [**53.5.3**] as soon as is practicable.
Proceeds of Crime Act 2002 s.337, as amended

53.5.2 The regulated sector

The money laundering rules apply only to the **regulated sector**, although those on terrorist financing apply more widely [**53.5.4**]. The regulated sector broadly comprises:

- **credit institutions**, such as banks;
- **financial institutions**, including **money service businesses** which transmit money by any means or cash cheques which are made payable to customers, **insurance companies** providing life assurance, some **insurance intermediaries** providing long-term insurance, persons whose regular business or occupation is the provision of an **investment service** to other persons or performing investment activities on a professional basis, and **collective investment undertakings** that market or offer units or shares;
- firms or individuals carrying out statutory **audit** work [**chapter 54**] or defined as statutory auditors under the **Companies Acts**, persons appointed as **insolvency** practitioners [**24.2.3**], firms or sole practitioners who by way of business provide **external accountancy** services to other persons, and firms or sole practitioners who by way of business provide advice about the **tax** affairs of other persons;
- **independent legal professionals**, which are firms or sole practitioners who provide **legal or notarial services** to other persons, involving buying or selling real property or business entities; managing a client's money or other assets; the opening of bank or other accounts; organising contributions necessary to create, operate or manage companies; or creating, operating or managing trusts, companies or similar structures;
- **trust or company service providers**, which are firms or sole practitioners who by way of business form companies or other legal persons [**3.1**]; act or arrange for another person to act as a company director or secretary, partner in a partnership, trustee or similar; or provide a registered or administrative address for others;
- carrying on **estate agency** work (but preparing or providing information for a home information pack is not regulated);
- dealing in **high value goods** (including as an auctioneer) where a transaction involves a payment or payments in cash of at least €15,000 (approximately £12,800 as at 1/8/09);
- operating a **casino**. *Proceeds of Crime Act 2002 sch.9 para.1,3, added by Proceeds of Crime Act 2002 (Business in the Regulated Sector & Supervisory Authorities) Order 2007 [SI 2007/3287]; Money Laundering Regulations 2007 [SI 2007/2157] reg.3(3)*

53.5.2.1   Relevant persons

Unless they qualify for the exclusion [**53.5.2.2**], an individual or body in the regulated sector to whom the **Money Laundering Regulations 2007** apply is a **relevant person**.   *Money Laundering Regulations 2007 [SI 2007/2157] regs.2(1),4(2)*

Industrial and provident societies which only issue share capital or take deposits from the public within the limits allowed by the **Industrial and Provident Societies Act 1965** are not relevant persons.   *ML Regs 2007 reg.4(1); Industrial & Provident Societies Act 1965 ss.6,7(3)*

53.5.2.2   Exclusion for occasional or very limited activities

An individual or body is not a **relevant person** if they engage in any of the above financial activities but it is not their main activity, and **all** of the following criteria are met:

- their total annual turnover from the financial activity is not more than £64,000 (as at 1/8/09);

- in relation to any customer, the financial activity is limited to no more than one transaction exceeding €1,000 (approximately £850 as at 1/8/09), regardless of whether the transaction is a single operation or a series of operations which appear to be linked;

- the financial activity does not exceed 5% of the person's annual turnover;

- the financial activity is ancillary and directly linked to the person's main activity; and

- the financial activity is provided only to customers of the person's main activity and is not offered to the public.   *ML Regs 2007 reg.4(2), sch.2 para.1*

This exclusion does not apply to dealers in high value goods, or where the financial activity is the transmission or remittance of money (or any representation of monetary value) by any means.

53.5.2.3   Voluntary organisations as relevant persons

The definition of regulated sector introduced in 2007 refers specifically to **firms** and to individuals or **sole practitioners**. Firm is defined as 'any entity, whether or not a legal person [**3.1**], that is not an individual'. It includes incorporated bodies, partnerships and unincorporated associations. This definition could include charities and other voluntary organisations. However, even if it does, most organisations would fall within the exclusion for financial activities that are occasional or limited [**53.5.2.2**].   *Proceeds of Crime Act 2002 sch.9 para.1(7)*

Where the activities are not occasional and limited, the definitions of the regulated sector say the work must be carried on **by way of business**. 'By way of business' is not defined in the legislation. HM Revenue and Customs says that registered charities which provide services that could be regulated are not relevant persons if the services are provided free of charge or for a nominal fee. Registered charities that charge more than a nominal fee, and other organisations regardless of whether or how much they charge, are therefore likely to be regulated unless their activities are within the occasional and limited exclusion.

Specialist legal advice should therefore be taken if the organisation provides financial activities that could be regulated, such as tax advice, setting up organisations, or receiving funds on behalf of other organisations; it is not eligible for the exclusion for occasional or very limited activity; and it charges its clients for the service, or has a contract [**52.1.2**] under which a local authority or other body pays for the provision of the service.

If the service is funded through donations and grants, it is unlikely to be treated as a business. But even if organisations providing financial activities are not covered by the rules, it may be sensible to operate as if they are [**53.5.3**].

Organisations which are explicitly set up to make a profit, including charities' trading subsidiaries [**51.2**] and some community interest companies [**3.4**], could be regulated if they provide financial activities as their main or a major part of their work and are not eligible for the exclusion for occasional activities – even if the profits from those activities are used for community or charitable purposes.

53.5.3 Responsibilities of relevant persons

Relevant persons [**53.5.2.1**] in regulated sectors must, before they can carry on their financial activities, register with the appropriate supervisory body. The supervisory body is HM Revenue and Customs for money service businesses, high value dealers, trust or company service providers [**53.5.2**], and accountancy service providers who are not registered with a designated professional body.

HMRC requires an organisation's governing body members and its money laundering nominated officer to pass a **fit and proper test** before the organisation can be registered to carry out financial activities.

Duties of relevant persons include complying with the registration requirements of their supervisory body, applying **customer** or **client due diligence** (KYC – 'know your customer') procedures to verify their customers' identity, appointing a **money laundering nominated officer**, setting up systems and procedures to forestall and prevent money laundering, and providing relevant individuals with training on money laundering and awareness of their procedures in relation to money laundering. Information about these duties is available from HMRC. Relevant persons who fail to comply with these duties can be fined or imprisoned.

53.5.4 Responsibilities of other organisations

Even if an organisation is not in the **regulated sector** [**53.5.2**] or if in the regulated sector is not a **relevant person** [**53.5.2.1**], it must still be aware of the risks of money laundering and terrorist financing.

Under Charity Commission guidance, a charity which receives donations or grants must satisfy itself as to the legitimacy of a large donation from an unknown donor, loans which involve repayment in cash, or donations or loans which require work to be done by a specified person or individual. If there is any reason for suspicion, the charity should refuse the donation or loan, or contact the Charity Commission for guidance [**48.3.2**]. Organisations which are not charities should comply with the same principles.

Funds must not be raised or passed on if they are for an organisation proscribed under the **Terrorism Act 2000** [**46.6.2**], or if the organisation has any reason to suspect that they may be used for terrorist purposes.

For organisations which provide goods or funds to individuals or organisations abroad, it may be difficult enough to monitor whether they have got to the right place and are being used as intended [**5.3.7**]. Particular diligence is needed where risk assessments have identified that the goods or funds could fall into terrorist hands or be used for terrorist purposes – or where there is a risk of the organisation being accused of its donations being used in this way. The Charity Commission has produced guidance on reducing such risks [**46.6.3**].

Resources: FINANCIAL PROCEDURES AND SECURITY

Good practice for charities and other organisations. Your organisation's accountant or auditor.

Community accountancy projects.

Charity Commission: www.charitycommission.gov.uk, 0845 300 0218, email via website.

Fraud. CIFAS: www.cifas.org.uk.

Home Office: www.crimereduction.gov.uk, 020 7035 4848, public.enquiries@homeoffice.gsi.gov.uk.

Identity theft. Home Office identity fraud steering committee: www.identitytheft.org.uk.

Money laundering. Consultative Committee of Accountancy Bodies: www.ccab.org.uk, admin@ccab.org.uk.

HM Revenue and Customs: www.hmrc.gov.uk/mlr/index.htm, 0845 010 9000, email via website.

Statute law. www.opsi.gov.uk and www.statutelaw.gov.uk.

Much but not all case law. www.bailii.org.

Updates cross-referenced to this book. www.rclh.co.uk.

Chapter 54
ANNUAL ACCOUNTS, REPORTS AND RETURNS

For sources of further information see end of chapter.

54.1 REPORTING REQUIREMENTS

Charities, companies and industrial and provident societies must comply with strict rules on annual accounts, the reports which accompany the accounts, and annual returns. Additional requirements may be imposed by the organisation's governing document or funders.

Non-charitable unincorporated associations and non-charitable trusts do not generally have to comply with statutory requirements, but do have to comply with their governing document and the requirements of funders.

Specific rules for registered social landlords (housing associations), NHS charities, credit unions and other organisations are not covered in this book.

54.2 CHARITIES

The rules on charity accounts, reports and audit are in the **Charities Act 1993** as amended by the **Charities Act 2006**, regulations, and the *Statement of recommended practice*: *Accounting and reporting by charities* (**charities SORP**). The Charity Commission provides free guidance, and books at various levels are available from publishers specialising in the voluntary sector and/or finance.

For information and advice specific to their situation, charities should consult their accountant or auditor or the Charity Commission. It is essential to ensure that the information is appropriate to the type of charity (unincorporated, or different types of incorporated charity), the charity's income level, and the type of accounts it prepares (receipts and payments, or accruals).

54.2.1 Financial year

In charities which are not companies or industrial and provident societies, the trustees set an **accounting reference date** (ARD). The first ARD must be between six and 18 months after the date of the charity's establishment, and the charity's **financial year** (FY) must then end within seven days before or after the ARD. *Charities (Accounts & Reports) Regulations 2008 [SI 2008/629], reg.3(4)*

Subsequent ARDs are then usually 12 months after the end of the previous FY, but if there is a good reason the charity trustees may set a **restricted financial year** ending on any date six to 18 months after the end of the previous FY. The reason for choosing a date other than 12 months after the end of the previous FY must be disclosed in the accounts. Such a date may not be chosen for two or more consecutive years without the consent of the Charity Commission.

Charitable companies and industrial and provident societies have different rules for determining their financial year [**54.3.1**, **54.4**].

54.2.2 Charities Act requirements

Unlike SORP [**54.2.3**], most Charities Act rules on charity annual accounts, reports and audit apply only to charities registered with the Charity Commission.

The chart below summarises the basic accounting and reporting requirements under the Charities Act and, where applicable, the Companies Act. The requirements are explained in this chapter. The chart does not apply to excepted charities which are not registered with the Commission, exempt charities, charities or charitable companies with subsidiaries, industrial and provident societies, or charities in Scotland and Northern Ireland.

FOR FINANCIAL YEARS ENDING ON OR AFTER I APRIL 2009
ENGLAND AND WALES ONLY

At the time of writing the rules are not known for CIOs or for IPSs registered with the Charity Commission.

Gross income	Assets	Accounts	Report	Scrutiny	A/c & rept to regulator	Return
Charities that are not companies or industrial and provident societies						
Not >10k	Any amount	R&P or charity accruals	Simplified or full trustees rept	No statutory requirement	To Char Comm if requested	Charity update form
Not >25k						Charity return
>25k-250k				Indep exam or statutory charity audit	To Char Comm	
>250k-500k	Not >3.26m	Charity accruals				
>500k-1m			Full trustees rept	Statutory charity audit		
>250k-1m	>3.26m					
>1m	Any amount					Charity return + SIR
Charitable companies						
Not >10k	Any amount	Company accruals (compliant with SORP)	Full trustees rept + directors rept *(can be combined)*	No statutory requirement	To Char Comm if requested; to Companies House	Charity update form + Company return
>10k-25k						Charity return +
>25k-250k				Indep exam or statutory charity audit	To Char Comm + Companies House	company return
>250k-500k	Not >3.26m					
>500k-1m				Statutory charity or company audit		
>250m-1m	>3.26m					
>1m	Any amount					Charity return + SIR, + company return
Turnover >6.5m & assets >3.26m				Statutory company audit		

> = 'more than'   k = thousand   m = million.

For financial years ending before 1 April 2009 the accounts thresholds for charities that were not companies were £10,000 (rather than £25,000) and £100,000 (rather than £250,000). The threshold for independent examination was £10,000 (rather than £25,000) and for statutory audit was £250,000 or £500,000, depending on the financial year. For financial years starting on or after 6 April 2008 the asset threshold was £2.8 million (rather than £3.26 million).

The Commission's publications in the CC15 series *Charity reporting and accounting* set out the requirements for accounts, reports and independent examination or audit. They include requirements for financial years ending before April 2009.

At the time of writing (mid 2009) the requirements for charitable incorporated organisations, and for industrial and provident societies registered with the Charity Commission, were not yet known. For industrial and provident societies not registered with the Commission, see **54.4**.

54.2.2.1 Charity groups

This book does not cover the accounting requirements for parent and subsidiary charities, charity groups [**9.4.2**] and the accounts of charities' trading companies. Advice should be sought from the charity's independent examiner or auditor.

54.2.2.2 Cross-border charities

Charities registered with both the Charity Commission and the Office of the Scottish Charity Register must send their accounts and an annual return to OSCR as well as the Commission. At the time of writing (mid 2009) the accounting and reporting framework was not yet available for charities registered with both the Charity Commission and the Charity Commission for Northern Ireland.

54.2.3 Charities SORP

The detailed provisions of the *Statement of recommended practice: Accounting and reporting by charities* (charities SORP) apply to virtually all charitable organisations in England and Wales, Scotland and Northern Ireland, even if they are not registered with the relevant charity regulator. The only exceptions are charities such as registered social landlords which have their own SORP.

The full SORP applies only if the charity prepares accounts on an accruals basis [**54.2.6**]. Unincorporated charities (trusts and associations) with income no more than £250,000 which prepare accounts on a receipts and payments basis [**54.2.5**] only have to comply with SORP rules on annual reports [**54.2.8**].

Although the SORP is only 'recommended' practice, regulations require charity accruals accounts to be prepared in accordance with SORP methods and principles unless doing so would produce a distorted view of the accounts. If SORP is not followed, this must be explained in the notes to the accounts.

Charities (Accounts & Reports) Regulations 2008 [SI 2008/629] regs.4,5

The SORP is reviewed annually and updated from time to time as general accounting practice requires. Up to date information is available from the Charity Commission.

54.2.4 Unrestricted, restricted, designated and endowment funds

A charity's annual accounts must have separate columns for **unrestricted** or **general funds**, which the trustees have discretion to decide how to use; **restricted funds**, which have been given to or raised by the charity for a specific purpose and may be used only for that purpose [**48.2**]; and **endowed** (sometimes called **capital**) **funds** [**58.8.1**] if applicable. Restricted and endowment funds may relate to **special trusts** [**9.2.3**].

Designated funds are not the same as restricted funds. Designated funds are received by the charity for general purposes, but the trustees have decided they will be used for a specific purpose. The decision is purely an internal matter, and can be changed by the trustees. With restricted funds, the trustees can use them for another purpose only if the donor agrees [**48.2**].

Designated funds should be set out in a note to the accounts with an explanation of their purpose.

54.2.4.1 Grants, donations and gifts

Grants, donations and gifts – whether money, other assets or in kind – are unrestricted if they are generally for the charity's primary purposes. If they are for a specific purpose, client group or geographic area, they are restricted income.

54.2.4.2 Fees, sales, contracts and service agreements

Income from fees or charges made for goods, services or facilities, including income from service agreements or contracts to provide services, should generally be treated as unrestricted. However, some so-called contracts or service agreements may in fact be grants [52.1] and therefore be restricted income. If there is any doubt about how to show such income in the accounts, advice should be taken from the charity's accountant, independent examiner or auditor.

54.2.4.3 Interest and dividends

Interest earned on bank accounts and income from other investments is general income if it is earned on general funds, or if earned on restricted funds it forms part of that fund unless the terms of the original restriction explicitly say otherwise. If it is earned on an endowment whose terms allow income from the fund to be spent on any of the charity's purposes, it is general income; if the fund is an endowment for a specific purpose whose income can be spent, the income is restricted and can only be spent for the fund's purpose. *Charities SORP 2005 para.69*

54.2.4.4 Expenditure

Expenditure out of income received for a restricted purpose or an endowment fund must be shown in those columns, and expenditure from general funds must be shown in the 'general' column. Transfers between columns must be shown gross and explained in notes to the accounts.

54.2.5 Receipts and payments accounts

For financial years ending on or after 1 April 2009, charities which are not companies or industrial and provident societies and have **gross income** of £250,000 or less may prepare either accruals accounts [54.2.6] or simplified annual accounts consisting of a **receipts and payments** (R&P) **account** and a **statement of assets and liabilities**. The Charity Commission provides a pack (CC16) with pro formas which may be used for these accounts. For financial years ending before 1 April 2009, the threshold was £100,000. *Charities Act 1993 s.42(3), amended by Charities Acts 1992 & 1993 (Substitution of Sums) Order 2009 [SI 2009/508]*

In R&P accounts, income is shown in the year it is received, and expenditure is shown in the year it is made. This is different from accruals accounts, where only income and expenditure which *applies to the year* is included – even if it is received or spent in a different year [54.2.6.1].

For the purpose of determining whether a charity can choose to prepare accounts on a receipts and payments basis, gross income is the income shown in its accounts for the year, excluding income which under the terms on which it is given, must be held as capital (also called endowment) and cannot be spent [58.8.1].

54.2.5.1 Changing to accruals accounts

Where the charity changes from receipts and payments to accruals accounting or *vice versa*, the previous year's accounts must generally be restated in the new format. Charities likely to reach the £250,000 threshold at which accruals accounts become necessary may find it advantageous to prepare them in that format even though it is not yet required. *Charities SORP 2005 para.31*

54.2.6 Accruals accounts

For financial years ending on or after 1 April 2009, charities with **gross income** over £250,000 must prepare **accruals accounts**. Gross income is the total incoming resources shown in the **statement of financial activities** [**54.2.6.3**], excluding income received as endowment, but including income transferred from endowment funds to be available for spending. The Charity Commission's CC17 pack includes pro formas which may in some (but not all) cases be used for these accounts. For financial years ending before 1 April 2009, the threshold was £100,000.

Charities Act 1993 s.42(3), amended by
Charities Acts 1992 & 1993 (Substitution of Sums) Order 2009 [SI 2009/508]

For charities which are not companies or industrial and provident societies, accruals accounts include a statement of financial activities (SoFA) [**54.2.6.3**] and a balance sheet [**54.2.6.9**]. For charitable companies they include a SoFA, an income and expenditure account [**54.2.6.8**] unless this is included in the SoFA, and a balance sheet. Corresponding figures for the previous year must be included.

It is beyond the scope of this book to consider the detail of full accruals accounts, but this summary should help trustees understand the accounts.

54.2.6.1 Accruals basis

Instead of simply counting the amounts received and the amounts spent in the period, accruals accounts are adjusted to show the income and expenditure which actually relates to the period. So if, for example, £50,000 is received this year as grants, but £8,000 is a late payment for the previous year and £12,000 is an advance payment for the next year, the accounts for this year would be adjusted to show only £30,000 as grant income. The £8,000 would have been shown as income in the previous year's accounts (even though it was not actually received during that year), and the £12,000 will be shown as income in the next year's accounts (even though it was actually received this year).

Accruals accounts must always be accompanied by a balance sheet [**54.2.6.9**] which shows the organisation's assets and liabilities at the end of the financial period covered by the accounts. In the example above £8,000 would have been shown as a current asset (an amount due to the organisation within one year) on the previous year's balance sheet, and £12,000 would be shown as a liability on this year's balance sheet (because the organisation could have to return it if it does not deliver the £12,000 worth of services for which it has received payment).

Accruals accounts prepared by commercial businesses are generally called **profit and loss accounts**, and if prepared by not for profit organisations are usually called **income and expenditure accounts**. Charities which prepare accruals accounts must do them as a **statement of financial activities** [**54.2.6.3**].

54.2.6.2 Material items

The SORP refers throughout to **material items**. Information is **material** if its misstatement or omission would reasonably be expected to influence a user of the accounts in relation to economic decisions based on the information. The trustees decide whether an item is material. If in doubt, it should be included – but irrelevant information, which creates clutter and could obscure material information, should not be included.

Charities SORP 2005 app.1 para.GL42

54.2.6.3 Statement of financial activities

Rather than using the conventional format for accruals accounts, charities must prepare a **statement of financial activities** (**SoFA**). The requirements are explained in the SORP and in the Charity Commission's CC17 *Accruals accounts pack*.

Charities SORP 2005 para.82-243

Instead of using the usual headings of 'income' and 'expenditure', a SoFA uses **incoming resources** and **resources expended**. Each heading has separate columns for unrestricted and restricted funds, endowment funds if relevant, and designated funds if the trustees wish [**54.2.2.1**]. Within this framework the main distinctions between a SoFA and a conventional I&E account are:

- a SoFA includes all incoming resources (money and the value of donated goods, services or facilities), whereas an I&E account shows only money;
- a SoFA includes all resources expended, including the value of donated goods sold or given away or services and facilities used, whereas an I&E account shows only money spent;

- an I&E account uses **natural categories** [**54.2.6.5**], but a SoFA prepared by a charity which requires a statutory audit must use **activity categories** [**54.2.6.4**, **54.2.6.5**] and charities below the audit threshold may use natural or activity categories;

- gains on revaluation of investments and buildings are included.

Charities SORP 2005 para.82-243

Material **disclosures** [**54.2.6.7**] must be included in notes to the SoFA.

54.2.6.4 Incoming resources

SoFA **activity categories** for incoming resources are:

- **voluntary income**: gifts and donations, including legacies, gifts in kind, donated services and facilities (but not the value of volunteer time), tax reclaimed under gift aid [**50.2.3**], membership subscriptions and sponsorships that are basically donations rather than payments for goods or services [**56.3.3**, **56.3.5**], grants for general purposes or for core funding;

- **activities for generating funds**: income from fundraising and from trading which is not primary purpose [**56.4.5**], including income from fundraising events, sales in shops, sponsorships for which the sponsor receives a benefit, income from providing goods or services that are not for the charity's beneficiaries, and rental income from property held for the charity's own use but temporarily not used by the charity;

- **investment income**: including bank and building society interest, dividends, rental income from properties held as investments, and tax reclaimable on the investment income;

- **incoming resources from charitable activities**: resources directly related to achieving the charity's objects, including contracts, fees and other income for **primary purpose trading** [**56.4.5**]; grants specifically for the provision of goods or services as part of charitable activities or services to beneficiaries; sales of goods or services provided by the charity's beneficiaries; income from non-investment properties let for the charity's purposes; and ancillary trading connected with any of the above;

- **other incoming resources**.

The incoming resources in each of the above rows should be divided across columns for unrestricted funds, restricted funds and (if applicable) endowment funds [**54.2.2.1**]. Resources from charitable activities should, if appropriate, be sub-divided onto separate rows for each type of activity.

The Charity Commission has guidance on which rows and columns various types of income or gifts in kind should be allocated to, and can provide advice. In particular, advice should be sought from the Commission or the organisation's independent examiner or auditor about how to show **performance related grants**, where payment of the grant is conditional on the charity providing a specified service, **legacies** 'in the pipeline' but where it is not clear when they will be received, and anything else where the accounting treatment is not straightforward.

54.2.6.5 Resources expended

In a receipts and payments or income and expenditure account, expenditure is usually shown in **natural categories** such as salaries, premises costs, office costs etc. Charities still need to keep their day to day accounts under these headings, but if the charity requires a statutory audit (gross income over £500,000 for financial years ending on or after 1 April 2009), the figures must be grouped in the SoFA into **activity categories** (also called **functional categories**), with the natural breakdowns shown in the notes to the SoFA.

Charities which do not need a statutory audit may use natural rather than activity categories in their annual accounts, regardless of whether they prepare receipts and payments or accruals accounts.

The activity categories set out in the SORP are:

- **costs of generating voluntary income**: costs of bringing in donations, legacies and other income in the 'voluntary income' incoming resources line;

- **fundraising trading costs**: to bring in the income on the 'activities for generating funds' line;
- **investment management costs**: costs of investment advice, managing and administering investments, collecting rents, investment property repairs and maintenance;
- **charitable expenditure**: the provision of services, grants, facilities, goods or other activities furthering the charity's objects, including salaries, administration, management and related costs;
- **governance costs**: the general costs of running the organisation itself, as opposed to the costs involved in raising funds, providing charitable services etc – includes AGMs, governing body meetings and other meetings of the organisation itself, governing body recruitment and training, legal advice about constitutional and statutory requirements, preparing charity/company accounts, the costs of audit or independent examination etc;
- **other resources expended**.

For an organisation which carries out more than one charitable activity, the charitable expenditure section should be subdivided into the various activities, for example day care, advice, respite care.

Expenditure covering more than one category – for example, the salary of a manager who spends part of her time managing day care, part managing respite care, part fundraising and part dealing with trustee matters – should be allocated on a reasonable and consistent basis to the relevant resources expended categories. The basis for the allocation should be explained in the notes.

As with incoming resources, the Charity Commission or the organisation's independent examiner or auditor should be consulted if there is any uncertainty about how an expended resource should be shown in the SoFA.

54.2.6.6 Donated services and facilities

Donated incoming resources such as free rent or printing or savings on reduced-rate facilities should be included in the SoFA if they are quantifiable and material, and the charity would otherwise have had to pay for them. A corresponding 'resources expended' entry must be made.

The value of volunteers' time should not be included as an incoming resource or a resource expended, but their contribution should be included in the notes to the accounts or in the trustees' report. Reimbursement of volunteers' expenses should be shown under the appropriate expenditure heading (for example charitable expenditure if the volunteers are providing services to beneficiaries or carrying out other charitable work; fundraising trading costs if they are working in the charity's shop; governance costs if they are carrying out trustee duties).

54.2.6.7 SoFA disclosures

Where a statement of financial activities is prepared, the charities SORP requires certain information to be included in the SoFA or in the notes to the accounts. Charities must ensure this information is kept and is made known to the person preparing the annual accounts. The required disclosures are:

- all transactions, even if not material [**54.2.6.2**] with trustees and related parties (as defined in GL50 in the glossary to charities SORP 2005), including purchases, sales, leases, donations and the supply of services to or from the trustee or related party, remuneration and benefits, and trustees' expenses;
- staff costs, including costs paid by someone else such as the charity's trading company or an organisation that seconds staff to the charity;
- for charities subject to statutory audit [**54.2.7**], the fact that there are no staff earning more than £60,000, or the number of staff earning more than this (in bands of £10,000 from £60,000 upwards), plus specified information about pension contributions for employees earning more than £60,000;
- cost of audit or independent examination and other financial services such as taxation advice, consultancy, financial advice and accountancy;
- *ex gratia* payments [**53.3.1**];

- conduit funding [**48.5**] and other assets held on behalf of others;
- gifts in kind which have not yet been used;
- an analysis of movement of funds in relation to endowments, fixed assets and programme related investment. *Charities SORP 2005 para.216-243*

54.2.6.8 Summary income and expenditure account

A charity may have to prepare a **summary income and expenditure account** [**54.3.3**] as well as a SoFA if it is a company, or its governing document or funder requires it. A summary account is different from the summarised (abridged) accounts that may be included in publicity materials [**54.2.6.11**].

If the SoFA includes only revenue (money) transactions, the one set of accounts may meet requirements for both a SoFA and a summary I&E account.

The summary I&E account does not have to distinguish between restricted and unrestricted funds. *Charities SORP 2005 para.423-426*

54.2.6.9 Balance sheet

The balance sheet shows the charity's net worth on the last day of the financial year. It includes:

- **fixed assets**: tangible assets held for the charity to undertake its activities, and investment assets;
- **current assets**: stock and work in progress held at the end of the year, debtors (amounts owing to the charity due within one year from the balance sheet date), prepayments (amounts paid in advance by the charity), short-term investments and deposits that will be realised and not re-invested within the next year, cash in bank and in hand;
- **current liabilities**: creditors (amounts owing by the charity due within one year) and accruals (amounts that the charity has received in advance, and still has to provide the paid-for goods or services);
- **future liabilities**: creditors (amounts owing by the charity due more than one year from the balance sheet date), amounts set aside as provisions for future liabilities and charges. *Charities SORP 2005 para.244-350*

Current assets minus current liabilities equals **net current assets**, or **net current liabilities** if the amount if negative. Total assets (both fixed and current) minus total liabilities (both current and future) equals **net assets**. If the figure is negative there is a **net liability** and specialist advice should be sought as a matter of urgency.

The balance sheet must be signed by one or more trustees who have been authorised to sign, and must give the date on which the trustees approved the accounts.

54.2.6.10 Cashflow statement

A cashflow statement should be included if during the financial year, the charity met at least two of the following criteria: gross income of more than £6.5 million, balance sheet total of more than £3.26 million, weekly average of more than 50 employees. *Charities SORP 2005 para.351-355*

54.2.6.11 Branches and special trusts

An unincorporated charity must include within its main accounts all the income and expenditure of branches, projects or groups which are not separately registered as charities, and **special trusts** for which it holds funds [**9.2.3**]. The main accounts should also include supporters' or fundraising groups and similar groups which raise funds only for that charity [**9.2.5**].

Income and expenditure of branches, supporters' groups etc must be included in the main accounts gross, rather than net with the expenditure deducted from the income. The groups' assets and liabilities must also be included.

Charity branches which are separately registered with the Charity Commission and have their own charity numbers should not be included unless the Commission has defined them as subsidiary charities [**9.4.2**].

54.2.6.12 Summarised financial information and statements

The SORP distinguishes between **summarised financial statements** which are abridged versions of the SoFA and balance sheet, and **summarised financial information** which covers a specific aspect of the finances, such as an activity, region or branch. Summarised financial information might not be based on information in the annual accounts.

Charities SORP 2005 para.371-379

A **summarised financial statement** that is published or circulated in any way, including on a website, must give a fair and accurate summary of the full accounts. The summary must include a statement, signed on behalf of the trustees, explaining the nature of the information and including the details listed in charities SORP 2005 para.377. If the accounts from which the summary is taken have been examined or audited, the summary must include a statement by the examiner or auditor stating whether the statement is consistent with the full accounts.

Information in **summary financial information** must be consistent with the accounts and not be misleading. It should be accompanied by a statement on behalf of the trustees setting out the purpose of the information, whether or not it is from the full annual accounts, whether the full accounts have been examined or audited, and how the full accounts and report can be obtained.

54.2.7 Independent examination or audit

If the gross income of an unincorporated charity or charitable company is over £25,000 for financial years ending on or after 1 April 2009, it must have its accounts independently examined or audited. For financial years ending before 1 April 2009, the threshold was £10,000. At the time of writing (mid 2009), it is unclear whether the £25,000 threshold will also apply to charitable incorporated organisations and charitable industrial and provident societies.

If the charity's gross income is over £500,000, or is over £250,000 and the charity has assets of more than £3.26 million, it must have a **statutory charity audit** or, if it is a charitable company in this bracket, either a **statutory charity** or **company audit**. For financial years ending before 1 April 2009, the threshold was £250,000, or £100,000 with assets of more than £2.8 million. Charitable companies with annual income over £6.5 million and assets of more than £3.26 million must have a **statutory company audit** [54.3.7].

If an audit is not required under charity or company law but is required by the governing document, it may be possible to amend the governing document [7.5] to require 'such audit or examination (if any) as is required under the Charities Act 1993, [Companies Act 2006] or subsequent enactments'. The words in brackets should be included only if the charity is a company.

If funders require an audit but it is not required under charity or company law or the governing document, it may be possible to negotiate with them to have an independent examination instead.

A person carrying out statutory audits, or an independent examiner of charities with income over £250,000, must be a member of a specified professional body [55.4.1]. Requirements for appointing, changing or removing an examiner or auditor and their rights are covered in **chapter 55**. The Charity Commission provides information on the responsibilities and rights of examiners and auditors.

After examining or auditing the accounts, the examiner or auditor must make a statement in the required format stating that the accounts are satisfactory, or include a statement in the accounts if there is reason to believe that proper records were not kept, the accounts are not in accordance with the records, or there has been material expenditure or action outside the charity's objects or trusts.

Charities (Accounts & Reports) Regulations 2008 [SI 2008/629] regs.24-26,31

If the examiner or auditor expresses no concerns, the report is **unqualified**. If concerns are expressed, the report is **qualified**.

Under Charities Act **whistleblowing** provisions, an auditor or examiner must inform the Charity Commission in writing if he or she believes there are reasons for the Commission to institute an inquiry [4.5.9] or act for the protection of the charity.

Charities Act 1993 ss.44A,68A, inserted by Charities Act 2006 ss.29,33

54.2.8 Trustees' annual report

The Charity Commission increasingly uses the acronym **TAR** to refer to the statutory report on the accounts that the trustees have to produce each year to comply with charity law. This need not be the same as a more descriptive report or **annual review** produced for publicity purposes.

The trustees' annual report must include the charity's principal address, and details of all trustees at the time the report is signed plus any others who served during the financial year covered by the report. If the inclusion of the principal address or a trustee's name could put the trustee in personal danger, the Charity Commission can dispense with the need to include that person's name and/or the principal address. This provision does not apply to the statutory reports of charitable companies, where under company law details of all members of the governing body must be disclosed [**54.3.6.1**].*Charities (Accounts & Reports) Regulations 2008 [SI 2008/629] reg.40*
; Companies Act 2006 s.416(1)

Trustees of most charities which are not required to have a statutory audit [**54.2.7**] can produce a **simplified report**, using a pro forma available in CC16 or CC17 from the Charity Commission, or adapting the pro forma. Even if a statutory audit is not required, a simplified report cannot be produced by charitable companies, charities that are registered in Scotland as well as with the Charity Commission, charities that are required by other legislation to have their accounts audited, and certain other charities.

At the time of writing (mid 2009) it was expected that charitable incorporated organisations (CIOs) would also not be able to produce a simplified report.
Charities Act 2006 sch.7 pt.2 para.4

The Commission's pro forma for a simplified report includes sections on structure, governance and management; objectives and activities, including a short statement on how they meet the public benefit requirement [**5.3.1**]; achievements and performance; a financial review including a brief statement of the charity's reserves policy [**58.8.3**] and details of any material deficits; and optional information. It includes the statutory declaration that the trustees have had regard to the guidance issued by the Charity Commission on public benefit, and confirmation that there are no serious incidents [**4.5.8**] relating to the charity during the year that have not been reported to the Commission. *Charities (Accounts & Reports)*
Regulations 2008 [SI 2008/629] reg.40

A **full report** must include more details on objectives, activities, achievements and performance, any significant contribution of volunteers to these activities, a more detailed financial review including details of the charity's principal sources of income, and a statement of whether the trustees have considered major risks to the charity and are satisfied that systems are in place to manage those risks.

The full report should also include details of policies and procedures for trustee induction and training, or a statement that no such policies are in place. If applicable, it should include policies on grant making or the provision of other financial assistance to individuals or organisations, investment performance, investment policies including the extent to which social, environmental or ethical criteria are taken into account [**58.6**], the charity's plans for the future, and assets held by the charity or any of its trustees on behalf of another charity.
Charities (Accounts & Reports) Regulations 2008 [SI 2008/629] reg.40; Charities SORP 2005 para.41-50

The report, whether simplified or full, must be signed by one or more trustees who have been authorised to do so by the other trustees.

54.2.9 Providing reports to the Charity Commission and public

Charities registered with the Charity Commission and subject to examination or statutory audit [**54.2.7**] must submit their annual accounts and report to the Charity Commission within 10 months from the end of the financial year to which they apply. The documents are available for public inspection at Commission offices, and are also on the Commission website. Charities under the threshold at which examination or audit is required should not submit their accounts and report unless asked to do so by the Commission. *Charities Act 1993 s.45(3)*

Because of the risk of identity theft if signed accounts are on its website, the Commission no longer requires signatures on the accounts and reports it receives, provided the documents are an accurate copy of the signed original [**53.2.1**].

All charities, even if not registered, must provide a copy of their most recent annual accounts and report within two months to any member of the public who requests it in writing. A reasonable fee may be charged for this.   *Charities Act 1993*
s.47, amended by Charities Act 2006 sch.8 para.140

54.2.10   Charity annual updates and returns

A charity **annual return** is a form sent by the Charity Commission, which charities with gross income over £10,000 must fill in and return within 10 months from the end of its financial year. Charities whose annual income is £10,000 or less submit a simpler **update form**. Information from the update form or return is used to update the register of charities and the charity's entry on the Commission's website.   *Charities Act 1993 s.48*

The charity's entry on the Commission's website should be checked shortly after the annual accounts and return are submitted, to ensure the Commission has received them and this is recorded on the website. The information on the website should be checked for accuracy – data inputting errors are not unknown.

At the time of writing (mid 2009) it was expected that charitable incorporated organisations (CIOs) would have to submit annual returns even if their income is below £10,000.   *Charities Act 2006 sch.7 pt.2 para.5*

Charities with annual income over £1 million must submit a **summary information return** (SIR) with their return. Unlike the rest of the return the SIR is not a regulatory tool, but is intended to enable funders, members of the public and others to understand and compare charities' activities and achievements. All SIRs are on the Charity Commission's website.

Between returns, the Commission must be notified of any changes in the charity's correspondent, address or other details on the register of charities. Changes of trustees can be notified at any time via the Commission's website, but there is no obligation to notify such changes until the next return.   *Charities Act 1993 s.3(7)(b)*

54.2.11   Excepted and exempt charities

Charities exempt from registering with the Charity Commission [**8.1.2**] or excepted and not voluntarily registered [**8.1.3**] are covered by some, but not all, of the accounting and reporting regulations. Excepted charities which are voluntarily registered must comply with the same rules as any other registered charity.

54.2.11.1   Excepted charities not voluntarily registered

Unless they are covered by specific rules, for example for industrial and provident societies [**54.4.2**], excepted charities which are not voluntarily registered with the Charity Commission must prepare annual accounts (but not reports), are subject to the same rules on independent examination or audit [**54.2.7**], and must provide their accounts to the public [**54.2.9**]. They do not have to submit their accounts to the Commission unless requested to do so, and do not have to submit an annual return.   *Charities Act 1993 ss.46,47(2)*

54.2.11.2   Exempt charities

Charities exempt from registering with the Charity Commission must produce annual accounts and have them audited as required by any legislation which governs them, for example in relation to higher education institutions. The accounts must comply with SORP rules appropriate to their level of income.

If there is no legislation specifying otherwise, exempt charities must produce an income and expenditure account and balance sheet at least every 15 months, A trustees' report does not have to be prepared under charity law unless the Commission requests it, but is likely to be required under other legislation and/or SORP. Annual accounts do not need to be submitted to the Commission unless requested, but have to be provided to the public [**54.2.9**].   *Charities Act 1993 ss.46,47(2)*

54.3   COMPANIES

This book can only briefly summarise company law rules on accounts and reports. Basic information is available from Companies House, and for charitable companies from the Charity Commission. The company's accountant, independent examiner or auditor should be consulted for further information and advice.

54.3.1   Financial year

For companies incorporated on or after 1 April 1990, the **accounting reference date** (ARD) is the last day of the month in which the anniversary of incorporation occurs; for companies incorporated before this, the ARD is 31 March. The company can alter its ARD at any time provided it is not within five years of previously changing it. The change must be notified to Companies House on form **AA01**.   *Companies Act 2006 ss.391,392*

The directors can agree to end the company's **accounting reference period** – its financial year – on any date within seven days before or after the ARD.
Companies Act 2006 s.390(2)

A subsidiary undertaking's financial year must be the same as its parent company's [**9.4.1**], unless the directors of the parent company believe there are good reasons for it not to be.   *Companies Act 2006 s.390(5)*

54.3.2   Small, medium and large companies and groups

The rules on the form and content of individual and group accounts and the audit requirements are less onerous for small and medium-sized companies and groups.

For accounting purposes, a **small company** must meet at least two of the following criteria: **turnover** (total revenue income) not more than £6.5 million, balance sheet total not more than £3.26 million, weekly average number of employees not more than 50.   *Companies Act 2006 s.382, amended by Companies Act 2006 (Amendment)*
(Accounts & Reports) Regulations 2008 [SI 2008/393] reg.3

A **medium-sized company** must meet at least two of the following criteria: turnover not more than £25.9 million, balance sheet total not more than £12.9 million, weekly average number of employees not more than 250.
Companies Act 2006 s.465, amended by 2008 Regs reg.4

Slightly different thresholds apply for **small** and **medium-sized groups**.
Companies Act 2006 ss.383,466, amended by 2008 Regs regs.3,4

A company or group which does not meet the criteria for being medium-sized is a **large company** or **group**.

54.3.3   Charitable companies

The accounts of charitable companies are prepared in accordance with company law, but must also comply with the charities SORP [**54.2.3**] or explain why not. The SORP requires a statement of financial activities [**54.2.6.3**] which is different from the income and expenditure account format required under company law. If the SoFA includes only revenue transactions the SoFA and I&E accounts may be able to be combined, but if the SoFA includes non-revenue transactions, a separate **summary income and expenditure account** may be required in order to comply with Companies Act requirements.

Annual reports of charitable companies must comply with both charity and company law, but it is usually possible to combine the requirements in one report.

Although all charitable companies prepare their accounts under company law, they are subject to independent examination or audit under charity law [**54.2.7**] if they qualify as a small company [**54.3.2**]. Medium and large companies must be audited under company law.   *Charities Act 1993 ss.41(5), 42(7), 43(9), amended by Companies*
Act 2006 (Consequential Amendments etc) Order 2008 [SI 2008/948] sch.1 para.192(4)

54.3.4   Community interest companies

Community interest companies are subject to the same rules as other companies, but must submit a **community interest company report** to Companies House on form **CIC34** with the annual accounts. The obligation to provide a CIC report applies even if the company is exempt from submitting an ordinary directors' report. Details are available from the CIC regulator [see end of chapter].

Companies (Audit, Investigations & Community Enterprise) Act 2004 s.34
Community Interest Company Regulations 2005 [SI 2005/1788] regs.26-29

54.3.5   Annual accounts

The form of a company's accounts depends on whether it is an individual company or a parent [**9.4.1**]; whether it is small, medium or large [**54.3.2**]; whether it is charitable or not charitable [**54.3.3**]; and if it is not charitable, whether it prepares its accounts under the **Companies Act 2006** s.396 or international accounting standards (IAS). Charitable companies cannot use the IAS.

Companies Act 2006 s.395; Small Companies & Groups (Accounts & Directors' Report) Regulations 2008 [SI 2008/409]; Large & Medium-sized Companies & Groups (Accounts & Reports) Regulations 2008 [SI 2008/410]

In all cases the accounts must be approved by the directors, and the balance sheet must be signed by a director. If the accounts have been prepared under the provisions for small companies, a prominent statement to this effect must be above the signature.

Companies Act 2006 s.414

54.3.5.1   Individual accounts

Every company must produce annual **individual accounts** which must include a balance sheet [**54.2.6.9**] and a profit and loss account or, for a voluntary organisation, an income and expenditure account [**54.2.6.1**]. The accounts must be prepared in accordance with s.396 of the **Companies Act 2006** or in accordance with international accounting standards, and any non-compliance must be explained. The directors must not approve the accounts unless they are satisfied the accounts give a true and fair view of the company's or group's assets, liabilities, financial position and profit and loss.

Companies Act 2006 ss.392-397

54.3.5.2   Notes to the accounts

The notes to the accounts must include specified information. This includes details of remuneration in cash or in kind paid to the directors or connected persons [**15.2.5**], either by the company itself or by a third party paying a director or connected person for services provided to the company, and details of credit or advances provided to directors or guarantees provided by the company on behalf of directors.

Companies Act 2006 ss.412,413; Small Companies Regs 2008 sch.3;
Large & Medium-sized Companies Regulations 2008 sch.5

Small and medium companies must disclose the fees receivable by their auditors for the audit itself; large companies must disclose all fees receivable by their auditors for services provided by the auditors or their associates. All companies must disclose any liability limitation agreement with their auditor [**55.7**].

Companies
(Disclosure of Auditor Remuneration & Liability Limitation Agreements) Regulations 2008 [SI 2008/489]

Medium and large companies must include information about the weekly average number of employees during the year in total and in various categories, and the company's salary and pension costs if these are not included elsewhere in the accounts.

Companies Act 2006 s.411

54.3.5.3   Group accounts

If the company is a parent company [**9.4.1**], it may also have to prepare group accounts with a consolidated balance sheet and consolidated profit and loss (or income and expenditure) accounts for the parent and all its subsidiary undertakings. The rules for group accounts broadly follow those for individual accounts. This book does not cover group accounts.

Companies Act 2006 ss.398-408

54.3.6   Report of the directors

The directors must prepare a statutory report on the accounts which must be agreed by the board and signed on their behalf by a director or the company secretary.

Companies Act 2006 ss.416,419

The directors' statutory report may be a short report issued with the annual accounts. It is not necessarily the same as a descriptive **annual review** for publicity purposes. A descriptive report may be used to meet Companies Act requirements only if it contains all the information required under company legislation.

Charitable companies must produce statutory annual reports complying with both company and charity requirements [**54.2.8**]. The company and charity reports may be separate, but are normally combined.

54.3.6.1 Small companies

The report of the directors of a small company [**54.3.2**] must include:

- the names of everyone who, at any time during the financial year, was a director of the company;

- the main activities of the company during the year and any significant changes;

- details of donations to a political party or other political organisation or independent election candidate or any other political expenditure in or relating to the UK or another EU member state, if the total of all such donations was more than £2,000 during the year (political organisation, expenditure etc is defined in the same way as for the decision making process to agree such donations, **46.3**);

- the total of any contributions to a non-EU political party or parties;

- details of donations for charitable purposes, if the total of all such donations was more than £2,000 during the year;

- if the company had a weekly average of more than 250 employees during the year, statements of the company's policies on employing disabled people, continuing to employ and if necessary train people who become disabled during the period they are employed by the company, and training, career development and promotion of disabled employees;

- in a share company, details of the company's purchase or acquisition of its own shares;

- unless the company has taken advantage of an exemption from audit under the Companies Act [**54.3.7.1**], a statement that no director at the time the report is approved is aware of any relevant information that should have been made available to the auditor, and that each director has taken all steps that should be taken by a director to become aware of any such information;

- if the company has taken advantage of the accounting provisions for small companies, a statement to this effect in a prominent position above the signature.   *Companies Act 2006 ss.416,418,419; Small Companies & Groups (Accounts & Directors' Report) Regulations 2008 [SI 2008/409] sch.5*

54.3.6.2 Medium and large companies

The report of the directors of a medium [**54.3.2**] or large company must include the information above, as well as additional information including the value of land held by the company if this is significantly different from the amount shown on the balance sheet; risk management policies on the use of financial instruments; details of any important events affecting the company since the end of the financial year; likely future developments; research and development (if any) carried out by the company; branches outside the UK; and in share companies the amount (if any) that the directors recommend to be paid as dividends. If the average weekly number of employees within the UK is more than 250, the report must include a statement about how the company involves and consults employees, and how employees are made aware of financial and economic factors affecting the company.   *Companies Act 2006 s.416; Large & Medium-sized Companies & Groups (Accounts & Reports) Regulations 2008 [SI 2008/410] sch.7*

All medium and large companies must include within their report a **business review**, describing the company's development and performance during the year, the main risks and uncertainties faced by the company, and the position of the company's business at the end of the year. The review must include analysis of financial key performance indicators (KPIs), and in large companies must also include analysis of non-financial KPIs.   *Companies Act 2006 s.417*

54.3.6.3 Public and listed companies

Public limited companies [**3.3.1**] and companies listed on a stock exchange have additional reporting requirements, for example the duty of listed companies to report on their social and environmental impact and on corporate governance. These requirements are not included in this book.

54.3.7   Audit

Most small companies [**54.3.2**] are exempt from having to have an audit [**54.3.7.1**] under company law. But charitable companies, even if exempt under company law, must generally have an independent examination or audit under charity law or company law [**54.2.7**].

Medium and large companies, whether charitable or non-charitable, must have a statutory (full) audit under company law [**54.3.7.2**] unless they are dormant [**54.3.10**]. The nature of the audit and the type of report produced by the auditor depends on the size of the company.

A person carrying out company audits must be a member of a specified professional body [**55.3.2**]. The process of appointing, changing or removing a company auditor is closely regulated by the Companies Acts [**55.3**].

54.3.7.1   Exemption from audit

A company is generally exempt from audit under the Companies Act if it qualifies as a small company, with a turnover of not more than £6.5 million *and* a balance sheet total of not more than £3.26 million. Unlike the usual definition of a small company [**54.3.2**], number of employees is not included. A company which takes advantage of the exemption must state this on the balance sheet.

Companies Act 2006 ss.414,477-479, amended by Companies Act 2006 (Amendment)
(Accounts & Reports) Regulations 2008 [SI 2008/393] reg.5

The exemption does not apply if the company's articles of association require an audit. In this case the articles can be amended [**7.5.3**] to require 'such audit or reports (if any) as are required under the Companies Act 2006, [the Charities Act 1993] and subsequent enactments'. The bracketed words should be included only for charitable companies.

Even if a company is exempt from audit, 10% of the members of a company limited by guarantee, or members holding 10% of the value of a company's share capital in a company limited by shares, can require the company to have a statutory audit by giving notice in writing at the company's registered office at least one month before the end of the financial year.   *Companies Act 2006 s.476*

A charitable company, even if exempt under company law, is likely to need an independent examination or audit under charity law [**54.2.7**]. The accounts must say that the company is exempt from audit under the Companies Act.

54.3.7.2   Statutory audit

For a statutory audit, auditors must make a report stating whether, in their opinion, the accounts give a true and fair view of the financial situation and have been properly prepared. A report confirming this is **unqualified**. If the auditors cannot for any reason state that the accounts have been properly prepared and give a true and fair view, they must give a **qualified report**.   *Companies Act 2006 s.495*

The auditors must also indicate whether, in their opinion, the directors' report reflects the accounts.   *Companies Act 2006 s.496*

54.3.7.3   Approval

After being signed by the auditor, the accounts and report must be approved by the board. The balance sheet must be signed on their behalf by a company director [**54.3.3**], and the directors' report must be signed on their behalf by a director or the company secretary [**54.3.6**].

54.3.8   Filing, circulation and publication

Once the annual accounts and reports have been signed, every copy which is circulated or published in any way, including on the internet, must be complete and must include the names of the persons who signed the balance sheet, the directors' report and, if applicable, auditor's report.   *Companies Act 2006 ss.433,434*

54.3.8.1   Circulation to company members

The annual accounts, directors' report and, if there is one, auditor's report must be circulated to company members, holders of the company's debentures and everyone entitled to receive notice of general meetings. This must be done by the end of the period for filing the accounts and reports with Companies House [**54.3.8.3**] or, if earlier, the date the accounts are delivered to Companies House. In some cases a **summary financial statement** [**54.3.8.2**] can be circulated instead of the full accounts.   *Companies Act 2006 ss.423,424*

The accounts can be put on a website or circulated electronically if this has been agreed by the members in general, and by each member to whom they are provided by this method [**18.3**].

The accounts no longer need to be presented to (laid before) a general meeting unless this is required by the articles of association. The articles can be amended to remove the requirement [**7.5.3**].

The accounts are often said to be approved at the annual or other general meeting, but this approval by the company members is not necessary unless it is required under the articles of association. Under company law, the company members simply receive accounts which have already been approved by the directors. If company members do not like what the accounts show, they can question the directors, express their concern, pass a resolution calling for the directors to act differently, or ultimately remove the directors [**13.5.6**]. But they have no right to refuse to accept the accounts, unless the articles give them this right.

54.3.8.2   Summary financial statement

If the accounts have been audited, a **summary financial statement**, rather than the full accounts, may be supplied to members and others entitled to receive the accounts. Before this is done, persons entitled to receive the accounts must be consulted in a specified way about whether they are willing to receive a summary or want the full accounts. Failure to reply is taken as agreement to receive a summary.   *Companies Act 2006 ss.426-428; Companies (Summary Financial Statement)*
Regulations 2008 [2008/374]

The statement must include specified information, must make clear that it is a summary, and must indicate how the full accounts can be obtained.

Summary financial statements cannot be used – even with consent – if the articles of association require the full audited accounts to be circulated. In this case the articles can be amended [**7.5.3**].

54.3.8.3   Submission to Companies House

For financial years starting on or after 6 April 2008, the annual accounts, directors' report and auditor's report (if there is one) must be filed with Companies House within nine months from the end of the financial year. Where the end of the financial year is the last day of the month, the date by which they must be filed is the last day of the month nine months later.   *Companies Act 2006 ss.441-443*

Small companies [**54.3.2**] may submit **abbreviated accounts** consisting only of a balance sheet, without a profit and loss or income and expenditure account and without a directors' report. If the company is not eligible for exemption from audit, it must submit the auditor's report. Medium-sized companies must provide a profit and loss account and directors' report, but some items in the P&L account can be combined to shorten it. If the full accounts have been audited, abbreviated accounts must be accompanied by an auditor's statement that the company is eligible to submit abbreviated accounts.   *Companies Act 2006 ss.444,445,449*

Accounts and reports can be submitted on paper or online. If the accounts are not in the proper form, for example if a signature is missing, they are treated as not having been submitted on time. Companies House recommends that accounts are submitted several weeks early, so there is time to put right any problems.

Extensions are granted only if there is a very good reason, and not if the accounts are already late. Application is made to the companies administration branch at Companies House.

There are automatic penalties for the company ranging from £150 if the accounts are between one day and one month late, to £1,500 if they are more than six months late. In addition, the directors may be held personally liable and may have charges brought against them. *Companies (Late Filing Penalties) & Limited Liability Partnerships (Filing Periods & Late Filing Penalties) Regulations 2008 [SI 2008/497]*

Persistent lateness may lead to the company being struck off the register of companies [**24.4.2**]. It is very important to avoid this, as reinstatement is very costly and involves a court hearing. Being struck off may have other damaging consequences, including exposing members of the governing body to personal liability, and giving grounds for the termination of leases and other agreements.

54.3.8.4 Making accounts and reports available to the public

A company must make its accounts and reports available to company members and debenture holders free of charge. In addition, the accounts and reports are open to the public at Companies House, and copies may be requested by any member of the public. They are also available, for a small charge, via the Companies House website. *Companies Act 2006 s.431*

Companies House has arrangements to reduce the risk of corporate or individual identity theft from the details available in the accounts and reports [**53.2.1**].

Under charity law, the accounts and reports must be made available within two months to any member of the public who requests them. A reasonable fee may be charged. For charities which are obliged to send annual accounts and reports to the Charity Commission, the documents are available free of charge on the Commission's website. *Charities Act 1993 s.47(2), amended by Charities Act 2006 sch.8 para.140*

54.3.9 Non-statutory accounts

Summarised or abridged company accounts which do not include the full accounts, directors' report and auditor's report if there is one are called **non-statutory accounts**. If non-statutory accounts are published in any way, including on the internet, they must not include the auditor's report, and must include statements in a specified form. It is usually advisable to have summarised accounts prepared by the auditor. *Companies Act 2006 s.435*

54.3.10 Dormant companies

A company is dormant if there has been no accounting transaction during the financial year, apart from the company annual return filing fee and a few other exceptions. *Companies Act 2006 ss.480,1169*

A small company [**54.3.2**] which is dormant is exempt from the requirement to have its accounts audited, but must comply with all other company law requirements. This includes statutory records [**18.5**] and notifications to Companies House, submission of balance sheet and return to Companies House every year, and compliance with constitutional requirements such as election of directors.

Details are in GP2 *Life of a company: Annual requirements*, available from Companies House. This should be consulted and advice should be taken before making a company dormant.

54.3.11 Company annual returns

Every company must submit an annual return each year. This is a straightforward procedure designed to keep the register of companies up to date, and is separate from the requirement to submit the annual accounts and reports. From 1 October 2009 the required information changed, to enable company directors to provide a **service address** rather than a residential address [**18.5.4**], and to reflect other company law changes from that date. *Companies Act 2006 ss.854-856, amended by Companies Act 2006 (Annual Return & Service Addresses) Regulations 2008 [SI 2008/3000]*

Companies House notifies the company shortly before the return is due, and it can be submitted electronically or a paper form can be requested. The annual filing fee (as at 1/8/09) is £15 if the return is submitted electronically and £30 if it is on paper. Failure to file on time carries penalties.

Information about company annual returns is in GP2 *Life of a company: Annual requirements*, available from Companies House.

54.4 INDUSTRIAL AND PROVIDENT SOCIETIES

At the time of writing (mid 2009), the government had proposed renaming industrial and provident societies as **co-operatives** and **community benefit societies** [3.5]. In this book we still refer to IPSs.

Also at the time of writing most charitable IPSs, apart from registered social landlords, were ceasing to be exempt charities [8.1.2]. If their annual income was more than £100,000 they would have to register with the Charity Commission, and if their income was less than this they would become excepted charities [8.1.2, 54.2.11.1]. It was not clear whether the accounting requirements for IPSs registered with the Commission would be similar to those for charitable companies [54.3.3].

54.4.1 Financial year

An industrial and provident society's financial year must end between 31 August and 31 January unless it has authorisation from the Financial Services Authority for it to end at another time. At the time of writing (mid 2009) the government had consulted on allowing the financial year to end at any time.

Industrial & Provident Societies Act 1965 s.39(2),(3)

54.4.2 Annual accounts

IPSs must prepare an annual **revenue account** and **balance sheet**. The revenue account can cover the whole society, or there can be two or more revenue accounts dealing with specific aspects of the society's work. The balance sheet must cover the whole society. *Friendly & Industrial & Provident Societies Act 1968 s.3*

A society which has one or more subsidiaries must produce group accounts, although it is possible to apply to the Financial Services Authority to exclude one or more subsidiaries if there are good reasons for doing so. *FIPSA 1968 ss.13-15*

54.4.2.1 Audit or report

An IPS does not need an audit if the total of its receipts and payments combined in the financial year was not more than £5,000, the value of its assets at the end of the financial year was not more than £5,000, and the number of members was not more than 500. *FIPSA 1968 s.4(2)*

Other IPSs must in general have a full audit carried out by a qualified auditor. However, the members may pass a resolution at a general meeting not to have a full audit if the IPS's turnover for the year did not exceed £5.6 million (£250,000 for charitable IPSs), and the total value of its assets at the end of the financial year did not exceed £2.8 million. This provision does not apply to credit unions, registered social landlords, or an IPS which is or has a subsidiary.

FIPSA 1968 ss.4, 4A, amended by FIPSA 1968 (Audit Exemption) (Amendment) Order 2006 [SI 2006/265]

The resolution must be passed at a general meeting and is passed only if no more than 20% of the votes cast are against the resolution, *and* no more than 10% of the members eligible to vote, vote against the resolution. *FIPSA 1968 s.4A(2)*

If the resolution is passed and turnover was more than £90,000 in the previous financial year, the IPS must have a **reporting accountant** make a report on the accounts. This is less detailed than a full audit. *FIPSA 1968 s.9A*

54.4.2.2 Approval

The IPS's accounts, audited or reported on if required, must be approved by the committee and signed by the secretary and two directors acting on behalf of the committee. *FIPSA 1968 s.3A(1)*

54.4.2.3   Filing, circulation and publication

The accounts form part of the annual return [**54.4.3**] and must be sent to the Financial Services Authority each year with (if required) the accountant's or auditor's report. The accounts and return must be submitted within seven months from the end of the IPS's financial year.   *Industrial & Provident Societies Act 1965 s.39(1);*
Friendly & Industrial & Provident Societies Act 1968 s.11(1),(2)

The revenue account and balance sheet must not be circulated or published unless they have been audited or reported on (if required) and signed, and are accompanied by the relevant report.   *FIPSA 1968 s.3A*

A copy of the most recent balance sheet and relevant report must be on public display at the society's registered office.   *IPSA 1965 s.40*

Unless the governing document requires it, there is no obligation to send accounts to all members, but if any member or person interested in the funds of the society requests the accounts they must be sent free of charge.   *IPSA 1965 s.39(5);*
FIPSA 1968 ss.11(5),13(7)

54.4.3   Annual returns

An annual return must be submitted to the Financial Services Authority within seven months from the end of the financial year. There is no annual filing fee for IPS returns, but IPSs pay a **periodic fee** each year, invoiced by the Financial Services Authority in September. The fee ranges from £55 to £425 (as at 1/8/09), depending on the IPS's total assets.   *Industrial & Provident Societies Act 1965 s.39*

54.5   NON-CHARITABLE ASSOCIATIONS

There is no statutory obligation for a non-charitable unincorporated association to prepare accounts or have them audited, but this may be required by its governing document or funders. If the governing document does not require annual accounts, the governing body or the members at a general meeting may require the treasurer or any other person to prepare accounts (and it would be a good idea to amend the governing document [**7.5**] to make this an annual requirement). They may also require the accounts to be audited or to be examined by a suitable independent person [**55.6**], and might want to amend the governing document to require this as well.

Resources: ANNUAL ACCOUNTS, REPORTS AND RETURNS

Local community accountancy projects. Details from NAVCA: www.navca.org.uk, 0114 278 6636, navca@navca.org.uk.

Charity accounts, reports, independent examination and audit. Charity Commission: www.charitycommission.gov.uk, 0845 300 0218, email via website.

Charity Finance Directors' Group: www.cfdg.org.uk, 0845 345 3192, info@cfdg.org.uk.

Company accounts, reports and audit. Companies House: www.companieshouse.gov.uk, 0303 1234 500, enquiries@companieshouse.gov.uk.

Community interest companies. CIC regulator: www.cicregulator.gov.uk, 029 2034 6228, cicregulator@companieshouse.gov.uk.

Industrial and provident societies. Financial Services Authority Mutual Societies Registration: www.fsa.gov.uk (at the time of writing, access is via Doing business with the FSA / Small firms / Mutual societies), 0845 606 9966, mutualsann@fsa.gov.uk.

Statute law. www.opsi.gov.uk and www.statutelaw.gov.uk.

Much but not all case law. www.bailii.org.

Updates cross-referenced to this book. www.rclh.co.uk.

Chapter 55

AUDITORS AND INDEPENDENT EXAMINERS

For sources of further information see end of chapter 54.

55.1 THE NEED FOR AN AUDITOR

The accounts of many charities and other organisations are subject to independent **scrutiny**, either in the form of a full **statutory audit** [**54.2.7**, **54.3.7**, **54.4.2**] or in some cases a simpler **independent examination** or **reporting accountant's report** [**54.2.7**, **54.4.2**] rather than a statutory audit.

Even where there is no statutory obligation for independent scrutiny, it may be required by the organisation's governing document, members or funders. The members of a company or industrial and provident society always have a statutory right to require an independent examination, reporting accountant's report or audit, even if these are not required under statute or the governing document.

If there is are differing requirements – if, for example, the governing document or a funder requires a full audit when statute allows a simpler scrutiny or none at all, or *vice versa* – the higher requirement prevails. It may be possible to amend the governing document [**7.5**] to bring it into line with statutory requirements, or to negotiate with funders to change their requirement.

55.1.1 Choosing an examiner or auditor

The voluntary sector is a specialist area, with complex accounting and reporting provisions [**chapter 54**]. Auditors with a real knowledge of the sector are relatively rare, but organisations should make every effort to find one already familiar with the sector and with the type of work carried out by the organisation.

Eligibility to act as an independent examiner or to carry out **statutory audits** under charity, company or other law is defined in the legislation for each type of organisation, and is summarised in this chapter [**55.3.2**, **55.4.1**].

If there are differing requirements, such as the governing document or a funder requiring 'a qualified auditor' when under statute a non-qualified examiner would be sufficient, the higher requirement prevails but it may be possible to amend the governing document or negotiate with funders.

55.1.2 Cost

It is vital to obtain comparative quotes prior to appointment, and to find out what charges are made for additional services (for example, advice on VAT) and the basis for calculating them – but cost should not be the only basis for selection. Once an auditor, examiner or reporting accountant is appointed, they should be asked to provide a new quote each year, or changes in the fees should be monitored.

55.1.3 Expectations and role

The form and content of statutory audits are specified by law, and in **international standards on auditing** (IASs) and practice notes issued by the Auditing Practices Board. For charity independent examinations, the form and content is set out in charity law, and for reporting accountants' reports for industrial and provident societies, the rules are in IPS law. For other types of scrutiny, the form and content may be specified in the governing document or may simply be arranged between the organisation and the person carrying out the scrutiny.

Qualified auditors are required by auditing standards to provide a **terms of engagement** letter setting out the contract between the auditor and the organisation. This may seek to limit the role of the auditor, both to narrow the grounds on which the organisation could make a claim against the auditor for breach of contract or negligence [**55.7**], and to make clear the limits of the service provided. The terms of engagement must be carefully considered by the governing body, with particular attention given to the need for additional services.

Where the auditor or examiner is not professionally qualified, it is even more important that the governing body and person carrying out the scrutiny understand exactly what is expected. This should be set out in writing.

55.1.3.1 The auditor's role

The core of the auditor's role is ensuring that the accounts give a **true and fair view** of the organisation's financial affairs (or, for charity independent examinations, that the accounts are consistent with the financial records). Professional auditors must review the design and operation of internal controls [**53.1**], procedures for reviewing and assessing risk [**53.1.2**], and procedures for the prevention and detection of fraud [**53.1.3**], but there is no duty on the auditor to ensure any weaknesses are rectified. That responsibility rests with the governing body.

Charity auditors or independent examiners have to report deliberate or reckless misconduct in administering the charity to the Charity Commission [**54.2.7**]. For other types of audit, auditors should report fraud to the governing body – but the responsibility for detecting and preventing fraud rests with the governing body, not the auditor. The auditor will look at anti-fraud procedures, but unless the client organisation specifically requests it, will not be searching for fraud.

The provision of advice on tax and VAT matters does not generally fall within the scope of an audit, so if these are required this should be made clear.

The organisation should also clearly specify if it requires the auditor to carry out other tasks, such as filing the accounts with the Charity Commission and/or Companies House, or submitting the accounts to funders or other bodies. It is the responsibility of the governing body, not the auditor, to ensure this is done.

55.2 RIGHTS OF AUDITORS AND EXAMINERS

Auditors for companies, industrial and provident societies and charities have statutory rights to receive information and communicate with members,.

55.2.1 Companies and IPSs

Auditors for companies, and auditors and reporting accountants for industrial and provident societies, have a statutory right:

- to have access at all times to the organisation's books, accounts and all related documentation;

- to require relevant information and explanations from the organisation's directors, company/IPS secretary and employees (and it is an offence for them knowingly to make a misleading, false or deceptive statement to the auditor);

- if auditing a parent body, to require information and explanations from its subsidiary undertakings [9.4.1] and their auditors;

- to receive the same notices of general meetings and other documentation as company or IPS members receive;

- to attend general meetings, and to speak (but not vote) on any topic which concerns them as auditor. *Companies Act 2006 ss.499-502;*
Friendly & Industrial & Provident Societies Act 1968 ss.9(5)-(7),9B

55.2.2 Charities

Auditors or independent examiners carrying out a charity's statutory audit or examination have a right of access to any books, documents or other records which relate to the charity and which they consider necessary to inspect, and the right to require information and explanations from past or present charity trustees, holding or custodian trustees [20.4], officers [14.1] or employees.
Charities (Accounts & Reports) Regulations 2008 [SI 2008/629] reg.33

There is no statutory right to receive notice of a charitable association's general meetings or a charitable trust's trustee meetings, but it is good practice for the charity to provide this. Charitable companies and industrial and provident societies should comply with the rules for companies and IPSs [55.2.1].

55.3 COMPANY AUDITORS

The basic rules on company audits, exemption from the need to have a full audit or from the need to have any audit, and companies which are examined or audited under charity law rather than company law, are set out in 54.3.7.

55.3.1 Charitable companies

For financial years ending on or after 1 April 2009, for most charitable companies defined as small under company law [54.3.2]:

- the accounts continue to be prepared under company law, and have to comply with all relevant requirements of charities SORP [54.2.3]

- the accounts are independently examined or audited under charity law rather than company law;

- the examination/audit provisions are the same as for unincorporated charities [55.4];

- the company law provisions for appointment, resignation and removal of auditors should be followed [55.3.3-55.3.6]. *Charities Act 1993 ss.43-45,47,68,69, sch.5A,*
amended by Charities Act 2006 (Charitable Companies Audit & Group Accounts Provisions) Order 2008
[SI 2008/527] & Charities Acts 1992 & 1993 (Substitution of Sums) Order 2009 [SI 2009/508]

Charitable companies with income over £6.5 million and assets over £3.26 million must have a statutory company audit as set out below.

55.3.2 Eligibility

An individual, corporate body or partnership carrying out a statutory audit for a company must be a member of a recognised supervisory body, be eligible to be appointed as a company auditor under the rules of that body, and must not be ineligible for appointment because of a connection with the company, or with an officer or employee of the company. *Companies Act 2006 ss.1212,1214*

The recognised bodies are the Institute of Chartered Accountants in England and Wales, Institute of Chartered Accountants of Scotland, Institute of Chartered Accountants in Ireland, Association of Chartered Certified Accountants, and Association of Authorised Public Accountants. Members of the recognised bodies in Scotland and Ireland can carry out company audits in England and Wales.

55.3.3   **Appointment**

Unless the directors reasonably believe that an audit is unlikely to be required and pass a resolution not to appoint an auditor, an auditor or auditors must be appointed for each financial year of the company.   *Companies Act 2006 s. 485(1)*

The directors may appoint an auditor at any time during the company's first financial year, or following a period when the company was exempt from audit and did not have an auditor, or to fill a casual vacancy in the office of auditor.
Companies Act 2006 s.485(3)

In other situations, the statutory **period for appointing auditors** lasts for 28 days after the end of the time allowed for sending out copies of the company's annual accounts and reports for the previous year or, if earlier, the day on which the company's annual accounts and reports are actually sent out [**54.3.8**]. During this period, the company's members may appoint an auditor by ordinary resolution [**19.7.4**]. The members may also appoint an auditor by ordinary resolution if they did not do so during the period for appointing auditors, or if the directors did not appoint an auditor when they should have done so.   *Companies Act 2006 s.485(2)*

In some situations the resolution requires **special notice** [**19.7.4**].

55.3.3.1   Deemed reappointment

Where an auditor has been appointed by the company members – either at a general meeting or by written resolution – their term of office generally runs from 28 days after circulation of the accounts until the end of the corresponding period the following year. If a different auditor is not appointed during the 28-day period at the end of the year, the auditor is deemed to be reappointed.

The provision for **deemed reappointment** does not apply where the auditor was appointed by the directors, the company's articles require actual reappointment, members representing 5% of the company's voting rights (or a lower percentage if this is specified in the articles) give notice that the auditor should not be reappointed, or the directors have resolved that no auditor or auditors should be appointed for the financial year in question.   *Companies Act 2006 ss.487,488*

55.3.3.2   Appointment outside the statutory period

If a new auditor is to start at the end of the financial year (rather than during the year, which would be dealt with under removal provisions, **55.3.6**), their appointment may be done by written resolution or at a general meeting at any time during the financial year, or after the end of the year if a replacement has not been appointed and the current auditor is not deemed to have been reappointed [**55.3.3.1**].   *Companies Act 2006 ss.514,515*

The current auditor and proposed replacement must be sent a copy of the resolution, and the current auditor may make a statement of his or her case within 14 days. Any such statement must be circulated along with the written resolution [**19.10.2**] or notice of the general meeting, unless the company or a person aggrieved by the statement applies to the court for it not to be circulated. If the statement is received too late to be circulated with notice of the general meeting, it must be read out at the meeting.

If a written resolution is to be used to appoint the new auditor, the outgoing auditor has the right to require it to be done at a general meeting [**55.2.1**].

55.3.4   **Remuneration**

If the auditor is appointed or reappointed by the company members, the members must also agree by ordinary resolution the auditor's remuneration or how the remuneration is to be decided. Often the members delegate to the directors the right to set the remuneration. If the directors appoint the auditor, the directors decide the remuneration. Remuneration includes expenses and benefits in kind.
Companies Act 2006 s.492

The amount of remuneration for the audit must be disclosed in a note to the annual accounts. Large companies [**54.3.2**] must also disclose any fees paid to the auditor or an associate for other services during the year.   *Companies Act 2006 s.494;*
Companies (Disclosure of Auditor Remuneration & Liability Limitation Agreements) Regulations 2008 [SI 2008/489]

55.3.5   Resignation

An auditor has the right to resign at any time, regardless of any agreement with the company. To do this, the auditor must deposit at the company's registered office a notice of resignation, and either a statement of circumstances connected with the resignation that the auditor thinks should be brought to the attention of the members, or a statement that there are no such circumstances.

Companies Act 2006 ss.516,519

Within 14 days, the company must send a copy of the notice of resignation to Companies House. If the statement contains circumstances which the auditor thinks should be brought to the attention of members, it must be dealt with in the same way as a statement of circumstances when an auditor is being removed [**55.3.6**].

Companies Act 2006 s.517

The auditor has the right to require the directors to call a general meeting to receive and consider an explanation of the circumstances connected with the resignation. The provisions on attendance at general meetings and notification to Companies House are the same as for removal of an auditor.

Companies Act 2006 s.518

55.3.6   Removal

A company may remove its auditor at any time by ordinary resolution [**19.7.4**] at a general meeting, regardless of any agreement between them. However, there are safeguards to ensure that a whistleblowing auditor is not being removed as a way of concealing the company's bad practice.

Special notice [**19.7.4**] is needed to remove an auditor before the end of his or her term of office. As soon as it receives notice of a resolution to remove an auditor, the company must send it to the auditor who is proposed for removal and to any person being put forward as a replacement. It must also be sent within 14 days to Companies House. If the auditor is removed, Companies House must be informed within 14 days on form **AA03**.

Companies Act 2006 ss.510-512

An auditor proposed for removal has the right to make a statement of his or her case, which the company must circulate within 14 days to everyone to whom notice of the general meeting is sent (or has been sent). If the statement is received too late to be sent out, the auditor can require it to be read out at the meeting. Alternatively the company or any person aggrieved by the statement may apply to the court not to do this if they think the statement is being used 'to secure needless publicity for defamatory matter'.

Companies Act 2006 s.511

The auditor has the right to attend the general meeting at which his or her removal is proposed, and to speak on any matter which concerns him or her as auditor. Even after dismissal, an auditor has the right to receive notice of a general meeting at which his or her term of office would have ended had he or she not been removed, or at which it is proposed to appoint a replacement auditor. The dismissed auditor also has the right to receive all documents sent to company members for the meeting, and to attend and speak at the meeting on matters of concern to him or her as former auditor.

Companies Act 2006 ss.502,513

55.4   CHARITY EXAMINERS AND AUDITORS

For financial years ending on or after 1 April 2009, charitable companies, unincorporated associations and trusts must have [**54.2.7**]:

- an independent examination or statutory charity audit if their annual income is from £25,000 to £250,000, regardless of value of assets;
- an independent examination or statutory charity audit if income is from £250,000 to £500,000 and the value of assets is not more than £3.26 million;
- a statutory charity audit if income is over £500,000, or over £250,000 with assets valued at more than £3.26 million;
- for a charitable company with income over £6.5 million and assets valued at more than £3.26 million, a statutory company audit [**54.3.7, 55.3**] instead of a statutory charity audit.

The governing document or funders may require independent examination or audit even where this is not required by statute.

55.4.1 Eligibility

For financial years ending on or after 1 April 2009, if income is more than £500,000 or a charity under this amount has a statutory audit, a charity auditor must be eligible to be appointed as a statutory auditor for companies [**55.3.2**].

Charities Act 1993 s.43(1),(2), amended by Charities Act 2006 s.28
& Charities Acts 1992 & 1993 (Substitution of Sums) Order 2009 [SI 2009/508]

For independent examination of charities with income from £250,000 to £500,000, the examiner must be eligible to be appointed as a statutory auditor for companies [**55.3.2**], or must be a member the Association of Accounting Technicians, Association of International Accountants, Chartered Institute of Management Accountants, Institute of Chartered Secretaries and Administrators, or Chartered Institute of Public Finance and Accountancy, and be eligible under the rules of that body for appointment as a charity auditor. A fellow of the Association of Charity Independent Examiners is also eligible for appointment as an independent examiner in this income bracket.

Charities Act 1993 s.43(1)-(3B),
amended by Charities Act 2006 (Charitable Companies Audit & Group Accounts Provisions)
Order 2008 para.2 & Charities Acts 1992 & 1993 (Substitution of Sums) Order 2009 [SI 2009/508]

If income is not more than £250,000, an independent examiner does not have to be professionally qualified but must be 'an independent person who is reasonably believed by the trustees to have the requisite ability and practical experience to carry out a competent examination of the accounts'. The trustees need to be satisfied the examiner has this ability and experience.

Charities Act 1993 s.43(3)

An independent examiner should have no connection with the charity which might inhibit the impartial conduct of the examination. This means, at the very least, that the examiner should not be closely involved in the charity's administration, a major donor, a major beneficiary, or a close relative, business partner or employee of such a person.

Anyone appointed as an independent examiner should contact the Charity Commission or consult its website for the necessary information and instructions.

55.4.2 Appointment, resignation, removal and remuneration

There are no specific charity law procedures or regulations for the appointment, resignation or removal of a charity auditor or independent examiner, or how their remuneration is determined.

Charitable companies and industrial and provident societies which have a statutory audit should follow the relevant rules [**55.3, 55.5**], and should comply with the company/IPS rules on rights of auditors [**55.2**]. Other charitable companies and IPSs should, as a matter of good practice, comply with those rules as well. For other charities, if the governing document sets out procedures relating to the auditor, these must be followed.

Even where there is no statutory or constitutional requirement to do so, it is good practice to invite the auditor or examiner to general meetings.

55.5 INDUSTRIAL AND PROVIDENT SOCIETIES

If an industrial and provident society's turnover is less than £5.6 million (£250,000 for a charitable IPS) and the value of its assets is not more than £2.8 million, the members can pass a resolution to dispense with an audit [**54.4.2**]. If such a resolution is passed and turnover is more than £90,000, a **reporting accountant** must provide a report on the accounts.

Friendly & Industrial
& Provident Societies Act 1968 s.4A

Only a person eligible to audit companies [**55.3.2**] can act as an auditor or reporting accountant for an IPS, unless the IPS's income for the year was not more than £5,000, and at the end of the year its assets were not more than £5,000 and it had no more than 500 members. In this case, an audit or report can be carried out by two unqualified persons rather than a qualified auditor.

FIPSA 1968 ss.4,7

An IPS's rules must specify whether the auditor is appointed by the members at a general meeting or by the governing body.

A qualified auditor who has been appointed is automatically reappointed unless he or she is removed by a resolution at a general meeting, resigns in writing, or becomes incapable or ineligible because of a connection with the IPS or ceasing to be a qualified auditor; or if an IPS eligible to do so has passed a resolution to appoint two unqualified persons rather than a qualified auditor.

Friendly & Industrial & Provident Societies Act 1968 s.5

A resolution not to reappoint a qualified auditor or to appoint someone other than the existing auditor must be given to the IPS at least 28 days before the general meeting at which it will be considered, be sent immediately to the auditor concerned, and be sent to the members with the notice of the meeting or at least 14 days before the meeting, or be publicised in a newspaper or in some other way. If the auditor proposed as a replacement is not eligible to serve or states in writing that he or she does not want to be appointed, the meeting may reappoint the retiring auditor or appoint another person even though proper notice of this has not been given.

FIPSA 1968 s.6(1)-(4)

A retiring auditor has the right to make written representations which the society must make available to members, to attend and speak at the general meeting, and to insist that the representations are read out at the meeting. *FIPSA 1968 s.6(6),(7)*

At the time of writing (mid 2009) it is not clear whether charitable IPSs will, when they cease to be exempt charities [**8.1.2**], be audited under charity law or IPS law. Up to date advice should be sought from the Charity Commission.

55.6 NON-CHARITABLE ASSOCIATIONS

Non-charitable associations are bound only by the terms of their governing document, and by funders' requirements or resolutions passed by the members.

If the governing document does not require an audit or the equivalent of a charity independent examination, the members may pass a resolution requiring it, or may be able to amend the governing document [**7.5.1**] to make it a requirement.

55.7 LIABILITY OF AUDITORS

Auditors, independent examiners and reporting accountants may be liable if they are in breach of their contract (terms of engagement) or other agreement with the organisation [**55.1.3**].

If an auditor, examiner or reporting accountant is negligent (in breach of their duty of care), the organisation may be able to sue for loss. In certain circumstances, third parties who have relied to their detriment on inaccurate or misleading audit reports may have a claim against the auditor.

A company and its auditor can enter into a **liability limitation agreement**, under which they agree to limit the auditor's liability to the company. Such an agreement cannot be for more than 12 months, is valid only if it is fair and reasonable, and must generally be approved by the company members. Details of limitation liability agreements must be disclosed in notes to the annual accounts.

Companies Act 2006 ss.532-538; Companies (Disclosure of Auditor Remuneration & Liability Limitation Agreements) Regulations 2008 [SI 2008/489]

Resources: AUDITORS AND INDEPENDENT EXAMINERS

See end of **chapter 54**.

Statute law. www.opsi.gov.uk and www.statutelaw.gov.uk.

Much but not all case law. www.bailii.org.

Updates cross-referenced to this book. www.rclh.co.uk.

Chapter 56
CORPORATION TAX, INCOME TAX AND CAPITAL GAINS TAX

For sources of further information see end of chapter.

56.1 VOLUNTARY ORGANISATIONS AND TAX

Apart from genuine donations, grants and the 'donation' element of membership subscriptions, virtually all income received or profit made by voluntary organisations, including charities, is potentially subject to corporation, income and/or capital gains tax. However, there are substantial exemptions from these taxes for charities, and in some cases for community amateur sports clubs (CASCs) and other organisations. These exemptions generally apply only if the income or profits are used for charitable purposes or for the purposes of the CASC.

Information about all aspects of tax is available from HM Revenue and Customs (HMRC) [see end of chapter].

56.1.1 The range of taxes

As well as **corporation tax** or **income tax** on its profits or surplus [**56.2**] and corporation tax or **capital gains tax** on the increased value of its assets when it sells or disposes of them [**56.2.5**], a voluntary organisation may have to deal with

823

a wide range of other taxes. These include **employer's national insurance** contributions (NIC) [**30.4.6**]; **income tax** and **employee's NIC** deducted from employees' pay and paid to HMRC on behalf of the employees [**30.4**]; **value added tax** (VAT) or excise duty on goods or services it purchases [**57.1**]; VAT it charges on goods or services it provides [**57.1**]; **duty** on imported goods; **business rates** or **council tax** on property owned, occupied or used by the organisation [**63.2, 63.3**]; **stamp duty land tax** on some property transactions [**61.10.1**]; and **stamp duty** on transactions in shares [**58.7.2**].

56.1.1.1   Exemptions and extra-statutory concessions

Charities are generally exempt from all or part of these taxes, except VAT, import duty, and income tax and national insurance on wages.

In addition to the exemptions set out in legislation, there are a range of **extra-statutory concessions** (ESCs), which HMRC applies even though it does not have to. There is no appeal against HMRC's decision in cases involving ESCs, so activities where tax relief is granted by concession must precisely follow the rules.

56.1.1.2   Tax recovery

As well as exemptions from income or corporation tax on most of their income or profit, charities and registered community amateur sports clubs [**56.5**] are able to recover tax paid by individual donors on donations made under **gift aid** [**50.2.3**].

56.1.1.3   Tax relief

Under gift aid rules [**50.2.7**], businesses or non-charitable organisations, including community interest companies and charities' trading companies, which owe corporation tax on their profits can donate some or all of the profit and the tax due on it to a charity. The donor does not have to pay tax on the donated amount, and the charity has received the tax so does not recover it from HMRC.

56.1.1.4   Definition of 'company'

For corporation tax purposes, the term **company** includes not only all companies, including charitable and community interest companies, but also other incorporated bodies such as charitable incorporated organisations (CIOs), industrial and provident societies and organisations incorporated under royal charter, and also unincorporated associations.   *Income & Corporation Taxes Act 1988 s.832(1)*

56.1.2   Who is liable?

The liability for an organisation's tax payments depends on the organisation's legal structure and on how it is treated under tax law.

56.1.2.1   Incorporated organisations

A corporate body (company, charitable incorporated organisation or industrial and provident society) is liable for its own tax. Individual members of the governing body or organisation are unlikely to be held personally liable unless they are involved in tax evasion or fraud, or are negligent in dealing with the organisation's tax affairs.

56.1.2.2   Unincorporated associations

For unincorporated associations [**2.2**], tax assessments are issued in the name of the organisation and in the first instance the association is liable for its taxes. But unlike an incorporated body, an association's members do not have limited liability [**3.1.1**], and unpaid tax may be recovered from the treasurer, another officer or member(s) of the governing body. They then have a right to be indemnified (repaid) by the association if it has adequate assets.   *Taxes Management Act 1970 s.108(2)*

56.1.2.3   Trusts

In a body set up as a trust [**2.3**], the trustees are liable for the trust's taxes. They could be held personally liable if the trust does not or cannot pay.

56.1.2.4   Branches

Whether a branch or the parent organisation is liable to pay tax depends on the nature of the relationship. A legally separate branch [**9.2.2**] is liable for its own tax. If it is legally part of the parent body [**9.2.3**], the parent is ultimately liable.

56.1.2.5   Charities

Most charities are unlikely to have to pay income or corporation tax on income or profits, or capital gains tax on the sale of assets. If they do owe these or other taxes, liability depends on their legal structure [above].

Under their duty to act in their best interests of the charity and safeguard its assets [**15.6.3**, **15.6.5**], trustees should recover all taxes due to the charity, and must not pay tax unnecessarily. Trustees who fail to recover tax or claim reliefs could be personally required by the Charity Commission or court to indemnify (compensate) the charity for its loss. This is unlikely if the trustees have acted honestly, reasonably and with reasonable care. Trustee indemnity insurance [**23.10**] might provide cover in rare situations where trustees are made liable.

56.2   INCOME AND CORPORATION TAX

The principal **direct taxes** which affect voluntary organisations are:

- **income tax** on the income of trusts, covered by the **Income Tax Act 2007**;
- **capital gains tax** on the capital gains of trusts, covered by the **Taxation of Chargeable Gains Act 1992**;
- **corporation tax** on the profits and capital gains of all incorporated organisations [**56.1.1.4**] and unincorporated associations, covered by the **Income and Corporation Taxes Act 1988** and **Corporation Tax Act 2009**.

Charitable organisations are generally exempt from these taxes, provided they meet the criteria for exemption [**56.4**].

56.2.1   Registering for tax

Non-charities are likely to have to register with HM Revenue and Customs for corporation tax, although they may be treated as dormant it their taxable income is very small. Registration should be within three months of starting to operate.

Charities are unlikely to have to register if they have no taxable trading income, but should take advice from HMRC or an accountant.

Companies House sends all new companies a pack which includes **form CT41G** to register with HMRC for corporation tax, and **form CT41G dormant company insert** if the company does not intend to start operating immediately. Non-companies which need to register must contact HMRC for the form.

Charitable trusts register with HMRC for income tax rather than corporation tax if they have taxable income.

56.2.2   Tax rates

The rates for income tax, capital gains tax and corporation tax are subject to alteration in each year's Finance Act. Current rates are available from HMRC.

56.2.2.1   Companies, CIOs, IPSs and associations

For companies [**56.1.1.4** for definition] with profits up to £300,000, the corporation tax **small company rate** in 2009-10 is 21%. At the time of writing (mid 2009) this was expected to increase to 22% for tax year 2010-11.

For companies with profits above £300,000, the corporation tax **main rate** in 2009-10 is 28%. But there is **marginal small companies' relief** (MSCR) of 7/400th on profits between £300,000 and £1.5 million (the MSCR upper limit).

For groups of companies or organisations where one controls the other or both are under common control [**9.4**], the figures of £300,000 and £1.5 million are divided between group members, so the higher tax rates become payable sooner.

56.2.2.2 Trusts

For trusts, income tax for 2009-10 is payable at 20% **basic rate** or 40% **trust rate**, depending on the nature of the income. Charitable trusts are unlikely to have to pay income tax. *Income Tax Act 2007 ss.11,15*

56.2.3 Calculating taxable income or profits

Charitable organisations are unlikely to have to pay income tax or corporation tax, but non-charities which receive income from sources other than donations and grants may well have to, and trading companies will have to pay corporation tax on any taxable profits which are not donated to a charity under gift aid.

For corporation and income tax, profits or income are worked out differently depending on whether the organisation is defined as a company for tax purposes [**56.1.1.4**] or is a trust, and on the type of income. Investment income, for example, is treated differently for tax purposes from other types of income.

In addition, income for the purpose of calculating taxable income or profit is not the same as income for accounting purposes. Non-taxable income [**56.3**], such as grants and donations, is included in the ordinary annual accounts, but is excluded from tax accounts. Charities which prepare accruals accounts [**54.2.6**] must usually show all incoming resources, including gifts in kind and donated services, in annual accounts, but these are not shown in tax accounts.

Similarly, some expenditure may not be allowable against taxable income. It is not shown in the tax accounts, but must be shown in the ordinary accounts.

Complex rules govern what is or is not included as income for tax purposes or is a proper deduction or expenditure, and specialist advice should be sought.

56.2.3.1 Tax reliefs and allowances

A wide range of reliefs, credits and allowances can be set against income or profit, for example **capital allowances** on the purchase of equipment, an annual **investment allowance**, **research and development tax credits** and **business premises renovation allowance**. Information about these and other allowances is available from the organisation's accountant and from HMRC.

56.2.4 Losses

If a company makes a loss on trading (the charges it makes or the amounts it is paid for its goods and services), the loss may be set against profits in any area of operation in that accounting period. Any balance may be carried back against profits in accounting periods within the previous three years. If there is still a balance or no claim is made, the loss may be set against later profits in the same area of trade. Similar rules apply for charitable trusts. *Income & Corporation Taxes Act 1988 ss.393,393A,396, as amended; Income Tax Act 2007 ss.562,563*

56.2.5 Capital gains

A **capital** or **chargeable gain** arises when an asset which has increased in value is given away, sold, exchanged or disposed of in any way, other than in the course of a trade. (In a trade, the sale gives rise to profit rather than capital gain.) Tax is charged on the increase in value, with an allowance for gain due to inflation.

Companies as defined for tax purposes [**56.1.1.4**] pay tax on chargeable gains as part of corporation tax. Trusts pay **capital gains tax**. Charities are generally exempt from tax on capital or chargeable gains [**56.4.16**].

56.2.6 Submitting returns

Under **corporation tax self assessment**, a company as defined for tax purposes [**56.1.1.4**] with taxable profits or chargeable gains estimates and pays its tax not later than nine months after the end of its accounting period. Larger companies pay their estimated tax quarterly. All companies must file a statutory return within 12 months from the end of the accounting period, unless it is a charity with no taxable profits or chargeable gains and has not been sent a tax return by HMRC. Where a return is filed late, automatic penalties apply.

If the estimate is too low, the company has to pay the unpaid tax plus interest. If the estimate is too high, HMRC makes a repayment with interest. A return must be filed even if the company does not actually have to pay tax on its profits, for example because it has donated all of them to a charity under the gift aid scheme.

Trusts which have taxable income file **income tax returns** for each tax year (6 April to 5 April).

56.3 NON-TAXABLE INCOME

Certain income – donations, grants, some membership subscriptions – is not subject to tax regardless of whether the recipient organisation is charitable or non-charitable. Specialist advice may be necessary to clarify what is and is not taxable, especially in relation to different types of sponsorship or where it is not clear whether a 'service agreement' is actually a grant and therefore non-taxable or a contract needing to be treated as trading income [**52.1**].

56.3.1 Donations

Money, property, goods, shares, services, facilities, publicity or anything else received as a donation is not subject to corporation or income tax, provided the donor receives nothing more than a simple acknowledgement. If the donor receives a benefit of any kind or the donation is not 'pure profit' for the recipient, the donation may be subject to corporation or income tax, and possibly VAT [**57.11.1**].

The status of 'donation' is not jeopardised if the recipient organisation gives a sticker or 'flag' to acknowledge the donation, a small acknowledgement in an annual report or other publications, or a small plaque which is an acknowledgement of a gift rather than publicity for the donor. Specialist advice about the tax and VAT implications should be sought if a donor requires anything more than a simple acknowledgement, or before seeking 'donations' which give some sort of benefit to the donors such as displaying their logo.

Charities and community amateur sports clubs can maximise the value of donations by encouraging the use of gift aid [**50.2**]. Donors can reduce their own tax through payroll giving [**50.4**], gifts of land and shares [**50.5**] gifts by companies [**50.9**], and other tax-effective giving.

56.3.2 Sale of donated goods

The sale of donated goods is exempt from corporation and income tax in the same way as cash donations. In addition, the sale of donated goods is generally, but not always, zero rated for VAT [**57.11.3**]. Charities and community amateur sports clubs may be able to treat income from the sale of donated goods as a gift aid donation, and recover tax on it [**50.2.2**].

Profits from the sale of bought-in goods are subject to corporation or income tax, but for charities may fall within the exemption for small-scale trading [**56.4.7**]. Sales of bought-in goods may also be subject to VAT [**57.11.5**]. Organisations which sell both donated and bought-in goods must have systems to keep the income separate.

56.3.2.1 Goods donated to a charity but sold by a non-charity

A potential complication arises when goods donated to a charity are sold by its non-charitable trading company [**51.2**]. Because of the trustees' duty to safeguard a charity's assets [**15.6.5**], the charity cannot give an asset – the donated goods – to a non-charity, even where the charity owns the non-charity and will eventually get all or most of its profits. Options are for the goods to be donated to and sold by the charity, donated to and sold by the trading company, or donated to the charity then sold by the trading company as agent for the charity.

Where goods are donated to the trading company, it should be made clear on signs or other notices that all goods are donated to the trading company which donates all (or some) of its profits to the charity. If the agency arrangement is used, advice should be taken about the VAT implications.

56.3.2.2 Some profit to donor

The sale of 'donated' goods where some of the income is paid to the donor and the voluntary organisation keeps the remainder (for example some auctions and nearly new shops) does not generally qualify for the reliefs available for donated goods, but may in some cases. An organisation should not enter into such arrangements without taking advice from its solicitor or accountant, or HMRC.

56.3.3 Sponsorship

The term **sponsorship** is used in many ways. Sponsoring someone to do something such as running the marathon is a donation. Sponsorship by a business or individual where the sponsor receives only a simple acknowledgement, such as a small logo on an annual report, is also a donation, and is not subject to corporation or income tax. But if the sponsor receives significant publicity or any other benefit as a result of its sponsorship – for example the organisation using the sponsor's logo or corporate colours in a significant way or mentioning the sponsor's products or services, or by the sponsor getting use of the organisation's logo – the sponsorship income may be classed as taxable trading income [**56.4.4**]. It may also be subject to VAT [**57.11.2**], and must comply with the rules on commercial participation [**48.6.4**].

To reduce liability for tax and VAT, it may be possible to arrange for the sponsor to divide the payment, making a commercial payment to cover the value of the benefits and a donation to cover the non-business element of the sponsorship.

Allowing a product to be branded with the organisation's trademarked logo not only has tax and VAT implications; it may also involve the organisation in liability for faults in the product under product liability legislation [**21.2.3**]. Agreements for product sponsorship therefore need very careful drafting.

56.3.4 Grants

Grants received by voluntary organisations are not subject to corporation or income tax, unless they are to subsidise a non-charitable trading activity such as a charity shop or fundraising event.

A 'grant' which is actually a payment in exchange for a service [**52.1**] could be considered by HMRC to be trading income and subject to corporation or income tax, unless the service falls within the primary purpose [**56.4.5**] of the charity carrying it out. Even if it is not subject to tax, it could be subject to VAT [**57.10**].

56.3.5 Membership subscriptions

Membership subscriptions paid to voluntary organisations, whether charitable or non-charitable, are exempt from corporation or income tax provided they are basically a donation to the organisation, entitling the member only to rights under the constitution such as the right to attend and vote at general meetings [**12.1.5**].

If the subscription entitles the member to any benefits, it is a trading activity. Any profit is potentially taxable, but there are a number of exemptions for both charities and non-charities. If some of the benefits are exempt and some not, the portion of the subscription that covers the non-exempt benefits is taxable.

Special rules apply to subscriptions to trade associations, professional associations and some other bodies.

Even subscriptions which are exempt from corporation and income tax may in some situations be subject to VAT [**57.10.1**].

56.3.5.1 Charities

If a membership subscription is paid to a charity, any profit is exempt from tax provided the benefits are directly related to the charity's primary purpose [**56.4.5**], for example being able to attend arts workshops run by an arts charity, and the profits are used for the charity's charitable purposes. A gift aid donation may be used to pay membership subscriptions to a charity provided the value of any benefits is not more than the allowed proportion of the donation [**50.2.1**].

56.3.5.2 Non-charities

In non-charities where the members have a constitutional right to a share of the organisation's profits, a membership subscription may be exempt from tax as **mutual trading** [**56.6.2**]. Otherwise any profit on the subscription is subject to tax. Non-charities in this situation may want to structure their subscription rates in a way that reduces the likelihood of taxable profit arising.

56.4 TAX EXEMPTIONS FOR CHARITIES

Apart from donations, grants and other income which is explicitly not subject to tax [**56.3**], a charity's income or profit is taxable unless a tax exemption or extra-statutory concession applies to that type of income or profit, and the income or profit which would otherwise be taxable is used only for the charity's charitable purposes. Trading or other activities which are not exempt from tax should be carried out through a trading company [**51.2**].

56.4.1 Charities and charitable purposes SHORTENED TO HERE

For tax purposes, a **charity** is defined as 'any body of persons or trust established for charitable purposes only', a **charitable company** is 'any body of persons established for charitable purposes only', and a **charitable trust** is a trust established for charitable purposes only.

Income & Corporation Taxes Act 1988 s.506(1), amended by Income Tax Act 2007 sch.1 para.95; Income Tax Act 2007 s.519

An organisation registered with the Charity Commission is conclusively presumed to be a charity, and will be treated as such by HMRC. The definition of charity is different in Scotland and in Northern Ireland [**4.4.6**], and any organisation which is registered with the Office of the Scottish Charity Regulator (OSCR) or the Charity Commission for Northern Ireland (CCNI), but would not be eligible for registration with the Charity Commission, should contact HMRC about its tax status.

Charities Act 2006 s.80(4),(6)

Charities which are exempt [**8.1.2**] from registration with the Charity Commission, or are excepted [**8.1.3**] and have not registered voluntarily, apply to HMRC for recognition of their charitable status and an HMRC charity reference number.

A charity registered with the Charity Commission, OSCR or CCNI which has taxable income or will recover tax through gift aid [**50.2**] should apply to HMRC [see end of chapter] for an HMRC charity registration number. This is different from the charity registration number given by the charity registration body.

56.4.2 Exemptions and extra-statutory concessions

The tax exemptions for charitable companies [see **56.1.1.4** for definition of 'company' in this context] are set out in the **Income and Corporation Taxes Act 1988** s.505 as amended, for charitable trusts in the **Income Tax Act 2007**, and in various extra-statutory concessions [**56.1.1.1**]. These cover most potential sources of income for charities and charitable purposes. But the exemptions are specific and carefully defined, and do not cover all sources of income.

A few exemptions and extra-statutory concessions are also available for non-charities, in very specific situations.

The organisation's solicitor or accountant or HMRC should be consulted if there is any doubt at all about whether income is eligible for exemption.

56.4.3 Charitable/qualifying expenditure

To qualify for exemption, the taxable income or profit must be used only for the charity's charitable purposes. This was formerly called **qualifying expenditure**, and for corporation tax purposes is now called **charitable expenditure**.

Income & Corporation Taxes Act 1988 s.506, as amended; Income Tax Act 2007 s.527(5)

Charitable expenditure includes costs of the charity's charitable activities or assets used in the activities; grants from the charity to another charity to fulfil the charitable purposes of the donor charity; reasonable administrative, management and fundraising costs; interest or other finance costs on the above; making qualifying investments and qualifying loans [**56.4.3.2**]; and other expenditure defined as charitable in the relevant tax legislation.

Payments to bodies outside the UK are charitable expenditure only if the charity has taken reasonable steps to ensure that the payment will be used for charitable purposes [**56.8.3**].

56.4.3.1 Endangering tax relief

Tax relief may be endangered or lost if income or profit is used for non-charitable expenditure, which could include HMRC considering that the level of administrative, management or fundraising expenses is unreasonable and treating it as non-charitable expenditure. If income is used to raise further money in a way which is not itself charitable or eligible for tax relief, for example by subsidising fundraising events or funding a trading subsidiary's losses [**51.4**], this could also endanger tax relief, as could income simply being accumulated because no immediate use can be found for it (rather than being accumulated for a clearly defined objective within the charitable purposes). Another risk to tax relief arises if the charity undertakes certain transactions with **substantial donors** [**50.7**].

56.4.3.2 Qualifying investments and loans

To be eligible for tax relief, surplus income must be invested in **qualifying investments** or loans. Qualifying investments are bank deposit and building society accounts, local authority and government bonds, shares and securities of companies quoted on a recognised stock exchange, unit trusts and certificates of deposit, interests in land (excluding mortgages), common investment funds and common deposit funds established for charities, and uncertificated eligible debt security units. The board of HM Revenue and Customs can approve other investments, including mortgages, if they are made for the benefit of the charity and not for the avoidance of tax. All investments made by a charity must be within its investment powers [**58.1**].   *Income & Corporation Taxes Act 1988 s.506(4),(5), sch.20 pt.1, as amended; Income Tax Act 2007 ss.558-561*

Qualifying loans include loans to another UK charity to be used for charitable purposes, loans to beneficiaries of the charity which are made in furtherance of the charity's purposes, and other loans approved by HMRC.

Tax relief on income, gain or profit used for non-qualifying purposes may be denied or restricted. The most common non-qualifying investments or loans are to a charity's own trading subsidiary [**51.4.4**, **51.4.5**] and other unlisted companies.

56.4.3.3 De minimis

There is no legal protection from tax for charities where any of the income, gain or profit is not eligible for tax exemption – even if the non-qualifying amounts are small. However, if a non-qualifying expenditure is very small in both absolute and relative terms, HMRC may not raise a tax assessment.

56.4.4 Trading income and profits

In tax terms, **trading** is defined as 'every trade, manufacture, adventure or concern in the nature of trade'.   *Income & Corporation Taxes Act 1988 s.832(1)*

This far from helpful definition is an old one, and has been subject to much litigation about what is or is not truly a trade. Whatever its imperfections, this definition is likely to cover most situations in which a voluntary organisation charges for goods, services, facilities, publicity, use of its name or logo, admission to events or other benefits, or is paid to provide these.

Trading may include many activities which are not typically thought of as such, for example making a charge for photocopying or training courses, charging day centre users for meals or activities, or making a management charge for helping an organisation or project. For more about what is and is not trading, see **51.1.2**.

Trading carried out by charities, and in some cases carried out by non-charitable voluntary organisations, may be covered by an exemption or extra-statutory concession [**56.4.2**]. But where there is no exemption or ESC, all profit arising from the trading is subject to tax. This applies regardless of whether the trading is intended primarily to meet a community need, primarily to raise money for the voluntary organisation, or both. The profit will be subject to tax regardless of whether the organisation making the profit is charitable or non-charitable, whether the price or fee is set with the intention of breaking even, making a small profit or making a substantial profit, and whether payment is made by the end user or by a third party. The trading may be subject to tax even if it is not subject to VAT [**chapter 57**].

56.4.4.1 Reducing tax liability

Where its trading falls outside the exemptions and extra-statutory concessions, a charity should generally set up a non-charitable trading company, which donates some or all of its profits and the tax due on those profits to the charity under gift aid [**51.2**].

Similarly, a non-charitable voluntary organisation might be able to set up a charity to undertake the properly charitable aspects of its work [**9.4.2**]. The non-charity can then either ensure that the profits arise in the charity or donate the profits to the charity under gift aid, and thus avoid tax on those profits.

56.4.4.2 Volunteer time and gifts in kind

If an organisation has taxable income, it may be able to set against it the value of volunteer time, rent-free accommodation, free services etc which it has received and would otherwise have had to pay for in order to carry out the taxable activities. Advice should be taken from the organisation's auditor or HMRC before making any such deduction.

56.4.4.3 Voluntary donations

Where trading is not eligible for an exemption or extra-statutory concession, tax can be reduced by charging only a small amount for the goods, service or event (thus minimising taxable profits), and asking for a supplementary voluntary donation. To be non-taxable the donation element must genuinely be voluntary, so cannot be obligatory or entitle the donor to additional benefits. Specific rules apply where a voluntary donation is suggested for a fundraising event [**57.11.8**].

56.4.5 Primary purpose/charitable trading

Profits from trading by a charitable company as defined for tax purposes [**56.1.1.4**] are exempt from corporation tax, and income from trading by a charitable trust is exempt from income tax, if the trade is actually carrying out a primary purpose of the charity or the work is carried out mainly by the beneficiaries of the charity, and the profits or income are used for charitable expenditure [**56.4.3**]. *Income & Corporation Taxes Act 1988 s.505(1)(e); Income Tax Act 2007 s.525*

This type of trading is generally referred to as **primary purpose trading**, but under the **Income Tax Act 2007** is called **charitable trade**.

Primary purpose is defined by reference to the charity's objects as set out in its governing document [**5.1**]. Primary purpose trading must *directly* achieve these objects, so the wording of the objects clause is crucial. The exemption applies, for example, to charging beneficiaries or service users for charitable services or for goods directly related to the charity's purposes (such as selling mobility aids to people with a mobility disability); contracting with a local authority to provide services to the charity's beneficiaries; a charity whose objects include improving the efficiency of other charities charging consultancy fees for services provided to those charities; a heritage charity charging admission to its properties; selling publications which advance the charity's objects; selling goods produced mainly by beneficiaries, or charging for services provided mainly by beneficiaries.

In relation to work carried out by beneficiaries, 'mainly' means 'probably ... more than half'. The 'probably' means that advice should be sought if there is any doubt. *Fawcett Properties Ltd v Buckingham County Council [1960] 3 All ER 503*

Even if charitable trading is exempt from corporation and income tax, it may be subject to VAT [**57.6**].

56.4.5.1 Ancillary trading

The primary purpose exemption applies as well to trading activities which are not in themselves charitable, but which are undertaken as an integral part of carrying out charitable trading. This is called **ancillary trading**. Examples are a bar or cafe open only to people attending the charity's charitable activities or using its charitable services (because they may need or want to eat while they are there), or renting accommodation to students attending a college.

56.4.5.2 Mixed trading

The boundary between charitable and ancillary trading – which are eligible for tax relief – and other trading depends on the wording of the charity's objects and the nature of the trading. For example, for a charitable theatre:

- charging admission to its plays is charitable trading to achieve its **primary purpose** (the education of the public in the arts, or something similar);
- charging for advertisements in the theatre programme, and the sale of pre-theatre drinks, programmes and ice cream to theatre-goers are **ancillary** to the charitable trading;
- opening the bar all day or when there is no performance is **non-charitable**.

Where trading is **mixed** – partly charitable/ancillary and partly non-charitable – the non-charitable trading may be covered by the exemption for small-scale trading [**56.4.7**]. If it is not, expenditure on that portion of the trading will not be **charitable expenditure** [**56.4.3**] and the income relating to it will be subject to tax. In most cases the taxable trading should be carried out within a trading company [**51.2**] rather than within the charity.   *Income & Corporation Taxes Act 1988 s.506(3), amended by Finance Act 2006 s.55*

56.4.6 Fundraising events

Fundraising events are a form of trading even if the money is being raised for charitable purposes, but the profits from fundraising events may be exempt from both tax and VAT [**57.11.8**]. The provisions for exemption from corporation tax are in HMRC **extra-statutory concession C4**, and those for exemption from income tax are in the **Income Tax Act 2007** s.529. Other events may be exempt from corporation or income tax, but not VAT, under the tax exemption for small trading [**56.4.7**].

Where the profits from a fundraising event are subject to corporation or income tax, it may be possible to reduce tax by asking for part of the fee or admission charge as a (genuinely) voluntary donation [**57.11.8**].

56.4.7 Small trading exemptions

Non-charitable trading activities which do not fall within another exemption are exempt from corporation and income tax provided they are carried out by a charity which uses the profits solely for its charitable purposes, and the total turnover from all the activities does not exceed the annual **requisite limit**.
Finance Act 2000 s.46, as amended; Income Tax Act 2007 ss.526,528

The annual requisite limit is the larger of £5,000; or 25% of the charity's total incoming resources for the year, subject to a maximum limit of £50,000. Incoming resources means the total receipts of the charity from all sources [**54.2.6**].

If trading income exceeds the requisite limit, it may still be exempt from tax if the charity can show that at the start of the tax year, it expected the turnover to be lower than it turned out to be, or it expected the charity's incoming resources to be higher than they turned out to be. HMRC will look at budgets, relevant figures for previous years, minutes of relevant meetings and similar documentation.

56.4.8 Lotteries and competitions

Proceeds from charity raffles and lotteries (including tombolas, draws etc) are exempt from corporation and income tax provided the lottery is an incidental non-commercial lottery [**49.6.3**], a small society lottery [**49.6.7**] or a large society lottery [**49.6.8**], and the income is used solely for charitable purposes.
Income & Corporation Taxes Act 1988 s.505(1)(f), as amended; Income Tax Act 2007 s.530

The exemption applies to lotteries run by a charity or run by a charity's trading subsidiary where the charity is registered as the society under the Gambling Act.

Lottery ticket sales are exempt from VAT [**57.11.4**]. Proceeds from a competition, where participants win on the basis of merit or skill, are subject to corporation or income tax and may also be subject to VAT.

56.4.9 Income from property

Tax is normally payable on rent and other profits arising from land and buildings. But rents or profits from land or buildings vested [**20.4.5**] in any person for charitable purposes are exempt from corporation and income tax provided the income is used for charitable purposes only. This exemption applies only to revenue income, not to capital sums received from selling or developing land [**56.4.10**].

Income & Corporation Taxes Act 1988 s.505(1)(a), as amended; Income Tax Act 2007 s.531

Even if a charity is exempt from corporation or income tax on rents or other income from its property, the provision of other services, such as room bookings or conference facilities, may be subject to tax as a trading activity unless it falls within an exemption for charitable or small trading.

Rents and other property income may be subject to VAT [**57.15**].

56.4.10 Sale and development of land

Under tax anti-avoidance provisions, profits from the sale or development of land may be subject to tax, even for charities. This is a highly specialist area requiring legal and financial advice.

Income & Corporation Taxes Act 1988 ss.776,777, as amended; Income Tax Act 2007 ss.757-759

56.4.11 Investment income

Interest on deposits at UK banks and building societies is subject to tax which, under anti-avoidance provisions, is generally deducted before the organisation receives the interest. Interest on government bonds and similar securities is also generally paid net of tax. Dividends from UK companies are paid net of tax.

56.4.11.1 Exemptions for charities

Provided the income arises from a qualifying investment [**56.4.3.2**] and is used only for charitable purposes, charities are eligible for exemption from corporation or income tax on interest, dividends and other distributions on shares, and profits on the disposal of some securities.

Income & Corporation Taxes Act 1988 s.505(1)(c), as amended; Income Tax Act 2007 s.532

If tax is deducted at source before the charity receives the income, the charity should seek to recover the tax from HMRC.

A charity may ask a bank or building society to pay interest gross, without deduction of tax, and may ask the Bank of England to pay interest gross on government bonds.

56.4.11.2 Places of worship

Public revenue dividends on securities held in the names of trustees are exempt from corporation or income tax if the dividends are used solely for the repair of a cathedral, college, church, or chapel, or any building used solely for worship. Public revenue dividends are income from securities which is payable from the public revenues of the UK, or securities issued by or on behalf of a government or public or local authority in a country outside the UK.

Income & Corporation Taxes Act 1988 s.505(1)(d), as amended; Income Tax Act 2007 s.533

56.4.12 Annual payments

Payments are exempt from corporation or income tax provided the payment is annual (even, in some cases, if the money is paid at intervals of less than a year), it is pure income or profit in the hand of the recipient with no element of current cost needed to generate the income, and it is used for charitable purposes.

Annual payments include interest, some royalties [**56.4.14**], and a range of other payments. Information is available from solicitors, accountants and HMRC.

Income & Corporation Taxes Act 1988 s.505(1)(c), as amended; Income Tax Act 2007 s.536(c)

56.4.13 Payments from one charity to another

If a charitable company as defined for tax purposes [**56.1.1.4**] receives from another charity in the UK a payment which is not for goods or services or does not cover the full cost of the goods or services paid for, and if the income is not exempt from tax under any of the other exemptions, it is treated for corporation tax purposes as an annual payment [above] and is exempt in that way. For charitable trusts, such a payment is exempt from income tax without having to be treated as an annual payment, provided the income is used solely for charitable purposes.

Income & Corporation Taxes Act 1988 s.505(2); Income Tax Act 2007 s.523

56.4.14 Intellectual property

Income from a licence to exploit an organisation's intellectual property, for example the right to use its name, logo or copyright, is subject to tax as a trading profit unless it is eligible for the small trade exemption [**56.4.7**] or is classed as an annual payment [**56.4.12**]. This is a difficult area and advice should be taken in each case.

Lawrence v Inland Revenue Commissioners [1940] 23 TC 333

Copyright royalties forming part of the income of a publishing trade are taxed as trading profits, unless they are charitable trading or are eligible for the small trade exemption. Other copyright royalties, for example inherited copyright, are normally taxed as an annual payment and are eligible for relief if paid to a charity. Income from royalties on patents is not eligible for tax relief, even when paid to a charity, unless it is from charitable trading.

Even where they might be exempt from corporation or income tax, royalties and other intellectual property income may be subject to VAT.

56.4.15 Income from overseas

Income paid to UK charities from abroad may be exempt as yearly interest and other annual payments [**56.4.12**], or charitable trading [**56.4.5**]. In practice, HMRC also exempts other overseas income, particularly rents and bank interest.

A UK charity which receives income from which foreign taxes have been withheld may be able to recover the tax from the relevant tax authorities. HMRC Charities can advise on this, and can provide standard repayment claim forms.

Income from investment in offshore funds is exempt from tax if used for charitable purposes.

Income & Corporation Taxes Act 1988 s.761(6), to be replaced by regulations under Finance Act 2008 s.41; Income Tax Act 2007 s.535

56.4.16 Capital gains

A **capital** or **chargeable gain** [**56.2.5**] by a charity is exempt from tax provided the gain is used for charitable purposes [**56.4.3**]. The exemption is available even if the remaining proceeds from the sale (those additional to the gain) are used for non-charitable purposes.

Taxation of Chargeable Gains Act 1992 s.256; Income Tax Act 2007 s.539

Where the asset sold is part of a charity's permanent endowment [**58.8.2**], the terms of the endowment may require the gain to be reinvested in similar assets, rather than being used for charitable purposes. This does not negate exemption.

56.5 EXEMPTIONS FOR COMMUNITY AMATEUR SPORTS CLUBS

Community amateur sports clubs registered with HM Revenue and Customs [**1.8**] rather than with the Charity Commission are exempt from corporation tax on interest received, capital gains, trading profits where turnover from the trade is less than £30,000, and income from property where the gross income is less than £20,000. To be eligible for tax exemption, the income must be used to provide facilities for, or promoting participation in, one or more sports that are eligible under CASC legislation. Where trading turnover or income from property exceeds the limits, the whole amount is taxable, not just the excess.

Finance Act 2002 sch.18 paras.4-8,16(b), as amended

Sports clubs registered with the Charity Commission are eligible for the same tax reliefs as other charities [**56.4**].

56.6   EXEMPTIONS FOR NON-CHARITIES

Organisations which are neither charities nor HMRC-registered community amateur sports clubs generally pay corporation tax on virtually all their income or profits, unless it arises from donations, grants, the sale of donated goods or the non-taxable element of membership subscriptions [**56.3**]; fundraising events covered by extra-statutory concession C4 provided the profits are all used for charitable purposes [**56.4.6**]; lotteries where the non-charity is a charity's trading company [**56.4.8**]; and mutual trading [**56.6.2**]. Information about the tax status of non-charities is in HMRC IR46 *Clubs, societies and voluntary associations*.

56.6.1   Small tax liabilities

Non-charities are subject to tax on all other income or profit, but in practice HMRC does not collect **small tax liabilities** where the organisation or club is run exclusively for the benefit of its own members, and its annual corporation tax liability is not expected to exceed £100. In this case HMRC treats the organisation as dormant and does not issue tax return notices, but reviews the organisation's status at least every five years.

An organisation treated as dormant under these provisions must contact HMRC if during any tax year it has or expects to have trading losses which could be set against tax, capital assets that are being disposed of, or payments from which tax is deductible and payable to HMRC.

56.6.2   Mutual trading

In some non-charitable membership organisations the members are entitled, under the constitution, to a share of the organisation's profits. Where this applies and the members pay for goods or services from the organisation in their capacity as members, it is called **mutual trading**. Examples might be the sale of drinks and food to the members of a members' club, or a sport club's fees for members to use its facilities.

Even if the members do not actually take their share in the profits, the profits from mutual trading are not subject to corporation tax. Income from 'temporary members' is not taxable provided they have the same privileges as full members.

If non-members pay for goods or services, or if the members pay for goods or services which are not directly related to their involvement as members (for example hiring the facilities for a private party, or buying t-shirts or mugs), the profits are taxable. Sales to signed-in guests are sometimes allowed tax-free by concession, provided the organisation is only open to members and guests, and the guests are not allowed to buy alcohol.

Even if mutual trading is not subject to corporation tax, it may be subject to VAT.

56.6.3   Industrial and provident societies

Under **HMRC extra-statutory concession C5**, industrial and provident societies which have made a trading loss in an earlier year can offset the loss against investment income arising in a later year.

56.6.4   Scientific research organisations

A non-charitable research and development organisation can claim most of the tax reliefs that charities enjoy [**56.4**], provided its object is undertaking research and development which may lead to an extension of a type or types of trade, and it does not distribute its profits to its members. *Income & Corporation Taxes Act 1988 s.508, as amended*

56.7   TAX AND OUTGOINGS

Tax is affected not only by the source of income and whether the organisation is or is not charitable, but also by the way income is used. Tax exemptions for charities are available only if the relevant income is used for **charitable expenditure**

[**56.4.1**], and for all organisations complex rules govern which expenditures can be set against income. This section looks at some of the tax issues relating to an organisation's expenditure or other outgoings.

56.7.1 Running costs of membership organisations

The running costs of membership organisations are assumed to be covered by membership subscriptions. As this income is not subject to tax [**56.3.5**], the costs of running the organisation cannot be claimed as a tax deduction.

If the organisation receives taxable income from trading activities, the costs of running these activities can be deducted from the trading income.

56.7.2 Grants to other organisations

Grants made by a charity to another voluntary organisation are generally outside the scope of tax, provided the grant is within the donor charity's primary purpose. But if a grant is made for any other purpose or in order to avoid tax, it will not be eligible for the exemptions and the income used for the grant will be subject to corporation or income tax.

56.7.3 Donations and grants to individuals

In considering donations or grants to individuals, attention must be given to the tax consequences for the recipient [**53.3.4**] as well as the donating organisation.

One-off or regular donations, grants, bursaries, scholarships etc provided by charities to an individual as a way of achieving its charitable purposes normally have no tax consequences for the donating organisation.

If the donating organisation is not a charity but is a club, society, residents' association or similar body run for the benefit of its own members, payments to individuals have no tax consequences for the organisation if they are made out of the organisation's untaxed income (received from subscriptions, mutual trading, donations etc – see **56.6**). If the payments are made out of taxable income (received, for example, from trading activities), they cannot be set against the income as a way of reducing corporation tax liability.

56.7.4 Payment of interest

Where an organisation pays interest on a loan, it may be required to deduct basic rate income tax and pay the tax to HMRC on form **CT61** within 14 days of the end of the quarter in which the interest is paid. This does not apply where the loan is made by a UK bank or is a hire purchase agreement, or where one company is paying interest to another company. Advice should be sought from HMRC before paying interest on any loan to which deduction of interest might apply.

56.8 OVERSEAS TAX ISSUES

Some aspects of the taxation of income received from abroad are dealt with above [**56.4.15**]. Many other complex tax issues, generally requiring specialist advice, arise for charities which operate overseas, receive income from abroad or make expenditure abroad.

56.8.1 Europe

Although VAT may in due course be harmonised across Europe, the EU has at the time of writing (mid 2009) adopted no directives on harmonisation of direct tax (income, corporation and capital gains tax). If such a directive is ever adopted, it could have very serious implications for voluntary organisations.

56.8.2 Fundraising

Generally a UK charity raising funds abroad needs to register a local charity or not for profit organisation if it wishes to take advantage of any tax exemption in that country. In some cases this may not be necessary within the EU [**50.1.1**].

56.8.3   Making payments abroad

If a UK charity makes charitable payments abroad, it is subject to the special requirements of the Charity Commission [5.3.7] and general rules on the prevention of money laundering [53.6], as well as the tax requirement that payments made to bodies outside the UK only count as qualifying expenditure if the charity has taken all reasonable steps to ensure that the payment will be applied for charitable purposes [56.4.1].

*Income & Corporation Taxes Act 1988 s.506(3);
Income Tax Act 2007 s.547*

To ensure that funds used for the payments are not subject to tax, the organisation should have a written agreement with the overseas recipient stating that the funds must be used for a purpose which is legally charitable under UK law, and must have appropriate reporting and monitoring procedures in place. In some situations, it may be advisable to obtain HMRC approval in advance.

56.8.4   Overseas charities operating in the UK

If a charity is not based in the UK but operates or fundraises here, it may suffer significant tax disadvantages:

- tax on UK income such as interest will be deducted at source, and it will not be able to recover the tax;
- it will not be able to use gift aid to recover tax paid by donors;
- it will not be eligible for the tax exemptions which are available only to charities.

Overseas charities suffer particular disadvantages if they are based in a country which does not have a double taxation agreement with other countries, for example an offshore tax haven such as the Cayman Islands. Because there are no reciprocal agreements, tax withheld on income is not recoverable in either country.

These disadvantages can normally be overcome by setting up a UK registered charity. The overseas charity will need to ensure that the UK charity qualifies for registration here, especially if a significant number of its governing body members are based abroad [4.4.5].

These arrangements may not be necessary if the overseas charity is based in the EU [50.1.1].

Resources: CORPORATION, INCOME AND CAPITAL GAINS TAX

Community accountancy projects.

Corporation, income and capital gains tax. HM Revenue & Customs: www.hmrc.gov.uk, 0845 010 9000, enquiries.estn@hmrc.gsi.gov.uk.

Business Link: www.businesslink.gov.uk.

Charity tax reliefs & exemptions. HMRC Charities: www.hmrc.gov.uk/charities/index.htm, 0845 302 0203, email via website.

Charity Tax Group: www.ctrg.org.uk, info@charitytax.info.

Charity Finance Directors' Group: www.cfdg.org.uk, 0845 345 3192, info@cfdg.org.uk.

Statute law. www.opsi.gov.uk and www.statutelaw.gov.uk.

Much but not all case law. www.bailii.org.

Updates cross-referenced to this book. www.rclh.co.uk.

Chapter 57

VALUE ADDED TAX

For sources of further information see end of chapter.

57.1   VOLUNTARY ORGANISATIONS AND VAT

Organisations which ignore VAT do so at their peril. An organisation (including a charity) which does not register when it has to will face substantial penalties, and if it does not register voluntarily when it would be advisable to do so, it may lose the opportunity to claim back some VAT it has paid. Even if an organisation does not have to register, it may pay unnecessary VAT if it does not know about the reliefs available to charities and other organisations.

With proper planning, voluntary organisations can often make substantial savings on VAT. This chapter provides an introduction, but cannot cover all the possibilities and is not a substitute for specialist advice. In particular it does not cover goods or services provided outside the UK.

Information about all aspects of VAT is available in *The VAT guide* (HMRC notice 700) and numerous other free publications from HM Revenue and Customs [see end of chapter], *A Practical Guide to VAT for Charities* by Kate Sayer (Directory of Social Change), and more detailed technical guides.

57.1.1 How VAT works

Unlike corporation tax, income tax and capital gains tax [**chapter 56**], VAT is not a tax on profits, income or gains, but on the **supply** of goods or services. The **value** of the supply is taxed, so VAT may apply even if the goods or services are supplied free of charge or make no profit.

Charities and other voluntary organisations generally pay VAT in the same way as everyone else, and are subject to the same rules as anyone else on registering for VAT and charging VAT on some or all of the goods and services they provide. An organisation registered for VAT may recover some or all of the VAT it pays.

57.1.1.1 Basic principles

The basic principles of VAT are:

- all goods, services, facilities and anything else provided, purchased or received by the organisation, including by mail order or via the internet, are **supplies**;
- a supply is either **non-business [57.6.1]** or **business [57.6.2]**;
- a business supply is either **exempt [57.7]** or **taxable [57.8]**;
- a taxable supply is subject to VAT at **zero [57.8.1]**, **reduced [57.8.3]** or **standard rate [57.8.2]**;
- when an organisation (or anyone else) purchases anything, it pays **input tax** (on supplies coming into the organisation) unless the supply is non-business, exempt or zero rated or is purchased from a supplier who is not registered for VAT;
- charities and some other voluntary organisations are eligible for a few zero ratings on goods or services they purchase which would normally be standard rated [**57.5**]. It is important to be aware of these **reliefs**, as they are available even if the organisation is not registered for VAT;
- if the organisation makes taxable supplies whose total value in any 12-month period is more than the registration threshold (£68,000 in 2009-10), it must register for VAT [**57.2.1**], charge **output tax** (tax on what goes out of the organisation) on its taxable supplies and pay the output tax it collects to HMRC;
- if the value of its taxable supplies is below the threshold it can register voluntarily [**57.2.2**];
- if it is registered it can recover input tax on some or in some cases all of the goods and services it purchases;
- if some of its supplies are taxable and some are non-business or exempt, it may only be able to recover the portion of input tax which has been paid on goods or services which were used for the provision of taxable supplies [**57.9**].

Other EU member states do not treat charities and voluntary organisations in the same way that they are treated for VAT purposes in the UK. If VAT is harmonised across the EU, it is likely to be disadvantageous for UK charities.

57.1.2 Assessing whether to register

Assessing whether an organisation has to register for VAT or should consider doing so voluntarily is not a once and for all matter, but something which must be constantly monitored. Many organisations assume their independent examiner or auditor will alert them to the need to register, but this is not generally included in their terms of engagement [**55.1.3**], and in any case they may lack specialist expertise in this complex area.

If it appears at any time that the organisation should be registered for VAT, advice should be taken immediately from its accountant or auditor, or HM Revenue and Customs. *Penalties for failing to register are severe.*

If the organisation does not have to register because all its income is **non-business** in VAT terms [**57.6.1**] or **exempt** from VAT [**57.7**], the people involved should be aware of the need to re-assess the situation if the organisation starts receiving income for goods or services which are defined as **taxable supplies** [**57.6.1**], for example if it starts providing services under a contract rather than under grant funding, or if it starts organising large-scale fundraising events or charging clients for services. Another trigger is if it starts providing goods or services which are not exempt, or in some cases if it uses the profits from the provision of exempt goods or services to subsidise other work [**57.10.6**].

If the organisation provides taxable supplies [**57.8**] but does not have to register because their value is below the registration threshold [**57.2.1**], it should consider whether to register voluntarily [**57.2.2**]. If it does not register, it should monitor the value of its taxable supplies on a monthly basis and be prepared to register as soon as required to do so.

57.1.3 Charities and irrecoverable VAT

Supplies funded by grants, donations and legacies are **non-business** [**57.6.1**] and therefore outside the scope of VAT. The income does not count towards the threshold for VAT registration, and **input VAT** – the VAT on goods and services purchased to make these supplies – cannot be recovered. This puts charities and other voluntary organisations at a significant disadvantage compared with commercial businesses, or even compared with organisations whose services are provided under contract rather than with grant funding.

Many other supplies provided by charities, such as welfare, care and health services [**57.10.2**], childcare [**57.10.5**] and training [**57.10.6**], are **business supplies** but are **exempt** from VAT [**57.7**]. The income does not count towards the registration threshold, and input tax on goods and services purchased to make these supplies cannot be recovered unless the organisation can take advantage of the *de minimis* rules or **partial exemption** [**57.9**].

Some supplies are always exempt; others are exempt only if provided by a charity. Where all suppliers are exempt they are all disadvantaged by not being able to recover input tax, but where only some suppliers, such as charities, are exempt they are disadvantaged in relation to other suppliers.

The amount of irrecoverable VAT paid by the sector is not balanced by the small number of **tax reliefs** [**57.5**] or **zero ratings** [**57.8.1**] that are available only to charities and in some cases other voluntary organisations. Organisations such as the **Charity Tax Group** and the **Charity Finance Directors' Group** [see end of chapter] have campaigned for many years for charities and other voluntary organisations to be able to recover some or all of their irrecoverable VAT.

57.2 REGISTRATION

To determine whether an organisation has to register for VAT, the value of all taxable supplies [**57.8**] – zero, reduced and standard rated – is totalled. Exempt [**57.7**] and non-business [**57.6.1**] supplies are not included, nor is income from the disposal of capital assets such as office furniture, computers, vehicles etc.

57.2.1 Compulsory registration

The rules on VAT registration are in HMRC notice 700/1 *Should I be registered for VAT?* An organisation must register within one month:

- if at the end of any month, the value of taxable supplies in the UK in the previous 12 months is above the threshold (£68,000 in 2009-10) unless evidence can be given that supplies in the next 12 months are not expected to exceed the deregistration threshold (£66,000 in 2009-10); or

- if at any time, there are reasonable grounds to believe that the value of taxable supplies in the next 30 days will exceed the threshold.

Value Added Tax Act 1994 sch.1 para.1

Separate rules apply for supplies between the UK and EU members states, the sale of certain assets, and taxable supplies made in the UK by someone who is not resident here. These are not covered in this book.

An organisation registers for VAT by submitting the required form (usually **VAT1**) online or to the appropriate registration office, along with evidence to show when it reached or expects to reach the threshold and that it did not or will not reach the threshold before this.

VAT registration is in the name of a **taxable person**. In this context 'person' means not only a human person or incorporated body [**3.1**], but also an unincorporated association [**2.2**]. A trust [**2.3**] registers in its own name but HMRC must be notified of the names of trustees and all subsequent changes.

VAT can usually be recovered on goods and services purchased in the six months prior to registration and on assets held at the time of registration, but only to the extent that the VAT relates to the supply of taxable goods or services. Advice should be sought about this.

57.2.2 Voluntary registration

An organisation which makes taxable supplies whose value is below the registration threshold [**57.2.1**] can choose to register voluntarily. It will then have to charge VAT on its taxable supplies, unless they are zero rated. It will be able to recover the VAT it has paid out on goods and services related to the provision of the taxable supplies, and may also be able to recover VAT on its exempt supplies if they meet the *de minimis* criteria [**57.9.2**].

Before registering voluntarily, the organisation should take specialist advice to ensure the benefits will outweigh the additional administrative costs, and to ensure that VAT charges will not have negative effects on its members, clients or other purchasers of its goods or services.

57.2.3 Branches

Branches or sections of an organisation which are legally separate [**9.2.3**] are generally treated separately for VAT purposes. If branches or sections are legally part of the main organisation [**9.2.2**], all their taxable income is added together to determine whether registration is necessary. If the main organisation registers, the branches will have to charge VAT on the taxable goods and services they provide, and will be able to recover the VAT they pay on goods or services they purchase to make their taxable supplies.

57.2.4 Group registration

Two or more bodies under common control as defined for company law purposes [**9.4.1**] – such as a charitable company and its trading company – can register as a **VAT group**. This is explained in HMRC notice 700/2 *Group and divisional registration*. An unincorporated organisation which controls a company cannot register as a group.

Group registration means only one VAT return has to be submitted, and there is no need to charge VAT on intra-group supplies. This could be an advantage where one part of the group is not registered for VAT and is therefore unable to recover the VAT it has to pay to other parts of the group.

The disadvantage is that all members of a group are jointly and severally liable for the VAT. If one part of a group fails, the other part(s) of the group would have to meet its VAT liability. The Charity Commission's view is that meeting such a liability is not a misapplication of charity funds, provided the charity entered into the registration honestly and reasonably at a time when it appeared to be in the best interests of the charity. A charity setting up or joining a VAT group should therefore ensure that it records the advice and discussions leading to the decision to create the group.

57.2.5   Deregistration

An organisation may deregister, if it wishes to, if the value of taxable supplies in any 12-month period falls below the deregistration threshold (£66,000 in 2009-10). If the organisation holds assets and stock on which it has recovered VAT, it may have to repay to HMRC some of this VAT. This depends on what the assets and stock are, how they were obtained, why the registration is being cancelled, and whether the repayable VAT would be more than £1,000. Information about deregistering is in HMRC notice 700/11 *Cancelling your registration*.

57.3   VAT RECORDS AND RETURNS

After registration the organisation must:

- charge VAT at the appropriate rate on all its taxable supplies;
- issue tax invoices on paper or electronically for all taxable (including zero rated) goods and services supplied, including those sold via the internet, showing the required details;
- obtain VAT receipts for all expenditure on which it is eligible to recover VAT;
- keep financial records showing the VAT on goods or services provided or sold by the organisation (**output tax**) and the VAT on goods or services purchased by or provided to the organisation (**input tax**);
- fill in and submit a quarterly or annual return, as appropriate;
- pay to HMRC the VAT owing if the output tax is more than the input tax;
- keep all VAT records for at least six years from the end of the year to which they apply.

Record keeping rules are set out in HMRC notice 700/21 *Keeping VAT records* and 700/63 *Electronic invoicing*.   *Value Added Tax Regulations 1995 [SI 1995/2518]*
regs.A13,13-20,24-43, .as amended

Errors of up to £10,000 or 1% of turnover to a maximum of £50,000, whichever is larger, must be corrected on the next return after they are discovered. Errors larger than this must be notified immediately to HMRC. There is a four-year cap on recovering VAT that has been overpaid to HMRC.

The **flat rate**, **cash accounting** or **annual accounting schemes** [below] can reduce VAT paperwork. Details of these schemes and their pros and cons are available from HMRC and Business Link [see end of chapter]. In addition, various schemes are available for retailers, as set out in HMRC notice 727 *Retail schemes*.

57.3.1   Flat rate scheme

A **flat rate scheme** is open to organisations whose estimated annual taxable turnover (excluding VAT) or estimated annual business income (including VAT) for the next year is no more than the thresholds applicable at the time (as at 1/7/09, £150,000 and £187,500). Details are in HMRC notice 733 *Flat rate scheme for small businesses*.   *Value Added Tax Regulations 1995 [SI 1995/2518] regs.55A-55V, inserted by*
VAT (Amendment) (No.2) Regulations 2002 [SI 2002/1142] reg.7, & as amended

Organisations on the scheme do not have to identify or separately record the VAT on sales and purchases. They simply record all their supplies, including exempt supplies, and apply a flat rate percentage which has been agreed with HMRC. Input tax can be claimed separately on the purchase of capital expenditure goods that cost £2,000 or more.

This scheme generally results in having to pay less VAT to HMRC, as well as reduced costs for bookkeeping, but is not suitable for organisations which make mixed zero rate, exempt and/or non-business supplies.

57.3.2   Cash accounting

Usually VAT is accounted for on the date the goods or services are supplied, not the date payment is made or received. But if the value of all taxable supplies made by an organisation is expected to be less than £1.35 million (as at 1/8/09) for the next 12 months and once on the scheme remains less than £1.6 million, the organisation can choose to use the **cash accounting scheme**. With this, the organisation accounts for input VAT on the date it pays for goods and services, and output VAT on the date it actually receives the payment. This can make bookkeeping more straightforward. Details are in HMRC notice 731 *Cash accounting*.

Value Added Tax Regulations 1995 [SI 1995/2518] regs.56-65, as amended

57.3.3 Annual accounting

Usually VAT returns are made quarterly, but organisations eligible for cash accounting can opt instead or in addition for **annual accounting**. Instead of making quarterly returns, the organisation pays a fixed VAT amount in nine monthly or three quarterly payments during the year, then completes a single return at the end of the year and either pays any VAT still due or receives a refund if VAT has been overpaid during the year. This is explained in HMRC notice 732 *Annual accounting*.

VAT Regs 1995 regs.49-55, as amended

57.3.4 Anti-avoidance schemes

Many schemes seek to reduce the effects of VAT. Some of these are acceptable to HMRC, but others are **listed** or **hallmarked** and are not acceptable. Organisations with business income over £600,000 may need to notify such schemes to HMRC. Details are in HMRC notice 700/8.

57.4 APPEALS AGAINST HMRC DECISIONS

Disagreements on VAT which cannot be settled with the local VAT office may be appealed to the **tax chamber** in the first-tier tribunal [**64.7**]. Appeals must be lodged with the tribunal within 30 days of the date of the VAT office's decision, although this period can be extended. If the organisation has already asked the VAT office to reconsider its decision and the decision is confirmed, the appeal must be lodged with the tribunal within 21 days of the confirmation.

57.5 RELIEFS FOR CHARITIES AND OTHER ORGANISATIONS

Information specifically about how charities are affected by VAT, both as purchasers and suppliers of goods and services, is in HMRC notice 701/1 *Charities*.

In general charities and other voluntary organisations have to pay VAT in the same way as anyone else, and can recover all or part of it only if they are registered for VAT [**57.2**]. However all charities, even if they are not registered for VAT, are entitled to a few **reliefs** from VAT on goods or services they purchase. The reliefs include advertising [**57.12.1**]; fundraising materials [**57.11.6**]; some disability-related goods [**57.10.3**]; some vehicles, medical and scientific goods [**57.10.2.1**]; rescue and first aid equipment [**57.10.2.2**]; building works [**57.14**]; and some goods purchased in the EU [**57.5.1**]. Some of these reliefs are also available for other voluntary organisations.

The relief takes the form of **zero rating** (0% VAT) on goods or services purchased by the organisation which would normally be standard rated. These reliefs do not exist in other EU states and are under threat from VAT harmonisation.

The organisation usually has to provide a declaration on its headed paper to the supplier at the time it orders or purchases the goods or services, confirming it is eligible for zero rating. The supplier then charges VAT at zero rate instead of standard rate. It is the purchaser's responsibility to provide the declaration. The supplier is not obliged to find out whether the purchaser is eligible for relief, or to make the declaration available to the purchaser.

The wordings for the declarations are in the relevant VAT notices from HMRC. If in doubt about whether a zero rating applies, check with a specialist advisor and/or HMRC. There are penalties for making an incorrect declaration.

Another relief entitles charities to **reduced rate** (5%) rather than standard rate VAT on gas and electricity [**57.15.4**].

57.5.1   Goods purchased in the EU

A VAT-registered organisation buying goods in another EU member state does not pay VAT when it imports the goods. Instead, it accounts for the VAT at the relevant UK rate when it fills in its next VAT return. A VAT-registered UK charity or other body eligible to purchase the goods listed above at zero rate can account for the goods at zero rate on its VAT return.

An organisation which is not VAT-registered pays VAT at the rate in the country where the goods are purchased. It cannot take advantage of UK zero ratings.

If an organisation spends more than the VAT threshold (£68,000 in 2009-10) on goods (but not services) purchased from other EU member states in any year, it is required to register for VAT, even if this would not otherwise be necessary.

57.6   SUPPLIES

All goods, services and facilities provided by an organisation are **supplies**, even if the supply is funded completely by grants and donations, or no charge is made for it, or it is produced or provided by volunteers or by a charity's beneficiaries.

Supplies are either **non-business** or **business**. For VAT purposes, these terms have nothing to do with whether the supplier operates on a for profit or not for profit basis. The terms refer to whether something is outside the scope of VAT (a **non-business supply**), or within the VAT net (a **business supply**).

57.6.1   Non-business supplies

For VAT purposes, a supply is non-business *only* if it is defined as such in the VAT legislation. Non-business supplies include services provided free of charge by voluntary organisations, except in some cases national museums which waive all admission charges [**57.10.7.1**]; some, but not all, goods and services provided to members of an organisation and funded by their membership subscription [**57.10.1**]; and welfare services and related goods supplied by charities consistently below cost to distressed people [**57.10.2.5**] for the relief of their distress. Other non-business supplies are listed in the relevant sections in this chapter.

57.6.1.1   If all supplies are non-business

Non-business supplies are outside the scope of VAT and are completely ignored for VAT purposes. If all of an organisation's supplies are non-business, it cannot register for VAT, and will not have to charge output VAT on any goods or services it provides. It will not be able to recover input VAT on its purchases, but may be eligible to make some purchases at 0% VAT [**57.5**].

57.6.1.2   If some supplies are non-business

Where some supplies are non-business and some are business (exempt or taxable), the organisation is making **mixed supplies**, and may have to register for VAT or be able to register voluntarily [**57.9**].

57.6.2   Business supplies

For VAT purposes, a **business** is any trade, profession or vocation which is not explicitly defined as non-business. It includes services provided to members by clubs, associations and organisations.   *Value Added Tax Act 1994 s.94*

The definition includes charities and other voluntary organisations which provide goods or services for which a charge is made, even if the charge is only nominal and does not cover the full cost of the goods or services, and regardless of whether the charge is made to the end user, to a third party purchaser (such as a local authority), or both. In some cases an organisation can be a business even if the goods or services are provided free of charge.

Among the criteria that are used to assess whether an activity is a business supply are whether the quarterly or annual value has a 'certain measure of substance', and whether the activity is carried out with reasonable continuity rather than only occasionally, is conducted on sound business principles, and primarily provides goods or services for which a charge is made and which are broadly similar to goods or services provided by commercial businesses.

57.6.2.1 If some or all supplies are business supplies

If some or all of a charity's or other organisation's supplies are business supplies, it needs to consider whether supplies are **exempt** [**57.7**] or **taxable** [**57.8**]. If the supplies are taxable, it may have to register for VAT [**57.2.1**] or may choose to register voluntarily [**57.2.2**]. Regardless of whether it registers, it may be eligible for zero rating on some goods and services it purchases or receives [**57.5**].

57.6.3 Services provided under contracts and service agreements

Before entering into a contract or service agreement [**52.1**] to provide services, in particular to or on behalf of a public sector body, organisations should take specialist advice about the VAT implications. The same applies when entering into a grant which could be construed as a payment for a service.

HM Revenue and Customs may regard something called a contract or service agreement as a grant and therefore non-business and outside the scope of VAT, or may regard it as a business supply within the scope of VAT. VAT, tax and contract law are all different, so something may be a business supply for VAT purposes but not be subject to corporation or income tax – and something which is neither a business supply nor subject to tax may still be a contract for the purposes of contract law.

Criteria used by HMRC to distinguish between grants and contracts include who defines the activities or services that will be provided, whether the funder imposes conditions on the recipient organisation, and whether there is a legally enforceable agreement between the parties.   *Bath Festivals Trust Ltd v Revenue & Customs [2008] UKVAT V20840*

It is essential to ensure all contracts or service agreements include a clause enabling the organisation to charge VAT to the purchaser [**52.5.5**] if it needs to, and to ensure the VAT situation is clear before the contract starts.

57.6.3.1 Services not provided to or on behalf of purchaser

Where a service is provided to the final users and not to the local authority, health authority or other purchaser, HMRC has said in some cases that there is not a business supply to the purchaser. In the case of a citizens advice bureau, for example, the CAB makes supplies to the clients which are free, and therefore non-business [**57.10.2.6**], and some VAT tribunals have ruled that there is no supply to the local authority which funds/purchases the service under a service agreement or contract.   *Hillingdon Legal Resources Centre Ltd v Customs & Excise [1991] VAT Tr 39; CAB (2000) VAT tribunal 16411 (unreported)*

In another decision, the tribunal ruled that even if a voluntary organisation's funding comes primarily from local and central government contracts, the fact that it relies on donations to top up the funding means that it is not operating as a business.   *Quarriers v Revenue & Customs [2008] UKVAT V20660, V20670*

However, in other similar situations HMRC has said that there is in fact a business supply to the purchaser/funder, even if services are provided direct to the final users or are funded is partly through donations. Specialist advice is therefore essential in each situation.

57.6.3.2 Services provided on behalf of purchaser

Where the local authority or a similar body has a statutory duty to provide a service and enters into a contract with an organisation to provide the service on its behalf, the service is a business supply. If the service is provided under a grant or service agreement, HMRC will look closely at the actual arrangement and is likely to say that these arrangements, whatever they are called, are a business supply between the organisation and the local authority – even though the service is actually being provided direct to the final users.   *Edinburgh Leisure & others v Customs & Excise [2004] UKVAT V18784*

57.6.3.3 Services directly purchased by purchaser

Where a local authority or other body purchases a specified number of places (for example in a nursery or training workshop) or pays for services to be provided to specified individuals, this is a business supply from the provider to the purchaser.

57.6.4 Place of supply

Whether VAT is charged on goods and services – and the rate at which it is charged – depends on the **place of supply**. This is based on whether the goods or services are being provided to a country within or outside the European Union, whether they are purchased via the internet or other electronic media, where services (but not goods) are physically provided, and whether goods or services are being supplied to a VAT-registered organisation or to an individual or organisation that is not registered for VAT. Basic information is in HMRC notices 700/15 *The ins and outs of VAT* and 741 *Place of supply of services*. Some of the place of supply rules will change on 1 January 2010.

57.7 EXEMPT SUPPLIES

All **business supplies** are either **exempt** from VAT or **taxable** for VAT. Exemption from VAT is completely separate from exemption from corporation or income tax [**56.4-56.6**]. An activity which is exempt from corporation or income tax may nonetheless be taxable for VAT purposes.

If everything an organisation provides is exempt, or is a combination of exempt plus non-business [**57.6.1**], it will not be able to register for VAT. Because it is not registered it cannot recover VAT on its purchases, but it may be eligible for zero rating on some goods or services it purchases or receives [**57.5**].

Complex analysis may be necessary to determine whether a supply is exempt. For example, if a charity is contracted to manage a local authority children's home [**57.10.5**], is it providing services for children, which are exempt, or is it providing management services to the local authority, which are taxable?

Where supplies are partly exempt (or partly exempt plus non-business) and partly taxable, the organisation is providing **mixed supplies** [**57.9**].

57.8 TAXABLE SUPPLIES

If goods or services are not defined as **non-business** [**57.6.1**] or **exempt** [**57.7**], they are **taxable** at **zero**, **reduced** or **standard** rate.

57.8.1 Zero rate

Some supplies are taxable at **zero rate**. To a purchaser the effect is the same as if they were non-business or exempt: there is no VAT on them. But to the supplier, there are significant differences. The value of zero rated goods and services is included in the total when determining whether the organisation has reached the registration threshold [**57.2.1**], but the value of non-business and exempt supplies is not. A VAT-registered organisation can recover the VAT paid on goods or services purchased for the purposes of making zero rated supplies, but not for making non-business or in most cases exempt supplies [**57.9**].

VAT-registered organisations whose supplies are all or mostly zero rated have the best of all worlds: they do not have to charge VAT to their clients or customers, *and* they can recover all or most of the VAT they pay out.

57.8.2 Standard rate

All goods, services and other supplies, including those provided by charities, are **standard rated** unless they are defined in VAT legislation or regulations as non-business [**57.6.1**], exempt from VAT [**57.7**], zero rated [**57.8.1**] or reduced rated [**57.8.3**]. The standard rate is 15% for goods and services provided until the end of 2009, and 17.5% for goods or services provided on or after 1 January 2010.

An organisation making standard rated supplies may be obliged to register for VAT [**57.2.1**], or may choose to register voluntarily [**57.2.2**]. If it is registered it must charge VAT to clients, purchasers or customers who buy standard or reduced rated goods or services. It is also able to recover all or some of the VAT it pays when it purchases goods or services.

57.8.3   Reduced rate

Some supplies, including the supply of fuel and power to homes and charities [**57.15.4**], the supply of energy saving materials for buildings [**57.14.4**] and some modifications of homes to meet the needs of older people [**57.10.4**], are **reduced rate**. The reduced rate of VAT is 5%.

A European Commission directive allows (but does not require) member states to apply reduced rate to certain labour-intensive or locally supplied services such as domestic care services, restaurant meals, gardening and bicycle repairs. At the time of writing (mid 2009) the directive had not been adopted in the UK.

57.9   MIXED SUPPLIES AND PARTIAL EXEMPTION

Many VAT-registered organisations provide **mixed supplies** – non-business [**57.6.1**] and/or exempt [**57.7**] together with taxable supplies. Such an organisation is **partly exempt**, and can generally recover VAT only on purchases relating to taxable activities. The rules are in HMRC notice 706 *Partial exemption*.

The organisation should ensure that purchases of goods and services are allocated to the activities they are for. If a purchase (for example, telephone or photocopying costs) relates to non-business or exempt activities as well as taxable activities, these costs will have to be apportioned to the different VAT categories.

57.9.1   Non-business supplies

VAT cannot be recovered on goods or services used to make **non-business** supplies [**57.6.1**]. VAT therefore cannot be recovered on the portion of the purchase which is to be used for services funded solely by grants, donations etc, services provided free by charities, goods used partly for private rather than business purposes, or other non-business activities.

Lennartz accounting regulations apply when purchasing land or goods which will be used partly for non-business purposes and will be held by the organisation for a significant period. These allow the organisation to recover all the VAT at the time of purchase, then pay back the proportion relating to non-business use annually over five or 10 years. The rules are explained in HMRC info sheet 14/07 *Assets used partly for non-business purposes*.   *Value Added Tax Regulations 1995*
[SI 1995/2518] regs.116A-116N, inserted by VAT (Amendment) (No.7) Regulations 2007 [SI 2007/3099]

57.9.2   Exempt supplies: de minimis rule

VAT on goods or services which are used to make **exempt** supplies cannot in general be recovered, but there is an exception if the amount of input tax relating to the exempt supplies is *de minimis* (basically, 'not worth bothering about').

A VAT-registered organisation within the *de minimis* limit can recover the VAT it has paid on goods or services used to make the exempt supplies. The VAT can be recovered if input tax relating to exempt supplies in the tax period does not exceed the *de minimis* limit (as at 1/8/09, an average of £625 per month), and is no greater than half the total input tax in the period.   *Value Added Tax Regulations 1995*
[SI 1995/2518] reg.106, amended by VAT (Amendment) Regulations 2002 [SI 2002/1074] reg.4

An organisation which has exempt input VAT over the *de minimis* limit cannot recover any of the input VAT relating to its exempt supplies, and there is no equivalent *de minimis* limit for purchases relating to non-business supplies.

57.9.3   Partial exemption

If the organisation makes mixed exempt and taxable business supplies and does not meet the *de minimis* criteria, it can recover input VAT only on the portion used to make taxable supplies. The portion that can be recovered will be based on a partial exemption method. *Value Added Tax Act 1994 s.26; Value Added Tax Regulations 1995 [SI 1995/2518] regs.99-110, as amended*

This may be the HMRC **standard method**, or a **special method** agreed with HMRC. A special method could be based on the percentage of income the organisation receives for each type of activity, the cost of providing each activity, the number of staff employed in each activity, or any other reasonable basis agreed with HMRC. The method is used to apportion residual input VAT (the VAT on overheads etc) after VAT on purchases has been directly attributed to activities.

Whatever method is used, an annual adjustment is required at the end of the tax year (end of March, April or May depending on the organisation's VAT quarter) which evens out variable exempt activity during the year.

Because of the complexities of mixed supplies and partial exemption, advice should be sought from an accountant who specialises in charities and other voluntary organisations.

57.10 VAT ON THE ORGANISATION'S SERVICES

This book cannot cover all aspects of VAT, but set out below are the supplies that are likely to be of most concern to a voluntary organisation new to VAT. For more information see the HMRC website [see end of chapter] and *A Practical Guide to VAT for Charities*, published by the Directory of Social Change.

57.10.1 Membership subscriptions and services

The rules on membership subscriptions and other VAT rules for membership organisations are in HMRC notice 701/5 *Clubs and associations*.

Where a subscription is simply a means of raising funds for the organisation and does not entitle the member to rights or benefits, it is **non-business [57.6.1]**.

Where services are provided to an organisation's members in return for membership subscriptions, these are **business supplies [57.6.2]**. They are **exempt [57.7]** if they are to not for profit organisations whose objects are 'in the public domain' and are political, religious, patriotic, philosophical or philanthropic or of a civic nature, or to trade unions, professional associations, learned societies and some trade associations. To be exempt the subscription must entitle the member only to the right to participate in the organisation's management, for example by voting at general meetings; the right to receive reports on its activities; and/or the right to receive benefits which relate to the aims of the organisation, are provided in return for the subscription, and do not include any right of admission to premises, events or performances for which non-members have to pay. *Value Added Tax Act 1994 sch.9 gp.9 item 1, amended by VAT (Subscriptions to Trade Unions, Professional & Other Public Interest Bodies) Order 1999 [SI 1999/2384]*

The VAT status of membership benefits which do not meet these criteria depends on the benefits. That portion of the membership subscription may be **exempt**, if it entitles the member to exempt supplies such as access to some cultural services [**57.10.7.2**], **zero rated** if it entitles the member to zero rate supplies such as a printed newsletter [**57.12.2**], or **standard rated** for benefits which are not exempt or zero rated, such as access to a members-only section of the organisation's website, or a newsletter provided electronically rather than on paper.

Where the subscription entitles the member to a single package of benefits, the VAT status is generally based on the **principal benefit**. If there are ancillary benefits in different VAT categories, HMRC extra-statutory concession 3.35 allows (but does not require) the VAT to be apportioned to reflect the categories.

57.10.2 Health, welfare and care services

Services for health, welfare and care may be **exempt**, **zero rated** or **standard rated**, depending on the nature of the service and in some cases, on who is supplying it. Goods such as adapted vehicles may also be rated differently depending on the nature of the goods and who is supplying them.

57.10.2.1   Vehicles, medical and scientific equipment

Zero rating [57.8.1] applies to the purchase of some vehicles and equipment by or for charities which provide care or medical or surgical treatment for people who are chronically sick or disabled, non-profit research institutes, hospitals and health authorities.   *Value Added Tax Act 1994 sch.8 gp.15 items 3-10, as amended*

Under HMRC extra-statutory concession 3.19, zero rating is also available to charities whose sole object is the provision of care services to meet the personal needs of people with disabilities, and charities which provide transport services predominantly to people with disabilities.

Further information is in VAT notice 701/6 *Charity funded equipment for medical, veterinary etc uses* and information sheet 8/98 *Charities: Supply, repair and maintenance of relevant goods*. The declarations to claim zero rating are in *701/6 Supplement*.

57.10.2.2   Rescue and first aid equipment

For charities providing sea rescue or assistance, lifeboats and lifeboat equipment are **zero rated [57.8.1]**.   *VATA 1994 sch.8 gp.8 item 3*

Equipment supplied solely for rescue or first aid services by a charitable institution providing such services is eligible for zero rating in the same way as medical and scientific equipment **[57.10.2.1]**. Under HMRC extra-statutory concession 3.25, resuscitation training models may be zero rated. In some situations warning sirens may also be eligible for zero rating.

57.10.2.3   Medicinal products, drugs and chemicals

Medicinal products can be **zero rated [57.8.1]** when supplied to a charity engaged in the treatment or care of people or animals, medical or veterinary research, or testing the efficiency of medicinal products for use by the charity. Drugs and chemicals for medical research can be zero rated when supplied to a charity engaged in medical or veterinary research. Details are in VAT leaflet 701/1 *Charities* and the declaration to claim zero rating is in *701/6 Supplement*.
                    VATA 1994 sch.8 gp.15 items 9,10

Condoms supplied to a charity that provides sexual health advice and contraception are eligible for zero rating as medicinal products. Other contraceptive products may be **exempt [57.10.2.4]** or **reduced rate [57.8.3]**.   *VATA 1994 sch.7A gp.8, inserted by VAT (Reduced Rate) Order 2006 [SI 2006/1472]*

57.10.2.4   Health services

Care or medical or surgical treatment in hospitals or state regulated institutions, and all medical services by recognised medical practitioners and by persons working under their direct supervision, are always **exempt [57.7]**. Provision of transport services for people who are sick or injured, in vehicles specifically designed for the purpose, is also exempt. Details are in HMRC notices 701/31 *Health institutions* and 701/57 *Health professionals*.   *VATA 1994 sch.9 gp.7 items 1-5,11, as amended*

57.10.2.5   Welfare and care services, protection of children

Welfare services and related goods are **exempt [57.7]** if they are supplied by a charity, a state-regulated private welfare institution or agency (for example a commercial or non-charitable domiciliary care agency or independent fostering agency), or a public body. A supply is eligible for this exemption if it involves 'the provision of care, treatment or instruction designed to promote the physical or mental welfare of elderly, sick, distressed or disabled persons'. The same exemption applies to the care or protection of children and young persons. Further information about exemption for welfare services is in HMRC notice 701/2 *Welfare*.
                    VATA 1994 sch.9 gp.7 item 9, as amended; notes 6-8, as amended

In the case of a local Age Concern, provision of welfare services to elderly people was confirmed as being exempt **[57.10.2.5]** even though the services were paid for under contracts with county councils and primary care trusts.   *Age Concern Leicestershire v Revenue & Customs [2008] UKVAT V20762*

Welfare services and related goods which would normally be exempt from VAT can be – but do not have to be – treated as **non-business [57.6.1]** if they are provided by a charity, are for the relief of distress, and are provided consistently below cost to the distressed individual. This provision does not apply where services are provided below cost to a local authority or similar purchaser of services, or where services are provided by a body which is not a charity.

Welfare and care services and related goods which are not exempt or non-business are **standard rated** [**57.8.2**].

57.10.2.6   Welfare advice and information

The provision of welfare information and advice is **exempt** if it is part of a course or other exempt educational supply [**57.10.6.1**]. Where it is provided by a charity or state-regulated private welfare institution or agency solely for the benefit of a particular individual or according to an individual's personal circumstances, it is an exempt welfare supply [**57.10.2.5**].

Where the information or advice is provided free of charge to an individual, it is **non-business** [**57.6.1**].

Where information or advice connected with or intended to promote the physical or mental welfare of elderly, sick, distressed or disabled persons or the care and protection of children and young people is provided by a charity or state-regulated private welfare institution or agency, and is neither exempt nor non-business, it is subject to VAT at **reduced rate** [**57.8.3**].   *Value Added Tax Act 1994 sch.7A gp.9 item 1,*
inserted by VAT (Reduced Rate) Order 2006 [SI 2006/1472]

Information about welfare advice and information is in HMRC notice 701/2 *Welfare*.

57.10.3   Disability-related goods and services

Charities and in some cases other voluntary organisations are entitled to zero rating on the purchase of some goods for use by people with disabilities, or for use in providing services to people with disabilities [**57.10.2.1**].

57.10.3.1   For blind and visually impaired people

Zero rating [**57.8.1**] is available to charities and other voluntary organisations on some sound recording equipment supplied to charities caring for or producing sound recordings for people who are blind or severely visually impaired, and radios and cassette recorders supplied to charities for free loan to blind and severely visually impaired people. Further information is in HMRC notice 701/1 *Charities*, and the declaration to claim zero rating in *701/6 Supplement*.

Value Added Tax Act 1994 sch.8 gp.4

57.10.3.2   For chronically sick and disabled people

If a charity purchases specially designed equipment which it intends to make available, either free or for a charge, to people who are chronically sick or disabled for their domestic or personal use, the purchase is **zero rated** [**57.8.1**]. Details and the declarations are in HMRC notices 701/7 *VAT reliefs for disabled people* and 701/59 *Motor vehicles for disabled people*.   *VATA 1994 sch.8 gp.12, as amended*

57.10.4   Goods and services for persons 60 or over

Reduced rate VAT [**57.8.3**] applies to the installation, or supply and installation, of mobility aids in domestic accommodation occupied by a person who is 60 or over at the time of the supply. The person for whom the aid is intended should make a declaration of eligibility for the supplier or installer. Information is in HMRC notice 708 *Buildings and construction*.

57.10.5   Services for children and young people

57.10.5.1   Care and protection

Services for the care and protection of specific children and young people, rather than children in general, are **exempt** [**57.7**] if they are provided by a charity, a state-regulated private welfare institution or agency or a public body [**57.10.2.5**]. Information about this exemption is in HMRC notice 701/2 *Welfare*.

VATA 1994 sch.9 gp.7 item 9, as amended; notes 6-8, as amended

In some circumstances, HMRC has ruled that children's care and protection services provided by charities may be **non-business** [**57.6.1**] rather than exempt. A charity wishing to take advantage of this ruling should seek specialist advice.

Customs & Excise Commissioners v Yarburgh Children's Trust [2002] STC 207;;
Customs & Excise v St Paul's Community Project Ltd [2004] EWHC 2490 (Ch)

Activity based after-school clubs such as dance classes and football clubs that do not have to be registered with Ofsted, even if they are for under-eights, may be **exempt** as a sports club [**57.10.8**]. If not exempt, they are **standard rated**.

57.10.5.2 Youth clubs

Facilities provided to members of youth clubs or associations of youth clubs in exchange for their subscription are **exempt** [**57.7**]. Entertainment, food, drink and purely recreational holidays are taxable at the appropriate rate. Details are in HMRC notice 701/35 *Youth clubs*. *Value Added Tax Act 1994 sch.9 gp.6 item 6, note 6*

Single-sport clubs, such as football clubs, are not youth clubs but may be exempt as sports clubs [**57.10.8**].

57.10.6 Education, research and training

Education, research and training are **exempt** [**57.7**] when provided by an eligible body. **Eligible bodies** are schools, universities, colleges etc, charities and other voluntary organisations, not for profit research institutes, and bodies which teach English as a foreign language. The latter are exempt only for the English language teaching part of their work. *Value Added Tax Act 1994 sch.9 gp.6, as amended*

Where services are provided by a charity or other non-profit-distributing body, they must be supplied on an **otherwise than for profit** basis in order to be exempt. This means that any surplus or profit made on the supply must be used only for the same type of supply. If the profit is used for any other purpose, the original supply is not exempt.

57.10.6.1 Education

Eligible bodies [above] are **exempt** from having to charge VAT on education of a type provided in schools or universities; vocational training [**57.10.6.3**]; examination services; and conference facilities, accommodation, catering etc when supplied to another eligible body for an exempt educational purpose. Details are in HMRC 701/30 *Education and vocational training*. *VATA 1994 sch.9 gp.6, as amended*

57.10.6.2 Research

Research is **exempt** [**57.7**] if it is provided by one eligible body [**57.10.6**] to another; otherwise it is **standard rated**. Where research is funded by a public body, its VAT treatment depends on whether it is grant funded or commissioned. If it is grant funded, it is **non-business** [**57.6.1**] and therefore outside the scope of VAT. Where it is commissioned – by a public body, or anyone other than an eligible body as defined above – it is **standard rated**. Research that is part grant funded and part commissioned is a **mixed supply** [**57.9**]. More information is in VAT information sheet 04/08 *Supplies of government grant funded research*.

57.10.6.3 Vocational training

Vocational training provided by an eligible body [**57.10.6**] is **exempt** [**57.7**]. This includes training, retraining or providing work experience for any trade, profession or employment, or for voluntary work connected with education, health, safety, welfare or activities of a charitable nature. *VATA 1994 sch.9 gp.6 note 3, as amended*

57.10.6.4 Distance learning

Distance learning provided by charities and other eligible bodies [**57.10.6**], comprising written materials, face to face tuition, website learning etc is a single **exempt** educational supply [**57.7**], rather than a mixed supply of exempt education and zero rated printed matter. *College of Estate Management v Customs & Excise [2005] UKHL 62*

57.10.7 Cultural activities

Free admission to cultural facilities or activities is generally **non-business** [**57.6.1**], as are voluntary donations [**57.11.8.8**] from people who attend. Where an admission or similar fee is charged, it may be **exempt** or **standard rated**, depending on the nature of the organisation and its activities.

57.10.7.1 National and university museums and galleries

National and university museums and galleries on a special list of eligible institutions, which waive all admission charges to their major collections and open the collections to the public for at least 30 hours per week, can **recover VAT** on their running costs, even though those costs are **non-business**. Museums and galleries which are not on the list cannot recover VAT on running costs.

Value Added Tax Act 1994 s.33A, inserted by Finance Act 2001 s.98; VAT (Refund of Tax to Museums & Galleries) (Amendment) Order 2005 [SI 2005/1993]

57.10.7.2 Cultural services

Public bodies and eligible bodies are **exempt** [**57.7**] from VAT on their admission charges to museums, galleries, art exhibitions and zoos, and to theatrical, musical and dance performances of a cultural nature. An **eligible body** is one which is prevented by its governing document from distributing its profits, operates on a **otherwise than for profit** basis [**57.10.6**], and is managed and administered 'on a voluntary basis'. The exemption is explained in HMRC notice 701/47 *Culture*. *VATA 1994 sch.9 gp.13, inserted by VAT (Cultural Services) Order 1996 [SI 1996/1256]*

Cultural organisations can be eligible for exemption even if they have salaried managers or paid governing body members, provided that such payments are allowed by the governing document [**16.3**] and comply with specified criteria. HMRC guidance is in notice 701/47 and in reference brief 27/07 *VAT cultural exemption: Clarification of 'direct or indirect financial interest'*.

Bournemouth Symphony Orchestra v HM Revenue & Customs, & HM Revenue & Customs v Longborough Festival Opera [2006] EWCA Civ 1281

The exemption on admission to performances applies only to live performances. *Chichester Cinema at New Park Ltd v Revenue & Customs [2005] UKVAT V19344*

57.10.8 Sport and physical education

Sporting and physical education services are **exempt** from VAT [**57.7**] if they are supplied by non-profit-distributing bodies. The bodies may be membership bodies providing the services to members who are granted membership of at least three months, or non-membership bodies providing the services to any individuals. Supplies not meeting these criteria are **standard rated**. Further details are in HMRC notice 701/45 *Sport*. *Value Added Tax Act 1994 sch.9 gp.10, as amended*

57.10.9 Spiritual welfare

The rules on **exemption** for welfare and care [**57.10.2.5**] apply to the provision of spiritual welfare by a religious institution as part of a course of instruction or a retreat, but not if the primary intention of the course or retreat is to provide recreation or a holiday. *Value Added Tax Act 1994 sch.9 gp.7 item 9, note 6(c), as amended*

The provision of places of worship and religious services is a **non-business** supply [**57.6.1**]. Goods and services incidental to the provision of spiritual welfare, provided by a religious community to its resident members in return for a subscription or other payment required as a condition of membership, are **exempt** [**57.7**] if provided by a charity. *VATA 1994 sch.9 gp.7 item 10*

57.10.10 Grant making and grant administration

The provision of grants is **non-business** [**57.6.1**] and outside the scope of VAT. But there may be VAT implications where an organisation administers grants as an intermediary, such as a council for voluntary service receiving a grant to pass on to other organisations, or a community foundation receiving a donation. The **Community Foundation Network** [see end of chapter] has guidelines for organisations which administer grants on behalf of funders or donors.

Where the intermediary's trustees have ultimate control over who receives the funding – even if within a framework set by the original donor or funder – both the receipt of the original grant or donation and the donations that are made to the ultimate recipients are non-business. If the intermediary retains part of the money or charges an administration fee, this is also non-business.

However, where the funds are **flow-through**, with the original donor or funder determining whom they should be passed on to or needing to approve the intermediary's decisions, the intermediary is providing a grant making service to the original donor or funder and any fee or charge for the service is **standard rated**.

Care is needed when an intermediary acts as the lead body or accountable body for a consortium bid [**11.3.1**] and receives a grant which will be passed on to other organisations. If the intermediary is in effect sub-contracting provision of services to the recipient organisations, those services may then be subject to VAT at **standard rate** unless they are exempt.

For other issues in administering grants on behalf of third parties, see **48.5**.

57.10.11 Food and drink

The supply of much food and drink is **zero rated** [**57.8.1**], but prepared foods or foods supplied in catering are **standard rated**. Catering includes, but is not limited to, supplies of food or drink for consumption on the premises where they are supplied, and hot take-away food. The rules are in VAT notices 701/1 *Charities*, 701/14 *Food*, and 709/1 *Catering and take-away food*.

Sales of food and drink by charities from trolleys, canteens or shops are **exempt** if the sales are connected with the welfare of people in hospital etc [**57.10.2.5**]. These sales are not exempt if they are not connected with such welfare, are made to staff, or are sales of excisable goods such as tobacco and alcoholic drinks.

Value Added Tax Act 1994 sch.9 gp.7 item 9, as amended; note 7

57.11 FUNDRAISING AND SPONSORSHIP

The costs involved in fundraising are generally standard rated, although some zero ratings and exemptions are available for charities, and in some cases for other voluntary organisations or for bodies which raise funds for charities and voluntary organisations. The zero ratings and exemptions are very specific and are narrowly applied.

57.11.1 Donations and grants

The receipt of donations, legacies, grants, sponsorship and other voluntary contributions is **non-business** [**57.6.1**], provided no supply is made to the donor other than a simple acknowledgement such as a mention in an annual report.

Where the donor or funder requires, is promised or expects to receive something in return, the 'donation' becomes payment for a business supply which in most cases will be **standard rated**. This includes, for example, a 'donation' for use of the recipient organisation's name, logo or copyright material, or the recipient organisation providing publicity, tickets or other benefits in return for a 'donation'.

Showing a corporate donor's logo on the recipient's materials or website makes a donation standard rated, but in practice HMRC does not enforce this if the logo is small and clearly intended as an acknowledgement rather than as publicity for the donor. But a link to a donor's website is likely to be treated as standard rated.

57.11.1.1 Donations by SMS text message

When a donation is made by text message there is no VAT on the donation itself, but **standard rate** VAT applies to any charge made by the mobile phone company to the subscriber for the text messaging service. At the time of writing (mid 2009), the mobile phone companies were introducing a system to distinguish donations from other premium rate texts, which would enable them to charge VAT on their own charges, but not on the portion that will go to the charity.

57.11.2 Sponsorship

Sponsorship may refer to funds received from businesses, individuals and others who wish to support an organisation, or to donations made to show support for an individual who is participating in an event. In both cases, if the sponsorship is a genuine donation it is **non-business**, but as soon as it is or can be perceived as a payment in return for something, it may become subject to VAT. Details are in HMRC notice 701/41 *Sponsorship*.

57.11.2.1 Sponsorship for an organisation, event, publication etc

Where a sponsor requires, is promised or expects to receive something in return, it is likely to be payment for a **standard rated** business supply [**57.11.1**], unless it is sponsorship for a **qualifying fundraising event** [**57.11.8.6**].

57.11.2.2 Sponsorship of individuals

Sponsorship where an individual asks 'sponsors' to make donations in recognition of something done by the individual, such as taking part in a sponsored walk, is generally a pure donation and therefore **non-business** with no VAT implications.

However, where an individual agrees with the recipient organisation to collect a minimum amount of sponsorship in return for the right to participate in the event, this part of the sponsorship becomes an entry fee. If the event is an **exempt fundraising event** [**57.11.8**], the entry fee element of the sponsorship is exempt from VAT and there are no VAT implications. But if the event is not eligible for exemption, the entry fee element of the sponsorship is **standard rated**.

If participants in events receive benefits such as free travel, accommodation and gifts, the organiser may need to charge VAT on that element of the sponsorship. HMRC allows some benefits – such as t-shirts to identify event participants, training advice, light refreshments etc – to be provided without incurring VAT.

57.11.3 Donated goods

The sale, hiring out or expert of donated goods by a charity, or by an individual or organisation which has a written agreement to transfer all the profits to a charity, is **zero rated** [**57.8.1**]. The goods must be offered for sale or hire either to the general public, or exclusively to people with disabilities or people receiving means-tested benefits. *Value Added Tax Act 1994 sch.8 gp.15 items 1,1A, as amended*

Under HMRC extra-statutory concession 3.21, sales by a charity are also zero rated where the goods are of such poor quality or so unsafe that they cannot be offered to the public, and are therefore sold on as scrap or for use as rags. This concession covers only the sale of items that are unsuitable for sale – not items that were offered for sale but were not purchased.

Other sales or hire of donated goods are **standard rated**.

Goods donated by a VAT-registered donor are zero rated, so the donor does not have to account for VAT on the goods. *VATA 1994 sch.8 gp.15 item 2, as amended*

57.11.3.1 Animals as donated goods

Charities for the rehousing of animals may receive animals from individual donors, or from local authorities which have collected them as strays. The sale of these animals by the charity is **zero rated** [**57.8.1**]. *Gablesfarm Dogs & Cats Home v HM Revenue & Customs [2008] UKVAT V20519*

57.11.4 Lotteries and competitions

The sale of lottery and raffle tickets [**49.6**] is **exempt** [**57.7**]. Where winning a prize is dependent on any element of skill, it becomes a competition and the entrance fee is **standard rated** [**49.7**]. *Value Added Tax Act 1994 sch.9 gp.4 item 2*

57.11.5 Fundraising goods

The sale of calendars, t-shirts, mugs and other items sold for fundraising purposes is **standard rated**, unless they are being sold at an exempt fundraising event [**57.11.8**] or are **zero rated** anyway, such as books.

57.11.6 Fundraising materials

Collection boxes, items such as lapel stickers, and stationery purchased by charities to be used specifically for fundraising appeals are eligible for **zero rating** [**57.8.1**] under HMRC extra-statutory concession 3.3.

The only stationery items eligible for zero rating under this concession are collecting envelopes which ask for donations of money, similar envelopes used by religious organisations in their planned giving schemes, pre-printed letters appealing solely for money for the charity, and envelopes used in conjunction with appeal letters and for forwarding donations, provided they are over-printed with an appeal request related to the appeal contained in the letter.

To be eligible for zero rating, collecting boxes and buckets must be tamper-proof and must include the name of the charity in a permanent form. Ordinary household buckets cannot be zero rated, but special tamper-proof lids used to seal such buckets are zero rated.

Lapel stickers, pins, badges, ribbons, artificial flowers (if they are the charity's symbol) and other small items designed to be worn on lapels or similar are zero rated, provided they are of nominal value. 'Nominal value' means they are given free to donors or in return for a suggested donation of no more than £1, and cost the charity considerably less than £1.

Other items – including wristbands – are not zero rated, even if they are just a larger version of a lapel item. If such items are freely available in return for a donation of any amount they are **non-business** [**57.6.1**]; if the item is sold for a specified minimum or fixed amount, it is **standard rated**.

Zero rating is not available for general stationery, raffle tickets, or other fundraising materials. If a charity buys its own materials to make stickers etc, the materials are not zero rated.

Further information and a suggested declaration are in HMRC notice 701/58 *Charity advertising and goods connected with collecting donations.*

57.11.7 Sale of advertising

The supply of advertisements in a charity's programmes, brochures etc is normally **standard rated**, but the sale of advertising space in brochures or programmes for a fundraising event is **exempt** [**57.7**]. The sale of advertising space in a charity's other programmes and brochures (not for fundraising events) can be treated as **non-business** [**57.6.1**], provided at least 50% of the advertisements are from private individuals rather than commercial businesses. The sale of advertising space in fundraising or other programmes etc is **zero rated** [**57.8.1**] if sold to another charity. Information is in HMRC notice 701/1 *Charities*.

57.11.8 Fundraising events

In general, fundraising events are subject to VAT. But fundraising events are **exempt** from VAT [**57.7**] and also from corporation or income tax [**56.4.6**] if they meet a number of criteria, which are set out in HMRC notice CWL4 *Fund raising events*. *Value Added Tax Act 1994 sch.9 gp.12, amended by VAT (Fund Raising Events by Charities & Other Qualifying Bodies) Order 2000 [SI 2000/802]*

Unlike the exemption from corporation and income tax, exemption from VAT is not necessarily advantageous. It means that organisations registered for VAT will not have to charge VAT on tickets, goods sold at the event and sponsorship for the event – but they cannot recover VAT on the expenses of the event.

57.11.8.1 Qualifying bodies

A fundraising event is exempt from VAT if it is a **qualifying event** [**57.11.8.4**] and is held by a charity or charities holding the event to raise money for charitable purposes, a corporate body wholly owned by a charity which has agreed in writing to transfer all of its profits (from all sources, not just from the event) to the charity [**51.7**], or a non-profit-making organisation which is a qualifying body holding the event to raise money exclusively for its own benefit. **Qualifying bodies** are those with political, religious, philanthropic, philosophical or patriotic objects or objects of a civic nature; trade unions, professional associations, learned societies, bodies established primarily to provide facilities for participating in sport and recreation, and cultural bodies that are eligible for the exemption for cultural services [**57.10.7.2**]. *Value Added Tax Act 1994 sch.9 gp.12*

Specialist advice should be taken before involving a charity's trading company in exempt events, particularly where the company is VAT-registered. Exempt income from the event may reduce the company's ability to recover some input tax, unless the exempt income falls within the *de minimis* provision or a partial exemption agreement [**57.9**]. Participation in exempt events also requires the trading company to transfer *all* its profits, from all sources, to the charity, which can leave the company without adequate operating capital.

57.11.8.2 Joint events

If two or more qualifying bodies [**57.11.8.1**] enter into an informal agreement to organise an event, each qualifies for the exemption. If the agreement is more formal and creates a separate legal partnership [**11.3.2**], the new entity is exempt only if it is itself a qualifying body.

57.11.8.3 Events organised by others

VAT exemption applies when a qualifying body enters into a written agreement with an agent or promoter to organise an event on its behalf. If the agent or promoter charges a fee or retains any of the event income to cover its own expenses, this is treated as payment for its agency services and is subject to VAT.

Income is not exempt from VAT if an event is organised by an individual or individuals or a non-qualifying body which has not entered into an agency agreement.

57.11.8.4 Qualifying events

The exemption applies to a wide range of events, such as discos and dances, live performances and other events which have a paying audience, film showings, fairs and festivals, exhibitions, bazaars, jumble sales, car boot sales, good as new sales, auctions of bought in goods (an auction of donated goods is **zero rated**; see **57.8.1**); sporting participation (including spectators) such as sponsored walks, sporting performances, participation in contests or games of skill, fireworks displays, fundraising dinners, and fundraising events held on the internet or through other electronic media. This is not an exhaustive list, and organisers of other types of event should contact their VAT advisor or HMRC.

To be exempt from VAT, it must be clear that the event is being held for the benefit of a charity or other voluntary organisation. All tickets and publicity material must clearly state that it is a fundraising event, or is in aid of a particular organisation or organisations. Where the funds are being raised for a registered charity or charities, this must be made clear [**18.1.5**].

Minutes and other internal documents should be retained in case HMRC needs evidence that the event was genuinely organised as a fundraising activity.

57.11.8.5 Number of events

The above events are qualifying events only if no more than 15 events of a similar type are held in the same location during the organisation's financial year – or if more than 15 events of a similar type are held in the same location, the gross income from them is not more than £1,000 per week. If these limits are breached, *none* of the events is exempt. For events on the internet, the charity's entire website is treated as one 'location'.

A two- or three-day event with a single admission ticket is only one event, but a series of events on separate dates count as separate events.

Even if the event meets the above criteria, it might not be exempt from VAT if it is commercially organised, very large and likely to make large profits. An organisation arranging this sort of event, or any other where it is not clear that VAT exemption applies, should take specialist advice.

57.11.8.6 VAT treatment of income at events

Donations made at or in relation to a qualifying event are, like all donations, **non-business** [57.6.1] and outside the scope of VAT. Income at or in relation to the event that would normally be **zero rated** [57.8.1], such as the sale of programmes or brochures, advertising sold to other charities, the sale of donated goods and the sale of young children's clothing, remains zero rated.

All other income from a qualifying event is **exempt** [57.7], including admission charges, the sale of advertising to businesses, sales of normally standard rated goods by the charity or qualifying body at the event, and sponsorship directly connected with the event even if the sponsor receives publicity in return.

57.11.8.7 Non-qualifying events

For a non-qualifying event, income which would normally be **standard rated** remains standard rated. If the organisation is VAT registered it will have to charge VAT on tickets, advertising, souvenirs etc. This increases the cost to customers, but enables the organisation to recover the VAT it has paid in organising the event, purchasing the souvenirs etc.

57.11.8.8 Voluntary donations

A VAT-registered organisation which wants to reduce the amount of VAT it has to charge on admission tickets can set a low admission price, with a voluntary additional donation. The donation element is **non-business** [57.6.1] and there is no VAT on it provided it is genuinely optional and it is clearly stated on all publicity, including tickets, that anyone paying the minimum amount will be admitted to the event or will receive the stated goods or service even if they do not pay the donation element. Donors must be free to choose how much to give, even if the organisation has indicated a desired amount, and the additional payment must not give the person any particular benefit, such as a better seat at a concert.

For film or theatre performances, concerts, sporting fixtures and similar events, the minimum charge must not be less than the usual price for a commercial event of the same type. For dances, dinners and similar events, the total of the basic minimum charges made must not be less than the total costs incurred in arranging the event.

HMRC officers can and do check that the criteria are met by the organiser.

57.11.9 Fundraising challenge events

Fundraising events that involve participation in sport or in endurance events such as charity challenge events [49.5] are generally **exempt** from VAT if they meet the criteria for fundraising events [57.11.8]. However, the exemption does not apply if the event includes the provision of bought-in accommodation, more than two nights' accommodation from the charity's own resources, or a package of travel and accommodation.

If the event does not meet the criteria for exemption, specialist advice should be sought. In some cases the charity may come within the **tour operator's margin scheme** (TOMS). TOMS rules will change from 1 January 2010.

Information about TOMS is in HMRC notice 709/5, and information about the general VAT treatment of challenge and similar events is in 701/1 *Charities*.

57.11.10 Fundraising costs

In the Tron Theatre case, a so-called donation to get a seat named in the theatre was held to be payment for a **business supply** [57.6.2]. The theatre company therefore had to charge VAT to the supporters who paid for seat names – but was able to recover VAT on the costs of running the fundraising scheme.

Customs & Excise Commissioners v Tron Theatre Limited [1994] STC 177

When the Church of England Children's Society subsequently argued that the same principle should apply to recruiting supporters, the high court ruled that carrying out fundraising is a business activity, and that where funds are being raised totally or partially to enable a charity to carry out its business activities, the VAT on that portion of the fundraising costs can be recovered. This applies only where the organisation is raising money to provide goods or services which are themselves subject to VAT, and where the charity is registered for VAT.

Church of England Children's Society v HM Revenue & Customs [2005] EWHC 1692 (Ch)

57.12 ADVERTISING AND PRINTED MATERIALS

57.12.1 Advertising placed by charities

Zero rating [**57.8.1**]applies to all advertisements, including job recruitment advertisements, placed by a charity in any media – print, radio, television, cinema, internet or other – and services connected with the design and production of the advertisement. *Value Added Tax Act 1994 sch.8 gp.15 items 8–8C, notes 10A-10C, as amended*

Zero rating applies only if the advertising is in someone else's – not the charity's – publication, website, time or space, and does not apply where design and production are done in-house by the charity, even if the advertisement will be placed externally. It does not apply to fees paid to an internet service provider to host a website.

Advertising targeted to specific individuals rather than to the public is not covered, so zero rating is not available under these rules for direct mailing, telephone fundraising, or emails. However, under other rules zero rating is available for some fundraising materials [**57.11.6**] and printing [**57.12.2**].

Further information and a suggested form of declaration are in HMRC notice 701/58 *Charity advertising and goods connected with collecting donations*. If VAT has been paid on items which could have been zero rated, the charity can make a declaration asking the printer, publication, agency etc for a credit note. There are penalties for wrongly claiming zero rating.

57.12.1.1 Other zero ratings

Some leaflets and other printed materials are always zero rated [**57.12.2**]. If an item is eligible for both zero ratings it may be better to use the one for charities, because this also allows for zero rating of the artwork, typesetting etc.

57.12.2 Printed matter

Zero rating [**57.8.1**] applies to the production of printed matter, regardless of whether the item is printed, photocopied or in braille, and also applies to its sale. Printed matter includes books, booklets, brochures and pamphlets; newspapers, journals and periodicals; children's picture books and painting books; printed, duplicated or manuscript music; and maps, charts and topographical plans. Leaflets are zero rated provided at least 50 are supplied and any portion intended to be completed, detached and returned takes up less than 25% of the whole leaflet. It may be possible to get HMRC consent for zero rating when this portion takes up more than 25%. *Value Added Tax Act 1994 sch.8 gp.3*

Zero rating applies to preparation of the artwork, typesetting etc when these are provided by the supplier of the item itself, but if they are provided by anyone else they are **standard rated**.

Special rules apply to printed materials which are partly zero rated and partly standard rated, and advice should be sought.

Posters are **standard rated** unless they are eligible for zero rating as charity advertising [**57.12.1**]. Materials downloaded from the internet or provided as PDFs, on audio or video cassettes or CD or in other electronic formats are standard rated, even if they would be zero rated if provided on paper.

Details are in HMRC notice 701/10 *Zero-rating of books etc*. As these zero ratings are available to everyone, not only charities, there are no declarations. A printer who charges VAT on items eligible for zero rating can be asked to re-issue the invoice with VAT at 0% rather than standard rate – but it may be sensible to have a copy of 701/10 with you when you do so, with the relevant section highlighted.

57.13   MANAGEMENT AND ADMINISTRATIVE SERVICES

Many voluntary organisations provide management or administrative services to other organisations, which may be subject to VAT.

57.13.1   Provision of staff

Some organisations employ staff then provide them to another organisation, charging a management or administration fee to the receiving organisation and sometimes also paying the employee and recharging the receiving organisation for the employee's salary, national insurance, pension and related costs. An organisation which provides employees in this way, but is not an employment agency, is an **employment business [25.5.3]**.

Until 31 March 2009 it was possible to arrange matters so that only the management fee charged by an employment agency or employment business was subject to VAT, but since then the full charge to the receiving organisation – including for salary and linked costs – is **standard rated**.

Specialist advice should be sought from a solicitor or accountant about whether it is possible to reduce the VAT burden. For example, it may be possible for a charity and its trading company to employ staff under a joint contract of employment or similar arrangements [**25.4**], or for a charitable company and its trading company to form a VAT group and not have to charge VAT to each other [**57.2.4**].

If another organisation acts as a payroll agent and calculates PAYE but does not actually pay the salaries, it only has to charge its administration fee which is subject to VAT at standard rate.

57.13.2   Postage, packing and delivery charges

Where postage and packing (p&p) or delivery is an essential part of the service of providing an item (for example, if the item is ordered online), the supply of the goods and the delivery are treated as a **single supply** rather than two separate supplies. This means the VAT rate for the p&p or delivery is **the same as for the goods**. This applies regardless of whether the p&p or delivery charge is included in the price of the item or is additional to it.

So on an order for books or other items which are zero rated [**57.12.2**], the element of the price that covers p&p or delivery is zero rated. On an order for items which are themselves standard rated, the element of the price that covers p&p or delivery is standard rated.

Where p&p or delivery is separate from the contract to purchase goods (for example, when something is purchased at a shop and the shop agrees to send the goods for an additional charge), the goods and delivery are treated as **multiple supplies**. The p&p or delivery charge is **standard rated** unless it is to a place outside the UK, in which case it is usually **zero rated**.

Further information is in HMRC notice 700/24 *Postage and delivery charges*.

57.13.3   Freelance/consultant expenses

The principle of **single supply** applies when a consultant, freelance worker or other contractor who is VAT registered charges a client for photocopying, postage, fares or other expenses that are integral to the provision of their work. When the consultant paid for them the postage and fares were exempt, and the photocopying may have been zero rated. But the consultant charges the client for the overall service, including photocopying, fares etc, and the overall service is standard rated, even if the elements are itemised separately on the invoice.

57.13.4   Investment managers' fees

A VAT-registered charity which uses investment income to support its business activities [**57.6.2**] may be able to recover VAT on part of the fees charged by its investment managers, on the same principle as recovering some fundraising costs [**57.11.10**]. A charity to whom this might apply should consult its VAT advisor.

57.13.5 Road fuel

A VAT-registered organisation can recover VAT on road fuel, provided the fuel is used in the provision of **taxable supplies** [**57.8**], and provided it has a VAT invoice for the purchase. This applies regardless of whether the fuel is purchased by the organisation, or is purchased by employees, volunteers, self employed people or anyone else with the organisation reimbursing them either as a direct reimbursement or through a per-mile payment [**30.4.10**].

Where road fuel is purchased by an organisation and provided to employees or others for private use, it can recover VAT only on the portion used for taxable purposes. This can be based on the actual proportion, or on a fixed **fuel scale charge**. This is based on the vehicle's CO_2 rating. *Value Added Tax Act 1994 s.57, as amended*

Information is in HMRC notice 700/64 *Motoring expenses*.

57.14 BUILDING CONSTRUCTION, ALTERATION AND REPAIR

VAT on anything to do with buildings or land is particularly complex and always requires specialist advice. Further information and the certificates for zero rating are in HMRC notices 708 *Buildings and construction* and 742 *Land and property*.

57.14.1 Construction and conversion

Relief from VAT in the form of **zero rating** [**57.8.1**] on construction and on some services connected with the construction is available if the building is to be used as a **dwelling** or dwellings, or for a **relevant residential purpose** or a **relevant charitable purpose**. Conversion of non-residential premises to relevant residential or charitable purposes is also zero rated. *Value Added Tax Act 1994 sch.8 gp.5*

Dwellings are buildings used as domestic homes or accommodation, including short-term accommodation.

Relevant residential purposes are the provision of residential accommodation for children, students, pupils or members of the armed forces; some care homes; hospices; premises such as monasteries where followers of a recognised faith or religious order live and worship; and institutions such as nurses' homes which are the sole or main residence for at least 90% of their residents. Hospitals, prisons, and hotels or similar premises are not relevant residential premises.

Relevant charitable purposes are purposes carried out by a charity which are defined as **non-business** in VAT terms [**57.6.1**], or are the purposes of a village hall or similar building, such as a community centre or sports pavilion, providing social or recreational facilities for a local community with any economic activities incidental to that use. Economic activities in which the local community participates directly, such as a jumble sale or plays performed by an amateur dramatic group for which tickets are sold, do not threaten zero rating, but other business activities, including lettings, could. For new buildings, a certain amount of commercial use is allowed by concession [**57.14.1.1**].

To obtain zero rating, the organisation constructing or converting a building must provide certificates of eligibility to suppliers. It is very important to take advice before providing these certificates.

57.14.1.1 New buildings

Provided a new self contained building will be used for a relevant charitable or residential purpose [above], **zero rating** is available for services purchased in the course of construction (but not the separate services of architects, surveyors or persons acting as consultants or in a supervisory capacity); materials, hardware and other goods provided as part of the zero rated services; and the sale of the freehold or the grant of a lease for a period exceeding 21 years. *Value Added Tax Act 1994 sch.8 gp.5, as amended*

For charities which can zero rate their building works, substantial savings can be made by entering into **design and build** schemes. This ensures that all the professional fees are then effectively zero rated. The same effect can be achieved by carrying out property development through a trading company. This should be done only with appropriate professional advice.

Under HMRC extra-statutory concession 3.29, zero rating was available for a new building even if it was partly used for business use, provided that at least 90% of use – as defined by floor space, time, or number or people using the building – is solely for relevant charitable purposes. This concession was withdrawn from 1 July 2009, and replaced by a requirement for 95% of the use – defined in any reasonable way – to be for relevant charitable purposes, During a transitional period until 30 June 2010 organisations may use either the old or new provisions. The related 'switching areas' and 'look through' concessions were also withdrawn on 1 July 2009. Organisations should consult their VAT advisor or HMRC before relying on either the former concession or the new rule to obtain zero rating.

If the building changes to a non-qualifying use or is disposed of within 10 years, the VAT saved may be payable. *Value Added Tax Act 1994 sch.10 paras.36,37, amended by VAT (Buildings & Land) Order 2008 [SI 2008/1146]*

57.14.1.2 Existing buildings

For existing buildings, **zero rating** [**57.8.1**] is available:

- for certain works to enable disabled access [**57.10.3.2**] or to assist mobility of elderly people [**57.10.4**];
- to charities, for services purchased in the course of constructing an annexe or extension with internal access to an existing building, provided the annexe has its own primary access and is capable of functioning independently of the existing building, and provided the building is used for a relevant charitable or relevant residential purpose [**57.14.1**];
- for sale or grant of a lease for more than 21 years by the person converting all or part of a non-residential building into a building intended solely for a relevant residential purpose;
- to registered social landlords, for conversion services when a non-residential building is converted for a relevant residential purpose.

Value Added Tax Act 1994 sch.8 gp.5, as amended

Zero rating is available by concession to charities which convert a non-residential building for a relevant residential purpose, and which are prevented by legal constraints from selling converted property.

Other renovations are generally **standard rated**. But if no more than one perimeter wall is left standing it is treated as a new building and the works are therefore zero rated [**57.14.1.1**]. HMRC will sometimes class a refurbished building as 'new' even if more of the old building remains; agreement for this needs to be obtained at the planning stage so the project can be costed properly.

57.14.1.3 When zero rating is not available

Under the **Lennartz rules** [**57.9.1**], if zero rating is not available on the purchase or construction of new buildings, a charity can use a **VAT saving scheme** which enables it to recover all the VAT at the time of purchase or construction, then pay the portion applicable to business use back to HMRC over 10 years. If zero rating is not available on renovations, a charity can recover the VAT it has paid on the renovation, then repay it to HMRC over 10 years. Specialist advice should be sought before using the Lennartz provisions. *Whitechapel Art Gallery v Revenue & Customs [2008] UKVAT V20720*

57.14.2 Housing regeneration

Reduced rate VAT [**57.8.3**] is available for some other building works, including renovating dwellings that have been empty for at least two years, or converting property into housing, a dwelling into a care home, or a house into multiple occupancy. *Value Added Tax Act 1994 sch.7A gp.6,7, as amended*

57.14.3 Protected buildings and places of worship

Zero rating [**57.8.1**] is available for approved alterations to a listed building or scheduled monument, but not for repairs or maintenance. Additional rules apply where a listed building is used as a dwelling. *Value Added Tax Act 1994 sch.8 gp.6, as amended*

Under a special scheme for listed churches and places of worship, the Department for Culture, Media and Sport makes grants to faith groups equivalent to the VAT they have paid on repairs and maintenance to the fabric of the building, repairs to fixtures and fittings such as clocks, pews, bells and pipe organs, and architects' and surveyors' fees related to the repairs.

A similar scheme, also administered by DCMS, rebates to charities and faith groups the VAT incurred in repairing and maintaining memorials, statues and similar constructions.

These schemes will be reviewed in 2011, unless the European Commission agrees before then that **reduced rate** VAT [**57.8.3**] can be charged for such repairs and maintenance.

57.14.4 Energy saving materials

Reduced rate VAT [**57.8.3**] applies to installation (but not DIY installation) of specified energy saving materials in all homes, including residential homes, and in buildings used for qualifying charitable purposes [**57.14.1**].

Value Added Tax Act 1994 sch.7A gp.2, as amended

Reduced rate also applies to installation, maintenance and repair of central heating systems in the homes of qualifying pensioners, if funded under a government grant scheme; grant-funded installation of heating systems in the homes of 'less well off' people; and installation of security measures such as locks and smoke alarms in the homes of qualifying pensioners, when installed at the same time as energy saving materials or central heating systems. *VATA 1994 sch.7A gp.3, as amended*

Further information is in HMRC notice 708/6 *Energy-saving materials*.

57.15 PROPERTY AND RENTAL

Most rents and property disposals are **exempt** from VAT [**57.7**], unless the landlord or owner opts to charge VAT [**57.15.3**] in which case they are **standard rated**. Difficult issues are raised by rent-free periods, reverse premiums and surrenders, and in the situation where someone builds property for itself or supplies land to itself. HMRC notice 742 *Land and property* provides basic information, but VAT relating to property is complex and it is essential to get specialist advice.

57.15.1 Premises bookings

Hiring out premises is **exempt** [**57.7**], but if the charge covers services other than pure rent (for example caretaking or use of audio-visual equipment), that portion of the charge may be **standard rated**. *Value Added Tax Act 1994 sch.9 gp.1*

In some situations the organisation can choose to waive the exemption on premises hire charges [**57.15.3**].

57.15.2 Rental income

Rent on residential dwellings and property used for a relevant residential or charitable purpose [**57.14.1**] or the disposal of such property is **exempt** from VAT [**57.7**]. *Value Added Tax Act 1994 sch.9 gp.1*

Rental income from other premises is also generally exempt, as are most disposals of premises other than the sale of newly constructed buildings. In order for rental income to be exempt, there must be a **licence** to occupy land. The criteria for determining whether a licence exists for VAT purposes are not the same as determining whether a licence exists in relation to property rights [**60.5**].

If other people have the right to use the same space at the same time, a licence may not exist and the rental income will be **standard rated** rather than exempt. An example is a shared office where neither business has its own specified space.

Where there is (or will be) a licence to occupy commercial premises, and the premises will be wholly or mainly used for standard rated or zero rated purposes, the landlord can choose to charge VAT [**57.15.3**].

57.15.3   Opting to tax

A landlord or owner of property can choose to charge VAT on rent. This is called **opting to tax**, or **electing to waive exemption**. Basic information is in HMRC notice 742A, *Opting to tax land and buildings.*   *Value Added Tax Act 1994 sch.10 para.1-34, replaced by Value Added Tax (Buildings & Land) Order 2008 [SI 2008/1146] art.2*

If an option to tax is in place, all supplies relating to those premises, including their construction or sale, are **standard rated** rather than exempt.

Opting to tax enables the landlord to recover VAT on the purchase of goods and services relating to the premises, but it makes rents higher. This does not affect VAT-registered tenants, who can recover the VAT they pay on the rent. But it will negatively affect tenants who are not VAT-registered or who can recover only part of their VAT. It is essential to take professional advice before opting to tax, or if the organisation's landlord can opt to tax [**62.2.3**].

The decision to tax must be notified to HMRC in writing within 30 days. After a three-month period during which the decision can be changed, it is generally irrevocable for 20 years.

57.15.3.1   Disapplication for premises used for charitable purposes

Before entering into a rental agreement where an option to tax is in place, a charity may apply for the option to tax to be **disapplied**. It can do this in relation to non-office premises used for **relevant charitable purposes** [**57.14.1**], but cannot apply for VAT to be disapplied in relation to premises used for fundraising and general administration, or for exempt [**57.7**] or taxable [**57.8**] activities. If the premises are used for relevant charitable purposes as well as other purposes and the use for other purposes is less than 5% of the total (10% until 1 July 2010), the charity can still apply for disapplication.   *Value Added Tax Act 1994 sch.10 para.7 replaced by Value Added Tax (Buildings & Land) Order 2008 [SI 2008/1146] art.2*

The charity must notify the landlord that the premises will be used for relevant charitable purposes by supplying a certificate before the supply takes place.

57.15.4   Fuel and power

Reduced rate VAT [**57.8.3**] applies to the supply of fuel and power to buildings where at least 60% of the building is used for domestic purposes or for non-business [**57.6.1**] charitable purposes, or regardless of the use of the premises, if only a small amount of fuel or power is supplied.   *Value Added Tax Act 1994 sch.7A gp.1, as amended*

Other supplies of fuel or power are **standard rated**. An organisation which pays for gas and electricity direct to a landlord may be paying full VAT even though it is eligible for reduced rate. In this situation it may be advantageous to negotiate with the landlord to install meters and pay separately for fuel and power.

Organisations which pay standard rate VAT on fuel may also have to pay **climate change levy** on their fuel use.

VAT rules on fuel and power are in HMRC notice 701/19 *Fuel and power*.

Resources: VAT

HM Revenue & Customs: www.hmrc.gov.uk, 0845 010 9000, enquiries.estn@hmrc.gsi.gov.uk.

Business Link: www.businesslink.gov.uk.

Charity Finance Directors' Group: www.cfdg.org.uk, 0845 345 3192, info@cfdg.org.uk.

Charity Tax Group: www.ctrg.org.uk, info@charitytax.info.

Grant administration & VAT. Community Foundation Network: www.communityfoundations.org.uk, 020 7713 9326, network@communityfoundations.org.uk.

Statute law. www.opsi.gov.uk and www.statutelaw.gov.uk.

Much but not all case law. www.bailii.org.

Updates cross-referenced to this book. www.rclh.co.uk.

Chapter 58

INVESTMENT AND RESERVES

For sources of further information see end of chapter.

58.1   INVESTMENT DUTIES AND POWERS

In this chapter, the term **investments** is generally used to refer to stocks and shares, money, land, and any investment assets expected to produce income or a capital return. The Charity Commission's CC14 *Investment of charitable funds: Basic principles* [see end of chapter] includes an explanation of different types of investment and the rules on investment by charities. Investment is a particularly complex area, and appropriate professional advice should always be sought.

An organisation may generally invest only to the extent that it has constitutional or statutory power to do so [**58.1.2**, **58.1.3**], and must comply with any restrictions imposed by the governing document or by law. Investing outside the powers granted by statute or the governing document, or failing to comply with investment duties, is a breach of trust and may also be a breach of statutory duty, for which the trustees may be held personally liable.

The organisation's governing body may authorise investments or a particular investment policy, provided it is not contrary to statute or the governing document.

58.1.1   Who is a trustee?

The extent of the power to invest depends largely on whether the investment is technically being made by a **trustee**. In relation to much of the law relating to trustee duties when investing, a **trustee** is different from a **charity trustee**.

A **charity trustee** is a member of the governing body of *any* charity, whether unincorporated or incorporated [**13.1.7**]. But in relation to duties when investing, a **trustee** is a member of the governing body of a trust [**2.3.1**], regardless of whether it is charitable or non-charitable; a member of the governing body of a charitable unincorporated association [**2.2.1**], a body established by royal charter [**3.6**] or governed by a Charity Commission scheme [**2.5**]; or a person who holds money, land or other property as a holding or custodian trustee [**20.4.4, 20.4.2**] on behalf of individuals, a charitable or non-charitable trust or an unincorporated association.

58.1.2   Powers and duties of trustees

All trustees as defined above have statutory and common law duties and powers in relation to investments. These are governed primarily by their governing document and the **Trustee Act 2000**, with some duties and powers under the **Trustee Act 1925**, **Settled Land Act 1925**, and **Trustee Investments Act 1961**.

Directors of companies (including charitable and community interest companies), charitable incorporated organisations and industrial and provident societies are not trustees in relation to their investment duties, even if they are charity trustees. However, the Charity Commission's view is that charity trustees should comply with the **Trustee Act 2000**, even if the duties do not explicitly apply.

58.1.2.1   Statutory duty of care

A statutory duty of care under the **Trustee Act 2000** must be exercised in relation to investment in stocks, shares and similar investments, and land. The statutory duty does not explicitly apply to purchases of items of value such as works of art, since these are not strictly investments.

The statutory duty of care obliges trustees to exercise such care and skill as is reasonable in the circumstances, taking into account any special knowledge or experience that the trustee has or holds himself or herself out as having. A person acting as a trustee in the course of a business or profession must exercise a duty of care that it is reasonable to expect of a person acting in the course of that kind of business or profession.   *Trustee Act 2000 s.1*

The duty of care applies when investing and reviewing investments; acquiring land or exercising powers in relation to land; setting investment criteria; selecting investment advisors or choosing to do without advice; selecting agents, nominees and custodians [**20.4, 20.5**]; and determining and reviewing the terms and policies under which agents, nominees and custodians are to act.   *Trustee Act 2000 sch.1*

58.1.2.2   General duty of care

In addition to the trustees' statutory duty of care [above], trustees who are **charity trustees** have a duty to invest in the best interests of the beneficiaries [**15.6.3**], to maximise the financial return on the investments [**15.6.5**] and to minimise the risks to which the organisation is exposed. This duty overrides the trustees' personal views or priorities, and may have implications for charities wishing to invest ethically [**58.6.2**].   *Cowan v Scargill [1985] Ch 270*

The obligation to maximise the financial return means that charity trustees who do not invest surplus income, or who put it into an account where it does not earn proper interest, could be in breach of trust.   *Inland Revenue Commissioners v Helen Slater Charitable Trust Ltd [1981] STC 471*

58.1.2.3   Delegation

Although trustees have a general duty to act personally and collectively [**15.6.8, 15.6.9**], they may in some situations delegate investment decisions [**58.3.2**].

58.1.2.4   Investment powers: trusts and charitable associations

If the governing document of a trust, whether charitable or non-charitable, or charitable unincorporated association permits 'any investment for the time being authorised by law' or 'authorised by the Trustee Investments Act 1961' (or similar wording) the trustees may make any kind of investment, provided they act in accordance with the duties imposed by the **Trustee Act 2000**. But if the governing document contains restrictions on investment, those restrictions will apply.

A charitable trust or association whose governing document includes an amendment power may alter the governing document to modify powers of investment. Prior written consent must be obtained from the Charity Commission [**7.5.1**].   *Re Jewish Orphanage Charity Endowment Trusts [1960] 1 WLR 344;*
Soldiers', Sailors' & Airmen's Family Association v Attorney General [1968] 1 WLR 313

If a trust, whether charitable or non-charitable, or charitable association does not have an amendment power, the Charity Commission or court may grant or vary powers of investment. The Commission can also give one-off consent for the acquisition of particular investments.

58.1.2.5 Investment powers: non-charitable associations

The investment powers of non-charitable associations are governed by their governing document and by any directions given by the association's members or by funders or donors. It may be possible to widen the powers by amendment [**7.5.1**].

If a non-charitable association's investments are held by holding or custodian trustees [**20.4.4**, **20.4.2**], investment powers are governed by the **Trustee Act 2000** unless the deed appointing the trustees specifies otherwise.

58.1.2.6 Investment in land

Subject to their duty of care and to any restrictions in their governing document, trustees have power to acquire freehold or leasehold land in the UK as an investment or for any other reasons, and to invest by lending on a mortgage of land in the UK.
Trustee Act 2000 ss.3,8

Charity trustees should consider the issues set out in the Charity Commission's CC14 *Investment of charitable funds*. Sales or lettings of charity land must comply with the **Charities Act 1993** [**60.12**].

58.1.2.7 Standard investment criteria

Trustees have a statutory duty to have regard to **standard investment criteria**. These criteria are the suitability of acquiring or retaining that type or class of investment, whether the particular investment is a suitable one within that asset class, and the need for diversification [**58.3.3**], insofar as it is appropriate.

Before making any investment, trustees must generally obtain and consider professional investment advice [**58.3.1**], unless they reasonably conclude that it is unnecessary or inappropriate.
Trustee Act 2000 ss.4,5

The investment restrictions in the **Trustee Investments Act 1961** were repealed by the **Trustee Act 2000**. Provided they act within their duty of care, any other duties and any requirements in their governing document, trustees are free to invest as they choose.

58.1.3 Investment powers and duties in incorporated bodies

Governing body members of charitable and non-charitable companies, charitable incorporated organisations and industrial and provident societies are not subject to the duties and do not have the powers set out in the **Trustee Act 2000**. However, they have other statutory and constitutional duties and powers.

58.1.3.1 Companies

Company directors have statutory duties to promote the success of the company and to exercise reasonable care, skill and diligence [**15.3.2**, **15.3.4**]. These duties are not quite as high as the duties of trustees under the **Trustee Act 2000**, but directors investing on behalf of a company should treat them equally seriously.

The directors' powers to invest are limited to those given in the memorandum or articles of association. If the powers are limited, they may be amended [**7.5.3**].

58.1.3.2 Charitable incorporated organisations

Trustees of charitable incorporated organisations (CIOs) have a statutory duty to exercise such care and skill as is reasonable in the circumstances, taking into account any special knowledge or experience that the trustee has or holds himself or herself out as having. For a person acting as a trustee in the course of a business or profession, the duty of care requires particular regard to any special knowledge or experience that it is reasonable to expect of a person acting in the course of that kind of business or profession.
*Charities Act 1993 sch.5B para.10,
inserted by Charities Act 2006 sch.7 para.2*

58.1.3.3   Industrial and provident societies

Directors of industrial and provident societies must exercise fiduciary duty and duty of care when investing [**15.4**]. Unless its rules state otherwise, an industrial and provident society has statutory power to invest in a range of investments, including the shares of other IPSs. The IPS's rules may extend the statutory powers.

Industrial & Provident Societies Act 1965 s.31, as amended

58.2   HOLDING INVESTMENTS

The way investments are held depends on the organisation's legal structure, the size and nature of its investment portfolio, the need to control and facilitate transactions, and the need to avoid repeated transfers when the trustee body changes.

If the trustees of a charitable trust or association have incorporated the trustee body [**2.4**], the trustee body generally holds the investments. Otherwise trustees have a statutory power, subject to their duty of care [**58.1.2.1**], to appoint **nominees** (holding trustees [**20.4.4**] or a custodian trustee [**20.4.2**]) or **custodians** [**20.4.3**] to hold their investments. If the organisation is charitable, the trustees should follow the published Charity Commission guidance [see end of chapter] in selecting a nominee or custodian. The functions of such nominees or custodians must be regularly reviewed.

Trustee Act 2000 ss.19,20,22

Companies, charitable incorporated organisations and industrial and provident societies can, as incorporated bodies, hold investments in their own name [**3.1.1**]. There is no need to appoint a nominee or custodian, although the organisation may do so if its governing document gives it this power.

58.3   INVESTMENT DECISIONS

The duty of care in relation to investments includes a duty to take advice unless there is good reason not to, and restrictions on delegation of decision making.

58.3.1   Advice

Trustees as defined in the **Trustee Act 2000** [**58.1.1**] must seek professional advice before investing and must consider the advice before making investment decisions, unless they consider it unnecessary or inappropriate to take such advice.

Trustee Act 2000 s.5

Trustees or members of the governing bodies of companies (including community interest companies), charitable incorporated organisations and industrial and provident societies may, provided it is not prohibited by the governing document and provided they exercise the appropriate duty of care [**58.1.2**, **58.1.3**], undertake investment themselves without seeking outside advice, where they reasonably believe such advice is not needed.

While taking advice may not be a strict legal requirement for companies, CIOs, IPSs and non-charitable associations, they have a general duty of care so it is generally sensible for them to seek and consider such advice.

Investment advice should be impartial and be given by someone with sufficient experience of the type of organisation and investment. Evidence of appropriate care taken in the selection of advisors should be preserved, and the terms of appointment and any instructions to the advisors should be in writing and retained. All investment advice should be in writing.

58.3.2   Delegation

Governing bodies may employ a stockbroker, financial advisor, accountant, solicitor or bank to act in an advisory capacity, advising about investments but leaving the final decision to the governing body. But a governing body which wishes to delegate the right to make investment decisions or manage its investments may do so only if this is allowed.

58.3.2.1 Statutory power to delegate

Trustees as defined in the **Trustee Act 2000** [**58.1.1**] have a statutory power to delegate some investment management responsibilities to stockbrokers and similar professionals, unless this is prohibited by the governing document. Before delegating such powers, trustees must draw up a written policy statement to ensure the agent acts in the best interests of the organisation. This policy statement must be regularly reviewed, and revised if necessary. Trustees must also assess whether the agent has complied with the statement.   *Trustee Act 2000 ss.15,22*

If the governing document contains restrictions on delegation, it can be amended in the usual way [**7.5.1**].

58.3.2.2 Constitutional power to delegate

A company or industrial and provident society can delegate investment decision making and management only if its governing document allows this. If necessary, the governing document may be amended [**7.5.3-7.5.5**]. At the time of writing (mid 2009) it was not clear whether charitable incorporated organisations will be able to delegate unless the governing document prohibits this, or will be able to delegate only if the governing document allows.

The power to delegate should include safeguards allowing delegation only to qualified professionals, requiring them to act only in accordance with the organisation's agreed investment policy, and requiring them to report back regularly to the governing body.

58.3.2.3 Investment managers

If delegation of investment decision making and management is allowed and the governing body exercises the appropriate duty of care, the governing body can hire a stockbroker, financial advisor or institutional fund manager as a **discretionary manager**, who will select investments within an overall policy set by the organisation, manage the investments, and monitor and report on performance.

Such an arrangement takes a considerable administrative and management burden off the members of the governing body. A manager is likely to act as a nominee [**20.4.4**] and hold the investments in its name, or arrange for a bank or other third party to act as nominee. A manager is also likely to take day to day investment decisions, and to handle collection of dividends, response to rights issues [**59.6**], and perhaps tax recovery from HM Revenue and Customs [**56.4.11**].

Investment decisions should be delegated on clear written terms only to persons regulated under the **Financial Services and Market Act 2000**. Periodicals such as *Charity Finance* provide information about the performance and charging policies of investment managers and common investment funds.

58.3.3 Diversification

Whether investing directly or through an investment manager, trustees as defined under the **Trustee Act 2000** [**58.1.1**] must have regard to the spread of investments and how well they meet the standard investment criteria [**58.1.2.7**]. Even where the spread is achieved by investment in a common investment fund [**58.4.2**] or unit trust, consideration should be given to the spread between differing asset classes.

Highly speculative investments should be avoided, because their potentially higher returns are likely to be linked to substantial risks.

Specialist investments such as futures options or foreign currency deposits are not suitable unless advised for a specific purpose. Charity trustees concerned about particular investments recommended to them may seek the Charity Commission's prior approval for the investment.

58.3.4 Reviewing and assessing performance

Trustees must regularly review the performance of investments, agents and custodians, and should ensure their records show they have done this and the reasons for decisions. Such review will require looking again at the situation and aims of the organisation and its investment policy, all within the framework of the standard investment criteria [**58.1.2.7**].   *Trustee Act 2000 s.4(2)*

Even where a charitable organisation does not have to comply with the **Trustee Act** or has explicit investment powers so wide that it can invest in high risk ventures, the duty of prudence [**15.6.5**] applies. Operating with less care than is required under the Trustee Act could be a breach of that duty of prudence.

Nestlé v National Westminster Bank [1992] EWCA Civ 12; Bartlett v Barclays Trust Co [1980] Ch 515

Part of the process of drawing up an investment policy [**58.6**] is deciding how to assess the performance of the investments. Investments may be assessed against standard indices such as those produced by FTSE, or against specialist indices which measure the returns of charitable funds. No index should be chosen unless the governing body is satisfied that it provides an appropriate indicator for the organisation's investment objectives. Professional advice may be needed before selecting the index against which to monitor.

58.4   FORMS OF INVESTMENT

The main forms of investment are:

- bank and building society **deposits** [**58.4.1**], providing income in the form of interest;
- **bonds**, which may be issued by governments or public bodies (and are called **gilts**) or by companies, and are a form of loan by the investor with interest payable at specified intervals and the loan repayable at the end of the period;
- **equity**, stocks and shares purchased on the stock exchange, which provide income in the form of dividends (a share of profits) and capital growth if the shares have increased in value when they are sold;
- **private equity**, shares offered directly to investors rather than being sold on a stock exchange;
- **venture capital** or **risk capital**, a form of private equity in which investors invest in new businesses;
- **pooled investments** such as unit trusts and common investment funds [**58.4.2**], where many organisations or individuals invest jointly;
- **property** (land or buildings) used as an investment rather than for the organisation's own use, providing income as rents and capital growth if it has increased in value when it is sold [**58.1.2.6**];
- **speculative purchase of assets** [**58.4.4**] such as currency or works of art, in the hope of capital growth if the value has increased when it is sold;
- financial instruments such as **derivatives** and **hedge funds** [**58.4.4**], which are purchased in the hope of capital growth or as a protection against risk.

58.4.1   Cash deposits

The deposit of small to medium sums requires prudence but is more a matter of practicalities, balancing accessibility, rate of return, and the cost of transactions. A promise of unusually high rates of return needs to be treated with considerable care.

In a worst case situation, such as happened when some banks failed in 2008, the **Financial Services Compensation Scheme** [see end of chapter] generally protects a customer's deposits, but only up to a specified limit. At the time of writing (mid 2009) this was £50,000 per customer per institution. Organisations should check that their deposits are covered by this scheme. Larger depositors will generally wish to spread their deposits and risk, and should take advice from investment managers who are registered with the Financial Services Authority.

58.4.2   Common investment funds and common deposit funds

Common investment funds (CIFs) are pooled investment schemes for charities, similar to unit trusts. All charities have a statutory right to participate in CIFs unless this is prohibited by their governing document or they do not qualify

as a participant under the CIF's rules. Some CIFs seek high income, while others seek to balance income and long-term growth. *Charities Act 1993 s.24,*
amended by Charities Act 2006 s.23(1)

CIFs allow an investment to be diversified over a much wider portfolio than would be economic for smaller charities, and investors have access to advice from an experienced fund manager. Other advantages are that the purchase and sale of investments is simpler and cheaper than buying them individually, there is less paperwork than holding individual investments, and income is paid gross so it is not necessary to reclaim tax from HM Revenue and Customs [**56.4.11**].

For non-charities, **unit trusts** provide similar advantages.

Common deposit funds (CDFs) operate like bank accounts but enable the investor's funds to be placed in a range of bank and building society accounts.
Charities Act 1993 s.25, amended by Charities Act 2006 s.23(2)

At the time of writing (mid 2009) CIFs and CDFs are regulated by the Charity Commission, but the government was consulting on transferring regulation to the Financial Services Authority and on creating a new form of collective investment for charities, to be regulated by the FSA.

Although CIFs and CDFs are likely to be suitable for many smaller charities, they need to be reviewed regularly to ensure they remain appropriate.

58.4.3 Pool charities

The Charity Commission can, through a **pooling scheme**, create a **pool charity** to manage the investments of two or more charities. The scheme has the advantage of allowing charities to pool their funds for investment purposes, in a way that may enable the trustees to reduce the overall costs of share dealing, reduce risk by achieving a more diversified portfolio, and use professional fund management more effectively. However, the participating charities and the pool charity must all have exactly the same trustees. If a participating charity subsequently has different trustees, it does not have to withdraw its funds from the pool charity but can no longer contribute to it.

Information about pool charities is in the Charity Commission's operating guidance OG49 [see end of chapter]. *Financial Services & Markets Act 2000 (Exemption Order) 2001*
[SI 2001/1201] schedule para.44

58.4.4 Speculative investment and derivatives

Because of the obligation for charity trustees and other trustees to avoid speculative investments, they generally should not purchase assets such as works of art and foreign currency with a view to making a gain from their eventual sale. This does not prevent organisations from purchasing assets as part of their primary purpose (for example museums purchasing works of art) or purchasing foreign currency which they need to carry out their work, and subsequently selling it.

Charity trustees and other trustees should also generally avoid financial instruments which are based on capital growth and are purchased in the hope of this, or as a protection against risk.

Derivatives (futures, forwards, options and swaps) are financial instruments whose value depends on movements in stock markets or money markets or on other specified variables. They can be used to reduce risk or as speculative investments. A typical example is purchasing an option today to sell shares in six months at today's price, as protection against the value falling between now and then.

It may be appropriate for an organisation to purchase derivatives, particularly to protect against a change in the value of assets or currency, but it should always obtain and consider professional advice and, if a charity, follow the Charity Commission guidelines in CC14 *Investment of charitable funds*.

Hedge funds are pooled funds which take advantage of rapid changes in derivatives and a range of complex financial techniques. As with derivatives, advice is essential as is, for charities, compliance with CC14.

58.5 PROGRAMME RELATED OR SOCIAL INVESTMENT

Social or **programme related investment** (SI or PRI) is not investment in the sense of using funds to generate income, but involves the provision of funds as a way of directly advancing the organisation's purpose. SI or PRI overlap with, but are not the same as, ethical or socially responsible investment [**58.6.2**].

Traditionally, a charity or voluntary organisation wanting to advance its own work through another organisation made a grant to that organisation. Now, it may take a more entrepreneurial approach, such as making an interest-free or low interest loan (a **soft loan**), or making an equity investment with a much lower expectation of return than with ordinary shares. An example would be an economic regeneration charity making a loan at a low rate of interest to a charity which provides employment training, or purchasing shares in a community interest company that provides such training even though the dividends that can be paid by the CIC are capped [**3.4.3**] and thus are likely to be lower than the charity would get from commercial investment.

Provided that the organisation is acting within its powers, such investment generally creates no problems. But if endowment or restricted reserves rather than current income is to be used, careful thought must be given to the balance between the benefits and risk of loss, and the impact of loss on future beneficiaries.

Independent advice should generally be sought, and charities should follow the Charity Commission's guidance on social investment.

58.6 DEVELOPING AN INVESTMENT POLICY

To be able to show that they have invested prudently, the governing body must develop a coherent approach to investment. This starts from an analysis of the reasons for holding investments, which may be:

- **provision for short-term expenditure**, where the funds will be spent in the relatively near future on running costs, provision of services, grant making or capital expenditure;

- **provision for longer term expenditure**, where the funds are put aside for an expected but not immediate expenditure such as redecoration of premises, long-term expansion plans or a predicted cycle of future expenditure needs;

- creation of a **semi-permanent fund**, where the intention is to keep the capital intact for a specified period or until the governing body decides otherwise, while using the income from the fund to meet expenditure;

- creation of a **permanent endowment**, a permanent investment fund where use of the capital is prohibited by the terms under which the funds are held, and the income might or might not be able to be expended; and/or

- creation of reserves to meet **pension obligations to staff** [**30.6.4**] or potential **pension scheme exit obligations** [**30.6.5**].

The purposes for which the assets are held will determine which types of investment are appropriate, and whether the investment income (interest or dividends) will be withdrawn or reinvested.

Charities are limited in their ability to create permanent endowments or to accumulate funds for general purposes, unless they have clear plans for how they will be used [**58.8.3**].

Larger charities are required to indicate in their annual reports the investment policy and objectives, including the extent, if any, to which social, environmental or ethical considerations are taken into account [**58.6.2**].

58.6.1 Investment strategy

An analysis of the reasons for investment may reveal that different pools of funds need to be created, with different strategies. Key issues are likely to include:

- **liquidity**: whether the money needs to be readily accessible;
- **access**: whether withdrawals are likely to be occasional or frequent;

- **growth**: the desired level of growth, and over what period;
- **risk**: the level of acceptable risk, and in particular whether the risk of a reduction in the value of the invested funds is acceptable;
- **income**: whether a regular income is needed and if so, how often.

The strategies should be written into one or more investment policies. Strategies and policies must be reviewed regularly to ensure they are being properly implemented, are fulfilling their objectives, and remain relevant. This may involve obtaining professional advice on appropriate measures to assess success [**58.3.4**].

58.6.2 Ethical and socially responsible investment

Charitable organisations have a general duty to invest in the best interests of the beneficiaries [**15.6.3**] and must generally get the highest return possible, taking into account their need for liquidity and security of funds. Ethical, environmental or social considerations may be taken into account only in limited circumstances.

Non-charitable organisations are generally free, subject to the duties of trustees if these apply [**58.1.1**], to create their own guidelines for investment, either as part of the governing document or as policy decisions by the governing body or the organisation's members.

Information about issues arising from **ethical** or **socially responsible investment** (SRI) and the ethical behaviour of specific companies is available from **EIRIS** and other organisations [see end of chapter].

58.6.2.1 Guidelines for trustees

In a case brought against the commissioners of the Church of England, the bishop of Oxford argued that their policy of investing in arms companies and companies which perpetuated apartheid in South Africa was against the ethical principles of the church and was therefore in breach of trust and should cease. The judgment in this case set out guidelines for ethical investment:

- ethical criteria, if used, must be based on the needs of the beneficiaries of the charity, not on the trustees' views;
- generally, the key criterion must be obtaining the best secure return on the investment;
- investments which impede the furtherance of the charity's objects may be excluded, for example a charity for alcohol abusers could exclude investment in breweries or companies owning pubs;
- where large numbers of investments are excluded and the financial risks for the charity are therefore greater, the arguments in favour of excluding those investments must be proportionately stronger;
- in justifying ethical exclusions the trustees cannot simply implement the directions of the membership, if those directions are contrary to their legal duties as trustees. *Harries v Church Commissioners for England [1993] 2 All ER 300*

58.6.2.2 Ethical and socially responsible investment policies

Before drawing up an investment policy which excludes any investments, the governing body must be absolutely clear what they mean by each restriction and must take advice from an investment advisor about the potential impact on investment returns.

If the impact is likely to be negative, the charity may have to take a less principled approach. For example, an absolute ban on investment in any company involved in the manufacture or supply of arms or other military equipment would exclude a high proportion of the larger UK companies. The impact of such a restriction might be reduced by specifying, for example, that companies are excluded only if a certain proportion of their turnover is linked to military supplies.

Thought should be given to what happens if a previously suitable investment becomes unsuitable. If its policy is very tightly defined, an organisation may need to disinvest very quickly if a company moves into prohibited work, and shares may have to be sold at a disadvantageous time.

58.6.2.3 Positive policies

Instead of or in addition to excluding certain investments (a negative policy), some policies actively encourage investment in certain types of enterprise (a positive policy). The same underlying principles applies: the primary concern must be to maximise the return to the charity. Different principles apply for programme related or social investment [**58.5**].

58.6.2.4 Ethical unit trusts

Ethical unit trusts enable organisations to tailor their ethical investments without having to investigate dozens of companies. In deciding to invest in ethical unit trusts, the same principles apply as for other types of ethical investment.

58.7 PRACTICAL MATTERS

As well as ensuring that decisions about investments are properly made and regularly reviewed, the governing body must also ensure that practical matters relating to the investments are adequately dealt with.

58.7.1 Security and procedures

Regardless of who holds or manages the investments, appropriate procedures must be in place to ensure effective communication and security, and to ensure all investment income is received and is allocated appropriately, and where applicable, tax is recovered promptly [**56.4.11**]. Investment income must be monitored and reconciled against the investment certificates actually held. Disposals must be carefully controlled, particularly ensuring that multiple signatories are required and if possible requiring separate signatories for the disposal of assets and the control of the certificate representing those assets.

58.7.2 Stamp duty

The transfer of stocks and shares is generally subject to **stamp duty** or **stamp duty reserve tax**. At the time of writing (mid 2009) the rate for each is 0.5%. Charities are exempt from these duties. Information about stamp duties is available from HM Revenue and Customs.

58.7.3 Tax

Investment income is subject to income tax or corporation tax, but when received by charities is generally exempt from tax [**56.4.11**]. Tax is generally deducted at source, before the income is paid to the investor or reinvested, and charities should seek to recover the tax from HM Revenue and Customs.

Gains from the sale of investments are subject to tax on the gain [**56.2.5**] but charities are exempt from tax if the gain is used for their charitable purposes [**56.4.1**].

58.8 RESERVES

The term **reserves** may refer to money held by an organisation, or to the value of shares, stocks and bonds. Reserves are sometimes called **accumulated funds**.

58.8.1 Types of reserves

Reserves are divided into:
- **general or unrestricted reserves**, which can be used for any purpose at the discretion of the organisation;
- **designated reserves**, being held for a specific purpose decided by the organisation, but which could be used for another purpose;
- **restricted reserves** or **restricted funds**, being held for a specific purpose specified by the donor or by the terms of the appeal, and which can be used only for that purpose [**48.2**];

- **permanent funds**, sometimes called a **capital fund** or **permanent endowment**, a form of restricted fund where the organisation is prohibited from spending the capital and can only spend the income from it;
- **expendable endowment**, a capital fund which the trustees have power to convert into income, and then spend for the purposes of the endowment.

Reserves held for general or designated purposes are sometimes called **administrative retention**, because the governing body makes a managerial or administrative decision to hold on to those reserves.

58.8.1.1 Incorporated charities with permanent endowment

The Charity Commission's view is that permanent endowment cannot be held by a charitable company or charitable industrial and provident society, but must be held by a separate, unincorporated **special trust** [**9.4.2**]. A similar rule is likely to apply to charitable incorporated organisations (CIOs).

If the incorporated body is wound up, the special trust continues to exist or is wound up in the same way as an unincorporated charity with permanent endowment [**24.9.1**].

58.8.2 Expending permanent endowment

58.8.2.1 Income and capital growth

The **income** generated by permanent endowment can be spent, provided this is not prohibited by the terms on which the endowment is held and provided it is spent only for the purposes set out in the endowment.

Capital growth earned by permanent endowment must be added to the endowment. Where a charity is allowed to spend both the income and capital growth from a permanent endowment, this is called a **total return** approach to investment. If the original terms of the endowment do not allow this, the charity Commission may make a scheme [**4.5.5**] or order [**4.5.4**] permitting it.

58.8.2.2 The endowment

Capital held as permanent endowment cannot, in general, be spent, and if it is an asset such as a building or a work of art, cannot be sold. However, the trustees of some unincorporated charities holding permanent endowment can resolve to spend the capital or, in the case of an asset, resolve to sell it and spend the proceeds, if they believe that the purposes for which the permanent endowment is held can be more effectively carried out if the capital as well as the income can be spent.

Such a decision may be made by the trustees if the charity holding the endowment had gross income of not more than £1,000 in the last financial year, or the market value of the permanent endowment is not more than £10,000, or regardless of income or market value, the permanent endowment was given by more than one person or institution and for more than one common purpose. In other unincorporated charities, the trustees' decision must be approved by the Charity Commission. *Charities Act 1993 ss.75, 75A, inserted by Charities Act 2006 s.43*

58.8.3 Reserves policy

An organisation's auditor should be able to advise on a realistic assessment of needs and appropriate levels of reserves to meet those needs. Examples of appropriate reasons for holding reserves include future purchases of major equipment or premises, a major future development, safeguarding against anticipated and unanticipated fluctuations in income and expenditure, or receiving an unexpectedly large legacy or other major donation and not wanting to spend it all at once.

Based on this assessment of needs, the organisation should develop a reserves policy setting out why the organisation needs reserves; what level of reserves it seeks to hold for general purposes (often stated in terms of a specified number of months' operating costs); what designated reserves the governing body wishes to hold, and for what purposes; whether any restricted and permanent reserves should be held, and for what purposes; how the reserves will be built up; the form in which the various funds should be held; how the income earned by reserves is to be used; and how the policy and its application will be monitored and reviewed.

The reserves policy must be very closely linked to the investment policy [**58.6**].

58.8.3.1   Charities and reserves

Charity trustees are obliged to use a charity's income and funds for its charitable purposes. But this does not mean that charities are not allowed to build up reserves. The governing document or the terms on which restricted funds are held may allow, or even require, the charity to build up reserves. Even if the governing document says nothing about reserves, there is an implied power to ensure the organisation has enough to meet its operating costs for a reasonable period, and to hold reserves for future general or specific (designated) charitable expenditure.

The Charity Commission's guidance on reserves (CC19) and research on reserves (RS13) recognises that there is wide variation in the needs of charities, and does not set out a recommended level. However, its operational guidance suggests that reserves would be 'too high' if they were more than three years' gross expenditure, unless the charity could justify the higher amount. If charity trustees allow excessive reserves to accumulate without a reason, the Commission may seek an explanation and can require the charity to spend some of its reserves to meet its charitable purposes.

But even where a charity's reserves are well within what the Commission would consider to be acceptable and good practice, funders may consider the reserves are too high. It is important for organisations to be able to challenge such funders and grant makers, by having a clear and reasonable reserves policy.

If excessive funds are held, HM Revenue and Customs could require tax to be paid on the income held as reserves and/or the income from the reserves, because the income is not being used for charitable purposes [**56.4.1**]. If there is a specific reason for wanting to accumulate reserves which might be considered excessive, the Charity Commission may make an order [**4.5.4**] allowing this.

58.8.4   Accounting for reserves

Charities must show general funds, restricted funds and capital (permanent) funds separately in their accounts [**54.2.4**]. Non-charitable organisations do not have to make this distinction in their accounts, but may choose to do so because it gives a more accurate picture of the organisation's financial position.

Resources: INVESTMENT AND RESERVES

Investment by charities; charity reserves. Charity Commission: www.charitycommission.gov.uk, 0845 300 0128, email via website.

Charities Aid Foundation: www.cafonline.org, 0870 264 3296, email via website.

Ethical investment. Ethical Investment Research Service: www.eiris.org, 020 7840 5700, ethics@eiris.org.

Charity SRI: www.charitysri.org, 020 7840 5738, charitysri@eiris.org.

Protection for bank deposits. Financial Services Compensation Scheme: www.fscs.org.uk, 020 7892 7300, enquiries@fscs.org.uk.

Regulation. Financial Services Authority: www.fsa.gov.uk, 0845 606 1234, email via website.

Statute law. www.opsi.gov.uk and www.statutelaw.gov.uk.

Much but not all case law. www.bailii.org.

Updates cross-referenced to this book. www.rclh.co.uk.

Chapter 59
BORROWING

For sources of further information see end of chapter.

59.1 BORROWING POWERS AND RESTRICTIONS

A voluntary organisation may borrow money only if it has power to do so. This will depend on the organisation's legal structure, whether it is a charity, and the powers granted under its governing document.

A few organisations have a statutory power to borrow, but for most the power must be explicit in their governing document [**7.4.4**]. The terms of the power must be read carefully to ensure that any proposed borrowing is allowed. The clause may, for example, give the organisation the right 'to borrow money and charge all or any part of the property of the organisation for the repayment of the money so borrowed'. This allows the organisation to use its assets as security for a loan, but does not allow it to guarantee a loan taken out by another organisation, such as its trading subsidiary [**51.4.5**]. Unless the power to borrow is absolutely clear, it is essential to get legal and financial advice before borrowing.

Loans to and investment in eligible community organisations through **community development finance institutions** are eligible for **community investment tax relief** [**50.10**].

59.1.1 Incorporated bodies

A company's governing document nearly always includes either a specific borrowing power, or a broad general power under which a power to borrow can be implied. If it does not, it should be amended in the usual way [**7.5.3-7.5.5**] before undertaking any borrowing. Where there is a general power but not a specific power to borrow, lenders may insist on a specific power to borrow being added.

The governing document may occasionally contain restrictions or prohibition on borrowing without specific consent, for example from the Charity Commission or the organisation's members.

An industrial and provident society's rules must state whether it has power to borrow, and whether there is any limit on the borrowing and on how the loan can be secured. The rules often contain limitations on the rate of interest to be paid on borrowing. If the specified rate of interest is unrealistically low, an application should be made to Mutual Societies Registration at the Financial Services Authority [end of **chapter 1**] to vary the restriction. *Industrial & Provident Societies Act 1965 sch.1 para.8*

59.1.2   Unincorporated organisations

Where an unincorporated association has statutory power or power under its governing document to borrow, the individual(s) who sign the borrowing agreement, those who authorise the borrowing and/or the members of the governing body at the time the debt is due to be repaid could potentially be held personally liable if the organisation is unable to meet the repayment terms of its borrowing [**22.5.3**].

It may be possible to create a borrowing arrangement in which the lender agrees to limit its right to repayment of principal and interest to the extent of the funds of the organisation [**22.7.5**]. This means that if the organisation does not have enough funds, the lender does not get repaid. Commercial lenders, in particular, are unlikely to be willing to agree to this limitation on their right to be repaid.

59.1.2.1   Unincorporated associations

Unincorporated associations defined by statute as literary or scientific institutions have a statutory right to borrow money on the security of their property in order to pay costs related to the property.   *Literary & Scientific Institutions Act 1854 s.19*

Apart from this, a non-charitable association can borrow money, commit its members to repaying a loan, or use the association's property as security for a loan (including a mortgage) only if the power to do so is explicit in the governing document or is given by the members [**22.5.3**]. Unless the governing document explicitly allows borrowing, approval of the association's members should be obtained before small-scale borrowing such as a temporary small overdraft, and the constitution must be amended before any substantial borrowing [**7.5.1**].

59.1.2.2   Trusts and charitable associations

Trustees of a charitable or non-charitable trust, or of a charitable association, have statutory powers to borrow for acquisition of land and for repair and maintenance of land and buildings they own.   *Trusts of Land & Appointment of Trustees Act 1996 s.6*

A trust or charitable association may borrow for other purposes only if the governing document includes power to do so. It may be possible to amend the governing document [**7.5.1**] to provide this power.

59.1.3   Charities

Trustees of all charities, whether incorporated or unincorporated, have a duty to act prudently and exercise their duty of care [**15.6.7**], and must comply with Charities Act requirements prior to taking out a mortgage and other borrowing using a charity's land or buildings as security [**61.11.1**].

An unincorporated charity has a statutory power to borrow and to charge (mortgage) property [**59.1.2.2**]. The Charity Commission considers that this power extends to unsecured borrowing where no security over property is required, but some commercial lending organisations still insist on an explicit power.

A corporate charity cannot rely on the statutory power, and its memorandum or articles of association must contain an express power to borrow.

Where a charity's governing document does not contain a power to borrow, the Charity Commission may make an order [**4.5.4**] to grant authority for a particular borrowing or, if there is no constitutional or statutory power to amend, may make an order to amend the governing document [**7.5**].

59.1.4   Borrowing and Islamic law

The collection and payment of interest is prohibited by **sharia** (Islamic law). Islamic banks and an increasing number of mainstream financial institutions provide mortgages and loans consistent with sharia principles.

These arrangements may not be covered by the standard borrowing powers in a charity's governing document. Islamic charities which wish to use sharia arrangements should consult the Charity Commission to ensure they have the necessary power, or to obtain an order from the Commission [**4.5.4**].

59.2   OVERDRAFTS

An **overdraft** facility provided by a bank is a simple form of loan. An overdraft is not for any specific period, and the bank may withdraw the facility and require immediate repayment at any time. If the organisation expects to need the facility for a significant and predictable period, it may be advisable to enter into a loan agreement. This removes the risk of being required to pay the amount unexpectedly, and may also offer lower rates of interest.

Banks are unlikely to allow a significant overdraft or loan without seeking security in the form of a charge on the organisation's assets [**59.5**] or a guarantee [**59.5.3**]. Where security over land is required, the provisions of the **Charities Act 1993** must be complied with [**61.11.1**].

59.3   CREDIT FINANCE

Especially when acquiring equipment, an organisation may obtain credit through **credit finance**. The major forms of this are hire purchase, finance leases and operating leases. Credit finance is a form of borrowing, and organisations can enter into it only if they have power to do so [**59.1**].

59.3.1   Types of finance

Hire purchase is a contract allowing the purchaser to use an asset while paying for it over time. The seller retains title until payment is complete. Only when the final payment is made does the purchaser acquire legal title.

With a **finance lease**, the asset is still owned by the finance house or other lessor at the end of the lease period, but the finance agreement may allow the organisation to acquire ownership of the asset for a reduced price or to hire it for a further period for a nominal sum.

With an **operating lease**, the organisation obtains a limited right to use the asset through the hire period. At the end of the period the lease is renewed or the asset is returned to the owner.

59.3.2   Implications

Each form of finance has different financial and tax implications. These are beyond the scope of this book, and organisations are strongly advised to take advice before entering into any significant credit finance.

An agreement for any type of finance is likely to be subject to comprehensive and sometimes onerous standard terms imposed by the hiring or leasing company. These must always be carefully considered before the agreement is accepted. Although the terms are standard, they are in fact frequently negotiable [**21.3.2**].

Few forms of credit finance can be terminated without substantial penalty, so all such agreements must be treated with considerable caution – regardless of the verbal assurances which might be given.

The legislation which protects consumers who use these forms of finance to purchase goods does not generally apply to organisations, which are assumed to be operating as commercial bodies rather than as individual consumers. However, some protection may in some cases be obtained under consumer protection legislation [**21.2.3**, **21.2.7**].

59.3.2.1   Authorisation

Many organisations and businesses have experienced very serious problems with credit finance, particularly with equipment leases, entered into without proper authorisation and without proper attention given to the small print [**21.3.2**].

It is vital to establish a clear policy setting out who is authorised to make decisions about whether to enter into credit finance, who can agree the terms, and who can sign the agreement. Any such policy is a purely internal matter within the organisation, and if an unauthorised person enters into a contract, it is binding on the organisation provided the person acting on behalf of the organisation appears to the other party to be authorised [**21.1.3**]. However, if the organisation has a clear policy about who can and cannot enter into agreements, it may be able to claim compensation from the person who took the unauthorised action.

59.4   UNSECURED LOANS

An **unsecured loan** does not give the lender any direct charge on (right of recourse to) the organisation's assets if the loan is not repaid. The loan may be given by a bank or other financial institution, or by an individual or organisation.

A voluntary organisation which receives loans from individuals or bodies which are not financial institutions should take advice to ensure it does not contravene the regulations on money lending, money laundering [**53.6**] and financial services. The lenders may also need to take advice.

59.4.1   Loan agreements

Key issues when entering into a loan are the amount of the loan, the conditions that must be satisfied before the loan can be drawn down, repayment terms, provision for payment and calculation of interest, and any special provisions, such as higher interest if payment is late. The repayment arrangements are particularly important, and the organisation must be confident it will have adequate funds when repayment is due.

For substantial loans, legal advice should be sought before signing any agreement, to ensure the organisation's interests are protected and, in the case of unincorporated organisations, to try to reduce the potential risk to individual members of the governing body [**2.2.4**].

59.4.1.1   Interest-free loans

An organisation's supporters may be willing to provide interest-free loans. There may be a temptation to 'keep it simple and informal' for loans such as this, especially if they are short term, but all borrowings should be carefully documented.

If an interest-free loan is made to a charity and is intended for investment rather than immediate use, HM Revenue and Customs must be satisfied that the lender has not made the loan as a way of avoiding tax on the investment income. To comply with this, the loan agreement should make clear that the lender has no right to specify how the loan is to be invested or how the income earned from the investment is to be used.   *Income Tax (Trading & Other Income) Act 2005 ss.620,628*

59.4.1.2   Loans from governing body members

There are no restrictions on members of a governing body making interest-free loans to their organisation, but the lender and other governing body members need to document them and be aware of potential conflicts of interest [**15.2**] and rules governing transactions with company directors [**15.3.6**].

In relation to loans on which interest will be charged, the prohibition on charity governing bodies members and connected persons [**15.2.5**] gaining personal benefit [**15.6.6**] means that they can charge interest to the charity only if the charity's governing document explicitly allows them to receive interest on such loans, or if the Charity Commission has specifically authorised the payment.

Where a charity's governing document allows payment of interest to governing body members and specifies a maximum rate, it can be amended only with the prior written consent of the Charity Commission. If the governing document does not specify a maximum rate, the governing body may decide, but should take account of other sources of finance and rates available. The person(s) making the loan must not take part in any discussion or decision about the loan terms and conditions.

In non-charities with power to borrow, interest may be paid to members of the governing body unless the governing document prohibits such payment. The governing document may set a maximum interest rate for such loans.

59.4.1.3   Soft loans

The terms **soft loan** and **soft financing** are used for loans with interest at below the market rate, and/or with other benefits such as a longer repayment period, or even provision to write off the loan if a project fails. At the time of writing (early 2009) the government was committed to increasing the amount of loan funding to charities, other voluntary organisations and social enterprises, and a number of loan initiatives had been set up.

Where such loans are made with public sector funds the rules on **state aid** [**48.4.2**] may apply, and organisations which are offered such loans should take advice about this.

The rules on power to borrow, and the duties of prudence and care, apply to interest-free and soft loans in the same way as to commercial loans.

59.5   SECURED LOANS

Few lenders, except an organisation's wealthy supporters, are likely to make a substantial loan to an organisation without requiring security or **collateral**. This is likely to be in the form of a **charge** over the organisation's land and buildings (a **mortgage**), a charge over its other assets (**debentures**), a promise from a third party to cover the debt if the organisation defaults (**guarantee**) or a **retention of title** to goods supplied on credit [**59.3**]. A charge gives the lender the right to the asset if the borrower does not repay the loan.

Mortgages and charges granted by a company and some retentions of title must be registered within 21 days at Companies House, and records of mortgages and charges must be kept in the company's **register of charges** [**18.5.11**]. When some or all of the mortgage or charge has been repaid, Companies House must be notified on the appropriate form and the register of charges must be updated.

Charges on the assets of an industrial and provident society, and subsequent changes in the amount owing, must be notified to the Financial Services Authority [**18.6.4**]. There is no obligation for an IPS to keep a register of charges, but it is good practice to do so.

At the time of writing (mid 2009), the rules on registration of charges on the assets of industrial and provident societies registered with the Charity Commission and charitable incorporated organisations (CIOs) had not been finalised.

59.5.1   Mortgages

For substantial loans, a mortgage is likely to be the lender's preferred form of security. If the **mortgagor** (the borrower) defaults, the **mortgagee** (the lender) can sue the mortgagor, take possession of and sell the mortgaged property, foreclose (transfer ownership of the property to the lender), or exercise a statutory power to sell the mortgaged property. Lenders can also appoint a receiver to manage the mortgaged property and take the income from it, or may have power to grant leases after taking possession of the property.

Detailed rules apply to mortgages granted by charitable organisations [**61.11.1**].

59.5.2   Debentures

Companies of any type, charitable incorporated organisations (CIOs) and industrial and provident societies may enter into a form of charge over assets such as equipment, stocks of publications or other items, money in bank accounts, money owed to the organisation, and intellectual property rights. This type of charge is called a **debenture** or **debt stock**.

Unlike shareholders, who invest by buying a part of a company [**59.6**], holders of debentures simply lend money to the organisation for a fixed period at a fixed rate of interest, with their loan secured against the organisation's assets. A **fixed charge** is a charge on a specific asset or assets. A **floating charge** is a charge on the assets held from time to time, such as stock or money due to the organisation.

Most banks routinely secure overdrafts and loans to incorporated organisations with a standard form of debenture. If the organisation becomes insolvent, this gives the bank the first rights to the organisation's assets which are subject to a fixed charge [**24.10.5**, **24.10.6**], with power to appoint a **receiver** who will take possession of the organisation's assets and dispose of them.

59.5.3 Guarantees

A bank or other lender may seek personal **guarantees** from individuals or other organisations before lending to an organisation which has few assets. Guarantees may also be required by lenders to an unincorporated association or trust, which by its nature cannot own assets in its own right [**2.2.4**, **2.3.9**]. Because the assets are vested in trustees [**20.4.1**], the organisation may find it difficult to grant security over the assets.

The organisation needs to think very carefully before asking anyone to provide a guarantee, since it imposes on the guarantor potentially onerous obligations, not only for the loan itself but also often for interest and legal costs. Similarly, any individual or organisation asked to provide a guarantee should consider it carefully, and especially consider the worst case situation where the organisation defaults on the loan. It is advisable for any potential guarantor to obtain independent legal advice.

An organisation guaranteeing another organisation's loan is potentially liable for the borrowing, so can give a guarantee only if it would itself have the power to make that borrowing.

59.5.4 Clawback

Providers of funding or donors of assets may make their funding or donation subject to provisions requiring repayment in full or part if the funds, the assets bought with them, or donated assets cease to be used for the purposes for which they were provided, or the assets are disposed of. Similar provisions may apply where an asset such as a community building has been transferred to an organisation, and the asset is disposed of or is no longer used for the intended purpose. These arrangements are frequently called **clawbacks**, and can greatly reduce or negate the value of the asset as **collateral** which can be borrowed against.

Clawback arrangements are not strictly borrowing, and will often not fall within an organisation's ordinary borrowing powers. The powers may need to be amended in order to grant any charge or mortgage necessary to secure the clawback.

In relation to assets provided by public sector bodies, the government now accepts that they can be used as collateral, and that income generated through the sale of such an asset can be kept by the organisation provided it will be used to achieve the same general outcomes as originally agreed. Information about these arrangements is available from the Development Trusts Association and Community Matters [see end of chapter].

Unless carefully worded, clawback provisions can have unintended consequences. A provision entitling the original donor to the full value of the property if it is sold, for example, would entitle the donor to claw back not only the original value, but also the value of any subsequent improvements made by the organisation from its own funds. Legal advice should always be sought before entering into clawback arrangements, especially for major assets.

59.6 EQUITY FINANCE AND OTHER FINANCE

Equity finance is where a business raises funds by inviting others to invest in the business by purchasing **shares** or **stock**, with a view to receiving a share of the profits. Investors receive their share of any profit through **dividends**. Holders of **ordinary shares** are company members and have a right to take part in certain decisions about the company [**12.4.1**]. Holders of **preferred shares** generally do not have a right to take part in decisions, but are entitled to a higher dividend which is often fixed.

59.6.1   Sale of shares

Organisations set up as companies limited by shares – including charity trading subsidiaries – can raise funds by issuing shares, subject to any restrictions in their governing document. Community interest companies limited by shares can also issue shares, but there is a cap on the dividends that can be paid [**3.4.3**]. Companies limited by guarantee cannot issue shares.

Public limited companies (plc's) raise funds from the public by selling shares listed on a stock exchange. Shares of private limited companies (Ltd) cannot be offered to the public at large but may be offered to limited classes of investors. The offer and sale of shares must comply with rules governing **financial promotions**.   *Financial Services & Markets Act 2000 (Financial Promotion) Order 2005 [SI 2005/1529]*

Industrial and provident societies can raise funds by issuing shares and paying dividends to investors. At the time of writing (mid 2009) it was not clear whether charitable IPSs will be able to continue to do so or will have to convert their shares to loan stock when they register with the Charity Commission [**8.1.2**].

59.6.2   Other forms of finance

Variants of equity finance, based on partnership and profit sharing, have been devised to meet the requirements of Islamic law [**59.1.4**].

Other variants based on the sharing of risk and profit, such as **venture capital** and **risk capital**, are available as investments for new businesses.

Debt finance means raising funds by issuing **bonds**, which are repayable to the holder after a specified period. Interest is paid to the holder during and at the end of the period. An example is the first bond issue by a charity, in 2003, by Golden Lane Housing, a charitable subsidiary of Mencap. It used the income from the bond issue to buy homes for people with learning disabilities, using the income from rents to fund the interest and repayments.

59.6.2.1   Quasi equity

Charities and other voluntary organisations often have insecure income, or start new ventures which may not become profitable or even cover their costs. If they could issue shares [above] as a way of raising funds, dividends would only have to be paid to shareholders if the organisation makes a profit. But because this is not an option, they may need to raise funds by way of loan – which must be repaid, usually with interest, even if they do not have the funds to do so.

As a way of reducing both the pressure to repay and the risk of personal liability for governing body members if the organisation cannot repay, some social lenders are adapting their repayment schedules so they share some of the organisational uncertainty. Instead of fixed repayments at specified times, repayments are linked to the organisation's revenue or profit over a specified period, and can be capped at a specific figure. These arrangements are sometimes called **revenue participation agreements**, or because they can mimic equity finance they may be called **'quasi equity'**. The lender shares the risk, in that it will not be repaid or will be repaid more slowly if income does not come in as anticipated.

Resources: BORROWING

Borrowing by charities. Charity Commission: www.charitycommission.gov.uk, 0845 300 0218, email via website.

Clawback. Community Matters: www.communitymatters.org.uk, 020 7837 7887, communitymatters@communitymatters.org.uk.

Development Trusts Association: www.dta.org.uk, 0845 458 8336, info@dta.org.uk.

Statute law. www.opsi.gov.uk and www.statutelaw.gov.uk.

Much but not all case law. www.bailii.org.

Updates cross-referenced to this book. www.rclh.co.uk.

The decision to buy freehold land or take on a long lease involves the organisation in substantial expenditure and a long-term commitment which may be overlaid with ancient rights and covenants. Even a shorter lease or licence may involve the organisation in a myriad of obligations, some of which could extend long after the organisation leaves the property.

'Land' and 'property' means the land itself, as well as buildings and some objects on the land.

Part VII covers some of the main issues relating to property.

Chapter 60

LAND OWNERSHIP AND TENURE

60.1 VOLUNTARY ORGANISATIONS AND PROPERTY

The law in relation to land is very old and complex, encompassing not only statute and common law but also the specific rights and restrictions set out in the title documents or contract, with special rules for charity land. Even what may appear to be a simple transaction is likely to have potentially complex implications. Mistakes can be costly, so legal advice should always be sought before buying or selling land, or entering into a lease or licence as either landlord or tenant.

Chapter 61 explains how freeholds and leases are acquired and disposed of, and **chapter 62** explains typical business leases.

The most important land rights are **freehold** (ownership) [**60.3**]; **lease**, also referred to as **tenancy** (exclusive right of occupation) [**60.4**]; and **easements** (rights over the land of another) [**60.7.1**]. Only freeholds and leases are **legal estates** and give rights to the land. A **licence** [**60.5**] is not legal estate; it is only a contract or permission.
Law of Property Act 1925 s.1

In legal terms, **land** or **realty** usually mean land plus the buildings and other structures on it, but may mean just the land. **Property** is often used in a broader sense, to cover all of the organisation's assets, so it will sometimes be necessary to clarify whether 'property' refers only to buildings and land, or to everything owned by the organisation.

Tenure refers to the relationship between the landlord and a tenant – the way the land is held.

60.2   POWERS RELATING TO PROPERTY

To acquire or dispose of property, an organisation must have appropriate powers, which may be included in the governing document [**7.4.5**] or given by statute. Registered social landlords are subject to special restrictions when dealing with property. These are not covered in this book.

60.2.1   Companies

Companies generally have in their memorandum or articles of association full powers to buy, sell, take on lease, mortgage and develop property; to alter, build, maintain, and equip buildings; to sell property or dispose of it in other ways; and/or to make regulations relating to any property.

These powers may be explicit, or may be implicit in a general power 'to do anything lawful to attain the organisation's objects'. Legal advice should be taken before entering into a property transaction if the memorandum or articles do not contain either the relevant power or a general power. If property is being purchased as an investment – to earn income from it rather than to use it for the organisation's activities – explicit power to invest may be necessary [**58.1.3**].

Charitable companies are also subject to charity law rules on property [**60.2.4**].

60.2.2   Industrial and provident societies

Unless its rules indicate otherwise, industrial and provident societies have all the powers relating to real property set out above. Charitable IPSs which are registered with the Charity Commission or are excepted from registration [**8.1.3**] must comply with the Charities Act rules on property in the same way as any other charity [**60.2.4**]. IPSs exempt from registration [**8.1.2**] are not bound by most Charities Act rules, but do have to include the required statement in documents relating to mortgages and transfer of property [**61.11.1, 61.12.4**].

Industrial & Provident Societies Act 1965 s.30(1); Charities Act 1993 ss.36(10)(a),37(1),38(7)

60.2.3   Trusts and unincorporated associations

Unless their governing document specifies otherwise, trusts and charitable associations have a statutory power, subject to a duty of care [**58.1.2**], to acquire freehold or leasehold land in the UK as an investment, for occupation by beneficiaries or for any other reason, and have the same rights in relation to the land as any other owner. This statutory power is in addition to any other powers specified in the governing document. If the organisation is charitable, it must comply with charity law requirements [**60.2.4**].   *Trustee Act 2000 ss.1,2,8*

If a trust or charitable association will ever want to acquire land outside the UK, the governing document should include power to do so.

The power of a non-charitable unincorporated association to undertake property transactions is governed by its governing document.

60.2.4   Charities

Powers relating to property will generally be implied (assumed to exist) if use of land is necessary to achieve the charity's objects.   *Rosemary Simmons Memorial Housing Association Limited v United Dominion Trust Limited [1987] 1 All ER 281*

Beyond, this, charities' powers depend on their legal structure [above] and governing document, and are subject to duties under trust and statute law.

The normal duties of charity trustees [**15.6**] apply to all land transactions by charities. This normally means obtaining and acting on appropriate professional advice. This could include a structural survey, advice on the value of the property or level of rent, and legal advice as to the suitability of the title for the purpose intended, planning permission, and burdensome covenants or restrictions [**60.7**].

If proper advice is not taken and the charity suffers a loss on a property transaction, the trustees could be held by the Charity Commission or court to be in breach of trust, and could be personally required to make good the loss to the charity.

In addition to the general duty of prudence [**15.6.5**, **15.6.7**] and the duty of care when investing [**58.1.2**], special rules apply to mortgages [**61.11.1**], selling or disposing of land or surrendering a lease [**61.12**], and selling or disposing of permanent endowment [**61.13**].

60.3 FREEHOLD

In legal terms a **freehold** gives rights to the land forever, but the title may be subject to a wide range of restrictions and obligations affecting the land or endowing it with additional rights [**60.7**].

60.3.1 'Squatters' rights'

A freeholder can be deprived of ownership though **adverse possession** (colloquially called **squatters' rights**), if a squatter or series of squatters has occupied land which is not registered with the Land Registry [**60.6.3**] for a continuous period of at least 12 years, or if registered land was occupied by squatters for at least 12 years prior to 13 October 2003 and is still occupied by them.

Limitation Act 1980 s.15

Since 13 October 2003, a squatter who has occupied land for 10 years can apply to the Land Registry. The Land Registry notifies the registered owner (**proprietor**), and if the registered owner objects to the application, the Land Registry will reject it unless rather limited provisions apply. *Land Registration Act 2002 ss.96-98*

If the squatter's application is dismissed, the registered owner should bring possession proceedings within two years. Failure to do so gives the squatter a further right to apply for adverse possession.

An organisation which is a proprietor of registered land should ensure that its address for service of notices by the Land Registry is fully up to date.

60.4 LEASES AND TENANCIES

A **lease** or **tenancy** is the right, granted to a **tenant**, to occupy a freeholder's land for a defined period or a succession of periods, combining a contractual relationship with a property relationship. It is in effect a right of temporary ownership, subject to obligations and conditions that are contractual in nature. For long leases the tenant may be called a **leaseholder**.

If the person granting the lease (the **lessor** or **landlord**) is a tenant of the freeholder, the lease can be known as a **sub-lease** or **underlease**. If the 'sub-lessor' has an underlease, the new lease is sometimes called a **sub-underlease**.

If there is a defined period for the lease, this is known as the **term**. The interest retained by the freeholder – the right to re-occupy the land when the lease has expired – is the **reversion**.

The relationship of landlord and tenant is primarily governed by what the two parties agree, but many statutory and other rules affect the relationship. The detailed terms of a typical business lease are dealt with in **62.2**.

60.4.1 Personal liability

60.4.1.1 Unincorporated associations and trusts

In an unincorporated association or trust [**chapter 2**], the signatories – and potentially other individuals in the organisation or named in the lease as acting on behalf of the organisation – are personally liable for ensuring the terms of the lease are complied with, unless the lease states otherwise. They may be personally liable for payment of rent, any obligation to repair, and all other obligations.

Individuals who are held to be personally liable have a right to be indemnified (compensated) by the organisation [**22.7.8**] if the organisation has funds to do so. In some cases they may be able to make a claim against other members of the governing body or members of the organisation [**22.2.3**].

The landlord may be willing to agree that the liability of the signatories will not be greater than the organisation's ability to indemnify them [**22.7.5**]. If this is not possible, each signatory should take independent legal advice before signing a lease on behalf of a trust or unincorporated association.

60.4.1.2 Incorporated organisations

When entering into a lease with a company, industrial and provident society, charitable incorporated organisation or other incorporated body with limited liability [**3.1.1**], the landlord stands to lose out if the organisation becomes insolvent. A landlord may therefore require **guarantors** for a lease [**62.2.3**]. Generally governing body members or others should not agree to guarantee leases, and if they do, it should only be after taking independent legal advice. Where there is no guarantor, the landlord may ask for a **rent deposit** instead [**62.2.3**].

60.4.2 Lease formalities

Leases for three years or less at a market rent may be created verbally, or take the form of a formal or informal written agreement. For fixed terms of more than three years, a lease must be signed as a deed [**20.3**].   *Law of Property Act 1925 ss.53,54*

Leases are often drawn up in duplicate with one copy, the lease, signed by the landlord and the other copy, the **counterpart**, signed by the tenant.

60.4.2.1 Premiums and rent

Tenants may pay the landlord for the lease in a variety of ways. Even where the landlord does not expect payment of rent the lease will usually specify that a peppercorn is payable annually (**peppercorn rent**). Where there is rent it may be nominal, only a few hundred pounds a year, or a more substantial rent up to a full market rent (**rack rent**), generally with regular increases.

Where the rent is nominal or a peppercorn, the landlord often expects an initial capital payment (a **fine** or **premium**) or another obligation such as constructing a building on the land or delivering a service from it [**62.2.1**].

60.4.3 Exclusive possession

Tenants have **exclusive possession**, giving them the right to sole use of the property and the right to exclude everyone else, including the landlord. Exclusive possession is the most important feature that differentiates a lease from an occupational **licence** [**60.5**]. However, even leases generally provide for many exceptions to exclusive possession by the tenant, such as a landlord's right of inspection and rights of access in an emergency or to do work on other land.

60.4.4 Changes in tenant or landlord

Once the landlord lets the land the tenant may, unless prevented by the terms of the lease, **assign** (transfer) the lease to another person [**62.2.7**].

Alternatively a tenant may, unless prevented by the terms of the lease, retain the lease but sub-let all or part of the property. The new lease is then a **sub-lease** [**60.9**].

Freeholders may sell their interest in the reversion [**60.4**]. The purchaser becomes the landlord, and the right to possession of the land reverts to the new freeholder when the original lease expires.

60.4.4.1 Leases granted before 1 January 1996

A tenant who entered into a lease before 1 January 1996 and subsequently assigns (transfers) it effectively guarantees all of the obligations of all assignees of the lease until it expires. For a landlord to protect its right to make the original tenant liable in this way, it must notify the original tenant of mounting arrears for which they may be liable. If this is not done within six months of when the arrears become due, the landlord loses the right to claim those arrears from the original tenant.   *Landlord & Tenant (Covenants) Act 1995 ss.16-18*

An original tenant who pays the arrears of a defaulting assignee has a right to be granted an **overriding lease**. The original tenant becomes the assignee's landlord. Although this makes the original tenant once again directly liable to the landlord, the original tenant can enforce the collection of rent from the defaulting assignee or forfeit (end) the lease.   *Landlord & Tenant (Covenants) Act 1995 ss.19,20*

60.4.4.2 Leases granted from 1 January 1996

For leases from 1 January 1996, unless granted as the result of an agreement, option or court order prior to that date, the original tenant is released from its obligations after the lease has been assigned to a new tenant unless the lease specifies otherwise. Leases granted after that date may – or may not – include provisions giving the landlord the right to require the outgoing tenant to guarantee the new tenant's obligations through an **authorised guarantee agreement**. If this guarantee is in place, the outgoing tenant remains liable until the new tenant assigns to yet another new tenant. When this happens, the original outgoing tenant is released from any obligation under the lease.   *LT(C)A 1995 ss.5,11-16*

As with pre-1996 leases, in order to be liable the former tenant must be informed within six months of any liability for arrears of a later tenant. If it pays these arrears, the former tenant has the right to be granted an overriding lease.

60.4.4.3 Liability of landlords before and after 1 January 1996

Unless excluded under the terms of the lease, the original landlord of a lease entered into before 1 January 1996 is liable for the landlord covenants [for example **61.2.9**] until the lease expires.

The original landlord of a lease entered into on or after 1 January 1996 may also remain liable for landlord covenants until the lease expires, even if the lease is assigned to another landlord. However, the original landlord's liability to tenants can be contractually limited to the period while it is actually the landlord under the lease.   *London Diocesan Fund & others v Avonridge Property Company Ltd [2005] UKHL 70*

60.4.5 Tenancies with security

Statutory provisions for business leases (any non-residential tenancy, even if granted to a charity or other non-business) generally entitle the tenant to a new tenancy as of right on expiry or termination of the original [**62.6**]. Non-residential tenancies include part residential/part business tenancies, such as flats above and let with shops, and live/work units. The statutory security provisions do not apply to licences [**60.5**] or tenancies at will [**60.4.6.3**], or to tenancies that fall within specified exclusions [**60.4.6**].

The security provisions apply only to property actually occupied by the tenant for the purposes of its activities, and where the activities are carried on by the tenant. Thus security of tenure is not available for parts of the premises sub-let to or used by other organisations, or even a subsidiary of the tenant.

Different provisions apply to 'pure' residential tenancies. These are beyond the scope of this book.

60.4.5.1 Term of years

A lease for a **term of years** means a lease granted for a fixed period, although it may contain provisions for early termination [**62.7.2**, **62.7.3**]. If the provisions for security of tenure apply, the lease continues on the same terms at the end of the fixed period, until the expiry of a notice given by the landlord or tenant pursuant to the **Landlord and Tenant Act 1954** ss.24-28 [**62.6**].

60.4.5.2 Periodic tenancy

A **periodic tenancy** consists of a succession of short periods, each from a week to as much as a year. A periodic tenancy continues until terminated by the landlord or tenant. If the security of tenure provisions apply, the tenancy continues on the same terms until a notice to quit from the tenant or the expiry of a notice from the landlord pursuant to the **Landlord and Tenant Act 1954**, and will continue thereafter if the tenant applies to the court for a new lease [**62.6**].

| 60.4.5.3 | Continuation tenancy |

A **continuation tenancy** is created when a lease for a term of years or a periodic tenancy [**60.4.5.2**] is continued past its expiry or termination. The tenant 'holds over' rather than leaving at the end of the term, and the tenancy can be ended only by the procedures specified in the **Landlord and Tenant Act 1954**. Where a tenant holds over it will be on the same terms, but for business tenants either party can apply to have a new interim rent fixed [**62.6**].

60.4.6 Tenancies without security

Certain types of business tenancy do not have statutory security of tenure. These include short fixed-term tenancies, tenancies where the landlord and tenant agree to exclude security of tenure following the appropriate procedure under the **Landlord and Tenant Act 1954**, and tenancies at will.

| 60.4.6.1 | Short-term tenancy |

For business tenancies, security of tenure is not created where a fixed-term tenancy for six months or less is granted, without any provision for renewal beyond the six months, and the total period of occupation by the tenant under a formal lease or otherwise does not exceed 12 months. If a fixed-term tenancy is granted that will bring the total occupation by the tenant over the 12-month limit, that lease will be subject to the terms of the Act. *Landlord & Tenant Act 1954 s.43*

| 60.4.6.2 | Exclusion of security of tenure by agreement |

The provisions of the **Landlord and Tenant Act 1954** ss.24-28 can be excluded through a statutory procedure, under which the tenant has no right to statutory continuation of the tenancy at the end of the term, or to statutory compensation which might otherwise be available, or to apply to the court for a new lease. Any such agreement will usually be included in the lease itself.

For the agreement to be valid, the tenancy must be for a fixed term and not be a periodic tenancy [**60.4.5.1**], and the landlord must serve notice on the tenant in statutory form prior to the grant of the tenancy. The statutory form contains information regarding the rights the tenant will be giving up by entering into a lease subject to the exclusion agreement. *Landlord & Tenant Act 1954 s.38A, inserted by Regulatory Reform (Business Tenancies) (England & Wales) Order 2003 [SI 2003/3096]*

The tenant, or someone authorised by the tenant to act on its behalf, must make a declaration in a prescribed form, confirming that the tenant has read and understood the notice. If the lease is completed less than 14 days after the service of the notice, the declaration must be signed by the person declaring in the presence of an independent solicitor. In other cases, the declaration may simply be signed by such person without the involvement of a solicitor.

The clause in the lease containing the agreement to exclude the Act must refer to the service of the notice and the making of the declaration.

The procedures must be completed prior to the grant of the tenancy. Any error in the procedure, even if minor, could give the tenant rights that were intended to be excluded, so landlords should seek legal advice before using these provisions.

If it is later agreed that the tenant will stay on after the end of the term, the whole procedure should be repeated and a new fixed term granted before the term expires. Otherwise, the tenant may obtain a periodic tenancy with security.

| 60.4.6.3 | Tenancy at will |

A **tenancy at will** is a right of occupation that can be ended immediately by either side, without having to give a period of notice. It may be used or arise by implication, for example where tenants surrender their lease but cannot move out on the due date and the landlord allows them to remain, or where a tenancy does not have security of tenure and the lease expires while a new lease is still in the course of negotiation.

60.5   LICENCES

A **licence** is a permission to use property, but unlike a freehold or lease it is not a legal estate. The term can be used for a very temporary occupation such as the right to erect a market stall for the day, or may be a long-term arrangement very similar to a lease. Often but not always the owner, rather than the occupant, is responsible for repairs, insurances and rates, and either side can terminate on short notice.

60.5.1   Lease or licence?

It can be difficult to ascertain whether an occupying organisation has a lease or a mere contractual right to occupy (a licence). An agreement that gives the occupier exclusive possession of property may be a lease even if it is called a licence – but not all agreements giving the occupier exclusive possession are leases. Specialist legal advice is likely to be needed to clarify the relationship.

The issue is important because, for example:

- a licence does not create any security of tenure [**60.4.5**] under the **Landlord and Tenant Act 1954** ss.24-28 [**60.4.5**], and a licensor does not have the wide range of remedies open to a landlord under a tenancy [**62.4**];
- a lease is likely to be transferrable, but a licence is not;
- a lease may be registrable at the Land Registry [**60.6.3**], but not a licence;
- a lease may be liable to stamp duty land tax [**61.10**], but not a licence;
- the grant of a lease is subject to the **Charities Act 1993** s.36 [**61.12**], but the grant of a licence is not;
- a landlord under a tenancy has a right to seize goods by way of security for non-payment of rent [**62.4.3**], but a licensor cannot do this.

60.6   LAND OWNERSHIP AND REGISTRATION

An incorporated organisation can own land, including leases, in the name of the organisation, but unincorporated bodies cannot. Legal advice should be taken before undertaking any actions involving land ownership or its registration.

60.6.1   How land is held

60.6.1.1   Incorporated organisations

A company limited by guarantee, company limited by shares, charitable incorporated organisation or industrial and provident society is a legal person [**3.1.1**] and can own a freehold or lease in its own name.

60.6.1.2   Incorporated trustee bodies

The trustees of an unincorporated charity may apply to the Charity Commission to incorporate the governing body (the charity trustees), without incorporating the charity as a whole [**2.4**]. This enables the charity to hold land in the name of the incorporated trustee body. This type of incorporated body does not have limited liability, and trustees will still be personally liable [**60.4.1.1**].

60.6.1.3   Unincorporated trusts and associations

An unincorporated association or trust which has not incorporated its trustees [**60.6.1.2**] is not a legal person and is unable to hold or rent property in its own name. The title to any freehold property owned or lease held by the organisation must be vested in individuals (called **holding trustees** if their only function is to hold property) [**20.4.4**], or in a corporate body as a trustee or **custodian trustee** [**20.4.2**]. The **Official Custodian for Charities** [4.5.3] can also hold land for charities. Unless the governing document requires property to be held in a particular way, the governing body can decide.

Entries in the land register [**60.6.3**] and unregistered leases must be in the name(s) of the individuals or corporate body holding the property, and should say that the property is held on behalf of the organisation. This makes clear that the individuals or corporate body hold the **legal title**, but the organisation is the **beneficial owner** with sole right to use and benefit from the property. For more about how unincorporated bodies hold property, see **20.4**.

60.6.2   Title deeds

For some freehold properties and long leases, ownership is still shown by a collection of **title deeds** showing a succession of transfers of the property through **conveyances** (or assignments in the case of leases), together with other documents such as grants, rights of way and mortgages. Now, however, property ownership and rights are generally shown on the land register at the Land Registry [below], and the old deeds are no longer required.

60.6.3   Land register

The **land register**, maintained by the Land Registry [see end of chapter], covers freehold properties, leases of more than seven years, and charges and other matters affecting them. Failure to register ownership or rights over land promptly can lead to a loss of those rights, although some documents relating to registered leases (for example formal permissions given by the landlord under the terms of the lease) are not generally notified to the Land Registry or referred to in the register.   *Land Registration Act 2002*

Land that is not already registered does not have to be until it is sold, mortgaged, gifted, or (from 6 April 2009) when land held in trust is vested [**20.4**] in a new trustee. Registration must take place within two months. Land which does not have to be registered can be registered voluntarily. One advantage for landowners is that this generally gives them enhanced rights to take action in case of a claim for adverse possession [**60.3.1**]. The Land Registry hopes that by 2012, all land in England and Wales that is capable of registration will be registered.

Land Registration Act 2002 (Amendment) Order 2000 [SI 2000/2072]

At the time of writing (mid 2009), leases of seven years or less and periodic tenancies [**60.4.5.2**] cannot be registered.

The register must indicate whether the land is held by or in trust for a charity, and whether the charity is an exempt or non-exempt charity [**8.1.2**]. If land comes to be owned by a charity without a transfer taking place, or if an exempt charity becomes non-exempt, the trustees must apply for a restriction to be inserted in the land title at the Land Registry.   *Charities Act 1993 s.37(7),(8),(10)*

Register entries are listed on the Land Registry website, and are available to anyone electronically and on paper, for a small fee. Documents that the register refers to, such as mortgages, are available on paper, even if the document is marked 'confidential'. Where disclosure of information in a document could cause substantial unwarranted damage or distress to an individual or could prejudice commercial interests, the property owner or an interested party may apply to have the document declared an **exempt information document** (EID). An expurgated version of an EID is made publicly available, but in some cases the person requesting the document can apply for the full document to be disclosed.

60.6.4   Land charges register

For unregistered interests in land, including leases for seven years or less, the **land charges register** lists some rights affecting the land, including mortgages, contracts for sale (estate contracts, see **61.6.1**), restrictive covenants and easements [**60.7**]. The land charges register is becoming of less importance as more land is registered with the Land Registry [above]. If a right which should have been registered was not registered, the right does not generally bind the new owner when the land is sold or a lease is assigned.

60.7 PROPERTY RIGHTS AND RESTRICTIONS

Most property rights date back centuries and are enshrined in common law; others arise from statute law, the title deeds or lease provisions. Some of the most common rights and restrictions are explained here. At the time of writing (mid 2009) the Law Commission had consulted on modernising and simplifying the law on easements, restrictive covenants and other property rights and restrictions.

60.7.1 Easements

An **easement** is a right in favour of a third party landowner, generally the occupier of neighbouring land. A typical example is a right of way. An easement may be created by deed but may also arise because of long use (**prescription**) or be implied in some special circumstances. On any sale, the benefit of such rights generally pass to the new owners unless they are explicitly excluded.

The land with the right is called the **dominant land**, and the land subject to the right is the **servient land**. Easements are traditionally very hard to lose accidentally, even if they are not exercised for many years.

60.7.2 Right to light

After 20 years of uninterrupted exposure to natural light, the windows of a building may acquire a right to continue to receive light. This may prevent an adjoining landowner putting up a building which cuts off all or part of that light, or may enable the person owning the right of light to be compensated by the person wishing to put up the building.

Prescription Act 1832 s.3

To prevent a **right to light** being acquired, the neighbouring owner may take steps under the **Rights of Light Act 1959** or obstruct by way of statutory notice the access to light in the 20 years after construction.

60.7.3 Rights of way

A **right of way** may be in the form of an easement [**60.7.1**] benefiting one or more pieces of land. It will have been created by deed or by **implication**, as when a landowner sells a landlocked piece of land and the law implies a **right of access** over the vendor's retained land.

Law of Property Act 1925 s.62

The other form of right of way is a **public right of way**. This may have been created by ancient usage, custom, implied grant, agreement under the **Highways Act 1980**, or **dedication**. Where a highway has been used by the public for 20 years it is presumed to be dedicated – unless there is a clear indication that this was not intended – and it becomes a permanent public highway.

60.7.4 Right to park

A right of way gives a right to get from point A to point B across a piece of land, but not a right to stop for any length of time. The **right to park** is an easement that gives the right to leave a vehicle on the land.

60.7.5 Restrictive covenants

Land is frequently the subject of **restrictive covenants**. These are restrictions which benefit neighbouring land, for example preventing the site being used for non-residential purposes. A restriction may be of almost any nature so long as it is capable of being for the benefit of the neighbouring or nearby land and is of a negative rather than positive nature. Restrictive covenants continue indefinitely, although their transfer, particularly when land is sub-divided, is complex.

If covenants no longer have any useful purpose, application to have them removed (discharged) or modified may be made to the **lands tribunal** [see end of chapter]. This is generally done only if the restriction is obsolete or prevents reasonable use, and if the person with the benefit of the covenant is not losing any practical advantage. Occasionally a restrictive covenant is ended even where the person with the benefit is disadvantaged, if money is an adequate compensation.

Law of Property Act 1925 s.84

The lands tribunal will become part of the **land, property and housing chamber** in the first-tier tribunal [**64.7**].

60.7.6   Positive covenants

Land is sometimes subject to **positive covenants** – an obligation to do, rather than not do, something. Positive covenants can generally be enforced only between the parties who originally made the agreement.

60.7.7   Boundaries and party walls

The legal ownership and indeed the position of boundaries is often hard to ascertain. In normal circumstances, there is no obligation on anyone to mark the boundary, put up any fence or maintain it.

Boundaries are not guaranteed by the Land Registry. The Ordnance Survey maps on which land registration is based are too small-scale to guarantee boundaries, and the Land Registry does not in any event investigate the position to an exact level of detail. The relinquishing or acquisition of small parcels of land where owners agree or adjust boundaries to settle a dispute is not necessarily subject to the same statutory formalities as in other circumstances where land changes hands. In addition, small portions of land adjacent to boundaries may be acquired by what amounts to adverse possession [**60.3.1**] in certain circumstances.

The position regarding unregistered land is often even more obscure, with the land described with reference to out of date or inaccurate plans. Issues about the extent of unregistered land can usually be best addressed by a voluntary application for Land Registry registration [**60.6.3**]. This should crystallise any issue relating to the general boundaries of the land. The general clarification of boundaries that registered title provides will often outweigh the legal costs of making the application, although as indicated above the exact boundaries cannot necessarily be confirmed through registration.

If a boundary wall exists it may be a shared **party wall**, and any dealings with or work on it are subject to special rules. In particular, anyone intending to build on a boundary or to repair a party wall or fence must notify the adjoining owner. Anyone intending to carry out an excavation within three metres, or in some cases six metres, of a building or buildings must notify the owner(s), even if there is no party wall or there is land or a building between.   *Party Wall etc Act 1996*

Although a party wall is divided vertically, each side has a right of support.

Law of Property Act 1925 s.38

60.7.8   Access to neighbouring land

When access to adjoining land is needed to carry out basic preservation works and there is no easement [**60.7.1**] allowing access, application for an **access order** can be made to the county court. This does not include access to carry out rebuilding, alteration or improvement. An order might not be made if it would cause undue hardship or interference, and if made may be subject to conditions including payment of a reasonable price for the right of access.

Access to Neighbouring Land Act 1992 s.1

60.7.9   Fixtures and fittings

An object on land may be a building or other object considered to be part of the land itself, a **fixture** attached to the land or building, or a **chattel** (moveable property) attached to the land or building.

When land is purchased it includes the fixtures but not the chattels, and this may lead to disputes as to what is a fixture and what is a chattel. The degree, permanence and purpose of the attachment are significant. An object attached to facilitate enjoyment of the object, such as a picture screwed to the wall, is a chattel, but decorated wooden panels forming part of the design of the building would be fixtures.

Where a tenant has fixed an object to the building, the law is likely to agree that the tenant may remove it if this can be done without causing damage. These are sometimes known as **tenant's fixtures**. However if a tenant installs fixtures which cannot be removed without causing damage, such as a central heating system, these can become **landlord's fixtures**. Removal of landlord's fixtures could constitute theft from the landlord.

60.8 MULTIPLE OWNERS

A freehold or lease may be owned solely by one person or organisation, or jointly by two or more. Multiple ownership of a freehold or lease may be a joint tenancy or tenancy in common. These are technically **trusts of land**, and are subject to statutory provisions.   *Trusts of Land & Appointment of Trustees Act 1996*

60.8.1 Joint tenancy

With a **joint tenancy**, all the owners of a freehold or lease own the whole, with none of the owners having rights to a distinct portion. If one owner dies the right of survivorship applies, and the property automatically becomes the property of the surviving owner or owners. Where one owner is a corporate body which is dissolved, the body will be treated as owning a distinct share by value. The liquidator will dispose of the share or it will be *bona vacantia* [**24.4.2**] and will be vested in the Crown.   *Law of Property Act 1925 s.36*

60.8.2 Tenancy in common

A **tenancy in common** is much more frequently used for multiple ownership by organisations. If individuals or organisations own a property as tenants in common, each owns a share in the net value. The shares do not need to be equal, and each party is free to dispose of its share. The size of the shares should be set out in an agreement or deed between the tenants in common.

The death or dissolution of an owner does not lead to the other owners acquiring that share. The share passes under the deceased owner's will if the owner is an individual, or as part of the process of distributing its assets if it is an organisation which has been dissolved [**24.1**].   *Law of Property Act 1925 s.34*

60.8.3 Issues and problems

Joint owners or tenants should draw up, on the basis of legal advice, an agreement for their shared occupation. This covers, for example, share of ownership, mutual obligations, share of income, share of maintenance and other costs, input into decisions about usage or sub-letting, the right to force a sale or other disposal of the property, and procedures to resolve disputes. Without such an agreement, it will generally be assumed that the parties own as tenants in common in shares equal to their contribution to the purchase price.

Most jointly held leases provide that the parties entering into the lease are jointly and severally liable [**22.2.3**]. This means that each tenant is liable to the landlord for the whole of the obligations under the lease, for example to pay the whole rent. Each has a right to recover from the other tenant(s) if it pays more than its share, but this right means little if the other tenants are unable to pay.

A jointly held lease requires the agreement of both or all parties for any rent review or change in the lease, and also requires the consent of both or all organisations if the lease is to be handed back to the landlord by consent (**surrendered**) [**61.7.3**]. Where, however, there is a periodic tenancy granted to joint tenants, any one of those tenants can serve an effective notice to quit, bringing the tenancy to an end. This is subject to any other statutory obligations [**60.4.5.2**].

60.9 SUB-LETTING

The complexities of joint tenancies and tenancies in common mean that it is usually advisable to avoid jointly held leases, and to opt instead for one organisation to take the lease of the whole and to grant the others a sub-lease of part. A lease will generally set out very clearly their mutual rights and obligations, and avoids the complex agreements needed for jointly held leases.

When sub-letting, the owner of the lease must decide whether to grant a sub-tenancy with security of tenure [**60.4.5**] or to ensure no security of tenure arises [**60.4.6**]. Alternatively under limited circumstances, the owner of the lease may decide to grant a licence or tenancy at will [**60.5, 60.4.6.3**].

A charity is under a legal duty to make the best use of its resources [**15.6.5, 61.12**]. It should be satisfied that it is obtaining the best return from its property that is reasonably obtainable, unless a convincing argument within the Charities Act criteria [**61.12**] can be made that it is in the best interests of the charity and its beneficiaries not to do so. Examples are letting to a beneficiary, or to another charitable body to advance the letting organisation's charitable objectives. In some cases Charity Commission consent may be required before proceeding.

The Charities Act requirements apply to all tenancies granted by charities, whether secure or without security. Technically they do not apply to licences, but trustees must obtain an appropriate return from use of the charity's assets.

Several other issues need to be considered before sharing or sub-letting premises:

- whether the proposed letting or licence is in breach of the terms of the organisation's own lease or any covenants in its title;
- whether there are planning issues [**63.10.1**];
- the term to be granted and what provisions for early termination (if any) each side requires;
- whether the sub-let will affect exemption from non-domestic rates [**63.2**], or cause the premises to be re-rated as separate units with a possible increase in the total amount of rates payable;
- whether a service charge is to be made [**62.2.3**], and how these costs will be apportioned between the letting organisation and the tenant;
- tax implications [**56.4.9**];
- VAT implications, in particular whether to elect to charge VAT [**57.15**];
- who will take responsibility for the arrangements and obtain appropriate legal advice on the documentation.

Sometimes an established organisation informally offers the use of its premises to new groups 'to tide you over till you find your own place' or 'for the duration of the campaign'. Even arrangements such as these should be put into writing, and legal advice taken to ensure security of tenure is not unintentionally created.

Resources: PROPERTY

Advice for charities and community groups. Charity Property Help: www.charitypropertyhelp.com, 0870 333 1600, propertyhelp@rics.org.

Ethical Property Foundation: www.ethicalproperty.org.uk, 020 7065 0760, mail@ethicalproperty.org.uk.

Acquiring & disposing of charity land. Charity Commission: www.charitycommission.gov.uk, 0845 300 0218, email via website.

Business leases. *Code for leasing business premises in England and Wales:* www.leasingbusinesspremises.co.uk.

Service charges in commercial property: code of practice: www.servicechargecode.co.uk.

Property Litigation Association: www.pla.org.uk, 020 8883 1700, email via website.

Community asset transfers. Asset Transfer Unit: www.atu.org.uk, 0845 345 4564, info@atu.org.uk.

Land registration. Land Registry: www.landregistry.gov.uk, local office telephone numbers available on website.

Managing community premises. ACRE: www.acre.org.uk, 01285 653477, acre@acre.org.uk.

Community Matters: www.communitymatters.org.uk, 020 7837 7887, communitymatters@communitymatters.org.uk.

Stamp duty land tax. HM Revenue & Customs: www.hmrc.gov.uk/so/sdlt/index.htm, 0845 603 0135.

Lands chamber of the upper tribunal: www.landstribunal.gov.uk, 020 7612 9710, lands@tribunals.gsi.gov.uk.

Statute law. www.opsi.gov.uk and www.statutelaw.gov.uk.

Much but not all case law. www.bailii.org.

Updates cross-referenced to this book. www.rclh.co.uk.

Chapter 61

ACQUIRING AND DISPOSING OF PROPERTY

*For sources of further information see end of **chapter 60**.*

61.1 PROPERTY TRANSACTIONS

This chapter looks at steps that an organisation typically goes through in purchasing a **freehold** [**60.3**], taking on a **lease** [**60.4**], or disposing of a freehold or lease. For a short tenancy or a **licence** [**60.5**] some of these steps may be omitted, but care should be taken before doing so, because most are designed to protect the potential purchaser or tenant. In most circumstances, organisations should not attempt to undertake a property transaction without advice from an experienced solicitor. If the solicitor is not experienced in dealing with charities, charities should also get information about charity law requirements from the Charity Commission [see end of **chapter 60**].

61.1.1   Typical stages in acquiring property

The stages in acquiring property vary depending on whether it is a freehold, lease, short tenancy or licence. However, once a property has been identified and heads of terms [**61.4**] agreed, the process is likely to involve the following procedures – set out here as an example in relation to an office lease:

- a **survey** [**61.3.7**], especially if there is an uncapped service charge liability;
- the tenant's solicitor undertaking various **property searches** [**61.5**];
- the tenant's solicitor raising various **enquiries** of the landlord's solicitors;
- the tenant's solicitor considering a **draft form** of lease;
- the tenant's solicitor **advising** the tenant on the results of searches and replies to enquiries, and the terms of the lease;
- the tenant's solicitor **negotiating** the terms of the lease with the landlord's solicitor and agreeing a **final form** of lease;
- the solicitors completing the lease by dating and **exchanging** copies signed by their respective clients;
- the tenant's solicitor preparing a **stamp duty land tax** return [**61.10.1**] if applicable, and sending it to the tenant for checking and signing;
- if applicable, the tenant's solicitors arranging for **registration** of the lease at the Land Registry [**60.6.3**].

A number of other documents and procedures may apply, such as **deposit deeds**, **licences for alteration**, or consent from a superior landlord. The time scale can vary enormously, from a few weeks to many months, and may be difficult to estimate at the outset.

Where the remaining term of an existing lease is being assigned [**62.2.7**], some of the above steps are unnecessary or inappropriate. For example, there may be little scope for renegotiating the fundamental terms of the lease with the landlord, and any negotiations are likely to take place with the existing tenant.

A tenant should take legal advice before deciding to exercise a right to terminate an existing lease or licence by giving notice to the current landlord (a **break clause**). It may be risky to give notice on current premises before contracts for the new lease are exchanged, but leaving it this late may mean that the tenant must continue paying rent on the old lease for a considerable period.

61.2   SAFEGUARDS

The traditional approach to risk when buying property is known as *caveat emptor* – the principle that it is up to the buyer to find any problem. This generally applies to land transactions, but has to a large extent been modified by statute and by the standardisation of conveyancing documents.

61.2.1   Misrepresentation or misdescription of the property

If a seller makes a statement knowing or not caring that the statement is false, and the purchaser relies on that statement, the purchaser can seek to have the contract rescinded [**21.6.5**]. If successful, the parties are put back as if the conveyance had not taken place.   *Misrepresentation Act 1967*

Even an innocent or negligent misstatement might give rise to a claim for damages. However, leases and contracts for sale of property usually provide that certain representations not actually written into the contract or lease do not give rise to a claim.

In general it is not an offence *not* to give full information about non-residential property. For example there is no obligation to disclose matters such as lack of planning permission or physical defects – but if asked, the seller cannot give false or misleading information. Certain information, such as a defect in the title of the seller, does have to be disclosed.

A false or misleading claim by a property developer or estate agent may constitute a criminal offence.   *Property Misdescriptions Act 1991*

61.2.2 Implied covenants

A lease or deed may include **express** (explicit) **covenants** granting or restricting certain rights in relation to the property [**60.7.5**, **60.7.6**]. In addition, a property may be subject to **implied covenants**. An implied covenant is a promise which the court will assume exists, even if it is not explicit.

61.2.2.1 Covenants for title

Covenants for title imply promises into the contract, transfer, lease or mortgage about the nature of the owner's or landlord's ownership. The extent of the implied covenants depends on whether the transfer is expressed to be **with full title guarantee** or **with limited title guarantee**. If these phrases are omitted, from the contract or lease, covenants for title will not be implied.

Law of Property (Miscellaneous Provisions) Act 1994

With full title guarantee implies that the owner or landlord has a right to convey the property; the owner or landlord will do whatever is necessary to vest the land in (formally transfer it to) the purchaser or tenant; the property is free from any rights exercisable by third parties, except those that the owner or landlord does not know about and could not reasonably be expected to know about; since the last sale the owner or landlord has not created an encumbrance or **charge** (mortgage or other claim on the property) to which the sale will be subject, or let anyone else do so, and is not aware of any such encumbrance or charge; and where a lease is being assigned (transferred), the lease still continues and is not voidable because of any breach of the tenant's covenants [**62.2.2**].

Law of Property (Miscellaneous Provisions) Act 1994 ss.2-4

The owner or landlord will not be liable in any case where the purchaser or tenant had actual knowledge of the facts or the sale was subject to the particular matter in question.

With limited title guarantee means that the covenants are slightly more limited. In either case, the covenants may be amended by particular provisions.

61.2.2.2 Quiet enjoyment and derogation from grant

All leases contain an implied covenant that the landlord will not **derogate** from the grant of the lease, and will not affect a tenant's **quiet enjoyment** of the property. **Quiet enjoyment** refers to the tenant's physical use of the premises. An example of interference with a tenant's right to quiet enjoyment is when a landlord unduly restricts a right included in the lease of access to the premises.

Derogation from grant is similar to this, but usually refers to an interference arising from how a landlord uses their own retained neighbouring land. The emphasis is on an act by the landlord. If the premises are unusable at the beginning of the tenancy this is not a derogation from a grant, because it was up to the tenant to be aware of the unsuitability prior to signing the lease.

61.2.2.3 Covenants implied to make an agreement work

In certain very limited circumstances, covenants may be implied in a contract or lease. This will happen only if the covenant is fair and obvious, does not contradict any agreed term, and is necessary to the business effectiveness of the contract or lease.

61.3 INITIAL STEPS IN ACQUIRING PROPERTY

A prospective purchaser or tenant first needs to ensure that they have the power to acquire property, confirm the property is indeed as they think it is, and determine whether the asking price or rent is reasonable.

61.3.1 Power to acquire property

Prior to embarking on any purchase or lease, the governing body must ensure it has the necessary power to buy or lease property [**60.2**], and if the organisation is unincorporated they will need to clarify how the property is to be held [**60.6.1**].

61.3.2 Charities Act requirements

If the organisation is legally charitable – regardless of whether it is or is not registered with the Charity Commission – it must comply with specific requirements when acquiring or disposing of property [**61.11.1**, **61.12**]. These are summarised in the Commission's CC33 *Acquiring land*, and further guidance should be sought from specialist solicitors or the Commission.

61.3.3 Conflict of interest

Governing body members must consider whether any actual or perceived conflict of interest arises in relation to themselves or persons connected with them [**15.2**]. Trustees of all charities, whether registered with the Charity Commission or not, must comply with their duties to avoid conflict of interest [**15.6.4**] and not to profit [**15.6.6**], and company directors must ensure Companies Act requirements are observed [**15.3.5**].

61.3.4 Community asset transfers

Under a government programme to encourage community management and ownership of public assets, redundant and under-utilised local authority buildings and land are being transferred to charities and other voluntary organisations. Property might be leased, sold at below a market rate, sold at a market rate, or gifted to an organisation or partnership body. Information is available from the Asset Transfer Unit [see end of **chapter 60**].

Any organisation considering taking on such property should take independent advice about the legal implications, including whether the disposal of the land by the public body is subject to the rules on **state aid** [**48.4.2**].

61.3.5 Mixed use property

Where the property has a residential element, such as retail or office premises with flats above, solicitors should always advise a purchaser whether the occupiers of the flats might have rights of first refusal to buy that interest [**61.14**].

61.3.6 Valuation

A price or rent should generally not be agreed without first obtaining professional valuation advice from a surveyor or a qualified and experienced estate agent. Purchase prices and rents offered are often highly speculative and open to considerable negotiation.

61.3.7 Inspection and survey

The potential purchaser or tenant should undertake a careful and methodical inspection of the property, noting any matters which may need further investigation. These might include, for example, evidence of recent building works which would have needed planning and building regulation approval, a path at the back over which others might have a right of way, evidence that anyone other than the seller is occupying or using the premises and thus might have rights to the premises, the need for rights over other land, such as a fire escape over the roof or other shared facilities, access for people with disabilities [**42.7**], or evidence of the presence of asbestos or other environmentally sensitive materials.

For virtually all freeholds and the majority of leases, the potential purchaser or tenant should have a **structural survey** of the building and land. Where undeveloped land is being developed or a new development is planned, an **environmental survey** [**61.5.7**] should be undertaken.

61.3.7.1 Potential liabilities revealed by the survey

Before doing a survey for a lease or tenancy, the surveyor should have a full copy of the lease, because the terms set out in the lease will affect his or her report. The majority of leases of buildings are **full repairing** leases [**62.2.4**], under which repair can extend to full replacement, for example of a roof. The words '**keep in good repair**' in a lease mean put into good repair and then keep it in that condition. A surveyor can help ensure the potential tenant is fully aware of the condition of the premises and potential costs of repair and maintenance.

In addition, the obligation commonly found in leases requiring a tenant to comply with statutory obligations could result in significant liability for remediation of environmental problems, and/or for provision of access and adaptations for disabled people [**42.7.2**].

If defects are revealed by the survey or the tenant is likely to face significant costs for statutory compliance, a potential tenant or purchaser may seek to require the landlord to carry out repairs or improvements, or may seek a rent-free period, reduction of rent, a **reverse premium** (the landlord or assigning tenant paying a capital sum to the incoming tenant) or a price reduction.

61.4 HEADS OF TERMS

At some stage the seller and purchaser or the landlord and tenant will strike a deal, generally through their solicitors. The main terms may then be set down in a non-binding document called **heads of terms**. This is often drawn up by the agents selling or letting the property. It is very important to get professional advice on heads of terms, because subsequent variation can be difficult.

The *Code for leasing business premises in England and Wales* [see end of **chapter 60**], prepared by organisations representing landlords, tenants and commercial property professionals, is a useful checklist when negotiating a new lease or a renewal. It contains a landlord code, occupier's guide, and model heads of terms.

61.4.1 Freehold

The heads of terms for a freehold purchase are generally very short, consisting of the price, size of deposit and suggested completion date. The completion date may later be varied. Additional terms may be included such as fittings [**60.7.9**], works to be undertaken prior to completion, or events on which completion is conditional [**61.9**].

61.4.2 Lease or tenancy

Heads of terms for a lease or tenancy should be more detailed, with each issue thought about and carefully negotiated. Issues commonly covered are:

- amount of **rent**, what it includes, and length of any rent-free period (if agreement on rent cannot be reached, a compromise may be a low starting rent, stepping up during the period to the first rent review);
- whether there is any restriction on the landlord's right to charge **VAT** on the rent [**57.15.3**];
- **rent reviews**, their timing, whether they are upwards only or reviewable upwards or downwards, and any special methods of review [**62.2.10**];
- length of the **term** of the lease, whether the lease has **security of tenure** under the **Landlord and Tenant Act 1954** ss.24-28 [**60.4.5**], and if so, whether the tenant's right to renew the lease at the end of the term is excluded [**60.4.6**, **62.6**];
- any right of early **termination** [**62.7.2**, **62.7.3**] by the tenant or landlord;
- any restrictions on the tenant's right to **sub-let**, share or assign the lease [**62.2.7**];
- **uses** of the property allowed by the lease [**62.2.5**];
- **additional rights** such as car parking or use of common facilities;
- whether any **repairing obligation** is full [**62.2.4**], internal only, or limited, for example to keeping the property 'wind- and water-tight' or 'in its current condition';
- **service charge**, any limitations on increases, and what it includes [**62.2.3**];
- who will **insure** the property [**23.6.1**, **62.2.6**];
- whether a **deposit** is required as security for performing lease obligations, and if so, conditions for return of the deposit [**62.2.3**];

- who will pay **legal and surveyor's costs**, including costs of the superior landlords (tenants are increasingly resisting attempts to make them pay the landlord's costs);
- desired **time limits** for exchange of contracts or completion;
- **works of repair**, **fitting out** or **alteration** to be carried out by either party before or after completion;
- any **precondition to completion**, such as a grant of planning permission or consent of a superior landlord to change of use;
- **references** to be provided.

If the organisation does not have limited liability [**2.1**], the lease signatories and others on the governing body or in the organisation could be held personally liable. To reduce this risk, a clause can be included in the lease, specifying that the signatories and others are liable only to the extent of the organisation's resources [**60.4.1**]. If an organisation is considering taking on a long lease or one with substantial obligations, this may be the time to consider incorporation [**3.1.1**].

If the organisation has limited liability, the landlord may require a deposit, or a guarantor or guarantors [**62.2.3**]. A guarantor is personally liable if the organisation cannot or will not perform its obligations under the lease.

61.4.3 VAT

VAT rules on property transactions are complex [**57.15**], and advice is essential. Typically the purchase price, premium and/or rent and service charge as specified in the contract or lease are exclusive of VAT. This means that if the transaction is subject to VAT, VAT at the current rate will be added to the stated price or may, at the landlord's option, be added to the rent during a course of the lease.

Charities may be able to require that VAT is not charged on the basis that they are using the property for a relevant charitable purpose [**57.15.3**]. Otherwise, any organisation which cannot recover VAT must be absolutely clear whether VAT will or may be added, and must budget accordingly.

61.5 INVESTIGATING TITLE

One of the key steps which must be taken by a purchaser or tenant to protect itself is the professional examination, by the organisation's solicitor, of the title being proffered in the lease or sale. The solicitor also undertakes other enquiries relating to the property.

61.5.1 Evidence of title

The evidence of title usually consists of official copies of land register entries [**60.6.3**] and documents that the land register refers to. Sometimes there will be additional documents not mentioned on the land register, or matters mentioned in title deeds [**60.6.2**]. The title will indicate any covenants, restrictions or burdensome obligations [**60.7**], any mortgage on the land, any third party's consent needed for the transaction, and other important matters affecting the land.

61.5.2 Enquiries before contract

The purchasing organisation's solicitor raises a series of questions with the seller or landlord. The solicitor should be briefed on any points which are important to the organisation, or which have arisen as a result of their inspection. Where replies from a seller or landlord are uninformative or evasive, the organisation's solicitor should be asked to press for clearer answers.

61.5.3 Local search

A local search is a formal enquiry to the local authority where the land is located. The search reveals what has been registered on the **local land charges register**. This contains a limited amount of information about the property, for example details of some planning permissions, or whether the local authority has a charge over the property for the recovery of an improvement grant. It is not the same as the land charges register [**60.6.4**] or land register [**60.6.3**].

The local search also raises standard questions such as whether there are any notices relating to public health matters or proposed road or rail developments nearby. The enquiries are limited in scope, and do not give information about planning permissions granted for neighbouring property or major local redevelopment. It is important to look carefully at the answers and where necessary to ask the solicitor to seek further information.

A visit to the planning office often reveals more information, so an organisation concerned about local development should visit or ask the solicitor to do so.

61.5.4 Lawful use

The local search will reveal some or all planning permissions [**63.10.1**]. However, many buildings came into use prior to planning legislation, and the search may reveal little. The local authority will generally confirm its view of the current use, but that view has no weight in law.

If required, the authority can be asked to issue a **certificate of lawful use** [**63.10.2**] for an established use, which provides protection for continued use of the land for particular purposes. This is legally conclusive at the time it is issued, being equivalent to a planning permission. However, if the land is not used for this purpose or is used for a different purpose over an extended period, the certificate of lawful use may cease to apply.

Town & Country Planning Act 1990 s.191;
M&M (Land) Ltd v Secretary of State for Communities & Local Government [2007] EWHC 489 (Admin)

The local authority may also provide a history of all planning applications in respect of the property. This usefully reveals what the authority has refused permission for as well as what it has granted.

61.5.5 Building and fire regulations

If the building was recently erected or there is any indication that it has been altered or extended, evidence of compliance with building regulations must be obtained. The previous owner's or landlord's fire risk assessments [**40.8**], surveys and reports on the management of asbestos [**40.7.1**], files relating to compliance with the **Construction (Design and Management) Regulations** [**40.7.4**], and similar records should also be obtained.

For matters involving building regulations or fire safety, there is an overlap of responsibility between the surveyor and the solicitor, and the organisation should be clear who is supposed to resolve outstanding matters in these areas.

61.5.6 Plans

At some stage the solicitor will generally send the potential purchaser or tenant the plans to the property. The organisation should check any plan against its own understanding of what is being sold or let. Plans are a very frequent source of error, partly because it is not standard practice for the solicitor investigating title to visit the site unless specifically requested to do so. The solicitor may thus not have a full idea of what to look out for while investigating title.

61.5.7 Other enquiries

It is now common practice for solicitors to undertake an **environmental search** from an agency that compiles information from various sources. These cover previous environmentally sensitive uses and general environmental conditions; a search confirming availability of public water supply and sewerage facilities; and a **chancel repair search**, to reveal any obligation to contribute to church repairs. If it is known that the site produced hazardous waste, a **hazardous waste search** will be carried out to determine how much hazardous waste the premises have produced in the previous 12 months, and the implications under the **Hazardous Waste Regulations** [**63.12.4**].

If appropriate, the solicitor may also make enquiries to ascertain whether there is any danger of subsidence or flooding, or may check whether any of the land involved is registered as a common. Mining searches may be carried out in areas where there has been coal, tin or other types of mining.

61.5.8 Title insurance

Title insurance may be obtained where the investigation of title has revealed defects in the title, such as a long-ignored covenant preventing land being used for its current purpose. Such insurance may cover any loss in value of the property arising from such defects and/or the cost of defending legal proceedings.

61.6 CONTRACTS AND AGREEMENTS

Prior to exchange of the final contracts [**61.7**] or transfer of the freehold or lease, the parties may enter into a variety of preliminary contracts or agreements.

Contracts for land transactions must be in writing, and legal advice should be taken to ensure proper documentation.   *Law of Property (Miscellaneous Provisions) Act 1989 s.2*

In very limited circumstances, the court may enforce rights over land without a written contract. An example is where by agreement a tenant has started to occupy the property, perhaps paying rent and making improvements, and it would be unfair to allow the landlord to assert that the tenant had no rights because there was nothing in writing. This type of restriction on the exercise of strict legal rights on the grounds of unfairness is known as **proprietary estoppel**. Such a situation can create considerable legal difficulty and should be avoided.

61.6.1 Estate contracts

Instead of an immediate sale or grant of a lease, the parties may enter into a contract for this to happen later (an **estate contract**). The contract may be **absolute**, with the parties bound to put it into effect on a particular date, or **conditional**, with the parties bound to proceed only if a specified event occurs. Such a condition might be outline or detailed planning permission being given for a change of use, or a satisfactory survey. Conditional contracts need very careful drafting so that it is absolutely clear whether the condition has been fulfilled.

61.6.2 Building agreements

A **building agreement** is a form of contract by which the purchaser or prospective tenant agrees with the owner or landlord that following the completion of building works on the site, the property will be sold or a lease granted. The agreement may provide that the owner, a third party, or the purchaser or incoming tenant actually undertakes the building works. It normally contains detailed provisions for the works.

The process of developing land can be undertaken without a building agreement by proceeding straight to the grant of a lease, often referred to as a **building lease**. Under such an arrangement, the incoming tenant is normally obliged to construct, within a strict timetable, a building on the site.

61.6.3 Lockout/exclusivity agreements

A seller may agree with a purchaser not to offer the property to anyone else or hold negotiations for a period. Considerable litigation has occurred about such 'lockout' or exclusivity agreements, and neither party should enter into one without legal advice.

61.7 EXCHANGE OF CONTRACTS

Normally a contract provides for the lease to be granted or the sale to be completed at a later date (the **completion date**), but simultaneous exchange of contracts and completion is not uncommon.

Exchange of contracts generally refers to the date on which the contract binding the parties to enter into the sale or lease comes into force. Typically the contract is drawn up in duplicate, with one copy signed by the seller or landlord and the other (the **counterpart**) signed by the purchaser or tenant. The two copies are then exchanged and dated on the day on which it is agreed that the parties will be henceforth bound.

Prior to that date, correspondence between the parties and their lawyers or agents may be headed **subject to contract**, to ensure that a legally binding contract is not created until the parties have agreed and signed the final agreement.

Since the contract will legally bind the parties, it should not be exchanged until all searches, surveys and enquiries have been undertaken; necessary planning permissions have been obtained, unless the contract is conditional on this; any necessary funding or mortgage has been fully secured, unless the contract is conditional on this; the Charities Act requirements have been complied with [**61.11.1**, **61.12**] if either the purchaser/tenant or seller/landlord is a charity; and property insurance is in place [below].

Contracts normally use or incorporate standard terms, of which the most widely used are set out in the **standard conditions of sale**. These terms cover in detail a very wide range of possibilities.

61.7.1 Insurance

Normal property insurance arrangements need to be put in place for damage or liability to third parties from the time of exchange of contracts until completion of the purchase or taking on the lease. It must be clear whether this is the responsibility of the seller/landlord or the purchaser/prospective tenant.

61.7.2 Deposit

Where a purchase price or premium [**60.4.2**] is to be paid, the contract usually provides for a deposit, typically 10%, to be paid when contracts are exchanged.

An estate agent may seek payment of a small deposit before exchange of contracts. Such payment should not usually be made. If it is made, there should be a clear agreement that it is returnable if the transaction does not go forward.

61.7.3 Late completion or non-completion

If the purchaser or tenant fails to complete as specified in the contract, the seller normally becomes entitled to interest on the purchase price. The potential purchaser or tenant risks losing their deposit and may face a claim for damages.

A failure by the landlord or freeholder to complete may allow the tenant or purchaser to withdraw, or to apply to the court for an order requiring the transaction to be completed (**specific performance**) and damages.

61.7.4 Auctions

In a sale by auction, the contract is made when the auctioneer accepts the highest bid. The contract terms are set out in the auction particulars. All the purchaser's preliminary investigations [**61.3**] will have had to be done prior to bidding.

61.7.5 Options and rights of first refusal

A deed, contract or provision in a lease may give a right or obligation which comes into effect at a later date, for example a right to a grant of a further lease at the end of the first lease, or the right to purchase the reversion [**60.4**] if the landlord ever wishes to sell it. To be fully binding, these rights must be registered on the land register [**60.6.3**], or on the land charges register [**60.6.4**] if the lease is not on the land register. If options are not registered, a third party may not be affected by them.

Options and rights of first refusal need careful drafting, not least because a badly worded option could create a **perpetually renewable lease**.

Law of Property Act 1922 s.145,sch.15

61.8 BEFORE COMPLETION

61.8.1 Searches

If the transaction has to be registered with the Land Registry [**60.6.3**], searches will be made there to ensure there has been no change in the position on the title since copies of the title documents were produced prior to exchange.

61.8.2 Early occupation

Often the parties wish to allow the purchaser or tenant into occupation before completion. This can be done under the terms of the contract or under a separate agreement, normally a licence [**60.5**], or a tenancy at will or short fixed-term lease [**60.4.6**].

Access should not be given or taken unless all the terms have been agreed and in the case of a lease the full wording has been agreed. Resolving any outstanding matters can be extremely difficult once possession has been given.

Where a tenant is assigning or sub-letting, completion may be delayed by the lack of a superior landlord's consent. The current tenant may want to allow the new sub-tenant to move in while waiting for the consent, but if this is done it is likely to be a breach of covenant, entitling the landlord to forfeit (end) the current tenant's lease [**62.4.2**].

61.9 COMPLETION

If a lease, assignment or transfer is required for the completion, it will need to be properly executed [**20.1.3**]. If the property is being purchased with the aid of a mortgage [**61.11**], this will usually be completed simultaneously with completion of the sale or the grant of the lease.

61.9.1 Payment

Completion is normally arranged by telephone, with the monies being sent by post or electronic transfer. Payment is normally by banker's draft or an inter-bank transfer of funds. Only if the amount involved is small might an ordinary cheque be accepted.

At completion of a lease any premium is due, along with the rent and service charge, if any, for the first period, and any required contribution towards insurance. There may also be a contribution towards the landlord's legal costs, sometimes a contribution towards the landlord's surveyor's costs and perhaps also a contribution to one or more superior landlords' costs.

61.10 AFTER COMPLETION

Further procedures must be carried out after the freehold has been transferred or the lease has been granted or transferred.

61.10.1 Stamp duty land tax

Land transactions are generally subject to **stamp duty land tax** unless they involve a licence to use or occupy land [**60.5**] or a tenancy at will [**60.4.6**], or are otherwise exempt from SDLT. Information about SDLT is available from HM Revenue and Customs [see end of **chapter 60**].

For many land transactions, a **land transaction return** must be filed with HMRC by the purchaser or tenant at the time of the land transaction. When the return has been processed, HMRC issues a **land transaction return certificate**. This is needed to register the transaction at the Land Registry [**60.6.3**]. The SDLT has to be paid within 30 days of the **effective date** (the date the transaction comes into effect).

If a purchaser takes possession of all or nearly all the property or pays a substantial amount of the consideration for the property, the transaction needs to be notified and SDLT can become payable at this point even if the land is not transferred or the lease granted until a later date. At that later date, further notification is required and additional SDLT may become payable.

61.10.1.1 SDLT relief for charities

There are various reliefs from stamp duty land tax, including if the purchaser is a charity and it intends to hold the land for **qualifying charitable purposes**. This means that it will be used only in furtherance of the charitable purposes of the purchaser or of another charity, or will be held as an investment from which all the profits are applied to the charitable purposes of the purchaser.

Finance Act 2003 s.68, sch.8

Even if eligible for relief from SDLT, the charity may still be obliged to make a land transaction return, and will be liable for a penalty if it is not made on time.

SDLT becomes chargeable if a **disqualifying event** occurs within three years beginning with the effective date of the transaction, or in connection with arrangements made before the end of that period. A disqualifying event occurs if the purchaser ceases to be established for charitable purposes only, or if the property, or any interest or right derived from it, is used or held by the purchaser for anything other than qualifying charitable purposes.

If a lease is assigned to another party which is not itself exempt from SDLT, the new tenant will be liable for SDLT as if the assignment were a new lease.

Finance Act 2003 sch.17A para.11, as amended

61.10.2 Land registration

Where the transaction involves registered land or the creation of a registrable interest in land, the Land Registry must be notified [**60.6.3**].

61.10.3 Notification to landlord

In some cases, typically where a sub-lease or underlease is being granted or a lease is being assigned, there may be an obligation to notify the superior landlord formally about the details of the transaction, and to pay a small fee.

61.10.4 Safe storage

Finally, any original documents must be stored safely. Frequently the solicitor arranges this. The organisation should retain a complete set of copies for its records, and keep a note of where the originals are stored. The organisation should also retain copies of Land Registry entries, and planning and other consents.

61.11 MORTGAGES AND CHARGES

A **mortgage** or **charge** [**59.5.1**] is a security against property. The security may be for a loan or another obligation, such as an agreement to repay grant funding if an organisation defaults on the grant conditions.

Mortgages or charges must be registered at the Land Registry. Companies and industrial and provident societies which mortgage or charge land must register the charge within 21 days with, respectively, Companies House [**18.5.11**] or Mutual Societies Registration [**18.6.4**]. Charitable incorporated organisations (CIOs) will have to register mortgages and charges with the Charity Commission.

61.11.1 Charities and mortgages

Prior to using land as security for the repayment of a loan, security for repayment in default of grant conditions (sometimes called **clawback**), or security for any purchase, a registered or excepted [**8.1.3**] charity must obtain and consider proper written advice about the charge. If advice is not taken, land held by or for a charity can be mortgaged only by order of the court or Charity Commission. Exempt charities [**8.1.2**] do not have a statutory obligation under charity law to take advice, but it is likely to be advisable to do so and may be required under other law.

Charities Act 1993 s.38, amended by Charities Act 2006 s.27

The advice must be in writing from a person who has no financial interest in the loan or grant, and who the trustees reasonably believe to be qualified by his or her ability and practical experience in financial matters. In the case of a loan or grant, the advice must consider whether the loan or grant is necessary to enable the charity to carry out the particular course of action for which the loan is sought, whether the terms of the proposed loan or grant are reasonable, and whether the charity has the ability to repay the loan or grant on those terms.

In any other case, for example where there is a mortgage to secure a right to share a proportion of the eventual sale proceeds of the property, the advice must consider whether it is reasonable for the charity trustees to undertake to discharge the obligation, having regard to charity's purposes.

A mortgage may be extended to cover additional sums subsequently secured on the same property, for example if additional money is borrowed. The charity trustees must not undertake any such liability unless they have first considered advice as above.

Advice is not necessary if the charity has special or general authority under statute to mortgage its property [**59.1**], for example the right of registered social landlords to enter into transactions.   *Housing Act 1996 s.8*

61.11.1.1   Statement on mortgage documents

For all charities, including exempt charities [**8.1.2**], the loan document must state that the land is held by or in trust for a charity; whether the charity is an exempt charity; whether the charity has special or general authority to take out the loan or grant; and if the charity is not an exempt charity and does not have special or general authority, that it has obtained an order of the court or the Charity Commission or has taken and considered advice as required. A loan to a charity which does not comply with these conditions may in some circumstances not be valid or enforceable.   *Charities Act 1993 s.39, amended by Land Registration Act 2002 s.133,sch.11*

61.12   DISPOSAL OF CHARITY LAND

Non-charities are governed only by their governing document, company law duties if applicable, and the general law in selling, leasing or disposing of land, but charities must comply with special rules. Charity Commission booklet CC28 *Sales, leases, transfers or mortgages: What trustees need to know about disposing of charity land* sets out the basic requirements.

61.12.1   Power to dispose of land

Trustees must be satisfied that the charity has power to dispose of land. This may be explicit in the governing document [**7.4.5**], or be implied within a general power in the governing document [**7.4.3**]. In the case of charitable trusts, such a power may be implied by statute.   *Trusts of Land & Appointment of Trustees Act 1996 s.6(1)*

Even where the governing document includes power or it can be implied by statute, there may be specific restrictions on certain types of transaction.

Unless charity trustees are certain they have the necessary power, an experienced solicitor or the Charity Commission should be consulted. A Charity Commission scheme [**4.5.5**] may be necessary to authorise the transaction.

61.12.2   Connected persons

A registered or excepted [**8.1.3**] charity's land (including a lease) can be sold, leased or otherwise disposed of to a charity trustee or other **connected person** only if the Charity Commission or court is satisfied it is in the best interests of the charity and makes an order [**4.5.4**] allowing it. Without such consent, the disposition is voidable (can be invalidated) or may be void from the start, even if the trustee retires from her or his post before the disposal.   *Charities Act 1993 s.36(1)*

The definition of connected person in this context is different from other definitions under charity and company law [**15.2.5**].

61.12.3   Leases of seven years or less

If a registered or excepted charity is granting a lease of not more than seven years to a **non-connected** person [15.2.5] and is not asking for a premium or fine [60.4.2], it does not need to get an order provided that prior to entering the lease or agreement for the lease, the governing body obtains and considers the advice of a person they reasonably believe to have the requisite ability and practical experience to provide them with competent advice on the proposed lease; and having considered the advice, they are satisfied that the terms of the lease are the best that can reasonably be obtained.   *Charities Act 1993 s.36(5)*

61.12.4   Other dispositions of land

A registered or excepted charity may grant a lease for longer than seven years, sell or otherwise dispose of land without a court or Charity Commission order only if the disposition is to a non-connected person [15.2.5], and the trustees have obtained and considered a surveyor's written report prior to the exchange of contracts, have advertised the property as advised by the surveyor, and are satisfied that the terms of the sale or lease are the best that can reasonably be obtained.
                                                                    Charities Act 1993 s.36(3)

The surveyor must be a fellow or professional associate of the Royal Institution of Chartered Surveyors (RICS) or the Incorporated Society of Valuers and Auctioneers. The trustees must reasonably believe the surveyor has the ability and experience to undertake a valuation of this particular sort of land and the particular area in question.   *Charities Act 1993 s.36(4)*

The surveyor must act exclusively for the charity and must prepare a written report complying with detailed regulations.   *Charities (Qualified Surveyors' Reports)*
                                                              Regulations 1992 [SI 1992/2980]

Unless the surveyor advises otherwise, the trustees must advertise the proposed sale or lease in the manner specified in the report.

If the trustees do not comply with the requirements for a surveyor's report and advertising, or do not feel the terms are the best they can reasonably obtain, they must obtain a Charity Commission or court order before selling or leasing the property. The Commission is unlikely to make an order without very good reason.

61.12.5   Exceptional situations

An order need not be obtained before a disposition by a registered or excepted charity:

- where a sale is made under any court order, Act of Parliament or specially established scheme;
- where a lease is granted at less than the best rent to a beneficiary of a charity, for the purposes of the charity (for example, a charity for elderly people providing low-rent housing for their beneficiaries); or
- where the disposition is made by one charity to another charity, the first charity is not seeking to transact on the best terms reasonably obtainable, and the objects and powers of the first charity permit such a disposition.
                                                                    Charities Act 1993 s.36(9)

These exceptions *do not* mean that a charity can automatically let or sell at below market value to any other person or charity. This can be done only if it is clear that a transaction on such a basis furthers the interests of the charity.

61.12.6   Special trusts

Land held on trusts (conditions) which stipulate that it must be used for the purposes or a particular purpose of a charity is called **specie land**. Where specie land is being disposed of, the trustees must generally place public notices before the exchange of contracts, giving the opportunity for representations to be made for at least one month. This requirement does not apply if the property being sold or leased will be replaced with other property which will be held on the same trusts, or is being let for not more than two years, or is being disposed of under the exceptional situations mentioned above.   *Charities Act 1993 s.36(6),(7)*

61.12.7 Other requirements

Disposals by registered social landlords, parish or community councils, schools, churches and certain other organisations are covered by specific legislation, as are disposals of open spaces.

61.13 DISPOSAL OF PERMANENT ENDOWMENT

Permanent endowment is property where either the property can be sold but the proceeds of sale must be retained as capital and not spent, or where there is a **special trust** requiring the property to be used indefinitely for a specific purpose. The Charity Commission may in either case relax, amend or remove such requirements. The circumstances in which this may be possible are explained in guidance on the Charity Commission website.

61.14 DISPOSAL OF MIXED-USE PREMISES

Where at least half of the square footage of a property consists of residential flats (for example where there are flats above commercial premises), and at least half of those flats are occupied on leases for more than 21 years, right to buy leases, or tenancies still protected under the **Rent Act 1977**, then it is likely that before there is a disposal of the freehold of the building (or other specified interests) it must be first offered for sale to the tenants. A failure to give a right of first refusal to the tenants is an offence, and gives the tenants a right to require the actual purchaser to re-convey the freehold to the tenants for the same price that the purchaser paid for it.

Landlord & Tenant Act 1987 ss.1-20

61.15 REVERSION OF SITES

Sites donated under the **School Sites Act 1841**, **Literary and Scientific Institutions Act 1854** or **Places of Worship Sites Act 1873** are subject to special rules under which the land, even if owned by the organisation, is held in trust for the donor or his/her estate. This means that if the land ceases to be used for the original purpose for which it was donated, the donor or estate has forever a claim on the proceeds of any sale of the land (but not on the land itself).

Trustees of charities whose land could have been donated under one of these Acts should take specialist advice before changing the use of the property – even if it is to be used for a similar charitable purpose – or selling the land. *Reverter of Sites Act 1987; Fraser & another v Canterbury Diocesan Board of Finance & others [2005] UKHL 65*

Resources: ACQUIRING AND DISPOSING OF PROPERTY

See end of **chapter 60**.

Statute law. www.opsi.gov.uk and www.statutelaw.gov.uk.

Much but not all case law. www.bailii.org.

Updates cross-referenced to this book. www.rclh.co.uk.

Chapter 62
BUSINESS LEASES

*For sources of further information see end of **chapter 60**.*

62.1   BEFORE ENTERING INTO A LEASE

Leases are technical legal documents and the tenant and landlord should each seek advice before entering into one. For the process of entering into a lease, see **chapter 61**. The *Code for leasing business premises in England and Wales* [**61.4**] provides a framework for lease negotiations.

Leases are prepared by landlords in a way that protects themselves, but the terms are negotiable and tenants should be wary of unsuitable or unfair terms. They should also ensure that any promise or assurance previously given by the landlord or its agent is explicitly incorporated into the lease.

Many leases on offer for offices are on **full repairing and insuring** terms (FRI). The tenants pay all the costs arising from the premises, either directly through their obligations to keep the building in repair, decorated and clean, or indirectly through service charges or other obligations to contribute towards costs incurred by the landlord. Before entering into a lease or tenancy agreement, organisations need to be fully aware of the potential costs over the duration of the lease, and during preliminary negotiations should seek to persuade the landlord to limit the extent of these liabilities.

62.2   A TYPICAL LEASE

There is no standard wording or layout for leases, although the code for leasing business premises [above] sets out a framework that many landlords now follow. The typical contents of an office lease are outlined here.

62.2.1   Introductory matters

The first part of the lease includes the date and details of the landlord, tenant and any guarantor [**62.2.3.5**]. If the landlord is not the freeholder, the lease may be called a sub-lease or underlease [**60.4.4**].

62.2.1.1   Definitions

The **definitions** section is very important, because words are sometimes defined in an unusual or far-reaching way which has important effects on clauses later in the lease. Defined words are likely to start with a capital letter in the lease, to show that they are being used in the specific way defined in this section.

62.2.1.2   Interpretation

Particularly important in the **interpretation** section is the typical provision that two or more tenants are **jointly and severally** (separately) **liable**. This means that each tenant is individually liable for all the obligations, without any obligation on the landlord to pursue any of the other joint tenants [**22.2.3**].

62.2.1.3   Term and extent of premises

The length of the lease, the formal words by which the landlord grants the lease to the tenant, and the definition of the property granted (usually described as 'the Premises') are often included in the same clause.

A more detailed description of the property may be included in a schedule attached to the lease, or the description may refer to an attached plan. Plans for a lease that is compulsorily registrable at the Land Registry [**60.6.3**] must be as far as possible to scale (1:500 to 1:1250 for urban properties), accurately show the position and extent of the property including unclear boundaries, and include a north point. At the time of writing (mid 2009) this includes leases for a term of more than seven years, but is likely in future to be extended to shorter leases. Plans are a frequent source of error and should be carefully checked.

62.2.1.4   Rights, exceptions and reservations

These sections will generally specify the rights granted to the tenant, and that the grant is subject to certain exceptions and the reservation of benefits for the landlord, particularly where the landlord owns adjacent property. The details are often set out in a schedule. Rights typically granted to the tenant include a right of way, rights over escape routes, a right of support from adjoining buildings, use of common facilities such as toilets and lifts, use of parking or loading spaces, rights of running pipes and wiring, and right of access to the landlord's neighbouring property in order to undertake inspection or repair to the premises.

Common law implies that the tenant gets the benefit of any rights enjoyed by the premises at the time the lease is taken on. But most modern leases exclude this implication, so all necessary rights, however obvious they may seem, should be spelled out.

An **exceptions and reservations** clause prevents the tenant getting the benefit of rights which might otherwise be implied, and gives rights to the landlord.

Rights excepted from the tenant typically include the right of light [**60.7.2**]. Excepting the right of light gives the landlord the right to develop adjoining premises. Rights reserved to the landlord typically include the right to run pipes and wiring through the premises, and right of access to the premises in order to inspect or do works to the landlord's adjacent property.

62.2.1.5   Rent

The rent payable under the lease is also usually included in the initial clause or clauses. In addition to the normal rent, a modern lease is likely to reserve as rent all other sums due from the tenant to the landlord under the lease, for example the service charge or a contribution to insurance or business rates. A landlord can use special methods such as **distress** (also called **distraint**) to recover unpaid rent, so it is in the landlord's interest to define all monies as rent.

When **commercial rent arrears recovery** (CRAR) [**62.4.3**] replaces distress (expected April 2012), it will apply only to actual rent, and not to other payments such as service charges. Where these are included in a total 'rent', CRAR will apply only to the amount that reasonably relates to possession of the premises.

Tribunals, Courts & Enforcement Act 2007 s.76 [expected 1/4/12]

However, it may be easier for the landlord to forfeit (terminate) the lease if sums reserved as rent are not paid than to go through the CRAR procedure, so it is in the landlord's interest to ensure that all monies are technically defined as rent, even if they would not conventionally be thought of in that way.

62.2.1.6   Premium or fine

Some leases require the tenant to pay a capital sum, known as a **premium** or **fine**, for the grant of the lease. This may happen where the lease is being granted for a long period, or there is a great demand for the particular premises and the landlord seeks an immediate cash payment. It may also happen where the lease has a rent below market rent, either intentionally where the landlord seeks only a nominal rent, or on assignment because upward movement of rents since the last rent review means rent is below the current market level.

If the premises are in poor condition or the rent is over the market level, the tenant may require a payment to move in – a **reverse premium** – as compensation, or may negotiate a rent-free period.

62.2.2   Tenant's covenants

The longest section in the lease is generally the **covenants** (promises) by the tenant. Typical covenants cover rent and other payments, maintenance and repair, use of the premises, restrictions on disposal of the lease, and insurance. In these covenants the landlord may seek to ensure that every possible obligation, cost or liability which arises is the responsibility of the tenant.

In addition to the covenants listed here, there may be a host of other restrictions or requirements. This is because, in general, a tenant will be able to do what it wants to with the premises unless an act is specifically excluded. Every lease, and every clause in it, needs careful consideration.

62.2.2.1   Limitation of liability

A tenant's liability is generally unlimited. A tenant which does not have limited liability [**2.1**] may seek to limit liability to the extent of the assets of the organisation [**22.7.5**], so that lease signatories or members of the organisation's governing body do not become personally liable. Landlords are likely to be reluctant to agree this, and may require a **guarantor** [**62.2.3.5**] or **deposit 62.2.3.6**]. Organisations should resist pressure to provide personal guarantors, and anyone asked to be a guarantor should refuse, or take independent legal advice before agreeing.

62.2.3   Rent and other payments

The tenant's first covenant is usually to pay the rent or reviewed rent [**62.2.10**] specified in the lease. The landlord's right to charge VAT may be mentioned here and/or in a separate clause [**62.2.3.4**]. Other clauses will detail other sums payable by the tenant, such as business rates, water charges, a share of insurance, service charge, taxes and other outgoings. These clauses are often very wide in scope, and tenants may find themselves liable for large sums in addition to rent.

Special tax provisions may apply when rent is paid to a landlord based overseas. Information is available from the local office of HM Revenue and Customs.

62.2.3.1   Service charge

The **service charge** clause will deal with what the service charge includes and how it is calculated, whether the tenant must make interim payments before the full cost is known, whether interest is charged if the landlord borrows money to finance works covered under the service charge, and what accounts and evidence of the expenditure are to be provided to the tenant.

The clause will indicate whether there is a **cap** (limit) on the annual amount payable. This may say, for example, that service charge will not increase by more than, say, the retail price index, or particular items of major repair may be excluded. Unless so specified, there is no limit on future increases. If this is the case, the clause needs to be considered particularly carefully to ensure it is reasonable. In the absence of a reasonable cap, major repairs or renovations such as re-roofing or a new lift can result in a huge service charge.

The Royal Institution of Chartered Surveyors' code on commercial property service charges [see end of **chapter 60**] provides a framework for good practice in setting and managing service charges in business leases.

62.2.3.2   Sinking fund

Some leases provide for the landlord to set a service charge of more than is spent, and place the balance in a **reserve fund** or **sinking fund** to cover large occasional costs such as lift replacement or re-roofing. If this is not done, a tenant at the time of major repairs may have to bear its share of the full cost of a large repair, even though its lease is short or about to expire.

To protect themselves, tenants should have a full survey done so that potential major repairs are highlighted [**61.3.7**], or seek limitation on the maximum service charge liability. They should also seek to ensure that this fund is held **on trust**, so that it cannot be used for any other purposes, and if the landlord goes into liquidation the funds are not available to meet the demands of its creditors.

62.2.3.3   Landlord's costs

The clause on landlord's costs typically obliges the tenant to pay, in a variety of situations, not only the landlord's solicitor's costs but also the costs of surveyors and other experts, and court and bailiffs' fees. The tenant should seek to limit obligations and at least try to agree to pay only 'reasonable and proper costs'.

62.2.3.4   VAT

Modern leases generally explicitly state that VAT is payable in addition to any other sums [**61.4.3**]. Generally for non-residential accommodation the landlord is free to elect to charge VAT at any time, unless the tenant manages to agree a specific provision preventing this or the tenant is a charity using the premises for a relevant charitable purpose [**57.15.3**]. If charged, VAT will be added to the rent.

62.2.3.5   Guarantors

In many situations a landlord will be reluctant to grant a lease to a body with limited liability [**3.1.1**] or limited assets without some sort of guarantee of the tenant's obligations, or other security.

A **guarantor** has been described as **a fool with a pen**, because the role is potentially extremely onerous and once taken on cannot normally be terminated. In most cases the guarantor has no control over potential liabilities, nor is there any obligation for the guarantor to be kept informed as they arise. In addition to an obligation to meet the rent – which may increase substantially during the term – the guarantor will be obliged to honour the tenant's other obligations, including obligations for repairs and even a possible obligation to rebuild the entire premises [**62.2.4**]. Guarantors should therefore be separately advised from the tenant about the implications of the obligations they are taking on.

It has become increasingly common for tenants to refuse to provide guarantors, and to provide a rent deposit [**62.2.3.6**] instead. It is particularly inappropriate for individuals to guarantee the liabilities of voluntary organisations.

62.2.3.6   Deposits

An alternative to guarantors which may be more attractive from a tenant's point of view and has some advantages for a landlord is a **deposit**. This is often referred to as a **rent deposit** but the wording generally provides that the deposit is available to meet any claim by the landlord under the lease. Issues which need to be agreed are the amount of the deposit, whether it is increased when rent is increased at rent review, whether there is a time limit on the deposit after which the tenant is entitled to its return, and what happens to the deposit if the lease is assigned. *Landlord & Tenant (Covenants) Act 1995 ss.5-8*

The tenant should seek to ensure that the deposit is held by the landlord on trust [**62.2.3.2**].

62.2.4 Maintenance, repair and alteration

The repair clause needs to be read carefully, in conjunction with the definition of the premises [**62.2.1.3**] and the terms of the lease as a whole, to see exactly what falls within the tenant's obligation to repair. The clause may, for example, oblige the tenant 'to repair, renew, replace and rebuild'. This could require a tenant who rents a building in unsound condition to replace it completely if ordinary repairs are not possible.

The phrase 'to **keep in good repair**' is often misunderstood. It is in fact an example of a **full repairing lease**, and creates an obligation to put the premises into good repair even if they were in poor repair when they were taken over.

A repairing clause may be moderated by excluding liability for **fair wear and tear** or **inherent defects**, such as faults in the original design.

If the tenant is only required to keep the building in no better condition than it was in at the start of the lease, a schedule describing the original state of disrepair should be prepared. This often includes a survey prepared by a surveyor, usually supported by photographs.

It is usual for a lease to include a clause that if the tenant does not carry out works of repair etc, the landlord can enter the premises to carry out the works on the tenant's behalf, and recover the cost of doing so from the tenant.

Associated with, although technically separate from, the repairing clause is the obligation usually found in leases to give back the premises to the landlord in a **good state of repair** [**62.4.4**].

62.2.4.1 Shared facilities

The tenant is likely to be required to pay a share of the repair, rebuilding or replacement costs for any shared facility such as party walls, drains or access road. If it is agreed that the service charge should be capped, the tenant should ensure that this type of potential cost is also included within the cap.

62.2.4.2 Fitting out

The landlord may seek to oblige the tenant to fit out the premises for use or to make improvements. A tenant must ensure that the cost of this is covered by a reduced initial rent or rent-free period or, where appropriate, that any increase in rent following a rent review will be based on the value of the premises disregarding some or all of the improvements.

62.2.4.3 Decoration

A decoration clause requires the tenant to redecorate some or all of the premises, usually with differing timescales for the interior and exterior. The landlord's consent may be required to change the colour or to make other decorating changes.

62.2.4.4 Alterations

The lease may totally prohibit alterations, or allow some degree of freedom, for example to install non-structural partitions. If the lease requires the landlord's consent, the landlord is under a statutory duty not to withhold consent unreasonably, but the landlord is likely to require the tenant to pay all the costs associated with the consent. If surveyors or engineers are involved, these costs can be significant. It is therefore best to get any consent for the work written into the lease. *Landlord & Tenant Act 1927 s.19(2)*

In limited circumstances there is a statutory right to carry out alterations even if these are absolutely prohibited by the lease, provided that a defined procedure is followed by the tenant. *Landlord & Tenant Act 1927 ss.1-3*

62.2.4.5 Compliance with statute

The lease generally requires the tenant to comply with a range of statutes such as the **Health and Safety at Work Act**, **Disability Discrimination Act** and any orders or notices delivered by statutory authorities. This could involve the tenant in very expensive works such as installing an external fire escape, upgrading fire alarms, or improving access for people with disabilities. The likelihood of such costs arising should be investigated before taking the lease [**61.3.6**].

62.2.4.6 Planning permission

Normally the tenant is allowed to apply for planning permission only with the landlord's consent. If such consent is likely to be needed immediately, it should be dealt with before the lease is granted. If it is likely to be needed in future, an exception should be added to the clause to allow such an application.

62.2.4.7 Access

The landlord will want rights of access to the premises for various purposes. The tenant needs to consider whether these are reasonable. If possible, rights should be restricted to circumstances where it is absolutely essential for the landlord to have access.

62.2.5 Use of premises

The **user clause** limits the ways in which the premises may be used. The uses must be wide enough to include all of the tenant's activities not only at the start of the tenancy but at any time during its likely length including any renewal, as well as use by potential assignees or sub-tenants.

If the tenant may want to move before the end of the lease and cannot surrender the lease (return it to the landlord), it will have to try to find someone to take an assignment [**62.2.7**]. If the permitted use is very narrow, it is likely to be difficult to find an assignee. Tenants who might be in this situation should seek to include a wide permitted use in the lease.

User clauses may allow additional or alternative uses with the landlord's consent. Except in limited cases the landlord cannot require payment of money as a condition of giving such consent.   *Landlord & Tenant Act 1927 s.19(3)*

62.2.5.1 Permitted use and the rent review

If the rent is to be reviewed by reference to market rents [**62.2.10**], it is normally assumed that the use permitted is that allowed by the lease. If the use permitted is very narrow, the market rent will generally be lower; if it is wide, the market rent will be higher.

Some rent review clauses require the valuer to assume that the premises are available for any use or a variety of uses specified in the rent review clause, rather than those specified in the tenant's covenant. In this case, there is no advantage for the tenant in accepting a narrow user clause.

62.2.5.2 Regulations

For a building which has multiple occupants or for buildings forming part of an estate, a landlord frequently reserves the right to impose additional detailed rules for the good management of the estate. This may be reasonable if the rules are limited to those necessary for good estate management.

62.2.6 Indemnity and insurance

An indemnity clause generally requires the tenant to pay costs or losses arising out of any claim within the premises, for example a claim arising from a person being injured on the stairs. The tenant should take out appropriate insurances [**chapter 23**]. The requirements may be very wide, and the tenant should seek written confirmation from its broker that its insurances cover all the liabilities.

62.2.6.1 Buildings insurance

Generally the lease requires the ground and building – but not the tenant's contents or fittings – to be insured by the landlord, who will then require the tenant to contribute a share of the insurance premium. The lease may prohibit the tenant from insuring the building, in order to protect the landlord against its own insurers refusing to pay on a claim on the grounds that the tenant's insurers should meet the claim.

However, even where the landlord has taken on an obligation to insure, it may have insured against only limited risks, such as fire and flood. A tenant who is obliged to put and keep the building in repair would then find itself liable if the building is damaged through an uninsured risk, such as a car crashing into it.

To avoid this happening, the lease should specify that the landlord is obliged to insure the building against all normal risks, or should not prevent the tenant from insuring the building. The tenant should insist on seeing the landlord's insurance [**23.6.1**], and should consider what is covered and what remains uninsured. If some risks are uninsured, the tenant needs to consider insuring against these. The tenant should also seek to ensure that the lease obliges the landlord to inform the tenant of any change in the insurance provision.

The lease is likely to oblige the tenant to comply with the landlord's insurer's requirements. These may involve purchasing equipment or making modifications to the premises. The lease will forbid doing or allowing anyone to do anything which invalidates the insurance.

62.2.6.2 Uninsured risks

A landlord may decide not to insure against certain risks because of the cost, or insurance may not be available to cover certain risks. Insurance against flood damage, for example, may not be available in a flood plain area. A tenant with a full repairing lease could find itself liable for substantial repairs or even a complete rebuilding, unless the lease excludes its liability for all or part of the costs of repairs or rebuilding in these situations. Tenants should take specialist advice about appropriate lease clauses to ensure they do not become liable for major uninsured or uninsurable losses.

Under the Commercial Landlords Accreditation Scheme code of practice, tenants are entitled to terminate their lease if the premises become unusable after damage caused by an uninsurable risk. However, this applies only if the landlord is a member of the scheme and uses its logo.

62.2.6.3 Rent during rebuilding

The tenant remains liable to pay rent even if the building is destroyed or uninhabitable, unless the lease contains a proviso suspending or waiving rent in these circumstances. The waiver period is generally limited to two or three years, and will be covered by insurance taken out by the landlord. If there is no waiver of rent, the tenant should take out insurance to cover the rent during any period of liability when the building is uninhabitable.

62.2.7 Assignment

If there is no restriction in the lease, the tenant is free to assign, sub-let, underlet or mortgage the property without any consents [**60.4.4**]. However, most leases impose some restrictions.

62.2.7.1 Assignment and sub-letting

The tenant may be prevented from sharing the premises, or from assigning or underletting part of them. Without this restriction, the landlord could end up with a multiplicity of tenants if the original tenant went into liquidation or did not renew the lease of the whole premises. Landlords are more likely to agree to sharing or sub-letting if the sub-tenant is not given security of tenure [**60.4.6**] or if the sub-tenant is a branch or subsidiary of the tenant.

A tenant may have a right to assign the whole and perhaps also to underlet the whole. Generally only in short leases or in special circumstances are these rights excluded. However, the landlord's consent is generally required to such assignment or sub-let [below].

The lease frequently includes detailed provisions designed to provide additional protection for the landlord following assignment, such as the right to require the new tenant to provide guarantors or a deposit and to enter into direct covenants with the landlord.

62.2.7.2 Landlord's consent

If a covenant requires the landlord's consent for assignment or sub-letting, the law implies that the consent should not be unreasonably withheld, and the landlord must give its decision within a reasonable time. *Landlord & Tenant Act 1927 s.19; Landlord & Tenant Act 1988 s.1(3)*

Case law on what is 'reasonable' in giving consent generally turns on whether the landlord's neighbouring properties or its reversionary interest in the property [**60.4**] will be affected, and whether the proposed tenant is a responsible or respectable person or organisation capable of meeting the financial obligations on the part of the tenant under the lease.

In relation to time, landlords should generally make a decision within days or weeks, rather than waiting months. *NCR v Riverland Portfolio No.1 Ltd [2005] EWCA Civ 312*

An assignment or sub-letting which requires the landlord's consent but takes place without it is legally valid. However, the breach of the covenant to obtain consent means the landlord can terminate the lease or apply to court for the lease to be re-transferred to the original tenant.

62.2.7.3 Authorised guarantee agreement

The lease may require a tenant who subsequently assigns the lease to provide an **authorised guarantee agreement** [**60.4.4**]. If such an agreement is in place, the tenant is liable for defaults by its assignee.

62.2.7.4 Mortgage

If the premises are being let at less than market rent because a fine or premium has been paid [**62.2.1.6**], or if inflation in market rents subsequently leaves the lease rent behind, the lease is a valuable asset which the tenant may wish to charge as security for borrowings.

But landlords may put restrictions on the property being mortgaged or charged, because if they decide to forfeit the lease [**62.2.11**] they may face the prospect of the person holding the charge applying to the court to reverse the forfeiture in order to preserve their security. Whether this restriction is important depends on whether the lease has a value on the open market.

If the tenant is contemplating charging or mortgaging the property, the forfeiture provisions need to be examined carefully. These are often worded in a way which renders the lease worthless as security for a charge.

62.2.8 Break clause

A **break clause** gives the tenant, the landlord or either of them the right to terminate the lease before expiry, on giving the specified period of notice. Organisations are often persuaded by property agents that if the tenant has a break option, the landlord should have one too. This may appear logical but can put the tenant at a significant disadvantage.

Whether it is fair for the tenant to have a break clause at all will depend on the surrounding circumstances, particularly lease terms such as the length of the term, the existence of rent review provisions and the extent of the tenant's rights to assign the lease or sub-let.

Whether or not the landlord can successfully exercise its break clause might also depend upon consideration of whether the lease is a **protected business lease** [**60.4.5**].

Legal advice should always be taken when considering how to exercise a break clause. Break clauses often have to be exercised within strict time limits, so it is vital that diary arrangements are in place and that all lease conditions relating to giving notice are strictly observed.

62.2.9 Landlord's covenants

In contrast to the tenant's covenants, the landlord's covenants are often very brief, frequently no more than allowing the tenant peacefully to enjoy occupation of the premises [below]. But they may include a variety of other obligations.

Where such obligations are included, the landlord may wish to qualify them. This might be done, for example, by making its obligations dependent on the tenant not only paying the rent but also observing the other terms of the lease; by expressing its obligations not in the absolute terms normally imposed on tenants but in terms such as 'use reasonable endeavours'; or by limiting the obligations to the period in which the landlord owns the reversion [**60.4**], thus escaping liability if it assigns its reversionary interest. If the landlord is an unincorporated organisation, it may limit the personal liability of the lease signatories and members of the governing body to the amount of the organisation's assets [**22.7.5**].

Under a **full repairing and insuring lease**, the landlord seeks to ensure that it is able to recover from the tenant all the costs of complying with its own obligations, so that its rental income is not eroded by the rising costs of compliance.

62.2.9.1 Quiet enjoyment

A covenant for **quiet enjoyment** prevents the landlord from physically interfering with the property or harassing the tenant [**61.2.2**]. The right of quiet enjoyment can be limited, for example if the landlord makes clear that someone else has a right of way over the land.

62.2.9.2 Insurance

Leases generally provide for the landlord to insure the premises. The tenant should ensure that the landlord's obligation to insure is wide enough to cover all likely occurrences [**62.2.6**].

Where the tenant is liable for repairs [**62.2.4**] it must be absolutely clear whose insurance covers repairs caused by damage to or destruction of the building. This clause should include a proviso that the tenant is not liable for rent or repair if the landlord receives a compensatory payment from its own insurer.

Tenants negotiating leases should ensure that they have a right to copies of relevant insurance policies held by the landlord [**23.6.1**].

62.2.9.3 Destruction of premises

One issue which may be covered in a lease is what happens if, following destruction of the premises, the landlord cannot or does not wish to reconstruct the premises. The landlord generally seeks to include a provision that it has a right to all the insurance money. The tenant needs to consider whether it should be entitled to a share – which will be the case if the tenant has paid a premium – and if so, should seek to include a provision for fair shares to be decided by an independent arbitrator. A right for the tenant to surrender the lease or for the landlord to terminate if the premises are destroyed may also be included.

If the premises are going to be rebuilt, the lease should allow for waiver of rent during the rebuilding (and the landlord's insurance should cover this), or the tenant should take our insurance to cover the rent [**62.2.6.3**].

62.2.9.4 Repairs

Unless the tenant has taken on all the obligations of repairing the building [**62.2.4**], the tenant will be dependent on the landlord carrying out works to common parts, the main structure, roofs, accessories etc. It is very important for the landlord's obligations for such repairs to be spelled out in appropriate detail. If this obligation is not written in it will only rarely be implied, and the tenant may have no right to make a claim for losses caused by lack of repair.

62.2.9.5 Management and other services

Particularly in multiple occupancy buildings, the tenant may be dependent on the landlord for a range of other services, including cleaning, lighting and heating common parts, reception, common kitchens, toilets and a variety of other facilities. A clear obligation on the landlord to provide these needs to be included.

62.2.10 Rent review

Many leases, particularly those for more than three to five years, contain provisions for the rent to be reviewed. This may be in the form of a **review to market rent [62.3]**. Alternatively the lease may link the new rent to an indicator such as the retail price index (RPI) or the turnover or profitability of the tenant, or simply provide for a fixed percentage increase. The implications of any such indicator need careful consideration. The RPI, for example, has on occasion increased much faster than commercial rents.

For voluntary organisations, the tenant's funding may dictate the sort of reviews it can accept. It may be essential for it to negotiate for the right to surrender [**62.7.3**] if the rent is reviewed to a level it can no longer afford. Landlords generally resist such rights if they can.

A key issue in a rent review clause is whether the review is **upwards only**, requiring the new rent to be the same as or higher than the current rent, or is **reviewable either way**, allowing for a lower rent if market rents have dropped.

62.2.10.1 Assumptions for the review

Where rent is to be reviewed to market rent, the review clause will set out the assumptions on which the review is to be based (creating what is usually called the **hypothetical lease**). Even quite small variations in wording may have significant impact [**62.3**].

Improvements carried out by the tenant during the period of the current lease are generally excluded from the review, provided the tenant has received all necessary consents from the landlord and provided the improvements were not required under the lease. If this assumption is included, there may need to be explicit provision as to whether improvements by the tenant during an earlier lease or under a contract prior to the grant of the lease [**61.6.1**] will be considered.

All the assumptions need to be looked at carefully to see if they are fair. In particular, tenants should realise that the more beneficial the terms of the hypothetical lease are to them, the higher the reviewed rent will be.

62.2.10.2 Time limits

Time limits are important in any property transaction, but may have particular bearing on rent reviews. For example, some leases contain a provision that if the landlord serves a notice on the tenant suggesting an increased rent and the tenant fails to serve a counter notice rejecting it within a time limit, the new rent is whatever has been specified by the landlord even if it is well above market rent.

A key issue in negotiating time limits is whether the party affected loses its rights if the time limit is not met. If the time limit is to be strict in this way, the clause generally states that '**time is of the essence**'. Even if time is not of the essence, it may be possible for one party to make it of the essence by writing to the other setting a deadline specifying that time is of the essence in meeting that deadline.

Review clauses tend to allow the rent to be agreed a reasonable time prior to the rent review date, or in many cases at any date thereafter. This can have serious consequences for the tenant. If the landlord takes no steps to activate the rent review on the due date, the tenant may feel a certain sense of relief. Such relief is misplaced, because unless there is a limit on when the landlord can activate the review, it may be activated several years later.

Modern review clauses generally provide that no matter how long the gap between the rent review date and the actual review, the new rent is backdated to the review date. In addition, many clauses provide that interest is payable on the backdated rent as if it was rent in arrears. A delayed rent review could therefore create a large payment for the tenant. To avoid the risk of a retrospective claim, both the tenant and landlord should have the right to initiate the rent review.

62.2.11 Forfeiture

Leases contain a clause specifying circumstances which give rise to a landlord's right to **forfeit** (end the lease) [**62.4.2**]. Generally the right to forfeit is given for any breach of any of the tenant's covenants [**62.2.2**], or the rent being unpaid for a defined period even if no demand has been made for the rent.

Forfeiture clauses frequently allow forfeiture if the tenant becomes insolvent or bankrupt, or suffers any of a wide range of events which indicate that it is about to become insolvent [**24.2**]. Such provisions generally make it impossible to use the lease as security for any loan.

Landlords may also seek provisions allowing them to forfeit the lease if a guarantor [**62.2.3.5**] becomes bankrupt. Tenants should seek to resist such provisions.

62.2.12 Provisos

The main part of a lease normally ends with a series of miscellaneous provisions. These may cover, for example, the service of notices, interest payable on late payments, what happens to property left behind when the tenant leaves, exclusion from the lease of any representations made by the landlord prior to the grant of the lease, exclusion of the normal rule that acceptance of rent by the landlord waives any previous breach [**62.4.2.1**] (although this clause is legally unenforceable), special provision for early surrender of the lease [**62.7.3**], and if the organisation is a charity, any clause required by the Charities Acts [**61.12**].

62.2.13 Execution

Unless it is for three years or less at a full market rent without any fine or premium, a lease must be executed as a deed [**20.3**]. If there is a plan of the property it should be signed by the lease signatories, but the signatures do not have to be witnessed as they do for a deed.

62.3 RENT REVIEW PROCEDURES

Rent reviews during a lease are subject to the exact wording of the lease [**62.2.10**], and time limits must be strictly followed [**62.2.10.2**]. In a **review to market rent**, a typical procedure is for the landlord to serve a notice specifying the desired new rent. In a majority of cases the rent is then agreed by negotiation.

62.3.1 Arbitration or review by expert

If the landlord and tenant cannot reach agreement, the parties agree a suitable **arbitrator** [**65.2.5**] or **expert** [**65.2.4**] to assess a new rent. A clause in the lease normally provides that if they cannot agree an arbitrator, one will be appointed by a neutral party such as the president of the Royal Institution of Chartered Surveyors. If the lease does not specify that an arbitrator must be appointed, the landlord and tenant may agree to a rent review by a professional acting as an expert, a less formal procedure than arbitration.

The arbitrator or expert assesses market rent on the basis of **comparables**. This is evidence of similar lettings within recent months, which gives an indication of the current market level. Normally both landlord and tenant employ solicitors or surveyors to gather information on comparables and make the arguments about rent level.

At an arbitrator's rent review hearing, the parties may be represented by solicitors and are likely to call surveyors to give expert evidence on comparable rent levels. If evidence is being submitted about rent levels which the parties have not dealt with directly themselves or through their surveyors, proper evidence of the rent level together with a copy of the lease must be submitted to the arbitrator.

62.3.2   **After the rent review**

After the rent is fixed, whether by agreement, arbitration or an expert, a **rent memorandum** setting out the new rent is normally signed by both parties, with a copy attached to the lease and to the counterpart held by the landlord.

62.4   **LANDLORD'S REMEDIES**

Because of the historical nature of the landlord/tenant relationship, a landlord has substantially more ways of enforcing its rights than under a simple contract.

62.4.1   **Suing**

The landlord may sue the tenant for rent or other sums due. For leases granted before 1 January 1996 the landlord may be able to sue not only the current tenant but also the original tenant, provided the landlord serves a **default notice** on the original tenant in a prescribed form within six months of the money becoming due [**60.4.4**]. For leases granted on or after 1 January 1996 the original tenant is not automatically liable for the default of a subsequent tenant, but could be liable if it entered into an **authorised guarantee agreement** [**60.4.4**] when it assigned the lease to the new tenant.

62.4.2   **Forfeiture**

Most leases grant to a landlord a right to end (**forfeit**) a lease where the tenant is in breach of a covenant. To do this, the landlord must take possession or obtain a possession order. There are a number of statutory restrictions on forfeiture, contained primarily in the **Law of Property Act 1925** s.146.

Forfeiture of a lease will also bring to an end any sub-leases that are in existence in relation to the premises.

62.4.2.1   Waiver

The landlord will lose its right to forfeit if it does something which **waives** the tenant's breach which gave rise to that right. Waiver is an act which acknowledges a continuing tenancy, and cannot be contractually overridden [**62.2.12**].

Demanding or accepting rent is a common act of waiver, since rent can only be demanded or accepted if the tenancy is still in existence. Another action which waives is taking a court action for rent due after the right to forfeit arose.

Whether the right to forfeit has in fact been waived depends in part upon the nature of the covenant breached. If the landlord obtained the right to forfeit because the tenant breached a covenant of a **continuing** nature, such as the repairing or user covenant, then despite the waiver the landlord 'regains' the right to forfeit if the breach continues. If the tenant's breach was of a non-continuing nature, such as failure to pay a particular rent instalment, there must be a further breach of covenant before the landlord regains the right to forfeit.

62.4.2.2   Method of forfeiture

The landlord can exercise its right to forfeit by taking proceedings through the court, or by **peaceable re-entry** where the landlord simply changes the locks, goes back into possession of the premises and thereafter excludes the tenant.

In either case, the landlord must first generally serve on the tenant a notice under the **Law of Property Act 1925** s.146 specifying the breach, requiring its remedy if it is capable of remedy, and requiring the tenant to make compensation in money for the breach. Such a notice is not required if the only default is rent arrears. A **section 146 notice** may well look like yet another letter, and may contain no indication that the landlord intends to forfeit.

If the tenant fails to meet the requirements set out in any notice or the breach is not capable of being remedied, the landlord can go forward with the forfeiture. If the landlord takes court proceedings the court has discretion, having regard to all the circumstances, to prevent the forfeiture. If the landlord has already forfeited, the court may allow the tenant back into occupation (be granted **relief from forfeiture**). If this happens, the landlord will be entitled to recover its reasonable expenses properly incurred in connection with serving the section 146 notice.

A third party, such as a sub-tenant or a mortgagee, can apply for relief from forfeiture, on whatever terms a court thinks fit.

62.4.2.3 Forfeiture for failure to repair

If a landlord seeks to forfeit because the tenant has not put or kept the property in repair, and if the lease was originally for a term of more than seven years and there are still more than three years to run, the section 146 notice must advise the tenant of its right to serve a counter notice claiming the benefit of the **Leasehold Property (Repairs) Act 1938**. If the tenant serves such a counter-notice, the landlord must obtain the leave of the court before enforcing its right to re-enter.

Leasehold Property (Repairs) Act 1938 s.1

62.4.2.4 Forfeiture for rent arrears

If forfeiture is sought for non-payment of rent, it is not necessary for the landlord to serve a section 146 notice. However, even after forfeiture the court has a right to give the tenant relief from forfeiture, and normally does so if the tenant applies to the court within six months and is able to pay the arrears.

Law of Property Act 1925 s.146(11)

62.4.3 Distress / commercial rent arrears recovery

A landlord can, without a court order, ask bailiffs to go onto the premises and seize the tenant's goods as soon as the tenant is in arrears. This is called **distress** or **distraint**.

Distress will be abolished (expected April 2012) and for premises used solely for commercial purposes will be replaced by **commercial rent arrears recovery** (CRAR). The type of debts for which CRAR can be used will be narrower than for distress [**62.2.1.5**], and unlike distress CRAR will not be able to be exercised until a notice of enforcement has been served upon the tenant. CRAR can only be exercised by an **enforcement agent** (currently known as a **bailiff**). Complex rules will apply and specialist advice should be sought.

Tribunals, Courts & Enforcement Act 2007 ss.71-87, sch.12 [expected 1/4/12]

62.4.4 Disrepair and schedule of dilapidations

62.4.4.1 During tenancy

The landlord may inspect the property at any time, serve a **schedule of dilapidations** (a list of alleged defects in repair, or unauthorised alterations) and require the tenant to rectify them. Most leases allow the landlord to enter the premises and do the works itself if the tenant fails to take action. It may be possible for the tenant to dispute some or all of the items on the schedule.

62.4.4.2 At end of tenancy

At, or shortly before, the end of a tenancy the landlord will often send its surveyor to prepare a schedule of dilapidations. It is not uncommon for the landlord's or surveyor's schedule simply to list all the defects in the premises, regardless of whether these amount to a breach of a tenant's covenant in the lease [**62.2.4**]. In addition, the surveyor may overstate what is wrong or include trivial matters, or the pricing of the items may be open to argument.

62.4.5 Damages

Damages are compensation awarded by the court for the landlord's loss. In relation to dilapidations they may be the cost of putting right the tenant's defaults, plus loss of rent if re-letting is delayed. Damages for lack of repair are limited to the damage to the value of the landlord's interest in the property on reversion [**60.4**]. In some circumstances these can be evidenced by the cost to the landlord of carrying out works of reinstatement if these have, in fact, been completed. A claim for damages may not be available where the landlord is going to demolish or refurbish at the end of the term, and therefore any disrepair will not affect the value of the landlord's interest. An unscrupulous landlord may nonetheless try to obtain compensation, and the tenant may find it difficult to discover the landlord's intentions for the building.   *Landlord & Tenant Act 1927 s.18*

In any event, the sums claimed are in practice open to negotiation. If the claim is substantial, advice should be sought from a surveyor or solicitor. The Property Litigation Association [see end of **chapter 60**] has a **dilapidations protocol** for the exchange of evidence about dilapidations before proceedings are brought.

62.4.6 Specific performance

The court may order the tenant to discharge its obligations under the lease, for example to carry out repairs. However, this remedy is at the discretion of the court. The court may refuse an order which would require detailed supervision, and award damages instead. A notable example of this is the court's refusal to compel a tenant to keep trading from premises against its wishes, even if the lease contains a 'keep open' covenant.   *Co-operative Insurance Society Ltd v Argyll Stores Ltd [1997] UKHL17*

62.4.7 Injunction and damages

If the landlord wishes to stop particular behaviour by the tenant, it may apply to the court for an injunction ordering the behaviour to cease and may claim damages. This is at the court's discretion.

62.4.8 Action by landlord

Most leases reserve a right for the landlord to enter and carry out works if the tenant fails to observe the terms of the lease. Generally this covers repairs, but it may cover other areas such as ending nuisances. If no right is reserved, the landlord will not generally be able to come onto the premises, and doing so would constitute trespass.

62.4.9 Other consequences

A tenant's breach may have other consequences. It may, for example, allow the landlord to withdraw money from the deposit, trigger an action against a guarantor, cause the tenant to lose rights under the lease, or in the case of a lease within the **Landlord and Tenant Act 1954** ss.24-28 [**62.6**] result in a loss of the right to a new lease at the end of the lease term. An example is where the tenant has a right to surrender [**62.7.3**], but the lease provides that this is conditional on the tenant having observed all the covenants and conditions in the lease.

62.5 TENANT'S REMEDIES

The tenant is much less well provided for by the law, and has no rights equivalent to forfeiture or distress. A tenant has to rely therefore on court action or one of the few other available remedies.

62.5.1 Court action

If the landlord breaches an obligation in the lease or implied by the law [**61.2.2**], the tenant may be able to get an injunction to restrain further breaches and compensation for any damage or loss caused. For example, if the landlord does not fulfil a covenant to repair and the tenant's goods are damaged as a result, the tenant will be able to require the landlord to repair and to provide compensation for the loss of goods and for any loss arising directly from the damage.

62.5.2 Set off

If the tenant has a clear and quantifiable claim against the landlord, the tenant may be able to **set off** the sums due to the tenant from the landlord against any claim by the landlord for rent or in proceedings. Many modern leases explicitly deprive the tenant of the right of set off, so advice should be taken before setting any sums due from the landlord against sums due to the landlord.

62.5.3 Self help

If a landlord is in breach of its obligations, a tenant might itself take the required action. For example, a tenant might undertake repairs which are the landlord's responsibility, and then set off the cost against future rent. This remedy should be used with considerable caution and only after advice. The tenant must particularly be careful not to trespass on land it has no legal right to enter.

62.5.4 Receiver

The high court has power to appoint a receiver of the property. This is an unusual step but might be taken where the landlord cannot be located or has failed to comply with orders to carry out vital repairs.

62.5.5 Repudiation

It has been accepted by the courts that where the landlord is in breach of the terms of a lease, the lease may in some situations be **repudiated** (cancelled) by a tenant on normal contractual principles [**21.6.6**]. This is despite the fact that a lease is an interest in land, which normally could not be terminated in this way. However, because of the nature of the landlord/tenant relationship, repudiation is only likely to be possible in the case of extremely serious breaches. Case law on repudiation is unclear, but the possibility of such action could be raised as a way of exerting pressure on a landlord to remedy a breach.

62.6 SECURITY OF TENURE

A tenant of premises used for business purposes (including not for profit purposes) may be entitled to a new tenancy as of right on the expiry or termination of the original. This security of tenure applies not only to premises, but also to open ground if this is used for the purposes of the business, for example a car park.

To obtain the new tenancy, the original tenancy must meet defined criteria [**60.4.5**], certain procedural steps must be taken by the tenant within fixed time limits, and the landlord must not have successfully established a ground of opposition to the grant of a new lease.   *Landlord & Tenant Act 1954 ss.23-46*

This security is in addition to the security inherent in most fixed-term leases or tenancies, which unless there is a landlord's break right generally cannot be terminated by the landlord prior to their expiry if the tenant observes their terms.

A tenant who does not have statutory security of tenure, generally because the relevant provisions of the **Landlord and Tenant Act 1954** have been excluded by agreement [**60.4.6**], will not have the right to apply to the court for a new lease. and will have to agree any renewal with the landlord. This may enable the landlord to extract from a tenant more than the market rent at a renewal, by taking advantage of the tenant's wish to avoid the expense and inconvenience of finding and moving to new premises.

62.6.1 Procedure at expiry of a lease

A tenant who does not want the lease to continue can simply vacate the premises by the termination date, in which case the tenancy will automatically expire.

62.6.1.1 Continuation tenancy

If the tenant in a business tenancy to which the Act applies remains in occupation and neither the landlord nor tenant takes any action when the original lease term expires, the tenant remains a tenant despite the expiry of the lease. The tenant **holds over** under the protection of the Act, and the tenancy becomes a **continuation tenancy** on the same terms as the old tenancy, including the same rent. However, both the landlord and the tenant have a right to apply to the court to set a new **interim rent**.   *Landlord & Tenant Act 1954 s.24A*

62.6.1.2   Section 25, 26 or 27 notice

If either party is not happy with a continuation tenancy, either the landlord or tenant can serve notice ending the original or continuation tenancy or proposing a new tenancy. These notices are:

- a **section 25 notice** given by the landlord, indicating that it is willing to grant a new tenancy and the terms for the tenancy, or that it is not willing to grant a new tenancy and its reasons for opposing it;
- a **section 26 request** given by the tenant, requesting a new tenancy and the proposed terms for the tenancy;
- a **section 27 notice**. If a fixed-term tenancy is coming to an end, a tenant can give three months' notice expiring on the termination date of the lease. Alternatively, the tenant can just leave on or before the date without giving notice. If the tenant is holding over in a continuation tenancy [**62.6.1.1**], it will have to give three months' notice to terminate, whether or not it is in occupation.

Landlord & Tenant Act 1954 ss.25-27, amended by Regulatory Reform (Business Tenancies)
(England & Wales) Order 2003 [SI 2003/3096]

A section 25 notice or section 26 request must be in a specified form; preprinted forms are available from legal stationers or via the internet. The notice or request must specify a date between six and 12 months after the date of the notice, by which time any court application for a new lease must generally be made.

A section 26 request should be given between six and 12 months before the end of any fixed term. In order to ensure that the procedure commences at the earliest possible point, organisations wishing to proceed in this way should begin planning approximately 15 months before the current lease ends.

The whole procedure is complex and must be carried out within strict time limits, so it is very important to take advice at all stages. For example, the landlord for the purposes of the 1954 Act is not necessarily the person to whom the tenant is currently paying rent, but may be that person's landlord or the landlord superior to both of these.

62.6.1.3   Court application

Following service of a section 25 notice or section 26 request, either the landlord or the tenant may apply to the court for a new tenancy at any time before the expiry of the notice. This time period can be extended by written agreement, provided this is done before the date specified in the notice.

62.6.1.4   Interim rent

Either party can apply for an interim rent to be fixed and will do so if they think that the existing rent is (in the case of a landlord) below market rent or (in the case of a tenant) above market rent.

62.6.1.5   Grounds for opposition

The only permissible grounds for a landlord's objection to granting a new tenancy are:

- breach by the tenant of its repairing obligation [**62.2.4**], persistent delay in paying the rent, or breach of another substantial lease obligation;
- the landlord has offered and is willing to provide alternative accommodation which is suitable;
- the tenancy was created by sub-letting part of a property and the landlord will be able to get more rent by letting as one unit;
- the landlord intends to demolish or substantially reconstruct the premises; or
- the landlord intends to occupy the premises itself. This ground can be used only if the landlord purchased the premises at least five years prior to the end of the tenancy, and at all times since the purchase the tenants have occupied under a tenancy or successive tenancies which fall within the Act.

Landlord & Tenant Act 1954 s.30(1)

In the absence of a negotiated settlement, the question of whether the landlord has established its ground or grounds of opposition must be decided by a court.

62.6.1.6   Negotiation

The terms of a new lease are often resolved by negotiation. Even after a landlord or tenant has issued proceedings, they may agree some or all outstanding matters, and these issues do not need to be the subject of a court judgment. However, once proceedings have been issued, it is rare for a court to permit parties to negotiate indefinitely. The court will usually at the outset of proceedings order a time-table for exchange of evidence to bring the litigation to a trial. Compliance with this timetable can be time-consuming and costly. Early agreement is therefore sensible if possible. A tenant can withdraw from the proceedings, but may have to pay the landlord's solicitor's legal costs as well as its own.

62.6.2   The new lease

If the landlord does not oppose the grant of a new lease, its grounds for opposition are found to be invalid or it fails to comply with the procedural requirements, the court will grant the tenant a new lease for the premises occupied by the tenant for its business, for a term of up to 15 years. If the tenant has sub-let part of its premises it will not be entitled as of right to a tenancy for all of the original premises, although the landlord can insist upon the tenant taking such a lease so that the landlord avoids having an increased number of tenants.

Generally the new lease follows the old, but the court has wide discretion to vary this. The court also fixes the new market rent. *Landlord & Tenant Act 1954 ss.32-34*

62.6.3   Compensation

If a new tenancy is not granted because the landlord opposed it on grounds of wanting to let the property as one unit, planning to demolish or reconstruct, or wanting to occupy the premises itself, the outgoing tenant may in some cases be entitled to compensation. This will be based on the rateable value and how long the tenant has been in occupation. *Landlord & Tenant Act 1954 s.37*

Tenants may also have a statutory right to compensation for improvements they have made to the property. To qualify, the tenant must comply with strict time limits and procedural requirements in serving a notice on the landlord prior to making the improvements, and at the end of the tenancy. Compensation is the lesser of the net addition to the value of the property directly attributable to the improvement, or the cost of the improvement. There is provision for reference to the court if compensation cannot be agreed. *Landlord & Tenant Act 1927 ss.1-3,9*

62.7   ENDING A TENANCY

The principal ways in which a tenancy comes to an end are:

- the original term granted has expired;
- the lease or tenancy agreement gives one or other party the right to end the lease;
- the landlord accepts a surrender from the tenant;
- the tenant purchases the freehold and the tenancy ends as it is merged with the larger freehold interest;
- the landlord forfeits the lease because the tenant is in breach of its obligations under the lease [**62.4.2**];
- either the landlord or the tenant terminates a periodic tenancy by a notice to quit;
- a section 25 or section 27 statutory notice is served [**62.6.1.2**];
- in certain cases where a demolition order, closing order or derelict land order has been made by the court;
- there is a total destruction of the premises and the site on which they rest, for example by sea erosion;
- the lease is disclaimed by a liquidator of a tenant company or trustee in bankruptcy of an individual tenant (including a tenant that is a trustee) under the **Insolvency Act 1986** ss.178-182 and 317-321.

A tenant cannot end a fixed-term lease prior to its expiry if there is no specific provision allowing it, and the landlord does not wish to accept a surrender. When taking on a lease with no break clause [**62.2.8**], the tenant should consider carefully exactly how long the premises are needed for, and whether it will be possible to dispose of the premises before then by assignment or sub-letting.

62.7.1   Expiry

At the end of a tenancy with security [**62.6**] the tenant may either continue in occupation under the Act [**62.6.1.2**], give notice to the landlord [**62.6.1.2**], or vacate the premises ending the tenancy. Tenants without security are obliged to vacate unless the landlord and tenant agree a renewal. A prudent landlord should refuse to accept rent from a tenant which is unlawfully 'holding over' (continuing in occupation), in order to avoid the accidental creation of a new tenancy.

62.7.2   Notice under lease

Where the lease or tenancy agreement allows, a party may have the right to end the term. This is often called a **break clause** [**62.2.8**].

62.7.3   Surrender

A lease may be **surrendered** (given back to the landlord):

- by voluntary agreement between the parties;
- by operation of law, for example when a tenant takes a longer lease before the old lease expires, and the old lease is deemed to have been surrendered and replaced by the new lease, or when surrender can be implied from unequivocal actions, for example if the tenant gives up possession and the landlord accepts the keys and takes over occupation;
- because the lease provides for surrender, for example that the tenant must offer to surrender before seeking to assign the lease.

Formal surrender must be by deed [**20.3**]. In an implied surrender the situation may be unclear, so it is preferable for the agreement to be made formally.

Law of Property Act 1925 ss.52,53

A surrender by a registered or excepted charity is a disposal for the purposes of the **Charities Act 1993** s.36, and valuation advice or a Charity Commission order may be necessary [**61.12**].

62.7.4   Notice to quit

A continuation [**62.6.1**] or periodic [**60.4.5**] tenancy may be terminated by a **notice to quit**. The amount of notice required and the date on which it must expire are governed by complex common law rules. The notice requirements of the **Landlord and Tenant Act 1954** ss.25 and 27 [**62.6.1.2**] must be observed.

Resources: BUSINESS LEASES

See end of **chapter 60**.

Statute law. www.opsi.gov.uk and www.statutelaw.gov.uk.

Much but not all case law. www.bailii.org.

Updates cross-referenced to this book. www.rclh.co.uk.

Chapter 63
PROPERTY MANAGEMENT AND THE ENVIRONMENT

For sources of further information see end of chapter.

63.1 MANAGING PROPERTY

Responsibility for the various aspects of property management should be allocated to named individuals, in order to ensure that the organisation's activities do not breach the terms of its freehold, lease or licence [**60.3-60.5**], and to ensure that vital time limits such as those for rent reviews [**62.3**] or continuation of a lease [**62.6.1**] are not missed. Individuals with these responsibilities must have appropriate experience and training, have access to professional advisors, and maintain a diary highlighting key dates.

As an organisation's property management becomes more complex, a decision needs to be made about whether to use its own staff or outside professionals. If the decision is to use in-house staff, the costs of hiring qualified persons or training unqualified staff should not be underestimated. Property management is complex and highly technical, and small mistakes can have large consequences.

An outside person can be appointed to manage the organisation's property only if the organisation has power to appoint an agent. Trusts and charitable associations have power to do so under the **Trustee Act 2000** [**20.5.1**]; other organisations must have power to appoint agents under their governing document [**7.4.6**].

63.2 NON-DOMESTIC RATES

Property which is not used solely for residential purposes is subject to **non-domestic rates** (also called **business rates**). Refuges, hostels and other properties used solely for accommodation are subject to council tax [**63.3**]. Where a property is used primarily for residential purposes but also as an office or for other non-domestic purposes, the valuation officer decides whether to charge a business rate for the non-domestic part of the premises.

Information about business rates and rate relief is available from Business Link [see end of chapter].

63.2.1 Valuation of property

Business rates are based on the **rateable value** of the property. This is the annual rent the property could be let at on the open market on a particular date on full repairing and insuring terms [**62.2.4**], as assessed by the Valuation Office Agency every five years, or when a building is first built or brought into a separate rating assessment. This method of valuation means that an historic building which is very expensive to maintain might have a very low or even zero rateable value. Rateable values can be checked on the VOA website [see end of chapter].

Buildings in a poor state of repair are valued for rating purposes as if they were in a reasonable state of repair.

An appeal can be made within six months of any change in valuation. Many firms of surveyors have rating departments, and may handle an appeal on a 'no reduction, no fee' basis. During the appeal period, rates must be paid based on the valuation officer's valuation.

63.2.2 The rate

The business rate for a property is its rateable value times the **national multiplier** (also called the **uniform business rate**). The national multiplier is set each year by the government, except for the City of London which has a separate procedure and sets its own multiplier.

A lease will set out whether the landlord or tenant is responsible for paying rates [**62.2.3**]. If the landlord is responsible, the lease will state whether the landlord can recover the amount from the tenant.

63.2.2.1 Business rate supplement

From 2010, county councils, unitary authorities and the Greater London Authority have power to charge a **business rate supplement** of up to 2p in the pound, to help fund economic development projects. Charities and similar organisations and empty properties with no liability for non-domestic rates [below], and properties with a rateable value below an amount specified in regulations, will be exempt from the supplement.   *Business Rate Supplements Act 2009 ss.1,11*

63.2.3 Rate relief

Charities, many other not for profit organisations, small businesses and empty properties may be eligible for relief from some or all business rates. The reliefs must be applied for; even where they are mandatory, they are not automatic.

63.2.3.1 100% mandatory relief

Registered places of public religious worship are fully exempt from rates, as are their administrative offices, halls and similar buildings used in connection with a place of worship. 'Similar buildings' has been widely interpreted to include church-owned buildings used for youth clubs, recreation and accommodation.
Local Government Finance Act 1988 sch.5 para.11, amended by Local Government Act 2003 s.68;
Glasgow City Corporation v Johnstone [1965] AC 609

Full rate relief is also available for premises used wholly for training, day care etc for people who are or have been ill or are disabled, welfare services for disabled people, and workshops and other employment-related facilities for disabled people.

Rating (Disabled Persons) Act 1978

If only part (but at least half) of the premises is used for these purposes, the rate relief may be proportionately reduced.

63.2.3.2 80% mandatory relief

A property is entitled to 80% relief from rates if the ratepayer is a registered, excepted [**8.1.3**] or exempt [**8.1.2**] charity and the property is used wholly or mainly for charitable purposes, or if the ratepayer is registered with HM Revenue and Customs as a community amateur sports club [**1.8**]. It may also receive discretionary relief [below].

Local Government Finance Act 1988 ss.43(6), 45(5),(6), amended by Local Government Act 2003 s.64

63.2.3.3 Discretionary relief

The local authority may, at its discretion, allow relief to a charity or registered community amateur sports club on all or some of the remaining 20% of the rate. Charity trustees are obliged to safeguard their charity's assets and not pay unnecessary taxes, so they must apply for mandatory and discretionary rate relief.

Local Government Finance Act 1988 ss.47,48, amended by Local Government Act 2003 s.64

Rating authorities may also grant discretionary relief of up to 100% to not for profit organisations using property for educational, social welfare, philanthropic, religious, literary, artistic or scientific purposes; and not for profit clubs, societies or other organisations using property for recreational purposes.

LGFA 1988 s.47(2)

Criteria used in deciding eligibility for discretionary rate relief include whether the organisation encourages young, elderly or disabled people and people from ethnic minorities to take part; provides education or training; makes its facilities widely available; and/or is actively involved in local or national organisations.

Rating authorities must give notice to the ratepayer of changes in relief. In cases of hardship, the authority has power to reduce or return non-domestic rates.

63.2.3.4 Mixed use

Rate relief for charities is available only for premises actually used for charitable purposes, and not for related purposes such as fundraising. Administration and management are classed as 'charitable' when they are directed to the achievement of charitable objects. Premises used partly for charitable purposes (including relevant administration and management) and partly for other purposes are eligible for rate relief if use is mainly charitable.

63.2.3.5 Charity shops

Shops run by charities are eligible for the same reliefs as charities, provided they are used wholly or mainly for the sale of goods donated to a charity, and the proceeds of sales minus expenses are paid to the charity.

Local Government & Finance Act 1988 s.64(10)

Shops run by a charity's trading company may be entitled to the relief, provided the other conditions are satisfied and the charity can be regarded as acting as agent of the trading company in the sale of the donated goods. Guidance is available in the Charity Commission's CC35 *Trustees, trading and tax*.

63.2.3.6 Small businesses

A business with a single property whose rateable value is below £5,000 (as at 1/8/09) is eligible for 50% mandatory relief. The relief is decreased by 1% for every £100 of rateable value from £5,000 to £9,999. Where the business has more than one property, the additional properties must not have individual rateable values of more than £2,200, and the rateable value of all the properties added together must be less than £15,000 or £21,500 in London. Only the main property is eligible for this relief.

Non-Domestic Rating (Small Business Rate Relief) (England) Order 2004 [SI 2004/3315], as amended

Different rules apply in Wales.

63.2.3.7   Empty property

Empty office and retail premises are eligible for full rate relief for the first three months of becoming vacant, and industrial and warehouse premises and listed buildings [**63.11.1**] for the first six months. Thereafter full rates are payable. Empty property with rateable value below £15,000 (as at 1/8/09) or property where occupation is prevented by law or by a public authority is exempt from rates.   *Local Government Finance Act 1944 ss.44A-47, amended by Rating (Empty Properties) Act 2007*
& Non-Domestic Rating (Unoccupied Property) (England) Regulations 2009 [SI 2009/353]

Empty property occupied by charities and community amateur sports clubs [**1.8**] is eligible for 100% rate relief, provided it appears that it will next be used wholly or mainly for charitable purposes or the purposes of the CASC. But property held by a charity as an investment is subject to the same rules as non-charity property.

Properties which are partly vacant and would be eligible for relief if unoccupied are eligible for a reduction in rates.

63.3   COUNCIL TAX

Council tax is a tax on property used for residential purposes, assessed according to eight bands A to H on an open market valuation as at 1 April 1991. The tax is set by the local authority each year and is broadly proportionate to these band valuations. Information about council tax is available from the Valuation Office Agency [see end of chapter] and the local authority.

Liability generally rests with the occupier of the dwelling but the owner, rather than the occupiers, is liable if the property is a hostel, residential care home, nursing home, religious community, student hall of residence, dwelling occupied solely by students, residence of a minister of religion, a house in multiple occupation, or occupied by staff who live there in order to carry out work for an owner who lives elsewhere.

Certain persons are disregarded for the purposes of council tax, and there is a discount for properties occupied by only one person, or by one person and a disregarded person or persons.

An organisation liable for council tax on its dwellings needs to be clear whether and if so how it will recover the tax from occupiers.

Empty dwellings are exempt from council tax for up to six months. Dwellings undergoing substantial structural alterations or repair works are exempt during the works and for six months after substantial completion of the works.

63.3.1   Dwellings for disabled people

Where a dwelling is specially adapted for use by a physically disabled person, any increase in value created by the adaptations is ignored in determining the value for council tax purposes. In addition, the property may be assessed as if it is in the band immediately below the band it is actually in, if it meets specified criteria and is not already in the lowest valuation band.

63.4   WATER CHARGES

Water charges cover water supply, drainage of waste water from sinks and toilets, surface water drainage, and highways water drainage. The charges are payable by the occupier of the premises (whether residential or business) or by the owner of properties in multiple occupancy. For non-domestic premises, water supply and waste water drainage charges are based on the rateable value of the property. At the time of writing (mid 2009), charges for surface and highways drainage may be based on either rateable value or site area, but from 2010 were expected to be based on site area. Churches, charities and community organisations which would be significantly affected by this change were campaigning against charges based on site area.

63.5 LIABILITY TO AND FOR PEOPLE ON THE PROPERTY

Anyone who owns, controls or occupies land or buildings has a wide range of obligations to prevent **visitors** – invitees or licensees who come onto the premises with permission – from being injured. Many of these obligations also extend to **trespassers** who are on the premises without permission.

A landlord has a **duty of care** [**22.6.1**] to put right any defects in premises which it has an obligation or right to remedy. Where the tenant is under an obligation to repair [**62.2.4**] but fails to comply with this, the landlord is not liable to the tenant for the defect, nor is the landlord liable to the tenant where the property is apparently 'unsafe' but is not actually in disrepair (for example if new safety standards have developed since the property was constructed). However, a landlord may be liable to third parties if it has a legal power to put right the defect if the tenant defaults.

Defective Premises Act 1972 s.4

If a lease, tenancy or contract gives the tenant's invitees or licensees the right to use common parts still in the landlord's occupation, the landlord has a duty to see that such people are safe while using the common areas.

An occupier owes a greater duty of care if it is aware that children are likely to come onto the premises. A duty of care cannot be modified or restricted in relation to claims for personal injury or death arising from the occupier's negligence [**22.7.6**]. In relation to other possible claims, for example for property damage, liability can only be restricted to the extent that it is reasonable to do so, such as a disclaimer of liability sign in a car park.

Occupiers' Liability Act 1957 s.1;
Unfair Contract Terms Act 1977 s.2

For any organisation which has employees, duties in relation to premises also arise under health and safety legislation [**chapter 40**].

The liabilities arising from these duties should be insured against by taking out public liability insurance [**23.5.1**]. In addition, an organisation hosting an event should ensure that those providing facilities or entertainment on its behalf or on its premises are fully insured [**22.6.4**].

63.5.1 Landlord's liability for acts of tenants

A landlord can be liable to visitors to a tenant's premises, if the landlord does not seek to ensure the tenant does not create a hazard. An example is a florist's shop in a railway station, where a person slipped on flower petals that had not been cleared away. Had the railway company not admonished the florist to keep the floor around its shop clear, it could be been held liable to the person who was injured.

Piccolo v Larkstock Ltd (t/a Chiltern Flowers), Chiltern Railway Co Ltd & others [2008] EWCA Civ 647

63.5.2 Liability under contract or licence

A contract or licence arises if the organisation charges or receives consideration (something of value) for the use of its premises. Examples include charging for entry to a fête (licence to enter for the fête), hiring out land for a car boot sale (licences to bring cars onto the land and to attend the sale), or charging a room hire fee for a training course on the organisation's premises (licences to the course organiser, the trainer and the students). This type of contract does not have to be written; it is implied when someone pays for the use of land or premises.

Thought needs to be given to the exact terms under which entry is allowed. These terms and conditions may be imposed by putting up a clear sign at the point of entry, printing them on an admission ticket, or asking the person to enter into a formal agreement embodying those terms [**63.8**].

In any agreement, including one governing use of premises, liability for causing personal injury or death cannot be excluded [**22.7.6**]. Public liability insurance should be taken out to cover such claims [**23.5.1**]. The hire agreement should state whether this is the responsibility of the licensee or the landlord.

Other claims which may arise from a licensee's occupation include loss or damage to property, or financial loss. These can be excluded in the contract [**22.7.5**], and the organisation needs to consider whether to do this or to take out insurance to cover such claims. The court may rule that unfair exclusions are invalid [**21.2.7**].

In addition, the organisation may need to reserve a right to terminate the licence prematurely or take action within the licence, for example reserving a right to exclude individuals because of unacceptable behaviour or to terminate the booking.

63.5.3 Trespassers and squatters

A person on premises without permission, even for a few minutes, is a **trespasser**. Consent to enter is implied in many situations or may be explicit under a licence, but may be withdrawn before or after the person has entered. For example an organisation implies by its 'open' sign a licence to enter, but a staff member may revoke the licence by asking a visitor to leave.

Invitees and licensees have no right to remain on the property outside the terms of a licence agreement. They are trespassers if they come onto property outside these terms, or refuse to leave when properly asked to do so.

The person with the right of occupation may use reasonable force to eject a trespasser who does not leave when asked to do so [**47.7.1**], but it is usually better to call the police in these circumstances. However, simple trespass is a civil wrong rather than a crime [**22.6.1**], and the police may refuse to become involved.

Squatting is a trespass where a person goes into occupation of premises or land. Squatters may be evicted through the civil courts using a speedy procedure under the civil procedure rules.

Even where a person is a trespasser or squatter, the occupier can be liable for injury caused by the state of the premises or by something the occupier has done or not done. The duty to trespassers is less than the duty to people who have a right to be on the premises, but occupiers should nonetheless take reasonable steps to reduce the risk of injury to anyone, especially children, who might get onto the land or into buildings or other structures. *Occupiers' Liability Act 1984*

63.5.4 Right to roam

Ramblers have a **right to roam** in 'open country' (land that is primarily mountain, moor, heath or down) and registered common land, but only on foot and only for the purposes of open-air recreation. There are restrictions for specified areas, for example golf courses and land near dwellings. It is unlawful to put up 'no trespassing' or similar signs on land where there is a right to roam. Information about the right to roam is available from Natural England and the Countryside Council for Wales [see end of chapter]. *Countryside & Rights of Way Act 2000*

The landowner and any occupier have a duty of care but this is even lower than to trespassers, as it does not cover risks arising from a natural feature of the landscape. The law explicitly states that the right to roam should not be seen by the courts as imposing an undue burden on occupiers. *Occupiers' Liability Act 1984 ss.1,1A, amended by Countryside & Rights of Way Act 2000*

63.5.5 Drug use on premises

Occupiers of premises must not knowingly 'permit or suffer' the production, attempted production, supply or attempted supply of any controlled drug, preparation of opium for smoking, or smoking of cannabis or prepared opium. *Misuse of Drugs Act 1971 s.8*

It is not enough for an organisation to have a policy saying it does not allow the sale, distribution, preparation or use of illegal substances; it must take active steps to prevent these activities. In addition, it may be unlawful for staff or others to comply with a confidentiality policy that prevents disclosure of names to the police [**43.1.2**], even where it is a condition of their contract of employment that they comply with it. *R v Brock & Wyner [2000] EWCA Crim 85*

Permitting possession of controlled drugs, or working with people who are under the influence of controlled drugs, is not an offence.

63.5.6 Banning people from premises

A person who does not pay an admission or similar charge has a right to be on premises only if the owner or occupier of the premises allows, and can be asked to leave at any time for any reason. However, where an organisation is providing public services and users of those services have access to the premises, a person may in some situations have an implied right to be on the premises unless they have explicitly been warned that they will be banned. *Wandsworth London Borough Council v A [1999] 1 WLR 1246*

Where people pay for the right to be on the premises, it is advisable to clearly reserve the right to require a person to leave, for example by a clause on the ticket or by displaying a notice. Whether a person has paid or not, refusal to leave within a reasonable time when asked makes the person a trespasser [**63.5.3**].

63.6 ACCESS AND SAFETY

63.6.1 Disability access

The **Disability Discrimination Act 1995** requires all employers to make reasonable adaptations to premises to enable a specific person with a disability to be appointed or to remain employed [**28.7.4**]. In addition, providers of goods, services and facilities, even if they have no employees, must take reasonable steps to remove, alter or provide reasonable means of avoiding physical features that make it impossible or unreasonably difficult for disabled people in general to use the goods, services or facilities, unless they are provided by a reasonable alternative method [**42.7.2**].

Those who manage or let premises must comply with similar obligations to their tenants, but are not required to remove or alter physical features – unless they are obliged to do so anyway, because of duties to service users or employees.

63.6.2 Safety and security

If the organisation has any employees, the premises where they work must be healthy and safe as required under the **Health and Safety at Work Act 1974** [**chapter 40**]. Organisations without employees do not have a statutory duty to comply with the Act but because of their duty of care [**63.5**], should comply insofar as they reasonably can. Owners, tenants and occupiers of premises, even without employees, must ensure fire safety [**40.8**].

Advice should be sought from the local police crime prevention officer about how to make premises secure. Failure to ensure that premises and contents are secure could invalidate some insurances [**23.6**], and could breach the governing body's duty of care [**15.3.4**] and duty to safeguard the organisation's assets [**15.6.5**].

The noise made by alarms is controlled under the **Control of Noise (Code of Practice on Noise from Audible Intruder Alarms) Order 1981** *[SI 1981/1829]* and the **Clean Neighbourhoods and Environment Act 2005** ss.69-81.

A guard dog cannot be used unless warning notices are clearly displayed, and the dog is under the handler's control or is secured. *Guard Dogs Act 1975*

63.7 HOUSES IN MULTIPLE OCCUPATION

Properties occupied by more than one household must meet minimum standards on facilities such as toilets, annual gas safety checks, electrical safety and smoke alarms. In addition, a **house** (or flat or building) **in multiple occupation** (HMO) is likely to need to be licensed by the local authority if it is occupied by at least three people making up two or more households, and has at least one amenity, such as toilet, bathroom or kitchen, which is shared by two or more households. A household can be a single person, a family, or a couple living together. Domestic refuges and houses let to students or migrant workers are HMOs. *Housing Act 2004 ss.254-259*

Houses or blocks of flats which are less than three storeys, or are occupied by fewer than five people, are not covered by the mandatory licensing requirements, but some local authorities may require them to register. Two-person flatshares, buildings occupied by a resident landlord with up to two lodgers or tenants, and some other premises are exempt.

Failure to licence premises which should be licensed is a criminal offence, with a fine of up to £20,000. The local housing authority can apply to a **residential property tribunal** for repayment of any benefits paid towards the rent while the premises were unlicensed. If the local housing authority has been granted a rent repayment order, or the landlord has been convicted of the offence, the tenant may also be entitled to a rent repayment order. *Housing Act 2004 ss.72,73*

While premises that should be licensed are unlicensed, the landlord will not be able to serve statutory notice for a tenant to leave on or after the expiry of an assured shorthold tenancy.

The residential property tribunal will become part of the **land, property and housing chamber** in the first-tier tribunal [**64.7**].

63.8   HIRING OUT PREMISES

When an organisation becomes involved in hiring out rooms, halls, playing fields or any other facility, it is creating a licence for use of the facilities [**60.5**]. It is advisable to put this into writing prior to the commencement of any hiring. Organisations such as Community Matters and ACRE [see end of **chapter 60**] can provide model hiring agreements, but every agreement should be carefully checked to ensure it reflects the particular situation and activities involved.

Insurance is vital. It is sensible for the organisation to extend its own public liability insurance [**23.5.1**] to cover the hirer, and not to rely on the hirer's duty to indemnify the organisation which may be included in the hire agreement.

If the hiring involves providing more than normal furnishings – for example if it includes the use of catering facilities or training equipment – it could constitute a trading activity and be subject to tax and VAT.

For licences granted for longer term occupation, see **60.5**.

63.9   WORKING FROM HOME

Many voluntary organisations operate from the home of a governing body member, employee or volunteer, or an organisation may agree that employees or volunteers can undertake some or all of their duties from home. Even if the amount of work or the space it takes up is insignificant, a number of issues should be considered by the organisation and by anyone working at home.

A company's name must be displayed outside its registered office and any place where its statutory records are kept [**17.1.3**], even if it is a residential address.

63.9.1   Contract of employment

If an employee will be working regularly from home, the statement of particulars [**26.7**] or contract of employment should be amended to reflect this. As well as place of work, the new contract might need to include provisions for expenses that can be claimed; an allowance for business rates [**63.9.6**], heat, light and use of phone lines [**30.4.9**]; the employer's right to enter the premises to install or maintain equipment or carry out risk assessments; the employee's obligation to keep the employer's equipment and confidential information secure and to return the property on request or when employment is terminated; and the employer's right to review or cancel the arrangement at any time or at specified intervals.

63.9.2   Insurance

People working from home have a duty of disclosure [**23.3.3**] to their insurer. They should ensure that their insurance policies, and those of their landlord if they are tenants, are not invalidated because of the work. Contents insurance may not cover equipment or goods used partly or solely for work purposes, and a special policy or an extension to a domestic policy may be necessary.

An employer should ensure that its employer's liability insurance or insurance covering volunteers [**23.4.1**] covers activities based outside its main premises. If equipment or goods owned by the organisation are used at the worker's home, it should be absolutely clear who is responsible for insuring them in the worker's home and in transit.

63.9.3 Health and safety

The organisation has a duty of care and statutory duties to ensure the place of work – wherever it may be, including at the staff member's home – is safe and will not have negative effects on the health or safety of staff [**40.2.1**].

Regulations governing the use of equipment apply with the same force if it is used at home, regardless of whether it is supplied by the employer or worker.

63.9.4 Breach of covenant

Most leases for residential premises contain covenants [**60.7.5**] preventing the premises being used for other purposes. Many freehold residential properties also have restrictive covenants on the title limiting their use to residential, and these could be enforced by owners of neighbouring property. A landlord or a neighbour with power to enforce a restrictive covenant may obtain an injunction to prevent work use of the flat or house.

In the case of a lease or tenancy, the landlord might seek to forfeit (end) the lease [**62.4.2**]. Provided the work ceases, the courts are unlikely to allow forfeiture if a long lease has been purchased for a premium [**62.2.1**]. But for a monthly or weekly tenancy or a licence, the landlord is more likely to be successful.

63.9.5 Planning permission

Limited work activities undertaken at home may not be extensive enough to constitute development as defined in the Planning Acts [**63.10.1.2**]. However, extensive use of a home for the activities of an organisation may well constitute development requiring planning consent.

If home-based activities involve large quantities of post, visits from the public or clients, or any nuisance to neighbours, complaints may be made to the planning authorities. The authorities may then seek to end the use by means of an enforcement or stop notice [**63.10.7**].

63.9.6 Tax and rates

Extensive working from home, especially if part of the premises is used solely for work purposes, could breach mortgage terms and lead to withdrawal of the loan. It could also have significant effects on tax and rates, with part of the premises assessed for business rates, and/or capital gains tax payable on the part used for work purposes when the dwelling is sold.

A person working at home should seek advice from an accountant before claiming a portion of rent or mortgage as a business expenditure for tax purposes. Specialist advice should also be sought if customers or clients will visit the premises, if there will be a sign or advertising outside the premises, if the work will involve equipment not normally found in homes, or if structural alterations are to be made to allow the premises to be used for work purposes.

63.10 PLANNING LAW

Ascertaining current planning use is a key task [**63.10.1.1**] when buying or taking on premises, but the impact of the legislation is much broader than this.

63.10.1 Planning permission

Planning permission is needed for most **development** [**63.10.1.2**] of property and some **changes of use**. It is obtained through the local authority's planning department. General information is available from the government's planning portal website, and advice for voluntary organisations is available from Planning Aid [see end of chapter].

63.10.1.1 Land use classes

There are 19 classes of land use divided into four broad categories. Details are on the Planningportal website [see end of chapter]. Some uses, such as theatres, hostels providing no significant element of care and homes in multiple paying occupation are *sui generis*. This means they are in separate classes of their own, rather than within a use class. *Town & Country Planning (Use Classes) Order 1987 [SI 1987/764], as amended*

63.10.1.2 Definition of 'development'

Development is defined as carrying out building, engineering, mining or other operations on land or making any material change in the use of any building or land. *Town & Country Planning Act 1990 s.55(1), as amended*

Anything which involves development needs planning permission, unless it falls within an exception. The main exceptions are maintenance, improvements or alterations which affect only the interior or have no material effect on the external appearance (but specified internal changes such as construction of mezzanine floors are not excepted); use of a building or land within the grounds of a dwelling for any purpose incidental to its enjoyment; use of land for agriculture or forestry; and change of use within a use class [above].

Further exceptions include developments within a dwelling house, minor operations such as fencing, access ways and exterior painting and decoration, and certain changes of use. At the time of writing (mid 2009) the government had proposed allowing households to install small-scale renewable technologies, such as solar panels and wind turbines, without planning permission, subject to safeguards and standards to ensure there is little or no impact on neighbours.

Listed buildings [**63.11.1**] are covered by separate rules.

63.10.1.3 Restricted developments

All new buildings, other than some limited extensions to dwellings, are developments requiring permission, and some demolition also falls within the definition of development. Building operations which require planning permission have been widely defined and include, for example, putting up a portacabin, erecting a translucent roof over a patio, and attaching a radio aerial to the exterior of a building. At the time of writing (mid 2009) the government had proposed reducing the number of small-scale developments requiring full planning permission.

Hoardings and external fascia signs, hanging signs or illuminated signs generally need planning permission. *Town & Country Planning (Control of Advertisements) Regulations 2007 [SI 2007/783]*

Material changes of use have been very widely defined. There has been much litigation about it, and guidance should generally be sought.

63.10.2 Lawful use

If a development has taken place without planning permission, the local authority may take enforcement proceedings [**63.10.7**]. However, action cannot be taken if the breach was a change of use to a dwelling or building/development works more than four years previously, or it was another type of change of use and occurred more than 10 years previously. *Town & Country Planning Act 1990 ss.171B*

It is possible to apply for a **certificate of lawful use** for an established or proposed use or development [**61.5.4**]. *TCPA 1990 ss.191,192*

63.10.3 Development plans

Regional and local planning authorities have an obligation to draw up long-term plans for their area. These must be referred to when making decisions about individual planning applications. *Planning & Compulsory Purchase Act 2004 s.38, amended by Planning Act 2008 s.180*

An organisation which intends to develop land it owns or occupies should become involved in the development planning process. Otherwise it may find that land it wants to use has been designated for different purposes under the plans.

63.10.4 Planning agreements and planning gains

Local planning authorities are allowed to control development either by imposing conditions within the planning permission or by entering into separate **section 106 agreements**, for example where a developer is obliged to provide a community facility as part of the development. These agreements will be replaced by the community infrastructure levy [**63.10.5**].

Town & Country Planning Act 1990 ss.106-106B, as amended

Organisations carrying out development may be asked to enter into a section 106 agreement. This can impose burdensome obligations, so needs careful consideration. The organisation should ensure that the obligations are reasonable and that the organisation is no longer bound by them if the property is sold.

63.10.5 Community infrastructure levy

From 6 April 2010, local authorities have power to charge a **community infrastructure levy** (CIL) to landowners and developers who create new buildings or make any changes to existing buildings. CIL replaces section 106 agreements and will be used to help fund community infrastructure such as roads, schools and hospitals. At the time of writing (mid 2009) detailed regulations for the CIL were being consulted on. Each authority will be able to choose whether to implement it and the level of the charge, after consultation with developers and the local community. Information is available from the Department for Communities and Local Government [see end of chapter].

Planning Act 2008 ss.205-225

Charities will be exempt from CIL in relation to developments that will be used wholly or mainly for charitable purposes. Regulations may exempt charitable institutions from CIL on other charity developments, such as those used primarily for fundraising.

Planning Act 2008 s.210

63.10.6 Objecting to planning applications

Developments may be announced by a notice on the site, or neighbours immediately adjacent or across the road might be directly notified. Major developments are listed on local authority websites and must be advertised in local newspapers.

Objection may be made by letter or petition, or objectors may be allowed to speak at planning meetings. Effective objections are based on a thorough understanding of relevant planning law, the local plan, environmental issues and issues of architectural merit. It is usually helpful to involve a solicitor and/or planning consultants at an early stage.

63.10.7 Enforcement

63.10.7.1 Planning contravention notices

Planning is enforced by the local authority, frequently starting with the service of a **planning contravention notice** if it appears to the local authority that there has been a breach of planning control.

Town & Country Planning Act 1990 ss.171C-171D

The recipient must respond within 21 days, giving information about how the property is being used. The notice constitutes a halfway house between discussions with the planning authority about an alleged breach and enforcement of an actual breach, and gives the local authority more information on which to decide what action to take.

An organisation receiving such a notice should immediately take professional advice. Failure to respond within 21 days is punishable by a substantial fine, as is providing a misleading response.

63.10.7.2 Breach of condition notice

A **breach of condition** notice is served when a condition attached to a planning permission has not been complied with. Failure to comply with a notice can give rise to an unlimited fine, unless the recipient took reasonable measures to comply with the conditions or is no longer in control of the land. There is no right of appeal.

Town & Country Planning Act 1990 s.187A

63.10.7.3 Injunctions and enforcement notices

Where it appears to a local authority that there has been a breach of planning control, the authority has a choice of possible remedies:

- applying to the court for an **injunction** requiring action to be taken or activities to be stopped;

- serving an **enforcement notice** on the owner or occupier, requiring the breach to be remedied within a specified time unless the notice is appealed against by public enquiry or via written representations;

- serving a **stop notice**, which takes effect within three to 28 days and immediately blocks continued use. But if the local authority wrongly serves a stop notice, the person served may be entitled to compensation. *Town & Country Planning Act 1990 ss.172,187B*

63.10.8 Other action

Development of land might also give rise to a landlord taking action for breach of the terms of the lease; a claim under the **Public Health Acts**, **Control of Pollution Act 1974** particularly ss.60 and 61, **Environmental Protection Act 1990** ss.79 and 82, or under the law of nuisance [**22.6.1**]. There may also be public pressure on the organisation to cease a use.

63.11 CONSERVATION

In addition to ordinary planning regulations, a variety of conservation measures may be used to protect buildings and the environment. Alterations to or development of listed buildings or conservation areas require a separate application for listed building and/or conservation area consent, in addition to an application for planning permission.

At the time of writing (mid 2009) the government had consulted on a **heritage protection bill** to provide a single system of national designation for listed buildings, scheduled monuments and registered parks, gardens and battlefields. It would merge conservation area consent with planning permission, and extend the range of marine historic assets that can be protected. Information is available from the Department for Culture, Media and Sport.

63.11.1 Listed buildings

Buildings are listed if they are of special architectural or historic interest. This may include both their intrinsic worth and their association with important events. Grounds or specific items attached to the building may also be protected.
Planning (Listed Buildings & Conservation Areas) Act 1990

It is an offence to demolish, alter or extend a listed building without consent from the local planning authority. Consent for alterations may have conditions attached. If these involve undertaking works in a particular way or using particular materials, the cost of maintenance or alterations may be hugely increased.

63.11.2 Conservation areas

Local authorities have a duty to consider whether any part of their area is of special or historic interest, and can designate that area as a **conservation area**. Within a conservation area demolition is more strictly controlled, and some rights to carry out development [**63.10.1.2**] are restricted. *Planning (Listed Buildings & Conservation Areas) Act 1990 s.69(1)*

Development is strictly controlled in areas designated as a national park or an area of outstanding natural beauty, and the Norfolk and Suffolk Broads.

63.11.3 Town and village greens

Land registered as a **town green** or **village green** is protected from development. A town or village green can be registered if a significant number of local residents have lawfully used it for recreational purposes for at least 20 years, and it is still being used for these purposes or the use ceased before 6 April 2007 and not more than five years has lapsed since the use ceased. Where the use ceases on or after 6 April 2007, application for registration must be made within two years.

Commons Act 2006 s.15

63.11.4 Tree preservation

If a tree is protected by a **tree preservation order** or is in a conservation area, it is an offence to cut, uproot, top or lop it without permission from the local authority. *Town & Country Planning Act 1990 s.198, amended by Planning Act 2008 s.192*

63.12 ENVIRONMENTAL PROTECTION

63.12.1 Environmental information

Public authorities and bodies carrying out environmental work under the control of a public authority are required to make public environmental information if asked to do so. The information must generally be provided within 20 working days of the request. There are exceptions for information which it is not in the public interest to disclose, but the general presumption is that information should be disclosed. Exceptions also apply to some data on emissions, and personal data about individuals, for which any request must be under the Data Protection Act [**43.3.5**]. *Environmental Information Regulations 2004 [SI 2004/3391]*

63.12.2 Biodiversity

Public sector bodies have a duty consider how to conserve and protect biodiversity (the variety of plant and animal species) in the work they do. Voluntary organisations do not have a statutory obligation to do this, but it may be a condition of contracts or grants from public sector bodies. *Natural Environment & Rural Communities Act 2006 s.40*

63.12.3 Energy efficiency

63.12.3.1 Carbon dioxide emissions

From April 2010, organisations whose annual energy consumption during 2008 was greater than 6,000MWh must comply with the **carbon reduction commitment** (CRC) scheme. This is a **cap and trade** scheme under which organisations set their own emission targets within limits set by the government, are granted allowances called **carbon emission reduction credits**, and then are able to buy and sell allowances via an auction process. There will be a self certification process for monitoring, reporting and verifying energy use. Information is available from DEFRA [see end of chapter].

63.12.3.2 Energy efficiency

Energy performance certificates show the amount of carbon used by the energy demands within a commercial building, or the energy efficiency of a dwelling (both on a scale of A-G, with A being the best). They include recommendations for improvement, and are valid for 10 years. *Energy Performance of Buildings (Certificates & Inspections) (England & Wales) Regulations 2007 [SI 2007/991]*

EPCs are required on construction, sale or rental, or if gas, electricity or water services are modified in an existing building. When a building is sold or let the seller or landlord must provide a valid EPC free of charge to the prospective buyer or tenant.

Buildings over 1,000 square metres occupied by a public authority or an institution (which could include voluntary organisations) providing a public service to a large number of people must display in a prominent position, where the public can see it, a **display energy certificate**. This shows the actual energy usage of the building and is valid for one year. The requirement to show a display energy certificate is likely to be extended to other buildings such as shops and hotels.

63.12.4 Pollution

Pollution of the air, land or water, including pollution by noise or heat, is a statutory nuisance. *Environmental Protection Act 1990*

Specialist advice should be sought by any organisation which is responsible for an industrial or unusual process which causes or could cause pollution, or where an organisation occupies or manages property on which there are potentially polluting substances. Even if the organisation takes care to ensure these substances do not cause pollution, it could be held liable if pollution occurs as the result of acts of vandals or other third parties.

Hazardous Waste (England & Wales) Regulations 2005 [SI 2005/894], as amended

63.12.4.1 Contaminated land and waters

Local authorities are required to identify contaminated land where there is some actual or potential hazard to health or the environment, and have powers to require land owners to clean up contaminated sites. Where contamination is an issue it is possible to carry out specialist surveys, for example of the soil and subsoil.　　*Environmental Protection Act 1990 ss.78A-78YC (pt.IIA), inserted by Environment Act 1995 s.57*

At the time of writing (mid 2009), the **Water Act 2003** s.86 had made similar provisions for contaminated waters but had not been implemented.

Information about contaminated land and waters is available from DEFRA [see end of chapter].

63.12.4.2 Ozone depleting substances

Organisations which use refrigeration, air conditioning equipment or firefighting equipment should check with suppliers to find out whether they contain ozone depleting substances such as CFCs, HCFCs or halogens. Strict rules apply to the disposal of such items. Information is available from DEFRA [see end of chapter].

Environmental Protection (Controls on Ozone-Depleting Substances) Regulations 2002 [SI 2002/528]

63.12.5 Noise

The emission of noise prejudicial to health or which creates a nuisance is a statutory nuisance. Local authorities may impose conditions relating to noise on planning permission for new buildings, or may issue noise abatement notices. Where a noise abatement notice is not complied with, the local authority may seize and remove any equipment which it believes is being or has been used in the emission of the noise in question.　　*Environmental Protection Act 1990 ss.79,80; Noise Act 1996 s.10(7)*

63.12.6 Waste management and recycling

Waste management – the deposit, transport, treatment, disposal or recovery of waste – is strictly controlled under the **Environmental Protection Act 1990** as amended, **Waste Management Licensing Regulations 1994** *[SI 1994/1056]* as amended, **Environment Act 1995** as amended, **Clean Neighbourhoods and Environment Act 2005**, and regulations on specific types of waste.

63.12.6.1 Environmental permits

An **environmental permit** may be required for waste operations, covering waste management and pollution prevention and control. Information is available from the Environment Agency, Waste Watch and NetRegs [see end of chapter]. At the time of writing (mid 2009) the governing was considering requiring permits for composting, unless carried out by a household. Information about this is available from the Community Composting Network.　　*Environmental Permitting (England & Wales) Regulations 2007 [SI 2007/3538]*

Details of recycling sites, other disposal sites and carriers for various types of waste are on the NetRegs and Waste Directory for All Business websites.

In disposing of paper, computers, computer disks and other electronic media which might contain confidential or sensitive information, issues around data protection and information security must be considered [**43.1.6**].

63.12.6.2 Waste collection and disposal charges

Local authorities must collect and dispose of household waste. 'Household' includes places of places of public religious worship and halls or similar buildings used for the purposes of the church or other religious groups. The local authority cannot charge for either collection or disposal of waste from these premises.

'Household' also includes premises occupied by a charity (other than a church, church hall or similar) and wholly or mainly used for charitable purposes, halls or other premises used mainly for public meetings, residential hostels, residential homes, and premises forming part of an educational establishment, hospital or nursing home. The local authority can charge for collection of waste from these premises, but not for disposal.   *Controlled Waste Regulations 1992 [1992/588]*

The Department for Environment, Food and Rural Affairs confirmed in September 2006 that waste from charity shops is also in this category. Information is available from the Association of Charity Shops [see end of **chapter 50**].

Other waste, including waste from non-charitable clubs, societies and other organisations which operate for the benefit of their members, is normally collected by commercial contractors.

63.12.6.3   Packaging

Businesses which produce more than 50 tonnes of packaging (including items sent as unsolicited direct mail) per year and have a turnover of more than £2 million must register with the Environment Agency [see end of chapter] or a recycling compliance scheme, and must recycle a specified proportion of packaging. The producer responsibility obligations in the regulations do not apply to charities entitled to general income tax relief [**55.5.1**], but could affect trading companies involved in large-scale mailings or the sale of packaged products.
Producer Responsibility Obligations (Packaging Waste) Regulations 2007 [SI 2007/871]

63.12.6.4   Electrical waste

The **Waste Electrical and Electronic Equipment Regulations 2006** (WEEE) apply to computers, monitors, printers, mobile phones and similar equipment, as well as household products. Manufacturers and importers of such equipment are required to finance the collection, treatment and recovery of waste electrical equipment, by joining a producer compliance scheme.

Distributors – including charities that pass on computers and other equipment to other organisations or individuals – must allow customers to return their waste equipment free of charge. This is done through a national distributor takeback scheme, with a network of designated collection facilities where consumers can return their used items for recycling or re-use. Distributors must provide information, through posters or leaflets with purchases, on how purchasers or consumers can dispose of waste equipment.   *Waste Electrical & Electronic Equipment Regulations 2006 [2006/3289]*

Information is available from the Department for Business, Innovation and Skills [see end of chapter]. At the time of writing (mid 2009) the European Commission was considering significant changes to the WEEE rules.

63.12.6.5   Batteries

Retailers who sell 32kg or more of portable batteries or accumulators (rechargeable batteries) in a year must, from 1 February 2010, take the batteries back instore free of charge. They must then be collected by a waste contractor or waste management company or be taken to an authorised collection facility. Separate rules apply to industrial and automotive batteries, and to producers who place portable batteries on the UK market for the first time.   *Waste Batteries & Accumulators Regulations 2009 [SI 2009/890]*

All battery users should dispose of batteries separately from other waste, either by putting them in a battery box and arranging for its collection by a waste contractor or a waste management company, or by taking them to a recycling facility.

63.12.6.6   Hazardous waste

Hazardous waste poses a danger to people, animals or the environment, and includes everyday items which contain dangerous chemicals such as lead batteries, computer monitors, televisions and fluorescent tubes as well as more obviously hazardous wastes such as asbestos and industrial chemicals. Other wastes, such as ink and paint, may need to be assessed to determine if they are hazardous.
List of Wastes (England) Regulations 2005 [SI 2005/895];
List of Wastes (Wales) Regulations 2005 [SI 2005/1820]

All organisations have a duty of care to dispose of hazardous waste properly. Many premises which produce hazardous waste or from which hazardous waste is removed must be registered with the Environment Agency. Offices, shops, charities and certain other premises are generally exempt from registration if they produce less than 500kg of hazardous waste per year. This is roughly equivalent to 25 small televisions or computer monitors, or 12 domestic refrigerators.

Hazardous Waste (England & Wales) Regulations 2005 [SI 2005/894] reg.30,
amended by Hazardous Waste (England & Wales) (Amendment) Regulations 2009 [SI 2009/507] reg.11

Even organisations which do not need to register are required to keep records of hazardous waste removed from or delivered to their premises.

Information is available from the Environment Agency [see end of chapter].

63.12.6.7 Non-hazardous waste

Organisations have a duty to reduce the amount of waste that is sent to landfill sites, either by recycling their non-hazardous waste, treating it before it is collected and disposed of, or ensuring it will be recycled or treated by their waste collection contractor. Treatment must reduce the volume of the waste, reduce its hazardous nature, facilitate its handling, or enhance its recovery. Liquids cannot be sent to landfill sites. Information is available from the Environment Agency.

Landfill (England & Wales) Regulations 2002 [SI 2002/1559], as amended

63.12.6.8 Construction sites

For any construction project where the estimated cost is more than £300,000, a **site waste management plan** must be drawn up, showing how building waste and other waste products will be removed from the site. Information is available from the Environment Agency. *Site Waste Management Plans Regulations 2008 [SI 2008/314]*

Resources: PROPERTY MANAGEMENT AND THE ENVIRONMENT

Business rates and rate relief. Business Link: www.business.link.gov.uk, 0845 600 9 006.

Valuation Office Agency: www.voa.gov.uk, 0845 602 1507.

Charity Commission: www.charitycommission.gov.uk, 0845 300 0218, email via website.

Environmental issues and waste. Department for Environment, Food and Rural Affairs: www.defra.gov.uk, 08459 33 55 77, helpline@defra.gsi.gov.uk.

Community Compost Network: www.communitycompost.org, 0114 258 0483, info@communitycompost.org.

Environment Agency: www.environment-agency.gov.uk, 08708 506 506, enquiries@environment-agency.gov.uk.

NetRegs: www.netregs.org.uk.

Waste Watch: www.wastewatch.org.uk, 020 7549 0300, info@wastewatch.org.uk.

Waste Directory for All Business: www.wastedirectory.org.uk, email via website.

Department for Business, Innovation & Skills: www.bis.gov.uk, 020 7215 5000, enquiries@bis.gsi.gov.uk.

Planning. Local authority planning department.

Department for Communities and Local Government: www.communities.gov.uk, 020 7944 4400, contactus@communities.gov.uk.

Planning portal: www.planningportal.gov.uk.

Planning Aid: www.planningaid.rtpi.org.uk, 0121 693 1201, info@planningaid.rtpi.org.uk.

Right to roam. Natural England: www.naturalengland.org.uk, 0845 600 3078, enquiries@naturalengland.org.uk.

Countryside Council for Wales: www.ccw.gov.uk, 0845 1306229, info@ccw.gov.uk.

Statute law. www.opsi.gov.uk and www.statutelaw.gov.uk.

Much but not all case law. www.bailii.org.

Updates cross-referenced to this book. www.rclh.co.uk.

To understand how the law affects voluntary organisations, it can be helpful to understand where the law comes from and how it operates. Part VIII explains this, and provides advice on finding a solicitor and finding out more about legal and related matters.

Chapter 64

HOW THE LAW WORKS

For sources of further information see end of chapter.

64.1   TYPES OF LAW

The law is divided into public and private law. **Public law** governs the behaviour of the state and of people towards the state, while **private law** governs the rights and obligations of individuals and groups and their relationships with each other.

64.1.1   Public law

Most **public law** comes from legislation and delegated legislation. Many public law powers are exercised by the criminal courts and by tribunals.

64.1.1.1   Judicial review

The decisions of bodies exercising public functions – or the way in which decisions are made – may be subject to **judicial review** by the courts. Examples include community groups challenging a local authority's decision to summarily cut grants with no consultation or even notice period [**48.4.3**], and Age Concern's challenge to the government's right to impose a mandatory retirement age [**28.6.1**]. Information for organisations which want to challenge decisions by public bodies is available from the **Public Law Project** [see end of chapter].

64.1.2   Private law

Within **private law**, legal action is brought by and against individuals or corporate bodies, and the courts award suitable remedies [**64.6.2**]. Private law is often referred to as **civil law**.

The main areas of private law are **contract law**, which deals with agreements which are intended to be legally binding [**chapter 21**]; **property law**, dealing with the ownership and possession of property [**chapters 60-62**]; **trust law**, dealing with persons holding property on behalf of others [**2.3**]; **tort**, which covers rights to compensation other than from breaches of contract or trust, such as negligence, libel and trespass [**22.6**]; and **family law**, covering marriage and civil partnerships, divorce rights, children's rights, and parents' rights and duties.

64.2 SOURCES OF LAW

Many countries have written constitutions setting down the structure of the state and the rights of people within the state. In the UK there is no formal constitution (technically, power still resides with the monarch), and many rights arise from the common law [below] or the principles of **equity** [**64.2.3**] rather than from formally enacted statute law.

64.2.1 Common law

From the reign of Henry II (1154-1189) judges' decisions were recorded and came to be used as **precedents**. In time this became a formal system with the preceding cases creating a uniform body of the **common law**, with all judges bound to follow a precedent if the facts were the same in the case before them.

64.2.1.1 Precedents

Precedents still form the basis of common law, with lower courts generally bound to follow precedents set previously by higher courts in similar cases. The ranking of the main courts [**64.5.1**, **64.6.1**] in English law is:

- **county courts** and **magistrates courts**, whose decisions do not set legal precedents;
- **crown courts** and the **high court**;
- **courts of appeal**;
- **supreme court**, replacing from 1 October 2009 the appellate (appeals) function of the House of Lords.

In cases involving European Union law, decisions of the **European court of justice** [**64.2.7.4**] are binding on all other courts, including the supreme court.

With the implementation of the **Human Rights Act 1998** [**64.3**], decisions made in foreign courts on related issues and decisions in the **European court of human rights** [**64.2.7.5**] may be taken into account.

64.2.1.2 Case reporting

Case decisions are recorded in a variety of journals and specialist publications known as **law reports**. When referring to cases in law reports there is a standard format for the case name, the year in which it was reported, an abbreviation of the law report in which the case was published, and the page number.

Increasingly, cases are also referred to by a **neutral citation** which is based on the court in which the case was heard, rather than the journals in which it was reported. The format for neutral citation is the case name, the year of the decision, an abbreviation of the court in which the case was heard, and the case number. In this book we use neutral citation if it is available.

The **British and Irish Legal Information Institute** (BAILII) website [see end of chapter] provides free public access to hundreds of thousands of decisions.

64.2.2 Civil law countries

Elsewhere in Europe, law is generally based not on common law but on legislated codes, of which the most famous is the Code Napoléon. Systems based on such codes are referred to as **civil law**. In Britain the term **civil** is generally used to distinguish cases involving claims [**64.1.2**] from criminal cases.

64.2.3 Equity

Historically, common law remedies were based on payment of money **damages** to compensate the wronged party. But sometimes damages were not appropriate. To deal with these cases a separate system of courts, derived from the ecclesiastical courts, evolved alongside the common law courts. Parties unhappy with the decisions of the common law courts or in situations where damages would not have been an appropriate remedy could take their cases to this **court of chancery**.

The chancery court based its judgments on **equity** (from the Latin *aequitas*, fairness) and made orders requiring acts to be done (**specific performance**) or not to be done (**injunctions**). It was this court that originally developed the trust rules that form the basis of charity law [**2.3**].

Since the **Judicature Acts 1873-75**, equity and the common law have been dealt with in the same courts and are now dealt with as a unified body of law.

64.2.4 Statute law

Statutes are laws enacted by Parliament. English law is rooted in the doctrine of **parliamentary sovereignty** – the supremacy of Parliament over all courts. This means that Acts of Parliament are superior to all other English sources of law, and that a statute cannot be challenged under English law as illegal or unconstitutional, but stands until repealed by Parliament.

Since the UK joined the European Community (now the European Union) in 1973, some EU law overrides English law, and the European court of justice has on some issues been able to overrule both Parliament and the courts [**64.2.7.4**]. Contrary to popular belief, it rarely does.

Under the **Human Rights Act 1998**, parts of the **European convention on human rights** are part of UK law. If the UK courts fail to give a remedy for breach of a convention right or Parliament fails to amend legislation incompatible with the convention, a person or organisation whose rights have been breached can petition the European court of human rights [**64.2.7.5**].

64.2.4.1 Enactment

Proposed laws are put forward as **bills**. A bill is debated by the House of Lords of House of Commons, depending on where it is proposed, and is either rejected or goes forward to a committee which discusses it and makes amendments. The House then votes on whether to accept the bill, reject it or make further amendments. If accepted it goes to the other House, and goes through the same process.

After being passed by both Houses of Parliament (except for finance bills, which do not need consent of the Lords), the bill is given **royal assent** and becomes an **Act of Parliament**. An Act takes effect immediately unless it contains a clause stating that it does not come into effect until a later date.

The progress of bills can be tracked on the Parliament website, and Acts are on the Office of Public Sector Information (OPSI) and statute law database websites [see end of chapter].

64.2.4.2 Interpretation

The courts must accept statute law, but must interpret it in a way which is compatible with the **European convention on human rights** [**64.3.1**], and may declare legislation incompatible with the convention. Parliament is not obliged to change the law to make it compatible, but if it wishes to do so there is a fast track procedure. Until it is changed, the law remains in force even though it is incompatible with the rights granted under the convention.

Ambiguities in the wording of statute law provide scope for interpretation. When there is doubt over meaning, the courts consider Parliament's intention in introducing the law, and may consult Hansard, the record of parliamentary debates.

64.2.4.3 Secondary legislation

Many Acts do not set out the detail of the law, leaving this to be done by supplementary **statutory instruments** (SIs) made under the Act. Statutory instruments are laid before Parliament but are not passed in the same way as Acts. Draft and final statutory instruments are on the Office of Public Sector Information (OPSI) website [see end of chapter].

64.2.5   Delegated law

Parliament can give other bodies the power to make binding laws within a specific framework. An Act, for example, may give the relevant secretary of state power to make regulations (statutory instruments) relating to that Act, or may give local authorities power to make by-laws on local matters.

64.2.6   Devolution

This book does not cover the law of Scotland or Northern Ireland, and does not cover the law of Wales where it is different from English law. Information about the law in these nations is available from Scottish Council for Voluntary Organisations, Northern Ireland Council for Voluntary Action, and Wales Council for Voluntary Action [see end of **chapter 1**].

64.2.7   European law

Depending on their nature, laws of the European Union may apply to all or some member states, and may or may not need to be enacted by the individual states.

European **regulations** are EU laws which apply immediately in all member states. They are binding without reference to national governments.

Decisions are binding only on a named state, individual, company or group, and are most often used to grant exemption from a piece of legislation. They sometimes need legislation by the state involved.

Directives are orders to the governments of all member states to enact a particular law within a prescribed time. If a member state does not do so, the European court of justice can enforce the law.

64.2.7.1   European commission

Commissioners forming the **European commission** are nominated by their national governments, but are independent of those governments. The commission is the only European body which can initiate legislation.

64.2.7.2   Council of ministers

The **council of ministers** is made up of a delegate, normally the foreign minister, from each member state. When the council is debating a particular subject, the delegates are each country's minister for that subject; for example when the council is debating agriculture, it is composed of each member state's minister of agriculture. Delegates to the council represent their own governments.

As the delegates are full-time ministers in their own countries and have little time for European work, the **committee of permanent representatives**, made up of permanent delegates from each member state, considers commission proposals on behalf of the council.

Final decisions on whether to pass legislation rest with the council. It votes by qualified majority voting (with each delegate's vote weighted according to the size of their state's population) but certain decisions require unanimity.

64.2.7.3   European parliament

The **European parliament** is made up of elected representatives (**MEPs**) from each member state. The number from each state is based on its population.

The European parliament shares legislative power with the council of ministers. It can amend or delay the budget and can dismiss the entire commission (but not individual members), but otherwise acts primarily as an advisory body, with few powers.

64.2.7.4   European court of justice

The duty of the **European court of justice** (ECJ) is to ensure that member states uphold the laws of the European Union. It is composed of one judge from each member state, plus one additional judge. Judges must be 'independent beyond doubt', and do not represent national interests.

The parties to any case requiring an interpretation of European law which reaches a court from which there is no appeal (in the UK the supreme court) may submit the case to the ECJ. ECJ decisions must be accepted by all member states.

64.2.7.5   European court of human rights

The European court of human rights, based in Strasbourg, is not part of the EU. Its role is to enforce the European convention on human rights [**64.3**].

64.3   HUMAN RIGHTS

The **Human Rights Act 1998** introduced into UK law most of the substantive rights embodied in the **European convention on human rights** (ECHR). The UK had been a signatory to the convention for nearly 50 years, and cases could be taken from the UK to the **European court of human rights**. But now:

- all acts of public authorities [**64.3.2.1**] must be compatible with convention rights;   *Human Rights Act 1998 s.6*
- individuals, associations and corporate bodies have the right to bring a claim in the UK courts against a public authority or a private body carrying out a public function [**64.3.2.2**], for breach of a convention right;   *HRA s.7*
- government ministers must declare that each new bill is compatible with the convention, or must indicate that the government wishes to proceed with the bill even though a statement of compatibility cannot be made;   *HRA s.19*
- when hearing cases on any matter, courts and tribunals must interpret all legislation consistently with convention rights, and must take into account judgments of the European court of human rights and other relevant decisions;
                                                                                  HRA ss.2,3
- certain courts can declare existing legislation incompatible with the convention, and it can be reviewed by Parliament on a fast track basis.   *HRA ss.4,10*

Claims under the Human Rights Act can be brought only against public authorities or private bodies carrying out public functions [**64.3.2**]. But all legislation, even in relation to purely private relationships such as between a private landlord and tenant, must be interpreted consistently with the convention.

Information about the Human Rights Act and the convention is available from the Ministry of Justice, the **British Institute of Human Rights**, **Justice**, and **Liberty**'s voluntary sector advice service [see end of chapter].

64.3.1   Convention rights

Rights under the European convention on human rights are set out in articles and additional protocols. The rights granted by incorporation into UK law are:
                                                                 Human Rights Act 1998 sch.1

- **Article 2**: right to life;
- **Article 3**: prohibition of torture, inhuman and degrading treatment or punishment;
- **Article 4**: prohibition of slavery and forced or compulsory labour;
- **Article 5**: right to liberty and security of person;
- **Article 6**: right to a fair and public trial or hearing in the determination of a person's civil rights and obligations or criminal charges against a person;
- **Article 7**: no punishment without law (the right not to be found guilty for an action or inaction which was not a criminal offence at the time it happened);
- **Article 8**: right to respect for private and family life, home and correspondence;
- **Article 9**: freedom of thought, conscience and religion, including freedom to manifest religion or belief, in public or private, through worship, teaching, practice and observance;
- **Article 10**: freedom of expression, including freedom to hold opinions and to receive and impart information and ideas without interference by public authority and regardless of frontiers;

- **Article 11**: freedom of peaceable assembly and freedom of association;
- **Article 12**: right to marry and found a family;
- **Article 14**: prohibition of discrimination in the exercise of other convention rights;
- **Protocol 1 Article 1**: protection of property and peaceful enjoyment of possessions;
- **Protocol 1 Article 2**: right to education;
- **Protocol 1 Article 3**: right to free elections.

Protocol 13, abolition of the death penalty in all circumstances, has replaced protocol 6, abolition of the death penalty except in time of war.

Human Rights Act 1998 (Amendment) Order 2004 [SI 2004/1474]

64.3.1.1   Absolute rights

The right to life, the prohibition of torture and of inhuman and degrading treatment or punishment, the prohibition of slavery, and no punishment without law are **absolute rights**, also called **unqualified rights**. However, the convention sets out exceptions. The right to life, for example, is not breached if it is absolutely necessary to use force in specified circumstances such as protecting a person from unlawful violence or lawfully arresting a person.

64.3.1.2   Limited rights

For some rights, the convention sets out circumstances in which the right may be **limited**. These rights are the prohibition of forced or compulsory labour, the right to liberty and security, the right to a public trial (but not the right to a fair trial), the right to marry and found a family, and the right to education.

The allowed limitations are very specific, and may not be exceeded. The right to a public trial (article 6), for example, may be limited by the exclusion of press and the public from all or part of a trial if this is necessary to protect the interest of juveniles or the private life of the parties.

64.3.1.3   Qualified rights

The main **qualified rights** are the rights to respect for private and family life, home and correspondence; freedom of thought, conscience and religion; freedom of expression; and freedom of assembly and association. The government may pass laws to limit these rights, but only if such limitation or qualification is necessary in a democratic society and meets other criteria set out in the convention.

For example, laws may be passed allowing restriction to the right to freedom of expression (article 10), if this is necessary for national security, public safety, the prevention of disorder or crime, protecting the reputation or rights of others, or preventing the disclosure of information received in confidence.

64.3.2   Public authorities

Public authorities are prohibited from acting incompatibly with convention rights, and it is only against a public authority that a person may bring a claim for breach of a convention right. A public authority is any body, organisation or individual 'certain of whose functions are functions of a public nature'.

Human Rights Act 1998 ss.6-8

64.3.2.1   Pure public authorities

Bodies such as the courts, government departments, executive agencies, the police and local authorities, are clearly public authorities. They are sometimes called **pure public authorities**.

64.3.2.2   Functional public authorities

Many other bodies are quasi-public or private, but carry out some **public functions**. They are sometimes called **quasi public authorities**, **functional public authorities** or **hybrid bodies**. They are public authorities in relation to their public functions, but private bodies in relation to other functions. This differentiation is very complex, and decisions in cases about this are inconsistent.

Where a charity or other private body carries out functions that are explicitly delegated to it by statute (such as NSPCC carrying out some child protection work), it is a public authority in relation to those functions.

Where a public sector body sets up a charity or other private body to take over a function – such as a housing association set up to take council housing – the private body is likely to be carrying out a public function. *Donoghue v Poplar Housing & Regeneration Community Association Ltd & another [2001] EWCA Civ 595*

Where a public body contracts out a service which it has a public duty to provide and which is essentially public, rather than private or commercial, in nature, the service may be found to be a public function. An example is a private company contracted to manage and regulate street markets – which are clearly public – on behalf of the local authority. *Hampshire County Council v Graham Beer (t/a Hammer Trout Farm) [2003] EWCA Civ 1056*

But in a case involving residential care for disabled people, the charity running the homes was held not to be carrying out a public function, even though it was providing services under a contract with the local authority that the authority would otherwise have had to provide. This approach was subsequently confirmed by the House of Lords. *Leonard Cheshire Foundation & another, R v [2002] EWCA Civ 366; YL v Birmingham City Council & others [2007] UKHL 27*

The Leonard Cheshire and Birmingham decisions created the anomalous position where a person receiving a service direct from the public sector body had a right to bring a claim against it under the Human Rights Act, but could not bring such a claim where the public sector body had contracted out the service. To remedy this, all charities and other private bodies providing care home accommodation and nursing or personal care under arrangements made with a statutory body have been defined by statute as exercising a function of a public nature under the **Human Rights Act 1998** s.6(3)(b). *Health & Social Care Act 2008 s.145*

A case under the Human Rights Act can be brought against a charity, voluntary organisation or other 'hybrid' body only in relation to its public functions – not in relation to its private acts. In December 2008 the Cabinet Office said the government would consult on whether the HRA should explicitly cover charities delivering public services.

64.3.2.3 Bodies which are not pure or functional public authorities

Even where an activity funded or purchased by a public sector body is not a public function, the public authority will itself be exercising a public function in grant funding or purchasing the service, and will almost certainly have a duty to ensure it is carried out in ways that are consistent with the convention. Grant and contract conditions may therefore require grant recipients to act compatibly with the convention. Even if this is not required by funders, it is good practice.

64.3.2.4 Bringing a claim

Only a 'victim' – a person whose rights have been breached – can bring a claim under the Human Rights Act. This includes individuals, groups of individuals, unincorporated associations and corporate bodies. Claims must usually be brought within 12 months.

In addition to an HRA claim – or instead of one, where an HRA claim is not possible – a person may bring a claim against an organisation for breach of any other rights. The courts must interpret these rights compatibly with convention rights.

64.4 PERSONNEL OF THE LAW

Legal work is carried out not only by solicitors and barristers, but by a range of other personnel. An understanding of their role can be helpful in understanding and making the best use of the legal system.

64.4.1 Solicitors

Solicitors provide legal advice, deal with legal paperwork, and represent clients in county courts and magistrates courts, and in crown courts when dealing with appeals or sentencing from cases in county and magistrates courts. A small number of solicitors are authorised to appear in the higher courts.

Solicitors in England and Wales are regulated by the Law Society. Solicitors may practise alone, in partnerships or increasingly as limited liability partnerships. In selecting a solicitor, it is important to try to find one with appropriate experience and expertise [see **64.8.4** for how to find a solicitor].

64.4.2 Legal executives and paralegals

Legal executives work with solicitors' firms, and must have considerable practical and formal training before admission into the Institute of Legal Executives. They can give legal advice if they are working under the authority of a solicitor.

The term **paralegal** is sometimes used synonymously with legal executives, but paralegal encompasses a wide variety of personnel who may or may not have any formal training or qualification.

64.4.3 Barristers

Barristers must act alone and not enter into partnerships, although they share offices known as **chambers**. They are regulated by the Bar Council. They usually specialise in a particular field of law, and may appear in any court. Barristers are generally engaged through solicitors, but direct access by clients is possible.

After 10 years, a barrister can apply to become a **QC** or queen's counsel (when the monarch is a king, the title is king's counsel). This is called **taking silk**, because of the silk robes QCs wear in court. A barrister who is not a QC is referred to as a **junior barrister** whatever his or her age and level of experience.

64.4.4 Justices, magistrates and judges

The majority of **judges** are still drawn from among barristers but increasingly, particularly in the lower courts, some are solicitors.

Magistrates courts and youth courts are presided over either by lay people who undertake the role on an unpaid basis (**justices of the peace** or JPs) or lawyers who are paid for the work (**stipendiary magistrates**). Lay justices are assisted by a legally qualified clerk who advises on the law.

64.4.5 Prosecution

In the past, the police generally decided whether to prosecute for a crime. This function is now undertaken by a government department, the crown prosecution service, which is staffed by lawyers.

64.4.6 Law officers and lord chancellor

The **attorney general** is a member of the government who has practised as a senior barrister. Where cases are of constitutional importance, the attorney general represents the crown (the state) in civil cases and acts as prosecutor in criminal cases. The attorney general supervises the **director of public prosecutions**, advises the government on legal issues and answers questions in Parliament on legal issues. The **solicitor general** acts as the attorney general's deputy.

At the time of writing (mid 2009) the government had proposed a **constitutional renewal bill** that would remove in most situations the attorney general's right to give direction to prosecutors in individual cases.

The **lord chancellor** is the secretary of state for justice and head of the Ministry of Justice.

64.5 ENFORCEMENT OF CRIMINAL LAW

Crimes are considered to be offences not only against individuals, but also against the community and the state. Criminal law is enforced by the state through the criminal courts. The state or occasionally a private individual brings the action, and the court decides on guilt and administers sanctions, usually based on punishment, to offenders.

64.5.1 Criminal courts

64.5.1.1 Magistrates courts

Each geographical area has its own **magistrates court**, which deals with the vast majority of criminal cases in the area. These courts deal with summary trials (not triable by a jury) for minor offences which carry a penalty of not more than six months' imprisonment or a fine; preliminary matters, such as bail, on more serious cases which are being sent to the crown court for trial by jury; and a wide variety of other functions. Magistrates courts are bound by precedents set in the higher courts, but their own decisions do not set any precedents.

Defendants may appeal to the crown court against their sentence, or to the divisional court of the Queen's bench division [**64.6.1.2**] on points of law.

64.5.1.2 Youth courts

The **youth courts** deal with offenders under the age of 18.

64.5.1.3 Crown court

The **crown court** sits in a number of locations throughout England and Wales, and is able to try cases committed anywhere in England or Wales. The best known is the central criminal court or Old Bailey. The crown court deals with appeals against convictions or sentencing from cases tried in the magistrates courts, passing sentence on people found guilty by magistrates when the magistrates do not have jurisdiction to pass an appropriate sentence, and hearing cases triable by judge and jury.

The crown court is bound by decisions of the Queen's bench division of the high court [**64.6.1.2**], the court of appeal (criminal division) and the House of Lords and supreme court.

64.5.1.4 Court of appeal (criminal division)

The **court of appeal** (criminal division) hears appeals against decisions of the crown court. Appeals on points of law are always heard, but appeals against a sentence are only heard by leave (consent) of the court. Victims of crime or those acting on their behalf can appeal for a light sentence to be extended. The court can quash (overturn) a decision, make the sentence longer or shorter, or order a retrial.

The appeal court is not bound by its own precedents, but it is bound by decisions of the House of Lords and supreme court.

64.5.1.5 House of Lords / supreme court

The **House of Lords** has been the highest court in the UK, but from 1 October 2009 its judicial functions have been taken over by a new **supreme court of the UK**. The supreme court hears appeals if the courts certify that a point of law of public importance is involved and leave to appeal is granted. The court is not bound by precedent when making decisions.

Although the supreme court is the highest court, its decisions may be overturned by the European court of justice if the case involves European Union law [**64.2.7.4**], or the European court of human rights if the case involves the European convention on human rights [**64.2.7.5**].

64.5.2 Criminal sentencing

Sentences – usually punishments – are imposed when a person is found guilty of having committed a criminal offence. The rules for sentencing in criminal cases are laid down in the **Powers of Criminal Courts (Sentencing) Act 2000** and the **Criminal Justice Act 2003**. These are expanded in sentencing guidelines which are available on the sentencing guidelines website [see end of chapter].

An offender sentenced to custody of one year or more must generally be released after serving half the sentence, but will remain on **licence** until the end of the sentence, and can be returned to prison if the licence conditions are breached. For some sexual and violent offences the licence period can be extended even beyond the period of the sentence.

64.5.3   Anti-social behaviour orders

The **Anti-Social Behaviour Act 2003** gave the magistrates courts power to make orders against individuals involved in anti-social behaviour. The making of an order is not a criminal conviction or a sentence, but the result of breaking an order can be a criminal charge leading to imprisonment.

64.6   ENFORCEMENT OF CIVIL LAW

The **civil courts** deal with claims for remedies such as compensation.

64.6.1   Civil courts

64.6.1.1   County courts

The work of **county courts** is carried out by district judges or the more senior circuit judges. Claims under £5,000 are dealt with under the **small claims** procedure, with a **fast track** procedure for those between £5,000 and £15,000. The court may hear larger claims if both parties agree. Some claims can be made online, through the **money claims online** website [see end of chapter].

County courts are bound by the decisions of the high court, the court of appeal (civil division) and the House of Lords and supreme court. Their own decisions do not create precedents.

64.6.1.2   High court

The **high court of justice**, usually called the **high court**, deals with contract and tort [**22.6**] claims worth more than £15,000 (£50,000 for personal injury claims), and certain specialised claims such as libel.

The high court is divided into the **family division**, which deals with marriage and divorce, civil partnerships and dissolution, custody of children, guardianship and adoption of children; the **chancery division**, which deals with company law, property, trusts, mortgages, taxation, administration of the estates of the dead, and probate disputes; and the **Queen's bench division**. This deals with all other civil matters, mainly contract and tort. It hears applications for *habeas corpus* and hears appeals from magistrates courts on points of criminal law.

Specialist courts exist within the Queen's bench division, such as the **commercial court**, dealing with banking and insurance matters, and the **admiralty court**, for admiralty matters.

At the time of writing (mid 2009) there was speculation that the chancery and Queen's bench divisions would be combined.

The high court is bound by its own past decisions (except for the divisional court of the Queen's bench division, which is not bound by its own past decisions on criminal matters), and by decisions of the court of appeal (civil division), the House of Lords and the supreme court.

64.6.1.3   Court of appeal (civil division)

The **court of appeal** (civil division) hears appeals from the county courts and high court on matters of fact or law, and deals with questions on legal matters arising from tribunals. Unlike the criminal division, the civil division of the court of appeal is bound by its own precedents, but it is not bound by decisions of the criminal division. It is also bound by decisions of the House of Lords and supreme court.

64.6.1.4   House of Lords / supreme court

From 1 October 2009, the judicial functions of the House of Lords in relation to civil matters have been taken over by the **supreme court of the UK [64.5.1.5]**. This is the final court of appeal, except in the limited circumstances where it is possible to appeal to the European court of justice or European court of human rights.

64.6.2   **Civil remedies**

The most common remedies in civil cases are orders to do or stop doing something (**specific performance** or **injunctions**), or **damages** to provide financial compensation. Civil remedies are explained in **65.4.7**, and remedies in relation to contract law in **21.7**.

Orders may also be made in **judicial review** cases **[64.1.1.1]**, where the court reviews quasi-judicial or administrative decisions of public bodies.

64.7   **TRIBUNALS**

Tribunals are boards – not courts – to which Parliament grants a judicial function. From November 2008 most tribunals are being phased into a new unified system, consisting of a **first-tier tribunal** and an **upper tribunal**, each made up of **chambers**. The upper tribunal deals with appeals and judicial reviews.

Tribunals, Courts & Enforcement Act 2007 pt. I

As of 1 September 2009 the first tier includes the **social entitlement chamber** (asylum support, social security and child support, and criminal injuries compensation); the **health, education and social care chamber** (care standards, mental health, and special educational needs and disability); the **war pensions and armed forces compensation chamber**; the **tax chamber** (tax, VAT and duties), and the **general regulatory chamber** (charity, consumer credit, estate agents and some transport functions from 1 September 2009; information, gambling, claims management and immigration services from January 2010). A **land, property and housing chamber** will be added, and other chambers will be added in due course.   *First-tier Tribunal & Upper Tribunal (Chambers) Order 2008 [SI 2008/2684];*
First-tier Tribunal & Upper Tribunal (Chambers) (Amendment) Order 2009 [SI 2009/196];
(Amendment No.2) Order 2009 [SI 2009/1021]; (Amendment No.3) Order 2009 [SI 2009/1590]

The above list does not cover all responsibilities of the chambers.

The three upper tribunal chambers cover **administrative appeals**, **lands**, and **tax and chancery**.

Information about the chambers, claims and appeals is available from the Tribunals Service [see end of chapter]. At the time of writing (mid 2009) there were no plans to bring the employment and employment appeal tribunal [**chapter 37**] into the unified system.

64.8   **FINDING LEGAL HELP**

A book such as this can highlight areas of concern and explain general points, but cannot replace a professional advisor. This is why we have emphasised, throughout the book, the importance of seeking advice.

Voluntary organisations are at the crossroads of an unusually complex set of rules and laws. They have to deal with the general law – employment, data protection, health and safety, intellectual property, contracts and everything else – in the same way in the same way as a comparable sized business. On top of this, the interaction of charity law, special tax and VAT rules, complexities of their own unusual internal structures and governing documents, and rapidly changing government policies mean that the voluntary sector has a very particular need for expert and up to date advice.

Organisations should make an effort to seek out advisors with voluntary sector experience and specialist expertise.

64.8.1   Support organisations

For straightforward issues, information and advice may be available from voluntary sector support organisations such as the National Council for Voluntary Organisations, Wales Council for Voluntary Action, Scottish Council for Voluntary Organisations, and Northern Ireland Council for Voluntary Action. Information and advice for community associations, especially those running community centres and similar premises, is available from Community Matters, and for organisations in rural areas from Action with Communities in Rural England (ACRE). For details of all organisations, see end of **chapter 1**.

Local councils for voluntary service may be able to provide advice to local organisations. Details are available from the National Association for Voluntary and Community Action. Some CVSs have specialist advice services for accountancy and/or employment law.

Umbrella bodies and federations can often provide information on legal matters to their member organisations. Law centres and citizens advice bureaux may be able to advise on some matters, but many do not advise employers on employment matters, even where the employer is a management committee or board of trustees of a voluntary organisation. Some areas have community accountancy projects which can provide advice and practical help on financial matters.

64.8.2   Legal update services

Voluntary sector specialist solicitors, accountancy firms and other advisors may provide newsletters or internet-based update services. The authors of this book have such services:

- Russell-Cooke LLP: 020 8789 9111, www.russell-cooke.co.uk
- Sandy Adirondack: 020 7232 0726, www.sandy-a.co.uk.

64.8.3   Regulated claims management services

Only persons who are authorised or exempt from authorisation under the **Compensation Act 2006** can provide **regulated claims management services**. Regulated claims are those for compensation in relation to employment, personal injury (including work-related injury, disease or disability), criminal injuries, industrial injuries disablement benefit, housing disrepair, or financial products and services.

Compensation Act 2006 s.4; Compensation (Regulated Claims Management Services) Order 2006 [SI 2006/3319] reg.4(3)

Among the services that can be provided only by an authorised or exempt person are advertising or marketing to claimants or potential claimants; advising claimants or potential claimants in relation to their claim or potential claim; referring the person or case to another person, including a solicitor, if the referral is made in return for or in expectation of a fee or reward; and representing a claimant in any way.

Compensation Order 2006 reg.4(2)

Authorisation is obtained through the claims management regulation unit in the Ministry of Justice [see end of chapter]. Breach of the authorisation requirements can lead to imprisonment.

Among those who are **exempt** from authorisation are legal practitioners acting under the professional rules to which they are subject; charities and not for profit advice agencies; individuals acting otherwise than in the course of business and without reward (this includes volunteers, as well as individuals acting solely in a personal capacity); trade unions certified as independent [**36.3.2**], subject to compliance with a code of practice; student unions; and persons who give or prepare to give evidence.

Compensation (Exemptions) Order 2007 [SI 2007/209]

Organisations which are paid or rewarded for referring cases to solicitors or claims management businesses, but which refer only a small number of cases as an incidental part of their work and do not carry out other regulated services, are likely to be **exempt introducers**. They do not need to be authorised, but need to comply with the rules on advertising, marketing and soliciting business.

Organisations seeking advice on compensation-related claims should ensure they use only practising solicitors and legal practitioners, authorised individuals, or individuals or organisations that are exempt from authorisation.

Organisations which themselves provide advice or representation on these issues should be satisfied that they meet the criteria for exemption, or should become authorised.

64.8.4 Finding a solicitor

The Law Society [see end of chapter] can provide names of practising solicitors and law firms with charity expertise, and legal directories listing solicitors and law firms and their areas of expertise are available online and in reference libraries. Voluntary sector periodicals such as *Charity Finance* and *Third Sector* carry advertisements for a range of professionals. Names can also be obtained from other organisations which have used solicitors or accountants for similar matters.

Even where a solicitor or accountant advertises in a reputable voluntary sector publication or is recommended by another organisation, it may be sensible to ask for and take up references.

64.8.4.1 Pro bono services

Organisations such as the **Bar Pro Bono Unit**, **LawWorks**, **Professionals4free**, **ProHelp** and **Advocates for International Development** [see end of chapter] can often match organisations with legal, accounting and other professionals willing to offer their services free of charge. However the fact that a service is being provided free does not remove the need to ensure the person is suitably experienced in the relevant areas.

64.8.5 Choosing a solicitor

Value is more important than price, particularly in legal services. Where charges are based on time, cost will depend on hourly charging rates and the time spent. More experienced or specialist advisers with higher hourly rates may in fact be less costly for any given piece of work, because they are able to complete a task more quickly. Some firms' rates may be based on high overheads to provide facilities which are not necessary for some clients. The culture of a firm may be important in determining how aggressively time is recorded and charged.

There are substantial benefits from a continuing cooperative relationship with one firm, because of increased understanding and the customisation of services over time. On the other hand, using more than one advisor can provide competition, avoid complacency and allow a 'horses for courses' approach.

It is good practice to ensure that costs estimates are provided and regularly updated. The identity of personnel proposed to provide services should also be discussed and agreed.

64.8.6 Terms of appointment

Solicitors provide detailed **terms of appointment**. These should be examined carefully to ensure that the service specified includes all the required work. The terms of appointment will also specify payment conditions. Most professionals are willing to organise payments in a way that does not put pressure on the client's cashflow if this is requested in advance.

64.8.7 Disputes

Dissatisfaction with service or the bill should be discussed thoroughly with the person who provided the service or delivered the bill. If this is unsatisfactory, it should be raised at a higher level within the firm. Most firms will be prepared to offer a reduction or compensation if there is a genuine problem with the service they have provided.

For work which does not involve the courts, a client can require solicitors to obtain a **remuneration certificate** from the Legal Complaints Service confirming that the bill is or is not reasonable. A deposit of 50% of the amount due must be made. Where the client is served with a notice drawing its attention to the right to require a remuneration certificate, the right is lost if action is not taken within 30 days.

Where the disputed bill involves court proceedings, the client can apply to have a detailed **assessment of costs** by the court. At a formal hearing a court official examines the work done by the solicitor and approves or otherwise the bill. The client has a chance to make its comments at the hearing.

The **Law Society of England and Wales**, which is responsible for solicitors, is made up of three independent units. The **Solicitors Regulation Authority** deals with all regulatory and disciplinary matters; the **Legal Complaints Service** is for members of the public wishing to make a complaint about solicitors; and the Law Society itself concentrates on representing solicitors. The Legal Complaints Service is part of the Law Society but operates independently. The service will be replaced by a fully independent **Office for Legal Complaints**, expected to be operational in autumn 2010 or soon thereafter.

Legal Services Act 2007 s.114, sch.15

Complaints of negligence against solicitors are made through the courts. Advice should be taken from a different solicitor before bringing legal action for negligence against a solicitor.

Resources: HOW THE LAW WORKS

Courts. Courts Service: www.hmcourts-service.gov.uk.

Ministry of Justice: www.justice.gov.uk, 020 7210 8500, general.queries@justice.gsi.gov.uk.

Money Claims Online: www.moneyclaim.gov.uk, 08456 015935, customerservice.mcol@hmcourts-service.gsi.gov.uk.

Sentencing guidelines website: www.sentencing-guidelines.gov.uk, 020 7084 8130, info@sentencing-guidelines.gsi.gov.uk.

Tribunals Service: www.tribunals.gov.uk.

Solicitors and legal advice. Law Society: www.lawsociety.org.uk, 020 7242 1222, contact@lawsociety.org.uk.

Legal Complaints Service: www.legalcomplaints.org.uk, 0845 608 6565, enquiries@legalcomplaints.org.uk.

Solicitors Regulation Authority: www.sra.org.uk, 0870 606 2555, contactcentre@sra.org.uk.

Claims Management Regulation Monitoring & Compliance Unit: www.claimsregulation.gov.uk, 0845 450 6858, info@claimregulation.gov.uk.

Pro bono. Advocates for International Development: www.a4id.org, 020 7772 5988, info@a4id.org.

Bar Pro Bono Unit: www.barprobono.org.uk, 020 7611 9500, enquiries@barprobono.org.uk.

LawWorks for Community Groups: www.lawworks.org.uk, 020 7929 5601, email via website.

Professionals4free: www.professionals4free.org.uk.

ProHelp: www.prohelp.org.uk.

Human rights. Ministry of Justice: see above.

British Institute of Human Rights: www.bihr.co.uk, 020 7848 1818, info@bihr.org.uk.

Justice: www.justice.org.uk, 020 7329 5100, admin@justice.org.uk.

Voluntary Sector Advice Service (Liberty): www.yourrights.org.uk/vas; 0845 122 8621, email via website.

Public law & judicial review. Public Law Project: www.publiclawproject.org.uk, 020 7697 2190, admin@publiclawproject.org.uk.

Bills. www.parliament.uk.

Statute law. www.opsi.gov.uk and www.statutelaw.gov.uk.

Much but not all case law. www.bailii.org.

Updates cross-referenced to this book. www.rclh.co.uk.

Chapter 65
DISPUTE RESOLUTION AND LITIGATION

For sources of further information see end of chapter.

65.1   DISPUTE PROCEDURES

Most disagreements and disputes are resolved informally and relatively amicably, and require no further action. But some require formal procedures within the organisation, intervention by an outside person, and/or legal action.

A contract or agreement between the parties may set out a procedure to be followed prior to legal action, to help resolve the matter. Before proceeding to action through the courts, the governing body must consider whether it has a power to conduct or settle litigation [**7.4.3**], and charities should consider specific issues relating to charity proceedings [**65.8**].

65.1.1   Time limits

Many methods of resolving disputes, especially if the courts are involved, have time limits. These are very strictly applied, and failure to comply generally means that the party loses its right to claim, and may involve liability to the other party.

65.2   ALTERNATIVE DISPUTE RESOLUTION

Alternative dispute resolution (ADR) involves a range of techniques to try to resolve disputes without having to take legal action through the courts.

Government policy is to encourage the use of mediation or arbitration to resolve government legal disputes, so it includes ADR clauses in all standard procurement contracts. Voluntary organisations which carry out work under public sector contracts may be required to agree to ADR clauses in their contracts.

Similarly, court procedure rules state clearly that litigation should be the last resort, and the 'parties should consider whether some form of ADR procedure would be more suitable than litigation'. Failure to use ADR can be taken into account when the court determines costs.

Information about ADR is available from the **ADR Now** website run by the Advice Services Alliance, the **Centre for Effective Dispute Resolution**, and the **National Mediation Helpline** [see end of chapter].

65.2.1 Complaints procedures

An effective internal complaints procedure can often allow issues to be resolved at an early stage. Aggrieved individuals who may want little more than to be heard and to receive an apology often feel they have no choice but to turn to the courts when this is not forthcoming. The governing body should receive regular reports on the number and type of complaints made through the organisation's internal complaints procedures, the outcome, and how many result in litigation.

65.2.2 Mediation

Mediation is an informal but structured process, a form of facilitated negotiation where one or more independent mediators help the disputants reach an agreed resolution. A mediator does not take sides or impose solutions.

If both parties agree, mediation clauses can be included in contracts to purchase or provide goods or services, leases and other contracts. Clauses can also be included in an organisation's internal procedures. The Centre for Effective Dispute Resolution [see end of chapter] can advise on appropriate wordings.

A successful mediation ends with a solution which the parties to the dispute are willing to accept. It is usually put in writing and signed by the parties, and may include a procedure for reviewing it to be sure it is working. A mediated settlement is generally legally binding and can, if necessary, be enforced in the courts.

If the parties cannot reach a mediated settlement, they retain the right to use arbitration or litigation.

ACAS, which provides dispute resolution services between employers and employees [**37.1.2**], makes a distinction between **conciliation**, where the employee has brought or could bring an employment tribunal claim against the employer, and **mediation**, which does not involve an actual or potential tribunal claim. For some unfair dismissal and other cases, ACAS offers arbitration [**37.2.3**].

65.2.3 Early neutral evaluation

Where mediation is not feasible because the differences between the parties are too great, but they do not want their dispute to be decided by an expert [**65.2.4**] or arbitrator [**65.2.5**], **early neutral evaluation** (ENE) may be an option. The parties appoint an independent person who assesses the strengths of each party's position. This can help the parties decide whether to settle through mediation or arbitration, or to take legal action.

65.2.4 Expert determination

In some situations a contract, lease or agreement may provide for resolution by an **expert**, or parties to a dispute may agree to use this method. This is more formal than mediation [**65.2.2**], but less formal than arbitration [**65.2.5**].

Experts are different from arbitrators in that they give their own opinion, rather than deciding between the parties' cases, and if they ask for or allow evidence to be submitted to them, there are no formal rules governing their procedures. In cases of a wrong decision a court can overturn an arbitrator's decision on the basis of misconduct or wrongly applying the law, but an independent expert can only be sued for negligence.

65.2.5 Arbitration

In **arbitration**, an arbitrator hears evidence from both parties and makes an award to one party or the other. Arbitration procedures are governed by the **Arbitration Act 1996**, and the arbitrator's decision is legally binding.

Arbitration is widely used in leases for fixing rents at rent review [**62.3.1**]. Contracts may also allow for arbitration. A typical clause is:

> Any dispute arising out of or in connection with this contract shall be referred to and finally resolved by an arbitrator agreed by the parties or, failing agreement, by an arbitrator appointed, on the application of either party, by the President or a Vice President of the Chartered Institute of Arbitrators.

Where an agreement contains a binding arbitration clause, either party can require arbitration prior to any court proceeding.

Arbitration is similar to litigation but is more private and generally quicker. It is more formal and judicial than mediation, and tends to be more expensive. The arbitrator will normally give a **reasoned award**, which is like the judgment of a court, if asked to. The arbitrator is paid by the parties to the dispute and generally does not release the award until the costs of the arbitration have been paid.

A decision by an arbitrator can generally be challenged in the courts only if it is alleged that the arbitrator made a mistake in law, and only if the court believes the issue is likely to have a substantial effect on the rights of the parties.

An arbitrator does not have to be qualified, but it is advisable for an arbitrator who is not qualified to take advice about the conduct of the arbitration. Qualified arbitrators may be contacted via the **Chartered Institute of Arbitrators** [see end of chapter].

65.2.6 Ombudsmen

For some areas of law there is an **ombudsman** to whom complaints can be made after complaints procedures have been followed or, where there are no complaints procedures, a reasonable effort has been made to resolve the dispute. The decision of an ombudsman is final.

65.3 CONSIDERING LITIGATION

Litigation is the process of making a formal legal claim against someone [**64.6**]. If the matter is not resolved between the parties, litigation ends in a court trial. Most cases settle before trial.

An organisation's decision to take legal action or to defend an action brought against itself should not be taken lightly. The process can be long, costly in time and money, and emotionally draining. On the other hand, the cost to the organisation may be even greater if such action is not taken.

A desire for justice may not be fulfilled by legal action. Technical considerations, the passage of time, the costs and the relative power of the parties can all conspire to produce results far short of 'justice'. Even where the **claimant** (the person bringing the action) obtains the judgment it seeks, it only has an order. The claimant, not the court, then has the task of enforcing the order, again through technical and sometimes frustrating procedures.

65.3.1 Before litigating

Before making a decision to proceed with litigation, factors which should be carefully considered within the organisation and with its legal advisor are:

- whether there is a legal right that can be enforced;
- whether mediation, arbitration or another form of alternative dispute resolution should be attempted, especially because failure to do so could have a potential impact on any subsequent award [**65.2**];
- whether, if judgment is obtained, the court will have power to provide an adequate remedy [**65.4.7**];
- whether the defendant is worth suing;
- whether the organisation has the legal power to litigate [**7.4.3**];
- the cost implications, including whether these are covered by insurance [**23.9.3**];
- how long the process might take;

- issues where the case involves charity proceedi
- the implications of diverting the time and ene~~~~~ ody
  members from the normal work of the organis~~~~~ trial
  itself but during all the preparations, meetings
- the public relations implications, which may be~~~~~ interfering with fundraising, or alienating supporters~~~~~ reducing
  the risk of similar problems, or demonstrating ;~~~~~ se).

A decision to enter – or not enter – into litigation~~~~~ by the governing body or under clear and explicit delegated auth

65.3.1.1 Choosing a legal advisor

Litigation is a formal affair, and quickly exposes~~~~~ experience in a legal
advisor [see **64.8.4** for how to find a solicitor]. Org~~~~~ ons should not be afraid
to ask whether a firm of solicitors has a litigation~~~~~ ialist, and to ask whether
they have experience in the relevant type of litigati .

Where a claim or potential claim could involve com pensation – for example in re-
~~~~~ here may be restrictions on who
~~~~~ in relation to that issue [**64.8.3**].
~~~~~ one other than a practising solicitor
~~~~~ profit advice centre or trade union, it
~~~~~ thorised to provide **regulated claims**
~~~~~ om authorisation.

~~~~~ widely and is not a reliable indicator of overall
~~~~~ een firms based on differing locations and re-
~~~~~ o experience and specialisation between solicitors
~~~~~ tigation team should have solicitors available with a
~~~~~ e.

~~~~~ lowest cost may be a false economy. An expensive but
~~~~~ citor may well end up costing less (and having a better
~~~~~ n a less expensive but less experienced solicitor.

~~~~~ tes where success or failure may depend on the weight of ex-
~~~~~ ge fees may be required by engineers, doctors, architects and
~~~~~ als.

~~~~~ is a contest, the amount of legal work will depend on the tactics
~~~~~ each side and cannot easily be determined in advance. Any estimates
~~~~~ dvance will be very provisional indeed.

~~~~~ d of costs and damages

~~~~~ losing party to a court action, unless he or she has a **certificate of public
~~~~~ nding** (legal aid), will have to meet his or her own legal costs [**65.4.8**], and
generally a portion of the other party's. This can range from a very limited
amount in small claims cases to up to 75% of the winner's costs in other cases, so
can add considerably to the loser's costs. Different cost rules apply in the employment and other tribunals.

Even if the winning party is awarded costs, these will not be for the full amount.
It is still likely to have to meet at least 25% of its own legal costs, and possibly
much more. So even winning can prove costly.

Where there are interim court hearings before the trial, it is usual for the party
who loses the application to have to pay some or all of the other side's costs, often
within 14 days of the hearing.

Defendants must also think seriously about the damages they could be ordered to
pay if they lose the case [**65.4.7.1**]. The claimant could also become liable for
damages if the defendant makes a counterclaim [**65.4.2.3**]. There is no limit on
damages in court cases, or in discrimination cases in the employment tribunal.

65.3.1.4   Indirect costs

There are also likely to be indirect costs such as locum staff to cover for staff involved in the case, and perhaps lost income if donors, funders, members or clients are antagonised by the proceedings.

65.3.1.5   Liability for costs

If an organisation is incorporated with limited liability [**3.1.2**], the organisation would be insolvent and would have to be wound up if it could not meet a costs liability. Defendants may ask the court to require an incorporated claimant to provide security for any costs that may be ordered against it.

If the organisation is unincorporated, any legal action will be brought against some or all governing body members [**22.2.2**], who could be held personally liable for any or all of the amount due. **Trustee indemnity insurance** [**23.10**] may be available to indemnify [compensate] any trustees who are held personally liable in certain types of cases.

If the organisation is an unincorporated trust and does not have trustee indemnity insurance covering potential costs, the governing body members should consider at the outset applying for a court order requiring the trust to indemnify them for costs and liabilities. This is called a **Beddoe** (or Beddoes) **order**, but it is not much use if the trust does not have funds to indemnify the trustees.

Chapters 22 and **23** include more about liability and insurance.

65.3.1.6   Issues for charities

The governing body of a charity has a primary duty to safeguard the charity's assets [**15.6.5**], and any decision to enter or not to enter into litigation must be in the best interests of the charity and its beneficiaries. Charities do not require the Charity Commission's consent to take or defend legal proceedings, but if the litigation is an unusual type, for example libel, or might involve substantial costs, the charity's trustees should seek the Commission's advice before proceeding.

65.3.1.7   Protective costs order

Where judicial review [**64.1.1**] of a decision by a public body is sought, the costs can be prohibitive. The courts recognise that there may be a wider public interest in some cases, and where this is the case may make a **protective costs order** capping the amount the applicant will have to pay. This enables an organisation (or individual) to proceed with the judicial review application without the risk of being required to pay the other party's substantial costs. The criteria for making a protective costs order were set out in cases involving the Child Poverty Action Group and Corner House Research. The Public Law Project [see end of **chapter 64**] can advise.   *Child Poverty Action Group, R (on the application of) v Lord Chancellors Department [1998] EWHC 151 (Admin); Corner House Research, R (on the application of) v Secretary of State for Trade & Industry [2005] EWCA Civ 192*

65.3.2   Deciding not to litigate

All these factors, and in particular the costs, mean that the vast majority of disputes or claims never lead to litigation. They are resolved through negotiation between the parties or through an alternative dispute resolution process [**65.2**], or the matter is simply dropped.

A **compromise agreement** is a legally binding agreement not to pursue legal action in the courts, in return for an apology, cash settlement or other settlement. Where a compromise agreement relates to a potential employment tribunal claim, it must follow specific rules [**37.2.2**].

65.4   THE LITIGATION PROCESS

No legal case is exactly like any other, and procedures and the course of the action vary greatly from case to case. In addition there are particular procedures for specialist sub-branches of litigation such as libel (one of the few types of civil case where jurors are involved), patent law and complex commercial matters.

The person who initiates the litigation is the **claimant** (previously called the **plaintiff**), and the person against whom the case is brought is the **defendant**. Both the claimant and defendant are **litigants**. There may be multiple claimants or defendants.

65.4.1 Preliminary stages

65.4.1.1 Consulting insurer

As soon as there is any possibility of litigation, the organisation should find out whether the matter falls within any of its insurance policies [**chapter 23**]. If the potential litigation is or may be covered by insurance, the insurer must be consulted immediately. Failure to consult the insurer immediately, any admission of liability or taking certain steps without the insurer's consent may release the insurance company from any obligation to cover the loss or costs.

If the issue is covered by insurance, it is likely that the insurance company will deal with all negotiations with the other party and will conduct any legal action against the other party. If the insurer is dealing with the matter, the organisation itself must not get involved in any discussions with the other party.

Where the insurance simply covers legal costs, the organisation can generally select its own solicitor and conduct the action. It may however need to obtain the insurer's consent for various steps.

65.4.1.2 Vexatious litigants

Where a person persistently brings claims which are frivolous or are intended to harass the other party, they can be banned from bringing any further claim without the consent of the court. The Courts Service [see end of **chapter 64**] maintains a list of vexatious litigants, and in some situations it may be worth checking to see if the potential claimant is on it.

65.4.1.3 Taking legal advice

The organisation may want at this stage to consult a solicitor or other legal advisor, or may decide to proceed further on its own. It is generally advisable to take legal advice sooner rather than later [**65.4.2.1**].

65.4.1.4 Documents

The organisation also needs to consider carefully what it puts into writing about the situation, even for its own use. Unless such documents fall within certain limits and are therefore privileged, they may have to be disclosed to the other side. This may weaken the organisation's case – but inability to provide relevant documents may also weaken its case [**65.4.3.1**]. Documents which may later be needed as evidence in a legal case must not be discarded, destroyed or altered.

65.4.1.5 Without prejudice communication

If there is a risk of litigation, nothing should be said or put in writing to the other party without legal advice or very careful thought. Unless specified otherwise, any communication with the other party is **open**, and the content of open discussions or correspondence can be disclosed in later court proceedings.

But by starting settlement offers – whether verbal or written – with the words **without prejudice**, the parties are able to hold discussions about settlement on the basis that these are **privileged** and neither side will be allowed to disclose what was said in these discussions or letters in later court proceedings. For example, an organisation in dispute with a computer company might offer without prejudice to accept £5,000 and a new computer. If the company refuses the offer, it cannot later at the trial say that the offer to accept £5,000 and a new computer is evidence of the level of loss suffered by the organisation.

Communications can be without prejudice only if they are part of a genuine attempt to settle the dispute. Other communications, even if they say they are without prejudice, may be open and can be disclosed in court.

In certain limited circumstances, without prejudice communications may later be disclosed to the court. For example, a computer company which makes a substantial settlement offer might indicate that if the organisation wins less than this as damages, the company will disclose the offer during arguments about who should bear the costs of the action. In this case, the company's offer would be made **without prejudice save as to costs**. After litigation has started there is a formal procedure for such offers, called a **part 36 offer**. Failure to accept a part 36 offer can have important consequences in costs and interest.

65.4.1.6 Agreeing an offer

If a without prejudice offer of settlement is unconditionally accepted, the correspondence or discussion then becomes open, and a binding agreement will be reached. This will be disclosable to the court.

65.4.1.7 Letter before action

If its demands are not met, the claimant generally writes a final **letter before action** giving a deadline after which it will commence proceedings. If such a letter is not written and the claimant commences proceedings without warning, the court might not award costs to the successful claimant, on the basis that a letter before action might have secured settlement without the need for proceedings.

For some types of claims, including personal injury, libel, professional negligence, judicial review and clinical negligence, pre-action protocols (procedures) set out the steps to be followed and the information that must be disclosed at this stage.

65.4.2 Starting the proceedings

65.4.2.1 Legal advice

Before starting or deciding to defend proceedings, the organisation will need to take advice from its solicitor, and may also seek a barrister's opinion. This may be expensive, but may be advisable because the solicitor may not have specialist expertise or may not have recent experience of litigation in the particular field. In addition, the process of writing the case down in order to instruct the barrister may provide a salutary concentration of the mind, and a barrister who is not involved in other ongoing relationships with the client, as a solicitor may be, may be more objective in his or her assessment of the likely outcome.

The solicitor may arrange a meeting with the barrister to clarify points or allow fuller discussion. This meeting is called a **conference**. The barrister's opinion may be given in writing, as an **advice**. A barrister's opinion is just that – an opinion – and does not provide an authoritative prediction of the outcome.

If advice is taken from anyone other than a practising solicitor, they may need to be authorised to provide this advice [**64.8.3**] or be exempt from authorisation.

65.4.2.2 Payment on account

A solicitor who instructs a barrister or expert becomes personally liable for ensuring they are paid. Most solicitors are therefore unwilling to incur liability for such costs unless the client has paid a sufficient sum into the client account held by the solicitor. Solicitors also generally ask for payment on account of costs to ensure their own fees are covered. Interest on these accounts belongs to the client.

65.4.2.3 Claim form

Proceedings are generally started when the claimant presents a **claim form** (formerly called a **writ** or **summons**) to the high court or a county court and pays a fee to the court. The claim form is then issued and must be **served** on (delivered to) the defendant. Strict rules apply to service of documents.

Generally with the claim form there will be an **acknowledgement of service** form, on which the defendant can indicate whether it intends to defend the proceedings. A defendant who wishes to defend then files its defence, and if it believes it has a claim against the claimant, may make a **counterclaim**. A fee is payable when making a counterclaim. The defendant may also join (bring) other parties into the action if it feels that they also have some sort of responsibility. Failure to respond to the claim form within the strict time limit may result in judgment being entered against the defendant in default of its response.

Documents filed with the court – the claim form, particulars of claim, defence, reply, counterclaim or any additional claim, and additional information – are in general available to the public, on request to the court and payment of a fee.

65.4.3 Before trial

When a defence is filed, the court issues **allocation questionnaires** for each party to complete and return to the court. This enables the court to allocate the case to the right track, and to make directions about how the case will be conducted. Cases are allocated to **small claims**, for most disputes worth less than £5,000; **fast track**, for claims between £5,000 and £15,000 where the trial is likely to last for one day or less; or **multi-track**, for claims over £15,000.

The high court can hear only claims over £15,000 (£50,000 for personal injury). County courts can deal with all cases, and will hear all except very large claims.

65.4.3.1 Disclosure

Each party is likely to be required to serve on the other a full list of the relevant documents which it holds. After the list has been served, the other party can inspect and take copies of those documents. This process is referred to as **disclosure** (formerly called **discovery**). It is very important, and both parties have a wide duty to preserve and disclose documents relevant to the case, even if the documents harm their position [**65.4.1.4**].

Documents which are **privileged** from disclosure do not need to be disclosed. Privilege may arise where communications between the parties are genuinely without prejudice [**65.4.1.5**], or where they are protected by **litigation privilege**. This protects communications between a client and lawyer, or between one of them and a third party, whose primary purpose is legal advice in relation to pending or contemplated litigation. Under **legal advice privilege**, confidential legal advice communications between the lawyer and client are privileged even if litigation is not involved, but communications with third parties are not.

Three Rivers District Council & others v Bank of England [2004] UKHL 4

65.4.3.2 Interim orders

In addition to these more routine steps, a party may apply to the court for an **interim order** to protect its position. If, for example, an organisation feels that neighbouring building works are damaging its buildings, it may seek an interim injunction to restrain further works. Except in very urgent cases or where prior notice might cause the defendant to pre-empt the effect of the order, prior notice of the application must be given to the other party.

Interim orders are powerful tools, even including a **search order** and orders forcing compliance with court rulings or earlier orders on pain of losing the case (an **unless order**: 'unless you do this, you will lose the case').

65.4.4 Settlement

Attempts to settle the matter may take place at any stage. As the date of trial approaches, the pressures for settlement may intensify, from within the organisation and/or from the other party, to avoid the cost and stress of the trial itself. A settlement reached before trial may be embodied in an order of the court consented to by both parties. This enables either party to take action if the other party fails to comply with what has been agreed.

65.4.5 Right of audience

Solicitors, barristers and others who have a right to speak for a party in court or at a tribunal are said to have a **right of audience** in the court. Each court or tribunal has its own rules about who has this right.

Individuals can always represent themselves. Organisations are generally allowed to be represented by a staff member or other unqualified person, but this must be confirmed beforehand. In some types of cases, non-lawyers can represent litigants only if they are authorised to do so or are exempt from authorisation [**64.8.3**].

65.4.6   Trial

The trial usually opens with the claimant, either directly or through its solicitor, barrister or other advocate (person representing it), opening the proceedings and calling witnesses in support of its claim. After each witness has given evidence, the defendant is able to cross-examine. If the cross-examination reveals new issues, the claimant may be able to re-examine the witnesses on these new issues. The defendant similarly presents its evidence, then both parties sum up.

65.4.7   Judgment and remedies

After summarising the facts, the judge gives a judgment and may make an order, referred to as the **remedy**, which will be set out in a written judgment of the court. The most common remedies are orders requiring **payment**; orders authorising **possession** of a property (land or building); **injunctions** requiring a party to perform an action or prohibiting a party from performing an action [for example **21.7.7**]; **specific performance** orders requiring a party to carry out a contract [**21.7.6**] or take some other specific action; and **damages** [below].

65.4.7.1   Damages

Damages are financial compensation for the wrongs suffered, with the object of placing the party in the same financial position as if the contract had been fulfilled, or the tort (wrong) or breach of statutory duty had not been committed.

If the court feels that the claimant was wronged but has not suffered any loss or has not suffered substantially, it may award only token **nominal damages**.

Aggravated damages are extra damages if the court feels that the injury was aggravated by the defendant's conduct or motives.

Very rarely, high **exemplary damages** may be awarded where the court considers that the defendant committed the wrong for self serving reasons or to make a profit, and the profit will exceed the claimant's loss – for example where a landlord evicts a tenant in order to rent at a better price. Exemplary damages may also be awarded to punish oppressive, unconstitutional or arbitrary acts by government. It is unusual for the court to award aggravated or exemplary damages, and they should not be claimed in ordinary contract or tort claims.

Rookes v Barnard (No.1) [1964] UKHL 1

Where the full loss is not known – typically in medical or accident cases – a provisional award may be made before the final assessment of the full amount.

65.4.8   Assessment and award of costs

The court generally awards **costs** to the winner of the case, so in addition to any other remedy, the loser is ordered to pay the legal costs of the winner. But the costs do not cover the winner's full costs. The proportion to be paid by the loser is either agreed between the parties or is assessed by the court. A judge may make a summary assessment of the costs at the end of a short hearing, or a court official may undertake a detailed assessment of costs. In normal circumstances, this is 50% to 75% of the actual cost paid by the winning party.

Costs covered by the losing party are referred to as **party and party costs**. The actual cost paid by the winner, in the form of a bill from its own solicitor, is called **solicitor and own client costs**.

Costs are normally awarded against the loser, unless the loser is funded through legal aid [**65.5.3**]. Costs may be reduced or lowered where the loser has offered to settle prior to judgment or paid a sum into the court at a figure at or above the final judgment, or the loser may receive costs from the winner in respect of awards of costs made in preliminary hearings.

The award of costs is discretionary. In a case where there are many issues and each party wins on some of them, the judge may order each party to pay costs for the issues that they lost, or may simply say that each side must pay its own costs.

65.4.8.1   Security for costs

In certain circumstances, foreign or incorporated claimants may be required to provide security for the defendant's costs, to prevent a successful defendant being unable to enforce an award of costs.

65.4.9   Enforcement

Obtaining judgment merely gives the person in whose favour it has been given an order of the court for the remedy. The court does not, except in very unusual circumstances, take any steps to enforce the order. It is up to the winning party to decide whether and how to do this.

The terminology and some of the rules for enforcement will be changed under the **Tribunals, Courts and Enforcement Act 2007**. At the time of writing (mid 2009), a date had not been set for these changes to come into effect.

65.4.9.1   Execution / enforcement

If the party against whom judgment is given fails to obey the order of the court, for example does not make the payment within the specified time, the person in whose favour judgment has been given may apply for a **warrant of execution** (to be renamed a **warrant of control**). Under this process, court **bailiffs** (to be renamed **enforcement agents**) enter the premises of the person against whom judgment has been given. If the judgment is for money they seize goods on the premises sufficient to meet the money judgment, or if the order is for possession they take possession of the premises.   *Tribunals, Courts & Enforcement Act 2007 s.62, sch.12*

Execution (to be renamed **enforcement**) cannot be levied against specified categories of goods, for example personal clothing and tools of the debtor's trade.

Execution/enforcement is effective where the individual or organisation can be traced and has significant saleable property. But problems can arise if the bailiffs/enforcement agents gain entry to the premises, or if the property on the premises may not be owned by the person against whom judgment was given.

The bailiffs/enforcement agents generally first take **walking possession** by seizing control of the goods but not actually removing them from the premises. The creditor is then given a short period of time before the goods are removed.

65.4.9.2   Court orders

If the person against whom judgment has been given has money in a bank or other accounts, the court will make a **third party debt order** requiring the bank to pay the money over. This was formerly known as a **garnishee order**.

If the person owns property or shares, the court may make a **charging order** to put a charge (similar to a mortgage) over them.

If the person against whom judgment has been given is employed, the court may order the employer to deduct amounts from the person's salary and pay them to the court to satisfy the judgment. This is called **attachment of earnings**.

65.4.9.3   Bankruptcy or winding up

If a judgment of £750 or more remains unmet, this provides grounds for an application to wind up an organisation [**24.5.1**] or to bankrupt an individual. This creates a completely separate case and requires a new set of proceedings.

65.4.9.4   Contempt

Where an injunction or other direct order of the court is disobeyed, the court can impose a fine or imprisonment for contempt of court.

65.4.10   Appeals

In many cases it is possible to appeal, provided strict time limits are met. However, the further up the court system a matter progresses [**64.6.1**], the more constraints are imposed requiring leave (permission) to be given before appeals are taken. This is done to prevent the courts becoming clogged with appeals with little chance of success.

65.5 COVERING THE COSTS

65.5.1 Insurance

Legal expenses insurance [23.9.3] covers the costs of litigation. An organisation with this insurance must generally contact the insurer before taking any steps towards settlement or litigation [**65.4.1.1**]. Insurance policies are also available to cover damages arising from a very wide range of claims [**chapter 23**].

After the event insurance may be obtained to finance a case where there is a high prospect of success. If the case is lost, the insurer pays the other side's costs and in some cases the loser's costs. The insurer will require sufficient information to enable it to assess the risk, and the premium may be substantial.

65.5.2 Conditional fees

Some solicitors now offer **conditional fees**, sometimes called **no win no fee**. These means that the client only pays fees if the case is won, although it may have to pay disbursements (the solicitor's expenses).

Conditional fees and after the event insurance are frequently used in personal injury litigation. Their use in other contexts is recent, and they are generally unlikely to be suitable or available to voluntary organisations.

65.5.3 Certificate of public funding (legal aid)

The **Community Legal Service Fund** may meet the reasonable fees of solicitors and barristers acting for individuals who meet the criteria for a **certificate of public funding** (**legal aid**). This involves rigorous means tested financial criteria, and tests as to the merits of their case. Public funding is generally not available for organisations, or for governing body members who are being sued as a representative of an organisation rather than in their individual capacity.

Public funding from the Community Legal Service Fund is not available for all types of action. In particular it does not cover libel, or cases where conditional fees may be available, such as most personal injury cases. It is not available for tribunals, but does cover advice and preparation for a tribunal hearing.

Information about eligibility for legal aid, and free legal information and advice for people who qualify for legal aid, are available from **Community Legal Advice** [see end of chapter].

The courts do not, in normal circumstances, enforce costs awards against publicly funded litigants [**65.4.8**]. So if an organisation brings an action against such an individual, the organisation will have to meet its own costs even if it wins the case. This may be a consideration in deciding whether to continue with an action.

65.6 DO IT YOURSELF LITIGATION

In actions involving small claims of up to £5,000 in a county court, a less formal procedure is used, and generally solicitors' costs are not awarded to the winning party. This is to encourage individuals to undertake their own proceedings.

Organisations can undertake actions larger than this without a solicitor, but the potential difficulties should not be underestimated. Where an organisation routinely needs to make claims which are unlikely to be contested – for example, recovering rent arrears from property let out – it may be sensible to train staff to conduct routine litigation. Qualified legal advice should be available, and procedures should be in place to transfer cases to solicitors if they become complex.

65.7 TRIBUNAL PROCEDURE

Procedures in **tribunals** [**64.7**] are generally similar to court procedures, but are less formal. Tribunals were developed to reduce the need for expensive legal representation, so do not generally make costs awards in favour of the winner. But proceedings may be complex, and it is usually sensible for the organisation to be legally represented. For employment tribunal procedures, see **37.3**.

Tribunals rarely have direct powers of enforcement, so court action will be needed if an award is not complied with.

Appeals may initially be to the upper tribunal, but the final appeal is generally to the courts.

65.8 CHARITY PROCEEDINGS

Charity proceedings are a very limited type of legal action where the court is asked to exercise its jurisdiction over the way a charity operates. Charity proceedings cover matters relating to charitable status, such as an appeal against the Charity Commission's refusal to register a charity [**8.2.10**], a challenge to a Charity Commission order [**4.5.4**], an application by the trustees to have the court decide matters relating to its governing document, claims involving trustees' breach of trust [**22.4**], and claims that trustees have acted unconstitutionally [**15.6.2**].

Charity proceedings can be brought only by one or more of the charity's trustees, the charity itself if it is incorporated, two or more people living in the charity's area of benefit [**5.1**] if it is a local charity, or a person 'interested in the charity'.

Charities Act 1993 s.33(1)

There have been a number of cases about who is a 'person interested in the charity'. This would probably not include ordinary members of the public, and even a founder or substantial donor would probably not be an 'interested person' unless he or she was also a trustee.

Bradshaw v University College of Wales [1987] 3 All ER 200

But parents of children attending a school run by a charity, and a local authority where the charity owned land have been found to be interested persons.

Gunning v Buckfast Abbey Trustees [1994] TLR 327; Re Hampton Fuel Allotment: Richmond upon Thames London Borough Council v Rogers [1988] 2 All ER 761

Cases that will be brought in the charity tribunal, such as appeals against refusal to register a charity, do not require Charity Commission consent. For other charity proceedings, registered and excepted charities [**8.1.1**, **8.1.3**] must obtain the Charity Commission's permission to proceed. If the Commission refuses, consent must be obtained from a chancery division judge of the high court. Charities themselves may be subject to proceedings brought by the attorney general or the Charity Commission.

Charities Act 1993 ss.32,33

To protect themselves from personal liability in charity proceedings, trustees of charitable trusts may seek a **Beddoe order** [**65.3.1.5**], and governing body members of any charity may seek section 29 guidance from the Commission [**4.5.2**].

Resources: DISPUTE RESOLUTION AND LITIGATION

Alternative dispute resolution. ACAS: www.acas.org.uk, 08457 47 47 47.

ADR Now (Advice Services Alliance): www.adrnow.org.uk.

Centre for Effective Dispute Resolution: www.cedr.co.uk, 020 7536 6000, info@cedr.com.

Chartered Institute of Arbitrators: www.arbitrators.org, 020 7421 7444, info@arbitrators.org.

National Mediation Helpline: www.nationalmediationhelpline.co.uk, 0845 60 30 809, email via website.

Legal aid. Community Legal Advice: www.communitylegaladvice.org.uk, 0845 345 4 345.

Solicitors and legal advisors. See end of **chapter 64**.

Statute law. www.opsi.gov.uk and www.statutelaw.gov.uk.

Much but not all case law. www.bailii.org.

Updates cross-references to this book. www.rclh.co.uk.

TABLE OF STATUTES
AND STATUTORY INSTRUMENTS

EUROPEAN LEGISLATION

TABLE OF CASES

NEUTRAL CITATIONS

Most recent cases are referenced by a neutral citation, showing the court in which they were decided. The neutral citations included in this table of cases are:

ECHR	European court of human rights		EWHC (QB)	Queen's Bench division
ET	Employment tribunal		EWHC (TCC)	Technology & construction court
EWCA Civ	Court of appeal (civil division)		EUECJ	European court of justice
EWCA Crim	Court of appeal (criminal division)		ScotCS	Scottish court of session
EWHC	High court		UKEAT	Employment appeal tribunal
EWHC (Admin)	Administrative court		UKHL	House of Lords
EWHC (Ch)	Chancery division		UKVAT	VAT tribunal
EWHC (Exch)	Exchequer court			

LAW REPORTS

Older cases, and recent cases for which there is no neutral citation, are referenced to the law journals in which they are reported. To find the full name for a law journal, you can use the Cardiff index to legal abbreviations, at www.legalabbrevs.cardiff.ac.uk.

INDEX

H